Traditional Storytelling Today

An International Sourcebook

Traditional Storytelling Today

An International Sourcebook

Edited by
Margaret Read MacDonald

Contributing Editors
John H. McDowell
Linda Dégh
Barre Toelken

FITZROY DEARBORN PUBLISHERS
CHICAGO · LONDON

For information write to:

FITZROY DEARBORN PUBLISHERS
919 North Michigan Avenue
Chicago, Illinois 60611
USA

or

310 Regent Street
London W1R 5AJ
England

Cataloging-in-Publication Data is available from the Library of Congress and the British Library

ISBN 1–57958–011–4

First published in the USA and UK 1999

Typeset by Print Means, Inc., New York, New York
Printed by Maple-Vail, Binghamton, New York
Cover designed by Peter Aristedes, Chicago Advertising and Design, Inc., Chicago, Illinois

To scholars of every age who have devoted hours, days, years to the collection, transcription, translation, and publication of our world's folktales. Thank you for caring enough to try to preserve story. Thank you for caring enough to share with the world. May a wise future bring honor on your names.

Contents

EDITOR'S NOTE   xiii

ACKNOWLEDGMENTS   xv

ESSAYS
Sub-Saharan Africa

Hunters' Narratives   3
Stephen Belcher

Central African Epics   6
Stephen Belcher

To Make Our World a Gentler, More Compassionate World   9
Raouf Mama

The Fulani Epics   13
Christiane Seydou

The Ga Folktale: Context, Themes, and Techniques   18
Abu Shardow Abarry

The Igbo Folk Epic   25
Chukwuma Azuonye

Igbo Stories and Storytelling   33
Chukwuma Azuonye

The Meaning of the "Meaningless" Refrain in Igbo Folk Songs and Storytelling Events   41
Chukwuma Azuonye

The Dogon Creation Story   48
Chukwumu Azuonye

The Storytelling Event Among the Igede of Nigeria   54
Ode Ogede

Ju/'hoan Folktales and Storytelling: Context and Variability   59
Megan Biesele

Storytelling: A Thread of Life Within the Kamba Community   65
Vincent Muli Wa Kituku

Narrative Performance in a Changing World: The Case of the "Storytellers" in Kenya   68
Ezekiel B. Alembi

The Meditation of Time, the Wisdom of the Teller, the Void of the World   71
Sory Camara

Asia

The Chantefable Tradition of Suzhou
Mark Bender
85

Antiphonal Epics of the Miao (Hmong) of Guizhou, China
Mark Bender
88

Rajasthani Hero Legends
Lindsey Harlan
91

Two Contemporary Performances of Savitri in Pune, India
Lee-Ellen Marvin
94

Saneguruji Storytelling Academy: Transformation of Domestic Storytelling in India
Lee-Ellen Marvin
98

Storytelling in Middle-Class Indian Families
Lee-Ellen Marvin
102

A System of Narrative Performances in Middle India
Joyce Burkhalter Flueckiger
106

Indonesian Storytellers and Storytelling
James Danandjaja
110

Religious Tales and Storytelling in Japan
Richard W. Anderson
114

Still Telling in Japan: Traditional Folktellers
Cathy Spagnoli
119

P'ansori, the Ancient Korean Art of Storytelling
Chan E. Park
122

Enduring Scars: Cautionary Tales Among the Senoi Semai,
a Peaceable People of West Malaysia
Robert Knox Dentan
130

Professional Storytelling in West Sumatra
Nigel Phillips
134

The Tradition of Storytelling in Malaysia
Mohammed Taib Osman
138

Thet Siang Performance in Isaan
Wajuppa Tossa
142

Storytelling: A Means to Maintain a Disappearing Language and Culture
in Northeast Thailand
Wajuppa Tossa
144

Australia and the Pacific

Nallawilli-Sit Down (and Listen): The Dreamtime Stories—An Oral Tradition
Pauline E. Campbell-McLeod
155

Ka Ola Hou ʻAna o ka ʻŌlelo Hawaiʻi i ka Haʻi ʻAna o ka Moʻolelo i Kēia Au Hou:
The Revival of the Hawaiian Language in Contemporary Storytelling
Kuʻualoha Meyer-Hoʻomanawanui
160

A Gossamer of Wisdom   171
Hinekahukura Barrett-Aranui

Tale Telling on a Polynesian Atoll   176
Michael Lieber

Europe

The Albanian World in the Folk Teller's Stories   181
Ramadan Sokoli

Basque Storytelling and the Living Oral Tradition   185
Linda White

Present-Day Storytelling in Northeastern Bulgaria   190
Yordanka Kotseva

Storytelling in Croatia   203
Ljiljana Marks

Traditional Legends in Contemporary Estonian Folklore   207
Ülo Valk

Factors Influencing the Formulation of Narration   212
Annikki Kaivola-Bregenhøj

New Storytellers in France   227
Veronika Görög-Karady

Storytelling in Spanish Galicia   230
Kristin Bervig Valentine and Eugene Valentine

Traditional Storytelling Today in the East of Northern Germany   234
Siegfried Neumann

Märchen 2000: Taking Care of the Fairy Tale in Germany   239
Sabine Wienker-Piepho

Greek-Albanian (Arvanítika) Interactive Storytelling
and the Legitimation of Critical Discourse   247
Lukas D. Tsitsipis

Aspects of Narrative Tradition in a Greek Gypsy Community   252
Diane Tong

Folklore Repertoires: Male, Female   257
Ilona Nagy

Traditional Storytelling in Ireland in the Twentieth Century   264
Patricia Lysaght

A Storyteller's Growing Consciousness   273
Inta Gale Carpenter

Once Upon a Time in Vale Judeu   281
Isabel Cardigos

Women's Stories Among Indigenous Peoples of the Russian Far East   285
Kira Van Deusen

Storytelling Traditions in Scotland   289
Barbara McDermitt

"Our Stories Are Not Just for Entertainment:
Lives and Stories Among the Travelling People of Scotland   301
Donald Braid

Storytelling in the Rhythm of People's Everyday Life:
An Investigation into Contemporary Slovakia   310
Gabriela Kiliánová

Problems in Translation and Storytelling Using Switzerland as Example   316
Barbara Gobrecht

Middle East and North Africa

Egyptian Peep-Show Storytelling   325
Kamal el dien Hussien

Narrating Epics in Iran   326
Mahmoud Omidsalar and Teresa Omidsalar

Stories About a Moroccan Storyteller   341
Deborah A. Kapchan

Storytelling in Palestine   344
Ibrahim Muhawi

Matrilineal Myths, Herbal Healing, and Gender in Tuareg Culture   348
Susan Rasmussen

Tunisian Storytelling Today   356
Sabra Webber

Native America

Storytelling and Teaching: A Cree Example   365
Kay Stone

What's in an Ending? Indian Storytelling of the Inland Northwest   369
Rodney Frey

Analysis of a Hupa Storytelling Event   371
Ruth Seiman Bennett

Traditional Storytelling at San Juan Pueblo   381
Sue-Ellen Jacobs and Esther Martinez (P'oe Tsawa)

Lushootseed Language and Story Revival   383
Vi (taqʷšəblu) Hilbert

North America

Where Have All the Märchen Gone?:
Or Don't They Tell Those Little Stories in the Ozarks Any More?   387
W.K. McNeil

Jack Tales   394
Carl Lindahl

Cowboy Poetry and Other Occupational Folk Poetry 398
Jens Lund

Del Ringer and His Tales of Salmon River, Idaho 403
Marjorie Bennett

Fifty Functions of Storytelling 408
Margaret Read MacDonald

"If We Don't Joke with Each Other, We Won't Have No Fun, Will We?"
Storytelling in the Richard Family of Rangeley, Maine 416
Margaret Yocom

Stories of Emergency Medical Responders 428
Timothy R. Tangherlini

Storytelling Style and Community Codes Among the Swiss Volhynian Mennonites 434
John McCabe-Juhnke

Storytellers and the Art of Storytelling in the Mexican Culture 442
Rosario S. Morales

Traditional Storytelling Among French Newfoundlanders 448
Gerald Thomas

Logger Poetry 453
Jens Lund

South America
Argentinian Folktale: A Genetic Approach 459
Maria Palleiro

The Art of Bahamian Narration 465
Daniel J. Crowley

"Fattening" in Belizean Creole Storytelling 467
Ervin Beck

Holding on to the Past: Maya Storytelling in Belize 471
David Pendergast

Function and Performance of the Chilean Folktale Today 475
Manuel Dannemann

Lira Popular in Chile: Between Traditional Poetry and Popular Urban Versifying 478
Marcela Orellana

Discourse and Storytelling in Otavalo Song: Resonance and Dissonance in San Juanitos 486
Linda D'Amico

Guaranitic Storytelling 490
Martha Blache

We Are the Real People: Tzotzil-Tzeltal Maya Storytelling on the Stage 494
Robert Laughlin

Fragments From the Past: The Politics of Storytelling in Morelos, Mexico 498
JoAnn Martin

Storytelling and Mental Representation Among Totonac Indians (Mexico)   502
Annamária Lammel

Exemplary Ancestors and Pernicious Spirits: Sibundoy Concepts of Cultural Evolution   513
John H. McDowell

Saramaka Maroon Folktales in Comparative Afro-American Perspective   522
Richard Price and Sally Price

The Art of Storytelling: Field Observations in Venezuela   528
Daniel Mato

Theory
Children's Telling of Ghost Stories   539
Sylvia Grider

Organizational Storytelling   544
Richard Raspa

The Role of Traditional Stories in Language Teaching and Learning   548
Martha S. Bean

The Storytelling Revival   552
Joseph Sobol

Preadolescent Girls' Storytelling   559
Elizabeth Tucker

An Analysis of Five Interviews with Storylisteners to Determine
How They Perceive the Listening Experience   563
Brian Sturm

Urban Legends   572
Jan Harold Brunvand

Cross-Culture, Cross-Class, Crossed Wires:
A Case Analysis of an Etic/Emic Storytelling Event   577
Wendy Welch

The Nature of Women's Storytelling   580
Linda Dégh

NOTES ON CONTRIBUTORS AND EDITORS   587

INDEX   605

Editor's Note

Storytelling, is it alive and well? Dead or dying? Has it returned to the sheltered (and largely undocumented) bosom of the family? Or has it simply jumped to a new host in the revivalist teller? Each of the essays presented here provides a possible answer to this question.

I had hoped to show in this collection that traditional storytelling is far from dead. Sadly, several tellers who grew up listening to traditional tellers report that this telling of their youth is no more. Others report that telling in certain venues—the home, for example—*does* continue, and others write of revivalist tellers who have given themselves the task of "taking care" of the folktale. Lee-Ellen Marvin discovered storytelling to children very much alive behind the closed doors of the middle-class Indian family home. Sabine Wienker-Piepho finds revivalist tellers caring for and reviving märchen telling in Germany. Raouf Mama writes of the demise of the type of home storytelling he experienced in his youth, blaming this loss on the advent of television and the fast pace of modern life.

Although the traditions of telling tales in the home and the small community may be waning in many locales, the telling of stories in schools, libraries, churches, community centers, parks, and hospitals seems to be thriving. The National Storytelling Association, based in the United States, has more than 5,000 members, and this clearly represents only a fraction of those individuals actually engaged in storytelling activity today.

Certainly the tradition of the *traveling* storyteller is thriving. Joseph Sobol writes of professional tellers in the United States, where hundreds of tellers earn their living by telling stories. Most tour widely throughout the United States and the world in order to earn this living.

Those of us who are a part of this traveling storyteller network and anyone who has lurked on the storyteller's listserv Storytell@venus.twu.edu can attest to the internationalism of the revivalist movement. In almost every country individuals are assuming the role of "storyteller" and beginning to nurture audiences and other tellers both in their own communities and abroad. In November 1998, tellers in São Paulo and Rio de Janeiro, Brazil, planned "Tellabration" events in which tellers from 10 countries told in 10 different languages.

The "Tellabration" movement was started by the National Association for the Preservation and Perpetuation of Storytelling (now the National Storytelling Association) in Jonesborough, Tennessee, to encourage tellers all around the globe to tell stories on one day in November—a worldwide celebration of story that its founder, J.G. Pinkerton, dubbed "Tellabration!" Although the village teller so coveted in our story mythology may have vanished with the village life that made his or her profession possible, the act of telling and the nurturing of the tale is perhaps as important to the human condition as ever. The tradition of telling tales is simply adapting itself to an electronic age. Both tales and tellers are thriving in today's global village.

In soliciting articles for this collection, I hoped to provide a format in which scholars who had experienced traditional storytelling events could share information about the content, context, and function of these events. I suggested that they discuss performance style, audience response, teller repertoire, or any other area that interested them. Some hit my suggested topics squarely, others selected more specific points to address. All shed interesting light on the state of traditional telling today.

You will find brief biographical information about the scholars at the end of this book. Working with these biographies, I was struck by the scholars' intense commitment to documenting story. You see here the fruit of many lifetimes devoted to listening, recording, and considering the art of the storyteller. Many have documented the traditions of their youth, others have spent years getting to know the traditions of another culture. This collection is but a glimpse into their many researches. I asked each scholar to provide a bibliography for further exploration. You will find these suggestions for "Further Reading" at the end of each essay. I hope you will use the lists and the information in the general index to explore the remarkable research of these and other scholars.

May you find this collection an exciting entrée into the amazement of our world's ongoing telling of tales.

Margaret Read MacDonald

Acknowledgments

Thanks to Linda Dégh, Jan Brunvand, Jens Lund, John McDowell, Harold Scheub, and Barre Toelken for encouragement and assistance with this enormous project.

For research assistance during the search for contributors I thank Julie MacDonald Martin and Nat Whitman. For translation I am extremely grateful to Winifred Jaeger, Jennifer MacDonald Whitman, and Catherine Racine.

Thank you to the Interlibrary Loan staff of the King County Library System in Bellevue, Washington, for bringing so many books to my door. And of course thanks to my long-suffering husband, Jim MacDonald, who must live amid the piles of books and manuscripts during the years it takes to complete such a project.

Sub-Saharan Africa

Hunters' Narratives

Stephen Belcher

Belcher shows us the figure of the hunter as brave adventurer. He discusses stories and epics centering on the hunter.

Hunting Groups in Africa

Hunting and foraging were central economic activities for many African people. Indeed, they are the original human activities, displaced and limited by developments such as pastoralism and agriculture, and until quite recently, parts of Africa offered groups who still subsisted in this manner. The best known may be the Khoi-San peoples of the Kalahari Desert in Southern Africa and the various pygmy groups of the central African rain forests, who have become almost legendary as living embodiments of a primordial way of life, but across the continent we find smaller, specialized hunting groups now assimilated into sedentary societies, preserving the traditions of a former way of life. Sometimes these groups retain a specific ethnic or professional identity within the larger culture. Elsewhere, hunting has become the profession of specialized groups whose members are subject to initiation and ritual constraints. Everywhere, hunting is associated with power of some sort, and hunters are figures of legend and adventure. They are credited not only with courage and skill, the qualities required to explore the unknown bush and to face large and fierce animals, but also with great occult knowledge and power, which are required to overcome the dangers of the unseen world and to protect men who deal in the death of other creatures.

Hunters' Narratives

Hunters' narratives thus range from the collective traditions of hunters' groups (all Khoi-San narratives, in some sense, might be termed hunters' narratives) to the specialized recitations of the hunters' associations to the folktales about hunters told by the nonspecialist. Hunters' narratives may also be incorporated into larger narratives: the Mongo cycle of the hero Lianja (central Zaire) includes a number of etiologic legends about certain techniques of hunting that also warn about the consequences of overhunting and the Sunjata epic of Mali also includes references to hunting, including one extended episode (the "Buffalo-Woman of Du").

Few hunters' narratives detail the technical or practical aspects of hunting save to describe their origin in etiologic myths. The narratives center rather on the social condition of the hunter and establish an equivalence between the human order in which the hunter lives and the natural and chaotic order in which he risks his life. A typical story line involves the confrontation of the hunter by some extraordinary beast, whose power is demonstrated by the defeat or humiliation of a series of lesser antagonists. The hunter, however, is not always victorious. In one story, recorded in Côte d'Ivoire, the elephant Kowulen kills the hunter Bamori, and one grisly Bamana (Mali) hunter's piece consists of a dialogue between a vulture, a hyena, and a wild pig over the carcass of a hunter. The hunter does usually win, however, and often his wife is brought into the story. Conjugal relations are a particularly attractive theme. One widespread story tells how the animals resolved to trap a too-successful hunter and sent one of their number, in the guise of a beautiful woman, to seduce him. Disregarding the warnings from his mother (or another), the hunter follows the animal-woman into the

3

bush and is almost killed, but he escapes thanks to secrets he had not revealed or to help from home. Another story requires that the hunter's wife help discover the secrets to the power of some monstrous beast through a partial seduction. Seydou Camara's *Kambili* is an example. The figure of the hunter thus becomes the vehicle for an opposition between the ordered world of human society and the dangers of nonsocial chaos. In many cases, the hunter becomes a primordial culture hero, differentiating the human world from that of the animals. This is the achievement of Kaggen (Mantis) in the Kalahari, and there is a certain resonance between his activities and adventures and those of more limited figures such as Moussa Gname or Fara Makan, the protagonists of different cycles of narratives collected along the Niger River at the turn of the twentieth century (Dupuis-Yacouba). Moussa Gname and Fara Makan move through a mythical world but are not its creators and shapers in the way that Kaggen is. The adventures of Moussa Gname are presented as a loose cycle that may overlap with the neighboring Mande hunters' traditions, in which the specialized performer's repertoire supposedly covers the stories of some forty-five master hunters. So far, however, no such complete cycle has been published.

Hunters' Songs

The most complex examples of hunters' verbal art come from the associations found in West Africa, where the varying traditions of hunters' poetry and incantations have been compounded with traditions of ceremonial song and, in certain cases, with epic narratives. A typical occasion nowadays seems to be the funeral of a senior hunter, and hunters' dirges have been recorded for the Yoruba, the Akan, and a number of Mande groups (Ajuwon). The Mande associations in particular have carried hunters' music out of its specialized context, and it is now a bestselling genre of popular music (in part, perhaps, because of the democratic organization of hunters' societies, in contrast to the socially stratified system outside the associations). Mande hunters' songs can also expand to become epic recitations, and a number of such recitations have been recorded and published from all parts of the Mande world: from northern Côte d'Ivoire, from Mali, from The Gambia. The late hunters' bard Seydou Camara is particularly well documented, but there are examples from other performers as well.

The Mande Hunters' Epic

The performance of a Mande hunters' epic (for which there exists the best information) occurs in a number of contexts and, increasingly, may simply serve as entertainment. The mastersinger (who may or may not play his own instrument, a form of harp-lute known as the *donso-ngoni*) is accompanied by colleagues or apprentices. One serves as a respondent, answering each line or rhythmic unit with an interjection or comment; others may play instruments. Charles Bird identified three modes of performance or vocal style while working with Seydou Camara. The first is the basic narrative, the second the song mode (lyric digressions to the narrative), and the third the "praise-proverb" mode, in which the performer strings together aphorisms, proverbs, and especially observations on the condition of the hunter and the burdens of his status. The third of these modes is not so obvious in the published texts of other performers, but at least one researcher, Karim Traore, while working with another prominent hunters' bard, Bala Jimbe Diakhite, found that in an evening's performance the narrative was almost never completed: the story was lost in the singing. The popularity of hunters' music and the democratic structure of the association may explain why modern pop music figures such as Salif Keita have turned to this style for inspiration and a certain measure of legitimation.

The Future

As the pace and the extent of modernization increases, it seems certain that the specialized narrations and song-genres of hunters will be absorbed into the larger culture, leaving the residual image of a bygone era and a certain set of narrative modes and stock figures. A recent movie such as *Guimba the Tyrant* (from Mali) turns the hunter into something of a folk hero: a virtuous master of the occult who finally defeats the corrupt ruler.

Further Reading

Ajuwon, Bade, *Funeral Dirges of Yoruba Hunters,* New York: NOK, 1982

Bird, Charles, "Heroic Songs of the Mande Hunters," in *African Folklore,* edited by Richard Mercer Dorson, New York: Anchor, 1972

Camara, Seydou, *Kambili,* edited and translated by Charles Bird, Bourama Soumaoro, Gerald

Cashion, and Mamadou Kante, Bloomington: Indiana University Linguistics Club, 1974

Cashion, Gerald, *Hunters of the Mande: A Behavioral Code and Worldview Derived from the Study of Their Folklore*, 2 volumes (Ph.D. diss., Indiana University), 1984

Cisse, Youssouf Tata, *La confrérie des chasseurs Malinké et Bambara: mythes, rites, et récits initiatiques*, Paris: Editions Nouvelles du Sud, 1994

Dupuis, Auguste Victor, *Les Gow, ou chasseurs du Niger*, Paris: Ernest Leroux, 1911; reprint, Nendeln: Kraus Reprint, 1974

Frobenius, Leo, *Dämonen des Sudan: Allerhand Religiöse Verdictungen*, Atlantis VII, Jena, Germany: Eugen Diederich, 1924

Herskovits, Melville, and Frances Herskovits, *Dahomean Narrative*, Evanston, Illinois: Northwestern University Press, 1958

Thoyer-Rozat, Annik, ed. and trans., *Chants de chasseurs du Mali*, volumes 1 and 2 by Mamadu Jara, volume 3 by Ndugacé Samaké, Paris: Thoyer-Rozat, 1978

Van der Post, Laurens, *The Heart of the Hunter*, New York: Morrow, 1961; Harmondsworth, England: Penguin, 1965

Central African Epics

Stephen Belcher

Stephen Belcher discusses elements of epic tradition from several central African cultures. He provides information on performance, context, and epic content.

Examples of Central African Epic

The narrative traditions of central Africa offer a grouping united by features of content and performance style that, owing to their length, their poetry, and their importance to the culture, are generally termed epic. Examples would include, from Congo (the former Zaire), the Mwindo epics of the BaNyanga, the Lega epics, and the Lianja cycle of the Mongo; other regions offer the Jeki la Nzambe of the Duala (Cameroon) and Ozidi of the Ijo (Nigeria). The *mvett* tradition of Cameroon and Gabon is also closely related in style.

These epics are the productions of specialists, often initiates into a spirit cult; the apprenticeship-initiation serves as training (observation and imitation of the master), as protection from the occult energies that are released in any performance, and as regulation of the creative process that inspires the poet. Boyer provides the fullest study of the performer's world for the Fang *be-bom-mvett*. The performances are also to be distinguished from ordinary folktales, narrated under a variety of circumstances, and from the output of specialized historical traditionalists such as were found in Rwanda and other kingdoms. The epics involve a team of performers, centered upon the master singer (male or female, although relatively few women's performances have been documented) and including musicians and other singers. Performances are typically public and festive events, although venues and occasions may vary. Among the Duala of the Cameroon, *Jeki* is now performed at wakes and funerals because it is a lengthy production that lasts most of the night and so simplifies the task of arranging entertainment. Among the Ba-Nyanga, Biebuyck has reported a far more sedate but intense variety of solo performance around the fires of hunting camps as a counterpart to the dramatic public spectacle recorded in a village. Performances typically mix a spoken narrative with frequent lyrical intrusions. The songs may be short onomatopoetic embellishments evoking the identity of a character or an activity such as paddling or running, or they may be extended meditations upon the poet's condition and the state of the world and only loosely related to the narrative (the *Mvet* of Zwe Nguema offers excellent examples of the latter). Other performance possibilities, not reflected in published texts and recordings, include dances in which the audience may engage and a high degree of mimetic action by the performer. Many passages of the *Ozidi Saga*, for instance, consist of dialogue between the hero and his antagonist, while the audience reactions and comments attest to effective nonverbal actions by the performer.

The length and scope of the performances will vary. Although the many adventures associated with the different heroes can be strung into a loose narrative sequence (a biographical pattern augmented with stories about the ancestors), it appears very rare for such a complete sequence to be performed—and in some cases it is explicitly claimed that the cycle has no end. A performance thus involves the selection of episodes to be presented in the time allowed. There are exceptions to this rule, such as the *Ozidi Saga*, which is presented as a complete sequence over a period of seven nights. Among the Fang, a *mvet* performance typically lasts an entire night; in this case, the performer, working without a fixed plot, develops as many threads as necessary in the course of the evening and then resolves them, sometimes abruptly, as the performance comes to a close. Generally, however, the model seems to be one of selection of appropriate and popular episodes from the cycle, according to the time allotted.

The hero is typically a precocious, often posthumous, child who springs from the womb (or sometimes the leg) ready to take on all comers and to avenge his (or his mother's) wrongs. He is usually assisted by a female relative: a sister, an aunt, or a grandmother, who provides instruction and magical support. His adventures constitute a series of confrontations, tests, and ordeals that may take him below the earth to the land of the spirits, over the waters, or into the sky. He works with magic rather than brute strength; the magic is often embodied in a talisman such as an amulet (the *ngalo* of Jeki) or a tool/weapon (Mwindo's conga-scepter) and may be invoked through songs. The hero's accomplishments, ultimately, establish a way of life, and in many regards he might be considered a culture hero. However, he often also shows signs of being a trickster, and there is some overlap between the adventures of a Lianja or a Mwindo and other (non-epic) tricksters such as Hlakanyaka of the Zulu. Nor is the hero always considered admirable; his power is often associated with arrogance. The mythical content of these adventures is strong, and the hero appears far more a demiurge than an ancestor.

The Fang *Mvett*

A related but distinct category of narratives is found among the Fang peoples on either side of the Cameroon-Gabon border. This genre is locally termed the *mvett*, and the word covers the instrument (a bamboo chordophone) and the genre of narrative-poetic performance. In most regards the performance style of the *mvett* seems identical to that of the other regional epics; the difference lies principally in the content. *Mvett* traditions are centered on a past mythical world dominated by two clans: the immortals of Engong, led by the powerful Akoma Mba, and the mortals of Oku. The plots develop from frictions and conflicts between these two groups. There appear to be no established story lines but rather a common set of recurring characters and narrative tropes. Romantic liaisons and the adventures of a traveling couple are a staple device, as are magical duels among the men over the women. Magic of various sorts plays a central role in the genre and may represent an artistic challenge for the performer (a competition of special effects); it also seems to be the mechanism for integrating modern elements into the stories. Plots will develop, over the course of a night's presentation, according to the performer's inspiration and audience interest, and will tend to be resolved abruptly as morning brings the performance to a close. The powers of Akoma Mba are essential for this method of closure, as he serves as a deus ex machina who appears to end the story. An interesting extension of the medium of the *mvett* is the work of Tsira Ndong Ndoutoume, who has produced literary examples of the *mvett*.

Further Reading

Austen, Ralph, *The Elusive Epic: Performance, Text and History in the Oral Narrative of Jeki La Njambé (Cameroon Coast)*, Atlanta, Georgia: African Studies Association Press, 1995

Bekombo, Manga, ed., *Défis et Prodiges: La fantastique histoire de Djèki-la-Njambé*, Paris: Classiques Africains, 1993

Biebuyck, Daniel, "The Epic as a Genre in Congo Oral Literature," in *African Folklore*, edited by Richard Mercer Dorson, New York: Anchor, 1972

———, *Hero and Chief: Epic Literature from the Banyanga Zaire Republic*, Berkeley: University of California Press, 1978

Biebuyck, Daniel, and Kahombo C. Mateene, *The Mwindo Epic*, Berkeley: University of California Press, 1969; London: University of California Press, 1971

Boyer, Pascal, *Barricades Mystérieuses et Pièges à Pensée: Introduction à l'analyse des épopées Fang*, Paris: Société d'Ethnologie, 1988

Clark-Bekederemo, J.P., *The Ozidi Saga*, Washington, D.C.: Howard University Press, 1991

Ndong Ndoutoume, Tsira, *Le Mvett*, Paris: Présence Africaine, volume 1, 1970; volume 2, 1975

N'Sanda Wamenka, *Récits épiques des Lega du Zaïre*, volumes 135 and 136 of Annales Sciences Humaine, Niamey, Niger: Agence de coopération culturelle et technique, 1992

Pepper, Herbert, and Paul P. de Wolf, eds., *Un Mvet de Zwé Nguéma: Chant épique fang,* Classiques africains, Paris: Armand Colin, 1972

Rop, A. de, *Lianja: L'épopée des Móngo,* Brussels, Belgium: Academie Royale des Sciences d'Outre-mer, 1964

To Make Our World a Gentler, More Compassionate World

Raouf Mama

Raouf Mama notes those storytelling traditions that continue in Benin and decries the loss of traditional telling in the home. He makes an impassioned plea for the need for story in today's world.

Storytelling in the Household

When I look back over the years of my childhood, memories of storytelling evenings in my household always bring the flicker of a smile to my face, and my heart sings with bittersweet joy. There was no television in those days, nor had the poison of the colonial educational system started to seep into our minds, and storytelling commanded the love and allegiance of my generation. I remember sitting with my brothers, my sisters, and other relatives in the living room or in our yard after the evening meal and listening while my mother, my stepmother, a relative, or a friend of the family led us, with splendid eloquence, through the wonderworld of stories of long ago.

We were treated to a wide range of stories: trickster tales, explanatory (*pourquoi*) tales, ghost stories, spiritual tales, dilemma stories, and stories about kings, children, orphans, and twins. All the stories had morals—they sounded a warning against the perils of hatred, envy, cruelty, greed, pride, prejudice, arrogance, sloth, and dishonesty. On the other hand, they pointed to the rewards of love, compassion, self-sacrifice, courage, patience, respect for the elderly, reverence for the sacred, and discretion.

In those stories, human beings, beasts, plants, and spirits interacted on a daily basis. It was common for animals, trees, and spirits to take human form to test, to punish, to hurt, or to help and reward human beings. Orphans, twins, and Yogbo the Glutton were familiar characters in those stories. Orphans were usually abused by their stepmothers, but they enjoyed supernatural protection and always conquered adversity. Twins were mysterious, unpredictable, and never given to idle chatter. They were demigods. Yogbo the Glutton, with his enormous appetite, was forever preying on children, fools, and anyone who let him. He was immune to violence, and he almost always escaped death. The only way to get the better of him was through cunning. My book *Why Goats Smell Bad and Other Stories from Benin* offers a representative sample of stories from my country.

Children were not supposed to tell stories during our storytelling evenings—that was the preserve of grown-ups—but we were encouraged to ask questions and make comments for purposes of clarification. In opening a story, the storyteller would compare it to a bird taking flight. Wherever the story alighted would be its setting, and whomever it alighted on was the main character. At the end of the story would follow a debate during which everyone had a chance to comment on its moral and establish connections between the story and real-life experiences. The questions, the comments, and the debates that followed the stories made storytelling a lively conversation between storyteller and audience.

The Decline of Storytelling in the Home

In the space of 12 years—from 1960, when Benin was granted independence, to 1972, the year of the

Beninese revolution—storytelling evenings in Beninese homes declined considerably. Today, that time-honored tradition has gone out of existence. Much of the blame for this must be laid on the colonial educational system, which sought to make the Beninese look down on his native tongue, customs and traditions, culture, and folklore. We were taught that we were primitive and that we had no history, no stories worth telling, and no civilization. In addition to the educational system, the ascendancy of television, the stresses and strains of urbanization, and increasing economic hardship have played a part in the demise of the tradition of storytelling evenings in Beninese households. And with its passing, a valuable educational tool and an important source of entertainment have been lost.

To be sure, people go on telling stories in my country. Folktales are often featured on our national radio. Our singers, both traditional and modern, retell our stories and myths in their songs. Our diviners, generally called *Bokonon* or *Babalawo,* often tell stories as part of their divination. Each sign of the *Ifa* oracle has a story attached to it, and some of our *Ifa* priests are accomplished storytellers. But storytelling evenings in Beninese households that bring together children and adults—men and women—in a ritualistic sharing of folktales and myths are a thing of the past!

Before the whirlwind of colonial conquest broke in on my people, storytelling was an important means of preserving cultural tradition and a potent tool for instructing the young and preparing them for adult life. It served as a source of inspiration in fashioning a moral code and gave the whole community a sense of belonging. It provided a thread connecting the living, the dead, and the unborn. In undermining our pride in our culture, customs, and traditions, in cutting us off from our storytellers, the colonial power put chains around our minds that can be broken only through a process of reeducation, a process that Ngugi wa Thiong'o eloquently expounds in *Decolonising the Mind.* The retrieval of our folktales from oblivion and the reawakening of the Beninese people, especially the young, to the folktales' timeless beauty and power are inescapable parts of the task of decolonization to which my country must settle down if she is to fulfill her destiny.

The Importance of Preserving and Retelling Folktales

A realization of the necessity of preserving and retelling the folktales from my country came to me when I was a graduate student at the University of Michigan and working on my dissertation on images of Africa and Africans in Western literature. Most of the novels and stories I read were shot through with prejudice. Most of the images were distorted—untrue to African culture and the African personality. I could not recognize myself or any of the people I knew in Conrad's *Heart of Darkness,* nor could I agree with the omniscient narrator in Conrad's "An Outpost of Progress" when he said that the language spoken by the Africans was "one of the impossible languages" that civilized men sometimes hear in their dreams. I was equally troubled by the narrator's description of the town of Fada and its people in Joyce Cary's *Mister Johnson:*

> Poverty and ignorance, the absolute government of jealous savages, conservative as only the savage can be, have kept it at the frontier of civilization. Its people would not know the change if time jumped back fifty thousand years. They live like mice or rats on a palace floor; all the magnificence and variety of the arts, the ideas, the learning and the battles of civilization go on over their heads and they do not even imagine them. (p. 99)

My dissatisfaction found support in the writings of Chinua Achebe, Ngugi Wa Thiong'o, British historian Basil Davidson, and others. For example, in an essay titled "The Novelist as a Teacher," Chinua Achebe argues that it is the responsibility of the African scholar or writer to teach his or her fellow Africans that "their past—with all its imperfections—was not one long night of savagery from which the first Europeans acting on God's behalf delivered them" (*Hopes and Impediments,* p. 45).

The more I read, the more urgent Chinua Achebe's call sounds in my ears. But what could I do in answer to the call? Then I realized that I could lend a voice to the stories of my people, for those stories present men, women, and children whose humanity stood in contrast to the savagery put forward as the defining feature of Africans in most of the expatriate works I had read. I had heard the lies told by foreigners about my fellow Africans, I knew some of our stories, and I had the training and the tools I would need to make them come alive. To have heard the call and to have done nothing would have been an unpardonable dereliction of duty.

Thus, I started recording and retelling in English some of my country's folktales. As a storyteller, I draw inspiration from the storytellers of my childhood—my mother, my stepmother, my grandfather, my grandmother, and many others. That is why, like them, I start my stories with the metaphor of the bird taking flight: "My story takes flight, over countries and kingdoms of long ago and alights on. . . ."

Retelling in English or French oral stories that I have heard in my mother tongues, Fon and Yoruba, is fraught with difficulty. I have to find in English or French words and idioms to express ideas and concepts that are not readily translatable. I have to convey to men, women, and children unfamiliar with my culture and my country most of the sights, sounds, and smells implicit in the stories I am sharing with them. Furthermore, I have to find a way of enlisting, whenever possible, the participation of my audience in my retelling of a story, for audience participation is crucial to my childhood experience of storytelling. Unless I fulfill all these conditions, I will be unfaithful to the unique tradition I seek to uphold.

Whenever I tell a story from my country, my goal is to share some of my culture with my audience, to point out to them some of the moral and ethical values by which my people have lived through the centuries and how they have coped with change. Above all, I try to make them see the fundamental human similarities that lie beyond differences of culture, race, color, religion, and political creed.

In her introduction to *Favorite Folktales from around the World*, Jane Yolen lays her finger on what I consider one of the essential virtues of storytelling: "Folktales are powerful, they are a journey and a joining. In a tale we meet new places, new peoples, and new ideas. And they become our places, our peoples, our ideas." Julius Lester makes a similar point in his foreword to *Black Folktales*: "Folktales," he suggests, "are stories that give people a way of communicating with each other about each other."

To travel to new places, meet new peoples, acquire new ideas, and tell each other about each other—therein perhaps lies the source of the power of storytelling. Through the stories we tell each other, we can set back the frontier of ignorance and darkness. We can strike a blow against prejudice. We can help tame the savagery within the human breast and make our world a gentler, more compassionate world. Folktales remind us again and again that despite all our differences we are bound up in a common destiny, that the human race has one color, which is the color of blood.

What James Baldwin said about the blues in "Sonny's Blues," one of the greatest short stories ever written, applies to folktales as well: "They were not about anything very new. . . . For while the tale of how we suffer, and how we are delighted, how we may triumph is never new, it always must be told. There isn't any other tale to tell."

Thus, it is important that we listen to each other's stories with our inner ears, for only then, as George Eliot observes in *Middlemarch*, can we hear "the roar on the other side of silence" and only then can we really live out the ideal of the world as a global village. But we cannot listen to each other's stories unless we quicken our awareness of the vital importance of our oral traditions. We must learn anew and teach our children and our children's children the stories that are part of our cultural heritage. Unless we do, our lives will be barren, and our hearts will ache.

The storyteller has a primordial role to play in the task of education and reeducation that lies ahead. By virtue of his position, the storyteller stands shoulder to shoulder with the writer, the poet, and the artist as the sensitive point of his or her people's conscience. In the best tradition of storytelling, the storyteller must find "where the laughter lies, like gold in the rock" (Margaret Laurence, "Godman's Master"); he or she must give the audience a sense of belonging; he or she must "strengthen flagging courage and inspire hope in hours of despair"(Bertrand Russell, "A Free Man's Worship"). In the magic circle of the storyteller's art, the listener catches a distant glimpse of "the whole drama of the human heart, with its laughter and tears, its fulfillments and failures"(Rabindranath Tagore, "Poet Yeats").

The Revival of the Storytelling Tradition

The revival of the storytelling tradition in the United States, Britain, and many other parts of the Western world is one of the most hopeful cultural trends of our time. The countless storytelling festivals, workshops, and conferences that take place in those countries every year symbolize a cultural reawakening that has yet to come to my people and the peoples of Africa. In the meantime, our elderly are dying off, taking with them some of our best folktales. "When an old person dies, it is as though a whole library has gone up in smoke," the saying goes. To this day, hundreds of oral stories exist of which no record remains except in the memories of our elderly. Of far greater importance, however, is the revival of the storytelling tradition as an educational tool, a source of moral guidance, and a valuable means of entertainment.

But there can be no revival unless our storytellers, like our writers, our poets, and our artists, feel a deep commitment to their craft, unless they have faith in their vision and are sustained by an inner power stronger than the fear of hostility or persecution and deeper than the desire for material rewards.

Now, a tendency exists in the United States and other parts of the Western world to trivialize storytelling and a belief that storytelling is just for children. Nothing could be farther from the truth. Like food, water, and air, like hope, faith, and love, storytelling is for everyone. If the truth be told, grown-ups are in greater need of stories because of all their hurts, hang-ups, pride, fears, and hatreds.

By virtue of its healing power, its potential for lowering some of the barriers dividing humankind against itself, and its strength as a multicultural learning and teaching tool, storytelling is a great and noble calling.

As an African storyteller from Benin, I rejoice in my position as a modern-day griot engaged in the struggle to save from permanent loss one of the richest folklore traditions in Africa. Furthermore, I feel myself especially blessed for the opportunity I have been given to play a part in countering the curse of prejudice, racism, and bigotry that has haunted the human race since the dawn of history.

Further Reading

Achebe, Chinua, *Hopes and Impediments: Selected Essays,* London: Heinemann, 1988; New York: Doubleday, 1989

Courlander, Harold, and George Herzog, *The Cow-Tail Switch, and Other West African Stories,* New York: Holt, 1947

Lester, Julius, *Black Folktales,* New York: Baron, 1969

Mama, Raouf, *"Why Goats Smell Bad" and Other Stories from Benin,* North Haven, Connecticut: Linnet, 1998

Ngugi Wa Thiong'o, *Decolonising the Mind: The Politics of Language in African Literature,* Portsmouth, New Hampshire: Heinemann, 1986; London: Currey, 1986

The Fulani Epics

Christiane Seydou

Christiane Seydou discusses features of the Fulani epic, examines specific epic types in Senegal and Mali, and points out the importance of the motto in epic.

Distribution of the Fulani (Fulbe) Peoples and Common Features of the Fulani Epic

The Fulani (singular, Pullo), or Fulbe, are present everywhere in the Sahelian zone of the African continent, from Senegal in the west to southern Sudan in the east and to the Central African Republic in the south. Varying according to the place and time, communities have been more or less numerous and have occupied different situations among other peoples, from small groups of herdsmen who even now lead a nomadic life (e.g., the Wodaabe in Niger) to the vast nation-states of the eighteenth and nineteenth centuries that were wiped out by the colonial conquest (Futa Jalon in Guinea, Sokoto in Nigeria, Adamawa in Cameroon, Massina in Mali, and the Tukulor empire in Senegal). The variety of circumstances that the Fulani communities have experienced has undoubtedly left its mark on their ways of thinking and of living, but it has not impaired their awareness of sharing a common culture and—in spite of dialectal differences—a common language (called Pulaar or Fulfulde) classified as an Atlantic branch of Nigero-Congolese languages. Their literary production is extremely rich in oral forms, dominated by poetry and epic, as well as in written forms; from Islamic influences they have acquired a tradition of scholarly literature written in Adjami script. On the ideological plane, the Fulani envision their culture as resting on three pillars (even though, often enough, this is a matter of mental representation rather than of hard facts): herdsmanship, *pulaaku* (the emblematic Fulani code of ethical, social, and psychological behavior), and Islam.

All three elements are apparent in the main trends of Fulani epics:

1. epics of a historical-legendary type, based on a truly historical foundation, reconstrued and reinterpreted so as to comply with the literary rules of the genre

2. epics of a "corporative" type, produced by groups living in a close relation with the world of nature (fishermen, hunters, cattle raisers)

3. epics extolling the achievements of jihad heroes.

Best known are the epics recorded in Senegal and Mali. In Senegal, the epic genre draws on all three lines of inspiration, while in Mali, the historical type comes foremost. On a social plane, this literary genre appears to be related to a type of social organization common to all human societies in West Africa, where it flourishes. These societies are based on a hierarchical system of personal status and a class system having three tiers: those who were born free, those who were captured or who were born in bondage, and the "caste people." This last class covers the whole range of craftsmen, including those who specialize in the musical and verbal arts, usually called griots—some of whom are specifically the authorized depositories of the epic legacy.

It should be noted that the epic genre, present as it is in the western part of the Fulani area, is strangely absent from the eastern part. It is even unfamiliar to groups that are still completely nomadic, faithful to their ageless way of living and only superficially influenced by Islam, such as the Wodaabe of Niger, whose social organization is based on lineage and knows no castes. The same absence has been noted in the sedentary communities in Adamawa (Cameroon), where a reformist brand of Islam became the rule at the time when a new empire instigated a rigidly structured social and political regime. This absence can be explained by several reasons. One is the sociocultural situation of the non-Fulani populations living there, who had no griots or epics. Another reason is the political-religious power of the Fulani, who were determined, in the name of orthodoxy, to unify society by canceling clan names and mitigating the effects of the caste system. They felt that the values extolled by the epic were incompatible with the virtues advocated by religion.

In contrast to this situation, in those regions of the Fulani area where the epic genre is alive, there is an obvious awareness of the leading role played by the epic in passing down the cultural heritage to future generations. The epic's mere persistence and its resistance to the impact of modernity—especially in its musical component—testify to the importance of the values it conveys.

These epic stories have many features, both of content and of form, in common with stories prevailing all over the world. In terms of contents, they are narrative texts telling of emblematic characters engaged in heroic actions that embody those ideological features with which the community identifies itself. Characteristics of their form are several: a clearly typified mode of declamation combining rhythm and stressed syllables that may evoke poetry (although it is prose); a musical accompaniment on string instruments (a prevalent feature all through the world's epic production); a "formula" style, either in the characters' mottoes, in place-names, or in certain conventional narrative motifs; action that is structured into separate episodes ultimately making up a gest but with each episode being self-contained in a recurrent pattern leading to an acme, an agonistic situation whose outcome brings the action to an end.

The specificity of these epics is that they are "acts of speech" in oral form, in which one cannot separate the text from its special mode of declamation and from the status of those who participate in its enunciation—the whole process being both a product and a testimony of the sociocultural context. Their main characteristic lies in the semantic purpose: they are essentially meaningful. Characters and events illustrate the main ideological trends that make up the identity values lying at the root of the community. In this respect, this is the most important literary genre, both culturally and politically. The semantic purpose would be aimless, however, if it were not matched with a pragmatic purpose: to evoke in the audience—through a carefully staged expression especially targeted to that end—an intense collective excitement that rekindles not only the awareness of the ideological foundations of the community but also a longing for the perpetuation of these values.

The Fulani Epic in Senegal

In Senegal, the epic is alive among both the Fulani and their Wolof neighbors. Given the fact that both Fulani and Tukulor societies include, besides their craftsmen's castes, some well-typified professional groups, such as Sebbe (warriors), Subalbe (fishermen), and Toorobbe (persons endowed with political and religious powers), Tukulor society is more elaborate than elsewhere because of the historical existence of al-Hajj Umar, the founder of the Tukulor empire in the nineteenth century.

The Historical-Legendary Epic

The best-known gest in this class is that of Samba Gelajo Jegi (of the Denyanke dynasty, founded by Koli Tengella around the middle of the sixteenth century). The troubled historical events of that time were reconstrued in the epic, which elaborates on Samba's adventures along a somewhat stereotyped pattern and shows him to be the victim of an uncle, the usurper of the power that should have been Samba's. The latter recovers it thanks to a magic weapon offered by a water jinni and to an army of Moorish allies. This invincible hero will only be killed through a woman's treachery. Samba Gelajo is the archetypal Fulani epic hero embodying the *pulaaku* virtues: unyielding pride, boundless courage, a keen sense of honor, and independence. Furthermore, it should be noted that the story itself is rich in unexpected events and adventures (which brings to mind the Malinke Sunjata epic) quite to the contrary of the corporative type of epic, which has a much less eventful development.

The Corporative Epic
The Pekaafi of the Subalbe. (The Subalbe is a social and professional class of fishermen among the Haalpulaar'en, or pularophones.) This type differs from the others on several counts: it is sung without instrumental accompaniment, not by a griot but by a singer from a special clan (the Jeeybe), and it is combined with specific ceremonial exercises. The *Pekaan* tells of the winning fights of the heroes who represent this group—but also, quite often, of their lost battles against a devastating hippopotamus, a monster jinni, and so forth. Such incidents are told in the general context of a ritual crocodile hunt, in which technical skill needs the support of magic powers (such as happens every time a man must placate those supernatural powers that are implicated in his predatory activity over the environment). The core of such stories is simple and straightforward, along the minimal pattern of epic adventures: the hero is challenged to face the enemy in an ultimate fight, a pattern also common to cattle breeders' stories.

Daari of cattle breeders. The Fulani cattle breeders' *Daari* can be considered in parallel with the fishermen's *Pekaan* only because both maintain a professional relation to nature and the animal world. In fact, the difference between these texts and historical-legendary epics lies only in their subject matter. They tell of the heroic cycles of characters who lived in the second half of the nineteenth century—Ama Sam Polel, Gelel Yero, Gumallo, Hammel Tiam, and others—but they deal only with cattle thefts, for various reasons a very common activity at that time in that region, mentioned in the epics only as a pretense for extolling the *pulaaku.* The characters are all peers who are often separated only by having their origins in different Fulani groups (Jengelbe and Yalalbe, for instance). The heroic feat of taking someone else's herd is justified only by the desire to gain celebrity by outdoing one's peers, not in wealth but in terms of courage, and thus in fame. Such stories, containing very little action but emphasizing psychological features, are the most revealing examples of what the Fulani people hold as ideal behavior. A parallel can be drawn between them and some episodes of the Massina epic, in Mali.

The Religious Epic
El Hadj Omar Tall, a historic Tukulor character who expanded his empire from Futa Toro to Mali, is the hero of an epic cycle recounting his conquests in the name of jihad. Apart from the traditional interpretation given by griots, however, there is a scholarly rendering that has taken the form of *qacida,* after the Arabian poetic form, and is sung without instrumental accompaniment. One example is the work of the well-known poet Mohammadu Aliyu Caam, who used the information collected from historical chronicles by learned people and developed them into an epic poem of considerable length that, when sung to an audience, extols this national hero and makes him familiar to everybody.

The Fulani Epic in Massina (Mali)
The Massina area in Mali, which the Fulani have called the "navel" of the Fulani world, is particularly representative of the Fulani culture: cattle breeding is practiced largely, if not on a nomadic basis, at least by transhumance over large expanses; Islam is deeply rooted and maintains numerous teaching centers of long standing; literary production is extremely rich and varied, in both narrative forms and poetry—the successive layers of cultural heritage have thrived there; and as regards epics, they are so famous that they have overflowed to the east and west of the area.

Although the Massina Fulani have a long historical tradition, the characters in these epic texts date back only to the last two centuries. The historical type of epic is predominant and has two strains that can be identified: a legendary type extolling pre-Islamic heroes and a type inspired by historical chronicles dealing with the *Dîna,* the founding of the Fulani empire in Massina by Seku Amadu in the beginning of the nineteenth century. In these gests, the characters are therefore either "Arbe's sons" (the heroes of the time when Fulani local powers were vassals of the Bambara kingdom) or warriors fighting for Seku Amadu at the time of the *Dîna.*

Although both groups are faithful to the Fulani ideal in all their actions, it is still among the former that this ideal is illustrated in the most striking manner. Actually, these heroes are well characterized, each having one dominant virtue: Silamaka has courage along with discretion and finesse; Ham-Bodejo is extremely courageous, to the point of being cruel, so proud that he easily takes offense and so sensitive about his honor as to ignore all humanitarian scruples. Bubu Ardo Galo is so proud and attached to the noble ideal that he cannot yield to any type of law, even God's, if it gets in the way of human dignity. They all nurture a keen sense of independence that finds all sorts of outlets, in various degrees and in different fields—from the most obvious to the most hidden, from the political to the psychological and ethical planes. This is the driving force in a range of situations that give rise to epic stories. Some touch upon universal themes, such as rebellion against an overlord and refusal to pay tribute (Silamaka and Pullori), revolt against the imposition of Islamic rule as it contravenes Fulani customary law (Bubu Ardo Galo), or a decision to carry out a revenge for the sake of a young Fulani woman's mother who has been slighted (a frequent excuse taken by several heroes to justify their attacks upon a Bambara chief). Less familiar, however, are other epic situations that are more genial to their culture—for instance, the many episodes telling of opponents who are not enemies (neither by tradition nor owing to specific circumstances) but companions of similar origin and social class; honor demands that peers and opponents who respect one another should fight it out.

There are numerous examples of such unmotivated and welcome provocations that only serve the literary purpose of challenging the heroes to fulfill themselves by revealing their Fulani identity. The common pattern guiding their actions is one of the most constant features in all the epics: the core is a transgression (rejection of a compelling law, or constraint, or behavioral norm, and so forth) usually deriving from a challenge (called by another person or by the hero himself) and leading to an agonistic situation, the keystone of the drama: the situation resulting from the very nature of the hero serves the purpose of revealing his nature while offering a symbolic illustration of the basic constituents of the ideological identity of the Fulani community.

A feature common to all epic heroes, especially noticeable in Fulani epics, is the paroxysmal character of their personalities and deeds. They are—and must remain—impossible to emulate. They are not models to be copied; their behavior is excessive. The epic has no pedagogic or exemplary ambition: it conveys in an emblematic and symbolic way an ideological identity endowed with a powerful drive to stimulate a general awareness of this ideology and to provoke the will to realize or reactivate the identity values. This driving force is partly supported by the declamatory form of the text and its musical accompaniment but mostly by the very status of the speaker.

The Motto

The Fulani epic, with its compulsory musical accompaniment, is in fact directly related to an important cultural element: the motto. In traditional Fulani society one of the main functions of the *maabo* griot was to play on his lute the musical motto of his "master," the head of a family to which, from father to son, he was bound in a very peculiar relationship of alliance and clientship. This relationship was founded on mutual dependence: economic dependence for the griot, social and psychological dependence for the "master." It is said that, through the motto, the *maabo nanngi* takes (or seizes) his "master"; a listener feels himself overwhelmed by the hearing of his motto, which is a means of emblematic and glorifying designation. This musical motto has a corresponding verbal motto, a concise, pithy and metaphoric formula that is a sublimated definition of the person and identifies him in an ideal manner.

To the musician's talent the griot adds the mastery of words. By the power of words and his specific status, the *maabo* wields with the motto a means of influencing not only the personality of the person whom he addresses but even his destiny; indeed, by declaiming to him the motto or by playing it on his lute, he compels the person to conform to the ideal image given of him. And through the exaltation produced by the motto, the *maabo* forces the "master" into fulfilling his most authentic self. Many anecdotes and episodes of epic narrative illustrate this.

The epic narrative is sustained from beginning to end in its declamation by a musical theme, which is nothing but the hero's motto; each melodic theme has a proper name. On this canvas, woven at will from an infinite number of variations on the basic theme, are grafted at times motifs common to the whole range of epic texts—muster drums, military cavalcades, vultures feeding on the dead on the battlefield—and at other times more personal and less conventional interpretations, kinds of original descriptive tableaux in which language sometimes gives way to music.

The paramount importance of the musical motto in the epic of this society as well as in that of the neighboring Bambara society is such that people hold that there can be no epic for a person who has not won his own motto: only those who have deserved a motto can be celebrated.

The very concept of the epic genre, in fact, comprises this fundamental constituent element: the musical expression (or, more accurately, instrumental music) of the lute *(hoddu)*. For even though the text has a well-determined structure and the hero a specific type of behavior, this is still not sufficient to define completely the narrative genre as epic. It absolutely requires its musical accompaniment, supplied by the lute. The *Pekaan*, in Senegal, is the only epic that does not call upon an instrumental accompaniment, a fact that may be explained partly by the fact that this text is a component in a complex ceremony in which effects of a different order assume the function otherwise played by music. Both the griot and his audience consider, moreover, that the lute "speaks." The lute, however, can do more than merely "speak," as can the words of the griot, which "take hold" of the person whom they address. The lute, then, exercises a power, an influence over every listener. In fact, by their emblematic character the melodies played on the lute, in evoking in the listeners a shared emotion or an internalized exaltation, plunge them into a sort of fervent communion, into the celebration of the cultural identity that the heroes embody.

In this society the epic, just like the personal motto for individuals, seems to function as a collective motto, the epic narrative being an extended metaphor of what constitutes the distinctive identity of the Fulani people: *the pulaaku.*

Translated by Nicole Lévy

Further Reading

Ba, Amadou-Hampâté, and Lilyan Kesteloot, "Silâmaka, épopée Peule," *L'Homme* 8:1 (1968)

Caam, Mohammadu Aliyu, *La Vie d'El Hadj Omar, Qacida en poular transcription, traduction, notes et glossaire par Henri Gaden,* Travaux et Mémoires de l'Institut d'Ethnologie 21, Paris: Institut d'ethnologie, 1935

Correra, Issagha, *Samba Guéladio: épopée Peule du Fuuta Tooro,* Initiations et Études Africaines, Dakar, Senegal: Université de Dakar, 1992

Johnson, John William, Thomas Hale, and Stephen Belcher eds., *Oral Epics from Africa: Vibrant Voices from a Vast Continent,* Bloomington: Indiana University Press, 1997

Kesteloot, Lilyan, and Bassirou Dieng, *Les épopées d'Afrique Noire,* Paris: Karthala Editions UNESCO, 1997

Ly, Amadou, *L'épopée de Samba Guéladio Diégui,* Paris, Silex-Unesco, 1990

Meyer, Gérard, *Récits épiques Toucouleurs: La Vache, le Livre, la Lance,* Paris: Karthala-A.C.C.T., 1991

Ndongo, Siré Mamadou, *Le Fantang: Poèmes Mythiques des Bergers Peuls,* Paris: Karthala, 1986

Ngaide, Mamadou Lamine, *Le Vent de la Razzia, ou, Les aventures de Amadou Sam Polel et de Goumalel: Deux Récits épiques peuls et français, enregistrés auprès de Sidi Mbothiel, du village de Fété Bowé, Matam,* Dakar, Senegal: IFAN, Departement des littératures africaines, 1983

Seydou, Christiane, ed., *La Geste de Ham-Bodêdio: ou, Hama le Rouge,* Classiques Africains 18, Paris: A. Colin, 1976

————, "Jeu de pions, jeu des armes. Le combat singulier dans l'épopée peule," *Cahiers de Litterature Orale, no32, Epopées* (1992)

Sy, Amadou Abel, *Seul Contre Tous, Deux Récits épiques des pêcheurs du Fouta Toro,* Traditions Orales, Dakar, Senegal: Nouvelles Editions Africaines, 1978

Tinguidji, *Silâmaka et Poullôri: Récit épique Peul,* edited by Christiane Seydou, Classiques Africains 13, Paris: A. Colin, 1972

The Ga Folktale: Context, Themes, and Techniques

Abu Shardow Abarry

Abu Shardow Abarry analyzes the context, themes, and techniques of Adesa Ga storytelling.

Introduction

The folktale is probably the most popular genre in Ga oral prose narratives. Although the folktale is often associated with legends and myths because of the generic affinity with these genres, Ga folktales are significantly different from other folk genres. Myths, for example, are generally held in high esteem by the people because they feature recognizable gods, ancestral spirits, and other supernatural beings as major characters (Bascom 1965). As such, myths are regarded as explanatory systems rather than literal historical accounts of humankind's relationship with God and the mystery of life, creation, and nature. Legends too are used in theology and ritual; for they also contain stories about certain past personalities and episodes. But the past dealt with in legends is less remote than the past that myths describe. Legends are considered to be serious, sacred, and "true," but less so than myths. In contrast to these forms, folktales are considered to be basically fictions that recounts the adventures or experiences of tricksters, humans, animals, ogres, deities, and supernatural beings. However, the distinctions noted among myths, legends, and folktales are not watertight because of the degree of overlap that exists between the sacred and the profane and among various categories of African oral literature (Okpewho 1992). In what follows below I focus on the Ga folktale, the various situational contexts in which it is performed, its major thematic issues, and the techniques by which it is performed.

Context

Storytelling among the Ga is mainly an adult activity but children may also participate depending upon their age and conduct as well as the tale type and context.[1] Since storytelling sessions are also family and community meeting times, proper conduct demands deference to the older members present. Children who participate see this not only as entertainment but also as an opportunity to learn narrative techniques and community values. Professionalism, in the Eurocentric sense, does not exist, though some individuals or groups have become recognized for their special talents and expertise, which consist of a good command of language, a repertoire of tales, sound knowledge of traditional history, a sense of the dramatic, and good narrative skills. Such semiprofessional individuals and groups are usually invited to perform on special occasions such as a festival, a family reunion, or a wake.

Tales are conventionally performed in the evening or at night because this is the time when most people are free from work and ready for relaxation and entertainment. Moreover, the night provides an ideal fantasy-inducing aura that emanates from the spiritual brightness of the moon, the wistful twinkling of the stars, and the flow of the evening log fire. Today, folktales are performed in living rooms and elementary school classrooms in addition to the traditional neighborhood and courtyard locations.[2] There are no fixed times for beginning and ending the performance. Once there is a storyteller and a considerable number of interested people, a session can begin. As the night matures, individuals, depending upon their own dispositions and commitments, continue to add to the growing audience. Other individuals may begin to leave in the course of the session after listening to particular episodes; the audience will gradually reduce in this way until it becomes meaningless to continue. Generally, though, the session is brought to an end through consensus after a reasonable period of storytelling, regardless of the time or the size of the remaining audience.

Themes

The main themes depicted in Ga folktales include relationships between spouses; qualities of leadership; the negative effects of selfishness, foolishness, falsehood, treachery, and witchcraft; and the rewards of loyalty, honesty, wisdom, courage, and hard work. Generally, such themes are presented realistically, but they are occasionally given a fantastic dimension. For instance, characters may assume the form and language of other creatures. This is so because the stories are set in a world in which the existential barriers between humans, animals, spirits, and even inanimate things are dispensed with, making it possible for all these entities to interact on the same plane (Jahn 1961).

Even when the characters are not human, they are imbued with human qualities, and are regarded for all practical purposes as human surrogates. This is true of virtually all parts of the African continent (Owomoyela 1979). For example, among the human characters, certain types recur: the jealous wife, the neighborhood gossip, the wicked stepparent, and the disobedient child. Because the animal characters are often well-known types, their very names have become synonyms in regular speech for the qualities they represent. For example, Monkey is renowned for opportunism and quick wit; Hare, Rabbit, Tortoise, or Spider for cunning and rascality; Elephant and Hippopotamus for their considerable strength and small brains; and Dog for greed. Because the characters represent such stock roles, it is very easy for the audience to discern and follow the dramas in each tale and at times to guess the outcome as soon as the characters are announced.

Though these Ga stories are performed mainly for entertainment, they also contain moral, social, and religious instruction. The tales validate Dundes's (1965) observation that such aspects of folklore help to educate the young, create a group's sense of solidarity, and provide a vehicle for social protest. Because the characters used in the tales represent both positive and negative human qualities, outcomes of dramatic conflicts indicate the values approved by the community and thus influence members toward desirable action. This moral intent is so important that the storytellers and members of their audiences often pause during the performance to moralize and sermonize. Most tales, therefore, tend to end on a moral note: "this is why you should not blab indiscreetly about what you see," or "why you should not be too stubborn or vainglorious."

Techniques

The complete realization of the Ga tale relies on the manipulation of a number of narrative techniques and strategies not only by the storyteller but also by the spectator-participants. These consist of effective use of speech, cultural crafts, improvisation, humor, and call and response. Unlike the written folktale, these strategies and other resources of the oral tale can be adequately appreciated only within the context of performance.[3]

The actual storytelling normally begins after a brief period of free-for-all communal riddle telling. When this is over, the narrator takes his position, usually at the center of the circle of people or at the open end of the horseshoe formed by the participants. He or she usually begins with an opening formula:

Ntaii ye loo'nka tan nye?
Shall I narrate to you or shall I not?

And the whole gathering responds:

Won hele bo no
We are listening

or

Tan Wo
Narrate to us.

This rhetorical formula establishes initial rapport between the narrator and the audience. Having engaged their attention, the narrator then plunges directly into the action but first hints at what the story is about: "Once there was famine in the world," or "All the animals decided to go on a journey," or "Once there was a beautiful queen." The story moves gradually through various episodes to a climax and finally to the denouement. All the while intermittent singing and dancing characterize the performance. At the end of the story, the narrator states the moral and then utters the closing formula:

Ke 'na ekoe nka tan nyetoi asee
If I had any, I've narrated them behind your
    ears.

This formula indicates that the narrator has formally come to the end of the narration of a particular story. By saying the stories are told "behind" rather than "into" the audience's ears, the narrator reminds them that the truths of the stories are metaphorical and symbolic, not literal, and should be taken as such. One story follows another far into the night. The session ends with the audience chanting playfully the closing formula: "*kakalika jee m'to: asee*" (cockroach, get off my ears), symbolizing once again the pure fantastic and unrealistic dimensions of the stories to be discarded (see table).

The narrator's techniques are generally rhetorical and self-expressive. Beginning with the effective use of the opening formula, the narrator tries to involve the audience in the action of the story. He or she may direct a remark to a member of the audience; he or she sometimes arouses their emotions, causing them to react to dramatic points like jokes, funny words, ridiculous exaggerations, or mimicry. He or she also uses simple language, but monotony is avoided by the intermittent use of ideophones, dramatic delivery, and dialogue in addition to the singing and dancing that permeate the narration. Repetition of words, phrases, or even sentences is fairly common. Alongside parallel phrasing and lists of various people and objects, the repetitions help to bring out the dramatic significance of certain episodes and give structural unity to the narration. Intermittently, the narrator uses direct speech when the character, voice, and behavior pattern of the protagonist can be represented dramatically. For instance, Annanu the Spider is said to speak "through his

nose," and the narrator must learn to switch easily from normal to nasalized speech whenever the situation demands it. Another important device is the effective use of common exclamations of surprise, shock, or admiration. For instance, to express surprise, the narrator merely gives out a direct frantic yell "Yes!" Other devices include onomatopoeia, which is freely used to capture the sound of falling persons, beasts, or objects—"He came crashing on the floor *oba*"—and nonverbal cues such as raising the eyebrows or leaving the mouth momentarily agape to suggest surprise or shock. To suggest sorrow, deep reflection, or mental conflicts, the narrator may rest his chin in his right palm, letting out short moaning sounds—"Hm! Hm! Hm! Hm!"

The Audience

The foregoing are some of the rhetorical and poetic techniques the narrator uses to make the narration interesting, memorable, and unique. But without the active participation of the audience, the tale will not be deemed "real" and the performances will be meaningless. It is the symbiotic interaction between the narrator and the audience that yields some of those categories by which the art may be evaluated.

The narrator is generally open to guidance from the audience regarding delineation of plot. This is not to suggest the existence of a "correct" version of texts. It only means that there are certain sequential landmarks, episodes, and characters that are considered to be vital and to which the narrator must adhere. The critical apparatus of the audience functions actively throughout the performance; they evaluate the tale as it develops and will habitually condemn the narrator for some careless oversight or exhort and applaud him or her for some particularly good craftsmanship. The narrator is assessed on the basis of his or her skill of delivery as well as his or her ability to unify the plot and the moral and those problems of explanation with which a story may end. They also evaluate how well the narrator fleshes out the skeletal theme of the plot using vivid and apt descriptions, songs, gestures, mimicry, variations in speech, and tone and how successfully the narrator is able to hold the attention of the audience to the end.

Songs

Another interesting factor that helps to reveal the symbiotic relationship between the narrator and the audience and the significance of this symbiosis in the performance is the songs that normally punctuate the narration. When at any stage in the narration someone in the audience wishes to introduce a song, he or she does so by saying aloud the interruptive formula "*Gbi le me ye jen! Gbi le mi ye jen!*" (I was there that day! I was there that day!) The interrupter sings the first line of the song he or she wishes to introduce, after which the group joins in and keeps time. After a reasonable period of singing and dancing, another member of the audience may shout out the connective formula "*Moanu nko! Maanu nko!*" "*Maanu nko!*" is obviously a corruption of the Akan phrase "*Mu wo ano nko*" (Let your mouth go). That is, "Continue with your story." This is a rhetorical formula by which the gathering allows the narrator to pick up the thread of the story without destroying the organic unity of the performance.

Songs that are featured in the performance seem to follow three main descriptive patterns. The first pattern consists of songs that are integral to the story. Such songs, usually sung by the narrator with the audience serving as the chorus, may promote the plot, remark on specific incidents, clarify the sentiments and emotions of particular characters, or signal the approach of climactic points. A good example of such verse occurs in the following story about Spider (Annanu), and Hyena (Kootse).

Spider, once upon a time, saw a very beautiful princess whom he wanted to marry. But when he put in his proposal, he was told she was already engaged to Hyena. Spider boasted before the king and all the court that Hyena was unworthy of such a beauty, since Hyena was his horse. The king was outraged, and soon after Spider left, he sent for Hyena and warned that unless he disproved what Spider had said about him, he would lose the hand of the princess to Spider. Hyena rushed out furiously in hot pursuit of Spider. When Hyena caught him, Spider denied ever saying anything like that to the king. But, not convinced, Hyena insisted that Spider should come along with him to the palace to make his denial public before the king and his court. Spider agreed; but a short distance away from the palace, he feigned physical incapacity and cajoled Hyena into allowing him to ride on his back. As they made their entry into the palace, Spider began singing:

Narrator: *Kootsc 'mkpongo ni-cc*
Chorus: *Won ba nonn*
    Be nyenna nonn

Narrator: *'Mkee kootse 'mkpongo mi-ee*
Chorus: *Wonba nonn*
    Be nyena nonn

Narrator: Hyena is my horse
Chorus: We are coming swiftly
    You are witnesses now

Narrator: I say Hyena is my horse
Chorus: We are coming swiftly
    You are witnesses now

As the narrator sings, he goes through the motions of horse riding, pushing, whipping, bobbing, jabbing on poor Hyena to the amusement of the gathering who, complimenting the dramatic irony, sing, clap, stamp, and dance excitedly to the end, in which Spider is declared by the king to be the most worthy of the Princess's hand since he has proved that Hyena is indeed his horse.

If Spider is the witty trickster, he is also fallible and sometimes gets cheated or outwitted. There is a story that tells how, in spite of his selfish possessiveness, he was deceived and cuckolded by his wife, Konole. Konole fell in love with a handsome man she met at the marketplace one day. She arranged for him to come and visit her in disguise. She told Spider that the visitor was her "aunt" from a distant country. Eager to please his supposed in-law, Spider offered the master bedroom to Konole and the "aunt," asking them to spend the night together while he retired into the guest room. At this juncture, the narrator sings the first line of a song, and the whole gathering join in and keep time:

Anaanu gnale moko so eno-ee
Anaanu gnale moko so eno-ee
Anaanu gnale moko so eno-ee
    Kurdwe! Kurdwe! Kurdwe!

Somebody is squatting on the Spider's wife
Somebody is squatting on the Spider's wife
Somebody is squatting on the Spider's wife
    Kurdwe! Kurdwe! Kurdwe!

What is to be noted here is the effective use of rhetoric, dramatic irony, and the call on us to imagine the sexual act between Konole and her lover in the master bedroom. The dancing and the strong consonant sounds in the alliterative "*Kurdwe! Kurdwe! Kurdwe!*" are skillfully used to capture the physical motion and rhythm of orgiastic copulation. The song and dance, therefore, advances the scene without being explicitly vulgar or obscene.

The second pattern of songs tends to be critical of the narrator's performance. When the narrator seems completely confused about the main outlines of a story or the logical sequence of events, the gathering may break into a song of censure:

Odesa otaa nee? Are you telling your own tale?
Kaa male   Don't tell lies
Odesa otaa nee? Are you telling your own tale?
Kaa male   Don't tell lies
Amala bgeo mo One may be killed by lies
Kaa male   Don't tell lies

Another song may warn the narrator that he or she is sticking too closely to the main outlines of the story, and because his narration lacks humor and appropriate improvisation it is dull and boring:

Boo ohe modeng, boo ohe modeng, boo ohe modeng,
Boo ohe modeng
Nko baahi ija bodientse -ee
Boo ohe modeng

Osee - yie!
Yee - yie!
Bo ohe modeng
Nko baahi ija bodietse -ee
Bo ohe modeng.
Noko baa gnoo ija bodientse -ee
No ohe modeng,

Try hard, try hard, try hard
Try hard
Whether your thing will be good depends on you
Whether your thing will be exciting depends on you
Try hard.

Osee - yie!
Yee - yie!
Whether a thing will be good depends on you
Try hard.
Whether a thing will be exciting depends on you
Try hard.

The third pattern consists of songs that are mainly ornamental but that also provide a means of rests in which the narrator can catch his or her breath without breaking the flow or cohesiveness

of the tale. Such songs have the added function of providing comic relief, especially after a very frightening or sad episode:

Adung dunaa ewo dunn
    Himama!
Aya wo kane aa kwe
    Himama!
Osono
    Himama!
Kuryen! Yen! Yen!
    Himama!
Kuryen! Yen! Yen!
    Himama!

The monkey's ass is dark
    Himama!
Let's get light to come and look
    Himama!
Oil lamp
    Himama!
Kuryen! Yen! Yen!
    Himama!
Kuryen! Yen! Yen!
    Himama!

or:

She, miyi ohami - ee
Ataa kwami shee miyi ohami - ee
Eshe le bunzu
Shee mshi ohami - ee
Ataa kwami she mihi ohami - ee
Eshe le kue kwe.

Shave the hair off my head
Ataa kwami, shave the hair off my head
He shaved it *bunzu* [untidily]

    Shave off my pubic hair
    Ataa kwami shave off my pubic hair
    He shaved it *kue kue* [unevenly]

There are yet other song groups that refer to the historical origins or ethnic identity of some folktale-telling groups that also indicate who the hero of the tales would be. Such songs, like signature tunes, are usually sung at the very beginning and ending of the performance, with many repetitions, miming, and dancing:

Osee - yie!
Yee - yie!

Ananse - oo!
Hu-m-m-m!
Wojee shonn ko - ee
Wojee shonn ko - ee
Awomei woje shonn ko - ee
Ataa mei wojee shonn ko - ee
Tete kpeshi webu' ji wo.

Ose - yie!
Yee - yie!
Spider - oo!
Hu-m-m-m!
Spider - oo
Hu-m-m-m!
Where we come from isn't that far
Where we come from isn't that far
Folks, where we come from isn't that far
We are Tettch Kpeshie's people.

The songs, then, are not mere haphazard interpolations. They function in the structural, thematic, critical, aesthetic, and identification dimensions of the art. They are a genuine rhetorical device that helps not only to reveal the symbiotic relationship between the narrator and the audience but also to sustain the vitality and the organic unity of the whole performance.

Conclusion

The foregoing has been a descriptive analysis of the context, themes, and techniques of Adesa, Ga storytelling. Adesa is a complex genre by which the social and moral fabric of society is reinforced and perpetuated.[4] It is a dramatic art form in which the performers, that is both the narrator and the audience, are completely free to create and interpret within traditionally established guidelines. Tradition requires adherence to conventional patterns of tales and knowledge of their technical aspects: opening, interruptive, resumptive, and closing formulas; sequential landmarks; and ability to sustain audience interest. Both the narrator and the audience are equally creative and skillful, using fantasy, the human and animal world, and rhetoric to create atmosphere, characterization, movement, and humor. Personalization, improvisation, word choice, repetition, songs, and ideophones contribute to the underlying aesthetic principle of the Ga folktale performance.

In spite of its time-honored social, moral, and aesthetic values, the Ga storytelling tradition is now fighting for its survival. For one thing, pow-

erful new entertainment sources such as the cinema, video theaters, discos, dance halls, and bars now entice those who in the past were the stable audience of the genre. Because of the increasing rate of migration to the greater Accra region from other parts of the country, neighborhoods that were once exclusively or predominantly Ga speaking are now changing, and the size of the Adesa's traditional audience is shrinking. Although efforts are being made to address these issues by incorporating storytelling in the curricula of schools, a much more comprehensive plan of action is needed by governmental and local administrators, educators, and urban planners in order to help preserve this significant genre.

Components and Sequence of Ga Folktale Performance

1. Opening Formula	Narrator
2. Response Formula	Audience
3. Beginning of Story	Narrator
4. Interruptive Formula	Audience
5. Song(s)	Audience
6. Connective Formula	Audience
7. Resumption of Story	Narrator
8. Closing Formula	Narrator
9. Closing Response	Audience

Notes

1. The Ga are a cognatic Kwa speaking people who inhabit a series of coastal towns and inland villages in southeastern Ghana, including Accra, the country's capital. The Ga language is one of the major national languages taught at schools and spoken on radio and television. Since 1981 aspects of the data on which this paper is based have been discussed at various conferences, including the University of Ibadan Annual Literature Conference (Nigeria), the Annual African Literature Association Conference (United States), and the first Oral Literature in Ghana Conference (Ghana).

2. Such contexts will identify the storytelling as "formal" rather than "informal," which is

held usually indoors, with fewer participants, mostly family members and friends.

3. Ruth Finnegan provides a detailed discussion of the significance of performance for the actualization of a tale in *Oral Literature in Africa*, London: Clarendon, 1970.

4. But it is not as complex as folktale genres observed by Ben-Amos among Benin storytellers.

Further Reading

Bascom, William, "The Forms of Folklore: Prose Narratives," *Journal of American Folklore* 78 (1965)

Ben-Amos, Dan, *Sweet Words: Storytelling Events in Benin*, Philadelphia: Institute for the Study of Human Issues, 1975

Dundes, Alan, *The Study of Folklore*, Englewood Cliffs, New Jersey: Prentice-Hall, 1965

Finnegan, Ruth, *Oral Literature in Africa*, London: Clarendon, 1970

Jahn, Janheinz, *Muntu: An Outline of the New African Culture*, New York: Grove, 1961

Okpewho, Isidore, *African Oral Literature: Backgrounds, Character, and Continuity*, Bloomington: Indiana University Press, 1992

Owomoyela, Oyekan, *African Literatures: An Introduction*, Waltham, Massachusetts: Brandeis University, African Studies Association, 1979

The Igbo Folk Epic

Chukwuma Azuonye

Chukwuma Azuonye discusses the Igbo folk epic and suggests fallacies in the Eurocentric approaches of some epic scholars.

Fallacies in Epic Scholarship

Four fallacies recur in the existing scholarship on heroic narrative poetry, otherwise known as the epic. The first is that the epic, indeed all heroic poetry, flourishes only in centralized, monarchical societies and that it is essentially an aristocratic genre of traditional poetry featuring mainly royalty and their aristocratic courtiers and is sustained by the patronage of royal courts. The second is that the epic is invariably a monumental narrative of great length, composed in elevated style by means of formulas or recurrent metrical units that serve more as aide-mémoire, filling lines and half-lines in the essentially mechanical process of oral-formulaic composition in performance rather than as semantic units creating culture-specific images of things or fully individuated human personalities. From this fetishization of *verse,* or metrical composition, and of *length,* or the elevated style in the conception of the epic, emerge the third and fourth fallacies, namely, that the epic is invariably a verse or metrical composition and that heroic narrative poems of brief compass, the so-called epic songs or heroic lays manifested in, for example, the Eddic lays of northern Europe and the briefer heroic songs of pre-Homeric Myceanean antiquity and elsewhere, are not epics per se but epics in formation, ancestors of the epic, or epic fragments. Until very recently, the epic has been ruled out of existence in the storytelling traditions of many peoples of the world, especially in Africa, because of these fallacies. Chief among those whose heritage of epic poetry has been either

misunderstood or denied are nonaristocratic and traditionally republican people, such as the 25 million Igbo people of southeastern Nigeria. This article discusses the types of heroic narrative poetry that have been found to exist in Igbo culture and that, on the basis of the most universal and inalienable features of the genre, cannot but be recognized as folk epics. The admission of these forms as epics will no doubt have important implications for the comparative understanding of the nature of the genre and its future definition.

Major Categories of Heroic Narrative Performance

Two major categories of heroic narrative performances have been found to flourish among the Igbo. The first is a product of warfaring culture and forms part of a complex of traditional war music, *iri-aha,* found especially among the Cross River Igbo of the extreme southeastern corner of Igbo country on the frontiers with the neighboring Efik-Ibibio and Ekoi peoples of Akwa-Ibom and Cross River states of Nigeria. The second is a product of peace and a culture of prosperity belonging to the tradition of *ita* (romantic stories), often described by both the tellers and the hearers as *ntu* (lies), which form part of work and leisure, especially among the fishing and farming communities of the Anambra Igbo of the extreme northwestern corner of Igbo country in the Omambala River basin close to the lower Niger. The former comprises heroic narrative "songs" of brief compass, whereas the later comprises heroic narrative "recitations" of great length, some of which take several days (and, sometimes claimed, weeks) to perform. Whereas the respective Cross River and Anambra traditions epitomize these categories,

25

variants of the two categories are found elsewhere in Igbo culture. For example, briefer forms of romantic heroic tales that share roughly the same kind of ambience and themes as the monumental recitations of the Anambra Igbo have been recorded among the Western Igbo of Delta State, west of the lower Niger (Okpewho, 1990, 1992), where they are sung rather than recited.

Typical examples of the briefer forms of heroic narrative "songs" (the Cross River Igbo type) are the narrative varieties of the war songs (*abu-aha*) of the Ohafia Igbo, a formerly warlike but now mainly agricultural and trading community of 25 village-groups located on the Cross River in the southern terminus of the great ridge and escarpment that traverses Igbo country from Enugu to Arochukwu. No specific local terminology exists for these narrative songs, but several descriptive phrases are constantly used when referring either to their form (most commonly *ububuo*, narrative) or their content (e.g., *akuko-aka*, stories of the past; *akuko-ali*, stories of the land; *akuko-ndi-ikike-Ohafia*, stories of Ohafia heroes; or *akuko-mgbe-ichin*, stories of the time of the ancestors). Besides the narrative songs, *abu-aha* includes a repertoire of traditional battle songs, commonly called *ikperikpe ogu* (battle rhythms), and invocative war songs, often described as *itu-afa* (praise naming). The battle songs form part of the paraphernalia of traditional warfare and, in their original forms, presumably were chanted by warriors on their way to battle, in battle, or on their victorious returns from battle. Today, they are performed as lyrical accompaniments of a well-known type of war dance (frequently staged on important social and cultural occasions) that comprises dramatic reenactments of typical battle scenes and movements. One of the victory songs in this repertoire, like many other battle songs, metaphorically describes the defeated enemy whose members have been captured alive as a leopard trapped in a hunt:

> The leopard has been trapped!
> > Come, let us go home, come let us go!
> The leopard has been trapped!
> > Come, let us go home, come let us go!
> Don't you know, the leopard has been trapped!
> > Come, let us go home, come let us go! . . .

The invocative songs comprise strings of names and praise names, with compact allusions to the legends of the great heroes as well as to myths, both creation and customary ones. They bear the unmistakable imprint of the traditional ritual ceremonies that, according to the literature, were usually performed before warriors went to battle to fortify their morale or immediately on their return to cleanse them from their deeds of blood. The following are the opening lines of an example of the former type, performed today as part of the reenactment of war in the Ohafia war dance:

> He that would shudder before a corpse, let him
> > retreat!
> He that would shudder before a corpse, I say,
> > let him retreat!
> Ajadu Uma Ajadu, pray drink wine for me.
> Mkpawe Imaga Odo, pray drink wine for me.
> Adukuru Mmon, son of Udumoke,
> Wherever you may be, we are at wine.
> Kamalu, son of Ngwo, man of Agala-Nde-
> > Odo-Ukiiwe,
> Come, drink wine for me and soothe my voice,
> For the night that falls on *afo* must dawn on
> > *nkwo*.
> My great father Awa Afaka, he-that-goes-to-
> > battle-with-a-farming-knife,
> Man of Udegbe-Ezhi-Anunu,
> Pray, we are at wine.
> Come, dip your lip in my wine,
> For lip dipped in wine is wine itself.
> > (Azuonye, 1990a)

By contrast to the battle songs and the invocations, the narrative war songs represent the drama of the emergence of the apical ancestral warriors as the great heroes of the land. Most of the heroes are war heroes, and their action is located in head-hunting and slave-raiding forays into the territories of their Ibibio and Ekoi neighbors or into the Igbo heartland. Historians have mistaken as mercenarism the people's apparent love of warfare, especially with regard to their alliance (*ukwuzi*) with their immediate Igbo neighbors to the south, the Aro, who masterminded the supply of slaves to European dealers on the coast. However, from the traditions of the Ohafia people themselves, their heroes, called *ufiem*, epitomize their people's historical need for security within the borders of lands cut off from the rest of Igbo country and open to hostile Ibibio and Ekoi neighbors. Over the generations, the ability to overpower an enemy in battle or single combat came to be seen not only as desirable but as a sine qua non for social recognition. Those who failed to show a head that they won in battle in their youthful days were denied social privileges, and such humiliating sanctions also drastically affected their spouses. Not surprisingly, most of the heroes of the texts belong to the order of young men spurred by this heroic ethos to engage in warfare or head-hunting to earn the *ufiem* title. Otherwise, they are heroes who have already earned the title but are spurred on by the special conceptions of manhood and honor that are the hallmark of heroes across the world to come out in defense of the honor of their people. *Amoogu,* one of the most popular of the epics, recounts fortitude of an unlikely hero: an unknown young man from the smallest of the 25 village-groups who alone is able to accomplish the test of endurance, namely, charging 12 guns while seated naked in a nest of soldier ants, a feat that one must accomplish before the Ohafia people can overcome a rival community, Aliike, led by a magical hero, the short-armed dwarf named Omi-iko. In *Egbele,* the young hero is persuaded by his concerned uncle to break with his thrice-bereaved mother, who dresses him like a little girl to protect him from the dangers of war. Fortunately, he returns triumphant with a live captive. His mother's song of joy at his reception is said to be the origin of the art of singing war songs. Interestingly, women are highly visible in these tales-in-song not as fair maidens to be won or defended by the men but as warriors in their own right and prime movers of action. In *Nne Mgbaafo,* a young woman in love takes the risk of dressing up like a warrior and venturing into the enemy Ibibio territory in search of her husband, who has been lost in battle. In most versions of the epic, she rescues him before he is sold into slavery. In a few versions, she recovers her husband's dead body and gives it a befitting burial. In *Inyan Olugu,* a humiliated wife of an *ujo* is forced by her deprivations to lure her husband into enemy territory, where she herself overpowers and kills four men in an ambush and delivers their chopped-off heads to her husband to take home in triumph as his own. She earns the title *ogbu-etuwi-di-ya* (she-that-kills-and-gives-the-honor-to-her-husband). Included in the repertoire are more pristine hunter-heroes, such as the hero of *Elibe Aja* who kills a man-eating leopard that harries Aro country but in a later encounter is himself killed when his gun explodes in a cavern. Other heroes include sporting heroes, great dancers, and modern political heroes and statesmen in the Nigeria-Biafra conflict of the 1960s. Other texts are myths and fables that focus on moral issues in a world that appears to be much the same as the world of the heroes.

Aesthetic Principles

The poetry is mainly in the form of chant, with moments of intense lyrical, oratorical, and ritual expression in the modes of song, recitation, and what appears to be ordinary speech. It is usually delivered in high speech, with the singer moving rapidly from one hero to another. Brevity and clarity are valued for their own sakes and out of deference to the republican ethos, which calls for the celebration not of one extraordinarily large cult figure but of heroes representing as many peoples and communities in Ohafia as possible. This and other underlying aesthetic principles are constantly invoked by both the artists and their audiences in oral literary criticism that is voiced in the course of performances or that can be elicited through in-depth interviews.

Other traditional aesthetic principles that are voiced in oral literary criticism are functionality, authenticity, and variety. Studying these principles is of great value because it enables us to better appreciate several features of the genre that can easily be misinterpreted in the light of exocultural literary theories and analytical models. Apart from the light they cast on the compact brevity and multivariety of heroic tales in the repertoires of the bards in this oral tradition, these principles help us to better appreciate the nature and function of the repeated phrases or formulas that constitute the main linguistic-stylistic resources used by the bards in the complex process of composition that takes place during oral performance. For Milman Parry and Albert Lord (the architects of the modern oral-formulaic theory, which revolutionized the study of the epic from the 1930s) and their followers, formulas—as manifested in repeated phrases in the Homeric epics that are similar to those found in the Yugoslavic oral epics and recorded in the field and studied by them—are viewed as metrical units with no particularized meaning, whether with reference to persons, places, or things. Rather, they are seen as generic in that they evoke generalized images of heroic reality that can be applied to any actor in the heroic world. Their more important function is to fill metrical slots (lines and half-lines) in the narrative gestalt. By contrast, in the Igbo epics the function of formulas seems to go beyond mere metrical necessity. These repeated phrases are mostly in the form of epithets (mostly praise names) that identify heroes in terms of their distinctive physical or psychological attributes; associations with ancestors, other heroes, communities, or other groups in the heroic world; and the circumstances of their emergence as heroes. Thus, for example, we have the following recurrent types: *Obirhazu-ka-ozo-agba,* "Hunchback-that-runs-faster-than-his-peers" (descriptive epithet); *Nwa-Nne-m-Orieji,* "Son-of-my-great-mother-Orieji" (associative epithet); and *Omerende-ekpu-ole,* "Terror-of-silver-merchants" (mythopoeic or historical epithet). The allusions in these epithets are not only often particularized but also required by tradition to be in accord with popular myths and legends about the heroes invoked. Other repeated phrases in the texts are verbal formatives (focus formulas) that serve to focus attention on particular types of themes. For example, the passage of time is almost always indicated by the phrase *ya rua hi* ("it went past a year"); movement from place to place by *wo ga-aga ogo mmuo* ("they went past their village"); cautious, stealthy movement by *wo jewe mbelege mbelege* ("they went *mbelege mbelege*"); and departure by *ya zhia ali zon oto turu* ("he/she rose from the ground and set off"). Thus, it appears that we can find parallels to generic formulas of the types described by Parry and Lord in the focus of the formulas.

At first sight, the monumental forms of heroic narrative "recitations" (the Anambra Igbo type) might appear to be plain prose narrative—one of the reasons that texts of this kind have been denied recognition as epics in Eurocentric scholarly circles. However, the verbal texture of the narratives is basically recitative and eloquently poetic in terms of inner structure. The recitative fabric is varied by chanted and spoken passages in the song that add lyrical, oratorical, and liturgical tones to the narration. Here, for example, are the opening lines of the epic of Ameke Okoye recorded in Aguleri in 1983:

      (*Three beats of* ubom)

      Narrator: Ehee-e!

      I, Jeveizu Okaavo,

      Of Okpu Ivite Aguleri,

      I am the one that tells the tale of Ameke Okoye;

5   I am the one that recounts his story

      Inside Nigeria;

      I am that very person

      That tells the stories of the heroes

      Of old.

10   That is what I am about to get into

      And expound.

      (*Three beats of* ubom)

      (*Song*)   Uooo, people of Oba-na-Iduu ooo!

                  Uooo, people of Oba-na-Iduu ooo!

                  Uooo, people of Oba-na-Iduu ooo!

15   Let him that is inside not come out again,

                  For that person that weaves trouble is out!

                  Let him that is outside go in quickly,

                  For that person that weaves trouble is out!

                  Iduu oooo!

      (*I beat of* ubom)

20   (*Chant*)   Hmmmm! Hmmmm! Hmmmm! Hmmmm!

                  Ooooo! Ooooo! Ooooo! Ooooo!

                  That day spirits went for the ranking of heroes!

                  That day Chukwu called for the ranking of heroes, eo!

25 That day Chukwu called for the ranking of heroes in the square of public
gathering!

That day Chukwu called for the ranking of heroes in the square of public
gathering

My child, do not go for the ranking of heroes, for there can be no ranking,
In the square of public gathering!

Didn't Okaavo, the spirit, tell him not to go, and he said he would go for the
ranking of heroes in the square of public gathering

30 Didn't Ojaali, the spirit, tell him not to go, and he said he would go for the
ranking of heroes in the square of public gathering!

(*Pause*)
(*Chant*) We've come, whatever will happen, let it happen;
That was the undoing of Nduba of Ikelionwu, Ikelionwu,
What will happen will happen as it happened to Nduba of Ikelionwu,

35 Was it not Nduba of Ikelionwu that begot Ikelionwu Mbaamali,
Hence Ikelionwu did not know what to do with Mbaamali?
Ikelionwu enacted a law in their land,
Saying that lest the novice should know *mpama* in Ikelionwu,
If the novice knows the mask, if the novice knows the mask,

40 Much later he will join the masquerade society.
If the novice knows Mbaamali of Ikelionwu,
It means that he has become powerless.
O hero, Mbaamali of Ikelionwu, welcome!
Hmmm, iyoooo, oooo oooo-m!

45 Iduu, I salute you!
Spectators: Welcome!
Narrator: Hmmmm.
We've now gone into it.

50 (*Chant*) That day the hero was preparing for war in heaven;
That day the hero was preparing for war in the house of
the sky-dweller, Enu-nyili-mba!

That day the hero was preparing for the house of
the house of the sky-dweller, Enu-nyili-mba!

My child, you joker, by which route will you (get to the point from
which you will) ascend the stairs?

But the hero said that, come morning, he would mount the stairs.

55 Didn't Ojaali, the spirit, tell him not to go, for there was no road out there, but
he said he could go!

Didn't Okaavo, the spirit, tell him not to go, for there was no road
out there, but he said he could go and return!

My child, do not go to the house of the sky-dweller, for it has no road, but he
said he would go and return!

The hero said that, come morning, he would ascend the stairs,
go and return.

Hmmm! Iyoo ooo, ho-oo-oooo!

60 Let us go to the house of Enu-nyili-mba—
The man that lives in heaven.
This is how it went.
Obuora Udechukwu,
It's beginning is this:

65   This world began
        And people lay about in the world,
        That is, all things created by God.
        They stayed like that,
        Stayed on and on and on.
70   No one knew what planted *aku-ubili, aku-ubili* planted itself.
        People came out one day—
        Sheets of paper from heaven
        Came scattering upon the earth,
75   Paper on which something was written.
        From above, it scattered on these people's town;
        From above, it scattered on these people's town—
        All over the world.
80   Those who knew how to read, whosoever picked up a sheet,
        Gazing at it a while,
        He would start to weep,
        Saying: What is this
        What is it that we (the inhabitants) of the world have done
85   That this man, Enu-nyili-mba, who lives in heaven
        Should write us this kind of letter,
        If you took the letter to your kinsman who knew how to read,
        Gazing at it a while,
        He would start to weep.
90   What he wrote in the letter
        Was that he said
        That is he, Enu-nyili-mba,
        That he had fixed a feast for himself
        Saying that this feast he had fixed for himself,
95   Where he lived in heaven,
        That it was for seven weeks he would hold it,
        And this feast he would hold for seven weeks,
        That all things truly human abounding on this earth born of people's breath,
        That a commandment he was handing down to everyone that lived in this world
             who was a human being conceived and born, was this:
100   Nobody should drink water;
        And nobody should eat food;
        And nobody should chew tooth-stick;
        And nobody should eat palm nuts.
        Until he completed the seven-week feast.
105   But if anyone turned a deaf ear and drank water there on earth,
        That he would see that person from heaven
        And he would kill him off.
                    (Azuonye and Udechukwu, 1984)

An Origin Among Fishermen

The monumental character of the Anambra epics seems to be a concomitant of the kind of social and cultural environment out of which it is believed to have emerged. Local informants agree that fishing, for which the Anambra region is famous, provided the original setting for the epics. During the rainy season (April through September), the Anambra River would from time to time overflow its banks, a phenomenon that the people call *iji*. After each *iji*, a large haul of fish called *azu-ogba* would be stranded on the shores when the waters suddenly receded. In the past, before the introduction of refrigeration, fish harvests each day had to be smoked before dawn to preserve the fish. To keep the fishermen awake while the smoking was going on, gifted storytellers would tell fantastic stories (*ita*) or lies (*ntu*) that invariably figured superhuman persons of extraordinary strength and size who fought and overcame monsters to maintain the peace and prosperity of the land. Deliberately sensational and replete with hyperbolic images, these stories were generally episodic and suspenseful. Over time, these stories are said to have fused into single, monumental tales, each of which took several days to tell.

Ameke Okoye

Ameke Okoye, from one of whose versions the above excerpt is taken, is among the most popular of these epics. The gigantic hero performs 20 great tasks and in the end overcomes the cruel sky-dwelling sadist who brings so much grief to humankind on earth. Another popular epic, *Ojaadili,* presents a refiguration of the great wrestler Ojaadili, who emerges as champion in the lands of humans, animals, and spirits; however, by contrast to the folktale in which he perishes when he is moved by hubris to challenge his own personal god (*chi*), Ojaadili the epic hero returns triumphant from his victories in spiritland to avenge the persecution of his father by a cruel king who sadistically plucks one of his teeth every year at his annual royal festival. Restoring sanity to the land, he enslaves the cruel king and his family and sets up large-scale farms to feed the deprived people. In another popular epic, Ozoemena Ndive, the hero, a child prodigy, disturbs a forest that is inhabited by monsters of all direction. This fascinating epic recounts the hero's seven-year flight from the most uncompromising of these monsters, Nduye-Nduye, a flight that takes him across the face of the earth and exposes him to various arts and sciences that he brings home to his people.

Romantic Epic

By contrast to the Cross River epics, which like the Mandinka epic of Sunjata are essentially historical, the Anambra epics are romantic ones, comparable to (among others) the *Ozidi* saga of the Izon (Ijo) of the Niger River delta, *Kambili* of Mali, *Mwindo* of Baganya in Zaire, *Lianja* of the Congo, and *Moneblum* (The Blue Man). Whereas the fantastic is severely limited in the historical epics, magic and fantasy seem to be the essence of the romantic epics, and whereas the historical epics are herocentric, focusing their narration on the moments of heroic emergence or on single actions that define the status of their protagonists as heroes, the ro-

mantic epics are informed by the heroic monomyth and seem to embody the totality of the "traits" and "incidents" of the archetypal hero pattern, from prebirth and birth to death and after-death. Thus, the stories conventionally begin with the hero's grandparents and progress through prophecies of the hero's birth, unusual fatherhood, miraculous conception, unusual career in the womb, his birth and the signs of wonder accompanying it, his prodigious childhood, journeys, labors and miracles, transfiguration, passion, and disappearance from the face of the earth, be it into heaven or the land of spirits or into nothing, but not without leaving a mark of his heroic presence on earth.

Heroic, Narrative, and Poetic

Three features are shared in common by the two major categories of traditional performances in Igbo culture examined in this article. They are heroic, narrative, and poetic. These three features are the essence of the epic, the inalienable features that are shared with the Homeric *Iliad* and *Odyssey* and with other worldwide manifestations of the genre, such as the *Aeneid,* the Indian *Mahabarata,* the Eddic lays of northern Europe, the French *Song of Roland,* the Mandinkan *Sunjata,* the *Mwindo* of the Baganya (Zaire), the Malian *Kambili,* the *Ozidi* saga of the Izon (Ijo) of the Niger River delta, and even the artificial Finnish epic *Kalevala,* created by Lonnront. The social context, be it aristocratic or nonaristocratic, does not seem material to the concept of the hero, who is essentially a person of extraordinary physical, moral, spiritual, or intellectual capabilities who emerges in times of crisis to bring salvation to his people. Alternatively, he might be an embodiment of a modus vivendi on which the people's survival and progress in difficult circumstances depends. Thus, inasmuch as heroes exist in aristocratic societies, heroes abound in peasant cultures as well. In addition, it appears that verse, be it metrical or nonmetrical, is by no means an inalienable property of the epic. Poetry rather than verse seems the inalienable medium, and poetry can exist in verse, prose, or an admixture of the two. Indeed, four modes or styles of vocalization—recitation, speech, song, and chant—have been found to be employed in such compositions in Africa and elsewhere, and Igbo folk epics of the two categories examined here use these two poetic modes, the Anambra type being mainly in recitation and speech modes with song and chant interludes and the Cross River type being mainly in song and chant modes with recitation and speech interludes. Length and historical content seem to be variable rather than fixed and to be inalienable properties of the folk epic.

Further Reading

Almqvist, Bo, Séamas Ó Catháin, and Pádraig Ó Héalaí, eds., *The Heroic Process: Form, Function, and Fantasy in Folk Epic: The Proceedings of the International Folk Epic Conference, University College, Dublin, 2–6 September 1985*, Dublin, Ireland: Glendale, 1987

Azuonye, Chukwuma, "The Heroic Age of the Ohafia Igbo: Its Evolution and Socio-Cultural Consequences," *Geneve-Afrique/Geneva-Africa* 28:1 (1990)

——, "Oral Literary Criticism and the Performance of the Igbo Epic," *Oral Tradition* 9:1 (March 1994)

——, "The Romantic Epics of the Anambra Igbo," *International Folklore Review* 7 (1990)

Azuonye, Chukwuma, and Obiora Udechukwu, "*Enu-Nyili-Mba*: An Encounter in the *Ameke Okoye* Epic as Performed by Jeveizu Okaavo of Aguleri," *Uwa Ndi Igbo: Journal of Igbo Life and Culture* 1 (1994)

Lord, Albert Bates, *The Singer of Tales*, Cambridge, Massachusetts: Harvard University Press, 1960

Okpewho, Isidore, *The Epic in Africa: Toward a Poetics of the Oral Performance*, New York: Columbia University Press, 1979

Parry, Milman, "The Traditional Epithet in Homer," in *The Making of Homeric Verse: The Collected Papers of Milman Parry*, edited by Adam Parry, Oxford: Clarendon, 1971; New York: Arno, 1980

Igbo Stories and Storytelling

Chukwuma Azuonye

Chukwuma Azuonye discusses various forms of ákúkó-àlà (stories of the land) and ákúkó-ífò (stories of the imagination). He concludes with examples of storytelling as communal theater.

Introduction

The Igbo people of southeastern Nigeria have one of the most thematically and stylistically varied traditions of storytelling in Africa. Little wonder that storytellers of Igbo origin dominate the modern African literary scene. Among these are such pioneering and world acclaimed novelists as Chinua Achebe, Cyprain Ekwensi, John Munonye, and Elechi Amadi. Igbo culture has also produced outstanding women writers, notably Flora Nwapa and Buchi Emecheta. In several interviews as well as in the many stories-within-the-story told in their works, these writers have again and again paid tribute to generations of little-known orators, historians, and raconteurs whose wish-fulfillment fantasies, gossips, dreams, visions, lies, projections, eyewitness accounts, memoirs, and recreations of historical reality have passed into common currency both as humor and as myths to live by.

As in everything in Igbo culture, stories are paradoxical structures of the imagination that flourish both as open communicative events and as coded messages. As open communicative events, they are called *ákúkó* and form part of everyday discourse. Thus, in some parts of the Igbo world, the word *úbùbó* is used to refer to both stories and ordinary conversation. As coded messages, they are called *ílú*, a term that also applies to proverbs, exempla, parables, allegories, and other forms of similitude, including some categories of riddles and even such analogical figures of speech as metaphor and simile.

But whatever may be their specific forms, manifestations or contexts, stories in Igbo culture fall into two broad categories, namely *ákúkó-àlà* (stories of the land) and *ákúkó-ífò* (stories of the imagination). *Ákúkó-àlà* comprise stories that are told as true accounts of past events. These are commonly viewed as men's stories because they deal with questions pertaining to land (*àlà*) in all senses of the word, questions that are traditionally regarded as falling within the men's domain in the delicate pattern of division of roles and responsibilities that exists in Igbo culture. *Ákúkó-ífò* stories are told as imaginative recreations of reality, the main purpose of that is the reaffirmation of the mores and values which govern social relationships. These stories are commonly seen as women's stories because they are bound up with nurturing responsibilities that traditionally fall within the women's domain.

On the face of it, the dichotomy between *ákúkó-ífò* and *ákúkó-àlà* might appear to indicate a simple distinction between "history" and "fiction" on the one hand and between a narrative genre of a higher order and one of a lower order on the other hand. But this, in reality, does not appear to be the case. What seems indicated rather is the paradoxical tension between patriarchy and matriarchy in Igbo culture. Igbo culture appears, on the surface, to be patriarchal: men control rulership, succession, and inheritance exclusively. But when one looks closely, evidence of dual organization with a balanced devolution of certain important social and ritual responsibilities to women appears rather clear. Men control the land, but the land is womanhood and motherhood deified; its nurturing feminity is symbolized and idolized in the figure of the earth-goddess Àlà, the supreme guardian and controller of the pattern of relationships that holds people together as members of a living community. Thus, while *ákúkó-àlà* comprises stories that refer to the visible economic and political parameters related to men's control of the land, *ákúkó-ífò* comprises stories that refer to the invisible moral and ethical bases of human coexistence on the land.

Content, Contexts, and Performance of *Ákúkó-Álà*

It seem clear that there are at least four distinct categories of stories that come within the term *ákúkó-àlà*. First, we have stories pertaining to *àlà* (land, earth, or soil) in its purely geographic or geologic sense; stories about the planet Earth, its hills, valleys, rivers, forests, and everything living and nonliving found on it. These are essentially creation or origin stories. It would appear, however, that there is no all-compassing Igbo story of creation, like the biblical or the Dogon creation stories. There are allusions to a time "when the heavens were the playground of squirrels" (*mgbé élū bū àlà òsá*), a time when the earth was so soft that the chameleon learned to walk slowly and cautiously so as not to sink into the porous earth, a time when "there was only one lizard on earth" (*mgbé ngwèré dí ótù*), or a time when the whole earth was so covered with water (the great flood) that the hornbill (*Òkpókō*) was forced to bury his dead mother inside his own head. Beyond these scattered universal motifs, Igbo tales about creation and the origins of things are local and circumscribed. Each community sees itself as the center of the world and spins yarns about phenomena in such a way as to suggest that everything has been called into being in the service of its own people. Thus hills, rivers, and forests appear, move, and disappear as blessing or punishment for the actions of members of the community. The motif of the river that changed its course leaving a deep, dry valley is one common topographic motif. Usually, the river (a deity) decides to flow away (through another village) because it is frequently abused, neglected, or denied its due sacrifice by the people. The story has been told of practically all the major rivers of Igboland—Ìmo, Ùráàsi, Ìdemíli, etc. Other cycles of stories about creation and the origins of things refer to the origins of night and day, the origins of the seasons, the origins of the four-day Igbo market week (*Èké, Óriè, Àfò,* and *Nkwó*), the origins of the rays of the sun, the origins of the full and half moon, the origins of death, and so forth.

Àlà in an Economic and Political Sense

The second and third categories of *ákúkó-àlà* are concerned with *àlà*, both in the circumscribed economic sense as capital (farmland, residential estate, and such) and in the wider political sense as a settled community with territorial integrity (fatherland, motherland, country or nation). In both of these senses, *àlà* refers to any piece of land that individuals or groups of people claim as their own and in which they have a vested interest to protect, expand, and if possible pass on as a legacy to their descendants. What we have here are two universal categories of legends—ancestral and heroic.

One of the main cycles of Igbo ancestral legends presents superhuman ancestors. Thus, among the Nri of the central Igbo area where an ancient civilization dating to circa 1000 was excavated in the 1960s, the supreme god, Chúkwú, is said to have sent the great culture hero Èrì and his wife Namuku from heaven, the sky. Another common motif is that of a race of supernatural giant or dwarf ancestors who have left their indelible footprints on rock, like Ónójá nwá Òbólí among the Northern Igbo of Nsukka. In other legends, the founding fathers or mothers are represented as autochthonous—meaning, as having sprung from the earth; grown out of the soil, rocks, or grains of sand; issued mysteriously from a lake, pond, sea, river, or the stream that waters the land; or else materialized from thin air or in wind or storm. The ancestress of Nnobi, on the Ìdémmíli River, among the Northern Igbo of Anambra State, is a typical example of the autochthonous founder believed to have sprung from the river (Amadiume, 1987). Other autochthonous founders are represented as having grown out of plant, tree, or vegetable matter.

A third group of ancestors and ancestresses are represented as heroic immigrants from one or the other of the four cardinal points or from a great kingdom, emporium, or civilization. Commonly, Ìdúù, or the ancient kingdom of Benin, is mentioned as the original homeland, as it is in the ancestral legend of the Onicha (Onitsha) Igbo on the lower Niger. But in some cases, it is asserted that Igbo is a corruption of "Hebrew," suggesting migration from ancient Palestine. We find this motif in the ancestral legend of the warlike Cross River Igbo of Ohafia, who also claim Benin origins in some of their epics. In a few other cases, Igbo ancestral legends refer to helpful animals, some of whom appear as the real or foster parents of the great founders. Such animals now have an honored position in the people's religious rituals as totems. Occasionally, the founders of the land may be represented as exiles or refugees from a neighboring group (in the Aro case, the Ibibio and the Ekoi) or as a settled class of migrant laborers or professionals. But this occurs only when it is deemed strategically valuable for upholding a people's self-respect and vested interests, as in the origin legends of the Cross River Aro of Arochukwu, who championed the 17th- and 18th-century slave trade through their infamous oracle of Chúkwú. Rarely does any group go so far as to ascribe to its forebears the status of captives, hostages, or slaves. In practice, every effort is made to conceal such a background no matter how blatantly it is proclaimed by rival communities. The telling of stories of the land emerges as a powerful instrument in communal self-assertion and in intercommunal rivalry.

Contested Space

In the third category of *ákúkó-àlà*, we have stories about contested space—about the successive generations of men and women on whose shoulders lie the burden of ensuring the power and survival of the land. We may call these actors "heroes," but in many respects the English term "hero" is inadequate to convey the full range of the meaning of the word, *díkē* (master of strength, or better still master or controller of forces) that the Igbo actually use to characterize this special breed of people. Whereas the English term is invariably used to describe a person who applies his extraordinary physical, moral, spiritual, and intellectual capabilities toward some positive end, the Igbo idea of *díkē* includes the opposite—the villain—a person of equally extraordinary capabilities whose actions are more destructive than constructive (for a comprehensive survey of this phenomenon, see Azuonye and Nwoga, forthcoming). Thus, in the end, the corpus of Igbo stories pertaining to the *díkē* are essentially stories about superhuman actors, be they heroes or villains. Beyond the archetypal man of action (the warrior), such superhuman beings are celebrated in a wide variety of other domains—wrestling, hunting, farming, householding, communal leadership, medicine, and oratory. In each case, the hero or villain is identified as *dí* (master or controller of) or *òkà* (one who excels in his particular domain). Thus, for example, we have the following types: *dí-ji* (master of yams), *dí-mgbá* (master

of wrestling), *dí-ntā* (master of the hunt); *dí-égbè* (master of the gun), or *òká-ókwú* (one who excels in the use of words), etc. In his celebrated novel *Things Fall Apart,* Chinua Achebe paints a picture of a great man of action, Okonkwo, who typifies the Igbo idea of *díkē* in the domains of wrestling, warfaring, farming, and householding, both their heroic and villainous aspects.

Laws of the Land

In the fourth major category of *ákúkó-àlà*, we have stories about the customs of the land, which for the Igbo are known as "the laws of the land" (*òménàálà*)—the unerring sacred rules of conduct ordained and superintended by the supreme mother that nurtures all creation, the earth-goddess Àlà. These stories incorporate references to the origins of communal beliefs, totems, taboos, customs, and institutions. In this sense, stories of the land are true myths, that is, myths as social charter that embody the ideals and espirit de corps of a living community.

How far these stories have grown out of memoirs and eyewitness accounts is rather difficult to ascertain. Quite often, narrators of *ákúkó-àlà* cite their fathers or elders as authorities for the stories they tell about their people and their land. But a little inquiry will confirm Carl von Sydow's model that argues that in the oral tradition folk memories of events decompose over time into memorates or formulaic patterns closer to but somewhat different from the actual event. The memorates themselves will further decompose over time into fabulates or formulaic patterns that are far removed from the truth and that include several universal fictional elements. Humorous tales or jokes, widely known today as *sòrómchìá* (laugh-with-me), seem to be part of the memorate-fabulate continuum. Thus, it seems appropriate to include them in any discussion of stories of the land. In essence, they hold a mirror up to significant events and happenings at transitional moments between one historical epoch to another, for example, the transition from a traditional, nontechnological social order to a modern, technological one. Laughable errors arise from inability to adapt to change. In a popular joke, an illiterate wife of a western-educated man learns that she must address visitors, as appropriate, with the following phrases: "Welcome, sirs," "Please have a seat," "What would you like to drink?" and "Good-bye." But when the visitors arrive in her husband's absence, she meets them at the door and repeats all four phrases parrotwise, much to their baffled amusement. In more traditional jokes, other forms of ironic discrepancies in behavior or morality are depicted. Thus, in a shaggy-dog type, Mbe (Tortoise), arrested for theft, pleads with his embarrassed children: "It's all your fault: I taught you not to steal but did any of you bother to teach me not to steal too?"

Humor is of course one of the most powerful ingredients of lively speech events in everyday social life. Described as *íkpā úbùbò* (the weaving or gathering of discourse), every conversational act is conceived as involving a certain degree of creative effort. Not surprisingly, Chinua Achebe (1964) ranks what he calls "serious conversation" with "oratory" *(ókwú-nkà)* as belonging to the highest order of artistic use of language among the Igbo. Apart from elaborate exchange of greetings and salutations by colorful titles or praise-names, even casual conversations involve the exchange of witticisms, the garnishing of discourse with similitude (*ílú*, including proverbs, fables, exempla and related rhetorical devices), the creation and application of condensed stories-within-the-story to reinforce arguments, and a whole range of other rhetorical features, all of which are most ably reproduced in the dialogues of Achebe's own novels. Oratory, then, is the primary medium for the transmission of *ákúkó-àlà*. Among its primary contexts are funerals, judicial or arbitration gatherings, public disputation, marriage ceremonies, and private family meetings in which the orator, as *ókwú-nlà* (master of words) or *ònú-nā-ékwúrúòhà* (mouth-that-speaks-for-all) must offer condolences, pass judgement, inspire or arouse passions, negotiate bride prices with in-laws, or offer advice through homilies to the young by invoking and manipulating words and allusions to relevant aspects of the stories of the land.

Apart from oratory and its rhetorical constituents (proverbs and other forms of *ílú*), the Igbo folk epic and other forms of traditional verse and traditional drama (dances, masked plays, folk festivals, and ceremonial rituals) constitute formal and theatrical contexts for the transmission of *ákúkó-àlà*.

Ordinarily, stories of the land survive in capsular and memorable forms in the very names of every autonomous local community and its constituent village groups and villages. The great majority of such names are genealogical and in-variably include references to the putative ancestor or ancestors of the people, for example, Umu-Duru (children or offspring of Duru), Umu-Chúkwú (children or offspring of Chúkwú), Nde-Izuogu (people of Izuogu), and so forth. A subclass of such names is devoted to invoking totemic animal-ancestors or helpers, for example, Nookwa or Ana-Okwa (land of Okwa, the Bushfowl), Nnewi or Ana-Ewi (land of Ewi, the Hare), and Loodu or Ala Odu (land of Odu, the Bushrat). Others are ethnonyms, identifying the group as distinct from others by reason of one or more social, economic, or cultural attributes, for example, Isu-Ikwu-Ato (Isusu, or mutual benefit group, of three matriclans); Aru-Chúkwú (Spear of Chúkwú, meaning weapons or agents of the supreme god, Chúkwú), and so forth. A host of other names are geographic and refer to location in one of the four cardinal points, topography (hill or valley), soil type (clay or gravel people), and the like, for example, Ugwu-Oba (Oba Hill), Ugwu-Eke (Eke Hill), Nde-Agbo (People of the valley), Ihi-Ala (People of the slope), Ota-Nchara (Place of gravel), Ota-Nzu (Place of chalk), Ihitte or Ibitte (Located on the left), Ikenga (Located on the right), Etiti (Center), Uzo-Agba (Gravel road), and Aba (Farm settlement).

Content, Contexts, and Performance of *Ákúkó-Ífò*

As in the case of *ákúkó-àlà*, the key to a proper appreciation of the content, contexts, and distinctive performance features of *ákúkó-ífò* is the key word, *ífò*. The etymology of *ífò* is rather obscure. But its semantic range includes fiction, relaxation, night entertainment, storytelling, flights of fancy, imaginative fantasy, and the like. In some Igbo communities, the term *ntu* (lies) is used to stress the fabulous elements in the story. Sometimes, as in the Anambra River basin, this term is used side by side with another term, *ita* (historical romance), which includes the people's highly elaborate, poetic-dramatic epic narratives (see "The Igbo Folk Epic"). But generally speaking, *ífò* seems to denote a special gathering of the family circle beside a fire or under the moonlight for storytelling events—a mixed program that includes the singing of songs with choric refrains (nursery rhymes), the telling of riddles, proverb-quoting competitions and other forms of verbal dueling such as tongue-twisting. In the following, Emenanjo (1978, ix–x) gives us a compendious description of a typical *ífò*:

Story-telling was one of the principal avenues for informal education and entertainment in the traditional Igbo society. Folk-tales were usually told in the evenings after the days' chores, or on the way to or from streams to fetch water, or the bush-farm to collect fire-wood or farm produce. In a typical evening the children usually congregated at agreed points, usually in the village square when there was moonlight or in the houses of women or children who were more favorable to or liked by children, and, of course, had an inexhaustible store of interesting and varied folk-tales and the ability to tell these in the most spectacular manner. Often elders, more usually women than men, and older children, more usually female than male, stayed around either to organize the little children or to correct an erring teller. Thus while the presence of these older people might be felt it is never obtrusive.

Ákúkó-ífò comprises four categories of stories: stories set in the animal world, stories set in the human world, stories set in the supernatural or spirit world (cosmological stories, didactic or moralizing stories), and formulaic stories.

At the center of the stories set in the animal world is the trickster hero, Mbe (Tortoise). Thus the Igbo often say, *Ilu agha Mbe* (there is no story without the tortoise), and in some parts of Igboland, animal stories are simply called *nnambesi* (great father *mbe* the tortoise said). The central theme of these stories is the triumph of the mind over brute force. Mbe (Tortoise) epitomizes the survival of the fittest in a dark world of hunting and gathering, in which the big and the strong are constantly bent on edging out the weak and the small and seizing a lion's share of everything. Mbe is the archetypal representative of the small and weak who is able to survive in such a world through mental agility. In encounters with big and strong animals like the leopard, the lion, and the elephant, Mbe always comes out the winner. But there are limitations to the positive evaluation the folk are prepared to accord intellectual agility. Does it go to the head of the hero? Does it make him selfish and overbearing? Such an excess is subjected to the same kind of punishment as is brute force. Mbe the trickster turns out to be as much a villain as he is a hero. In one story, he goes about collecting all the wisdom in the world in a calabash in order to keep it all to himself. But in the denouement he dies shamefully in an act of su-

preme folly. Even with the calabash of wisdom hanging around his neck, he lets himself fall head-long from a tall palm tree in order to crush a wasp perched on his head.

In many respects, these stories set in the animal world may be viewed as allegories of history. The animals appear as thinly disguised representations of various types of people in a wide variety of social, cultural, and historical roles and situations. Such representations even go far back into prehistoric realities and evoke memories of evolutionary patterns or life in more primitive times of hunting and gathering. These stories reflect some significant moments in the transitions to a more heroic (albeit savage) order, to the struggle for the establishment of a social charter, the rule of law and civilized values, and the triumph of mind over brute force.

Stories set in the human world assume the existence of a settled, civilized social order but one troubled by the perennial human foibles of greed, envy, rivalry, oppression, and intolerance. Its heroes are socially disadvantaged but virtuous actors who survive through the goodness of their hearts or by dint of poetic justice. In the family circle, co-wife rivalry often results in the triumph of the hated wife: she bears the king's or her husband's much-cherished only son or is blessed with riches when her son or daughter returns alive from the river of thunder and lightning to which she is invariably sent by a jealous co-wife bent on her destruction. The oppressed orphan is rescued and made wealthy by a dead relative, usually his or her own mother. The wise and obedient younger sibling survives when the foolish and the disobedient perish. A beautiful girl who rejects all human suitors ends up marrying a monster dressed in borrowed human parts and rich apparels. In the larger community—the great kingdom—a cruel and sadistic king is overthrown and humiliated by a low-born popular hero. Usually the wicked and the vicious must undergo a journey during which they must show a change of heart, suffer catharsis, or perish.

Stories set in the supernatural world invariably involve encounters between the living and the denizens of the spirit world, who are represented as monsters with social organizations similar to those of humans but with quaint personal attributes and manners. Usually, the spirits speak through the nose in guttural tones, are addicted to human flesh and the cocoyam, may possess several heads or half-bodies or evince other forms of deformity, are expert wrestlers, and live around in fires, either underground, in a dark forest, or in a vaguely defined land of spirits that lies across seven seas and seven deserts, separated from the human world by a deep gully. Descriptions of these spirits show clearly that they are seen not merely as ghosts of the dead but as beings of a different but vaguely humanoid species. Rather like the aliens of modern science fiction, they at times seem to betray memories of prehistoric humanoid peoples who may have coexisted for a while with modern human types before their final disappearance.

The Igbo have sometimes been represented in the literature as a people with little or no interest in the heavens or the cosmos beyond the earth. But the Igbo *ákúkó-ífò* includes a fairly remarkable, albeit scanty, body of cosmological stories that are concerned with the stars, the moon, the sun, and other heavenly bodies. In one such tale, the sun and the moon were once husband and wife. But following a long and bitter quarrel, the sun slashed the moon's head with a machete (creating the half-moon); but before this, the moon had struck the sun's face with a broom, creating the rays that we still see today. Interesting as these stories might be as indications that the Igbo did in fact contemplate the stars and the cosmos beyond the earth, they are rightly regarded not as myths but as didactic or moralizing stories, since what is ultimately emphasized is not so much the etiological element as the morals drawn at the end. Other "why so" or "how come" stories that focus on the characteristic features of animals, plants, and other phenomena are in the same sense better seen as didactic and moralizing tales than as true myths.

Other cycles of stories told as *ákúkó-ífò* are formula stories of the order of cumulative tales, catch-tales (stories in which the narrator describes his own death in the end), and other types that are distinguishable by their formal features but which otherwise belong thematically to one or the other of the above major categories.

Storytelling as Communal Theater

Igbo storytelling events have been rightly seen as communal theater. The storyteller invariably involves his audience and uses devices and techniques that help to reinforce a sense of drama and participation. First, there is a stylized opening repartee that is designed to transport the audience from the everyday world to the wonderful world of imaginative fancy. This opening repartee begins with a number of set opening formulas and then blossoms into a string of picturesque proverbs to which the audience must respond with appropriate parallels or complements. In one such repartee, we have the following:

Storyteller: *O tiii!* (She has come to put . . . !)
Spectators: *Oyo!* (Let it fall . . . !)
Storyteller: *O tiii!* (She has come to put . . . !)
Spectators: *Oyo!* (Let it fall . . . !)
Storyteller: If it happens here.
Spectators: We're there.
Storyteller: If it happens there.
Spectators: We're there.
Storyteller: When a dog carries a bag.
Spectators: Feces finish in the bush.
Storyteller: A forest in which a hen's toe is pierced by a thorn.
Spectators: No one can venture into it.
Storyteller: A woman that climbs a tree.
Spectators: A shooting war befits her more.
Storyteller: Once upon a time . . .
Spectators: And a certain time reached . . .

Thereafter, the story begins. The narrator may decide to adopt an eyewitness perspective, presenting the story as part of his own experiences in the course of an adventure through the mythical land of Iduu n'Oba. Iduu, as earlier mentioned, is often associated with the ancient kingdom of Benin, hence the reference to the Oba (King of Benin); but it would appear that in Igbo fabledom—more generally speaking—Iduu refers to the mythical world of fancy in which anything can happen. In stories in which the personal experience of the eyewitness is used, actions and incidents may be presented as one would present a commentary from a grandstand. At the end of the story the storyteller would normally sign off with the phrase, "That is where I reached and then came back," and the audience would respond: "Welcome." In other instances, the story, personified, runs and runs and catches the narrator or its main subject matter; and, at the end, it runs and runs off course, leaving the narrator to come back home to the spectators chorus of "Welcome."

Igbo stories are commonly of the order of chantefables. In the main body of the story, the storyteller uses songs with choric refrains to which the spectators respond in chorus to highlight points of intense emotion. Prophetic warnings by birds and other helpful figures come through dramatically using song. So too do the griefs, excitement, and joys of the heroes. Apostrophic, amplificatory, topical, complementary, inchoate, onomatopoeic, ideophonic, or lyrical (see "The Meaning of the 'Meaningless' Refrain in Igbo Folk Songs and Storytelling Events") the choric refrains add color, gaiety, somberness, and a wide variety of tones and mood to the drama of the storytelling event.

The dramatic presentation of events is enhanced by the use of arrestingly vivid sound images with strings of onomatopoeia and ideophones as their primary vehicles. In the following excerpt, such a string of onomatopoeia and ideophones, combined with repetition, parallelism, appropriate dialogue, and pithy answers to questions from the audience about cultural contexts and magical action, help to give volume, velocity, and sound to the evocation of a wrestling match between the wrestling hero Àkátámìkéògù, who is aided by his grandmother and one of his spirit adversaries, Órìé:

Storyteller: (claps) They rose, *fiam fiam fiam fiam fiam fiam fiam*. . . . They arrived at the boundary between the land of humans and the land of spirits. That is, the boundary . . .
Spectator: Is there really such a place called the boundary between the land of humans and the land of spirits?
Storyteller: Yes! There is!
Spectator: Really?
Storyteller: Yes! Eke-nwa-mmuo! It is called Eke-nwa-mmuo. He moved on and on!!!
Spectator: I don't know where they call Eke-nwa-mmuo.
Storyteller: Eke-nwa-mmuo. That is where people went when they died mysteriously in those days. So he moved on *viam viam viam viam viam viam viam*. . . .
Spectator: People used to go there in the olden times?
Storyteller: Yes.
Spectator: To ask questions? They usually took some pieces of white chalk? Do, remind me how?
Another Spectator: Wait, let's finish with this (story)!
Storyteller: Let me get on with my story. So, they journeyed on *viam viam viam viam viam viam viam*. . . . When they arrived at the boundary between the land of humans and the land of spirits, she told him it was time. And told him to get ready. She pulled off her human skin.
Spectators: Hee!
Storyteller: She stretched her hands across, gathered the skin off. . . . Then this one (Àkátámìkéògù) came, pulled off his human skin. . . . He pulled off his human skin, stretched his hand across, collected the skin of a spirit and wore it. They moved on. As they moved *viam viam viam viam viam viam viam*, who did they encounter first? Órìé! For Órìé was the youngest. . . . Órìé was at a place tending his yam tendrils, at such a time as now.
Spectator: Órìé? Was this Órìé market which people go to now?
Storyteller: Yes! He is a deity!
Spectator: So, Órìé was the youngest?
Storyteller: Yes! The youngest. He saw him. For he was a huge man. "Who are those moving forth?" He told Órìé that if he (Àkátámìkéògù) caught him . . . that he should stand still there, for both of them would wrestle! He replied, "It is a challenge!" And he told him that if he defeated him, he should carry his household property. But if he defeated him (Órìé), he and his kinsmen would share his meat for food. And he replied, "It is a challenge!" (Clapping his hands). He came out, and they wrestled, *girigi girigi girigi!* They wrestled, wrestled, and wrestled. The old woman looked around and there was no one in sight. She raised her voice. . . . For she did not pass through the street. She passed through the forest. She raised her voice from the forest and cried:
Àkátámìkéògù!
Unusual man of strength!
Àkátámìkéògù!

Unusual man of strength!
Stick up to wrestling,
Triumphs in wrestling
Unusual man of strength!
Kpam! Vruuuu! Tuai! He landed Órìé on the ground *gbiririm!* Órìé broke into pieces.
    (Chukwukere, 1993, 316–318)

The use of similar histrionic devices are amply evident in the Ogwashi-Uku narratives discussed and amply illustrated by Okpewho (1992). Other histrionic features of the storytelling events include: sharp character counterpoint and parallelism, the reversal of fortunes, situational or dramatic irony, and suspense and pathos.

Conclusion

Summing up the value of stories and storytelling in Igbo culture, the Old Man in the Abazon delegation to the military dictator Sam in Achebe's *Anthills of the Savannah* asserts:

the story . . . outlives the sound of war-drums and the exploits of brave fighters. It is the story . . . that saves our progeny from blundering like blind beggars into the spikes of the cactus fence. The story is our escort; without it, we are blind. Does the blind man own his escort? No, neither do we the story; rather it is the story that owns and directs us. It is the thing that makes us different from cattle; it is the mark on the face that sets one people apart from their neighbors. (Achebe, 1987, 114)

Igbo stories and storytelling are not only one of the most powerful forms of artistic verbal behavior in Igbo culture, but they are also the very soul of the culture. Stories nourish, strengthen, and validate social norms and vital social relationships. Above all they serve as dynamic instruments for maintaining cultural continuity, especially through their ideological recreations of the past that empower the present.

Further Reading

Achebe, Chinua, "Forward," in *Traditional Oral Texts*, volume 1 of *A Selection of African Prose*, edited by Wilfred H. Whiteley, Oxford: Clarendon, 1964

Amadiume, Ifi, *Male Daughters and Female Husbands: Gender and Sex in an African Society*, London and Atlantic Highlands, New Jersey: Zed, 1987

Azikiwe, Nnamdi, *Mythology in Onitsha Society* (Master's thesis, University of Pennsylvania), 1933

Azuonye, Chukwuma, "Igbo Enwe Eze: Monarchical Power vs the Democratic Ideal in Igbo Oral Narratives," in *Power, Marginality and African Oral Literature*, edited by Graham Furniss and Elizabeth Gunner, Cambridge and New York: Cambridge University Press, 1995

——, "Igbo Oral Literature," in *Groundwork of Igbo History*, edited by Adiele E. Afigbo, Lagos, Nigeria: Vista, 1992

——, "Morphology of the Igbo Folktale: Ethnographic, Historiographic and Aesthetic Implications," *Folklore* 101:1 (1990)

——, "Power, Marginality and Womanbeing in Igbo Oral Narratives," in *Power and Powerlessness of Women in West African Orality*, edited by Raoul Granqvist and Nnadozie Inyama, Umea, Sweden: Umea University, 1992

Azuonye, Chukwuma, and Donatus Nwoga, eds., *The Hero in Igbo Life and Literature*, Enugu, Nigeria: Fourth Dimension, forthcoming

Chukwukere, F. Ngozi, *Igbo Folktales About Women: Features and Ideological Implications* (Master's project report, University of Nigeria), 1993

Ugochukwu, C.N., T. Meniru, and P. Oguine, *Omalinze: A Book of Igbo Folk-Tales*, edited by E.N. Emenanjo, New York: Oxford University Press, 1977

The Meaning of the "Meaningless" Refrain in Igbo Folk Songs and Storytelling Events

Chukwuma Azuonye

Here Chukwuma Azuonye ponders the possible meanings of the "meaningless" refrains in Igbo folk songs that are sung during storytelling events.

A Bird Refrain

The refrains in folk songs that are often sung in chorus by the audience in folk storytelling events often have been described as "meaningless" or "nonsense" phrases largely because they comprise strings of sounds that supposedly do not have any current lexical status. But when one listens between the lines of some of the texts in which such descriptions occur, one is often struck by the wide range of expressive value that the so-called meaningless refrains have been recognized to carry. Indeed, when one closely examines these refrains, one finds that they are not only the most archaic and meaningful elements of the folk songs but by far the most critical in defining the lyrical quality and musicality of the songs. Isidore Okpewho (1992) comes more or less to these conclusions after examining the refrain of the following Igbo folk song, which he recalls from his childhood:

> Little bird, little bird
> *Tuluzamzam tuluzam*
> What are you doing there?
> *Tuluzamzam tuluzam*

> I'm up there fetching wood
> *Tuluzamzam tuluzam*
> After fetching what will you do?
> *Tuluzamzam tuluzam*
> After fetching I'll light a fire
> *Tuluzamzam tuluzam*

Of the so-called nonsense phrase (*Tuluzamzam tuluzam*), Okpewho writes:

> Such sounds are usually left untranslated—rightly, perhaps—because there is no obvious meaning or function to them other than to complete the rhythmic beat of the song. But it is equally possible that those sounds have been derived from a close observation of the habits of little birds and are employed as a vivid phonological way of representing the "personality" of the bird in this particular dialogue.

Okpewho concludes:

> On a more serious level, it has been charged that these ideophones or nonsense sounds are frequently found in "primitive" languages in their infancy of development. Again, it could be argued that some of these sounds have long lost their currency and that we no longer know their exact meanings because the language has developed well beyond them. On the whole,

41

however, it is safer to see ideophones and similar sound as proof of their users' sensitive feeling for language, a deep sensitive attachment to sounds and their power of vivid suggestion or representation.

Later, in this article, we shall see that—notwithstanding the validity of Okpewho's argument—the repeated phrase (*Tuluzamzam tuluzam*) in the song is not a case of a meaningless syllable, but a typical example of an onomatopoeic refrain, one that imitates sounds made by people, animals, and objects in the natural and cultural environment. Often other patterns of meaning in the folk song text (and in the larger narrative or liturgical text in which it is embedded) draw from, and are informed by, the fundamental meaning contained in the refrain.

While these claims will be illustrated in this article chiefly with reference to the folk songs and folktales of the Igbo people of southeastern Nigeria, it is assumed throughout that the emergent paradigms will be applicable to the choric refrain in other cultures, not only in Africa but elsewhere across the world as well. As T.V.F. Brogan and Laurence Perrine have noted in their contribution on the subject to *The New Princeton Encyclopedia of Poetry and Poetics*, "the full comparative study of refrains remains to be written" (p. 1018).

In order to present the so-called meaningless refrain in its proper perspective as part of a general pattern of meanings, it is necessary to outline and examine all the major categories of refrains that have been observed in the Igbo folk song, including those with unmistakable meanings. Eight main categories present themselves readily from the texts of performances that are available to us. These may be described as follows: (a) apostrophic refrains; (b) echo or parrot refrains; (c) complementary refrains; (d) exclamatory words; (e) theme or topical refrains; (f) onomatopoeic refrains; (g) ideophonic refrains; and (h) lyrical refrains. As we shall see presently, it is within the domain of ideophonic and lyrical refrains that the great majority of the so-called meaningless or nonsense phrases will be located.

Apostrophic Refrains

Apostrophic refrains are the most elementary and, presumably, the most archaic category of refrains. They range from simple interjections or exclamations that use all vowel sounds and na-

sals in the language (a! e! i! i! o! o! u! u! m! n! n!) to various patterns of combination and reduplication of these same sounds. Most common is the vocal exclamation, "O!" (Oh! Ou!), which, in Igbo, as in most other languages, is used to call attention to oneself or to something, or to express emotions ranging from surprise and admiration to fear, doubt, disapproval, or excitement. This is illustrated in the following song from the popular tale of "Omalinze," in which the hated wife bears the king's only male offspring. Here, the discovery of the king's unknown son, where he is being fostered by a pauper, provokes a song of praise and rejoicing with an apostrophic refrain:

> *Omalinze, Omalinze, Okoro oma*
> O, Omalinze!
> *Omalinze, Omalinze, Okoro oma*
> O, Omalinze! . . .
> *Nwa nze, Nwa nze, Nwa nze,*
> *Okoro oma*
> O, Omalinze!

> Omalinze, Omalinze, lovely man
> Oh, Omalinze!
> Omalinze, Omalinze, lovely man
> Oh, Omalinze!
> Lordly son, lordly son, lordly son,
> *lovely man*
> Oh, Omalinze!

Often, for melodic effects and as a means of maintaining quantitative symmetry between the solo and the refrain, the apostrophic phrase includes *melismata*, or different notes sung to one syllable, as in the following lines from the popular folk ballad "Nwakadiukporo." This is a cumulative tale that recounts a linked chain of tragic happenings that ensue when a breadfruit falls and kills the beautiful village girl for whom the ballad is named:

> *Gini, gini ga-emere m ukwa nu O!*
> *È-é-ē, Nwaakadiukporo!*
> *Gini, gini ga-emere m ukwa nu O!*
> *È-é-ē, Nwaakadiukporo!*
> *Ukwa mere gini?*
> *Ukwa kugburu Nwaakadiukporo,*
> *È-é-ē, Nwaakadiukporo!*

> What, O! what will happen to this breadfruit?
> *È-é-ē, Nwaakadiukporo!*

What, O! what will happen to this breadfruit?
È-é-ē, Nwaakadiukporo!
Breadfruit did what?
Breadfruit that killed Nwaakadiukporo,
È-é-ē, Nwaakadiukporo!

One of the major theories of the origins of human language suggests that interjections and exclamations, such as the above, that express a wide range of emotions—joy, grief, anger, excitement, fear, and love—lie at the very base of poetic communication. The idea of the lyrical impulse as the root of the emergence of primitive song has grown out of the assumption that humankind has an innate capacity to produce such emotion-toned sounds, which, in the course of time, crystallized in traditional form as codes for elegiac and rhapsodic song. Beyond simple exclamations (e.g., a!, e!, i!, o!, etc.) and their reduplications (e.g., a-a-a-a!, aa-aa!, a-aaa! aaa-a!, etc.) or *melismata* (such as we have seen in the Ballad of Nwaakadiukporo) that involve lyrical variations of the tones of a reduplicated sound (e.g., áàá ááá!, etc.), apostrophic refrains, like their manifestations in ordinary speech, are tonological gestalt tone-patterns with specific domains of meaning into which the singer or the speaker can fit in any vowel sound or nasal. Thus, for example, we can fit any vowel or nasal sound into the gestalt form (High-Low-High-Downstep) and the resultant sounds (e.g., áàáā!; éèéē!; îíî!; óòóō!; úùúū!) will always be connotative of a sudden flash of regret.

Exclamatory Words

In addition to vocal exclamations and *melismata*, Igbo folksingers make use of a rich repertoire of exclamatory words and phrases that have established themselves firmly, both in everyday speech and in formal religious and magical rituals, as codes for expressing certain kinds of emotion. Like "Alas!" in English, the exclamatory words *Hawee!* and *Ewu!* are interjections that express grief or regret that we find as refrains in funeral and satirical songs, either independently or as part of apostrophes addressed to death itself or to the dead. By the same token, interjections such as *Tufía!*, *Ihaa!*, and *Ise!* function as a ritual formula with specific connotations when used as refrains in a folk song. *Tufía!* is an interjection that connotes spitting off something in disgust; *Ihaa!* expresses affirmation or a plea for affirmation (as in the English "hear, hear!"); while *Ise!* (literally

"five") connotes ritual power and features frequently in ritual chants as the equivalent of the Judeo-Christian "Amen."

Interjections such as these occur frequently in Igbo ritual and satiric songs. In ballads and other types of folk songs, they serve as formulae to highlight the ritual seriousness of certain kinds of action. Thus, in a popular folktale, a group of animals going for a hunt discover a tree full of ripe berries but agree not to touch the fruits until after the hunt. But as is his wont, Mbe (Tortoise) the trickster would not leave the fruits alone. On the pretext of going to toilet, he returned to the tree and ate up most of the fruits (without plucking them from the tree) and managed to fill them all with feces. When the animals returned to the tree at the end of the hunt and discovered the outrage, they agreed that each and every one of them should swear an oath to clear himself. The oath is in the form of a song:

Umu njeee, umu njeee, jere nta,
Hii-i-hii!
Umu njeee, umu njeee, jere nta,
Hii-i-hii!
Ake m kpatukwa utu, okpa m
  kpatukwa utu chara acha,
Hii-i-hii!
Mmm, Omenuko ha alachaala

Travelers, Travelers that went a-hunting,
  Hii-i-hii!
Travelers, Travelers that went a-hunting,
  Hii-i-hii!
If my hands touched the fruits, if my legs
  touched the fruits that have ripened,
  Hii-i-hii!
Mmm, Omenuko and others have all gone
  home!

At the end of the song, each animal must jump over a pit. The culprit alone would be trapped by the charm placed in the pit. The refrain here ("*Hii-i-hii*") is a variation of the ritual interjection, "*Ihaa*" which is frequently heard in oath-taking rituals as a code of acquiescence to the terms of the oath. (The significance of the last line is rather obscure, but it may be mentioned in passing that Omenuko is the hero of an Igbo historical novel by Pita Nwana [1933]. The novel tells the story of a poor village boy who becomes a wealthy merchant. He must go into exile after he commits the outrage of selling his apprentices into slavery to make up for the losses he incurred when his goods fell into the rapids of a river when the bridge on which they were crossing collapsed.)

Echo or Parrot Refrains

Echo or parrot refrains are meaningful units which simply reecho, by repetition or parallelism, either the actual words or the meaning of the preceding solo lines. Refrains of this type range from single words and phrases to whole lines to verses of two or more lines. In the following song, an oppressed orphan, aided by his dead mother, conjures his magic palm tree to grow shorter so that he might harvest the fruits:

> *Nwa nkwu m sughu sughu . . .*
> *Sughu sughu!*
> *Nwa nkwu m sughu sughu . . .*
> *Sughu sughu!*

> My little palm tree, grow shorter, grow shorter
> Grow shorter, grow shorter!
> My little palm tree, grow shorter, grow shorter
> Grow shorter, grow shorter!

When verses are involved, we have instances of the traditional "shout" that was carried over to the New World.

Onomatopoeic Refrains

Onomatopoeic refrains are of the order of sound images. They are always complementary rhythmic units that add color and vividness to the song through the verbal imitation of sounds in the natural and cultural environment. In some cases, what may appear to the outsider as mere gibberish may indeed be a whole song comprising onomatopoeic patterns that reenact the sound of music and the thumping of dancing feet as in the following:

> *Tiiii-ro tiro*
> *Egwu na-agba n'obodo agu:*
> *Tijam jam!*

> *Tiiii-ro tiro*
> A dance is grinding in leopardstown:
> *Tijam jam!*

> *Tiiii-ro tiro*
> *Egwu na-agba n'obodo agu:*
> *Tijam jam!*

> *Tiiii-ro tiro*
> A dance is grinding in leopardstown:
> *Tijam jam!*

Similarly, we can hear the sound made by the drum of plenty in the refrain of the following verse:

> *Kwam putu kpam putu!*
> *Igba nri na ofe!*
> *Kwam putu kpam putu!*
> *Igba nri na ofe*!

> *Kwam putu kpam putu!*
> Drum of food and soup!
> *Kwam putu kpam putu!*
> Drum of food and soup!

And in the following, the solo imitates the beating of wooden drums (*ekwe*) while the choric refrain imitates the sound of the accompanying pot drum (*udu*) and maracas (*oyo*):

> *Kpom kpororom, kpom kpororom,*
> *Dum uyom uyom dum uyom!*
> *Kpom kpororom, kpom kpororom,*
> *Dum uyom uyom dum uyom!*

> *Kpom kpororom, kpom kpororom,*
> *Dum uyom uyom dum uyom!*
> *Kpom kpororom, kpom kpororom,*
> *Dum uyom uyom dum uyom!*

> *Ewu tara akara ike adighi ya*
> *Dum uyom uyom dum uyom!*

> A goat that has eaten beancakes has no
>   strength,
> *Dum uyom uyom dum uyom!*

By the same token, the guttural sound made by spirits is evident in the refrain ("*Hioro hioro*") that we hear in several songs through which one fiend or another threatens his human would-be victim.

Birds, both domestic and wild, figure frequently in Igbo songs and are often apostrophized. In such lyrics, onomatopoeic refrains that imitate the characteristic cries or other noises made by the animals that are being addressed help to underline the mood of the song. In the following lyric, the contrast is between the noisy gnawing of the squirrel and the death of its mother:

> *Osa na-ata akwu o!*

Charatam chatam!
Osa na-ata akwu o!
Charatam chatam!
I na-ata akwu o?
E gbuo ha nne gi o!
Charatam chatam!

Squirrel that is eating palm fruits,
Charatam chatam!
Squirrel that is eating palm fruits
Charatam chatam!
Are you eating palm fruits?
They have killed your mother!
Charatam chatam!

Onomatopoeic refrains are not limited to the re-production of sounds produced by people, animals, and objects in the natural and cultural environment. They also function as myth-creative devices that enable the singer to evoke an eerie atmosphere through the creation of imaginative patterns of sounds that suggest other realms of existence, such as the spirit world. In the following, the strangeness of the sound made by the horn of life and death that is blown by a spirit-woman who is pursuing two brothers fleeing from her ravenous claws is evoked by the refrain (*ndofuro ro-ro-ro-ro-ro*):

Opi ukwu, opi nta
Biko hwugbuoro umu nne abo na omiko,
Ndofuro ro-ro-ro ro-ro, ndofuro!
Ji mmam ha rikwere,
Ndofuro ro-ro-ro ro-ro, ndofuro!
Ede mmam ha rikwere,
Ndofuro ro-ro-ro ro-ro, ndofuro!

Big horn, small horn,
Pray, have mercy, blow to death two brothers
Ndofuro ro-ro-ro ro-ro, ndofuro!
Spirit yam, they ate,
Ndofuro ro-ro-ro ro-ro, ndofuro!
Spirit cocoyam, they ate.
Ndofuro ro-ro-ro ro-ro, ndofuro!

Similarly, in the refrain of another song, the horn of a fierce spirit pursuing his human victim has the menacing sound, *Temu lemu gene ntumulu gene tumu!* And in the hero tale of the great wrestler, Ojaadili, who throws spirits in a wrestling match in their own land, the refrain onomatopoeically reenacts the sound of the wrestling drums: *Ngoro ngoro didi ngoro!*

Ideophonic Refrains

Inasmuch as onomatopoeia is sometimes confused with ideophones, onomatopoeic refrains are apt to be confused with their very close relative, ideophonic refrains. But whereas onomatopoeia is a verbal pattern that imitates specific types of sounds, ideophones are gestalt sound patterns that provide subtle suggestions of the quality, duration, and intensity of phenomena. Thus, a steady flicker of light from the distance on a dark night would be described with the sound *keri keri;* the speedy movement of a stalwart going to war or a wrestling match is described as *viam viam viam viam viam!* or *flam flam flam flam flam!*; the smoothness of a shiny object is described as *muru muru.* By the same token, *vuruuu* describes the agility with which a fierce lion or leopard pounces upon his prey, while *jijiji* or *kwekwekwe* describes the suddenness of the body of a frightened actant shaking in the face of danger. A whole class of refrains in Igbo folk songs are of the order of this class of phonoaesthetic device. In one refrain, the wicked laughter of a heartless co-wife when her frightened rival knocks persistently at her closed door is described as *mgbafiri kotoo mgba mgba;* in another, the callousness with which a monstrous vulture swallowed the hero's mother together with her market commodities is depicted as *chafuru kpoto mkpo!*; and in variants of the story of the oppressed orphan, the hero's persistent and desperate weeping as he performs his tedious chores is evoked through the ideophonic refrains, *milize lizenze* or *zeezeelize Nwoye o zeze ze elize!* Similarly, when the king's lost son in the tale of "Omalinze" makes a revealing contact with his father's dog, his weeping is rendered as *Nnyàa, nyààko!* Ideophonic refrains are the so-called "meaningless" refrains par excellence; the popular assumption that they are meaningless derives from the fact that the verbal patterns involved are usually not lexical entities but are ideophones.

Lyrical Refrains

Closely related to, and, perhaps, substantially much the same as ideophonic refrains are lyrical refrains, a distinct class of refrains that make use of special lyrical formulae or codes, all of which are restricted to lyrical poetry and which we may aptly describe as lyremes. These archaic expressions generally invoke mood and atmosphere. Analysis of the contexts of their use reveal that each refrain belongs to a special mood category, such as elegiac, rhapsodic, or apostrophic. They have become an intrinsic part of the vocabulary of the song. The following are among the most common of these lyrical refrains that we find in Igbo elegiac songs—songs in which the atmosphere is predominantly one of grief, regret, or desperation: *Nda* (*Ndawere nda; Ndawerere werere nda*); *Une* (*Inine; Ineene; Une, unembele une*); *Shamala* (or *Samala; Samara; Ramala*); *Mbele* (*Mbene; Ajambele*); *Mbeneke* (*Bene; Tumbeneke; Tungenene*); *Awanjenje* (*Awandegele*); *Nturuzam* (*Turuzizi; Turuzi; Turuzanza; Tuzanza*); *Kparanuma* (*Kpalanuma*); and *Zamiriza* (*Zamirize; Nzamiriza; Awanzamirinza*). While there are no known lexical glosses to any of these sounds, it seems rather clear that each of them, like regular words in the lexicon, has dialectal and even idiolectal variants (the items in parentheses). It therefore seems right to assign them the meanings that seem clearly defined by the contexts in which they are used, for example, as lyrical codes for grief.

There is a whole class of lyremes in which the matrix of the apparently meaningless pattern of sounds is in fact a word that denotes a specific emotion (pity, fear, excitement, etc.) or describes a specific type of action or situation (movement through a forest, slow movement, etc.). Thus, in the refrain *ndo rima rima ndo rima* (Ugonna, 1980) and its many variants, such as *ndoghorighioma* and *ndo ndoo-o ndo ndo,* the matrix is the word *ndo* (denoting pity or sorrow). By the same token, *awa njenje* or its variant (*awa nje*) contains two meaningful matrices, namely *awa* from -*wa*- (to wade through a forest) and *nje* from -*je*- (to be on a journey). The lyreme thus literally means "wading through a forest, journeying and journeying." Not surprisingly this lyreme almost invariably occurs in songs that evoke the idea of an adventurous journey through a thick forest. In other significant instances, the matrix *awa* (wading through a forest) combines with such lyremes as *nzamiriza* (connoting harrowing and tear-provoking confrontations) to evoke the idea of an adventurous journey that takes the hero through harrowing, tearful confrontations such as encounters with dreadful many-headed spirits. It may be possible in the future to undertake a more detailed analysis of other lyremes that at present seem to defy such analysis.

Complementary Refrains

Complementary refrains may be regarded as half-lines that serve to complete the sense or meaning of the first half-line of a solo. Such complementary half-lines may be variable or fixed. In the following game song, the complementary refrain is fixed. It focuses on the overriding theme of the dispensable and replaceable abominable child, who must be thrown away or sold into slavery:

> *Tufuonu nwa mere aru o!* . . .
> *E ru echi amuta ozo!*
> *Refuonu nwa mere aru o!* . . .
> *E ru echi amuta ozo o!*

> Throw away the abominable child! . . .
> Tomorrow another will be born!
> Sell away the thieving child! . . .
> Tomorrow another will be born!

But, in another example, a lullaby, the complementary refrain is variable. Each new variant stresses a new strategy for lulling or coaxing the child to sleep:

> *Nwata m ku na-aka O!* . . .
> *Rahuru m ura!*
> *Nwata m ku na-aka O!* . . .
> *Rahuru m ura!*
> *O buru ji gi o* . . .
> *Mu enye gi ya!* . . .
> *O buru ede gi o.* . .
> *Mu enye gi ya o!*
> *Rahu ura ma oke*
>   *anyui gi nsi n'anya o!* . . .
> *Rahuru m ura!*

> O Child I'm carrying in my arms . . .
> Sleep for me!
> O Child I'm carrying in my arms . . .
> Sleep for me!
> If it's your yam . . .
> I'll give it to you!
> If it's your cocoyam . . .
> I'll give it to you!
> Sleep, lest a rat shits into your eyes . . .
> Sleep for me!

Theme or Topical Refrains

Theme or topical refrains are equivalent to the "Burden" in European folk songs. In this category of refrains, the main theme or subject matter of the song is reiterated throughout its performance. In the folk ballad or narrative folk song, the theme refrain is usually the name of the hero or heroine. Two examples that come readily to mind are the ballads of Nwaakadiukporo and Omalinze (Omalungwo or Omaraugo). The former is a cumulative or incremental ballad that begins with an apostrophe to the breadfruit tree whose fruit falls and kills the heroine:

Gini, gini ga-emere m ukwa nu O!
È-é-ē, Nwaakadiukporo!
Gini, gini ga-emere m ukwa nu O!
È-é-ē, Nwaakadiukporo!
Ukwa mere gini?
Ukwa kugburu Nwaakadiukporo!
È-é-ē, Nwaakadiukporo!
Gini, gini ga-emere m mkpo nu O!
È-é-ē, Nwaakadiukporo!
Gini, gini ga-emere m mkpo nu O!
È-é-ē, Nwaakadiukporo!
Mkpo mere gini?
Mkpo mawara ukwa!
Ukwa mere gini?
Ukwa kugburu Nwaakadiukporo,
È-é-ē, Nwaakadiukporo!

What, oh what will happen to this breadfruit?
È-é-ē, Nwaakadiukporo!
What, oh what will happen to this breadfruit?
È-é-ē, Nwaakadiukporo!
Breadfruit that did what?
Breadfruit that killed Nwaakadiukporo,
È-é-ē, Nwaakadiukporo!
What, oh what will happen to this stake?
È-é-ē, Nwaakadiukporo!
What, oh what will happen to this stake?
È-é-ē, Nwaakadiukporo!
Stake that did what?
Stake that split the breadfruit.
Breadfruit that did what?
Breadfruit that killed Nwaakadiukporo,
È-é-ē, Nwaakadiukporo!

There is no space to consider further examples. The material considered so far seems to show quite clearly that no refrain in the Igbo tradition on which we have focused can rightly be described as "meaningless." Every single sound that forms part of the idiom of the folk song seems to have some connotation, specific meaning, or symbolic value, no matter how unrelated they may seem to be to words in current language. Needless to say, further in-depth investigation of comparable manifestations of this important but hitherto neglected area of the expressive use of language in folk songs and storytelling events may yield meaningful results.

Further Reading

Egudu, Romanus, and Donatus I. Nwoga, comps., *Poetic Heritage: Igbo Traditional Verse*, Enugu, Nigeria: Nwankwo-Ifejika, 1971; also published as *Igbo Traditional Verse*, London: Heinemann, 1973

Ndiot, Innocent, *The Role of the Chorus in Igbo Folksongs and Folktales with Special Reference to Osisioma Ngwa* (Bachelor's long essay, University of Nigeria), 1983

Ogbalu, F. Chidozie, *Mbem na Egwu Igbo* [Igbo Songs and Poems], Yaba Lagos: Macmillan, 1978

——, *Onitsha Province Nursery Rhymes . . . Shamara*, University Publishing, n.d.

——, *Western Igbo Nursery Rhymes: Nda*, University Publishing, n.d.

——, *Zamiriza: A Collection of Igbo Traditional Poems*, University Publishing, n.d.

Okpewho, Isidore, *African Oral Literature: Backgrounds, Character, and Continuity*, Bloomington: Indiana University Press, 1992

Ugochukwu, C.N., T. Meniru, and P. Oguine, *Omalinze: A Book of Igbo Folk-tales*, edited by E.N. Emenanjo, New York: Oxford University Press, 1977

Ugonna, Nnabuenyi, ed., *Abu na Egwuregwu Odinala Igbo*, Ikeja: Longman Nigeria, 1980

The Dogon Creation Story

Chukwumu Azuonye

Here, Chukwumu Azuonye outlines and analyzes the creation story of the Dogon people and explains its relationship to the star Sirius.

The Seed of the World

The creation story of the Dogon people of the Bandiagara cliffs in southern Mali and the plains of northern Burkina Faso in the area of the Niger bend in West Africa is one of the most elaborate and fascinating traditional explanations of the origins of the world and of human culture. Unlike biblical and similar stories of creation in other African oral traditions, in the Dogon creation story the idea of an all-powerful and all-knowing divine creator is subordinated to an evolutionary process in which God (Amma) emerges as a supernatural but imperfect progenitor. In place of the traditional idea of creation out of nothing, the Dogon creation story offers through the magic of the divine logos a more scientific explanation that anticipates the modern big bang theory. In the Dogon creation story, we can see a projection into the cosmos of ideas that essentially belong to reproductive biology. Underlying these ideas is what appears to be some knowledge of the role of chromosomes and of DNA in the formation of every new life, as formulated in modern genetics.

The story begins with the idea of the seed of the world. Described by the Dogon as *kize uze* (the smallest of things), this tiny seed floated quietly through the dark emptiness of space before the birth of our galaxy, the Milky Way. Although it is as small as the smallest cultivated seed in Dogon culture, namely *fonio* or *digiteria exelis,* it

contains the potential for the existence of all reality. In the course of its flotation, it suddenly begins to expand under the pressure of internal vibrations. This happens at the point in space where the Dogstar, Sirius A (Digiteria) and its dwarf companion, Sirius B, are now located. Today, these twin stars occupy an important place on the Dogon ritual calendar. The all-important Dogon ritual of renewal, Sigui, which takes place every 60 years, follows the time it takes Sirius B to complete one orbit around Sirius A, a fact which has since been confirmed, with only a few minor differences, by modern science.

With the intensification of the internal vibrations within it, the seed of the world expands and expands until it reaches the utmost limits of the universe, forming an oval mass that the Dogon describe as the egg of the world (*aduno tal*) or the womb of the world, using the term *me* (which can be glossed as placenta or amnion) to describe its contents. The transformation of the seed of the world into the egg or womb of the world takes place in seven stages. Unwinding like a spiral from its point of origin, each of the seven stages of its expansion is longer than the preceding one. In Dogon iconography, this unwinding process is represented by a zigzag line called *ozu tonolo.* Other ritual drawings depict the seven-stage unwinding process as culminating in the prefiguration of the human shape. We can see from these drawings (Fig. 1) that the first and sixth vibrations represent the human legs, the second and the fifth the hands, the third and the fourth head, while the seventh represents the genitals (the male penis or the female clitoris):

At the seventh vibration, the enveloping sheath breaks releasing all creation into space, just as young lives are released into the world from an egg.

An interesting and significant aspect (from the perspective of modern science) of the Dogon view of the processes within the egg of the world before creation is the notion that the egg of the world contained a master plan for creation. This master plan is composed of images or signs called *yala*. Each *yala* contains a model or code of all the instructions needed for the creation of each and every thing now known to exist in the universe, and all these, according to the Dogon, are grouped into 22 basic categories.

Amma, the supreme being, is among the first of the 22 categories of beings (deities) who emerged to become fully differentiated self-conscious beings. As god of creation, he set out to complete the work of creation. But he does so, not as an omniscient and all-powerful God, but, through procreation, as a great father figure with all the imperfections of humankind.

Lacking foreknowledge of things, he must also proceed by trial and error. His first task was to procreate a divine model for humankind, Nommo. Nommo would be a pair of androgynous twins. Each pair would comprise two persons, one basically female but with balancing male attributes, the other basically male but with balancing female attributes. Through further procreation between the twin Nommo, the ancestors of humankind would come into being. Their offspring, like themselves, would preferably come as twins or as individual male and female beings with complementary female and male attributes like themselves. But, unfortunately, Amma's first attempt at procreating the Nommo proved to be a failure.

At first Amma was thwarted by the aggressive masculinity of the model earth (then still suspended in the heavens). As he approached the primordial female Earth in sexual foreplay, a termite hill, Earth's clitoris, rose aggressively like a gigantic penis. Amma was forced into a struggle to subdue this aggressiveness. In cutting down the earth's clitoris, he set down the rule that subsequent generations have followed through clitoridectomy (female circumcision) to subdue the potential of the female clitoris to compete with the male penis. After this, Amma succeeded in copulating with the earth; but unfortunately, the struggle with the earth's maleness had already marred this first sexual union. The offspring was the jackal, Dyougou

Figure 1: First Seven Vibrations of the Egg of the World (after Griaule and Dieterlen, 1954)

Serou, rather than the perfect model of creation, the twin Nommo, that was intended.

Dyougou Serou was a male being without any complementary female elements. In time, this all-male being raped his own mother, Earth. The result was a breed of incomplete beings that have survived in the universal order as evil beings of various kinds. Seized with shame over his misdeeds, Dyougou Serou spent the rest of his life in restless disgrace. Dogon sculpture represents him in several cringing poses with his hands covering his face (Laude, 1973; Imperato, 1978; Goldwater, 1959; and Ezra, *Art of the Dogon*, 1988). In time he suffered an antibirth by dissolving back into his mother, the earth's, vagina. But his evil offspring have survived to trouble the world.

The Dyougou Serou episode is only one of several versions of the explanation of the origins of evil in the Dogon creation story. In other versions, the origin of evil is attributed to a being known as Ogo, who, paradoxically, is an offspring of one of the pair of perfect Nommo born of Amma's second mating with the now circumcised earth. While still in the womb, the male person (Ogo) in one of the androgynous pair of twin Nommo tore his way out into space before the appointed time of his birth, leaving his female counterpart behind. He emerged carrying with him a piece of his own placenta. Outside the world-womb, this piece of placenta became his own earth. In addition to stealing a piece of his own placenta, he also stole some of the *fonio*, which Amma had intended to give to perfect humanity to plant for their sustenance on the pure earth. Ogo is thus also known in Dogon mythology as Yo Ogo (the thief Ogo) or Yurugu.

But Ogo's rebellion was in vain. The earth he created in such haste before his birth at full term was an impure earth in which nothing good or complete could thrive because of its denial of the female essence. In frustration, Ogo returned to heaven to search for his soul sister but discovered that Amma had retrieved her and placed her in the world-womb under the charge of the remaining twin Nommo. Ogo then returned to the dark and desolate world he had created with such reckless haste. There, Amma turned him into the pale fox as a punishment for his misdeeds. The single, all-male incomplete beings born of his incest with his mother's placenta who now peopled the earth have survived as the breed of evil beings that still trouble humankind. At this point the Dyougou Serou and the Yurugu versions of the Dogon creation story can be seen to merge.

Now, the impure earth of Yurugu or Dyougou Serou must be cleansed or created anew. To do this, Amma sacrificed the complete twin (male and female) Nommo of the other half of the placenta. These heavenly Nommo had been born at full term. Their bodies and blood were scattered over the cardinal points of the earth. Then the pieces were gathered together, resurrected in heaven, and sent back to the earth to remove all impurities. Earlier, Amma had created the sky and the stars to perfection through these sacrificed and resurrected perfect twin Nommos. They would now create a new earth, a world which, like the sky and the stars, would be perfect. They came down from the sky in a gigantic boat or ark which the Dogon describe as the "Boat of the World," or "the Ark of the World."

The "Boat of the World" is also described by the Dogon as the "Granary of the Master of Pure Earth." It contained everything needed to created a *gana duge* (a world in harmony). Piloted by the two heavenly Nommos, who now took the guise of blacksmiths, the Boat of the World finally came to rest in the present location of the earth, where it instantly became a new earth. This new earth was complete, formed according to Amma's order. Up until then the universe was in total darkness. Now light appeared for the first time. Water also appeared in the form of rain to clean and purify the earth, making it ready for the first ancestors of human beings.

With the descent of the boat of the heavenly Nommo came not only the separation of earth from other worlds, but also the separation of night from day and the appearance of the cycle of the moon (months), seasons, years, and generations. Social life was organized and the artistic

and technological foundations of civilization were laid by the Nommo turned blacksmiths.

Though he was an evil being, one of Ogo's actions for which he is still remembered in Dogon rituals today was the theft of a piece of the sun. Through this act, he brought fire to the world. With fire already present on earth, the Master Blacksmith introduced the major forms of art and technology for which the Dogon have been known for centuries. First, he taught humans how to weave. Then he instructed them in music and the making of the harp-lute and other musical instruments. After that, he taught them how to make various agricultural and household implements. The first ancestors of human beings appeared soon after the descent of the Boat of the World and its transformation into pure earth. The Dogon creation story says that there were four male ancestors: Amma Seru, Lébé Seru, Binu Seru, and Dyougou Serou (each with a female companion, his sister and wife). These four twins were born of four other pairs of Nommo which came from the four cardinal points—east, west, north and south—at the time of the descent of the Boat of the World. As they came from the four ends of the world, the four pairs or eight ancestors brought with them eight seeds. These seeds were sown in the new, pure, and fertilized earth. Out of each seed, a new seed grew.

The arrival of the eight ancestors signalled the blossoming of civilization on the new earth. This was not a civilization in which human life would be measured in terms of material success or the erection of tall architectural buildings and machines of destruction. It was rather a civilization governed by ideas about the completeness and meaningfulness of human life that run throughout the Dogon creation story.

The Dogon creation story as recounted above is only one of several versions of the myth found in Dogon culture. There are a wide variety of other versions, some far more evolutionary than the foregoing. Others are more creationist and represent Amma creating through the divine logos. Some of these versions may have been influenced by creation myths from other cultures. Nor are myths of this kind peculiar to Dogon culture. Similar myths seem to be widespread among the 44 or so ethnic groups that make up the Mande cluster in the area of West Africa that stretches from the Fouta Djallon to the Niger Bend and from the Atlantic Ocean to the Sahel. Possible links with ancient Egyptian mythology have been explored (Temple, 1976). But, in the end, the Dogon creation story is best understood as a reflection of the advanced scientific knowledge of the people and as the fundamental basis of their philosophy, worldview, and religion.

On the advances in scientific knowledge of the Dogon in their creation story, Marcel Griaule and Germaine Dieterlen (1954), two pioneering students of Dogon thought and religion, have written as follows: "All these images seem to relate to an effort of discovery, an attempt to apprehend the infinitely small at its point of departure towards the immeasurably vast. In fact, the order of the heavens, as it is observed and understood by the Dogon, is no more than a projection, infinitely expanded, of events and phenomena which occur in the infinitely small."

We shall see that the Dogon creation story explains the creation of the universe in the light of their knowledge of how life is procreated, that is, the reproduction of life in the womb. Thus we have images of the egg of the world, the womb of the world, the placenta, the amnion, the sperm, etc. If this is so, then the 22 basic categories cannot be understood outside the biology of human reproduction. The *yala* may refer to a supergenetic code, and the 22 *yala* signs may refer to 22 of the 23 pairs of chromosomes that carry the genes of the codes of life. Indeed, the Dogon speak of 22 pairs of basic categories, each comprising a male and a female. Twenty-two of the 23 chromosomes in the human body comprise male and female elements. It is also known that the 22 are grouped into four sections. The DNA is controlled by four bases: adenine, thymine, guanine, and cytosine. These correspondences are far too close to be ignored. Myth is not all fantasy; it is also a symbolic expression of the facts of life. This reality is clearly embedded in the Dogon creation story.

As both the reflection of and main pillar of Dogon philosophy and religion, the full meaning of the Dogon creation story can only be acquired by initiated elders as part of what the Dogon regard as *so dayi* (clear speech, or advanced knowledge of world order arrived at through progressive lifelong revelation and initiation). This initiation begins with *gid so* (front speech, or elementary knowledge) and proceeds like formal schooling through the intermediate stages of *benne so* (side speech) and *bolo so* (back speech) to *so dayi*.

An example of *so dayi* in print is Marcel Griaule's book, *Conversations with Ogotemmêli* (1965), in which the blind hunter and sage,

Ogotemmêli, reveals the framework of the Dogon system of thought and religion in a series of recorded interviews. Similar revelations have come from other sages, among them Tierno Bokar (Bâ and Cardaire, 1957) and Yèbène Dolo (Ezra, 1988b). From these and from more recent sources, we now know that the secret knowledge that constitutes Dogon philosophy is based on solid scientific knowledge of the universe and that it is founded on four major pillars. Stated briefly, these are: first, the idea that the universe is a system of forces (dynamism); second, the idea that everything in the existence comes in pairs or twins (dualism); third, the idea that human beings are the centerpiece of all creation and hence that everything in the universe exists in human interest (anthropocentricism); and, finally, the idea that everything in the universe is a miniature of the whole (microcosmicism).

For the Dogon, the vital force, *nyama*, which they see as pervading the universe, became personified in Amma, the creator. From Amma, this force has been transmitted to all beings. Humans received it through the Nommo and through the first human ancestors begotten by the Nommo. At death, *nyama* is let loose and must be contained in some way or it may cause harm. The Dogon do this by making *dege* (images) into which the *nyama* of the dead must be channeled. The main rituals of the Dogon are thus concerned with maintaining the continuity of *nyama* in its positive forms and with controlling all its negative manifestations.

Dogon religion reflects the four pillars of the people's philosophy. It seeks to control the flow of the life force, *nyama*, in the interest of humankind as the center of all creation. In the visible aspects of Dogon religion—in its rituals, altars, and major icons, such as carved images of gods and other powers (*dege*), care is taken to represent the principle of twinness associated with cosmic harmony, and one is at every stage reminded of the fact that in the smallest of things will be found the image of the universe, which in turn reflects the form and functioning of the human body.

Two main aspects of this religion stand out clearly. One is the directness of the relationship between every Dogon person and the creator, Amma. The second is the existence of a similar direct relationship between individuals and the community with other major bearers of *nyama*, through four fundamental cults: the totemic cult (Binu), the cult of the earth deity (Lébé), the cult of ancestors, and the cult of masks (*imina*).

Rites and other practices associated with all these aspects of Dogon religion involve first, the use of statues (*dege*) that represent the object of worship; second, the chanting of invocations or hymns (*toro*) that praise and petition the objects of worship in order of seniority (beginning with Amma) and that place them in the story of creation and of the maintenance of world order; third, the sacrifice of an animal or the making of an offering, usually on an altar (called *ama* after the creator, or *omono*). The altar usually comprises or includes a statue that shows the supplicant in one pose or another statue that indicates the need for which the sacrifice or offering is being made. The use of altars of this kind in Dogon religion is of special interest since they separate the Dogon and other Mande religious practices from what finds elsewhere in Africa.

The supreme god of Dogon religion, Amma Tongo, the creator, is not the withdrawn high god of the kind found in the religions and myths of many other African cultures. Amma, the source of life and rain, is ever present. The source of all *nyama*, he must be called upon directly over all key problems of life. Since all sacrifices ultimately go to him, altars are generally called *ama* after him. In all rituals, including those addressed to other powers, the *toro* (hymn or invocation to the divinities) that is chanted must begin by invoking the power and seniority of Amma and move from there down to the least important powers, namely human ancestors.

Although Amma is seen as the source of all *nyama*, he is by no means all-knowing, all-seeing, or all-good. It must be recalled that Amma himself is said in the Dogon creation story to have made some serious mistakes in the creation of the world. Amma is thus a supreme god who like human beings is subject to forgetfulness, mischief, and other caprices. Because of this belief in the fallibility of the supreme god, the Dogon feel the need to keep their petitions constantly in his view. This is where the statues that represent the petitioner in a pose that represents his or her needs come in. As a Dogon proverb tells us, "One cannot always pray and kneel at the altar, but the statue can." The *dege* statues thus help to keep petitions constantly in the view of the imperfect god. In prayers or sacrificial offerings of blood or millet, the petitioner would take off his or her clothes and take the pose of the statue. This also happens in rituals associated with Nommo, the ancestors, and the other fundamental cults.

Other major objects found in and around Dogon altars include a leather string with a *duge* (a bead or stone) that represents the egg of the world and a *bundo* (a small clay vessel) for libations.

Daily life in traditional Dogon society is made up of a series of colorful rites that maintain the continuity of the people's idea of the organization of the world. Other rites are rites of renewal whose purpose is to renew the life force (*nyama*) that flows with the blood in every human being and is part of the vital energy that controls human society at all levels and the universe at large.

The Dogon rites of continuity are of two types. The first are rites of passage of the kind found in all cultures across the world that mark key moments in the traditional life cycle from birth to death. The most representative of these rites of passage are funeral ceremonies, which are connected with beliefs in the continuity of the life force beyond death. The second type of rites of continuity consists of ceremonies that form part of four primary cults in Dogon culture, namely the cults of Binu, Lébé, Amma, and Dyougou. The most representative of these are the rites connected with the cult of Binu.

The Dogon funeral ceremony is the high point of a series of rites of passage that begin with birth and naming ceremonies and include initiation and marriage ceremonies. The cult of Binu exists to promote growth in the widest sense of the word and so do the rites associated with it.

The most important of the rites of renewal in Dogon culture is the very elaborate Sigui ceremony held every 60 years to mark the passage of one generation and the beginning of another. Another important ceremony of renewal comprises the death anniversaries, called Dama, held every year to mark the doings of one or more persons who died in the previous year.

The timing of the ceremony of Sigui is tied up with Dogon knowledge about the Dog Star, Sirius A, and the movements of its smaller but heavier companion around it. The Dogon believe that the big bang which led to the explosion and expansion of the seed of the world into the egg out of which everything in the world emerged began at the present location of Sirius. It takes Sirius B 60 years to orbit round Sirius A, and the Dogon believe that this period of time represents a significant span which affects the life of the world. People who were born during the last Sigui are on the threshold of old age while those who were old men at the last Sigui are either dead or on their way to the spirit world. The 60-year period thus represents a major shift in generations and of the life of the world. It is therefore an excellent occasion to make sacrifices and invoke powerful forces for the renewal of the world. In essence, the Sigui ceremony reenacts the story of creation.

The annual death anniversaries are less elaborate but no less colorful or less connected with the Dogon story of the origins of the world order. Today, there are three kinds of Dama. The first is a general Dama, held in honor of several persons who died in the previous year. The second is a special grand Dama, held in honor of one great personality. The third is a special adapted Dama that is performed as theater.

It must be stated in conclusion that controversy surrounds much of the above reconstruction of the Dogon creation story, especially with regard to its scientific and philosophical underpinnings. The Hamitic myth which holds that no black race has ever created any complex structures of the imagination has misled some scholars (such as Temple, 1976) to seek explanations for the Dogon's advanced knowledge first (without success) in European and Arab sources, and ultimately in ancient Egyptian sources. Temple ends up settling for extraterrestrial visits from the region of Sirius A and B. But today, as old-fashioned stereotypes about Africa disappear in the face of more intimate knowledge of the continent and its culture, the Dogon creation story and the worldview, science, and philosophy that inform and are informed by it have come to gain better acceptance as one of the most original and fascinating mythic explanations of the universe, of our world, and of human culture.

Further Reading

Azuonye, Chukwuma, *Dogon*, New York: Rosen, 1996

Bâ, Amadou Hampaté, and Marcel Cardaire, *Tierno Bokar, le sage de Bandiagara*, Paris: Présence Africaine, 1957

DeMott, Barbara, *Dogon Masks: A Structural Study of Form and Meaning*, Ann Arbor, Michigan: UMI Research, 1982

Ezra, Kate, ed., *African Arts* special issue 21:4 (August 1988)

——, *Art of the Dogon: Selections from the Lester Wunderman Collection*, New York: Metropolitan Museum of Art, 1988

Goldwater, Robert, "Introduction," in *Sculpture from Three African Tribes: Senufo, Baga, Dogon: [Exhibition] Spring 1959*, New York: Museum of Primitive Art, 1959

Griaule, Marcel, *Conversations with Ogotemmêli: An Introduction to Dogon Religious Ideas*, London: Oxford University Press for the International African Institute, 1965; New York: Oxford University Press for the International African Institute, 1970

Griaule, Marcel, and Germaine Dieterlen, "The Dogon of the French Sudan," in *African Worlds: Studies in the Cosmological Ideas and Social Values of African Peoples*, edited by Daryll Forde, London: Oxford University Press, 1954; New York: Oxford University Press, 1960

——, *Le Renard Pâle*, Paris: Institut d'Ethnologie, 1965; as *The Pale Fox*, Chino Valley, Arizona: Continuum Foundation, 1986

Imperato, Pascal James, *Dogon Cliff Dwellers: The Art of Mali's Mountain People*, New York: L. Kahan Gallery/African Arts, 1978

Laude, Jean, *African Art of the Dogon: The Myths of the Cliff Dwellers*, New York: Brooklyn Museum/Viking, 1973

Pern, Stephen, *Masked Dancers of West Africa: The Dogon*, Amsterdam, The Netherlands: Time-Life, 1982

Roy, Christopher, *The Dogon of Mali and Upper Volta/Die Dogon von Mali und Ober-Volta*, Munich, Germany: Jahn Gallery, 1983

Temple, R.K.G., *The Sirius Mystery*, New York: St. Martin's, 1976; London: Futura, 1976

The Storytelling Event Among the Igede of Nigeria

Ode Ogede

After showing us a typical evening of hearthside storytelling, Ode Ogede displays a sample tale text and discusses the didactic uses of such tales with the family.

The Commencement of an Evening's Storytelling

On a cool and moonlit night in December 1981, the members of Ode Agbike's family sat by a log fire in their home in Uchenyim village of the Ibilla clan. The majority of them have been busy all day harvesting crops—mostly yams and water yams—from the farm. After the evening meal, the head of the household announced that there was a pressing family matter to be discussed. Everyone waited for him to announce the subject. Shortly afterward, he called each of his wives and commended her for the work she did that day on the farm. On this particular day, only one family member had gone shopping, and she was thanked for that, while the efforts of another family member who had spent the day working hard to bring firewood home from the bush were also recognized. Afterward, he thanked the older children individually for the part each played in the family's work.

It is extremely important to bear in mind that the man had called his wives and children in their order of seniority. Every member present understood that this was a ritual of daily life that must be observed, and had the man chosen to omit it, he would have been reminded of it by one of the senior persons in the household. After mutual agreement was reached on the issue raised for discussion, the family members took turns telling folktales, one of which follows.

The Story of a Girl Who Disobeyed Her Parents

A long time ago, a mother lived with her only daughter. She was a stubborn girl who always disobeyed her mother. One day the mother needed to leave this daughter all by herself in the house. Before she left home, the mother told her daughter she was traveling to a very distant market. "I will be away all day. Do not leave the house for any reason whatsoever," the mother warned.

When the mother got ready to leave home, she repeated, "Don't leave this house until this food I am putting on the fire is done."

The mother filled a cooking pot with stones disguised as food. She then showed her daughter a big bundle of firewood. "Now, there is the fire-wood you are to use in cooking this food."

She also gave her daughter other detailed cooking instructions. "Do periodically watch out also for the water; when it dries out, do not forget to add some more," the mother said.

It was not very long after her mother's departure that several of the girl's friends arrived in a group at her home.

"What are you doing today?" one of them asked. She related that the group was going to the big forest to search for firewood and mushrooms. "Won't you come along with us?" asked the group.

The stubborn girl replied to her friends that she would have loved to go with them but could not. "My mother is away and she has left food on the fire for me to cook," she explained.

Upon hearing this, her friends smiled. "We can help you cook this food quickly, and then we can all go out together," they offered.

The stubborn girl's friends deceived her. They fanned the fire rapidly. Secretly, one of them went to the garden near the fireplace, where she collected the leaves of *cocoayam*. Secretly, she opened the pot and spread a thin layer of these leaves over the stones. A moment later, she asked the stubborn girl to go check the food and see.

As soon as the *ojeh* (a piece of iron rod used for testing food) touched the soft leaves of *cocoayam*, the girl was deceived into believing the food was cooked. She rushed into her mother's hut, fetched a cutlass as well as the basket for collecting mushrooms, and left the house in the company of her friends.

When the girls got to the edge of the forest, they found a huge log of firewood. They tried to cut it out—*Ka ka ka ka ka ka*—but it proved to be too hard for their tender hands. The girls decided to journey further into the forest.

They journeyed *la la la la la* into a very deep part of the forest. Mushrooms covered everywhere and the girls scrambled to pick them up. The stubborn girl was very smart, and it did not take her long to gather a generous amount. But while she busied herself collecting heaps of mushrooms *pia pia pia, pia pia pia*, she got lost in the rhythm of work and went deeper and deeper, far beyond the safe zones, into the heart of the forest, completely oblivious that she had strayed from the company of her friends.

When she finally looked up, she discovered to her consternation that she was alone in the thick and dark forest, as her friends had abandoned her. The thick forest was getting darker by the second! Cold shivers ran through the spine of the stubborn girl. She did not know what to do. The more she tried to find her way out of the darkness that was enveloping her by the second, the further into the thick forest her efforts took her. And the stubborn girl was seized by a great terror. It did not take long before ideas began to cross her mind that she might never see her home again. She was overwhelmed by regret over her original act of disobedience. "If only I had listened to Mother," she cried.

The stubborn girl began to send out a loud call to her friends, but none of them was within hearing distance of her any longer. In fact, all she could hear was her own voice as it echoed and echoed through the depth and breadth of the dark, terrifying, and lonely forest.

It turned out that a ghost disguised as an old woman was collecting firewood close by. Upon hearing the girl's human voice, it decided to respond. The ghost appeared and offered to rescue her, but instead it took the poor girl into captivity.

The ending of this tale, which is well known throughout Igedeland, is a fine example of the didactic structure of traditional Igede folktales, which have varied and numerous endings that enable their narrators to stress messages that may be of interest to them at any particular time.

In the version stressed at Ode Agbike's residence on the night in question, the girl suffers greatly in the home of the ghost, where she is daily made to drink a cupful of the secretions that endlessly gush out of the ulcers on one of the legs of her hostess. She endeavors eventually to make her escape.

During the escape attempt, however, she is hotly pursued by the ghost. The stubborn girl is about to reach the safety of her mother's hut when the ghost catches up with her. There is an ensuing struggle, and the injury the girl receives is the great curve of the human spine—which is re-ally the mark of the wounds left by the fingernails of the ghost as it reached out unsuccessfully to grab the fleeing girl from the back.

The scenario described above is an appropriate one with which to study the storytelling event among this minority group occupying the southern fringe of Nigeria's Benue State. It illustrates a pattern that is typically repeated, night after night, month after month, and year after year, by virtually every family in the community. Note the stress on the punishment for disobedience; it fits in with this particular family's need to instruct its young ones to obey their elders.

The Tale as Vehicle for Intergenerational Communication

Typically, at an Igede storytelling session such as the one that I witnessed at Agbike's home, all the participants—men and women, girls and boys, adults and children—sit around the family hearth. Every member present understands that the storytelling occasion is a time not only for recreation but also for fruitful and harmonious dialogue among family members.

The traditional Igede society is gerontocratic, and the respect that the people have for age is such that they have few occasions when people of different age groups ever get together. Storytelling provides one of the rare occasions when people in the community can break free of the dichotomization that is the normal order of their lives. Conducted in an informal setting, where all barriers of age and gender are broken, storytelling occasions allow the participants to interact in an astonishingly free manner. The Igede storytelling brings family members together in a way few other events do.

Typically, the narrator will begin with the formula "*ojah nyam piri piri piri ka ch*'" (My story journeys all the way to light upon), before naming the topic. This formula is a signal that all are entering the domain of storytelling—a playtime when all the players in the game have attained equality because all the barriers of age and even gender have been temporarily suspended. In Igede there are no defined criteria that qualify a person to be a performer. The only requirement is that he or she have a tale and a style captivating enough to hold the attention of the audience. Everyone is a potential narrator.

More often than not, however, it is boys who have reached puberty who show the greatest interest in storytelling performances. On this particular night at Ode Agbike's home he himself did not lead the storytelling that followed. He remained seated within the hearth throughout the entire duration of the performances, but it was evident that, even though he exerted no visible authority over those activities, his presence played a big role in the discipline of all the participants.

Conversation (*Ojah*) and Storytelling (*Ujwoh*)

Ujwoh is the name that the Igede give to the folktale narrative, as distinct from *ojah* (gossip or conversation). The distinction is important, since *ujwoh* is pure fiction, whereas *ojah* is based substantially on facts or on events that are believed to be true. Whereas people *j'ojah* (i.e., converse) essentially to share information, they *j'ujwoh* (i.e., tell a tale) not primarily for recreational purposes

but with a didactic intent. Essentially, the idea is to use depravities in the bizarre world, where animals, ghosts, ogres, and humans interact freely, to cast light on events in the normal human world, and to use macabre stories to teach appropriate modes of human conduct, morals, and other values.

Storytelling occupies a special place in the lives of the Igede. The storytelling is accompanied by riddle sessions as well as by games like hide-and-seek, by singing and dancing, and by snacks like roast corn, groundnuts, and peanuts. Storytelling is not only an occasion for relaxation, merrymaking, and imaginative adventure but also a time for education. Because it usually takes place only after dinner, when family members have completed the day's work, storytelling is also a primary venue for conflict resolution. Commenting on the emancipating role of carnival during the European Middle Ages, Mikhail Bakhtin writes that "carnival celebrates temporary liberation from the prevailing truth of the established order; it marks the suspension of all hierarchical rank, privileges, norms and prohibitions. Carnival was the true feast of time, the feast of becoming, change and renewal" (p. 109). The traditional storytelling event does for the Igede precisely what the carnival did for the Russians during the European Middle Ages.

Nighttime for Storytelling

Nighttime is the standard Igede setting for storytelling. People are forbidden to engage in storytelling at any other time, especially during the day. For instance, it is believed that whoever breaks the taboo will be visited by grave misfortunes. The efficacy of social conditioning can be measured by the fact that an average child grows up believing that if he or she narrates or listens to a folktale narrated in the daytime, he or she will have his or her head melted.

Although this stipulation is undoubtedly part of society's way of checking indolence among its members, in fact anyone who wishes to perform stories during the day will have no audience, since most people will be working in the fields far away from their homes.

Nighttime is the appropriate time for storytelling for other reasons as well. For one thing, it is cooler at night in the tropics, and therefore it is more enjoyable to tell stories at this time. For another, since darkness is the natural abode of ogres, spirits, and supernatural beings, it tends to add to the awesome powers of such creatures as ghosts, hares, elephants, leopards, tigers, baboons and monkeys, whose exploits in somber forests the stories almost always relate. The obscurity of the night creates the chilling atmosphere necessary for the assimilation of the lessons conveyed through the tales.

The Importance of the Hearth in Igede Society

It is not insignificant that in Igede people must sit around the hearth during storytelling. The Igede are exceptionally attached to the family home. Since the Igede regard the family home as something inherited from the ancestors, they regard it as a place of permanent domicile. Thus, the idea of parting permanently with a family home, in just such a way as Westerners do, say, by selling the home and moving to a new place, is alien to the Igede.

For the Igede the family hearth is the place where the ancestral presence is most noticeably felt, the seat of knowledge. At the hearth family history, secrets, and other activities can be related confidently because the protective power of the ancestors is there. Family members who go their separate ways during the day return to meet at the hearth to share with kith and kin the knowledge they have gained on their different paths. The adults know that when they tell stories, they are passing on traditional knowledge to the young ones in the same way as they themselves learned it from their own predecessors, and the new generation in turn will pass on the heritage to those yet to be born.

This awareness—that during storytelling sessions one is engaged in an activity in which one's ancestors, sitting on the same spot, had been engaged years before, and in which one's own children and their own children will engage in the future—is what makes the Igede view storytelling by the hearth as a family heritage. As a matter of fact, the Igede family storytelling resembles a club or association, for to this activity no outsider may ever be admitted fully.

Because the traditional Igede society is very conservative in outlook, every family encourages its members regularly to participate at its nightly storytelling performances. Indeed, the most savage insult that any young person can receive is that, after the evening meal, the child never allowed his or her hands to get dry by the mother's fireplace before rushing to pay a neighbor a visit.

Should such an allegation be substantiated, it means that the guilty individual has not received a proper upbringing. The result of one refusing to partake of the wisdom disseminated in one's family is always calamitous: since every family teaches the wisdom that its members require for dealing with their own peculiar life challenges, the Igede believe that one does not benefit much from lessons taught in a family to which one does not belong. In fact, as far as the Igede are concerned, lessons taught outside one's household can only result in serious and irreversible alienation.

The Moral Functions of the Tale

The subjects of Igede folktales are numerous. They include such issues as the evils of—as well as the price paid for—lack of discipline, intolerance, laziness, pride, jealousy, theft, wickedness, greed, and selfishness, to mention only key topics, and the virtues and rewards of modesty, moderation, self-denial, hard work, perseverance, fellow feeling, honesty, and so on. From this list, it should be clear that the tales cover all the life goals of the community. Thus, if during a given day in a family a particular child exhibits an attitude that requires correction, then this problem will be surely addressed squarely with a folktale.

This was precisely what happened at Ode Agbike's home. On that day his suggestion to one of his daughters to share a possession with a family member had met with considerable opposition; and so during the night's storytelling, he decided to include a folktale in which liberality was rewarded and self-centeredness and greed were punished severely. It happens that the lesson of the performance sank so deeply that the offending girl repented of her misbehavior instantly.

I noticed that Igede folktales have the elastic potential to explain several situations simultaneously. More significant was that, even when the same tale was told at separate occasions by two different families, each inevitably shifted the points of moral emphasis in the story to meet its own peculiar interests. Thus, the insistence that the individual is best served by education received in the home makes sense; since the experiences of any two families will not coincide exactly on any particular day, it is wise for people to listen to the tales told within their family, where they can best learn the tools they need for dealing with the world. It is in this sense that the practices of Igede storytellers also conform perfectly to that elaborated by Walter Benjamin: "The storyteller takes what he tells from experience—his own or that reported by others. And he in turn makes it the experience of those who are listening to his tale" (p. 87).

Audience Influence on Telling

I discovered that the participation of the audience in the narratives had great significance. Audiences get involved passionately because the tales cover situations to which they all can relate directly. Audience involvement takes the form of choral responses to the songs that accompany the storytelling, mimicry, and even outright interruptions—such as *"Iwe Ka"* ("You got it wrong"), *"A chl ohe d' eji le"* ("You have omitted a part")—which often draw disputed reactions, self-justifications, and other excuses from the main narrator.

The activities of the audiences thus show that, although the tales are undoubtedly the common property of the community, what lends freshness to each performance is the social dynamism generated and the interplay of human interaction leading to the upholding of social mores. The literary devices like proverbs, ideophones, mimicry, metaphors, similes, anecdotes, and so on, which

the narrators employ as part of their effort to speed up and deepen the imbibing of the messages, give a reflection of the narrators' determination to maintain the burden of the social contract. Ogede's *Art, Society, and Performance* gives details of these devices as well as more information on the Igede people in general.

Although a full elucidation of the role these devices play in the narratives awaits another forum, it is pertinent that I conclude this brief report by observing that the devices are not merely modes of utterance but a set of cultural practices that ensure the survival of the community.

Further Reading

Bakhtin, Mikhail, *Rabelais and His World*, translated by Helene Iswolsky, Cambridge, Massachusetts: MIT Press, 1968

Benjamin, Walter, *Illuminations*, New York: Harcourt, Brace & World, 1968; London: Cape, 1970

Ogede, Ode, *Art, Society, and Performance: Igede Praise Poetry*, Gainesville, Florida: University Press of Florida, 1997

Ju/'hoan Folktales and Storytelling: Context and Variability

Megan Biesele

Megan Biesele discusses individual variation in Ju/'hoan storytelling. She provides four versions of the tale explaining how death came to man and suggests ways in which one variant explicates Ju/'hoan life.

Context and Variability

Combining anthropological and folkloristic approaches creates a powerful, holistic lens through which to view a storytelling tradition. A major contribution made by anthropology to the study of folklore is a recognition of the mutually reinforcing metaphors of belief as understood from other media in the same cultural community. A major contribution of folklore to anthropology, in turn, is an insistence on performance context, which is the best way to get at the range of specifics within individual and group repertoires. Both disciplines have been converging in our generation of scholarship toward paying full attention, at last, to the individual as the place where tradition has its life. Both, however, still struggle with tenacious scholarly legacies that prompt the search for core beliefs and basic forms that are thought somehow to float free of context.

It is difficult to overemphasize the variability, both among individuals and at different times for the same individuals, in some oral traditions. Ju/'hoan (and all African San) folklore is one tradition lately characterized as highly variable. (Guenther's *Foragers, Tricksters, and Trancers*

makes interesting comment on this). Perhaps this realization has come because of the sheer weight of variants amassed over more than a century by energetic researchers, all of whom were looking for authoritative versions. I and Mathias Guenther, along with Sigrid Schmidt (Damara and Nama tradition), are privileged to find ourselves toward the end of this century of research: in effect, we have benefited from the work of a collectivity spread over time. In fact, many oral traditions may contain comparable variability and ambiguity and, as intertextual forms, are best apprehended by a collective effort at understanding. Those who stand at the end of a long history of cultural experience in a certain area of the world have many resources on which to draw for a balanced picture.

This paper draws on the work of a line of folklore researchers in Southern Africa that goes back more than 120 years, to the work of Wilhelm and Dorothea Bleek and Lucy Lloyd. It also draws, in my own case, on more than 25 years of anthropology, folklore, and grassroots political work with the Ju/'hoan San. Yet even now, each new day of experience when I return to Namibia or Botswana adds dazzling detail and dimension to my own understanding of Ju/'hoan folklore and belief. Setting something on paper about specific Ju/'hoan folktales, therefore, must be seen for what it is, the freezing of a moment in time, one that could and would be elaborated by new moments in the company of any Ju/'hoan storyteller.

Khoisan Storytelling

Ju/'hoan storytelling must be seen in the context of a vast, interconnected patchwork of Khoi and San storytelling communities extending over much of southern Africa (Barnard). Although isolation has to some extent characterized their lives, the San hunter-gatherers have also been great travelers and great gleaners of neighboring traditions. In some cases, they take the stories of nearby pastoralists (with whom they have a range of uneasy relationships) and turn them to their own social advantage. Even the Bible stories heard from missionaries become incorporated into their repertoires and are invested with San flavors and meanings. The Khoisan, or "click," languages they speak (Ju/'hoan or !Kung is one of six main Khoisan languages) tend to isolate their own verbal traditions from non-Khoisan groups, but this isolation does not necessarily happen the other way around. Many San people speak multiple click languages along with two or three languages of the Bantu, who are pastoralists, as well, with perhaps a European language or two thrown in for good measure. This verbal agility is in direct measure to the degree to which the San have had to accommodate themselves to more aggressive settlers and their economies.

There is clearly great variation among the cultural traditions of the various San groups. Across Namibia, Botswana, Angola, Zimbabwe, and Zambia today is spread a complex, interpenetrating patchwork of systems of belief and storytelling practice. Not long ago this patchwork was even more vast, extending across South Africa as well. Thus it is almost impossible to discuss San folklore without referring to specific groups, to specific places and historical times, and even to individuals within storytelling communities.

Individuals and Tradition

There is diversity of belief between groups and within single groups. Explanations for this diversity include some of the forces that also account for the wide variations among San languages. Also, creative individuals may exert tremendous influence in the shaping of local tradition and practice. For instance, local conceptions of God's appearance are greatly influenced by accounts of local healers who have "visited the sky" while in a trance. Another instance of the effect of a single individual concerns the Giraffe Medicine Dance, which is widely spread across eastern Namibia and western Botswana. Beh N!a'an (Old Beh)

"received the first Giraffe Song from God" when she was in middle life. When she died, only a few years ago, the song and its attendant medicine dance had spread across hundreds of kilometers of Africa to become the single most popular healing tradition among the San of three or more language families.

According to other Ju/'hoan people and to Beh herself, she was alone in the bush one day. She saw a herd of giraffes running before an approaching thunderstorm. The rolling beat of their hooves grew louder and mingled in her head with the sound of sudden rain. Then a song she had never heard before came to her entire, as a whole composition, and she began to sing it. "Anyone with sense would know it was a medicine song," people said. Beh went home and taught the song to her husband. They sang and danced it together. Her husband then taught it to others. There are elderly Ju/'hoan people who can trace those through whom the song moved as it spread from Namibia into Botswana. The Giraffe medicine tradition, stemming from a single inspired individual, virtually supplanted the earlier Gemsbok dance over vast areas of the Kalahari. This change occurred within living memory, in the second half of an otherwise ordinary woman's life.

In the realm of storytelling, individual variation is perhaps even more obvious. In a number of publications (Biesele, "Anyone With Sense Would Know," *Women Like Meat*, "Different People Just Have Different Minds") I profiled individual storytellers and the particular styles and emphases used by each in recounting "the same" tale, showing how they achieved their effects with well-known and widespread stories such as the heroine tale, the tale of the origin of the healing trance, and that of the source of mortality (the Moon and the Hare). Initially, I was amazed at the Protean nature of Ju/'hoan tradition, even within the small geographic space and few years in which I had the chance to experience it. Later, I came to realize that this variability reflected something very basic about Ju/'hoan life: tolerance for others' points of view. I came to see the varying expressive form of Ju/'hoan stories as a fabulous reflecting mirror for the great theme of Ju/'hoan (and San) culture—the theme of equality and of fairness to each individual.

Here, however, was the twist on what I, an American, thought I understood about individuality. Since great degrees of latitude were allowed in expressing "the same" story, the differences among individual storytellers were somehow experienced by their listeners as *not being in competition with each other*. No matter how flamboyant the storytellers' language and imagery, their lenient storytelling rules found a way to contain what might otherwise emerge as self-aggrandizement. In this context, individualism could be celebrated without becoming divisive.

Plot and Variation

But what are the mechanisms of such a tradition? Plot elements in Ju/'hoan stories are well known to people of all ages owing to years of repetition. The basic events that advance the plots form part of a shared repertoire. Because these plots are well known to all, they provide a well of reference from which all versions ultimately take their power. The storytellers' variations on the plot do not violate the basic themes illustrated; they merely range widely in the expressive means to make the story both memorable and reflective of an individual's own creative power. In a way, the tradition as a whole explores the ramifications of plots by turning them over and over to see how many intellectual changes may be rung upon them. This is true intertextuality: the tradition exists only in the dialogue among and endless number of variants.

Over the next pages are presented four versions of the Moon and the Hare story, each told to me by Ju/'hoan women, each successive one more elaborate than the last. Guenther devoted an entire chapter of *Foragers, Tricksters, and Trancers* to the variations on this story of the origin of mortality, yet there are profound themes and issues, especially in the fourth version by !Unn/obe N!a'an, not even touched upon in Guenther's encyclopedic chapter. I say this not to demonstrate that Guenther's account is limited, but rather to celebrate with him the fact that this storytelling tradition is virtually limitless in its implications.

Let us turn now to Di//xao's version.

Di//xao's Version

This is the story of the moon and the hare. The moon said to the hare, "Hey! Let it be that when a person dies, he'll live again. He won't just die: he'll come back to life."

The hare answered, "No. When a person dies he will smell bad. And he will never get up again."

The moon asked him, "And what about you, the hare, if you die: don't you think you will get up again?"

"Yes, even if I died, I don't think I'll ever get up again," said the hare.

So they began to argue, and to fight. The moon took a shoe and struck the hare's upper lip. Then they separated. The hare went one way, the moon went the other, into the east. The moon became the moon, and hung in the sky. The hare became an animal. And they were separate from then on.

//Ukxa N!a'an's Version

When the moon died, it returned to life again, to pass again across the sky. "Everyone will do as I do," said the moon. "When a person has died, don't think that he will just die and lie there and rot. Take heed, follow what I, the moon do: I die and then live again, and die again only to live again. Everyone should do as I do."

But the hare contradicted the moon. "No!" he said. "A person is born and he must die also. When he rots he will smell bad."

The moon argued with him, and said, "Watch me. I'm going to die and then I'll come alive again. Watch me and learn, and then we can both do it." But the hare refused. So the moon split his mouth open. The hare became the split-mouth hare that people chase.

The moon and the hare argued with each other and harangued each other. The moon said, "Take my advice . . . a person will die and yet return." But the hare refused, so the moon took a hatchet and split his mouth. Then the hare scratched the moon's face in return. The two of them fought back and forth. The hare scratched the moon's face! That's why you can still see marks on the moon's face, because the hare scratched it and the scratches festered. When the hare had spoiled the moon's face, the two of them separated. They spent the next day separate, and the day after that. That's how their anger rose and they fought, chopping each others' mouths and clawing each others' faces.

/Xoan N!a'an's Story

The moon said to the hare, "When a person dies, he will go away for awhile and then return."

And the hare said, "No, I don't like that idea. How could a person who comes back from the dead possibly smell good?" That's what the hare said.

But the moon said a dead person would smell good when he returned. He said that if a person died he would come back to life. Like the moon, he would die but return again as the moon did when the people in the west threw his shoulder blade back to the east and he came to life again. That's what the moon said, that when a person died he would go away and return. He would return, would return to his own people.

But the hare said, "A person will just die and not return!"

The moon again refused and said, "Corpses will smell good after death. Dead men will die and then return, as I do." That's what the moon does, dies and then swells again and hangs in the sky. You've seen him yourself.

The moon's words were good, but the hare spoke badly. The moon keeps his word and always returns when we think he has died. But the hare with the split mouth is surely a terrible thing. That day the hare scratched the moon's face with his claws. And the moon took an ax and chopped the hare's lip until it split. Yes, that little hare is bad.

!Unn/obe's Version

Long ago the animals of today were people and lived together like people. And the big moon we'll see tomorrow night was also a person and lived with the others. Sometimes the moon disappears and the next day we say he has died. But he always comes back. They all lived together, and the moon died. Everyone said, "Oo, our old man has died. Who will take care of us now that the old man is dead?"

So they stayed and stayed at that place and finally moved on. The little water hole where they were drinking stood there and they lived near it. When the water dried up they went and lived beyond it. They camped in a new place and the *n/n* berries ripened in their abandoned camp. The *n/n* ripened, so they left their new camp and came back to gather it. They came and picked it and picked it and brought it home. They picked it and brought it home.

One day they were gathering the *n/n*. One of the women was a hare: the hare, the little hare was a woman, a *ju/wa* woman who lived with the others. They all went gathering *n/n* together. When they entered the field of *n/n* bushes the others deceived the hare, telling her, "What we do is to eat the *n/n* that is red and collect the *n/n* that is white. Now, you gather that way too. Don't pick red fruits and put them in your kaross." In this way they deceived her. So she ate the red ones and collected the unripe ones, ate the ripe and collected the unripe.

When their karosses were full, the women brought their loads down to the little water hole and sat beside it. Then they said, "Hare, take off your kaross and let us see what you've gathered." So she took it off and was horrified to see that they were unripe. But the other women said, "Is this the only one of us who has gathered well, and the rest of us have collected bad ones?" They took their karosses off and their *n/n* were beautiful and ripe.

Then the hare said, "you white, white, white (diseased) crotches! Why have you done this to me?" The others replied, "Dump out your unripe *n/n* and go back for more. We'll sit here and wait for you. Now go gather *n/n* and then come back and we'll leave together."

So the hare dumped out her fruit and went collecting again. The other women said, "Let's not wait for her. Let's just go on home. Why should we sit and wait here?" Then one of them said to the others, "Now you all piss. And tell your piss that it should call out to the hare. The piss should answer when the hare calls." When they had finished pissing, they left.

Meanwhile the hare had gone off collecting. She dug up a big *!k ma* root and returned, munching on it. She was listening for their talk, but heard nothing. So she called out. And the piss answered her. But when she got there, she couldn't see anyone. Again she called out, and the piss answered, but she still saw no one. While she was looking around she heard a chopping sound. The old moon had managed to find a knobkerrie somewhere and was sitting in the doorway of his grave, where they had buried him. He was widening the entrance. He sat there and chopped at it with his stick *"//a! //a! //a! //a!"*

"Who is this?" wondered the hare. "Someone else?" She looked around for him. She searched for him and didn't find him. She was about to pass by but the moon said, "Yi!" And the hare turned to look. The moon said, "Come here!" She stood still in fear. But the moon called from where he was, saying, "Come here quickly and bring me what you're eating, that *!k ma* you're carrying."

The hare said to herself, "Who can this be? This man died long ago!" But she came a little closer. She came about as close as to the door of this house [4 feet] and stuck the *!k ma* on a stick and gave it to him. The moon refused it, saying, "Come on, I won't do anything to you. Now just come and give it to me. What could I possibly do to you?" But the hare kept her distance.

Just then some other people went by; they were moving to a new camp. The hare felt bolder and stepped forward to hand the old man the *!k ma*. The moon took hold of it and pulled the hare into the hole after him. He said, "Are you afraid of me? Where do you think I've been all this time that you should fear me so? I'm still alive, and am the same person you knew before. I'm not going to hurt you, I just want to tell you something. I came to tell you, so you could take the message to the others over there, those who are passing by just now. If I send you as my messenger will you do that for me?"

The hare answered, "Yes, of course." So the moon said, "Then run. Run to them and tell them that any person who dies will do as I have done and will return to life. He will die and be reborn. He won't just die; no, he will die and return, die and come to life again. In this way, people will live forever and not die." The hare answered, "I understand, I'll take the message."

"Have you understood me thoroughly? Will you tell them just what I've said?"

"Yes, I understand perfectly," answered the hare. So she ran and ran after the people. She came as close to them as those houses standing over there [100 feet] and called out to them so that they stopped. Then the hare said, "The old moon says that when you die you will just die and go away and won't ever be alive again. And he says that dead people's remains will rot and smell foul." The people asked themselves, "Where does this person come from, talking like this?" The hare said, "That's what the old moon told me to tell you. He said, 'You're going to die. Don't you dare come back to life.'" And the hare turned and went away. The people asked each other, "Who is this who has brought us such news?"

Meanwhile the hare went back to the moon. She wanted to hurry back and tell him she had delivered the message and returned. She entered the hole and came to him. "What message did you take to them?" he asked. "Like you said, I told them that they would die and not return, and that the remains of dead people smell foul."

So the moon came to her, took an axe and split her lip with it, so that hares' mouths are split that way today. The hare took off the gemsbok kaross she wore and started a fire and held the kaross over it. Then she threw it over the moon's face. That's why the moon's face is streaked with dirt. She made the kaross sooty, and when she had covered the moon's face with it, she ran away. The moon took the kaross off, but the streaks remained on his face. That's what the moon and the hare did to each other.

The Great Themes

There are at least three "pan-Khoisan" folktales in southern Africa of which many variants have been collected: the origin of death, trickster tales, and tales relating women's achievement of sexual maturity to the health of the environment and to social harmony. Themes appearing in the origin-of-death version told by !Unn/obe—all of whose stories in the collection *"Women Like Meat"* were longer and more elaborate than those of other storytellers—move the story in the direction of one of the two other "pan-Khoisan" folktales, that of menarche and its implications.

Only rarely in my years of listening to Ju/'hoan folktales have I heard the great themes strung together like this. But when they were, the experience was like a glimpse of eternity. Suddenly the seamless, circular world of imaginary reality emerged, and it appeared that all the stories were part of one great web of meaning thoroughly familiar to the storytellers and their listeners through many forms of repetition.

The Moon and Hare stories we have been looking at are ubiquitous, existing in as many as 70 known versions. Tricksters are also universal in Khoisan oral tradition and, as Guenther points out, approximately 400 tales and variants involving tricksters have been recorded. A third widespread story is that of the unwise or disobedient maiden whose violation of various proscriptions at the time of celebration of her first menstruation unleashes disaster upon her people and their surroundings.

In !Unn/obe's story, alone among the versions of the Moon and Hare story known to either myself or Guenther, the great themes of mortality and of menarcheal violations—many of which involve environmental knowledge and respect—are brought together. The critical difference between ripe red berries and unripe white ones, together with the suggestion of illicit sexual ambush that occurs when the naive girl is deceived by her wiser comrades, lift the story of the origin of death into another plane, one where knowledge and right relationships are seen as essential to the continuation of life as Ju/'hoansi know it. Here the perversity of the hare seen in other versions receives meaningful context, and there is a sense of tragic progression toward the inevitable.

The Message of Equality

I felt lucky to get !Unn/obe's tale on tape. She, like other storytellers, lived in a social matrix where respect for individual points of view allowed for a flowering of expressive styles, a creative meshing of episodes for maximum impact and meaning. Her story existed in an intertextual exchange with all the other versions experienced in the lifetimes of her listeners; in fact, it seemed that the stories flowed seamlessly into one another as facets of a collectively authored expressive world. I came gradually, over the course of years of working with the stories, to see that social agreement as mediated orally is a much more complex combination of many individual understandings of the world than I had dreamed at the outset. In the Ju/'hoan case, social agreement coalesced around the message of equality implied in the very lenience of their tradition.

By broadening our grasp of oral communicative processes such as these in a folklore tradition,

we can humanize what we understand of even the prehistoric world. Present and past human culture anywhere seems to exist most vitally on its performed cutting edge, where the moment-to-moment decisions of specific individuals, in the context of the social expectations surrounding them, continue to make new meaning of all the old repertoires, all the time.

This is as true for so-called traditional cultures as for the modern industrial ones we imagine to be uniquely characterized by endless change. The challenge of social life is engagement of individual minds in agreements and understanding. And in an expressive tradition, engagement of personal expressiveness is inseparable from communal commitment to ideas, beliefs, and courses of social action.

Further Reading

Barnard, Alan, *Hunters and Herders of Southern Africa: A Comparative Ethnography of the Khoisan Peoples,* Cambridge and New York: Cambridge University Press, 1992

Biesele, Megan, "'Anyone with Sense Would Know': Tradition and Creativity in !Kung Narrative and Song," in *Contemporary Studies on Khoisan*, edited by Rainer Vossen and Klaus Keuthmann, Hamburg, West Germany: Helmut Buske Verlag, 1986

——, "'Different People Just Have Different Minds': A Personal Attempt to Understand Ju/'hoan Storytelling Aesthetics," *Current Writing: Text and Reception in Southern Africa* 7:2 (October 1995)

——, *"Women Like Meat": The Folklore and Foraging Ideology of the Kalahari Ju/'hoan,* Bloomington: Indiana University Press, 1993; Johannesburg, South Africa: Witwatersrand University Press, 1993

Bleek, Wilhelm H.I., and Lucy C. Lloyd, eds., *Specimens of Bushman Folklore,* London: G. Allen, 1911; facsimile reprint, Cape Town, South Africa: Struik, 1968

Guenther, Mathias, *Foragers, Tricksters and Trancers: Structure and Anti-Structure in Bushman Religion,* Bloomington: Indiana University Press, n.d.

Schmidt, Sigrid, *Als die Tiere noch Menschen Waren: Urzeit- und Trickstergeschichten der Damara und Nama in Namibia,* Afrika Erzahlt Band 3, Cologne, Germany: Rüdiger Köppe Verlag, 1995

Storytelling: A Thread of Life Within the Kamba Community

Vincent Muli Wa Kitumba

Here Vincent Muli Wa Kitumba discusses the use of Kamba story for moral instruction of children.

Lessons from Story

The first life lesson I learned, *why we should not kill other creatures,* was in stories. Story after story portrayed the connectivity of life, animals, and plants. A tribe's escape from attacks perpetuated by tribal archrivals was possible because of rides provided by animals. The message was embedded in folktales. Trees and shrubs mysteriously provided protective cover that enemies could not uncover. Children who left home alone found shelter and nourishment from a tree that had the magic power of keeping the "ghosts" off until grown-ups came home.

The myth on the origin of death was explained through the story of Chameleon and Raven. Chameleon was to tell people to live forever, but he took a long time before delivering the good news. Fast flying Raven delivered his news, "People should die and go as deep as the roots of the mangrove roots."

For centuries the Kamba community of Kenya has had a most accurate and efficient teaching system. One area, however, where its teaching gift is magnificently portrayed is in storytelling. The mystery and reality of life were mystified or unfolded in stories. The oral tradition in Kamba culture is a means of teaching history and customs, for passing on legends and beliefs, and for explaining the natural and the supernatural worlds.

Life lessons were passed on to me in the form of stories. Thankfully, my mother (Mama) was my main storyteller. My grandparents and teachers at times enriched my life, too, with stories.

Dramatic movements, vocal variation, ritual songs, and animal sounds are just some of the fabrics of the folktales. Morals, ethics, motivation, education, sense of belonging, natural resource conservation awareness, and mind-testing skills are integrated in Kamba folktales. Traditionally, folktales were passed from one generation to another, sometimes with modifications that depicted changing times, places, or a way of life.

Growing up, I listened to and was nurtured by these folk stories. For an inspiration to strive harder in school, my Mama used to say, "*Kasili Kaaiwe ni kisithe onavala isithe syanenganawe niusue,*" meaning "the hamster never got a tail even though tails were distributed by his grandmother." This was a lesson on why one should not take for granted the opportunities within reach.

Stories about folk heroes like Mwatu Wa Ngoma (a warrior who led Kamba fighters against the Masai people) and Syokimau (a prophetess who prophesied the coming of Europeans to Ukambani) are comparative icons to our modern leaders. Children learned values of good and humane leadership from these folk heroes and heroines. The existence of supernatural powers was explored and reasserted.

Young girls learned about "Itumbi ya Nyaa," an ostrich's egg story. The ostrich's egg was a traditional Kamba symbol of delicate grace, beauty and femininity, and wholeness (my own interpretation). The story encompassed the behavioral and social belonging of young girls, thus giving them a sense of identity.

When my second grade teacher told us about "Musumbi Kitundumo," King Thunder, and how he dug a sweet potato ground and found gold, we learned that work, patience, and hope would help us in "plowing" through the books (our ground) for golden nuggets of education.

Folktales provided children with a very fertile ground for the imagination to play, to expand, to explore, and to experience the possibilities that exist in dreams only. Folktales bred the imagination to be productive, to be inventive, and to be elastic, allowing the children to see what they had not seen before. They gave a freshness, apart from the daily grind of sameness. Folktales invigorated that which would be stale without them.

The Kamba people knew that in folktales there was common background in diverse perceptions. Listening and speaking skills and sequential memory were significantly developed by stories. With stories, folks with wounded souls had their hopes restored. Lifelong values were fostered without insulting the intelligence of the listeners or excluding anyone in stories.

The flavor and beauty of Kamba folktales seemed to be in harmony with the surroundings. The background of crying children, songs of men on their way home after a great day capped with a calabash of traditional beer, the smell of acacia branches, the bleating of sheep and goats, noises from insects and wild animals, and nearby dance rhythms from circumcision candidates played a significant role in bringing out the wholeness of Kamba folktales.

People elicited the message of a story from their own life experiences and age levels. Sometimes the teller would develop a lead for listeners to see it from his or her perspective.

Here is a traditional Kamba folktale I use often in various settings. It is called "The Hamster Tail," and my mother told it to me when I was seven years old. I use a fly whisk (made from a cow or buffalo's tail) as a "whole tail" prop.

Once upon a time, before the famine of "Peeling off the Brain," all animals lived together in a place called "Gets Dark Early." There was plenty of food, and the animals lived in harmony.

One time, there was a very severe famine, "Peeling off the Brain." This caused some animals to change their lifestyle, which was a great surprise to the other animals. Flies started biting other animals. *[With children audiences, at this point I ask, "How many of you have seen a fly?" This gets their attention and is interactive because everyone puts up their hands.]*

The animals met to decide what they would do about the flies. That is when one woman of the hamsters' clan said she had made tails for keeping off the flies. She told the animals to go back to their homes and wait for her to announce the day she was to distribute the tails. *[Audience participation comes in here when I ask, "Who has ever seen hamster?" When the hands are up, I ask, "How big is the tail?" They show all kinds of sizes, but I pick the one portraying the shortest. Sometimes, I ask, "Why is it so short?" I have heard all theories, kids have no problem responding.]*

One hamster went to that woman, because she was his grandmother, to be given a tail. When he arrived, he told her, "Grandmother, I heard you are the one distributing tails. I have come to you to get mine."

The grandmother answered, "My grandchild, come very early in the morning the day after tomorrow, and I will give you your tail."

On the day the hamster was to get his tail, he did not arrive at the time he had been told to arrive by his grandmother. He thought that because his grandmother was the one distributing tails, he could never miss getting a tail. Because it was late in the day when he finally arrived, the hamster was told, "Sleep my grandchild, and tomorrow I will give you a tail if there are any remaining. Since you did not show up early today, I gave out all of them."

On the following morning, the grandmother looked around and found only a small broken piece of a tail and told her grandchild, "Take this small broken piece of a tail which is all that is left and put it on while I search for a whole tail for you." Up to the present time, the hamster's grandmother has never found a whole tail.[1] *[At this last sentence, I stretch out my fly whisk for the audience to see what the hamster would have gotten.]*

This story has guaranteed attentive audiences on many occasions. Some leads into this story follow. There is "no free lunch." Being surrounded by opportunities is not a guarantee that we will benefit from them unless we do what it takes to positively pursue them. There is no guarantee we will have the same fortunes as our parents. We have to do as our heroes did, for example, stay in school, have a vision or goal and work toward it, stay away from destructive habits, and detest bad associations. This lead works well with young audiences.

For adults, I twist the lead to the critical lessons on the importance of setting and achieving goals. Goals have to be specific (to get a tail for keeping away flies). Promptness is important in achieving goals (very early in the morning the day after tomorrow). Goals must be measurable (whole tail). Finally, to achieve goals there must be an action initiated by the benefactor (waking up and going to grandmother's place).

In Kamba people's communication, a story is the point. External influences, mainly Western education, religion, and work orientations have significantly impacted the Kamba way of life. Fathers left homes to work for taxes, something whose origin and use were unknown to them. Children were put in schools. Members of the community were introduced to new ways of worship with a particular day devoted to religion.

These factors changed the environment in which folktales were shared while members of a family were working together, or when warming themselves with the heat of burning acacia branches, or when just passing time.

These changes were so drastic that in 1967, when I was in second grade, I was punished for speaking Kikamba, my mother tongue, in school. The new education system forcefully discouraged perpetuation of Kamba traditions that included folktales. In addition, all national examinations were in English instead of Swahili, which was not emphasized as a national language should be.

My mother is Kasiva (or Ng'a Maele as she is referred to by most members of my dad's family,

of course, we, her children, call her Mama). At times she would tell me a story or sing a song as we were planting crops, cultivating, or harvesting. As I grew up, I started to realize that most of her stories were either motivational or contained a moral message or warning. The stories were short, humorous, and educational. With such inclusive teaching techniques, the intelligence of the learner was not insulted.

Kasiva, my oldest daughter, from the age of two and a half (she is now 13 years old) developed a natural taste for my folk songs. I didn't translate the songs when singing, but I told her the meaning. My other two daughters, Mbinya (eight) and Ndinda (five), love the folktales that I pass on to them using a language (English) they understand. The interest my children have had in folk songs and folktales has reconnected my past with the present. For more than 20 years, folklore was not an integral part of my life. In short, my daughters have been my teachers. They rekindled the rich heritage in me that has been silent for a long time. I have also affirmed that every adult needs to teach a child. That's how adults learn.

Note

1. Adapted from *East African Folktales: From the Voice of Mukamba,* by Vincent Muli Wa Kituku, Little Rock, Arkansas: August House, 1997.

Further Reading

Kituku, Vincent Muli Wa, *East African Folktales: From the Voice of Mukamba,* Little Rock, Arkansas: August House, 1997
——, *Sukulu Ite Nguta: The School with No Walls: Where Lifelong Lessons Begin,* Boise, Idaho: V. Kituku, 1997
Kituku, Vincent Muli Wa, and Felisa Galang Tyler, *Multicultural Folktales for All Ages,* 1998

Narrative Performance in a Changing World: The Case of the "Storytellers" in Kenya

Ezekiel B. Alembi

Ezekiel B. Alembi discusses the work of a theatrical storytelling troupe, the Storytellers. Using modern theatrical techniques, they bring traditional stories to theaters and schools.

Foundation of the Storytellers

Using the Storytellers as a case study, this article sets out to examine narrative performance in a changing world. The Storytellers are a semiprofessional theater company in Nairobi; the group is the only one of its kind in Kenya that is committed to the performance of oral narratives. In setting up the company, the Storytellers were responding to a need for the revival of an ancient custom, but they were also aware that, to ensure its survival, it had to be adapted to suit contemporary audiences.

Although they first performed earlier in 1992, the Storytellers were not registered as a professional performing company until June of that year. The group is based at the Kenya Cultural Centre in Nairobi and has three objectives: to entertain, to educate, and to create environmental awareness.

In order to achieve these objectives, the company makes a point of performing on Kenyan national days, which include Madaraka Day on June 1, Moi Day on October 10, Kenyatta Day on October 20, and Jamhuri Day on December 12. These celebrations bring together huge crowds from all walks of Kenyan life as well as expatriate communities and the diplomatic corps. Entertainment for these celebrations is always carefully selected, one of the criteria being excellence of presentation. The fact that the Storytellers have continued to be invited indicates that they are an outstanding troupe.

The Storytellers were also guest artists at a memorial festival held at the University of Nairobi, October 7–9, 1992, in memory of the late Jane Nandwa and Owuor Anyumba, who were among the founders of oral literature as a discipline in Kenya.

As a rule, the Storytellers' performances are staged in the Kenya National Theatre or in the auditorium of the French Cultural Centre, but the troupe also visits schools and kindergartens all over the country. They receive no financial backing from either the state or private sponsors and must rely on gate takings for their funding.

The founding members were seven graduates of the Nairobi Theatre Academy, which is Kenya's only theater school. Since then, the group has expanded by recruiting new members from Kenya's most promising theatrical talent. This has been done mainly through auditions so that candidates must prove their worth before being accepted. The company also contracts guest artists to work with them from time to time and, if these artists show the necessary talent and express a desire to become members, it is the Storytellers' policy to incorporate them into the company.

Several organizations have become associate members of the Storytellers. These include the Kenya Cultural Centre, the French Cultural Centre, the Kenya Oral Literature Association, the Goethe-Institut, numerous schools and kindergartens, Kenya Breweries, and Safari Park. When it comes to electing officers, however, only full members are eligible to vote or stand as candidates. An executive committee consisting of chairman, vice chairman, secretary, assistant secretary, treasurer, and five other members is elected by secret ballot at the annual general meeting.

Structure of Performances

The Storytellers are well aware that what pleased audiences of the past will not appeal to the more sophisticated audiences of modern times, and, what is more, that the success of any performance revolves around audience reaction. Consequently, they have seen the advantage of employing modern theater technology to enhance the presentation of their folk narratives.

The traditional narrative performance of stories in Kenya was generally delivered by an elderly person before a fire in a village compound prior to the evening meal. The traditional arena in the compound has been replaced by modern theater buildings; the bonfire and shining stars have been replaced by elaborate electric lighting systems; the chorus of frogs and night insects has been superseded by electronic sound effects; and the traditional performers, who were often elderly, have been supplanted by young, academy-trained men and women.

The audience is no longer made up of simple village folk who have no written language. Nowadays the audience comes mainly from urban areas and might include intellectuals, politicians, and clergy in addition to families and businesspeople.

Traditionally, people attended in order to be kept amused until the evening meal was prepared, but today there is a host of other reasons. A university professor may have set an assignment on the production in question so that his students have little option but to attend. Couples might attend for an evening out. A mother might deem it a suitable venue for a family outing, so the father feels obliged to go along. These are all people with varying degrees of exposure to the outside world, varying standards of education, and varying interests, yet in order to succeed, the performer must please them all. The Storytellers have responded to this challenge by introducing narrative changes to their narrative performances.

Modern audiences are accustomed to plays divided into acts and scenes and featuring a number of characters. The Storytellers have been successful in adapting the characterization of their narratives to accommodate this taste. No longer does one performer deliver the complete story. Instead, different actors are appointed to different parts. Such variety of characters serves to animate the performance and is, therefore, more likely to have audience appeal.

Another successful innovation is the use of modern costume. For instance, a hare dressed in jeans, hat, and spectacles adds more humor to a performance than does an actor relying solely on gesture and voice. Similarly, the use of masks has made a tremendous impact on characterization, especially when impersonating animals. The actors are immediately transformed into the personalities depicted by the masks they assume, and all their mannerisms are dictated by them.

When performing in theaters, the Storytellers have access to all the latest lighting and sound equipment, and they have not been afraid to use it. This has added new dimensions to an ancient craft, enabling it to hold its own in the modern world of theater.

It is obvious from the foregoing that the Storytellers have made radical departures from the traditional art of storytelling as it was known in ancient time and is still practiced in some isolated villages today. Nevertheless, it has been a positive departure, because it has kept alive a tradition which might otherwise have been lost to urban Kenyans who, while living in such multinational settings as Nairobi, are in danger of losing their ethnic identity.

Summary and Conclusion

In this paper, we have looked at narrative performance in a changing world, using the Storytellers, a professional Nairobi-based company, as a case study. In seeking to adapt traditional storytelling to modern theater, the Storytellers have recast their presentations to embrace modern theater technology and appeal to the tastes of today's audiences. This is a radical departure from the traditional narrative performance.

Contemporary society, having adopted Western ways and intermingled with cosmopolitan society, demands a more sophisticated type of entertainment than that previously enjoyed by illiterate communities. The sustainability of narrative performance has largely depended on its dynamic culture; it has only to meet the challenges of changing times in order to ensure its survival as a theatrical art form. The Storytellers have faced this challenge head-on and, with the introduction of new dimensions and use of up-to-date technology, they have succeeded in bringing the art of narrative performance into the twentieth century.

In conclusion, it is to be hoped that this paper will inspire theatrical groups the world over to follow the example of the Storytellers in reviving an ancient art form that must, at some time in history, have been common to them all. While preserving the original framework, we must dare to be innovative and adaptable because, like language itself, storytelling is a living thing and therefore ever-changing.

Further Reading

Finnegan, Ruth, *Oral Literature in Africa*, London: Clarendon, 1970

Kabira, Wanjiku Mukabi, *The Oral Artist*, Nairobi, Kenya: Heinemann Educational, 1983

Kabira, Wanjiku Mukabi, and Karega Mutahi, *Gikuyu Oral Literature*, Nairobi: Heinemann Kenya, 1988

The Meditation of Time, the Wisdom of the Teller, the Void of the World

Sory Camara

Sory Camara reveals the world of the Mandenkan narrator in a mystical recounting from a cultural insider's experience.

The Narration

The Mandenkan narration implies the end of all subsistence activities and of all liturgical dramas that support and ensure their existence. These are the elements that embody concern for the continuation of life. Subsistence activities drive human beings to such a close bond with the world that there is no backing out, no space between ourselves and the world. Ritual dramas use these elements to mystify death and grant us access to an eternity that does not require us to shed our bodies or to step out of the river of time.

Through the spoken word, the men of narration strive to free themselves from all subjugation and laws imposed by the physical world so they can contemplate and describe every part of it. In so doing, they question the priority of subsistence and the urgency it demands, and they free themselves from the authority of social convention.

This is how the Mandenkan tellers discover that the world of "make" and "make believe" affects only those who can barely see beyond the borders of the present moment. They reject such confinement and the servitude it engenders. They refuse to give in to the despair that they know can sooner or later subdue them. The spirit of this theme can be heard in the following song of the heroic mother whose only son was taken away by men to be subjected to ordeals of initiation:

Speed the drum
Drummer
Yesterday is past
Those locked within the present
Do not know tomorrow!

What is she saying? "May our hearts not stop beating like the drums at a feast where news of danger is announced. Life is a path cleared through the savanna of peril. There is no peril other than living itself." The teller could serenely conclude this song in the following way:

N Maaba Taala ka dinko min jaga
A fango le si wo dinko fa
Alan N ka N sumun sa
Sumungo te Laakira

The pit which the Great Forefather of Rapture
   has dug
It is he, himself, who will refill this pit
Let us now talk
There is no conversation in the Great Beyond

The pit in question is the abyss of need and the thirst that provokes our quest through the world. If N Maaba Taala in his generous wisdom occupies himself by filling in the pit, he can give the members of the caravan a chance to stop now and then so they can turn around to consider the road they have traveled, go over the events of the journey, and find a grain of vision or *Jeerikeso.*

Sumungo

Indeed, it is to illuminate this spark over the blind processions of existence that the Mandenka come together on the nights of the hot season to begin *sumungo,* the "Conversation" narratives.

Sumungo, or the narrative action, essentially contains three sections:

1. the narration purely spoken allows the teller's improvised text to be understood;
2. the prologue and the epilogue consist of formulas consecrated by tradition;
3. the sung portions are sung by the chorus, which is composed of the teller and all who assist him.

The prologue and the epilogue never change and have been transmitted from generation to generation from time immemorial. There is no invention here. One is content to repeat with pride that which is given and which seeks to dazzle the ignorant ones who listen. These apparent acts of vanity are really the formulas, the keys, that will unlock the meaning of the coded text of the narration. The Mandenka do not explain their stories or myths. Like masters of mystery, they deliver esoteric formulas to their unenlightened disciples while protecting the essence of the teachings from being divulged. Epilogues and prologues are the keys to the hermeneutics of oral traditions, and it is thanks to these keys that we have attempted for years to open and patiently travel the universe of the Mandenkan narrative.

The narration purely spoken is composed of two parts:

1. The words of the narrator: these include the text and the dialogue improvised by the teller;
2. The enchantments of the chorus: these are the traditionally sung portions.

The words of the narrator give full rein to his inspiration and imagination. This is the moment in which he reveals his mastery of drama and dialogue, his genius for the fantastic, and his acoustic brilliance and virtuosity in the art of sound and rhythm.

The enchantments of the chorus are manifest during the sung portions of the narrative when the *taali's* paroxysmal moment occurs. These songs come from a long tradition. The melody is recognizable and the words remain identical from one region to another throughout the countries inhabited by the Mandenka in West Africa. The identical nature of these songs is connected to the hermeneutic function they share with the prologue and the epilogue. Finally, these are the moments during which the ethic of the body's mastery is most rigorously demonstrated. (This subject will be discussed later in this essay.)

During the sung portions, the teller sings the refrain and the audience sings the couplets. Here the art of the teller consists of passing without a pause from the spoken word to song. In this manner the teller facilitates the shift from words to music, the original form of speech.[1] From this point on the narration appears to be a community endeavor.

The narrative community is fully operational in the Mandenkan narration because it is essentially and exclusively a collective act. This act is initiated by the word of the teller, the *Taalilaala.* His words are authenticated by the witness, the *Seerango,* and are supported and exalted by the song of the chorus, which is composed of the listeners, the *Donkililamutala.* This is the collective work of narration that the Mandenka call *sumungo,* or "conversations."

The witness (*Seerango*) plays an important role in the hermeneutics of the narration. He is the one who authenticates the words of the teller. Consequently, he frequently responds:

Uhun! Yes!
I tomya! You are right!
Naamu! That's it!
Fang Fang! The same! The same! Listen! What you are saying is exactly what happened![2]

If the witness is talented, he will agree with the teller by responding with relevant comments, proverbs, and wise sayings.[3] It is through the witness that the teller addresses his public and to him that the teller's words are first transmitted before being yielded to the next teller.

The transmission of the word is the golden rule of narration. The teller, or *Taalilaala,* only keeps the word for the time it takes for him to recite one or two stories. If he hogs the word, the elders will intervene and interrupt him. The narrative word is to be shared and may not be monopolized. The interruption is sufficiently humiliating to dissuade further breaches of this law. At the end of his recitation, the *Taalilaala* transmits the word to a person of his choice before returning to the communal narrative. The new teller takes his turn in the narrative action before passing the word on to a third. Thanks to this thread a narrative net is woven.

This subtle net of narrative transmission resembles a spider's web. Just as flying insects are caught in the suspended web, so too are the volatile inspirations of the listeners who are captured in the thread of the narrative word. But unlike the spider and the flying insects that are caught in its web, the web of narrative inspiration is spun by both the teller of the moment and all who assist him. They weave together, each one taking turns as the teller-weaver, each one receiving and offering in his turn the narrative word. As a hunter of thoughts, each teller captures everyone else's thoughts in the net of rapture and through the enchantments of his speech. Then he yields his place and exposes his own mind in turn to another abductor of thoughts.

The Feats of Tellers and Their Fantastic Narratives

Capturing the minds of each of the listeners, the voice of the teller steals them away from the heaviness of the world to a fluid universe. Radiating out to the narrative assembly, the teller's voice creates waves of thought in the pool of souls that flow through and around the listeners without obstacle or border. Besides listening to this unique voice, each listener contemplates the disposition of his own heart and focuses on the tension of his *nijulo*, his "cords of life." Thus, from a word or a sound each listener creates an ever-changing universe. All through the narration infinite universes are created and pour into one another, emerging one from the other like ocean waves. Here one enters a mystical time where illuminated beings, such as the Buddha, illuminate the souls of disciples.[4]

Knowing that everyone is a potential Buddha and that everyone is not illuminated at the same time, one can recognize successive narrators as Buddhas of successive cosmic periods. Each member of the narrative community achieves the status of a prophet who is rewarded by the brilliance of vision, who preaches the word to others, and who is eclipsed by another preacher in the following period. Each of these tellers comes from preceding periods. Thus, we can compare the narrative community to a body of water from which emerge the deepest waves that surface to follow the light, remembering one another, driving one another away, and merging with one another into infinity.

But all beings who are touched by the grace of illumination and who want to convert the mass of blind disciples to the light always address themselves to one gifted disciple in particular. This disciple who gives the reply to the master is represented here as *Seerango*, the narrator's witness.

Their communal activity can be compared to cast-net fishing. The casting net is a cone-shaped net that the fisherman holds in his left hand by means of a lasso attached to a central knot. With his right hand he picks up the net, swings it in a circle above his head and throws it. The casting net fans open in the air and falls on the fish, taking them by surprise. Then with the left hand he pulls the rope that will close the net around the fish. The right hand then passes over the left, seizes the cord and pulls. Then the left hand lets go, passes again over the right, seizes the lasso farther down and pulls the net until, hand over hand, the net full of fish is pulled in.

The casting net is like the net of narrative words pulled by the combined actions of *Taalilaala*, the teller, represented by the left hand, and by *Seerango*, the witness, represented by the right. The spirits of the listeners are the silver fish shining and wriggling in the light of contemplation. But unlike real cast-net fishing which is practiced only by a caste of fishermen known as *somono*, all the listeners of the narrative are called to become the fishers of souls.

> *N taali ferr . . . ka la Saran tingo la*
> My Taali ferr . . . on the forehead of Saran

This is the magic formula that the Mandenka use to transmit the word to each other:

Ferr . . . evokes the flight of a bird: *Taalila nyama Kônôndingo* means "the little bird-spirit of the narration." So, just as birds of the physical world fly from branch to branch fertilizing the blooms on the trees, so does the spirit of narration move from the mind of one listener to another, opening whorls of inspiration in a spring meadow of souls. This is how a forest of stories can grow from a little pollen of thought.

To accomplish this feat, the narrator strips his words of dangerous proliferations and polemic because such language can create a defensive barrier. Shielded by the armor of rigid definitions, words can be used to exclude and dismiss others.

Thanks to his marvelous vocals and his acoustic and rhythmic genius, the narrator seizes his armored warriors to meld them into an alloy of pure metal that flows and shines on the incandescent hearth of utterance. When the human word is reduced to its native fluidity as song is modulated by rhythm, it finds again a suggestive power that can arouse the strings of the soul into harmony with the movements of the cosmos. The words of the *taali* (common usage) attempt to resonate with the *Jen Sigo,* the "song of the world," but they hardly succeed. Only the words of the *Kumbenjalo*—the griots of the hunting assemblies—are supposed to succeed. These words, called *Wulajan julo* or "The Distant Chords," are songs accompanied by a *simbingo*[5] or lute.

In sum, the *taali* are not the popular reincarnations of this inspired mystical art. Still, the art of the *taali* has the same essence as the art of the *Kumbenjalo.* By skillfully combining the spoken word and song with deft arrangements of sound and rhythm, the *taali's* aim is not to represent the shape of objects and beings, but to suggest their specific movements.

This music insinuates itself into the soul and creates waves of emotion similar to the rhythms of vital physical movement. As these rhythms accelerate and decelerate they tend to lead the entire body into the dance. The bodies of the narrator and his listeners are always at the point of trembling. In fact, the sung episode of the *taali* are called *donkilo,* "invitation to the dance." But the aesthetic and the ethic of the narration forbids those who give themselves to this subtle art from making expressive gestures. Everything must remain purely vocal. The teller and the listeners remain seated, imperturbably still. All movements aroused by the voice are confined inside the participants.

Unable to find a way out of the body, these emotions transform into immaterial phenomena that open the way for their flowering into the universe of beings of the word. Here we are in the presence of original poetry, the moment of *sondome* when "one can listen in the heart."[6] Yet to listen in the heart is also "to contemplate the vision itself," *ka jeeri je,* according to the formula of the tellers, because this kind of music leaves a trace in the heart of the listener similar to that left by a light on photographic film.

To use an allegory familiar to the Mandenka, one could say that the trace of *bankekumo,* "the creating word," is identical to the beds plowed onto the slopes of hills and over alluvial plains by torrents born of sudden tornadoes. These beds stay dry during the sunny season but when he sees them, the man who recalls the times when they streamed immediately refills them with flowing water. The Mandenka also call these empty beds *woyo* or "streaming," the name given to the raw torrents of winter.

These beds are like the furrows of narrative language itself plowed into the alluvial earth of souls and waiting to be flooded by the river of illuminations and visions. The moment he begins the narration, each teller is like a mystic who, entering into concentration, yields to the light of vision or *jeeri yelen.* As soon as he speaks, the teller illuminates darkened souls as a Buddha illuminates his assembled disciples.

The Universe Revealed by the Narration
Like the Buddha, the Mandenka teller offers nothing that can be seen or grasped through the senses or conceptual intelligence. He reveals no imaginary universe although he appears to create one that flickers throughout the narration like the fugitive flames of wildfire. This stripping down frees a miraculous force that carries away these precarious structures of discourse and speculation, the diluvial waves, the palisades, the huts and their inhabitants.

If the teller offers nothing to see and nothing that speaks to reason, it is only so that each member of the audience can produce in his heart a universe that is perpetually transforming. The movements of this transforming universe shift according to the state of the ever-changing soul, the evolution of the narration, and the vocal genius of the narrator. For this reason, the words of the teller and his theater of light can dispense with props to bring characters to life on the stage of the void. Nor does the narrator act out characters and other ordinary signs of tangible existence.

Only a few indications are needed to identify the protagonists because the teller only needs to sublimate, not incarnate. It is enough for him to evoke the king who has lost his royal treasure, or the youth with empty hands, or the white-haired little old lady living isolated from humanity. Dramas animated by such archetypes come to life on the vacant stage of possibilities that are suggested by the environment itself. Thus, the village or savanna each with its lack of privacy may arouse fantasies of danger and isolation as well as premonitions of the drying up of life.

It is in areas absolutely uninhabited before the word that apparitions appear and disappear, converge and diverge. Spontaneous ascensions occur that look just like whirlwinds of dust rising on scorching days, and torrential rains fall like rain in the winter season. Here anything can happen as it does in a celestial dream where the stars threading through the nocturnal firmament are born in the dawn of this demanding life and fade before the vigilant mind falls asleep.

At the spectral door of narration waiting for the mirages, that moment when everything arrives without ever having gone away, we embark in sedentary little boats on the great river of words. Meanwhile the river, constantly churning the foam on the shore of thought, brings back those who have gone away and carries away the funeral effigies without requiring us to leave our beds. Here space is the pure effect of time, a flow of evanescence in which the appearance and disappearance of things last only while they are produced by the creative act of the narration.

The spaces where vision opens to the light of the visionary soul precede the movement of beings and things, and fade after their passage, leaving nothing more than subtle traces in the golden dust of pure worlds of speech.

This is the absolute reign of time that is mobilized first by desires, *lahio,* and the wills of individuals, *sago,* then quickly converted into acts, *waalio.* The acts create the causes and conditions that produce space and its accidents, its beings and things.

The process of desire is exactly what the teller acts out. Humans always desire, and when they stop desiring they stop acting. When they give up acting they stop talking to go into silence, until one after another, their fading thoughts fall into the abyss of attention and are completely extinguished. All things are extinguished in the void of consciousness and this is without doubt the state the narration aims to create. In effect, *ke taali la* means "release the grasp."[7] The teller takes the silver fish of the contemplation of vision only to throw them back in the water once he has made them shimmer in the minds of his listeners.

"There, where I took this, there is where I will leave it," concludes the teller before he stops speaking. In this way, the whole universe that has been raised up by the word vanishes into the night of slumber and forgetfulness. For the world, like the universe of tales, is only a momentary mirage.

The Time and Place of Narration or the Paradoxical Position of the Narrator

Contemplating the world from the same perspective, the teller opens the narration by affirming with the same certainty:

Bi ma dunnya da
Bi me dunnya ban

Today did not create the world
Today does not exhaust the world

Today, "that which will happen," "the moment that is coming," does not begin time but is the result of ongoing birth. Nor does today exhaust time, for it is perpetually transforming.

Taking them as fiction, the teller recognizes neither the present, the past, nor the future because the past was another "today," and tomorrow will be a new "today." Like fragile little islands newly revealed and just as quickly engulfed by the ocean of time, all "todays" are highly improbable. The present is a mirage born of the thirst to survive in the desert of existence.

From where does he speak, this man who tells the story of the world? What language does he use? He speaks the language of time because there is no language outside of time. Does he not risk betraying himself and appearing to be a mythomaniac when he speaks of time while living in it? Yet he presents himself just as he is! Under these conditions how can he realize his goal of demystifying the temporal world if he rejects his own words?

Fuulu Faala Fukho: Plateau of the Narrative Contemplation

To answer these questions we must start by considering the reference point of the teller. One of the formulas used to close a narration says:

Here is the little I have seen
Before the before
Under the foliage of the silk-cotton tree on the
Plateau of Fuulu Faala
Again today
When the children go there
They glean grains of gold and grains of silver

—You have contemplated the vision! Attest to it.

The narration situates the teller on Fuulu Faala Fukho, the Plateau of Contemplation. Now, this plateau exists nowhere in this world, nor in any world, but is the avatar of Jeng Dalaba, the Great Cosmic Pool, which takes shape in the dream of N Maaba Taala, the Very Ancient Forefather of the Rapture. It was by looking into this pool that the generation of human activists dissipated the mists and affirmed the substance. This was during the time of Folo Folo, Before the Before when the ages had not yet formed. Jiba Maana Folo, the Great Flaming Primordial Wave, held in her breast the howling swell of undulating ages. Fuulu Faala drifted along on its side, like a cloud of unknowing.

It was the human generation, watching from the entrails of the Ancestral Python as it crossed the Great Cosmic Pool, that was the witness of everything that happened at that time. The human generation has kept the memory.[8] But when the teller speaks of that time in the words of today, he admits he is lying because he wants us to understand he is using allegories, parables, and metaphors. It is this testimony and this memory of the creation of the universe that provide the source of human genius, and commemorate *Seerango,* the one who authenticates the words of today's tellers. Because each soul is the receptacle of this memory, the teller needs no proof besides that which he himself provides. All the listeners bear witness in silence to the truth of his word. When he speaks, someone among them will stand up and say: "It is true! I was there!" This is the function of *Seerango.*

Seerango, the Metallic Blackbird

Seerango, or Konjobi Seerango, is a bird from the savanna, a black bird with a fiery beak known as the Metallic Blackbird. When a hunter glimpses Seerango off in a distant stand of bamboo yellowed by the summer season, he immediately imagines a buffalo there. This bird lives off insects he pecks from the buffalo's hide, so these two animals are paired in the mind of the Mandenka because the dark plummage of the Seerango announces the presence of an unseen buffalo to the distant hunter. Seerango is the sign.

Mandenkan mythology tells a strange history that explains the source of the companionship between the buffalo and the bird. It seems that in the time of Folo Folo, the feminine spirit MaaJaaba

conceived and brought forth Mandalakaanya, who was an unformed being. MaaJaaba journeyed to obscure places and ages that still slumbered, searching for a craftsman capable of giving Mandalakaanya a living form. At last she found a colony of Seerango and begged the guide of the Metallic Blackbirds to come to her aid. He agreed. With the help of his beak he completed his first work of sculpture and surgery, because what is sometimes called *Kuro* (stone) by certain Masters of the Path contained the life force. Seerango sculpted a buffalo out of the unformed mass. Buffalo, who was born from the wound, became the grandfather of angry beings. He charged into the savanna of bamboo and roared, "I will throw anyone who tries to follow me into the field of death!"

Thus we discover that the bird who today merely signals the presence of Buffalo is really the craftsman who gave him shape and movement. Perched on Buffalo, Seerango is the creator's signature on his work.

Seerango and the buffalo represent the paradoxical connection of man to the world that nourishes him. But the narrator rebels against such deceptive visions of existential concerns by affirming what already exists in this nourishing world:

I carried my mother on my back
And my father ran along beside me

As the village avatar of the Metallic Blackbird, the teller remembers another time before the existence of this world with its fading generation, dwindling nourishment, and death. During that time, there was the witness.

If the teller remembers he is present in that other world, then he is not of this one and need not resolve himself to living like a resigned and burdened prisoner of a world where subsistence is overdue. Because this world of nourishment, marked by the worry of maintaining lives promised to corruption—that field where every action must perpetually be started anew—is overdue!

This fluctuating world is precarious for the man of narration. He is the one in that moment of remote awareness who is lost in the ocean of the ages, a place overflowing with anxiety. Anxiety creates activism and activism gives birth to despair. Like all desperate acts that cannot achieve their goals, activism takes aim at its own object. Condemned to shortsightedness and insularity, the endeavors of activism today are limited by the narrow strictures of the moment. These endeavors that attempt to tame the raging ocean of the temporal world are merely the foam upon it.

Contemplative, the man of narration is a vigilant witness to the shaking of the ages, and he never ceases remembering:

Bi ma dunnya da
Bi ma dunnya ban

Today did not create the world
Today does not exhaust the world.

He spells it out for those who would try to find a way around this rock of certainty:

Bi ma dunnya da
Bi dama fanan me dunnya ban

Today did not create the world
Many todays would not have been able to exhaust the world

Unlike activists confined to action, busy trying to extract some measure of power or joy, the narrator meditates. He withdraws from situations compromised by action for the sole purpose of considering time, the only reality that gives birth to every mirage of the thirst for life.

Also, his ethic renounces the break-in of thoughts that give birth to actions that tie men to the world of desire. As opposed to the break-and-entry of activism, the narrative meditation is pure revelation that brings to the surface moments of obscurity flowing through the underground of time.

This narrative exposes these moments one by one to the light of the contemplation of Jeerige Yelen's vision without removing them from the current that carries them along. The narrative meditation works like a sudden diversion that passes under a flash of its own watchfulness to join, without detour, the uninterrupted flow of centuries. The narrative neither takes nor adds anything to the passing world but instantly illuminates its passage. The contemplation of vision attempts to unveil the strand that threads the moments of time.

We remember that the narrator is the one who takes, who exposes to the light of vision, then, releasing his grasp, puts down what he took.[9] Demba Sussokho, Master of the Path of Tambacounda, ends his narration with these words:

There where I have taken this
There is where I put it back

Sometimes he says:

There where I have seen this
There is where I put it back

These words establish the equivalence between seeing and taking that makes the narration nothing other than a snapshot of "the shadow" or *Ji-ija*. This word describes the projected shadow that flows out or withdraws, that dims or pales as it is influenced by the light and the accidents of the terrain where the narrative occurs.

The name of this shadow is "shadow without intelligence" because it is enslaved by the world. Yet, the shadow's fluid, subtle, and impalpable nature is witness to another ineffable reality: the spirit itself. This pure luminosity nestled in the body, and forever shining its rays through the nest of the body, projects a translucent image like the dancing reflection of light in a wave. The Mandenka call this *sawura*.

Thus, shadow, which means reflection, indicates the spiritual essence beyond the physical substance of beings. This is the essence targeted by the narrative word even though it must be spoken in terms of tangible reality.

The "Lies" of Narration

While speaking to those subjected to the world of physical obsessions and vital necessities, the teller uses a confection of words. Here in the speech of the narration is where the lies and the mytho-mania dwell. The word is susceptible to affection, and the teller, willing as he is to express the nature of things, leaves the ineluctable imprint of his word on the well-worn path of appearances, that fraudulent path of dramatic confabulations. The detour made by this path should not utterly compromise the essence of reality. The narrator warns his listeners: "I am the Grandfather of liars!" But he only tricks those who want to be tricked because his words do not falsify reality; they simply suggest it in a circuitous way; they indicate it.[10]

After seeing the essence revealed beneath the veiled fable and the ornaments of words, the Master of the Way of Tambacounda says:

N taali Furundun ferenden:
My grasp Furundun ferenden!

Balancing from the right and the left the net of metaphors and allegories through which he presents "his grasp," the teller frees the live fish of the contemplation of vision. The fish, barely glimpsed, flees in the current escaping all capture: *Furundun ferenden!*

There is nothing left but the effect of dazzling clarity in a dimming mind.

There where I have taken this,
There is where I put it back

But from where does the teller take this except from his spirit? Because the *taalis* are interior events, pure objects of thought expressed in exterior terms. Here, interior and exterior are confused. The world of the spirit has no boundaries or confines, and whatever the teller takes from within himself is confirmed by the listeners even though they are outside of him. This reflection of inner and outer emerges from a universal source of memory brought to life by the narration. What is being actualized are moments that the vigilant narrative spirit illuminates through the course of time.

No one can hoard or save what the course of time manifests, and wise is he who releases his grasp before time can tear it away. He is the one who will avoid the pain that bruises the living. This is the pain of regret and nostalgia that detains those who are waiting to leave and brings back those who have died in the infernal cycle of rebirth.

The one who does not resolve to renounce the world,
Is the one who cannot put down the burden of the world
Never
He will carry the load of worry
Until he reaches the Great Beyond
He will see light nowhere!

The narrator is the one who practices renunciation. Taking and releasing his grasp each night of the solar season his whole life through, he secretly hopes he will not have too much trouble releasing his grasp when the time comes for the ultimate surrender. Perhaps he will be able to jump across Ji kuuma Mining mining, the Turbulant Current of Bitter Waters of unlived lives yet to come. So, it is thanks to *taalila* that the man who navigates the dizzying floods can hope to find the ford of

the contemplation of vision and so leave this world of slavish desires.

Taalila enters into narration as he entered into life. He prospers in narration as he prospered in life. He falls in love with narration as he fell in love with life, and he releases the narration of the narration so he may one day release his life. Thus, abandoning the misguided paths that are mirages of existence, he will set down his burden the way he has so often set down the narrative word. According to the formula of Djeli Mahan Djebahate, the Master of the Path of Kidougou:

Alan n ka kumo la jan
Dugu bata tala

For now let us set down the word here
The earth is divided

The "divided earth" represents that moment in the middle of the night when the earth is divided between the reigns of shadow and sun; two kingdoms with opposing manifestations of power. Far from being mutually exclusive, this apparent opposition implies a bond of alternation that cannot be reduced to the simple succession of two incompatible manifestations occurring at the same time. Having reached its zenith, sunlight projects shadows and can blind anyone who tries to stare at it; the sun is a blinding force. Similarly, in the depths of night there are always a few stars shining in the firmament, so the eye can fully open and see the tiniest firefly without the pupil being damaged. In reality, night and day are contrasts of the same phenomenon: change, the revolutions and metamorphoses of time. The passage of time from one state to another involves one intervening infinitesimal moment that is the fulcrum for the lever that tips things from one universe into another.

It is this "center" that distinguishes and connects the two contrasting reigns. The Mandenka call it *Temante dula*, "the center equidistant to all centers,"[11] the equivalent of the center of a circle. The center point gives rise to both the circumference and to a point of observation from which all points on the circle can be seen. This is the observatory of the revolution of ages, the place where the spirit, contemplating the two worlds of shadow and light, wakens and watches.[12]

The contemplative is the memory of the night that lies ahead and the prophetic vision of the coming day. He is the one who knows and who watches for that transitory moment in the middle of the night. He is the awareness of the passage itself.

Meanwhile, the activist has been trying in vain to make a royal kingdom of the day. Stripped of his conquests by the exhaustion of his resources and the onset of night, he sleeps. He will not waken until the first glimmers of day. Forgetting what he sloughed off in the night, he will renew his vain attempts at conquest as if nothing had happened in the interim. This is how he spends his life, forgetting the ruptures and deprivations created by time. Every day the uproar of action yields to the amazement of the night. So the momentary gains that the present brings in its apogee, and carries away in its decadence, are painful and leave all its conquerors diminished. The griot sings:

So it is true, so it is false
The song of the divided earth suits the old
    rooster
Tears flow in the wake of profit
But activism forgets the warning.
The torpors of sleep will carry away the bitter
    memories and at the start of day everything
    will begin as before.

Unlike the being that is reborn at each moment of these forgotten extinctions, the teller is similar to the old rooster. He releases himself from the conquests of the day. He also releases himself from the grip of nocturnal words that might distract him at the crucial moment of the revolution of time; the instant when "the earth is divided." Before this moment, the teller stops all physical activity and all thought so he can watch from the emptiness of a mind purified of disturbance. His task is to be present at the instant of passage and to escape from the two worlds—the one of blindess pulled by action and the one of dissipation that gives rise to all those stunning words and scattered thoughts. He does not want to miss the boat that is leaving to cross the swirling bitter waters for Heradugu, the Land of Peace. So he watches for the moment he can unshackle himself from the entrancements of the world and the burdens of desire and finally fan his spirit, *ka yili tofonyo.*

Fanning itself in the fresh breath of wakefulness, the spirit discovers that the gloomy chain of life is trammeled with threads of light that reveal the "caravan of words of silence." This is the caravan petrified in the desert by acts of servitude.

The middle of the night is the moment of communion when the breath of awakening melts the petrified caravan and restores the void to the desert. But to yield in this moment of vigilance is for most humans a distant hope, because the human soul is a universe of obsession and dread. The soul cannot withstand the void; its nights are peopled with activities of the day and preoccupations of the day to come. Thus, the spirit risks being obscured by its agitating thoughts and tends to favor inaction when the moment arrives for the world to divide.

The Time of Action and the Moment of Narration

While waiting, one must preserve hope to enter the quietude of the "moonlight of conversations," *Sumunkaro koyo,* which will liberate us for a moment from the worry of our days and our enslavement to action.

Today did not create the world
Today does not end the world.
So let us talk
There is no salvation in the affairs of today.
There is no salvation in the *lakira!*[13]

"Today," which neither creates nor begins nor ends the world is the moment of action for the man working against time, acting against time, to endure the world of the physical body. But the affairs of today bring no salvation.

Still, all hope of salvation is not lost. Despite everything, today still remains a chance, if not the only chance for salvation, and we must seize it now or never. Every "today" gives the traveler of life the chance to stop, to regroup, to consider the events of the journey, the chance for *sumungo.*

These conversations are generated by the desire to free oneself from the bonds of life, unload the burden of existence, and grasp the true nature of things born in the passing ages. Today and only today can we realize salvation by yielding to the vision of the word or vision by the word, *kkumajeeri,* thanks to the narrative conversation. Other than this, there is no conversation. Lakira Goréh is the Park of the Great Beyond that the Masters of the Path say is never full and never empty. This is the only place where the fruits of action taken in this world mature, and where the roots of future action germinate.

It is today we can yield to *Jeerikeso,* the grain of vision. Only this is the real event: the advent of man, witness to the shaking of the ages and the consolidation of the world of action. The advent of man who had the vision of all things before incarnating into the nest of the body, Balo Nyaa. I speak of Jeerije Mahan, Mahan of the Contemplation of Vision,[14] whose arrival is commemorated by the Words Most Ancient that occasionally burst through the *taalis:*

The words most ancient
Are as the grains
You sow before the rains
The earth is warmed by the sun
The rain moistens the ground
The water of the earth penetrates the grains
The grains become the grasses
Then become the millet
So you, to whom I come to speak these most
  ancient words
You are the earth
I have sown in you the grain of the word
The water of your life must penetrate the grain
For the germination of the word to take place

Salvation comes from the infinite germination of the word which alone can match the expansion of time. Only in this particularly fertile universe can humanity be freed today from the tyrannical power of the affairs of the world. This event can only take place in contemplation away from the bustle and blindness of worldly enterprises, and assumes the end of all physical activity.[15]

The "today" of the teller is that moment when he reveals the mirage of present action. From the narrative perspective, the present action of conquest is the desire for forgetfulness. Man's amnesia cuts him off from the past, and blindness conceals his future. Walking through the winds of sand, the conqueror of the world lives "Today" far too late compared to the beginning of the world and far too soon compared to the end. In sum, his existence is far too ephemeral compared to its duration. His consciousness is a sequence of events that become highly improbable even as they take flight. His inconsistant vigil is constantly overwhelmed by the events of his existence, his thinking struck with native instability. Thus, he evades each moment of his life. His spirit lives nowhere in his present, which is the only moment granted by the ages of deprivation, expropriation, and eviction.

Notes

1. Also, "to say" a word or "to play" an instrument are translated by one and the same Mandenkan verb, *fo: ka kuma fo,* "to proffer the word;" *ka kora fo,* "to play the kora."

2. *Naamu* is said to be an Arabic variation of the Mandenkan expression *Fang Fanr* (The same, the same!). It might also be thought that *Naamu* is a derivation of the Mandenkan *Naamo,* meaning custom or tradition. So this could also be translated as, "You speak according to custom, according to tradition!" From this expression comes a designation for the Witness: *Naamunamula,* who responds, "Naamu! Naamu!" In the same way, *Uhun* (yes) is from *Uhundurulila,* meaning "who acquiesces with yes."

3. Sory Camara, "Field of Life, Sowing of Speech, Harvest of Acts," *Oral Tradition* 9:1 (March 1994).

4. Sutra: "So, among the beings of Trisahasramahasahasralokadahatu and of the ten regions, everyone had the impression that the Buddha preached the law for himself and not for the other men."

   Sastra: Question, The Buddha appeared simultaneously in the same form to all the beings of Trisahasramahasahasralokadahatu and of the ten regions, so how is it that all of these beings see him sitting before them preaching the law?

   Answer, The miraculous force of the Buddha is two-fold. 1. Sitting in the same place, he preaches the law in such a way that all beings see him from afar and hear him from afar. 2. Staying in the same place, he preaches the law in such a way that each particular being sees the Buddha in front of him preaching the law. In the same way, shadows look like a body of water at the break of day. (*Nagarjuana: Traite de la Grande Vertu de la Sagesse,* vol. 1, p. 525)

   Trisahasramahasahasralokadahatu rests on space. On top of the space, the circle of wind; on top of the wind, (the circle) of waters; on top of the waters, the (golden) earth; on the earth, humanity. (*Nagarajuana: Traité de la Grande Vertu de la Sagesse,* vol. 1, p. 449)

5. An instrument with seven strings strung onto a calabash with an extended arm, the *simbing* looks like a *kora* and is supposedly the archetype for it.

6. *son* = heart; *do* = in; *me* = to hear, to listen in the heart

7. This term is composed of *taalli* and signifies the act of taking of grasping, and of the verb *laala*, which means to extend, to put down, to expose. The narrator is the one who takes, who exposes to the light of vision, then, releasing his grasp, puts down what he took. Taalilaala is the one who "releases his grasp."

8. Camara, "Field of Life, Sowing of Speech, Harvest of Speech."

9. The *bodhi* is light (*abhasa*) and has absolutely no object (*L'Enseignement de Vimalakirti,* p. 197). This is a domain where we consider nongrasping but where we willingly manifest the journey of existence. Such is the domain of the boddhisattva (*L'Enseignement de Vimalakirti,* p. 237).

10. So Manjursi prince heir to the licchavi Vimalkirti, Son of the Family, how will the boddhisattva follow his voice in the dharma of the Buddha?

   Vimalkirti answers, Manjursi, it is in following the deviation that the boddhisattva follows his voice in the dharma of the Buddha.

   Manjursi continues, how does the boddhisattva follow the deviation? Vimalakirti answers: The boddhisattva commits the five sins of immediate retribution except for wickedness, noisiness and hatred . . . the voice of error (moha), but he possesses in all ways, the clarity of wisdom (*L'Enseignement de Vimalakirti,* pp. 285–286).

11. *Temante dula* literally means "the middle place between the middle."

12. Finally the Buddha resides forever in the middle way, *Madhhyagati.* Having come to the Tusita, the boddhisattva stays in the Madhyadesa, "the middle country." It is in the middle of the night (*madhyame yama*) that he comes down from the sky (*avatara*). It is in the middle of the night that he leaves the country of *Kia p'i lo p'o* (*Kapilavastu*) and that after having travelled the middle path (*madhyatna pratipad*), attained the supreme and perfect illumination (*anuttarasamyaksamhodhi*). It is the middle way that he preaches to humanity. Finally, it is in the middle of the night that he enters eternal nirvana. Because he liked these "middle" ways, stays he in the middle of heaven.

13. *Bi ma dunnya da*
    Da me dunnya ban
    Alan n kan un sumun sa
    Kisin' te bikuwo la
    Summungo te Lakira

14. Sory Camara, *Paroles très Anciennes, ou, Le Mythe de l'Acomplissement de l'Homme,* Grenoble, France: Pensée Sauvage, 1982.

15. For the sage this implies a closure of words, those sons of inadvertence that leave the door open for thoughts to fly away.

Translated by Catherine Racine from a longer article titled "La Meditation du temps, la sagesse de conteur, la vacuité du monde"

Further Reading

Camara, Sory, "Fantasmagorie mythique et prodige rituel ou les sentiers de la maitrise du temps," *Anthropos* 87:1–3 (1992)

———, "Field of Life, Sowing of Speech, Harvest of Acts," translated by Lee Haring, *Oral Tradition* 9:1 (1994)

———, *Gens de la Parole: Essai sur la Condition et le Rôle des Griots dans la Société Malinké,* Bordeaux, France: Université, Faculté des lettres et sciences humaines, 1969

———, *Paroles très Anciennes, ou, Le Mythe de l'Acomplissement de l'Homme,* Grenoble, France: Pensée Sauvage, 1982

Asia

The Chantefable Tradition of Suzhou

Mark Bender

The art of tanci, Suzhou chantefable, is described by Mark Bender. He discusses performance devices, shows us the story house setting, and notes a possible future for this performance art.

Suzhou

Suzhou is an ancient city located in the delta of China's longest river, the Yangtze. Long ago the capital of the state of Wu, the city became known for its scenic canals, gardens, and temples as well as its silk and handicraft industries. By the fifteenth century it was a major center for the arts, literature, and popular entertainments. Among these entertainments were two closely related styles of professional storytelling still popular among older people today. Both are performed in special story houses where audiences, mostly retired males, gather daily to listen to the performances while they sip green tea. Besides Suzhou, the arts have a following in Shanghai, Wuxi, and other cities and towns in the region.

Pingtan

Pinghua

The two styles of storytelling are known collectively as *pingtan*. This term is a combination of parts of the terms *pinghua* (straight storytelling) and *tanci* (plucked verses). *Pinghua* is a style of narrative in which a sole storyteller narrates a tale. This performer uses no musical instruments and singing makes up little, if any, of his act. His tools of the trade are a folding fan, a handkerchief, and a small block of wood called an awakening block, which is rapped on the table at the beginning of performances and used to highlight points in the action as the story unfolds. The stories told concern war, heroes, or virtuous outlaws; in the past a story could take up to a year to tell in sessions of about two hours per day. Since 1949, when the performing arts came under the management and patronage of the Chinese government, the story lengths have been reduced to two weeks. Related styles of *pinghua* (sometimes called *pingshu*) storytelling are performed in the nearby city of Yangzhou, in Beijing, and as far up the Yangtze river as Szechwan province.

Tanci

The second style of Suzhou storytelling is *tanci*. This style can conveniently be called Suzhou chantefable, although the form differs considerably from European styles of chantefable. Suzhou chantefable is a sophisticated form of narrative entertainment that combines speaking, singing, and instrumental music in a form that is in some sense a synthesis of musical drama and narrative.

Although some storytellers do perform solo, and on some occasions three or more may collaborate to tell a tale, the most popular style of presentation today involves the cooperation of two storytellers. The duo usually consists of a male lead and a female assistant, although same-gender pairs are also common. The lead plays a three-stringed Chinese banjo (a *sanxian),* accompanied by the assistant, who plays a four-stringed, pear-shaped lute (a *pipa).*

In a typical performance, the audience gathers at about 1:00 in the afternoon in the story house, having bought tickets at the door and having received a glass with a pinch of green tea in the bottom. After the "guests" settle themselves, they may chat with friends and help each other pour boiling water into their tea. At about 1:30, the performance begins as the storytellers, dressed in traditional Chinese gowns, take their seats at the storytelling table on the small stage. Briefly tuning their instruments, the storytellers announce and then proceed to sing what is known as an opening ballad—a short narrative, or sometimes a lyric, that concerns a famous historical figure, a love story, or some beautiful scene reminiscent of images from Chinese classical poetry. One famous opening ballad concerns Hua Mulan, a young woman who in ancient times disguised herself as a young man so that she could take her father's place in fighting against northern invaders from the steppes.

After the ballad, the storytellers set their instruments aside and, sitting on the edges of the high-backed chairs in very erect formal postures, continue to tell the main story—which, often, they began several days before and have related episode by episode each day, somewhat in the form of television soap operas. Although there are dozens of stories that have been performed over the last few centuries, there are a handful of very famous ones with names like *The Pearl Pagoda, The Three Smiles, The Jade Dragonfly, The Story of the White Snake,* and *The Engraved Gold Phoenix.* Love between a gifted scholar and a lovely, talented woman is a prevalent theme in the chantefable repertoire.

In the 1950s, many of the traditional stories were censored, with lascivious or "feudal" content being forbidden. During the period of political turmoil between 1966 and 1976, performances were almost totally banned, except when used for propaganda purposes. As the arts revived in the early 1980s, many of the performers of the most famous stories were aged, and younger performers often lacked the level of training to satisfy audiences. Thus, today most of the stories performed daily are less famous ones, and new stories—usually set in ancient times—are still being written for performance. Well-known episodes from the most famous stories, however, are often heard at storytelling contests or extracts sometimes used as opening ballads and played on popular storytelling radio shows.

Performance Devices

In the course of performance, the storytellers employ a wide range of vocal registers. The most basic one is the role of the narrator, usually spoken by the lead. This way of speaking allows the storyteller to assume an omniscient perspective on the unfolding story—although the storytellers will sometimes break this frame and comment on the act of narration, as if they are observing themselves in action. This is only one of the many lively tricks used by the performers to keep audience interest. Besides narration, another major feature of delivery is the use of dialogue. Storytellers shift in and out of dramatic roles as they relate the story, adopting stylized registers of speech for each of the character roles they adopt. These roles, borrowed from a southern form of traditional drama called *kunju,* include the young male scholar, the young elite woman, old elite males and females, and socially lower characters, such as maids. When performers bring out the characters in the stories, they assume specific voice registers and employ stylized gestures and movements associated with the general character role. The language used in the roles of the elite characters is different from the Suzhou dialect used in the narration; it is an obsolete form of Mandarin once used by imperial officials as a lingua franca and preserved in forms of drama and storytelling today. Thus, in these dramatic roles, the Suzhou storytelling arts are quite similar to drama, although the performances are framed within a narrative form.

The music of the Suzhou chantefable tradition is one of its most inviting and enduring aspects. It has seen great development in the twentieth century, beginning in Shanghai in the 1930s. Young performers like Jiang Yuequan combined influences as diverse as Beijing opera and Bing Crosby to enliven the chantefable music for the new medium of radio. (Even today, the largest storytelling audience, numbering in the millions, is delivered via radio.) By the 1950s, more than a dozen recognized styles of music had emerged, although most can be traced to two major styles dating from the nineteenth century. Along with the opening ballads, passages in song make up a significant part of chantefable storytelling sessions. The musical passages are always accompanied by lyrics, many sung in a register used for the revealing of hidden feelings. Since the sexes were not as free to mingle in ancient times as today, the exploration of these secret thoughts and feelings adds suspense and heightens interest in the story, especially when related by mixed-gender pairs of performers.

In addition to the narration of the frame story, the dramatic encounters of characters, and the musical passages, the storytellers make wide use of inserted narratives, jokes, and humorous asides in their performances. In many cases, these insertions may refer to contemporary events and customs—hairstyles, brand names, watches, cars, and Western-style fast food—drawing the mundane world of the audience into the story frame. Many devices are used to hold audience interest. For instance, conversations between characters may take place at rapid speed, with wild articulation of the voices adding to the excitement. In many episodes plot development is minimal, the concentration being on the elaboration of scene, character, and event. The storytellers may spend an entire episode in which lower characters attempt to figure out the mood of the emperor or empress that day and how best to approach them without losing their heads. In one episode from *The Pearl Pagoda*, the heroine takes hours of storytelling time to walk down a flight of stairs to meet her beau, much of the time spent probing her inner feelings as she descends step by step. Alternating between sitting and standing, speaking and singing, and movement and stillness, and shifting constantly among an array of voice registers and narrative perspectives, the performers enthrall their audiences—and, if they are lucky, bring them back day after day of the engagement.

The Future of the Story House

In the 1980s and 1990s, storytellers have had to compete with the growing electronic mass media in China, and most young people have little idea of these arts beyond what they might see briefly on television. In order to survive, many story houses show videos to audiences of young people when storytelling is not scheduled. Although government patronage is still quite strong (there is a government-sponsored storytelling school in Suzhou), many performers and audience members are concerned about the fate of the arts and are especially worried over the lack of young performers to replace the middle-aged and older ones active today. One note of hope is that, as the concept of retirement communities in China expands, new venues for storytelling seem to be emerging. In some cases, new story houses have actually been built within these communities.

Further Reading

Bender, Mark, *"Zaisheng Yuan" and "Meng Lijun": Performance, Context, and Form of Two Tanci* (Ph.D. diss., Ohio State University), 1995

Blader, Susan, "Yan Chasan Thrice Tested: Printed Novel to Oral Tale," *Chinoperl Papers* 8 (1983)

Tsao, Pen-yeh, *The Music of Su-chou T'an-tz'u: Elements of the Chinese Southern Singing-Narrative*, Hong Kong: Chinese University Press, 1988

Antiphonal Epics of the Miao (Hmong) of Guizhou, China

Mark Bender

Mark Bender discusses the antiphonal singing of Miao creation myth and provides a sample text.

Antiphonal Singing, a Common Folk Song Style

Antiphonal singing, in which lyrics are sung in turn by two or more singers, is a common style of folk song in many parts of China. Throughout the south, large antiphonal singing festivals are still held among millions of people belonging to such ethnic nationalities as the Zhuang, Yi, Yao, Miao, Molao, Dong, and Tujia. Rice farming on hillside fields is the traditional way of life for most of these peoples. The language families they represent include Tai, Tibeto-Burman, and Miao-Yao.

About 5 million members of the Miao nationality live in the southern provinces of Guizhou, Hunan, Yunnan, Szechwan, and Guangxi. They refer to themselves as Hmong, Hmu, or other names in dialects of their own language. Among the many styles of antiphonal singing popular among the Miao nationality in Guizhou are the love songs used by young people while courting. Every stage in the process is pursued with lengthy, and often humorous, exchanges in song. In another common simuation, guests at a home may be greeted or sent off with songs and are expected to reply in kind. Persons stopping to chat on a hillside path may choose song as their medium of conversation. In certain areas, court cases were carried out in song.

Bu Mai: A Festival

Among certain groups of the Miao nationality living in the southeast corner of Guizhou, near the town of Taijiang, there is a tradition in which creation epics are sung antiphonally at huge song gatherings which are part of cyclical rituals held every five, seven, or twelve years, depending on the locale. That festival is called *bu mai* in the local language, meaning a sacrifice to the ancestors. These ancestors are not human but rather mythical beings such as the creator figure, Mother Butterfly, and the culture hero/trickster, Jang Vang. During these events, water buffalo are sacrificed, and activities include dancing, singing, feasting, and the staging of very involved rituals involving the making and use of sacred drums in which the ancestors are said to live.

The singers perform in pairs and the event takes the form of a contest—one pair of singers competing against another pair. The singers are seated across from each other at a table outdoors, with audience members crowding closely around them. Pairs of men or women may sing. Duos often travel from village to village during slack times in the agricultural cycle looking for singers with whom to duel in song. A pair of singers performs the lyrics in duet, making up the lyrics as they go. They know the story, and each is adept at following the other's cues. It is common practice to sing two lines and then pause to consult in whispers before proceeding. In some cases pairs of singers may hardly know each other, yet often they are able to sing lyrics simultaneously as if they regularly practiced together. In some cases, the singing may last three days and three nights, the singers stopping only occasionally to rest and to fortify themselves with roast duck and grain alcohol.

Creating the Sun and Moon: A Sample Text

The structure of the songs, which have five-syllable lines, is based on a question-and-answer format. Sung to a pentatonic tune that varies throughout the region, a passage of song is performed and then ended with a question. The opposing side recapitulates much of what their competitors have just sung and then proceeds to answer the question, which is often of a "who," "what," "where," or "how" type. For instance, in a passage in the epics concerning the creation of the tools for melting the metals to make the suns and moons, the following questions are asked and then answered:

Side A:
Who made the jeweler's crucibles
for melting the suns and moons?

Side B:
If they were crucibles for making silver jewelry, they would be made by the Han people. Today we melt gold and silver in crucibles to make jewelry for the girls—to give to the girls so they can marry. That's how it's done today.
But what about the crucibles for making the suns and moons?

Side A:
It was Grandma Yu who made them.
She brought them to create the suns and moons; to make the suns and moons to hang up in the sky. What were the tongs patterned after?

Side B:
A crab's claw was used as the pattern—that's how the tongs were made.
What did the tong rivets look like?

Side A:
The rivets looked just like leeches. When the leeches contracted they became rivets.

(By way of explanation, the Han people are China's majority ethnic group. They are often neighbors of other ethnic groups in Guizhou. It is a custom in some Miao nationality areas for young women to be given lavish sets of silver jewelry [neck rings, crowns, bracelets, huge lockets, and so forth] as part of their dowry in marriage. Blacksmith and metalworking shops are still common in many rural areas of China. Metal is melted inside a ceramic crucible set in the glowing coals of the smithy's forge.) This passage gives some sense of the imaginative style of metaphor used in the epics. Here tools and items from the natural world in the present are linked to processes in the mythic past.

The content of the epics centers around mythic ages of creation, beginning in an age before even the ancestors were created. An early grandfather and grandmother are born after Grandpa Xong Jang builds a small bridge. (Everything in the Miao myths seems to be "born" by something. In some villages today, ceremonial bridges are placed in front of shrines to local earth gods for barren women to kneel on as they pray for children.) The mythic grandmother gives birth to the various metals, including gold and silver. These precious metals are eventually used to build the pillars that hold up the sky and to make a number of suns and moons. After the earth begins melting because of the numerous suns in the sky, a hero stands in the top of a great tree and shoots all but one sun down with a bow and arrow.

"Song of the Ancient Sweet Gum"

A section of the epics called "Song of the Ancient Sweet Gum" concerns the birth of the creator figure, Butterfly Mother, a mythic butterfly who mates with Wave Foam on the river and gives birth to a great number of mythic creatures, including the Thunder God and the culture hero/trickster, Jang Vang, the ancestor of humankind. Eventually Jang Vang and the Thunder God fall into conflict, and the latter floods the earth in a rage. Jang Vang and his sister survive the flood in a floating calabash, and he eventually tricks her into marrying him. She gives birth to a ball of flesh named Gho Do, which is hacked to bits by an enraged Jang Vang. The pieces are collected in nine manure buckets and spread throughout the mountains, turning into the various peoples inhabiting southeast Guizhou. This account of the brother and sister surviving the flood and creating humans through incestuous activity is a common one among various ethnic groups in southern China and parts of Southeast Asia.

Other epics are also performed antiphonally among the Miao nationality in southeast Guizhou, among them the story of Zhang Xiumei, a Miao revolutionary during the time of the Taiping Rebellion in the mid-nineteenth century. A number of the epics have been collected and published in China by researchers including Jin Dan, Ma Xueliang, and Tian Bing.

Further Reading

Bender, Mark, "'Felling the Ancient Sweetgum': Antiphonal Epics of the Miao of Southeast Guizhou," *Chinoperl Papers* 15 (1990)

——, "*Hxak Hmub:* An Introduction to an Antiphonal Myth Cycle of Miao," *Contributions to Southeast Asian Ethnography* 7 (1988)

Rajasthani Hero Legends

Lindsey Harlan

Lindsey Harlan discusses the Rajasthani folk hero, in particular Rana Pratap. The epics are told by men, women, and the shamans (bhopas) who tend the shrines of these heroes.

Heroes of Rajasthan

Journalists and employees of the tourist industry in India and abroad have often compared the state of Rajasthan to America's Wild West. Waxing eloquent on the romantic ruggedness of Rajasthan's rocky crests and the beauty of its vast desert, magazines and brochures have often portrayed these features as apt props for Rajasthani tales of martial adventure. Typically noting that the state's name means "land of kings," the accounts tend to extol the virtues of heroic Rajputs, literally, "sons of princes" (which is to say members of the dominant caste), from whose ranks come many of the Rajput heroes throughout India. Celebrated by the British for their chivalry and courage—if also berated for their failure to accept British domination—the Rajputs have recently come to be represented by the popular media as horse-loving cowboys. In their accounts, heavily mustached and turbaned Rajput warriors rescue cows from rustlers (typically members of tribal groups or Muslims) and defend the land from outlaws (again, tribe members or Muslims) and rival Rajputs.

As the cowboy has epitomized the bravado and masculinity of the United States, the Rajput has embodied martial esprit and virility. The term for hero, *vir* (cognate of virility) also means simply "man," of which the hero is the finest or most perfect example. In popular journalism, Hindu tracts, and political rhetoric, Rajputs are also frequently depicted as chivalrous defenders of India against foreign conquerors and as the guardians of Hindutva (Hindu-ness). Stories of sword-wielding Rajput monarchs abound in the popular comic books found in bookstalls in Rajasthan and in major urban centers such as Delhi and Bombay. These colorful cartoon narratives, which also celebrate heroes from Sanskrit mythology and recent political history, serve to standardize elements of heroic legend and invest protagonists with widely shared value orientations, including the importance of duty, courage, justice, loyalty, and sacrifice.

Rana Pratap

Within Rajasthan, legends of heroic Rajputs abound. It is helpful to sort them into two categories, the first composed of heroes who are much revered but not ritually worshiped, and the second consisting of heroes who are ritually worshiped after achieving death in battle. Heroes much admired but devoid of rite and cult include many of the kings and generals from Rajasthani history. A prime example is Rana Pratap, who has been portrayed throughout the twentieth century as an archetypal patriot. The ruler of the Mewar, a kingdom in southern Rajasthan, Pratap led his army to fight the vastly superior forces of the Mogul emperor on the battleground at Haldigati, now a much-visited tourist destination. Hemmed in on the ledge of a riverbank, Pratap fended off myriad assailants before being rescued by his courageous horse, Chetak, who leaped across the river, saving Pratap but perishing upon impact. Chetak's elaborate memorial pavilion at Haldigati remains an object of veneration. The express train between the cities of Jaipur, the state capital, and Udaipur, the erstwhile capital of Mewar, bears his name, as do Chetak Circle, which is a prominent feature of Udaipur's topography, and many local businesses.

The legend of Pratap and his loyal horse was preserved in the *Annals and Antiquities of Rajasthan*, written in 1829 by the British political agent James Tod, a celebrated raconteur of Mewari history and legend. His version of Pratap's rescue has become authoritative for Mewari Rajputs today. In the twentieth century the legend of the "freedom fighter" Pratap has been deployed in the political speeches of nationalists agitating for independence from British rule and, more recently, in the rhetoric of right-wing Hindu movements. It has also been recounted as highly condensed narrative in tourist brochures, often featuring photographs of the equestrian Pratap statue that graces the highest hillcrest of Udaipur. Learned by urban children from history books and comics, the legend has also made its way into at least one village's performance of Ram Lila, a dramatic performance of the Ramayana, a pan-Indian epic recounting the life of the hero Rama (the god Vishnu incarnate).

Heroic Ancestors

Unlike Pratap, who was not slain, many heroes died violently and thereby achieved divinity. In many Rajasthani families, especially Rajput families but also some belonging to lower castes, descendants pass on to successive generations narratives about heroic ancestors who sacrificed their lives fighting. Descendants bask in the reflected light of ancient heroic glory in this land dominated by Rajputs and renowned for its martial ethos. At social gatherings Rajputs often narrate heroic deeds of their ancestors; heroic heritage is one determinant of familial status within the Rajput community. In centuries past songs of ancestral heroism were sung by bards composing rhyming couplets (*doha*), but in recent decades earning a living as a singer of tales has become increasingly difficult: without kings, patronage has diminished radically.

In Rajput households today, heroic narratives are preserved not only by men in the *patrihne* but also by daughters and, especially, wives. The demise of royalty and aristocracy since Independence has meant that few families have been able to retain professional priests to attend their shrines for deities and ancestors. At the same time the institution of *parda*, which among Rajputs once mandated segregation of women into *zanana*s, or women's quarters, has relaxed, allowing women access to shrines once tended by men. Women are now typically responsible for ensuring that all the deities worshiped by a family—from gods and goddesses to ancestors, *satimata*s (women who achieved divinity by immolating themselves on their husbands' pyres), and heroes—receive routine veneration. Knowing what offerings are required by each divinity, women have taught their children their rituals and narratives. Often women's accounts reflect their concern with and responsibility for performing rituals. Their narratives are often framed by details of iconography and ritual veneration, topics also given great attention in the hero songs women perform at *ratijaga*, or "wake," rituals, which occur on auspicious occasions such as weddings and births. Men's narratives, on the other hand, are usually more concerned with the specifics of history and with the details of heroic struggle and the achievement of glory. In fact, women often refer to their husband's versions as more *itihasik*, or historical.

Jhumjharji, *Bhomiya,* and *Sagasji*

The heroes whose battles and deaths are celebrated in the narratives of descendants are frequently addressed and referred to by epithet. Three such epithets predominate. *Jhumjharji* (struggler) refers to a decapitated hero who struggles on to avenge his decapitation by killing many adversaries. The *bhomiya*, understood by devotees as a protector of the earth, may or may not die in the manner of a *jhumjharji;* he must die in battle but not necessarily lose his head. The term is frequently employed in Marwar district (which includes Jodhpur) whereas the term *jhumjharji* predominates around Mewar and areas to the east.

The *sagasji* is a hero who dies after being ambushed. Often his assailants are blood relatives who do not wish him to succeed his father as king or who fear that he will depose his father. The most famous *sagasji* shrine is the Sagasji Bavji temple in the royal rose garden in Udaipur. This prince and his brother, the legend goes, were assassinated by order of the king, who had been told (some versions say erroneously) that the heir-apparent was misbehaving in the harem. The streets in the neighborhoods near the palace contain many smaller shrines where priests and devotees tell of royal intrigue.

Narratives of the Bhopas

Some hero shrines draw large numbers of devotees who are not necessarily descendants. Most such shrines are tended by shamans (*bhopa*s) whom the heroes possess and through whom the heroes cure. Shamans' narratives are inevitably much longer than ancestral narratives and tend to reflect divergent perspectives. Although the heroes worshiped at such shrines are typically Rajput, the shamans hail from a variety of backgrounds, and some belong to very low-status castes. Their narratives frequently stress the hero's inattention to rules of ritual purity, his availability to all pilgrims, and his special relationship to his familial *kuldevi* (lineage goddess), who is then homologized to one or another pan-Indian goddess, such as Durga. Some narratives about heroes worshiped at well-known shrines are printed along with *arati*s, songs of praise, for the heroes and perhaps also for their goddesses.

Kalaji Rathor and Other Rajasthani Heroes

One of the best-known Rajput heroes venerated in Rajasthan is the *jhumjharji* Kalaji Rathor, a warrior who, devotees say, defended the gates of the fortress at Chittor during the sack of Chittor by the Moghul emperor Akbar. The two main shrines for Kalaji, located about 60 miles from each other, are said to be constructed atop the final resting places of Kalaji's head and body. A popular printed pamphlet narrating Kalaji's story in couplets was written by Shil Sharma, a Brahman from Udaipur: it stresses the importance of ritual perfection and purity. The shaman who tends the shrine is also a Brahman. The narrative related by the Rajput shaman tending Kalaji's shrine at Rundela (Place of the Body) downplays such themes and stresses the mysterious or tantric powers of the hero, who was given divine wisdom by his guru, Bhairava, a pan-Indian deity who guards the gates of many goddess shrines.

Some Rajasthani heroes have been the subject of oral epics. One example is *Pabuji*, which narrates the divine birth, martial exploits, and apotheosis of a Rajput prince. It has been suggested that the epic is a greatly expanded *bhomiya* narrative. Of particular interest is its incorporation of *ratijaa* songs (or rather the male performers' renditions of women's wake songs), including one

for *bhomiyaji*. Other notable epics include those for Gogaji (who dies of snakebite and who also figures in the epic *Pabuji*), Gopi Cand (a member of the Nath community), Dev Narayan (a hero from the Gujar community), and Dhola-Maru (accounts of whose adventures are also performed by puppeteers). As noted, not all such epics are devoted to Rajput heroes, but they incorporate martial motifs and formulas that reflect a history of Rajasthani warfare, much of it conducted by Rajput warriors. There is ongoing debate about the value of classifying such epics according to existing ethnopoetic schemata; singling out the martial, sacrificial, and romantic elements of each and labeling the epics according to the perceived predominance of one element or another is a strategy that has seemed to scholars increasingly problematic. All hold in common a martial ethos, of which Rajput warriors are often rendered exemplars. Performers have variously rendered this ethos according to their own aesthetic and strategic agendas.

Further Reading

Blackburn, Stuart H., et al., *Oral Epics in India,* Berkeley: University of California Press, 1989

Harlan, Lindsey, *Religion and Rajput Women: The Ethic of Protection in Contemporary Narratives,* Berkeley: University of California Press, 1992

Rudolph, Susanne, and Lloyd Rudolph, *Essays on Rajputana: Reflections on History, Culture, and Administration,* New Delhi, India: Concept, 1984

Schomer, Karine, et al., *The Idea of Rajasthan: Explorations in Regional Identity,* 2 volumes, New Delhi, India, and Columbia, Missouri: Manohar, 1994

Smith, John D., *The Epic of Pabuji: A Study, Transcription and Translation,* Cambridge and New York: Cambridge University Press, 1992

Tod, James, *Annals and Antiquities of Rajasthan,* 2 volumes, London: Smith, Elder, 1829; New York: Dutton, 1914

Two Contemporary Performances of Savitri in Pune, India

Lee-Ellen Marvin

Lee-Ellen Marvin summarizes the Savitri tale and shows us two uses of the Savitri story by women, a reading of the tale among women in a home, and a temple presentation by a female performer. Marvin also discusses the metaphoric interpretation of this story by one young woman.

Vatasavitri: Savitri's Fast

In the city of Pune, about a five-hour drive from Bombay in the Indian state of Maharashtra, during the late morning of the day of the full moon in late June 1994, two women dressed in their finest saris. They prepared a brass plate with milk, rice, *kum-kum* (a red powder used to make forehead dots), tiny glass bangles, beads, and incense. Two small brass lamps were filled with ghee and fresh wicks. It was the day of Vatasavitri (Savitri's Fast), a ritual performed by married women on the full moon in early summer. This is a very popular ritual in Maharashtra, and many women were making the same preparations that day.

As an unmarried woman living with the family for six weeks, my preparations consited of loading film in a camera. The elder woman, Mrs. Shah, I called "mother"; the younger woman, her daughter-in-law, was "sister"; her young son called me *masi*—"mother's sister." We left their clean, four-room apartment and walked out of the modern housing complex, down the busy city road toward a small temple dedicated to "the goddess." The four of us approached a banyan tree close to the temple. About 10 women were

crouched at the base of the tree, conducting *pujas* (prayer rituals). Another 10 women stood nearby. Everyone was dressed in richly colored saris and bright jewelry—signs that they were all married women. We joined this group around the tree. The married women poured milk, lit lamps, and sprinkled rice. Their offerings made, they each tied a long thread onto the trunk of the tree and wound it around the banyan several times. For the rest of the day the women fasted, eating only milk and fruit, without salt. When asked why, they told me that this was a day to pray "for the husband's long life."

Reading the Savitri Story

In the afternoon of the same day, Mrs. Shah and her daughter-in-law gathered with other women in their housing complex to read the story of Savitri to each other. Savitri was a pious wife who fasted and prayed for an entire year to save her doomed husband. When death came for him, by a fall from a banyan tree, she followed Yama-raj, the God of Death, into the land of the dead. Her devotion to her husband was so strong that Yama offered her a boon, as long as she did not ask for her husband's life. She asked, first, for the good health of her husband's parents. Yama granted her wishes, but she continued to follow her husband's soul into death. "Whatever happens, I have no place in heaven without my husband, so I'm going to come with you," she said. Yama granted another boon, if only she would turn back. She asked for her own parents to be given 100 sons. "Done," replied Yama, "now return to your own life and don't follow me anymore." Nevertheless, Savitri followed Yama and her husband's soul away from life. Finally, she was offered one last boon. She asked for "100 strong sons" of her own. "Granted," said Yama. But Savitri followed him once more. She asked, "How can I have 100 sons if my husband is dead?" Yama-raj realized that he had been tricked. He reversed fate and returned life to Savitri's husband.

The story of Savitri is very old: the earliest written version of it comes from the *Mahabharata,* a major Sanskrit epic. It has been translated into many of India's major regional languages and published in numerous collections of Hindu religious tales. The story has inspired many literary and popular reworkings, from the Amar Chitra Katha comic-book edition to the poetic and extremely philosophical adaptation by the mystic Sri. Aurobindo. The story is of a type called "women's tales" by south Indian poet and folklorist A.K. Ramanujan, in that it begins with a search for a husband and a marriage, progresses quickly to a separation of husband and wife, and ends in reunion. In the story, Savitri is a model of the ideal Hindu wife, one who follows her husband into death rather than continue without him. For all that Savitri is dutiful, however, she is also strong, bold, and persistent. She is no martyr. As feminist scholar Rajeswari Rajan says, "her journey to the nether world is a trial that is at least undertaken to some purpose: she not only reclaims her husband, but herself comes back to the living."

A few days after Vatasavitri, with the help of a translator, I asked Mrs. Shah to tell me the story of Savitri. She told nearly the entire story from memory until the very end, when she consulted a book to check on the proper order of Savitri's wishes. When asked why the story was read and not told on the day of the *puja* itself, Mrs. Shah said that it was read to ensure that the story be told without any mistakes because "Vatasavitri was God's day and the story is God's story."

Domestic Performances by Women

A.K. Ramanujan defined two arenas of Kannada folklore performance (from the Indian state of Kerala): the *puram* (the public) and *akam* (the domestic). This is a useful distinction when looking at performance throughout India. Public performances, often restricted to men, are enriched with music, dance, and puppetry; domestic performances, by both women and men, have no such enrichments. Mrs. Shah's telling of the Savitri story was a good example of domestic performance. It was told in an conversational tone, without overt performative elements, such as character voices or dramatic changes in pitch and pace.

Her act of reading the story on Vatasavitri, as opposed to telling it, should not be seen as representing a loss of the role of storytelling in the home. This coexistence of written and oral practice has often been observed in Indian culture. By reading the story, Mrs. Shah assumed the role of mediator between text and voice, God and person. However, in the past, the role of literate mediator has been reserved for male Brahmans. Today, in urban, middle-class cities, literate women have achieved a similar mediating position within the realm of their domestic rituals. The act of reading and consulting a published text of the story, however, does raise concerns about the loss of alternate oral versions of the Savitri story. Ramanujan found that women's tales, told in domestic settings, frequently offered an "alternative set of values and attitudes" compared to public performances and classic Sanskrit literature. Historians have observed that these unique cultural expressions are often lost when women gain access to formal education.

A *Kirtan* Performance of the Savitri Story

On the same day that Mrs. Shah read from an official published version, a public performance of the Savitri story was given through the genre of *kirtan,* a kind of religious discourse. *Kirtan*s are usually performed by men in public places, such as outdoor parks, festivals, and temples, and are enriched with music, song, movement, and lively interaction with the audience. The practice of *kirtan* emerged from *Bhakti,* a movement of Hinduism from about the sixteenth century that emphasized a direct, and often romantic, relationship with God. *Bhakti* teachers bypassed the authority of Brahman priests by encouraging their followers to find their relationship with God in their own ways. They also undercut the special mediator role of the Brahman priests by translating Sanskrit texts into local, contemporary languages.

At a small temple in a middle-class neighborhood, the *kirtankar* (performer of *kirtan*) stood at one end of a large hall. The listeners sat on the floor, mostly senior and middle-aged women, many in the white or pale saris of widowhood. Three elderly men sat in chairs and benches along one wall. Behind the *kirtankar* sat three singers, a harmonium player, a cymbal player, and a drummer. She spoke without amplification, using large gestures, frequent changes in vocal dynamics and pitch, and vivid facial expressions. She occasionally posed rhetorical questions to the audience, to which the women murmured response. My translator commented that she spoke in an old poetic style of Marathi (the regional language). Passages of speech lasting three to five minutes were separated by song, during which the singers and musicians joined in after two or three lines. The 90-minute performance gradually involved more vigorous singing and finally simple dancing by the *kirtankar*. The conclusion was marked with a full prostration before the portrait of Satguru Maharaj, the temple's guru, to fast, vigorous music and singing. Still singing, the audience rose to receive blessings from the *kirtankar*.

Savitri as Allegory

During an interview a few days later, Asha Bhide, a young woman associated with the temple, spoke about the group's beloved female guru, Satguru Maharaj. She had taught them that *kirtan* is a form of devotion to God and encouraged women to perform because the competent performance of *kirtan* is possible for anyone who has realized God within the self. Mrs. Bhide retold the story of Savitri. There were only slight differences in her version compared to Mrs. Shah's. After telling the story, however, Mrs. Bhide provided an interpretation of the story, one that transformed the entire story into an allegory. She said, "the banyan tree is actually our body. And Savitri is our basic nature. . . . So when she asks for the first boon, she says, 'Let my father-in-law have sight.' By 'father-in-law' she means 'ego'." In this allegorical interpretation, the boons Savitri asked for are all requests for the personal ability to worship God, to remove blindness so that one may see God everywhere, and to have health so that one may pray to God until the last breath. Desire for 100 sons is a metaphor for progress of the soul through the rounds of birth and death. The story and the ritual fast thus entail a search for the progression of the soul itself. As Mrs. Bhide said, "That's why you fast. These are the things for which you fast. And, of course, for the husband's life."

The most literal and well-known interpretation of the Savitri fast is for the husband's long life, but, in this community of women, that interpretation was reduced to an almost ironic afterthought. In this case Savitri is understood to be a coded narrative. Asha Bhide's interpretation provides the key to what Jo Radnor and Susan Lanser would describe as "metaphoric indirection," the most common form of coding in women's folklore. In particular, the interpretive key translates the story as an expressed desire for the spiritual development—even liberation—of the individual. It transcends devotion and sacrifice to the husband, even as the story itself is told unchanged.

As social systems change, expressive and creative traditions change in response. Scholars have shown how women's alternative voices may be lost in modern education and cultural reform. Literate women, in the homes, are obliged to perform the sacred narratives as found in authorized, published versions. However, the Savitri *kirtan* suggests that alternative voices can reemerge in specialized public arenas. Under cover of pious religious practice, away from their homes, women can make and perform alternative interpretations of these same official narratives.

Further Reading

Appadurai, Arjun, Frank Korom, and Margaret Mills, eds., *Gender, Genre, and Power in South Asian Expressive Traditions*, Philadelphia: University of Pennsylvania Press, 1991

Blackburn, Stuart, and A.K. Ramanujan, eds., *Another Harmony: New Essays on the Folklore of India*, Berkeley: University of California Press, 1986

Chitre, Dilip, ed., *Says Tuka: Selected Poetry of Tukaram*, New York and New Delhi, India: Penguin, 1991

Collinson, L.A., *Savitri: A Tale and a Vision*, Calcutta, India: Writers Workshop, 1987

Dandekar, G.N., "The Last Kirtan of Gadge Baba," in *The Experience of Hinduism: Essays on Religion in Maharashtra*, edited by Maxine Berntsen and Eleanor Zelliot, Albany: State University of New York Press, 1988

Feldhaus, A., and E. Zelliot, "Marathi Religions," in volume 190 of *The Encyclopedia of Religions*, New York: Macmillan, 1987

Grima, Benedicte, "The Role of Suffering in Women's Performance of *Paxto*," in *Gender, Genre, and Power in South Asian Expressive Traditions*, edited by Arjun Appadurai, Frank Korom, and Margaret Mills, Philadelphia: University of Pennsylvania Press, 1991

Kumar, Nita, "Oranges for Girls," in *Women as Subjects: South Asian Histories,* edited by Nita Kumar, Charlottesville: University Press of Virginia, 1994

Mani, Lata, "Contentious Traditions," in *Recasting Women: Essays in Colonial History,* edited by Kumkum Sangari and Sudesh Vaid, New Delhi, India: Kali for Women, 1989; also published as *Recasting Women: Essays in Indian Colonial History,* New Brunswick, New Jersey: Rutgers University Press, 1990

Minault, Gail, "Others Voices, Other Rooms: The View from the Zenana," in *Women as Subjects: South Asian Histories,* edited by Nita Kumar, Charlottesville: University Press of Virginia, 1994

Radner, Joan N., and Susan Lanser, "Strategies of Coding in Women's Cultures," in *Feminist Messages: Coding in Women's Folk Culture,* edited by Joan Radner, Urbana: University of Illinois Press, 1993

Raheja, Gloria, and Ann Gold, *Listen to the Heron's Words: Reimagining Gender and Kinship in North India,* Berkeley: University of California Press, 1994

Ramanujan, A.K., "Toward a Counter-System: Women's Tales," in *Gender, Genre, and Power in South Asian Expressive Traditions,* edited by Arjun Appadurai, Frank Korom, and Margaret Mills, Philadelphia: University of Pennsylvania Press, 1991

Ramanujan, A.K., "Two Realms of Kannada Folklore," in *Another Harmony: New Essays on the Folklore of India,* edited by Stuart Blackburn and A.K. Ramanujan, Berkeley: University of California Press, 1986

Saneguruji Storytelling Academy, Transformation of Domestic Storytelling in India

Lee-Ellen Marvin

Lee-Ellen Marvin discusses aims and tactics of the Saneguruji Storytelling Academy in Pune, India. The academy strives to bring moral and instructional tales to schools and families. Although the academy leaders hold that storytelling in the home in India is now dead, Marvin finds evidence that a tradition of telling tales to small children is still alive.

An Academy to Revive the Art of Storytelling

The Saneguruji Storytelling Academy is a small organization in the city of Pune, India, dedicated to promoting storytelling in schools and families. A close look at the organization's history, ideals, repertoire and performance reveals a way of telling stories that combines contemporary and traditional approaches aimed at developing good citizens in a modern nation. Calling on images of grandmother and Gandhi, courageous soldier and scientist, the members of the Saneguruji Storytelling Academy have created a repertoire of stories performed in the style of Indian household storytelling.

While researching family-based storytelling in India during the summer of 1994, I was introduced to a schoolteacher and member of the academy. We felt that we had something in common. The leaders of the academy were well aware of storytelling practices in schools, libraries, and theaters of the United States—often called the "storytelling revival"—and as a professional storyteller, I wanted to know about this group that was consciously reviving storytelling in India. Three special gatherings of the academy's members were arranged so that we could get to know each other. In addition to being graciously welcomed and assisted in my research, I was asked to share a few stories myself and to talk about storytelling in the United States. The exchange was rich for all of us. For me, the result was an opportunity to look at the process of reviving lost traditions in contemporary society: When are traditions lost, and why do we choose to revive them? What changes under the revival process, what survives, and what parts of the old tradition are consciously abandoned for new times?

The academy was founded in the 1950s (soon after India gained its independence from Great Britain) by Gajanan Kelkar, a retired government administrator. It is currently coordinated by Anile Godbole, a full-time typesetter and stenographer with a Ph.D. in educational psychology. Its major activities are conducting voluntary workshops through the state of Maharastra for schoolteachers and publishing booklets of stories appropriate for telling to schoolchildren. The organization has offered more than 200 workshops, conducted by its members on a volunteer basis, since the late 1970s. In connection with the workshops it has also held public performances for tens of thousands of schoolchildren. Workshops and performances are conducted in Marathi, the regional language of the state of Maharastra. The academy does not have any formal office or meeting space of its own. The meetings with members took place in Mr. Kelkar's and Mr. Godbole's homes.

The Influence of Mahatma Gandhi's Thought on the Storytelling Academy

Mr. Kelkar named his storytelling organization after Sane, a Maharastrian storyteller and a freedom fighter—an active participant in Mahatma Gandhi's movement for Indian independence. "Guru" means "teacher" in many of India's languages, and "Ji" is a term of honor; thus the name Saneguruji Storytelling Academy. According to Mr. Kelkar, after independence was achieved, Sane traveled from village to village telling children stories from the well-known epics, *Ramayana* and *Mahabharata,* and about the many struggles for independence against British colonial rule. The academy's logo is a detailed line drawing that depicts Sane sitting on the ground, one knee bent up and the other wrapped around. "He sat on the ground to tell his stories, like a grandmother, see?" Mr. Kelkar said, pointing out that particular posture.

Not surprisingly, given the group's choice of role model, it is possible to recognize some elements of Gandhi's approach to political change in the academy. Storytelling promotes independence and self-sufficiency, important themes in Gandhi's political activism. It is a means of entertaining and educating without reliance on the larger institutions of radio, film, or television. Storytelling is also a nonviolent means of persuasion. Mr. Kelkar thinks of the storytelling academy as "moral movement" for children, youngsters, and adults. Mr. Godbole pursued a Ph.D. in educational psychology to research this particular topic. The academy members were particularly interested in the role of storytelling in "moral development" of young listeners. They emphasize the importance of telling stories that demonstrate integrity, honesty, and love. They sought out stories with positive "character building" effects on the listeners. Mr. Godbole pointed out that direct commentary on the moral meaning of the story is not helpful. "We consciously avoid preaching. Children also don't like it." Rather than enforcing moral behavior in children, stories ideally *demonstrate* moral behavior.

The story repertoire of the academy focused on real-life stories: biographies of great men of the twentieth century, such as Gandhi, Churchill, and Roosevelt; war and spy stories; struggles of the Indian independence movement; great discoveries in science; and selections from English literature. Märchen (fables and folktales) were not a prominent element of the repertoire. The members explained to me that "children will not be interested in long, long ago." Fantasy stories were reserved for young children, and from the relative unimportance of fantasy stories in the repertoire, it seems probable that the academy is not very much concerned about storytelling for children up to the age of about 9 or 10.

A Decision Not to Tell from the Hindu Epics

When asked about the possible inclusion of episodes of the famous Hindu myths—a major component of home-based storytelling in India—there was a hesitation. Mr. Kelkar and Mr. Godbole recommended careful selection of a few episodes of the myths, perhaps transformed into stories with modern settings. Giving a specific example, Mr. Kelkar said, "There should be no telling of the removal of Draupadi's sari in the marketplace." This famous episode from the epic *Mahabharata* is one of several crucial mythic touchstones in the lives of modern Indian women. It serves as metaphor for experiences of shame, exposure, and public betrayal as well as for moments of trust and faith in the redemption of the innocent by God. Mr. Kelkar said, "India is going down because of these old mythological stories. We have to remove it." Mr. Kelkar admits that the group did tell mythological stories in its beginning years of the 1950s, but "times have changed." Another member, a woman, said that such a tale should never be a part of school education because it was "immodest." Immodesty, however, might not be the major concern because the story hinges on the importance of a woman maintaining modesty. Rather, "communalism"— the Indian term for ethnic and religious conflict— is the problem. The best-known mythic epics of India are Hindu. The popularity of televised adaptations of these mythic narratives reflect not just an interest in Indian traditions but also a powerful political movement toward "Hindutva," the promotion of Hinduism as India's national religion, to the exclusion of other religions, particularly a long and complicated history of Islam. Telling these stories would contribute to some of the most explosive divisiveness confronting the nation of India today. During the struggle for independence, Gandhi frequently quoted passages from the *Ramcaritmanas*. The academy's adjustment of its repertoire reflects an awareness of the political subtext of religion in India and continued support of Gandhi's desire for a secular nation, even when that means setting aside the acknowledged masterpieces of Indian literature.

Aesthetics of Storytelling

The members of the academy were able to articulate several aesthetic ideals for effective and appropriate storytelling. Their design of the workshop series provided a framework for organizing these ideals around themes such as beginnings and endings, repertoire and selection, preparing, and acting. Summarizing some of the themes, Mr. Kelkar advised that one should "make the beginning catchy, with an effective stance," and also that "the end of the story should be crisp, like a good biscuit." He advocated the use of "simple words, not difficult ones, with a fast and flowing pace." Even as "acting," or dramatization of the story, was seen as a component of performance, Mr. Kelkar emphasized that it should be constrained to what would be recognized as "natural and genuine, everyday expressions."

During a special meeting of the academy members, one of the members, Mrs. Halbe, a principal for an English medium high school, provided a storytelling demonstration. (An English medium school is one in which all of the classes are taught in English, with Marathi, the dominant regional language, and Hindi, the national language, taught as foreign language subjects.) She stood up in a corner of the small room and waited while Mr. Godbole asked for quiet from the group. Quiet achieved, Mrs. Halbe introduced the story as one appropriate for children 10 to 12 years old. The source of the story and the identity of its central character were not revealed until the end. She told the story with her hands mostly clasped at her waist, sometimes released for simple gestures. Her voice varied moderately in pitch, volume, and tone, never more than would be found in normal conversation. The story was of a boy who had borrowed a book, accidentally left it in the rain, confessed his mistake, and worked to pay for a replacement of the book. The boy addressed his teacher as "Sir," as in Indian schools. Mrs. Halbe included a Sanskrit proverb to illustrate a particular point. The audience murmured approval for the proverb and for the main charac-

ter's good behavior, for example, wanting to tell the truth. The story was ended with the triumphant announcement, "And that boy was Abraham Lincoln!" In many ways, Mrs. Halbe's demonstration fulfilled the articulated ideals of the Saneguruji Storytelling Academy. Her story of Abraham Lincoln provided a model of moral behavior. It was a biography of a famous political leader, one that could be placed into a recognizable historical period. Her dramatization of the story was subtle, her physical gestures minimized. Overall, her use of voice, body, and gesture was constrained to the level of expression found in everyday conversation.

Middle-Class Home Storytelling: Dying or Thriving?

The storytelling style of the academy closely matches that of middle-class, home-based storytelling in India. Mr. Kelkar and Mr. Godbole both said that they learned how to tell stories from the traditions of their grandmothers. In interviews, middle-class residents of Pune recalled for me the storytelling of their childhood homes. Grandmothers—particularly the father's mother—held the role of family storyteller in a joint household or extended family. They were expected to tell stories to small children in the evenings; mothers were expected to be too busy with household chores to have time for stories. In fact, close questioning also revealed that other members of the family told stories, including fathers, mothers, uncles, aunts, and older siblings. It seems that, although the paternal grandmother was given the special role and honor of being the family storyteller, no one else was barred from the act. The repertoire for household storytelling ranged from episodes of the great epics, legends of the feast and fast days, humorous folktales, and Panchatantra fables to Western literary works by Charles Dickens and novellas from ladies' magazines. The style of storytelling was described as "simple" or "plain," using language and gestures as might be found in an ordinary conversation within the family.

I found that storytelling in Indian families is still a common practice, much as reading aloud is in common to American families. Some of my informants expressed worries that this practice was dying under the influence of television and the decline of the joint family, but everyone continued the practice of telling stories to their own young children and grandchildren. Surprisingly, although I found plenty of family storytelling during my short stay, it was seen as a lost art by the academy members. "Today, storytelling in Indian families is dead," Mr. Kelkar firmly stated. "Not dying, but dead." Mr. Kelkar based his claim on the general decrease in numbers of middle-class families with "joint" or extended-family arrangements and the recent and dramatic increase of television viewing (especially since the mid-1980s, when cable and satellite systems became widely available). What does seem to be missing from Indian family life is storytelling for older children and between adults. During interviews, however, few people recalled many times in past generations when storytelling was a form of evening entertainment for the entire family. Rather, storytelling was and still is an activity performed by adults for the youngest members of the family, before they learn to read.

Literacy is and has been very important to middle-class families in India. For the past three or four generations, as far back as interviews with contemporary informants could reveal, school-age children in middle-class families have been encouraged to read by themselves as soon as they are able. With the possible exception of the Bengali publishing industry (Bengali being another regional language of India, with a particularly rich literary heritage), there are not many picture books in India for reading aloud to young children. If anything of storytelling has been lost, therefore, it appears to have been storytelling for adults and older children. But this kind of storytelling was possibly lost with the development of the literate middle-class of India's cities, well before television.

The Saneguruji Storytelling Academy has developed a way of telling stories in the style of the prosaic, quixotic tradition of storytelling in Indian households based on real-life stories from modern times. This combination of new and old is shaped by a double-edged anxiety over tradition. On one side, the tradition of storytelling itself in Indian families is lamented as a thing of the past. On the other side, the core of the domestic storytelling repertoire from Hindu families—the myths, legends, fairy tales, and fables—has been rejected as no longer serving, as endangering the development of the nation. Combining the character of grandmother storyteller and a figure of Indian nationalism, the academy not only revives storytelling as an important cultural resource but also reforms it.

Ironically, this revival and reformation cannot take place until traditional storytelling is declared dead. What is overlooked in this revival is the "grandmother storyteller"—the life perspectives that older women bring to children through stories. Women's perspectives and unique interpretations of the domestic storytelling repertoire are being lost twice—not only in the declaration of their loss, but also in the declaration of their inappropriateness. Fortunately, parents and grandparents, especially grandmothers, continue to fulfill children's demands for stories. At the same time, this humble style of storytelling is finding its way into Maharastrian classrooms and community centers, where concern about the needs of the larger society challenge storytellers to find new stories for new times.

Further Reading

Kulke, Hermann, and Dietmar Rothermund, *A History of India*, Totowa, New Jersey: Barnes & Noble, 1986; London: Croom Helm, 1986

Rose, Kalima, *Where Women Are Leaders: The SEWA Movement in India*, London and Atlantic Highlands, New Jersey: Zed, 1992

Veer, Peter van der, *Religious Nationalism: Hindus and Muslims in India*, Berkeley: University of California Press, 1994

Storytelling in Middle-Class Indian Families

Lee-Ellen Marvin

Lee-Ellen Marvin discusses her observations of storytelling in a middle-class Indian family. From these observations and from interviews, she concludes that storytelling to young children is still practiced in Indian homes, often with the grandmother in the role of storyteller.

Research Methods

There is a tendency to think of storytelling as inevitably lost to modernity, and it is generally true that when people work away from the home and farm, when children go to school, and when television invades family gathering places, then storytelling appears to be irrelevant as a means of entertainment and cultural maintenance. Stories are still told, but shorter anecdotes and jokes are preferred among adults. The fantastic stories of kings and queens are relegated to the children's hour and/or replaced by the magic of professional performers. However, it would be a mistake to assume that the shifting of cultural practices under the force of progress is exactly the same in all cultures. This essay explores the current status of storytelling in well-educated, middle-class families in India and suggests that expanded literacy does not necessarily mean the end of storytelling.

This essay is based on fieldwork conducted in Pune, India, a large and modern city about a five-hour drive from Bombay, in the state of Maharastra. During my six-week stay, I lived with a small "joint," or extended, family, headed by Mr. K.G. Shah. As is customary in India, I referred to the members of this family by kinship position, as if I were a daughter to Mr. and Mrs. Shah. Thus, this couple in their 80s were my mother and father, "Babuji and Mamiji." Their 30-year-old son was my brother, "Bhai," and his wife my sister, "Bahen." Their son was two-and-a-half years old, and he called me "Massi," or mother's sister.

During those six weeks, I both interviewed and recorded stories told by ten people: seven women and three men. Their ages ranged from 20 to the late 80s. I consider these families to be "middle-class" because one or more members of each family have educational, technical, office, or retail jobs and because three generations of women in these families are educated to at least the level of high school graduation.

Caste identity was not presented as an important characteristic during the interviews. Identity based on region, however, made manifest by language, was frequently mentioned. In India more than 200 languages are spoken, and 50 years of government effort to make Hindi the national language have not been successful. Each state in India has a "state language," and when middle-class professional families travel to different parts of India they maintain their "mother tongue" as an aspect of their family's identity. Thus one women I interviewed was raised in the state of Gujarat, but her parents were from southern India. She identifies herself as Tamil but is a fluent speaker of Gujarati, Marathi, Hindi, English, and other languages. Of the other people I interviewed, five were Gujarati and four were Maharastrian. As I could speak neither Hindi, Gujarati, nor Marathi, during many of these interviews I worked with a translator/assistant, a Gujarati woman in her early 20s, who was able to give me on-the-spot translations into English.

I asked the interviewees about storytelling in their families as they were growing up and as their children were growing up. In particular, I asked who told stories, when stories were most likely to be told, what kinds of stories were told to children of different ages, and which stories were favorites of particular people. Aside from this general set of questions, the interviews were open-ended. Some of the collaborators had lived in villages and described for me village-wide storytelling and theatrical events and professional storytellers. The others had grown up in large cities where community events seemed to be centered on particular religious communities.

Many people told me that storytelling was no longer practiced in the home because television had taken over the evening entertainments. However, it was clear that people regularly told stories to young children, much as North American parents read books to children every day. In one case, a man admitted that he would certainly tell stories to his grandchildren if he had any, but at the present time his grown sons were not yet married. Perhaps storytelling is overlooked simply because it is such a regular activity between adults and children.

Storytelling Genres in Indian Families

My informants reported an impressive range of story genres told in their families. In almost all cases, their repertoires included a few episodes from the sacred epics (Ramayana and Mahabharata), stories of the incarnations of Vishnu and Krishna, legends associated with festival and fast days, saints' tales, animal fables, fairy tales, and folktales. Less frequently, these repertoires also included regional histories, Panchatantra fables. Ghost stories were also mentioned. Some also mentioned hearing European fairy tales, retold episodes from English literature—especially from the novels of Charles Dickens—biographies of famous men, and romantic novellas from women's magazines.

Some of my collaborators correlated particular story genres with particular age groups. The general pattern of age-appropriate stories in Indian households began with short animal fables for children as young as two and three years old. For children aged three to five, stories with moral lessons were chosen, and six- and seven-year-old children were told stories of the clever and the foolish, the meek and the powerful, "to teach that you need not use strength everywhere, you can use wits some of the times." Individual episodes of the great epics and the life of Krishna were shared with children who were seven years old and older. Stories also were edited to suit the age level of the listener. Krishna stories could be too "philosophical" but had good adventures that young children enjoyed. "The philosophy can come later, when the child is grown," said Babuji and Mamiji.

During these interviews, no one mentioned to me the still very active practice of telling special stories on days associated with religious fasts. These fasts are usually observed by women who do not work outside the home, so it would be logical to include them as a part of family storytelling. Perhaps because they are conducted primarily by adult women, often with women from other households, they are not considered a part of the family's practices. The best known example of such a ritual in Maharastra is the "Vatasavitri," which I report on in another essay in this book (see "Two Contemporary Performances of Savitri in Pune, India"). Kirin Narayan and Anne Mackenzie Pearson have studied women's fasting and storytelling extensively.

Books in Indian Households

It is generally expected that once a child is old enough to read, storytelling ceases. Those children who continue to enjoy and ask for stories past the age of seven or eight are considered unusual and are gently teased. Storytelling is the primary form of conveying stories to young children, and there are few picture books for reading aloud, such as one finds in American homes. In India, children's books are for children to read silently.

However, many people use books as sources for their storytelling. Families own published versions of the Panchatantra fables, legends associated with religious holidays, and regional translations of the Ramayana and Mahabharata. These are used by adults to study stories before telling them aloud. This use of texts might appear to be a small, semantic difference in approach when compared to the American picture-book tradition, but it renders an entirely different set of relationships between the child and the story, the child and the adult, and the adult and the story. In Indian families, there is no book that the adult and child look at together. Instead, the Indian child watches an adult's face and hands during the storytelling, and the adult, likewise, watches the child.

Text sources provide access to stories that extend beyond the family repertoire. One informant said that she knew relatively few stories because "my reading is not fast like my mother-in-law." Printed versions of religious stories were treated as authoritative texts. When I asked informants to tell me stories, some suggested that I go find the text versions of the stories because they no longer remembered the tales accurately. Babuji, my host father, was anxious to tell me the story of the Ramayana and confidently launched into the epic, starting at the beginning. When he failed to remember some details, he consulted a Gujarati translation of a Sanskrit text. Another informant opened a book of Maharastrian saints' tales, read the first few lines aloud but soon departed from the page, telling me the stories directly without reading, his hand resting on the page.

Performance Styles

I asked whether family storytellers had any particular style of performance. The answer was almost unanimously, "No, they told the stories plainly." In support of this claim, the storytelling I heard was very simple. There were no character voices or dramatic use of volume or pitch. I noticed only the slightest shifts in pitch and pacing as the storytellers approached the climatic scenes of the stories. There is a quality to this storytelling that avoids any sense of dramatic performance, thus making it an accessible form of communication, available to any member of the family. In contrast, public storytelling performances in India are often quite elaborate, incorporating music, dance, and vivid characterizations. Such differences between public and domestic performance styles were of particular interest to the poet and folklorist A.K. Ramanujan, who observed this same sort of simplicity and accessibility in domestic storytelling in the Kannada region of India.

Grandmothers as Storytellers

When asked, "Who told these stories to you?" all of my informants spoke first of their grandmothers. "Grandmothers have time to tell stories," they explained, and, "mothers have too much housework to do." One woman in her 40s with two adolescent daughters told me:

And what happens, for ladies in India, middle-class, they work so much in the day. So when they go in the bed, means they are also very sleepy! [Laughs] Naturally. So in that time, whatever story they can tell, they tell. . . . Because for mother-in-law, she don't have any work in the house.

Given the number of chores for all Indian women in any reasonably sized household, the idea that "mother was too busy" didn't seem to fully explain the idealization of grandmother as storyteller in the family. The role of mother is so deeply idealized, why does it not include the practice of storytelling? Insight might be found in R.K. Narayan's memoirs of his grandmother, in which he described the circumstances of her storytelling:

My grandmother Ammani was a busy person. She performed a variety of tasks all through the day, cooking and running the house for her two sons, gardening, counseling neighbors . . . settling disputes, studying horoscopes and arranging matrimonial alliances. At the end of the day she settled on a swing . . . chewing betel, she was completely relaxed at that hour.

This portrait is of a busy woman—it contradicts the premise that grandmothers have much free time. However, the portrait is also of a woman with a measure of authority in her day-to-day life. She is prominent enough to be an arbitrator and marriage counselor, and somehow she also finds time to tell stories to a small grandchild. Storytelling must have been expected of her, a facet of her responsibilities as a grandmother. At the same time, this scene of a relaxed woman chewing betel nut suggests that storytelling was one of the privileges of her position in the family.

In my own host family, where I could observe spontaneous storytelling, both Mamiji, the grandmother, and Bahen, her daughter-in-law, told stories, but Bahen's storytelling was limited to private moments with her young son, while Mamiji told stories to the entire family or while other family members could listen. The repertoire of the young woman was limited to animal fables, by necessity, given the age of her solitary audience member; the repertoire of the older woman included episodic adventures from the sacred narratives. The strong voice and rapid pace used for storytelling was the same voice she used throughout the day. Mamiji was in a position within the family structure to be a principal storyteller, not just because she had free time but because she had the authority as the senior woman in the family.

An interview with a middle-aged woman was interrupted by her formidable mother-in-law, a retired gynecologist and Sanskrit scholar. The younger woman was saying that she found the epics to be complicated and difficult to tell, that they weren't very practical, and that the fantastic elements of these myths were not "convincing." The older woman interrupted loudly, telling her daughter-in-law that she was not knowledgeable enough about the epics to say such things. The younger woman acquiesced to her mother-in-law's forceful opinions with silence. Here, the grandmother confidently proclaimed her authority to speak about the Sanskrit myths.

Where does this authority for grandmothers as storytellers come from? It could be explained as simple respect for the elderly, but it also reflects a position of authority among women within the family structure. A woman is an outsider within her husband's home until her son marries and brings a new bride into the household. It is then that the senior woman becomes an insider and she gains the authority over the new outsider. It might be that grandmothers are accorded the position of storyteller because they have both proven their procreative abilities and passed through their fertile life stage; thus, as menopausal women, they are no longer a threatening agent of feminine sexual power and energy. A senior woman who is a grandmother need no longer establish her worth nor need she control her energies with self-restraint and suffering. A woman undergoing menses is "not to go near God," as the women in my host family warned me, nor to perform rituals, but menopausal women suffer no such restraints. No one said that a menstruating women should refrain from telling stories, but as women restrict their activities during their menstrual periods, they also restrict their storytelling. If that is the case, menopausal women's voices are quite unrestricted within their homes and families.

Although grandmothers are given the role of storyteller within Indian families, any family member can and does tell stories. When I asked people to recall specific experiences from their childhood, they spoke of fathers, mothers, older siblings, aunts, uncles, and grandfathers sharing stories. In some cases, there were no grandmothers to tell stories, especially when families lived long distances away from the grandparents.

Conclusion

Although it is no longer a regular form of entertainment for adults, storytelling survives in middle-class Indian families as an activity to do with young children. Through stories, adults teach children basic principles for moral living and introduce them to important religious figures. Books provide a reliable source of stories to tell aloud, but reading aloud is a rare activity. While stories can be told by anyone, the family structure gives special responsibilities and privileges to the grandmother as primary storyteller. It is possible that storytelling will continue to hold a special place in the lives of Indian families for as long as the joint family structure is seen as the ideal arrangement.

Further Reading

Narayan, Kirin, *Mondays on the Dark Night of the Moon: Himalayan Foothill Folktales,* New York: Oxford University Press, 1997

Pearson, Anne Mackenzie, *"Because It Gives Me Peace of Mind": Ritual Fasts in the Religious Lives of Hindu Women,* Albany: State University of New York Press, 1996

Raheja, Gloria Goodwin, and Ann Gold, *Listen to the Heron's Words: Reimagining Gender and Kinship in North India,* Berkeley: University of California Press, 1994

Ramanujan, A.K., "Two Realms of Kannada Folklore," in *Another Harmony: New Essays on the Folklore of India,* edited by Stuart Blackburn and A.K. Ramanujan, Berkeley: University of California Press, 1986

A System of Narrative Performances in Middle India

Joyce Burkhalter Flueckiger

Joyce Burkhalter Flueckiger discusses genres of Chhattisgarhi stories, those typical of the Chhattisgarh region on the eastern borders of Madhya Pradesh.

Chhattisgarhi Stories

Traditional storytelling falls within several distinguishable repertoires in the Chhattisgarh region of middle India (on the eastern borders of the province of Madhya Pradesh). Performers and audiences, however, most strongly assert one particular performance repertoire: that identified with the region as Chhattisgarhi, as opposed to pan-Indian genres, which include genres such as the widely performed Hindi variant of the Ramayana epic. The distinction of genres within the regional repertoire is based primarily on the social identities of those who perform and hear the stories and songs, identities that coincide with the regional community itself, or with specific caste, age, and gender groups within that broad folklore community. Other generic distinctions based primarily on form or context, such as folktale/epic/song, public or private performance genres, or those performed by professional, semiprofessional, or nonprofessional storytellers, are further drawn primarily by folklorists. This essay focuses on the repertoire of stories identified with the region itself—Chhattisgarhi stories, narratives that both reflect the ethos of and give identity *to* the region. The repertoire of which these narratives are a part offers alternative ideologies of gender, fate, hierarchy, and power to those articulated in pan-Indian, Brahmanic textual traditions identified by Chhattisgarhi performers as *shastric*.

The geographic region identified as Chhattisgarh consists of a large, rice-growing plain and the surrounding hill regions; historically, the latter helped to isolate Chhattisgarh from surrounding regions and to create a politically and historically defined region. The Chhattisgarhi dialect of eastern Hindi also contributes to regional identity. Another major factor contributing to an identifiable cultural ethos is the high percentage of the region's tribal (*adivasi*) population. Although, on the plains, *adivasi* groups have been integrated into local caste hierarchies, have adopted many pan-Indian Hindu practices, and no longer speak their tribal dialects, they have retained many of their own traditions in some modified way. These include marriage practices, jewelry, tattooing practices, dress, festivals, and verbal and material folklore. Many of the traditions identified specifically with the region are attributed to these *adivasi* groups.

For someone familiar with north Indian social patterns and practices, the status and roles of women in Chhattisgarh are particularly striking. Their relative freedom of movement and associated perception of increased status are most noticeable in the absence of strict physical veiling (purdah), face covering, and physical seclusion, except among members of the highest castes (most of whose families immigrated from the north into Chhattisgarh). The roles and status of women may be related to both the influence of the *adivasi* population and the higher percentage of female labor participation in the rice-growing plains of Chhattisgarh compared to that of women in the wheat-growing north. Chhattisgarhi folklore reflects these roles of women and contributes to constructions of gender in the region that offer alternatives to Brahmanic, textual models for gender.

Narratives identified as specifically Chhattisgarhi are most often performed by professional and semiprofessional storytellers or by nonprofessional performers in the public context of community-based ritual or dance. That is, they do not include stories told by individuals in private, domestic contexts, such as bedtime folktales told by a grandmother to her grandchildren. Further, stories of this publicly performed repertoire are most often sung. Although there are Chhattisgarhi words that distinguish story and song (*kahani* or *katha* and *git*, respectively), these are not the basis for indigenous generic distinction in the regional repertoire, since publicly performed stories are sung and many lyrical songs are contextualized by narrative.

The Epic Traditions of Candaini and Pandvani

Two narrative traditions, and the stylistic modes in which they are performed, are closely associated with the region of Chhattisgarh: the epic traditions of Candaini and Pandvani. These two traditions are often paired when performers or audiences, or both, list genres associated with the region or in indigenous commentaries about Chhattisgarhi folklore. The performance community with which these narratives are identified is more inclusive both geographically and socially than that of any other genre from the regionally identified repertoire. Candaini is often referred to as "our story," a "Chhattisgarhi story," a narrative that captures what is perceived to be a unique cultural ethos.

Candaini and Pandvani are associated with each other more because of this regional identification than through form or thematic content. Candaini is a love story that tells of the elopement of the hero Lorik and heroine Candaini, both from the cowherding Raut caste. That the narrative is situated at this level on the social hierarchy, rather than among martial and other high castes, is one factor that marks it as a regional, rather than pan-Indian, narrative. The villages, rivers, and forests of the narrative are locally identified, the heroine wears uniquely Chhattisgarhi jewelry

and clothing, and numerous narrative motifs (such as ritual friendships between persons on different levels of the caste hierarchy) are drawn from customs and institutions unique to the region. The heroine Candaini is the dominant character in the pair of lovers and initiates much of the primary epic action. In several episodes, she actually saves or protects the hero rather than the reverse. Candaini is a resourceful, independent woman, rather than being portrayed as property to be exchanged and protected, as women often are in many epic traditions sung in north India, as well as in the Hindi variant of the Ramayana.

Pandvani, on the other hand, is a regional performance genre of the pan-Indian epic tradition of *Mahabharata,* a martial epic whose main characters are of the warrior caste and who battle over land and succession to the throne, not love. Although the narrative story line itself is not unique to the region, one singer explained to me that Pandvani is "Chhattisgarhi; it is sung from the heart," distinguishing this performance style from the television serialization of the *Mahabharata* that was drawn from the *shastras* (authoritative religious texts that represent the pan-Indian tradition). A popular young female Pandvani singer, Ritu Varma, ends her Pandvani performances with a song declaring her identity as a "Chhattisgarhi daughter" and the wombs of Chhattisgarhi mothers as carriers of the Pandava heroes.

Part of what gives Candaini and Pandvani, two rather dissimilar narrative traditions, their regional identification and dialogic relationship with each other are their shared performance contexts, their broad social base of audiences and performers, performance styles, and shared narrative formulas and motifs drawn from the local cultural context. Neither narrative tradition is performed in ritual contexts that might be restricted by caste or gender, though Candaini and Pandvani performances may be sponsored to help celebrate a ritual occasion such as a festival or marriage or simply presented as independent entertainment events. Troupes are usually multi-caste. Likewise, audiences of both genres represent the caste spectrum of particular villages or urban neighborhoods in which they are performed. Both traditions have followed a remarkably similar course of stylistic development. Initially, both were sung a cappella, with a lead singer and single respondent, or *ragi* (one who carries the tune). Within the last 20 years, both genres have experimented with style, adding instrumentation, more singers, and sometimes dramatization.

Both men and women are drawn into audiences, but, traditionally, performers of Candaini and Pandvani have been male, as is typical of professional performance throughout India (with significant exceptions). However, in recent years, a handful of individual female performers have begun to sing both Candaini and Pandvani professionally, such as the above-mentioned Ritu Varma. They have gained meteoric popularity because of their unusual position as professional, public female performers. Several audience members asserted, "Who *wouldn't* go to hear a woman? There's more entertainment in that!" These women perform locally but have also represented Chhattisgarh in countrywide government-sponsored folk performance competitions and festivals of India in Europe, Japan, and the United States. The innovative participation of female performers has infused Pandvani and Candaini traditions with new energy at a time when sponsorship and frequency of such folk performances is threatened by increased literacy and the proliferation of television and movie theaters. Audiences for these narrative traditions are drawn by their unique performance styles and association with things ethnic. For middle-class urban audiences of these epic traditions, the regional dialect of Chhattisgarhi in which they are performed may not be totally intelligible, but their performance style (including the village dress and jewelry of their performers and the musical instruments used in accompaniment) and images drawn from lower-caste village life seem to elicit a nostalgia for an idealized, simpler past.

Bas Git Performance

Other publicly performed narrative genres are not named for their narrative content, such as Candaini and Pandvani, but by performance styles that can be associated with a wide variety of narratives. The genre of *bas git* (song of the bamboo flute) is identified by the accompanying instrument, a bamboo flute four to five feet long, and is traditionally performed by men of the cowherding caste; the songs may be narrative or lyrical. I recorded two *adivasi* women performing what they identified as *bas git*. They sang one-to-two-hour narratives without any instrumentation, but their voices imitated the drone of the flute. These women were well known locally for their unique ability to imitate the flute, their narrative skill, the range of narratives over which they had control (unusual for nonprofes-

sionals), and their willingness to perform for small audiences outside of their families. The Chhattisgarhi system of narrative performance is flexible and often allows for innovation and individual creativity.

Kathani Kuha

The *kathani kuha* (teller of stories) is another narrative genre in the Chhattisgarhi repertoire that highlights individual creativity. The term identifies the performer himself, not his narratives; his repertoire theoretically is unbounded and idiosyncratic, drawing on both religious narrative traditions (such as *purana*s) and domestically performed folktales. What distinguishes the *kathani kuha* as a professional is the style in which he performs (song, dance, and spoken narrative interwoven), the skill with which he joins tale to tale to create an extended narrative of several hours, and the village-wide audiences before which he performs. As a professional, the *kathani kuha* is able to localize and regionalize almost any folk story, framing it within a local geography, indigenizing the voices of characters, often linking story to story through the use of local geography or regional motifs shared across genres in the regional repertoire (again, a common one being that of ritual friendships).

Sua Nac

The Chhattisgarhi narrative repertoire also includes song and dance traditions performed by groups of nonprofessional women in a ritual context, many of which carry narrative traditions less well known than the narratives of Candaini and Pandvani but which audiences identify as Chhattisgarhi because of either performance style or shared narrative motifs. One such genre is the *sua nac*, or parrot dance, performed during the fall harvest season. The auspicious dance of female land laborers in the courtyards of landowners (and more recently on streets of urban commercial districts) transforms newly harvested paddy into the goddess of wealth herself, Lakshmi. The narratives told through the songs of *sua nac*, however, often portray a very different female world than the auspicious one seen through the dance; the sung narratives often include tales of the sufferings of a new bride in the home of her in-laws, or a young wife whose husband leaves on a long journey, leaving her alone in the foreign land of her in-laws. These narrative motifs resonate with the lived experience of Chhattisgarhi women and find their way into a wide spectrum of folktales and songs, including those of the *kathani kuha.*

The bounded regional repertoire represented by the narrative genres described above present to us a strikingly female-centered world. Female performers and or characters are active and articulate and frequently challenge or defy Brahmanic (frequently male) expectations of gender. In this performance world, men, too, confound gender roles: a male storyteller assumes a mother's voice in noticing the subtle early signs of her daughter's pregnancy; a male character takes on female disguise to protect himself in an all-female kingdom in which he is seemingly helpless; men appropriate a particular female genre to displace its defiant voice. This play of gender and genre in the Chhattisgarhi repertoire contributes to the construction of a particular regional cultural ethos and is key to its understanding.

Further Reading

Blackburn, Stuart, et al., eds., *Oral Epics in India,* Berkeley: University of California Press, 1989

Elwin, Verrier, *Folk-songs of Chhattisgarh,* London, New York, and Bombay, India: Oxford University Press, 1946

——, *Folk-tales of Mahakoshal,* London: Oxford University Press, 1944; reprinted, New York: Arno, 1980

Flueckiger, Joyce Burkhalter, *Gender and Genre in the Folklore of Middle India,* Ithaca, New York: Cornell University Press, 1996

——, "'He Should Have Worn a Sari': A 'Failed' Performance of a Central Indian Oral Epic," *The Drama Review* 32:1 (Spring 1988)

Flueckiger, Joyce Burkhalter, and Laurie J. Sears, eds., *Boundaries of the Text: Epic Performances in South and Southeast Asia,* Ann Arbor: Center for South and Southeast Asian Studies, University of Michigan, 1991

Indonesian Storytellers and Storytelling

James Danandjaja

James Danandjaja discusses several forms of Indonesian storytelling: the didong of Sumatra, the Minangkabau kaba, the hoho of Nias, and the kentrung of East Java.

A Brief Introduction to the Indonesian Archipelago

Indonesia (before World War II, known as the Netherlands East Indies) comprises more than 3,000 islands stretching from Sumatra to West Irian, or Irian Jaya (the former Netherlands New Guinea), for a distance of some 3,400 miles. This represents an area comparable, in Europe, to that of an area reaching from west of Ireland to east of the Caspian Sea; in the United States, the region represented would reach from the Atlantic coast to the Pacific. Accounting for half the territory of Southeast Asia, the land area of Indonesia is exceeded in all of Asia only by India and China.

Indonesian history encompasses a succession of invasions from sea travelers. Chinese and Indian merchants and priests were followed by the Arabs, who were succeeded by the Portuguese, English, and Dutch, each bearing a distinctive culture. Most recently occupied by the Japanese, Indonesia has been heavily influenced by the Dutch and, later, by the United States.

Of the 3,000 islands, five account for 90 percent of the nation's land area: Sulawesi (formerly known as Celebes), Kalimantan (the part of Borneo belonging to Indonesia—the southern and central portions of that island), West Irian, and Java. Java extends 750 miles from west to east and is roughly equal in size to the state of New York. It makes up just 6 percent of the total land area of Indonesia, yet it supports well over half the Indonesian people (Peacock, 3).

The population of Indonesia in 1997 was more than 200,000,000. According to James L. Peacock, it consists of around 300 ethnic groups, the most important of which, owing to their roles in history, are the Javanese, Sundanese, Balinese, Toba Batak, Minangkabau, Atjehnese, Makassarese, Buginese, Ambonese, and Chinese (Peacock, 94).

From these facts one can see that it is impossible to include here all the arts of the storyteller and of storytelling in Indonesia. This article will concentrate only on storytelling from certain ethnic groups: the Gayonese (from central Aceh in northern Sumatra), the Minangkabau (from western Sumatra), the Ono Niha (native to the island of Nias, off the west coast of northern Sumatra), the Sundanese (from western Java), and the Javanese (from eastern Java).

Amateur, Semiprofessional, and Professional Storytellers

Indonesian storytellers can be divided into three groups: amateurs, semiprofessionals, and professionals. The amateurs are the parents, grandparents, older siblings, and nannies in the family group; the semiprofessionals are rural storytellers; and the professionals are the urban storytellers or court storytellers that in Java are called the *dalang*.

Stories for little children are told mostly after dinner, with the children sitting around the teller, and seldom while they are tucked in bed. In Java the story might be about the trickster Sang Kancil (mouse deer) or Bawang Merah and Bawang Putih, which contains the Cinderella theme and, according to Murti Bunanta (p. 96), also the theme of "kind and unkind girls." It is interesting to note that Indonesian children, especially those from rural areas, are not restricted from hearing the storytelling for the grown-ups, which takes place at night from about 9:00 to sunup. In many of the traditional ethnic groups there is no special bedtime for little children in the Western sense. Thus, children often sleep on a parent's lap while watching a storytelling performance. There is no separate bed for most Indonesian village children; they sleep with their parents.

Didong Performers in Sumatra: Group Story Singing in Competition

According to M. Junus Melalatoa (vol. 2, pp. 283–284), among the Gayo people of central Aceh in northern Sumatra, there is a folk performance that consists of storytelling that is sung and accompanied by special body movement. The performance is enacted by 25 to 35 persons, all male. The story is in the form of poetry. The performers sit in a circle, each holding a small pillow. The pillow is beaten rhythmically with the right palm. The performing is done simultaneously by two groups in a kind of a match. In the old days each group (*kelop* or *ulu*) represented the member of a clan. Each group had a special name, such as Biak Cacak, Ceding Ayu, Sinar Pagi, Dewantara, or Laki-laki. In 1980 there were 89 *didong* groups in Gayo Lut.

In every *didong* group there are several members called *ceh* and other members called *penungun*. The *ceh* is the master because he is not only a poet but also the composer of the song used in the *didong* and the singer of the tale. In a *didong* group there are several *ceh* ranked according to ability. Thus there is the chief *ceh (ceh kul)*, the second *ceh (ceh due)*, and so on. In the past the *didong* singer disseminated to the audience knowledge of the customs of the Gayo people. Later, performance become the vehicle for a match between the *didong* of different clans. The motive was to defend the goodness of their own customs. In more recent times it became the means to disseminate the history of the clan, the Five Principles of the Indonesian Republic (*Panca Sila*), sociocultural and technological development, environmental preservation, and so on. The *didong* is an expression of fine art. The *ceh* composes his own poetry, and the message is very deep but bit-

ing. The poetry must be composed instantly on the spot. By accomplishing this, the *ceh* will overcome his opponent.

Kaba Storytelling by the Minangkabau

Among the Minangkabau, the art of storytelling is called *kaba,* the storyteller is called *tukang kaba,* and the telling of the story is called *bakaba.* The story is accompanied by a bamboo flute called a *saluang* and a miniature cello called a *rebab*. During a performance the *tukang kaba* sits on the ground of the arena with his legs folded while the audience sits around him. The *kaba* is performed all night during a life-cycle ceremony. Some *kaba* are also performed as part of a folk theater called *rangdai*. In this performance, the *kaba* is not in the form of storytelling only but is supplemented with visual aids such as acting and martial art dancing (*silat*). The *kaba* has many functions—for example, as a recreational, pedagogical device to educate the audience about local customs and Muslim religious teaching. It can also be a means of social protest. The story is told in a humorous or heartrending way, and the text is poetic (Udin et al., quoted in Melalatoa, 575). In modern times the *kaba* is available on audiotape and is sold commercially.

The *Hoho* of Nias

Among the Ono Niha of the island of Nias there is a kind of storytelling that is called *hoho*. The storytelling technique is similar to that of the Gayonese *didong*, that is, not recited but sung, and the text is in the form of poetry. The story is in the form of myths concerning the origin of the Ono Niha clan and similar themes. The *tukang hoho* hold hands in a circle with the other players, swaying their bodies back and forth while chanting a monotonous song about the genesis of the people. They sing of the origin of the universe, the origin of the gods, the first human couple, and the origin of their clan and villages (Danandjaja and Koentjaraningrat, 52).

The Sundanese *Pantun, Wawacan,* and *Wayang Golek*

The Sundanese of West Java have a type of folk narrative called *pantun* stories. These stories take the form of Sundanese traditional ballads concerning the tale of the kings, and heroes from the ancient Sundanese kingdoms of Galuh and Pejajaran. Most often mentioned in the ballads is the king, or *prabu*, of Siliwangi. This ballad is cherished by the Sundanese audience because it relates to the grandeur of their past. In addition to the *pantun*, the Sundanese have other folk narratives such as the *wayang golek* (wooden puppet) stories and the *wawacan*, also called *beluk*. The *pantun* stories are concerned with the stories of the Sundanese indigenous heroes; the *wayang golek* stories are concerned with the Hindu heroes of the epics of Mahabharata and Ramayana; and the *wawacan* are about the heroes of the Sundanese Muslims. The tellers of these forms are called, respectively, the *tukang pantun*, the *dalang*, and the *tukang wawacan*. The *pantun* and the *wayang* are sung by one person, and the *wawacan* stories, by two. One person recites one verse, and the other sings it.

The stories are not only about the king of Siliwangi but also about the folk hero Sang Kuriang (the Sundanese Oedipus) and the adventures of Si Kebayan (the Sundanese *Tijl Ülen Spiegel*).

The *Kentrung* of East Java

Among the Javanese of East Java there is a kind of storytelling called the *kentrung*, sometimes also called *templing, tumpling, thumpling, kempling* or *jemblung*. This kind of storytelling is mostly from the rural areas. The storyteller of the *kentrung* is called the *dalang kentrung*; if he performs in the street he is called the *tukang kentrung*. The *dalang kentrung* and *tukang kentrung* can be of either sex. The first storyteller who studied intensively for his Ph.D. thesis is Suripan Sadi Hutomo. The stories told in the *kentrung* are mostly in the form of local legends of villages in East Java, such as "The Birth of Joko Tarub," "The Birth of Nabi Musa," "The Birth of Nabi Yusup," and others. These legends are told during the *tingkeban* ceremony (a ceremony for the seventh month of pregnancy). The Javanese people believe that the telling of these legends causes the baby to acquire the virtues of the prophets. On the occasion of the detachment of the umbilical cord from the baby, the *dalang* would narrate the legends of Lukman Hakim, Lokayanti, Prabu Rara, Ahmad Muhamad Aji Saka, and Joko Tingkir (Hutomo, 31).

The instrument accompanying the *kentrung* is called the *rebana*, or tambourine, and from the sound made by this instrument (rendered as "trung-trung") came the name of *kentrung*. Similarly onomatopoeic are the names *templing*, from the sound made by a small tambourine ("pling-pling-pling"), and *jemblung*, from the sound made by a larger tambourine ("blung-blung-blung"). There is, however, another explanation suggesting that the name of the *jemblung* is derived from the main character of the Menak stories, Jemblung Marmadi, who has a barrel-shaped belly. (The Menak story is a cycle concerning the Arab and Javanese Muslim saints.)

The function of the stories is to preach Muslim or Javanese morals and ethics. The god Dewata Cengkar, Raha Medhang Kamulan, loves to eat human flesh, the symbol of evil and covetousness in the world. The case of Aji Saka overcoming Dewata Cengkar represents evilness and covetousness, which must be destroyed. The legend of Joko Tingkir shows that a low-born peasant boy, if he has strong will and is able to overcome temptations in life, may reach a high position in his society. Joko Tingkir is a famous folk hero among Javanese youth. The legend is enacted not only in the *kentrung* play but also in *ketoprak* folk theater. For the circumcision ceremony, the Javanese *Santri* (strict Muslims) and the *Abangan* (less strict Muslims) love to perform the stories that have many fighting scenes or popular themes. For the wedding ceremony, the stories chosen are "the Joko Tarub" (which has the tale type "Swan Maiden"), or the "Pertimah," the "Murtasyah," and "Sarahwulan." The stories of these three goddesses symbolize the faithfulness of married women in accordance with Muslim morality. The goddess Pertimah (Fatimah) is especially beloved because, as she was the daughter of the Prophet Muhammad, her deeds serve as the example for young Javanese women. For the *ruwatan* (exorcism) ceremony, the story must be "Betara Kala" or "Dewata Cengkar." According to *abangan* Javanese belief, an only child of either sex, the only son among many daughters, or the only daughter among many sons is considered unclean and must go through an exorcism ceremony. Without this ceremony the child would be eaten by the demon Kala and would always be in poor health or unlucky. During the *ruwatan*, a *wayang* play or *kentrung* play must be enacted, and the story performed must be "Lairé Betara Kala" (the birth of the demon Kala). For the *santri* Javanese, the *Betara Kala* is *Dewata Cengkar*, and the god Wisnu, who for this occasion is believed to come to earth and act as the *dalang* Purwa Jati, is Aji Saka.

To enhance the dramatic effect of the tale—during such episodes as battle scenes, for example—the *tukang kentrung* beats vigorously the tambourine or *kendang,* a long Javanese drum that has two heads.

Apprentice *Kentrung*

To transmit the *kentrung* art, a well-known *tukang kentrung* takes a child as his or her *cantrik* (apprentice). There are three ways to be an apprentice of the art of *kentrung:* as an ordinary servant, as a *panjak,* and as a real apprentice. In the first case, a person initially works as a servant who not only assists a *tukang kentrung* during the performances by performing such services as carrying the musical instrument but also does household chores. For his work he receives food, lodging and wages. By being close to a *tukang kentrung,* he or she becomes familiar with the art of performing *kentrung,* and later, if he or she is smart enough, becomes a *tukang kentrung* as well. A *panjak* is an assistant to the *tukang kentrung* and is employed because he has the ability to play the instrument, which he mastered by working with a *wayang* company. A real apprentice is usually someone related to the *tukang kentrung,* and often the apprentice is the *tukang kentrung*'s own children (Hutomo, 35–37).

Further Reading

Bunanta, Murti, *Problematik Penulisan Cerita Rakyat untuk Anak di Indonesia: Telaah Penyajian dengan Contoh Dongeng bertipe Cerita "Cinderella" dan "The Kind and the Unkind Girls", Bawang Putih dan Bawang Merah* (Ph.D. diss., University of Indonesia), 1997

Danandjaja, James, and Koentjaraningrat, "Penduduk Kepulauan sebelah Barat Sumatera," in *Manusia dan Kebudajaan di Indonesia,* edited by Koentjaraningrat, Jakarta, Indonesia: Penerbit Djambatan, 1971

Hutomo, Suripan Sadi, *Cerita Kentrung Sarahwulan di Tuban,* Jakarta, Indonesia: Pusat Pembinaan dan Pengembangan Bahasa, 1993

Melalatoa, M. Junus, *Ensiklopedi Suku Bangsa di Indonesia,* Jakarta, Indonesia: Departemen Pendidikan dan Kebudayaan RI, 1995

Peacock, James L., *Indonesia: An Anthropological Perspective,* Pacific Palisades, California: Goodyear, 1973

Udin, Syamsuddin, et al., *Identifikasi Tema dan Amanat Kaba Minangkabau,* Jakarta, Indonesia: Departemen Pendidikan dan Kebudayaan, 1989

Religious Tales and Storytelling in Japan*

Richard W. Anderson

Richard W. Anderson discusses early collections containing Buddhist tales and notes their possible use by itinerant priests. He explains Barbara Ruch's argument that these priest storytellers were the originators of a Japanese national literature during the Muromachi period. Anderson then turns to an examination of New Religion and the use of personal story in these sects.

Early Traditional Histories and Religious Storytelling

The two earliest histories of Japan, the *Nihon shoki* (Aston) and the *Kojiki* (Phillippi), which were compiled in the early eighth century, record the myths and legends of the creation of Japan by the gods, the histories of the first rulers of Japan, and, most importantly, the genealogies of politically important families and clans and their relation to specific deities. It is recorded in these histories that much of the material included was obtained from people who were trained to memorize and pass down orally the traditions, history, and legends from earlier times. These histories, especially the *Nihon shoki,* are unusual because they give different variants of the same story from other written records or other narrators of the ancient stories.

The telling of stories other than official histories occurs in many different contexts in Japan. Some of the most interesting areas of study in Japan are those of stories that have a religious content and of stories that are told in a religious context. Religious tales and storytelling are important for two primary reasons: a plethora of extant printed materials exists dating from the early ninth century to the present, and such stories have had a great influence on the creation of a national literature.

The amount of material related to religious tales or storytelling is prodigious. Surveys of extant tale collections from the Heian (794–1185) and Kamakura (1185–1333) periods reveal that more than half of the collections contain purely Buddhist material, while in the mixed collections containing both secular and Buddhist tales, the latter outnumber the former two to one (Mills, p. 5). The predominance of Buddhist tales in later collections—that is, from the mid-fourteenth century on—tends to decline somewhat but is by no means insignificant. From this later period, and even up to and including the Tokugawa period (1600–1867), the earlier collections were often recopied and continued to be disseminated. Religious tale literature, admittedly of a different sort, has seen a resurgence in popularity in contemporary Japan owing to the rise of the New Religions in the middle of the nineteenth century.

Early Tale Collections

In a partial listing of tale collections from the Heian and Kamakura periods, D.E. Mills lists almost 50 different titles (pp. 437–438). The earliest collection, entitled the *Nihon ryōiki,* was

---

compiled in the 820s and contains 116 Buddhist tales and legends (Nakamura). Other collections of purely Buddhist tales are the *Dainihonkoku Hokekyōkenki,* which was compiled in the mid-eleventh century and contains 129 tales focusing primarily on the influence of the Lotus Sutra in people's lives (Dykstra), and the *Shasekishū,* compiled by Mugū Ichien in the late thirteenth century (Morrell). Two important tale collections that contain both Buddhist and secular tales are the *Konjaku monogatari,* which was compiled in the early twelfth century and contains 1,039 tales, making it one of the greatest tale collections in the world (Kelsey; Kobayashi; Ury), and the *Uji shūi monogatari,* compiled in the early thirteenth century and containing 197 tales (Mills).

The reasons for making these collections varied. A number of the collections were made in imitation of Chinese models to demonstrate that not only had Buddhist teachings entered Japan, but Japanese tales of the efficacy of Buddhist teachings existed independently in Japan, negating the need to use foreign (i.e., Chinese) narratives (Mills, pp. 6–7; Nakamura, pp. 99–102). Other collections were made for the religious edification of individuals—for example, the *Sambō-e,* which was compiled by a court noble for a young princess who was the daughter of the emperor (Mills, pp. 8–9)—or "for the betterment—both spiritual and social—of its audience," as W. Michael Kelsey argues was the case for the *Konjaku Monogatari* (p. 2).

Since all of the tales in these collections were written, it is obvious that they were not intended for the masses, who could not read. That does not mean, however, that these tales did not reach or come from the lower classes nor that they had no influence upon them. A number of compilers state clearly in their introductions that the tales circulated in the oral tradition and were collected from all levels of society (see, for example, Nakamura, pp. 42, 102). It has been noted by numerous scholars that the tales in these collections have two basic characteristics: they are written in a simple style illustrating Buddhist doctrine in easy-to-understand terms, and the tales tend to illustrate the rewards and punishments meted out to believers and nonbelievers in the present life (see, for example, Goodwin, pp. 56–59).

These observations have led to speculation that the texts were used by itinerant storytellers—that is, priests who traveled around the country trying to convert nonbelievers or to collect funds for the restoration of old temples, the building of new ones, the making of Buddhist statues, and the copying of sutras. The latter activity of soliciting funds *(kanjin* in Japanese) began in the late seventh century and was carried on into the Tokugawa period by itinerant priests called *hijiri* (Goodwin). In their attempts to collect funds and construction material, the *kanjin hijiri* would tell tales that focused on the rewards obtained in this life by people who helped propagate Buddhist teachings through donations to support priests, the chanting or writing of sutras, or the making of statues or construction of temples.

Besides tales from collections, the *hijiri* also used *engi,* the story of the founding of a temple and other miraculous tales associated with the temple, personages, or statues at the temple that was requesting aid. Often these *engi* were accompanied by *emaki* (illustrated manuscripts) that the priest would use to illustrate the story while he told it (Goodwin, p. 57; Ruch). Since many of these tale collections, *engi* and *emaki,* were copied and used by itinerant priests well into the nineteenth century, numerous copies of such materials are extant and provide fertile research materials for the historical development of religious storytelling.

The Creation of a National Literature

Barbara Ruch has argued persuasively that during the Muromachi period (1392–1568) these itinerant priest storytellers were the originators of a national literature in Japan that was fundamentally different from the literature of the previous period. Ruch claims that there were two types of Muromachi literature. The first type was a literature written by and for educated elites with specific rules and aesthetic principles that were strictly observed. The second type of literature had "no history of aesthetic codes [and] no body of criticism upon which practitioners based their activities. Their primary aim was to draw the listener deeply into an orally delivered narrative and to cause, above all, an emotional response in an audience" (p. 284). This latter form of literature, Ruch argues, was a "vocal literature" that was intended primarily not for elite audiences but for a wider audience that did not make rigid aesthetic demands. Ruch uses the term "vocal literature" as opposed to "oral literature," claiming that the former refers to a spoken literature in a literate society, whereas the latter term is generally reserved for a spoken literature in an illiterate society.

It was the itinerant priests who created, recited, and spread these tales but, as Ruch demonstrates, an important shift in themes took place in the thirteenth and fourteenth centuries—away from tales of love that were popular in court literature and toward tales of "the suffering and salvation of military heroes and deities as well as themes that reveal the anxieties and concerns of the new turbulent age" (p. 290). It was this new vocal literature, with its new heroes and themes, that was spread throughout Japan and came to be embraced by most Japanese. Ruch claims that "[f]or the first time Japan in the Muromachi period came to share one body of heroes and heroines, one sense of pathos, a consciousness as to what constitutes tragedy, a more or less unified attitude toward such problems as suffering, resignation, self-sacrifice, the transience of the individual yet the immutability of the social order. Even a national ethic, a national sentiment, was formed that was without question the product of the religio-secular missionary-jongleur of the fourteenth and fifteenth centuries." (pp. 293–294).

Japanese New Religions and Taiken (Personal Narratives)

With the overthrow in 1867 of the Tokugawa shogunate, the military rulers of Japan for 250 years, Japan entered a period of social and cultural upheaval. With regard to religion, the new government attempted to control and impose its will in a number of ways. The two most important were an attempt to separate Shinto and Buddhism and elevate Shinto to a state cult centered on the emperor and an attempt to eliminate "superstitious" beliefs and practices (Hardacre; Ketelaar). It was during this time that the New Religions began to appear and prosper. New Religions are "religious groups that have come into being during or since the closing years of the Tokugawa period, have their spiritual center in the person and purportedly unique teachings of a founder who comes from the common people, and are oriented toward the gaining of new members from among the masses" (Arai, p. 94). With the rise of these New Religions, the government's carefully laid plans to guide and control religious thought and behavior away from superstition and to separate religions began to unravel.

The reasons for the rise of the New Religions are numerous, but the most commonly cited one is the social crisis explanation (McFarland, pp. 39–70; Thomsen, pp. 18–20). This explanation claims that the rapid economic and social changes that Japan experienced during the previous 150 years disrupted people's lives to such an extent that many Japanese sought comfort in tradition-based New Religions—that is, new religious groups whose teachings were based primarily on Shinto or Buddhist beliefs, or both, and practices with strong thaumaturgic elements. Healing has been central to all New Religions in Japan—initially, healing of physical ailments, which over time often changes to a focus on healing of problems in human relations. Most New Religions discovered very early in their development that one of the most effective ways to proselytize prospective new members was to have an enthusiastic member relate a *taiken,* a narrative of personal experiences with the religion and how it had promoted physical or emotional healing and a changed life (Anderson, *Personal Narratives*; "Vengeful Ancestors"; "Social Drama and Iconicity"). To the best of my knowledge, all Japanese New Religions—and there are more than 1,000—request that adherents give oral presentation of *taiken* at training sessions and recruitment meetings (see, for example, Anderson, "To Open the Hearts of People"). These oral versions are often recorded, edited, and published in monthly magazines and newspapers.

Religious storytelling is therefore alive and well in Japan today, but, as can be seen, some major shifts have taken place. Contemporary tales relate an adherent's personal experience, not some miraculous tale of a statue, temple, or priest, and the tellers of the tales are ordinary people (mostly women), not priests.

There are probably a number of reasons for this shift in content, narrator, and gender. Arguably, one of the main reasons for this change is the increased emphasis placed on recruiting new adherents. Priests in the older established sects of Buddhism did not, and still do not today, proselytize actively. They did not have to proselytize because families had ties to a Buddhist temple that extended back over generations, since family graves were located at the temple. The priests at Shinto shrines did not proselytize since people were affiliated with a particular shrine simply because they lived in the neighboring area. The New Religions obviously did not have such claims on people's religious affiliations and therefore had to go out and actively recruit new members. Most of these new groups discovered that one of the best ways of gaining new members was to have an adherent tell an emotional testimony, explaining in some detail how painful life was prior to joining the group, then the beneficial changes wrought after the adherent joined the New Religion and internalized the teachings. These narratives of personal experience told by adherents present in easy-to-understand terms the basic teachings of the group and the benefits that a prospective or new member can expect to receive. The telling of this narrative also binds the narrator more closely to the group and demonstrates a commitment to the group and its teachings.

Another interesting aspect of this shift from priests to adherents telling tales is that the vast majority of narrators today are female. There are a number of reasons for this shift in gender of the narrators in the New Religions. One of the most important reasons is that participants at meetings, especially on weekdays, are overwhelmingly female. The explanation for the predominance of women, according to adherents, is quite simple: men are busy working and therefore do not have the requisite free time to spend at such meetings. A second parallel reason put forward is that most of the New Religions focus much of their attention on the family and the elimination of various problems in human relations that can upset the family. Narratives of strife between husband and wife, wife and mother-in-law, and parents and child therefore predominate. Since the husband and father's energy is directed outward, away from the family and toward providing materially for the family, the responsibility of family harmony and well-being falls primarily on the wife and mother. Her life and actions, therefore, must be the opposite of those of her husband—that is, directed inward toward the family. The narratives of strife inside the family and the overcoming of these problems through the teachings of the religion seem naturally to fall into her domain.

A 1,200-Year-Old Tradition of Religious Storytelling Continues

Religious storytelling and tales with a religious content have a history more than 1,200 years long in Japan. Throughout this long history, religious storytelling and the tales themselves have been used by a variety of people for a number of different purposes: for example, to impart basic religious teachings, to help people achieve enlightenment or a better birth in the next life, to solicit funds for a variety of religious purposes, to proselytize among the masses, and to bind new mem-

bers more closely to a group. The primary narrators of these tales have shifted during this long period from priests to adherents in the New Religions. As for what the future holds in store for religious storytelling and tales in Japan, we can be sure of only one thing, and that is that the Buddhist concept of *mujo* (impermanence, change) will continue to ensure, as it has in the past, that the narrators, tales, and their roles in society will not remain the same.

Further Reading

Anderson, Richard W., "Social Drama and Iconicity: Personal Narratives in Japanese New Religions," *Journal of Folklore Research* 32:3 (1995)

——, *Taiken: Personal Narratives and Japanese New Religions* (Ph.D. diss., Indiana University), 1988

——, "To Open the Hearts of People: Experience Narratives and Zenrinkai Training Sessions," *Japanese Journal of Religious Studies* 19:4 (1992)

——, "Vengeful Ancestors and Animal Spirits: Personal Narratives of the Supernatural in a Japanese New Religion," *Western Folklore* 54:2 (April 1995)

Arai, Ken, "New Religious Movements," in *Japanese Religion. A Survey by the Agency for Cultural Affairs*, edited by Hori Ichirō et al., Tokyo: Kodansha, 1972

Aston, W.G., trans., *Nihongi: Chronicles of Japan from the Earliest Times to A.D. 697*, London: Kegan Paul, Trench, Trübner, 1896; New York: Dutton, 1924

Chingen, *Miraculous Tales of the Lotus Sutra from Ancient Japan: The Dainihonkoku Hokekyōkenki of Priest Chingen*, translated by Yoshiko K. Dykstra, Hirakata City, Japan: Intercultural Research Institute, Kansai University of Foreign Studies, 1983; Honolulu: University of Hawaii Press, 1987

Goodwin, Janet R., *Alms and Vagabonds: Buddhist Temples and Popular Patronage in Medieval Japan*, Honolulu: University of Hawaii Press, 1994

Hardacre, Helen, *Shintō and the State, 1868–1988*, Princeton, New Jersey: Princeton University Press, 1989; Oxford: Princeton University Press, 1991

Kelsey, W. Michael, *Konjaku Monogatari-shu*, Boston: Twayne, 1982

Ketelaar, James Edward, *Of Heretics and Martyrs in Meiji Japan: Buddhism and Its Persecution,* Princeton, New Jersey: Princeton University Press, 1990

Kobayashi Hiroko, *The Human Comedy of Heian Japan: A Study of the Secular Stories in the Twelfth-Century Collection of Tales, Konjaku Monogatarishū,* Tokyo: Center for East Asian Cultural Studies, 1979

Mills, D.E., trans., *A Collection of Tales from Uji: A Study and Translation of Uji Shûi Monogatari,* Cambridge: Cambridge University Press, 1970

Mujū Ichien, *Sand and Pebbles (Shasekishu): The Tales of Mujū Ichien, A Voice for Pluralism in Kamakura Buddhism,* translated by Robert E. Morrell, Albany: State University of New York Press, 1985

Nakamura, Kyoko Motomochi, trans., *Miraculous Stories from the Japanese Buddhist Tradition: The Nihon Ryoiki of the Monk Kyōkai,* Cambridge, Massachusetts: Harvard University Press, 1973; new edition, Surrey, England: Curzon, 1997

Philippi, Donald, trans., *Kojiki,* Tokyo: University of Tokyo Press, 1968; Princeton, New Jersey: Princeton University Press, 1969

Ruch, Barbara, "Medieval Jongleurs and the Making of a National Literature," in *Japan in the Muromachi Age,* edited by John Whitney Hall and Toyoda Takeshi, Berkeley: University of California Press, 1977

Ury, Marian, *Tales of Times Now Past: Sixty-Two Stories from a Medieval Japanese Collection,* Berkeley: University of California Press, 1979

Still Telling in Japan: Traditional Folktellers

Cathy Spagnoli

In 1992 Cathy Spagnoli toured Japan on a fellowship from the Japan Foundation in pursuit of traditional storytellers. She discusses several tellers and their motivations for continuing the folktelling tradition.

The feeling of closeness, of caring was so important, it made every story special. People have told stories for ages. Why? Because a story has a heart, a spirit which we need.
—Asai Masako, storyteller

I remember my grandmother holding me and whispering stories to me as we laid down to sleep. —Shirane Keiko, storyteller

Warm memories of shared stories are held by many Japanese today because traditional storytelling was a valued pastime in an older Japan. A farming economy allowed for slow winter evenings when the family gathered around the *irori* fireplace, and words became wings with which to soar. But factories grew, needing labor, and hard times hit the farms, sending young listeners to the cities. The invasion of television and the pressure of a very competitive school system further weakened the folktelling tradition. Fortunately, through the efforts of dedicated scholars, collectors, librarians, and other storytellers, a renewed interest in storytelling has flourished of late in folklore societies, home and public libraries, community centers, and college classrooms.

Today, story collectors throughout Japan continue to seek out traditional tales and tellers. Inada Kazuko and Koji, from Okayama, have published several story collections much used as sources for modern storytellers; writer/folklore scholar Matsutani Miyoko of Tokyo collects and shares stories in person and through her publications; Kubota Zentaro, a lively, retired educator from Kochi, publishes regional tales in local dialects; high school teacher Abe Toshio, in Hokkaido, leads a folklore society as he, too, gathers tales. There are numerous other dedicated collectors in local education boards, women's groups, and community centers across Japan. Yet still, for some groups like the indigenous Ainu of Hokkaido island, it is almost too late.

"We have lost so much over the years," said Ogawa Ryukichi, Ainu spokesperson. "Our language was banned for years in this century. The only elders who remember the old tales are weak and many are in nursing homes. We have almost lost our stories, so Shirasawa Nabe [an 86-year-old Ainu storyteller, one of the few remaining] is very special to us. We try to preserve her energy so that she can teach us."

According to Shirasawasan, "Our houses were far apart, so it was wonderful to gather together some nights, after working all day, and tell stories. I heard so many tales then, when I was 5, 6, and 7. I told them as well, yet I forgot so many too. . . . My father once told me I would be important in preserving our culture. But I didn't listen to him. I married and was then so busy just trying to survive."

Luckily, a young scholar some years ago contacted her during his research on the Ainu language. Soon after, in a meeting of Ainu elders, Shirasawasan told a *yukara*, an Ainu epic, for the first time in decades. "Everyone was thrilled to hear the real thing," she said. Ever since then, she has shared the stories she recalls, even though she has lost many of the old words.

During her singing of part of a *yukara*, Shirasawasan's eyes gaze at the floor. Her voice chants soft words, richly repeated. Her hands sing a rhythm, too, the right fist tapping lightly against the left palm. The song moves the listeners in time from the storyteller's small home today to the older, prouder times of Ainu hunters free in their land, sharing their tales.

The images of the *yukara* come to life. The goddess of fire sews day and night, hears a bird's warning call, dons shoes to walk on water, and journeys to bring home her wandering husband. At last, after much trouble, the couple returns home together and the goddess once again sews day and night while her husband carves peacefully. Too soon, the chanting stopped, and it was again 1992.

Weeks later, in a tall apartment building in Koriyama city in Fukushima prefecture, Sakonji Masae, one of Japan's youngest traditional tellers, had gathered local tellers.

"I don't want to learn any new stories, or to teach others to tell their tales," she said. "I only want to share my grandmother's stories with many listeners. I heard them when I was young, as we drifted to sleep. My grandmother said she was too busy to share stories with my father when he was little, and my brother wasn't very interested in her stories, so she passed everything to me."

Sakonjisan keeps the tales alive by using the same words, sounds, and emotions that her grandmother did, adapting the quiet style of telling used by her grandmother as the two relaxed at bedtime. Her repertoire includes tall tales of lazy men, funny stories that turn out to be dreams, tales of tricky *tengu* creatures, and several popular tales of kind and greedy neighbors. She is often asked to tell in community centers, libraries, and for folklore festivals. Six years ago Sakonjisan put 32 of these oral tales into a book to honor her late son and her grandmother.

Tales passed on from another grandmother to her family are told in Yamagata prefecture as well. There, in the shadow of a sacred mountain, in an old farmhouse that appears to float on rice fields, lives 84-year-old storyteller Ito Takeyo. Above her Buddhist altar, a scroll with careful calligraphy advises, "Have big ears to hear and a small mouth to speak little as you listen with kind eyes."

She tells listeners her stories in a quiet voice, her hands content with small gestures, her face sliding often into smiles. Her words flow out as her son, his eyes closed, urges her on with frequent responses ("Hah, ah ra, ra . . ."). Her stories are told in a strong dialect, for a sense of place is very important to Itosan and to other traditional tellers, too. This feeling of homeland, of *furusato*, is passed on through story choice and through the words and nuances of local dialect.

Her repertoire of more than 100 tales includes ghost stories, tales of tricky monkeys, love stories, and local legends from her beautiful region. Local legends are some of the most often told, and yet least translated, Japanese stories. The powerful pull of one's homeland is passed on through story words born from and defining the stones, waters, landforms, and statues of the land. Traditional tellers are able to relate the legends of each rock, tree, and hill in their local regions.

Itosan's son tells his tales a little more loudly, a little more quickly, and just as warmly. During an annual snow festival in nearby Shinjo city, mother and son share traditional tales together with the youngest storyteller in their extended family, a 14-year-old girl, Itosan's granddaughter. One tale she tells is a version of the story of the boy with the very long name. Itosan's lips move silently with words that flow from a distant past through this child into tomorrow. Itosan has indeed taught her children to tell well.

Further south in Tohoku region, a story heartland of Japan, another teller teaches others to tell. Once a year, in an old home complete with dark beams and an *irori*, under the painted eyes of 3,000 wooden dolls proudly displayed, more than 50 men and women gather. There, in Koriyama city, Yokoyama Sachiko leads a six-week storytelling course. She tells tales as she teaches—one minute in a loud, comic style, the next in a very quiet style, her voice taking on the huskiness of a much older woman. Comments on finding and telling stories complement the stories, and at the end of each session, her students, too, share their tales.

Yokoyama Sachiko is a very active traditional teller, traveling throughout her prefecture and across the country as she shares tales heard in childhood and gathered since. Although she heard stories often in her family as she grew up during wartime Japan, she was pulled into public telling only when her youngest son died at 20 in an accident.

"I realized then that I never had enough time for him, to tell him stories. I was so busy helping my husband's printing business, too eager to just make a good living. After my son's death, I made a vow to his spirit that I would share with other children all the stories I should have told him."

Yokoyamasan now travels widely telling those tales in community centers, theaters, schools, after-school programs, and over the radio. She calls herself Ohanashi no Obasan, "Storytelling Aunt," hoping to be the older storytelling relative that many of today's youngsters no longer have nearby. Unlike some traditional tellers, though, she is as comfortable with 500 listeners as she is with five. Her style changes to suit the audience, but her dress is usually the traditional loose pants and jackets of a farmer, often hand-dyed by artists in her hometown. She often shows traditional tools and items to help modern children imagine Japan as it was.

Yokoyamasan collects stories as well, especially from her home near Fukushima city—painful ghost stories, funny folktales, and even legends as small and as suspect as one behind the name of her town, Yanagawa: Two men stood on opposite banks of a river. One called, "Ya," the other answered, "Na," and this exchange, added to *kawa* (river), became Yanagawa.

Yokoyamasan is one of the few traditional tellers today teaching Japanese children to tell tales. Her young storytellers gather weekly in a lovely old farmhouse museum and share stories around the traditional *irori*. She also works with a group of middle school and high school storytellers. Fourteen-year-old Yoko, one of her students and the proud teller of 30 tales, shares what she has learned from Yokoyamasan, who looks to the past with an eye on the future: "Choose a story that you like, and not because of tradition or what others think!"

Many stories, traditional and modern, are now being shared in Japan. The traditional tellers introduced here are part of a larger storytelling movement that includes storytelling in theaters, public and home libraries, mothers' groups, schools, community centers, and elsewhere. In many of these settings, and in their own homes, numbers of older tellers are sought out by newer storytellers and listeners eager to learn. Thus, while robots build cars and video games flourish in Japan today, the words of traditional tellers are still heard, their words reaching all those who wish to hear.

Further Reading

Adams, Robert J., *Social Identity of a Japanese Storyteller* (Ph.D. diss., Indiana University), 1972

Dorson, Richard, *Folk Legends of Japan*, Rutland, Vermont, and Tokyo: Charles Tuttle, 1961

Inada, Koji and Kazuko, *Nihon Mukashi Banashi Hyaku Sen,* Tokyo: Sanseido, 1983

Kayano, Shigeru, *Our Land was a Forest: An Ainu Memoir,* translated by Kyoko Selden and Lily Selden, Boulder, Colorado: Westview, 1994

Mayer, Fanny Hagin, ed., *Ancient Tales in Modern Japan,* Bloomington: Indiana University Press, 1985

——, ed., *The Yanagita Kunio Guide to the Japanese Folk Tale,* Bloomington: Indiana University Press, 1986

Morioka, Heinz, and Miyoko Sasaki, *Rakugo, The Popular Narrative Art of Japan,* Cambridge, Massachusetts: Council on East Asian Studies at Harvard University, 1990

Philippi, Donald, *Songs of Gods, Songs of Humans: The Epic Tradition of the Ainu,* Princeton, New Jersey: Princeton University Press, 1979

Seki, Keigo, ed., *Folktales of Japan,* Chicago: University of Chicago Press, 1963; London: Routledge and K. Paul, 1963

Wheeler, Post, *Tales from the Japanese Storytellers,* Rutland, Vermont: Charles Tuttle, 1976

P'ansori, the Ancient Korean Art of Storytelling

Chan E. Park

Chan E. Park gives a brief history of Korean p'ansori, discusses features of p'ansori performance, and speaks of the discipline of the performer and the transmission of this tradition. He includes summaries of five p'ansori tales.

P'ansori—from *p'an* (performance, performance space, or performative occasion) and *sori* (sound, voice, or singing)—is a solo-singer type of storytelling that surfaced as a distinctive artistry about three centuries ago in the southwestern part of the Korean peninsula. Its discovery goes back to the mid-eighteenth century, when a government official stationed in Chŏlla province one day witnessed in his village a performance of the Song of Ch'unhyang, one of the most popular stories performed. He later recorded the narrative, the first transcription of its kind.

The conventional performance of *p'ansori* takes place on a straw mat upon which the singer stands, moves around, or sits, while a drummer is seated to the left of the singer. The singer alternates between stylized speaking (*aniri*) and singing (*sori*) to tell the tales of the ancient times, stories that take between three and eight hours if delivered in their entireties. They are sung (with detailed description of the scene, including the thoughts and actions of the characters) and spoken (with plot summaries, scene changes, and commentaries), which serves as a necessary break from the strenuous singing. The drummer beats the barrel-shaped drum called a *puk* on the right side with a smooth birch drumstick in his right hand, coordinated with his left palm and fingers on the left side. As the singing progresses, the drummer frequently emits a stylized cry of encouragement (*chwimsae*) that blends with the singing and the accompanying rhythm. The members of the audience follow suit and add their own cries, showing both performers their appreciation for their energy and expertise.

Traditionally, the success of a *p'ansori* performance has been evaluated according to such categories as the performer's presence, narrative content, vocal virtuosity, and dramatic gesture, as articulated in the Song of the Kwangdae (circa 1875), composed by the nineteenth-century critic Sin Chaehyo (1812–84). Most essential is the strength of the voice that, through lifelong discipline, has attained the power of portraying even the most intimate details of the story. The narrative richness of the *p'ansori* voice is further accentuated by its aesthetic of minimalism, manifest in its theatrical simplicity: the very subdued costumes of the performers, the bare straw-mat stage, the stylistic gesturing, and the creation of imaginary scenery and ambiance by the use of a folding fan made of bamboo ribs and rice paper.

History

The evolution of *p'ansori* can be discussed in the following sequence: emergence before the eighteenth century, proliferation and gentrification in the nineteenth century, theatrical experimentation, sociocultural challenges in the form's encounter with modernity, and efforts of preservation and transmission in the twentieth century. Because *p'ansori* was developed and transmitted orally, no written documents about its origin have been cited, but it has been established that *p'ansori* emerged as a marketplace entertainment from the periphery of the native shamanistic ritual practice called *kut*. The early singers were among the folk performing artists, *kwangdae*, whose important artistic function included providing musical accompaniment for *kut*. In shaping the basic performance structure of *p'ansori*, they closely incorporated elements of the ritual music and chanting while blending in the multiple vocal, lyric, and narrative traditions of the time.

It was in the nineteenth century that *p'ansori* reached its heyday with the emergence of generations of brilliant singers, each singer possessing a distinctive style of singing. They contributed to the expansion of its repertoire and the redefinition of its standard of excellence. This occurred in tandem with sociocultural changes that promoted the development of folk culture away from the dictates of neo-Confucian practices; those practices nurtured only persons of sociopolitical privilege. Disenchanted with the Confucian rhetoric that seemed useless in the face of governmental corruption and national danger, many among the aristocratic literati joined the writers and artists in promoting a popular culture grounded in native folk aesthetics. Many of them participated in further contextualizing and canonizing *p'ansori* by collaborating with the talented singers. In the process, they helped select five narratives (from the 12 that were popular at the time) that similarly represented the five Confucian cardinal virtues: filial piety, chastity, loyalty, respect for older siblings, and faith between friends. The literati went further, matching the linguistic and narrative revision on the selected five to the elitist patrons' ideology and level of appreciation. As a result, *p'ansori* narratives came to offer an interesting blend of multiple cosmologies, values, themes, and narrative styles.

Toward the latter part of the nineteenth century, women began to enter what had been the male-only territory of the *p'ansori* discipline. In retrospect, the participation of both genders appears to have been the dawn of an era of theatrical experimentation. The turn of the century marked an important development: the birth of *ch'angg k* (singing theater), performed by multiple singers playing their respective roles. Supported by Emperor Kojong (reigned 1864–1907)

himself, *ch'anggŭk* was launched, and many prominent singers participated. Their efforts to innovate a dramatic format on the national level, however, were discouraged and restricted by the ensuing cultural persecution by the Japanese imperial police, which continued until the Japanese surrender at the end of World War II. Nor did it help that silent films and Western music and drama were welcomed and gained dominance. In the aftermath of the Korean War (1950–53) it was the Korean government that took on the mission of preserving the traditional folk heritage. Today, the art of *p'ansori* is designated as the intangible national treasure Number Five; its prominent singers are human national treasures. Their official mission is to help preserve the art by transmitting it to the next generation, while the creative perpetuation of *p'ansori* in modern times remains a topic of serious discussion.

Synopses of the Five Traditional *P'ansori* Narratives, Retold by Chan Park

Song of Ch'unhyang. Around the beginning of Emperor Sukchong's reign (1674–1720), there is a young gentleman staying in Namwŏn: Yi Mongnyong, the handsome, intelligent, and gallant son of the new magistrate from Seoul. On a brilliant spring day Mongnyong has an urge to take a stroll. He closes his book and rides out to the scenic Kwanghallu pavilion, escorted by his servant Pangja. There he sees in the distance, amid flowers and willow branches, a beautiful maiden on a swing. Her name is Ch'unhyang. It is love at first sight. That night, Mongnyong visits Ch'unhyang's house and succeeds in persuading Ch'unhyang's mother, Wŏlmae, a retired court entertainer, to let them marry. The two exchange nuptial vows. According to neo-Confucian social practice, however, it was unthinkable for a son of a nobleman to take a lover before taking the state examination, nor could he wed anyone but a girl from a noble family, and in a proper ceremony. Nevertheless, their love deepens and time flies.

The magistrate is promoted to a higher position in Seoul, and Mongnyong, like a good son, must accompany his parents back. Pledging to meet again, the lovers have a sad farewell.

A new magistrate by the name of Pyŏn Hakto arrives. Hearing of Ch'unhyang and her beauty, he had petitioned to serve the township of Namwŏn. Immediately following his inauguration, Magistrate Pyŏn begins to harass Ch'unhyang to serve him. She refuses, saying that she is already married, and the magistrate orders her torture and imprisonment. She is to be beheaded on the magistrate's birthday, with her execution the highlight of the banquet entertainment.

Meanwhile, Mongnyong applies himself wholeheartedly to his scholarship and wins the first-place honor in the state examination. The king dubs him with the royal insignia to serve the state as royal inspector incognito. Mongnyong leads his secret officers to Namwŏn, righting wrongs along the way. On the eve of Ch'unhyang's execution, Mongnyong, incognito in threadbare attire, turns up at her door. Wŏlmae, who has been praying fervently for his return so that her daughter's life might be spared, despairs at his beggar-like state. His return as an official higher than the new magistrate would have been the only recourse, and now that hope is gone. That night, at the prison, the lovers meet.

In the middle of the birthday banquet for the magistrate, a loud call announcing the presence of the royal inspector incognito is sounded. Havoc erupts; the magistrate and all his guests scatter, looking for places to hide. Justice is delivered as the royal inspector orders punishment for the corrupt officials and freedom for the innocent. Ch'unhyang, too, is brought before the royal inspector. He asks her if she will serve him instead of the magistrate. Unaware that he is Mongnyong, she criticizes him as being no better than the corrupt magistrate. He produces before Ch'unhyang the jade ring she gave him as a token of unchanging love when they separated. She sees the ring, sees Mongnyong, and the story ends with a happy celebration.

Song of Hŭngbu. In a country place where Kyŏngsang, Chŏlla, and Ch'unch'ŏng provinces meet, there live two brothers, Nolbu and Hŏngbu. The younger brother, Hŭngbu, is good, but the older brother, Nolbu, is obnoxious and greedy. According to the Confucian custom, Nolbu inherits everything from their father, including the responsibility of looking after the entire family, but he is not the kind of person to care for anyone else. One winter day, he chases Hŭngbu and his family out into the cold.

After much wandering Hŭngbu and the family settle in a valley among the homeless. The traditional education of a nobleman consisted of learning prose writing and poetry recital, not survival skills, and with the mother having no means to support 11 children and another on its way, life is hard. The children cry for food and fight for scraps of blanket to keep themselves from freezing. They are on the verge of starvation when they are visited by a Taoist monk. Instead of collecting alms, the monk takes Hŭngbu deep into the valley, points to an auspicious building site, and then disappears. Hŭngbu builds a hut and moves his family there. Life seems a bit more bearable.

One spring day, a pair of swallows fly in and build their nest under Hŭngbu's eaves. Soon, two baby swallows hatch. One of them falls and breaks its legs while practicing flying. Kind Hŭngbu and his wife treat it with utmost care and put it back in the nest. Autumn comes, and all the birds prepare for their journey to their winter homes in the south. Hŭngbu's swallow soars up high and circles the sky in farewell to kind Hŭngbu and his family.

It is the week of homecoming in the great Kingdom of the Swallows. Millions of swallows fly in from all over the world to report their arrivals. Hŭngbu's swallow limps in and recounts his birth in Korea, his leg injury, and his survival thanks to kind Hŭngbu. Greatly impressed, the Swallow King produces a magic gourd seed for Hŭngbu's swallow to take back to Hŭngbu the following spring. The next spring, Hŭngbu's swallow returns with the gourd seed and, with thankful heart, Hŭngbu plants the seed behind his house. In the fall, it yields three huge gourds. One fine day, the family gathers in their courtyard and sees the gourds open. Out pours money, gold, silver, silk, and rice, and they become the wealthiest people in the country.

The rumor that Hŭngbu has become the wealthiest man in the country reaches Nolbu. Seething with jealousy, he comes over one day to see for himself. Having heard the whole story of the swallow and the magic seed, Nolbu is determined to make himself richer than his brother. He catches a dozen swallows and, one by one, breaks and bandages their legs. Next spring, he, too, receives a magic gourd seed. He plants it and harvests three huge gourds in the fall. As they are sawed open, instead of jewels and rice, demons and goblins hop out amid oozing feces and shrill curses. Nolbu becomes destitute overnight. Good Hŭngbu, however, takes in Nolbu and his family to share his wealth and his living quarters, and they live happily ever after.

Historical background to Song of the Red Cliff. Toward the end of the later Han Dynasty, the political power of China was divided among warlords, and the land was looted by bandits. The emperors in the capital were mere puppets in the triangles of power struggle between the eunuchs, relatives of the dowager queens, and the scholar-gentry. As a son of an adopted son of a eunuch, Cao Cao had no family background to boast of, yet, through a series of conquests and brilliant strategic manipulations, especially against the Yellow Turbans, he rose to the position of prime minister for the puppet emperor. With the imperial authority behind him, he brought one warlord after another to surrender until all of northern China came under his control.

In the meantime, situated in the southwest was Liu Bei, who, although but a minor official, retained his pride as a descendant of Liu Bang, founder of the Han Dynasty, and he felt it was his responsibility to restore the Han court. Meanwhile, Sun Quan was in control of the eastern territory south of the Yangtze River. In A.D. 208 Cao Cao led his 830,000-man army southward in order to fight the allied forces of Liu Bei and Sun Quan, who posed the last hindrance to his unification of China. The background of the Song of the Red Cliff is the river battle at Red Cliff (Chibi), on the Yangtze in modern Anhui province, in which Cao Cao suffered devastating defeat.

Song of the Red Cliff. Liu Bei, having lost his trustworthy strategist Xu Yuan Zhi to a snare contrived by Cao Cao, seeks the counsel of Zhuge Liang, a tactical genius recommended by the departing Xu. After Liu makes three humble visits that are known as the Three Visits to the Grass Hut, his supplication wins the heart of this wisest man of the time.

The next episode is the Battle of Powangp'o, in which Liu Bei, with Zhuge Liang's help, wins a minor battle. It is followed by Zhuge Liang's visit to Sun Quan's headquarters to reveal one of his clever ruses to instigate Sun's adviser Zhou Yu to join the battle against Cao Cao.

Next comes the eve of the Battle of the Red Cliff. Cao Cao's soldiers are homesick, drunk, and anticipating a bloody battle. Meanwhile, Zhuge Liang performs a ritual prayer to heaven to bring about the southeasterly wind, which would not normally come in the middle of winter. Heaven responds by sending the southeasterly wind, with which Zhuge Liang destroys Cao Cao's force.

The Battle of Red Cliff ends in Cao Cao's utter defeat. In his retreat, Cao Cao is captured on Hwa Rongdao path by Guan Yu, a noble warrior who, remembering a previous favor, releases Cao Cao.

Song of Sim Ch'ŏng. In Peace Blossom Village in Hwangju district lives a blind man by the name of Sim Hakkyu and his good wife, Kwak-ssi. She is diligent and resourceful and takes care of her husband with the utmost devotion. They do not have a son to carry on Sim's name, however, so they pray for one. At last they beget a child, but to their great disappointment, it is a girl. They name her Ch'ŏng. Kwak-ssi, weakened by the birth, falls ill and dies, and Blind Man Sim is left alone to care for the newborn baby. Thanks to the kind women of the village who take turns nursing her, Sim Ch'ŏng grows into a beautiful girl with a filial heart, and Blind Man Sim finds joy and happiness in watching her blossom.

Sim Ch'ŏng turns 15. Having heard of her beauty and virtue, Lady Chang, widow of the late Minister Chang, one day sends for Ch'ŏng to come to her mansion in Arcadia Village. While Ch'ŏng enjoys her visit with Lady Chang the sun sets. Blind Man Sim is home alone, awaiting Ch'ŏng's return. Cold, hungry, and worried, he gropes his way out into the drifting snow to look for Ch'ŏng. He slips into an icy stream and is about to drown when a Buddhist monk passing by pulls him out of the water. The monk tells Blind Man Sim that omnipotent Lord Buddha will help him regain his sight if he prays and donates 300 straw sacks of rice to his temple. In spite of his penniless state, Blind Man Sim pledges to donate the proposed sum. Home again, he sorely regrets his thoughtless blunder, but the pledge is final, and offering false commitment to Lord Buddha would be unpardonable.

When Ch'ŏng returns home and hears what has happened, she comforts her father not to despair. From that day on, she prays to her guardian spirits to help procure the sacrificial rice. One day, a group of merchant sailors enters the village, announcing loudly that they will pay any price for a sacrificial maiden to be offered to the Dragon King of the four oceans. (In the ancient times, human sacrifice was a way of insuring a safe and prosperous journey.) Ch'ŏng commits herself to the deal in return for the delivery of the sacrificial rice her father has promised to the temple. Blind Man Sim, unaware of this tragedy until the morning of her departure, is beside himself with anger, remorse, and grief, and he breaks down pitifully. Leaving behind her grief-stricken father and the sympathetic villagers, Sim Ch'ŏng follows the sailors to the sea. At the appointed hour she throws herself into the raging waters of Imdangsu and is heard of no more.

Virtuous deeds do not pass unnoticed by omniscient heaven. Sim Ch'ŏng is sent back to float on the surface of the sea in a magical lotus bud. The sailors, on their way back from yet another profitable journey, approach the water of Imdangsu, reminiscing mournfully about the life and death of beautiful Sim Ch'ŏng. Suddenly, they see the magical lotus bud floating afar. Meanwhile, the recently widowed emperor of the country has, instead of remarrying, cultivated a hand at horticulture by growing plants from all over the world. He beams with delight when the captain presents him with the mysterious lotus bud from sea. One night, as the emperor strolls in his flower garden, the lotus bud opens into a marvelous flower and Sim Ch'ŏng emerges from within. She becomes his empress to enjoy his love, wealth, and luxury. She misses her father badly, however, and the emperor, to help his empress find her father, decrees that all the blind men of the country be invited to a royal banquet 100 days long.

Since Ch'ŏng's departure, Blind Man Sim has lived in grief and remorse until a woman by the name of Ppaengdꞓgine appears and marries him. Blind Man Sim is happy again in his newly found love, but on the road to the capital banquet, his wife takes everything and runs off with a younger blind man. After a lengthy journey filled with adventures, Blind Man Sim arrives at the banquet. A commotion erupts as his name is announced. Several officers rush out to escort him to the inner palace, where Empress Ch'ŏng waits anxiously for him. At long last the father and the daughter have a dramatic reunion. In the intensity of his surprise and joy, Blind Man Sim regains his sight. Wonders do not cease: one by one, all the blind people of the country regain their sight, blessed by Empress Ch'ŏng's filial piety, which moved heaven. The story ends with great jubilation.

Song of the Underwater Palace. The Dragon King of the Underwater Palace is bedridden with a grave illness, and all the medicine in the world cannot cure him. One day a Taoist monk appears from the sky and, having told the king that the only cure is a hare's liver, disappears. None among the members of the king's aquatic cabinet has the courage or integrity to venture to the land to find a hare and bring it to the king, but loyal Pyŏlchubu, a turtle, volunteers for the difficult task.

After a lengthy journey through the icy waves, Pyŏlchubu the turtle reaches land. Shivering, he crawls into a valley where all the world's animals are holding an election to determine who among them should be the most respected. Thanking heaven for the occasion, Pyŏlchubu calls out from his hiding place, "Mr. Hare!" Because his chin is frozen hard from navigating through the cold water, however, the words come out as "Mr. Tiger!" He ends up inviting the tiger, and it is only with wit superior to that of his captor that he narrowly escapes his death. Finally, he encounters a hare and allures him to come with him to the Underwater Palace, where he, the turtle, tells the hare he will be made at least the chief of police.

The vainglorious hare follows Pyŏlchubu to the Underwater Palace, only to discover that he has been tricked. Gathering himself together, he tells the Dragon King that, regrettably, he has left his liver in his dwelling in the mountain, and he needs to be taken back so that he can bring his liver to the palace. Thoroughly convinced, the Dragon King orders Pyŏlchubu to fetch him back to the land. Pyŏlchubu is no fool, but he dares not contradict his king.

Safely back on land, the hare insults Pyŏlchubu profusely and colorfully before hopping away. In his flighty celebration, the hare gets caught again, this time in the grip of an eagle. Again, the hare outsmarts his captor and survives. Meanwhile, Pyŏlchubu's loyal heart moves heaven, and he is awarded the heavenly medicine with which to cure his king.

The Three Vital Aspects of *P'ansori* Singing

In the discussion of *p'ansori*'s musical structure, three concepts have surfaced as the most essential elements: rhythmic cycles, melodic paths, and overall vocal expressiveness. These important musical elements are deftly coordinated in accordance with the general principles of yin and yang—that is, the complements of high and low, long and short, clear and murky, tensed and relaxed, and sorrowful and merry. Termed *changdan* (long and short), rhythmic cycles are a set of rhythmic patterns that prescribes the tone, the pace, and the dramatic mood in each song. The following is a table of rhythmic cycles frequently distinguished in *p'ansori* singing.

Rhythmic cycle	Beats per phrase	Dramatic effects
Chinyang	slow six beats, frequently forms four-phrase lyrical line	doleful, peaceful, or magnanimous
Semach'I	a bit faster than *chinyang*	*chinyang* with added resolution and dynamism
Chungmori	medium 12 beats, stress on the ninth beat	peaceful or sorrowful
Chungjungmori	faster 12 beats, stresses on the first, fourth, seventh, and tenth beat	dynamic, comic, or hurried
Chajinmori	medium or faster four beats	dynamic, comic, undulating
Hwimori	fast four beat	sweeping or chasing
Ŏnmori	medium ten beats in two five-beat parts	crosswise or asymmetrical, a mysterious appearance
Tanmori	medium six beats, the first half of *chungmori*	finalizing, adopted in the final summary of a narrative

In *p'ansori* singing the pace and the flow of dramatic mood prescribed by the rhythmic cycles find a channel in the intricately complex melodic paths. The most fundamental are the following three interrelated and often interchangeable concepts: the melodic modes (*cho*), the specific style of singing (*che*), and individual narrative or vocal innovation (*tŏnŭm*).

Of the extant melodic modes, thes most frequently adopted are *ujo* and *kyemyŏnjo*, terms that originally referred to a set of modes in court music. They have helped define the course of folk melodies in vocal and instrumental music alike. The ambiance of *ujo* is described by the singers as grand, magnanimous, and masculine, and that of *kyemyŏnjo* is doleful, nostalgic, and feminine.

Two of the best-known styles of singing are the Eastern School (*Tongp'yŏnche*) and the Western School (*Sŏp'yŏnche*). The division between the schools is demarcated by the Sŏmjin River, which flows through the hills and plains of Chŏlla province. The two schools grew apart from one another in the nineteenth century. Centered in the townships of Unbong, Kurye, Sunch'ang to the east of the river, the Eastern School was established by the singers trained in the style of the nineteenth-century singer Song Hŭngnok. West of the river, Posŏng, Kwangju, and Naju became the center of the Western School by singers following the style of another nineteenth-century singer, Pak Yujŏn. The Eastern School of singing manifests the strength and stately bravery of *ujo*, and the Western school adopts *kyemyŏnjo*, pronounced in the doleful melodic movements that linger at sentence endings.

Throughout the centuries following the birth of *p'ansori*, anonymity has been ascribed to the singers who have contributed their narrative or vocal innovation (*tŏnŭm*) to help build the existing canon. It was formerly customary during performance, however, for singers to cite the name of a specific singer known to have composed the segment. Such practice is rarely observed today. *P'ansori* performance is less an intimate storytelling than a classical musical presentation. Furthermore, the future of *p'ansori* has been invested in the preservation of its antique heritage rather than in its existence as a creative storytelling in the changing social context. Accordingly, its narrative and musical creativity has been waning, making the composition of new *tŏnŭm* an atypical and inauthentic phenomenon.

The culmination of the musical venture lies in the overall realization of the unique *p'ansori* vocal expressiveness, termed *sŏngŭm* (the music of the voice). The *p'ansori* aesthetic, grounded in the principle of yin and yang, requires a voice capable of projecting all ranges of pitch, tone, and movement—high and low, clear and murky, slow and swift, and comic and sad, regardless of the singer's gender. A well-trained *p'ansori* voice is invariably husky, resonant with strength and subtlety simultaneously. Corresponding to both vocal mechanism and vocal aesthetics, the concept of *sŏngŭm* defies simple definition. The concept is further complicated as the term is applied to explaining such metaphysical concepts as *imyŏn* (the picture within), the poetic or dramatic imagery portrayed by the voice. Several categories are used to evaluate the vocal strength of individual singers: inherent vocal or tonal quality, authentic discipline, and tonal and rhythmic variation that reveals the interpretive as well as aesthetic sensibility of the singer. In sum, *sŏngŭm* is the culmination of the singer's vocal skill, dynamism, and artistic sensibility. It refers to all vocal qualities the singer is born with and has cultivated through discipline. So how does one acquire such a voice?

Discipline and Transmission

The discipline in *p'ansori* singing is a lifelong process of *tŭgŭm*, translatable as "the attainment of the voice." Throughout the history of the art, many aspiring practitioners underwent all-too-rigorous—life-threatening, at times—ways of training focused on cultivating an accomplished voice that resonated with energy and pathos. Once the singer was finished with the initial stage of apprenticeship under a master singer, he found a study site away from the distractions of civilization and close to nature. Some singers harmonized their voices with the murmuring of water by the streams; some befriended waterfalls so that they might be heard above the thundering of the falling water; and some entered caves to hear the echoes of their own voices. Their progress was monitored by none but the sights and sounds of nature: the sighing winds, the dripping rain, the falling leaves, and the silent poetry in flowering, wilting, and snowing. The legendary self-regimentation by the singers of the past has generated popular tales about them that border between myth and reality; for example, the point at which the vocal chords began bleeding supposedly signified a turning point in the singer's rites of passage. Today, rare are singers who would go so far as to shun the temptations of modern life for a long time in exchange for the genuine voice. Furthermore, the availability of recording technology and mass communication has accelerated the demise of the traditional ways in which *p'ansori* is transmitted to the next generation. As a modern substitute, however, many of the master singers today hold a summer camp away from the city, usually in a Buddhist temple in the mountains.

Who are the learners of *p'ansori* today? In traditional Korean society *p'ansori* and the other folk performing arts were thought of as being practiced only among the social outcasts—the males referred to as *kwangdae* and females as *kisaeng* (a traditional female court entertainer). The stigma still continues, but to a lesser degree. Today, the students of *p'ansori* are much more diverse. They include students aspiring to major in *p'ansori*, college *p'ansori* clubs, housewives, senior citizens, working professionals, and folklorists. These amateur practitioners will also help shape the performative identity of *p'ansori* in the next century. Since its designation as a national treasure and its prominent singers as human national treasures, *p'ansori* has been canonized as a classical art to be preserved "as is." From the storyteller's point of view, an even more appealing task would be rehabilitating *p'ansori* as a popular art of storytelling that reflects the zeitgeist of a changing era.

Further Reading

Killick, Andrew P., "Putting P'ansori on the Stage: A Re-study in Honor of Marshall R. Pihl," *Korea Journal* 37:1 (Spring 1997)

Kim Hung-gyu, *Understanding Korean Literature*, Armonk, New York: Sharpe, 1997

Kim Kichung, *An Introduction to Classical Korean Literature*, Armonk, New York: Sharpe, 1996

Kim Woo Ok, *P'ansori: An Indigenous Theater of Korea* (Ph.D. diss., New York University), 1980

Park, Chan E., "P'ansori in Trans-National Context: The Global Transmission of Korean Performance Tradition," *Korean Culture* (Summer/Fall 1998)

———, "Playful Reconstruction of Gender in P'ansori," in *Korean Studies* 22, University of Hawaii Press, 1998

———, "Why Recitative, Instead of Just Speaking or Singing, in P'ansori Storytelling?," Selected Proceedings of the 3rd PACKS Conference, University of Sydney

Park, Chan E., et al., *The Ch'anggŭk of Korea*, collection of four *ch'anggŭk* subtitles in English, Seoul, South Korea: National Theatre, 1995

Park-Miller, Chan Eung, *P'ansori Performed: From Strawmat to Proscenium and Back* (Ph.D. diss., University of Hawaii), 1995

"Performance of P'ansori and Ch'angguk in Translation," Proceedings *Translating and Teaching Korean Literature,* for International Korean Literature Association, University of Hawaii Center for Korean Studies, 1992

Pihl, Marshall R., "Korea in the Bardic Tradition: P'ansori as an Oral Art," *Korean Studies Forum* 2 (Spring/Summer 1977)

——, *The Korean Singer of Tales,* Cambridge, Massachusetts: Council on East Asian Studies, Harvard University Press, 1994

——, *The Tale of Sim Ch'ŏng: A Korean Oral Narrative* (Ph.D. diss., Harvard University), 1974

Seo Dae-seok (Sô Taesôk), "Issues in P'ansori Research," in *Seoul Journal of Korean Studies,* volume 1, Seoul, South Korea: Seoul National University, 1988

Skillend, W.E., "The Story of Sim Ch'ong," in *Korean Classical Literature: An Anthology,* edited by Chung Chong-wha, London and New York: Kegan Paul International, 1989

Song Bang-song, *"Kwangdae ka:* A Source Material for the P'ansori Tradition," *Korea Journal* 16:8 (August 1976)

Um, Hae-kyung, *Making P'ansori: Korean Musical Drama* (Ph.D. diss., Queen's University of Belfast, Northern Ireland), 1992

Enduring Scars: Cautionary Tales Among the Senoi Semai, a Peaceable People of West Malaysia

Robert Knox Dentan

Robert Knox Dentan shows uses of two cautionary tale genres by the Senoi Semai of Malaysia. Dentan first discusses the use of organ-snatcher tales to keep children away from strangers then tells of the Semai response to frightening thunderstorms through story and propitiatory action.

> *Luka hilang tinggal parut*
> (Wounds disappear, scars last).
> —Malay proverb

> His Father, who was self-controlled,
> Bade all the children round attend
> To James' miserable end,
> And always keep a-hold of Nurse
> For fear of finding something worse.
> —Hilaire Belloc, "Jim Who Ran Away
> from His Nurse and Was Eaten by a Lion,"
> in *Selected Cautionary Verses*

Dealing with Fear

The pervasive fear of stranger pedophiles in the United States has far less basis in fact than the fear of kidnappers among the Semai of West Malaysia. For at least a century Malay slavers and their agents raided Semai settlements, stealing children and often killing the adults, whose lives seemed valueless to them. Semai react to their history much as people in the United States react to the sensationalist, prurient television programs: by fantasizing horrors.

This history, endlessly revivified, is not all there is to Semai fear, of course. The fear's persistence after slaving died out needs explaining. Rational fear—distrust, suspicion, caution—would affect anyone subjected to the standard government policy for the Semai. Instead of slaying and slaughter the Semai now endure careless dispossession and genocide. For the Semai, trust, faith, or carelessness would be stupid. The stealing of children or their organs is a concrete metaphor for what the state does.

Stories rationalize this fear. Older adults, men more often then women, sit around telling stories and drinking tea or coffee in the evening, when the day is cool and most work is over. Younger adults listen to the stories with some skepticism. "I enjoy listening to old folks tell these stories," said 30-year-old Bah 'Apel. "I get a kick out of comparing one version with another." The people most sensitive to these stories, however, are Semai children, who sometimes hear them as bedtime stories told by elder siblings or other caretaking relatives. Two types of these stories are those about organ snatchers and those about storms.

Organ Nappers (1990): Cautionary Tales for Children, Fearsome Rumors for Adults

In 1990 we took our long-suffering and intelligent daughter Elizabeth (Wa' Lisbet in Semai) to live with us along the Teew Warr in the mountains. The family we lived with treated her much like one of their own children. Cat, her Semai "mom," and 'Ilah, Cat's younger sister, told Lisbet the sort of story they tell children, warning her of the dangers that face children. As a result, the first complete Semai phrases our daughter learned were references to *maay* (people or strangers) who *-koh kuy* (chop off heads), *-klooh mad* (claw out eyes), and *-blah nɔɔs* (slash hearts). These evil people, she learned, lurked around the settlement.

Like Semai children, upon hearing the stories for the first time Lisbet would weep with sorrow for the protagonists and fear for herself. "They should weep, they should be afraid," said Cat. "We tell stories in the evening. My mother's mother used to tell stories that made even grown-ups weep. Like the story of Tailorbird, which lasts all night. We have many many stories."

Indeed, tellers may modify the story to make sure the listener identifies with a particular character. For example, Youngest Son, the standard hero of Semai tales, always became Youngest Daughter when people were telling stories to Lisbet. The stories are stripped down, yet the thin description is sufficient for its end and lets any narrator, not just skilled ones, produce the desired effect of making children fear, and especially of making them fear strangers:

"You tell Wa' Lisbet she shouldn't get on his motorbike with the Malay [whom the Bureau of Indigenous People's Affairs had licensed to market the people's crops]. He'll take her to Tapah, and there... [knowing look]. He always gives her things to eat [finger symbolically slitting throat]. We can't *srngɔ* her [warn her; literally, 'make her fear']. You have to do it."

The tales keep fear alive. For example, one day Cat, 'Ilah, and Bun, their aunt, were chatting about "headchoppers." A couple—a Malay man and a Bengali woman—had come to a settlement at the sixth milestone of the Cameron Highlands Road and threatened the headman, said 'Ilah.

"That's the sort of thing that happens when you live near a city like Tapah," responded Cat, 'Ilah's oldest sister, in her usual soft, jittery staccato. Cat was sitting cross-legged, weaving a mat with precise repetitive movements, never looking up. She had become a compulsive worker after a botched cesarean section by a Malay doctor at the Orang Asli Hospital made it impossible for her to do the heavy work other women do, such as collecting firewood or fruit. "You have headchoppers at the first and sixth milestone, and in Tapah."

'Ilah, with Wa' Lisbet on her lap, agreed and added earnestly, "They don't come up here often, but it's the first thing we think about when we see Pale People [Europeans]. They shoot people. No use going up against them with your bare hands, and no use blowpiping them either. They shoot you anyway. We need to watch Wa' Lisbet so they don't snatch her." At supper a week later Cat relayed a report from her younger brother's wife, who heard it from someone in a settlement a dozen miles downriver. She said, "They say some *mnaleh* [nubile Semai girls] near Kampar [a valley town] are part of a headchopper gang who steal people's eyes and sell them to rich Malays and Chinese. The Bureau [of Indigenous People's Affairs] made a report. Anybody going to Kampar should watch out."

"Especially men," said 'Ilah to me and to Cat's oldest boy, Faisul, a very hip 15-year-old *litaw* [adolescent man, presumed to be lecherous] who paints his face and wears his hair long like Malay rock stars. Normally, one would trust *mnaleh* not to hurt people.

The next morning a group of women setting out to collect firewood ran into the schoolteacher and his family—two adults and two children—coming downstream. The two little groups spent 45 minutes sitting by the roadside eating betel and exchanging misinformation about "eyegougers." There were three eyegougers, said the teacher: a Malay, a Bengali, and a Chinese, like a Baha'i missionary team. They put eyes and hearts in a Styrofoam cooler and shipped them overseas. By the end of the day, people in our settlement were carrying machetes or blowpipes wherever they went.

Cat's husband, Lwey, seemed unperturbed. Puffing on his stubby homemade pipe in his kitchen, he advised his wife's younger brother Panda' to take a blowpipe with him if he went off by himself. "Maybe you should take a machete, too. And a spear. And a club. Do you have a gun? And a machine gun. And a tank."

Panda' and a group of other *litaw* met under Alang's house to plan how to defend the settlement against the "heartslashers," discussing who would hold what position and which weapons they would carry. "Then we'll see who's afraid and who isn't," said Panda', apparently quoting from the epic tale of how the Semai defeated the genocidal Rawas, which Panda''s father could recite. Like many *litaw* schemes, however, this one did not get off the ground.

The next morning at breakfast in the house of Cat and Lwey, people heard someone outside warning a child about eyegougers. On Bun's lap sat her granddaughter, Wa' Mnjuun', about seven years old. Mnjuun', unused to Pale People, clung tightly to her grandmother, who smiled and said to her, "That's right. There are people who gouge out the eyes of our people and sell them to Pale People like Lisbet's father. Maybe he wants a pair for Lisbet."

"That's true. Your grandma herself bought her left eye in Tapah," I said, making Bun smile.

"They tie you up," said Cat seriously, adding a detail I had not heard before, "then they claw your eyes out."

"They particularly like little girls' eyes," added Lwey, glaring directly at Wa' Mnjuun'. By this time the little girl was clinging so tightly to her grandmother that she almost vanished into her.

"Pale People especially," said Bun grimly, indicating me with her chin. "This one buys eyes all the time." Mnjuun' buried her face in her grandmother's plump shoulder, and the old woman gave us a faint smile.

Lwey and Faisul grinned widely. That night, however, out frog hunting by torchlight, Lwey, Faisul, Panda', and one of Panda''s *litaw* younger brothers began talking about headchoppers, each racheting up the others' fears. The shadows along the river teemed with menace and sinister rustlings. There seemed to be someone with a flashlight up on the road that passes through the settlement, but it was too far away to see who it was, or if it was human. Finally it seemed only prudent to come home, although they had caught only half a dozen little frogs.

The fear lasted several weeks and then was replaced by worry that the Bureau was going to relocate the settlement downstream, in another settlement where people were bound to resent being crowded by outsiders. The Bureau denied the rumor. "We are not the Los Angeles Police Department," wrote the director general, who was subsequently removed for corruption. Such forced relocations are common, however.

Conclusion

There is no doubt that the women loved Lisbet. It was obvious in every look and gesture. They said

what other Semai say: that to -srngɔh children protected them from evil by making them stay close to adults who could look after them. That is, after all, what the fuss about "stranger danger" in U.S. schools and homes is about, and it is at least as rational. Semai children, however, have a much wider range of laps and hugs at their disposal than do children in the United States, so they suffer less from adults' obsessive fears. For a child on someone's lap, getting a hug after hearing the stories time and time and again, the stories seem to arouse a certain frisson of horror and titillation, as do U.S. horror movies.

Still, there is a cruelty lurking in both sets of cautionary tales. Lisbet's tears made 'Ilah glance at the other Semai women. They all smiled, probably because the weeping was cute. With obvious enjoyment, the adults would comfort the weeping child as she sought safety on a familiar lap. This reassurance, however, was nonverbal. No one said, "It's just a story."

Thunderstorms (1962): Telling Tales to Shame the Monster God

Black as oil smoke, a thunderhead appears seaward of the settlement, moving toward it, spreading into flat darkness that swallows the sky. Chilly, unsettling breezes snake through the wet, overheated air, not even as definite as breezes but like the cold touch of something inexorable approaching. People gather up their children and throw the hearth coals out the door. They gather together in little clumps under their houses, trying to stay warm by the coals, listening to the assault-rifle clatter of the approaching rain. Here it comes. No stopping it. No place to run and hide. It's really dark and chilly now.

Suddenly the squall hits like a waterfall: hard to stand up in, let alone see one's way. Great shuddering rolls of thunder alternate with tom-tomming monochromatic explosions of brightness that illuminate nothing. In the jungle the lightning rips and crashes, followed by the increasing slow screech and snap of wood fibers splintering and tearing away from each other, as an immense wind-stricken rain forest giant totters, leans—ripping away the lianas and rattans that bind it to the lesser trees around it—and falls, pulling down to destruction the smaller trees entangled with it and crushing everything—little trees, houses, people—in the path of its dying fall.

Huddling under their houses for protection from falling trees, adults -srngɔh the children. A mother puts her child's hands over its eyes or over its ears to block out the thunder and lightning, saying "*Sng'ɔh! Sng'ɔh!*" Grown-ups nag the children to -*ctɔh.* slash their shins and throw the blood into the rain and fog, crying "*Tlaac! Tlaac!*" The verb *-trlaac* refers to the loss of self-control or violation of the natural order that can bring on a thunderstorm. "If we don't *ctɔh,* this whole place will be flat to the ground, covered with mud—and us underneath it," says a woman. "Why don't *you* do it?" asks her child, nine-year-old Wa' Prankuup, refusing. (A person may tear out a bit of his hair and rush into the whirling rain to club it with a pestle, crying "Ow ow ow!") A young man with a spear rushes out from under his house into the storm; he is just a shadow seen through shoots of pounding rain—stabbing, stabbing, stabbing—then he suddenly slumps and returns, dragging his spear behind him. What's he doing? He is afraid. But what's he fighting? Wind.

The Semai visualize Nkuu', the thunder god, as a large black animal, horribly black, sometimes slashed with white or flame red—a Malayan sun-bear, a giant ape or monkey with a huge throat pouch that grows or swells and releases quickly, making a noise: BUU! When he suddenly raises his huge arms, bolt lightning flashes; when he licks his fingers, sheet lightning. He descends to smash trees and houses, to punish and torment humankind.

This great dark monster slashed with ghostly brightness, this vast, violent horror that overwhelms all fragile human intimate love, this evil ferocious destroyer god, is so grotesquely stupid as to be a figure of fun; he knows it and is ashamed. The Semai despise him as well as fear him. They tell stories about his gross stupidity: how, carrying his child to the grave wrapped in a mat, he let the corpse fall and buried just the mat. The corpse can still be seen as a mountain along the Rias River; the Public Works Department is mining it for gravel. The people tell how, when Nkuu' tried to seduce his little brother's wife by disguising his own penis as a phallic toadstool, the little brother burnt the toadstool. Along the Teew Warr in 1991, anti-storm exhortations reminded Nkuu' how Brahman shat up and down his back; no one in the settlement remembered the story; but they knew the enduring shame might make the monster flee.

Conclusion

Nkuu' stories create a dark circus of ferocity, fear, and hunger, simple stupidity and uncontrolled desire. Nkuu' is feral, unsocialized, bereft of self-control. He is considered as being like Malays or the state: fearsome but stupid. Offering blood and pounding one's hair and crying out in pain are to fool him, people say. He paints his face with the blood or enjoys the pain because he thinks the hurt is horrible. His desire to hurt makes him stupid; his stupidity makes him desire to hurt. In these tales, wanting to hurt, he hurts himself.

Both the Nkuu' stories and the organ-snatcher stories make people feel that the world is a dangerous place outside one's own settlement, away from one's own decent fellows. This sort of conjured fear does not need a lot of reinforcement. Most people in the United States—estimates range up to 85 percent—have never experienced a violent crime, but one would never know based on the general fear of violent crime. Unlike people in the United States, the Semai cannot hide from the evils they see gathering around them, but they are no less vigilant in training their children to fear and distrust everyone. They teach them how to use their brains to resist and to fool Nkuu', and they recognize, as many people in the United States do not, that violence is stupid as well as scary.

Further Reading

Dentan, Robert Knox, "Against the Kingdom of the Beast: An Introduction to Semai Theology, Pre-Aryan Religion and the Dynamics of Abjection," in *Tribal Communities in the Malay World: Historical, Cultural and Social Perspectives,* London: Kegan Paul, forthcoming

———, "The Persistence of Received Truth: How the Malaysian Ruling Claws Constructs Orang Asli," in *Indigenous Peoples and the State: Politics, Land, and Ethnicity in the Malayan Peninsula and Borneo,* edited by Robert Winzeler, Monograph 46/Yale University Southeast Asia Studies, New Haven, Connecticut: Yale University Southeast Asia Studies, 1997

———, *The Semai: A Nonviolent People of Malaya,* Fieldwork edition, New York: Holt, Rinehart and Winston, 1979

Dentan, Robert Knox, Kirk Endicott, M. Barry Hooker, and Alberto Gomes, *Malaysia and the "Original People": A Case Study of the Impact of Development on Indigenous Peoples,* Cultural Survival Studies in Ethnicity and Change, Boston: Allyn and Bacon, 1997

Professional Storytelling in West Sumatra

Nigel Phillips

Nigel Phillips describes three Minangkabau narrative forms: sijobang, dendang Pauah, and rabab Pasisia Salatan, including information about singers, story content, and performance.

The Minangkabau

The Indonesian province of West Sumatra, home of the Minangkabau ethnic group, lies halfway down the west coast of Sumatra. It consists of a mountainous interior and a low-lying coastal strip, where the capital, Padang, is situated. The province's population is about 3 million, but, as a result of emigration (*merantau*), many Minangkabau also live in other parts of Indonesia. Like most Indonesians, the Minangkabau are Muslims. Their language, Minangkabau, is closely related to Indonesian, the national language. The Minangkabau still practice traditional forms of verbal art, of which the most important are ceremonial speech-making, the singing of rhymed verses called *pantun*, and the singing of stories.

Early Storytelling

The earliest evidence of storytelling in West Sumatra is provided by the written versions of oral tales, known as *kaba*, that were obtained by Dutch colonial government officials in the nineteenth century. From their editions of these stories we learn that at that time there were many oral tales, which differed in popularity from place to place. Storytellers called *tukang kaba* would be "generously received" when they sang the tales at feasts, and their audiences would respond with sighs or laughter. The tales were made up of lines of eight or nine syllables, interspersed with *pantun*, and the singer would vary the story from one performance to the next.

Some idea of how far storytelling has changed since the nineteenth century may be gained from a brief review of three narrative forms practiced today: *sijobang,* a story found in the interior of West Sumatra, and *dendang Pauah* and *rabab Pasisia Salatan,* two styles of storytelling popular on the coast.

Sijobang

Sijobang is a long story dating back at least to the nineteenth century (there are manuscripts of it from that time) that is performed in the inland district of Lima Puluh Kota. It is about a prince, Anggun Nan Tungga, who sails away to seek his five missing uncles and, at the same time, obtains 120 rare objects that his fiancée, Gondoriah, has requested as a condition of marriage. He succeeds in both his quests, but only by agreeing to marry his uncle's daughter. Gondoriah learns of the marriage and, when he returns, rejects him. She turns into a gibbon and he into a dolphin.

Sijobang is sung to entertain those present at weddings and such festivities as circumcisions and installations of lineage heads. On such occasions the performance takes place in the host's house, but *sijobang* may also be sung less formally to entertain customers in coffee shops.

The singers, called *tukang sijobang,* are peasant farmers. They receive a modest fee that for most of them is a useful supplement to their main livelihood, although for the few singers who are disabled, it may be more important. In the mid-1970s there were at least 18 active *tukang sijobang* in the area. All were men; although there had recently been two female singers, the traveling and late nights were said to conflict with a woman's domestic life.

A novice singer learns the story partly by listening to his teacher, usually a *tukang sijobang*, recite the story and, perhaps more importantly, by hearing performances given by his teacher and other singers. He begins by learning the most popular parts of the tale and adds the rest later, taking—it is said—about three years to learn the entire story. A few *tukang sijobang* accompany themselves by strumming a steel-stringed instrument called a *kucapi*, but most simply tap a box of matches against the floor to mark the rhythm.

The language of *sijobang* contains words and constructions not heard in everyday speech and is considered to have a special, literary character. The words are divided into phrases of about eight to ten syllables. Like many other forms of oral literature, *sijobang* has a wordy style, fixed epithets, formulaic phrases, and stock scenes, which ease both performance and listening. It also contains many parallelisms in which the sense of one line is repeated in different words in the next, a skill in which *tukang sijobang* take pride. Performances of the "same" episode vary from one occasion to the next.

A *sijobang* performance usually begins at about 9:00 in the evening. Before beginning the story proper, the *tukang sijobang* spends at least half an hour singing *pantun*, which are a traditional kind of rhyming verse, usually in quatrains. Some of the *pantun* express respect for the guests, others are humorous, and yet others are about love. After this the singer begins whichever episode of the story has been requested by the host and proceeds, pausing only for coffee and cigarettes every hour or so, to sing until dawn. The preliminary *pantun* receive a louder response from the audience than does the story itself, during which most of those present appear to pay little attention to the singing: they talk, eat, drink, play cards, and come and go. When most of the guests have left or fallen asleep, however, a small group of men remains, listening and making occasional comments until the end. If sung in full, the story is said to take seven nights, but *sijobang* performances usually last only one night.

Some of the more strictly religious Minangkabau disapprove somewhat of *sijobang* and other *kaba* performances because they involve staying up all night and are therefore associated with the world of the *parewa*, a class of unemployed and undisciplined young men. Another criticism is that these entertainments give boys and girls opportunities to meet without supervision. To avoid giving offense, storytellers make sure to begin their performances after the last obligatory prayers of the day and to end them before dawn prayers.

Dendang Pauah

Dendang Pauah (Pauh singing) is the favorite form of storytelling in the area round Pauh on the outskirts of Padang. There are about 12 *dendang Pauah* stories. Unlike *sijobang*, which recounts the adventures—natural and supernatural—of a prince in days of yore, *dendang Pauah* stories are about the changing fortunes and (usually unhappy) personal relationships of ordinary people. Sometimes the stories are located in West Sumatra but often elsewhere in Indonesia and are set in the not-very-remote past, often in the period of Dutch rule before World War II. The *dendang Pauah* date back to at least the 1930s, when the oldest singer still living today began to perform. A typical story is "Kaba Urang Bonjo" (A Tale of People from Bonjol): Rawina, the daughter of a rich family in Bonjol, marries against her parents' wishes. When she is pregnant, her husband leaves her to marry again. Now reduced to poverty, Rawina abandons her baby son to be brought up by an official in the colonial government. The boy, ignorant of his parentage, grows up and becomes a doctor. He is on duty in a hospital in Padang, when Rawina, who knows that he is her son, is brought to the hospital after a road accident. After revealing that she is his real mother, she dies in his arms.

Like *sijobang*, *dendang Pauah* is sung at weddings and similar traditional celebrations but also in connection with features of modern life, such as birth control and indoctrination programs. It is also broadcast on local radio, and a number of the stories have been commercially recorded on cassettes, usually six or seven per story.

Dendang Pauah is performed by a singer (*tukang dendang*) accompanied by a flute player (*tukang saluang*). Sometimes there are two singers who take turns. In 1993 there were 18 active *tukang dendang*, all of whom originated from Pauh. In occupation they range from poorly paid laborers to office workers. All are men, as are the flute players: religious and social attitudes do not favor female participation. An apprentice storyteller learns by listening to performances by his teacher, a practicing *tukang dendang* who is often a member of the same lineage. After about six years, the apprentice will be able to perform an entire story on his own.

Whereas *sijobang* is a continuous stream of blank verse, *dendang Pauah* is a series of *pantun* verses, most being quatrains, although many are six lines long and some even longer. Because the meaning of a *pantun* is concentrated in its second half (the first half merely foreshadows it in rhyme), the language of *pantun* is terse and even elliptical. There is thus no room for the parallelisms, pairs of synonyms, and long terms of address that make the diction of *sijobang* so wordy and so easy to follow. However, although it is a relatively condensed form, *dendang Pauah* is saved from opacity by the fact that *tukang dendang* sing more slowly than *tukang sijobang*, pausing not only between lines but also for several seconds between verses, the gaps being filled by the flute player. *Dendang Pauah* does, however, resemble *sijobang* in containing many stock elements—for example, the lines and half lines composing the first halves of *pantun*—but also recurrent scenes like eating, sleeping, and traveling. Its richness in traditional imagery is said to make the language of *dendang Pauah* particularly attractive to older members of the audience.

A performance starts with several minutes of solo flute playing. The singer then joins in; there follows, as in *sijobang*, about 45 minutes of introductory *pantun*, in which the singer explains the reasons for the performance and makes respectful comments about the host and guests. He then begins the story and continues to sing it, with breaks for rest and refreshment, until just before the time for dawn prayers. There are six tunes, each supposed to correspond to a different stage in the story. One in particular, which is sung without flute accompaniment, is used for very emotional passages and always at the end of the performance. Although few of those present give the performance their full attention, those who do listen are more responsive than a *sijobang* audience, usually shouting comments in the gaps between *pantun*. The main reason they shout is probably that they are egged on by one or more aficionados known as *sipatuang sirah* (red dragonflies), who are afterwards rewarded by the singer with a small sum of money. Another factor may be that during the performance the singer often addresses members of the audience by name.

Rabab Pasisia Salatan

Rabab Pasisia Salatan or *rabab Pasisia* (South Coast viol or coast viol) is a style of storytelling that originates from the coastal area south of Padang, but it is also popular in other parts of West Sumatra. *Rabab* refers to the violin, held upright, on which the singer (*tukang rabab*) accompanies himself. The stories told in this style include old tales in the *sijobang* mold, but many are recently composed stories set in modern times. An example of these from Suryadi is *Zamzami dan Marlaini* (Zamzami and Marlaini), in which the father of the eponymous brother and sister abandons his first wife and takes a second, who then reduces him to penury. Meanwhile, his distraught first wife leaves their two children and travels to a distant town, where she scrapes together a living by selling fruit. The children are adopted by two different kindhearted couples and lose touch with each other. However, they both prosper, Zamzami in the police and Marlaini by marrying a civil servant. Finally, a series of chances reunites parents and children and they are reconciled. Many *rabab Pasisia* stories are about the hardships involved in *merantau*, the custom whereby young Minangkabau men leave their home villages to seek their fortunes.

Like *sijobang* and *dendang Pauah*, *rabab Pasisia* is performed by invited and paid singers at weddings and similar events, but it is also sung by itinerant performers in markets and other public places in return for money from bystanders. The singers (*tukang rabab*), who are all men, originate both from the southern coastal district and from the Padang area. The most successful of them are invited to sing in towns and cities outside West Sumatra. They also perform on the radio and make recordings on cassettes, usually four or five per story.

A typical performance of *rabab Pasisia* begins with a few minutes of violin playing in which the *tukang rabab* is sometimes accompanied on a *rabano* (a shallow one-headed drum). This is followed by the singing of *pantun*, which begin deferentially and then turn to the usual topics of love, melancholy, and humor. This *pantun* singing is so popular that interludes of it are interspersed between the sections of the story, and it takes up a much bigger part of the night's entertainment than happens in *sijobang* and *dendang Pauah*. As in the other two types of entertainment, the story is not usually completed in a single night. The audience, which is predominantly male, pays varying amounts of attention, but as always there is a core of interested listeners who applaud or comment, especially in the breaks in the narrative that occur every few lines.

Like *sijobang*, *rabab Pasisia* stories consist of a series of roughly nine-syllable phrases, and like both the forms of *kaba* already discussed, they contain many stock elements, ranging from half lines to whole scenes. Compared with *sijobang*, however, the diction is less repetitive and there is a higher proportion of action to speech, with the result that the story advances more rapidly. In keeping with their contemporary subject matter, some of the idiom of *rabab Pasisia* stories is also modern and close to conversational style, but much of the diction is still taken from a traditional stock shared by older *kaba*. Some of the *pantun* tunes are taken from music that is currently popular, but most of the *pantun* and the whole *kaba* are sung to traditional melodies.

Continuity and Change

Judging by the brief descriptions above, professional storytelling in West Sumatra has not, in general outline at least, changed very much since the nineteenth century. Stories still have a local popularity, although radio, cassettes, and easier travel have made them more widely known than before. Singers still perform on festive occasions to responsive audiences and are rewarded for their work, and they still use a nine-syllable metrical unit, sing *pantun*, and vary their performances. Within this general continuity, however, some changes have taken place. While *sijobang* and the older *rabab Pasisia* stories are reminiscent of nineteenth-century stories in content and language, *dendang Pauah* is more modern in both respects, although it still uses the traditional *pantun* form. The new *rabab Pasisia* stories, with their up-to-date settings, more fast-moving plots, more colloquial language, and elements of pop music, have taken an even greater step towards modernity while still remaining recognizably traditional in language, meter, and music.

Further Reading

Phillips, Nigel, *Sijobang: Sung Narrative Poetry of West Sumatra*, Cambridge and New York: Cambridge University Press, 1981

——, "Some Ideas Expressed in a Minangkabau Oral Story," *Tenggara* 21/22 (1988)

——, "Two Variant Forms of Minangkabau Kaba," in *Variation, Transformation and Meaning: Studies on Indonesian Literatures in Honour of A. Teeuw*, edited by J.J. Ras and S.O. Robson, Leiden, The Netherlands: KITLV, 1991

Suryadi, ed., *Dendang Pauah: Cerita Orang Lubuk Sikaping*, Jakarta: Yayasan Obor Indonesia, 1993

——, *Dendang Pauah: sastra lisan Minangkabau* (unpublished master's thesis, Andalas University, Padang), 1991

——, ed., *Rebab Pesisir Selatan: Zamzami dan Marlaini*, Jakarta: Yayasan Obor Indonesia, 1993

Wieringa, Edin, "The *Kaba Zamzami jo Marlaini*: Continuity, Adaptation, and Change in Minangkabau Oral Storytelling," *Indonesia and the Malay World* 73 (1997)

Yampolsky, Philip, *Night Music of West Sumatra: Saluang, Rabab Pariaman, Dendang Pauah*, compact disc recorded and compiled by Philip Yampolsky and annotated by Hanefi and Philip Yampolsky, Washington, D.C.: Smithsonian/Folkways Recordings, 1994

The Tradition of Storytelling in Malaysia

Mohammed Taib Osman

The "Great Tradition" and the "Little Tradition"

Oral tradition was once vibrant among the native people of insular Southeast Asia, of which Malaysia, as a national entity as constituted today, formed a part. The Malay Peninsula and the Bornean territories of Sabah and Sarawak, which today form the Federation of Malaysia, were part and parcel of the historical experience and cultural pattern of insular Southeast Asia until the twentieth century. Historically, the island world was characterized by the establishment of harbor principalities at strategic geographical locations on the seacoast. These principalities engaged in interinsular or intercontinental trade and established government and religious or learned centers. Most important for the purposes of this essay, these were the loci of the "Great Tradition" for the population. Throughout history, these city-states (as we call them because they emerged or submerged as kingdoms, sultanates, or even empires, such as the Sriwijaya, Majapahit, and Malacca) had provided cultural leadership. In the hinterland, the populations had less contact with the outside world, but in various degrees they had symbiotic relations with the coastal principalities and formed the "Little Tradition." The written, or book, tradition developed in the centers of the Great Tradition because they were also the religious and learned centers for the propagation of the Hindu and, later, the Islamic religions and cultures. These two religions had a dominant influence on the people and their civilization, the former from the first century A.D. to the twelfth century and the latter from then up to today.

The traditional oral storytelling and related cultural beliefs and practices that are still observed today, although perhaps transformed and reduced in significance in the lives of people, are the legacy of this Little Tradition. However, no clear-cut demarcation exists between the Little Tradition and Great Tradition, and much that is found in one is reflective of or derived from the other. This is especially true of Malay-Indonesian society as it has emerged from traditional society into the twentieth century, during which time literacy was still limited. A favorite pastime among the genteel womenfolk of the feudal elite (*bangsawan* class) and the emerging mercantile families involved listening to the stories (*hikayat*) or rhymed poems (*syair*) recited from manuscripts or lithographed pieces by raconteurs. In Malay literary tradition, the *hikayat* (prose) consists normally of tales of foreign provenance from Hindustani or Tamil repertoire or the treasures of Islamic literature, consisting mainly of religious and moral stories from Arabian sources or romances and heroic tales of Persian origin. These stories must have been translated mainly into Malay, which had been the lingua franca of the island world and the cultural language used in most of the royal courts. When lithography was introduced in the wake of the European colonial foothold in the region, these *hikayat* found allies in propagating their popularity through technology. Even folktales that existed exclusively in the oral tradition were lithographed to be turned into books.

Storytelling in Sabah and Sarawak

However, the Little Tradition continued in different degrees into the twentieth century. As long as the people's way of life in the interior had not been transformed drastically as modernization made its incursion into the countryside, oral storytelling remained a vibrant tradition with the religious rituals and other observances that are still practiced today. Among the indigenous groups of Sabah and Sarawak and despite vigorous Christian evangelistic activities, age-old traditions remained. By the 1950s and at least until the 1960s, the Ibans of Sarawak were still actively holding the "miring" ritual, *gawai* observances, and the ceremonial smoking of skulls hanging from their longhouses, a relic of bygone head-hunting days. The tales of cultural heroes such as Pulang Gana, Senggalang Burung, Seragunting, and Keling and Kumang were still told to children by the fireside in the *ruai* (common veranda) of the longhouses. However, these tales are being preserved more assuredly by publishing them as school readers by the government-sponsored Borneo Literature Bureau. These tales are still told because the exploits of these heroes embody the values dear to the Ibans' way of life: the spirit of corporate life and proximity to the natural world. The Kayan and Kenyah, who dwell in the upper region of Sarawak, have a vibrant epic-telling tradition that is elaborate and specialized. The epic reciter must be skilled, use a special language, and occupy a distinctive position in the community. However, the epic telling is also communal because the audience is expected to participate by reciting the chorus lines (*nyabei*), which are learned in the process of being socialized in the community. Different styles of storytelling are adopted for different categories (e.g., epics and ordinary tales). Storytelling in Sabah is similar in pattern to Sarawak, being fragmented and closely related to its cultural and religious foundations, as the groups developed autochthonous traditions. Among the Dusuns and their subgroups, the tales they recite at rituals normally refer to their beliefs in the spirit world. The creation myths are narratives that validate their beliefs and rituals. Among groups that have embraced Islam (the Bajau, Tausug, Illanun, and Orang Sungai), their tales reveal cultural borrowing from the repertoire of the Great Tradition in insular Southeast Asia. The ubiquitous trickster mouse-deer is found among the Bajau and the Dusun, among the latter with local adaptations. However, in Sabah and Sarawak a definitive Great Tradition is lacking, with the exception of the Brunei sultanate, whose influence on the interior groups is limited. The repertoire of tales and the tradition of storytelling in the two territories show greater autochthonousness than in peninsular Malaysia.

The Malay Sultanates

Among the Malays of the peninsula and the Sabah and Sarawak who had been under the influence of the Brunei sultanate, the oral or folk tradition is truly the Little Tradition compared to the Great Tradition of the Malay sultanates. Although existing as separate political entities, the Malay sultanates, which dotted the coastline of the island archipelago since Islam gained a foothold in the region beginning in the thirteenth century A.D. and overcame the old Hindu kingdoms, belong to a single cultural and religious entity. As such, the folk or oral tradition of the Malays is not much different from that of the Sabah and Sarawak interior peoples. The former contains some features of Malay Islamic civilization of the archipelago, whereas the latter is a whole tradition by itself, although the influence of the Malay Great Tradition is felt to some extent. Although the Great Tradition was centered in the Malay sultanates that were the centers for maritime trade, religious learning and propagation, cultural and literary activities, and political leadership, the Little Tradition of the village folk held on steadfastly to the older stratum of cultural traditions while adjusting to the demands and appeals of Islam and elite traditions.

The Storyteller

Although storytelling can be said to be a distinctive folk tradition, its fortune is bound with the rest of the folk traditions of rural Malay life. The mainstay of this way of life is the *pawang* and *bomoh*, whereas the storyteller, or *penglipur lara* (soother of woes), occupies a lesser position. The *pawang* is a ritual specialist, an expert in life's activities (e.g., gathering honey or agricultural venture), and a diviner; the *bomoh* is an expert curer, be it in the herbal or the spiritual domain. However, the roles of *pawang*, *bomoh*, and storyteller are often found in one individual, especially when the folk life was disappearing in the face of modernization and development in the twentieth century. Such life would have gone unrecorded and would have disappeared for good had the scholar not intervened.

Colonial scholars such as Hugh Clifford, W.E. Maxwell, Walter William Skeat, R.J. Wilkinson, and Richard Winstead, besides their official duties, recorded and studied storytelling among Malays while the art was still vibrant, especially in the nineteenth and early twentieth centuries. Clifford, who still had the opportunity to witness storytelling as a favorite pastime among the Malays, states:

> Bayan the Paraquet (i.e., the raconteur) was what is technically termed a Penglipur Lara— "Soother of Cares"—a class of men which is fast dying in the Peninsula. . . . These people are simply the wandering bards and minstrels, who find their place in an independent Malay state. . . . They learn by rote some oldworld tale, which has been transmitted by word of mouth through countless generations, and they wander from village to village, singing it for pay to the unlettered people, to whom these songs and stories represent the only literature which comes within their experience . . .

The account (especially the last part) might have been exaggerated or colored, as it came from a colonial administrator. As long as a mosque, or *balai,* was present, the villagers would have been familiar with Islamic elements of literature. Maxwell, another colonial officer and one who recorded oral storytelling in the nineteenth century, states:

> To the Malays, the skillful raconteur, who can hold his audience enthralled with the adventures of his hero and heroine, or with elaborate descriptions of the magnificence of the palaces and courts of mythical rajas is the Penglipur Lara . . .

By the 1950s, young Malay scholars who had graduated in Malay studies at the local university had joined the scholarly interest in Malay folk traditions. These scholars discovered that the repertoire (collected by colonial scholars and given permanence through the publication as school readers) was much larger in scope, ubiquitous, and still fresh in the mind of the raconteurs in the village communities, and they gained new insights from their studies. For example, they found that storytelling had manifested itself in different traditions in different communities. In Kelantan, the institutionalized storytelling is found among the

blind storyteller called Awang Selampit or Tok Selampit, who intones his tales to the accompaniment of his *rebab,* a two-stringed elaborately crafted fiddle with an equally ornamented bow. His repertoire consists of long tales of adventures of kings, princes, and spirits. Tok Selampit, as a professional storyteller, is a prominent feature of Kelantan folk culture and vies with other artists, such as *dalang* (the manipulator of the carved leather figures) of the shadow play, *wayang kulit* or *tukang karut* (the lead of the chanting group) of the Dikir Barat ensemble, or the prima donna of Makyong dance drama. In Perlis was Awang Batil, who chanted his romances to a tune while drumming his fingers on a bowl or pot so as to give rhythm to his tale. Sometimes, as practiced in upriver Pahang and Terengganu, the storyteller recites his or her tale unaccompanied by any instrument but, rather, intones with a distinctive tune.

The more skilled are often referred to as Tukang Cerita, a class of storyteller that appears to be more professional in approach. The lady Tukang Cerita, from whom in the 1970s I recorded a number of long romances that lasted a few nights in Hulu Tembeling in the upper reaches of Pahang River, both had a wide repertoire and used distinctive devices in her art. For example, her romances were organized around salient episodes, such as battles, festivals (weddings), and partings between main characters or their meeting or reuniting. Thus, a particular romance can be extended or shortened according to the episodes she chooses to recite. Another device is the embellishment of actions (battles), materials (dresses or armaments), or the feelings and countenances of characters (love, hate, or anger). Usually, such Tukang Cerita would ply their trade at night, as would be true of other cultural and religious activities in the village communities. The nonprofessionals are the Tukang Cerita who tell animal tales, tall tales, and funny anecdotes or popularly known tales strictly for whiling the time away around campfires while on expeditions to gather jungle produce, such as rattan or fish.

Repertoire

The repertoire of the Malay storytellers as unearthed by the colonial scholars in the nineteenth and early twentieth centuries shows a legacy of the civilizations that had been part of Malay life. The distant animistic past has left the mythology of the spirit world, tales of origin, and etiological and animal stories. These found expression in explanatory tales of nature and geographical landmarks and help explain unusual events, such as the unsolved disappearance of villagers and etiological animal tales. Contacts with the civilization of India must have been varied, as testified by the tales reflecting that civilization. The Sanskrit or Tamil literary collections, such as *Kartha Sarit Sagara* or *Panchatanderan,* must have bequeathed the widespread animal and humorous stories recorded by the colonial scholars. These tales are sometimes adapted to local coloring and assume local characteristics. The ubiquitous mouse-deer, or Sang Kancil, around whom is spun the animal trickster motif, is found all over the Malay world. The humorous stories "Pak Belalang," "Pak Kadok," "Pak Pandir," "Lebai Malang," and "Si Luncai" might seem local in character, but the plots are identifiable as coming from the great Indian collections of animal and humorous tales. The epic *Ramayana* has found expression in the Great Tradition of the Malays as the written adapted romance called *Hikayat Seri Rama,* an almost faithful rendering of the original Sanskrit epic. However, this epic has also filtered to the folk or oral tradition (as recorded by the colonial scholar) and is also known as *Hikayat Seri Rama,* but with a distinctive touch of the Malay folk story. Not only are the characters and place names far removed from the original—as "Maharaja Duwana" for "Rawana," "Tuan Puteri Sekumtum Bunga" for "Sita," and "Kacapuri" for the "abode of Duwana"—but the plots and episodes tend to follow the formula of the more indigenous folk romances, such as *Malim Deman* or *Awang Sulong Merah Muda.* Some of these tales can be traced to the migration of the Malays from other parts of the archipelago (e.g., Sumatra or Java). The latter provides a rich repertoire of the *Panji* cycle, popular among the Malay folk for its adventurous and amorous plots.

Absorption of the Islamic Tradition into the Folk Tradition

Although the Islamic tradition was confined mainly to the Great Tradition with its emphasis on correct belief and practices (of which the ruling authority is the arbiter and emanating source, as in the royal centers in the past or in religious departments in the modern state), aspects of that tradition have filtered down into village life and become part of the folk tradition. Activities such as *dikir* (chanting praises for the greatness of Allah and His Prophet) have spawned activities such as *dikir rebana* (the chanting of *dikir* to the accompaniment of one-faced hand drums) and *ratib saman* (chanting of *dikir* with dancelike steps and hand movements, a spin-off from a mystic [*tarekat*] practice). Popular Muslim theology and tales of history and romances have trickled down to the folk tradition—stories of retribution in purgatory for earthly misdeeds and irreligious behavior; tales about the exemplary life of Prophet Muhammad and other prophets in Islam and their performance of miracles (*mu'jizat*); heroic exploits of Muslims in history such as Saiyidina Ali, Prophet Muhammad's son-in-law and companion; and the ethical and just examples shown by Muslim rulers in the past—and are often told orally by the preachers in the countryside. However, as literacy spread, as compulsory education up to middle or secondary school was introduced by the government, and as radio and television and now the computer dominate life in Malaysia, traditional storytelling has became a cultural anachronism. The new media have tried to keep storytelling alive as an educational and communicative device, but it is different from the cultural legacy that has outlived its purpose.

Further Reading

Mohammed Taib Osman, "Myths, Legends and Folk Tales in Malay Culture," in *Bunga Rampai: Aspects of Malay Culture,* Kuala Lumpur, Malaysia: Dewan Bahasa dan Pustaka, 1984

Winstedt, Richard Olof, *A History of Classical Malay Literature,* Singapore: Malayan Branch, Royal Asiatic Society, 1961; New York: Oxford University Press, 1969s

Thet Siang Performance in Isaan*

Wajuppa Tossa

Thet Siang, a contemporary style of religious narration performed by monks, is described by Isaan (northeastern Thailand) scholar Wajuppa Tossa.

Storytelling Tradition in Isaan

For centuries storytelling has been important in all levels of society among the Isaan people of northeast Thailand, who speak a related group of dialects. When a baby is born fellow villagers visit, entertaining themselves by reading stories from palm-leaf manuscripts, reciting or singing verse stories, or narrating tales in prose. Mothers sing lullabies that often tell stories. Grandparents and parents recount folktales to entertain children and to teach them proper conduct and morals. Children tell stories to each other. At social gatherings such as Buddhist merit-making ceremonies, wedding receptions, ordination ceremonies, and wakes, storytelling or story-singing is a major form of entertainment.

The Buddha used many stories known as the *jataka* tales to illustrate his teachings. One of these, called "Thet Mahachaart" or "Bun Phawet," tells the story of the Buddha's incarnation as Prince Vessantara. It is told in almost every Isaan village for one day (24 hours) every year in the fourth lunar month. If a devotee can participate in the entire ceremony from the procession of painted scrolls to the temple through the entire

sermon, it is believed he or she will gain a life in the age of the next Buddha, when everyone will be equally healthy, prosperous, and peaceful.

The Performance of *Thet Siang*

Once performed as a serious reading aloud by a monk or a series of monks, "Bun Phawet" has been transformed within the past 30 years by the addition of new performance styles and melodies. The changes have pleased audiences and kept them listening from beginning to end.

Thet siang (the sermon of voices) is a style of religious narration in which three to six monks assume different dramatic parts. The performance begins with a summary of the story chanted by the leader both in Pali, the Buddhist language, and in the local Isaan language. Each monk chants the role of his character in a different tune.

Although a recent innovation, the sermon helps preserve the Isaan language and literature. The monks who perform *thet siang* are students of an old Isaan language as well as of ancient forms of Pali and Thai, and they memorize old verse stories and compose new ones. *Thet siang* performances are now held in private homes on religious and festive occasions as well as at temples. At least 23 groups of monks perform almost every day in the Isaan region and in central Thailand. Part of the money earned from perfor-

---

*Reprinted with permission from *Smithsonian Institution 1994 Festival of American Folklife*, Washington, D.C.: Smithsonian Institution, 1994, p. 52

142

mances is used for improving the monks' living quarters, building new temple meeting halls, and constructing temple water tanks.

The more popular *thet siang* is, and the more the beauty of the old Isaan language and poetry is heard, the less, it is hoped, will be the feeling of cultural inferiority among the speakers of Isaan dialects, particularly the Lao. And it is also to be hoped that the moral content in performances of *thet siang* will enable us all, including the monks, to rise above human lust and greed.

Further Reading

Tossa, Wajuppa, *Phadaeng Nang Ai: A Translation of a Thai/Isan Folk Epic in Verse*, Lewisburg, Pennsylvania: Bucknell University Press, 1990; London: Associated University Presses, 1990

——, *Pya Khankhaak, the Toad King: A Translation of an Isan Fertility Myth in Verse*, Lewisburg, Pennsylvania: Bucknell University Press, 1996; London: Associated University Presses, 1996

Storytelling: A Means to Maintain a Disappearing Language and Culture in Northeast Thailand

Wajuppa Tossa

Wajuppa Tossa discusses a project to engender pride in local language and culture through storytelling. Her project includes the training of a core of university student tellers, visits to elementary schools in 19 school districts, and pre- and posttests to assess changes in children's attitudes toward local dialects.

Prejudices Against Local Dialects

The program I discuss was executed from our base in the Western Language Department at Mahasarakham University. Mahasarakham is a small province in Isan, the northeast region of Thailand. For some time I have been translating into English northeastern Thai literature that is virtually unknown to most of the population of Thailand. Even in the northeast region itself, only a handful of people know this rich and varied body of literature.

My learning of the richness of Isan literature began only recently and by accident. I went to study at Drew University in New Jersey in 1982 under the premise that I would get a tuition waiver and then be placed in the work-study program. A professor let me stay with his family without charge for the first year. After the first semester, the university was going to take away that grant because I had only one "A" in my record, and that is not acceptable for a doctoral student.

Thus, I needed to find extra funding. I asked an American friend to write up a translation project proposal for a grant for which I would be the translator. We proposed to translate 10 northeast Thai verse tales into English verse in two years. We did not get the grant, but I discovered the wonder and greatness of this northeast Thai literature. Thus, I chose the most unique folk epic, *Phadaeng Nang Ai,* to translate as my dissertation and at the same time sent out grant proposals to several foundations, including the Witter Brynner Foundation for Poetry. I was granted permission to undertake the project with financial support from the Witter Brynner Foundation for Poetry. When I finished the project, it was published by Bucknell University Press. At that time I wanted to continue translating because I knew of many more excellent stories.

By translating these stories into English, I hoped to let my own people see that their minority literature is in the language spoken by major-power countries so that they would value their own literature more. At that time, my purpose was simply to publish and preserve the literature, which is disappearing. Through my work on my second book of translation, *Phya Khankhaak,* I discovered that the language of my mother tongue, Lao, is endangered. This text is an ancient fertility myth of the northeast, and I had trouble

144

understanding the language because I had never been taught Lao in school. The language of instruction in schools at all levels is Central Thai, and the only languages taught in school were official Thai and English.

When I completed the translation, I returned home and talked in Lao to my niece and nephews, who answered me in official Thai. Then, one day I talked to twin babies in Lao because I know that their parents are from the northeast and that their babysitters are from the same area. However, the babysitters told me, "Please don't speak to the babies in Lao, their parents forbid that. Please speak to them in Thai." I began to feel upset. If no one speaks the language, it will die. Thus, I began thinking of ways to save the language from extinction

A Brief History of Thailand with Reference to Its Many Dialects

Thailand is divided into five regions: the central and the east, whose people speak the Bangkok Thai language, with a few other Central Thai dialects; the south, whose people speak Paktai and a few other dialects; the north, whose people speak Khammuang and a few other dialects; and the northeast, whose people speak Lao and a few other Lao and Khmer dialects. Thailand has almost 100 dialects overall. The prototype of most of these dialects is Tai, which was recorded on a language map of Southeast Asia in David Wyatt's *Thailand: A Short History*. By the eighth century A.D., five groups were known.

The Tai languages have gradually been modified and further developed. Depending on logistics, environment, and surroundings, Tai-language groups adopted and borrowed words from several sources, including Pali, Sanskrit, and Mon through Buddhism; Khmer through controlling and being controlled by the Khmer Empire; and Chinese through trade. The Tai-speaking peoples' early history has remained a subject of controversy to historians and linguists. Only during the 1200s and 1300s did the Tai peoples' history become clear. Yet, they were scattered around mainland Southeast Asia as autonomous kingdoms, each of which might have had its own spoken language. By the 1500s, four major Tai-language groups existed: Central Thai in the Siamese Ayuthya kingdom, Khammuang in the northern Lanna kingdom, Lao in Lan Sang kingdom, and Paktai in the lower-peninsular Ayuthya kingdom. At this time, Burma had come to exist through consoli-

dating small kingdoms and states, such as Pagan, Pyu, and Hemsawatti.

The Tai kingdoms during the late 1500s until the late 1700s were intermittently attacked by Burma. The Lanna kingdom fell into Burmese control in 1558 and has never recovered as an independent kingdom. The Lan Sang kingdom enjoyed independence until 1694, when, on the death of King Suriyavongsa, it was split into three smaller kingdoms—Vientiane, Luang Phrabang, and Campassak—because of internal conflicts. The central Tai kingdom of Ayuthya, referred to as the Siamese kingdom, was also intermittently attacked and taken over by Burma, once in 1569 and then in 1767. After the second fall of the Ayuthya kingdom to Burma, King Taksin established the new capital in Thonburi in 1767. During his reign, all three kingdoms of Lan Sang were under the control of the Siamese kingdom, with Chao Phraya Chakri and his brother as commanders.

In 1782, Chao Phraya Chakri took over and established the present Chakri dynasty with the capital city in Bangkok. In his reign, all small kingdoms became one. During this time, people from the other side of the Mekong River were resettled in several parts of what is now Thailand. Many Siamese nobles were installed in several major cities in the northeast for political reasons.

There was no evidence of a language policy in this reign. I assume that people were free to speak their own dialects. No formal education existed. Only males were allowed to learn to read and write through their ordination as Buddhist monks or novices or their becoming the temple boys who served the monks. They learned to read palm-leaf texts and to copy these texts in their own local scripts using a metal stylus and charcoal dust mixed with some kind of plant resin. In the north, boys or monks learned Pali, Sanskrit, Tham, Yuan, and Lanna scripts. In the northeast, boys or monks learned similar scripts, and some modern Thai scholars learned old Lao script, so-called Thai *noi* script. The subjects of these palm-leaf texts included Buddhism, animistic rites, folk and herbal medicine, astrology, political or administrative strategies, history or chronicles, and literature of all kinds.

By the reign of King Rama II (1809–24), the kingdom remained the same, with the exception of a few signs of revolt in the northeast and the south. Trouble arose during the reign of King Rama III (1824–51). In 1827, Cao Anu of Vientiane tried to attack Bangkok but was counterattacked; Vientiane was destroyed in 1828. From this time on, the influence of Bangkok over the northeast increased. The resettlement of people from the other side of the Mekong River was undertaken seriously. New towns were created with the installation of Bangkok officials in these towns. Again, no evidence of a language policy could be found in these towns.

Beginning in 1830, several attacks and counterattacks of the southern Malay cities occurred. These continued until 1841, when the Siamese government decided to let go of the Malay cities.

Trouble in Cambodia between 1833 and 1846 was more serious because of Vietnamese support and intervention. Afterward, three Cambodian princes began to make trouble. One prince was supported by the Vietnamese, and two were supported by the Siamese. After the Vietnamese-supported prince died, one of the Siamese-supported princes ascended the throne. Thus, Cambodia was once again influenced by Siam.

By 1851 and the early twentieth century, the Tai peoples were victims of European colonization. Many of the Siamese territories were severed and fell into the hands of Britain and France. The threat of disunity in the country became evident during the reigns of King Rama IV and King Rama V. King Rama IV developed publishing and printing businesses to help educate the Siamese people. Many notable reforms took place, but the drastic changes (the reforms of 1888–92), including education and language policies, came during the reign of King Rama V.

During this reign, the government passed a law that made the Central Thai language the one and only official language. All other languages spoken by the people in the country were considered foreign. Village schools were opened to replace the temple schools, and both boys and girls could attend school. This reform began to take place in all regions of Siam at the same time. Every school must use "standardized syllabi and textbooks developed by the Ministry of Public Instruction in Bangkok. They introduced rural youth, not only to basic literacy in a standardized script and language [what has come to be called 'Bangkok Thai'] in place of local scripts and dialects, but also to modern Western-style mathematics and science. . . . " The idea that every Siamese, no matter where he or she lived, was a subject of a single king and belonged to one single body politic was reinforced everywhere. Gradually, fewer people could read and write their own regional languages.

The policy of "Bangkok Thai" as the only required language for both official and instructional purposes worked extremely well during this time because of government support. The minister of public instruction stated that "in the areas where two languages were in use," as in the north and northeast, the "local language may be taught, but only education in (central) Thai may be supported by the government" (Wyatt, *Politics of Reform,* p. 333). More Bangkok-trained teachers and educational commissioners were sent to provinces to strengthen the policy.

In 1908, the Ministry of the Interior began to take part in the language policy. It was reported to the king that the affluent population of Phuket sent their children to local Chinese schools, to Penang, or to Singapore for education. This was an economic threat to the government, which thus saw the need to assimilate the Chinese population into Thai society. The government offered financial support to those Chinese schools "on the condition that such schools offer Thai instruction" (p. 338). At this time, the language policy was considered a matter of national security. The king "issued a strong order" to Chaopraya Wichitwong to "consult with the Ministry of Interior, get to work on it, . . . and do not let up until it is done" (p. 338).

The foundation of the language policy established during this reign has undergone very little change through time. Even today, the language policy is enforced by the Ministry of the Interior and the number one decision maker on language policy the Ministry of Defense.

The importance of the Central Thai language was again strengthened by an act in 1914 that enforced standard Thai writing during the reign of King Rama VI (1910–25), during whose reign Siam became Thailand. The policy of Bangkok Thai as a single official language continued to take firm hold on the language policy as time passed. However, in rural areas few people could still read and write local scripts. Ancient palm-leaf manuscripts were still plentiful both at peoples' homes and in the temple until the reign of King Rama VIII (1935–46), three years after Thailand became a country under constitutional monarchy. Throughout Siamese and Thai history, Siam was under absolute monarchy (until 1932).

Use of Dialects Prohibited

During the government of Plaek Phiboon-songkhram (1938–46), the government prohibited the use of any local dialect and ordered abbots to burn old palm-leaf manuscripts. David Wyatt reported this in 1987 from an interview with the abbot of Wat Si Khom Kham in Phayao.

In the 1960s, threats of separatist movements in northeast and southern Thailand occurred. Thus, the question of language was again brought to the government's attention. The enforcement of Central Thai as the only language of instruction was even stronger. The Ministry of Defense began

> to safeguard the country's interests by making sure that its internal and external security will not be threatened by any language issue in certain sensitive areas, for example, where speakers of minority or foreign languages may use a language barrier as an instrument to attain their political aims. Hence, any language policy concerning learning, teaching or studying minority or foreign languages which may threaten peace must be brought to the attention of the Ministry's Security Council, whose consideration of that language policy virtually finalizes the issue. (Noss, ed., pp. 75–76)

Other institutions that deal with language policy and implementation are, in order of significance, the Ministry of the Interior, the Ministry of Education, the Bureau of University Affairs, the National Education Council, and the Royal Institute. The Ministry of the Interior supervises official personnel at the provincial levels. These officials include governors, district officials, and all administrative personnel in every province in Thailand. This ministry makes sure that the policy that is finalized by the Ministry of Defense is implemented at all levels in each province. The Ministry of Education "ensures that a uniform standard of the national language is promulgated throughout the country" (p. 77) through the Teacher Training Department, Educational Techniques Department, Curriculum Development Center, and the government textbook publishers (Khurusapha). The Bureau of University Affairs "approve[s] and academically supervise[s] universities" (p. 78) on language teaching, learning, and research at the undergraduate and graduate levels according to the policy outlined by the Ministry of Defense. The National Education Council "is the overall coordinating agency for education in Thailand" (p. 78). Finally, the Royal Institute is "the place where the purification and standardization of the national language are being looked after" (p. 79).

Besides the national language, the only foreign language that was allowed to be taught in schools was English. Children began learning English in fifth grade. The reasons were twofold: "(1) English would be needed as a tool language by those students going on to higher education; (2) for those students who did not continue their education, English would enhance their employment possibilities no matter when they left school" (p. 9).

In 1976, English was taken out of the elementary school curriculum and became only an elective in secondary schools because, as the government stated, "all Thai citizens should be given the opportunity to learn Thai [Central Thai] and use it proficiently and correctly" (p. 9).

Change in Language Policy

In 1978, Thai language policy was slightly changed. The classification of languages was adjusted. Now four types of languages exist: "(1) national language (Standard Thai); (2) foreign languages; (3) regional languages (in our sense, mainly the three provincial varieties of Thai spoken in the north, northeast, and south); and (4) minority languages. This is the first time that the government recognized any other languages existing in Thailand. In this same year, five principles of educational (and official) language policy were enunciated:

1. *Education:* The psychology of foreign language learning, the acquisition of the mother tongue as a springboard for foreign language learning, motivation, readiness, teacher preparation, et cetera should be considered.
2. *National Security:* The teaching of Thai should be compulsory and begin early.
3. *Racial Integration:* The teaching and learning of Thai as an avenue to national integration should be required at all levels.
4. *Information Dissemination:* English is the most widely used international language for academic and occupational purposes.
5. *International Relations:* Languages of all friendly nations are regarded as having the same status (pp. 10–11).

Noss makes an interesting remark here that although the existence of regional languages is recognized, "provincial Thai varieties and minority languages are not specifically mentioned in the five principles" (p. 11).

Because regional and minority languages are omitted from the national principles altogether, Central Thai has become even more dominating. People of other languages have gradually assimilated Central Thai terms and grammar into their own regional or minority languages. In schools, teachers had been trained to use only official Thai and to teach only in official Thai. These teachers in turn forced children to speak only official Thai in school. Other languages have been considered inferior, and people were discouraged from speaking the language of their heritage. If they do speak the language of their heritage, or if they speak official Thai with a local intonation, they will be punished or ridiculed by the teachers and their classmates. As in schools, official Thai is the language used in government offices.

Mass Media and Language

In the past, when the mass media were not as developed, the attempt to overrule all local or regional languages was not as successful. Children would speak local languages at home and official Thai elsewhere. Children in that generation became bilingual. Now, as the mass media have become more available to the public, children have begun to imitate the language of movie and television stars. Parents begin to speak Central Thai at home with their children, who they hope will do better or become more accepted at school. More children in the younger generation are becoming monolingual—they speak only Central Thai. Once the language is not spoken, literature, rituals, and social mores unique to the region begin to disappear. This loss of the diversity in language and culture is happening in all three regions of Thailand: the north, the south, and the northeast. Only a handful of scholars in each region have begun to recognize the loss of the rich cultural diversity of the country.

A few Buddhist monks both from the north and the northeast quietly began the revival movement. They began to recollect ancient palm-leaf manuscripts and to transcribe them into modern Thai script so that the younger generation could read them. A handful of universities began to disguise these transcribed texts into a curriculum called Thai Studies. Other than that, no effort has been made to teach these ancient texts in the original language, partly because younger professors do not read and write these texts.

The monks' efforts were partially successful. Some of these ancient texts became known to educators. Still, the texts are not popular among most people because a negative attitude about them has been implanted in the younger generation for a long time. When they pick up these texts to read them, they read them in Bangkok Thai intonation. The beauty of the original language is lost, and many of these terms make no sense to these young readers, who no longer speak the language.

The Storytelling Project Is Planned

As a person from northeast Thailand (which recently has been named Isan to distinguish the region from Laos), I discovered this distressing fact only through my translation of Isan literature. Because I have been trained in school to speak and read only Central Thai language texts, I have used many Central Thai words in speaking the Isan language (almost identical to the Lao language spoken in southern Lao PDR), which is spoken in the northeast. I found it difficult to translate the ancient text *Phya Khankhaak, the Toad King* (an ancient fertility myth), as I had to spend a lot of time tackling the meanings of ancient words. After I finished the project, I decided to begin my work to preserve the Isan languages and culture.

First, in 1993, I did a small survey of the knowledge of Isan language and literature among the first-grade children in Mahasarakham municipality. With some colleagues, I conducted a survey at the demonstration school at the Teachers' College, which is a school run by the Mahasarakham Municipal Office and the largest elementary school under the jurisdiction of the Ministry of Education. More than 50 percent of these children do not understand the Isan local language, and less than 20 percent could recognize the titles of works of Isan literature. Most of them cited Western fairy tales, such as "Little Red Riding Hood" and "Cinderella," as Isan folktales. Some even cited modern television drama series as Isan folktales. From the results of this survey, I realize that we are facing a great loss. Within the next 20 years, young adults from northeast Thailand will speak only Central Thai. The beauty of these hundreds of dialects will be lost. Soon, Isan people from urban areas will not be able to communicate with those from the rural areas.

Thus, I began to put together a grant proposal to seek funding for a project that would preserve the languages and cultures of various ethnic languages in Isan. Perhaps, later, I could raise the interest of scholars from other parts of Thailand to do the same.

My plan was to recruit interested university students at my university and train them to collect Isan folktales from different resources: palm-leaf texts, books, chronicles, and interviews with the elders. We would train them to be successful storytellers and then take them to the largest school in each province in northeast Thailand to tell stories to children in the local language spoken in each province. At that time, we would ask the children to go back to their parents and grandparents to learn some stories that they know. After some period of time, we would go out to the same school and hold a storytelling session by children from that school. Small prizes might be given to the storytellers as reinforcement. In the summer, we would hold a storytelling camp for children participating in the storytelling project.

We gained support from the Fulbright Foundation, which sent a folklore scholar and professional storyteller to train the university students in storytelling techniques. The James Thompson Foundation of Thailand gave stipends to our storytellers through the three years of the project. The project began in September 1995 and ended in August 1998. Every summer, we organized a storytelling camp for children along with a workshop for interested scholars on storytelling techniques. After the project is completed, the summer storytelling camp is expected to continue.

We trust that the project will be successful, as storytelling is enjoyable for people of all ages. The organizers and participants of the storytelling project are from the highest and most respected institution in Thailand. Because of their respect and admiration, teachers and children in elementary schools might feel that it is all right to speak the local language and become interested in reviving storytelling in their own dialect and searching for stories that might be lost or forgotten. With the success of the project, the language, literature, and rituals inherent in the use of the language will be maintained. Children will learn to speak, read, and write the mainstream language and literature while maintaining fluency in speaking their local dialects. The ultimate goal of this project is to try to push these local dialects into the educational system so that these dialects are taught in school. Ultimately, children are expected to be bi- or multilingual.

First Phase of the Storytelling Project

The storytelling project began in September 1995. We recruited 20 students (6 graduates and 14 un-

dergraduates) and arranged a time to meet with them about three times a week during September and October 1995. In November, Dr. Margaret Read MacDonald, a Fulbright scholar, arrived to begin the training. Students were trained to be sensitive story collectors and storytellers. We met as a large group and as smaller groups and learned to tell stories in lively styles as a single teller, in tandem telling, and as a story theater. The stories that we learned were Thai folktales from Dr. MacDonald's collection. She told a story in English that I translated into Lao simultaneously as if we were tandem telling the story. Then we asked the students to tell the story in the language with which they felt most comfortable, in most cases Lao.

One assignment for the students was to find folktales from folktale collections and from interviewing storytellers from their communities. Then they were to share their stories in class. I would translate the stories as they were being told for Dr. MacDonald, who would choose appropriate stories and then shape them to make them performable. Then she retold each story in English, and I translated it in tandem format. The students then practiced telling the story in their own language. Dr. MacDonald also searched for Isan folktales from folktale collections at the university library. One graduate student helped her translate the stories and would teach each story to the class after she had worked on it.

We learned to tell stories with few or no props. We used our three instruments: voice, facial expressions, and body movements. After two months of training, we took the students to tell stories in nearby schools.

Our storytelling was by no means traditional, but most of our stories were. We made the telling lively and the audience participatory. This kind of storytelling was new, so we could hold the children's attention and interest. Before we began targeting schools where we would tell stories, we held a storytelling conference in which our students had another chance to tell stories to adults. We had participants from all regions of the country and from Laos. It was so successful that we still maintain ties with these seminar participants. We have made this storytelling an annual event.

A Survey of Children's Attitudes and an Encouragement to Tell

After the summer and in the first semester of 1996, we prepared survey questions to find out the children's experience with local dialects and folk literature. In November 1996, we traveled to 22 provincial city schools. At each school we had the teachers give survey forms to the first-grade children (4,933 in all), told stories to these first-grade children and to the whole school assembly, and gave a storytelling workshop to teachers after classes were over.

We believe that if a dying language and culture are to be maintained and revitalized, everyone must take part. Thus, we tried to get both parents and teachers involved, not only the children. At the performance, we told three or four short folktales in tandem and one in story-theater format. Then we encouraged the children to collect stories from home to share with us next time. We also encouraged teachers to help us follow up by asking the children every one or two weeks which stories they had learned from home. If the children wanted to tell stories, the teachers would help them rehearse. In this way, everyone would be involved in preserving Isan folk literature that might otherwise be forgotten. The children might feel that these stories were important. If they liked the stories and the way that we told the stories in dialects, they might have better attitudes toward local dialects and literature.

Although we tried to involve everyone in the process of preserving local languages and culture, our focus was on the children. Thus, in our second visit we asked students to volunteer to tell their stories to us. We left for about a year before we returned to the schools to do the same activities and to listen to representative children tell their stories to us. We hoped that the children would choose to tell the stories that they learned from home and to do so in local dialects. We were delighted to find 129 young storytellers among the 4,933. Among these children, 81.6 percent told folktales that they learned from home, and 75.96 percent told stories in local dialects. The stories that the children told were unique, such as the "Golden Conch Shell," which is similar to the "Golden Turtle Prince." Some stories were so tellable that we adapted them from the children's tellings and added them to our troupe's repertoire. These included "When Xiangmiang Is Outwitted," "Three Animals" (similar to "Three Friends" by Phra Inta), and "The Miser Bird" ("Nok Khee Thi"). These stories are now being shared all over Isan, thanks to these children who learned the stories from their communities.

We set up our hypotheses, namely, that after we told them fun stories in local dialects and after we encouraged them to collect stories from their communities, the number of children who knew local dialects and literature would increase and that their attitudes toward local dialects and literature would improve as well.

Analyzing the Data

After the two visits, we gathered and analyzed the data and compared the results of the two surveys. Some of our hypotheses were proved correct and others incorrect. In terms of dialects, the results were not what we had expected. Even after we had demonstrated to the children how much fun it was to tell stories in local dialects, the number of children who knew dialects did not increase but dropped quite drastically. Before we told stories to the children, 71.85 percent knew Lao, a major dialect spoken in Isan. In the second survey, the number of children dropped to 67.27 percent.

It was puzzling that the number should drop so drastically. Looking back at the surveys, we found five factors that might have caused the decrease. First, the test might have been too difficult for the children, who had been studying for only three months. They might not have understood what "know Isan dialects" meant in the survey. They might have thought that knowing three to five words in first grade could justify "know Isan dialects." Then, when they were in second grade and their reading skills should have been better, "know Isan dialects" for them might be more clear in terms of what it meant to be able to speak and tell stories in Isan dialects instead of in Thai with a mix of three or four words in Isan dialects. This tells us that, in the future, we might need to explain definitions of key concepts to both the teachers and the children before they take the test.

Second, as the children had just begun studying, many of them might not have been able to even read. In the first few schools in which we did the survey, we gave the questions to the children to read and to mark the answer sheets. When we examined the answers, we found that they did not answer some questions and, thus, that we would need to use fewer questions than we had expected. Later, we asked the teachers to read the questions to the children and had the children only mark the answer sheets. We were able to obtain complete answer sheets as we had expected.

Third, we were resigned to the fact that we could not expect the children to learn local dialects that they had no occasion or chance to use in one year after listening to our storytelling performance only once. Other influences were stronger and more regular. In school, children were not allowed to speak local dialects. At home, they spoke Thai; as evidenced in our survey, 54.53 percent of the children's families spoke Thai rather than the local dialects.

Fourth, Thai children spend a lot of time watching television. Thai was the only language used, let alone the fact that they wanted to imitate their idol stars and singers, who always speak Thai regardless of where they come from.

Fifth, our own storytelling team might have had limitations. We were not able to speak all the dialects mentioned in the survey. We could tell stories only in Lao, Khmer, Khorat, Yo, and Phutai.

Although the number of children who knew local dialects decreased, we were quite pleased with their attitudes toward local dialects. In the first survey, 76.5 percent of the children were proud to speak local dialects, and in the second survey the number rose to 86.18 percent, 81.69 percent of whom could not speak the local dialects but wished that they could in the first survey and 81.35 percent of whom wished that they could in the second survey; 75.66 percent of the children agreed that Thai people should be able to speak a dialect as well as Standard and official Thai, and this number rose to 83.13 percent in the second survey. In the first survey, 53.61 percent of the children felt embarrassed speaking any local dialect, but after they had more storytelling experience the number decreased to 51.50 percent. In the first survey, 38.41 percent of the children thought that Thai people should speak only one language (Standard and official Thai). However, in the second visit their attitudes improved, and the number of students with negative attitudes dropped to 23.40 percent.

After examining the data related to dialects, we studied those related to local literature or folktales. We were quite delighted that 45.76 percent of the children knew the 12 items listed in our first survey. After listening to our stories and being encouraged to learn more stories from home, the number of children that knew the 12 items listed rose to 54.24 percent.

Findings of the children's attitudes toward local folktales, like that of the dialects, are most satisfactory. They prove our hypotheses accurate. For the first survey, 74.91 percent of the children agreed that everyone should know at least one local folktale, and the number rose significantly in the second survey, to 84.13 percent. In the first survey, 85.36 percent of the children liked to ask their parents, grandparents, and elders to tell them stories. After our project's storytelling team told the children stories, 95.07 percent of the children agreed with this statement. Before our visit, 90.77 percent of the children felt that stories could teach moral lessons; after our visit, 97.53 percent agreed with this statement.

For those who did not have good opinions of local folktales and storytelling, their attitudes improved after being exposed to our storytelling experience. In the first survey, 31.74 percent of the children felt that local folktales and storytelling are old-fashioned. However, after hearing our stories, the number dropped to 21.63 percent. Before our visit, 29.59 percent of the children thought that local folktales and storytelling were of no value, but after we exposed them to local folktales and storytelling, the number dropped to 21.58 percent.

Unlike the language, folktales have always been in the children's lives. From our survey, 71.70 percent of the children still have storytelling at home with their parents, grandparents, aunts, uncles, brothers, and sisters. No one has ever forbidden them from listening to or telling stories. Thus, it is quite appropriate that their knowledge and attitudes toward the folktales should improve.

However, if we do not encourage storytelling among adults and children, the art might disappear, as the age of mass media and technological information advances. We have tried to organize more storytelling events in and out of educational settings so that people will be constantly excited about storytelling. Three events have become annual affairs at Mahasarakham University.

Each February we organize a nationwide storytelling workshop and conference for teachers, educators, and interested individuals. For each of three years, we have attracted more than 50 participants. We hope that these participants will carry on the work of preserving local dialects and literature. We keep in touch with these participants and receive encouraging reports from most of them on how they spread our ideas of preserving local dialects and literature.

Each year we organize summer storytelling camps for both parents and children in April. For each of two years, at least 50 pairs of parents and children have attended the camps.

Another activity that Dr. MacDonald helped introduce and set up for us has become another annual event. "Tellabration," a celebration of storytelling around the world, is held around the third week of November. We offer a short workshop, a storytelling demonstration by the members of the university storytelling association and internationally known storytellers, and a storytelling contest. The two contests we have held included at least 20 young storytellers who were most enthusiastic to help us carry on the storytelling tradition and to collect and preserve these stories through adapting them for lively performances. These young people have become our "junior staff." They were active camp leaders for the 1998 summer storytelling camp and are eager to continue helping us with storytelling events. We plan to continue "Tellabration."

With the mostly favorable statistical results of the project and with the fruitful and soul-satisfying storytelling activities that have sprung from the mother project, I think we are on the right track in using storytelling as a way to revitalize the use of local dialects among the people. The results might not always be clear in the short term, but if we are consistent and determined, we can reach our goal of making people see the significance of both local dialects and literature. Ultimately, we might be able to push both storytelling and local dialects into formal and respected courses in schools at all levels.

Further Reading

Gonzalez, Andrew B., *An Overview of Language Issues in South-East Asia, 1950–1980,* New York and Singapore: Oxford University Press, 1984

Tossa, Wajuppa, *Phadaeng Nang Ai: A Translation of a Thai-Isan Folk Epic in Verse,* Lewisburg, Pennsylvania: Bucknell University Press, 1990; London: Associated University Presses, 1990

——, translator, *"Phya Khankhaak, the Toad King": A Translation of an Isan Fertility Myth in Verse,* transcribed by Phra 'Ariyanuwat, Lewisburg, Pennsylvania: Bucknell University Press, 1996; London: Associated University Presses, 1996

Tossa, Wajuppa, and Margaret Read MacDonald, *Nithan Phunban Kap Kanlaonithan: Folktales and Storytelling,* Mahasarakham, Thailand: Storytelling Project, Mahasarakham University, 1996

Vathanaprida, Supaporn, *Thai Tales: Folktales of Thailand,* edited by Margaret Read MacDonald, Englewood, Colorado: Libraries Unlimited, 1994

Wyatt, David K., *The Politics of Reform in Thailand: Education in the Reign of King Chulalongkorn,* New Haven, Connecticut: Yale University Press, 1969

——, *Thailand: A Short History,* New Haven, Connecticut: Yale University Press, 1984; London: Yale University Press, 1986

Australia and the Pacific

Nallawilli-Sit Down (and Listen): The Dreamtime Stories—An Oral Tradition*

Pauline E. Campbell-McLeod

Pauline Campbell-McLeod discusses the great antiquity of the Aborigine Dreamtime story tradition and its continuance through the present into the future. She shares two stories with the permission of her elders and points out the many lessons contained in such stories.

The Aboriginal Peoples, Custodians of the Australian Landmass

Within the indigenous cultures of Australia, now known as Aboriginal Australia, the oral tradition is a very intricate part of the history, culture, and customs of the people. This group of people is widely recognized as the oldest continual culture on earth, dating back to the beginning of time.

In the presentation of the oral tradition in Aboriginal Australia art, dance, music, and storytelling in their diverse forms are used. Sadly, over the last 200 years, the oral art forms have been looked at separately, rather than as part of a whole cultural entity, by the Australians who immigrated from elsewhere and have tried to form an understanding of my people's culture. This has resulted in a fragmented overview of Aboriginal Australia.

In the early 1900s a scientist trying to describe a religion within Aboriginal Australia coined the words "the Dreamtime," and since then that phrase has come to mean the all-encompassing mystical period of Aboriginal beginning. All to do with that mystical period—the art, stories, the songs, and the dances—became well known as part of the Dreamtime, but it is still little understood and very hard to explain.

If one goes beyond the emotions of the exotic, mystical, and primitive descriptions of Aboriginal people and looks at a few fundamentals, a better understanding of the culture and the Dreamtime can be gained.

Since time began, the Aborigines have been in Australia. It is a popular belief that the Aborigines migrated to Australia some 40,000 years ago, but that theory is now being disproved by recent archaeological discoveries. We are the custodians of the landmass known as Australia. The original people lived a seminomadic way of life based on oral tradition, existing as hunters and gatherers who traded or bartered their excess produce.

Symbolic languages were used throughout Aboriginal Australia, but a written language was never developed or used. No man-made monoliths, cities, or towns were formed. We lived by the lore of the various creator spirits and ancestral spirits of the diverse landscapes, the sky and the creatures and plants of Australia. The people worshiped no deity or gods nor possessed an organized religion such as there exists throughout the world today.

---

*Stories are retold with permission.

The Dreamtime Stories

The Dreamtime is part of the oral tradition and is only one aspect of the very complex spiritual belief system of Aboriginal culture. An important point to note is that the Dreamtime, in the Aboriginal culture, is known as the Dreaming (which in itself becomes more profound and significant to the culture when one is learning it).

The Dreamtime stories are the verbal form of the Dreaming; the art is the visual form; the customs are the practical form; the music is the acoustic form; the totems are one spiritual form; the lore is the cultural form; the land is the physical form. To take one away would fragment the whole and make it difficult, if not impossible, to comprehend.

The stories of the Dreaming are more than myths, legends, fables, parables, or quaint stories. They are definitely not fairy tales for the amusement of children but are more the oral textbooks of the people's accumulated knowledge and wisdom from when time began.

The structure and form of a traditional Dreaming story is unique and cannot be copied easily. An oral Dreaming story of 10 minutes' length can cover several topics and subjects and be suitable for all age groups at one time. For instance, 20 to 40 lessons can be found in one story, teaching such topics and subject matters as the spiritual belief system, customs, animal behavior and psychology, a land map of the region, hunting and gathering skills, cultural norms, moral behavior, survival skills, and food resources. They are structured for the understanding of all age groups, from preschoolers through generational barriers to elders; all in one story.

Because there are approximately 700 Aboriginal nations (language groups), there are 700 ways, for instance, of How the Kangaroo Got Her Pouch (which vary according to the land region and the creature's habitat). Every genre of storytelling and hundreds of categories are used within the Dreaming stories of Aboriginal Australia: stories such as horror stories, babies' stories, adults' stories, children's stories, women's stories (both public and secret), men's stories (both public and secret), love stories, comedy and tragedy, parables, spiritual (public and secret) and sacred stories, and mystical stories.

The Dreaming stories do not have dates. What was important for the story to become part of the oral tradition was not time but the event that occurred and that affected the people, the land, and the culture.

The lessons within a Dreaming story are not taught, but they are learned as a person grows to maturity. People hear a story over and over throughout their lives, and slowly, as they learn the story along with all the lessons that come with it, it becomes part of their memories and way of life. When the time comes for them to pass the stories on to the next generation, it can be done correctly, keeping the stories in their entirety without distortion, thus keeping the oral tradition alive.

The traditional oral storyteller, in the retelling of a Dreaming story, can use virtually every form of theater known to pass on the culture to the next generation. Solo performers or troupes can use music or song or simply tell a story without any aids. In addition, the story may be told in the form of plays, pantomimes, dances, or visual art. Facial expressions, hand movements, vocal variety, mime—both vocal and physical—were, and still are, very important in the presentation of a Dreaming story.

Looking at the Dreaming stories as part of the cultural education system within Aboriginal Australia, the oral tradition seems to be far more accurate than any written form of history. There is no cutting or editing in the oral system, owing to the strict requirements of traditional storytelling, cultural lore, and custodianship and the individual's personal knowledge. That is why in Aboriginal culture the oral tradition is considered far more accurate and important than any form of written history.

According to my research, traditional Dreaming stories have creatures now extinct, including the kangaroo that existed some 15,000 years ago during the megafauna period of world history and the devil dingo of at least 5,000 years ago. Stories account for the invention of weapons (the boomerang, at least 15,000 to 25,000 years ago). Giant lizard stories relate to the age of the dinosaurs, and the story of the birth of the platypus tells of a time at least 1,000,000 years ago. A Dreaming story tells of how death came into the world (date unknown), and another, of the birth of the sun (date also unknown).

The Dreamtime did not stop with the European invasion in 1788, but new Dreaming stories came into being—stories of islands pushed along by clouds (sailing ships of the 1700s), of invasion by strange men, ghosts, or evil spirits from across the seas (1788–1950s), and of four-footed, hoofed, monstrous creatures with two heads that stink like bunyips and defile nature (men on horses) of 200-30 years ago.

There are tales of sights that could only be described by the sounds they made, as there is no word in any of our languages that could describe such creature—for example, the Chuggasshhhh-chuggashhhh (paddleboats, used on the Murray River) from 160 to 50 years ago. The stories of flying ships (airplanes, from the 1940s) amazed and terrified those people of the interior who had never seen them.

There are horror stories of deaths in custody (1880–1990s) and sad stories of removed or stolen children (1800–1976), which is the most recent Dreaming story (better known to my people as the Screamtime/Nightmare period of our history).

The Dreamtime is the period of creation, change, and learning. It is the period during which the very essence of nature—human nature—came to an understanding. This understanding was made up of that which is required to be able to live in peace and harmony with all around you and to understand differences and changes. The lessons of this period of enlightenment are encapsulated within the Dreaming and passed on to the next generation in the oral traditions.

The Little Black Snake:
A Giant Lizard Story

Here is a story with more than 40 different lessons for all age groups. This story comes from the days of the megafauna, when giant lizards roamed the land region of the flat plains (Riverina) of New South Wales, southwest Queensland, and the southeast part of South Australia. In this latter region there are no black snakes but brown ones, so the variation there is the Little Brown Snake. The nations of this region are Wiradjuri, Nari Nari, Wadi Wadi, Yorta Yorta, Madi Madi, Kurinji, Barindji, Danggali, Meru, Wandjiwalgu, Barltindji, Wergaia, and Wongaibon. A variation of the story is told in a language unique to each nation and locality.

The Little Black Snake: A Plains Story of New South Wales. When the world was young, in the long ago, the little black snake was a harmless creature that never ever hurt anyone. He lived in the time of the giant wombats, giant kangaroos, giant emus, and the most vicious and poisonous of all, the giant lizards. These giant goannas were six meters [19 feet] long—they were big and poisonous, and they loved eating people.

But they didn't eat just any kind of person— never the small folks first, but the big folks. The bigger they were, the better—and they could eat something like 30 people a day. Then they would start on the little snacks for in between.

It got so bad that people could not go into the bush by themselves, because if they did, they would rarely come home because of the giant goannas. Everyone had to go into the bush in groups.

It got so bad that the animals became worried. They held the biggest meeting ever. The big red kangaroo, the spokes-animal for all the creatures in Australia, stood up in front of everyone and said, "We have to do something about these giant goannas. The way they are eating our people, soon they'll be all gone—then what will they eat?"

Just then someone called out. "Us! They will eat us next!"

"That's right," said the kangaroo, "that's right. They will eat us next. What can we do about it? Has anyone got any ideas how we can get rid of giant goannas? Maybe we can make them harmless."

Suddenly the little black snake piped up and said, "Me! Me! Me! I will do battle against the giant goanna!"

And when everyone turned around to see who had spoken, and they saw the little black snake, they all laughed at him. "What can you do?" they asked. "You're small, you've got no arms or legs, and you crawl on your belly. Go away and leave it to us bigger animals. We'll know what to do with giant goannas."

Well . . . that was the cruelest thing anyone could have done. That little black snake got so embarrassed, he bolted into the bush crying, saying things like, "It's not fair. Just because I am small, it doesn't mean I don't know what I am talking about."

As he was crying the little black snake came across the giant goannas' camp by accident. But he was not scared; he went right into the middle of that camp and stood up to the giant goannas, saying, "Good day! Can I stay here for the night, please?"

"And who are you?" asked the giant goannas.

"Oh! I am a little black snake and I am harmless; I don't hurt anyone and I don't taste any good either!"

"And where are you going?" asked the giant goannas.

"I am just looking for a place where I will be left alone," answered the little black snake.

"Yeh! We are all looking for that!" said the giant goannas. "Okay, you can stay here the night. Just don't get in our way!"

And with that they all turned around and went to sleep.

Later that night, when the moon was high and there was no sound in the bush whatsoever, one of the giant goannas got up and went for a walk. The little black snake followed close behind and saw the giant goanna come across a lone traveler. That man was told not to go into the bush alone, but there is always someone who doesn't listen. Now the giant goanna had found his midnight snack.

He pounced on the man, threw him over his back, and took him back to his camp, where the little black snake was pretending to be asleep.

The giant goanna didn't care. He kicked the snake out of his way, threw down his victim, and pulled out a poison satchel.

One drop of this poison and man or animal would be paralyzed from the head down; nobody would be able to move. Meanwhile, the giant goanna decided what he would eat first.

The nose? No. The toes? No. The arms? Yes. The arms? No. No, the legs? Yes. The legs first.

And while the giant goanna decided what he would eat first, he put down the poison satchel.

As soon as he done that, the little black snake opened his mouth as wide as he could. He uncoiled himself and darted for the poison satchel, grabbed it in his mouth, and bolted into the bush.

It happened so quickly that the giant goanna didn't know what to do. He went after the little black snake but he was too slow, so he returned to his last meal.

Meanwhile, that little black snake traveled as fast as his belly would let him, and soon he came across the camp of all the animals. They were still having their meeting.

Well, the little black snake, he went right to the center of that meeting and cried out, "Hey everybody, have a look at what I've got!"

Well, everyone turned around to see who was making such a commotion. When they looked, they saw the little black snake, and in his mouth was the poison satchel from the giant goannas.

The animals gathered around the little black snake and said, "How did you do that? Weren't you scared?" "Tell us all about it!" "Was he big, did he chase you and almost get your tail?"

Well, the questions went on for ages, then the kangaroo became impatient and said, "Okay. Okay, we know that you are a brave and clever little black snake. Now, I tell you what to do, you spit out that poison satchel and toss it into the river, so it will flow out of this land forever."

The kangaroo waited, but nothing happened.

"Go on!" she said to the little black snake. "Throw it into the river."

But the little black snake had other thoughts and said, "Don't you come near me! I am the one who got the poison satchel from the giant goanna. If any of you come near me, I will bite you!" And with that the little black snake bolted into the bush.

Well . . . everyone just sat there and said, "Did you see that?" "Did you hear that?" "What a crazy little black snake!" "One bite from him and you will be gone forever!" "I wouldn't disturb him for all the wombats in Australia."

And it's true. From that day to this, no one, no man or animal, disturbs the little black snake, because he still has the poison satchel from the giant goannas in his mouth.

And what happened to those giant goannas?

Well . . . after the fight with the little black snake, the giant goannas became smaller and weaker, generation after generation.

And that is how the little black snake became poisonous.

As mentioned earlier, the storyteller does not tell what the lessons within the story are but rather draws the listeners' attention to the facts, letting them search for the truths hidden within the story.

The Little Flying Fox: A New South Wales North Coast Story

In this story of the little flying fox there are 16 to 20 lessons. Once again, it is not the storyteller's responsibility to tell you what they are but the listener's task to find the lessons hidden within the story.

The Little Flying Fox. Have you ever seen a flying fox? Well . . . he has a body of a bat and the head of a fox, he only eats the fruit of a tree, and when he is on the ground he screeches and hollers and gets underfoot and trips people all the time.

Away back in the Dreamtime the little flying fox thought he was a bird and not a bat. It was during the time when the Great Spirit came down to earth to teach all the birds how to be birds: things like how to fly, how to sing, how to make nests and lay eggs and do all those bird-y things.

When the little flying fox went over to the Great Spirit, getting underfoot, tripping him, and screaming out, "Teach me! Teach me! Teach me how to be a bird!," the Great Spirit said, "Hey, flying fox, you are not a bird. You are a bat. Wait over there, and when I am finished with all the birds, I will teach you how to be a bat."

But the little flying fox wouldn't listen; he kept getting under the feet of the Great Spirit, tripping him, screaming out, "Teach me! Teach me! Teach me how to be a bird! I've got wings—I can fly, teach me how to be a bird, right now!"

Well . . . the Great Spirit looked at the little flying fox and said, "Flying fox, you are not a bird but a bat. You wait over there, and when I am finished with all the birds, I will teach you everything you need to know about how to be a bat."

But the little flying fox just would not listen; he kept on getting under the feet of the Great Spirit, tripping him, screaming out, "You teach me! Teach me how to be a bird. I've got wings! I can fly! You teach me how to be a bird right now, or I'll hold my breath until I turn blue!"

And he held his breath, slowly turning blue.

"Flying fox!" cried the Great Spirit, "That is no way to behave. Now I must teach you a lesson."

The Great Spirit went over to the little flying fox and picked him up by his feet, then went to the nearest branch of a tree and hung the little flying fox upside down in the branch of the tree. Not the right way round, like all the birds . . . but upside down! And the Great Spirit left him there and went back to all the birds to teach them everything they needed to know about how to be birds.

Meanwhile, the little flying fox was so embarrassed about being hung upside down that he held his hands together, clicking his thumbs, saying to anyone who would listen, "I don't care, I could hang upside down all the time, if I wanted to!"

When the Great Spirit was finished with all the birds; he went over to where the little flying fox was hanging in the tree and asked, "Flying fox, have you learned your lesson? Do you know that you are not a bird, but a bat?"

Well . . . the little flying fox was so cheeky, he said, "I don't care. I can hang upside down all the time if I want to. I still think I am a bird, you know!"

When the Great Spirit heard that, he said, "Okay, flying fox, if that's the way you are going to be, than that's the way you will be. From now on and forever, you will hang upside down in the branches of trees, firstly, to remind you that you are a bat and not a bird, and secondly, to keep you from getting underfoot."

And from that day to this, all flying foxes hang upside down in the branches of trees, because of that cheeky little fellow, way back in the Dreaming. . . .

Ka Ola Hou 'Ana o ka 'Ōlelo Hawai'i i ka Ha'i 'Ana o ka Mo'olelo i Kēia Au Hou: The Revival of the Hawaiian Language in Contemporary Storytelling

Ku'ualoha Meyer-Ho'omanawanui

Ku'ualoha Meyer-Ho'omanawanui discusses aspects of the Hawaiian language and notes the recent revival of language and story through dramatic productions, hula, language festivals, and storytelling events.

I ka 'ōlelo no ke ola, i ka 'ōlelo no ka make.
In the language is life, in the language is death.
—Traditional Hawaiian proverb

Aloha mai, aloha kākou. I greet you in the manner of my ancestors and as a genealogical descendant of Kaua'i island, O'ahu island, and Hawai'i island; as a *wahine kanaka maoli*, a native Hawaiian woman and scholar; and as a *haku 'ōlelo Hawai'i a mea ha'i ōlelo Hawai'i*, a Hawaiian storyteller and Hawaiian-language speaker.

People unfamiliar with Hawai'i are often surprised to learn that a native population of people, *kanaka maoli* (native Hawaiians), exists here, complete with our own language, culture, and social system, who have survived (by and large) over 200 years of colonization and oppression (primarily by the United States). They are even more surprised to learn that native Hawaiians have continued to struggle, resist, and fight for the retention and/or revival of all aspects of our indigenous culture, including (but not limited to) self-identity; political sovereignty and self-determination; land, water, and access rights; and language and cultural issues. One aspect of our native struggle that I address in this paper is the revival of *ka 'ōlelo Hawai'i* (the native Hawaiian language) and its application in contemporary *ha'i 'ōlelo* (storytelling).

The main point of this article is to demonstrate the importance of the Hawaiian language to activities such as storytelling and the relationship of language to the Hawaiian concept of *mana* (life force, spiritual energy, or power). Most people outside the Hawaiian-language community in Hawai'i are unfamiliar with the importance of the language to anything, let alone storytelling, despite the fact that the Hawaiian language is one of the two official languages of the state (the other being English) and that Hawaiian is the native language of the indigenous people of Hawai'i. Thus, pressure is being exerted constantly by government and business leaders to erode the language and culture and to streamline Hawai'i into a more American mold in an effort to make Hawai'i nothing more than "southern California with palm trees."

Local politicians and businesspeople are not alone in their efforts to manipulate, transform, and, in effect, control traditional Hawaiian culture and values. Hollywood and other outside venues have also done their fair share to damage the perception of native traditions through their ignorance and ethnocentrism over the decades. Thus, in presenting this topic from a culturally correct and native perspective, a great deal of background information must be put forth before I even address the issue of storytelling.

Two metaphors are indigenous to the traditional way of Hawaiian thinking, and I would like to present my *mana'o* (thoughts) to you about Hawaiian-language storytelling through these metaphors, which are, first, the *ha* (the breath of life), the spiritual essence at the core of the second, *aloha* (love) and the *lei,* often thought of as a lovely garland of flowers one wears around one's neck but entailing so much more.

O Ka 'Ōlelo Ka Mea Nui (The Importance of Language)

Language holds a central role in native cultures as it "demonstrates the uniqueness of a people, carrying with it centuries of shared experience, literature, history, traditions and reinforcing these through daily use" (Kimura, p. 173). The link between *'Ōlelo Hawai'i* (Hawaiian language) and *mo'omeheu Hawai'i* (Hawaiian culture) is an example of this thought, as *'Ōlelo Hawai'i* is "inextricably tied to the definition and identity of the Hawaiian people" (p. 173). This connection is demonstrated in three primary ways: "the necessity of language to human activity in order to identify it as human [like storytelling] (or, in a narrower perspective, Hawaiian); the importance of subtlety, personality, and detail, that is, nicety in expression (also called *kaona*); and the power of the word" (p. 175).

First, language is important because activities are identified in the native language and imply specifics that do not always translate into another language (such as English). One example is *hula,* the native Hawaiian dance form. *Hula* is a dance form specific to Hawai'i and Hawaiian culture; there are specific steps, hand gestures, body movements, costuming restrictions, and musical

implements that either makes a dance *hula* or does not. In other words, the word *hula* does not translate to a more general and generic term such as "dance." In addition, many words and phrases in the Hawaiian language are used to identify specific dance movements that are not easily replicated in English. For example, when the "basic steps" of *hula* are taught, each step has a name that implies a specific movement: a *hela* is the pointing of the left or right foot at a 45-degree angle to the front and side of the body, which rests on the ball of the extended foot with the heel slightly raised off the ground and all five toes squarely planted on the ground. One's body weight rests on the opposite hip and with that knee bent; the foot is then returned to the original position, and the step is repeated with the other foot (Pukui and Elbert, p. 64). An *'uwehe* is the lifting of the left or right foot slightly from the ground; with both knees bent, the dancer taps that foot down, thrusts both knees outward from the body, and snaps them back closed again (usually this is repeated with the tapping of the opposite foot, followed by the same outward, then snapping, inward motion of the knees).

Other names are attached to specific motions (*lele 'uwehe, kaholo, 'ami, 'ami kūkū, kawelu, 'ōniu,* and so on); once the dancer understands the movements for each step, the *ho'opa'a* (chanter) can call out the step in any order ("*'uwehe, hela, kaholo, hela, 'ami,*" and so on), and the dancer, familiar with the technical terms, can execute each step with precision. This is only one small example of the importance of language to human activity.

The word for "word" in Hawaiian is *hua 'ōlelo: hua* (fruit) + *'ōlelo* (language) = the thought that "a word is the fruit of speaking." Individual words are selected by the storyteller or speaker and strung together into a coherent, exciting, and wonderful story in the same way that flowers are carefully selected and strung together into a beautiful lei. Every word has double, triple, or quadruple meanings, which Hawaiians call *kaona,* that add subtlety and impact to the telling of the story. One example, found printed on the cover of the October 8, 1868, issue of the newspaper *Ke Au 'Oko'a* ("The Independent") is an *oli pana* (chant of praise). This *oli pana,* titled "No 'Ke Au 'Oko'a'" ("For [the newspaper] 'The New Era'"), is 12 *paukū* (stanzas) long. The second *paukū* states:

Aia ma laila nā kaʻao
A na wai i kākau?
He mea no ka naʻauao
ʻAʻole he lālau.

There [in the paper] are the stories
Who are the writers?
The ones who are knowledgeable
Not the blundering ignorant ones.

It then names several of the writers, including noted Hawaiian scholar Samuel M. Kamakau, and their works. The tenth *paukū* makes reference to another author, Moses Manu, whose *moʻolelo* "Riva Home" ("River Home") was being printed as a serial in the paper:

Eia aʻe no Riva Home
Ke keiki o ka noke
He wiliau a he hone
I ka pua o ka loke.

Here indeed is Riva Home [River Home]
The child of persistence
Stirring up trouble and mischief
For the blossom of the rose.

This *paukū* contains a classic example of Hawaiian *kaona;* "Ka pua o ka loke" refers to the heroine of the *moʻolelo*, Rose Blossom (or Rose); it is also a reference to the author, who hails from Kīpahulu on the island of Māui, as does the *loke* (rose), which is the "island flower" of Māui.[1] Manu himself is the *pua*, the flower (the product or native of Māui), as the rose blossom is the product of the rose bush.[2]

Hua ʻōlelo can also be strung together in storytelling, as in the following example:

Hānau ka iʻa, hānau ka Naiʻa i ke kai la holo
Hānau ka Manō, hānau ka Moano i ke kai la holo
Hānau ka Mau, hānau ka Maumau i ke kai la holo
Hānau ka Nana, hānau ka Mana i ke kai la holo
Hānau ka Nake, hānau ka Make i ke kai la holo
Hānau ka Napa, hānau ka Nala i ke kai la holo
Hānau ka Pala, hānau ke Kala i ke kai la holo
Hānau ka Paka, hānau ka Pāpā i ke kai la holo

Hānau ke Kalakala, hānau ka Huluhulu i ke kai la holo
Hānau ka Halahala, hānau ka Palapala i ke kai la holo

Born is the fish, born the Porpoise in the sea, swimming
Born is the Shark, born the Goatfish in the sea, swimming
Born is the Mau, born the Maumau in the sea, swimming
Born is the Nana, born the Mana in the sea, swimming
Born is the Nake, born the Make in the sea, swimming
Born is the Napa, born the Nala in the sea, swimming
Born is the Pala, born the Sturgeon in the sea, swimming
Born is the Paka eel, born the green crab in the sea, swimming

Born is the Kalakala, born the sea slug in the sea, swimming
Born is the Halahala, born the Palapala in the sea, swimming.
(Beckwith, p. 191; English translation and regularized text by Kuʻualoha Hoʻomanawanui)[3]

The above 10 lines are taken from the second *wā* (epoch, era, or, in this written form, chapter) of a 2,108-line Hawaiian creation chant titled the *Kumulipo* ("Source of Deep Darkness"). This chant was composed in the seventeenth century and chanted at the birth of high *aliʻi* (chief) Kalaninui ʻIamamao (the great supreme chief from afar) by the *kahuna* (religious leaders) of his chiefly parents. The purpose of the chant was to connect the birth of this new chief to the beginning of time, establishing his place in the universe as the supreme ruler over it. It begins with the establishment of the heavens and earth from chaos and darkness and proceeds through several eras with birth lists of different species in a way similar to Darwin's theory of evolution. On the surface, it looks like a fairly straightforward evolutionary account—with simpler sea creatures being born, then moving to creatures of the land that get larger and larger (rat, dog, and pig)—and culminates in the birth of man. However, the *Kumulipo* is not merely a scientific theory but also a wonderful, complex work of poetry to be savored. In the first line of this section, the birth of the *iʻa* (fish) is paired with the emergence of the *nai'a* (dolphin). In the Western mind, this is an illogical pairing, as we are trained as Western scholars to move from the smallest and simplest life form to the largest and most complex. Is the dolphin not one of the larger, more complex sea creatures? Moreover, it is a mammal and not even a fish! However, there is a poetic structure at work here that comes alive through the *hā* (the breath) in its oral recitation. The first is the repetitive structure: "Hānau ka[4] (mea), hānau ka (mea) i ke kai la holo." This translates to "Born was the (species), born was the (species) in the sea, [and went] swimming [away]." When one is memorizing over 2,000 lines of a chant, this simple device of a repetitive formula makes the task much easier than memorizing the thought in a prose or narrative form. The second is the rhythmic form: *i'a* rhymes with *nai'a,* *manō* with *moano,* *mau* with *maumau,* and so on. Thus, a Hawaiian style of logic is revealed: The *hua 'ōlelo* are selected and strung together for their rhythmic value, which also assists the storyteller as a memory aid in both the memorization and the recitation process. This reinforces Kimura's argument that "Hawaiian culture placed great emphasis on language as the means of human artistic development" (p. 175). It also demonstrates the important role of language: a poetic recitation of the Kumulipo would be impossible in English, simply because "fish" rhymes with "dolphin" as closely as "shark" rhymes with "goatfish." The English interpretation serves its purpose of enlightening a non-Hawaiian-speaking audience, but the poetry is lost.

Another example is in the telling of *mo'olelo* because Hawaiians emphasize different elements in storytelling than do Westerners. For example, Hawaiian w*ahi pana* (stories about places) place a great emphasis on the storyteller's knowledge of a place, which was revealed in the detailed setting of the *mo'olelo.* This is done through the use of place names in both poetic and nonpoetic ways.

Like the Kumulipo, place names within the *mo'olelo* were poetic, as "in their imaginations people ally the place with amusement and affection to the wondrous events of the past" (Elbert, p. 124). One example from the Pele epic is the little islet of Mokoli'i, which sits off the coast of Kualoa Beach Park near the boundary between the Ko'olauloa and Ko'olaupoko districts on the windward side of the island of O'ahu. *Moko* is an older form of the word *mo'o* (dragon, water serpent, lizard), and *li'i* is "small" or "tiny." Thus, the name is rendered as "Little Lizard." It refers

to a *mo'o* of the area slain by Pele's younger and most favored sister, Hi'iakaikapoliopele (Hi'iaka-in-the-bosom-of-Pele), who was on her way from the volcano to the island of Kaua'i to fetch Pele's lover, Lohi'au. When Hi'iaka slayed the dragon, part of its body fell into the bay; the island represents the tip of the *mo'o*'s tail, which is sticking up out of the water.[5] Today, this island is incorrectly labeled "Chinaman's Hat" or "Keone's Poi Pounder" because of its shape, which approximates these two items.

Wahi pana (Hawaiian place names) also have a second nonpoetic use, namely, their listing of place names, or at least their prominent inclusion, in the plot of the story. Here, "the teller becomes a reporter of detail rather than a reteller of adventure. To the outsider, such detailed lists of places are boring, but not so to the narrator or [the] Hawaiian audience. Listed in travel guide order, the places are a witness both to the story's veracity and the teller's memory" (p. 124).

One example is the following passage from the story of Laenihi, a fish-goddess on her way to find her brother a wife. In this short paragraph, 18 *wahi pana* (place names) are mentioned in the course of Laenihi's travels from the island of Moloka'i to the islands of Maui and then Hawai'i:

Holo maila 'o Laenihi i ke ahiahi, a hiki i Haleolono ma Pāla'au, i Moloka'i, ua ka ua. Kā hāhā 'o hope no ka hikiwawe loa. Ma laila aku a Hanaka'ie'ie, ma Kahikinui i Honua'ula ma Māui, 'ōlapa ka uila. Kā hāhā hou 'o hope no ka 'emo 'ole loa. Mai Māui aku a 'Umiwai, ma Kohala i Hawai'i, ku'i ka hekili; ma laila aku a Pōlolikamanu, ma waho o Mahiki i Hāmākua, nei ke ōla'i. Ma laila aku a hala 'o Hilo, a komo i loko o Pana'ewa, a hiki i Kūkulu ma waho o Puna, kahe ka wai 'ula. A laila, no'ono'o 'o hope nei, ua loa'a 'o Kamalā-lāwalu. (Fornander, p. 233; Hawaiian text regularized by Ku'ualoha Ho'omanawanui)

In the evening Laenihi set out going to Hale-o-Lono ("House of Lono") at Pā-lā'au ("Wooden Fence") on [the island of] Moloka'i ("Twisted Leaders"), [where] it was raining. The people behind were astonished at the great speed [at which she traveled]. From there [she traveled] on to Hanaka'ie'ie ("The *ka'ie'ie* vine bay") at Kahiki-nui ("The great Kahiki") at Honua-'ula ("Red earth") on Māui [where]

the lightning flashed. The people behind were astonished [at the speed with which she traveled], quick as a flash. From Māui to ʻUmi-wai ("Chief ʻUmi's water"), at Kohala on Hawaiʻi-the thunder roared; from there to Pololi-ka-manu ("The bird is hungry"), beyond Mahiki ("Lizard") at Hāmākua-the earth quaked. From there past Hilo, entering within Panaʻewa and on to Kukulu outside Puna-the red water ran. Then the people behind thought that Kamalālāiwalu had been found.[6]
(translation by Kuʻualoha Hoʻomanawanui)

Again, the fact that the place names are presented in the Hawaiian language lends a poetic sense that is not present in English. Kimura's view on this is that "the Hawaiian attention to detail . . . sound[s] silly in English . . . [as] it cannot be done properly in that medium" (p. 177). This is also a testament to the Hawaiian connection to the ʻāina (the land), which is traditionally viewed as an ancestor through our Earth Mother, Papahānaumoku, "the foundation (*papa*) that gives birth (*hānau*) to the land (*moku*).[7] Reference to the ʻāina in storytelling is called *aloha ʻāina* (love for the land) and is an integral part of Hawaiian storytelling in its various forms. Elbert says that

there are probably thousands of *aloha ʻāi-na* sayings. They name illustrious chiefs and places, important rains, seas, winds, and distinctive features. Speakers of Hawaiian never tire of hearing them over and over, and on hearing them one recalls his own grandmother or older relative who used to say them, and one has heard some of them in songs. They thus reinforce ties to family as well as to places, and are a link with a past. . . . Even more cogent than the association of *aloha ʻāi-na* sayings with friends and relatives were the ties with the land and the seas . . . opportunity was on the land and in the sea. The present and the future lay in the gardens, fishing grounds, and surfing sites. This attachment to the land and the sea was reflected in the poetic *aloha ʻāi-na* sayings. (pp. 121–122)

Thus, once again we see the importance of the native language, as the mere mention of a specific place name recalls to the educated mind the countless number of *moʻolelo* associated with that place, preserving both the name and the story of the area.

Ka Wā Kaumaha: The Decline of the Hawaiian Language in the Period after Contact, 1778–1958

In Hawaiian culture, the word *mana* has many meanings but is most often applied to one's spirit or soul. *Mana* is "supernatural or divine power [or] authority" (Pukui and Elbert, p. 235). It is a term often applied to charismatic leaders who are said to possess powerful *mana*. English has no direct equivalent because, unlike the English synonyms "charisma" and "spirit/soul," inanimate things or concepts can also possess *mana*. Trees have *mana*, as do rocks and geographic places and as do words and the speaking of language.

All people communicate through language. In its most common form, language is spoken. Spoken language is reinforced with gesture, which in turn can be codified into what we call sign language. Both spoken and sign language can be reduced to written symbols and represented on paper, forming the basis of written language, which is learned and passed on in the practice of reading and writing.

One of the main pastimes of both the spoken and the written language, regardless of cultural, social, or political constructs, is the telling of stories, that is, the creation or re-creation of a story for the purpose of entertaining and/or informing an audience. Storytellers were employed in traditional oral cultures. In traditional, preliterate Hawaiian society (i.e., pre-1820s), stories were told by *mea haʻi ʻōlelo* (storytellers) and by *mea oli* (chanters) and/or *ʻōlapa* (*hula* dancers) in a *halau hula* (school or troupe that performed the traditional native dance, called the *hula*). During traditional times, storytelling festivals or events could last all night long or days on end. Storytelling was especially entertaining in the family or community because of the *kaona* (nuances) that could be woven into the chosen tale. In other words, the clever storyteller carefully selected words and metaphors in his or her telling so that not everyone in the audience would necessarily "get it" at the same level. For example, a reference to sexual activity could be viewed in such a way that the mature and knowing adult would understand the metaphor but not a child or sexually immature person. Thus, the native language was an important cultural element in the telling of stories to a native audience.

Native life changed drastically after the invasion of white Europeans and Americans, beginning with British explorer Captain James Cook in

1778. Cook's "discovery" of the Hawaiian Islands and her native inhabitants opened up Hawai'i to the onslaught of the outside world. Foreign diseases ravaged the population physically; new political philosophies and religious ideologies ravaged the population culturally and spiritually; alien species of plants and animals smothered the land and choked the sea; and the introduction of capitalism turned the native economy on its head.

In 1820, a small company of Calvinist missionaries arrived in Hawai'i from New England. Their white, conservative, Protestant values had a far-reaching and devastating influence on Hawaiian culture and society for decades to come. On a positive note, these American Calvinist missionaries are credited with creating a Hawaiian alphabet, which allowed the Hawaiian language—up to now, strictly a spoken language—to be expanded into a written form. On the other hand, these missionaries and their descendants were quite blatantly racist and anti-Hawaiian and did everything in their power to wipe out the native population and subjugate them to American authority, including outlawing social custom and practice (such as the dancing of *hula* and the speaking of the Hawaiian language) and orchestrating the overthrow of the Hawaiian monarchy in 1893.

Hawaiian language was freely spoken throughout traditional times, surviving well through the first 40 years or so of Western contact. Early explorers, such as Cook, and even the first missionary companies in the 1820s and 1830s were relatively fluent in the Hawaiian language. But as Hawai'i became progressively "civilized" in foreign ways, American nationals exerted strong pressure to make English the main vehicle for daily life. By the turn of the twentieth century, a new "language," called "Hawaiian creole"—a blend of Hawaiian, English, and immigrant languages of the sugar plantations (i.e., Japanese, Chinese, Portuguese, and Filipino), commonly referred to as "pidgin"—began to replace the native Hawaiian language. Although the goal of white society was for "standard" American English to prevail, their efforts were resisted by the native Hawaiians, plantation immigrants, and merchant classes; still, the result was the demise of *ka 'ōlelo Hawai'i*. Most Hawaiians in the first half of the twentieth century turned away from their language and social customs to blend into the "melting pot" propaganda that was put forth at this time. The failure of the *kanaka maoli* to thrive in this social experiment planted some of the first

seeds of colonial backlash and political resistance to Americanization by the native people. Thus, the dawn of statehood in 1959 saw the birth of a renewed interest by the native people in their traditional culture that has become known as the period of the "Hawaiian cultural renaissance."

Ka Huli 'ana (The Changing Tide): Hawaiian Cultural Renaissance, 1960s to the Present

Although examples of protest against the westernization of culture and American political authority are evident throughout Hawai'i's contact with the West, a strong grassroots effort has been growing since the late 1960s. This period, the so-called Hawaiian cultural renaissance, is marked by unprecedented political activism and protest in the Hawaiian community. Interest has flourished for *nā mea* Hawai'i (things Hawaiian), which is viewed by some as a backlash against statehood and the continued encroachment of American culture, values, and ideals on the Hawaiian population. Music and dance turned away from the Hollywood-inspired *"hapa-haole"* (part Hawaiian, part foreign), in which white, cellophane-skirted women danced to jazzy tunes, and back to more traditional ways. Hawaiian-language lyrics were backed up by *ki hō'alu* (slack-key guitar), and *'ukulele; hula kahiko* (ancient, traditional dance) was revived through competitions and exhibitions such as the Meff ie Monarch, Prince Lot, and Kamehameha Day *hula* festivals. As more and more Hawaiians actively began searching for their cultural "roots," the groundwork was laid for the blossoming of the culture in the 1970s and 1980s. This era is highlighted by the creation of the Protect Kaho'olawe 'Ohana (PKO), dedicated to halting federal military bombing and returning to Hawaiian control the small, uninhabited island of Kaho'olawe off the south coast of the island of Māui; the establishment of the Polynesian Voyaging Society and the successful maiden voyage of the traditional double-hulled voyaging canoe *Hōkūle'a* from Hawai'i to Tahiti and back in 1976;[8] the creation a decade later of the Pūnana Leo and Kula Kaiāpuni Hawaiian Language Immersion Schools (preschool through high school); and the increase of Hawaiian-language classes at the college level.[9] With the struggle to reestablish a native Hawaiian-speaking population in the 1980s, not until the 1990s could the performance/storytelling aspect of the language be more widely implemented—and successfully so.

Hawaiian storytelling has always been more than just a single storyteller on a stage. In traditional times, *oli* (chant) and *hula* (dance) were often the main vehicles of storytelling. The main part of storytelling in these contexts is the Hawaiian language. This differs from many other cultural dances, especially Euro-American forms (such as ballet, jazz, blues, rock and roll, and hip-hop) in that the primary impetus of the dance is not the beat or rhythm of the music but the presence of the spoken words. Dances are choreographed to the words of the song or chant and timed to the beat; without the spoken words, no meaningful choreography would (or could) exist. Because the *hula* has come from the traditional past, it is rare, and, in fact, it is considered distasteful by serious *hula* practitioners and cultural experts to see *hula* performed to songs written in English (and I am unaware of *hula* chants written in any other language, although Japanese is creeping in). I mention this simply because, like the singing troubadours of Europe's past, Hawaiian music is another popular storytelling vehicle, although English songs composed in the Hawaiian musical style (as well as *hapa haole*, or part-English, part-Hawaiian lyrics) have been around since at least the 1880s (but more so from the 1920s to the present).

Although *hula* festivals have been popular and regularly held since the 1960s, they are not the best examples of language revival in storytelling for two main reasons. First, each *halau* is allowed to perform only one *hula*. Individually performed *hula* do not tell a complete story. More often than not, they are only a fragment of a longer story, and the telling of the story is thus incomplete. Second, *hālau* are allowed to freely choose what *mele* they will perform, and, for obvious reasons, one does necessarily lead to the next. Thus, the "storytelling" through the *hula* competitions is fragmented. However, in recent years, Hawaiian-language storytelling has broken new ground outside the regular *hula* arena.

Ka Ha'i 'Ana O Nā Mo'olelo Maoli (Native Storytelling): Holo Mai Pele and Kalauaiko'olau

Kaluaiko'olau: In 1994, Hā'ili'ōpua Baker, a theater student at the University of Hawai'i at Mānoa, wrote a script for a dramatic play in the Hawaiian language for her senior project. Titled *Kaluaiko'olau*, the name of the lead character, this play is a historical biography based on the actual events surrounding a native Hawaiian man in the

1890s from the island of Kaua'i. Ko'olau, as he is often referred to, contracted leprosy, a greatly dreaded disease of the time, and defied government orders of exile away from his family on the remote peninsula of Kalaupapa on the island of Moloka'i. Branded an outlaw by the Americans who controlled the government after the Hawaiian monarchy was overthrown by force and regaled as a hero by Hawaiians for his antigovernment stance, Kaluaiko'olau was an important political figure and cultural icon for Hawaiians of his time, and he remains one for Hawaiians today.

Kaluaiko'olau was an important milestone in the reestablishment of *ka 'ōlelo Hawai'i* as a primary vehicle for storytelling, as no other dramatic presentation before it had ever been produced by the University of Hawai'i's Theater and Drama Department. It was the first to be staged in the Lab Theater; despite successful reviews and sold-out performances, the Theater Department refused to allow it be presented on the main stage of the University's Kennedy Theater. Since then, this presentation has successfully toured other venues around the state. A follow-up play, *Mōhala ka Lehua* (Blossoming of the Lehua Flower), also conducted entirely in Hawaiian, has been successful in the Lab Theater as well.

Holo Mai Pele: In 1995, after lengthy research and preparation, Hilo's Hālau o Kekuhi, under the direction of sisters Pua Kanaka'ole Kanahele and Nālani Kanaka'ole Zane, premiered a groundbreaking *hula*-storytelling event. Titled *Holo Mai Pele* (Pele's Journey), which is also the name of a particular Pele chant, it was the first modern attempt to join the different segments of the traditional Pele epic into one cohesive performance. This event presented the myth of Pele in its proper chronological order, from her birth in Kahiki (the ancient Hawaiian homeland) to her eviction from the island and her subsequent journey to Hawai'i. Once here, the story continues: how she establishes her home at Halema'ma'u crater on Hawai'i island; how her spirit "dream travels" to the island of Kaua'i, where she meets her mortal lover, Lohi'au; and how, on her return, she invests her youngest sister, Hi'iakaikapoliopele, with the responsibility of bringing Lohi'au back to Pele at the volcano.

Told partly through narrative, partly through *oli* (chanting), and partly through the dramatic and bombastic *hula 'aiha'a* (traditional Hawaiian dance), it is an enthralling and mesmerizing experience. With the exception of a brief introduction to each segment by a narrator, in English, the entire performance relies on the Hawaiian language, especially with the chants and *hula* segments that form the main body of the production.

Like *Kaluaiko‘olau, Holo Mai Pele* has successfully toured around the state of Hawai‘i to rave reviews and sold-out performances. To the critics and disbelievers, the widespread success of these two dramatic storytelling events clearly demonstrates that the Hawaiian language is being revitalized.

Na Ha‘i ‘Ōlelo ‘O Ko‘a (Different Venues of Hawaiian-Language Storytelling)

Besides the more traditional venues of Hawaiian storytelling, there has been experimentation with pulling Hawaiian language into new forms. Two that have been performed in the past few years have been European-style opera and Japanese Kabuki theater. In both, the structure of the original style has been retained. However, the differences have been in the subject (all from Hawaiian history and mythology) and presentation (incorporating Hawaiian language, song, costume, and dance).

The Hawai‘i Children’s Opera Chorus, under the direction of Nola Nahulu and assisted by Malia Ka‘ai (with the support of the City and County of Honolulu), has presented two such operas: *Kahalaopuna* and *Lā’eikawai.* Both are goddesses from Hawai‘i’s mythical past whose stories intersect with each other. Although the plot and characterization of the stories presented here were retained in these productions, unfortunately many of the songs presented were sung in the English language. Although Hawaiian language was not highlighted, it is not difficult to imagine future productions (or a revamping of these productions) to utilize the language in an operatic form. After all, European-style opera performed in the Hawaiian language was a regular feature in Honolulu during the nineteenth-century Victorian period in Hawai‘i.

In a different venue, the life stories of two historical chiefly figures, Keoua and ‘Umialiloa, were presented primarily by the members of Kumu John Lake’s *hālau* in the Kabuki style. Although the action was dramatized through traditional Kabuki theater, the language featured in both events was ka ‘ōlelo Hawai‘i.

On August 12, 1998, *Ka Pā Hula Hawai’i,* under the direction of *kumu hula* Kaha‘i Topolinsky, presented a *hula* drama titled *Lā Ho‘olilo* (Day of

Loss) in commemoration of the one-hundredth anniversary of the annexation of Hawai‘i to the United States. Although depicted in U.S. history books as a day of great celebration and honor for native Hawaiians, to native Hawaiians the annexation of Hawai‘i to the United States was a tremendous blow to most of the native population, who worked so hard to regain Hawaiian sovereignty and independence and to restore the Hawaiian monarchy.[10]

Topolinsky’s production, no doubt inspired by *Holo Mai Pele,* incorporated *hula,* chant, storytelling, and reenactments of historical events into a dramatic, cultural, and overall impressive event, especially because of the prominent role that the Hawaiian language played in this touching production.

Nā Mea ‘E A ‘E ‘O Ka Ha‘i Mo‘olelo ‘Ana (Other Venues of Traditional Storytelling)

Although the storytelling events discussed in the previous section have been incredibly successful and in demand, they have been special presentations that are not planned to be made into ongoing or annual events. However, as the success of each of these unique events spreads and more people learn or return to ‘Ōlelo Hawai‘i, these types of storytelling events undoubtedly will become more common in Hawai‘i’s cultural arts and entertainment scenes. Although these events have thus far been one-time-only presentations, other, smaller events held regularly around the islands have been dedicated to fostering Hawaiian-language storytelling. Here are a few examples.

Mission House Museum. The Mission House Museum in Honolulu on O‘ahu has held an annual open-house and storytelling event the past several years. Last year, it added a Hawaiian-language storytelling component. This is only fitting, as the missionaries who originally built and lived in the structure over a century ago were themselves immersed in learning the language to better communicate with the native Hawaiian population. This has also given young storytellers from the Hawaiian language and Hawaiian studies programs at the University of Hawai‘i’s Mānoa campus additional venues at which to hone their storytelling skills.

Lā Kūkahekahe: Lā Kūkahekahe (“Day of Pleasant Conversation”) is called by other names around the state, but the idea in each is similar: the promotion of the Hawaiian language and the practice of Hawaiian culture through ‘ōlelo Ha-

wai'i. Lā Kūkahi are usually day-long events sponsored by the Hawaiian language programs at both the university and the various community colleges that encourage people to speak Hawaiian. Food booths, games, arts and crafts demonstrations, and entertainment are features. Hawaiian-language storytelling is a regular feature of the entertainment (which also includes music and *hula*).

Talk Story Festival: The Island Talk Story Festival is an annual event sponsored by the City and County of Honolulu Department of Parks and Recreation. It is usually held in October at the McCoy Pavilion at Ala Moana Beach Park. Lasting several days, the festival brings together storytellers from different cultures and communities throughout the state. A stage dedicated to Hawaiian storytelling is often featured. In the past few years, Hawaiian storytellers have slowly begun to include more *'ōlelo Hawai'i* in their storytelling. Some individuals have even told short *mo'olelo* completely in the Hawaiian language. It is foreseeable that this aspect of the festival will be expanded in the future as the popularity of the Hawaiian language and the number of people able to speak and understand it continue to grow.

Nā Mea I Ka Manawa Hope (Future Events)

After the success of *Holo Mai Pele,* Pua Kanaka'ole Kanahele and other well-known and well-respected *kumu hula* (*hula* teachers) formed a *hui* (coalition) called Ilio'ulaokalani (Red Dog of the Heavens) to protect native Hawaiian gathering rights, which were threatened in 1998 by proposed legislation in the state government. As part of the activities of this politically and culturally active *hui,* a storytelling event similar to *Holo Mai Pele* is currently being planned. Titled *Keaomelemele* after a Hawaiian goddess embodied in the golden clouds at sunset, this production is tentatively scheduled for the year 2000. This much anticipated event will break new ground and set a higher cultural standard for *hula* and storytelling for generations to come.

After the success of *Kaluaiko'olau,* Hā 'ili 'ōpua and Kaliko Baker have had success with a play about the adventures of the Hawaiian demigod Māui (*Māuiakamalo,* or Māui-of-the loin cloth) that also was performed entirely in the Hawaiian language and that toured statewide. Plans are being made to produce other storytelling events entirely in the Hawaiian language: at least one about another popular figure in Hawaiian myth (the pig-god Kamapua'a) and another original production.

Ha'ina 'Ia Mai 'Ana Ka Puana (Conclusion)

Ha'ina 'ia mai 'ana ka puana (Thus the story is told). Although a standard opening to a Hawaiian *mo'olelo* (e.g., "Once upon a time") does not exist, Hawaiian *mo'olelo,* as told through *mele,* frequently conclude with this line. The stories of my Hawaiian ancestors were passed down through oral tradition for countless centuries, and for over 100 years many stories have been preserved on paper in the Hawaiian-language newspapers—a legacy to Hawaiians of this generation of our illustrious storytelling past. These stories survive through the *ha* (the breath of life), the essence of *aloha* (love), which nurtures them in laughs and whispers.

Notes

1. Although each state has a designated flower (Hawai'i's is the hibiscus), each island in Hawai'i also has a flower or lei associated with it: Kaua'i's is the *maile and mokihana,* O'ahu's is the *'ilima,* Hawai'i's is the *lehua,* Lāna'i's is the *kaunaoa,* Moloka'i's is the *kukui,* Kaho'olawe's is the *hinahina,* Ni'ihau's is the *pūpūu o Ni'ihau* (Ni'ihau shells, as there is little vegetation on this arid island), and Māui's is the *loke,* or rose (for more detailed information, consult the *Atlas of Hawai'i,* by O.A. Bushnell).

2. The word *pua* is used metaphorically for "offspring" in other ways as well: as a *pua* (flower) is the offspring or product of a plant, so a *pua* (baby fish) is the offspring or product of a mature fish. *Lei,* or garlands of flowers one wears about one's neck, are made from *pua;* thus, children are often referred to as *ku'u pua* or *ku'u lei* (my beloved flower, or my beloved *lei*).

3. The *kahakō,* or macron, which elongates vowel sounds, and the *'okina,* or glottal stop ('), which separates two vowel sounds, punctuating them as in "oh-oh," are the two diacritical marks recognized in the Hawaiian language. Prior to the 1970s, these sounds were recognized, but no consistent standard of marking them was ever agreed on. Thus, most texts recorded prior to this time did not incorporate these markings. The exclusion of diacritical marks can be confusing to the

reader, as marked and unmarked (or variably marked) words can have different meanings, for example, *pau* (completed), *pa'u* (sooty, dirty), *pā'u* (ink for tattooing), and *pā'ū* (woman's garment). However, since the 1970s their value to traditional Hawaiian texts has been understood, and contemporary scholars and language experts have utilized them more consistently in their own writing and in analyses of older texts. Although some argue that old texts should be left alone because vagueness is sometimes the goal of the original author (a form of *kaona*) and because we cannot, in good conscience, ascribe a meaning to a word that was written in a context different from one in which we might understand it, I chose to utilize the diacritical marks to help clarify meanings. Where obscurity is perhaps intentional and where a double meaning is implied, I will note it.

Beckwith's Kumulipo study is based on several nineteenth-century texts: one commissioned by King David Kalākaua in 1881 and published in Hawaiian and German; a Hawaiian version (1902) by Joseph Kukahi, a member of Kalākaua's court, that was later reprinted in the magazine *Aloha: An English and Hawaiian Magazine* (vol. 1, June 15–September 1, 1928); and an English translation of the Hawaiian text by Kalākaua's sister, Queen Lili'uokalani (1897) (Beckwith, p. 253).

4. You might notice that the word *hānau* is followed sometimes by *ka* and other times by *ke*. They both mean "the" in Hawaiian: *ka* is the normal use, except with words beginning in *k*, *e*, *a*, or *o*. *Nā* is the plural form of "the" for all words, but in this type of grammatical structure the *ka/ke* form is preferred.

5. One of the most accessible sources of this story, albeit not the best, is Nathaniel B. Emerson's *Pele and Hiiaka, a Myth from Hawaii* (1915). Emerson based his story on several previously published versions by native Hawaiian authors from 1860 to 1906. With only one exception, these *mo'olelo* were printed in the Hawaiian language and thus are inaccessible today to non-Hawaiian-language speakers. The sole English-language version was published in 1883 in the newspaper *Pacific-Commercial Daily Advertiser.* Titled "Hi'iaka: A Hawaiian Legend by a Hawaiian Native," the author's name was given only as "Kaili." Emerson, who

was of American descent, was raised in the islands and was a fluent speaker of the Hawaiian language. Today, most Hawaiian scholars agree that although Emerson has, in previous generations, been upheld as a preserver of Hawaiian traditions, he was little more than a plagiarist who capitalized on his knowledge of the language and his connections in the Hawaiian community by publishing English renditions of sacred stories and selling them for money. Unfortunately, because many people today do not speak, read, or understand Hawaiian, Emerson's English-language versions are relied on as "authoritative" texts, which they are not.

6. Not all place names are translated because not all are known. Translations here are taken from Pukui, Elbert, and Mookini, *Place Names of Hawai'i.*

7. For a more in-depth study of this concept, see Kame'eleihiwa, *Native Land and Foreign Desires.*

8. Since this time, the *Hōkūle'a* has made several successful voyages to other areas of the Pacific. In addition, several other traditional Polynesian voyaging canoes have been built (see Finney, *Voyage of Rediscovery: A Cultural Odyssey Through Polynesia*).

9. See Kimura.

10. Recently, Hawaiian researcher and scholar Noenoe Silva traveled to Washington, D.C., and uncovered one of two known antiannexation petitions in the National Archives. Titled "Palapala Ho'opi'i Ho'ohui 'āina" ("Petition against Annexation"), it was taken from island to island by members of the Hui Aloha 'Āina, a Hawaiian patriotic league formed shortly after the overthrow of the Hawaiian monarchy in 1893. Dedicated to the restoration of Hawaiian sovereignty, the Hui successfully attained over 21,000 signatures on its petition, most of which were native Hawaiian. A similar petition was sent around by the Hui Kālai 'āina, a similar patriotic league. Its petition was signed by over 17,000 native Hawaiians. Together, these petitions were signed by 38,000 native Hawaiians, an impressive number, especially because the population of native Hawaiians at the time was a mere 40,000. For more insight into this period of Hawaiian history, see Silva and Minton, comps., "Kū'ē: The Hui Aloha 'Āina Anti-annexation Petitions, 1897–1898."

Further Reading

Beckwith, Martha W., ed. and trans., *The Kumulipo, a Hawaiian Creation Chant*, Chicago: University of Chicago Press, 1951

Daws, Gavan, O.A. Bushnell, and Andrew Berger, *The Illustrated Atlas of Hawai'i*, Norfolk Island, Australia: Island Heritage, 1970; second edition, Honolulu, Hawaii: Island Heritage, 1980

Elbert, Samuel H., "Connotative Values of Hawaiian Place Names," in *Directions in Pacific Traditional Literature: Essays in Honor of Katharine Luomala*, edited by Adrienne L. Kaeppler and Harry Nimmo, Honolulu, Hawaii: Bishop Museum, 1976

Finney, Ben, *Voyage of Rediscovery: A Cultural Odyssey Through Polynesia*, Berkeley: University of California Press, 1994

Fornander, Abraham, comp., "Legend of Halemano," in *Fornander Collection of Hawaiian Antiquities and Folk-lore*, Honolulu, Hawaii: Bishop Museum, 1916; reprint, Millwood, New York: Kraus Reprint, 1985

Hālau o Kekuhi, *Holo Mai Pele*, Kahului, Hawaii: Maui Arts and Cultural Center, 1995

Kame'eleihiwa, Lilikalā, *Native Land and Foreign Desires*, Honolulu, Hawaii: Bishop Museum, 1992

Kimura, Larry K., "Native Hawaiian Culture," in *Native Hawaiian Study Commission Report*, Washington, D.C.: United States Government Printing Office, 1985

Pukui, Mary Kawena, *'Ōlelo No'eau: Hawaiian Proverbs and Poetical Sayings*, Honolulu, Hawaii: Bishop Museum, 1983

Pukui, Mary Kawena, and Samuel H. Elbert, *Hawaiian Dictionary: Hawaiian-English, English-Hawaiian*, revised edition, Honolulu: University of Hawai'i Press, 1986

Pukui, Mary Kawena, Samuel H. Elbert, and Esther T. Mookini, *Place Names of Hawai'i*, Honolulu: University of Hawai'i Press, 1981

Silva, Noenoe, and Nālani Minton, "Kū'ē: The Hui Aloha 'Āina Anti-Annexation Petitions, 1897–1898," unpublished paper, compiled 1998

A Gossamer of Wisdom

Hinekahukura Barrett-Aranui

Maori elder Hinekahukura Barrett-Aranui discusses her ancestral wharenui (meetinghouse), Te Tookanganui-a-noho, at Te Kuiti in the King Country. She shows how men and women earn the right to speak the communities' stories and the great responsibility they then assume.

Maori Tradition

In a cultured race, stories, myths, legends, lyrics, and poetry reflect oral traditions; buildings, carvings, weaving, and sculptures are the artistic portraits; and the games and dances are the kinetic aesthetic expression. Indigenous peoples throughout the world are ingenious in creating the reflections, portraits, and expressions that complement their environments and ways of being. When time is taken to observe and experience different cultures one finds that each has vast accumulations of interesting ways of demonstrating the profound wisdom of its people. In New Zealand one recognizes the true value of myths and legends when one sees the solidarity with which the Maori people of New Zealand have withstood the tests of time and have also felt the stoicism of some tribes as they sought compensation for past disparities.

Myths and legends have captivated my interest since childhood. In my more mature years I have realized the brilliant logic of my ancestors, who interlaced the wisdom of their people in a gossamer of Maori myths obscured under the rafters of their ancestral houses.

For eons oral traditions have been a medium for learning. Myths and legends abound in every group of people in the world. For many of these groups oral tradition is the primary method of retaining and maintaining their histories, genealog-

ical records, philosophies, and truths. The Maori people were ingenious in the art of storytelling and used this medium to convey information that contributed to community growth and development. Maori generally were comfortable using their myths to facilitate a process of conflict resolution, so it is not surprising to find that they were experts in using a narrative approach to life. This approach built upon the images in the stories that give their lives meaning, and an approach to counseling that builds upon this perspective has an appeal to people from a background of oral traditions.

This essay draws from facets of Maori life vignettes discussed and experienced over 65 years of my life. It emphasizes the importance of gender, age, and origin of individuals within *whanau* (family), *hapu* (subtribe), and *iwi* (tribe). The responsibilities borne by each person or group are clearly defined within Maori society. The genealogy, history, arts, and lifeblood of a people are some of the intrinsic values that are respected and treasured.

An attempt is made here to trace the effects of the woven threads of myths and legends in shaping the fabric of Maori lifestyle. Further exploration reveals the tactile treasures within the *wharenui* (meetinghouse), situated on the Ngaati Maniapoto ancestral *papakaainga* (village grounds). My hope is that readers will reach an understanding of how drawing upon myths and legends within the meetinghouse has played an important part in the weaving of protocol, education, discipline, and guidance for the future of the tribe of Maniapoto. Under the facade of the performing arts, the tactile treasures and eloquence of poetic language of the elders is an entanglement of wisdom that is still untapped. Joseph Campbell suggests that myths are the "clues to the potentialities of human life." New Zealand's colonizing history attempted to bury some of the clues beneath Western regimes of truth, but Maori tradition is deeply ingrained.

The Maori are tribal people, and the concept of *whanaungatanga* (interrelationships) is still very strong. I am affiliated to four major subtribal groups, each of which has strong roots in the main tribe of Ngaati Maniapoto. Maori tradition accepts that one may write in detail about one's own people because one understands that the tribe has a way of being that was molded by one's forefathers. I cannot and certainly dare not attempt to describe another tribe's way of being. I therefore write as a descendant of subtribes of Ngaati Maniapoto, a tribe named after Maniapoto, an ancestral figure of the 1400s and 1500s. I offer a viewpoint influenced by my female status, age, and subtribal responsibilities. As a female I chose to research, observe, and discuss with male colleagues the motives behind male interaction within Maniapoto tribal protocols. The role of the male differs from but seems to complement the role of the female within the tribe.

Therefore, the roles of the male and female as they work on their ancestral platforms will be observed together and valued for the dignity they bring to the tribe and family network.

Traditionally Maori people narrated their stories. Different trigger, or "clue," techniques were employed to trigger their memories. The techniques and stories became woven into a gossamer that became a remarkable reservoir of wisdom for the people. The professional arts of *whaikorero* (speech making), *waiata* (songs), *whakatauki* (proverbs), *haka* and *waiata-a-ringa* (posture dancing), *whakairo* (carving), *kowhaiwhai* (scroll painting), *moko* (tattoo), and *raranga* (weaving), besides *korero purakau* (storytelling) and everyday activities, became "clues" for retrieving historical and traditional information. These techniques give a distinctive quality to traditional customs that are unique to the Maori. These intrinsic arts enclose a myriad of clues that prompt one to retrieve those fascinating myths. In walking through the portals of the ancestral meetinghouse and standing on the speaking platform of the ancestors, one may then begin to understand the reverence that Maniapoto people have for Te Tookanganui-a-noho, their ancestral house.

Te Wharenui
Te Wharenui
Ko Pukenui te maunga,
Ko Mangaokewa te awa,
Ko Maniapoto te rangatira.
Ko Te Tookanganui-a-noho te Kuititanga o nga maunga,
te Kuititanga o nga whakaaro,
te Kuititanga o Ngaati Maniapoto.

Pukenui Mountain stands sentinel,
Mangaokewa River provides sustenance,
Maniapoto was the paragon of leadership.
Tookanganui-a-noho stands in the shelter of converging mountains,
where the decisions were discussed and set,
within the stronghold of the tribe of Maniapoto.

Te Tookanganui-a-noho, the *wharenui* to which I am affiliated, sits in Te Kuiti, a town some 50 miles south of the city of Hamilton and in the heart of the King Country. This is the stronghold of the Maniapoto tribe, a section of descendants from the ancestors who sailed the Pacific Ocean in the Tainui canoe. Maniapoto is one unit of the four major tribes connected to the Tainui federation. The King Country was so named when King Taawhiao, the second Maori king, set his top hat

on an area of the map of New Zealand and claimed the land under his hat as the King Country. He later placed an embargo on the area when he decided to go into exile after the land wars of the 1860s. The King Country was his birthplace, and he returned to his ancestors to be protected and cared for. During his exile he invited Te Kooti, a Maori renegade of the times, to stay with him in Te Kuiti during his exile. Years later, after having been pardoned, Te Kooti commissioned his own people to build this meetinghouse in payment for the sanctuary and hospitality he received from King Taawhiao and the people of Maniapoto. This house stands as an act of appreciation, a historical focal point, a collection of stories, an expression of arts, a citadel for the universal knowledge of the cosmos of which we are all a part, and what was a refuge in later years for the people who had given Te Kooti sanctuary. This, then, is Maniapoto's respected treasure, a treasure protected and maintained by Ngaati Rora, a subtribe of Maniapoto, a treasure trove of history and art with which the people of Maniapoto identify strongly.

The *wharenui* faces east, and behind it on a hill, resting in the *urupa* (cemetery), are the *tuupuna* (ancient ones) who called, spoke, strode, postured, worked, laughed, and cried on the *marae atea* (forecourt). Immediately to the north of the *marae,* Highway 3 wends its way north to Hamilton and Auckland, and south to New Plymouth and Wellington. East of the complex, stretching north and south, is the railway with its yards. Beyond and around the complex are the shopping areas, schools, service buildings, parks, hospital, and residential areas that shelter and service the more than 5,000 inhabitants of Te Kuiti.

To the right of the *wharenui* stands a large structure. Naumai, the *wharekai* (dining hall and kitchen), epitomizes the support and hospitality offered by Ngaati Maniapoto. Between the two buildings, at the back, are the ablution blocks, and in front is the Maori queen's residence, used on special occasions. Surrounding this complex are stone walls and a high hedge. The slope between the *wharenui* and the *urupa* has been landscaped and bears a floral border for the service entrance. Herein reposes Te Tookanganui-a-noho, with its reservoir of wisdom.

Carved, or "written," on the front *maihi* (bargeboards) is the "sculptured history" of the meetinghouse and its people. The scrollwork on the *tahuuhuu* (ridgepole) declares the emblem of the subtribe, the custodians of the complex. The *tukutuku* (lattice) panels reflect the stories of the founding of this meetinghouse. As one quietly walks through the *kuaha* (portals) one observes a continuation of the same carved scrolls and woven panels seen outside. The symbols reflect the traditions of the past and present. From each side of the ridgepole on the ceiling descend the symbolically painted *heke* (rafters) of the meeting-

house. The rafters represent ethereal threads, meshing strongly from the ridgepole above to the *poupou* (upright posts) below. The posts as refined sculptures symbolize the ancestors, and the lattice panels between are pages of history. One does not need an explanation of the reason chosen ancestors support the house of Ngaati Maniapoto, because the images encompass the gifts that each of these leaders have bestowed upon the people. The overall picture symbolizes the link between Ranginui (Sky Father) and Papatuanuku (Earth Mother), the spiritual and the physical; the esoteric and the exoteric. The meetinghouse is a wonderful collection of visual arts that when told, interpreted, and clarified, relate figuratively to the origins of ancestors and the colorful life patterns they molded for posterity.

The ancestors were the warriors and mothers that made history in the King Country and abroad. Their combined skills and strengths make up the *punawairua* (spiritual wellspring) from which descendants were able to draw strength during their life journeys. The three *poutokomanawa* (central poles) support the meetinghouse just as the *kaumatua* (elders) support the purpose of the gatherings held in the complex. The gallery of photographs attached to different panels conveys the *aroha* (respect and love) that the living still observe for their respected elders. On the front and back walls are carvings of esoteric characters of the cosmos and the spirit world. These characters symbolize the blueprints of Maori *tikanga* (life patterns). The *waka* (canoe) commanders of early migrations and the mythical characters of stories walk side by side in the display of scrolls and patterns. These metaphoric characters are part of the oral traditions, the intended designs for human behavior according to the Maori world. Carved into the post that reflects each one's image are the cunning of Tamate-Kapua to find food; the ingenuity of Maaui-Tikitiki-a-Taaranga to achieve the impossible; the creativity of Kinohaku and her weaving skills; the charisma of Tuhoe and his spirituality; the brilliance of Maniapoto's strategies in times of peace and war; and many others. Each one bequeathed a legacy, as reflected in the carvings.

Male and Female Roles on the *Marae*

Males and females have different roles and responsibilities when they are in the complex. Everyone is expected to offer their skills. This is particularly noticeable during the three-to-four-day periods of *tangi* (mourning). The smooth running of activities during these periods is a spectacle to admire. The empathy, warmth, and support given and received by everyone in all situations become realistic expressions of love. Children, adolescents, adults, and elders unconditionally practice their caring skills during this period. Grief is visible and shared physically. Grief is real, and compassion is practiced and accepted. Personal conflicts become trivial, as the priority is to support the *whanau pani* (bereaved family).

In the meetinghouse, where the body of the deceased is placed during mourning, one observes a variety of narratives being played out. Some are visual, others are enacted, and some are told as stories. The carvings and the speeches exude a warm atmosphere in which one pauses and takes time to recharge one's spirit. The carvings are not just for aesthetic pleasure. They portray caricatures of ancestors who are one's role models. The artists and speakers transform the images and stories that affirm the people without formal structures and boundaries. Speeches, stories, songs, and general chatter radiate a warm and recuperative tone to *manaaki* (support) the family in their grief.

The living breathe life into the ceremonies on the *marae*, and it is the responsibility of the *koroua* and *kuia* (male and female elders) to guide the processes by cuing in to the traditional strands carved and spoken within the *wharenui*. They work with the people to bring meaning into their shattered lives. The stories carved and painted within the walls of the *wharenui* hold the secrets and treasures that the *kaumatua* of the tribe know, respect, and refer to constantly. Let us now observe the special roles of the *kuia* and *koroua* during the *marae* ceremonies.

When the female elder is appointed to be keeper of the house she already understands the immense responsibility that she will need to carry with integrity. Her apprenticeship has been rigorous. She knows what happens in the "back." She has served food and washed dishes there as an adolescent. She has cooked her specialties as a mother. As a grandma she has trained youth to serve, and she has organized meals for 10 and meals for thousands. She therefore has a working knowledge of the hospitality offered in and around the dining room. Now she needs to revisit all the stories within the meetinghouse. Those stories will help her guide, lead, delegate, and control

from the unobtrusive position of the *kuia*. Her new position is set. Few indeed reach this point; but when they do, one word from the *kuia* is sufficient to move the local community into action. Depending on the importance of the gathering, she will invite members of her subtribe to support the purpose of the gathering.

The male elder has a different role but is still intertwined with the role of the female elder. As the central posts stand inside to support the meetinghouse, so do these two elders stand together outside to support their people. Together, the elders organize, *karanga* (call), *korero* (speak), and *waiata* (sing) for the *tangata whenua* (host group). The *kuia's* voice is the first to be heard as she sends her call to the *manuhiri* (visitors). She has the ability to reach into the emotional depths of each one. Her poignant voice pierces the heart, her words of compassion reach the soul, and she envelops the people with a mantle of affection. She has learned well how to use the genealogies and literature from within the meetinghouse to begin the process of bonding. With that part of the process complete, the male elder stands on his *turangawaewae* (turf), from where he will deliver his *whaikorero* (speech of welcome). He has taken the cue from the *kuia* and continues to expound the *whakapapa* (genealogies). He weaves the new groups to the family during the speech to complete the process of bonding.

Like the female, the male elder has undergone his own apprenticeship. He, too, has served food and washed his share of dishes. He has hunted with his father for food that must grace the tables. As an adolescent he has fished, cultivated potatoes and *kumera* (sweet potatoes), and gathered his share of seafood. Preparation of the *hangi* (earth oven) to cook for large groups has been mastered. He knows what happens in the "back." He is then invited to the "front" to join the elders.

For a period of time an apprentice is not allowed to say anything. He knows, however, that one day he will be called upon to speak. In the beginning the elders model the speeches and the stances, and there is a constant feedback of information as to the references in each spoken innuendo. The *wero* (challenges), the *whakautu* (replies) by eloquent speakers who speak on behalf of their tribal groups, are heard. No school's teaching is as rigorous as the teaching of these skills by the elders. The apprentice undergoes a training that will prepare him for life. He reflects upon myths and legends from within the meeting-house; he recites *whakatauki* (proverbs); he ob-serves, hears, and practices the *wero* (thrust), *karo* (parry), and *haka* (posturing) by the elo-quent speakers in quiet approval. When given the nod, he is ready. Supported by his elders, perhaps two or three of them, his speaking role is clearly set. In the inner sanctum of the elders he learns to be humble before he can begin to lead, delegate, mediate, and protect the prestige of his tribe.

During my research I have had recurring vi-sions of faces of past elders who gave so much of their wisdom in the stories they related to me as a child, a child who now writes about them. Stories were told to encourage my sense of tribal dignity; to comfort me as a child; to sort justice for human frailties; to affirm me, the child who knew not the ways of the white man's world; to explain to a young woman the origins of humanity; and to of-fer a spiritual haven to comfort my often dis-tressed soul. Within my ancestral house I have found an accumulation of myths and legends. The stories are amusing, romantic, historical, uplift-ing, and figurative. The privilege has been mine to hear, feel, and glean so much wisdom ensconced within the ancestral house, but the stories belong to the people. The narration of stories waits for the moment when an elder speaks, a mother tells a story, or someone takes up the task of recording the chronicles of Maniapoto treasures that abound within the ancestral house. That will no doubt be a labor of love that will be done at a later date. I am eternally grateful and acknowl-edge the gifts handed down by my revered elders, and I honor the ancestral house, which has with-stood the tests of time, the elements, and human eccentricities. May you always stand as a bulwark for the people of Maniapoto.

Sources

Ngaati Maniapoto Elders
Anderson, Ripeka
Anderson, Rua
*Aranui, Otia and Pani
*Barrett, Hira and Wairata
*Chapman, Mio and Mokau
*Coffin, Charlie
*Crown, Te Kore
Muraahi, Erana and George
Muraahi, Maehe
Nelson, Thomas and *Rangi
Pairama, Kapu and *Turi
Rauputu, Haara and *Wiari
Rawiri, Heemi and Iris

Other Elders
Hohepa, Hiko (from Te Arawa)
Karetu, Tiimoti (from Ngaati Kahungunu)
Melbourne, Hirini (from Tuhoe)
Milroy, Wharehuia (from Tuhoe)
*Rangihau, John (from Tuhoe)
*Rei, Patariki (from Aote)
Waikerepuu, Huirangi (from Ngaati Ruanui)

Further Reading
Campbell, Joseph, *The Power of Myth*, New York: Doubleday, 1988
Jones, Pei Te Hurinui, *Celebration for Tookanganui a Noho*, King Country Chronicle

---

*Deceased

Tale Telling on a Polynesian Atoll

Michael Lieber

Michael Lieber discusses the telling of tales in Porakied village on Pohnpei Island in Micronesia. He describes an event during which the Kapingamarangi people, resettled to this island from their own in 1919, tell traditional tales; then he discusses the more usual lack of such occasions.

Traditional Tale Telling in Porakied Village

My first experience with collecting tales in their natural contexts was in 1965 in Porakied village, a resettled colony of Kapingamarangi people transplanted from the atoll of Kapingamarangi to Pohnpei Island in Micronesia. Kapingamarangi (hereafter called Kapinga) people, although located in Micronesia, are Polynesians who established a resettled colony on Pohnpei in 1919 after a devastating famine. Their village had grown to a population of 270 people by the time I arrived there in July 1965.

I was working on the Pacific Resettled Communities Project, a comparative study of resettled communities in Oceania. My task was to compare the resettled community with the parent community on the atoll. I had been in Porakied village for five months and could communicate in the Kapingamarangi language by then, although not fluently. I had been busy documenting festivities of the Christmas holiday, which would end with the much-anticipated New Year's Day, when people would clown, drink, dance, and in general raise hell. It was New Year's Eve, and although there was a sense of anticipation in the air, there was nothing much planned for the evening.

People were meandering toward the communal house that stood in the center of the village square. As darkness fell, people outside the house were suddenly quiet, straining to hear what was going on inside. An old man had begun to sing a chant about a fishing expedition, and a few people joined in. Then someone asked another old man to tell a story, and he obliged with a traditional folktale. What followed was a round-robin, with every person present telling a tale or singing a chant. I had no tape recorder then, so I had to make do with scribbling inadequate translations as the tales were being performed. The session continued until early the next morning. Although my cramped hands and inadequate fluency rendered my notes rather useless for transcription purposes, those notes turned out to be valuable for understanding tale-telling contexts.

People there were disappointed that I had not tape-recorded the session, so I promised to find a machine and some tape and to record them the next night. For three nights I let the tape recorder run as people told stories and sang chants. I took that opportunity to ask people whether the round-robin was an annual event and was shocked to learn that it was not. One older man remembered a similar event during the Christmas holiday many years before but, like this one, it was spontaneous.

In my subsequent research, which continued off and on until 1990, I encountered the telling of traditional Kapinga tales only in the privacy of households and in one other public context—during the Christmas holidays in another resettled homestead community on Pohnpei—and occasionally in a homestead group on Oroluk, a tiny atoll that Kapinga people used for copra growing and turtle farming. Oroluk is an interesting, although rare, sort of case. This atoll, with a single islet no larger than a few acres but rich in its productive capacity, is 180 miles west and south of Pohnpei and was uninhabited until the 1940s. The Japanese colonial administration stationed a few people there to make copra, and in 1954 the U.S. administration on Pohnpei gave Kapinga settlers permission to use the atoll to grow copra and to farm turtles. Groups of a dozen or more people, mainly males, would spend six months on the atoll living on the supplies they brought and whatever they could grow and catch. Among the early homesteading crews were a mix of older and younger men who would entertain one another at night with personal anecdotes and stories. The older men taught stories and chants to the younger men, and the latter told stories they had heard from Pingelapese, Ngatikese, Mokilese, Chuukese, and other islanders who had been their classmates in school. Two of these younger men performed ancient ritual chants learned on Oroluk at the round-robin, a point to which I will return.

Public Tale Telling: The "Right" Version

In the household context, old people tell the old tales to entertain and pacify the children they are baby-sitting. Public tale telling is, according to Kapinga people with whom I talked, a rarity. But why?

What I have learned about public tale-telling contexts is that there are certain sorts of occasions when people might tell tales but no occasions when they are expected to tell them. Tale telling, in other words, is improbable relative to other sorts of possible interactions.

To explain why this should be the case is to confront local epistemology and the local theory of the text. Put simply, to memorize something is one thing and to know it is another. Anyone can memorize something, but using what one has memorized presupposes the right to use it. Until one acquires the right of use, one is not said to know the text. For example, in pre-Christian times, every boy was taught a set of chants used to appease spirits of the deep that might be encountered while fishing beyond the reef. These chants had to be memorized to be performed without error. Boys would never actually use the chants until they were eligible to take a canoe out to deep water (i.e., until they were in their 40s or older). Only then were they said to "know" the chants. Knowing something means making it one's own. The word "know" is a verb, and it is only used as a noun when it follows a personal pronoun. All knowledge, in other words, is personal knowledge, better glossed as "information." People are secretive about revealing personal information, and they will do so only when it is to their personal advantage to do so. Sharing personal knowledge invites gratuitous criticism from others, usually directed toward details that others consider incorrect. An example or two will make this clear.

When it was known in Porakied village that I was recording chants and stories on tape, several people in the village and others on the atoll of Kapingamarangi wanted to listen to the tapes. I obliged. This was a big mistake. It was equivalent to telling people what an informant had told me in confidence. Every rendition of every tale was greeted with derision by the listeners. Comments were on the order of "What a child, [she] doesn't know it!" (of a 65-year-old woman) and "Where did he learn that, in a tree?"

On another occasion I was recording a woman's version of a well-known Kapinga tale when her husband happened by. He listened for a few moments and then cut her off sharply with a few humiliating remarks. He then proceeded to tell me the "right" version of the tale. This sort of carping over details is typical of any display of knowledge by almost anyone, whether it is of fishing techniques, land histories, construction techniques, mat-making techniques, basketry, or something else. One has to suffer through an enormous amount of criticism on the way to becoming knowledgeable, much less expert, at anything.

Knowledgeable people, for this reason, are almost always older people whose persistence has won them the right to know. There is a difference, however, between knowledge of techniques and knowledge of formula-like chants, tales, directions to particular fishing spots, and land histories—that is, techniques and texts are different classes of knowledge. Techniques demand accuracy; texts demand precision. A mistake in a fishing technique can always be corrected on the next try, but on encountering a spirit on the water, one gets only one shot at chanting the formula of appeasement, and it has to be right or disaster will follow. The details of genealogy of a plot of land determine who has what land rights, so the *kai* (story) of the land is a text that carries high stakes.

Folktales are a category of texts learned within the family, as are certain ritual chants and directions to fishing spots. There is some evidence that folktale texts were considered family property, one child in a sibling set inheriting the right to tell them. This has two related implications for folktale texts and contexts. Because the household context is the one in which a raconteur has the least chance of being challenged, most people hear and learn folktales in this context. This being the case, there is a good deal of variation in tale renditions from one family to another, particularly in small details of the text (e.g., the names of specific places where events are said to occur, identities of minor characters, and some variation in the ordering of tale events). Given that children hear the renditions from their older relatives who have the right to tell them, children assume the authenticity of the text. People are largely unaware of the variability in text versions until they hear by chance that of another family, which they naturally assume must be incorrect. Why, then, would anyone venture to tell their version of a folktale in a public context in any event? How does one explain the round-robin, rare though it may be?

From precolonial times to the present, there have been special times—brief periods of an evening or a day—called *goaa heihei noo* (time of doing freely without restriction). In pre-Christian times these were days when it was certain that the temple spirits, who usually came to the atoll to sleep in the temple and left again in the early morning, would not return to the island that day. This was a day of revelry and rule breaking. For example, couples could marry without parental permission. Men could claim drift logs (for canoes) that were normally considered the property of the high priest. Men and women could eat together in a large feast, followed by a ritual orgy. After conversion to Christianity, New Year's Day became the day of revelry on which people could get away with public drunkenness, playing prac-

tical jokes (such as throwing water on one another), dancing in public, and general buffoonery. Behavior that is usually frowned on is tolerated on this day. Normal restrictions are relaxed, and the village is said to be "open" at this time. One can even get away with telling a traditional folktale in public.

Yet, even in the relaxed circumstance of an open village, it seems that some rules still hold. Garbled as my notes were on the Great Tale-Telling Orgy of 1965, they were quite clear on the point that the right to know remained undiluted in its hegemonic sway. Every one of the known traditional Kapinga tales told that night was recounted by people in their 50s and older. All of the tales told by people younger than that were without exception tales of non-Kapinga origin— tales from other islands (announced as such) and European folktales, such as the story of Dick Whittington's cat. The lone exception to this pattern was the instance of two young men who had been on Oroluk and were asked to perform ritual chants they had learned there. They refused these requests until the old man who had taught them the chants encouraged them to sing them.

The natural contexts within which folklorists are encouraged to collect tales are, in the Kapinga communities, contexts of the politics of interpersonal, intra- and interfamily, and village life. The stakes in these political contexts are, at a minimum, personal reputations, which are tokens of people's public careers. These political contexts are shaped in turn by an inchoate but omnipresent local epistemology. I conclude with some confidence that, outside the family circle, the public context of traditional tale telling is best described and understood as a minefield.

Further Reading

Emory, Kenneth Pike, *Kapingamarangi: Social and Religious Life of a Polynesian Atoll*, Honolulu, Hawaii: Bernice Bishop Museum, 1965

Lieber, Michael D., *More Than a Living: Fishing and the Social Order on a Polynesian Atoll*, Boulder, Colorado: Westview, 1994

Europe

The Albanian World in the Folk Teller's Stories

Ramadan Sokoli

Here Ramadan Sokoli discusses the many uses of folk literature in Albania.

A Varied Tradition

The Albanian folk tradition is rich in tales and legends. In this beautiful and tragic land, in a mountainous terrain close to the coasts of the Adriatic Sea in the southwestern Balkans, many kinds of impressive stories have flourished. In every region, storytellers have elaborated numerous subjects, motifs, and chimerical elements in their tales and legends. The inexhaustible mines of these ethnocultural traditions are found in the remote mountainous regions, where crystal-clear new fantasies emerged from the rocks, where until the twentieth century the sun, the "beauty of the sky," was worshipped, and where the local population swears "on the sunlight." Folk scholars who roam across those areas and meet highlanders who have lived in beautiful landscapes washed in sunlight and blue sky find themselves in the grip of overwhelming feelings.

In the varied universe of Albanian oral stories, where rational and irrational creatures perform, the tales, legends, myths, lays intermingle. They reflect the ability of the people to attach objects to well-chosen images and idealize through fantasy human deeds and natural phenomena. The characters include genuine human beings, deities, semideities, monsters, and supernatural beings in the shapes of men, animals, and plants. Those characters that reflect the grief and suffering, the dreams and everyday concerns, the joys and afflictions of the Albanian people are the favorites in this body of literature.

The courage of the heroes and their self-sacrifices emerge as central themes in these tales, in addition to their hope for a bright future and love of life. In the fight between obscurity and light, between virtues and vices, between the good and the bad, the heroes triumph in most cases.

The folktales describe observations from everyday life. Consequently, useful advice or teaching instructions are found there—present also are sarcastic remarks or ironical and satirical elements that are permeated by feelings of derision about different weaknesses that at times are presented in strange shapes like the distortions in concave and convex mirrors. Although most of the folk stories have originated from observations and experiences of real life, they are not devoid of combinations of the artifices of the elaborated fantasy. It is well-known that the fabulous elements related either to natural phenomena or to living creatures are one of the essential features of folk storytelling. Some of these creatures have been carried over from the ancient cults, the pagan beliefs of our forefathers. Many folk legends are related to the *murana,* the walls set up in areas where outstanding events have taken place. From this point of view, even the stones that have faced up to the storms of time have a great deal to relate, and in particular those rocks that resemble human or animal shapes and monsters. Admiration of them has stirred the people's fantasy. Worth mentioning is the rock block called the "frozen young ladies," and the "old lady" turned into stone by the March frosts.

Some legends circulate in specific regions and other legends are told all over the country. One such tale is the legend of the cuckoo's metamorphosis, in which a former young lady turns into a fowl.

Alongside folk stories about given objects and places, we have stories about renowned historical events that bring in the echo of past times. "Arber's Great Year" has left a deep impression in the Albanian people's recollection. Memories of this glorious period during which the Albanian people, through impressive resistance, faced up to the fifteenth-century invasion of Ottoman hordes are found in castles and caves as well as on rocks and springs of water. Particularly impressive are the legends about the "lake of flowers" in the Lura Highlands, where they say the Arbeereshi brave ladies drowned themselves rather than allow the Ottoman invaders to take them alive. You will hear impressive legends about the waters of the springs opened by Skanderbeg's sword, stories about rocks that this Albanian national hero has allegedly rolled over against the enemy armies. We also have the stories about the shape of the heel of Skanderbeg's horse, a shape that allegedly left its imprint in the rock when Skanderbeg rode from one side of the abyss onto the other. Skanderbeg has always been present in Albania; his figure has been highlighted in the amazing stories handed over from one generation of folk storytellers to the next. This presence is felt especially in the areas where the hero carried out more intensive activity: they say there where the wind blows, the outcry of Skanderbeg's call for attack on the enemies is heard. Strangely both those who tell these stories and those who listen to them believe these exaggerated stories. Accompanied by the tune of the lute and a two-stringed musical instrument these deeds gain in emotional force and have been handed over from one generation to the next while being enriched in new details.

Despite the wonderful elements depicting impossible deeds that go beyond people's physical possibilities, in essence these folk stories carry an idealized truth that could be viewed as the vital crystallization of the freedom-loving spirit and as the triumph of immortal glory over material death.

In the Albanian people's spiritual heritage you can see pearls that shine marvelously. Alongside the simple ones that are developed in small proportions and have few vital elements (and that is why they have been left in the shade), others carry images of scenes that take place in breathtaking heights and depths. One of them, for example, is the legend of fratricide of the two giants that turned into two mountains: Tomorr and Shpirag, in southern Albania. Some legends are chanted in verses. So, for example, the tale of the "snake bridegroom" or the "legend of muration" of a human being entombed in the foundations of a building is not only related as a story but is also sung to the tune of the players of the two-stringed musical instrument in northern Albania and in Kosova, in the same way that the epic-lyrical ballads were sung.

The Rozafa legend, the legend of muration, is one of the most impressive legends that has come down to our days. This legend, which sings of the history of the building of the Shkodre Castle, underlines the idea of the sacrifice of the wife (the wife of the youngest brother of the three brothers who were building the castle), who agrees to be murated in the castle walls so that they could stand. The three brothers built the walls during the day and during the night they were razed to the ground. This went on for quite a long time. Her behest was to leave one of her eyes outside the wall so that she could see her baby, to leave one of her arms outside of the wall so that she could lull the baby to sleep, and to leave one of her breasts outside of the wall so that she could feed the baby. The spring of water, found at the place where one of the breasts of the young mother was left outside of the wall, has been a source of inspiration for foreign and local writers who have picked up this legend in their works: novels, stories, and plays.

We have also "Kostandin and Doruntina" (southern Albanian), one of the marvelous Albanian ballads. It tells of the rising of the youngest brother from the grave in order not to renege on his word given to his mother that he would make sure that his married sister in a faraway place would pay a visit to her family. This has not only been handed over from one generation of folk storytellers to the next, but has also been embodied in one of the well-known novels by the great Ismail Kadare. This has been the motif on which many stories and plays have been based.

Under the conditions of the five-century-long Ottoman invasion, Albania was declared a cursed country in which Albanians were not entitled to build houses of more than two stories. Education in the Albanian language was forbidden. It is understood what a great role the folk storytellers have played in preserving the heritage of the ethnocultural values. More often than not their meaning and message was in a straightforward language that everyone understood and that captured the children's minds and imagination.

Bearers of folk tradition and folk storytellers and their attitudes deserve special attention. Every bearer of folk tradition carries in him something general and at the same time something personal that distinguishes him both in terms of the way he relates his story and the means he uses to tell it.

Shadow Play

Folk storytellers, including the grandfathers and grandmothers, were the ones who enlivened the family milieus. The most favorable occasions were offered by the cold season when the people, especially the peasants, got around the fireplace during the winter nights. The light of fire projected all kinds of shadows with which the storytellers played in order to entertain those present, the children in particular. By producing different images against the light of the fire they projected silhouettes of two dimensions that moved on the wall surface. So, in that scene without a setting and without perspective appeared the "greyhound and rabbit," the "cat and mouse," the "stork and frog," the "fox and drake," the "wolf and lamb," and other grotesque figures accompanied by onomatopoeic imitations, with different words and explanations that the children admired with immense pleasure. Their very fantasy completed the simplicity that the means of expression limited so very much.

Puppet Shows

Puppet shows take up a conspicuous place. The types of folk puppets differ more or less according to the regions and social strata. The quality of the material used to make puppets (wood, clay, metal, tanned hide, and cloth) also influenced their types. The stick puppets are the most simple ones. The symbiosis "puppet-man" constitutes a category in itself. Another example is "the old lady twisting bobbin." This is a genuine twisting bobbin that during the play represents a given character, usually the "bride" or the "bridegroom." Both of these characters are played by the same person, often a woman, who uses the movements and positions of the twisting bobbin accompanied by conversations, questions, and answers, in which case the voice is changed accordingly. Another figure is the one called "the bride with the husband on the back." Both characters of this subject are played by the same person: the performer is dressed in man's clothes in the upper part of the body, and in lady's clothes in the lower part. A big puppet lopped in the middle is attached at the performer's belt, for example, some sort of mannekin resembling a womanly bust. The puppet is firmly tied to the performer's sides in a perpendicular position with his body. Dressed in slacks filled up with straw, hanging down like a riders' legs, the puppet gives the impression of a bent woman carrying her husband on her back. The storytellers' movements or conversations in the course of this show present both the man and the woman during the unfolding of the story.

Before the 1930s, one of the most attractive entertainments in wedding parties in Shkodra, a city in northern Albania, was this: a "master" was lying flat on his back on the floor; he covered himself from head to toe with a sheet leaving out only his hands that carried the puppets, which he moved to the rhythm of a piece of music played by the musicians present. The movements and actions of the puppets were accompanied with the words that the performer (storyteller) pronounced, with the words spoken in different voices—husky, nasal, or guttural.

Until several decades ago, in the mountainous regions of Lura, northeastern Albania, the wedding parties or other celebrations were accompanied by puppet shows that had a different setting. Once the musical instruments started to play, a person covered from head to toe in a carpet entered the areas where there were people gathering, walking to the musical rhythm. When he reached the center of the gathering he stood up and held his hands out. In his hands he carried puppets that he moved over his head according to the actions of the different characters. In these shows fantastic subjects (usually satirical) were described with great humor. Their humorous effect was produced by the funny abrupt expression and the intonation of the voice, the improvised twaddles of intricate words or distortions in the pronunciations, and meaningless chattering. The jokes used in these shows were called by the people "humorous play." In this well-chosen description lies their essence. Generally speaking, the audience in these shows were not passive onlookers, but they frequently broke in, cooperating with the action as the play unfolded. This involvement of the audience in the traditional shows is characteristic of and essential to Albanian folk creativity.

The Albanian ethnocultural tradition has many subjects and motifs in common with the traditions of other peoples. The geographical position of our country close to Mediterranean civilization, at the crossroads between the East and the West, has enabled such a phenomenon: through the centuries Albania was overrun by different peoples from all over the world who have left visible traces. On the other hand each invading culture has obtained something from here.

Balkan people have developed mutual relationships with their neighbors as they have shared historical experiences, which is but natural of good neighborliness. Unfortunately, however, this neighborliness has not always been peaceful. On the contrary! However, motifs and elements in common, for example, with Aesop's tales were depicted long ago in Albanian folklore. Until the turn of the twentieth century the legend of the "loyal wife," a motif of the Homeric Penelope, and the legend of "the young man married to his mother," a motif of Edip, were told in the highlands of northern Albania. I would like to point out that at that time, when the Albanian high-landers had no formal education, this phenomenon was not a reflection of something that they might have read in books.

Several motifs of legends are widespread both in Albanian folklore and in the traditions of the neighboring peoples. With regard to the ballad of muration, for example, different opinions exist, which I do not think are fit to be handled in this piece of writing.

Folk creativity has justly been called our national heritage. In the past this heritage made up for the lack of schools. During the many-centuries-long yoke it molded generations of people with the experience and wisdom of their forefathers and protected them against the assimilation process. By way of ethnocultural traditions it is possible to penetrate deep into the worldview of the Albanian people and to clarify several vague issues of the history of the Albanian society and nation.

Our times are bringing about vigorous changes in the country's life, enveloping in its whirlwind the ethnocultural field as well. With each passing day many values of the Albanian national heritage are being damaged or lost. Concerned scholars are faced with the task of taking greater care to study and guard this valuable heritage against extinction.

Translated by Pranvera Xhelo

Basque Storytelling and the Living Oral Tradition

Linda White

White comments on the origins of Basque written literature, defines six forms of Basque oral literature, and discusses three living forms: pastorales (theaters with dancing or singing), bertsolaritza *(the art of improvising verses to music), and storytelling. White also discusses specific Basque supernatural characters such as the* sorgina, jentilak, basajauna, lamina, *and* Mari.

The Basque Language, Euskara

Storytelling within Basque culture is one aspect of an ancient oral tradition that survives and flourishes today in the Basque country. Euskal Herria, as the region is called in the Basque language (Euskara), occupies a small area in the north of Spain and south of France, in the Pyrenees. The Basque people (*euskaldunak*) speak a non–Indo-European language but live in a diglossic situation. That is, Basque and the majority languages, Spanish and French, coexist in the same territory. This has been the case in the Basque country for centuries. It is estimated that from 20 to 25 percent of the population speaks Euskara today.

Until the twentieth century the Basque language had no standardized system of spelling. In addition, there are several dialects of Basque, and until the creation of Unified Basque (or Euskara Batua) in the mid-1900s, Basques from the different provinces (Araba, Bizkaia, Gipuzkoa, and Nafarroa in Spain; Behe-Nafarroa, Lapurdi, and Zuberoa in France) had trouble understanding each others' spoken and written words.

Basque culture has traditionally been an oral one. Written literature came late to the Basque country. Since other languages were used for all official purposes, and because so few people would read anything written in Basque, those with something to say tended to say it in Spanish or French. The first book written in Basque, in 1545, was Bernat Dechepare's *Linguae Vasconum Primitiae* (note the Latin title). Dechepare was a priest, and his motivations for writing in Basque were religious ones. The Council of Trent (1545–63) generated a flurry of writings on religious topics throughout the Basque country, but the vast majority were written on the French side of the border in the dialects of those provinces. Not until the eighteenth century did the tide turn; then more Basque books were written in the south than in the north. Religious themes and religious writers predominated for the first 300 years of written Basque literature. Only in the last 150 years has the laity become the majority of those who write in Basque.

Six Genres of Basque Oral Literature

Storytelling is part of the Basque oral tradition. Although written literature came relatively late to Euskal Herria, oral literature was alive and well, and very popular with the people. We can identify various genres of oral literature:

1. epic poems inspired by early historical events. When we apply the term "epic poem" to an early Basque composition, we are assuming a

great deal. Since no poem in its entirety has come down to us, we are assuming that some works were long enough to be considered epic poems, even though we do not have the whole poem;

2. *eresiak,* elegies for the living and the dead, songs of praise or mourning invented to commemorate the passing of a loved one or other important personage;
3. *Kopla zaharrak,* or "old couplets," snatches of ancient verses of four lines each;
4. pastorales, a form of theater with dancing, music, and singing;
5. *bertsolaritza,* or the art of the Basque troubadour, the art of improvising verses to music and singing them extemporaneously;
6. storytelling, the traditional means of passing fables, legends, and stories from generation to generation.

The first three genres on the list are no longer created. We know they existed because certain individuals wrote down remembered fragments of them to save them for posterity. One such individual was Esteban de Garibay (1533–99), royal historian, or *Cronista de Su Majestad,* to the king of Spain.

The last three—storytelling, pastorales, and *bertsolaritza*—are still active art forms. Although storytelling was considered a dying art during the first half of the twentieth century, it is experiencing a revival today.

Basque Storytelling

If the *bertsolari's* (Basque troubadour's) goal is to create something new, the Basque storyteller's goal is to pass on the traditions and legends of his or her people. The traditional storyteller in the Basque country does not embellish or alter the content of the stories, if it can be helped. Only the performance of them varies, owing to differences in voice, location, atmosphere, and audience.

Basque culture is full of old tales, as all cultures are, but most of the Basque tales have not yet been repackaged à la Disney into a single homogenized version. José Miguel de Barandiarán (1889–1991) spent much of his 102 years collecting the old stories by visiting those who told them and recording their oral product as carefully as he could. The results of his painstaking labors are collected in volume after volume, and selections of the stories and legends are available in English as well in Barandiarán Irizar's *A View from the Witch's Cave.* He wrote about the mythology, archaeology, anthropology, culture, and history of the Basque people. He also produced a book on Basque witchcraft.

In a culture that has traditionally been an oral one, the art of storytelling itself appears to be taken for granted. Barandiarán mentions little or nothing about the techniques of telling stories. He focuses for the most part on the content of the stories, legends, and fables that he recorded, and he uses the word "story" to include both the content and the telling. He says, "Story is all popular narration in which characters, setting and time are indeterminate" (*Obras Completas,* p. 239). These stories begin with special formulas, such as *"Munduan asko bezela"* (Like many in the world) and *"Antxiñen munduen asko lez"* (Like many in the world in the old days). They also often end with special formulas, such as

Oi ala bazan,
sartu deilla kalabazan,
d'ata deilla
Bitoriko plazan.
(If this was the way it happened,
jump into a pumpkin
and jump out
in the plaza of Vitoria.)
(Barandiarán Irizar, *View,* p. 28)

and

Egia bada, sakelan zar; gezurra bada, atera ez deilla.
(If it's true, put it in your pocket; if it's false, don't let it out.)
(Barandiarán, *Obras,* p. 240)

Barandiarán makes a distinction between stories and legends. In legends, the characters and settings are specified, often with local landmarks and individuals' names.

In previous centuries, grandmothers would tell stories to entertain their grandchildren, but adults would also attend the telling, especially in the days before radio and television. In the Basque country, although print media was available, it was inevitably in Spanish or French, so those who spoke nothing but Basque were even more limited with regard to the printed word.

Women would also tell stories to keep themselves awake and alert while spinning, a task they often performed in groups, and this custom helped preserve many of the old legends until the twentieth century, when Barandiarán began writing them down.

Although writing down the stories as people told them preserves the content of the stories and legends, when we read them we lose the rest of the storytelling experience: the teller's voice and mannerisms, the responses of fellow listeners, and the joy of hearing the key phrases repeated over and over again.

Today, there is a resurgence of storytelling in the Basque country. Although it is not yet as healthy an oral art as *bertsolaritza*, interest is growing, due to the abiding public fascination with all activities that promote the Basque language.

Basque Characters in the Old Stories

One universal character that appears in many Basque stories is the *sorgina*, or witch. Many people, however, do not realize that the modern American image of the witch owes a great deal to the Basque witch of legend. Even today, one can visit the caves of Zugarramurdi, where witches were known to have held their covens, or *akelarreak*. Those witches, of course, were undoubtedly the remnants of the pre-Christian religion of the area. Thirty-one witches were brought before the Spanish Inquisition's auto-da-fé at Logroño, Spain, in 1610, and 25 of those were from the villages of Zugarramurdi and nearby Urdax (Henningsen, p. 27). Witches were common characters throughout the Basque country, and they have survived in stories down through the centuries. Basque women view witches somewhat differently than does traditional Christian legend, and more than one female friend has confided in me that the women of her family still believe in the powers of the witch. As they say in Basque, "One should not believe that they exist, but one should not say that they do not exist."

"The Witches of Xuritegui" is an example of a witch story told by Dominica Giltzu of Zugarramurdi in 1941:

According to the story, when she was a little girl María de Larraburu had in her house a servant from Lesaca. This was nearly 70 years ago.

One day the servant decided to go to Lesaca to visit her family. Since there was no clock in the house, she got the hours mixed up and set off on her journey at night, thinking that it was almost dawn. But before she reached Xuritegi'ko Borda [a farm in Sara], she spied a group of witches dancing to the music of the *txistu* [flute] and drum.

The witches shouted an invitation, "Come dance with us!"

But the servant was very frightened, and instead of joining them she ran away from there as fast as she could. (Barandiarán Irizar, *View*, p. 125)

Many of the most popular stories told in the Basque country are the old folktales which contain characters who, like the witch, are part of the mythos of the Basque country. Julio Caro Baroja identifies four different historical phases for the construction of these tales: the prehistoric, the matriarchal/agricultural, the pastoral, and the pre-Christian (p. 7). The latter era had tremendous influence on the tales and characters as they appear today. Certain characters appear over and over, such as *jentilak, basajaunak, laminak,* and most famous of all, Mari (Anbotoko Anderea).

Jentilak are big men with amazing strength. (The singular of *jentilak* is *jentila.*) Their voices are like a lion's roar or a peal of thunder. Animals run from them in fear, and the ground shakes when they walk.

The *basajauna* looks manlike, but he is much bigger and taller than any man. He also has incredible strength and energy. The *basajauna*'s body is covered with hair, and long hair falls in front to his knees, covering his face, chest, and belly. *Basajaunak* live in the woods, and they work the land for a living. Legend says they taught man how to cultivate grain. The *basajauna* was the first blacksmith (ironworker) and the first miller. *Basajaunak* are the spirit protectors of sheep, and they shout in the mountains when a storm is approaching so the shepherds will take in their flocks. It is said that when the sheep shake their bells, *basajauna* is nearby.

A *lamina* was a spirit that appeared with the body of a woman and often the feet of a duck or a chicken, or even a goat in some locations. Even their name varies from site to site, *lami, lamin,* and *lamiña* being the most widespread. *Laminak* are usually female spirits, but in Lapurdi and Behe-Nafarroa both genders occur. Some say their skin is copper in color, and others say they live underground. Among other tasks attributed to them, they spin with a distaff, they build dolmens and bridges, and they wash clothes in the night. A *lamina* is often sighted with a gold comb.

An old story about a *lamina* in love:

A young man from the Korrione house near Mondragón saw a *lamina* at the mouth of the cave called Kobaundi. He fell in love with her, and they agreed to marry, on the condition that the young man could guess her age. He went home and told his problem to a friendly neighbor, who then went to the cave, where she stood with her back to the entrance, bent over, and peered at the cave between her own legs. The *lamina* came out, saw the woman, and cried, "I've never seen such a thing in all my 105 years!" And so the young man discovered the age of his fiancée. But next he observed that she had the feet of a duck and realized she wasn't human, so they could not marry. He died of a broken heart, and the *lamina* followed the funeral procession all the way to the church of Garagarza. (Barandiarán Irizar, *View*, p.107)

Mari is the leader or the queen of all the other spirits. She is female, and she has many names, often associated with where she has been sighted. Some of her names are Anbotoko Anderea (the Lady of Anboto), Marije Kobako (Mari of the Cave), and Aralarko Damea (the Lady of Aralar) (Barandiarán, *Obras*, pp. 157–158). Mari can appear in various guises, but they are all female. Some of her forms include a lady seated on a cart crossing the sky, pulled by four horses (in Amezqueta); the figure of a woman giving off flames (in Zaldivia) and seen crossing the sky in a horizontal position (in Bedoña); a lady mounted on a ram (in Oñate and Cegama); and a woman whose head is encircled by the full moon (in Azcoitia).

She can also appear as a horse, a female calf, a tree trunk shaped like a woman, a gust of wind, a white cloud, a rainbow, and a ball of fire. Regardless of what form she takes, however, everyone agrees she is female.

Mari dwells inside the earth, and she makes appearances at cavern mouths or in deep ravines (Barandiarán, *Obras*, p. 160). Some say she changes dwellings, spending seven years at a time in different caves (such as Anboto, Oiz, Mugarra, Aralar, Aizkorri, and Murumendi).

There are other characters who populate Basque stories, but these are the most famous and the most frequent.

Pastorales

The pastorales are a form of theater, but they are traditionally included in oral literature in Basque culture because the verses (sung by the actors to a background of music and dance) were passed down from performance to performance in an oral fashion. Villages in the province of Zuberoa took turns presenting the pastorale every year, and as a result, each village would put on a pastorale about once a generation (or every 30 years).

Today, the pastorale is still a community-wide event, but instead of moving from village to village, people from several villages get together to present the pastorales. They are performed in the summer months in order to attract the tourist trade. New pastorales are being created by artists such as Pedro Bordazaharre (known as "Etxahun Iruri") and Junes Casenave.

Bertsolaritza

The *bertsolari*, or Basque troubadour, is another aspect of Basque oral literature that is alive and well. While storytelling in the home declined as a means of cultural transmission and entertainment, the *bertsolaris* were going strong, performing in taverns, at weddings, and during public festivals. Today the *bertsolaris* are organized, and they compete regularly in elimination rounds for the title or *txapelketa* that is awarded every year.

A *bertsolari* creates extemporaneous verses (within about three seconds of being assigned a topic) and then sings them (to an assigned melody) before an audience. The Basques call *bertsolaritza* a "word sport," and it is a very popular art form. The goals of the *bertsolari* are to create new and fleeting verses about subjects of interest to an audience, to be the voice of the people, to express feelings and points of view on their behalf that ordinary citizens may not feel capable of stating as well as they would wish.

For more on the *bertsolari*, see Aulestia, *Improvisational Poetry from the Basque Country*.

Further Reading

Aulestia, Gorka, *Improvisational Poetry from the Basque Country*, Reno, Nevada, and London: University of Nevada Press, 1993

Barandiarán, José Miguel de, *Obras Completas*, Bilbao, Spain: La Gran Enciclopedia Vasca, 1972

Barandiarán Irizar, Luis de, ed., *A View from the Witch's Cave: Folktales of the Pyrenees*, Reno: University of Nevada Press, 1991

Barbier, Jean, *Légendes du pays Basque, d'après la tradition*, Paris: Delgrave, 1931

Cantón, B. Beatriz, María Nieves Díaz, and María Cristina de Pablo, *Euskal Herriko Bertsolariak*, Donostia, Spain: Kriselu, 1992

Caro Baroja, Julio, *Mitos vascos y mitos sobre los vascos*, San Sebastián, Spain: Txertoa, 1985

Henningsen, Gustav, *The Witches' Advocate: Basque Witchcraft and the Spanish Inquisition, 1609–1614*, Reno: University of Nevada Press, 1980

Present-Day Storytelling in Northeastern Bulgaria*

Yordanka Kotseva

Yordanka Kotseva notes several Aarne-Thompson tale types common in Bulgarian folk narrative, examines features of the story text, and discusses the function of storytelling in the life of the community.

The Study of Bulgarian Folk Narrative

It is common knowledge that on a local scale, Bulgarian folk narrative has been documented, published, and studied insufficiently and unevenly. Some parts of Bulgaria are particularly poorly studied. Among them is northeastern Bulgaria, which has to date remained almost terra incognita for the researcher of the folk narrative.[1]

Discharging a long-overdue duty of Bulgarian folklorists, a qualified team of the Institute for Folklore with the Bulgarian Academy of Sciences began systematic work in 1987 toward the recording and study of folk narratives in northeastern Bulgaria. The observations and conclusions included in this presentation are the initial summary of the material collected in the region of Razgrad in the period 1987–90. Attention has been focused mainly on revealing the contents and volume of the folk narrative. Also considered are matters related to characteristics of the folk narrative under present conditions and to the change of its functions, nature, and place in the culture of today (Kotseva, "Folklornata prikazka"; Kotseva, "Glassovete vi chouvam").

Genre Composition and Subject Matter

The folktales told in the region of Razgrad include the basic genres of Bulgarian folk narrative: tales about animals, fairy tales, legends, and novella-like tales. The core of the local comic narrative is made up of what are called stories of everyday life, a variety of story writing and jokes (classified separately as an independent narrative genre).

The tales and parables about animals (also plants, objects, and so on) belong, owing to their functional characteristics, to the category of tales for children. They are comparatively well represented in the local narrative tradition. Among the tales about wild beasts, particularly popular is the one about the fox. This tale actually mixes together several plots: the fox stealing fish; the wolf fishing with his tail; the fox, having covered his head with bread dough, lying that his brains were spilling; the wolf helping the "sick" fox (the sick one carrying the healthy one); and the fox killing the wolf by weaving a closed basket with the wolf in it and then kicking the basket into the river or gully. This last plot is characteristic of the narrative tradition in the village of Dryanovets

*This article was first published in *Regionalni Prouchvanija na Bulgarskija Folklor: T.3. Folklornite Traditsii na Severoiztochna Bulgaria,* Sofia, Bulgaria: 1993, pp. 6–21. (Regional Studies of Bulgarian Folklore, vol. 3, The Folk Traditions in Northeastern Bulgaria, Sofia, Bulgaria: 1993).

and the town of Senovo and has not been recorded anywhere else in Bulgaria. The theme of retribution and settling of accounts with the fox features in other narratives. He is outwitted by the hedgehog, who counters the fox's numerous tricks by his own three tried and tested tricks (AT 106). The fox is also outwitted by man; the fox appears in one and the same tale as a helper of humans and as the victim of their ingratitude. Interesting in this respect is the variant of the tale "Priest, Bear and Fox" that comes from the town of Senovo. This variant, by its numerous details linked in a streamlined story, completes the general Bulgarian picture of the AT 154 international type of story. The tale about the wolf and the children (AT 123) in the narrative repertoire of the Kapantsi ethnic group has also been recorded in an original anthropomorphic variant— a little girl bearing the onomatopoeic name Djungur Savka (Hullabaloo Savka) or Koundovelka (a distaff full of wool) appears in the role of the children and is swallowed by the wolf (or, alternatively, a bear). In this case, too, the character of the bear is associated with other plots, including the plots of the bad word (AT 159B), the granny and her granddaughters Yakoushka, Mekoushka, and Tvurdoushka (Toughy, Softy, and Hardy), and the troubles that a sly hare causes to the bear (AT 36). A favorite tale for children in the villages near Razgrad is the one about the damned little he-goat and the tiny pestering thing that drove the child out of the fox's house (AT 212). An original tale not recorded anywhere else in Bulgaria is the one about the little house made of straw (or reeds), common in the village of Tserovets and in Senovo, in which the idea of the loyalty of animals to humans and of human criminal cruelty to them is convincingly implied in a chain of episodes built after the same pattern.

The animal tales that are a constant component of the narrative repertoire of adults (especially of women, where their vitality is considerably more outspoken) most often have the ring of guileless, entertaining stories of the adventures of animals and people. They suggest delicately, without obtrusion, some basic maxims of life and serve successfully in a mother's daily work in educating her children. The elements, fairy and archaic in origin, are often hidden under the coating of realistic details and motivations of everyday life. In terms of composition, the tales of animals share the basic qualities of the genre: they are often built upon a single episode or upon several independent episodes united around a common personage, according to the principle of cumulation. Examples are the original local tales about the little house of straw (or reeds) and about the little girl with the little bell in the town of Senovo (cf. EB 24).

Characterized by outspoken emotionality, the local tales about animals are specific in terms of intonation as well. A woman telling the stories evinces tenderness and love for children, which seem to pour forth from her every word (not only as a result of the high frequency of diminutive forms and appellations), from every look and gesture. Of great importance in the creation of entertainment value in the stories are word coinage, expressive language (including even swear words), and rhythmic phrases, particularly emphasized in some types of plots or individual variants. Verse-like additions are important as well (they are constant, for instance, in the tales about the he-goat), and that rhythmic organization in the story brings it close to the pastime rhymes of children. These linguistic characteristics are also discernible in some of the favorite fairy tales in the region of Razgrad, which have turned into folkloric classics for children for the local people; for instance, the tale about the little cockerel (AT 715, 715A) has become one such classic. It was not an accident that I heard the beginning of that tale in a spontaneous female performance, almost a chorus, during my first visit in 1990 to the village of Krivnya. It went: "Once upon a time there was one little cockerel, with one little leg, with one little wing, with one little eye, with half a little beak, with half a little tail. . . ."

There is no doubt, however, that the most representative part of the local folk narrative repertoire is that composed of the fairy tales. (Incidentally, in the hierarchy of values the point of view is also of importance.) We managed to record quite a few international and original types of plots. In fact, some of the most popular types of plots in the Bulgarian repertoire of fairy tales are represented by the greatest number of variants, such as those of the valiant man and the three girls from the netherworld (AT 301, 300), the twin brothers (AT 303), the king's daughter and her worn-out slippers (AT 306), the brother stag (AT 450), the golden girl (AT 480), and Cinderella (AT 501A). The main groups of plots of fairy tales (Meletinsky, p. 162) are present to this day in the local tradition, documented in other parts of Bulgaria in records of the nineteenth and twentieth centuries.

Following are the heroic tales of the type of dragon fighting (AT 300–303): the three brothers and the dragon that stole the golden apple; the orphan, a sworn brother of Avdji Mahmoud and Dal Akran (AT 301B); the scars of the kidnapper of the meat-eating bear (according to the variants of this type recorded mainly in western Bulgaria, the antagonist is a dragon); Bakla (Broad Beans) Wrestler and his wonderful sworn brothers who rescued his sister, abducted by a dragon; and the adventures of the two brothers and their helper animals. The archaic tales of adventures of children or teenagers in the forest have been presented in several plots: the three sisters who, in pursuit of an unwinding roll of wool, happen to find themselves in the cave of a bridegroom he-bear—a variant of the Bluebeard tale from the village of Dryanovets; the cannibal who murders his own children instead of the brothers of Tom Thumb (AT 327B); and the children abandoned by their parents in the forest or pursued by their cannibal parents (usually elaborated as an introduction to the tale of the little brother stag, AT 450). From among the thematic range of the stepdaughter and her stepmother, the most popular in the villages of the Razgrad region has turned out to be the tale about the golden girl (in two basic variants: with a horizontal and a vertical organization of space in the fairy tale). A specific variant of AT 480 has also been recorded in the village of Krivnya and in the town of Senovo in which an orphan who has happened to enter the house of a bear receives from the she-bear a pot full of gold coins for teaching her how to spin (cf. AT 1199A). At the same time, the tale of the stepdaughter in the mill, recorded in almost every population center in the Blagoevgrad region, for instance, is almost nonexistent in the Razgrad region. There is an enduring tradition of the tale about Mara Cinderella, told along with the introduction about the metamorphosis of the mother into a cow, which is typical for the tales of the Balkan peoples. The group of tales about premarital trials is comparatively poor, at least in our documentation so far. Noteworthy here is the tale about the Little Brat with his wonderful horses (AT 530), elaborated into a fairy novella by the skillful storyteller Atanassov (in the village of Kamenovo). The presence of the tale about the trials of the bridegrooms-to-be has also been

noted (AT 621); this tale shares the basic specificity of the Bulgarian model of this type, incorporating an episode about the birthmarks of the king's daughter in the novella-like tale (AT 850). So far, the stories about magic objects have been relatively poorly recorded. Noteworthy here, however, is the magnificently told variant of the story of the magic ring (AT 560) told by 10-year-old Nikolai G. Nenov, a fourth-grade pupil in the village of Svalenik, who had learned it from his grandfather along with other narrative pieces. Very few tales have been recorded about wonderful marital partners (AT 400, 425, and others). Standing out among them most prominently is the tale of the wood-nymph bride from the village of Koushkoundalevo. The endurance of this plot is also determined by the impact of literary pieces. (This also holds true about other plots of tales mentioned here, not only on a local but a national scale.)

During fieldwork we have also come across some plots that are less common in the repertoire of Bulgarian folktales: the vampire fiancée (AT 366); the Little Hunchback (a tale about two hunchbacks and the devils [AT 503] is told in the village of Ossenets); Draganka,[2] the little girl who got drowned into a pot of beans (AT 700B); the wonderful tree that grew out of a snake's bone; the stepson murdered by his stepmother and cooked into dried meat, later turning into a magic bird (AT 720),[3] and others.

The main characters in fairy tales in the Razgrad region are heroes with supernatural abilities, popular in the Bulgarian folktale tradition. Such heroes include those born by supernatural conception, like the valiant Baka Wrestler; Salty and Peppery, or Little Sultana and Peppery; a local Razgrad incarnation of the literary Tom Thumb or of Nahoudcheto (the Little Chick Pea) from the Macedonian tales; the son of the bear; the little boys with golden forelocks; the painted girl (cf. AT 898, EB 91); the beauty Gyul Yordana; and others.

Standing out amid the considerably larger group of characters who obtain magical power as a result of a preliminary trial to which they are subjected (tests of knowledge or skill, possession of extraordinary beauty or magnificent wedding presents) are the characters of the golden girl, of Ah, the disciple of the devil, and of the poor young man or maiden who learns the art of metamorphosis or the language of animals. The stories of these possessors of magical powers have already been recorded in other parts of Bulgaria. The beloved heroes of the fairy tales in the Razgrad region are the youngest brother or sister as well as the stepdaughter or stepson, the traditional performers of the part of a hero in the Bulgarian folktales.

Apart from the subject matter, the main characters, and the basic features of the composition, there are some distinctive stylistic characteristics preserved in the fairy tales recorded here. The introductory formula, marking the undefined fairy tale dating ("Once upon a time" and the like) are extended in a number of cases by reassurances as to the authenticity of the text (such as "This tale is an old one, dating back for years; my grandmother used to tell it, as did my mother and my grandfather"). In some cases these introductions are elaborated into whole episodes (conforming to the communicative situation, in which the folklorist is making a recording), which are interesting in view of the functional characteristics of the tale in retrospect. Here is an example of how Grandmother Ginka, from the village of Kamenovo, began the tale about the bride of the cloth-beam: "Once upon a time there was a woman; she was on her own, with a little boy of hers; and once upon a time there were no such things, none of them, there were only tales, and children used to listen to tales. So she had a little boy. . . ."

Worth mentioning also is the striving of some informants to show that they control the rituals of storytelling by using final formulas. These are variants of a few basic models. The final formulas most commonly encountered are typical of the Bulgarian fairy-tale style; the specific intonation and accompanying mimicry and gestures illustrate the return to the real world and the separation from the fairy world of the tale. Examples include the following: "and this is the end of the story"; "a clover and the story's over"; "and the story is already over"; "and the story was old and cold" (typical of the villages of Tserovets and Svalenik; it is also used by the Turkish population); and "Grandmother went to bring a drop and the story came to a stop." Extended final formulas are also used, although more rarely; these consist of elaborations upon the shorter ones, or they may incorporate new characters. Examples of such elaborations include the following: "And the story was old and cold. The sentinel brings clover and the story is over"; "There was a big wedding, they feasted and

drank, and the drums beating at his wedding could be heard even here. And if there is still anyone alive from his family, may they live on." Parallel final formulas also occur with the penetration of the mediation formulas, which introduce the character of the storyteller to the narration: "And I am telling you here her [or their] story [or stories]." In some cases the specification is still more convincing because the name of the narrator is also included: "Granny Yana tells them the story here." The formulas revealing prosperity and eternal life (that is, life to the present time) of the fairy-tale heroes also give rise to a lively response. This is how the story of Djangur (Hullabaloo) Savka ends (whereby the genetic proximity between type AT 123 and AT 333 is emphasized on the level of fairy-tale rituals): "And Savka came out again in one piece [from the belly of the wolf] as she had been—hale and hearty. And folks adorned her with knickknacks and necklaces, and they are living to this day." Upon the utterance of these words Elenka Angelova Mateeva, born in 1909, who attended the recording in silence, spontaneously added: "I've just met 'em,"[7] a response that was welcomed with laughter by the entire working bee (a gathering of neighborhood women who meet in the afternoon to do handiwork and talk).

The smallest number of recordings to date is that of the legendary tales. This fact is not surprising, considering the deliberate or unconscious pushing of legendary plots to the periphery of intellectual interest for years on end. Some of the most characteristic tales of this type have been recorded with their basic elements well preserved: "the three brothers and the lord" (AT 750D), sacrificing one's own child (cf. also AT 750), the ages of man and of the animals (AT 828), the greatest sinner (AT 822), and Saint Peter's sinful mother (AT 804). This type of folktale, relatively rare in Bulgaria, has been recorded in Senovo, in a laconic variant, almost without any details whatever; standing in place of the saint's mother, the heroine in this version is a common, tightfisted woman. Of interest to the researcher, however, is also the communicative tie-in of that text, which was told in direct association with a memory of the informant's relative. This relative had had a fit, and his experiences in the netherworld were being described, suggesting the idea of real, essential matters and actions deduced in a concise form in the widespread belief running like this: "It is only what you give out as a present here, in this world, that you have there in the netherworld!" Or, as Radka Todorova put it, "Whatever you happen to hand out yourself, in the netherworld will all be in front of you: were it a dish, a spoon, or even a piece of thread. When you die they would drop that same piece of thread to lead you out of hell with. . . ." The story itself continues after a short pause: "And one woman failed to give out anything. She was very tightfisted, very tightfisted was she, and never did she give out anything to anyone. . . ."[8]

Legendary tales, recorded in the region of Razgrad as well as in the other parts of Bulgaria, confirm that the actions described in the tales take place here on earth, even within the boundaries of a specific town or village. The elements of local toponymy are combined in the classical legendary tales with some mythical chronology (e.g., "When the Lord used to walk the earth. . ."), which has definite ethnic projections. It turns out, however, that it is precisely that type of chronology that is wavering owing to various reasons in the local tales. Upon my request to hear tales associated with the time when the Lord used to walk the earth, I was corrected by my informants in the following manner. Peter Stanev of the village of Tserovets, a colorful storyteller with an extensive repertoire of fairy and adventure tales, pointed out, "I am a churchgoer, myself, but I know of no stories about the Lord. There are parables. . . ."[9] But despite my insistence he told me not a single one. The above-quoted Radka Todorova, upon ending the tale about the woman with the sprig of onion, spontaneously continued to tell me the one about the Lord, the plowman, and the Weaver, quite naturally using the typical initial formula "Once upon a time, when the Lord used to walk the Earth, He happened to pass by a plowman." During my second visit, a few months later, I asked the same informant to tell me other tales about the Lord. She refused in no uncertain terms: "The Lord never walked the earth. Jesus and the saints did." Despite that assertion the storyteller, in an instantaneous association, immediately switched to the tale of offering one's own child as a sacrifice (Abraham's sacrifice), but she used a definitely realistic introduction: "Once a man set out in search of work from the village of Nikolovo to Rousse. While on his way, he saw an old man under a tree." Having wound up her story, Radka further explained (in answer to my questions) that she had known that tale "from within herself." The first part, relating to the man

who had set out in search of work, she had heard from her husband, who in turn had learned it from someone with whom he had stayed in the hospital in Rousse some 20 to 30 years before. Of the second part, about the hospitable family that had sacrificed their child, she said, "I have also heard it, it must've been some tale, but it's all I've remembered. And as I'm telling you, it's a bit from here and a bit from there. I patch it up to make it a tale. That's why I've added it up." The scope of this work does not allow me to enter into details of the "contradictions" in the style of the storyteller or in the specificities of the individual repertoire and manner of presentation. But the quotations given are indicative in outlining the specificity of legendary tales, the typical and incidental contaminations within which legendary plots exist in local narrative tradition.

The narrative repertoire of the Razgrad region does not lack novella tales, in their basic versions. Some of the most characteristic novelistic adventure plots in Bulgarian narrative tradition have been recorded, moreover in the interpretation of talented storytellers. Some characteristic plots are those of the scars of the king's daughter (AT 850), the clever maiden (AT 875), the trade of the king's son (who, according to the version from the village of Kamenovo, became a carpet weaver), the trial of woman's fidelity (AT 881, 882), and the trial of the fidelity of friends (AT 982).

The thematic series about highwaymen and robbers is represented by very diverse versions of the adventurous fairy tale (A 965B) rather than by a great variety of plots. Listed under that number in the international catalogue of fairy-tale plots features the tale about Haidouk Rada (Pretty, White-Skinned Rada), as the female storytellers call the girl with unconcealed fondness; the story is a special favorite among the ethnic Kapantsi. Rada, as the story goes, succeeded many times in escaping the highwaymen owing to her female ingenuity and her manly valor.

Grown-ups and children alike show keen interest in telling and listening to tales about the destiny and happiness of man. These are tales about death predetermined by a drop of water, by a thunderbolt, or by a frog (cf. AT 934–934A); about the bride chosen in advance by fate (AT 931A); about the sister who rescued her brother who had been fated to die on the day of his wedding (AT 934A, AT 460–462); about Boncho the peddler (type AT 930, discovered under that title in the village of Tserovets); and about the lad who was destined to murder his father and marry his mother (AT 931). The tale "When Suffering Is to Be Endured, in Youth or in Adulthood" (AT 938B)[12] is common among Christian Bulgarians and the Turkish population alike, and the versions show almost no differences in plot.

The series of didactic tales is well defined. It is represented alongside the plots known from primers and popular books for children (especially since the 1920s) about hardship that teaches lessons, about labor as the greatest wealth (AT 910B), and about the deceitful little shepherd (AT 1333). It is also represented by most diverse versions of the tales of wise advice: about the pieces of advice paid for (AT 910A, in a typical contamination of the Bulgarian tradition with the fairy-tale plot about the grateful dead man AT 507C), about the pieces of advice given by the father on his deathbed (AT 911),[13] about the misunderstood paternal advice (AT 910A), and some others.

The vitality of funny tales and jokes, noted repeatedly in folklore, is also borne out by our studies of folk narratives in the Razgrad region. Most versions are common there; they reflect the life of man in his family, treated moreover, as is natural for this genre, through the prism of human shortcomings (laziness, stupidity, fear, greed, gluttony, drunkenness, frivolity, and so on). Popular here as throughout the country are the tales about sly and lazy women, ingenious in withstanding their laziness, and the witty ways their husbands find to teach them better. Covering that thematic range are the tales about the lazy spinner (Motovila-vila) (AT 1465), about the slovenly woman who managed to spin but a single spindle (cf. AT 902), and about the beating of the mat (or the cat) as a means of fighting indolence. Of course, the tale about Bogdanka or Galenka (the pampered girl) is also common, and its tradition in the local repertoire (as well as in the nationwide Bulgarian repertoire) has been reinforced by repeated publications and authored renditions by A. Karallichev and Ran Bossilek as well as by the performances of school dramatic groups. This phenomenon could hardly be defined as novel, for one can detect it even in the childhoods of our informants (who are most often aged between 60 and 80). Quite a few of them in the village of Ossenets, in Krivnya, in Tserovets, and in Senovo remember with tenderness and pride "how they played" or "how she performed the part of Galenka."

Of the tales of fools, I shall note only the greatest number of versions recorded here—about the cooked dog Belcho (AT 1409), about Unborn Petko (AT 1450), about the forgotten word (AT 1687, 1696), which begins with the episode about the fool sent to buy some wool (for the stuffing of quilts)—which are typical of the narrative tradition of northeastern Bulgaria. (The story about the wool is based on a pun using the homonymy of the dialect word meaning "wool" with the word meaning "naught.") In the group of our finds, I would list tales seldom recorded anywhere in Bulgaria, like the tale about Ivancho, whose mother made him a bride out of a skein of yarn and called her Boika (the Bulgarian word "boi" means "beat, thrash").[14] A version of the plot of the deft thief, whose series of skillful deceits and thefts is successful thanks to the stupidity of his partners, has also been recorded in the town of Senovo[15] (cf. AT 1525).

Erotic tales and jokes make up a specific layer, archaic and at the same time persisting to the present in local comic narratives. In their presentation the sexual opposition is clear-cut: there are male and female tales. Although the tales collected so far are insufficient in number (owing also to the specific difficulties in their recording), the female tales recorded so far give grounds to consider the idea of the existence of a certain tradition of ritual female presentation of erotic tales (among women only during set periods in the year, most often on Midwives' Day, January 21). Among the most popular plots are those about the punished priest-seducer and the bride (AT 1730, 1536B); about the misbegotten child (AT 1424); about the man who liked boiled eggs; about the gifts of Naida (*naida* means "find"), acquired upon her getting her new name (an etiological story about a female sex organ); about the father-in-law and the shameless bride; and some others.

An original "game-like" version of the female tales is erotic fortune-telling (in the village of Krivnya). Unlike the female tales, the male ones have not yet been recorded or studied even as subject matter. Comparing them with the tales of the *Decameron*, Dimo Atanassov (from the village of Kamenovo) said that he knew more than 100 of them but refused to tell them. He said, "They are not to be told to everyone; they are told among men only or, just like that, among people who are familiar to each other, just for fun."[16] Obviously, the study of these tales, which are still under a powerful taboo, is a pending issue in Bulgarian folklore research.

Jokes naturally occupy an essential place in the lively narrative tradition of the population (rural and urban alike) in the Razgrad region. Observations to date have shown that the overwhelming majority of the jokes told here came into being on the basis of novella-like and anecdotal tales (as their version) in particular, although borrowings from the stock of motifs and characters from other folklore genres have also been identified. Like elsewhere in Bulgaria, here, too, jokes about family relations, about various shortcomings of the people, about lazy, stupid, fainthearted, greedy, lascivious, thickheaded men and women, about stutterers, about misunderstandings among deaf people, and so on, are still told and listened to with relish. Anecdotes of local rivalries are also popular (e.g., between representatives of the ethnic groups of mountain people and Kapantsi), as are jokes about gypsies. It is noteworthy, however, that, judging by a review of the records accumulated to date, the jokes related to Sly Peter and Nastradin Hodja are comparatively less common. Single versions of several tales have been recorded: "The Bagful of Lies"(taking part in this story are the two characters of these jokes, and Sly Peter is the one outwitted); a tale about Nastradin Hodja and the Jew (AT 1543); and one about the unjust sentences that he passed as a judge (AT 1534). The joke dealing with the bet for silence, told in other parts of the country as a bet between Sly Peter (or Nastradin Hodja) and his wife is also popular in the region of Razgrad, but the characters in it are anonymous—an old man and his wife.

At the same time, jokes and jocular tales about local heroes constitute a rather rich field (one as yet insufficiently investigated). There is such a comic figure (sometimes several) in almost every one of the population centers studied, and that figure in some cases combines the parts of the creators and discriminators of comic narratives on the one hand and of their hero on the other. For instance, in the village of Tserovets, people relish the anecdotes about Kolé Kouteto, about Granny Yanka, about the Bassan old lady and others[17] in the village of Ossenets—the funny sketches about the wise-cracker Elena Madzurova[18] and those told by her, the jokes told by Granny Kalina and Granddad Radko. It is worth mentioning that the name of Granddad Radko is associated with the widespread anecdote in Bulgarian comic narratives about Sly Peter (Nastradin Hodja) who, when asked to tell a lie, immediately announced

that his father had died and asked for money to bury him.[19]

Principles and Features of the Poetic Style

Some general characteristics stand out in the review of the contents of the dominant genre of folktale narratives in the Razgrad region. It evinces a clearly identifiable trend toward the adaptation of plots and motifs inherited from old times to modern conditions. The following specificities may be considered as a manifestation of the updating of folktales:

1. Naming of the characters. Probably because it is most unusual, it makes the strongest impact in the fairy tales. Moreover, this is used mostly without giving the impression of spontaneity by old and middle-aged informants. The names most commonly used are Ivancho and Penka (which enjoy special preference in the tales of the villages of Tserovets and Svalenik; Ivancho and Mariika (diminutives of Ivan and Maria) in the tales of type AT 327A, village of Dryanovets; Penka, Zlatanka, and Todorka (in the fairy tale about the golden girl, village of Tserovets and village of Ossenets); Tom Thumb (Palechko, AT 327, village of Kamenovo); Solnicho and Piperko, or Sultanka and Piperko (AT 700, Senovo, Ossenets); Draganka (AT 700B); Djangur (Hullabaloo) Savka and Koundouvelka (AT 123, Senovo); *haidout* (pretty) Rada/Penka (AT 956B, Senovo).

2. Location of the action, associating it with the local toponymy. This general tendency in the Bulgarian narrative tradition has been moderately interwoven in the tales of the Razgrad region, where it is subordinated to the goal of specification of the developments in the narrative, enhancing the sense of their authenticity. In legendary tales and in fairy tales, in tales of the novella type and in tales about animals, separate developments may acquire the respective local coloring by association with familiar villages—Krivnya, Tserovets, Nissovo, Ossenets, and so on—or with the rivers Lom and Danube.

3. Swift transitions (analogies) between the past time of the folktale and the present. These are manifested best in the novella-like tales and the anecdotes. This specific in growth of the folktale's past time into the present has been ascribed above all to the skillful storyteller and

the wary and witty listener, whose resourceful remarks and explanations update, in their own way, the antiquated plots. For instance, while telling the tale of the children bearing the extraordinary names What-I-Was, What-I-Am, and What-I-Shall-Be (AT 883C), the shepherd Ibryam Abdoullov builds the episode when the children are discovered by their father, the king, in the following manner: "Well now, the king, for a day or two, as he is a king and has the right to go anywhere—now Todor Zlvkov can go all over Bulgaria—struck up a friendship with the hunters going from village to village and hunting. . . . When the king heard the woman calling her children by their names, "Neidim! Neolum! Neoladjam!" (Come here, What-I-Was, What-I-Am, What-I-Shall-Be!)—for they were renamed in this way in Turkish—the king's curiosity was stirred up. The way we have now started to rename people—what shall I be—Yuri, the other Gagarin, don't you agree, for example, but at that time there were no such names. . . ."[20]

4. There is a tendency toward a novelistic transformation of the motifs as one of the methods of their adaptation to contemporary conditions. Through the infiltration of new lexical units, of concepts and ideas from contemporary life, "the old motifs change into new clothes." The wonderful tree that sprang up from the bones of the grateful serpent is playing and singing "like a radio"; the fairy-tale king "gets about calling a mobilization," while the husbands of his sisters-in-law "watch the military operations through binoculars"; the scabby person "disguises himself, putting on a doctor's outfit, taking the stethoscope, putting the earpieces in place, and pretending to be a doctor; then he goes to the sick king," to his father-in-law. Having come back home, the golden girl is asked by her father to wait until he "puts on the light," and the girl responds with a characteristic line repeated several times in the text of the tale: "I am myself a light, open the door!" In the tale about the adroit thief, the hero "got the job of a servant in a coffeehouse, where the boyars used to get together. The boy handed over the duck to the comrade of the boyar with the following words: 'Comrade, well, your comrade said that you would give me the money, here's even a token [his handkerchief], he gave it to me, in case you don't believe me'."

In the final episode of the same tale, the boyars promise half the kingdom to the man who would kidnap the sultan from Turkey. The hero is ready for that exploit, as well: "I'll bring the royal sultan down over here!"

The examples can be multiplied many times if it is our objective to present a collection of folkloric "pearls." However, even the above samples of the specific (sometimes grotesque) alloy of old and new in the lexicology of the folktale, and hence in the system of plots and images in the tales, is sufficiently convincing to reveal a familiar picture not only of Bulgarian outlines alone but also of the irresistible spontaneous adaptation of the language and the entire substance of the tale to modern conditions. What is the most interesting in these "anomalies" is that they are hard to notice, probably because they are completely normal and do not startle (almost) anyone in the process of storytelling. In this way, imperceptibly transgressing the canon of the traditional style, the tale seems to be ruining itself. Yet the limited quantity of collected material warrants but the most general inferences about the fate of the tale at present.

5. There are, however, opportunities for other observations—for example, about the place of the contemporary tale somewhere "between the oral tradition and the written word." Retold folktales that have undergone literary editing are commonly included in readers, school textbooks, periodicals, and popular collections and exert an influence that is perceptible, to varied extents, in the tales told in the region of Razgrad. That influence takes very diverse forms and nuances, from the emergence of new plots, characters, and motifs to the stabilization and revival of some narratives in the folkloric repertoire, as well as in the changes in the stylistic and language standards. The indisputable influence of the literary, written tradition can be detected, for instance, in the tales about the three brothers and the golden apple, the wood-nymph bride, the little brother beetle, the unborn maiden, the pampered Bogdanka, and the like. It is probably the "read" tale disseminated by literary channels that is one of the factors in the concrete period prompting the frequency of name-giving, of the christening of the otherwise nameless characters of the folk narrative. Some coincidences are not accidental: Ivancho and Mariika (Margaritka)

are among the commonly used names in the popular collections of literary renditions of Bulgarian and foreign folk narratives in Bulgaria, especially in the period from the end of the nineteenth century to about the 1940s. Other character names from narratives recorded in the Razgrad region give indications of the reception of the Grimm brothers' fairy tales in Bulgaria. Such is the case of the fairy tale about the girl Creamy (Kremka) conceived by cream, whose original is the Grimms' Rapunzel. The coincidences between the translated tale under that title[21] and those told in the village of Tserovets and Svalenik[22] are not only in the name of the heroine but in the overall makeup of the plot as well.

Some of the tales included in our documentation have direct links to popular books, such as, for instance, the fairy-tale novellas recorded in other parts of Bulgaria about Protopei the flag-bearer, the king's 40 sons, the loyal servant, and others. Here we encounter them in a set as the core of the repertoire of Dimo Atanassov, the skillful storyteller from the village of Kamenovo. If he remembers well that he had read in a book in 1925 the tale about Protopei, the novella about the white Ethiopian (AT 531) is associated in his mind with his "serving in the army," where he learned it. This is probably so, and the informant reproduces a text he had listened to but whose original source is literary (indications of this are the specific composition, the contaminations, and the very title of the piece). An interesting detail is that there was a popular book published in Bulgaria in 1896 under the title *White Ethiopian*,[23] which, in addition to the story about the white Negro that has similarities to the tale told by Dimo Atanassov going beyond the name of the hero alone, contains a translation of the Russian tale about Ivan, the czar's son, the Gray Wolf, the Fire Bird, and the beautiful Anastassia. That tale (with great similarity in the details) is also in the representative part of the repertoire of Dimo Atanassov that consists of 20 "tales of the simple folk" (in the words of the informant himself). What is more, he tells them in the same order[24] in which they appear in the book *White Ethiopian*.

Yarn Spinning in the Process of Communication

Besides the collection of texts—whose value is beyond any doubt in view of the formation of a more comprehensive idea of the Bulgarian repertoire of folktales in its local and regional variants—the observations and inquiries that parallel the recording of the tales contain some data about the process of communication in their telling. The generalization of these data outlines some of the fundamental situations of yarn spinning in the region of Razgrad from the 1920s to the present. Naturally, they do not differ much from those that are already generally known and that exist in other parts of the ethnic Bulgarian territory.

Most numerous are the data outlining the role of the family as the basic microcollective in handing down and preserving the narrative tradition. Most of the storytellers point to the family environment as the source of their repertoire. Many of them have unforgettable memories of the skill of yarn spinning and the inexhaustible repertoire of their grandmothers, grandfathers, mothers, and fathers. This is probably the reason that the family has remained to this day the last fortress of live communication through folktales; it is precisely here that they continue to resound, although "in a low key"—mostly a medium for the instruction and entertainment of children.

A number of data point to yarn spinning as an inseparable part of the life of society, of the intellectual world of the adults. Tales are most often told at working bees, at the mills and inns, in the coffeehouse and in the pub, in male company in the barracks, at meetings, during long journeys, in hospitals, and so on. More typical for the region is yarn spinning in male company during the winter nights (although in this case "tale" or "yarn" denotes a wider spectrum of narrative forms). Danka Ivanova Velkova said, "They would get together in the nighttime on some holiday during the winter, when there is no field work, and the old people would get together there (there were no old people at that time, but they seemed to me old, because I was very young) and they would get together, sit down, telling memories and tales. There were two of them from Ljublin, they would play some instrument: I think it was Granddad Gyotso, the husband of Granny Nidelya; they would spend the whole night till daybreak, they would make coffee and drink it; just men seated by the walls on woolen cushions, and they would meet the day in this way; just yarn spinning and cracking jokes. Well, yes, the women would get together at working bees in the houses, women only; this evening in the house of one of them, tomorrow night in another one's house, taking turns. They would spin, and then they would offer a treat of prunes and dried pears and apples there. No coffee at the working bees. They would sometimes boil corn, spin, tell tales and sing numerous songs."[25]

There is an interesting analogy with the data collected about communication through storytelling among the Turkish population. In this respect the information received from shepherd Ibryam Abdoullov, from the village of Svalenik, is particularly valuable. He is an exclusive master of the epic narratives (fairy tales and novella-like tales). "I've been spinning these yarns [the tales he tells are transmitted only by word of mouth, from man to man] when we get together several men to a friendly talk. I, for my part, have learned them from an old man no less than 50 years ago. That old man was 60 or 70, while I was a brat just like these children over there [meaning his grandchildren who were present during the recording]. I would look him in the eye. And then he would start examining me: 'Tell me what you've remembered!'" It is typical that the informant never told these stories to his wife and children. It was the first time that his grandchildren happened to be in the audience of listeners under the simulated situation of our fieldwork; never before had they heard the tales of their grandfather. Ibryam specially emphasized that at one time men used to gather to make merry, separately from the women. As the men got together they told each other different tales. They took turns and competed in yarn spinning. To tell tales, one has to be in the proper mood. Ibryam remembered sadly how many tales he once had known, and that sadness was evidently shared by a great many male and female storytellers in Bulgaria, judging from their responses: "My head was full as a bag, the way we fill them with stones. But when you don't use 'em [the tales]. . . , like a dish, when you don't wash it, it gets rusty."[26]

A considerable amount of data has been collected about the specific circumstances under which the separate folktale plots were learned (or told). Here is an example of some typical cases in the childhood, youth, and "manly years" of the fair-spoken Dimo Atanassov from the village of Kamenovo.

"But there was one tale I heard as early as 1928, we were in the fourth grade at school; we got together, a group of five, five boys from the neighborhood, we were pupils and we were weaving a rush mat for each one. . . . And one night while weaving rush mats Tsilyo's father, Dad Vassil—as there were no women with us, and we were there only boys and he was with us—he dampened the eider for us and set out telling us that story about the Scabby Fellow"[27] (cf. AT 530, 531, 314).

"I know this tale [referring to the tale about Ahmed, Mehmed, and Pretty Dounya/Gyuzeli—AT 514] from an old man; once we used to go grazing the horses; we would graze them in the nighttime, and one night he told it to us as we were sitting by the fire while grazing the stock; that was where he told us this tale and I have remembered it ever since. It was very long ago, I must have been 12 or 13 years of age, I was little still. He was from our village, but he was an apprentice; he was here, in our village, and to tell you the truth, I don't remember his name, apprentice he was in our village. And he was grazing the horses of his master over there where we were. We were sitting at a common fire. . . . And I have repeated this tale many a time, many times have I told it to the children, that's why I have remembered it—you see, I know it."[28]

Dimo had learned some of his best tales in the barracks while doing his military service. "Someone told it to me, I've not read it, this tale [referring to the Brave Tailor, AT 1640]. It was a very long time ago, once upon a time, in '36, while I was doing my military service in Turnovo. I was over there in Turnovo in the military school. And it was there that a boy told it to me."[29]

The same informant also spoke about the role of the anecdote and the joke during the preelection campaigns in 1934. "I know it, the story [about compliance] from a solicitor. At a meeting, a party meeting it was, when we were going to hold elections in '34. That solicitor, Angel Stoichev his name was, from Borzankevi, now it is Trubach, the village of Trubach, so he spoke, he was a member of Stefan Tsanov's wing; he delivered that speech and it came to the compliance of the people that were then ruling and those around them, and he told that joke about the sultan that I am telling you now, about the vizier. It was he that told it, I have heard it from him, that story. It was as early as in '34."[30]

Classical situations of yarn spinning, in conditions approximating those of today, have also been noted. Such a situation is created during travels, reproduced after the old model but with a more modern text. Obviously, the oral art of the yarn spinner cannot be regarded as something long lost; it is a fact that may still be investigated here and now in its respective modifications.

"We used to go there, I was working at the machine and agricultural station, I was bookkeeper of the team of tractor drivers, and they called us to a meeting in the afternoon. The meeting ended, it grew late, darkness fell, and we set out with the agronomist from the village of Ravnevo and the agronomist from our village that was, the two agronomists were both young men; they did not feel like walking, they wanted some vehicle to take them back. I was telling them, 'Come on, I'll tell you a story while we go, little by little, we'll get back'. We took a bite at the restaurant, had something to eat and started, and I began telling them that tale about Sergeant Protopei, and when we came to the end of the village, over there, next to the water fountain, I hadn't finished it, so we sat down on a tree trunk and I finished the tale off. . . . But I couldn't tell it, we walked for 20 kilometers and I couldn't finish the tale, so we sat down at the end, so I would wind it up."[31]

This fragmented exposition aimed primarily at revealing the contents of the local repertoire of tales and some of the ways of their dissemination does not give any place to the consideration of another substantial issue regarding the process of storytelling: the presentation, which is part and parcel of the question of the bearers of the tale, of the storytellers. I shall only point out that in our fieldwork we were lucky to come across and find a number of good storytellers with outstanding creative talent within the framework of the local narrative tradition. In the village of Tserovets alone there are three prominent storytellers: Maria Stancheva Dimitrova (born in 1924), mostly skilled in the comic narrative; Yana Gancheva Ganeva (born in 1923), whose fresh memory has retained quite a number of fairy-tale plots and who displays outstanding originality in the rendition of these plots (for instance, in her parodies of miracle tales); and Peter Stanchev Stanev (born in 1915), a colorful narrator of fairy tales for whom the working bees in his youth served as a school in which he mastered and presented his repertoire of tales. It is regrettable that now he is a typical example of a storyteller without an audience. Even excerpts from the interview with him are of undoubted scientific interest. He said, "When we went to the working bees, the maidens would stick around me pestering me all the time: 'Come, Peter, tell us!' I was like a mad horse in those days! Merrymaking—that is how

we used to pass our time!"; "I can't remember anything else—it is only when I hear a story that I never forget it. When I hear the others spin a yarn it is imprinted in my mind"; and, "I've never taken a book of tales to read."[32]

Dimo Stoyanov Atanassov (born in 1915) is almost universally known in the telling of folktales; he is "the living history of the village," as his fellow villagers lovingly call him. His repertoire derives from various sources, and books occupy a place of honor among them. He learned much during his travels around Bulgaria as well as during illnesses and stays in different hospitals (which served as modern centers for the exchange of narrative data of all sorts). Dimo would say about himself, "There is no town in Bulgaria I haven't been to. I have known all kinds of people and I have always learned from them." His comment regarding the truthfulness of his stories is very interesting indeed: "He, the Danish writer Andersen, devised the tales; I don't think them up, I've either read 'em or heard 'em." A number of other details round out the portrait of Granddad Dimo. He is a singer whose repertoire includes mostly long narrative songs, performed at feasts, during harvesting, and so on. He also partially uses the written word as a means of preserving the text (in the form of making lists with the titles of the plots featuring in his repertoire). Another component of his repertoire are his ledgers, containing quite varied data: a list of the Bulgarian rulers (with precise dating of the periods of their rule) from Khan Asparukh to King Boris and King Simeon II; a list of the United States presidents; and a list of Turkey's sultans. In a "meteorology ledger" he has been entering for years the relation between meteorological phenomena and some actions of birds, insects and animals.

Another source of local folktale creation, particularly as presented by women, is the town of Senovo. There, during a working bee (a spontaneously reconstructed situation of yarn spinning, in which the presence of the researcher had a definite impact), quite a few versions of international folktale plots, as well as of original local forms were recorded.

We have come across outstanding storytellers among the Turkish population, too. The dignified figure of Ibryam Abdoullov (born in 1925) stands out in the village of Svalenik. The core of his repertoire is in fairy tales and novella-like tales, presented by him with his typical epic bias toward repetition and sudden, witty transitions, making a bridge to the present day. I shall mention also a humble storyteller from the village of Staro Selishte, namely Fidana Raikova (born in 1924), who, during our single meeting "endowed us" (the expression is hers) with a rare folktale plot in Bulgaria about the magnificent fish in the part of the grateful deceased (AT 507C, EB 62), which was first recorded in this country in 1891.[33]

The recording of the tales of the Turkish population is valuable not only toward the completeness of folkloric documentation but also for the opportunities it opens up for most wide-ranging investigations aimed at elucidating the local specificity and penetrating the mechanism of creation of a common narrative repertoire among the different ethnic communities by way of the dynamic exchange of different narrative forms.

The general review of the folk narrative in the region of Razgrad presented here shows unambiguously that, although it began late, its scientific recording serves as a sound basis for the study of the nationwide Bulgarian narrative tradition as well as the investigation of one of the key problems of Balkan folkloric studies related to the Balkan community in the field of folktales (and of the folk narrative in general).

Notes

1. The observations and inferences, drawn on the basis of folkloric narratives collected in northeastern Bulgaria have been included in the studies of Rossitsa Angelova (Angelova 1963; Angelova 1964; Angelova 1976). R. Angelova's recordings, however, have not been handed over to the archives and have not been published.

2. The tale about Draganka recorded in Senovo (by Milena Benovska in 1990) has but two parallels in this country. Cf. *Collection of Folklore, Science and Letters* later to be referred to as Col. Folklore 16–17, p. 342, No. 2, Ochrid; a zoomorphic variant—a rat adopted by old people, cf. Shapkarev, K. *Sbornik ot Bulgarski narodni oumocvorenia.* Sofia, 1982, 11, Vol. 8, No. 190, Leriasko (in Bulgarian).

3. This type of fairy tale has not been recorded in this country before. Its appearance is probably associated with the reception of the respective tale of the Grimm brothers, but the questions related to its translation into Bulgarian and its spread call for further studies.

4. Arhiv na Instituta za Folkklore (Archive of the Institute for Folklore), further referred to as AIF, No. 60, p. 133, village of Kamenovo, Razgrad region. Informant Ginka Yordanova Atanasso, born in 1925, seventh-grade graduate, engaged in farming. Recorded by Yordanka Kotseva.

5. Yana Toncheva Toneva from the village of Tserovets (born in 1925, seventh-grade education, engaged in farming) winds up with this formula not only from the tales she had learned in her childhood but also from those learned from the radio, from gramophone records, and so on. We have encountered the same formula in the neighboring village of Svalenik, used by Ibryam Abdoullov, born in 1925, fourth-grade schooling, a shepherd. He winds up the story of the Ethiopian Off (AT 325) in the following manner: "And we are now telling their stories here." Recorded by Plamen Bochkov in 1988. Ibryam Abdoullov is a Turk, but he told his stories in Bulgarian.

6. AIF VIII, No. 23, p. 94, village of Tserovets, Rousse region. Recorded by Plamen Bochkov.

7. AIF 1, No. 60, p. 53, the town of Senovo. Informant Suba Nikolova Yovcheva, born in 1919, seventh-grade schooling, engaged in farming. Recorded by Yordanka Kotseva.

8. AIF 1, No. 61, p. 53, Senovo. Informant Radka Dimitrova Todorova, born in 1924 in the village of Glodzhevo, married in 1960 in Senovo, fourth-grade schooling, engaged in farming. Recorded by Yordanka Kotseva.

9. Informant Peter Stanchev Stanev, born in 1915, fourth-grade schooling, engaged in farming, village of Tserovets, Rousse region. Recorded by Yordanka Kotseva.

10. ATF No. 61, p. 66. Informant Radka Dimitrova Todorova. Recorded by Yordanka Kotseva in 1989.

11. AIF 1, No. 60, p. 349. Informant Radka Dirrtitrova Todorova. Recorded by Yordanka Kotseva in 1990.

12. Disseminated, though seldomly, in writing in the nineteenth and twentieth centuries, the tale features as early as in the collections of Damascenes (Ivanova, 1967).

13. So far this type of tale has been recorded in Bulgaria in one single version in the region of Topolovgrad (CBT, 1993: No. 915A). Clearly, fieldwork in northeastern Bulgaria brings out the existence of plots so far recorded in the nationwide repertoire only in single versions.

14. AIF 1, No. 60, p. 123, town of Senovo. Informant Ginka Yordanova Atanassova. Recorded by Yordanka Kotseva in 1990.
15. AIF 1, No. 61, p. 95. Informant Radka Dimitrova Todorova. Recorded by Yordanka Kotseva in 1989.
16. Excerpts from the inquiry of Dimo Stoyanov Atanassov, by Yordanka Kotseva in 1990, in the village of Kamenovo.
17. Told by Sister Mara (Maria Stancheva Dimitrova, born in 1925, fourth-grade schooling, engaged in farming), the renowned wisecracker in the village of Tserovets. A curious phenomenon are also the attempts to popularize her "funny sketches" by putting them into print (after the intervention of an editor) in periodical publications or in local amateur publications.
18. AIF 1, No. 64, p. 131, village of Ossenets, Razgrad region. Informant Ganka Nedelcheva Ganeva, born in 1932, primary education, engaged in farming and works as a servant. Recorded by Magdalena Elchinova in 1989.
19. Ibid, p.107, about Grandad Radko.
20. AIF VII, No. 23, p.7, village of Svalenik. Informant Ibryam Abdoullov, born in 1925, fourth-grade schooling, works as a shepherd. Recorded by Plamen Bochkov in 1988.
21. Kremka. Prikazki. Sofia, 1921. In other Bulgarian translations of the same tale, the girl in the tower gets analogous vegetational names: Blubell, Lettuce, Salad (Zvunche, Maroulka, Saladka).
22. AIF VIII, No. 20, p. 207, the village of Svalenik, Rousse region. Informant Nikolai Georgiev Nenov, born in 1977, fourth-grade pupil. Recorded by Yordanka Kotseva.
23. Doktorov, I. Byal Arapin. Published by Ivan Bozhinov, 1896 (in Bulgarian).
24. Phonoteque of the AIF 1990, village of Kamenovo, No. 5, II 5; No. 5, II 6. Recorded by Yordanka Kotseva.
25. Excerpts from the inquiry of Danka Ivanova Velkova, born in 1931, seventh-grade schooling, works as a milking woman, engaged in farming, village of Tserovets, Rousse region. Recorded by Yordanka Kotseva in 1988.
26. Ibid.
27. AIF 1, No. 60, p.36, village of Kamenovo.
28. Ibid., p. 5.
29. Ibid., p. 95.
30. Ibid., p. 139.
31. Ibid., p. 53.
32. Excerpts from the inquiry taken from Peter Stanchev Stanev, village of Tserovets, Rousse region. Recorded by Yordanka Kotseva in 1988.
33. Col. of Folklore, 5:2 (1891), p.143.

Further Reading

Aarne, Antti, *The Types of the Folktale: A Classification and Bibliography,* edited and translated by Stith Thompson, second revision, Helsinki, Finland: Academia Scientarum Fennica, 1961

Angelova-Georgieva, R., "Kum vuprossa za suvremennoto sustoyanie na bulgarskite narodni prikazki legendi i predaniya," *Izvestiya na Etnografskiya institut i muzei* 7 (1964)

——, "Legendi Suvremenno sustoyanie na bulgarskite narodni prikazki, predania," *Slavyanska filologiya* 5 (1963)

——, "Osnovni nassoki v zhiyota na Bulgarskata razkazna proza," in *Folklorut i narodnite traditsii v suvremennata natsionalna kultura,* volume 2 of Problemi na bulgarskiia folklore, Sofia, Bulgaria: Izd-vo na Bulgarskata akademiia na naukite, 1976

Daskalova, L., D. Dobreva, Y. Kotseva, and E. Mitseva, *CBT (Catalogue of Bulgarian Folk Tales) 1993,* Sofia, Bulgaria: 1993

Eberhard, Wolfram, and Pertev Nailî Boratav, *Typen Türkischer Volksmärchen,* Wiesbaden, West Germany: Steiner, 1953

Ivanova, Ana, *Troianski damaskin: Bulgarski pametnik ot XVII vek,* Sofia, Bulgaria: Izd-vo na Bulgarskata akademiia na naukite, 1967

Kotseva, Y., "Folklornata prikazka i suvremennite detsa," paper presented to the IX International Symposium on the Problems of Bulgarian Folklore, Stiven, 1989

——, "Glassovete vi chouvam (Zhenata. Kato razkazvach na folklorna proza)," *Bulgarski folklor* 4 (1989)

Meletinsky, E., "Struktourno-typologicheskoe izouchenie skazki," in *Morfologiia skazki,* edited by V. Propp, second edition, Moscow: 1969

Storytelling in Croatia

Ljiljana Marks

Ljiljana Marks presents an overview of Croatian folktale scholarship from the tenth century to the present day. She concludes with a note on changes in contemporary storytelling.

Croatia and Its Neighbors

Tales, legends, and other narrative genres from Croatia—which has a population of some 4,800,000 and shares borders with Slovenia, Italy, Hungary, Serbia, and Bosnia-Herzegovina—are denoted and determined by multiple and deeply interwoven historical links. These range from those that Croatia had in past centuries with Venice and Austria-Hungary, and those from the twentieth century, primarily from its shared life until 1991 as a part of Yugoslavia. Consequently, Croatian tales have had peripheral contacts and are interwoven with diverse traditions—for example, those of the Mediterranean, central Europe, Pannonia, and the Balkans. These are the sources of their profile and their distinctive quality. However, they cannot be distinguished only by these elements, nor can they be classified according to the usually uncertain origin of the tales. The only factor that makes storytelling specifically Croatian is the language in which the teller of the tale heard it, remembered it, and then passed it on in his local or broad community.

Medieval Sources of Croatian Tales

Written confirmation of Croatian oral stories can be found far back in the past. The legend of the migration of the Croats to their present homeland, led by four brothers and two sisters, is the oldest written testament to Croatian oral traditions. It is found in part of *De administrando imperio*, written by the Byzantine emperor Constantine VII Porphyrogenitus in the tenth century. Legends about the origins and names of individual settlements date from very early times—from between the twelfth and fourteenth centuries—and the continuity of these legends has been preserved almost to the present day, with contemporary writings concerning their alternatives published in more recent collections of stories and legends. Medieval chronicles of Dalmatian cities and religious tracts in Latin, Italian, and the Croatian language give legends about the patron saints of individual Dalmatian cities and about the miracles of healing and deliverance they performed. Among old apocryphal texts, often reflected in later oral tradition, there is an important dualistic story from two Croatian reviews written in the Croatian language in the distinctive Croatian Glagolitic script; the sources are the Petris collection (dating from 1468) and the *Žgombić* collection (from the sixteenth century). This story is one of the oldest known texts about the dualistic creation of animals and speaks of God creating Adam, while the devil created the bear, although only God could breathe life into it.

Many legends and stories from the era of Croatian medieval literature were written down in popular reviews of edifying and ecclesiastical rhetorical prose by priests and laymen from the Middle Ages until the late Baroque period. These were made up of largely freely recounted material from edifying stones, *exempla,* and European Roman Catholic authors, and their function was to stimulate religious feeling. Many of these tales were heard and adopted from sermons and were later transmitted mainly orally and became deeply rooted in Croatian oral tradition. They tell, for example, of the evil son who hid a roast capon from his father and, as punishment, a frog jumped out of the pan and glued itself to the son's cheek; of an ungrateful son whose mother laid a curse upon him that prevented the earth or the sea from accepting his body after death; of the monk who listened to a bird of paradise, thinking that its song lasted only a few moments when in fact a whole century passed; of a living man who returned after more than 100 years from the other world to his village—unaware that he had been away—and found it completely unrecognizable; and so on. A humorous story that is noted down is about a young man who had never seen a woman and who, when the devil showed him a goose, desired the goose, believing it to be a woman. Miracle stories and legends about the miracles performed by the Virgin lived on and were transmitted in various transformations in oral tradition (such as the fairy tale of the young girl without hands; the oral legend of the religious woman whom the mother of God replaces when her husband tries to sell her to the devil; and a parody of a legend about the sinful and repentant nun).

Renaissance and Baroque Sources

In Croatian Renaissance literature there are echoes of legends, most of which are etiological (about the origins of localities and their names): of the miraculous fern seed that can only be picked on the evening of Midsummer Day (St. John's Day); and of the godfather who stole another godfather's straw, so that the sign is still visible in the sky (Zoranić). The famous Italian Renaissance Giovanni Straparola collection of short stories dating from the sixteenth century, *Le Pacevoli notti* (*The Pleasant Night*), contains the tragic love story of Malgerito Spolatino (with roots in the ancient tale of Hero and Leander), set in the surroundings of the Croatian city of Dubrovnik; the same tale was told to the Czech travel writer Lobkovic as part of the local oral tradition from the Dubrovnik area (published in 1834).

Croatian Renaissance and Baroque writers from Dalmatia (e.g., Marin Držić, Juraj Baraković, Petar Zoranić, Sabo Bobaljević, Junije Palmotić) borrowed themes from oral narrative tradition (for example, about the absurd chemist, the fictitious payment to gain a fictitious profit, and the humorous story about the urinated pears) and motifs from local legends, beliefs, and anecdotes. They often mentioned the names of fantastic creatures from oral legends, adapting them to the literary styles of their time. They spoke of evil sprites, bloodsucking witches, spells, werewolves, mountain fairies, witches, and warlocks.

The Age of Enlightenment

During the Age of Enlightenment, two writers—J.W. Valvasor and G.F. Tommasini, writing in German and Italian respectively—testified to Croatian Istrian beliefs and stories. In northern Croatia, A. Baltazar Krčlić, a priest and chronicler, noted down legends on the foundation of the city of Zagreb, the capital of Croatia, and he also wrote in the *Annuae* chronicle, mainly as a skeptical witness, of local events, along with anecdotes and mythical legends current in the Zagreb of his time.

Pre-Romanticism

In the era of the awakening of pre-Romanticism, two writers were particularly interested in popular customs and in stories. The Italian travel writer and priest Alberto Fortis mentioned some orally transmitted legends in his 1774 *Viaggio in Dalmazia* (*Travels Through Dalmatia*): about two witches who roasted a human heart and about a quick-witted thief. Variants of these legends had been collected at mid-century in the same region through which Fortis traveled, the Dalmatian mountainous hinterland. Inspired by what had been written, Ivan Lovrić, a Croatian from the township of Sinj, wrote about Croatian popular customs and made notations of legends and descriptions of narrative situations in his book *Bilješke o putu po Dalmaciji* (*Notes About a Journey Through Dalmatia*), which was published in Venice in 1776. Both these works exerted a powerful influence on European Romantic literature.

With the national awakening of the Croats in the first half of the nineteenth century, systematic notation and research of folk tradition commenced, primarily of songs and later of stories. Ljudevit Gaj, the reformer of the Croatian literary language, wrote down from memory what he recalled of the legends of his native place and the first written Croatian fairy tale, about the stepmother and her stepdaughter. The questionnaire for the collection of information about popular culture that was printed in the first issue of the *Arkiv za povjestnicu jugoslavensku* (*Archive for Southern Slavic History*) in 1851 was intended as a stimulus for Croats to collect data about local history and culture and also oral tales and beliefs.

The responses, which were published in later issues, contained oral stories, beliefs (about fairies, witches, werewolves, pestilence, and bloodsucking witches), songs, and customs, and marked the beginning of the systematic collection and research of this material. At the same time, the eminent Croatian philologist Vatroslav Jagić published the results of his comparative philological and critical papers on oral stories, marking the beginning of work on their scientific study.

The first Croatian review of authentically notated tales was published in the Kajkavian dialect—one of the three Croatian dialects—in 1858, presenting material collected in the city of Varaždin (in northwestern Croatia) and its surroundings by Matija Valjavec, a high school teacher, who was Slovenian by birth. Authentic notations of stories were also published by later collectors, R. Plohl-Herdvigov and Rudolf Strohal. Fran Mikuličićc published largely stylized fairy tales from the Croatian littoral region in the Čakavian dialect. The stories in the Mijat Stojanovic collection were mainly freely restylized. Stories from Istria—the peninsula in the northern Adriatic—were noted down in the mid-nineteenth century but published only recently. Regional reviews of Croatian stories and legends, as well as less comprehensive notations, not always literally exact but rather stylized or adapted to literary language, were systematically published from 1886 onward in the editions of *Zbornik za narodni život i običaje južnih Slavena (Review of the Folk Life and Customs of the Southern Slavs).*

Folklore Studies in the Twentieth Century

Since 1962 the Institute for Ethnology and Folklore Research in Zagreb has been issuing its journal, *Narodna umjetnost (Croatian Journal of Ethnology and Folklore Research),* publishing, among other things, exact, contemporary notations of stories and legends recorded on tape all over Croatia. These collections—with introductory studies—have resulted from field research done by the institute's collaborators (Maja Bošković-Stulli, Divna Zečević, and Ljiljana Marks); apart from the texts, also given are information on the context of the storytelling, the narrators, variants of the stories, and classification according to the Aarne-Thompson catalog. Regional reviews are also published as separate editions—with material from Dalmatia, Istria, and the Neretva River region—as well as reviews of urban stories from Zagreb. A number of reviews

have been published of oral tales of ethnic Croats living in other countries (Slovakia, Austria, Hungary, and Romania).

Scientific papers about oral narrative genres—classical and modern—are also written and published: everyday and autobiographic narratives; urban horror stories; children's jokes; and traditional narratives from urban communities; narrative methods; meta-narrations; mimicry and motion during storytelling; regional characteristics; and the relationship between written and oral texts. Autobiographical genre papers on the stories of persons displaced in the recent 1991 war have been published in various journals (*Narodna umjetnost* [*Croatian Journal of Ethnology and Folklore Research*], *Etnološka tribina* [*Ethnology Tribune*], and the review *Fear, Death and Resistance*).

Historical and local particularities are found within internationally known narrative topics in Croatian stories—as in European stories in general. Actual historical characters appear, such as Emperor Diocletian, Empress Maria Theresa, Joseph II, Emperor Franz Joseph, and Miho Pracat, a rich transoceanic merchant from Dubrovnik. The real experiences of the narrator intertwine with the fictitious elements drawn from the story, particularly in stories of maritime adventures, sea sirens, and monsters, and on the wonders seen in distant, overseas lands, which are retold in the coastal parts of Croatia. Actual historical events such as the Peasant Uprising and wars conducted on Croatian territory are seen and interpreted through the eyes of the folk narrator, in some way creating oral history. Through its fictionalization, local legend gives a spiritual dimension to well-known places and preserves the history of long ago. For example, oral tradition in the surroundings of Split in Dalmatia nurtures memories of antiquity and the emperor Diocletian, just as legends from the Neretva River region are imbued with the marshland landscape and reminiscences about the ancient city of Narona.

Stories change from place to place and show variability; storytellers, male and female, make their individual contributions in each narration in an unending game between the more-or-less fixed model and its individual adaptation. Narrators enrich their stories with nontextual elements: gestures, mimicry, and movement, documented on video in modern notations. Authentic narrative situations are a rarity in Croatia today. Formerly, stories would be told at the winter dinner table or by the fire, on tournament days, when homemade brandy was being distilled, at bees, at cornhusking time, on return from work in the fields, at pasture, at feasts, in taverns, during army service, in the hospital, and so on. Shorter stories were also included in everyday conversation. Modern narrators largely remember stories from their childhood and pass them on to their grandchildren in the way they remember them.

Changes in the Storytelling Tradition

Stories have changed with the advancement of technology and alternative, diverse forms of communication, and some genres, such as fairy tales, are disappearing from active narrative practice or are being transformed, while new ones are also appearing. Along with traditional texts, texts that are read (in schoolbooks, newspapers, and magazines) are also transmitted orally in the towns and the villages. Television programs are recounted, usually the content of soap operas or serials that have fairy-tale elements; "terrible, authentic experiences" are narrated.

Stories, therefore, continue to be told; they are a part of human life and social interaction. Humankind's everyday stories are necessary as something that differs from everyday life.

Further Reading

Bošković-Stulli, Maja, *Kroatische Volksmärchen*, Düsseldorf, West Germany: Diederichs, 1975

———, ed., *U kralja od Norina: Priče, pjesme, zagonetke i poslovice s Neretve* [Of the King of Norin: Stories, songs, riddles and sayings from the Neretva River], Metković: Galerija "Stecak" Klek, 1987

———, ed., *Usmene pripovijetke i predaje* [Oral Tales and Legends], Zagreb, Croatia: Matica hrvatska, 1997

———, ed., *Zakopano zlato: Hrvatske usmene pripovijetke, predaje i legende iz Istre* [Buried Treasure: Croatian oral tales, and legends from Istria], Pula, Croatia: Cakavski sabor, 1986

———, *Žito posred mora: Usmene priče iz Dalmacije* [The Wheat in the Middle of the Sea: Oral Tales from Dalmatia], Split, Croatia: Knjizevni krug, 1993

Krauss, Friedrich S., *Sagen und Märchen der Südslaven. Zum grossen Teil aus ungedruckten Quellen*, Leipzig, East Germany: W. Friedrich, 1883–1884

Marks, Ljiljana, *Vekivečni Zagreb: Zagrebačke priče i predaje* [Tales and Legends from Zagreb], Zagreb, Croatia: AGM, 1994

Mikulicic, Fran, *Narodne pripovietke i pjesme iz Hrvatskog primorja. Pobilježio ih čakavštinom Fran Mikuličić* [Folk Tales and Songs from the Croatian Littoral. Noted down in the Čakavian dialect by Fran Mikuličić], Kraijevica: 1876; second edition, 1993

Plohl-Herdvigov, Rikardo Ferdinando, comp., *Hrvatske narodne pjesme* [Croatian Folk Songs and Stories], Varaždin, Croatia: Brozotiskom Platzera I Sina, 1869

Stojanović, Mijat, *Narodne pripoviedke. Sabrao i priredio za mladež Mijat Stojanović* [Folk Tales. Collected and prepared for young people by Mijat Stojanović], Zagreb, Croatia: 1879

Strohal, Rudolf, *Hrvatskih narodnih pripovijedaka knjiga I: Narodne pripovijetke iz sela Stativa* [Croatian Folk Tales Volume 1: Folk tales from the village of Stativa], Rijeka, Croatia: 1886

Strohal, Rudolf, *Hrvatskih narodnih pripovijedaka knjiga II: Narodne pripovijetke iz grada Karlovca, sela lokava, Delnica, i trgovišta Vrbovskoga* [Croatian Folk Tales Volume II: Folk tales from the city of Karlovac, the village of Lokve, Delnice and the market town of Vrbovsko], Karlovac, Croatia: 1901

Strohal, Rudolf, *Hrvatskih narodnih pripovijedaka knjiga III: Narodne pripovijetke iz grada Rijeke, trgovišta Mrkoplja i Ravne Gore, te sela Broda na Kupi i Ošarija* [Croatian Folk Tales Volume III: Folk tales from the city of Rijeka, the market towns of Mrkoplja and Ravna Gora, and the villages of Brod na Kupi and Oštarije], Karlovac, Croatia: 1904

Valjavec, Matija Kracmanov, *Narodne pripovjedke Skupio u i oko Varaždina* [Croatian Popular Tales from Varaždin and Vicinity], Varaždin, Croatia: stampo Josip pl. Platzera, 1858

Traditional Legends in Contemporary Estonian Folklore

Ülo Valk

After giving a brief background on Estonian folklore studies, Ülo Valk shows us supernatural legends from two contemporary female tellers in their 70s.

Folklore Studies in Estonia

Estonian folklore is well documented since the last decades of the nineteenth century, when the extensive collection of folklore began in Estonia. This coincided with the period of Russification and gained popularity as a form of protest against it. Oral traditions and mythology were used in the building of the national identity that led to the founding of the Estonian Republic in 1918. The revival and idealization of folk culture played a significant role during the period when the Communist empire collapsed and Estonia regained its independence in 1991. The collections of folklore are preserved in Tartu in the Estonian Folklore Archives, which contain more than 1,260,000 pages of manuscripts.

Philological approaches have dominated in Estonian folkloristics; it has become a scholarly tradition to work with the texts in the archives. Estonian folkloristics has been influenced by the historic-geographic method, known also as the Finnish school. One of the exponents and developers of this school was Walter Anderson, who held the chair of Estonian and Comparative Folklore at the University of Tartu in 1919–39. His authority has reached beyond this historical period. He remained a classic among folkloristics in Estonia after World War II, when folklore was taught on a more modest scale by his pupil and successor, Eduard Laugaste. Both the folklorists of the Estonian Folklore Archives and those of the University of Tartu organize annual fieldwork trips into old Estonian parishes. Urban folklore is recorded, too, but it is still less well documented than rural traditions.

Legends in Estonian Folklore

Many Estonian legends can be classified according to the catalogs of Antti Aarne (FFC 25) and Lauri Simonsuuri (FFC 182). The latter gives a systematic classification of Finnish legends, but, as the folk traditions there have close parallels in Estonian folklore, Simonsuuri's type numbers can be applied in many cases to Estonian folklore. Several types of migratory legends described by Reidar Christiansen (FFC 175) were known in Estonia as well. Most of the legends relate the encounters of men with the world of supernatural: witchcraft and wizards, the devil, water and forest spirits, revenants, whirlwinds, nightmares, werewolves, buried treasures, demonic treasure haulers (*kratt, pisuhänd*), the demon of plague, and so on. To a great extent these legends can no longer be recorded in living folklore, since interest dominants in the field of the supernatural have changed in both rural and urban settings. Contemporary Estonians rather tell about UFOs and aliens, telepathy, dream omens, astrology, miraculous powers of local healers, transmission of spiritual energy, reincarnation, the possibilities of communication with the dead, and so forth. There are several "esoteric" newspapers and journals that generally follow the "new age" line of thought. The supernatural world of the children's horror stories has its peculiarities (Kõiva); several international urban legends have reached Estonia as well (Kalmre).

Examples of Two Storytellers

During fieldwork in the southern Estonian countryside during August 1996, I met a woman who had amazing knowledge of the traditional legends, beliefs, customs, and songs. She had learned them from the local oral traditions, to a great extent from her stepmother. Emma B. was born in 1921 and lives in a remote farmhouse in a big forest in Rõuge parish. There are not many strangers who come to these out-of-the-way places, and therefore it is no wonder that a few miles from her home a Soviet nuclear military base was situated. Nowadays the missile shafts are empty and the system of underground fortifications is deserted, but the forest around it is still rich in mushrooms with extraordinary shape. Emma B. lives as a traditional Estonian peasant. She has suffered from the wars and political changes. Her first husband was killed by the Communists, her second husband by the Nazis. I visited her together with a colleague who had met her several times before, and therefore it was easy to make contact with her. She did not pay attention to the minidisc recorder being used, although later on she listened to the recordings with great interest. As the recording of these legends could be regarded as an authentic situation in which a memorized tale is told to a new listener, I give a word-for-word translation of three stories. Emma B. said that her stepmother believed in the truthfulness of the following stories; she herself has some doubt, which she sometimes expresses, as in the third example.

Oh yes, I remember, my stepmother told it. I do not know exactly but my [step]mother told me about it. [I don't know] who told her or how it actually happened. There was a woman whose husband died. He began to come back home in the evenings. Started to eat together with her at the table, the man was there now and again. She told another woman, "You know what is happening; my husband has started visiting home every night." The second woman advised, "You should let something

drop on the floor, then you can see what kind of feet he has." The woman let something fall—a spoon or a fork. One of his feet was a hoof of a horse. The woman was very scared and the man understood everything. He said to the woman, "Listen, everything from below your breasts will belong to me!" The woman was pregnant. Soon after the baby was born it died. Yes, that was the story.

Many Estonian legends illustrate the traditional Lutheran belief that the devil can hide himself in the guise of a dead person. A demonic revenant and the devil can both appear to the widow in Estonian folklore, and both interpretations of this legend are possible. Since the story was told together with other legends about the Evil One, Emma B. probably preferred the latter explanation, although the claiming of the unborn baby by the dead father is not impossible in folk belief. In Estonian popular religion the devil used to steal and exchange unbaptized children; even unborn babies were in danger from him. The legend also expresses the widespread belief that evil demons cannot hide their nature, although they try to appear in pleasant guises. Many Estonian legends tell about recognizing the anthropomorphic devil by some bestial or demonic token (horns, tail, red eyes, black or bloody teeth, and others). Checking the leg of an anthropomorphic demon or detecting him by a hoof is a traditional motif in several legends.

Wait a minute, there was another story. There was a fight at the tavern. There was a tavern in Konki valley. . . . I do not remember well. . . . My father told about it. I think that it was his father on his way home and he was passing by the tavern. There was something like a big hayrick that he encountered; it made a voice like, "Oh-oh-oh-oh!" The father said: "Hush-hush!" This thing passed by the father and rolled towards the tavern. That was the Old Devil (*vanakurat*) who went to incite [men to fight]. . . . If somebody is killed, he will get the soul. Yes, that was the story.

This legend conveys two traditional motifs of Estonian folklore. The first concerns the appearance of the devil, who is very often described as a moving and noise-making hayrick, which probably means a large, amorphous guise. Hayricks are typical in the Estonian landscape, and supernatural beings (mainly the restless dead) are often compared with them. Second, the legend illustrates the Christian belief in the connection of the devil with taverns, merrymaking, and his attempts to obtain human souls by inciting murders and suicides.

> I haven't heard that anything like that had happened here among our folk. These are all old tales. I do not know who was buried, probably a landlord or somebody like that. The horse was not able to draw the carriage; I don't know, perhaps there were even two horses. They could not go on. They put the horse's collar backwards around the neck. Could it be possible? Then the horses started to draw again. The Old Devil was there in the coffin, therefore the horses could not draw. That is another legend that was told. Backwards, I think, how can you bind the collar like that? It is not possible.

The Christian belief that dead sinners are taken by the devil was well known in Estonia. In many legends the Evil One is sitting invisibly on the coffin, which makes the hearse too heavy. An extraordinary weight is characteristic of several supernatural beings in Estonian folklore. They are sometimes detected only by this peculiarity. Weight can be connected with the concept of the load of sin that can sometimes be experienced, according to folk belief (the corpse of an evil person is heavy). Social criticism against evil landlords who are closely related to the devil is fairly typical in Estonian folklore.

These three legends express traditional beliefs about the devil, who is the dominant supernatural character of Christian folk religion. The Estonian Folklore Archives are rich in such legends, but only seldom can they still be recorded in oral traditions.

A Second Teller

Another storyteller is a woman who was born in 1924 and comes from the neighborhood of a small town in northern Estonia, where she lived since World War II. Renata K. used to work at home sewing clothes for customers; she is married and has three grown children. Her repertoire includes a few legends about the supernatural that are based on her life experience, as are most of her other stories. In December 1996 she told some stories during her husband's birthday party. Plenty of food and alcohol was offered to the

guests, which kept them sitting at the table for hours. Such informal gatherings of relatives and friends are excellent situations for storytelling. Listeners, four or five people of her age and two or three younger guests, followed her stories with great attention. Her presentation was so convincing that nobody expressed doubt or supplied any other, more rational, interpretation. It was impossible to note down the stories then. I therefore asked her to repeat them later on so that I could record everything. She agreed with pleasure, but I did not expect her to prepare a handwritten version of the stories that she used while speaking. This changed the style toward a literary elaboration containing many repetitions, which have been omitted here for the sake of clarity. The stories give an insight into the contemporary Estonian urban folk religion of the older generation.

> When I was young I did not believe in life beyond the grave but due to my experience I changed my mind: I now believe in the existence of the human spirit in the other world. I have heard and seen a spirit and talked with it. When my mother was ill I took care of her for more than a year. The mother who was dying said that if life beyond the grave exists she would give some kind of sign so that she could be recognized. "If you go to divide my property I will be there." Forty days after her death we went together with my sister to tidy up her house which was to be sold. About 15 glasses were standing on a table in the dining room. We were cleaning the bedroom; suddenly we heard the clatter of glasses. There were no strangers and no animals in the house. The sister was frightened and said, "That's mother!" I said, "Yes!" We went to the dining room and had the feeling that mother had hit the glasses with her hand. I said, "Probably mother does not like that we intended to throw away the glasses. Let's keep a few glasses as a memory." That's what we did.

Auditory supernatural experiences are often described in Estonian legends about the revenants and haunted houses. Relations between the members of a family used to be stronger in traditional Estonian peasants' culture than nowadays and were transferred to the world beyond. The composition of the first story is traditional: first a general thesis is given about the life beyond the grave and then a personal story is added that confirms that statement. Here, the interpretation of the supernatural experience is added immediately: the clatter of the glasses is said to be caused by the deceased mother who both proves her presence and stresses the need to commemorate the dead. In another story Renata K. tells about seeing the spirit (*vaim*) of her mother.

> It was midnight, I was in bed beside my husband. Suddenly I woke up, opened my eyes and some kind of energy (*vägi*) forced me to look towards the window. At this moment a shining shade entered through the window which soon took the appearance of my mother's face, head and shoulders. The lower part was like grey mist. It stood in front of the bed and said, "Now I know everything, I see everything, I feel sorry that I was unjust towards you." The mother had loved the sister more and therefore felt guilty after death. She came to beg my pardon. I looked at her and said, "Yes, mother, it is too late now. I have suffered a lot." Mother seemed to be offended and said, "We are here together with father." My husband heard the talk and asked, "What's up?" I said, "You see, mother is standing here in front of the bed." He did not see anything. Then mother transformed into mist and disappeared through the window. At this moment I saw a scene of a stony landscape and mountains. They were ascending a mountain together with father; I recognized their silhouettes.

Conflicts within families are reflected in many Estonian legends about the restless deceased who haunt the living. The story presents a typical situation in which a supernatural experience takes place in a dreamlike state of consciousness. This story about the unforgiving daughter is an introduction to the next story, which relates a demonic encounter.

> Two or three years passed. I think that my mother was wandering in this dark tunnel as I have read in literature. She cannot pass this tunnel and get into the light before redeeming her sins. She regarded it as her sin that she had not loved me as she loved the other daughter. Therefore she came to me to beg my pardon. But as I did not know it then I did not forgive her.

> It happened in the daytime; I was laying in my bed and resting. I saw that from the upper corner of the bedroom a shining shadow came which took the form of a human head; she had a black mask and a black wafting robe. She stood in the air above me and seized my throat with her hands without saying a word. But I recognized the features of my mother although she was wearing the mask. With my hands and legs I hit her and shouted, "Go away!" Then she turned into mist and left through the same corner.

The feeling of guilt and belief in the absolution of sins belongs to the traditional Lutheran mentality, expressed in many Estonian legends. The interpretation of this experience as an attack of the vengeful mother is determined by the first story. Final comments about "wandering in the dark tunnel" were added decades later when Renata K. read the esoteric newspapers that describe postmortem experiences. Traditionally, such dreamlike supernatural experiences, when one is attacked or suffocated in bed, are connected with the belief in nightmares (*luupainaja*) that is to some extent still alive in the Estonian countryside. Recognizing the nightmare, being able to move oneself, and uttering a sound are old forms of defense against it.

Conclusions

Jürgen Beyer, in his article on the history of storytelling around the Baltic Sea, has recently shown how the corpus of folk narratives and the concepts of genres developed through the centuries and how both drastically changed at the time of the Grimm brothers. A comparison of the repertoire of the two storytellers illustrates this statement. Emma B. still knows traditional migratory legends; Renata K.'s repertoire consists of personal stories such as those that dominate in contemporary Estonian religious folk narratives. We can trace the continuation of some beliefs (e.g., midnight as the proper time for supernatural experiences, black as the color of the demonic), some significant topics (the relationship between the living and dead members of a family), and expressions of the same mentality (guilt and the following punishment). Emma B.'s legends can be classified into definite tale types such as those described by Aarne, Simonsuuri, and Christiansen, which is not the case with Renata K.'s stories. Both storytellers, however, tell dramatic stories that rely upon folk belief.

My research at the folklore archives and my fieldwork experience confirm that male and female repertoires differ. Women tend to tell didactic stories that convey serious belief, as in the two cases presented above; men often neglect and contest the religious topics; they rather express their doubts and entertain the listeners. However, this is only a general tendency, not a universal rule. It also seems that the boundaries of the interpretation of a supernatural experience have nowadays become more limited; there used to be more diversity as regards the supernatural beings as models of explanation. However, personal narratives about the supernatural are told among different age groups, in both urban and rural settings. These stories have the same basic function as traditional legends; they confirm the reality of the divine and the demonic, exemplify social values and popular beliefs, and influence human behavior.

Further Reading

Beyer, Jürgen, "Prolegomena to a History of Story-Telling Around the Baltic Sea, c. 1550–1880," volume 4 of *Electronic Journal of Folklore* (http://haldjas.folklore.ee/folklore), 1997

Chesnutt, Michael, "The Great Crusader of Diffusionism: Walter Anderson and the Geographic-Historical Method," in volume 1 of *Studies in Folklore and Popular Religion,* edited by Ülo Valk, Tartu, Estonia: Department of Estonian and Comparative Folklore, University of Tartu, 1996

Kalmre, Eda, *Vorstivabrikutest kassitoiduni ehk mõnda linnalugudest,* Mängult-päriselt, Tänapäeva folkloorist II, Toim, Mare Kõiva, Tartu, Estonia: 1996

Kõiva, Mare, "In a Big Black Town There Was a Big Black House," *Journal of the Baltic Institute of Folklore* 2:1 (1997)

Factors Influencing the Formulation of Narration*

Annikki Kaivola-Bregenhøj

Annikki Kaivola-Bregenhøj examines the ways in which Finnish narrator Juho Oksanen structures his narratives.

Introduction

Folklore is no longer viewed as a true or a false copy of some background "original," but as a presentation the formulation of which is influenced by various factors, some of which favor constancy, others variation from one performance to the next. There are many such factors, and they can all be classified as "rules for reproduction."

The performance from memory by a folklore expert cannot be viewed in isolation, as having no connection with the other factors behind the production and regeneration of tradition. Obviously poems in Kalevala meter are "remembered" more easily by virtue of their meter than prose narratives, and a small-scale riddle with an image firmly attached to the answer is easier to recall word-for-word than some longer item. The special features of the genre and the performing context are almost inseparably tied up with the personality of the folklore expert and his method of memorizing (Kaivola-Bregenhøj 1985). When a narrator tells the same story on different occasions, he is by no means merely repeating an item of folklore he knows off by heart; instead he creates a new version, drawing on the facts and fragments stored in his memory.

Although the process by which folklore is produced does incorporate cognitive spheres that are difficult to approach, the folklorist is in a unique position to observe what happens when information stored in the mind is once again turned into a story, for example, through the act of telling. By analyzing versions of the same story repeated by a single narrator on various occasions the folklorist is able to indicate how the story is preserved in the memory, how it is reproduced, what is permanent and what is not. The interview situations can roughly be divided into two categories: the interview proper and the tape-recorded social gathering. The first refers to the informant interviewer cooperation, the second to an informal discourse involving more members of the research team and/or the informant's family.

The research material referred to here consists of interviews I conducted in 1968–71 while working in Sysmä in Central Finland as a member of a fieldwork team from the Finnish Literature Society. All the examples quoted are from tape recordings of one informant, Juho Oksanen. Before his retirement Juho Oksanen was a church sexton with a reputation for being a good narrator. I met him several times in the course of our fieldwork and was therefore able to observe the way he varied his narratives from one recording session to another. During the 20 hours on tape Juho Oksanen presented a total of 56 narratives or narra-

*Reprinted with permission from *Studia Fennica: Review of Finnish Linguistics and Ethnology* 33 (1989).

tive chains that were repeated on two to five occasions.

Many scholars from different fields have in recent years been approaching, via, e.g., memory research and pragmatics, the factors that influence the formulation of a narrative. Let us now take a look at the narrator, the listeners and various contexts, the factors that, according to my research material, clearly influence the way a story is verbalized on different occasions. I place these factors in five main categories: 1.) *Command of scheme:* the structural and contextual norms for producing a narrative are part of the narrator's competence. The narrator is then capable of constructive recreation and mere reproduction can be excluded. 2.) *The narrator:* the nature of his personality, his social status, and folklore preferences always leave their mark on his narrative. 3.) *The position of the narrative in the discourse* in turn determines how the narrative is begun and how much the narrator can expect his listeners to know already. 4.) *Pragmatic-textual features of separate interviews:* these manifest the changes that take place in the telling as the narrator and the interviewer get to know one another. 5.) *The listeners and the situation* impose their own demands, which may vary from one performance to the next; they must always be allowed for.

Let us now subject these different factors to closer scrutiny. Obviously they overlap in a narrative situation and acquire different emphasis from one telling to another. As a result the story varies, at least at verbal level, each time it is told.

Command of Scheme

The concept of scheme was created by cognitive psychological research and has been used as one means of analyzing the processes of observing, memorizing, and interpreting. The folklorist is most interested in schemes applicable to the analysis of narrative discourse. Terry Winograd divides discourse schemes into three categories: 1.) personal schemes—conventions for interactions between the participants in the communication, 2.) rhetorical schemes—conventions for laying out a reasoning sequence which the speaker wants the hearer to follow, and 3.) narrative schemes—conventions for connecting a sequence of utterances into a coherent text. We all have a large number of schemes for the presentation of different narratives (Winograd 1977, 8184). A scheme can also be defined as the listener's expectations concerning the narrative. The scheme is a

framework with gaps to be filled in, and it acts as the macrostructure of the narrative. The listener or reader immediately recognizes the story. He also expects it to have the episodic structure typical of the genre of discourse, the events to be in some temporal causal order, the story to have a principal character and the events reported to be interesting (Kintsch 1978, 82).

There is some variance in the terms used by scholars to denote the episodes in the narrative scheme and the size of the units into which a narrative is broken down. David E. Rumelhart, for example, breaks the narrative down into 18 elements (e.g., the plan, preaction, and action of the story, the internal and external reactions of the characters), and he further defines the relationships between them using six semantic predicates (e.g., some element of the story initiates, allows, or motivates another [Rumelhart 1975, 222]). I here define schematic elements in the manner of Walter Kintsch, who claims that each type of text has a different macrostructure, but that "simple stories are formed as a sequence of episodes, each episode consisting of an exposition, a complication, and a resolution. Embeddings are frequent, so that, for instance, the complication of one episode may consist of another whole episode. . . . Furthermore, a story may have a moral, usually in final position" (Kintsch 1977, 38).

The narratives told by my informant, Juho Oksanen, are for the most part chronicates, recollections, and legends representing varying degrees of the schematic command of folk narratives. In the best performances the schematic structure is like a firm ladder up which the narrative progresses step by step, in regular and easy fashion. The best example is his idiosyncratic story "Juho and the lord of the manor" (Appendix 1, Narrative 1), in the presentation of which each element of the scheme clearly occupies a set position. In this story the climax of the plot enhances the structural parallelism of the episodes (Episodes I and II, units 11–27 and 28–34). The way in which the reporting, the speech and the main characters are inserted into the scheme is also proof of a fine command of scheme.

Constructive regeneration may take the form of free variation on the scheme. The narrator then draws on his sense of scheme to produce a slightly different presentation to suit the demands of the situation or, say, his objectives on that particular occasion. But the narrator may also stumble into the story on some association, start with a schematically wrong sequence or mix up episodes. For the rest of his narrating he strives to find the "red thread." One may say that the verbalization of a text is then endangered. This occurred when Juho Oksanen presented the second version of the story of "Dean Renqvist on his way to visit the sick" (Appendix 1, Narrative 2, Performance 2). On the other hand a narrator may use repetition as a means of underlining a point in his story. But he may also wish to spotlight twists in the plot that he finds problematic. For example, telling a story about the supranormal may be psychologically difficult for a particular narrator, so he points this out either by means of repetition or by some other paralinguistic device, such as a chuckle.

Schematic variation is most obvious in contexts clearly differing in mood. In telling, for instance, the story about "Heikki and the authorities" (Appendix 1, Narrative 3) Juho Oksanen clearly applied divergent telling strategies. When he had only one listener, he was able to linger over the telling, building broad schematic episodes and packing them with information that was omitted on the other occasions. In telling the longest version he skillfully added details designed either as extra information for the listener (background to the minor characters, Performance 3, units 6–7) or to enrich the plot of the story (description of the principal character's internal reaction and brief outline of the situation, Performance 3, units 5 and 14). During social gatherings, when there were several people present and a party atmosphere, the narrator chose a different telling strategy. Then he eliminated all the padding from the plot and handled each schematic episode and contextual unit as succinctly as possible. On this occasion he made none of the spontaneous personal comments that had featured so large at the interview.

The narrator is familiar with the conventions of performing folklore and knows from experience that his listeners also have a sense of scheme. This means that a story can be understood even if the information given is incomplete. It does, however, go without saying that there is a vast difference between a story that *is* merely "understood" and one that is "a pleasure to listen to." The shortest version of the story about Heikki and the authorities comes to a premature halt because it completely lacks a resolution. The reason for the interruption did, however, lie with the audience, which broke out laughing before the narrator

even got to the point where the glass sticks to the policeman's fingers (Performance 4, unit 15). Being in two parts, the story had so much plot redundancy that the audience—who had heard it before—did not need to hear the end.

It got the point of the story and reacted immediately. The listeners indicated that there was nothing more to be said.

It is easy for the listener to deduce when the narrator is engaging in the creative variation of the scheme and when he fails to command the conventions of his genre. In the poorest performances of, e.g., "Dean Renqvist on his way to visit the sick" the narrator stumbles and tries again and again to structure his story (Appendix 1, Narrative 2, Performance 2). Once he does finally get started he presents a version that lacks the contentual unit vital for creating a bridge between the complication and the resolution episodes (cf. Performance 3, Lead-up to Resolution). In that same performance he also forgets to inform the listener in time of the persons involved in the story. The supranormal point of the story is lost, and the listener remains bewildered.

Errors are to some extent part of the essence of oral narrative. The narrator produces his story as he tells it and cannot as a rule plan it in advance. Nor can he vary it in the same way as, for instance, a writer creating text. It was quite common for the exposition and complication episodes to overlap in the stories told by Juho Oksanen (cf. Siikala 1984, 89). In presenting, for example, the story about Heikki and the authorities he did not mention all the background facts about the characters and the situation in the exposition and hurried ahead to the complication. Each time he was, however, forced to go back to the exposition (Narrative 3, Performance 3, units 1–3 and 6–7). Sometimes he was able to cover up for this blunder in an elegant manner, but at other times he was obliged to interrupt the course of events for a moment and to resort to unforeseen repetition. Such blunders are not, however, always evident to the listener, because the narrator has numerous paralinguistic means, such as facial expressions and tones of voice, of covering them up.

Sometimes the presentation in some quite different context of contentual material that really belongs to the exposition may seem intentional. It is important for the description of the main character in "Heikki and the authorities" to mention that he had magical power. If the narrator does so right at the start of the story (Narrative 3, Performances 3 and 4, unit 2), the listener is all set for the supranormal turn of events thus promised him. But in two performances—not included here—the narrator nevertheless saves (or forgets?) this piece of information until the climax of the story, when Heikki has just made the official look stupid by offering him a drink out of a glass that sticks to his fingers. In this case the contentual unit "he was a seer" acts as a comment explaining the point of the story.

The narrator's grasp of scheme may to begin with weaken if he has to deviate either from his genre or from a topic with which he is highly familiar to a completely new narrative theme. It is then common for the narrator to make a short pause, to hesitate, to grope for words and to falter before embarking on a new narrative episode. But as a rule the skillful narrator soon gathers all the threads together, so long as he is on familiar territory.

The Narrator

The personal contribution of the narrator to the shaping of things he has heard, experienced and read until the product is acceptable as part of his own repertoire is one of the most significant factors causing variation. This variation is particularly clear in the narrative tradition, more than any other. As soon as the would-be narrator hears a story, he forms his own interpretation of it. We may call this the first interpretation process, and in it the narrator forms his own attitude to what he has heard. Anna-Leena Siikala, in a study of the narrative tradition of a single Finnish parish, analyzed the variation brought about by the divergent views of different narrators on a series of events and the reasons for them (Siikala 1984). Two narrators may form two narrative versions of a given event that are completely different but that both fit into their own personal repertoires. The ultimate success of the story in no way depends on the correspondence between the narrator's interpretation and the original source of information (Clark and Clark 1977, 164).

Most narrators specialize in certain narrative genres. Some of the folklore assimilated by a narrator passes into his active repertoire and he readily presents it. But he also has a latent store of items that he may be able to recall when asked, e.g., by an interviewer. This material, familiar to the folklore expert but not presented spontaneously, may be completely alien to him as a person.

Here are a few examples to demonstrate how Juho Oksanen handled folklore motifs that did not belong to his repertoire. In the first example I asked him a completely stereotyped story well known to the local people about a giant who built a church:

AK: Have you ever heard about a giant in connection with this church?
JO: Yes, a giant woman carried over two cornerstones from Särkilahti on her way to milk the cows. *It's all just a tale, but a giant could no more carry stones like that in her skirt than any ordinary person, but there they are underneath the corners.*
AK: Well if it is just a tale, how do you think it started?
JO: *It's the way people think, they've got a lot of imagination, it's all a product of the imagination.*

Oksanen did, it is true, answer the question, but he did not make a story out of the familiar motifs. His comments (in italics) show that he did not consider the subject worth talking about.

In the second example the conversation touched on a church ghost well known in the local tradition, and I wanted to ask Juho Oksanen whether he also knew the story attached to it:

AK: Was the church ghost the sort people could ask for help?
JO: *I don't know, I wouldn't know, I didn't . . . I don't reckon anyone got talking to it.* There was a simple man, he was once working the organ bellows, and there was to be a rehearsal one evening, so I had left the church door open for them earlier in the day, and I said to the old man, "Will Uoti let us in? Wait a minute, I'll call out three times "Uoti, open the door!" Old Aaltonen, old Kustaa, there he was with his eyes popping out, and then I said, I pulled the door open and said: "He heard!" *That's the way stories get about.* He was a serious-minded fellow was old Aaltonen, he was never one for a joke, he never said a word.
AK: It was only a joke, but wasn't it founded on a tradition? I mean, you could have done it quite seriously.
JO: It's quite possible, and others have tried, *but I don't believe the door ever opened,* but I knew it would open because I'd left it open earlier in the day. *So . . . so, according to tradi-*

tion I carried it off, I'd heard they'd asked Uoti to open the door, so I did too, but . . .

The example shows that Juho Oksanen, who did not believe the legend and who did not therefore consider it worth telling, had devised a version of the subject to suit his own ends. The belief motif also served as the subject for a joke even when the original meaning of the folklore product had lost its topical relevance.

The world of values of narrators and their listeners has undergone rapid change, and this is reflected particularly clearly in the way primitive folk motifs are used to produce narratives and the way these are presented. Motifs can be used to produce variations that differ greatly from the form, content and meaning of the discourse serving as their model.

There was room in Juho Oksanen's repertoire for few stories on supranormal subjects. The rest of his active repertoire consisted of chronicates mostly of a historical nature and dealing with local events. It was with such stories that he was most at home. His status in the local social hierarchy unquestionably also imposed its own restrictions. Being the church sexton and an elected representative of the people on numerous official committees he was "almost gentry" and made his choice accordingly.

In addition to supranormal subjects, which he considered "of minor importance," Juho Oksanen avoided anecdotes of a suggestive nature, even going so far as to flatly refuse to tell any to a woman interviewer. When, after persuasion, he did on one occasion agree to tell my male colleague Pekka Laaksonen a few risqué anecdotes, he was shy and clumsy in his performance. This narrative genre did not suit him at all.

The Position of the Narrative in the Discourse

The position of a narrative in the discourse also helps to give it shape. While analyzing the repertoire of Juho Oksanen I examined the way in which telling linked up with its preceding linguistic context. There are two factors that are important here: what has previously been said and on whose initiative the story is taken up.

The links between a story and subjects that have previously been raised are evident in the text in a number of ways. If, for example, two stories are told on the same topic, the narrator can gloss over many details of the plot or background of the second because the listeners already know them. The closer the stories are to one another, the more the narrator can lean on the first. In performing "Heikki and the authorities" for the fourth time Juho Oksanen, for reasons of telling context, chose a brief presentation. Embarking on the second of the pair of stories, he cut the telling to a minimum, beginning with the words: *"So then he gave Lunström a taste of the liquor, to crown it all . . ."* (Narrative 3, Performance 4). Since the characters in the story, the setting, the plot, and the liquor were already familiar to the listeners, the narrator needed only to refer to them and thus gave the exposition of the story only the briefest of handlings. The topical links of a story with what has gone before may sometimes be manifest by means of pronouns. Continuing the conversation about the well-known Sysmä Dean Henrik Renqvist with a new story, Oksanen began: "Then we got a new curate, *this* Henrik Renqvist. . . ." By using a pronoun the narrator links the principal character in his new story with what has just been said. But a story does not always need to have any lexical signifiers indicating that the characters or topic are familiar. Sometimes the performance is simply cut short if the main character is already familiar to the audience. And vice versa: the exposition becomes drawn out if the narrator has to fill in the details of, e.g., the hero's origins and family.

In order to understand a story fully it is important to know who or what sparked off the narrative chain that yielded it. In answering a question addressed to him, the narrator may quickly have to produce a narrative he has had no time to plan. Wallace L. Chafe rightly speaks in this context of a "change of world," often accompanied by hesitation and stammering (Chafe 1980, 46–47). The logic of the story may suffer and there may be gaps that can only be filled by the listener familiar with both the conventions and motifs of the genre. If, on the other hand, the narrator launches on his performance spontaneously, he may have had the subject in mind for some time, and he has had time to recall it, sometimes even down to the verbalization he usually adopts.

When the discourse shifts at the narrator's initiative from one topic to another, he may have two subjects in mind at the same time. In this case he can quickly shift from one subject and story to another, without the listener even realizing. Transitions are usually easy to spot, for they are accompanied by schematic (beginning of a story), lexical (particles and pronouns), and paralinguistic (variations in voice volume and pitch, timing, etc.) signifiers. But if the narrator fails to use any of these signifiers, he may also leave his listeners momentarily in the dark.

If a story is part of a chain comprising several narrative entities on a uniform theme, it is presented at a faster tempo than separate stories. The pauses in between narratives are then short. The narrator must, through his performing technique, indicate to his listeners that he wishes to hold the floor for longer than usual. Since relating a chain may take far longer than the time normally allotted to one narrator, he must produce his narrative more quickly.

Pragmatic-Textual Features
of Separate Interviews

The researcher able to work with a given narrator for years on end may well find that the relationship between them gradually changes, and he will modify his interviewing technique accordingly. An explanation for the formulation of telling should ultimately also be sought by observing the differences in mood from one interview period to another. It is essential for the informant and the researcher to have a trusting relationship if an interview study is to succeed. As time progresses, they get to know one another extremely well; even so it may come as a surprise to the researcher to discover that the narrator knows him. It is often the case, at least temporarily, that the narrator selects a performing code he thinks will please the researcher.

The cooperation between Juho Oksanen and myself fell into three main periods differing somewhat in mood. The first summer was spent getting to know one another; we were both slightly on our guard, though we became more and more relaxed each time we met. I adopted an interviewing technique by which I asked him questions in fairly rapid succession, and he often commented on the truth of his narrative. The second period was one of less inhibited interaction, as a result of which Oksanen would sometimes guide his telling in whatever direction he wished. But I noted that he was on this occasion mentally prepared for his role of informant and kept quite a close check on his own performance. The previous autumn he had received an award for being a good narrator, and this possibly placed greater pressure on his telling. When speaking, people put across not only information but their own image, too (Tan-

nen 1984, 1). Oksanen's image as a narrator was clearly reinforced as our work progressed and this obviously pleased him. There is no single heading to cover the third interview period: *it* was much the same as the previous summer, but our interaction was marked by deeper acquaintance and friendship. Oksanen became less reserved as our work progressed, and he gradually realized that I was happy to listen to anything he might tell me.

The differences between the interview periods are evident from the text in two ways. They concerned on the one hand the special nature of the first performances at the contextual and linguistic level, and on the other hand the fact that the narratives seemed to have a clear tendency to get longer each time. When the narrator told a story for the first time, he knew it was new to the interviewer. This was manifest in his lexical choices. For example, when he first told me a long chain of chronicates about the municipal harvest surveys he was involved in after the war, he used the words "one" and "a certain" (referring in Finnish to an unknown person or thing) more often than on subsequent occasions. But the first performance might also be a test for the listener: what do you make of this story? On first telling the story about Heikki and the authorities Oksanen chuckled far more often than during the subsequent performances. The comic turns in the story were not the only source of laughter, for his chuckles either coincided with the supranormal twists in the plot, or they divided up the narrative and/or indicated that he had done his job and now awaited the listener's reaction. He wanted to be sure that I would not base my interpretation of his story and him as its performer merely on his words. It was most apparent that he wanted me to know that he himself did not fully believe in the possibility of supranormal twists in the plot.

Many of the stories told by Juho Oksanen grew in length from one performance to the next. I must at this point emphasize that at no time did I ask him to tell me a certain narrative again; his stories always arose spontaneously out of the conversation. During the third interview period he told me the longest versions of "Dean Renqvist on his way to visit the sick," "Juho and the lord of the manor," "Heikki and the authorities" (Appendix 1), and of two other stories not included here. As our work progressed, the stories became more and more polished in the narrator's mind and performances (cf. Dégh 1969, Pentikäinen 1980, and

Bauman 1986). The reason for this was undoubtedly that the stories became easier to recall and the expectations he attributed to me. But it also lay in the contextual diversion between interview and informal gathering to which I shall be returning later. My material clearly proves that a story does not by any means necessarily improve as it gets longer, for the narrator may begin to repeat himself. One thing is, however, certain, and that is that in the long versions the narrator had a chance to present not only the nucleus story but also his opinions on, say, the plot and its authenticity.

Sometimes the narrator has a chance to prepare for a meeting and to decide what story to tell. This was also the case with Oksanen, when he knew he could expect me the following day. The fact that he had prepared his story was usually immediately evident from his manner of speech and his voice. He would try to eliminate some of the dialect from his speech and certain elements would appear that were missing from his normal speech—grandiloquence, affectation, and an emphasis on certain words. He might also adopt a slower tempo. The prepared story was usually longer than the spontaneous one, because he would begin to philosophize, to make comparisons, and so on. The disadvantages of preparation were, however, as a rule soon overcome as soon as he got going and forgot he was supposed to be performing with dignity, avoiding any expressions he considered commonplace or unrefined.

The Listeners and the Situation

The listeners and the situation are closely connected to one another, for the mood of the situation is influenced by the number of listeners, their degree of familiarity, their social status, sex, etc. The listeners in turn behave differently at, for example, a church meeting attended by the vicar or over a cigarette with the men outside. I nevertheless intend to examine the influence of situation and listeners on the narrative separately.

The Situation

Situation can, first of all, be used to refer to the macro or cultural context providing the basic prerequisites for understanding a folklore item. Changes in the macrocontext transfer to folklore. Scholars have in the past few decades taken an interest in their reflection in popular traditions. Tradition is not altered suddenly, and changes are initially manifest as temporary variations on a

folklore item. It has been observed that meanings change more rapidly than motifs (Siikala 1984, 220). Scholars have also recorded the devices by which a narrator can update an item of folklore to meet the narrative needs of the present day (e.g., Hiiemäe 1980). My informant, Juho Oksanen, represented the narrator whose repertoire was clearly rooted in the agrarian and socially stratified culture that was vanishing from Sysmä in the late 1960s and early 1970s.

Situation is, however, most often used to refer to the microcontext or the social state of interaction in which folklore is transmitted from the narrator to the listener. Our folkloristic knowledge of situational variation is growing as the results of more interview studies are reported. Situationally oriented variation is often confined to a single occasion and takes the form of either the addition or the elimination of details felt to be unnecessary.

The telling situation quickly changes if there are other listeners in addition to the interviewer. My own recordings have proved that the trusting atmosphere prevailing during the interview becomes lighter, there are almost no pauses, the narrator makes fewer or no comments, the tempo increases, the narrator's voice becomes louder, and he laughs more when, instead of performing to a single folklorist, he has an audience consisting of, say, members of his family and other members of the fieldwork team. The serving of coffee—to say nothing of alcoholic drinks—alters the telling situation (cf. Hoppál 1980b).

The nucleus narrative itself seldom varies—it is difficult and even futile for the narrator to abandon his basic interpretation—but the point of the story and its presentation may differ greatly when the same story is told on two different occasions. In Appendix 2 I analyze two conversations in which Juho Oksanen repeated the story about Heikki and the authorities. At the interview (Appendix 2, Situation 1) neither I nor Oksanen's wife, present at the time, interrupted his narration, but during the social informal gathering (Situation 2) it was rare for anyone who began a story to finish it without the others chipping in with extra information or their own comments. It was also quite common for some of those present to start talking about something completely different (e.g., their own state of health or the handing round of coffee) while someone else was still speaking. Admittedly, people usually stopped to listen to a story that clearly stood out as an entity in itself. The second distinct difference between the situations concerned the discourse. At the interview (Appendix 2, Situation 1) most of the topics ran into one another, so that the narrative flowed onwards. During informal gathering (Situation 2) there was a smooth transition between topics only twice, for in most cases the conversation switched sharply from one subject to another. This proves that none of the people present had a chance to plan the course of the conversation, which rambled as dictated by the situation and the speaker of the moment.

The performances of "Heikki and the authorities" in the situations analyzed by me proved to be very different. Oksanen gave the fullest account of the story at the interview, making a number of situational additions and stressing various points (Appendix 1, Narrative 3, Performance 3). During social gathering the rapid shifts from one speaker to another and the attempts of the other people present to influence the course of the conversation, either adding information or guiding it in their own direction, forced Juho Oksanen to change his telling strategy. "Heikki and the authorities" got reduced to a story in which the plot is given a minimum of attention and from which all extra information and details have been eliminated (Performance 4).

It is, of course, impossible to generalize on the effect of the situation on the narrator and his performance, for this is ultimately influenced by his accustomed manner of performance, his personal qualities and special talent, and the differences that exist between genres. Juho Oksanen, who in his capacity as sexton had heard numerous clergymen speaking, was himself a good performer and an eminent speaker. On receiving the medal awarded by the Kalevala Society to good narrators he unexpectedly spoke on behalf of all those who had received medals. The academic ceremony and formality of the event seemed to inspire rather than to confuse him. He was used to being a speaker and a narrator, and he had greater difficulty in assuming the role of listener.

The Listeners

The observations made by folklorists on authentic contexts for the presentation of folklore inevitably stress the interaction between the performer and the listener. The narrator expects his audience to provide some sort of feedback in order to encourage him to continue and to spur him on to the best possible performance. Linda Dégh has pointed out how eager comments from the audience, disagree-

ment, and doubtful or even scornful remarks appeared to stimulate the fairytale teller. For these were an indication to the narrator of activeness on the part of his audience. Even the smallest signal from the audience may often influence a narrator and the shaping of his performance. It either helps him or disturbs him in producing his narrative. "The tale becomes more beautiful and colorful when the narrator feels that his listeners are with him, living each moment along with him; the more complete the audience cooperation, the more perfect becomes the tale" (Dégh 1969, 113II 9). Performances 3 and 4 of "Heikki and the authorities" are a clear demonstration of how the audience influenced the telling. On the third occasion Oksanen treated me to a lengthy version rich in detail, whereas the version produced for the fourth occasion, at his birthday party, was shorter than the others and was completely lacking in metaphrases. The reason for this was that the narrator sensed that his listeners might interrupt him, and he did not appear to welcome the thought. He also indicated by a change of voice that the doubt expressed by Tilda Oksanen did not please him and disturbed him.

The audience may sometimes be too familiar to a narrator. It already knows the story, and the narrator in turn knows how it usually reacts. A new listener, whose positive attitude may be interpreted by the narrator from his expressions and his questions, may inspire him to a longer and, in some cases, a better performance. The linguistic scholars have noticed that people choose a language to suit the needs of the genre and their listeners (Tannen 1982, 18).

Folklore communication also undergoes changes when used repeatedly by an in-group to which it is very familiar. There may be as many as three different variations of a folklore item in circulation at the same time, such as a full anecdote version, an isolated quotation from it, and a hybrid form combining features of full reproduction and allusion in a way that does not otherwise occur (Lehtipuro 1979, 103–105). An elliptical reference to the anecdote is sufficient for the in-group audience, which derives from it the same information as from the complete anecdote version. The interviewer is often offered a mixture of the quotation and the full version, and he has to press for "the whole story" before he gets to hear it (Lehtipuro 1979, 153–154).

The narrator's knowledge of and observations on the makeup of his audience, its preferences, and its social expectations of him influence an item of folklore. There has been talk of the roles existing between a performer and his audience as manifest in a telling situation (Abrahams 1976, 15). In Juho Oksanen's case these expectations are evident in both his choice of repertoire and in the variation of a folklore item: the most popular stories are polished to perfection while the less popular ones deteriorate or vanish entirely from his active repertoire. There were two completely idiosyncratic recurring narrative motifs in my narrator's repertoire. One was a recollection of the year he spent as a student player in the band of the Finnish Guards in 1904. These recollections recur in his recordings more frequently than any other. But closer inspection does, with a few splendid exceptions, reveal them as lacking uniformity in their narrative technique. The fact that they recurred was due to the interviewers' interest in such an unusual subject. The narration is, however, fragmentary, for apart from the interviews Oksanen probably did not tell of his experiences so often that they assumed the form of a story.

The other idiosyncrasy—the story about Juho and the lord of the manor—tells how the seven-year-old Juho met a local figure of note, Magnus Tandefelt, Lord of the Manor. This recollection, polished until it has become a story, appeared three times on tape, and each time the narrator embarked on it spontaneously. This childhood memory turns out to be a key story reflecting a rise in social status on the part of the narrator. According to his daughter Oksanen told this story rather often, and in the course of repetition it has acquired a form bordering on perfection (Appendix 1, Narrative 1). The disparate fates enjoyed by these two motifs in the narrator's repertoire is understandable when we know that Oksanen's audiences most often consisted of the local parishioners he met while carrying out his church duties and on his various committees, the people of the manor, and the clergy. He probably did not consider it fitting to tell these people the historically oriented story of the time he spent in the Finnish Guards while Finland was still under Russian rule. It had lost its topicality and was, perhaps, politically unsuitable. The cultural value of this subject had dwindled and the theme was remote from his listeners. People did not expect a churchman and a local figure to tell a story like that. By way of contrast, the story of the rise of the manor housekeeper's illegitimate son to the company of the men of influence in the church

and society was just what people liked to hear. In this story the values and life experiences of listeners and narrator came close to one another, and the story was easy to accept.

Conclusion

I have concentrated here on analyzing the factors that would, according to my own research material, appear to have the greatest influence on the formulation of a narrative. Since my analysis concerned the repertoire of a single narrator, I have passed over such macrocontext factors as the structure of society and the economy, which naturally ultimately influence the folk narrative at macrolevel.

In the analysis of the formulation of narrative at microlevel recurring stories are of primary importance, for through them it is possible to compare the influence of the situational and linguistic context, the narrator's competence and psychophysical state, the state of the interaction between the interviewer and the narrator and the audience on the final result in one and the same story. The frequency of performance in turn shapes the verbalization of the story. The linguists (such as Chafe 1979, 173–175) have noted that a story may, on being repeated several weeks later, have changed considerably from the original version. As a rule this is not, however, the case with the stories in a narrator's nucleus repertoire, but personal narratives, for instance, that have only been presented a couple of times (Shuman 1986) may undergo major variation. The most recent additions to Juho Oksanen's repertoire consisted of two short chronicates about local antiheroes. The stories were only just acquiring the features of legends, and there was great variation at the different levels of telling. The genre of the narrative sometimes varied from one performance to the next, to say nothing of the decisions taken at the level of verbalization. In the case of these chronicates the facts were not organized into a narrative until the subject was raised during the conversation, whereas the schematic outline of the old stories in the repertoire already existed in the narrator's mind. The core of the old stories did not vary. The themes had already been given form, though the point of the stories and the perfection of their performance would, like the number and nature of the narrator's comments, sometimes vary.

The repeated stories of the competent narrator are a form of creative narration adapted to suit the requirements of the situational and linguistic context and the expectations of the listeners. Each time it is performed a story becomes subjected to factors bringing about variation and invariability, and its verbalization depends on how they influence the narrator on that particular occasion.

Appendix 1: The Narratives

All the narratives are examples from Juho Oksanen's repertoire and were recorded at Sysmä in Central Finland in 1968–71. The tapes belong to the Sound Archive of the Finnish Literature Society.

Narrative 1: "Juho and the lord of the manor"
This story was recorded in summer 1968, 1969 and 1970. The narrator began all three variants spontaneously, without any prompting from me, and all the variants came at stages in the telling when we had been talking about social differences in Sysmä and life at the manors.

    Performance 1. Transition to new theme—Yes, I remember old Tandefelt very well, I came into contact with him when I was still only a little boy. Old Tandefelt of Virrat himself. My mother was housekeeper at Yskelä Manor, and *Exposition: 1–5 "Arrival"* 1. one winter's evening the bells rang and there was the swish of a sleigh 2. it draws up in front of Yskelä Manor, 3. and there's Tandefelt, the lord of the manor himself. 4. The maids, the dairy maids, the serving girls and the coachmen come running out 5. to drag the master out of the sleigh, it was some job. *Exposition: 6–10 "Reception"* 6. and when they got him inside, 7. I can still remember it, and I can still see it all 8. first he was dressed in great furs and there was a big scarf wound round his neck and waist, and it crossed over his chest, and when they got the big furs off, there were smaller furs underneath. 9. The old man must have given a sigh of relief to be rid of all this garb 10. and then he was taken up to his room. *Episode I: 11–27, which can be divided into the schematic elements: Exposition:11–12: 11.* Well, all the people in charge were questioned first as the master asked about the manor, and so on. *12.* The evenings are long in winter, *Complication: 13–14 Lead-up to Action: 13.* and then it was my turn, I was just a lad of seven. *14.* He took me between his knees and said to me: *Complication: 15–17: Climax: 15.* "So you're Johanna, I always thought you were a boy, but you're a girl." *16.* I didn't want to hear another word, and I pulled away, *17.* but he caught me by the tail of my coat and said: *Resolution: 18–25: 18.* "Here, no need to be angry, we all make mistakes," he said *19.* and he took a packet of sweets out of his pocket and gave them to me and said: *20.* "You've never had sweets like these." *21.* "Yes I have, lots of times," I said, "I've been given them by my mother." *22.* But then he had a watch in his pocket, a pocket watch, a silver watch, it was a real whopper and all in a case, I can still remember it. *23.* Well he put it up to my ear and said: *24.* "Can you hear anything?" *25.* "It's playing a tune," I said. *Coda: 26–27: 26.* It was playing a tune, it was a pocket watch but it had musical clockwork inside. *27.* I've asked these youngsters too, "Have you ever found it?" . . . well one remembered a watch like that and having seen it. *Episode II: 28–34, which can be divided into the schematic elements: Exposition: 28.* And so he spent the night there in the manor. Morning came. *Complication: 29 Lead-up to Action: 29.* He says, he asked to speak to me again, and he says: *Complication: 30–34: Climax: 30.* "Well, now, I've been using your house, I've spent the night here and eaten, and so on, so what do I owe you?" *31.* "It's not my house," I said, "it's the master's own house." *32.* There was a great argument, he didn't give in until *Resolution: 33–34: 33.* at last I said, in order to be free of the whole thing, I said five pennies for his stay, *34.* and he gave me that. *Resolution 35–39: 35.* And I was in high spirits, I ran into the kitchen and there was the coachman, I said: *36.* "The master gave me five pennies." *37.* "What for?" So I told him. *39.* "Well I never," he said, "you could at least have said a mark." (Chuckles)

Narrative 2: "Dean Renqvist on his way to visit the sick"
The narrator presented four variants of this story on three consecutive years. The poorest of the performances is the second, the best the third one:

    Performance 2: Moral—and so on, it's all fiction, isn't it, but about Renqvist . . . lots of things have been put down to him. *Resolution (1):* a fir tree *Complication (1):* the horse stopped short, refused to budge. *Lead-up to Resolution (1):* But when he looked through his ring *Resolution (2):* and then he saw *Groping for Exposition, Lead-up to Result:* So there was the Dean . . . or it may have been the bridle ring he looked through *Resolution (3):* And then he saw what was in the road, stopping the horse from going on. *Exposition:* Once it was like this . . . a priest was being taken to see a sick man *Complication (2):* but the horse stopped short in the middle.

Performance 3: Exposition—He was fetched to visit a sick man, *Complication:* But the horse suddenly stopped short, nothing would make it go on. What could it be? *Lead-up to Resolution:* The Dean takes off his ring and looks through it. *Resolution:* A fir tree being dragged across the road, right in front of the horse's nose. "We're too late now," says the Dean, "the sick man's dead." *Moral:* Legends they are, just legends . . . I don't believe them there's not much truth in them.

Narrative 3: "Heikki and the authorities"
This story was recorded each year from 1968 to 1971. The third performance is the longest and the fourth the shortest. The third performance began spontaneously and was presented at an interview at which only the narrator, his wife, and I were present. The fourth performance was a lively occasion and was given to a group consisting of ourselves and my colleague Pekka Laaksonen and the narrator's daughter Rauni Hakala. The course of these two telling situations is charted in Appendix 2.

Performance 3: Transition to new theme—(Annikki Kaivola): We had a bit of trouble with the tape recorder just now, and you were telling me the story about Heikki Iitempaasi, but now I'm afraid you'll have to repeat it because none of it went onto tape. NARRATIVE 1. *Exposition (1):* 1–3: 1. First of all they used to say his name was Hidenpaasi, or was it Iidempaasi, but I've sometimes heard it called Iitempaasi, and Heikki was the man we're talking about now. 2. He was a seer. 3. And over there at Vintturi they were brewing spirit, and it was a nice quiet place, and so this Heikki, he distilled his own hooch. *Complication (1):* 4–5: *Lead-up:* 4. but the authorities got to hear of it and they came to look into matters and to have a word with Heikki. 5. Well Heikki wasn't that perturbed, offered them *Exposition (2):* 6–7: 6. Proms was bailiff in those days and there had been Promses for ages, bailiffs for several generations, and people used to ask, "Who's the Proms in Sysmä these days?" . . . as the bailiff. 7. And old Lunström, his son was too, he was the policeman I knew, but this was old Lunström, the father of this last one, who was known as an overseer. There's a statue of him, up on the hill, by the church, it says he was a "prokfokt," or whatever that is, in Swedish. *Complication (2):* 8–9: *Lead-up:* 8. So off they go, and who do they come up against but Heikki, and 9. Heikki gave them a taste, Lunström, and *Complication:* 10–11: *Climax:* 10. Lunström tossed back the drink, he went to put the empty glass down on the table but it wouldn't leave his fingers. 11. "So what's all this," says our Heikki, he snatches the glass without a word, and there's nothing on the man's fingers, no resin or glue or anything. NARRATIVE 2. *Exposition:* 12. But then the talk turned to the still. Of course they found that too, there was nothing special about that, *Complication:* 13–14: *Lead-up:* 13. the bailiff and the overseer, they took the still with them and set off to carry it to the sleigh. 14. Heikki watched them carrying the still away. *Complication:* 15: *Climax (1):* but when the moment came to put the still on the sleigh, they couldn't get their hands free, there they were. *Moral:* 16–17. 16. Goodness knows what held it there 17. but that really is what people say, and *Complication:* 18–20: *Climax (2):* 18. Heikki had to go and help them, they called out to him, he had been watching all along. 19. "Come and fetch your still, we don't need it." 20. They couldn't get their fingers off it. *Resolution:* 21. Up came Heikki and grabbed his still and marched off with it, and that was that (chuckles). *Moral:* 22. That's what tradition says. The story spread far afield, and it's come to my hearing too. (Oksanen and I began to talk about the story.)

Performance 4: Transition to new theme—(Pekka Laaksonen): It was up in the north of this parish, up by Vintturi, a pretty wild spot. (Juho Oksanen): Oh, it's still sometimes called Sysmä's Petsamo. Vintturi, Sydänmaa . . . (Rauni Hakala): There's a good road up there now, a good surfaced road. (PL): Yes, it's good now. (JO): Sydänmaa they used to call it. "I'm from Sydänmaa," they say. (PL): Were they, I mean the people who lived there, were they in any way special, were they the sort of people who . . . *NARRATIVE 2: Exposition: 1–5: 1.* There was a fellow called Heikki Iitempaasi, and *2.* he was a real seer. *3.* It was the custom to brew spirit there, then *4.* the bailiff at that time was Lunström . . . no, Lunström was the policeman *5.* but the bailiff was Proms *Complication: 6–7: Lead-up: 6.* well there they found the stills and all the other gear, *7.* and they took the still and made to take it away on the sleigh *Complication: 8: Climax (1): 8.* but it was stuck fast to their fingers, they couldn't get their hands free. They tried. *Moral (Tilda Oksanen in the background):* Was that really true, I wonder . . . (JO): they tried . . . they assured everyone it was so *Complication: 9–11 Climax (2): 9.* At last they shouted to Heikki, *10.* "Come and fetch your still then." *11.* So he said, "Take it then, and while you're about it, hold on to it." *Resolution: 12.* So they kept it, but they couldn't get it and had to fetch it and take the still away. *Moral. (TO):* I don't really believe there's any truth in it. (JO): *13.* Well it's just a legend then if it isn't true. *NAR-RATIVE 2. Exposition and Complication: 14 Lead-up: 14.* So then he gave Lunström a taste of the hooch, and to crown it all *Complication: 15 Climax:* the glass stuck to Lunström's fingers (laughter). *Moral:* (TO): Such strange, strange things do happen sometimes (speaks at the same time in the background). (JO): Yes, in the olden days. It was Heikki Iitempaasi, he . . . (People all begin to talk.)

Appendix 2: The Telling Situations

Transitions from one topic to another and speakers during the two telling situations

The tables analyze a period of 30 minutes at two different telling situations in 1970 and 1971. TOPIC denotes the subject for discussion and TRANSITION indicates the point at which the topic either changed abruptly or moved on to a subject related to what has gone before. The arrows in the center indicate that two topics are contentually related. NARRATIVE EPISODES denotes the narrative entities in consecutive order. DETAILS OF TOPIC tells what was discussed. TOPIC IN-TRODUCED BY states the person who introduced the topic, and EPISODE INTRODUCED BY states whether the narrative entity began in reply to a question from the interviewer (AQ) or spon-taneously (BS, begins spontaneously; C, continues, or AQ,C, answers question and then contin-ues). Situation 2 also states the OTHER PARTICIPANTS in the conversation. The boldfacing indicates the person/people who had most to say. If the introducer of a topic is in bold, he not only introduced the subject but also talked about it himself.

SITUATION 1. 1970 RECORDING				
Duration 30 mins. Present: JO = Juho Oksanen, TO = Tilda Oksanen, AK = Annikki Kaivola				
TOPIC	NARRATIVE EPISODES	DETAILS OF TOPIC	TOPIC INTRO-DUCED BY	EPISODE INTRO-DUCED BY
TOPIC 1 marriage TRANSITION I	(1) Dean refuses to address marriage couple in familiar form // recorder off at JO's request // (2) marriage banns ↓		JO	C AQ
TOPIC 2 names for and status of women TRANSITION II	(3) names for women (4) churching of wives and fallen women ↓		JO	AQ, C C
TOPIC 3 narrator's father TRANSITION III	(5) narrator's father			C, AQ
return to TOPIC 2 TRANSITION IV	(6) churching (TO) ↑ (continued next day)		TO	C
TOPIC 4 moonshiner TRANSITION V	(7) Heikki and the authorities		JO	BS
TOPIC 5 master and farm hands of Moiska TRANSITION VI	(8) Moiska's "educated" (9) JO pacifies the Moiska farm hands ↓		AK	AQ
TOPIC 6 youthful pursuits TRANSITION VI	(10) Jo finger-pulling (11) JO goes dancing ↓		JO	AQ, C AQ
TOPIC 7 lads TRANSITION VII	(12) name for the Moiska "educated" (13) nicknames: Samper-Otto ↓		AK	AQ C
TOPIC 8 stingy master TRANSITION IX	(14) story learnt from Samper-Otto: Stingy Ala-Leppäkorpi (15) serving girl offers farm hand the meat (16) shoemaker urges apprentice to eat butter ↓		AK	AQ C C
TOPIC 9 whipping	(17) Samper-Otto's story of whipping post		AK	AQ, C

SITUATION 2. 1971 RECORDING Duration 30 mins. Present: JO = Juho Oksanen, TO = Tilda Oksanen, RH = Rauni Hakala, PL = Pekka Laaksonen, AK = Annikki Kaivola					
TOPIC	NARRATIVE EPISODES	DETAILS OF TOPIC	TOPIC INTRO- DUCED BY	EPISODE INTRO- DUCED BY	OTHER PARTI- CIPANTS
TOPIC 1 TRANSITION I	(1) looking at photos		?	?	
TOPIC 2 poem TRANSITION II	(2) JO reads a poem by a friend of his ↓		JO	BS	
TOPIC 3 name TRANSITION III	(3) discussion of friend's name // recorder off //		PL	AQ	JO, TO
TOPIC 4 house TRANSITION IV	(4) building the Oksanen's house		JO	BS	TO, PL
TOPIC 5 Tilda TRANSITION V	(5) how Juho met Tilda // recorder off //		AK	AQ	JO, TO
TOPIC 6 cats TRANSITION VI	(6) cats		?	JO, RH, PL, AK	
TOPIC 7 the Schildt family TRANSITION VII	(7) Mrs. Schildt remembered Juho's birthday (8) as a child JO forbidden to address the daughters of the Schildt manor in the familiar way (9) Onni Schildt always invited the Oksanens to his parties (10) the Schildt's adopted son lost all his money // recorder off //		JO C C 	BS C	TO, PL, AK TO, RH
TOPIC 8 bed for the night TRANSITION VIII	(11) The Möyhäläs came to the Oksanens' for the night late one evening (12) brought their own coffee pot and cups ↓		RH RH	BS C	JO JO
TOPIC 9 moonshiner TRANSITION IX	(13) Heikki and the authorities (14) Heikki's surname		PL	AQ, C AQ	JO, TO, RH PL, JO, TO RH
TOPIC 10 master and farm hands of Moiska	(15) Moiska's "educated" (16) the master of Moiska farm hands of came for help when the Moiska farm hands drove him out // tape ended in middle of story		JO	BS	

Further Reading

Abrahams, Roger D., *Genre Theory and Folkloristics*, Studia Fennica 20, Helsinki, Finland: 1976

Bauman, Richard, *Story, Performance, and Event: Contextual Studies of Oral Narrative*, Cambridge and New York: Cambridge University Press, 1986

Chafe, Wallace L., "The Deployment of Consciousness in the Production of a Narrative," in *The Pear Stories: Cognitive, Cultural, and Linguistic Aspects of Narrative Production*, edited by Wallace L. Chafe, Norwood, New Jersey: Ablex, 1980

———, "The Flow of Thought and the Flow of Language," in *Syntax and Semantics*, edited by Talmy Givón, New York: Academic, 1979

Clark, Herbert H., and Eve V. Clark, *Psychology and Language: An Introduction to Psycholinguistics*, New York: Harcourt Brace Jovanovich, 1977

Dégh, Linda, *Folktales and Society: Story-Telling in a Hungarian Peasant Community*, Bloomington: Indiana University Press, 1969

Hiiemäe, Mall, "Kertoja Puijaa Kuulijaa," in *Kertojat ja Kuulijat*, Kalevalaseuran Vuosikirja 60, Helsinki, Finland: Suomalaisen Kirjallisuuden Seura, 1980

Honko, Lauri, "Kertomusperinteen Tutkimustavat ja Niiden Tulevaisuus," in *Kertojat ja Kuulijat*, Kalevalaseuran Vuosikirja 60, Helsinki, Finland: Suomalaisen Kirjallisuuden Seura, 1980

Hoppál, Mihály, "Folk Narrative and Memory Processes," in *Folklore on Two Continents: Essays in Honor of Linda Dégh*, Bloomington, Indiana: Trickster, 1980

———, "Genre and Context in Narrative Event: Approaches to Verbal Semiotics," in *Genre, Structure and Reproduction in Oral Literature*, edited by Lauri Honko and Vilmos Voigt, Budapest, Hungary: Akadémiai Kiadó, 1980

Kaivola-Bregenhøj, Annikki, *Kertomus ja Kerronta*, SKS: Toimituksia 480, Helsinki, Finland: Suomalaisen Kirjallisuuden Seura, 1988

———, "Variaatio Kansanperinteessä," in *Muuntelu ja Kulttuuri*, edited by Päivikki Suojanen, Tampere, Finland: Myynti, Tampereen yliopiston julkaisujen myyntipiste, 1985

Kintsch, Walter, "Comprehension and Memory of Text," in *Handbook of Learning and Cognitive Processes*, volume 6, edited by W.K. Estes, Hillsdale, New Jersey: Erlbaum, 1978

———, "On Comprehending Stories," in *Cognitive Processes in Comprehension*, edited by Marcel Adam Just and Patricia A. Carpenter, Hillsdale, New Jersey: Erlbaum, 1977; London: Wiley, 1977

Lehtipuro, Outi, *Perinneyhteisö ja Kollektiivitraditio. Folkloristinen Yhteisöntutkimus*, manuscript, Turku, Finland: 1979

Pentikäinen, Juha, "Yksilö Perinteentutkimuksen Kohteena," in *Perinteentutkimuksen Perusteita*, edited by Outi Lehtipuro, Porvoo, Finland: Söderström, 1980

Rumelhart, David E., "Notes on a Schema for Stories," in *Representation and Understanding: Studies in Cognitive Science*, edited by Daniel Bobrow and Allan Collins, New York: Academic, 1975

Shuman, Amy, *Storytelling Rights: The Uses of Oral and Written Texts by Urban Adolescents*, Cambridge and New York: Cambridge University Press, 1986

Siikala, Anna-Leena, *Tarina ja Tulkinta: Tutkimus Kansankertojista*, SKS: Toimituksia 404, Helsinki, Finland: Suomalaisen Kirjallisuuden Seura, 1984

Tannen, Deborah, *Conversational Style: Analyzing Talk Among Friends*, Norwood, New Jersey: Ablex, 1984

———, "Oral and Literate Strategies in Spoken and Written Narratives," *Language* 58:1 (1982)

Winograd, Terry, "A Framework for Understanding Discourse," in *Cognitive Processes in Comprehension*, edited by Marcel Adam Just and Patricia A. Carpenter, Hillsdale, New Jersey: Erlbaum, 1977; London: Wiley, 1977

New Storytellers in France

Veronika Görög-Karady

Veronika Görög-Karady discusses the contemporary revival of storytelling in France and notes that modern storytelling cannot be said to be the direct descendant of traditional oral culture in that country.

Traditional Telling

In order to grasp the originality of the new vogue of storytelling in present-day France, it is worth considering more generally the social uses of the oral arts—among them tales—in traditional societies. In traditional societies, the meaning of oral narrative productions resides both in the texts themselves and in the dynamics of the relationships that connect them to their social framework; that is, to the immediate circumstances of their performance (the discursive context) on the one hand and to the cultural system at large on the other hand. Thus, traditional storytellers ignore the problems of tale repertory, since they have free access to the whole set of narratives of their community, which they know by having been initiated into it as native listeners. Obviously enough, they make choices in the range of tales at their disposal; for example, they relate some stories preferentially to others on the strength of personal taste. But the way traditional storytellers operate, up to the very formulation of essential narrative details, is strongly controlled by prevalent aesthetic canons that are commonly shared by both the storytellers and their audiences. Similarly, the places, venues, and occasions regarded as appropriate for the production of narratives are defined by rather strict rules known by all concerned.

The closely knit correspondence between community norms and the ways and means of the performance of oral art (its texts and contexts) manifests itself most clearly in times of rapid socioeconomic change that necessitate the transformation of customary repertories or even the disappearance of some genres. In Europe the risk of such radical breaks with tradition was often recognized by ethnographers and folklorists. Their involvement in the defense of regional or national values under menace regularly brought them to embark upon the systematic collection of pieces of oral literature. Ethnographers and folklorists thus became the agents who transcribed collective art (which they considered to be the epitome of popular culture) from oral to written forms. Most of these initial collectors proved in fact to be both gatherers and authors since they tended to adapt, rewrite, or reshuffle the narratives they had found in order to make them agreeable for contemporary educated readers. But because their writing was often published in popular almanacs, it was sometimes redirected to oral audiences. This function of folklore scholars—their contributions to the perpetuation and popularization of oral art—has continued to the present day.

Storytelling Revival in Urban Settings

The resumption of storytelling for the educated urban public dates back to the 1960s in western Europe, particularly in France. The reappearance of a wide range of styles of storytelling as a public performance is a return to a form of art that had been absent from the symbolic products of contemporary societies for over half a century. The interest in folktales was part of a major change in an aesthetic canon that privileged the rehabilitation of naive, popular, or spontaneous forms of arts over high culture. After a period of fascination with individualistic, erudite, innovative, and rationally developed forms of art, a significant demand for traditional craftsmanship has emerged among modern elites. The rehabilitation of simple ways brought about by the renewal of old-time practices in the arts has also constituted an attempt to counteract the alienating reality of late industrial societies. The revitalization of storytelling has involved an effort to democratize culture, since publicly performed oral narratives represent a collective cultural experience intended for all age groups and (at least in theory) all kinds of social audiences.

There is indeed practically no barrier between the storyteller and his or her usual public: the content of his or her messages derives from a commonly accessible stock; the artist resorts to relatively few narrative techniques; and an appreciation of the genre does not require any specific competence or education. Even the most traditional folktale can acquire a new meaning and articulate new messages when it is performed in a contemporary urban setting. Narrative genres lend themselves to virtually unlimited degrees of disruption and subversion of traditional meanings, and the literary act upon which they are based is still open to change.

The rehabilitation of oral culture has emerged in the context of larger societal and ideological trends, such as the growing awareness of environmental problems and anxiety about a loss of control over forces that are generated by complex technologies. Renewal of oral culture can also be linked to regional movements that have led to the rediscovery and reemphasis on ethnic identities; this ideological message can be conveyed by oral literature. The same movements and ideologies gave rise to the implementation of new cultural projects and the construction of hitherto nonexistent agencies of cultural diffusion that are favorable to storytelling sessions in modern urban or suburban settings. Because industrial societies long ago eliminated occasions to perform customary oral art, new institutional frameworks for such art must be invented and arranged. The role of the ever spreading network of public libraries, youth or community centers, senior citizens' programs, state-sponsored *Maisons de la culture,* etc., played a key role in launching the new fashion of storytelling.

The New Tellers

But the new storytellers cannot be regarded directly as offspring of tradition, a natural link in the "chain of cultural transmission," to quote storyteller Praline Gay-Para. New storytellers have to find and develop the texts they propose to their audiences, often a complex task indeed, since it comprises a truly creative process of bringing about an appropriate oral style of their own. Their performances are not spontaneous but are usually carefully arranged in advance, especially when the storytellers are unfamiliar with the audience and venue for their performance. Often born and educated in cities, new storytellers do not follow their own experience to bring their tales alive. The texts they find in books have been usually transliterated by collectors and editors, so that they must be readapted to the needs of an oral performance. This transposition into orality can be realized publicly before their audience by the storytellers or done ahead of their performance through rewriting. Storytellers tend to insist upon the length of time necessary for the process of personal reappropriation of tales they have read or heard. To put together his or her repertory, each performer may have recourse to tales that are told and published in his or her own tongue or extend the quest for sources into new geographic or linguistic areas. As a rule, French storytellers do not limit themselves to traditional French or francophone repertoires. Their genuine eclecticism in this field is often a matter of conviction. As one of them put it, "Nowadays, [because] travel and business [is] transacted on a worldwide basis, the storyteller is no longer obliged to be rooted solely in one territory." As it appears from several interviews, French storytellers even tend to refuse the function of perpetuating a traditional lore that pertains to an erstwhile rural world that is now vanished. Additionally many storytellers in France are immigrants or have an international cultural background. Because they perform in French, they transpose from one language to another elements of the specific oral tradition (texts, mimics, gestures, melodies) that they keep in their memories.

Among regular storytellers in France one can identify two main categories. Those who are librarians, writers, scholars, or senior citizens with various professional backgrounds tend to perform occasionally. Others are professionals who make a modest living from storytelling and the connected activity of teaching their art (mostly at weekend seminars and occasional summer schools). Though it is not easy to quantify their respective numbers, amounting to a total of several hundreds, the number of professionals does not exceed 60. Many professional storytellers started their adventure in oral art as participants of the 1968 generation that represented a kind of cultural revolution. Many of them gave up their earlier commitments—studies, regular jobs, trained professions—some time in the 1970s in order to become full-time storytellers. Their biographies and the motivations that led them to oral narrative art are extremely diverse. For some the beginning (or the failure) of an acting career (in a theater) was the point of initiation into narration. Others revolted against the constraints of written literature. For librarians and other agents of cultural popularization, storytelling was a logical extension of their professional activities. It helped them to widen the didactic and even political dimensions of their work. Others, as conscious heirs to an extant oral tradition, embarked upon storytelling in an effort to reclaim or reestablish a formerly existing public function.

The social origins of storytellers appear to be diverse as well. Some common aspects of their biographies are nevertheless striking. Those raised in middle-class milieus often demonstrate the rejection of bourgeois culture in their professional practice. Others, whose family education was a vehicle of the preservation and transmission of elements of traditional narrative, remain heavily indebted to their heritage. Several African and some Jewish storytellers in France owe their vocations to their family setting. For Africans narration is always a means of a customary self-assertion and exemplification of collective identity. For modern Jews storytelling may advance the rediscovery of a cultural legacy forgotten or repressed during the process of assimilation. In addition to factors that derive from social background, the calling to storytelling is often related to aspects of formal education, such as artistic training in music, drama, drawing, and painting. Primary ideological inspirations (antico-

lonialism, regionalism, pacifism, antiracism, feminism, ethnic revivalism, etc.) that storytellers receive from "spiritual families" who are politically active may also play a role in the birth of a storytelling career, especially when public narration is invested with ideological significance.

Depending on their professional status, most contemporary storytellers share the experience of a degree of insecurity about their remuneration and artistic career. But the market for their performances continues to grow, since their success brings about new demands for the genre.

It would be premature to attempt to answer the question that begs a response. Where is the movement of storytelling heading? The audiences for this cultural practice continue to spread, although folktales remain a marginal object of artistic performance in contemporary France. But in the long term this may change. The rehabilitation of storytelling on stage and by the audiovisual media is regarded as both a risk and a challenge. Most if not all professionals concerned are willing to take that risk. But will stories told on TV or in ordinary theaters be the same thing as they once were? Will they be received by and addressed to the same audiences as they are today?

Further Reading

Calame-Griaule, Geneviève, ed., *Le renouveam du conte: The Revival of Storytelling*, Paris: Centre National de la Recherche Scientifique, 1991

Görög-Karady, Veronika, "Qui conte en France aujourd'hui? Les nouveaux conteurs," in *Cahiers de littérature orale*, volume 11, Paris: Publications Langues'O, 1982

Röhrich, Lutz, and Sabine Wienker-Piepho, eds., *Storytelling in Contemporary Societies*, Tübingen, Germany: Günther Narr Verlag, 1990

Storytelling in Spanish Galicia

Kristin Bervig Valentine and Eugene Valentine

After Spanish dictator Generalissimo Francisco Franco died in 1975, restrictions against regionalism in the country were eased considerably. In Galicia, the northwest province of Spain, reprinted collections of traditional Galician stories and legends were once again available, giving official endorsement to local stories that had been communicated orally for centuries. This essay by Kristin Bervig Valentine and Eugene Valentine provides an example of one of the more popular stories in the oral tradition, that of the Santa Compaña.

Introduction to Spanish Galicia

Galicia, a semiautonomous region in northwest Spain, is bordered by the regions of Asturias and Castile-León on the east, the Bay of Biscay on the north, the Atlantic Ocean on the west, and Portugal on the south. Its coastline—breached by a number of sunken estuaries—has been likened to the fjords of Norway, its rainy weather to that of England and Ireland. The people speak Galego (Galician), a language related to Portuguese, although most Galicians also speak Castilian Spanish.

As we have described elsewhere (Valentine and Valentine 1992, 180), the earth in Galicia is greener and more fertile than the sun-parched lands of Andalucía or the windswept plains of Castile. The buildings of farm and town are constructed from the ubiquitous dark gray granite of the region. The air is cool and mists hang over the valleys. The spiritual and governmental center of Galicia is the city of Santiago de Compostela, a focus since the tenth century for Catholic pilgrims who come to see the legendary resting place of the bones of St. James the Great (Santiago).

Resurgence of Interest in Galician Folklore

During the dictatorship of Francisco Franco (1936–75), the Spanish government actively discouraged regional identities, except for the dominant Castilian one, as a way of uniting the country's disparate cultures. Regional languages and literatures, including Galician, were officially proscribed, although they continued to be spoken and read in private homes. Ironically, Franco was born in El Ferrol, Galicia, and was raised speaking Galician. Soon after he died in 1975, and, with the constitutional establishment of regional autonomy in 1978, long suppressed regionalism rose more strongly than ever as Basques, Catalonians, and Galicians reasserted their cultural individuality. An important element in the resurgence of Galician culture was, and continues to be, the teaching in schools of not only the Galician language, but also traditional folklore narratives written in Galician.

In 1982, when we arrived in Galicia for our first year of folklore fieldwork, we found bookstore windows displaying colorful paperback books containing Galician legends, proverbs, songs, history, and ethnological descriptions of life in the tiny rural settlements called *aldeas*. We eagerly bought the books and began to immerse ourselves in the stories, only to discover that almost all of these bright new book jackets camouflaged reprints or anthologies of pre-Franco collections of legends, folktales, and folk songs (see, for example, Feijóo y Montenegro 1966 and

Carré Alvarellos 1977). Since it is unlikely that Galicia's pre-1936 oral traditions would continue essentially unchanged as they were presented in print by these early collectors, what is being perpetuated in these reprints is seldom either the form or content of the oral tradition as it is currently being communicated in Galicia. The reprinted collections, however, are useful to contemporary folklore scholars for background against which currently told versions can be compared. And, fortunately, original folklore fieldwork is being conducted with greater frequency in the 1980s and 1990s (e.g., Cocho 1990, García Rodero 1995, Kelley 1994, Liste 1981, Mariño Ferro 1987, Rey-Henningsen 1994, Valentine and Valentine 1992, Valentine and Valentine 1997, and Valentine and Valentine 1998).

With this background in mind, it is useful to mention that when Galicians use the term *folklor,* they are usually referring specifically to music, dances, and costumes of the eighteenth and nineteenth centuries—genres preserved by reenactment at cultural festivals. They continue, however, to pass on other types of folklore, such as myths, legends, jokes, proverbs, personal narratives, family histories, urban folklore, and material folklore everywhere and at any time, especially in plazas and stores, over meals, and in café-bars. The following is only one of many examples of storytelling that could be cited (the translations are ours and the storyteller's names are, at their request, pseudonyms).

Stories of the *Santa Compaña*

One afternoon in 1990 in our apartment in La Coruña, a large, dynamic city on the northwest coast of Galicia, our friends Dóres Queixeiro Crego and her husband, Domingo Reboleiro Grandal, joined us for *una copita y charlar* (a drink and a chat). They had worked for 10 of their adult years in England and, in common with other Galician guest workers, saved as much as they could so as to return to Galicia and live comfortably. When we first met them, Domingo was a waiter at a popular local restaurant, and Dóres contracted to clean offices after business hours.

As our contribution to the afternoon social, we were prepared to offer Ribeiro wine and *aguardiente* (a strong local brandy), in addition to coffee and tea. From a nearby bakery, Eugene produced six chocolate-and-egg-white confections that would have made a baroque architect proud. We converted our work table into a tea table by covering it with a Galician lace tablecloth.

Dóres and Domingo arrived bearing two gifts—a white ceramic cup decorated with a map of Galicia and a ceramic plate on which was printed a popular Galician saying: *Eu non creo nas bruxas, pero habel-as hainas* ("I don't believe in witches, but they exist"). That saying triggered a discussion of good witches, bad witches, ghosts, and spirits. The conversation deviated only occasionally from these topics during the four hours we talked together in a potpourri of English, Galician, and Castilian Spanish.

We started off by looking at a map of Galicia to locate the birthplaces of our friends. Domingo showed us where to find his *aldea* of Castillos located inland in Lugo Province, and Dóres showed us her birthplace of Carnota on the western seacoast in La Coruña Province.

As part of a description of life in Castillos, Domingo talked about his father's brush with the *Santa Compaña* (a nocturnal procession of souls in torment, figures akin to zombies—the walking dead [see Becoña Iglesias 1982]). Most Galician folktale collections contain one or more stories about the actions of the *Santa Compaña,* described as at least five ghosts who each night roam from the church throughout the neighborhood (Fraguas y Fraguas 1973, 102). Domingo and Dóres animatedly alternated stories they'd heard about the *Santa Compaña.*

DOMINGO: My father loved to play cards. He would walk the five kilometers to Ferreira every night and play, and stay sometimes until 3:00 or 4:00 in the morning. Then he would walk back and work all day and do the same thing the next night. One early morning he was walking back to Castillos with a friend. You've seen the men who carry their umbrellas on their backs with the handle hooked in their collars? Yes, well, he had his umbrella like that and all of a sudden there was a huge ball of light that came between him and his friend. It really scared him and he wasn't sure whether to believe it or not but when he got home he saw that his umbrella and the side of his jacket was all burned to ashes. He said it was the *Santa Compaña.*

DÓRES: My father had an experience with the *Santa Compaña* too. He was walking along late one night on his way somewhere around Carnota and he felt a heavy weight on his shoulder. He looked behind him but nothing was there. He wasn't carrying anything but he was sweating as if he were carrying a heavy load. It really happened to him. And it must have been the *Santa Compaña*.

DOMINGO: In our village there was a family with a small girl child. The mother died. After she died, the father had to go back to work and he left the child at home. My mother told me that when the father got home, the child had a clean face and clean clothes. He asked her, "How did you get clean?" "My mother cleaned me," the little girl said. She said she was sure it was her mother. So the father went to the priest who said some special prayers for the resting of the soul of the mother. It was the restless spirit of the mother who had cleaned her child, but when the priest put the mother's soul to rest, the mother went away in peace. I don't know, but my mother said it was true.

Both storytellers related their narratives with intense voices and illustrated events with energetic clarifying gestures, making vivid such scenes as Domingo's father walking along the road with an umbrella hooked to the back of his coat collar. And both agreed with the oxymoronic popular Galician saying that while they did not believe in such things, they do exist.

As the plates, cups, and glasses were emptied and daylight began to fail, Domingo said to us, "You both like Galicia, yes?" We replied, almost in unison, "Yes, we do, very much, especially when we can share your experiences with you." Laughing, Domingo responded with an apt proverb: *En Galiza chove moito pero temos de todo* ("It rains a lot in Galicia, but we have everything"). Proverbs like this one, and the saying that was printed on the plate they had brought at the beginning of their visit, are constantly at the ready in Galician society, inviting the careful listener to partake of the culture.

Galicia Today

Galicia is considerably more prosperous today than at any point in this century. Galician men and women no longer have as much economic need as they did in the past to migrate to Northern and Central Europe or to the Americas to find work. At the same time, Galicia is considered by its citizens, and by Spaniards outside Galicia, to be a traditional, legend-filled culture. Like its stories, Galicia will have elements of both tradition and change as it enters the twenty-first century.

Further Reading

Barrio, Maruxa, and Enrique Harguindey, *Contos Populares*, Vigo, Spain: Galaxia, 1983

Becoña Iglesias, Elisardo, *La Santa Compaña, el Urco y los Muertos*, La Coruña, Spain: Magoygo, 1982

Bouza-Brey Trillo, Fermín, *Etnografía y Folklore de Galicia*, 2 volumes, edited by José Luis Bouza Álvarez, Vigo, Spain: Xerais de Galicia, 1982

Carré Alvarellos, Leandro, *Las Leyendas Tradicionales Gallegas*, Madrid, Spain: Espasa-Calpe, 1977

Cocho, Federico, *O Carnaval en Galicia*, Vigo, Spain: Xerais de Galicia, 1990

Feijóo y Montenegro, Benito Jerónimo, *Antología Popular*, Buenos Aires, Argentina: Ediciones Galicia del Centro Gallego de Buenos Aires, 1966

Fraguas y Fraguas, Antonio, *La Galicía Insólita: Tradiciones Gallegas*, La Coruña, Spain: Librigal, 1973

Frutos, Pedro de, *Leyendas Gallegas*, 2 volumes, Madrid, Spain: Tres-Catorce-Diecisiete, 1980-1981

García Rodero, Cristina, *España Oculta: Public Celebrations in Spain, 1974–1989*, Washington, D.C.: Smithsonian, 1995

Kelley, Heidi, "The Myth of Matriarchy: Symbols of Womanhood in Galician Regional Identity," *Anthropological Quarterly* 67:2 (April 1994)

Liste, Ana, *Galicia, Brujería, superstición y mística*, Madrid, Spain: Penthalon, 1981

Mariño Ferro, Xosé Ramón, *Las Romerías: Peregrinaciones y sus Símbolos*, Vigo, Spain: Xerais de Galicia, 1987

Rey-Henningsen, Marisa, *The World of the Ploughwoman: Folklore and Reality in Matriarchal Northwest Spain*, Helsinki, Finland: Suomalainen Tiedeakatemia, 1994

Sueiro, Jorge-Víctor, and Amparo Nieto, *Galicia: Romería Interminable*, Madrid, Spain: Penthalon, 1983

Valentine, Kristin B., and Eugene Valentine, "'Dead or Alive, You're Going to Teixido': The Teller and the Tale," in *Fiction and Social Research: By Ice or Fire*, edited by Stephen Banks and Anna Banks, Walnut Creek, California: AltaMira, 1998

———, "Folklore Figures in Spanish Galician *Carnaval*," *Southern Folklore* 54:3 (1997)

———, "Performing Culture Through Narrative: A Galician Woman Storyteller," in *Performance, Culture, and Identity*, edited by Elizabeth C. Fine and Jean Haskell Speer, Westport, Connecticut: Praeger, 1992

Traditional Storytelling Today in the East of Northern Germany

Siegfried Neumann

Drawing on research conducted in one area over a number of years beginning in 1939, Siegfried Neumann shows how the repertoire of storytellers in that area has changed.

Story Traditions in Mecklenburg and West Pomerania

The concept of storytelling is usually combined with the idea of legends, fairy tales, stories of heroes and saints, and comic tales—that is, with a small number of so-called classic categories of prose created by the people. It is commonly accepted that such stories have all along stood at the center of orally transmitted stories of the "people" (the "folk"). This is certainly based on an oversimplified viewpoint. This is so because life among the lower levels of society has at all times been determined primarily by work and the concerns about daily needs. As a result, conversation and telling are likely to have dealt with everyday topics. But until the recent past, hardly anything of these "everyday tellings" was written down. On the other hand, numerous subjects for legends, comic tales, and fairy tales have been transmitted from older literature, which is based in part on oral sources and which, through research, can be ascribed to folk tellings of specific social levels. For nineteenth-century Germany this would apply to large portions of the rural population who were mostly without opportunity for education and had practically no means of communication other than verbal exchange.

Mecklenburg and West Pomerania, where dialect was spoken almost exclusively, at least among the population of villages and small towns, can be counted as an area with a particularly rich folk storytelling tradition. From Mecklenburg, for instance, more than 30,000 legends, about 8,000 comic tales, and more than 2,000 fairy tales are in existence; these have been written down since the 1890s by the famous collector Richard Wossidlo and numerous helpers from word of mouth—from tellings by day laborers, servants, peasants, village artisans, etc., captured in the respective dialects of the tellers. These written materials, housed in the Wossidlo-Archiv in Rostock (Neumann, *Richard Wossidlo*), give a quite detailed picture of the art of storytelling in the low German area of the late nineteenth and early twentieth centuries.

Even then, there were always only a few persons who stood out as tellers of fairy tales, legends, and comic tales, although there was one in almost every place, while everyday happenings usually were passed along by word of mouth. A large part of the population was familiar with extant subjects of the "classic categories," at least from hearing about them, so that the involvement of passive tellers can be classified as relatively high. As the collections prove, this orally transmitted material served not only as one of the foremost means of social conversation but, to a high degree, as a mirror of the worldview among large segments of the people and as medium for social testimony (Neumann, *Der mecklenburgische Volksschwank*).

In the twentieth century, however, especially among urban populations, new opportunities for conversation and communication opened up, which curtailed telling by word of mouth within its functional implications. If today one wanted to focus attention primarily on the classic categories of folk prose and to narrow it down to its oral existence, one could barely find more than marginal evidence of the phenomenon of traditional storytelling. After World War II, however, Mecklenburg–West Pomerania and other parts of the country saw a reactivation of oral telling when local inhabitants, refugees, and displaced people not only exchanged regional stories but, in the telling, poured out their wartime and postwar experiences. Soon thereafter, however, every family was back to having its radio or newspaper, both of which offered more new information. As long as only a few people had television, there was a resurgence of neighbors gathering during leisure hours, but as soon as more television sets were available the gatherings were reduced to the family. The increase in reading generally took place on an individual basis. Additionally, with living quarters becoming more solitary and jobs becoming increasingly technical, the opportunities for telling and the human need for it were further reduced.

With the decline of everyday telling the knowledge of traditional tales also diminished. These days, if subjects of the classic categories are told in public, they do not generally recall something from memory but include, to the extent they find acceptance, the attraction of newness. In contrast to the folk song, which is constantly being reproduced by means of modern mass media and therefore, at least in popular thinking, has a continuing existence, folk prose generally requires recapitulation through telling so that the story material does not disappear from memory. Little attempt is made to remember stories because they are available in printed collections and can, if desired, be reproduced orally from these sources. In such cases a selection is always made depending on what will be most popular, so that generally only a small portion of the materials safeguarded in books is offered.

Nevertheless, there is still a lot of telling, and one must grasp, or at least record, the breadth and diversity of storytelling material to gain a true picture of the telling. To say whether there is continuity or lack thereof in today's storytelling, a comparison of the present findings with those of earlier centuries is necessary. For the sake of showing an overview I have chosen Mecklenburg as the geographic example for the passing on of

traditions because there, within Germany, the richest source material is available and has also been researched (Wossidlo, *Mecklenburgische Sagen;* Wossidlo-Neumann; Neumann, *Mecklenburgische Volksmärchen*), allowing a comparison with the results of my own collecting since the 1950s. Whenever within this area, after World War II, materials and contents of earlier genres of folk prose were passed along orally in villages and small towns, this telling often retained a definitely traditional flavor for many years. Yet, as early as the 1960s and 1970s, the picture had changed considerably from the time that Wossidlo made his collections.

Some Classic Categories of Folk Prose

The change from traditional materials and contents can best be demonstrated through the results of research into the classic categories of folk prose. Among them, the comic tale has so far shown the highest degree of vitality. The largest number of my informants (Neumann, "Volkserzähler unserer Tage") were tellers of comic tales who, at least in rural areas, defined traditional storytelling. The tellers were still relatively secure in the tales' transmittal and from there continued to tell what found the most acceptance: funny stories of farmers and their hired workers, masters and journeymen, rural and urban folk, clergymen, lovers, and spouses, and so forth. A comparison of new findings with the collected materials of Wossidlo shows that the thematic range and the diversity of motif among comic tales has shrunk only a little from the 1930s to the 1970s. Certainly, the individual stories were known to fewer people, and they were told less often than in the years before World War II, but they were told, even if primarily among the older generation. The example of the old laborer August Rust (Neumann, *Ein mecklenburgischer Volkserzähler*) can be considered typical as regards the gift of the storyteller, themes of the stories, and effect in his rural setting—even though the astounding volume of his repertoire of tales was in itself unusual. Which groups of funny tales would be brought up at the most diverse occasions—for instance, in tavern gatherings or at family or group festivities—would depend on the composition of the group of storytellers and the main topic of conversation. Usually, funny entertainment would stand in the foreground. Again and again, the attraction that could be drawn from this story material would lie not just in its comic nature.

Rather, as before, people found the greatest pleasure in the cutting remarks being handed out.

By the 1960s and 1970s, the oral tradition of legends had already diminished greatly, even in rural areas. Only a few elders could give information about the world of legends in their area. Often the content would deal with international travels that would be tied to hills, ravines, lakes, and so on, in nearby surroundings. But the content of these etiological or mystic legends was no longer believed; they had, with some exceptions, become stories of a more illustrative than informative character. In contrast, the historical consciousness and some memories of the older generation found expression in the legendary or anecdotal reports on the history of a given locality. A few older people who were knowledgeable in legends had grown into the roles of living chronicles. A sign of the status of oral tradition is that no person who stands out as knowledgeable in legends can be found any more, and most people who knew about legends are able to actually tell only a portion of them.

The old oral tradition of telling fairy tales was almost extinguished. At the beginning of the twentieth century, fairy tales were still alive in the countryside of Mecklenburg as storytelling material for adults, and they took on the character of the teller's ideology. In the 1960s and 1970s even 80-year-olds knew their fairy tales mostly from schoolbooks or through more recent literature, and they would tell stories only to children. While people with an oral tradition of comic tales or legends would repeat what they had heard (i.e., draw on their memory), the fairy tale book, particularly the collection by Grimm, had generally become both source as well as permanent aid to the memory. This does not exclude the fact that there were still remarkable women who told fairy tales (Neumann, *Eine mecklenburgische Märchenfrau*), but such storytellers were only exceptions, and their efforts at a storyteller's expressive presentation of "book fairy tales" were no longer spontaneous but already belonged to a type of conscious individual "protection of the inheritance" (Neumann, "Mecklenburgische Erzähler").

The legend, on the other hand, had totally disappeared from the fund of storytelling material. Even legends with funny aspects, like the ones repeatedly told to Wossidlo, could be remembered only by a few older people, and even then, 60 years or more ago, a schoolbook would often have been the source. One could occasionally hear comic tales or jokes that alter a personage of a legend so that the world of Christian belief is seen from a comical side (Neumann, *Armin*).

The Joke

In the meantime, this process of disappearance has continued. The loss in the classic categories of oral tradition is, however, not a measure of the reduction of oral perpetuation of artistically created storytelling material. Proof is provided by the genre of the joke, which more and more takes the central place in oral telling in almost all circles of the population. The need to hear the latest joke can be found everywhere, and, there being a shortage of jokes, one can find opportunities to tell them. Along with old and new themes and groups of jokes of all kinds, there are two types of jokes that determine the picture when stories are told: the sexual joke and the political joke. It seems that only a portion of the jokes that suddenly appear and circulate widely become the subject of transmittal over the years, to keep appearing anew as "traveling jokes." Often the punch line is "used up" after a short time, or the situation to which the joke referred no longer exists. Such jokes are no longer effective and are forgotten, but new ones arise daily and are disseminated, partly through newspapers or through joke books, but primarily by word of mouth. During the years of East Germany's existence, it was considered too dangerous to write down the political jokes that made the rounds. The collections that have appeared since the reunification in 1989, however, show very clearly to what extent jokes, in particular, can bear witness to general public opinion, and jokes can even act as barometer of changing political moods (Brednich).

Other Examples of Folk Prose

When one listens to people who in the course of a conversation fall into telling stories, jokes are of course only one part among other categories of folk prose. As it has been for years and years, the speakers are telling about everyday happenings that are of particular concern to them at that moment or are related in the context of the conversation. Such reports of happenings are based partly on personal experiences of the teller or of her family members or acquaintances or have been transmitted through them (Lehmann). In part, however, the materials have been remembered as particularly remarkable and are passed on orally, having been among the large number of reports offered daily by radio, newspapers, and magazines. What is being told is as diverse as the spectrum of human life, so that it is difficult to make an overview. But of the most important contents of the stories one can distinguish between stories about children and childhood, school and study anecdotes, family histories, stories about work in all kinds of professions, stories about illness, travel experiences, reports about soldiers and war, local anecdotes about particular happenings or about personages in villages and towns, and neighborhood gossip of all kinds, and in almost all cases the truth of the story is said to be guaranteed.

These mostly basic reports on happenings that one can hear almost daily have little in common with the poetic creations of comic tale or fairy tale. Their transformation into folklore or tradition, their acceptance as collective property, or their geographic dissemination—all essential elements of traditional folk creation—are more the exception than the rule. It is interesting to note, however, what out of all happenings has been considered remarkable enough to be reported. To start with (see Bausinger), one can combine into one group the reports on lucky happenings: stories of surprised lottery winners and of having one's life saved, for example. In these stories it is the happy ending, usually after former bad luck, or the fact of having survived great danger that make such experiences appear worth telling. A parallel can be drawn from much of this material to wish fulfillment and happy endings in fairy tales. A second group is made up of the likewise much-discussed reports on astounding occurrences such as natural catastrophes, accidents, and criminal offenses—stories in which, usually, a tragic coincidence affects human life, whereby the eventual mishap is often contrasted with former good fortune. Such stories betray a distant relationship to legends. The third large group can be made up of reports about funny everyday happenings, which are in close proximity to the joke because of their subject matter and sometimes become transformed into jokes.

These groups of everyday storytelling categories, differentiated by content and structure, become mixed to a large extent when viewed from a thematic standpoint. We find within each category—stories by grandparents, stories of the workplace, stories of war—some that are stark and serious, others with a funny bent, and some that have lucky or tragic endings. Many of these tellings occur today under the name of "modern legends," reported as being true even though as a rule they are fabricated and are considered as *Wandergut* (Brednich).

In addition, stories people tell after reading books or watching movies and television shows that made a special impression play a considerable role these days. Particularly in the countryside, one finds lively discussions of movie and television shows; and especially among youth, stories from movies that others have not seen make up a large portion of everyday talk. These are mostly simple summaries of the action in a movie, a transformation of more or less artistic experiences into everyday language—in each case, as long as the immediate impression lasts. But in this quick exchange of story material that does not have its origin in oral tradition there lies, without doubt, a characteristic of today's storytelling that is unthinkable without the influence of mass media.

In today's books, newspapers, radio programs, and movies, folk prose that has been handed down leads an established "second life" that has become almost more important than its existence in word-of-mouth transmittal. Many people in Mecklenburg, where they like to tell stories, learn about local retellings of legends, fairy tales, comic stories, and so forth, less by means of live tellings, as listeners, but through their publication in books and through literature. But even those who are still connected to oral tradition and tell stories, drawing on this fund, are generally other people than formerly. For many of the storytellers, from whose stories the collectors of the nineteenth and early twentieth centuries wrote their materials, the content of their stories constituted a considerable part of their intellectual world. Today this is true only in a limited way. People since the early twentieth century have gained a different horizon in education and experiences, and they have become intellectually more flexible. I have, however, gotten to know numerous storytellers, mostly elderly, who had a definitely spontaneous connection to their story material. For someone who tells comic tales or legends in this age, the appreciation for folk prose and the fun of presenting it has to find a place among a multitude of other interests. He satisfies his many-sided intellectual and cultural needs through light material as well as more demanding fare in television, movies, theater, different kinds of reading, and music of the most diverse kinds. Into this spectrum, with an individual idea of its value, enters the knowledge of folk storytelling and a person's relationship to it. Here it does make a difference whether both result from a direct relationship to the oral storytelling tradition or from printed anthologies of story material. Where, for instance, the telling of comic tales by word of mouth is still practiced, one can observe a spontaneous and natural relationship to the story material. On the other hand, the relationship that follows acquaintance through literature is usually influenced by certain criteria of taste or by cultural and political values (Neumann, "Volkserzählung heute"). It is difficult, however, to make definite statements in this connection since this problem has not yet been sufficiently researched.

Translated by Winifred Jaeger

Further Reading

Bausinger, Hermann, "Strukturen des alltäglichen Erzählens," *Fabula* 1 (1958)

Brednich, Rolf Wilhelm, "Deutschland, einig Vaterland? What Germans Narrated Before and After the Reunification," in *Folklore Processed: In Honour of Lauri Honko,* edited by Reimund Kvideland, Helsinki, Finland: Suomalaisen Kirjallisuuden Seura, 1992

——, *Das Huhn mit dem Gipsbein: neueste Sagenhafte Geschichten von heute,* München, Germany: Beck, 1994

Lehmann, Albrecht, "Erzählen eigener Erlebnisse im Alltag," *Zeitschrift für Volkskunde* 74 (1978)

Neumann, Siegfried, *Der mecklenburgische Volksschwank; Sein sozialer Gehalt und seine soziale Funktion,* Berlin: Akademie-Verlag, 1964

——, "Mecklenburgische Erzähler der Gegenwart und ihre Märchen," in *Märchen in unserer Zeit,* edited by Hans-Jörg Uther, München, Germany: Diederichs, 1990

——, comp., *Mecklenburgische Volksmärchen,* Berlin: Akademie-Verlag, 1971

——, comp., *Plattdeutsche Legenden und Legendenschwänke. Volkserzählgn aus Mecklenburg,* Berlin: Evangelische Verlagsanstalt, 1973

——, *Richard Wossidlo und das Wossidlo-Archiv in Rostock,* Rostock, East Germany: Wossidlo-Archiv, 1994

——, "Volkserzähler unserer Tage in Mecklenburg. Bemerkungen zur Erzähler-Forschung in der Gegenwart," *Deutsches Jahrbuch für Volkskunde* 15 (1969)

——, "Volkserzählung heute. Bemerkungen zu Existenzbedingungen und Daseinsformen der Volksdichtung in der Gegenwart," *Jahrbuch für Volkskunde und Kulturgeschichte* 23 (1980)

Peters, Bertha, *Eine mecklenburgische Märchenfrau: Bertha Peters erzählt Märchen, Schwänke und Geschichten,* edited by Siegfried Neumann, Berlin: Akademie-Verlag, 1974

Rust, August, *Ein mecklenburgischer Volkserzähler. Die Geschichten des August Rust,* edited by Siegfried Neumann, second edition, Berlin: Akademie-Verlag, 1970

Wossidlo, Richard, *Mecklenburgische Sagen: ein Volksbuch,* 2 volumes, Rostock, East Germany: Hinstorff, 1939

——, *Volksschwänke aus Mecklenburg: aus der Sammlung,* edited by Siegfried Neumann, third edition, Berlin: Akademie-Verlag, 1965

Märchen 2000: Taking Care of the Fairy Tale in Germany

Sabine Wienker-Piepho

Sabine Wienker-Piepho presents an overview of contemporary storytelling revival groups in Germany. While academic scholars are losing interest in the fairy tale, these groups have assigned themselves the task of "taking care" of the fairy tale.

Taking Care of the Fairy Tale

In Germany, the fairy tale (*Märchen*) is being cared for intensively. However, the expression "taking care" was not accepted there without criticism by friends of the fairy tale. Some suggested that in German, the term "taking care" (*gepflegt*) evokes connotations of sickness, chronic illness, or at best convalescence; only what is ill should require care, and certainly the fairy tale is not sick. On the contrary, according to self-proclaimed and accepted experts in the field, it belongs among the few really healthy traditions of narrative transmittal. Indeed, the fairy tale in Germany is enjoying the best of health. It has long since passed its period of convalescence, into which it had fallen after World War II and following severe attacks during the discourse of the 1968 movement.

There are two sides to this trend: On the one hand, the fairy tale is finding increasing acceptance in broad circles of the population; on the other hand, its importance seems to be diminishing at the few academic chairs for folklore at German universities.[1] Perhaps the fairy tale and its science belong to the so-called sinking cultural commodities, to use the tie-in with this much-discussed term by Hans Naumann; they are, in any event, "sinking scientific commodities." But whereto is the fairy tale in Germany sinking? To the place where it is *cared for*. The following essay is intended to describe these efforts at caring.[2]

Albert Wesselski was the first to speak of "caring for the fairy tale." He utilized this concept in 1931 in attempting a theory about fairy tales when he demanded that artists who are gifted in storytelling (people who are caring for fairy tales) commit themselves to the fairy tale lest it perish; for Wesselski, collectors, reporters, and fairy-tale field-workers—persons who are practically non-existent today[3]—are included in this group. Wesselski understood caring for the fairy tale to be "in the nature of an activity that will protect fairy tales transmitted in good condition and that wants to rehabilitate those transmitted in poor condition."[4] In a broader sense, one can sum up caring for the fairy tale as all efforts in maintaining or breathing new life into the fairy tale and its storytelling tradition. The most diverse organizations and private individuals within and outside of Germany have subscribed to this task of conserving, and thereby caring for, the fairy tale. Further, they have promoted the telling of fairy tales and generally have supported an exchange about fairy tales and their background. They are therefore responsible for the fact that the fairy tale as a genre and living form is presently enjoying a general boom. The goal of all this caring is to restore the fairy tale to the status of a generally available cultural good.

The conservation trend is visible in Germany not only in the large printings of fairy tales and analyses but also in the eager participation of broad audiences in the most diverse activities of different presenters on the theme of fairy tales. By the very names of the activities, the "sinking scientific commodities" referred to above become apparent. We are dealing not only with festivals but also with workshops, seminars, symposiums, meetings and conferences, study groups, and courses. Such semantic upgrading apparently draws its terminology from a university context and always connotes the idea of "work." The attempt to give the scene an academic slant, however, has rather had the effect of repelling many friends of fairy tales and lay researchers. These friends and lay people, who lack access to specialty archives and books and research materials in university libraries, and who additionally were angered by the highbrow nomenclature of international secondary literature, reacted with a "gut against the head" movement that rejected emphatically any turning of the fairy tale into a science (turning it into "head-matter"). This negative attitude—sometimes aggressive or radical—reaches its peak, for instance, in the centers for fairy tales (*Märchenzentren*). One such center is the Troubadour near Vlotho, Germany; its leader, a former mountain climber, has postulated theories about a seven-jointed "original fairy tale" and, for participation in paid courses, has given out certificates and lent magic paraphernalia to "people knowledgeable about fairy tales."

The general fairy tale boom is evident from the number of subscribers to specialty periodicals[5] and the increasing attention by the press.[6] The boom is also evident in studies that analyze acceptance and also include performances of fairy tales of the immediate present.[7]

The phenomenon of professional storytelling by people who are trained and paid for their performances, and who deal with stories that have become literature (sometimes called "folklore in secondary existence"),[8] was at first strongly promoted in the Eastern European countries. Fairy-tale performers were turned into "storytelling contests,"[9] and the winners were honored with prizes ("outstanding masters of folk art").[10] Similar forms of storytelling have also become firmly established and to some extent commercialized in the United States and throughout Western Europe, particularly in Germany.

Gesellschaft zur Pflege des Märchengutes der europäischen Volker

The fairy tale scene in Germany is dominated by a particular fairy tale society, which displays the said "caring" for the fairy tale on its banner. Its statutes say that the Europäische Märchengesellschaft (EMG) "is devoted to the task of protecting folk fairy tales and of raising them anew in the consciousness of the people."[11] It was founded in 1956 as the Gesellschaft zur Pflege des Märchengutes der europäischen Volker (Society for Taking Care of Fairy Tale Materials of European Peoples) and has expanded considerably the original purposes of the organization of offering a communications forum to fairy tale friends and specialists in an extranational setting. Its task is to motivate storytellers, hobbyists, field researchers, well-known persons in the fairy tale arena, and scholars from all faculties, as well as artists, to all sorts of fairy tale-related activities. They are supposed to examine critically modern tendencies. Further, they are supposed to tell fairy tales and ultimately exchange the results of research and experiences. The epithet "European" does not sit well with people at the administrative level; but in fact, communication has taken place exclusively in the German language, and fewer than 2 percent of members have been from countries in which German is not the main language. EMG members, expected to number about 2,500 at the turn of the twenty-first century, have received as a free annual benefit books that publish the results of the international conferences, summarized in German. In addition, the EMG has documented on cassettes the work of well-known storytellers, and it has maintained its own library with primary and secondary literature at its business office in Schloss Bentlage bei Rheine in Westphalia. Members have been informed about meetings, seminars, new publications, and personal news by way of bulletins.

The caring aspect of this institution was early on delineated from the side of research. For instance Kurt Ranke, in his study on the interdependency between oral and printed presentations of fairy tales, pointed out that the EMG—ranked second in size after the Goethe-Gesellschaft among "literary" organizations in Germany—was formerly called specifically the Society for *Taking Care* of Fairy Tale Materials of European Peoples.[12]

How has this "caring" manifested itself in meetings, and how have the "curators" structured them? Once a year, this organization holds its so-called annual meeting, which always has had a particular theme,[13] and which has gotten larger and more spectacular over time and has taken place in various localities. In the morning, participants attend three or four lectures given for members, to which German-speaking researchers from all over the world are invited. Meetings continue in sections in the afternoons, or there may be meditation on fairy tales or teaching of storytelling. During the evening, fairy tales are told simultaneously in various places and are sometimes enhanced with music or presented as artistic stage versions. There may also be storytelling in a tent called *Märchenjute,* put together by Pathfinders (Pfadfinder), which is related consciously or not to shamanistic traditions, with campfire, guitar music, and an appropriately romantic mood. A spring conference is also held regularly. This somewhat smaller event also is not tied to a particular venue: for example, in 1996 it was held in northern Italy, and in 1998 participants gathered on a ship that carried them to Norway and back. In addition, short programs take place throughout the year based on a large array of themes or particular goals. For a tidy fee, one can sign up for such educational short courses, which are conducted all over the country, mostly on weekends. There is still a need in the former East Germany to catch up in this regard; under the umbrella of the EMG, many local and regional groups have organized themselves there into what are usually called fairy tale circles (*Märchenkreise*).

Many members of this organization have approached the subject primarily through narrative practice. Next to providing information about fairy tales and presenting them to lay people, one of the most important branches of the renewal movement for fairy tales is caring for the *telling* of fairy tales. The telling is being undertaken more and more professionally in these organizations and is taught in well-attended and sometimes expensive courses for storytelling, some of which are supplemented by specialized and educational literature.[14] To that extent it seems that reality has caught up to the saying "The telling is the tale," coined in 1971 by Dan Ben Amos in a totally different context. It seems that a strong fascination is generated especially by storytellers in their middle years—men and women who, without any props, give themselves over to this seemingly easy, unassuming, and timeless art of solo performance. It is probably not without reason that oral delivery is so much appreciated, particularly in a highly technological society. This fairy-tale–like storytelling,[15] for which a kind of individualistic "teller ethos" has already been developed,[16] can be understood as an answer to the high-tech culture of our time, with all its loneliness and "going it alone." It exerts a strong attraction, not least because every storyteller—women by far in the majority—thinks that he or she could do it, too.

Problems arise frequently among circles of storytellers when original material is told in different ways and made to go along with real and local happenings of the present.[17] This debate appears to be specific to Germany. Although German people usually recite word-for-word and in an exceedingly conscientious manner when following the "Grimm type" or the German-language edition of international fairy tales (*Märchen der Weltliteratur* [MdW]), only a few presenters in other countries stress in the same sense an authentic rendition that is true to the written source.[18] Storytellers in the United States, for instance, appreciatively use sourcebooks that are laid out so that with the help of corresponding indexes one can easily find material that relates to given circumstances.[19]

In another vein, there is a successful method of caring for fairy tales within the EMG that recognizes the therapeutic value of storytelling (freeing yourself with storytelling) and therefore pushes use of fairy tales, both in telling and interpretation.[20] This trend in psychology is of course not restricted to the EMG. From a sociological standpoint, such acceptance rather takes place primarily against a background of self-fulfillment,[21] which plays a large role in Germany and occasionally reaches into the now also rampantly esoteric scene in eastern Germany, where fairy tales are likewise in vogue.[22]

Yet another forum for deliberation on fairy tales is the Volkshochschule, a specific German institution that allows adults to make up deficits in their education and even catch up with their Abitur (examination qualifying one for university admission). The Volkshochschulen can be found in all of the larger cities in the country and even in the former East Germany. They are financed with public funds, private donations, and admission fees. There is hardly one of these schools that does not, because of great demand, offer at least one fairy tale course per semester, regardless of what is offered and how and at what level it is taught.

The anthroposophic movement continues to enjoy a large following, and at the Goetheanum, its center in Dornach, Switzerland, near the Swiss-German border, it regularly undertakes meditative settings of fairy tales in eurythmic productions. These interpretations follow faithfully the methods indicated by Rudolf Steiner.

Märchen-Stiftung Walter Kahn

Like the EMG, the Märchen-Stiftung Walter Kahn, named after its founder, has expressed in its statutes the specific purpose of caring for folk fairy tales. This institution was organized in 1985 and today has DM 730,000 at its disposal. It bestows primarily a DM 10,000 fairy tale prize to persons and institutions for special achievements in artistic and/or scientific areas related to the folk fairy tale and, secondly, the Lutz-Röhrich Prize of DM 5,000 for the best submitted graduating paper in the field of research into storytelling and/or the science of fairy tales (per statutes). Walter Kahn's periodical *Märchenspiegel* (Fairy Tale Mirror), edited since 1997 by folklorist Sabine Wienker-Piepho, entered its ninth year of publication in 1998. Each quarterly issue contains approximately 35 pages and includes an English summary of feature articles for those who do not read German. At 1,800 copies, the circulation of this popular/scientific periodical is considerably higher than that of scientific periodicals such as *Fabula*. Once a year, *Märchenspiegel* also provides a schedule of events that, among other things, promotes the activities of the EMG. The authors contribute their work without pay, but in exceptional cases (such as for authors from Eastern Europe) an honorarium is paid, the amount being determined according to Kahn's estimation and judgment.

The Fairy Tale Museum

In a broad sense, the caring for fairy tales in Germany incorporates also the whole field of the fairy tale museum, an overview of which is hardly possible anymore (Grimm-Museum in Kassel, Märchen- und Wesersagenmuseum in Bad Oeynhausen); work performed on various Grimm memorials and collections (in Hanau, Steinau a.d. Strasse, Haldensleben, Bad Homburg); and the so-called fairy tale parks and the profit-oriented fairy tale tourism industry.[23] There, "folklorism," a substitute for true folklore, unfolds into a sometimes grotesque bloom. Fairy tale movies, electronic fairy tale computer games, and the presence of fairy tales on the Internet also contribute to the repopularization of classical materials and thereby indirectly to the caring for the fairy tale.[24] As it is, some German people, especially the young, know fairy tales only from Disney adaptations.[25] To that extent, through good or ill-intentioned transformations of this type, folk storytelling materials undergo the process of "folklorization,"[26] well known from other areas of folklore, and indeed appear in their second, or even third, lives.

An International Fairy Tale Revival Movement

Much criticism has been raised by international researchers of storytelling regarding a "pseudo-esoteric"[27] and also an "unconditional, eclectical way of dealing with fairy tales," which triggered the whole nostalgic revival.[28] From the side of science, on the other hand, the phenomenon was taken seriously. Finally, conferences and symposiums were held on international ground for the specific purpose of discussing current forms of acceptance and the topic of contemporary storytelling.[29] In 1998 the International Society for Folk Narrative Research (ISFNR) addressed itself in a section of its twelfth international conference on the theme of caring for the fairy tale. From this perspective, it becomes more and more obvious that this revival is gradually becoming institutionalized, not only in Germany but all over the world. There are dozens of storytelling societies (such as the National Association for the Preservation and Perpetuation of Storytelling [NAPPS] in Jonesborough, Tennessee; the Society for Storytelling in Canada; the Key of Storytellers in the United Kingdom; and the Maison du Conte, in France), many of which distribute publications of their own. These include the *National Storytelling Journal* of the NAPPS;[30] *Canadian Storytellers Directory,* published in Vancouver, British Columbia; *Ceremonia de Palabras; Quaderno de tradition y narration oral,* published in Graz, Austria; *Tale Trader,* the quarterly newsletter for the International Order of E.A.R.S., published in Louisville, Kentucky; *Storytelling Times* of the Washington Storyteller Theatre, in Washington, D.C.; *Storytelling Diary* of the British Society for Storytelling; *AMAC-Infos* of the Antenne Mobile d'Action Culturelle; *Op Verhaal Komen,* published in Amsterdam, The Netherlands;[31] and many others. Although people in Germany still consider the magical fairy tales of the "Grimm type" to be the real fairy tales and prefer fairy tales containing magic,[32] events conducted by these organizations include not only classic folk and/or artistic fairy tales but also all types of stories, such as legends, comical tales, myths, heroic tales, jokes, anecdotes. By way of commercially produced recordings and videocassettes of the stories, a renewed reinforcement takes place.

Taking care of the fairy tale in Germany—we see a lively mosaic reaching into the most diverse directions and levels. As this pluralism is sometimes described, people have always "laid many ladders up against the fairy tale," but it has never yet been shaken. On the contrary, in the year 2000 it will, thanks to the caring activities described above, be stable and healthy as seldom before.

Translated by Winifred Jaeger

Notes

1. Alarming symptoms are the closures of institutions (NIF and Copenhagen) as well as the freezing of positions in Zurich (the Schenda chair) and elsewhere. Since researchers of the generation of Lutz Röhrich entered emeritus status, fairy tale research is barely being carried on under altered conditions. All fairy tale research is concentrated more and more exclusively in Göttingen around the *Enzyklopädie des Märchens,* a project of the Akademie that is already beyond "halftime."

2. For the basis of this study, see Sabine Wienker-Piepho, "Märchenpflege," in *Enzyklopädie des Märchens: Handwörterbuch zur historischen und vergleichenden Erzählforschung,* vol. 9 (New York: de Gruyter, 1997).

3. The last great field researchers in Germany remembered mostly the so-called folklore of banished people. Among people who returned to be resettled (German nationals from former eastern areas), Johannes Künzig of Freiburg im Breisgau, for instance, was a good find. One of the last publications of this type was Alfred Cammann, *Deutsche Volksmärchen aus Russland und Rumänien: Bessarabien, Dobrudscha, Siebenbürgen, Ukraine, Krim, Mittelasien,* second edition (Göttingen, West Germany: Schwartz,1988).

4. Albert Wesselski, "Versuch einer Theorie des Märchens," *Prager Deutsche Studien 45* (1931): 139.

5. See the periodical *Märchenspiegel,* published by Märchen-Stiftung Walter Kahn.

6. For an examination of articles that have been published in German-language daily

newspapers on the subject of fairy tales, see Sabine Wienker-Piepho, "Presse und Märchen," in *Presseinformationen zum Thema Märchen* (Bayersoien: Märchen-Stiftung Walter Kahn, 1994), 3–18.

7. Katalin Horn, "Zeitgenössisches Märchenerzählen und Weltanschauung," *Fabula* 24:3–4 (1993): 201–210; Lutz Röhrich and Sabine Wienker-Piepho, eds., *Storytelling in Contemporary Societies* (Tübingen, Germany: Narr Verlag, 1990).

8. Dagmar Klimova, "Versuch einer Klassifikation des lebendigen Sagenerzählens," *Fabula* 9 (1967): 244–253.

9. Dorota Simonides, "Rezente Erscheinungsformen der Märchen in Polen," in *Märchen in unserer Zeit,* edited by Hans-Jörg Uther (Munich, Germany: Dioederichs, 1990), 115–130, particularly 124 ff.

10. Rudolf Schenda, *Von Mund zu Ohr: Bausteine zu einer Kulturgeschichte volkstümlichen Erzählens in Europa* (Göttingen, Germany: Vandenhoeck und Ruprecht, 1993, 237–238.

11. After a portrait in *". . . and so they're living still?" Märchen ins Auge gefass,* catalog of an exhibition by students at the University library in Freiburg, mach. (1990) 26.

12. Kurt Ranke, *Die Welt der einfachen Formen: Studien zur Motiv-, Wort- und Quellenkunde* (New York: de Gruyter, 1978), 56.

13. For instance, The Fairy Tale and the Arts; Fairy-Tale Children—Children's Fairy Tales; Fairy-Tale Magic—Magic Fairy Tales; Fairy Tales and Death; Time in Fairy Tales; Fairy Tales and Shamanism; Fairy Tales and Creation; Fairy Tale Tellers; the Storytelling Community; and Jokes, Humor and Drollery in Fairy Tales.

14. For instance, see Gail de Vos, *Storytelling for Young Adults: Techniques and Treasury* (Englewood, Colorado: Libraries Unlimited, 1991).

15. Linda Dégh, "Zur Rezeption der Grimmschen Märchen in den USA." in *Über Märchen für Kinder von heute: Essays zu ihrem Wandel und ihrer Funktion,* ed. Klaus Doderer (Weinheim, Germany: Belz, 1983), 116–128; Katalin Horn, "Storytellers in the German Federal Republic and in German Speaking Switzerland," in *Le renouveau du conte/The Revival of Storytelling,* ed. E. Calame-Griaule (Paris: Editions du centre national de la

recherche scientifique, 1991), 43–50; Sabine Wienker-Piepho, "Storytelling und Storyteller: Einige Bemerkungen zum zeitgenössischen Erzählen," *Märchenspiegel* 1 (1995): 4–6.

16. See, for instance, Johannes Merkel, *Erzählen, Die Wiederentdeckung einer vergessenen Kunst: Geschichten und Anregungen: Ein Handbuch* (Reinbek bei Hamburg, Germany: Rowohlt, 1982).

17. Walter Scherf, *Bedeutung und Funktion des Märchens* (Munich, West Germany: International Jugendbibliothek, 1982), especially 12–18.

18. Katalin Horn, "Authentizität der Volksmärchen," *Märchenspiegel Jubiläumsausgabe* (1995): 52–56; Jürgen Janning, "Textgebundenes Erzählen als sprachliche Sensibilisierung zum freien Erzählen," ibid., 56–59.

19. For instance, Margaret Read MacDonald, *The Storyteller's Sourcebook: A Subject, Title, and Motif Index to Folklore Collections for Children* (Detroit, Michigan: Gale Research/ Neal-Schuman, 1982).

20. Verena Kast, *Märchen als Therapie*, (Olten, Switzerland: Walter Verlag, 1986); Katalin Horn, "Lebenshilfe aus uralter Weisheit? Psychologische und popularpsychologische Märchenrezeption unter ihrem therapeutischen Aspekt," in *Märchen in unserer Zeit*, ed. Hans-Jörg Uther (Munich, Germany: Diederichs, 1990), 159–169; Brigitte Brun, Ernst W. Pedersen, and Marianne Runberg, *Symbols of the Soul: Therapy and Guidance Through Fairy Tales* (London and Philadelphia: Kingsley, 1992).

21. Gerhard Schulze, *Die Erlebnisgesellschaft: Kultursoziologie der Gegenwart* (New York: Campus, 1992), 312–321.

22. See Sabine Wienker-Piepho, "Junkfood for the Soul: Magic Storytelling During Esoteric Workshops in Germany," *Fabula* 34:3–4 (1993): 225–237.

23. M. Vater, "Die deutsche Märchenstrasse," in *Touristische Konzeption und volkskundliche Bezüge* (Göttingen, Germany: 1989); A. Di Maglio, "Le fiabe com attrazione turistic," in *La Strada delle fiabe Tedesca,* (Naples, Italy: 1991–92).

24. Christoph Schmitt, *Adaptionen klassischer Märchen im Kinder- und Familienfernsehen* (Frankfurt, Germany: Haag und Herchen, 1993); Willy Höfig, "Märchen als Vorlage für Film und Fernsehen," in *Märchen in unserer Zeit,* ed. Hans Jörg Uther (Munich, Germany: Diederichs, 1990), 39–55.

25. Jack Zipes, "Breaking the Disney Spell," in his *Fairy Tales as Myth/Myth as Fairy Tale* (Lexington: University of Kentucky, 1994), 72–95.

26. Hermann Strobach, "Folklorepflege-Folklorismus: Tendenzen, Probleme und Fragen," in *Jahrbuch für Volkskunde und Kulturgeschichte* 25:10 (1982): 9–52.

27. Sabine Wienker-Piepho, "Märchen und Esoterik: Die neue magisch-spirituelle Märchenwelle," in *Das selbstverständliche Wunder: Die Welt im Spiegel des Märchens* (Karlsruhe, Germany: Evangelischer Presseverband für Baden, 1996), 51–77.

28. Leander Petzoldt, "Tendenzen und Perspektiven der Volksprosaforschung: Die Sagenforschung nach 1945," *Rheinisches Jahrbuch für Volkskunde* 26 (1985–86): 70, 93–107.

29. For instance, Morten Nørgaard et al., eds., *The Telling of Stories: Approaches to a Traditional Craft: A Symposium* (Odense, Denmark: Odense University Press, 1990); E. Calame-Griaule, ed., *Le renouveau du conte/ The Revival of Storytelling,* (Paris: Edition du centre national de la recherche scientifique, 1991).

30. Kay F. Stone, "Oral Narration in Contemporary North America," in *Fairy Tales and Society: Illusion, Allusion, and Paradigm,* ed. Ruth B. Bottigheimer (Philadelphia: University of Pennsylvania Press, 1986), 20f, 23–31.

31. See Sabine Wienker-Piepho, "Storytelling und Storyteller: Einige Bemerkungen zum zeitgenössischen Erzählen," *Märchenspiegel* 1 (1995): 4–6.

32. See Kay F. Stone, "Once upon a Time Today: Grimm Tales for Contemporary Performers," in *The Reception of Grimm's Fairy Tales: Responses, Reactions, Revisions,* ed. Donald Haase (Detroit, Michigan: Wayne State University Press, 1993), 250–268. The dominance of magical fairy tales seems to be indicated by the fact that recently the Aarne-Thompson Type Index appeared in German (its usefulness to lay people has failed mostly in the English language); this index, however, covers only the 200 most important magical fairy tales of the group termed ordinary

(magic) tales. See also Dieter Röth, ed., *Kleines Typenverzeichnis* (Baltmannsweiler: Schneider, 1998).

Further Reading

Brun, Birgitte, Ernst W. Pedersen, and Marianne Runberg, *Symbols of the Soul: Therapy and Guidance Through Fairy Tales,* London and Philadelphia: Kingsley, 1992

Cammann, Alfred, *Deutsche Volksmärchen aus Russland und Rumänien: Bessarabien, Dobrudscha, Siebenbürgen, Ukraine, Krim, Mittelasien,* second edition, Göttingen, West Germany: Schwartz, 1988

Dégh, Linda, "Zur Rezeption der Grimmschen Märchen in den USA," in *Über Märchen für Kinder von heute: Essays zu ihrem Wandel und ihrer Funktion,* edited by Klaus Doderer, Weinheim, Germany: Beltz, 1983

De Vos, Gail, *Storytelling for Young Adults: Techniques and Treasury,* Englewood, Colorado: Libraries Unlimited, 1991

Di Maglio, A., "Le fiabe com attrazione turistic," in *La Strada delle fiabe Tedesca,* 1991–92

Höfig, Willy, "Märchen als Vorlage für Film und Fernsehen," in *Märchen in unserer Zeit,* edited by Hans-Jörg Uther, Munich, Germany: Diederichs, 1990

Horn, Katalin, "Authentizität der Volksmärchen," *Märchenspiegel Jubiläumsausgabe* (1995)

———, "Lebenshilfe aus uralter Weisheit? Psychologische und popularpsychologische Märchenrezeption unter ihrem therapeutischen Aspekt," in *Märchen in unserer Zeit,* edited by Hans-Jörg Uther, Munich, Germany: Diederichs, 1990

———, "Storytellers in the German Federal Republic and in German Speaking Switzerland," in *Le renouveau du conte/The Revival of Storytelling,* edited by E. Calame-Griaule, Paris: Editions du centre national de la recherche scientifique, 1991

———, "Zeitgenössisches Märchenerzählen und Weltanschauung," *Fabula* 34:3–4 (1993)

Janning, Jürgen, "Textgebundenes Erzählen als sprachliche Sensibilisierung zum freien Erzählen," *Märchenspiegel Jubiläumsausgabe* (1995)

Kast, Verena, *Märchen als Therapie,* Olten, Switzerland: Walter-Verlag, 1986; also published as *Folktales as Therapy,* New York: Fromm, 1995

Klimova, Dagmar, "Versuch einer Klassifikation des lebendigen Sagenerzählens," *Fabula* 9 (1967)

MacDonald, Margaret Read, *The Storyteller's Sourcebook: A Subject, Title, and Motif Index to Folklore Collections for Children,* Detroit, Michigan: Gale Research/Neal-Schuman, 1982

Merkel, Johannes, *Erzählen, Die Wiederentdeckung einer vergessenen Kunst: Geschichten und Anregungen: Ein Handbuch,* Reinbeck bei Hamburg: Rowohlt, 1982

Nøjgaard, Morten, et al., eds., *The Telling of Stories: Approaches to a Traditional Craft: A Symposium,* Odense, Denmark: Odense University Press, 1990

Petzoldt, Leander, "Tendenzen und Perspektiven der Volksprosaforschung: Die Sagenforschung nach 1945," *Rheinisches Jahrbuch für Volkskunde* 26 (1985–86)

Ranke, Kurt, *Die Welt der einfachen Formen: Studien zur Motiv-, Wort- und Quellenkunde,* New York: de Gruyter, 1978

Röhrich, Lutz, and Sabine Wienker-Piepho, eds., *Storytelling in Contemporary Societies,* Tübingen, Germany: Narr Verlag, 1990

Röth, Dieter, ed., *Kleines Typenverzeichnis,* Baltmannsweiler: Schneider, 1998

Schenda, Rudolf, *Von Mund zu Ohr: Bausteine zu einer Kulturgeschichte volkstümlichen Erzählens in Europa,* Göttingen, Germany: Vandenhoeck und Ruprecht, 1993

Scherf, Walter, *Bedeutung und Funktion des Märchens,* Munich, West Germany: International Jugendbibliothek, 1982

Schmitt, Christoph, *Adaptionen klassischer Märchen im Kinder- und Familienfernsehen,* Frankfurt, Germany: Haag und Herchen, 1993

Schulze, Gerhard, *Die Erlebnisgesellschaft: Kultursoziologie der Gegenwart,* New York: Campus, 1992

Simonides, Dorota, "Rezente Erscheinungs-formen der Märchen in Polen," in *Märchen in unserer Zeit,* edited by Hans-Jörg Uther, Munich, Germany: Diederichs, 1990

Stone, Kay F., "Once upon a Time Today: Grimm Tales for Contemporary Performers," in *The Reception of Grimm's Fairy Tales: Responses, Reactions, Revisions,* edited by Donald Haase, Detroit, Michigan: Wayne State University Press, 1993

Stone, Kay F., "Oral Narration in Contemporary North America," in *Fairy Tales and Society:*

Illusion, Allusion, and Paradigm, edited by Ruth B. Bottigheimer, Philadelphia: University of Pennsylvania Press, 1986

Strobach, Hermann, "Folklorepflege-Folklorismus: Tendenzen, Probleme und Fragen," *Jahrbuch für Volkskunde und Kulturgeschirk* 25:10 (1982)

Vater, M., "Die deutsche Märchenstrasse," in *Touristische Konzeption und volkskundliche Bezüge*, Göttingen, Germany, 1989

Wesselski, Albert, "Versuch einer Theorie des Märchens," *Prager Deutsche Studien* 24 (1931)

Wienker-Piepho, Sabine, "Junkfood for the Soul: Magic Storytelling During Esoteric Workshops in Germany," *Fabula* 34:3–4 (1993)

———, "Märchenpflege," in *Enzyklopädie des Märchens: Handwörterbuch zur historischen und vergleichenden Erzählforschung*, New York: de Gruyter, 1997

———, "Märchen und Esoterik. Die neue magisch-spirituelle Märchenwell," in *Das selbstverständliche Wunder: Die Welt im Spiegel des Märchens*, Karlsruhe, Germany: Evangelischer Presseverband für Baden, 1996

———, "Presse und Märchen," in *Presseinformationen zum Thema Märchen*, Bayersoien: Märchen-Stiftung Walter Kahn, 1994

———, "Storytelling und Storyteller: Einige Bemerkungen zum zeitgenössischen Erzählen," *Märchenspiegel* 1 (1995)

Zipes, Jack, "Breaking the Disney Spell," in his *Fairy Tale as Myth/Myth as Fairy Tale*, Lexington: University of Kentucky, 1994

Greek-Albanian (Arvanítika) Interactive Storytelling and the Legitimation of Critical Discourse

Lukas D. Tsitsipis

Lukas Tsitsipis analyzes the storytelling strategies of a small group of middle-aged and elderly women commenting on current behavior of young engaged couples. The women, from Arvanítika, in southern mainland Greece, speak both Arvanítika (a dialect of Albanian) and modern Greek. Tsitsipis includes their full text to explicate their use of code-switching between languages for effect.

Introduction

Herbert Marcuse (pp. 170–199) criticizes linguistics and analytic philosophy for taking as their object of study a language that is purged of the means for expressing any other contents than those furnished to people by the established society. He takes this as an index of lack of the critical stance—lack of negativity—that modern society requires most. This article suggests that such a critical stance is frequently included and performatively enacted in certain forms of traditional storytelling that juxtapose and negotiate points of view on traditional and nontraditional value systems.

Traditional storytelling and other genres of oral discourse, along with their participation frameworks, should be viewed as complex responses to specific sociostructural conditions and changes rather than as relics of a fossilized past. Leroy Vail and Landeg White give a criticism of ethnocentric and authoritative theories in their introduction. It is probably the vitality and creativity of storytelling that Walter Benjamin (p. 91) has in mind when he considers it a form of craft rather than art.

In what follows I examine an excerpt of Arvanítika (Greek-Albanian) interactive storytelling in modern Greece. In these stories the tellers bring into sharp contrast traditional and modern value systems, thus bringing into the foreground the critical negativity that Marcuse calls for in the center of their performances.

About the Arvanítiki Dialect and this Excerpt

Arvanítika is a variety of southern Albanian spoken in what is now Greece for more than four centuries. Arvanítika speakers, who are bilingual with modern Greek, have come under a long and complex ethnic-linguistic hegemony the results of which surface in their linguistic ideology concerning Greek and their threatened local dialect (Tsitsipis, "Coding," pp. 541–577). Arvanítika stories, the telling of which amounts to frequent code-switching between Greek and Albanian, range from one-speaker tellings (Tsitsipis, "Language Shift," pp. 61–86) to jointly constructed narratives. In the latter case the stories are not typically structured on the basis of a main plot line leading to a denouement. For a similar case, see Mannheim (in Becker and Mannheim, p. 243) on southern Peruvian Quechua conversational narratives.

The excerpt below is from a jointly constructed story-commentary on moral habits offered by middle-aged and elderly women from an Arvanítika community in southern mainland Greece. In an unprepared and politically unplanned manner dimensions of modernity are scrutinized and juxtaposed to moral-ideological alternatives. Speakers take a full responsibility for telling, interpreting, and commenting critically.

In the excerpt, switches to Greek are in capital letters. Turns at talk are numbered serially; lines approximate breath-taking pauses; commas are used sparingly to index very short pauses; parentheses are used either for message clarification purposes or to insert in the gloss syntactic material predictably missing from Arvanítika surface syntax. The slanted line in 8d indexes an uncertainty as to whether the second part of the utterance belongs to reported speech or to narrative voice.

For the representation of the Arvanítika sounds, the following conventions are adopted: j following a consonant indicates palatalization; an h after a consonant indicates a fricative sound, after an s palatalization and as an autonomous sound, the glottal fricative; ë stands for the schwa; ll indicates the velarized lateral, and rr the dental trill vibrant.

The Conversation

1.) Middle-aged-woman: *edhé pastái na, kljókje*
and after (the wedding) (she) would be beaten
túti báshkë naní
all together now
mínë bënjënë
they are doing fine

2.) Mrs. K.: *mírë zbënjënë po afú. . .*
they are not doing fine but. . .

3.) Old J.: *íshtë módha naní*
it's in fashion now

4.) Mrs. K.: *edhé martóneshin, stefanóseshin, íshnë djelj*
and got married, held the ceremony, were children
naní di vítra aravonjásur, tre vítra aravonjásur
now two years engaged, three years engaged

5.) Middle-aged woman: *ne, alá kánë dhíkjo, atá vítra g' alárghu*
yes, but they are right, those years from afar

6.) Mrs. K.: *díinë púnë, pa naní bënjën di tre vítra ravonjásur*
(they) knew the job, but now stay two three years engaged
éma jo túti SÍSHTO KAJÓ
but not all WHAT THE HELL
bjérënë e fljénë bashk po, po, po turp
fall and sleep together po, po, po shame
kalá djeljm jánë do dáljënë do ghlendísënjën
fine they're young they'll go out they'll have fun
váiza naní do véte do bjérë me revnjári
the girl now will go and fall (in bed) with the one (she is) engaged to
afú fljénë bäshkë bënet ajó pun?
since they sleep together is that job (appropriately) done?
afú zë dóra njichík , ku do ftásnjën pasandái?
since they touch the hand a little, where are they going to reach later?

7.) Old J.:   *naní dhjaforetiká shúmu moré*
now (things) very different guys

8.) Middle-aged woman: *ish një stratjótë edhé játi tërgói ghram:*
one was a soldier and (his) father sent a letter:
(a) *të bësh të marsh ádhja nga stratói të vis*
arrange to take an absence of leave from the army to come
(b) *pse t' arevonjása*
since I got you engaged
(c) *ku m' arevonjáse táta?*
who did you engage me with father?
(d) *cílja / émërënë núsës?*
which / the bride's name?
Thói
(he) said
(e) *e do vinj*
and I'll come
edhé váte në núsja
and went to the bride
nuk e nih cílja isht
didn't know who she is
kúa bílja e díi
whose daughter (he) knew
ALÁ PJA ÍTANE DHEN DIN ÍKSERE
BUT WHO SHE WAS (HE) DIDN'T KNOW

9.) Ms. K.:   *atá vítëra i bëinë fshéhura*
those years they did (things) them under cover
shtúar edhé púthëshin
standing and were kissing

10.) Another old woman: *kalá vromodhuljét íshnë*
fine they were bad things
al ' íshnë më të rrállë thómi
but they were more rare we claim

11.) Middle-aged woman: *naní jánë kjílrjo*
now they are gentlemen
atá vítra ga dhrómetë
those years from the streets
revonjárëtë shtúara edhé pútheshin
the engaged standing and were kissing
PERPÁTAGHAN LÉi TA VRÁDHJA
(THEY) WALKED SAYS AT NIGHT
edhé véj edhé núsa nga prápa, pútheshin
and the bride followed behind, were kissing
nëk isht turp? më mírë mbërdha
isn't it a shame? better (if they do things) inside

Analysis

In the excerpt above one notices a constant alternation between story frame and interpretive frame. Owing to the interfering commentary, however, the whole narrative linearity strikes an interlocutor not familiar with this storytelling technique as fragmentary. The story core provides the ground concepts around which a critical story-centered discussion ensues. The major point is the direction of critical blows at contemporary sexual morality. The positions adopted, however, do not constitute a one-dimensional view. The ideas expressed cover a range from negotiation to authoritative discourse. Thus, the speaker in turn number 8 provides a whole story in direct discourse. Reported speech becomes a powerful device offering the possibility of a different world line from the one carried by the succession of statements in the main narrative. The truth of such an embedded dialogue is less accessible to challenge by the interlocutors (see Hill, p. 118, and references therein). The related anecdote therefore culminates the first part of the interaction with a discourse that is sealed from questioning by attributing the represented events to traditional norms, resembling Bakhtin's "authoritative discourse." The teller supports this authoritative foregrounding through code-switching to Greek in order to qualify the significance of the statement. John J. Gumperz discusses this in his *Discourse Strategies* (p. 79).

Nevertheless, not all parts of this collaboratively constructed story are equally authoritative. Turns 1, 2, 3, 4, 5, 6, 7, 9, 10, and 11, structured around the reported speech pivot, fluctuate between criticizing and accepting norms of sexual conduct of the past and the present. Members of these communities have not been incorporated completely into the modern world, and thus sections of the local society are not a natural extension of the urban context. They retain features of "leaky" or "boundary" discourse, which allows them to view critically habits of a rapidly changing world, embedding it ideologically in a traditional frame of reference.

The beating of wives by their husbands in the past is criticized and the modern condition accepted (turn 1), but the current situation, as the narrative suggests, becomes the locus of negotiation (turns 2 and 3). Staying engaged for years without getting married is both scorned and upheld, as is the habit of today's young people of sleeping together before an official wedding takes place (turns 4, 5, 6, and 7).

The direct-discourse part of the story—that is the story within the story—as constructed dialogue (turn 8) provides a legitimation for the traditional point of view. This resolves temporarily the undecidability of the first part of negotiation. In turns 9, 10, and 11 the polyphonic structure of the interactive story resumes by juxtaposing arguments for and against people's habit of kissing and embracing in public places.

Traditional storytellers in this unity, as is also the case elsewhere, express and foreground performatively critical views built through a constant interplay between negotiation and authoritative discourse. Code-switching, reported speech, and other devices turn this piece into a performed story foregrounding its ability to be told and its value. (See Bauman for discussion of the performed story.)

Further Reading

Bakhtin, Mikhail M., *The Dialogic Imagination: Four Essays,* edited by Michael Holquist and translated by Caryl Emerson and Michael Holquist, Austin: University of Texas Press, 1981

Bauman, Richard, *Verbal Art as Performance,* Rowley, Massachusetts: Newbury House, 1977

Becker, Alton L., and Bruce Mannheim, "Culture Troping: Languages, Codes, and Texts," in *The Dialogic Emergence of Culture,* edited by Dennis Tedlock and Bruce Mannheim, Urbana: University of Illinois Press, 1995

Benjamin, Walter, *Illuminations,* New York: Harcourt, Brace & World, 1968; London: Cape, 1970

Gumperz, John J., *Discourse Strategies,* Cambridge and New York: Cambridge University Press, 1982

Hill, Jane H., "The Voices of Don Gabriel: Responsibility and Self in a Modern Mexicano Narrative," in *The Dialogic Emergence of Culture,* edited by Dennis Tedlock and Bruce Mannheim, Urbana: University of Illinois Press, 1995

Marcuse, Herbert, *One-Dimensional Man: Studies in the Ideology of Advanced Industrial Society,* London: Routledge and Kegan Paul, 1964; Boston: Beacon, 1991

Tsitsipis, Lukas D., "The Coding of Linguistic Ideology in Arvanítika (Albanian) Language Shift: Congruent and Contradictory Discourse," *Anthropological Linguistics* 37:4 (Winter 1995)

———, "Language Shift and Narrative Performance: On the Structure and Function of Arvanítika Narratives," *Language in Society* 17:1 (March 1988)

Vail, Leroy, and Landeg White, *Power and the Praise Poem: Southern African Voices in* *History,* Charlottesville: University Press of Virginia, 1991; London: Currey, 1991

Aspects of Narrative Tradition in a Greek Gypsy Community*

Diane Tong

Diane Tong discusses narrative traditions of a Greek Gypsy community of Thessaloníki.

An Overview of the Content and Scope of Gypsy Narrative Tradition

Most of the Greek Gypsies from whom the material presented here was collected live in Thessaloníki; a few of them have recently moved to Athens. They were born in small cities and towns in northern Greece, and their parents came to Greece from Turkey. Although many people in the community are bi- or trilingual (Romani/Greek or Romani/Greek/Turkish), Romani is the language they use for legends and folktales.

The Gypsies told me that their oral tradition is dying because everyone tends to spend the long winter evenings watching television instead of telling and listening to folktales; other evidence, however, would indicate that the tradition still has a certain amount of vitality. I wish to present here a brief overview of the content and scope of Gypsy narrative tradition in one of the many groups of Gypsies in Greece.

Over the past few years I have taped a number of examples of different kinds of narrative, both in Romani and in Greek. In addition to the folktales, which provide the most numerous and most complex material, there are several other types of oral tradition in this community, such as riddles, adages, and others; an example of a riddle is as follows:

> *Si man yek phen, kai jav voida avel. So si ? Si mi ŭcalin.*
> (I have a sister who goes wherever I do. What is it ? My shadow.)
>
> (A.D., female, age 27, Athens, 1985)

Riddles often appear in one Greek-Gypsy folktale genre in which the hero or heroine must solve the riddles (usually three of them) of the king and thereby save his or her own life and also win a royal marriage partner or a lot of money, or both.

The Personal Story

Another type of narrative is the personal story. Some of the people in this community have had dramatic and difficult lives and can narrate their stories very vividly. A somewhat ritualized and communal type of personal story is told when a group of mothers-in-law gathers and each in her turn tells stories that illustrate the laziness or ingratitude of her latest daughter-in-law. The daughters-in-law have the same storytelling tradition, but their stories illustrate the demanding and tyrannical behavior of their mothers-in-law.

---

*Reprinted from *Cahiers de Littérature Orale* 30 (1991)

All of this is a way of relieving the real pressures of everyday life in a poor community.

Yet another type of personal story that is, if not apocryphal, at least highly embellished, is the personal story about another person. I heard an elaborate "rags-to-riches" story during the summer of 1985 from an elderly man. It involved a poor Greek who, in answering a newspaper ad for a husband, was chosen by a millionaire woman from the United States and brought there to live happily like a king. This story was very much like a folktale, in both style and content, and my impression was that the storyteller very much wanted to believe that things like that could happen.

Legends

Greek Gypsies have many legends in which they attempt to explain their origins or elements of their lifestyle (which is markedly different from that of the people around them, at least in the case of the group I am discussing here). There are dozens of variations of these legends. One of the most common themes is an explanation of why the Gypsies do not have their own writing:

> Once there was a king and he had the Gypsy alphabet. He put it between some cabbage leaves, since in those days they didn't have bookshelves to put things on, and he fell asleep next to a spring. A donkey came along, drank some water, and ate the cabbage leaves along with our alphabet, and that's why we don't have an alphabet.
>
> (A.D., female, age 27, Athens, 1985)

A variation:

> Didn't God gather together the people till the tower was built up as high as they wanted it? He separated all the languages on pieces of paper. He took his pencil and gave the American the American dialect, the Italian Italian, the Greek Greek, the Bulgarian Bulgarian, etc. For the Gypsy, since he was last, there was no paper left. At exactly that moment, a child was passing by and gave him a watermelon rind. The Gypsy had his donkey with him. He took the watermelon rind and wrote down the alphabet. On the road as he was going along, the Gypsy decided to sit a while and rest. He saw a nice landscape, and got down to drink some water. The donkey moved a little and the watermelon

rind fell. The donkey was hungry—he hadn't been fed—and he ate the watermelon rind and from that moment our alphabet was lost.

> (Y.K., male, age 23, Thessaloníki, 1982)

In 1985 I met some Gypsy high school students in Thessaloníki who have become interested in writing Romani and in devising their own orthography, since the Greek alphabet cannot accurately represent a number of Romani phonemes. Another concern reflected in legends is why the Gypsies are scattered all over the world:

> I've heard that we come from India. There was a very good king there who loved the Gypsies. He used to go and admire the dances around the fire—they had violins and guitars and the girls would dance. He liked our people a lot. But when that king was conquered in a war— I don't know what race he was—the new king didn't love the Gypsies and began to chase them out of the country. They were forced to leave and go to I'm not sure what other country but there, because they had tents, and caravans, people began to chase them away. Since there were a large number of caravans, maybe 10,000, they were forced to disperse: for example, five caravans to France, five to Spain, five wherever, and we're scattered all over the world, and little by little . . . you see, we're only about two or three thousand here. . . .
>
> (V.T., male, age 32, Thessaloníki, 1985)

This legend seems to offer an explanation of more than origin: the speaker evidently fears that the Gypsy diaspora will be the eventual cause of their disappearance.

Another legend explains why it is that Gypsies eat hedgehog:

> There was once a king, and he summoned everyone to the palace to bring the best meat. And they each tried to bring their animals so that the king could try to see which was the best. They all brought different animals and then a Gypsy went inside with a hedgehog and the king tried it; it was the sweetest-tasting of all those animals. Finally the others wanted to kill the Gypsy who brought the hedgehog because now they wouldn't be able to sell their animals. They killed him, and from then on only we, the Gypsies, eat hedgehog.
>
> (P.K., adult male, Thessaloníki, 1982)

Although I have met Greeks who have also enjoyed eating hedgehog, the practice is generally looked upon with scorn. Reaction to this scorn is probably what motivated the above legend, which offers a rationale for a positive interpretation of the custom.

There is a story common throughout the Balkans—the Greek version is The Bridge of Arta—of which the Greek Gypsies have their own version, which does not, apparently, turn up in non-Gypsy sources. This story resembles both legend and folktale and tells how the master builder's wife becomes the foundation sacrifice so that the haunted bridge will stay built. The Gypsy version is called The Forty Brothers and the Bridge, and, in addition to the usual narrated version, there is a long and very passionate ballad. Paspati (pp. 621–623) was told another version of this story in which the husband, rather than his wife, is sacrificed.

It is a commonplace that bears repeating that it is impossible in written versions of folktales to do justice to their liveliness and variety when told by a gifted storyteller who is in the right mood. Tenderness, fury, and other emotions felt by the characters, along with the narrator's own feelings regarding the various incidents of the tale, are conveyed not only by words but also by tone of voice, expression, and gesture. There is also the participation of at least some of the other people present, who agree, clarify, and correct the storyteller, thus turning the storytelling into a communal event. One woman who was contributing such comments to someone else's tale remarked to me that her words were like the spice added to a dish of food.

The Folktale

The most complex and rich area of narrative tradition in this community is the folktale; as expected, there are many types of tales (from the slapstick farce to the "anti-fairy tale" to the romance) and many versions of each tale in the repertoire of different storytellers and in the same person's repertoire of different occasions. Both repetition and variation have appeal for the listener. As Luthi, whose main concern is with the aesthetic aspects of the folktale, observed (p. 73):

If the same listener wishes to hear the same fairytale several times—completely in contrast to the case, say, of the joke—shows that it sets in motion a pattern of internal experience, sets off a sequence of tension and relief of tension, of

concentration and relaxation, similar in effect to that of musical work, whose interest is also not exhausted by a single hearing and which one needs to hear time and again, since the effect is deepened through repeated listening.

The same author also proposes, again making an analogy to music, that "[T]he numerous repetitions and variations [within the folktale itself] . . . like the repetitions and variations in a piece of music, serve the purpose of the whole" (p. 56). I would like to emphasize that these folktales have political and psychological as well as aesthetic components, that Gypsies can be quite sensitive to these components, and that one of the attractions of folktales is in fact the interplay of the aesthetic, the political, and the psychological.

Before describing one story in detail, I would like to briefly mention the types of tales I have collected. The most specialized tales are those designed for specific occasions—for example, tales to be told only at a wake, for the purpose of consoling the family of the deceased. There is also the tale only told to small children at bedtime—the folktale version of the lullaby.

Many of the other tales have their counterparts in European folktale collections, both Gypsy and non-Gypsy, although there are also tales whose source seems to be Indian or Turco-Arabic. The origin of some of these tales is difficult to ascertain, since Greek and Turkish folktale plots are often identical. When such stories include Gypsy characters—sometimes as the main character and sometimes as bit players—the Gypsies are seen in a highly sympathetic light, unlike the usually negative portrayal of Gypsies found in non-Gypsy folktales. In one short folktale, an elderly couple is fooled by a crafty and dishonest *gajo;* the same story is told by the Greeks—but with the ethnicities reversed.

As in all communities with this kind of tradition, countless types of tales are represented: the comic (the wise and the foolish brother; the man and his simpleminded wife; the Gypsy and the giant); the episodic adventure tale, a good example of which is The Fearless One, a story, known also in Europe, of the man who needs to go out into the world to learn the meaning of fear; what one of the storytellers call the "thriller"—an example of which is the story of the animal bridegroom, with lots of scary sound effects and supernatural creatures; the anti-fairy tale (the story with an unhappy ending), as exemplified by the classic tale of the fisherman's greedy wife; and the romance. These categories contain numerous subcategories, all of which have been classified with great care by folklore scholars.

As anyone who has enjoyed listening to the tales will agree, the stories provide both entertainment and some kind of message. The message is usually implicit in the tale, and in fact there are differing and sometimes contradictory interpretations of folktales; occasionally, however, the narrator will spell out the message for the audience. The woman who told the story of the fisherman's greedy wife ended with the comment, "so, money isn't everything." At least one of the messages in tales where the hero is a Gypsy is that the hero is extraordinarily clever and flexible, unlike her or his powerful but stupid adversaries. After hearing a lively version of The Gypsy and the Giant in January 1985, a Gypsy woman interpreted the message as follows: "You see, the giant is the Greek and we are the Gypsy. And it means that no matter how much power the Greeks have, we're still smarter than they are." This is a political interpretation, following Atwood's eloquent definition of "political": "having to do with power: who's got it, who wants it, how it operates; in a word, who's allowed to do what to whom, who gets what from whom, who gets away with it and how" (p. 353), all issues of immediate interest to Greek Gypsies. This kind of message, of course, is not confined to the Gypsies alone. Baker Miller has pointed out that "It is not surprising . . . that a subordinate group resorts to disguised and indirect ways of acting and reacting . . . Folktales, black jokes, and women stories are often based on how the wily peasant or sharecropper outwitted the rich landowner, boss, or husband. The essence of the story rests on the fact that the overlord does not even know that he has been made a fool of" (p. 10).

The message in a romantic tale may not be quite so obvious, but it is there nonetheless. I taped one of these tales on a summer evening in 1985 in a friend's courtyard in the Gypsy quarter in Thessaloníki. There were 10 or 12 of us, mostly women and children, in addition to the storyteller, K., a woman of 35 who comes from a family of gifted storytellers. People in the community often comment on how one feels as though one is really there when K. tells a story. Unfortunately, the following partial summary of the plot of a long and complex folktale cannot convey the drama and irony of the original.

The story of the tailor's youngest daughter and K.'s vivid telling of it enchanted everyone who heard it, both those present that evening and the people for whom I later played the tape, Gypsies and non-Gypsies alike. One of the charms of this particular tale is that the main character is a dynamic, independent woman who uses her own intelligence and imagination to solve difficult problems and get what she wants.

K. began the story with a description of the king who, jealous of the rich and talented tailor, a widower with three beautiful daughters, sets for him what appears to be an impossible task: in three days he has to make the king a suit without measuring, cutting, or sewing, or he will have his head cut off. The tailor sits miserably on his aluminum chair—when he is happy he sits on his silver chair—so that when his daughters come home, they know that something is wrong. The youngest daughter, who is the protagonist of the story, finally persuades him to tell her what is bothering him and then proceeds to solve his problem. The tailor places a large round table outdoors and turns the material for the suit round and round on the table. When his deadline is approaching, the king arrives and questions him. The tailor says that the sun is bothering him, and could the king please remove the sun from the sky so that he can get on with the business of making the suit. The king, furious, screams out, "Are you serious? What's the sun, some kind of vase that you think I can move from place to place?" And the tailor answers, "And how do you think I can make a suit without measuring, cutting, or sewing?" The king thereupon realizes how ridiculous he has been and releases the tailor from his obligation. In this way the tailor's daughter successfully solved her father's problem, but the king comes up with a new one: he demands that the tailor find three women who are both pregnant and virgins. Back to the aluminum chair; the youngest daughter (who has meanwhile fallen in love with the king) claims once more that she can solve the problem. The three daughters stuff some cloth under their clothing and go off to be presented to the king. The king asks each daughter who the father of her unborn child is, and the youngest daughter names the king himself. ("Don't you remember?" she asks.) He is outraged and punishes her for her irreverence by throwing her into a horrible dungeon, where she spends the first year locked up during the day, going home to visit her family in the evening by means of a secret tunnel she has dug herself. At about this time the king announces that he will take a trip. The young woman rushes to her father and asks him to make her a dress. She arranges her hair in some new way so that she will be un-recognized by the king and boards a plane to the city to which the king is traveling by ship, taking a backgammon set with her. As soon as the king arrives, she stops him and challenges him to a game of backgammon, with her virginity as the prize. She loses the game and they spend the night in a hotel, where she actually does become preg-nant. The story continues with two similar trips; the heroine ends up losing three backgammon games and producing three children, all of whom are later recognized by the king, who forgives and marries the tailor's youngest daughter, the mother of his children.

There are two features of this story that people accustomed to literary rather than oral tradition invariably comment on. The first is what Lüthi has called the "modernization of props" (p. 69): in this case, the presence of an aluminum chair and the airplane. This blending of modern con-cepts into the folktale is one of the lively aspects of oral tradition that contrasts with the static quality of the literary tale. Another characteristic that is unusual to readers of tales is the lack of coyness about sexual matters. (See Zipes, pp. 48–

531 for a discussion of the role of the "moral san-itation man" from the Grimms to Walt Disney.) People who are used to the sanitized literary ver-sions of folktales would likely be surprised at the frank sexuality in some of the tales which is, in fact, typical of the Gypsies' general approach, as are their resourcefulness and imagination—quali-ties prominent in their everyday life as well as in their narrative tradition.

Further Reading

Atwood, Margaret, *Second Words: Selected Critical Prose,* Toronto, Ontario: Anansi, 1982; Boston: Beacon, 1984

Lüthi, Max, *The Fairytale as Art Form and Portrait of Man,* translated by Jon Erickson, Bloomington: Indiana University Press, 1984

Miller, Jean Baker, *Toward a New Psychology of Women,* Boston: Beacon, 1976; London: Lane, 1978

Paspates, Alexandros G., *Études sur les Tchinghianés, ou, Bohémiens de l'Empire Ottoman,* Constantinople: Antoine Koroméla, 1870

Zipes, Jack, *Fairy Tales and the Art of Subversion: The Classical Genre for Children and the Process of Civilization,* New York: Wildman, 1983; London: Heinemann, 1983

Folklore Repertoires: Male, Female

Ilona Nagy

Nagy examines the repertoires of three Hungarian siblings, two male and one female, and discusses differences in male and female tale interpretation.

Folktale Analysis

Folkloristic research in the past quarter-century has placed great emphasis on exploring the "biology" of folklore phenomena. The desire to know the transmissional processes requires a study of the persons of transmitter and receiver and of the communication arising between them—that is, the manifestation of folklore and the occasions of its performance. Focusing on the personalities of the storytellers in folk narrative research has a tradition of about 100 years and—at least in Hungary—has been regarded as a compulsory task for more than 50 years. The refined methods of folk narrative research, communication-centered research, the application of performance theory, and so on, have been present continuously since the early 1970s in the scholarly publications.

It is by now obvious that the phenomenon of folklore can be understood, to some extent, only through the combined use of a number of methods. In folktale research, complex investigations have frequently been made in the analysis of archive texts collected at the beginning of the century (Holbek, *Interpretation;* Herranen, "Blind Storyteller"; etc.). The magic tale had disappeared from oral tradition in some of the industrialized Western societies by the time this new interest had arisen in folkloristics and methods had been developed to satisfy the new demands. The context of the heard text is generally explored and the circumstances of the performance examined in presenting occasions when legends, recollections, jokes, or personal narratives were related (Hoppál, "Genre and Context"; Kaivola-Bregenhøj, "Folklore Narrators"; Stahl; etc.). Only more rarely could a magic tale told orally be subjected to analysis applying a variety of methods (Dégh, *Folktales and Society;* Pentikäinen; Bar-Itzhak; etc.).

This paper examines the repertoire of a woman storyteller and her two brothers and provides data for gaining an insight into the scenario of storytelling. A woman and two men who say that they learned most of their tales and knowledge of folklore from the same man, their own father, share this knowledge with a female folklorist. How characteristic of the individual is the knowledge stored in the memory? Is it determined by gender or by other personality traits? What can influence the way this knowledge is brought to the surface?

About the Collector

On five occasions I did fieldwork in my own native village, Nagyfödémes (now Velké Úlany, Slovakia) in 1987, 1988, 1989, 1992, and November 1994, each time for a week. I did research on a number of themes and one of these became the regular collecting of narratives related by Mrs. Károly Matlaha (née Etelka Manczal) and her brothers. I have distant relatives in the village: Etelka Manczal's son married my second cousin. Everyone in the village knows my family and my ancestors; it is worth noting that genealogy is still

257

the most popular folklore genre there. (Eighty percent of the 4,600 inhabitants are Hungarian. Everyone knows his or her own lineage for several generations back, including also those who were deported, moved away, or died. If a person is mentioned in the course of conversation, immediately listed are all the person's relatives and place of residence.) They received me as an acquaintance and relative but also as an intellectual from Budapest, the Hungarian capital, who lived in the village only until the age of two. They showed due respect, especially at first.

The Narrators

Etelka Manczal was born in Nagyfödémes in 1922. Her parents belonged to the landless poor of the village. Her father was widowed with four children and her mother with one: they married and had seven more children, one stillborn and one who died in infancy. Their father worked as a day laborer: there was no work at all in winter, and he was not always able to find work in summer. They lived in incredible poverty and from early childhood the children, too, worked on the neighboring estates. They did not have proper food or clothing or even acceptable beds. In the evenings their father, Szilveszter Manczal, sat by the open stove door—it was left open to give light so that they did not have to use the lamp—and, taking the smallest ones on his knee, told the children stories to distract their attention from food. He told stories in winter, too, when they went out to the forest to remove stumps; this was the only form of work available in winter. They received as pay every fifth stump removed, which they used for fuel. Tales were told during cornhusking too, but not only the children were present then. Their mother preferred to sing. They learned many songs from both parents: from an early age they went from house to house at Christmas, singing songs to collect a few coins. Their knowledge of folklore was then already a means of earning a living for them. Etelka's brother Feri (Ferenc, born 1926) was an amateur actor all his life and a popular groomsman at weddings. The family's bent for the arts was manifested not only in their storytelling talents. Besides having skill in role-playing, Etelka, for example, supplemented her income from the collective farm in the 1950s by painting houses; she would paint a kitchen at dawn before work and a room in the afternoon after work, but she was not content with the fashionable patterns of that time applied with a roller.

In each corner of the ceiling she painted a colored rose pattern, using a paper form and six colors. She is a small, fragile woman, and she painted standing on a chair placed on top of a table: because she used six colors she had to climb down from the chair six times in each corner. On the walls she also painted scenes with deer and pine trees because she found them very attractive, and she did not spare any effort. She raised her two children as a widow. Her husband died of war injuries and because of the political situation at that time she did not receive any aid. She told tales only to her children—this was the case with Feri, too—but adults also enjoyed listening to her humorous stories.

Józsi (József, born 1928, died 1989) was an exuberant humorist who was fond of erotic and even obscene jokes. He claimed that he had never been drunk, but he liked to spend time in the inn where he entertained the company. I visited him on only one occasion, in 1988.

There was also a fourth sibling in the village, born from the mother's first marriage—Mrs. Ferenc Pudmericzky (née Karolin Kovács, born 1920). She feels no bent at all for performance.

Members of the informal audience were also narrators: two or three women told stories themselves, constantly commenting on what they heard when the performance was the occasion of a social gathering.

Context and Performance

I made approximately 25 hours of tape recordings with the three siblings. My first meeting with Etelka was in 1987 on a Sunday afternoon in the pensioners' club. This was a place of informal conversations over cake and soft drinks. The few men sat in a separate room; the women outnumbered them. My appearance caused a minor sensation: they willingly answered my questions, many of them told stories, and they all clearly enjoyed it. We had to record Etelka's longer tales in an empty room because the conversation did not stop for the sake of the tale. The texts were precise but became a little restrained. From then on we always met in the home of my relative, Ilonka, who lived opposite her. This relative was her daughter's mother-in-law, a widow who lived alone. We did not disturb anyone there. Etelka lives with her son and his family (four generations). At least two widows and sometimes three sat with me in Ilonka's kitchen (in a poor but friendly peasant house in the part of the village where the landowner, Count Pálffy, distributed free building sites to his workers). A further social component of the context was that I was born into the wealthy branch of the family: I was never made to feel this tension, but it did exist and I had to resolve it gradually. During the 1940s my family was displaced. Those relatives who remained in the village were poorer at the time, so they had respect for me, not only as an educated woman from the city but also as a member of a once-respected family. They were aware of the fact that the mentality and norms were not the same in the two branches of the family and between the two social groups of the village. For example, my grandparents would not have paid any attention to fairy tales or untruths. They considered such stories useless. In fact, any such amusements were useless, because they had no connection to prayer and work.

Four or five women sat together in the evenings, sometimes until midnight, telling tales of persecuted heroines, belief legends and sacred legends, occasional jokes, and endless personal narratives and life stories. The principal narrator was naturally Etelka, right up until November 1994. By then we were on very intimate terms, and I had them invite Feri for an evening. A man who had prepared carefully for the occasion entered our circle; he was dressed elegantly and obviously wanted to do himself justice. Our evening became an extremely cheerful one. Etelka and Feri vied with each other in giving different performances of pieces in the repertoire of their father. Sexual jokes and dirty jokes also appeared, and each of the five participants told at least one. It must be noted that the four women were among the 15 most religious women in the village: they went to Mass and took communion daily. They did this on the following day too (but without confessing).

I had met Feri for the first time on the morning of the same day—I had visited him in his house where he lives alone, a widower. His children visit him regularly, and the village's social caregiver brings him lunch every day for a small payment. He was cleaning walnuts that he had gathered from trees by the roadside and was preparing for sale. He was proud of one of his sons, who works in the furniture factory in the neighboring town and makes "artistic" objects from wood. Feri himself learned several crafts and also knows how to work with wood: he makes flower stands and sells them in the market. Our discourse was only partly an interview: I decided to let him talk about himself or say what he wanted to. He would have preferred to sing, however, as he considers he has talent in that direction. Whenever he hears folk songs or Hungarian popular songs on the radio, he finds that he knows them all. As in Kodish's "Absent Gender, Silent Encounter," "He was waiting silently" for someone to visit him, too, one day with a microphone. A woman visited him. (In Kodish's discussion of the typical anthropological case, it is a woman who waits for a "collector" and a man arrives.)

Józsi was far from reserved at our first and last meeting. He was clearly proud that I had come to visit him, too, after his elder sister. He lived with his family, and his grandchild sometimes came into the room—which was elegantly furnished with modern furniture—but did not stay for long. Józsi really only wanted to jest: he told the obscene jokes he had picked up in the army and the inn lightly and also recounted his "amorous" adventures. I did not object. In this culture such behavior almost certainly had significance, and I wanted only to avoid the falsification of his folklore knowledge and the spontaneity of his performance by diverting him away from his favorite topics with questions.

It is possible to include in collections of folk narrative texts originating from oral tradition or written sources that make up the repertoire, both traditional and nontraditional, placing them side by side following the customary principles of classification. However, this does not give the reader of the texts a picture of how these texts were related by people living at the end of the twentieth century. The context of the performances therefore includes the mechanism whereby these are drawn out of the memory, the minute-by-minute scenario of the narrative occasion. The collector obviously influences what is said with his or her mere presence and even more with questions. If the collector succeeds in remaining unnoticed but is nevertheless able to activate the participants, authenticity can be approached. Without the appearance and interest of the collector, tales would not have been told in that community, but the texts still live intact in memory and can be reproduced in the course of the performances. This stock of narratives is not the stock of the people living in the village today but simply those of three members of a single family (others, mainly elder people, remember a few shorter tales). A number of people know belief legends and sacred legends, while many people know jokes and humorous stories. But the Manczal siblings who know tales also lived/live in the present; when they come together they discuss their everyday problems and concerns. The time we spent together was a game based on common agreement and turning to the past. They entered into the spirit of the occasion and strove to make it enjoyable, easing it with cheerfulness and jokes. The scenario follows the rhythm of breathing: the peak is always a tale, accompanied in an associative way by a short story. The association is set off by a central notion: another participant joins in until the associations are exhausted or a new focal core (notion, action, and so forth) sets off a new train of associations. The genres alternate until the series is broken off: this is resolved by the hostess offering food and drink, the discussion of current themes bringing the company abruptly out of the poetic world into the real world. Annikki Kaivola-Bregenhøj made similar observations when she examined the position of the narrative in the discourse: "There are two factors that are important here: what has previously been said and on whose initiative the story is taken up" ("Folklore Narrators," pp. 45–54).

Following is just one example: On November 17, 1994, in the kitchen of Ilonka (Mrs. Ernö Szabó, neé Ilona Sebök, my relative) was the full company, together with Feri. Etelka tells her "Rózsika" tale (The Stretching Tree, Aarne-Thompson Type 317). The "turul bird" transports the hero to the underworld, during which time he eats seven sheep. When there is none left he cuts a piece out of his own posterior on the way there and again on the way back. He takes away the princess.

Etelka Sebök: I once heard that when this was done, he said, well, he doesn't want the kingdom either, just the girl, but there's a problem, he hasn't got a "backside."

Ilona Nagy: And what happened then?

Etelka Sebök: Well, I don't know, do I? (laughs)

Ilona Nagy: (to Etelka Manczal) But what happened Aunt Etelka, if he knew that he would marry, but he didn't have a "backside"?

Etelka Manczal: *Well* he got married, he took her as his bride!

Ilona Nagy: Didn't he have to do something?

Etelka Manczal: There wasn't any operation then (laughter), they didn't have plastic surgery in those days!

Ilona Sebök: Have some wine! Can I fill your glass?

Ilona Nagy: Thank you, just a drop!

Ferenc Manczal: In the J RD (cooperative farm) . . . the hooligans went into the stables and they cut out the cow's two haunches and left the rest there. Just the two haunches.

Ilona Sebök: The hind parts.

Etelka Sebök: And the cow died.

Ferenc Manczal: And that's a true fact, because it happened here . . . now.

Ilona Sebök: Etus, will you have a drop?

Etelka Sebök: No, no, no.

Ferenc Manczal: That's not a tale.

Etelka Manczal: But that didn't grow back again . . .

Etelka Sebök: They ate it. (Laughs)

The following coarse joke was told by Izabella Szabó. This is not about the posterior, but about excrement. A statue of St. Anthony figures in the story.

Izabella Szabó: And the parish priest was preaching about St. Antony and it occurred to me that I know a joke about him, but I didn't dare to tell him.

Etelka Sebök: The parish priest told us that the ribbons on the wreaths used to be made of rag. And they say to the cemetery guard that the ribbons are missing from the wreath. Does he know anything about it? Yes, he says, I do. And does he know who took them, does he know that too? Well, tell us then! Do you want me to tell you or to show you too? How do you mean? I can. Show us then. So he unbuttoned himself and pulled down his trousers and there, sewn into his underpants, was Rest in Peace! (much laughter)

The transitions speak for themselves. A tale-telling gathering is a series of such associative links, but there are no forced changes of theme. As time passes there are more jokes and trivial themes. Riddles also appear to keep attention alive.

The participants in the tale-telling event are persons who know each other well; they are of the same age and identical social status. An internal analysis of their texts also shows that they are full of allusions that do not need to be explained among the group.

Male Repertoires

Józsi told two magic tales: The Magic Bird-Heart (AT 567), which he learned from his father, and The Man on a Quest for His Lost Wife (AT 400), which he heard at work from a foreman on a construction site. He also told a Stupid Ogre (in Hungarian folklore, Stupid Devil) tale, 15 jokes (10 of them dirty ones), 10 riddles or riddle tales, seven definitely obscene narratives, and six personal narratives, two of which were erotic and one definitely obscene (according to Mitchell, p. 318: "classical theme of penis-size competition"). He also sang an obscene song and another that blasphemed Jesus and St. Peter.

Feri also told two magic tales. First was an unusual version of The Stretching Tree (the hero does not climb a tree that reaches to the sky but goes down into the underworld on the back of a bird; nevertheless, they have to cross high mountains and oceans—either horizontally or vertically—and the hero kills the dragon and wins the princess) that he learned from his father. Second was a similarly unusual version of The Three Magic Objects (Fortunatus) (AT 566), also learned from his father. In addition to the formula tale There was a Wee Wee Woman (AT 2016), he told a combination of Crazy Mihók (MNK 1684) and Guarding the Door (AT 1653). He told seven Gypsy anecdotes (one very coarse) and two about priests, in the presence of the women. In general he entertained them with his humorous experiences, but when only the two of us were present he spoke of the more difficult periods in his life, the war and his experiences as a prisoner of war. We were alone when, with tears in his eyes, he sang a ballad of a murder, so moved was he by the tragedy as he performed it. He learned it from his mother, and he once sang it on a car journey to his 18-year-old granddaughter, who also burst into tears. He also sang a long wedding song in dance rhythm but claimed that as far as he could remember this was not sung at weddings.

Female Repertoire: Etelka

Etelka told a variant of the above form of AT 317 but with more detail; however, she left out the duel with the dragon (in both 1988 and 1994). The Three Magic Objects were actually three only in her version. Feri was content with the miraculous bag. Her five magic tales also include the Genoveva (MNK 714+), which she learned from a pulp booklet) the Singing Bone (AT 780) and The Kind and Unkind Girls (AT 480). She told three novella-like tales and Crazy Mihók (MNK 1684; Etelka called him András, and Feri called him "the foolish lad") several times. Her version of the story does not end with marriage; the second time she told it the girl leaves the foolish lad. I asked her, "She really didn't marry him? Why, would you have married him?" Everyone laughed at this. She also told three etiological tales that were actually animal tales (Why the Rabbit Has a Short Tale [AT 119A+], etc.), The Wolf and the Kids (AT 123), two numskull stories, nine sacred legends, of which seven were actually etiological legends, two belief legends, and nine jokes, two of them coarse. She related children's games, Christmas songs, the course of the Bethlehem play, and many hours of personal narratives. She sang two murder ballads, a legend ballad, and humorous songs.

Comparison of the Tellers' Repertoires

All three tellers repeatedly claimed that they had learned what they know from their father. However, it turned out that their repertoire is derived not only from him: all three, especially Józsi, also learned from others. As Linda Dégh says in her article "Conduit Theory" (p. 124), "Tradition does not flow without regulation from one person to another but runs within society through particular transmission conduits." Only similar personalities can be transmitters and receivers in the system of communication in which the messages are channeled through the appropriate conduits. An individual receives the messages through a number of conduits (Józsi's most likely came through the army barracks and numerous inns).

The conduit theory also leads to the conclusion that the father had the most influence on the personality of Etelka and the least on that of Józsi. The variations in the items found in the repertoire of both Etelka and Józsi function according to the differing gender rules. Etelka leaves out of accounts the rules of male crafts—for example, she has the devil hiding in the sack struck with hammers weighing 50, 100, and 150 quintals at the smithy, while Feri is content with weights of 5, 10, and 15 kilos; Etelka's hero hides behind the door to strike off the heads of the seven-headed dragon, while Feri makes him struggle and has the heroine offer him a drink to boost his strength before the combat. (Feri recently became a widower after a long and harmonious marriage; his heroines are always ready to cooperate.) A favorite item in the personal narratives that they recounted spontaneously tells how bread was baked once a week in their childhood: the difference between the male and female way of seeing this lies not only in the different roles they played in the work. Feri's greatest experience was the regular whitewashing after the baking. After bread was baked in the kitchen, their mother beat the wall with a rag dipped in paint to clean the opening in the chimney that allowed the smoke out. According to Feri, the children enjoyed this greatly because the blobs splashed on the wall excited their imaginations and they tried to make out what the different shapes represented.

Despite their different use of allomotifs, their attraction to different genres (Etelka is fond of legends, Feri is not), and the difference in their manner of performance (Etelka goes into greater detail, Feri uses words more sparingly), their repertoires resemble each other far more than those of the two men, Feri and Józsi. As Aili Nenola tells us in "Folklore and Gender, "both the repertoire and context of performers may be gender specific and reflect the gender system of the community in question—be it family, village or some other community." We can add that this is certainly true to some extent, but not entirely. The division of labor between men and women in the poor stratum of village society to which my storytellers belonged was not so strictly separated as in the closed community of farmers, which was better protected with rules. For this reason, the narrative texts reflect a relatively symmetrical and complementary state of the gender system. Inger Lövkrona discusses this in her "Gender and Sexuality." The jokes, even the erotic ones, tend to be aggressive

towards the minorities, Gypsies and Jews, which have an even more isolated position than formerly. This particularly applies to Józsi's repertoire, and his text sources are quite heterogeneous.

The repeated interviews that gradually shifted in the direction of spontaneity also changed the repertoire and the texts. There was a striking increase in coarse expressions and erotic themes (although Józsi showed no inhibitions, even on the first occasion). Although this certainly does not mean that the yardstick for the authenticity is a coarse style or erotic nature (all this is, in fact, foreign to some of the narrators), it nevertheless confirms the opinion that the texts preserved in archives do not always give a faithful picture of the folklore of a given community or person.

Further Reading

Abrahams, Roger D., "The Training of the Man of Words in Talking Sweet," *Language and Society* 1:1 (1972)

Bar-Itzak, Haya, "*Smeda Rmeda Who Destroys Her Luck with Her Own Hands:* A Jewish Moroccan Cinderella Tale in an Israeli Context," *Journal of Folklore Research* 30:2–3 (1993)

Bauman Richard, *Verbal Art as Performance,* Rowley, Massachusetts: Newbury House, 1978

Dégh, Linda, "Biologie des Erzählguts," in *Enzyklopädie des Märchens: Handwörterbuch zur historischen und vergleichenden Erzählforschung: Band 2,* New York: de Gruyter, 1979

——, "Conduit Theory," in *Enzyklopädie des Märchens: Handwörterbuch zur historischen und vergleichenden Erzählforschung: Band 3,* New York: de Gruyter, 1981

——, *Folktales and Society: Story-Telling in a Hungarian Peasant Community: Expanded Edition with a New Afterword,* Bloomington: Indiana University Press, 1989

——, "Frauenmärchen," in *Enzyklopädie des Märchens: Handwörterbuch zur historischen und vergleichenden Erzählforschung: Band 5,* New York: de Gruyter, 1987

Dégh, Linda, and Andrew Vázsonyi, "The Hypothesis of Multi-Conduit Transmission," in *Folklore: Performance and Communication,* edited by Dan Ben-Amos and Kenneth Goldstein, The Hague, The Netherlands: Mouton, 1975

Fox, Jennifer, "The Creator Gods: Romantic Nationalism and the Engenderment of Women in Folklore," *Journal of American Folklore* 100:398 (1987)

Georges, Robert A., "Toward an Understanding of Storytelling Events," *Journal of American Folklore* 82 (1969)

Haiding, Karl, "Träger des Volkserzählungen in unseren Tagen," *Österreichische Zeitschrift für Volkskunde* 56 (1954)

Herranen, Gun, "Aspects of a Blind Storyteller's Repertoire: Auditive Learning-Oral Tradition," in *Le conte, pourquoi? comment?/Folktales, Why and How?*, Paris: Éditions du Centre national de la recherche scientifique, 1984

———, "A Blind Storyteller's Perception of Reality," in *Telling Reality: Folklore Studies in Memory of Bengt Holbek*, edited by Michael Chesnutt, Copenhagen, Denmark: Department of Folklore, University of Copenhagen, 1993

———, "A Blind Storyteller's Repertoire," in *Nordic Folklore: Recent Studies*, edited by Reimund Kvideland and Henning K. Sehmsdorf, Bloomington: Indiana University Press, 1989

Holbek, Bengt, "Eine neue Methode zur Interpretation von Zaubermärchen," *Jahrbuch für Volkskunde und Kulturlgeschichte*, 1980

———, *Interpretation of Fairy Tales: Danish Folklore in a European Perspective*, Helsinki, Finland: Suomalainen Tiedeakatemia, 1987

Hoppál, Mihály, "Genre and Context in Narrative Event," in *Genre, Structure, and Reproduction in Oral Literature*, edited by Lauri Honko and Vilmos Voigt, Budapest, Hungary: Akadémiai Kiadó, 1980

Kaivola-Bregenhøj, Annikki, "Factors Influencing the Formulation of Narration," in *Studies in Oral Narrative*, edited by Anna-Leena Siikala, Helsinki, Finland: Suomalaisen Kirjallisuuden Seura, 1989

———, "Folklore Narrators," in *Studies in Oral Narrative*, edited by Anna-Leena Siikala, Helsinki, Finland: Suomalaisen Kirjallisuuden Seura, 1989

Kinnunen, Eeva-Liisa, "Women and Humour: Some Reflections," paper delivered at the 9th Finnish-Hungarian Folklore Symposium, Budapest, Hungary, October 26–27, 1993

Kodish, Debora, "Absent Gender, Absent Encounter," *Journal of American Folklore* 100:398 (1987)

Kovács, Tágnes, "A Bucovina Szekler Storyteller Today," in *Folklore on Two Continents: Essays in Honor of Linda Dégh*, edited by N. Burlakoff and Carl Lindahl, Bloomington, Indiana: Trickster, 1980

Lövkrona, Inger, "Gender and Sexuality in Pre-Industrial Society: Erotic Riddles," *Fabula* 34:3–4 (1993)

Mark, Vera, "Women and Text in Gascon Tall Tales," *Journal of American Folklore* 100:398 (1987)

Mitchell, Carol A., "The Sexual Perspective in the Appreciation and Interpretation of Jokes," *Western Folklore* 36 (1977)

Nenola, Aili, "Folklore and Gender," paper delivered at the 9th Finnish-Hungarian Folklore Symposium, Budapest, Hungary, October 26–27, 1993

Papamichael-Koutroubas, Anna J., "Paramythas and Paramython: Male and Female Storytellers," in *Papers* (8th Congress of the ISFNR), 4 volumes, edited by Reimund Kvideland and Torunn Selberg, Bergen, Norway: International Society for Folk Narrative Research, 1984

Pentikäinen, Juha, *Oral Repertoire and World View: An Anthropological Study of Marina Takalo's Life History*, Helsinki, Finland: Suomalainen Tiedeakatemia, 1978

Rey-Henningsen, Marisa, *The World of the Ploughwoman: Folklore and Reality in Matriarchal Northwest Spain*, Helsinki, Finland: Suomalainen Tiedeakatemia, 1994

Saltzman, Rachelle H., "Folklore, Feminism, and the Folk: Whose Lore Is It?," *Journal of American Folklore* 100:398 (1987)

Schenda, Rudolf, "Autobiographen erzählen Geschichten," *Zeitschrift für Volkskunde* 77 (1981)

Shenhar, Aliza, "Metafolkloristic Additions to Stories by the Artistic Narrator," *Folklore* 98:1 (1987)

Stahl, Sandra K.D., *Literary Folkloristics and the Personal Narrative*, Bloomington: Indiana University Press, 1989

Traditional Storytelling in Ireland in the Twentieth Century

Patricia Lysaght

Patricia Lysaght discusses the Irish storytelling tradition and introduces us to six tellers from this century whose large repertoires have been documented.

Background: The Narration of Tales

In Ireland the narration of tales as a form of entertainment is of venerable antiquity. In ancient times tales were told by the official *scéalaí*, or teller of tales, to kings and nobles at the great assemblies or fairs held at Teltown or Carman. The *scéalaí* had a large repertoire of tales, including narratives about the supernatural world based on ancient Celtic myth. In these mythological tales, the Tuatha Dé Danann (People of the Goddess Danu) are the principal otherworld race. Many of the characters in these tales are Irish manifestations of a Celtic pantheon of divine beings—for example, Danu of the Tuatha Dé Danann, who was an ancient Celtic land goddess.

As the occasion required, the *scéalaí* would also have told tales from the so-called Ulster Cycle, the oldest collection of heroic tales in Irish literature. The tales are based on an ancient people called the Ulaidh, for whom the province of Ulster is named, and feature Conchobhar Mac Nessa as their king and Cú Chulainn as their youthful hero. The central and basic story of the cycle is "Táin Bó Cuailnge" (Cattle Raid of Cooley), a version of which was probably committed to writing as early as the seventh century. The tales, which are set in the dawn of the Christian era in Ireland, portray a heroic, warrior society and provide a depiction of an Iron Age Celtic culture from the inside.

Stories from the Ulster Cycle are not very common in Irish oral tradition. Among the most popular are those that tell how Cú Chulainn (Hound of Culainn) got his name and how he slew in single combat his son Conlaí, whom he did not recognize. The latter story appears in a late ninth-century text, *Aided Oenfir Aoife* (Death of Aoife's Only Son), and is an Irish form of the international Romantic tale (Type 873) "The King Discovers His Unknown Son."

The best-known tale from the Ulster Cycle, in the literary and oral tradition, is probably the tragic love story of Déirdre and the Sons of Uisneach, the earliest-known text of which, entitled "Loingeas Mac n-Uislenn" (Exile of the Sons of Uisliu), dates from the ninth century. It concerns competition and enmity between an old and a young man for the hand of a young woman and resembles the romance of Tristan and Isolde on the Continent and the story of the elopement of Diarmaid with Gráinne in the Fianna Cycle of tales in Ireland and Scotland.

Stories of the Ulster Cycle were a very prestigious component of the *scéalaí's* repertoire, but he probably also would have told tales about Fionn Mac Cumhail and a roving band of warriors known as the Fianna. These Fianna (Ossianic) stories, which first appear in literary texts in about the eighth century, have been very popular in the literary and oral traditions of Ireland and Gaelic Scotland for more than a thousand years. The principal characters are Fionn Mac Cumhail, his son Óisín and grandson Oscar, the handsome Diarmaid Ó Duibhne with the love-spot, Goll Mac Móirne, and Caoilte Mac Rónáin.

One of the most enduring tales of the Fianna Cycle and beloved of traditional audiences in Gaelic-speaking areas of Ireland and Scotland down the centuries was the "Boyhood Deeds of Fionn MacCumhail" ("Mac-ghníomhartha Fhinn mhic Cumhail"). The "Pursuit of Diarmaid and Gráinne" ("Toraíocht Dhiarmada agus Gráinne"), the earliest surviving recension of which dates from the fifteenth century, was also a very popular Fianna tale. It has left traces in landscape features, such as the so-called Beds of Diarmaid and Gráinne—dolmens with their large bed-like, flat capstones—where the lovers were imagined to have slept during their seven-year-long pursuit by Fionn Mac Cumhail, and in many Irish and Scottish place-names. Fenian Lays (Laoithe Fiannaíochta), poetic compositions extolling the glories of nature and the excitement of the chase, were recited by old people in the Gaelic-speaking areas of Ireland and Scotland until well into the twentieth century.

There were, of course, many other genres of narrative that were probably the stock-in-trade of storytellers in medieval as in modern times, such as hero tales other than those of the Ulster and Fianna cycles, a large variety of romantic tales, märchen, genealogies, and an extensive catalog of legends, songs, prayers, rhymes, proverbs, and so on. The conventions of storytelling, too, such as the association of heroic tales with male storytellers and the tendency to perform these and other categories of longer tales at night and during the winter half of the year—from Samhain to Bealtane, November to May—show a certain continuity from the medieval period. It is the role and evaluation of the storyteller in society that has changed drastically over the centuries as a result of political, cultural, and social upheavals in Irish society, arising from the Elizabethan, Cromwellian, and Williamite conquests and land usurpations of the seventeenth century, the Act of Union of Ireland with Great Britain (1801), and the Great Famine of the mid-nineteenth century. In the resulting changed linguistic and social climates, in which the informed and the necessary mutual understanding and interchange between teller and listener gradually lost its vitality, the institution of storytelling became, over time, socially and culturally anachronistic and went into irretrievable decline.

In most parts of Ireland, therefore, in the late nineteenth and early twentieth centuries, the traditional storyteller no longer had an appreciative local audience for his tales. Nevertheless, some outstanding storytellers in the Gaeltacht, or Irish-speaking areas, not without difficulty held on to their repertoires, and their unique art and cultural inheritance were recognized and appreciated once again, as the nineteenth century drew to a close and Ireland gained national independence in the 1920s. They were, however, acknowledged largely by outsiders—by folklore collectors and by native and foreign scholars interested in the Irish language.

A survey of the repertoire of a number of these storytellers—men and women from the Gaeltacht or Irish-speaking areas of Ireland, as well as from the English-speaking areas—and of the attitudes of their contemporaries to their art will provide a glimpse of the former richness and glory of traditional storytelling in Ireland and of the altered status of the storyteller in Irish society in the twentieth century.

Seán Ó Conaill, Cill Rialaigh, County Kerry (1853–1931)

One such storyteller was Seán Ó Conaill, a native of the parish of Iveragh, county Kerry, in the southwest of Ireland. Born in 1853, this farmer and fisherman eeked out a living in the bleak, windswept, cliff-top village of Cill Rialaigh until his death in 1931. His remarkable repertoire was discovered by chance by Séamus Ó Duilearga in the 1920s, when he came to that part of county Kerry as a student of the Irish language. Over a period of some 10 years, he collected Seán Ó Conaill's repertoire—consisting of more than 150 folktales and legends, as well as songs, poems, prayers and other items—which he edited, annotated, and published in the 1940s.[1]

Here is how Seán Ó Conaill described night-visiting in his youth when tales were told:

When the long nights would come long ago, the people of this and another village would gather together every night sitting beside the fire or wherever they could find room in the house. Many a device they would resort to to shorten the night. The man who had a long tale, or the man who had the shorter tales (*eachtraithe*), used to be telling them. At that time people used to go earning their pay working in County Limerick, County Tipperary and County Cork, and many a tale they had when they would return, everyone with his own story, so that you would not notice the night passing. Often the cock would crow before you would think of going home.

I used to watch out for anyone with a story, and when the travellers (beggars) would come and one of them would stop in the village, we used to go to the house they stayed listening to them telling stories, and trying to pick them up from them. I had only to hear a story once to have it. These "Finn Tales"[2]—nobody knows who made them. We never got any account from anyone when they were made or who composed them. They are very fine things to shorten the night in company especially those which have plenty of action in them, for example, a hero's feats of valour. . . .[3]

In the beginning of my life when I was growing up I was very interested in the Finn tales (*scéalta fiannuíochta*) if I heard of anyone who could tell them. There was no one very near who could tell them but there was a man in the village called Micheál Ó Conaill, and he used to spend his time after Michaelmas going around the countryside making baskets (*cléibheanna*)—there were few people at that time able to make them—and he used to be away until Christmas. When he came home after his rounds he had a collection of tales to tell, and I would be well to the fore in the crowd listening to him, and whatever he said I took it from him.[4]

But even then, in his early youth, interest in storytelling as a form of entertainment was in decline:

So as I was growing up and taking things in, if I went out at night with anyone and heard a story, I would want to return again and again if someone would come with me, but those of my own age were not interested in stories; they preferred other kinds of amusement. . . .

And there came a time when stories and storytellers were no longer sought after, and when he was no longer being asked to tell tales:

Many though the tales be which I have told you I have forgotten as much again; that I as-

sure you is the truth. For fifty years I have not committed to memory a Finn tale. . . .[5]

If I had known thirty years ago [that people would be looking for stories] I would have more of them certainly, but nobody bothered about them, and the pastime then and what has become commonplace for many years past—music, dancing and drinking—makes poor company. Nobody came my way but an occasional withered old man to spend a while [of a night] talking to me. . . .[6]

Stiofán Ó hEalaoire, Baile Uí Choileáin, County Clare (1858–1944)

Another outstanding storyteller, whose art was unknown in his native area until he was "discovered" by Séamus Ó Duilearga in the 1930s, was Stiofán Ó hEalaoire (1858–1944) from northwest county Clare.[7] On August 15, 1930, Séamus Ó Duilearga recorded from him on the Ediphone recording machine[8] a version of the hero tale "Conall Gulban,"[9] which took him nearly one and a half hours to tell, even though he was speaking very fast. Like Seán Ó Conaill, in his youth, Stiofán Ó hEalaoire liked listening to the old men of the locality telling stories during the long winter nights as they gathered together in a neighbor's house. His father was also a great storyteller. Over a period of about 13 years (1930–43) Séamus Ó Duilearga collected Stiofán Ó hEalaoire's repertoire, and the published volume includes hero tales, tales of magic, *Novelle* (romantic tales), stories of tricksters, humorous tales and anecdotes, religious tales, a large variety of legends of various kinds, poems, anecdotes about poets, and other items.[10]

Éamon a Búrc, Aill na Brón, Cill Chiaráin, Connemara, County Galway (1866–1942)

As the folklore movement in Ireland gained momentum after the setting up of the Irish Folklore Commission in 1935, the deployment of field collectors meant that a clearer picture of the extent and status of storytelling activity could be more clearly ascertained. In west Connemara, county Galway, as in other parts of the Gaeltacht, or Irish-speaking areas, of the west of Ireland, there were still storytellers with large repertoires picked up from the previous generation, but for whom storytelling was not an intrinsic part of social life. One such was Éamon a Búrc (1866–1942), who was acknowledged as the best storyteller in his local area and described by Seán Ó Súlleabháin as "possibly the most accomplished narrator of folk-tales who has lived into our own time."[11]

Yet it was in the 1930s that Éamon a Búrc came to outside attention, when the folklore collector Liam Mac Coisdeala began to officially collect his repertoire on behalf of the Irish Folklore Commission. He was then over 60 years of age, and he told the collector that the work of collection should have started 40 or 50 years previously, when it would have been worthwhile doing it.[12]

Éamon a Búrc had a wide range of narratives, a representative sample of which has already been published:[13] tales of the Ulster and Fianna cycles, supernatural legends, and a large corpus of lore about his native place. But it was his ability to tell the multi-episodic hero tales that firmly secured his reputation as a gifted storyteller. One of these, "Eochair mac Rí in Éirinn" ("Eochair, a King's Son in Ireland"), which he told in October 1938, consists of about 30,000 words and appears to be the longest tale ever recorded from oral narration.[14] However, he told Liam Mac Coisdeala that he had never made a practice of storytelling as those who had come before him,[15] and thus, when collecting the long tales from him, such as the hero tales, Mac Coisdeala usually gave him a few days' space to recall the story.[16] Liam Mac Coisdeala believed that Éamon a Búrc told him some stories, especially the long hero tales, that he never told a second time.[17] It is fair to say that Liam Mac Coisdeala and folklore collectors revived the custom of storytelling in the area for a short period of time, something that the narrators understood very clearly. Indeed, Éamon a Búrc himself acknowledged this to Liam Mac Coisdeala when he was going off to collect folklore in another area: He told him that the stories and other traditional lore would be thrown aside until he came back again with his recording machine.[18]

Peig Sayers, An Blascaod Mór, and Baile Viocáire, County Kerry (1873–1958)

In the remote and windswept Great Blasket Island, lying in the Atlantic Ocean off the southwest coast of county Kerry, storytelling was still part of the social fabric of the people in the early decades of the twentieth century. In a society in which entertainment was still community-based, the custom of house visiting provided a structure for nighttime amusement, of which storytelling was a part.

In this community, too, the prestige of local storytellers was greatly enhanced by the recognition afforded them by foreign scholars who came

to the island to study the Irish language. Peig Sayers (1873–1958), who was born on the nearby mainland, but who spent a large part of her life on the island after her marriage, is an example of this. Even before the field-workers of the Irish Folklore Commission began to systematically collect her repertoire, a collection of her tales made by the Celtic scholar Kenneth Jackson between 1932 and 1937 had been published (1938). Her autobiographies had also been published—*Peig* in 1936[19] and, in 1939, *Macnamh Seana-Mhná* (*An Old Woman's Reflections*).[20]

These books, however, do not capture the vigor and genius of Peig Sayers as a storyteller, the extent of her repertoire, or the skill of her performance, as it was portrayed by the medievalist Robin Flower of London's British Museum in his book *The Western Island or The Great Blasket* (1944). Flower also extolled her outstanding command of the Irish language. It was, however, as her repertoire was being officially collected by the field staff of the Irish Folklore Commission after Peig Sayers returned to the mainland in 1942 that these aspects of her storytelling ability became more clearly discernible. Over a period of some nine years, Seósamh Ó Dálaigh collected an immense amount of tales, legends, and other traditional lore from her on behalf of the Irish Folklore Commission. At least 200 tales were collected from her, including three major Fianna tales and about a dozen international wonder tales, as well as animal tales, a category of the international folktale not too common in Irish oral tradition. A large portion of her repertoire consisted of *Novelle*, and she had a large collection of religious tales. She also had songs, cante-fables, proverbs, riddles, and a large corpus of lore about traditional life on the island and contiguous mainland.

The storytelling occasions when Peig Sayers, seated in front of the fire in her home, entranced her audience and the collecting sessions when just Sayers, her son, and the collector, Seósamh Ó Dálaigh, were present are vividly recalled in Ó Dálaigh's diary accounts of his collecting activities and in W.R. Rodger's introduction to *An Old Woman's Reflections*:[21]

> ". . . I wish I had the ability to describe the scene in Peig Sayers home in Dunquin on a winter's night when the stage was set for the *seanchaí*," writes Seósamh Ó Dálaigh to me. "The evening meal was over, the day's work done, the family rosary finished. On the hearth

glowed a small peat-fire and on the side-wall an oil-lamp gave a dim light. Peig dominated the scene, seated on a low chair right in front of the fire (this was most unusual in the locality; *bean a' ti,* the woman of the house, usually seated herself at the side) and smoking her pipe. Mícheál her brother-in-law sat with his vamps[22] to the fire on one side of her and Mike her son at the other. When the visitors arrived (for all gathered to the Sayers house when Peig was there to listen to her from supper-time till midnight) the chairs were moved back and the circle increased. News was swopped, and the news often gave the lead for the night's subject, death, fairies, weather, crops." All was grist to the mill, the sayings of the dead and the doings of the living, and Peig, as she warmed to her subject, would illustrate it richly from her repertoire of verse, proverb and story. . . .

Great artist and wise woman that she was, Peig would at once switch from gravity to gaiety, for she was a light-hearted woman, and her changes of mood and face were like the changes of running water. As she talked her hands would be working too; a little clap of the palms to cap a phrase, a flash of the thumb over the shoulder to mark a mystery, a hand hushed to mouth for mischief or whispered secrecy. "When the fun is at its height it is time to go," runs the Irish proverb; and when visitors went each night Peig would draw the ashes over the peat-embers to preserve the fire till morning, reciting her customary prayer: "I preserve the fire as Christ preserves all. Brigid at the two ends of the house, and Mary in the centre. The three angels and the three apostles who are highest in the Kingdom of Grace, guiding this house and its contents until day."[23]

Anna Nic an Luain, Na Cruacha Gorma, County Donegal (1884–1954)

In another remote area of Ireland—in county Donegal in the northwest of the country—another remarkable female storyteller lived. This was Anna Nic an Luain (1884–1954), who was born and reared, was married, and lived all her life in the town land of Cruach Thobraid, in an isolated and lonely mountain glen in southwest Donegal, extending only about five miles in length and lying in the shadow of the Blue Stacks, ten miles north of Donegal town. She married into the McLoone

clan (Clann Mhic an Luain), one of the principal families of the area, and they, together with their neighbors, constituted a small community of Irish language monoglots who had an extraordinary rich oral tradition in that language.

To this out-of-the-way place Seán Ó hEochaidh, a full-time collector with the Irish Folklore Commission, came in 1947 to record the traditions of this isolated and self-contained community. He spent nearly three years at the task and was very impressed with their rich store of traditions—their stories, songs, poetry, prayers, and Fianna lore. Some of the tradition-bearers and storytellers were, of course, more expert than others, and of the women, it was Anna Nic an Luain, a housewife in her early 60s, who excelled. Seán Ó hEochaidh, who spent a good deal of time during the period 1947–48 recording her traditions, considered her quite remarkable as a person and as a storyteller. She told him long stories, Fianna tales and international folktales, some of which took a full night to perform, as well as legends, including fairy legends, prayers, and much information on the material culture of the Blue Stacks area. She also "worded" or recited from memory, 200 songs, some of them containing more than 20 stanzas.[24] Anna Nic an Luain also had a remarkable collection of riddles, which Seán Ó hEochaidh recorded from her. Seán Ó hEochaidh described the repertoire, performance, and status in the community of Anna Nic an Luain thus:

> . . . She is as wonderful a woman as I ever met. I wrote down about two hundred songs from her, and as regards stories, traditional lore and other short items, there is no knowing how much I wrote down from her. Often while I was writing from her, I was reminded of a well of clear water in a great summer drought. The well would run dry today and tomorrow morning it would be full to the brim again. Thus it was with Anna. I would spend, perhaps, a whole day writing and taking down pieces of folklore of some kind from her, and I would be finished with her, it would appear, and if I went back the following day she would be ready again, and the well of knowledge would be brimming over.

He paints a most engaging picture of Anna Nic an Luain, who had no children of her own, sitting by the fire, surrounded by the neighboring children, whom she is entertaining with her store of riddles:

When I thought I was finished with her, I was passing by one night and I put my head in the door to her. She was sitting knitting in the chimney corner with a crowd of the children of the villages sitting around her, asking them riddles. . . . I listened to Anna asking the children the riddles, and, indeed, it wasn't long before I started writing. I wrote down every single one I heard from her; I came back again and again, and in the end I had one hundred and twenty riddles from Anna. . . .[25]

To Seán Ó hEochaidh, Anna Nic an Luain "was a woman of the old world" and in that old-world, remote place at the foot of the Blue Stacks in the 1940s and 1950s, the traditions of the old Gaelic world still prevailed, in community life, in language, and in the oral traditions of the people. Seán Ó hEochaidh states that "It was rare to go into Anna's house and not find that she had company. Often I saw the small kitchen full to the door, and that was her heart's desire."[26] She also had her share of international visitors, and as in other parts of the Irish-speaking areas, the presence of the collector brought the spotlight of external recognition to shine briefly and belatedly on the storytelling tradition of the area. Anna Nic an Luain died in 1954 aged three score and ten, and it is to be regretted that she did not, unlike Peig Sayers in the southwest, leave behind an account of her daily life in that remote glen in the heart of the Donegal highlands.

There were, of course, other storytellers with important repertoires from different parts of the Gaeltacht who came to the notice of the field collectors of the Irish Folklore Commission and the Department of Irish Folklore, some of whose store of tales have been published. I have already listed most of these in an earlier article.[27]

English-Speaking Areas

Although folklore-collecting activities in Ireland have been mainly concentrated in the Irish-speaking areas, collecting in the English-speaking parts of Ireland has also been carried out, although not as vigorously as in the former areas. Full-time field-worker Michael J. Murphy collected in the north of Ireland from 1941 until his retirement in 1983, and his collection of tales from various narrators include the following categories of international folktales as designated in Antti Aarne and Stith Thompson, *The Types of the Folktale* (1961): animal tales, ordinary folk-tales, religious tales, *Novelle,* tales of the stupid ogre, jokes and anecdotes, and some formula tales.[28] Other collectors also have been at work in the English-speaking areas: for example, James G. Delaney, who collected in the midlands of Ireland until his retirement. The remaining full-time collector, Tom Munnelly, is based in west county Clare, and although he is primarily a folk-song collector,[29] he has also assembled a very large collection of traditional narrative and lore of various kinds. Although the formal institution of storytelling is long since a thing of the past in west county Clare, it is a measure of the persistence of traditional themes and genres of the oral tradition in Ireland that such collections can still be made.

In this connection, I wish to mention in particular a storyteller with whom I have worked for many years. This is Jenny McGlynn (born 1939), from county Laois, in the midlands of Ireland.

It was only in the 1960s, after her marriage, that Jenny McGlynn became an active storyteller.[30] Her early home environment and local milieu had provided her with the traditional material, which, combined with various stimuli in her new surroundings after marriage, would enable her to emerge as a storyteller in her own right. Her family home was a "rambling house" where neighbors felt welcome to visit to while away the night telling stories and singing. Her new home was also a rambling house of some repute. Jenny McGlynn describes it in the following words:

It was a kind of rambling house and everyone rambled in. You see, we had no television or anything like that so there was no distraction. . . . And it was a place to go for a chat and a laugh and a cup of tea to break the monotony of the night. . . .[31]

It was in this environment that Jenny gradually began to perform her narratives for appreciative adult audiences. She describes storytelling sessions in the 1960s, when large groups of people gathered in the kitchen at night while she and her husband sat at either side of the fire; her husband would open the session by telling a story if the circumstances required it. Jenny, as the woman of the house, was often the only female present on these occasions, and when called upon by the predominantly male audience to contribute, she would do so if the theme under discussion was suitable. Her preferred genre was, and is, supernatural lore in all its variety and complexity, especially ghost lore, and she is regarded as an expert in this branch of tradition. At large sessions, she usually told only one story in order to give the others present an opportunity to participate. She also liked listening to the stories being told in order to "put her own word on them," using her creative skills to adapt them to her own style and her audience's taste, and to incorporate them into her repertoire.

Thus, Jenny McGlynn's narratives, which are firmly based on inherited, traditional lore, still have an audience, although a diminished one. This is also the case with various storytelling groups that have emerged in recent years and who provide public entertainment at home and abroad. Some have a limited repertoire, consisting of a certain number of short narratives based on traditional stories but adapted for modern audiences. Others mostly tell jokes based on the idiosyncrasies of rural people and communities. It is a measure of the persistence of a rural worldview, even among country people in the capital city and still among Irish immigrants abroad, and of various layers of traditional knowledge and lore, that these storytellers are popular as entertainers in Ireland as well as overseas in places where the Irish diaspora has reached.

Notes

1. Séamus Ó Duilearga, *Leabhar Sheáin Í Chonaill sgéalta agus seanchas ó íbh ráthach* (Dublin, Ireland: An Cumann Le Béaloideas Éireann/Folklore of Ireland Society, 1948); Republished 1964, and in 1977 by Comhairle Bhéaloideas Éireann/Folklore of Ireland Council. Translated by Maire MacNeill in Séamus Ó Duilearga, ed., *Seán Ó Conaill's Book* (Baile Átha Cliath: Comhairle Bhéaloideas Éireann/Folklore of Ireland Council, 1981).
2. These are the tales of the Fianna (Ossianic) Cycle described above.
3. Ó Duilearga, *Seán Ó Conaill's Book*, xviii.
4. Ibid., xx.
5. Ibid., xv.
6. Ibid., xxi.
7. Séamus Ó Duilearga, *Leabhar Stiofáin Uí Ealaoire* (Dublin, Ireland: Comhairle Bhéaloideas Éireann/Folklore of Ireland Council, 1981), xx.
8. The Ediphone was a clockwork wax-cylinder recording and transcribing apparatus used by collectors of the Irish Folklore Commission until the 1960s, when tape recorders became available for recording purposes.
9. This is one of the most popular hero tales in Ireland. It is also known in Gaelic Scotland. See Alan Bruford, *Gaelic Folk-Tales and Mediaeval Romances* (Dublin, Ireland: Folklore of Ireland Society, 1969).
10. Ó Duilearga, *Leabhar Stiofáin Uí Ealaoire.*
11. Seán Ó Súlleabháin, ed. and trans., *Folktales of Ireland* (Chicago: University of Chicago Press; London: Routledge and Kegan Paul, 1966), 262.
12. Peadar Ó Ceannabháin, ed., *Éamon a Búrc: Scéalta* [Eámon a Búrc: Stories], (Dublin, Ireland: An Clóchomhar, 1983), 16.
13. Ibid.
14. Caoimhín Ó Nualláin/Kevin O'Nolan, ed. and trans., *Eochair mac Rí in Éirinn/Eochair, a King's Son in Ireland* (Baile Átha Cliath: Comhairle Bhéaloideas Éireann/Folklore of Ireland Council, 1982), 9.
15. Liam Mac Coisdeala, "Im' Bhailitheoir Béaloideasa," *Béaloideas* 16 (1946): 150.
16. Ó Ceannabháin, op. cit., 18.
17. Ibid., 16.
18. Ibid.
19. Peig Sayers, *Peig .i. A Scéal Féin,* ed. Máire Ní Chinnéide (Dublin, Ireland: Clólucht an Talbóidigh, 1936). This has been translated by Bryan MacMahon in Peig Sayers, *Peig: The Autobiography of Peig Sayers of the Great Blasket Island* (Dublin, Ireland: Talbot, 1973).
20. *Macnamh Seana-Mhná,* ed. Máire Ní Chinnéide (Dublin, Ireland: Oifig an tSoláthair, 1939); it was translated by Séamus Ennis in Peig Sayers, *An Old Woman's Reflections* (London and New York: Oxford University Press, 1962). Another description of her life, by her son, is Micheál Ó Guithín, *Beatha Pheig Sayers* (Baile Átha Cliath: Foilseacháin Náisiúnta Teoranta, 1970).
21. Sayers, *An Old Woman's Reflections,* xii–xiv.
22. Stockinged feet.
23. For other versions of this prayer, see Diarmuid Ó Laoghaire, *Ár bPaidreacha Dúchais* [Our Traditional Prayers] (Dublin, Ireland: Foilseacháin Ábhair Spioradálta, 1975), 76–77.
24. In addition to the collection of riddles from Anna published in Seán Ó hEochaidh, "Tomhasannaí ó Thír Chonaill" [Riddles from Donegal], *Béaloideas* 19 (1950): 3–28, and five narratives from Anna published in Seán Ó hEochaidh, Máire Ní Néill, and Séamas Ó

Catháihn, *Fairy Legends from Donegal/
Síscéalta Ó Thír Chonaill* (Dublin, Ireland:
Comhairle Bhéaloideas Éireann, 1977), the
collection of narratives and traditional lore
from various tradition-bearers in the area of
the Blue Stack Mountains, county Donegal, in
Áine Ní Dhioraí, ed., *Na Cruacha: Scéalta
Agus Seanchas* (Dublin, Ireland: An
Clóchomhar, 1985) includes 23 items from
Anna consisting of Fianna lore; folktales of
various kinds; and fairy, ghost, and religious
lore; as well as children's games and a number
of songs.
25. Ó hEochaidh, 6–7 (my translation).
26. Ibid., 7.
27. See Patricia Lysaght and Douglas Hyde, in
Enzyklopädie des Märchens, Lief. 4/5, Berlin/
New York: Walter de Gruyter, 1990, 6:1429–
1431; Patricia Lysaght, "Ireland," in
*Enzyklopädie des Märchens: Handwörterbuch
zur historischen und vergleichenden
Erzählforschung* (New York: de Gruyter,
1991), 7:277–284. Some recent publications
are Cathal Póirtéir, ed., *Micí Sheáin Néill:
Scéalaí agus Scéalta* (Dublin, Ireland:
Coiscéim, 1993), representing County
Donegal; Áine Máire Ní Fhaoláin, ed., *Scéalta
agus Seanchas Phádraig Uí Ghrífín* (Kerry,
Ireland: An Sagart, 1995), representing
County Kerry; Máirtín Verling, ed., *Gort
Breac: Scéalta agus Seanchas ó Bhéarra*
(Dublin, Ireland: Coiscéim, 1996),
representing County Donegal.
28. Michael J. Murphy, *Now You're Talking:
Folk Tales from the North of Ireland* (Belfast,
Northern Ireland: Blackstaff, 1975).
29. See, for example, Tom Munnelly, *The Mount
Callan Garland: Songs from the Repertoire of
Tom Lenihan of Knockbrack, Miltown
Malbay, County Clare* (Dublin, Ireland:
Comhairle Bhéaloideas Éireann/Folklore of
Ireland Council, 1994).
30. For discussion of Jenny McGlynn's
background, repertoire, and worldview, see
Patricia Lysaght, "A Tradition Bearer in
Contemporary Ireland," in *Storytelling in
Contemporary Societies,* ed. Lutz Röhrich and
Sabine Wienker-Piepho (Tübingen, Germany:
G. Narr Verlag, 1990), 199–214; Patricia
Lysaght, "Fairylore from the Midlands of
Ireland," in *The Good People: New Fairylore
Essays,* ed. Peter Narváez (New York:
Garland, 1991), 22–46.
31. Lysaght, "Fairylore from the Midlands of
Ireland," 53.

Further Reading
Bourke, Éamon, *Eochair, mac Rí in Éirinn/
Eochair, A King's Son in Ireland,* Dublin,
Ireland: Comhairle Bhéaloideas Éireann,
University College, 1982
Bruford, Alan, *Gaelic Folk-tales and Mediaeval
Romances,* Dublin: Folklore of Ireland Society,
1969
Lysaght, Patricia, "Fairylore from the Midlands
of Ireland," in *The Good People: New
Fairylore Essays,* edited by Peter Narváez,
New York: Garland, 1991
———, "Ireland," in *Enzyklopädie des Märchens:
Handwörterbuch zur historischen und
vergleichenden Erzählforschung, Band 7,* New
York: de Gruyter, 1993
———, "A Tradition Bearer in Contemporary
Ireland," in *Storytelling in Contemporary
Societies,* edited by Lutz Röhrich and Sabine
Wienker-Piepho, Tübingen, Germany: G. Narr
Verlag, 1990
Mac Coisdeala, Liam, "Im' Bhailitheoir
Béaloideasa," *Béaloideas* 16 (1946)
Munnelly, Tom, *The Mount Callan Garland:
Songs from the Repertoire of Tom Lenihan of
Knockbrack, Miltown Malbay, County Clare,*
Dublin, Ireland: Comhairle Bhéaloideas
Éireann, 1994
Murphy, Michael J., *Now You're Talking: Folk
Tales from the North of Ireland,* Belfast,
Northern Ireland: Blackstaff, 1975
Ní Dhioraí, Áine, ed., *Na Cruacha: Scéalta Agus
Seanchas,* Dublin, Ireland: An Clóchomhar,
1985
Ní Fhaoláin, Áine Máire, ed., *Scéalta agus
Seanchas Phádraig Uí Ghrífín,* Kerry, Ireland:
An Sagart, 1995
Ó Ceannabháin, Peadar, ed., *Éamon a Búrc:
Scéalta* [Éamon a Búrc: Stories], Dublin,
Ireland: An Clóchomhar, 1983
Ó Duilearga, Séamus, *Leabhar Sheáin Í Chonaill
sgéalta agus seanchas ó íbh ráthach,* Dublin,
Ireland: An Cumann Le Béaloideas Éireann,
1948; reprint, Dublin, Ireland: Browne and
Nolan, 1964
———, *Leabhar Stiofáin Uí Ealaoire,* Dublin,
Ireland: Comhairle Bhéaloideas Éireann/
Folklore of Ireland Council,
1981

Ó Gaoithín, Micheál, *Beatha Pheig Sayers,* Dublin, Ireland: Foilseacháin Náisiúnta Teoranta, 1970

Ó hEaochaidh, Séan, "Tomhasannaí ó Thír Chonaill" [Riddles from Donegal], *Béaloideas* 19 (1949–1950)

Ó hEochaidh, Séan, Máire MacNéill, and Séamas Ó Catháin, *Fairy Legends from Donegal/ Síscéalta Ó Thír Chonaill,* Dublin, Ireland: Comhairle Bhéaloideas Éireann, 1977

Ó Laoghaire, Diarmuid, *Ár bPaidreacha Dúchais* [Our Traditional Prayers], Dublin, Ireland: Foilseacháin Ábhair Spioradálta, 1975

Ó Súilleabháin, Séan, ed. and trans., *Folktales of Ireland,* Chicago: University of Chicago Press, 1966; London: Routledge and Paul, 1966

Póirtéir, Cathal, ed., *Micí Sheáin Néill: Scéalaí agus Scéalta,* Dublin, Ireland: Coiscéim, 1994

Sayers, Peig, *Mactnam Seana-Mhná,* edited by Máire Ní Chinnéide, Dublin, Ireland: Oifig an tSoláthair, 1939

——, *An Old Woman's Reflections,* translated by Séamus Ennis, London and New York: Oxford University Press, 1962

——, *Peig: .i. A Scéal Féin,* edited by Máire Ní Chinnéide, Dublin, Ireland: Clólucht an Talbóidigh, 1936

——, *Peig: The Autobiography of Peig Sayers of the Great Blasket Island,* translated by Bryan MacMahon, Dublin, Ireland: Talbot, 1973

Verling, Máirtín, ed., *Gort Broc: Scéalta agus Seanchas ó Bhéarra,* Dublin, Ireland: Coiscéim, 1996

A Storyteller's Growing Consciousness

Inta Gale Carpenter

Here Inta Gale Carpenter examines the repertoire of her Latvian grandfather and his use of story.

Story as an Attention-Getting Device

Stories are attention-getters. In the midst of ordinary conversation, they call attention to themselves through conventions of structure and form and through a style of delivery that suggests that what is about to be told is of particular significance. Stories also call attention to storytellers, to those who command certain traditions and use them for their own purposes before an audience. Thus, storytelling is a means to personal power. Effective storytellers display their skills and proclaim their knowledge, not only as a way to entertain, inform, or instruct others but also as a way to seek a position of respect and authority for themselves.[1]

In an age when few sit down to listen to storytellers, individuals with an ear and disposition for narration must utilize often brief opportunities for capturing the attention of an audience. For the elderly, who quite unthinkingly might be shunted to the sidelines of family or social life, storytelling is a particularly pertinent, and poignant, means to identity and connection. It might well also be part of a developmental stage of life that is ushered in by the passage of years and the wish to take stock through a "life review."

Jānis Pḷavnieks, the Storyteller

In the 1970s, I witnessed these ideas in action when I collected my maternal grandfather's stories. Jānis Pḷavnieks, whom I always called Tētis (the Latvian word for "father"), agreed to help me fulfill requirements for a master's degree by allowing me to record his narrative repertoire. Our collaboration extended over a period of about two years, during which time we visited in my home in Bloomington, Indiana, and his in Indianapolis, Indiana. Recording continued even after my husband and I moved to Kentucky. I arranged for Tētis to record himself, and he eagerly complied, for storytelling had become thoroughly integrated into his everyday life.

When our collaboration began, he was 86 years old and long retired, with plenty of time, most of which he passed reading, aided by a thick magnifying glass. He lived with his wife, who was considerably more active than he, and with his daughter and son-in-law, who were still in the workforce. In the boredom of long days, often spent in solitude, my collecting proved immensely ego-lifting for him.

At first, he responded hesitantly to my queries. Our individual appraisals of the task at hand contrasted sharply. I considered him not only knowledgeable but also an able artist with noteworthy memory and performance skills, and I told him so. He discounted the anecdotes, jokes, and parables I sought, which I remembered hearing as I was growing up and on the basis of which I judged him with such respect. One time, when I asked him for a story I remembered his having told, he responded,

Tētis: Ah, yes, the one about the farmer . . . [but] that's all pretty inconsequential. You don't even need such stories.

Inta: No, I do. I want you to tell them to me.

Tētis: That's as you said, they are international anecdotes.

Inta: Yes, and that's the interesting thing, that you know a variation of them. They change from person to person and place to place.

Tētis: Yes. [A three-minute pause followed, and then he said:] When you live and think here in peace, then one or another thing comes to mind, some more serious story.

Inta: What do you mean?

Tētis: Nu, about Kronbergs [a story about a rich neighbor]. So, I guess it means that I can call myself a cosmopolitan individual, if I know one or two variations of stories told the world over.

When this conversation took place, I had been recording for several weeks. We were becoming comfortable with each other. He was beginning to admit a certain value to my goal of recording what he knew, and he was starting to take real pleasure in the telling and even more so in his knowledge of traditional stories and the alacrity with which he was remembering them. Soon enough, his tales came like rapid-fire. His initial self-deprecation dissipated, and he began to develop a growing consciousness of his artistry. It is this process of expanding self-appreciation that I wish to describe here, as well as my own growing appreciation of storytelling as a means of personal power and identity enhancement for the elderly.

Although a farmer by inclination, Jānis Pḷavnieks also worked as a steam-generator operator in a large paper factory in Latvia, as a member of a road-building crew in Russia, in a sawmill in a refugee camp in Germany, and as a nurseryman and janitor in the United States. He was born in Latvia on June 26, 1886, the third of four children. He grew up on a 70-acre family farm, called Lauksargi (Guardian of the Fields), in a tiny village of some 300 inhabitants and about 14 stores. Tētis regrets that his formal education was cut short after two winters of schooling. As a child, he had contracted scarlet fever and, after a very high fever, had lost the sight in his right eye. The doctor advised his family that if he strained his eye with too much reading, he could go blind. "You can't say my head was particularly good, but it's not bad either. But my sight is what held me back, the loss of my eye," he told me.

Between the two world wars, during Latvia's brief period of independence, Tētis and my grandmother, Anna, ran his family's farm, which he had inherited as the eldest son. They slowly improved it until they lived prosperously. In 1944, as both Russian and German bombs dropped all about them, they watched their house and barns full of grain and livestock burn. Then, as they had already done during World War I, they left Latvia. This time, they were accompanied by their daughter and granddaughter. I was born in Latvia just six weeks before their flight. Instead of going to Russia, they fled to Germany, where after the war they settled into various United Nations refugee camps for nearly five years. It was a time, he said, when "even an insignificant person's life passed in war alone."

My grandparents and mother ultimately chose to emigrate to the United States rather than return to a Communist-occupied homeland. Tētis was not disappointed by America, even though it remained a strange, largely unexplored country to him; he spoke its language only haltingly and befriended few of its natives. But America provided him with jobs and, consequently, with the earnings to buy a home and live comfortably and peacefully after the repeated destructions and departures of his early years.

The Storyteller's Style

Tētis undoubtedly heard and told his tales and anecdotes most often in the masculine company of work and tavern and card table. Quick to humor, strong-willed, intelligent, and curious, Tētis enjoyed being the center of attention. As recorded in *A Latvian Storyteller: The Repertoire of Jānis Pḷavnieks,* Tētis told animal tales, songs, riddles, puzzles, anecdotes, jokes, simple tales, folk poetry, and personal history narratives. Without a doubt, Tētis and I shaped the table of contents jointly, in terms of what I sought, what he wanted known, and what he wanted to share. Similarly, my mood and receptivity as audience affected the type and quantity and quality of performance.

The stories he told most typically were short and often humorous, with simple plots that were realistic in setting and event. Tētis told no fairy tales nor supernatural legends. The characters were those he might well have encountered every day in rural Latvia: the farmer, the farmhand, the farmwife (often silly), the student, the Jew, and the minister. Animal and human characters indulged in similar behaviors: they were often caught in foolish or compromising situations, or they managed to outwit their opponents. They were motivated by revenge, conceit, or stinginess; brought down by foolishness, greed, overconfidence, or possessiveness; or helped by wit, honesty, common sense, or self-control.

Although low-key and restrained in his narration, Tētis imbued his texts with an urgent tone that gave notice and commanded attention. He used gestures sparingly and without flourish. Whenever his story called for a distinct action, Tē tis followed through in an almost unconscious manner with the appropriate gesture. He rarely raised his voice but rather seemed to add emphasis through rhythm and repetition. Dialogue came easily to him, and he made abundant use of it, consistently rendering it in a colloquial, smooth flow.

His style was characterized by sentences that twisted and turned in on themselves, going forward and then retreating to include parenthetical material before proceeding once again. A sentence such as the following is entirely representative: "One day he crawls out of his house and sees under a nearby bush, squatting, shivering, frozen—a porcupine." Tenses changed from past to present and back again. Sentence fragments were given an independent status and emphasis. He rhythmically punctuated his sentences with sudden, brief, even single-word interjections, repetitions, or descriptions that tended to break up the forward momentum. Such rhythmic breaks included single words ("There is a variety on which such small balls grow—green."), evaluative comments ("Yes, nu, good."), short rhetorical questions ("What to do now?"), or brief repetitions ("The lord notices that sometimes the chauffeur also needs to go, but he does it very quickly, does it very quickly."). He used incremental threefold repetitions generously to describe, to build up plot, to structure sentences: for example, "The devil, he starts to run, runs all along the ditch, gets to the end."; "The other barons take him, and throw him out of the room, out of the game."; "But the other one was really stingy, would starve her servants, give them bad food."; "squatting, shivering, frozen"; "The potatoes grow and grow and grow."; and "Then she pulls, carries, drags the dog." Over half of Tētis's tales

exhibited opening formulas, some brief ("In olden times . . ." or, most frequently, "One fine day . . ."), some interrogative ("Do you know what happened?"), or some combination ("All in all it is said that in old times . . .").

Throughout the collecting, Tētis would comment on the aesthetics of certain tales. Some he found easy to tell; others, more difficult: "I never learned the fairy tales, about the glass mountain and such. Those were hard." He was sensitive to meanings lost because he had to translate them for me: "It is somehow more interesting, more effective in Russian," he said after finishing one story. His consistent initial impulse was to object to his wife's occasional suggestions for different phrasing or censoring of crude language. But although he often refused his wife's changes, he agreed that variation was acceptable. When I told him that in some versions of a tale he told, the wolf is killed, he disagreed, "No, why kill him?" but then added, "But you could tell it that way, too."

He indicated his favorites by his laughing enjoyment during the telling or with asides. Certain tales were "more piquant" or "a very big, long story." They were "believable" because their characters acted "sensibly" or "valuable" because they ridiculed foolish people, conveyed wise advice, or exercised people's minds. He told some stories dramatically, creating what Roger Abrahams has termed "aesthetic emotion" toward the characters on the part of listeners.[2]

He prided himself most of all on his memory of complicated mathematical kinds of problems, which he said had been shared "long, long ago" in Latvia, "when the old men—when lots of people would be together in a room on winter nights. It was before there were oil lamps and the light came from a kindling fire. They gathered, stooped together around the fire, and so they told riddles to one another." He compared these mathematical puzzles favorably with what a student might learn in school. Often while doing the monotonous task of plowing his fields, Tētis recalls, he would pose problems to himself and thus pass the time more quickly. When "educated people" (like me and others) fumbled and pondered unsuccessfully over solutions, he was delighted. He had not actively tackled these puzzles for many years, and he found that he "had forgotten the solutions. But once you start figuring, remembering, guessing to yourself, questioning yourself, then you remember," he said. "If you don't do that, then it dies and is gone." He had learned them from his father.

For the most part, Tētis was vague about his sources, saying it was hard to remember where each story was heard. Frankly, he was uninterested in the question. Some came from his father, others from teachers, neighbors, coworkers, and cronies. He enjoyed talking about the talents of other good storytellers and was interested in the process of learning and retaining traditions. He once objected to my calling his retention of mathematical puzzles an art. He retorted, "You have to know simple arithmetic, that's all. It's not an art. It's simple." He emphasized that the would-be narrator had to listen carefully wherever he was—at funerals, dinners, the market, or the tavern—for then "You picked up a thing or two. There was a friend in Baldone who ran a threshing machine, and I met him often. There were several there who had quick tongues. And I always paid attention to what they said." He would sometimes ask a friend to repeat a story he liked so that he could better commit it to memory.

Storytelling Sessions and Storytelling Events

Our work together moved through distinct phases. At first, I was my grandfather's primary audience, and I set the agenda by asking him to recall the stories I remembered from childhood. Soon enough, these began to flow in a constant and seemingly unending stream: verses of songs, riddles, proverbs, anecdotes, and even texts remembered from newspaper articles. But as our collaboration continued, my grandfather's audience expanded and he engaged in the process of documenting his stories; he began to set his own agendas as well.

Once "rummaging" is stimulated, writes Donald A. MacDonald, a good tradition bearer almost always has recollected something else to offer by the next visit.[3] Each time I came with a tape recorder, asking to "hear it all," and making it clear I had virtually unlimited time, Tētis was ready. He reacted in a pattern typical for elderly storytellers who are suddenly approached by eager collectors after not having had sustained contact with an active and appreciative audience for some time. Tētis entered what Kenneth Goldstein calls the "rummaging stage," during which he resurrected narratives recalled from times past with friends, relatives, and growing children. Even so, on at least two occasions, my grandmother stated that Tētis had forgotten so much of what she had heard him tell, particularly during their life in Russia between 1914 and 1918.

From my perspective, he shared an incredible array of texts and kept challenging himself to remember still more. When he found me to be a good listener and as he began to trust that my interest was enduring, he seemed to become mentally and emotionally more engaged in our activity. Some mornings, his first greeting to me was a text he had remembered as he "slept without sleeping at three or four in the morning." He recalled stories that definitely would not have been recorded had our collaboration been brief and our wish to deepen our growing relationship less intense.

Performing: The Storytelling Event

My interest in his storytelling renewed his own interest in "performing" before an audience.[4] With greater frequency and increasing delight in the good company of family and friends, he told stories simply because the moment was right, and he was able to contribute with texts interpretive of that "right" moment. He narrated from his own needs and desires, not because of one of our storytelling sessions.

One evening, when the family was gathered (and I was without a tape recorder), we were talking about my husband Bruce's interest in growing grapes. Because Bruce does not speak Latvian, in his presence the family usually switched to English, even though neither of my grandparents could converse in English with the speed and complexity of normal social talk. Although I would sometimes translate, for the most part, they were sidelined during these times and sat in silence. On the night I remember, Tētis had surmised the gist of our talk; it piqued his interest, for without warning, he began to tell a tale, addressing it specifically to Bruce. The family, of course, now focused on Tētis and listened to the narration, which I afterward translated for Bruce. Tētis told the fable of the fox and the sour grapes, and the point was well-taken: Bruce's enthusiasm for viticulture might benefit and even be tempered by actual rather than intellectual or leisure-time involvement. After a brief discussion of the meaning and application of the text, the conversation resumed, returned to English, and veered away from its focus on Tētis.

In the performance event, a specific topic of ongoing conversation prompted Tētis to tell this story. The artifice of the opening formula, the tone of his voice, the form itself, signaled to the family that a story was being told. Our attention turned to Tētis as he narrated the tale—or in other circumstances, applied a proverb, sang a song, tried to stump us with a mathematical puzzle. We integrated his performance into our conversation, either by verbal or nonverbal appreciation or prolonged discussion of its meaning. Sometimes, the text was accepted lightly or perhaps even shrugged off, in which case conversation resumed quickly. At other times, the family lingered on the message or on the execution. In any event, the text constituted a significant part of the momentary reality. During these times, my identity as collector was secondary to my identity as listener. What was primary was Tētis's growing confidence in his narrating powers as a basis from which to claim attention. In once again actively performing his traditional knowledge, Tētis demonstrated how he used the texts he had spoken into the recorder. In addition, he would recount things I had not yet heard. He achieved and realized new power and status through the effective performance of stories that revealed new dimensions of his worldview and his wit to us, sometimes informed and instructed us, and certainly enhanced our respect for him and his authority within the family circle.[5]

As I noticed him once again taking the spotlight, being actively involved in conversations and joining in them in ways that captured our attention, I began to differentiate his memory repertoire (which he offered during our times together) from his active-use repertoire. Two different, though related, phenomena seemed to be operating, almost side by side. The first was the storytelling session, which consisted of a number of successive tales told to a recording audience—in this case, me and often also my grandmother. During these sessions, my identity as collector overshadowed my identity as audience-listener, for contrary to my grandmother, who would sometimes co-narrate or critique, I was for the most part a passive recorder. Both Tētis and I were primarily concerned with documenting a maximum number of texts.

A second phenomenon was beginning to take place in the midst of ordinary conversation, one that Robert Georges termed a "storytelling event."[6] Looking back, I doubt that my grandfather was ever—before my request—a storyteller who told many tales at one sitting. The dinner-table storytelling seems much more characteristic than the collecting sessions I conducted, in which tale dutifully followed upon tale. By all accounts,

his repertoire lent itself to the quick introduction of stories at appropriate moments. For example, Tētis characteristically launched into an anecdote or brightened up his language with proverbs, proverbial phrases, and comparisons. At other times, he summarized a conversation in progress with an apt story or saying, or he provided another point of view, offered wise advice, or simply and humorously expanded on a topic at hand. In daily life, Tētis's repertoire actually appeared considerably larger than on tape and paper.

Even aside from whether or not Tētis benefited in personal status or power through the telling of tales, my realization that he was performing "artistic verbal communication"[7] required that I take into account all the dimensions of storytelling, that I recognize each storytelling event as unique and interpretively appropriate to that moment alone. Dan Ben-Amos has written that the unifying thread that joins jokes and myths, gestures and legends, costumes and music into the single category of knowledge we call "folklore" is the fact that it constitutes "artistic communication in small groups." The process of storytelling, he contends, intimately "unites the narrator, his story, and his audience as components of a single continuum."[8]

If in the early sessions Tētis had some freedom of expression in the face of my requests and my tape recorder, my guidance nevertheless propelled him toward narrating simple tales and anecdotes, perhaps riddles. Later, he began to rummage around in his mind for whatever else he could remember. Gradually, he reclaimed an identity as a performer who chose his texts to suit himself and to fit the momentary mood.

Sometimes during our recording sessions, he also broke through into performance. He would retell a text he and I had both enjoyed immensely during an initial telling, although in such instances, he might have given only a shorthand version. He seemed not so much interested in the text as in evoking and recapturing shared emotions: humor, joy, sorrow, amazement—whatever was momentarily brought back through the juxtaposition of the emotions generated at the first telling and now revisited through another telling. At these times, he was not transmitting text alone, or even performing for personal status, so much as he was re-creating the emotive power of storytelling. In effect, he was saying, "That was a good story." But more importantly, he was saying, "We had a good time."

Reminiscing: Narrator-Initiated Life Review

After several months of working together, my collecting seemed to propel Tētis into the past, not that of imagination and art, but of history. He began to tell me about Latvia, about his neighbors and relatives, and about places and events he recalled from long ago. These memories, it turned out, were the ones he most wanted to share and to record. Indeed, they may have been the ones he needed to share. At his age, personal, family, and community history occupied an important role in his life, giving him the opportunity to review his life and compose disparate parts into an acceptable whole. I was his most appropriate audience, for the stories were long, requiring hours of time. I was the one member of my family who knew little about this personal history. Luckily, I had plenty of time to listen to and record these stories that I had not imagined in my initial scheme of things. To my surprise and pleasure, he brought the artistry of the anecdote to this life history, turning his past into more of a series of short stories than dry, factual reports.

I first became aware of his ability to give form to the everyday details and events of his past when Tētis told me the story of his neighbor Grundmanis. I was fascinated by it and immediately struck by the narrative's reliance on certain märchen conventions. Tētis described the deeds of the youngest son, a blond, handsome soldier, bedecked in a silver and gold uniform, who enlists the support of the Russian czarina to recover the family home, which has been lost through the immoral behavior of his lazy, drunkard father and older brother. Tētis described the older brother as dark and black, himself admitting his perplexity at this striking contrast to the beautiful and fair younger brother. To Tētis, the story was pure history. To me, the story suggested the possibility that my grandfather's skills as narrator carried over to his personal reminiscences. He adeptly imbued memory with artifice, structure, and theme.

My enthusiasm was evident, and from the first story we moved to many more, all of which came quickly yet never fully exhausted the memories he had about his community in Latvia. He knew tales he never had a chance to share, for he would sometimes enticingly refer to them in a kind of expressive shorthand. For example, he mentioned, but never told, one about "the man who was skinned alive. . . ."

Tētis seemed naturally to structure certain life experiences in a more or less fixed form, with some memories becoming almost motif-like in their recurrence in his personal vision of life and of the people around him. Certain elements of shock, surprise, heroics, humor, terror, or coincidence captured his mind and helped him to remember and to construct a good story. Themes included personal and social disintegration, divine retribution, lucky escapes, and local characters. The stories often assumed the structuring of more established genres, echoing the threefold repetition, dramatic dialogues, and distinctive endings of fairy tales and legends.

Tētis's memories extended as far back as the Russo-Turkish War of 1877–78, about which he was told by an uncle, and moved forward to vividly describe the turbulent encounters with Germans and Russians during the 1905 revolution and the years of World War I and World War II. He dwelled at length on the family histories of several neighbors and drew a picture of discontinuity and dissolution that was almost metaphoric for the historical events of the world at large between 1905 and 1945. Home ownership jumps with unnatural speed from heir to heir. Verbal contracts are not honored. Family fortunes plummet. Friends abruptly disappear or are hunted down and shot by the current political enemy. Life, in Tētis's view, "just didn't prosper anymore." In his advanced years, it is perhaps not surprising that dissolution and decay seemed an appropriate image for life. What was significant was his ability to structure and give thematic unity to the disparate events he recalled.

He began with the years 1886–1937, describing his childhood, early adulthood, exile in Russia, and return to Latvia after World War I. I also recorded the years 1938–44 in other sessions, which focused particularly on the autumn of 1944, when the family fled Latvia for Germany, and during which Tētis dwelled especially on the productivity of the new nation. He also told about his wife's family and farm, during the period 1870–1930, and then returned to the intensive five years between 1944 and 1949, which included Soviet occupation, flight, and resettlement in refugee camps. I tried unsuccessfully to engage him in discussions of experiences in America. He resisted, with the result that he told a few anecdotes of his life in Shelby, North Carolina, and later in Indianapolis, but all in all, his version of 25 years in the United States was vague and incomplete.

Affirming a Friendship

The last stage of our collecting relationship was also initiated by Tētis. He set an agenda that both pleased me and took me aback. By this time, we were confirmed collaborators, who possessed an almost secret sense of the rich experiences and body of knowledge that had transpired between us and that united us. One day, he added yet another dimension to our deepening relationship by suggesting that we go down into our basement family room to record. We customarily would sit at the kitchen table. My grandmother was usually present, but she stayed busy with food preparations and never sat down with us. She nevertheless listened to our conversation and regularly contributed or commented on it. In the basement, no one was likely to interrupt, walk through, or overhear.

We walked down the steps, and once settled, with tape recorder running, he told me he wanted to tell me some stories of a slightly different order from what he had shared so far. He began to narrate a series of bawdy tales—far from obscene but still so dependent on a vocabulary unfamiliar to me in Latvian that I had to struggle for meaning. In some cases, I simply had to admit that I did not understand his point and dared to ask for explication. Telling such stories to me, his granddaughter, indicated the depth of trust and friendship he was bestowing upon me. Usually, cohorts share such stories, and rarely do they cross gender lines. His sharing these funny stories with me suggests not only that sexuality is not absent in old age but, more sadly, that his social network of peers had become very narrow, indeed, nonexistent.

We both laughed heartily at the jokes he told, although I also recall my occasional downright embarrassment at the narrated scenes and images. But mostly, I was honored. To me, Tētis had long ago become more than a grandfather—that is, a close relative, but someone I did not know as an individual. I had also by now come to recognize him as my teacher, and it is to him, in the end, that I owe my subsequent interest in the history and culture of Latvia. With this storytelling event in the basement, we also bonded as friends.

In 1980, when my thesis was published, Latvia was still under Soviet occupation and my grandfather's land was being worked as a collective farm. In 1990, Latvia regained its independence, and just a couple of years later, his son and children reclaimed the family farm, Lauksargi. Tētis would be pleased to know that in a real sense he has "returned" to Latvia through his stories. His granddaughter and her husband are building a house near the spot where the original farmhouse was bombed and burned. When she had questions about local history, she turned to a copy of *A Latvian Storyteller* for answers and found them. The impulse he had, to share his personal history for posterity, also served her well.

Our storytelling sessions served in many ways. They initiated a life review for my grandfather that helped him pass tiresome days and nights and, undoubtedly, also allowed him to come to terms with and make sense of his life. He educated me and provided information across time and space to his family in Latvia. But the process of storytelling also rejuvenated my grandfather. It proved to be more than an internal value-making life review. It also spurred him to risk performing again before audiences and to bridge generations by reaching out for a full friendship with his granddaughter. When I told Tētis that the thesis I had written about him would be published, he was exuberant. "You mean," he asked, "that I will be in libraries all over America?" "Yes," I answered.

Notes

1. See Roger D. Abrahams, "Personal Power and Social Restraint in the Definition of Folklore," in *Toward New Perspectives in Folklore*, ed. Américo Paredes and Richard Bauman (Austin: University of Texas Press, 1972).
2. Ibid., 18.
3. Donald A. MacDonald, "Fieldwork: Collecting Oral Literature," in *Folklore and Folklife*, ed. Richard M. Dorson (Chicago: University of Chicago Press, 1972), 427.
4. For a lucid treatment of storytelling as both narrative event and narrated event, see Richard Bauman, *Story, Performance, Event* (Cambridge: Cambridge University Press, 1986).
5. Abrahams, 28.
6. Robert Georges, "Toward an Understanding of Storytelling Events," *Journal of American Folklore* 82 (October–December 1969): 324.
7. Richard Bauman, *Verbal Art as Performance* (Prospect Heights, Illinois: Waveland Press, 1977).
8. Dan Ben-Amos, "Toward a Definition of Folklore in Context," in *Toward New Perspectives in Folklore*, ed. Américo Paredes and Richard Bauman (Austin: University of Texas Press, 1972), 6.

Further Reading

Abrahams, Roger D., "Personal Power and Social Restraint in the Definition of Folklore," in *Toward New Perspectives in Folklore,* edited by Américo Paredes and Richard Bauman, Austin: University of Texas Press, 1972

Bauman, Richard, *Story, Performance, and Event: Contextual Studies of Oral Narrative,* Cambridge and New York: Cambridge University Press, 1986

——, *Verbal Art as Performance,* Rowley, Massachusetts: Newbury House, 1978

Ben-Amos, Dan, "Toward a Definition of Folklore in Context," in *Toward New Perspectives in Folklore,* edited by Américo Paredes and Richard Bauman, Austin: University of Texas Press, 1972

Carpenter, Inta Gale, *Being Latvian in Exile: Folklore as Ideology* (Ph.D. diss., Indiana University), 1989

——, *A Latvian Storyteller: The Repertoire of Jānis Pḷavnieks,* New York: Arno, 1980

Georges, Robert, "Toward an Understanding of Storytelling Events," *Journal of American Folklore* 82 (1969)

Macdonald, Donald A., "Fieldwork: Collecting Oral Literature," in *Folklore and Folklife: An Introduction,* edited by Richard M. Dorson, Chicago: University of Chicago Press, 1972

Once Upon a Time in Vale Judeu

Isabel Cardigos

Isabel Cardigos discusses the repertoire of three elderly storytellers in the Algarve region of Portugal. She compares past use of story in the community with present lapse of interest in storytelling in the region.

Storytelling 40 Years Ago

Vale Judeu—the Valley of the Jew—is a village a few miles away from the sea in southern Portugal, the Algarve. Idália Custódio, a 59-year-old secondary school teacher who is the granddaughter of a local landowner, lived in Vale Judeau from the time she finished primary school until she was 21. She left the area to pursue studies that eventually led to a degree in Romance studies. During the 10 crucial years of transition from childhood to womanhood she lived as a villager in Vale Judeu. Because of an acute awareness of the radical changes that this locale has undergone since the halcyon days of her youth, she decided to record and transcribe the stories, ballads, prayers, and songs that her old friends in the village remember and graciously recite for her benefit and for posterity.

Forty years ago, Idália recalls, all the villagers of Vale Judeu lived off the land. The rich owned farms (*montes*) and the poor rented farmland from which to grow their livelihood. Vale Judeu was a close-knit community that did not look elsewhere for either work or leisure. This was before the advent of television; villagers relied on relatives and neighbors for entertainment. The winter evenings were spent in the kitchen by the hearth while the women busied their hands with the *empreita*—woven baskets made with palmetto leaves. The chatter often evolved into storytelling by the most gifted and authoritative among them while the younger ones listened. In the hot summer, the gatherings took place outside in the cool of the evening in the *eirado,* the yard next to the house where figs were laid to dry, or on the large round threshing floor, the *eira*. These gatherings were larger and the mood was different; the repartee invariably shaped itself into improvised rhyming contests—the *desgarradas*—sung by those who dared take up the challenge. Just as there were songs and chanted prayers for every task and every event, there was also a story about every known crook in the land: for the crossroads, for this tree, for that well, and so on. Everything was christened and made into lyrical or narrative discourse. Everything was both haunting and familiar.

Life, however, was hard in those days. Portugal lived under the oppression of a fascist regime that encouraged ignorance and alienation of the people in order to hold on to its power and close the country off from the rest of Europe. The more enlightened scholars were forbidden to teach and many of them were forced into exile. Most people were illiterate in the rural areas (even Dona Idália's primary schooling had to take place outside the village) and the "beauty of the plow" was praised, in opposition to any kind of technological development. Then the bloodless "April Revolution" of 1974 appeared as a miracle that brought democracy to the country, with its corollaries of freedom of thought, schooling for all, and access to the opportunities the industrialized world could offer.

The Tourist-Invaded Algarve of Today

The tourist industry has invaded the Algarve. It receives 3 million tourists from spring to fall. Most of the farms in Vale Judeu have either grown wild or have turned into developments. Undereducated residents of Vale Judeu now use the path their ancestors once used to fetch water in times of drought to travel to their jobs as cleaners and caterers in the thriving tourist resorts of the Algarve. Others have clerical positions in the prosperous towns of Loulé and Faro and identify more with their workmates in the more urban neighborhoods. When they drive home after work, it is usually only to eat, watch television, and go to bed. Villagers all now belong to much wider community circles, the widest and strongest being the world of Brazilian soap operas and Hollywood films, which are automatically associated with the wealthy tourists from whom they make their livelihood. The older inhabitants stay at home, and seem to be adapting themselves to an easier way of life. Obtaining food, water, light, and heat is no longer a problem, so why complain? Their generation is associated with the hard times of the past and backward social conditions, and younger people feel that they have nothing of value to impart. The younger generation finds itself living in a time of plenty. They have very little in common with the older folk, who keep quiet in their new passive submission to the all-powerful appeal of the television. Their stories, prayers, and songs are now discarded as meaningless and obsolete.

Idália Custódio Attempts to Preserve Folk Traditions

Well, this is not so for Idália, who once partook with her friends in the games, sang with them in the wakes that lasted all night long, and listened wide-eyed to the stories of the gifted tellers. The old villagers are suspicious of educated outsiders they do not know, who drop by uninvited to meddle with their old memories. But they trust Idália and they actually become quite excited when she telephones to announce that she is coming to listen to the stories that their own grandchildren ignore. If she turns up in the house of Dona Salvina, the word will spread around and Dona Boa Hora, Dona Glória, and Dona Prazeres will be there as well (and even some men), all eagerly recollecting their memories, looking forward to really having a good time with one another—almost as in the old days. We can ask ourselves if what they now come up with is—in Heda Jason's terminology[1]— artificially demonstrated or authentically performed. Do their words arise spontaneously in order to fulfill the functions they once had? If we

consider their prayers and songs, most of which arose in specific contexts that are now obsolete, the answer is no. In this case the women are demonstrating how they chanted to cure skin or joint ailments, to avoid being struck by lightning, to call for rain, to mark the time for planting or threshing, to help the deceased on their otherworldly journey, or to celebrate with the bridal pair on their wedding day. They demonstrate how the spoken—the power to bless, to curse, and to swear an oath—word had far more power than the written one. They are also willing to demonstrate because they trust that Dona Idália will publish their words in a book, which will give them the novel recognition of the written word.[2]

However, when it comes to storytelling, the context miraculously becomes the same as it once was, if only for an odd afternoon and among the older folks only. As before, they gather in one home to share stories and laugh together, enjoy the pleasure of remembered discourses with one another, and delight in the best renditions of their two best performers—Dona Salvina and Dona Boa Hora. These two women are responsible for 30 of the 40 stories that were published in Idália Custódio's book. The others contributed one or two tales each. We will mention just a handful of tales that Idália Custódio gathered.

Dona Salvina Baptista's Repertoire

Dona Salvina Baptista (61 years old at the time) is the most remarkable and prolific storyteller of the community. Her repertoire of over 20 well-defined tale types was inherited from her mother, who had learned it from both parents. Their skill in storytelling became legendary in the village. This is probably why Dona Salvina is the only female informant in the village who tells both hero and heroine tales. Nevertheless, she starts "The Dragon Slayer" (AT300) with "There was once a king who had an only daughter," a princess who refused to accept the king's offer to replace her as the dragon's victim. Only then does the hero appear on the scene. It is also curious that Dona Salvina lightens the guilt of the female villain in "The Faithless Sister" (AT315): her betrayal is caused by a giant who "hypnotizes" the otherwise innocent sister. The religious appropriation of folktales is particularly noticeable in Dona Salvina's repertoire. Two of her tales are used as a framework for ritual prayers—as the myth that explains the ritual: one is "The Devil in Noah's Ark" (AT825), a story that explains the origin of the morning ritual of reciting a prayer before taking any food and while washing hands and face, "so that the devil may not know what you are doing." The other one is an ecotype of "The Prince and the Storm" (AT934). At the crucial time when he is about to be struck by lightning the prince is taught a particular prayer that "since then is used against storms." In a Bluebeard-type tale the heroine is saved with the help of Our Lady, through a prayer on the eve of Her day. Another of Dona Salvina's religious tales—"The Man Who Was Burned Up and Lived Again" (AT788)—is the story of St. Thomas, "who had to die so as to be reborn and become a saint," is a very intriguing tale of reincarnation. Her repertoire also includes two distinct and well-developed versions of "The Search for the Lost Husband" (AT425). As with published Portuguese versions no harm ever comes to the second bride, whose marriage simply does not take place. In her wanderings, the heroine passes the houses of the mothers of the Sun, Moon, and Wind, who give her as magic tokens a walnut and two indigenous fruits of the Algarve, an almond and a pomegranate. This visit to the mothers of the Sun, Moon, and Wind is so well ingrained in the narratives of AT425 that, in his rendering of "The Search for the Golden Bird" (AT550), Mr. Estevão (75 years old) gives his hero the same journey, which is uncommon for a male protagonist in the Portuguese tradition. Mr. Estevão probably inherited the story from a woman.

Versions of "The Golden Childen" (AT707)

Mr. Ascenso, a 73-year-old villager, gives a curious appropriation of "The Golden Children" (AT707), known in Portugal as "The Children with a Star on their Foreheads." Mr. Ascenso's attention is focused on the children's father, a farmer's son who before his wife gives birth emigrates to Brazil—the land of riches to Portuguese peasants in the last century. The episode of the children's tasks is omitted from his version. When the father returns from Brazil he notices the children because, unlike everyone else, when they pass by his wife, who is buried up to the waist in front of his farmhouse, they refuse to spit upon the woman. He invites them in and tells them that they have to follow the rules of good manners in his home; that is, they should uncover their heads when sitting for lunch. He recognizes them when he sees a star on their foreheads, just as his wife had promised him they would before he left for

Brazil. When telling the same story, Dona Boa Hora follows a more traditional pattern and lengthens her narrative about the predicament of the forsaken queen and about the children's role in the recognition of her innocence.

The large number of jocular tales that appear in the published collections that portray a woman as an adulteress with a friar seem to have vanished from the repertoire of Vale Judeu. One of Dona Salvina's stories may allude to the past popularity of such tales: a husband becomes suspicious when, at night, he overhears his wife sighing for her dearest "João Dorido," which turns out to be her nickname for sleep—she suffers from insomnia. Nevertheless the gatherings are spiced with many jokes, many of them unclassifiable as they depend on puns and on the gusto of the performances.

All the tellers leave the gatherings enriched, refreshed and, Idália tells me, looking forward to the next one. For she is now the catalyst that makes tales happen again for a day before they sink back into oblivion.

A Quite Different Use of Storytelling in Contemporary Portugal

Vale Judeu is a typical case of what is happening with the oral tradition in the rural villages of Portugal. Storytelling has nearly vanished because of the appearance of new technologies that have restructured the communities into a more urban way of life. The developing new interests are devaluing and displacing the older ones. The ubiquitous habit of watching television seems to be the imported weed that is stifling a whole variety of regional wildflowers, except for those sufficiently resilient to grow in towns: café jokes and urban legends of UFOs, stolen organs, and poltergeists. An awareness is slowly spreading that something valuable is about to be lost, and a few universities now include a semester of oral literature in their humanities programs. Although there is no course as of yet on folk studies or on the verbal arts, the departments of education are now devoting much attention to the oral tradition and are gearing it toward primary school education. The storytelling hour is now a must in these schools. Some secondary schools in the Algarve are now pioneering the idea of bringing "little old grannies" to tell stories in the class, but most schoolteachers pick up the classic Portuguese folktale collections and read folktales to the students. Others, more enlightened, encourage the young to collect and transcribe stories. The art of storytelling is an odd curiosity that is beginning to be taken up in artistic and literary circles.

A feeling of nostalgia for the fast disappearing "real stuff" is a fair price we all have to pay for the end of rural Portuguese poverty and oppressive living conditions. Nevertheless it prevents people like myself from perceiving and appreciating what is presently taking its place in the verbal arts.[3]

Classified Corpus Included in Idália Custódio's Collection of Vale Judeu

1. AT15 "The Theft of Butter by Playing Godfather" and AT6 "Animal Captor Persuaded to Talk"
2. AT20 "Animals Eat One Another Up"
3. AT61 "The Fox Persuades the Cock to Cry with Closed Eyes"
4. AT122F "Wait Till I Am Fat Enough"
5. AT300 "The Dragon Slayer"
6. AT303 "The Twin Brothers"
7. AT312 Local version of "Bluebeard"
8. AT313 "The Girl as Helper in the Hero's Flight"
9. AT315 "The Faithless Sister"
10. AT408 "The Three Oranges"
11. AT425 "The Search for the Lost Husband" and 425A "The Animal Bridegroom"
12. AT425 and AT432 "The Prince as a Bird"
13. AT511 "The Little Red Ox"
14. AT550 "The Search for the Golden Bird"
15. AT550 and AT780 "The Singing Bone"
16. AT563 "The Table, the Stick, and the Ass"
17. AT571 "All Stick Together"
18. AT700 "Tom Thumb"
19. AT707 "The Golden Children"
20. AT709 "Snow White" and AT706 "The Maiden without Hands"
21. Robe 752 Etiological tales around the Flight to Egypt
22. AT756A "The Self-Righteous Hermit"
23. AT774C and AT774E "Peter Stories"
24. AT788 "The Man Who Was Burned Up and Lived Again"
25. Tubach 1486 "St. Augustine and Child Jesus"
26. AT825 "The Devil in Noah's Ark"
27. AT851 "The Princess Who Cannot Solve the Riddle"
28. AT875 "The Clever Peasant Girl"
29. AT884A "A Girl Disguised as a Man Is Wooed by the Queen"
30. AT891B "The King's Glove"
31. AT923 "Love Like Salt"
32. AT934 "The Prince and the Storm"
33. AT955 "The Robber Bridegroom"
34. AT956D "How the Girl Saves Herself When She Discovers a Robber Under Her Bed"
35. AT1457 "The Lisping Maidens"
36. AT1539 "Cleverness and Gullibility"
37. AT1567 "Hungry Servant Reproaches Stingy Master"
38. AT2019 "Louse and Flea Wish to Marry"
39. AT2023 "Little Ant Finds a Penny"
40. AT2075 "Tales in Which Animals Talk"

Repertoire of the Two Main Storytellers

Mrs. Salvina Baptista (born 1935): 1, 4, 5, 6, 7, 9, 11, 12, 21, 22, 23, 24, 25, 26, 28, 31, 32, 37
Mrs. Maria da Boa Hora Correia Casanova (b. 1925): 8, 10, 13, 15, 16, 19, 20, 29

Notes

1. Heda Jason, "The Authentic and the Spurious," *Estudos de Literatura Oral* 3 (1997): 75–79.
2. Idália F. Custódio and M. Aliete Galhoz, *Memória de Vale Judeu,* 2 vols. (Loulé: Câmara Municipal de Loulé, 1996, 1998).
3. My heartfelt thanks to Idália Farinho Custódio, whose generous cooperation gave rise to this paper, and to Bruce Byrd for his careful and sensitive revision of the text.

Further Reading

Custódio, Idália F., and M. Aliete Galhoz, *Memória de Vale Judeu,* 2 volumes, Loulé: Câmara Municipal de Loulé, 1996
Jason, Heda, "The Authentic and the Spurious," *Estudos de Literatura Oral* 3 (1997)

Women's Stories Among Indigenous Peoples of the Russian Far East

Kira Van Deusen

Kira Van Deusen discusses themes in women's storytelling in the Russian Far East. She draws conclusions from her experiences with Chukchi, Yupik, Nanai, Udegei, Ulchi, and Nivkh women. She suggests that tales chosen for narration deal with themes pertinent to the women's own lives.

Introduction

In the Russian Far East, as in many parts of the world, indigenous women are the principal carriers of culture and language. Even within a larger culture, however, women create subcultures with similarities on a deep level that defy geography, defining and celebrating women's achievements while enriching tradition as a whole. A major part of this subculture involves storytelling, both of traditional tales and of contemporary life stories. I would like to introduce here some aspects of women's storytelling I have met among indigenous people in northern Asia, in Chukotka and the Amur River region of the Russian Far East.

Like everyone in Siberia today, these women are experiencing a profound upheaval in values and their way of life. Traditionally herding, hunting, and fishing peoples, they have been subject to Russian invasion and colonization for 300 years. Their way of life was most severely compromised by Soviet collectivization. In the post-Soviet period yet another major transformation is taking place, involving adaptation to a market economy and revival of spiritual and cultural traditions.

From 1993 to 1996, I made voyages totaling six months to Chukotka in the far northeastern part of Russia, where I worked with Chukchi and Yupik people, and to the region around the Amur river in the southeast, with Nanai, Udegei, Ulchi, and Nivkh people. I listened to indigenous storytellers, most of whom are women. Many of the tellers are from the older generation. They tell in the native languages, translated by their relatives or even themselves. Others are in the middle generation—completely bilingual, telling their tales to me in Russian. This article looks at the kinds of stories told today: how they relate to tradition and to contemporary social, cultural, and economic change.

Magic Tales, Differences in Treatment by Women and by Men

I use the term "magic tale" instead of "fairy tale" to describe many of the stories I heard because it better describes the product of vision, of the inner world. In Siberian tradition storytellers are very similar to shamans, sharing the traditional healer's gifts of inner vision, inspiration, and the ability to cure illness and to predict the future. Tales of transformation and magic are based in the same worldview as the mystic journey of the shaman who restores lost souls and communicates with spirits of nature. Shamans and storytellers maintain contacts between the physical and spiritual worlds.

Women's tales differ from those told by men in the more active role played by women characters in them. Not only major female characters but also minor ones are more developed. Active heroines undergo transformation and use their wisdom and strength to heal and empower. Even in stories predominantly about men, the hero's wife or sister gives good advice, especially before the beginning of a journey. The antagonist's wife mediates to help the hero. When these same tales are told by men, the minor characters are often left out and heroines' male helpers are emphasized.

Another difference between men's and women's storytelling lies in the choice of material. Both men and women have always told legends, which are thought to be literally true, and magic tales, also true but more the product of vision. In the past women were the main tellers of the linear epic (also taken as true). This was different from Turkic and Mongolian cultures, where epic tellers were almost always men. Today, however, women tell more magic tales and men tell more legends. Men are also much occupied with studying history. Their speaking and writing debunks the Soviet ideological view of their past. As far as I know, today no one is telling heroic epics in this area.

Magic tales characteristically work in cycles—heroes and heroines have one name through many stories, plots overlap, motifs repeat. Although one tale is not exactly a sequel to the last, it may pick up on a different thread and carry it to a different outcome. Cycles of magic tales show the endless variety in human character and behavior. They often contain lessons about practical, environmental and spiritual matters, and can be tailored to meet the needs of a specific audience. They may be studies in character or allegories for current events. They are always multilayered vehicles for spiritual truth. Although tellers say they have learned tales precisely as told by their parents, it is understood that changes can be made and new tales and details created from the vision of the teller.

Legends, on the other hand, cannot be changed, and no matter how fantastic legendary events may seem, like a woman marrying a tiger, they are accepted as literal truth. Today the practical teaching tale, formed from magic tale or legend by a shift in emphasis, has become more predominant than it was in the past. It has come to eclipse much of the spiritual and historic function of storytelling, forbidden under the Soviet system.

Heroines

Each region has its own favorite heroine. In the north she is the girl who refuses to marry the man her father has in mind. After leaving home or being thrown out she goes on to marry an animal or to create a new culture on her own, becoming the ancestor of a clan and a way of life. In some tales she dies, perhaps to be reborn in another story. This heroine is a powerful embodiment of female creative power. In asserting her will, she undergoes a transformation that has much in common with shaman initiation.

In the Amur region the favorite heroine is Belye (among the Udegei) or Fudin (among the Nanai and Ulchi), known for her wisdom, creative energy, insight, and ability to protect her family through the spiritual use of amulets and embroidered clothing. She lives alone at the beginning of the tale and often joins forces with animals and with nature to accomplish her own transformation and goals. She helps her brothers in times of trouble and either possesses shamanic power or gives birth to shamans.

In tales I have heard, women are said to have married whales, bears, tigers, walrus, fish, snakes, puppies, and even a human skull and a hunting bag. The skull relates to the world of the ancestors, but the others show the intimate relationship of humans with the natural environment, their interdependence with the animal world, and the power of women to maintain this connection. The woman who marries an animal may carry on a clan when patrilineage is broken by war or epidemic.

The Function of Tales in Womens' Lives

I have identified several predominant themes among the many magic tales, stories from contemporary life, and legends that I heard over four years. Storytellers choose their tales based on internal questioning. To be compelling, the tale must answer some pertinent question for teller and audience or contribute to greater understanding of it. In spite of the fact that traditional tales remembered today have undergone severe processes of selection and reworking through the Soviet educational system, the teller's selection process still works in the same way, incorporating those changes. Stories carry and reinforce much-needed traditional values. They must speak to a need in contemporary people, or they would not be told.

In the outside world of social reality, today's women face problems of economic breakdown—many people have worked without pay for many months. For the first time there is unemployment. There is moral breakdown in the younger generation: robberies, murders, problems with alcohol abound. A different set of values required by the market as opposed to the socialist ideal causes confusion and breaks in communication between generations. The natural environment is severely damaged. Fewer resources must feed greater numbers of people. Marriage is under stress as men have lost work and succumb more often to alcohol and fighting. Women turn to their traditional strength in the family, acting as heads of households, dedicating their efforts to the health and education of children.

The kinds of problems heroines face in stories told today most often involve abusive or neglectful husbands and fathers, the need to take care of brothers, natural phenomena such as storms and epidemics, and the effects of human enemies and of evil spirits who attack unexpectedly.

I frequently heard stories about smart and stupid behavior, stories about selection of a marriage partner, tales of creation, including supernatural help, tales of abduction by evil spirits, and stories of how that evil can be overcome with courage, persistence, and resourcefulness. Truly evil behavior is often seen as completely inhuman. Bad husbands and envious sisters turn into monsters and evil spirits. All of those things are very pertinent in the face of economic change and in the process of cultural renewal.

Within the theme of smart and stupid behavior there are many stories showing good hunting practice, respectful treatment of animals and of one's fellows, adaptability to the unexpected behavior of weather and of people, and refusal to give up in the face of seemingly insurmountable difficulty. A man spent the winter in a bear's den; another was initiated by a tiger. Many tales show the contrast between the morality and intelligence of two brothers. There is a very strong belief that the good wins. Can it be that hunting in today's world relates to the new market economy? It is necessary to find a new arena for exercising skill in making a living, negotiating new perils.

The female equivalent of these hunting stories shows the ability of women to save the day, defeating evil powers through their wisdom and creative energy. Clothing embroidered with intricate patterns showing plants and animals is both physically and spiritually protective and plays an enormous role. One girl succeeds in climbing the ice mountain aided by the protective designs on her clothes. Another escapes evil spirits with the aid of her sewing tools and a magic horse. An embroi-dered mitt brings a person to life. In the north the preparation of skins and sewing of good outerwear is essential to survival, and clothes carry the strength of the animals they are made from. Today women are still using their hands to make beautiful goods and their wits to protect those near them.

In stories about the choice of marriage partners, there is preference for merit over wealth. Especially in Chukotka the male hero is usually an orphan who by rights should be cared for by his uncles but is not. Instead he receives supernatural aid, which, combined with his resourcefulness, makes him the most desirable of marriage partners. The desirable female partner is clever, hardworking, and above all, spiritually gifted. To a certain degree these preferences also show up in everyday life choices.

Besides the girl who lives alone or refuses to marry, creative artistry, and marriage with animals, another common theme in women's stories is an envious sister who creates problems for a woman and her child. This has echoes in today's ever-present squabbles within performing ensembles, where the most despicable behavior is described as "ambitious," putting oneself first.

In the course of their adventures, heroes and heroines have many kinds of helpers: the old woman who gives amulets and good advice; mice, spiders, reindeer and other animals; trees that bend down to help people cross rivers; human friends; and especially a woman's own children. Mutual aid is praised; the necessity of working together is emphasized. This is one value that traditional culture had in common with the Communist ideal, if not the practice. It is now being eroded by the value of looking after oneself in a market economy.

Storytelling Seeks Its Place in Today's Society

For a long time the elders have complained that nobody listens to them. They told their tales only to folklorists. A lot of this problem has to do with language, as today's elders are the last generation to speak the native languages fully, including the complex and poetic language of story. The middle generations are bilingual, while most of today's children and young people speak only Russian. Other reasons stories are little heard are the downgrading of native culture in schools, the demands of modern life, and the intrusion of television.

But during the course of my work over the years since perestroika, I notice that more and more local people now join me to listen to their elders. They want to find out how to perform rituals. There is a strong cultural emphasis today on working with children. Stories are also being used in theatrical context with children and are even cleverly reworked as games in which children take the roles of heroes. On a deeper level, there is a revival in traditional healing, aided by information from shamans and storytellers. Storytelling is undergoing a major change today, as is the whole society, but it still meets deep needs in both tellers and listeners. What form it takes in the future and how that will relate to tradition remains to be seen.

Further Reading

Fitzhugh, William W., and Aron Crowell, eds., *Crossroads of Continents: Cultures of Siberia and Alaska*, Washington, D.C.: Smithsonian Institution, 1988

Forsyth, James, *A History of the Peoples of Siberia: Russia's North Asian Colony, 1581–1990*, Cambridge and New York: Cambridge University Press, 1992

Riordan, James, *The Sun Maiden and the Crescent Moon: Siberian Folk Tales*, Edinburgh: Canongate, 1989; New York: Interlink, 1990

Van Deusen, Kira, "The Flying Tiger: Aboriginal Women Shamans, Storytellers and Embroidery Artists in the Russian Far East," *Shaman* 4:1–2 (1996)

——, "Protection and Empowerment: Clothing Symbolism in the Amur River Region of the Russian Far East," in *Braving the Cold: Continuity and Change in Arctic Clothing*, edited by Cunera Buijs and Jarich Oosten, Leiden, The Netherlands: Research School CNWS, School of Asian, African, and Amerindian Studies, 1997

——, *Raven and the Rock: Oral Traditions and Spiritual Ecology of Chukotka*, Seattle: University of Washington Press, 1999

——, "Ulchi Shamans," *Shaman* 5:2 (1997)

Zheleznova, Irina, *Northern Lights: Fairy Tales of the Peoples of the North*, Moscow: Progress, 1976

Storytelling Traditions in Scotland

Barbara McDermitt

Barbara McDermitt shows us several strands of contemporary storytelling in Scotland. Giving examples from traveler, Shetland, and urban traditions, she presents a picture of tellers intent on preserving their cultural heritage through shared story.

The Passing of Many Fine Storytellers and Attempts to Preserve and Revive the Storytelling Heritage

In the summer of 1978 I came across to Scotland from America to pursue a doctoral research project that consisted of a comparative study of storytellers and their repertoires from among the Scottish traveling people and the Appalachian mountaineers. Twenty years hence I am still living in this beautiful country and still enjoying the privilege of listening to excellent traditional storytelling. Yet when I first arrived at Edinburgh University's School of Scottish Studies those many years ago, the perception there was that traditional storytelling was thin on the ground and disappearing quickly. So many important master storytellers with rich repertoires had died either before I arrived or soon afterwards. Among them was Alasdair (Ailidh Dall) Stewart from Lairg, Sutherland, one of the greatest of the Gaelic traveler storytellers and whom Hamish Henderson extensively recorded in the mid and late 1950s. Another fine Gaelic storyteller of that period was Donald John Stewart from South Uist. Donald Archie MacDonald and other staff from the school spent many hours gathering his stories. Then there were Bruce Henderson and Tom Tul-

loch, old Shetlander storytellers whom Alan Bruford and others recorded in the 1960s and 1970s. And sadly, I also missed Jeannie Robertson, a Lowland traveler from Aberdeenshire who was an extraordinary traditional singer and storyteller loved and respected by her own people and non-travelers alike. Hamish's discovery of Jeannie and her relatives and friends in the 1950s opened the doors to a treasure trove of traditional stories that, unbeknown to the settled community, had been handed down and preserved by the Scots-speaking travelers. Remarkably, these stories included a staggering number of international wonder tales that had long been given up as lost to the oral tradition. Without a doubt these traveler stories represent the richest repertoire of international folktales found in the English language today.

The Scottish traveling people until modern times had always lived outside mainstream society in their own close-knit family units and so little was known about their beliefs, customs, and traditions. As far back as the Pictish pre-Christian period they lived a gypsylike existence, moving from campsite to campsite in the countryside. Even into modern times, travelers mingled as little as possible with those outside their culture. What Hamish was to discover was that storytelling and ballads were valuable parts of the heritage they passed on to their children. The same wonder tales, trickster tales, fairy legends, and ghost, witch, and devil stories once told two centuries before by the country folk in the evenings by the hearth were still being told by the travelers. But the travelers gave the stories a special character, adding cant and using their own racy turn of phrase and colorful, descriptive language that defined the stories as belonging to them.

Sadly, today, the traveling people's traditional ways are fast disappearing and the master storytellers among them are now few indeed. This serious breakdown of the culture started in the 1950s and 1960s when the government began to restrict traveler camping sites in the countryside, forcing families, against their will, to move into city council flats. The government also passed a law that required travelers to send their children to mainstream schools. This forced travelers to integrate even further with nontravelers, thus weakening the strong community ties they had held till then.

So with my arrival in the late 1970s I was already seeing the decline of oral traditions among the travelers as I set out to begin my fieldwork among them. Television had taken over as the main source of entertainment and the art of telling stories was no longer honored, especially by the younger ones. There was about my work, and that of other field collectors, a strong sense of urgency for fear that the once deep well of traveler traditions would dry up before our eyes.

But on the more positive side, there were still some strong-minded travelers who were determined to retain their traveler ways—their belief system, superstitions, music, and stories. These men and women, realizing that their talents as tradition-bearers were being rejected by their own people, went to find new audiences in an effort to save what remained of their culture. The School of Scottish Studies was quick to show their appreciation and invited them to perform for staff and students. Also, the Traditional Music and Song Association of Scotland (TMSA), credited with fostering the folk revival by organizing the first Folk Festival in Blairgowrie in 1966, eagerly opened their doors to these traditional artists. At Blairgowrie and following festivals travelers were invited not only to sing but also to tell their stories. First among them to appear on stage were Belle and Alec Stewart, their daughters Sheila and Cathy, Jeannie Robertson, her daughter Lizzie Higgins and her nephew Stanley Robertson, Willie MacPhee, and later Duncan Williamson and Betsy Whyte. In this manner traditional storytelling got its initial foothold among nontravelers who, for the most part, were unaware even of the existence of Scots folktales. They heard these master storytellers for the first time and were enthralled by the experience.

In the last twenty years, sadly, more excellent tradition-bearers have been lost to us. Nan McKinnon, a Gaelic singer and storyteller from the Isle of Vattersee, and Lowland traveler storytellers Betsy Whyte from Montrose, Auld Maggie Stewart from Aberdeen, John Stewart from Perthshire, Alec Stewart from Blairgowrie, and just this year his wife Belle, famed storyteller, singer, and songwriter, will all be remembered and cherished for their contribution toward keeping Scottish oral traditions alive. And the tradition is alive due to them and the few others who are still with us—Willie MacPhee, Stanley Robertson, Sheila Stewart, Duncan Williamson, and a recent addition, Duncan's grown son, Jimmy.

The recognition of storytelling by various folk festivals was followed in the mid and late 1980s with a new interest in storytelling expressed by school and library administrators. They began to see possible educational value in Scottish traditional stories told live to children. The Scottish Arts Council agreed that there just might be value in supporting storytellers in the schools. At this juncture there were only a few traveler storytellers—Willie, Duncan, Stanley, and Betsy Whyte—willing to "go public" beyond universities and the folk festival scene. There also began to appear Scots who were keen not only to hear the stories but also to learn the art of storytelling from the old traditional masters. Many of these individuals started to explore their own family and community roots and to research archival materials in order to offer old forgotten stories not necessarily found in the traveler repertoires. In fact storytelling began to take a new hold on the Scottish people. This was an exciting turn of affairs, but the trend, rather disjointed, had no center core. Then in 1990 a few people who were determined to give storytelling a higher profile in Scotland got together to establish the Scottish Storytelling Forum at the Netherbow Arts Centre in Edinburgh. The forum is a loose umbrella for storytellers and all those interested in the art. It is responsible for the annual Scottish International Storytelling Festival; the development and encouragement of storytelling groups throughout the country; the training of storytellers especially to work in schools, libraries, community centers, etc.; and the development of the Scottish Storytelling Centre at the Netherbow. The founder of the forum and its present chairman is Donald Smith. The thrust of the forum and the Storytelling Centre is to encourage traditional storytellers to tell their stories to wider audiences of all ages and to re-awaken an interest in others to help revive the art in a full, meaningful way that does honor to past historical roots and acknowledges present developments in Scotland's ever-changing human and political landscape. In short, the forum and its outreach programs are rekindling a genuine revival in the art of storytelling.

Scottish storytelling tradition today, with its roots firmly set in the past, has three major strands. There is the Highland and Heberdian Gaelic tradition, the Scots tradition in the Lowlands and up as far north as Shetland, and, coming into its own with new appreciation, the ever-evolving urban tradition.

Gaelic Storytelling Tradition

The Gaelic tradition has suffered the biggest loss over the years. According to Donald Archie MacDonald the first major setback for Gaelic storytelling in the Hebrides was the death of so many young men in World War I, men who would have been the next generation of storytellers and who would have kept the communities running as an environment in which storytelling could take place. Also, regrettably, of those young lads who did survive, many of them were forced to find work on the mainland, thus again draining communities of their potential storytellers. This same situation was repeated following World War II. But an added dilemma for storytelling was the coming of electricity to the far-flung island communities, bringing television in its wake. So not only were there fewer upcoming storytellers, but audiences were shrinking in favor of television and other new media entertainment. Another problem was the Gaelic language itself. Ever-decreasing numbers of young people became good Gaelic speakers. This paralleled a concurrent decline of the storytelling linguistic register in Gaelic in which important Gaelic words that make up the runs and formulae in the stories became too difficult for the young people to understand and so they just gave up. Also, by this time formal education was pervasive in communities so that young people were experiencing a shift in orientation. Then Sputnik opened outer space, thus, as far as young people were concerned, making the old hero stories redundant.

John Shaw has pointed out that Gaelic storytellers such as blind Ailidh Dall Stewart managed to hold on to stories because travelers were more isolated from mainstream society and therefore were left to their own devices. Although the traveler children back in the 1950s and 1960s had to attend schools, they still had an alternative life within their own community that helped define who they were and kept them keenly aware and respectful of their traditions and interested in hearing tales told by the like of Ailidh.

What is happening today in the Scottish world of Gaeldom? Following on the heels of a new Scots storytelling revival, the Gaels are waking up to the loss of their rich oral traditions and now want to reclaim them. Classes in the Gaelic language are now to be found at all levels from nursery school through university in both the Highlands and Lowlands. Young people and older people too, aware that their forebearers once held the richest story tradition in Scotland, are tentatively seeking help to reconnect with it. But as John Shaw points out, the problem is Gaelic traditional stories are of "high context" (Hall, 1976). A lot of prior knowledge is assumed—formulae, repeated runs, illusions behind expressions, proverb material, and related stories as in the Fin Cycle. Young people today are not story-language literate. This is a real difficulty. They have not had access to communal associations and a context that is shared between teller and audience. But there is hope. This picture is slowly being turned around through the help of the Scottish Storytelling Forum, the School of Scottish, and Sabhal Mor Ostaig (The Gaelic College) on the Isle of Skye. These organizations are behind projects already launched to help retrain Gaelic speakers in story language and context. In spring 1998 the Scottish Storytelling Centre offered its first storytelling workshop in Gaelic, and September 1998 saw the third storytelling gathering at Sabhal Mor Ostaig held exclusively in the Gaelic language.

Essie Stewart: Gaelic Traveler

Another crucial impetus for change is the appearance of a few Gaelic speakers who can still claim direct experience of oral Gaelic storytelling. Essie Stewart is such an example. Essie is the granddaughter of Ailidh Dall and grew up in her grandfather's home hearing his stories on a daily basis. According to Essie,

> Storytelling played a big part in my life when I was a child. No radio, no television in those days. It was a natural way of life for me. We were brought up with storytelling and thought

nothing of it. It was a sharing with the family, my mother and me and my cousins who lived near us. It was a bonding. Yes, it was very special. And the older I get the more special it becomes. I just wish I appreciated it more when I had it. Thank goodness so much [of Granda's stories] has been recorded by Hamish Henderson.

Essie, a grandmother now herself, has pledged to relearn Ailidh's stories. Thanks to Hamish, this master storyteller's entire repertoire is in the archives of the School of Scottish Studies, recorded both in Gaelic and English. Essie has already begun listening to the tapes and is now relearning lost stories. Her favorites are the long Irish epics like Ossian and "The Golden Birds of France." "And when I hear one of Granda's stories I can visualize him sitting on that stool and everyone sprawled out on the ground. And Hamish asking him to translate a saga and he said, 'Well, I'll try.' You see this is what evokes so many good memories when I listen to that tape." Her first thought in wanting to relearn the stories is to give her grandchildren an important part of their rightful heritage.

My grandsons are coming of an age that I think they would be interested. The time has come for me to sit them down and tell them their grandfather's stories. It's important I do this because when I go, that's it. It's the end of the line. I'm the last. No one else. If I don't do something and preserve what's left of it for future generations that's the end—now it's up to them. If I have the stories, they'll be there if they want them.

Though Essie's immediate family, her grown daughters, are proud to be travelers, she is saddened by the fact that so many other relatives are not keeping the traditions. "I have nieces and nephews, but they're married out with the traveling people and they are ashamed of their background, of what they are. But there you have it—modern times, modern families."

Now Essie wants to help other Gaelic speakers, be they within or outside her traveler culture, to regain their lost heritage. "I feel the same as Granda. I think (the stories) should be shared with everyone. Probably if it hadn't been for Hamish coming up to our camp they would never have been recorded. In fact I know they would

never have been recorded or preserved the way they are. They would have gotten lost. . . . I do want to rekindle the link (to my Granda)."

John Shaw feels, as do others, that with the new enthusiasm for spoken Gaelic and help from such individuals as Essie Stewart, the future of Gaelic storytelling looks bright, though it will take time to rekindle past links and it must be done correctly and honestly. As he said in a report for Comunn na Gaidhlig:

At the centre of Gaelic culture lies an extensive story of shared tradition passed down orally in communities over generations. It is a vernacular tradition, unsurpassed in its depth and quality in Europe today, combining the legacy of the oral heritage of ordinary folk with the lettered culture of the Gaelic nobility which ceased to be active some three centuries ago. The survival of Gaeldom's oral and musical heritage in its present form is regarded by scholars as remarkable, and is due primarily to the conscious effort of ordinary Gaels and their communities. (Shaw)

Scots Storytelling: Lowland Travelers

An equally important strand to traditional storytelling in Scotland concerns the Lowland Scots traveling people. Unlike Gaelic storytelling, in which there was a more obvious break with tradition, the picture is different for the Scots. A continuity, however fragile, has been maintained down to the present day. A few Lowland travelers from Aberdeen, Angus, Ayrshire, the North East, and Perthshire have been and are keeping the tradition alive. And even far north beyond the shores of mainland Scotland a Shetland story tradition just holding on by its fingertips seems ready to be reawakened.

Like their Gaelic cousins, Scots travelers for centuries past lived outside the settled community. In this way they, too, were able to hold on to their beliefs, superstitions, and oral traditions. According to Sheila Stewart:

Ye see, because traveller folk never blended into society we dinnae lose our identity. It was bad at the time because we suffered a lot, but now I'm glad because maybe I would o lost my identity.

Like the Gaels, the Scots travelers have experienced a decline of their way of life.

"A lot of travellers deny their heritage," says Stanley Robertson. "They went intae the scaldie society an rejected everything. Those left to honour the traditions are few an far between because a lot o them married oot of the culture."

Sheila Stewart agrees:

An all this outside world was seeping in during the period of the time I had to learn my culture (1950s and 1960s). An what's happening tae-day, travellers are losing their identity. . . . So many don't want to know the stories and don't want tae know the ballads. They're not interested. Give it twenty years from now an there will be no traveller culture left. There will be nobody speakin the language. They'll no be able tae tell ony stories. So me an Stanley an Duncan we're the last of the line.

Today's traveler storytellers, Gaelic and Scots, are very aware that they are the last of a special breed of tradition-bearers, if you will, the last custodians of their traditional culture. They know full well that if they do not share their stories and songs with as wide an audience as possible, they will be lost forever. To this end Duncan Williamson, with the help of his wife, Linda, has published a number of story collections from his rich repertoire of many, many hundreds of tales. Stanley Robertson has also produced several books containing his family memories and legends and stories of his life as a traveler. These publications and the two-part autobiography written by Betsy Whyte have gone far to alert the establishment of a live tradition in their midst that at one time long ago was shared by the whole of Scotland.

So now, encouraged by the Scottish Storytelling Forum and the Arts Council, Scots travelers are regular visitors at festivals, schools, universities, libraries, and community halls—anywhere appreciative adults and children want to gather to hear them. Mostly thanks to these raconteurs, a new generation of young people are learning the lost art of how to listen to and visualize the unfolding of a story, understand and delight in story language, and catch the nuances and hidden meanings that make the experience so very meaningful for teller and audience alike. This kind of listening skill is an art unto itself that in modern times has been almost forgotten, given the place in our lives of television, film, and videos.

Story Repertoires

Lowland Scottish story traditions do have some links with Gaelic/Irish storytelling, but the long Irish hero epics and myths as told by Gaels like Ailidh Dall never really became a part of the Scots tradition. This very old learned Gaelic tradition, with its scrupulous fidelity to how a particular story was told and so should be passed on and with its special attention to exact language, did not sit comfortably with the Scots' looser, more fluid style of delivery and story interpretation. For even travelers who claim to faithfully tell stories as they heard them have their own individual way of embellishment.

Scots storytelling where the constant reworking of the tale and its sort of re-creation for *that audience* is almost the leading characteristic. I think that is to do with social context and to do with class to some extent. It's a very democratic tradition. We make it anew. We can rework it for our own social context—an affirmation of the right of the community to make it their own to tell it in its own way. Whereas with the Gaels we see archaic formalities of language that retain the power of memory of how it was told to me and there's influence of a very learned tradition that originally was purely oral but has also been influenced by manuscript. (Donald Smith)

Because they fit into their more relaxed style of telling, Scots travelers favored the international märchen, some of which did reach them from Ireland, perhaps through Irish travelers, but for the most part came by way of Europe and the northern Scandinavian countries. But the Gaels and the Scots have always held in common the shorter, looser stories such as fairy legends, joke tales, Burker tales, and tales of the supernatural. Traveler children were treated to this wide variety of stories from a very early age. Sheila Stewart, like Essie, saw storytelling very much as an integral part of her childhood:

Storytelling, it was just a natural function when we were growing up. That was what we did. So it was just part o our life. Storytelling wasnae a separate thing. It was all with the one function like learning our cant language. We spoke cant all the time around the fire so the kids could pick it up. They did storytelling so they could pick it up. They did ballad singing. They did cantra, the mouth music. An it was all done an to us it wasnae onything great. It was just something natural in our family—like potty training. Once you learn you never forget.

Stanley Robertson's attitude toward the stories preserved in his family is that they are for everybody, not just travelers:

The country folk gave up this tellin of the stories. We kept them. They dinnae merely belong tae us. We were only the guardians of them—the caretakers. Now I'm tryin to bring traveller culture back intae the mainstream.

But he also acknowledges the importance of preserving the old stories in order that traveler culture is not lost altogether:

Storytelling [in my childhood] was escapism and entertainment an alternative education for the children cause there was nothin for ye when ye went back intae the scaldie community. Storytelling was a bonding process; it glued the family taegether and nothin can break intae the family when its sold like that. [Today] I must keep ma traveller beliefs because if I deny the things I grew up wi I would lose so much culture. Sae I preserve these [stories] as well in all ma family. I think its very important even if its jus for a folklore culture preservation.

All traveler storytellers speak about stories as a force that in the past bonded families and kept their culture alive. But they also recognize that today this tradition is an important link to that past, as explained by Jimmy Williamson:

Stories help keep our culture alive. Because the stories are told by just ordinary people. You can bring back a memory of someone who told you a story that can put you back in a situation where you were when you heard the story. You just need something to visualise the memory and bring back. Bring back that memory of the actual place, the site where you were camped. And that keeps your culture alive because you're remembering the culture as well as the people.

For some storytellers, like Stanley Robertson, the link can go even deeper than a memory:

[The stories, songs] it's ma living link between me an my forebearers. There's a closeness between me an ma folk. There's something I feel, the veil between me and them is a line separated by only such a thin memory. . . . When I'm asked tae sing in a hall, I ask Jeannie tae come tae me and she aaways comes . . . she fully takes over, her voices comes oot ma body, and ye ken when you were singin, her feelin came through me. . . . That closeness living link is there. The stories ken, I'm tellin stories, an goin back wi them, these people are with me. . . . Aul Bill comes through me. I feel him so close at times. An that's the spiritual thing.

And Sheila Stewart mirrors Stanley's experience:

An when I'm singing a ballad ma mother learned me, its ma mother singin through me. . . . The way I got told the stories, its no me tellin the stories, its my father and ma grandfather tellin them through me.

Scots traveler storytellers have definite ideas about how they should tell their stories regardless of whether the audience is composed of travelers or nontravelers. Sheila Stewart:

I don't care if I tell a story in front o the queen. I would tell it in the old traveller traditional style. I never change ma way o tellin the stories. But I use some embellishments. And the embellishments throw in cant words. I tell it the raw travellers' way. Sharin with scaldie makes me even more adamant to do it my own way. Because traveller people were never accepted by society anyway so why the hell should I change my culture for anybody. I give it to them my way, if they don't want it tough.

And Stanley Robertson:

An I try tae pass [my story tradition] on in its realness. Ye ken there is sometimes pretence. I speakit in Doric. I like tae tell the stories as I ken them, learned them. . . . It's ma spirit that I'm sharin with folk. It's very poignant inside me. Ken its deep and there's an inner beauty. An I try an paint this inner beauty so it touches other folks' lives.

Sheila uses the cant word "conyac" when she talks about expressing her "inner true feelings" of a song or story.

Jimmy Williamson pays tribute to the descriptive style of telling he learned from his grandmother that he feels is a crucial part of the story experience.

She'd have the standard words like the shenaghan would have like the words she used to start a Jack story. "He left his mother and father, packed his bag and took off to seek his fortune. He walked and he walked till the stones made holes in his feet and a bird's nest in his hair." That way she could spin out the tale. They all did that, every storyteller did. They had their own method. They had the bare skeleton of the story in here [points to his head] and they can build it up to suit the occasion. And I do the same. . . . My granny's stories are mostly in cant and you can stretch them out with the language.

These are very important comments made by Sheila, Stanley, and Jimmy. And they are reinforced by other traveler storytellers I have spoken to. These tradition-bearers are trying not to let stage performances for paying audiences adversely affect the genuineness of their storytelling. They are avoiding a danger Donald Smith expresses when he talks about the importance of retaining a story and storytelling authenticity.

And I think sometimes we have to listen very hard [to stories being told] because one of the dangers of smoothing out, ironing out some of the old inconsistencies and old imagery and incongruities in some of these really old stories is we may actually be losing something very, very important which is about a certain wisdom about how human life is in relation to Nature.

The Scots travelers realize this too and for the main part are holding to their principles of giving outsiders stories the old way, the true way, as they themselves heard them. But there is a difference. The functions of storytelling as a bonding mechanism and an education for the children no longer apply. Stanley Robertson:

Today we're sharing in a different way. We're now goin tae universities an colleges, an big audiences. But we've all now got a professionalism tae our storytellin. But its nae quite the same. It's nae the same teachin element it once was.

But the stories are at least still being told and being appreciated in new ways. Earlier in this chapter I quoted Sheila Stewart as saying she wouldn't be surprised if within twenty years there would be no traveler culture left, no cant language, no songs, no stories—a very pessimistic prediction. But on the other hand Sheila admitted that she regularly passed on her ballads and stories to her children when they were young and now is doing the same for her grandchildren, and what is more, she has taught them the cant language. And she says, "I know for a fact if I wasnae here [my children] would take up the tradition an carry it fully on."

Jimmy Williamson has quite recently started to publicly tell the stories he learned from his father Duncan and from his grandmother. He has passed the stories on to his son and daughter, liberally embellishing them with cant words as he heard them told to him. Jimmy's son learned the stories from his father and grandfather so well that he became a recognized storyteller at his school. As Jimmy said,

Every time [my son] would visit [his grandfather] he'd say, "Tell me a story." And he'd tell him a story and he would come back and tell it in his own words in the classroom, would sit there and tell stories in the middle of the floor. . . . He knows them—a lot of them, the bare bones—and not only that, he has a great mind for detail. . . . He's got the mind for it. He has a good memory.

So Jimmy's son makes three generations of storytellers within the Williamson family living today. A very promising sign indeed. Stanley Robertson's six grown children are also story literate, having heard stories from their father on a daily basis throughout their childhood.

When the children were little bairns they aaways got a story every night. An they used tae tell each other stories. We still tell stories— all of us. An ma wee grandbairns sometimes tell me stories I've tellt them. I aaways encourage the bairns. . . . Oh, aye, ma stories will be passed on. An if I wisnae here I'm sure ma family would tell them as granddad's stories. . . . These stories are my memorates of love for them. They will continue. Ma great, great, great grandchildren maybe [will] hear the same stories.

Though these storytellers are making sure their own offspring learn traveler cant and are steeped in story and ballad traditions, their mission to preserve and perpetuate their traditions takes them much further afield into mainstream society. Stanley:

I'm telling [stories] taeday because I know it is much needed. An there is an urgency on it because there are very few aul storytellers left. Television killed that aff—with television everything's done for them an its taken awa the art o conversation. . . . At least when they're in the company of a live storyteller their own creativity gets a chance to be exercised. An I think ma work in the schools is extremely important. I tell a story, I gie them a seed—now a lassie or laddie might become a storyteller an that's good. . . . When I tell stories in schools I aaways ask the bairns will ye tell this tae yir aunties, uncles, brothers, cousins, friends. An if they do that, ken, they've started the storytelling.

All the travelers I have spoken to have expressed pleasure in outsiders taking a serious interest in their stories, learning them and telling them. Sheila Stewart:

I think its brilliant [if nontravellers] pass on my storie. That's why I'm doing it. I don't want it tae die. . . . I think its wonderful if they're prepared tae learn the stories an sing the ballads, then I know our identity isn't lost. I'm doin it for ma people tae be recognised.

Here I think Stanley Robertson speaks for all the others:

I'm very happy. I feel I'm part o a living tradition. There's nae such a thing as a dead tradition. A lost tradition. You can get a lost tradition. But it's still there.

Scots Storytelling: Shetland

Though storytelling traditions in Shetland are very different than those on mainland Scotland—both Highland and Lowland—there are certain similarities. The traditions share in common an interest in

genealogy and the passing on of family history. When I first collected among the traveling people I was in awe at their ability to relate their family tree going back many generations and to include personal knowledge of their forebearers, most especially those with outstanding musical or storytelling skills. This knowledge, I was assured, is faithfully passed on even to this day as a way of honoring those family members who have gone before and as a way of keeping their memory alive. As Stanley Robertson has said, the line that separates him and them is only a thin memory. So an important part of both Gaelic and Scots traveler traditions is the sharing of family experiences.

As Sheila Stewart says:

[The true stories] are the raw stories of how travellers lived long ago, how they survived, the persecution, the ridicule. . . . An these are the tales o true life o travellers. An it needs tae be told. These true stories give travelling people like my family an identity.

Jimmy Williamson talks about true stories as "crac."

The wee pairsonal tales what happened tae cairtain pairsons, they don't classify them as stories. That's crac. The classic tales now—like Jack tales—they're less and less [at the campsite] because TV takes up the entertainment value. . . . But crac goes on. Crac is experiences, or exaggerated tales that can stretch tae make like fantasy things. That's still alive. You're interacting. I mean, the art of conversation isn't dead yet. They still like to crac.

In Shetland today there are two recognized traditional storytellers—Laurence Tulloch from the northern island of Yell and George Peterson from Brae in the center of Shetland. Interestingly, the two men have not met or shared stories together, but their experiences of storytelling are similar.

Both tradition-bearers describe storytelling today in Shetland much along the same lines as Jimmy Williamson describes the shape it takes in present-day traveler camps. As Laurence Tulloch says:

Storytelling here is seldom a formal business. You very seldom gather people to tell stories. But inevitably stories come out in conversation. People tell their reminiscences. I have friends I go visit and we sit and talk, tell stories, usually funny stories or reminiscences . . . . Well the way stories are told today. There's a bit of drinking an people sitting—talking the way we're talking—conversations develop into stories. Somebody will tell maybe something that happened to them in the course of their work, an somebody else will pipe up and say you're like the man that—and they'll tell a story. . . . And so on it goes. And you can have a whole night of storytelling an not a soul would realise it. Storytelling by the backdoor if you like.

Another similarity Shetland storytellers share with the travelers is the importance of genealogy. Laurence:

Passing on our genealogy is a way of keeping alive those who have died. The youngsters around here if I mention certain names they would know something about them because they have had me and others talking about them, even those that would be dead before they were even born. What you have to realise is if you keep an oral tradition like this alive then every generation passes along something and loses something and finds something new. It's ongoing.

According to George Peterson, genealogy has always been an important part of the Shetland storytelling tradition.

They told stories of daily experiences about happenings to local people present and past. These true stories were important to the community. They would go over a story, chew over it, get all the details like who were the relations. Then this would lead to the family tree. . . .

Laurence Tulloch came out of a strong storytelling tradition. Besides genealogy, he remembers as a child in the late 1940s and 1950s hearing the fairy stories (locally called "trowly" tales, like the Norwegian trowls), the odd supernatural tale, and humorous tales. His father, Tom Tulloch, was steeped in storytelling, and learned his stories from his mother, a maiden aunt, and a neighbor called Betty Spence. The three would gather of an afternoon and tell stories, but they called it "yarnin."

Yarnin was the word they used for it. An me father was interested in this and he had a good memory and he'd pick them up an then he liked to pass them on. . . . He would never go somewhere to tell stories to an audience. But he did tell them to the family and the children. He would tell stories all the time. It just seemed to be incidental. There would be a bit of conversation and he would say, "There was one time . . ." and he would then go into a story.

So storytelling for Laurence as he grew up was a natural happening rather than a formal special occasion activity. However, he also remembers when storytelling was an important part of the social fabric of the community.

Storytelling was definitely a part of the social life in those days. But we're going well back. . . . This business of meeting to knit and spin and tell stories together I saw the end of it in my time. . . . Electricity came to this island in something like 1966–67 and I can tell you that the coming of television was an absolute revolution in terms of entertainment and doing away with the older ways of doing things.

George, who is now a retired school teacher, also remembers storytelling in his childhood as social entertainment when visitors would come to the home, play their fiddles, and tell stories. But most of the stories George tells today he heard from his aunts and uncles who would visit at least twice a week.

Well once the lamp was up at night in the winter time, my mother would knit, but the men would sit and smoke and branch into stories and even the women visitors would knit and continue to tell stories. The women told stories as well as the men. I would be listening to all of this. It seemed to register on me subconsciously. That's how I remembered the stories.

The story repertoires learned by Laurence and George are similar. Wonder tales are not a part of the Shetland tradition. But most characteristic of the island are the popular stories of the trows indicating a strong Scandinavian influence on an island once owned by Norway. There are also stories of the supernatural, including seal stories and stories of witchcraft, historical tales about local people and events, and true stories about people at sea, about such topics as shipwrecks and the press gangs. And the true stories have always been considered as important as the make-believe ones to these storytellers.

In his teaching days, George would tell his stories to the children in his classes. He always told them in a half-Norse dialect, which he felt was important if the stories were to be passed on faithfully. Laurence, too, feels it is vital that the old stories be told in dialect as he himself heard them. He has begun telling these stories outside of Shetland and he says, "My real fear, my biggest worry there are some stories that really depend on dialect and people [outside] like the Netherbow wouldn't understand. The stories that rely heavily on dialect for me these are the most important ones."

Both Laurence and George feel that the Shetland stories must be preserved. George has passed on his stories not only to schoolchildren, but to his own children and his grandchildren.

These stories belong to Shetland as the Highlanders to the hills and dialect is also important because it stamps Shetlanders as being different from Arcadians. [I tell them] just for sheer enjoyment and to keep them alive for other generations. It's a cultural thing. [Stories] help to keep the roots of our culture alive.

Laurence has passed on his stories to his daughter in the hope that she will one day tell them. He has also put a number of them on tape and this tape has been picked up by many schools, so the children are getting to hear them. George continues to tell stories in schools at his end of the island, and in spring 1998, the Shetland Board of Education introduced storytelling training workshops for teachers, librarians, and parents for the first time. The response was an overwhelming success and now there are calls for more storytelling for children and for adults. There is even an effort afoot to start a storytelling club on the island. This could be the beginning of a new revival in Shetland. Let us hope so.

The Tradition of Urban Storytelling

There is a Scottish urban storytelling tradition, as exemplified in Glasgow, that is flourishing and developing. But just as Jimmy Williamson would not call crac "traditional" storytelling, so too city folk would not call their special brand of repartee storytelling, yet "story" is at the heart of it. This tradition can not claim to have within its frame of reference Irish epic sagas or international wonder tales or fairy legends or stories about trows. Rather, the urban tradition adheres to the relevance of the here and now more than the past, to the true rather than to fantasy. But like crac the true can and often is exaggerated to the very borderline of fantasy. According to Ewan McVicar, an active urban storyteller,

You tell stories against someone and they have to throw it back with another story and the story must always be based on truth. They have to have a truth in their core. But the pleasure of the event is using that core and spinning it out. But you can never stray far enough from the truth that they say that's not true. But you work it, embroider it, and build it for the sense of it and the glory of the narrative and the improvisational skill of it. And it is a style that has a name and its "patter." Glasgow patter. It's partly a way of using inventive language an invention of language, but its also a part of the spinning of the story.

This is a natural urban storytelling language and form of story expression enjoyed regularly by adults who would not call themselves storytellers, but rather players in a game of words. Patter is a powerful shared language, a very creative gift for words that fits comfortably within the urban setting. Again Ewan says,

The difference I see between the true story and the traditional story is the traditional story people have made a rounded shape to it and a satisfying ending. Real life seldom has a satisfying ending. . . . Really what the story's about is the journey. The observation about people, the comment on life. The things people will recognise with a wry smile or chuckle. The word play, the inventiveness. You can tell it is coming from somewhere and is not learned. That, I think, is more urban than country. . . . It is always being improvised and created.

Michael Kerins, also Glaswegian, is a particularly inventive storyteller. He blatantly reworks old traditional stories and he invents his own, most especially when he is telling stories to children or to specific urban adult audiences, and he uses his own brand of improvisational presentation. Michael talks about the importance of stories being made relevant for a given audience.

Speaking to me recently he said,

> I learned the old fairy legend of the two fisherman from you and it's now changed beyond recognition. But that's to do not with me changing that story. It's to do with that story becoming changed because the points of reference for a 1990s city-bound audience are quite different than the people who lived in Iona 500 years ago. . . . Essentially storytelling is the same. The Jack tales about the unhelpful landlord were points of reference for people of that time. And today the suburban myths of hitchhikers or stories of the Internet or college tales or whatever—these have to have a reference point to which the listener not the teller, because these are two different entities, to which the listener can take part in. . . . Recently I told a story of "Wee Tom and the Bank Robbers" [his invention] to an inner-city Glasgow class in which the police were not the heroes because the children had had bad experiences of the police. . . . Interesting how the story has to adapt for the audience.

And so when Michael reshapes a märchen or invents his own story his point of reference is the familiar city setting from which he also takes his streetwise story language, this being his way of drawing his audience directly into the story. His sources are eclectic. He takes his material from all around him—other stories he hears, his own experiences, his family history, the pub, the corner grocery store, the schoolyard, the playground, the church. His antennae are forever alert, ever ready to receive starting points for stories.

Both Ewan McVicar and Michael Kerins stress a "shared language" that enhances and enriches the urban stories. Also, as Donald Smith points out, equally important are the shared values.

> There's the shared values of things [in the urban tradition]—what serves the community and what doesn't serve the community . . . and shared humour that's hugely important because humour is one of the few gifts of the survivor. And you see these stories by and large come out of oppressed communities—the urban poor.

And so the stories reflect these values and humor in much the same way as the old traveler traditional stories reflected the values and humor of that community and were used as a form of educating traveler children into the accepted ways of their culture.

Summary

Storytelling today in Scotland is rich and varied. It is flourishing on all fronts and developing and changing. As George Peterson says,

> I'm still telling the same stories. I must admit that I've doctored one or two of them. . . . I've added a bit here and there—repeating a story word for word for generations, the tradition is killed stone dead if they do that. A storyteller has to keep a story alive and so a story changes from generation to generation just that little bit, that doesn't make it wrong.

So the many strands of Scottish storytelling are ever evolving. There are similarities between them, but also in a very exciting way, so too are there differences. Much of the latter is due to the creative role language plays in the expressing of each story tradition, be that language Gaelic, Scots, cant, Shetland Norse dialect, or Glaswegian street patter.

Donald Smith points out:

> What Scotland has is an incredible linguistic diversity for what is after all a small northern European nation. But its combination of geography and history with its contrast between the urban and the rural and the East of Scotland that looks to northern Europe and Scandinavia and the West that looks towards Ireland and America. So there are real community roots with linguistic diversity because the two go together.

And what is the future for the continuity of Scotland's story traditions? There is a tenacity in all this. The picture of diversity, survival, the new drive of ordinary people to search for story roots, a desire to come together to share and listen to stories—all this bodes well for the healthy continuity of story traditions. On the other hand, the real continuity is fragile. To ensure that it flourishes story listeners must remain alert and sensitive to story language, rhythm, and context, listening hard for the authentic while rejecting that which is fake, honoring storytellers who speak with the weight of their community or tradition rather than those who are basically professional performers and nothing else. In this way everyone helps to foster the revival of Scotland's storytelling traditions and even strengthen these traditions for future generations.

Personalities
The School of Scottish Studies, University of Edinburgh
John Shaw, senior lecturer

Donald Archie MacDonald, senior lecturer, retired

Alan Bruford, reader, deceased

Hamish Henderson, senior lecturer, retired

The Scottish Storytelling Forum, Netherbow Arts Centre
Donald Smith, chairman

Scottish Storytellers Recorded Between January 1998 and May 1998
Essie Stewart, Gaelic, traveler—Lairg, Sutherland

Sheila Stewart, Scots, traveler—Blairgowrie

Stanley Robertson, Scots, traveler—Aberdeenshire

Jimmy Williamson, Scots, traveler—Dumbarton

George Peterson, Shetlander—Brae

Laurence Tulloch, Shetlander—Yell

Ewan McVicar, Scots, urban—Glasgow/Linlithgow

Michael Kerins, Scots, urban—Glasgow

Further Reading

Bruford, Alan, ed., *The Green Man of Knowledge: And Other Scots Traditional Tales,* Aberdeen, Scotland: Aberdeen University Press, 1982

Bruford, Alan, and Donald A. MacDonald, eds., *Scottish Traditional Tales,* Edinburgh: Polygon, 1994

Hall, Edward Twitchell, *Beyond Culture,* Garden City, New York: Anchor, 1976

Robertson, Stanley, *Exodus to Alford,* Nairn, Scotland: Balnain, 1988

——, *Fish-Hooses,* Nairn, Scotland: Balnain, 1990

——, *Fish-Hooses 2,* Nairn, Scotland: Balnain, 1991

——, *Nyakim's Windows,* Nairn, Scotland: Balnain, 1989

Whyte, Betsy, *Red Rowans and Wild Honey,* Edinburgh: Canongate, 1990; London: Corgi, 1991

——, *The Yellow on the Broom: The Early Days of a Traveller Woman,* Edinburgh: Chambers, 1979; London: Futura, 1986

Williamson, Duncan, *The Broonie, Silkies and Fairies,* Edinburgh: Canongate, 1985; New York: Harmony, 1987

——, *Don't Look Back, Jack!: Scottish Traveller Tales,* Edinburgh: Canongate, 1990

——, *Fireside Tales of the Traveller Children,* Edinburgh: Canongate, 1983; New York: Harmony, 1983

——, *The Horsieman: Memories of a Traveller, 1928–58,* Edinburgh: Canongate, 1994

——, *May the Devil Walk Behind Ye!: Scottish Traveller Tales,* Edinburgh: Canongate, 1989

——, *Tales of the Seal People,* Edinburgh: Canongate, 1992; New York: Interlink, 1992

——, *Tell Me a Story for Christmas,* Edinburgh: Canongate, 1987

——, *A Thorn in the King's Foot: Folktales of the Scottish Travelling People,* New York and Harmondsworth, England: Penguin, 1987

"Our Stories Are Not Just for Entertainment": Lives and Stories Among the Travelling People of Scotland

Donald Braid

Donald Braid suggests ways in which Traveller narrative functions to maintain community, to link individuals with ancestors, and to traditionalize certain elements of their world.

About the Travellers

The people who call themselves the Travelling People of Scotland have been known by many names. They have been called tinkers because some Travellers used to make and sell tinware—"tink" being derived from the sound of hammer on tin. Their nomadic life inspired names such as the Gan-aboot folk (the going-about folk) or the mist-folk. A few scholars have used the term tinkler-gypsies—a term that emphasizes possible ties to the Gypsies found in England and other parts of Europe.

These names are important because they identify a minority cultural group in Scotland that shares significant beliefs and values. Travellers recognize themselves as a distinct group and maintain a strong sense of cultural identity, yet Traveller culture is far from homogeneous. Travellers tend to be very anarchical and individualistic. The comments in this article cannot, therefore, be understood as representative of a uniform Traveller identity. The comments do, however, reflect the views of the individuals I met during my field research. While these comments might be able to be generalized to Traveller cul-ture as a whole, such a conclusion needs to be based on further research.

Although questions about Traveller origins and their relationship to the Gypsy groups in Europe have never been adequately answered, the Travelling People have been present in Scotland since at least the 1500s. Because they have endured centuries of discrimination from non-Travellers, Travellers keep to themselves as much as possible and avoid contact with the settled folk, except where it is necessary or where mutual respect has enabled trusting relationships. Yet despite their intentional isolation, Travellers have always survived in relationship to the settled folk by exploiting the "cracks" in the settled economy. They make a living, for example, by doing itinerant farmwork, hawking various items or services door to door, dealing in scrap metal, or trading in secondhand cars. Approximately 17,000 Scottish Travellers live in the British Isles, a figure that includes 3,000–5,000 individuals who are primarily nomadic (Acton, p. 2; Gentleman, p. 14). (For more information about the Travelling People and Traveller life, see Gentleman and Swift or one of the recent auto-biographical accounts of Traveller life by Leitch, Whyte, and Williamson, *The Horsieman*.)

The Collection of Traveller Narratives

The Travelling People of Scotland have been known for well over a hundred years to be competent storytellers. Collector Joseph Campbell includes two stories in his collection *Popular Tales of the West Highlands* that he attributes to John MacDonald, a "travelling tinker." Of John MacDonald and his son Campbell comments, "they do not simply tell the story, but act it with changing voice and gesture, as if they took an interest in it, and entered into the spirit and fun of the tale"(p.179).

Those who studied Gypsies at the turn of the twentieth century made forays into Traveller culture and at times paid attention to narrative (e.g., Groome; McCormick). It is not until the 1950s, however, and the work of the School of Scottish Studies by fieldworkers Hamish Henderson, Maurice Flemming, and Farnham Rehfisch that the depth of Traveller narrative and song traditions was fully understood by outsiders. Henderson argues that this fieldwork had a dramatic effect on the study of Scottish folklore by revealing "the colossal wealth of folk tradition of every conceivable kind which had remained hidden in the tents—and city ghettos—of the travelling people" (p. 219).

This "discovery," coupled with the interest generated through the folk music revival, brought Traveller singers and storytellers—such as Duncan Williamson, Betsy Whyte, Willie MacPhee, Jeannie Robertson, Stanley Robertson, Belle Stewart, Sheila MacGregor, Cathie Higgins, and Lizzie Higgins—to public *ceilidh*s and concerts that celebrated Scottish traditional music and culture (see Munro). The consequent interest in Traveller storytelling inspired a number of collections of Traveller stories intended for general audiences (Bruford, *Green Man;* Douglas, *King o the Black Art;* MacColl and Seeger; and selected works of Robertson and of Williamson). This interest has also motivated scholarly works that explore Traveller storytelling (Bauman, *Three Guesses;* Braid; Bruford, "Storytellers"; Douglas; McDermitt; and Lucinda Williamson).

During my own field research among the Travellers, from 1985 to the present, I observed skillful narrative performances of a wide range of folktales, legends, and ballads—many of which have recognizable international analogues. It does not follow from this statement, however, that all Travellers are or would claim to be storytellers. Yet Traveller interactions are saturated with verbal interaction, or "crack," that includes many genres of discourse (cf. Glassie, p. 36). Although folktales are not as common as they once were, oral narrative forms are highly valued in many Traveller communities, and virtually everyone tells personal experience narratives.

Traveller stories, songs, and ballads cannot be understood as an isolated category of "things Travellers know." There is a deep sense of interconnection between Traveller narratives and Traveller lives. Traveller narratives provide a significant medium for knowledge and interaction in Traveller communities. These narratives are not so much "traditional" as they are a medium of traditions. They are a key element in a process that links past to the future, Traveller to Traveller, and Travellers to the world in which they live. What follows is a brief exploration of two aspects of the interconnection between Traveller narratives and Traveller lives by means of examining how narrative performances are used to link Travellers symbolically to each other over time and space and to significant elements of the world in which they live.

Connections Between Traveller Narratives and Traveller Lives

Traveller narrative performances often play a key role in the perception and maintenance of community. Travellers use narrative performances that index aspects of relationship or that replay interactions between individuals, to create, embody, and refresh the links that interconnect individuals to each other as a community. Experience narratives, for example, may bring news about those who are not present during the telling. These stories often take the form (for example) "Oh, did you hear about what happened to such-and-a-body?" Narratives may be used to remind listeners about past interactions that are relevant to current relationships: "We used to all leave here and go off to the potato gathering." Narratives may even introduce listeners to people they have never met: "I don't remember him [my grandfather] but my mother told me about him. She told me. . . ."

The act of performance also links individuals through the dynamics of the transmission process. The memory of the person from whom a story was learned, for example, often embodies significant meaning for Traveller tellers and listeners. This link between performance, memory, and relationship is vividly expressed in the comments of Betsy Whyte when she was asked by Alan Bruford how she remembers a story:

Well, ye're almost hearin yir mother tell it tae ye again,
the whole thing,
an when ye're sittin tellin these stories to yir ain bairn,
if yir mother's dead, the whole thing—
the feeling even comes back o yir mother tellin ye the story
an ye're full o emotion tellin your bairns the story.

A found it like that wi me an lots o ither . . . travelin folk anyway,
I don't know about anybody else,
but ye sit there an the whole thing comes right back:
instead o you tellin your mother [sc. bairns] the story,
you're sittin there listenin tae yir mother tellin you the story,
but the words are comin oot o your mouth.

> (Bruford, "Storytellers," 35–66)

Duncan Williamson commented that memories of the source of a story may be a very conscious motivation for performers to keep the memory of their ancestors alive and keep their own memory alive in the minds of future generations.

They knew in their own mind that they were also leaving something behind,
a treasure that we could treasure their memory by.
I mean Travelling people doesn't need to go and,
when their old people dies,
and buy a great granite tombstone
and put it in a graveyard to remember them by. . . .
They had the beautiful story told to them,
and the moment they told that story over again
they could picture in their mind . . .
　　　their father,
　　　　　their mother,
　　　　　　　their granny,
　　　　　　　　　their uncle,
who had told them the great story . . .
the picture in their mind would never die
as long as the stories remained with them.
And that's what the old people left with them.

> (Field recording of Duncan Williamson by Donald Braid, 1987, #1)

What emerges from these comments is a sense of narrative performance as inextricably intertwined with a vivid sense of connection or relationship with others. This sense of connection includes not only the previous teller and the members of the audience but also any other members of the Traveller community who are implicated in the transmission process (e.g., "This was your grandmother's story").

Whether through associative links generated through the transmission process, or relationships evoked by narrative content, Travellers use narrative performances to refresh or "remind" participants in the narrative event of the interrelationships among community members and therefore of the interconnecting webs that join them in community.

Traditionalizing Links to the Traveller World

Travellers similarly use narrative performances to create and traditionalize links between individuals and significant elements of the Traveller world. Key to understanding this process is the fact that narrative performances are doubly grounded in human events—they are grounded in both the event that is narrated (the narrated event) and in the event in which the narrative is performed (the performance event) (Bauman, *Story, Performance*). In performing a story, tellers bring these two events into relationship by reanimating and displaying the narrated event within the boundaries of the performance event. Whether the story being told is a fictional folktale or a personal experience narrative, tellers adapt this story creatively to fit the performance event. As part of this process, tellers must contextualize the narrated event by explicitly or implicitly commenting on how the narrated event is relevant to the ongoing dynamics of the performance event and to the participants in this event. Through

contextualization and careful choices as to what events are narrated and how they are narrated, tellers can focus attention on the narrated event as an object of analysis that is to be examined and interpreted.

Consider, for example, the following story I recorded from Bryce Whyte during an interview that focused on questions of Traveller identity. When Bryce told the story we were discussing the assumption many settled folk make that all Travellers are thieves.

I was blamed for stealing a bike too once,
by a boy at a bothy [building used as living quarters for farmworkers].
I says, "We'll see about that," I says.
"When I go up to," I says, "When I go up to the town," I says,
"I'm taking the police back with me,"
"Taking the police back," I says.

"Take your bike man?" I says.
"I don't need to take your bike."
I says, ". . . I have two bikes at home."
And
"Aye you took the bloody bike," he said to me.

And eh, I was away about a hundred yards down the road,
and I saw him coming like the hammers of hell after me.
I says, "What is the silly bugger needing now?"
You ken? to myself.
"What is the silly bugger needing now?"
I'd just a bike to myself at that time.

And he jumped off the bike.
He says, "Oh come here," he says.
"I want to speak to you."
I says, "What do you want now?" I says
        I says, "I'm going for the police to you."
And he says, "Oh, no, no."
And he says, he says, "I'm sorry," he says.
He said, "The bike," he says, "was lying round the back of the bothy."
You ken they used to cry them bothies where they would bide.
I says, "Well why the hell," I says,
"Did you no go round the bothy before you accused me," I says,
"of stealing the bike?"

So.
He says, "I'm sorry."
He says, "Come on back to the bothy and I'll give you something."
I said, "I'm no wanting nothing.
I don't want anything from you.
No not at all."
          (Field recording of Bryce White by Donald Braid, 1992, Tape #30)

Bryce frames this story as a personal experience that actually happened at some point in his life. We, the listeners, are invited to interpret this event and draw our own conclusions from the words and actions—and therefore the implicit identities—of the individuals in the narrated event. By replaying this experience in the interview, however, Bryce suggests this event is not unique but typical of the beliefs that settled people have about Travellers and behaviors that emerge when Travellers and non-Travellers interact. In following Bryce's story we are offered a chance to experience the kind of stereotyping and discrimination Travellers frequently encounter and to integrate this experience—including any emotional response, interpretation, and analysis—into our own understanding of the contexts with respect to which Traveller beliefs and values have been formed (see Braid 1996c). Consequently, for an outsider audience this narrative performance functions as a dynamic and reinterpretable experience of the world in which Travellers live their lives. For a Traveller audience it would serve as a confirmation or traditionalization of common experience.

This ability to use narrative performance to reanimate and focus attention on past events is what makes narrative performances such a potent medium for communicating and negotiating the meaning of lived experiences. It is also what leads many Travellers to use narrative performances as a resource for negotiating issues of identity and difference between Travellers and non-Travellers (see Braid 1996a).

The Cumulative Effect of Multiple Performances

In order to understand fully the role of narrative performances in Traveller life, however, it is important to consider the cumulative effect of multiple narrative performances. Within the course of daily life Travellers tell and hear many different stories in many different events. These performances effectively stitch together divergent lived experiences into a symbolic fabric. In combination with the "real world," this fabric provides a context with respect to which individuals reinterpret and resynthesize events in order to create their senses of worldview and identity. These reinterpretations draw on the past and present as resources and therefore directly influence future thought and action.

Duncan Williamson's *The Fox and the Crow*

Narrated events need not have actually happened to evoke links to other people or to significant elements of the lived world. The following folktale, for example, was recorded from Duncan Williamson in July 1976. The recording was made in Duncan's tent on Tarvit Farm, near Cupar in Fife, Scotland. Duncan's audience was composed of several small children, his granddaughters.

The Fox and the Crow
Well, this is a story about a fox and a crow. [Mhmm]
And
Once upon a time there were a fox, you see? [mhmm]
And och he was—
he had wandered here and wandered there
looking for something to eat.

But he couldnae get nothing to eat.
Oh, he was hungry as could be.
Chased by the hounds,
chased by the hunters and everything.
He was tired and wearied,
couldnae get a bite.

But anyways,
he says to his self,
he says, "This will never do," he says.
"I'll have to get something to eat," he says,
"or I'm gonnae die."

So he says, "there's only one cure for it.
I'll have to go to the village
and see if I can get something to eat."

So on this path leading down to the village, there was a tree.
And sitting on the branch of the tree was a crow.
And this crow had managed to get hold of a big lump of cheese,
oh a beautiful lump of cheese, you see?
And he had flown up the branch with it.
And he's sitting on the branch with it.
And he's sitting, and he's got his foot on it, you see?

When down comes mister fox,
trotting down, wearied and hungry.
And he looks up.
And he sees the crow sitting up the tree,
oh well out of reach,
with this lump of cheese.

He says to his self,
"That is a lovely lump of cheese.
I wish I had that."
He said, "That black bird has got it.
But," he says, "I'll never get it.
"But," he says, "I'll have to rake my brains to see what can I do,
to see if I can get that bit of cheese."

Now when the crow seen the fox,
the crow catched the cheese and put it in his beak,
so's it wouldnae fall, see?

When the fox come down the wee path under the branch
and he looks up.
And that's what he says to his self,
"I'm gonnae have that bit of cheese."

So he thought a plan.
"There's only one thing for it," he says.
I must," he said, "get that bit of cheese."

So he sits and he thinks
        and he thinks
                and he thinks
                        and he thinks
                                and he thinks.
And he looks up.
And he says,
he said, "I heard my father say a long time ago," he said
"that," he said, "'there were bonnie black birds flying about," he said.
"He said they cry them crows.
And they were 'the bonniest birds that ever I seen in my life.'

"But," he said, "I never saw one before.

And I think," he said, "to mysel, that that [is] one there now.
Man," he said, "that is a lovely bird.
And look at the way the sun is shining on it," he said.
"Look at its feathers!
    Look how black and glossy they are!
        And look at its lovely beak,
            and its lovely feet!
I wish I had a bird like that for a pet."

And the crow sat listening, you see?
But nope,
it never let the cheese go.

So the fox says, "I heard my father tell me a long time ago," he said,
"that these black birds," he said,
    "they called them crows,"
and he said, "they were the greatest singers in the world."
He said, "They could sing
and their singing could put you asleep."
And he said, "I never really heard one singing,
but I'd give anything if I could hear one of these birds singing."

So the crow couldnae stand this no longer.
And he opened his beak.
And he says, "Caaaaw, caaaw."
And the big lump of cheese fell.
And the fox picked it up.
And he ate it.

And he looks up at the crow.
He says, "See you,
    you black, dirty, silly bird," he said,
        "you silly black crow,"
he said, "I thought you were fly [clever]."
He said, "you're no fly."
He said, "its me who's fly," he said.
"I'm the fly fox," he said.
"I got your cheese,
and," he says, "you got nothing.
And," he said, "I'm on my way and I feel better now."
And that's the last of my wee story.
      (Duncan Williamson, recorded by Linda Williamson. Archived School of
        Scottish Studies SA76.107)

The Fox and the Crow is a version of an internationally known folktale (Aarne-Thompson 57). Yet, as Duncan tells the story, it is deeply integrated with the beliefs and values of Traveller culture. The opening lines of the story portray the fox as an outcast. He is tired, hungry, and persecuted by hunters. But the fox's wit triumphs over his predicament as he flatters the crow into foolishly dropping its supper. This story is not just about the character of foxes and crows. In a number of Traveller stories foxes and Travellers are linked through metaphor. From this vantage point the story is a metaphorical commentary on Traveller identity in contrast to the non-Traveller identity of the crow. The story emphasizes the crucial importance of wit and creativity in Travellers' struggle to survive in an unfriendly world. In following the dynamics of the narrated event, listeners experience the value of wit over all else. Although this lesson takes place in abstract terms, the listeners' experience of the narrated event, like lived experience, becomes a resource that can be used for deciding future actions.

The Fox and the Crow is also a story that has been nurtured by generations of Travellers. Duncan Williamson learned this story from his grandmother. He has told it to his children. They have told it to their children. This story is told in other families as well. Each performance of this folktale has the potential to evoke implicitly or explicitly the relationships that connect these individuals in families and in communities.

Traveller stories and storytelling traditions are not static but are changing along with the world in which Travellers live their lives. During one interview Duncan Williamson commented on the changes he has seen in his own lifetime:

Oh we don't have wir great outside fires [and] . . . carry ons any more.
But still in their little caravans and the little caravan sites
they have always close knit family get together[s] for the storytelling sessions.
And they'll say,
"This is a story, I remember my old grandfather telling this one.
This was one of my mother's old stories.
Minding my old uncle telling me this one."
And that's the way it goes on.
And then maybe the next time it'll be on somebody else's caravan.
And these stories will go on for ever more.
That's the way it was with the Travelling People.
And I hope it remains like that for a long long time to come.
(Duncan Williamson, recorded by Donald Braid, 1987, Tape #1)

The functions and meanings of these stories will also change over time—as they have always done. There will also be continuities with the past—as there have always been. As one Traveller in her 20s commented, "Storytelling will never die out."

Further Reading

Acton, Thomas, "Draft report to UNISAT/Etudes Tsiganes Research Project on Gypsies and Travellers: What Future in the Europe of 1993," unpublished manuscript; partially published as "Les définitions l'égales du Tsigane au Royaume-Uni," "Tsiganes d'Europe: circulation et enracinement," *Etudes Tsiganes* 39 (1993)

Bauman, Richard, "'I'll Give You Three Guesses': The Dynamics of Genre in the Riddle Tale," in *Untying the Knot: On Riddles and Enigmatic Modes,* edited by Galit Hasan-Rokem and David Shulman, New York: Oxford University Press, 1996

——, *Story, Performance, and Event: Contextual Studies of Oral Narrative,* Cambridge and New York: Cambridge University Press, 1986

Braid, Donald, "The Construction of Identity Through Narrative: Folklore and the Travelling People of Scotland," in *Romani Culture and Gypsy Identity,* edited by Thomas A. Acton and Gary Mundy, Hatfield, England: University of Hertfordshire Press, 1997

——, "The Negotiation of Cultural Identity Through Narrative," in *Texts and Identities: Proceedings of the Third Kentucky Conference on Narrative,* Lexington: University of Kentucky, College of Communications and Information Studies, 1995

——, *The Negotiation of Meaning and Identity in the Narratives of the Travelling People of Scotland* (Ph.D. diss., Indiana University), 1996

——, "Personal Narrative and Experiential Meaning," *Journal of American Folklore* 109:431 (1996)

——, "The Traveller and the Hare: Meaning, Function, and Form in the Recontextualization of Narrative," *Folklore Forum* 26:1–2 (1993)

Bruford, Alan, ed., *The Green Man of Knowledge: And Other Scots Traditional Tales,* Aberdeen, Scotland: Aberdeen University Press, 1982

——, "Storytellers and Storytelling," *Tocher* 31 (1979)

Campbell, J.F., *Popular Tales of the West Highlands,* 4 volumes, Edinburgh: Edmonston and Douglas, 1860; London: Gardner, 1890

Douglas, Sheila, "John Stewart—Storyteller: Three Stories from the Repertory of a Perthshire Storyteller," *ARV: Nordic Yearbook of Folklore* 37 (1981)

——, *The King o' the Black Art: A Study of the Tales of a Group of Perthshire Travellers in Their Social Context* (Ph.D. diss., University of Sterling), 1985

——, *The King o' the Black Art and Other Folk Tales,* Aberdeen, Scotland: Aberdeen University Press, 1987

Fraser, Angus, *The Gypsies,* Oxford and Cambridge, Massachusetts: Blackwell, 1992

Gentleman, Hugh, *Counting Travellers in Scotland: The 1992 Picture: Estimates of the Number, Distribution and Characteristics of Travelling People in Scotland in 1992, Based on a Count Undertaken for the Scottish Office,* Edinburgh: Scottish Office, Central Research Unit, 1993

Gentleman, Hugh, and Susan Swift, *Scotland's Travelling People: Problems and Solutions,* Edinburgh: H.M.S.O., 1971

Glassie, Henry, *Passing the Time in Ballymenone: Culture and History of an Ulster Community,* Philadelphia: University of Pennsylvania Press, 1982

Groome, Francis Hindes, *Gypsy Folk Tales,* reprint, Hatboro, Pennsylvania, and London: Folklore Associates, 1963

Henderson, Hamish, *Alias MacAlias: Writings on Songs, Folk and Literature,* Edinburgh: Polygon, 1992

MacColl, Ewan, and Peggy Seeger, *Till Doomsday in the Afternoon: The Folklore of a Family of Scots Travellers, the Stewarts of Blairgowrie,* Manchester, England, and Dover, New Hampshire: Manchester University Press, 1986

McCormick, Andrew, "Nan Gordon," *Journal of the Gypsy Lore Society,* New Series 1:3 (1908)

——, *The Tinkler-Gypsies,* Dumfries, Scotland: Maxwell, 1907; reprint, Darby, Pennsylvania: Norwood, 1973

McDermitt, Barbara, "The Belief System of a Scottish Traveller as Reflected in His Memorates, Legends and Tales," *ARV: Nordic Yearbook of Folklore* 37 (1981)

——, *A Comparison of a Scottish and American Storyteller and Their Märchen Repertoires* (Ph.D. diss., Edinburgh University), 1986

Munro, Ailie, "The Travelling People," in *The Folk Music Revival in Scotland,* London: Kahn and Averill, 1984; Darby, Pennsylvania: Norwood, 1989

Robertson, Stanley, *Exodus to Alford,* Nairn, Scotland: Balnain, 1988

——, *Nyakim's Windows,* Nairn, Scotland: Balnain, 1989

Stewart, Sandy, *The Book of Sandy Stewart,* edited by Roger Leitch, Edinburgh: Scottish Academic Press, 1988

Whyte, Betsy, *Red Rowans and Wild Honey,* Edinburgh: Canongate, 1990; London: Corgi, 1991

——, *The Yellow on the Broom,* Edinburgh: Chambers, 1979; reprint, London: Futura, 1986

Williamson, Duncan, *The Broonie, Silkies and Fairies,* Edinburgh: Canongate, 1985; New York: Harmony, 1987

——, *Don't Look Back, Jack!: Scottish Traveller Tales,* Edinburgh: Canongate, 1990

——, *Fireside Tales of the Traveller Children,* Edinburgh: Canongate, 1983; New York: Harmony, 1983

——, *The Genie and the Fisherman and Other Tales from the Travelling People,* Cambridge: Cambridge University Press, 1990; New York: Cambridge University Press, 1991

——, *The Horsieman: Memories of a Traveller, 1928–1958,* Edinburgh: Canongate, 1994

——, *May the Devil Walk Behind Ye!: Scottish Traveller Tales,* Edinburgh: Canongate, 1989

——, *Tales of the Seal People,* Edinburgh: Canongate, 1992; New York: Interlink, 1992

——, *Tell Me a Story for Christmas,* Edinburgh: Canongate, 1987

——, *A Thorn in the King's Foot: Folktales of the Scottish Travelling People,* New York and Harmondsworth, England: Penguin, 1987

Williamson, Linda, "What Storytelling Means to a Traveller: An Interview with Duncan Williamson, One of Scotland's Travelling People," *ARV: Nordic Yearbook of Folklore* 37 (1981)

Storytelling in the Rhythm of People's Everyday Life: An Investigation into Contemporary Slovakia

Gabriela Kiliánová

Gabriela Kiliánová discusses reasons for the survival of storytelling tradition in Kysuce, a mountain region of northwest Slovakia where she did fieldwork between 1974 and 1987. She describes three storytelling communities, one centering around two male tellers in their 60s and 70s, one centering on a humorous teller in his 50s and his crony, and a third group of three women who sew together in the evenings with friends.

Storytelling Continues in Kysuce, Northwest Slovakia

Between 1974 and 1987 I went almost every year to do fieldwork in Kysuce, a mountain region in Northwest Slovakia. This particular territory was to prove a very interesting terrain for folk narrative research. Following World War II fundamental changes occurred in the way people lived in the area. The advent of modernization, which began at the end of the 1950s, brought with it industrialization, urbanization, the collectivization of agriculture, the development of mass communication, and higher standards of education, which were eventually to transform the region.

Kysuce has always been primarily a rural area with few industrial centers, and until the end of the 1950s the main occupations of the indigenous population were agriculture and domestic industrial production (the production of home crafts).

This rural way of life survived in the villages for a long time, and, because the people's working life was largely bound up in their daily routine, it provided many opportunities for social meetings and social communication. Consequently, the division between work time and leisure time did not exist. The ritual of storytelling, which as a spontaneous and live oral expression is inextricably connected to interpersonal contact and small social groups, was a natural part of the rhythm of everyday life.

There were at least two reasons for this phenomenon: 1.) Storytelling, as will be shown in the following, represents one of the universal modes of mutual social contact amongst individuals within various societies, and thus it is always potentially present. 2.) Most cultural phenomena are kept alive better if they continue unabated, and this includes the phenomenon of storytelling. In Kysuce in the twentieth century, large population movements did not occur; and even after World War II the people in the region still lived in their original residences, in spite of the fact that they frequently traveled to remote industrial centers for work. This factor helped to maintain the continuity of generations of the population as well as the continuation of the transmission of cultural phenomena. However, fundamental changes to the way in which people met and interacted within their societies gradually took place. For example, the majority of men of a productive age, who had jobs outside their villages, stayed at their places of work, returning home only at weekends. The majority of women, however, remained and worked in the villages—in agriculture or in small, local industrial businesses. Only a minority of these women, mostly of the younger generation, traveled to work.

My research enquiries, which concentrated on narrative repertoire, were collected from narrators of all generations, men, women, and children, in which I observed natural storytelling situations and conducted interviews with narrators and their audiences. This paper will describe and identify the groups of narrators and their audiences, the content of their repertoire, the functions their narratives fulfilled, and the place that storytelling had in the rhythm of people's everyday life.

I had the opportunity to investigate the old generation, which lived almost their entire life in a traditional rural community; the middle generation, which was the bearer of the modernization processes after World War II; and the younger generation, who were born in the period when the main changes to the old rural way of life had taken place. I shall take as my example one village, Nová Bystrica, and examine the process therein.

My fieldwork in Nová Bystrica took place between 1981 and 1987. I interviewed 59 respondents and collected 485 texts. There had been 3,200 inhabitants in the village in 1981, but the population had declined slightly since then. The village was divided into so-called courtyards, which were small site units, built on land that belonged to one original settler or to one family. There were 36 courtyards in Nová Bystrica. In one courtyard lived between eight and 12 families, which in some cases were no longer related. The community-consciousness of one courtyard of inhabitants that was traditionally very strong in the past had survived at the time of my research. Contacts between neighbors in one courtyard provided a base for all social contacts, and the people in the village organized themselves around common work details according to the requirements of the courtyards. The village experienced a lot of out-migration to the United States from the beginning of the twentieth century. However, following the creation of the Czechoslovak Republic in 1918, emigration was directed toward Belgium, France, and Holland, where people worked as miners and agricultural workers. The main original occupation was farming, connected to diversified additional occupations

such as rafting, the peddling of fancy goods, which survived up to the 1950s. In the 1980s the majority of men worked in industry outside the district during the week. Only one small industrial business was located in the village, a shoemaker's workshop of 150 employees, mostly women.

Since the 1950s many men from Kysuce were employed in Ostravska, an industrial area with mining and smelting industry in northeastern Moravia. After the split of the Czechoslovak Federation on January 1, 1993, the Ostravsko area became the easternmost part of the Czech Republic, and Kysuce became a part of the Slovak Republic, complicating the mobility of itinerant workers.

Storytelling Repertoire in the Village of Nová Bystrica

During the 1980s I collected in this village almost 500 texts, which show the genre and theme composition of its local storytelling culture, including all oral narrative genres, but in a very disproportionate ratio. The majority of these collected texts include personal narratives and true stories (224 texts), followed by supernatural legends (143 texts), humorous stories (48 texts), and local and historical legends (41 texts). The smallest volume among the collection was that of tales (29 texts). The composition of this repertoire, with its emphasis on personal narratives, humorous narratives, and anecdotes and legends (mainly supernatural), and a minimum representation of tales, is by no means extraordinary or atypical within the Slovak context. Research into narrative repertoire in other Slovak areas have brought rather similar results (Gašparíková, *Slovenská*; Leščák; Michálek; Michálek and Irša). Further research in other European countries has also found a dominance of the indicated genres within the present storytelling repertoire (Gwyndaf; Neumann, "Volkserzählung heute," "Erlebnis Alltag"; Pomeranceva; Simonides; Šrámková; etc.).

From the sources of Nová Bystrica it was interesting to discover that, even in the 1980s, there still existed a rather rich and stable genre structure and that among the active narrators were men and women of the older, middle, and younger generations. The repertoire of storytelling mostly included many traditional narrative plots, which occurred generally in Slovakia, such as the cycle of traditional anecdotes about Gypsies (i.e., Aarne Thompson, 81B, 1626, 1810A, 1833B), historical legends surrounding the famous forest robber Jánošík and his followers, and stories about the sleeping army inside the hill.

A large number of narratives arose from legends, which focused mainly on stories about death and corpses, on strange omens and the circumstances of death, and on unexplainable magical coincidences, ghostly encounters, and incidents of bad luck. Alive in the people's memory were also legends about devils, torchbearers, witches, water sprites, and other spirits. Most narrators were familiar with motifs from the cycle of legendary tales on Christ's wanderings in the world with Saint Peter (i.e., Aarne Thompson 774C, 774F, 791, 822). This data on the storytelling repertoire in Slovakia was provided by the *Catalogue of Slovak Folk Prose I and II* and from my own research.

Personal narratives focused mainly on biographical themes (childhood, growing up, work, migration, tragedy, dramatic and comic life events, etc.); on historic themes (stories about World War I and World War II, the Slovak National Uprising, etc.); on local events (tragedies, fires, comic characters in the village, etc.). The storytelling repertoire of the village pointed to a continuity of the storytelling tradition and to the functioning of an inter-generation transmission even within the investigative period of the 1980s.

The Social Context of Storytelling Performances: Telling in the U Bereši Courtyard

The storytelling repertoire of the village of Nová Bystrica was transmitted in the 1980s because of regular storytelling performances, which generally had regular narrators and a captive audience. I shall give examples of certain storytelling communities, which I observed in the village from 1981 to 1983.

The storytelling community in the U Bereši courtyard developed around the storyteller Rudolf (born 1910), a widower, who lived with the family of his youngest daughter Anna (born 1947) and was one of the oldest people in the courtyard. At that time, Anna was a housewife bringing up four children. Her husband, an electrician, would for several weeks at a time go to work around the whole Czechoslovak territory. Anna's was an open, hospitable house, and visitors were welcomed by the family. Almost every afternoon the storyteller Ľudovít (born 1900) would come from the neighboring courtyard and,

depending on the weather, would either sit with village menfolk in front of the house or gather inside. Rudolf and Ľudovít lived all their lives in this one village and were naturally connected through their shared common experiences.

Among the storytelling community were three female neighbors (born 1900, 1910, and 1928), daughter Anna, her children, and other children, all of whom lived in the U Bereši courtyard. In this group storytellers divided their roles and themes respectively. Rudolf acted mainly as a storyteller cum personal observer. He usually narrated stories about the hardships of life in the past as well as memories of his childhood, his parents, and the events of war. He would also often relate stories about superstition alongside funny experiences from his repertoire, such as experiences from weddings, at which he was also esteemed as a musician. However, these funny stories of his were only supplementary to Ľudovít's narratives, which were strictly focused on humorous themes. Ľudovít's repertoire included numerous anecdotes from a cycle on gypsies (mainly on the gypsy-priest theme), as well as narratives about former local priests and his own personal comical conflicts with local youths and grown-ups.

Rudolf, a religious Roman Catholic, tolerated these narrations in silence. Similarly, Ľudovít listened to the supernatural legends performed by Rudolf, although he considered them to be unbelievable. Both storytellers respected each other because they did not want to stop the regular meetings, the main reason for which was the need to maintain mutual, informal social contacts. Discussions and storytelling strengthened social relations within the local group, which had an inter-generation function (compare Sirovátka). Another reason that bound this storytelling community together was the mutual appreciation of their storytelling mastery. Even so, Rudolf and Ľudovít, in separate interviews, also expressed a certain criticism of each other; for example, Rudolf took offense when Ľudovít made fun of the church and priests, and Ľudovít kept aloof of Rudolf's narrations of superstitious tales. Nevertheless, a mutual sympathy and an overall appreciation of storytelling qualities prevailed in their relations. Of the two storytellers Ľudovít, however, had the stronger personality. In the heat of their storytelling he would, on occasion, interrupt Rudolf's speech, sometimes finishing the story his partner had started or making witty asides to his storytelling. In this way he would change the tone of Rudolf's serious stories to a humorous level. This is nothing unusual if we understand that in dramatic folk narrations the comic and the tragic are always closely linked (see Bachtin). In performance, the interaction of humor and seriousness in the art of storytelling is a device that not only captures the attention of the audience but makes the story more interesting.

On working days in Nová Bystrica, a small group of men and women who were employed in the village would return home in the evening, providing the opportunity for Ľudovít to make fun of the passing women. To assist him in his banter he would involve two "fellow actors," the sisters Vilma (born 1944) and Mária (born 1941), who would often stop and join in the performance. In this way the storytelling would go in a different direction, as the women would make witty comments about work or some news from the village, whereupon they would exchange jokes and anecdotes, mainly with Ľudovít. The sisters also had an extensive repertoire of their own consisting of traditional narrations that they had learned as children from their uncle, another good storyteller. The women would also tell stories of superstition to support Rudolf's narrations, but it was always the two older men who were at the center of the storytelling activities. This particular storytelling community, however, was largely absent of men from the middle and younger generations for reasons referred to earlier—that virtually all such men from the U Bereši courtyard worked outside the village and came home only at weekends. When they did meet during their free time, they would prefer to play cards and share in common conversation, and they lacked the expressiveness and personality to indulge in storytelling.

Women Embroider and Tell Serious Tales

An example of the women's storytelling community is that of a group which used to meet in the house of narrator Alojzia (born 1907) in the U Holienky courtyard. Alojzia was a widow who lived alone, but she was frequently visited by her neighbors Anna (born 1931) and Jozefína (born 1906), who were sometimes joined by two or three other women. The main purpose of their meetings was embroidery, which was taught by Alojzia mostly during autumn and winter evenings. They would busy themselves in sewing and exchanging patterns and also indulge in storytelling, directed mainly by Alojzia, who was a storyteller with a strict and serious character. The main themes of

their narrations were drawn from stories from life and supernatural legends. During the course of my research I learned that the widow Alojzia was among the most important interpreters of supernatural legends in the village of Nová Bystrica. Her stories were sometimes completed by Anna, also a talented storyteller with a sense of humor. However, it seems that within this women's circle the narrations were never of a humorous theme, which points to the dominant influence of Alojzia's more serious nature. When, during my interview with her, I would try to lead the enquiry to humorous themes, she lost interest in the discussion, even dismissing humorous stories and anecdotes as being irrelevant. Her attitude derived from her understanding of social behavior: jokes and having fun were inappropriate for a woman and belonged to the realm of the male narrators. And, although I met with this response elsewhere, mostly among the older generation, this is not to say it was the prevailing situation. Observations in the village indicated that women as well as men were active interpreters of humorous stories, as in the U Bereši courtyard.

In the past women would also, on occasion, play an active role in providing social entertainment, although conservative critics would contradict this. At a wedding ceremony married women would improvise whole dramatic scenes of infidelity, in which they performed the role of the false bride or wronged lover, whereupon a good performance would elicit much laughter and admiration. Such dramatic charades took place in certain wedding ceremonies even in the 1970s and 1980s, and women also got involved in various forms of social entertainment—for example, during local festivals and Shrovetide. However, the research material collected shows that it was men who were the predominant humorists in storytelling communities, which met the audience's expectations entirely.

Humorous Tales in the U Talapky Courtyard

Another example of a male-dominated storytelling community was a group who were active in the U Talapky courtyard. In this courtyard lived a humorous storyteller by the name of Štefan (born 1920). He was frequently visited by his friend and neighbor Martin. Both of them were retired and associated themselves with the middle and older generations. Both men had earlier worked together in Ostravsko and, like Rudolf and

Ľudovít, shared common life experiences, but they were also of a similar temperament—happy by nature, with a good sense of humor.

Štefan had the main word in meetings, while his friend would act as a kind of prompter. And, as with the U Bereši storytelling community, U Talapky storytellers shifted from everyday discussions about recent events to associative memories recounting various stories or anecdotes. Having observed these "harmonious" storytellers I was able to see how in a group a well-known story could be interpreted, which in a way connects with the findings of K.V. Čistov (1967:34–35) when he studied the legends. During the flow of conversation, the storyteller did not interpret the whole story but simply took it to a suitable point (a motif or episode) in the narrative. The main purpose throughout was to make people laugh, and to this end, a conversation would interrupt the storyline so that the traditional story would be reinterpreted in a new context and the meaning would therefore assume a new dimension.

During my research in the U Talapky courtyard I realized again how important it is to listen to the storytellers' repertoire in a natural setting. Only by listening to the range and the order of the narratives can we discover the real meaning of the texts in the context being related by the narrator. This was especially so with the stories about superstition, which could be told in a humorous or a more serious context, either in the original version or as a parody, without any additional commentary. Observation of the storyteller shows time and again that the meaning of the same story can change according to different narrators and social contexts (compare also Kirschenblatt-Gimbett).

Thus far I have described the various groups of narrators in the village of Nová Bystrica who largely staged their performances for a receptive audience, but within the rhythm of people's everyday lives, storytelling could stem from an accident or unusual event, such as the following example that I witnessed. The real episode began when Rudolf's 10-year-old granddaughter returned from school one day with a group of friends and was bitten by a neighbor's dog in the U Bereši courtyard. When the excitement calmed down the child's mother and her neighbors began to administer treatment, while Rudolf meanwhile began to relate a couple of stories with dog themes. The first of these was recounted from his childhood: once, while playing with other children, he too was frightened by a dog and, in running away from the animal, fell and injured his leg, which was the reason he had a limp for the rest of his life. The second anecdote told how Rudolf's own dog once bit a policeman and what problems the storyteller had with that. Here was an example of how the artifice of storytelling was used as a device to lessen tension and cool tempers in a very subtle way. In other words, the narrative skill was the regulator of potential social conflict.

Values of the Storytelling Event

Various sources of research have shown the existence of a diversity of storytelling groups, and members of these groups were connected by local ties of friendship and family through the generations. People would meet mainly because of the basic social need to be together and to create some fun in their lives. Regular meetings such as these provided the opportunity to tell stories, although, as we have seen, the success of this depended upon the presence of a verbally gifted individual, the narrator. Only the narrator could transform everyday discussions into a story whereby the combination of the commonplace and legend assumed an aesthetic value. And although my empirical research material was limited to storytelling communities in one rural area of Slovakia, the described mechanism of repertoire transmission and the contexts into which the act of storytelling can enter have a wider validity.

Storytelling is, on the one hand, a form of entertainment, a performance during which the audience appreciates the artistic qualities of the narrators. Yet, on the other hand, storytelling is also a means of transferring information and knowledge. People are naturally interested in life stories and the life experiences of their relatives and friends as well as the events that occur in their immediate society. Storytelling recreates the past, and because of this it reestablishes and reinvents the identity of the local group, collectively and individually, as memory and reality (Fentress and Wickham, pp. 47 and following). Stories in themselves become real and guiding experiences, which help us to orient in the present. For these reasons storytelling remains important for people, and, however much the context, the frequency, and the techniques of storytelling might change, it does satisfy a permanent need in people.

Further Reading

Aarne, Antti, *The Types of the Folktale: A Classification and Bibliography,* edited and translated by Stith Thompson, second revision, Helsinki, Finland: Academia Scientarum Fennica, 1961

Bachtin, M.M., *François Rabelais a lidová kultura středověku a renesance* [François Rabelais and Folk Culture of Middle Ages and Renaissance], Prague, Czechoslovakia: Odeon, 1975

Čistov, K.V., "Problema kategorij ustnoj narodnoj prozy neskazočnogo charaktera," *Fabula* 9 (1967)

Fentress, James, and Chris Wickham, *Social Memory,* Oxford and Cambridge, Massachusetts: Blackwell, 1992

Gašparíková, Viera, *Katalóg slovenskej ludovej prózy/Catalogue of Slovak Folk Prose,* 2 volumes, Bratislava, Czechoslovakia: Národopisný ústav SAV, 1991, 1992

———, *Slovenská ludová próza a jej súčasné vývinové tendencie* [Slovak Folk Prose and Its Contemporary Development], Bratislava, Czechoslovakia: Národopisný ústav SAV, 1986

Gwyndaf, R., "Memorates, Chronicates and Anecdotes in Action," in *Papers,* volume 1, 8th Congress of the International Society for Folk Narrative Research, Bergen, Norway: Nordic Institute, 1984

Kiliánová, Gabriela, "Chapter XII: Folk Narrative," in *Slovakia: European Context of the Folk Culture,* edited by R. Stolicna, Veda, 1997

Kischenblatt-Gimbett, Barbara, "A Parable in Context: A Social Interactional Analysis of Storytelling Performance," in *Folklore: Performance and Communication,* edited by Dan Ben-Amos and Kenneth S. Goldstein, The Hague, The Netherlands: Mouton, 1975

Leščák, M., *Súčasný stav humoristického rozprávania na Spiši* [Contemporary Condition of Humorous Narration in Spiš] (Ph.D. diss., Komensky University), 1971

Michálek, J., "Ľudové rozprávanie" [Folk Narration], in *Stará Turá,* edited by Ján Michálek, Bratislava, Czechoslovakia: Obzor, 1983

Michálek, J., and R. Irša, "Ľudová prozaická tradícia" [Folk Narrative Tradition], in *Záhorská Bratislava,* edited by Ján Podolák, Bratislava, Czechoslovakia: Obzor, 1986

Neumann, Sigfried, "Erlebnis Alltag," in *Papers,* volume 2, 8th Congress of the International Society for Folk Narrative Research, Bergen, Norway: Nordic Institute, 1984

———, "Volkserzählung heute," in *Jahrbuch für Volkskunde und Kulturgeschichte,* Berlin: Akademie-Verlag, 1980

Pomeranceva, T.E.V., "Foľklornyj repertoár odnogo sela za sto let," in *Russkij foľklor 16*

Simonides, D., "O procesie zmian w folklorze slownym," in *Tradycja i przemiana,* edited by Zbigniew Jasiewicz, Poznan, Poland: Wydawn. Naukowe Uniwersytetu im. Adama Mickiewicza, 1978

Sirovátka, O., "Funkce folklóru v životě vesnice" [Function of Folklore in the Village Life], in *Revoluční proměny jihomoravského venkova,* edited by Václav Frolec, Brno, Czechoslovakia: Blok, 1980

Šrámková, M., "Proměny a současný stav lidového vyprávění" [Changes and Contemporary Condition of Folk Narration], in *Slovenský Národopis* 24, Bratislava, Czechoslovakia: Veda

Problems in Translation and Storytelling Using Switzerland as Example

Barbara Gobrecht

Barbara Gobrecht discusses problems inherent in translating. She uses examples from the translation of dialect to High German and from High German to dialect.

Language and Legends in Switzerland

For many people who do not belong to the Swiss Confederation, the vacation paradise with its mountains and lakes is fairy tale land and a land in which four languages are spoken: German, French, Italian, and Rhaeto-Romanish (Ladin). Both of these assumptions are incorrect.

Switzerland is a land of legends. Mountains, lakes, and the unpredictability of the weather again and again have inspired people to tell each other legends—some of blooming Alps that become accursed; of herds of cows that, in panic, throw themselves into an abyss; of treasures buried deep in mountain caves; and many others. Anyone who, while looking for fairy tales, opens an anthology, such as Hanns Bächtold's *Schweizer Märchen* or Johannes Jegerlehner's *Volksmärchen aus den Walliserbergen,* will most certainly, and regardless of its title, find more legends than fairy tales.

Wrong, also, is the assumption that four languages are spoken in the Swiss Confederation. There are at least five languages. In the German part of Switzerland everyone, from infants to the aged, from untrained workers to university professors, speaks Schwyzerdütsch. This Swiss-German has the function of a spoken national language.[1] Fairy tales for children and fairy tales for adults are, as a matter of course, told in dialect, regardless of whether the printed text of a respective collection is given in High German (Hochdeutsch) or in one of the many Swiss-German dialects.

Officially, there are only four languages in Switzerland. Of those, 65 percent of the population speak the German language, 18 percent the French language, 12 percent learn Italian as a first language, and only 1 percent learn Rhaeto-Romanic (Rhaeto-Romance, Ladin), which has a number of separate dialects. Wealth in fairy tales and high population numbers seem to stand in reverse proportion to each other. The Rhaeto-Romanic part of Switzerland in particular offers original storytelling personalities and a vast treasury of fairy tales that have been recorded by industrious field researchers and preserved (*aufgehoben* = lifted up and saved) in anthologies, just as "the Rhaeto-Romanic idioms have been endangered for a longer period and had to be protected."[2]

The canton of Tessin, as part of a much wider cultural area, has a strong alignment with Italy both in its language and in its fairy tale material. In contrast to the German part of Switzerland, speaking in dialect in the Tessin used to be "equated with a low educational level and social standing."[3] As a result, simple folk in fairy tales speak in dialect, while kings and princesses speak "high" Italian. For her collection *Märchen aus dem Tessin*, the fairy tale expert Pia Todorovic-

Strähl first had to transcribe the local storyteller's dialect into written Italian before she could translate that text into German.[4]

We are facing a problem that is already becoming delineated: The path of a Swiss fairy tale from the moment of its being written down until it appears in a printed version in German is a long road and often paved with many stumbling blocks, including the possibility of faulty sources. Such is the case of the difficult dialects of the Jura, where even the first step in the translation process—transcription into French—presents a problem.[5] In addition, the French-speaking North Jura, known as a land rich in fairy tales, dances out of step with the internationally known fairy tale types. North Jura's fairy tales of wonderful and humorous content, called *fôles* (from the Latin *fabula*), have only barely found their way into the large Swiss anthologies of fairy tales.

With seven-league boots we have rushed through the Rhaeto-Romanic, Italian, and French parts of Switzerland and now arrive in the German part of the country, familiar in its geography, linguistics, and cultural history. It cannot be denied, the German part of Switzerland is Grimm country. Most fairy tales show a clear connection to German fairy tales. Characteristic German-Swiss thoroughness is present not only in everyday matters but also in fairy tales, starting with the shiny cleanliness of the baking oven in Frau Holle's house (Mother Holle), up to the double-underlined moral at the end of the fairy tale about herding the hares.

Many German-Swiss fairy tale anthologies are geared toward an audience of children and believe they cannot forgo the moral of the story. We know from Katalin Horn's research on modern telling of fairy tales in German-speaking Switzerland[6] that indigenous tellers of fairy tales are charged with "an important role in the linguistic discovery of identity, particularly by children who have not quite mastered the written language." The Brothers Grimm had in mind a comparable audience for their children's stories and house fairy tales without, however, overemphasizing their moral usefulness. They refrained from using usual children's language and created an artistic style that may be called literature. One example for comparison, from "Der Wolf und die sieben jungen Geisslein" (The Wolf and the Seven Young Kids): "Not long thereafter the old goat came home from the woods. Oh, what a sight she found! . . . (*"Ach, was musste sie da erblicken!"*

[*Kinder- und Hausmärchen 5*]); "*Gli druf ist's Müetterli hei cho. Wos vo witem gseh hät, dass d'Hustüre offe-n-ist, isch es schuli verschrocke und wos erst na die Unornig gseh hät, wo de Wolf gmacht hät, häts denkt, da seig allweg öppis Dumms gange*" (Louise Müller and Hedwig Blesi, "Erzählungen und Märchen," in *Schweizer Mundart Für Kinder von 4–7 Jahren*, Zürich-Leipzig: 1928, p. 149).

In our short excursion through Switzerland, we have determined that fairy tales are more or less connected to the local language. But despite language barriers, there is also some connection in the fairy tale treasures of this multi-language country. Typical throughout the confederation are a number of fairy tale motifs and decorative features[7] that stem from historical experiences as well as experiences that are countrywide. Some developed from the long tradition of democracy, from the experience of landscape, but above all from bitter poverty.

In Swiss fairy tales there is frequent mention of someone having to hire himself out, of children being exposed, of emigrating, of distant travels, and repeatedly of the suffering from hunger. Even Betheli, the hard-working girl in several German-Swiss variants of Frau Holle (Mother Holle) was not made to *freeze*, but to become so *hungry* that "her *ears almost fell off*" (Hanns Bächtold, *Schweizer Märchen*, Basel, Switzerland: 1916, p. 176; Robert Wildhaber and Leza Uffer, *Schweizer Volksmärchen*, Düsseldorf-Cologne: 1971, p. 5; Hans Peter Treichler, *Märchen und Sagen der Schweiz*, Zürich-Wiesbaden: 1989, p. 98), or that "her ears *shook*" (*Kinder- und Hausmärchen aus der Schweiz, gesammelt von Otto Sutermeister, neu bearbeitet von Fritz Gafner*, Basel, Switzerland: 1977, p. 12); or that "her *nails* almost fell off her fingers and feet" (*Das Schweizer Märchenbuch, neu mitgeteilt von Curt-Englert-Faye*, Basel, Switzerland, 1971, p. 44). That sounds suspicious! Have the publishers copied from each other? And incorrectly, yet? We must follow up on these questions.

In collections on the subject that are described as Swiss fairy tales, one finds next to real fairy tales and genuine myths a range of mixed forms such as found in Grimm's *Kinder- und Hausmärchen*—comical tales, legends, etiologic tales, and so forth. They belong, to a large extent, to international storytelling material. Throughout Switzerland, not only in the German-speaking area, variants of "Frau Holle" (Mother Holle),

"Sneewittchen" (Snow White), "Aschenputtel" (Cinderella), and "Tischchendeckdich, Goldesel und Knüppel aus dem Sack" (The Magic Table, the Golden Donkey, and the Club in the Sack) appear with more than average frequency. "Tischchendeckdich, Goldesel und Knüppel aus dem Sack" has lost some of its detail on its travels through the Swiss cantons, especially when it had to overcome language changes in the Tessin and in Rätien (Walter Keller, *Tessiner Sagen und Volksmärchen*, Zurich, Switzerland: 1981, pp. 229–232; Pia Todorovic-Strähl and Ottavio Lurati, *Märchen aus dem Tessin* 22 [1984]; Leza Uffer, *Rätoromanische Märchen* 2 [1983]).

In transcription from dialects, in translation from one language into another, and during preparation for printing, there are always instances of making the original material worse in order to make it better, most frequently and noticeably in Switzerland, land of many languages. Texts that have undergone the "making worse before making better" treatment become traditional during their written and oral travels. That is how original material and stories worth preserving are created, but also how many irritating mixtures of form are added. Many a fairy tale that has been "told out" (*zerzählt*) gives the impression of being illogical.

With contamination of different story types, making original sources worse before making them better, and language problems, it is not without reason that researcher Ursula Brunold-Bigler admonishes publishers of Swiss fairy tale anthologies to be more critical about their sources.[8] Working critically with one's sources is often difficult or even tedious, but it can lead to exciting results. I have taken 22 magical fairy tales, all from collections that appeared between 1869 and 1994, and analyzed them microscopically, and I have analyzed an additional dozen favorite fairy tale anthologies. From this analysis, I have determined that Switzerland is and remains a land of legends, but the German-speaking Swiss knew how to turn this to their advantage by turning their relatively small fairy tale treasury into an extensive volume. They accomplished this by copying old texts, rewriting them, translating them, translating them back, working the material, and telling. Nevertheless, not a few publishers have vouched for the authenticity of their texts and the national characteristics of their informants, and they make assurances that the local dialects, even those written down from memory, have been reproduced in an unadulterated form.

Schwyzerdütsch Translation Problems

The question arises of how do storytellers recognize the *quality* of a text that has between transcribed from a different language or from a dialect into German? Is Karl Dedecius correct when he quotes Voltaire saying that translations are "like women, either beautiful but not faithful, or faithful but not exactly beautiful?"[9] I do not wish to bore anyone with theories about translations, we will stay with the *practice* of language and the requisites for storytelling.

In Switzerland, fairy tales usually are told in dialect and primarily are printed in the appropriate written language. The reverse also happens and is often particularly revealing. Swiss dialect is difficult to understand for many. The "high" German way of speaking by Swiss people—with their phonetic deviations, "Swissisms," unusual accentuation of foreign words,[10] the more relaxed tempo—occasionally draws a smile in Germany. Though we do not regard the velar *ch* (formed far back along the soft palate) as a pleasant sound,[11] that does not change the fact that Schwyzerdütsch, like no other language, is suited for the telling of fairy tales. Why?

Schwyzerdütsch is an unusually flexible, efficient language that offers the user a rich and differentiated "choice of words for daily living and for the expression of his feelings."[12] The Swiss-German dialects, which are different from one canton to another, distinguish themselves for their great vividness and strength, onomatopoeic word construction, and archaic expressions with which the user associates ideas such as "original, true, or suitable."[13] Schwyzerdütsch, the spoken mother tongue, is considered to be the language of the heart and of comfort (gemütlichkeit). A large majority of the German-Swiss population finds the dialect "more direct, warmer, more personal, more natural, and more free" than High German.[14] The relatively more informal everyday language, which is more than a dialect, fosters community in its use in the telling of fairy tales as well as in church. A pastor made this point: "When I am trying to lift people up to God, I use the standard language; however, if I want to bring our dear Lord down to the people, I speak in dialect."[15]

Let us look at the special ability of the Swiss-German to add the suffix -le, or -ele, almost randomly to any verb. For instance, from the German verb *plaudern* (to chat) one can create *plaudere* and *pläuderle,* a neat way to carry on this activity. The cumbersome and clumsy German word combination with the verb *werden* (to become) can be sidestepped by the verb itself in dialect: *hübscher werden* (to become more beautiful) is said as *hubschë*. The importance of onomatopoeic action words in storytelling is well known. The impression of a spontaneous experience, of lively and immediate telling is delivered by the verb in dialect through typical application of the "compound perfect"; the more distant written-language "imperfect" is no longer in use.[16]

To illustrate the problems in translating from German into dialect, and from dialect into German, let us concentrate on a known Swiss fairy tale. It came into Grimm's *Kinder- und Hausmärchen* (KHM) by way of Swiss informants, from Grimm by way of Otto Sutermeister's *Kinder- und Hausmärchen aus der Schweiz* back to its homeland, and then into the hands of studious translators and creative tellers of known stories. KHM 166, "Der starke Hans" (Strong Hans), appears with the Grimms in High German. We cannot here delve into detailed questions about the origin of the Swiss contributions to Grimm fairy tales, but we want to try to examine what happened to 166 with so much transcribing going on.

From among many observations, I would like to present here two of 16 translations of the fairy tale "Der starke Hans" (AT 650A and 301A), one of which I believe to be miserable (from dialect into a stilted written-language German) and an interesting one, though not without problems (from KHM 166 into Basel-German).

As early as 1869, Otto Sutermeister, the "Swiss Grimm," presented two variations of this fairy tale—which continues to be popular in Switzerland—one of them in High German and one in dialect. In 1977, a publisher in Basel decided to republish the Sutermeister fairy tales and, in view of the "reading problems with original dialects"[17] that would be presented, to reedit them. The reviser was to maintain a closeness to the dialect to ease later telling of stories in dialect. But what did Fritz Gafner do with Sutermeister's "Der Bueb mit dem isige Spazierstecke" (The boy with the iron walking staff)? He made him into a "Knabe mit dem eisernen Spazierstöcklein." This *stöcklein* (little walking stick) weighs, in both versions, ten hundredweights! No one other than the hero is able to lift it.

The Sutermeister version begins, "*Do hend d'Räuber die Frau gstohle, hend sie in e Höhli gschleikt, und do hed sie ihne muesse choche und wäsche.*" Gafner does replace the perfect of the

dialect version with the high language imperfect, but he forgets to translate the word *gstohle* (stolen) into written German; people are usually said to be abducted or kidnapped. The many periods create a staccato that holds back the flow of the telling. "*Aber unterwegs wurde sie von Räubern gestohlen. Die schleppten sie in ihre Höhle. Dort musste sie bleiben und für die Räuber kochen und waschen.*" (*Kinder- und Hausmärchen aus der Schweiz*, collected by Otto Sutermeister, revised by Fritz Gafner, Basel, Switzerland: 1977, p. 28).

The list of awkward use of language could go on and on. For instance, Gafner often turns Sutermeister's verbs, which give a lively impression, into bloodless creations. Unfortunately, he has undone the beauty and immediacy of the dialect version of the text and has been unable to make up for this loss with a transcription into correct High German. Gafner's translation is neither literature nor suited for storytelling.

Translating also means "thinking along" (*mitdenken*). Someone who has thought along and partly thought ahead is Curt Englert-Faye, whose voluminous fairy tale books are enormously popular in Switzerland but disdained by fairy tale researchers as not being worth citing.[18] In KHM 166, when Hans beats up the robbers he is 10 years old, a few hours later he is already 12. Englert-Faye has corrected this error in logic in his dialect version of the Grimm fairy tale. In an effort to turn German literary language into a Swiss fairy tale written in everyday dialect and to create a piece of writing suitable for oral delivery, he made small but striking changes in his translation, or refrained from making them.[19] He seasoned the original with all sorts of Swiss "ingredients," with invented interjections ("*Jo guet Nacht!*"), weighted adjectives ("*das fräch Männli*"), and local Swiss color (when the robbers play jazz).

One can argue about the sense of arbitrary additions by translators. In the case of Englert-Faye, the result is artificial emphasis on the oral character ("*künstliche Mündlichkeit*"). We know by now that even Wilhelm Grimm sought to give the impression that the *Kinder- und Hausmärchen* originated "directly with the oral storytelling material of the rural population."[20] He succeeded, for instance, by inserting proverbial expressions. But Grimm's formulations are still much too literary for Englert-Faye—not enough day-to-day language, too far above the commonplace, not inventive enough. When the Tannendreher (in

"Der starke Hans") "fell to the ground" in the original, Englert-Faye's translation says "*dä guet Tannedriller . . . an Bode pflymlet.*" For the "*zentnerschweren Spazierstab,*" the Swiss translator found the more appropriate expression "*e zimftige Stäcke.*" With Grimm "*machten sie sich einen Braten zurecht und waren guter Dinge*" was translated by Englert-Faye as, "*händ si die Sau am Fyr knuschplig brun brote, und die Drei händ yne bige, was numme yne gange-n-isch.*" Grimm: Hans "*tat seine Arbeit in der Küche, wie sich's gebührte*"; Englert-Faye: Hans "*het ene welle-n-eppis ganz bsunders gschmäckigs koche.*" It seems that Swiss cooking is done with more love and expertise.

As Jacob Grimm remarked,[21] translating (*Übersetzen*) also means to set across, to lead to the other shore. A good translation must bring the reader to the work or bring the work to the reader. A rewritten work may under certain circumstances seem unfamiliar, but it should not be more flat or more coarse than the original. Exactly that happened to the popular Swiss storyteller Trudi Gerster when she rewrote "Vogel Greif" [KHM 165] for children. When the feared Vogel Greif comes home and notices the smell of the hero, Grimm wrote it as:

Der Hans . . . lit unders Bett undere. Z'Obe
chunt der Vogelgrif häi, und wiener i d'Stube
chunt, so säit er: "Frau, i schmöke ne Christ."
"Jo," säit do d'Frau, "s'isch hüt äine do gsi,
aber er isch wieder furt;" und mit dem het der
Vogelgrif nut me gsäit.

But Trudi Gerster puts it like this:

So kroch Hans unter das grosse Himmelbett.
Kurz darauf hörte man draussen ein Trampeln
und ein lautes Gebrüll. Die Tür wurde aufgerissen und herein kam der Vogel Gryff. Er
schnupperte überall herum und knurrte:
"Frau, hier riecht's nach Mensch—wo ist er,
damit ich ihn fressen kann!" Seine Frau beruhigte ihn: "Sei still und geh schlafen! Es ist ein
Mensch dagewesen—aber er ist wieder fort!"
Der Vogel Gryff maulte: "Warum has du ihn
denn ziehn lassen? Du weisst doch, wie gern
ich die mag—auf Toast, mit Kräuterbutter.
Jetzt muss ich wider ohne Nachtessen ins Bett,
Donner und Doria!" (Trudi Gerster, *Schweizer Märchen für Kinder erzählt*, Basel, Switzerland: 1990, p. 151)

Onomatopoeic verbs, day-to-day language formulations, diminutions, expressions of power, and vivid scenes alone do not set the proper tone, the "fairy tale style," and the rhythm for storytelling. In the Grimm version, more is said with less. Trudi Gerster would, in my estimation, have done better with a word-for-word translation from the original dialect than with her attempt at rewriting.

Enough of critique. Translating is difficult—I know that from my own experience. Whoever wants to translate *well* must struggle with every word, find the appropriate picture, try to carry across proverbial expressions, and, wherever possible, take the storytelling rhythm into account. Anyone who wants to translate fairy tales should not only study variants and be critical of sources but also listen and pay close attention to good storytellers, preferably in German *and* in dialect.

Translated by Winifred Jaeger

Notes

1. Arthur Baur, *Schwyzertüütsch*, p. 7.
2. Ursula Brunold-Bigler, "Schweizer Märchensammler," in *Märchen und Märchenforschung in Europa: Ein Handbuch*, p. 233.
3. Pia Todorovic-Strähl, "Nachwort," in *Märchen aus dem Tessin*, p. 240.
4. Richard Waldmann, "Vorwort," ibid.; in his *Die Schweiz in ihren Märchen und Sennengeschichten*, p. 12.
5. Ursula Brunold-Bigler, "Schweizer Märchensammler," p. 232.
6. Katalin Horn, "Modernes Märchenerzählen in der deutschsprachigen Schweiz," in *Märchen und Märchenforschung in Europa: Ein Handbuch*, p. 240.
7. Max Lüthi, "Dekorative Züge," in *Enzyklopädie des Märchens 3*, pp. 380–385.
8. Ursula Brunold-Bigler, "Schweizer Märchensammler," in *Märchen und Märchenforschung in Europa: Ein Handbuch*, p. 232.
9. Karl Dedecius: *Vom Übersetzen: Theorie und Praxis*, p. 96.
10. Andreas Lötscher, *Schweizerdeutsch: Geschichte, Dialekte, Gebrauch*, p. 89.
11. Arthur Baur, *Was ist eigentlich Schweizerdeutsch?* Winterthur, Switzerland: Gemsberg, 1983, p. 24.
12. Andreas Lötscher: *Schweizerdeutsch: Geschichte, Dialekte, Gebrauch*, p. 119.

13. Daniel Erich Weber: *Sprach- und Mundartpflege in der deutschsprachigen Schweiz: Sprachnorm und Sprachdidaktik im zweisprachformigen Staat*, pp. 96–97.
14. Daniel Erich Weber, ibid., p. 99.
15. Cited after Peter Sieber and Horst Sitta, "Zur Sprachsituation in der Deutschschweiz," in their *Mundart und Standardsprache als Problem der Schule*, p. 22.
16. Andreas Lötscher, *Schweizerdeutsch: Geschichte, Dialekte, Gebrauch*, p. 118.
17. From the back cover, Friedrich Reinhardt, Verlag Basel: 1977.
18. Robert Wildhaber, "Sammlungen, Auswahlprinzipien und Anordnung," in *Schweizer Volksmarchen*, p. 256.
19. Anna La Roche, "Foreword," "7 über die aus Basel stammende Geschichte vom starken Hans" in: *Übertragung resp. Neugestaltung besorgt*.
20. Lutz Röhrich, "Volkspoesie ohne Volk. Wie 'münlich' sind sogenannte 'Volks-erzählungen?'," in *Volksdichtung zwischen Mündlichkeit und Schriftlichkeit*, pp. 49f.
21. Jacob Grimm, "Über das Pedantische in der deutschen Sprache," in *Das Problem des Übersetzens*, p. 111.

Further Reading

Baur, Arthur, *Schwyzertüütsch: Praktische Sprachlehre des Schweizerdeutschen: "Grüezi Mitenand"*, seventh edition, Winterthur, Switzerland: Gemsberg, 1981

Brunold-Bigler, Ursula, "Schweizer Märchensammler," in *Märchen und Märchenforschung in Europa: Ein Handbuch*, edited by D. Röth and W. Kahn, Frankfurt, Germany: Haag and Herchen, 1993

Dedecius, Karl, *Vom Übersetzen: Theorie und Praxis*, Frankfurt, West Germany: Suhrkamp, 1986

Grimm, Jacob, "Über das Pedantische in der deutschen Sprache," in *Das Problem des Übersetzens*, edited by H.J. Störig, Stuttgart, West Germany: Goverts, 1963

Horn, Katalin, "Modernes Märchenerzählen in der deutschsprachigen Schweiz," in *Märchen und Märchenforschung in Europa: Ein Handbuch*, Frankfurt, Germany: Haag and Herchen, 1993

La Roche, Anna, "7 über die aus Basel stammende Geschichte vom starken Hans in: Übertragung resp. Neugestaltung besorgt," Basel, Switzerland: 1940

Lötscher, Andreas, *Schweizerdeutsch: Geschichte, Dialekte, Gebrauch*, Stuttgart, West Germany: Huber, 1983

Lüthi, Max, "Dekorative Züge," in *Enzklopädie des Märchens 3*, Berlin and New York: 1981

Reinhart, Friedrich, Verlag Basel: 1977, back cover

Röhrich, Lutz, "Volkspoesie ohne Volk. Wie 'münlich' sind sogenannte 'Volks-erzählungen?'," in *Volksdichtung zwischen Mündlichkeit und Schriftlichkeit*, edited by Lutz Röhrich and Erika Lindig, Tübingen, West Germany: Narr, 1989

Sieber, Peter, and Horst Sitta, "Zur Sprachsituation in der Deutschschweiz," in *Mundart und Standardsprache als Problem der Schule*, Aarau, Switzerland: Verlag Sauerländer, 1986

Todorovic-Strähl, Pia, *Märchen aus dem Tessin*, Cologne, West Germany: Diederichs, 1984

Waldmann, Richard, *Die Schweiz in ihren Märchen und Sennengeschichten*, Cologne, West Germany: Diederichs, 1983

Weber, Daniel Erich, *Sprach- und Mundartpflege in der deutschsprachigen Schweiz: Sprachnorm und Sprachdidaktik im zweisprachformigen Staat*, Frauenfeld, Switzerland: Huber, 1984

Wildhaber, Robert, "Sammlungen Auswahlprinzipien und Anordnung," in *Schweizer Volksmärchen*, compiled by Robert Wildhaber and Leza Uffer, Düsseldorf, West Germany: Diederichs, 1971

Middle East
and
North Africa

Egyptian Peep-Show Storytelling

Kamal el dien Hussien

Kamal el dien Hussien discusses the tradition of storytelling via a peep-show box.

The *Sandouk el Donia*

One of the Egyptian storytelling traditions observed by researchers in the nineteenth century was the telling depending on one narrator telling the story by using a series of pictures. These pictures may be unrelated to the story narrated. The narrator uses in his performance a wooden box called *Sandouk El Donia* or *Sifira Aziza*. This is one of the folk shows involving some dramatic elements. The dramatic element is provided by the solo narrator, who rolls the pictures and moves toys while describing and commenting on the content of the picture in a monotonous way and a mechanical style. Sometimes the comment may differ from the content of the picture. Often the series of pictures consists of 20 different pictures. They depict heroes of the Egyptian epic (Al Seira) or sometimes pictures of movie stars.

The subject of narration is always about some parts of the Egyptian Seira of Abo Zeed El Helali and the characters of that Seira. The wooden box itself is designed as a big wall of a castle that has two towers, one on each side of the wall.

There are also three or four holes on the anterior side of the box. Their diameters are about 6 inches, and they each are covered with a concave glass lens to magnify the picture inside the box. In the roof of the box there is a small window to provide light inside the box. At each tower there is a plastic or a wooden toy dressed in a folkloric costume. This toy is moved by a wire in a hinging movement by the hand of the player or the narrator.

The player or the narrator calls to the children to watch his show moving his puppets before his performance. When the children come they sit on a wooden sofa in front of the holes in the box. Then the narrator drops a piece of curtain around the children to keep out outside light.

After that the narrator moves the pictures, which are arranged as strips inside the wooden box, rolled on two metal axles, one in each tower. On the top side of each tower there is a window in which a metal hand is joined to the axle. When the narrator moves the hand, the strips of pictures roll around the axle and move from side to side.

The narrator goes around with his box from one place to another, carrying it on his back, and whenever he meets some children, he puts it down. Then he starts his performance.

Indoor Performances for Festivals

Sometimes, on special occasions related to some religious festivals, the narrator presents his performance in a shop in a regular manner until the occasion is over. Instead of the daylight he uses a small gas lamp inside the box to give the suitable light for his pictures. This has always been done in exchange for money from the children.

Until the 1950s the phenomenon of the peep show could ordinarily be seen on the roads or in villages of Egypt. However, after the spread of television and videos even to the small cafeterias or cafés in small villages, that phenomenon began to disappear gradually.

Narrating Epics in Iran

Mahmoud Omidsalar and Teresa Omidsalar

Mahmoud and Teresa Omidsalar discuss the Iranian oral epic tradition from pre-Islamic times to the present. They take exception with scholars who suggest that an oral-formulaic tradition of extemporaneous versifying extends through centuries of Iranian storytelling.

The *Shâhnâma*

The Iranian national epic, called the *Shâhnâma*, is the most important text in Persian high literature. This epic was versified from a prose original in the tenth century A.D. by a poet called Ferdowsi. To the extent that the *Shâhnâma* narrates the legendary history of the country from the rule of the first primordial king to the Muslim conquest in the seventh century A.D., it has justifiably been called the "ethnic history of Iran." One authority proclaims it Persia's "cultural I.D." (Mînuvî, p. 14; and cf. pp. 18, 63), and another considers Ferdowsi's epic fundamental to "Iranian cultural identity" (Matini, pp. 119–122; and cf. Puhvel, pp. 117–118, 125).

Shâhnâma is by no means the only epic poem in Persian. Shortly after its composition in A.D. 1009, other poets began to versify a large number of other prose epics.[1] All of these later poems are heavily influenced by the *Shâhnâma*, and by the art of its poet. What is more, they bear a greater resemblance to the genre of the Greek and medieval romance rather than to the epic *per se*.

The oral epics, although largely based on the *Shâhnâma*, freely borrow episodes or motifs from the post-*Shâhnâma* epics. These borrowed elements are then woven into the main narrative as either digressions or elaboration. The outcome tends to be a rich mosaic of folk epic narrative, which is always told in prose. The prose narrative

of these tales, however, may be punctuated occasionally with verses taken from the *Shâhnâma* or from other classical poetry.

This essay concerns the history and character of the oral epics in Iran. It relies on the evidence of the primary sources and the native scholarship in Persian, which is not readily accessible to most Western folklorists. We have approached Iranian epic storytelling in terms of the Iranian culture itself rather than according to the Eurocentric presumptions about how epics are supposed to be narrated. We have provided historical and ethnographic evidence to demonstrate that Western preconceptions about the narration of oral epics do not apply to Iran, and we have further challenged the efficacy of converting this tradition to what can only be called Harvard's tribal religion of "Oral Formulaicism," hoping all along to rescue the massive Persian epic narrative from the tyranny of the Homeric tradition and its attendant Western scholarship.

To the extent that the Iranian oral epic narrative mirrors its literary counterpart, it has assumed some of the cultural importance of the literary poem. However, it also has important features of its own. First, it is the chief means by which the literary epic finds public expression. In other words, it serves as an interface between elite and folk literary traditions. It is the path through which a largely illiterate public finds access to the *Shâhnâma*. Second, like its literary counterpart, it is a focal point of cultural identity. Third, it provides Iranian folklore with a vast body of explanatory legends, which tell of how a thing, custom, or place came to be. Fourth, it establishes ideal as well as culturally acceptable models of behavior. Fifth, it provides an immense body of narratives that have served as objects of nonverbal art forms (e.g., painting and weaving).

In spite of the obvious importance of the oral epic tradition, little research of substance on the subject exists. What does exist is deficient in that most of it tends to evaluate the evidence of the primary sources incorrectly. A short review of the existing evidence might not be entirely fruitless.

Folk Epic in Pre-Islamic Times

The sacred book of the religion of ancient Iran, Zoroastrianism, is called the *Avesta,* which was first written down during the rule of the Achaemenid dynasty (559–321 B.C.). Only small parts of the original *Avesta* have come down to us. Of these, the *Yashts,* which are a series of hymns to the ancient Iranian gods, are among the oldest parts. These hymns contain frequent references to kings and heroes of ancient lore. These references are cursory and obscure. Unfortunate as this may be for scholarship, the obscure nature of these references implies that when the *Yashts* were composed the stories were so well known that a mere hint was sufficient to recall them to the listeners (Gershevitch, p. 23; cf. Nöldeke, 1930:5).

There is no doubt that the Iranian heroic narratives were widely transmitted by storytelling in the ancient period. The evidence of the ancient Greek texts supports this conclusion. Greek authors not only provide occasional references to specific tales but also allude to the function of these narratives in ancient Persian society. Aside from Diodorus's quotations from Ctesias's *Persica* (II.22.1–5; II.32), Xenophon (c. 428–354 B.C.) provides an eyewitness account of the prevalence of stories and songs in Persia. Apparently, these tales celebrated the deeds and heroism of Cyrus among Persians of the fifth century B.C. (I.ii.1, I.iv.25). In his description of the education of the Persian youth, Strabo (64 B.C.–after A.D. 24) tells of the social function of these tales:

> [Persians] use as teachers of science their wisest men, who also interweave their teachings with mythical elements . . . and rehearse *both with song and without song,* the deeds of both gods and of the noblest men. (Strabo, XV:3:18, italics added)[2]

If these accounts are accurate, then the recitation of heroic narratives must have fulfilled an educational function in the Persian society of that time (cf. Bascom, pp. 58–59 and 64). Before we leave this point, let us briefly discuss the merits of a claim about the manner of narration of the pre-Islamic epic tradition in Iran. This is the problem of the so-called poetic oral epic tradition in Iran, the performance of which is often placed in the mouth of a class of minstrels who were known by the title of *gôsân.*

Boyce has argued that the *gôsân*s were a group of professional singer-bards of the Parthian period (c. 171 B.C.–A.D. 227) and that they may have been active in transmitting the Iranian epic tradition. Boyce's suggestion is carried to fanciful extremes by the contemporary scholarship on the subject. Two unwarranted conclusions are drawn from her arguments: first, that the *gôsân*s were the chief transmitters of the Iranian epic tradition; and second, that the Iranian epic tradition was chiefly in song form, and that this tradition of singing epic tales survived even to the time of Ferdowsi and influenced not only his great poem but also Iranian epic storytelling in general (see, for example, Davidson, pp. 24–26).

The fallacy of the first assumption is self-evident. Aside from the fact that no clear textual evidence of the existence of such singer-storytellers exists, professional minstrels are not the same as singers of epic tales. Furthermore, even if we grant out of hand that some singers of epic songs existed in Iran, their existence is no proof that all epic narrative was transmitted by a "poetic oral tradition." Such an argument would be similar to proposing that because there are some professional race-car drivers in the United States, all of the driving in that country is of necessity accomplished by Mario Andretti's colleagues.

The error of the second assumption of the "formulaicists," namely that the Parthian *gôsân* tradition survived in Iranian culture, and was even maintained into Islamic times, flies in the face of the existing textual evidence.

The word *gôsân* (which is of uncertain etymology) is mentioned in the works of a number of Persian and Arab authors. All of these sources understand the word to mean a class of ancient minstrels that no longer exists. With only three exceptions, all Persian and Arab authors of the ninth and tenth centuries A.D. completely corrupt the form of the word. This corruption is found even in Persian Zoroastrian texts. For instance, the *Persian Rivâyat* speaks of a councillor in the court of the pre-Islamic King Anûshîrvân (A.D. 531–79) whose name is recorded as Yûnan. It appears that *yûnân* is a textual corruption of *gôsân,* and that the word *gôsân,* which was no longer current or understood even by Zoroastrians, was corrupted into a personal name Yûnân. Based on the orthographic similarity of *gôsân* and *yûnân* (spelled, respectively, *gws'n* and *ywn'n* in Persian), the corruption must have been purely textual. Now, had Persian speakers of the ninth and tenth century A.D., be they Muslims or Zoroastrians, understood who a *gôsân* was or what he actually did, they would not have misunderstood the word, nor would they have needed to reinterpret it as a personal name.

All this implies that the transmission of the Persian epic tales from the pre-Islamic times to the Islamic period was not achieved by a class of singers called *gôsân,* nor was it effected by sung poetry. As we shall see presently, there is no evidence to indicate that the Iranian epic tradition in its nonliterary oral form was transmitted in any way other than by prose narration. At most, the narration of the tales was embellished by occasional verses from the formal literature.

Another important foreign source about Iranian epic narrative is Moses Khorenats'i (fifth century A.D.), who is called *patmahayar,* or "father of history," in the Armenian tradition (Moses Khorenats'i, 1978:1). Moses was a scholar, a translator, and the author of a well-known history of the Armenian people and did not consider Persian tales to be at all suitable for Christians. He reproached those Armenians who enjoyed the narration of Persian stories in the following words:

> What then is your delight in the obscene and ridiculous fables . . . and why do you trouble us for those absurd and incoherent Persian stories, notorious for their imbecility? . . . What need have you of these false fables; what use are these senseless and stupid compositions? Surely they are not Greek fables, noble and polished and meaningful, which have hidden in themselves allegorically the meaning of events. But you ask us to explain the reason for their irrationality and to embellish what is unadorned. . . . But as it is the desire of your youthful years and immature understanding we shall provide them. (Moses Khorenats'i, 1978, pp. 126–127; 141–142)

Moses' account shows how prevalent Persian tales were among the Armenians of the fifth century A.D. If Moses' summaries are to be trusted, these tales must have been significantly different from their surviving literary form. Many of them, however, closely resemble the modern oral variants of a number of *Shâhnâma* tales. Two conclusions may be deduced from Moses' account. First, some of the existing oral versions of these tales may be dated to the time of Moses of Khoren in the fifth century A.D. Second, at that time these borrowed Persian stories competed with the religious narratives that Moses and other Christian Armenian authorities deemed more appropriate for their flocks to know. In this respect, the attitude of these patriarchs is similar to that of the early Muslim theocrats who felt that the Iranian epic tales distracted faithful Muslims from the more "suitable" religious narratives.

There is no doubt that telling of Iranian epic tales was attested among a number of non-Iranian peoples. We have already made mention of the prevalence of these pagan stories in Armenia. Let us now consider their dissemination among the Arabs of the seventh century A.D.

Naḍr Ibn Ḥârith, who was a cousin of the prophet Muḥammad, is often mentioned as an active transmitter of Iranian oral epic narratives in Arabia. However, his role and activities in this regard are significantly misunderstood. Most authorities on Iranian epic narrative since Nöldeke (1836–1930) state that Naḍr narrated stories that he had "heard and memorized" in the course of his commercial travels. He is said to have brought his memorized tales back to Mecca, where he narrated them at the mosque where the prophet preached. There is no doubt that by his narration of these tales Naḍr intended to compete with the founder of Islam, who often instructed his flocks by means of telling biblical narrative. Naḍr claimed that his Persian stories were more interesting than those told by the prophet Muḥammad, and he tried to lure the prophet's audience away by reciting Persian tales for them (Nöldeke, p. 19, n. 4; Ṣafâ, "Ishâra'i," pp. 9–10; 1363, pp. 45, 565; Mînuvî, p. 50; Lisân, p. 5).

The assumption that Naḍr had memorized these tales from some oral source that he encountered during his travels is incorrect. The fact is that the overwhelming majority of the classical Arabic and Persian texts that mention Naḍr's storytelling activities state that he had purchased books of Persian tales in his travels, and that it was from these books that he recited his tales. For instance, Abû Zakariyâ Yaḥyâ ibn Ziyâd al-Farrâ' (A.D. 761–822) writes that Naḍr "used to purchase books of Persians and Romans, and those of the people of Ḥayra" (vol. 2, p. 326). It is only Ibn Hishâm (d. A.D. 834) who speaks of his having learned his collection of Iranian epic narrative (pp. 191, 235). But obviously, even "learning" in Ibn Hishâm's account does not necessarily mean learning from oral sources. Naturally—since Naḍr either read aloud from written sources, or alternatively, narrated from memory that which he had previously read in books—the suggestion that his "performance" was an oral traditional performance is absurd. Placing Naḍr among the active bearers of oral tradition requires such a broad definition of oral tradition as to make the very concept meaningless. Either Naḍr read directly from books or his narration had an immediate written antecedent. Clearly, this is not what most scholars understand by "oral tradition," especially in its "oral formulaic" form.

In Classical Persian

Most references to narration of ancient heroic tales in classical Persian concern reading aloud from written sources rather than storytelling per se. However, these references are also misinterpreted and are often taken as evidence of an oral tradition of "epic singing" in Persia.

There is a new academic fad that interprets all reference to "books" and "reading from books" in connection with Persian epic literature as a formalized reference to oral tradition (e.g., Davidson; Davis, 1996). We find this interpretation unacceptable. Persian culture, in its classical period, was highly literary. It was drastically different from the essentially oral culture of western Europe in the Middle Ages.[3] Therefore, making absurd analogies with regard to the relationship of the oral and written traditions in these drastically different areas is unjustifiable.

A comparison of the data on the size and nature of the Iranian libraries with the book collections of western Europe of the seventh to thirteenth centuries A.D. shows how fundamentally different these civilizations were.[4] The Iranians of that time depended to a far greater extent on book learning and literary sources than did their Western counterparts. Therefore, when composers of classical Persian epics state that they obtained their tales from written sources, their statements may be taken as dependable, except when clear and convincing evidence to the contrary exists.

Be that as it may, whereas no evidence for singing of epic tales exists in Classical Persian sources,

proof of reading or telling of prose tales is not difficult to find. According to the *Shâhnâma*, during one of the hunting trips of King Bahrâm (reigned A.D. 421–38), his chamberlain and the high priest entertained him by reading stories of the ancient kings (Moscow edition, vol. 7, p. 325, lines 349–351). In another instance the king called for the "ancient book of heroic deeds: to be read to him by some knowledgeable person" (Moscow edition, vol. 7, p. 323, line 315; cf. vol. 7, p. 331, line 446).

The most explicit instance of how princes were entertained by readers of heroic tales is found in the episode of the rule of Khusrow Parvîz (d. A.D. 628): "He seated those who were literate [literally, "were writers and readers of things"] in front of his throne; and each in turn read to him the stories of the olden times" (Moscow edition, vol. 9, p. 197, lines 3161–62; cf. Khaleghi-Motlagh). This, of course, does not mean that no oral tradition of epic tales existed alongside the written one. According to the *Shâhnâma*, one of the tutors employed by the Arab king Mundhir for the education of his Persian ward, Prince Bahrâm, was charged with telling him legends of kings and wise men of yore (Moscow edition, vol. 7, p. 270, n. 34).[5]

The fact that the oral and written versions of the epic tales existed side by side is stated explicitly in the verse of a highly literate poet of the tenth century A.D., Munjîk of Tirmidh. Munjîk states that he both read heroic tales and listened to their narration from written sources: "Many versions of the tales of the Seven Trials, and the Brass Fortress did I read myself, and heard recited [to me] from the book [called] *Hazâr Afsân* "*A Thousand Stories*" (Lisân, p. 6). Similar evidence abounds in the verse of another poet of the early eleventh century A.D. (Farrukhî, p. 257, line 5108; p. 284, line 4955).

The oral and the literary epic traditions undoubtedly coexisted. However, the coexistence of these two traditions does not warrant the further conclusion that the composition of the literary epic tradition was in any way influenced by the oral epics. Indeed, greater evidence may be marshaled to show an opposite direction of influence. The oral epic tradition in Iran is heavily influenced by the literary tradition (cf. Richmond, pp. 181 ff; and Rosenberg, pp. 25–41).

The overall evidence of the classical Persian literature indicates that the written literary epic tradition was predominantly, although not exclusively, in verse. It was part of the elite literature and was occasionally read aloud for the entertainment or education of the noble and the commoner alike. By contrast, the oral tradition was exclusively in prose. It was never sung in the manner of the Homeric or Serbo-Croatian heroic lore, and it was narrated by diverse groups of people under varied circumstances and on different occasions. Let us address another typical problem in studies of epic storytelling in Iran.

References in classical Persian and Arabic sources to the tellers of epic tales should be disentangled from those that point to storytellers who specialized in the narration of religious or didactic accounts. Tellers of religious or didactic tales, called *qâṣṣ* or *quṣṣâs* in Arabic, were often poorly educated preachers who entertained the public in mosques or in bazaars with their didactic tales (Goldzieher, vol. 2, pp. 153–159). Some of these performers could also play musical instruments and did not hesitate to entertain their listeners with song.[6] Ibn Qutaiba (d. A.D. 715) refers to one such fellow in the eighth century A.D. who during one of his performances brought his audience to tears. He then produced a musical instrument from the folds of his robe, said, "Let us have a bit of joy after this sorrow," and proceeded to cheer them up by song (Ibn Qutaiba, vol. 4, p. 91). No doubt this man was not singing an epic tale. He thus could in no way have been a "singer of tales," nor could he have resembled either the Parthian *gôsân* or the Balkan *guslari*. Yet discussions of oral storytelling in Iran veritably bubble over with reference to this fellow and with insinuations that his art had some similarity to that of a singer of heroic tales (e.g., Lisân, p. 6; Zarrînkûb, p. 87; Mîrshukrâ'î, pp. 58–59).

The Iranian storytellers of the first few centuries of the Islamic period were usually called *muḥaddith* (Lisân, pp. 6–7). The best of these were employed by kings and were often literate individuals prized by their royal masters for their skillful recitative and performance capabilities. Most of them actually read stories from written sources, although they may also have recited from memory. One of them, a man by the name of Kârâsî, rose to the rank of governor under the Ghaznavids. Kârâsî was killed during a tax riot that broke out because of his oppressive rule in A.D. 1030 (Qazvînî, vol. 6, pp. 185–187; *Mujmal*, pp. 395–397; Mustawfî, p. 795; and cf. Lisân, p. 7).

The historian Bayhaqî (d. A.D. 1077) mentions both professional and lay storytellers in the entourages of kings. A talented teller of tales was given a reward equal to 16,000 gold coins for his skill (pp. 153–154). Although a number of references to these tellers of tales have been translated into English from classical Persian (Omidsalar; Page, pp. 14–17), many remain scattered in the writings of Iranian scholars (Lisân; Maḥjûb, "Sukhanvarî I" and "Introduction"; Ṣafâ).

Epic tales served several social functions. When told to princes they presented these autocrats with models of moderation and justice and provided a measure of protection against arbitrary excesses of absolute rulers. Bayhaqî quotes Ibn al-Muqaffaʿ (d. A.D. 759) as saying that the ancient Persian kings always kept wise men around to tell them the stories of the kings of yore so that they might emulate their conduct (p. 125). The same note is sounded in *The Book of Government*, by the grand vizier Niẓâm al-Mulk (d. A.D. 1092), according to which kings are encouraged to follow the example provided in such narratives (Asadî, p. 264; Niẓâm al-Mulk, pp. 190, 212; cf. *Qâbûsnâma*, p. 204).

Be that as it may, the aristocrats among the audience of these tales not only liked the epics (e.g., Niẓâmî-yi ʿArûḍî, p. 29) but also sought to model their lives and behavior on the lives and conduct of the epic personages as related by the storytellers. For instance, the Ghaznavid Sultan Maḥmûd once captured an onager during one of his trips and ordered it to be branded by the royal iron and released "because he had heard from storytellers that [the epic King] Bahrâm used to do so" (Bayhaqî, p. 505). Another ruler of this dynasty emulated the ancient kings of Iranian lore by hunting lions unaided and armed only with two spears (Bayhaqî, p. 151). According to the *Majma' al-Ansâb* (composed in A.D. 1332), two Iranian rulers, one of Turkish origin, and another an ethnic Iranian, died in battle while reciting verses from the *Shâhnâma*. Of these two, the former was the Turkish king Tughril born Arslân (died A.D. 1193). Tughril's psychological identification with the Iranian epic heroes is unmistakably communicated by the account of his death:

> [The king] bore his heavy mace, and roaming
>   up and down the battle front, recited the
>   following verses from the *Shâhnâma*:
> When the dust of that great army rose
> [And] our warriors turned pale [with fear]
> I took my massive mace
> And left the army behind.
> Mounted, I roared such a battle cry

That made the earth turn like the firmament. (Shabânkâra'î, p. 121)[7]

The second ruler was a native Iranian. He died in the following manner:

[The Prince] was riding a fine white steed. It is said that he recklessly rode into dangerous situations. Several times Nasîr al-Dîn Gûdarz, who was a great lord among the lords of the Shabânkâra, got hold of the reigns of his horse, and led him out of danger; but he rode back into battle [every time]. He fought while reciting verses from the *Shâhnâma*, until he attacked the heart of the enemy forces single handedly. He was swallowed up by the host, was struck by a blade, and was slain. (p. 169)

It is clear from the existing accounts that the best storytellers were highly prized by the Iranian royalty of the classical period. In contrast to the situation in western Europe, professional storytellers who were associated with the courts of kings and princes were no bucolic bards spinning crude tales of adventure for little pay, but highly cultured and lettered men themselves. They often belonged to the inner aristocratic circles. Prince Manûchihr ibn Qâbûs (reigned A.D. 1012–1029), for instance, sent one of his confidants, Ḥasan-i Muḥaddith (Hasan the Storyteller), to the court of Prince Mas`ûd (d. A.D. 1040) as a royal envoy. This fellow "served both as a storyteller, and a carrier of [private] messages [between the two princes]" (Bayhaqî, p. 162). Mention has already been made of King Maḥmûd's storyteller, Kârâsî, or Kârâstî, and his unfortunate fate as a governor.

The situation of the storytellers who entertained the general public was quite different. As we have already pointed out, most were despised by the literati, who spoke of them almost with contempt (e.g., *Baḥr al-Fawâ'id*, p. 94). Occasionally, however, the more skillful among these incurred the admiration of men of letters. Rashid al-Dîn al-Waṭwâṭ (d. A.D. 1177), who was a great poet, statesman, and scholar, briefly refers to the art of the Persian storyteller of the twelfth century in his handbook on poetry. Since his brief references have never been translated before, and since they represent the opinion of a great critic of that period, we shall quote them in full:

Persian storytellers say: So and So rode into battle; mounted upon an angry lion, holding a

serpent, he produced onyx (*jaz'*) from chrysolite, and Judas-Tree (*arghavân*) from lilies. By this they mean to liken the "steed" to an "angry lion," the "spear" to a "serpent," the "horse's hooves" to "chrysolite," "swords" to "lilies,"[8] and "blood" to the "Judas-Tree." (Waṭwâṭ, p. 45)

Elsewhere he writes:

As Persian storytellers say: the dust which was raised from the hooves of horses turned the firmament into the color of the earth; and the earth began to move like the firmament by the rushing of mounted warriors. (p. 47)

There is some evidence that tellers of Persian epic tales were employed rather early in Muslim history as tools of political propaganda. It is claimed that shortly after the murder of the prophet's grandson Imam Husayn in A.D. 680, the ruling Umayyad caliphs began to promote telling of Iranian epic tales by professional storytellers in bazaars and other public places, their Persian possessions. One Shi`ite authority claims that by so doing they sought to divert attention from the tragedy of the saint's martyrdom and aimed to discourage the narration of religious accounts bearing on his murder (Râzî, p. 67). One modern author has discovered a more political aim in the activities of these storytellers. He suggests that the narrators attempted to "encourage a spirit of resistance against the oppression of the ruling classes in their listeners, by providing a model of heroic conduct for the masses from the epic narratives" (Ṭâhirî, p. 1317). This view met the need of the leftist Iranian bourgeois.

Telling Epic Tales in Coffeehouses

Although the exact date of the appearance of coffee in Iran is not clear, we know that by the time of King `Abbâs II (A.D. 1642–66), coffeehouses were quite common. The coffeehouse was like a social club for diverse groups of people, especially the literati and the aristocracy. It was a large establishment, with clean, white walls and fine furnishings. Many were well lit at nights, and most had fountains pouring into rather large indoor pools. King `Abbâs II used to frequent coffeehouses, where he occasionally entertained some of his foreign dignitaries. Coffeehouse patrons often engaged in heated literary discussions, in some of which the king himself is reported to have taken part.

Epic poetry was recited in these establishments by performers who were themselves talented poets or critics. There were also those who told tales concerning the heroic deeds of religious figures. Generally, storytellers used to stand upon a step stool in the middle of the assembly and perform while holding a short cane with which they gesticulated (Falsafî, *Zindigânî-i,* pp. 261–266; cf. Falsafî, "Târikh-i," vol. 1/2, pp. 343, 353–356). Although many famous professional reciters of the *Shâhnâma,* as well as storytellers, are mentioned in the literature of the period (e.g., Naṣrâbâdî, pp. 145, 307, 324–325, 357, 379, 401, and 414), there exists absolutely no evidence of "singing" epic narratives in this period.

With the passage of time and the decline of the grandeur of the Safavid era, the coffeehouse underwent a fundamental change. It was no longer a social club where the cream of Persian intellectual and aristocratic society entertained themselves. It rather became a place frequented by customers of lower social rank and poorer education. Epic storytelling in coffeehouses evolved accordingly. It was no longer the recitation of Ferdowsi's verses from the *Shâhnâma* but a telling in prose of various folk epics. Indeed, the narration of tales taken from the actual *Shâhnâma* was, as we shall see presently, a relatively modern development, which may be traced only to the third decade of the twentieth century.

The Modern Period

Most narrators of epic tales in Iran have been amateurs. Recitation of the *Shâhnâma* or telling of episodes from the book in family gatherings was effected by someone who had a good speaking voice and who was able to recite with appropriate diction and finesse (Afshârî, pp. 475–476; Mîrshukrâ'î, pp. 60–61). Even in many coffeehouses, most epic storytelling was performed by direct reading from the *Shâhnâma* (e.g. Zarîrî, p. xxxii; Maḥjûb, 1966, p. iv). In large cities where professional epic storytelling was ordinarily performed, coffeehouses served as social clubs in which practitioners of certain trades gathered (Maḥjûb, p. 530, and p. 532, n.1; cf. Najmî, pp. 476–478). Those who directly recited from the *Shâhnâma* were addressed as *mîrzâ,* while those who performed epic stories as professional storytellers, were called *murshid* (Injavî-yi Shîrâzî, 1979, p. xv; Page, p. 43). However, the modern idea that epic tales were narrated in every coffeehouse by professional tellers has no basis in fact or evidence

and, like much of the modern scholarship on Persian epic narrative, is unalloyed romantic fancy. Most professional performances of epic tales were undertaken only in larger, more prominent establishments (Mîrshukrâ'î, p. 61).

Most professional storytelling performances took place during the winter months and typically around two or three o'clock in the afternoon (Shahrî, vol. 4, p. 494). Some coffeehouses, however, had performances throughout the year. Performance of long tales, the narration of which had to be broken down into manageable sessions, was called *naql* (telling), and the narrator of such tales was called *naqqâl* (storyteller). It is reported that a telling of the whole *Shâhnâma* took about three to four years (Shahrî, vol. 5, pp. 513, 515; cf. Page, p. 37).

Until the end of the Qajar period (1779–1924) most storytelling in coffeehouses involved narration of tales from a variety of books such as *Amîr Arsalân, Ḥusayn-i Kurd,* and more often *The Romance of Alexander* (Maḥjûb, 1966, pp. ii–iv; Najmî, p. 476). These tales, however, lost their appeal with the passage of time. One storyteller in the city of Shîrâz, for instance, reported that his audience did not appreciate the story of Ḥusayn-i Kurd because "they did not know it and would therefore not enjoy it"[9] (Page, p. 37).

It was not until sometime around 1929 that, by the order of the government, professional storytelling in coffeehouses was made to focus exclusively on the narration of the *Shâhnâma* tales (Maḥjûb, p. 531; Shahrî, vol. 5, pp. 510–511). This is a significant fact and shows how evidence of the modern history of professional storytelling in Iran contradicts the modern notions about it.

According to the contemporary scholars' romantic recreation of the past, "performance" of tales from the *Shâhnâma* in or out of coffeehouses has been an age-old tradition in Iran. Although this view is shared by many—including some who state it outright (e.g., Dûstkhâh, pp. xiv–xv) and others who merely imply the idea (e.g., Davidson, pp. 55–60)—ethnographic evidence and interviews with those who practiced the craft tell a different story. Let us quote the words of one of the most skillful Persian storytellers of this century as an example:

There is no dependable evidence about the history of the art of storytelling (*naqqâlî*). However, it appears that before the Safavid period (A.D. 1502–1779), this art did not exist in the manner that we know it now. The profession of storytelling in a fashion, more or less similar to what we practice now, began from the time of King Ismâ'il (A.D. 1501–24). . . . In the past it was mostly stories frosm *Iskandar Nâma* (The Romance of Alexander), *Mukhtâr Nâma* (a religious epic about the deeds of Mukhtâr ibn Abî `Ubaida, d. 686), *Abû Muslim Nâma* (The Romance of Abû Muslim), *Rumûz-i Ḥamza* (The Romance of Ḥamza), and more recently *Yatîm Nâma* (a collection of tales about Ḥusayn-i Kurd-i Shabistarî). Rarely, were any tales from the *Shâhnâma* narrated. (Zarîrî, p. 389)

Elsewhere in his memoirs, Zarîrî points out that in 1308 (i.e., A.D. 1929), when he began his career of professional storytelling:

There was no telling of stories from the *Shâhnâma*. The only thing narrated [that concerned the national epic at all] was a small chapbook called *Rustam Nâma* [The Book of Rustam], which dealt briefly with these tales that fall between the birth of Rustam and the death of Afrâsiyâb [in the *Shâhnâma*]. Even so, not many audiences were interested in listening to these tales. Indeed, most storytellers narrated tales from [other books]. Not a single line from the *Shâhnâma* was recited, because most storytellers were illiterate and narrated their tales from memory. . . . It was around 1308 (1929), or may be a year before or after that date—I don't rightly recall—that telling of non-*Shâhnâma* tales in coffeehouses was prohibited by the government. Only those performers who recited verses from the *Shâhnâma*, and could expound upon the book's verses were allowed to continue. [All] storytellers, however, were from time to time harassed by the police. (Zarîrî, pp. xxviii, xxxii)

It should be understood from the outset that narration of heroic tales in these places was not in verse, nor was the performance of them ever far removed from a written document. We know that even women who could read and write would occasionally read stories from some text to entertain their family members (Mîrshukrâ'î, pp. 60, 64). Zarîrî's observations in this regard are instructive: "I have often seen people gathering in dignified assemblies in coffeehouses around a literate person who entertained them by reading verses from

the *Shâhnâma*, until the arrival of the professional storyteller" (Zarîrî, p. xxxii; cf. Shahrî, vol. 5, p. 517; Mîrshukrâ'î, pp. 60–61; Mustawfî, vol. 3, pp. 407–408).

The most common term of address for storytellers is *murshid*. This is different from *naqqâl*, which means "storyteller" and is never used as a term of address. The term *murshid* has religious connotations and has come "to mean teacher, and by extension, someone who knows books and interprets them for others" (Page, pp. 43, 49, 50; cf. Najmî, pp. 476, 478). Indeed, we have evidence from the twelfth and thirteenth centuries that indicates that storytellers narrated as well as composed stories in writing. They often had a scribe who transcribed the tale as he heard it recited. We consider it quite likely that the scribe's transcription was later edited and reworked by the storyteller. Some of these "scribes" were also readers of written tales. This is evident in the name of one of them, namely the scribe of Bîghamî's *Dârâb Nâma* (in A.D. 1482), who was called Maḥmûd-i daftar khwân (Maḥmûd the lector) (Ṣafâ, vol. 1, p. xiv).

Every *naqqâl* possessed a written version of his tales, which he had committed to memory during his years of apprenticeship, to which he could refer, and the text of which he followed with greater or lesser fidelity. Moreover, during their apprenticeship with an experienced master, most were given large parts of the *Shâhnâma* to memorize (see, for example, Page, pp. 32, 36–37; Shahrî, vol. 5, p. 511).

Inability to read and write among the *naqqâl*s is a modern phenomenon that probably started after the Safavid period. Even the illiterate narrators, however, would arrange for someone to read the stories to them from a written source. They would then memorize these stories and narrate them for the audience. That being illiterate was a source of embarrassment for storytellers is implied in Zarîrî's statement:

[In the beginning], although well-known as a storyteller, I used to have a literate person read the scroll of the story, and after listening to it, and memorizing it, I used to pretend to the people—*barâ-yi mardum vânimûd mîkardam*—[that I've read it myself]. [This was] because like many other storytellers, I was illiterate. [Later] I purchased a first grade textbook . . . and gradually learned to read by asking those who were literate, to identify the letters of the alphabet for me. Soon, I learned to read and began to study many books [on my own]." (Zarîrî, p. xxviii)

As Page correctly observes, the evidence shows that epic storytelling in Iran "is not an inherited profession" (p. 48). Most storytellers come to this profession by twists and turns of fortune, or more likely, misfortune. The case of Zarîrî is worth quoting:

I was born in the city of Eṣfahân in 1909 and lost my parents in childhood. [That is,] a horrific famine hit Eṣfahân quite hard in 1916. [I remember] that there was a small window (literally, "hole") which led to the outside from every bakery; and [in order to stop looters from overrunning the store] bread was handed out to the paying customers from that window. But a hundred starving arms stretched out for every loaf of bread that made it out of the hole. Even if the customer could manage to grab hold of his loaf, the people jumped on him, forced the bread out of his hands; and lying on their bellies on the ground, devoured it. . . . I was the only member of my family who survived that famine. I sold my father's house early in my teens, and since I knew no trade, began to travel with wandering dervishes at the age of eleven. [During this time] I supported myself by singing religious praise poetry about the saints. (Zarîrî, p. xxvi)

Zarîrî came to storytelling after delving in a number of other professions, such as folk dentistry and folk medicine as well as compass making and bookbinding.

In a similar way, both of Page's storyteller informants came to their trade by choice rather than by inheritance. One was a tradesman who decided to become a *naqqâl* at the age of 28 (Page, pp. 32–33), and the other came to his profession through a more twisted path (pp. 35–36).

Rather than climbing on a step stool in the manner of the seventeenth-century performers, the modern storytellers sat upon a small chair and placed their "book" (really a scroll, called *ṭûmâr*) on a little table in front of them while they narrated (Shahrî, vol. 5, pp. 516–517; cf. Rahmânî, pp. 211, 216–217).

*Naqqâl*s were generally divided into three groups: those who had memorized a huge number of verses from the *Shâhnâma* and recited by declamation; those who mixed the verses of the epic

with other material in verse or prose; and those who relied on the tales of the *Shâhnâma*, but narrated these in prose with many changes. The performance of the third group was also called *ṭûmâr-khânî*, "reading from the scroll" (Shahrî, vol. 5, p. 511; cf. Mîrshukrâ'î, pp. 60–61). These scrolls were usually copied by poorly literate scribes during the performance and were later sold to other storytellers or to others who were interested in purchasing them (Zarîrî, pp. xvii–xviii). Most scrolls were filled with grammar and spelling errors.[10] It is important to note that, although some unlettered storytellers employed marginally literate individuals to read their scrolls to them, the majority of those who wrote down the performance of a storyteller did it for their own purposes.

Storytelling Techniques

The professional telling of stories took place in almost any public place where a crowd could gather. The earliest eyewitness account of public storytelling in classical Persian is found in the work of the historian Bayhaqî (A.D. 995–1077; for the English translation of the passage see Omidsalar, pp. 205–206). The great theologian al-Ghazzâlî (A.D. 1058–1111), in his *Kîmiyâ-yi Sa'âdat* [The Alchemy of Happiness], which is his own Persian translation of his encyclopedic Arabic work *Iḥyâ al-Ulûm al-Dîn* [The Quickening of the Sciences of Religion], gives some idea of the places and the manner of public storytelling performances:

Let it be known that in these days the world is filled with iniquitous [deeds] and the [learned] have given up all hope of improvement. . . . [A]s for [unlawful] customs, some take place in mosques, some in bazaars, some in public baths, and some in houses. (al-Ghazzâlî, p. 404)

Al-Ghazzâlî then goes on to specify that mosques were especially attractive to storytellers. This may have been because the performer would have had a ready-made audience in these places. He also gives us a glimpse of the manner and appearance of the storytellers of his time:

It is not permitted to gather a crowd around oneself and narrate stories in mosques or sell charms or other objects. One must expel those who tell stories in mosques if the contents of the stories are not found in dependable books of religious tradition, or are inaccurate. Expelling these [storytellers] was the custom of the ancients. As for those [of them] who adorn themselves and who are ruled by lust, and tell [their stories] in rhymed prose and sing them—even when young women are present in the assembly—such a deed is considered an unforgivable sin and is not permitted even outside the Mosque. (p. 406)

Al-Ghazzâlî's pious prohibition implies that two groups of storytellers existed in his time. First were those who narrated their tales in mosques but were not possessed of any outstanding characteristics. These were probably storytellers who told religious stories of miraculous deeds of prophets and saints. This group was called *qâṣṣ* (plural *quṣṣâṣ*) in Arabic. Second were narrators who either dressed in special costumes or "adorned themselves" in some fashion. They also embellished their tales by various rhetorical devices and told them in a mixture of prose and song, or in rhymed prose. It is important to note that al-Ghazzâlî does not object to telling stories in mosques per se. He merely rules that telling pagan narratives in these sanctuaries is illegal. More significantly for our purposes, however, his ruling implies that pagan tales were indeed told in mosques by narrators whose tales, manner of performance, and appearance were objectionable to him.

The most extensive discussion of storytelling performance is found in the *Futuwwat Nâma-yi Sulṭânî* [The Royal Book of Chivalry], which was composed by Mullâ Ḥusayn-i Kâshifî, surnamed Wâ`iẓ (d. A.D. 1504–05).[11] In his *Futuwwat Nâma*, Kâshifî collected a great deal of information about guilds and their social organization. One of these guilds is that of the entertainers. Storytellers belong to this guild. According to Kâshifî storytellers sat on a chair and occasionally held onto an ax while performing (pp. 302–303). He divides storytelling into two kinds: telling tales in prose and reciting versified tales. He then describes the following rules for storytelling:

If they ask, "How many are the rules of storytellers?" answer, "Eight." First, if he is a beginner, the storyteller must have studied the tale that he wants to tell with a master; and if he is experienced, he must have practiced it beforehand, so that he may not get stuck in telling it. Second, he must begin with eloquence, speak in an exciting manner, and not be plain or bor-

ing in his discourse. Third, one must know what kind of narration is fitting for what kind of assembly, and how much to simplify, and so on. The storyteller should narrate more of what his audience likes. Fourth, one should occasionally embellish one's prose by verse. However, one should be careful not to bore people with it; as the great ones have said, "Verse in storytelling is like salt in food; if it is not enough, the food will be bland, and if it is too much the dish will be salty." One must therefore keep to moderation. Fifth, one should not utter impossible statements, nor should one hyperbolize lest he should appear silly to his audience. Sixth, one should not make sarcastic or critical remarks lest he become an object of dislike. Seventh, one should not demand payment forcefully, nor should one pester the audience for it. Eighth, one must neither stop too soon, nor go on too late; but must always keep to the path of moderation.

If you are asked: "How many are the rules of reciting [narrative] poetry?" say: "They are six. First, one should recite melodically. Second, one should make the words penetrate the audience's hearts. Third, whenever one comes upon a difficult verse, one should explain it to the audience. Fourth, one should not bore the audience. Fifth, one should not implore the audience for payment, nor should one ask for too much. Sixth, one should mention the poet of the verse that one recites either at the beginning of his performance, or at its conclusion, and send blessing to his soul. (Kâshifî, pp. 304–305)

Storytellers in the modern period also followed most of these rules. Murshid `Abbâs-i Zarîrî, for instance, punctuates his prose narration of the story of Rustam and Suhrâb with verses from the *Shâhnâma* (e.g., pp. 4–5, 8–9, 24, 226–227, 353) as well as from other poets (e.g., pp. 116, 118–119, 219, 282, 317, 352).

The storyteller opens his performance in the name of God. This involves uttering the religious formula "*bismillâh al-raḥmân al-raḥîm*" [In the name of God, the merciful, the compassionate]. Different storytellers may utter other blessings, which may or may not rhyme with the traditional formula. Thus, one of Page's informants started by saying:

Besmellâh al-raḥmân al-raḥîm
Yâ rahmân o yâ raḥîm

Hast kelid-e dar-e ganj-e ḥakîm
Nâm-e khodâvand-e karîm o raḥîm
In the name of God, the merciful, the
   compassionate!
O merciful and compassionate [God]!
The key to the door of the sage's **treasure is**
The name of the kind and merciful **Lord**.
(Page, p. 57)

Although Page is correct in recording that all performances of epic tales begin with some sort of religious formula in praise of God, she confuses the issue by reading more into a simple act of traditional reverence when she writes:

The storyteller uses the opening words to unite himself to his audience. The *besmellâh* identifies all participants as Muslims engaged in a Muslim activity, in keeping with the religious functions of the meeting." (ibid.)

This explanation is, in our opinion, interpretive overkill. All beginnings in Muslim traditional settings require the utterance of the formulaic phrase "in the name of God." Devout Muslims are required to utter the formula even at the outset of sexual intercourse. That is, the husband is supposed to say *"besmellâh al-raḥmân al-raḥîm"* just before penetrating his wife. Similarly, a hunter is expected to recite the formula as he is about to shoot his prey, or release his hunting dog or his falcon; and sellers and buyers are expected to do the same as they engage in a commercial transaction. The utterance of the formula no more "unites" the storyteller with his audience than it unites the hunter with his prey, or the seller with the buyer. Sometimes, if we may borrow from Freud's wit, a *bismillâh* is only a *bismillâh*.

Page's reference to the two lines that begin the formula as "the first two hemistiches" (p. 57) is inaccurate and misleading. The word "hemistiches" implies poetry, whereas the formula to which she refers is clearly not in verse. This type of presentation encourages the Eurocentric interpretation of all epics as poetry. There is no Persian teller of epic stories, now or in the past, who has told his tale in extemporaneously composed verse. The so-called formula in Page's example is at best a piece of rhymed prose. The second two lines are in a well-known poetic meter; but if this is not an accident, then we are dealing here with no more than the common mixing of verse with prose as a narrative technique. In neither case is

there even a hint of extemporaneous composition detectable in this opening. In a similar way, Zarîrî starts an episode in the story of Rustam and Suhrâb by the following words: " `iqd-i jawâhir-i sukhan-i kuhan dar maḥḥal u môḍi`î bûd ki `arḍ kardîm" (the bejeweled chain of the ancient tale was at the part that we said . . .), and then he continues with his narrative (p. 362, and cf. pp. 391 and 409). Clearly the words *sukhan* and *kuhan* rhyme, and the sentence is therefore a piece of rhymed prose. However, no one who is familiar with the Persian language would ever confuse this with poetry.

This of course, does not mean that there are no poetic introductions in storytelling. There clearly are (e.g., Zarîrî, pp. 408–409). However, these verse introductions are not extemporaneous compositions by the storyteller; they are merely verses of different poets, strung together for their beauty's sake or because of the relevance of their theme to the theme of the episode that the storyteller is about to narrate.

The storyteller asks for money at the end of his performance. The request for payment has its own etiquette. For instance, Zarîrî, first asked the audience to recite a certain religious formula and then ended with the following words:

Just so you know, this story gets more beautiful day by day. The story grows so beautiful that no play and no novel can surpass it. The story is exceedingly excellent. The story is like poetry. Consider this: When they want to praise something in verse, if they simply say: "how good this is, how beautiful this is"; such a statement would have no poetic delicacy. But if they were to praise something by saying for instance: "Your hair is like a ton of amber." Obviously a person's hair can not be a ton of amber, or "Your face is like a field of flowers, your ruby lips a cellar full of red wine, and the beloved's hair a vast space of [ethereal] souls." These are all exaggerations. But if a poem lacks these things, it lacks poetic delicacy. Tales are the same. There should be a certain delicate hyperbole in stories in order for them to be beautiful. This story [of Rustam and Suhrâb] is very beautiful. God willing if the Lord gives us health [in the days to come], you will come here, and I will tell you the rest of it. And now, we will make our rounds. We will make our rounds because it is the tradition that has always been. May God almighty never dishonor the chivalrous man whose hand touches my hand [with payment]. Everyone, say Amen. (Zarîrî, p. 418)

Similar techniques of asking for payment, and of encouraging the audience to return for more in the future, are discernible in the text of *Samak-i `Ayyâr,* which is the earliest extant adventure story in the Persian language. This book, which was probably compiled from the narration of a professional storyteller some time in the twelfth century A.D., is full of important information about the culture of professional storytelling at that time.

The narrator of *Samak-i `Ayyâr* adopts a number of strategies in order to ask for payment. Sometimes he inserts his request in the middle of his narrative, by putting it in the mouth of one of the *dramatis personae* (e.g., Farâmarz, vol. 4, p. 108; vol. 5, p. 609). At other times he may break the narration at an exciting point and say to the audience, "those who want to know what happened to [so and so] should pay the storyteller [such and such] a sum of money, food, or say a prayer for him" (e.g., Farâmarz, vol. 4, p. 101; vol. 5, pp. 531–532).

Aside from asking for payment artfully, the teller of the story of *Samak-i `Ayyâr* employs a number of narrative techniques to keep his audience interested in his narration. One of his most interesting ploys is humorous irony. For instance, while describing how one of his *dramatis personae* kills a witch, he says: "[the hero] stepped forth, and without asking permission, beheaded the witch Sahâna, and Sahâna duly died because in those days it was often the case that those who were beheaded, also died" (Farâmarz, vol. 5, p. 585). In another scene, the Amazon Mardândukht seizes a hero, whom she lifts over her head. She then "swung him around her head, and so skillfully smashed him upon the ground that he was not hurt at all, except for the fact that no part of his body was left unharmed. Indeed, there was nothing wrong with him apart from the fact that he expired on the spot" (Farâmarz, vol. 5, p. 319).

Professional telling of epic tales in Iran is a defunct art form. It has neither the audience that it once enjoyed nor the popularity that it commanded in the past. Repeated official efforts to revive and promote it during the rule of the Pahlavi dynasty were never successful and managed only to reproduce a caricature of the once-thriving art. This was immediately obvious to all those observ-ers who witnessed the government-sponsored performances (Ṭâhirî, p. 1318). Let us end with the words of that great storyteller of the twentieth century, *murshid* Zarîrî, who eulogized his profession in these words:

In 1967 they invited your humble servant to the King `Abbâs Hotel, and even published my photograph in the newspapers several times; [with the caption that said] "the renowned storyteller of Esfahân, *murshid* `Abbâs-i Zarîrî narrates the story of the *Shâhnâma* for the foreign tourists in this place." All of the rich folks of the city and their wives showed up at the hotel to see me. However, none of them listened to the story. It was as though they had no idea what the *Shâhnâma* was. [I remember] one night [someone] even asked me: "was Tahmîna Rustam's mother or his wife?" I said: "No [dear], she was his wife." . . . In the past [the audience for our stories] was huge. Times were not like now, when everyone has a lot of distractions. In those days the Western musicians and the fake heroes of foreign [movies] had not mesmerized the population yet; and the people naturally liked the national stories and considered them important. Coffeehouse owners used to compete with one another over attracting skillful storytellers to their establishments. [Now] our art form is approaching dissemination. I have no hopes for the future, [nor] do I see a way to save this art. (Zarîrî, p. xxxiv, 390)

We can not imagine any set of circumstances under which the art of professional epic storytelling in Iran can ever be revived again.

Notes

1. These are *Garshâspnâma* or *The Book of Garshasp* (completed in A.D. 1065), *Bahmannâma* and *Kûshnâma,* or *The Book of Bahman* and *The Book of Kûsh,* composed sometime in the twelfth century A.D.; *Farâmarznâma,* or *The Book of Farâmarz,* circa the thirteenth century A.D. These were later followed by several inferior younger compositions such as *Burzûnâma, Shahriyârnâma, Jahângîrnâma,* and *Sâmnâma;* or the *Books of Burzû, Shahriyâr, Jahângîr,* and *Sâm,* respectively. Although the composition of these "epic" poems has been ascribed to some time between the tenth and thirteenth centuries

by a number of authorities (e.g., Ṣafâ, 1363, pp. 300–340; cf. Mohl, 39–50; Nöldeke, pp. 133–135; Molé), none of these poems appears to be of great age. Indeed, based on stylistic and internal linguistic evidence, the exposition of which may take us far afield, one may not assign any of them to a date before the seventeenth century, or perhaps even later.

2. We believe that Strabo's statement "both with song and without song" is merely a Hellenism, and that if the evidence of the later periods may be taken to indicate a pattern, the majority—if not all—of these tales were probably in prose.

3. "The notion of a chronological Middle Ages," writes Nicholaisen, "with its concomitant epithet medieval, is . . . essentially European in origin and application. Any exercise insisting on a double vision in matters concerning oral tradition in a medieval setting . . . is consequently, almost by definition, predestined to concentrate on and perhaps even to deal exclusively with the European scene" (Nicholaisen, p. 2).

4. Scattered data on the size and nature of Muslim libraries of Iran and elsewhere, with those of medieval European book collections are available in the literature which concerns history of these institutions (e.g., Afsaruddin; Hessel, pp. 9–28; 30–31; Johnson, pp. 95–107; and Naraghi). The literature shows a vast network of public and private libraries with holdings that, in some cases, ran into tens of thousands of volumes throughout the Muslim lands, especially in Iran. During the same period, western Europe's book collections were quite meager. Most had collections of less than 1,000 volumes. Given the difference in cultural circumstances between these areas, we consider drawing analogies between the intellectual environment of the Middle East and that of western Europe unjustified (see, e.g., Davis). Furthermore, following Nicholaisen, we consider the term "medieval," with all of its cultural and intellectual implications, to be applicable only to western Europe.

5. This verse is assigned to the critical apparatus by the Moscow editors for no clear reason.

6. It appears that these tellers of religious stories had a poor reputation among the literati of the time. Many classical authors considered them to be buffoons, and they published collections of anecdotes in which they ridiculed these simpleminded folk. Among the authors who wrote on storytellers, one may point to luminaries such as al-Jâhiz (A.D. 776–868), al-Râghib al-Isbahânî, who died sometime between A.D. 1005 and 1010 (not, as the *Encyclopaedia of Islam* states, in A.D. 1108); and above all Ibn al-Jawzî (d. A.D. 1200).

7. These verses are taken from the episode of the wars of the hero Sâm in the *Shâhnâma* (Khaleghi-Motlagh edition, vol. 1, p. 226, lines 894–895).

8. This is because of the bluish hue of a fine blade.

9. This statement further supports the well-known fact that people do not listen to storytelling in traditional settings because they want to "learn" the story but in order to enjoy the performance.

10. A number of sample pages from these scrolls are reproduced photographically in Zarîrî, pp. xix–xxv, xxix–xxxi, and xl–xli. The poor writing style of these reproductions shows the marginal literacy of their scribes.

11. Kâshifî is best known for his *Anwâr-I Suhailî [Lights of Canopus]*, a florid retelling of *Kalîla wa Dimna* (Rypka, pp. 313–314). The French translation of the *Lights of Canopus* is said to be one of La Fontaine's sources in composing his fables.

Further Reading

Afsaruddin, Asma, "The Great Library at Alexandria," *The American Journal of Economics and Sociology* 49:3 (1990)

Afshârî, Miran, "Haft lashkar yâ *Shâhnâma*-yi naqqâlân" [The seven armies, or the *Shâhnâma* of storytellers], *Farhang* 7 (1990)

al-Farrâ`, Abû Zakariya Yahyâ ibn Ziyâd, *Ma`ânî al-Qur`ân*, Cairo, Egypt: al-Dar al-Misriyah lil-Ta'lif wa-al-Tarjamah, 1966

Bahar, Muhammad Taquî, ed., *Mujmal al-Tawârîkh wa al-Qisas*, Tehran, Iran: Zavvâr, 1940

Bascom, William, "Four Functions of Folklore," *Journal of American Folklore* 67 (1954)

Bayhaqi, Abû al-Fadl, *'Uyûn al-Akhbâr* [History of Bayhaqî], edited by 'Ali Akbar Fayyâz, 2nd edition, Mashhad, Iran: Ferdowsi University Press, 1977

Bertels, Y.E., et al., eds., *Shâhnâma*, 9 volumes, Moscow: Dânish, 1960–71

Boyce, Mary, "The Parthian Gôsân and the Iranian Minstrel Tradition," *Journal of the Royal Asiatic Society* 18 (1957)

Davidson, Olga M., *Poet and Hero in the Persian Book of Kings*, Ithaca, New York: Cornell University Press, 1994

Falsafî, Nasr Allah, "Târikh-i qahva va qahvakhâna dar îrân" [History of Coffee and Coffeehouses in Iran], *Sukhan* 5:9 (1954)

———, *Zindigânî-i shâh `abbâs avval* [The life of King `Abbâs I], fifth edition, Tehran, Iran: Ilmi, 1992

Farâmarz ibn Khudâdâd Arrajani, *Samak-i `Ayyâr*, 5 volumes, edited by P. Khanlari, Tehran, Iran: Agah, 1984–91

Farrukhî, Salî ibn Jawlûgh, *Dîvân-i Farrukhî*, edited by M. Dabîrsiyâqî, Tehran, Iran: Tahûrî, 1990

Gershevitch, I., "Old Iranian Literature," in *Literatur*, Handbuch der Orientalistik, Leiden, The Netherlands: Brill, 1968

Hessel, Alfred, *A History of Libraries*, translated with supplementary material by Reuben Peiss, Washington D.C.: Scarecrow, 1950

Ibn Hishâm, *Sîra al-Nabî*, edited by Wüstenfeld, Gottingen, West Germany: Dieterichsche Universitats-Buchhandlung, 1858

Injavî-yi Shîrâzî, *Gul ba Sinôbar chi kard?* [Persian Tales], Tehran, Iran: Amir Kabîr, 1979

Johnson, E.D., *History of Libraries in the Western World*, second edition, Metuchen, New Jersey: Scarecrow, 1970

Kâshifî, Husayn, *Futuvat?Nâmah-'i Sultânî*, edited by M.J. Mahjûb, Tehran, Iran: Bunyad-i Farhang-i Iran, 1971

Khaleghi-Motlagh, J., "The Oral Traditions of Improvised Poetry and the Shâhnâma," *Iranshenasi* 9:1 (1997)

———, ed., *The Shahnameh*, 5 volumes, New York and Costa Mesa, California: Mazda, 1988–97 (ongoing edition)

Khânlarî, Parvîz Natîl, *Shahr-i Samak* [Samak's City], Tehran, Iran: Âgâh, 1985

Lisân, Husayn, "Shâhnâma khânî" [Narrating epic tales], *Hunar va Mardum* 14:159/160 (1976)

Mahjûb, Muhamad Ja'far, "Introduction," in *Amîr Arsalân*, written by Naqîb al-Mamâlik, edited by Muhammad Ja'far Mahjûb, Tehran, Iran, 1961

———, "Sukhanvarî I" [Poetic Verbal Dueling, part I], *Sukhan* 9:6 (1958)

Manûchihrî Damghani, Abu Najm Ahmad ibn Qaws̲, *Dîvân-i Manîchihrî Dâmghânî*, edited by Muhammad Dabîr Siyâqî, Tehran, Iran: Zavvâr, 1991

Matini, Jalâl, "Naqsh-i Firdôsî dar hifz-i huviyyat-i mâ îrâniyân" [Ferdowsi's role in protecting the national identity of us Iranians], in *Kongress 1000 Jahre persisches Nationalepos: Ferdowsi's Schahnameh*, edited by Ja'far Mihrgânî, Cologne, Germany: Mehr Verlag, 1990

Mînuvî, Mujtabâ, *Firdowsi va shi`r- û* [Ferdowsi and his poem], second printing, Tehran, Iran: Dihkhudâ, 1976

Mîrshukrâ'î, Muhammad, "*Shâhnâma* khânî az dîd-i mardumshinâsî" [Narrating epic tales: an anthropological view], *Hunar va Mardum* 14:165/166 (1976)

Mohl, Jules, "Dîbâcha" [Introductory Essay], in *Shâhnâma-'i Firdawsî*, edited by J. Mohl, Tehran, Iran: Sukhan, 1990

Molé, Marijan, "L'épopée iranienne après Firdosi," *Clio La Nouvelle* 5 (1953)

Mustawfî, ´Abd Allah, *Sharh-i zindigânî-'i man* [My memoirs], 3 volumes, Tehran, Iran: Zuvvar, 1992

Najmî, Nâsir, *Tihrân-i ´Ahd-i Nâsirî* [Tehrân Under the Rule of Nasir al-Dîn Shâh], Tehran, Iran: `Attâr, 1985

Naraghi, Ehsan, "The Islamic Antecedents of the Western Renaissance," *Diogenes* 44/1:173 (1996)

Nas̲râbâdî, Muhammad Tâhir, *Tazkirah-i Nasrâbâdî*, edited by Hasan Vahîd Dastgirdî, Tehran, Iran: Ibn Sina, 1938

Nicholaisen, W.F.H., *Oral Tradition in the Middle Ages*, Binghamton, New York: Medieval and Renaissance Texts and Studies, 1995

Niz̲âm al-Mulk, *Siyar al-Mulûk*, edited by Hubert Darke, third printing, Tehran, Iran: Scientific and Cultural Publications, 1994

Nöldeke, Theodor, *Nöldeke's "The Iranian National Epic,"* or *The Shahnamah*, Bombay, India: K.R. Cama Oriental Institute, 1930; reprinted as *The Iranian National Epic, or, The Shahnamah*, translated by Leonid Th. Bogdanov, Philadelphia: Porcupine, 1979

Omidsalar, Mahmoud, "Storytellers in Classical Persian Texts," *Journal of American Folklore* 97:384 (April–June 1984)

Page, Mary Ellen, *"Naqqali" and Ferdowsi: Creativity in the Iranian National Tradition* (Ph.D. diss., University of Pennsylvania), 1977

Puhvel, Jaan, *Comparative Mythology*, Baltimore, Maryland: Johns Hopkins University Press, 1987

Râzî, `Abd al-Jalîl, *Kitâb al-Naqd,* 3 volumes, edited by Mir Jalâl al-Dîn Muhaddith, Tehran, Iran: EAAM, 1979

Richmond, Wintrhop Edson, "The Textual Transmission of Folklore," *Norveg* 4 (1954)

Rosenberg, Bruce A., *Folklore and Literature, Rival Siblings,* Knoxville: University of Tennessee Press, 1991

Rypka, Jan, *History of Iranian Literature,* edited by Karl Jahn, Dordrecht, The Netherlands: D. Reidel, 1968

Safâ, Zabîhullâh, *Hamâsa surâ'î dar îrân* [Epic poetry in Iran], Tehran, Iran: Amir Kabîr, 1984

——, "Ishâra'î kûtâh ba dâstânguzârî va dâstânguzârân tâ dôrân-i safavî" [A short note on story telling and storytellers until the Safavid era], *Kelk* 61:64 (1995)

Shabânkârahî, Muhammad ibn ´Alî ibn Muhammad, *Majma´ al-Ansâb,* edited by Mir Hâshim Muhaddis, Tehran, Iran: Amir Kabîr, 1984

Shahrî, Ja'far, *Târikh-i ijtimâ´î-i tihrân dar qarn-i sizdahum* [Social history of Tehran in the twentieth century], 6 volumes, Tehran, Iran: Intisharat-i Isma´iliyan,1988

Sorûshyâr, Jamshîd, "Hwsy'n-hws'r," *Râhnumâ-yi Kitâb* 20:8/10 (1977)

Ṭâhirî, Hûshang,"Guzârishî az sivvumîn jashn-i tûs" [Reporting from the third Tûs festival], *Sukhan* 25:12 (1977)

Tarsûsî, Abu Tahir Muhammad ibn Hasan, *Dârâb namih-i Tarsûsî,* edited by Zabih Allah Safâ, Tehran, Iran: Bungah-i Tarjumih va Nashr-i Kitab, 1965

Uncâlâ, Ervad Manockji Rustamjî , ed., *Dârâb Hormazyâr Rivâyât,* 2 volumes, Bombay: British India Press, 1922

Zarîrî, Murshid ´Abbas, *Dâstân-i Rustam va Suhrâb: Rivâyat-i Niqalan* [The Story of Rostam and Sohrab], edited by Jalîl Dûstkhâh, Tehran, Iran: Tûs, 1990

Zarrînkûb, ´Abd al-Husayn, *Az guzashtah-´i adabî-i îrân* [From Iran's literary past], Tehran, Iran: al-Hudâ, 1996

Stories About a Moroccan Storyteller

Deborah A. Kapchan

Here Deborah A. Kapchan examines questions raised when dealing with informants who trade in untruths.

Lies Are Synonymous with Fiction

The following is a story about a storyteller in a marketplace in Morocco. You don't have to believe it. I don't vouch for its facticity or truth. As Moulay Abdellah has told me on several occasions, 98 percent of his stories are lies. Why should my story be any different?

"The day I don't see you all here listening to me is the day that I know you've gotten smart," Moulay Abdellah tells his audience of old men in the marketplace. They sit on pieces of cardboard on the rocky dirt that slopes down toward the plain, flies lighting on their calloused feet and swollen toes. "But as long as you keep coming, I'll keep telling you stories." This is the way that Moulay Abdellah has the last laugh at his audience and at me. More important, perhaps, is the way that my work with Moulay Abdellah has made me rethink the assumptions of sincerity on which genres of ethnographic inquiry, such as the life history, are based. In the marketplace (or in interactions with marketplace performers—*musha'widin*, or charlatans) lies are the assumed modus operandi; they are a performative art, a selling strategy, and a way to pass the time (Gilsenan). In Moulay Abdellah's dialect, lies are synonymous with fiction. This is not to say that there is no sincerity in his or other marketplace interactions. It is to assert that divining the intentions[1] (*niya*) of the actor is imperative to any

interaction wherein the dynamics of fabrication are in full play (Bauman 1986, p. 201; Duranti).

Until recently, most case studies have been studies in narration, whether the patient Dora's confessional narratives to Freud or the artistic narration of folklore genres to ethnographers (but see Desjarlais 1992). Through all the various readings of these texts, there is an implicit acceptance of their sincerity, if not their veracity. What happens, however, when lies conflate with fact and any notion of "the real" is untenable? In a context where, as William Carlos Williams asserts, "only the imagination is real," notions of sincerity—whether in narrative or in empirical experience—are confounded and, I suggest, ethnographic authority is undermined in the process (Kirshenblatt-Gimblett).

The Sincerity Principle

When working with a self-proclaimed charlatan the ethnographer can no longer assume the "sincerity principle" to be at work (Grice). Not only is the veracity of the narrative called into question, so is the sincerity of its *narration*: the story world and the storytelling world collapse into each other (Bauman 1986; Shuman; Young). There is an element of irony in these interactions that does not necessarily exist in the telling of oral history, personal memorate, or genres with a more explicit relation to the real. Tricksters use the ethnographers for their own ends and the ethnographers watch themselves being used, let themselves be taken, become knowing dupes. It is a winking ethnography wherein storytelling becomes an end in itself and not a means toward another (cf. Behar). What, after all, is to be gained from interrogating fabrication?

As Moulay Abdellah tells it, he owes his career to lies. He ran away from his home in Marrakech when he was in mid-adolescence upon finding out by accident that he was adopted. Deeply wounded by the realization that his identity was based on a deliberately maintained deception, he went to Casablanca and got a job busing tables and cleaning a cafe. The few dirhams he made during the day were spent on going to the cinema. Almost every evening he was there, watching films from India and Egypt. But he also did not waste time going to the local *halqa*, the public space for performance. He had grown up listening to storytellers and praise-singers in the main square in Marrakech. Now he decided, he could do as well. Forced to live by his wits ("my master" he says, "was poverty"), Moulay Abdellah would recount the plots of Indian and Egyptian romance and war films that he had seen the night before, changing the names and places of the story line, localizing them for a Moroccan audience.

The dictionary says a charlatan is "a mere talking pretender: a quack." There is also, however, something of the impostor here. A charlatan is one who affects different stances, who confounds with the counterfeit. Possessing only surfaces, the charlatan is a sciolist, a half-scholar, making a living by pretense and words.

Moulay Abdellah is now an epic storyteller in a midsize town in the Middle Atlas Mountains. He arrives in the marketplace every day at about the time of the afternoon call to prayer. Sitting on an old wooden box, he recounts the heroic tales of 'Antar to a circle of about 40 unemployed and aging men. He resides in a quarter below the *suq*, in a brick-converted shantytown. He has opted for permanence, but only after a quarter century of wandering. Although he is a storyteller now, he was once an itinerant salesman of nonprescription medicine following the market circuit in southeastern Morocco. He tells me how it was common practice to hold a tire gauge against the foreheads of clients, and, when the needle began to wiggle, divine their ailments and prescribe a remedy consisting of "pills" sold for twice their cost in a pharmacy—common medicines like Actifed and antacids.

"You can play with a person from the get-go. You can play with him a second time and a third, until, perhaps he'll wake up a little . . . wake up

with his head. I came here to this town and I would go out and sell medicines. I went to a market. It's called Ouled Yaani. I just got settled and started, like that. I put down the goods [the "trust," *amana*]. I remained there. I started working and someone came and stood next to me. He had a goat on his shoulder. He came wanting to sell that goat and buy provisions for his family. He said to me, like this . . . He saw me talking about head colds, . . . and about rheumatism. When he told me this and that, I stuck a tire gage that I had up to his forehead and looked at that needle. And I told him, "My friend, you have mixed-up blood and you have one pure kidney; but the other one is dirty. Your blood doesn't circulate [well]. I got him to talking and it happened that I hit the nail on the head. I took the goat and I took the 400 [riyals] that he had. And I gave him three injections of Actifed and two pills of Ruwuzid."

He tells me this with a mixture of pride and embarrassment, proud of his wiliness, yet aware of his lack of scruples. Yet he is quick to turn his trickery into pedagogy: "It teaches people to be wary of other's intentions," he asserts. Like burns teach people about fire. "Wear your size and it will fit you," he asserts. "If you wear a size that's too big, it will become an embarrassment. If you wear something too small it's a double embarrassment."

Interrogating Fabrication

What is to be gained from interrogating fabrication? A partial response is found in the way in which ethnographers know and project the world. (For the sake of analytic elegance, we might name it the transference of trope.) As ethnographers enter into the ethos of their interlocutors, they tend to use native metaphor to describe lived experience; thus, Paul Stoller, who works with griots, has suggested that, like griots, "ethnographers must negotiate and renegotiate their social roles across a maze of cultural boundaries," changing their discourse and genre to fit the context, the content, and the audience (p. 358). Robert Desjarlais, whose case study with a Nepalese shaman breaks ethnographic ground in centering his narrative in the bodies and emotions of his informants, considers the ethnographer a diviner of sorts, someone who must intuit the tacit, somatic experience of others and translate it into an idiom understandable for the reader.[2] Behar transforms herself "from a listener into a storyteller" in the act of writing a life history (p. 13), and Abu-Lughod asserts that storytelling is the least injurious of all ethnographic genres. At work here is a transference symptomatic of the disjunctive experience of fieldwork, the move toward otherness, the relinquishing of an always malleable self into another idiom.

Given the self-reflexive intentions of this type of rhetorical strategy, might we consider the ethnographer as charlatan? Scandalous. Yet it is just such a trope that may unhinge ethnographic representation from its authoritative stance. If, to paraphrase Lacan, all we do is lie, how does the ground of ethnographic case studies shift? What is to be gained from interrogating fabrication? Only a story. It is just this simple "truth" that breaks the case study out of its encasement.

Notes

1. Says Duranti of the (Western) classic view of truth and intentionality, "Social actors understand each other's wants, beliefs, feelings, recollections, and so on through a set of conversational maxims (cf. Grice 1975), which instruct them on how to package information in utterances and on how to process what others say." (Duranti, Alessandro. 1993. "Truth and Intentionality: An Ethnographic Critique." *Cultural Anthropology* 8 (2):219.
2. "The function of the diviner, in sum, is to transcend the boundaries between Yolmo bodies and thus to breach the borders between tacit and apparent realms of experience." (1992: 182). This, asserts Desjarlais, is the work of translation, the work of ethnography. "Like a well-told tale, a good divination emits flickers of meaning and connotation, the portent of which is filled in by (and so engages) its listeners." (1992: 182)

Further Reading

Abu-Lughod, Lila, *Writing Women's Worlds: Bedouin Stories*, Berkeley and London: University of California Press, 1993

Bauman, Richard, *Story, Performance, and Event: Contextual Studies of Oral Narrative*, Cambridge and New York: Cambridge University Press, 1986

Behar, Ruth, *Translated Woman: Crossing the Border with Esperanza's Story*, Boston: Beacon, 1993

Desjarlais, Robert R., *Body and Emotion: The Aesthetics of Illness and Healing in the Nepal Himalayas*, Philadelphia: University of Pennsylvania Press, 1992

Duranti, Alessandro, "Truth and Intentionality: An Ethnographic Critique," *Cuadernos Americanos* 8:2 (1993)

Gilsenan, Michael, "Lying, Honor and Contradiction," in *Transaction and Meaning: Directions in the Anthropology of Exchange and Symbolic Behavior*, Philadelphia: Institute for the Study of Human Issues, 1976

Grice, Paul, "Logic and Conversation," in *Speech Acts*, volume 3 of *Syntax and Semantics*, edited by Peter Cole and Jerry Morgan, New York: Academic Press, 1975

Shuman, Amy, *Storytelling Rights: The Uses of Oral and Written Texts by Urban Adolescents*, Cambridge and New York: Cambridge University Press, 1986

Stoller, Paul, "Ethnographies as Texts/ Ethnographers as Griots," *American Ethnologist* 21:2 (1994)

Young, Katharine Galloway, *Taleworlds and Storyrealms: The Phenomenology of Narrative*, Boston: Nijhoff, 1987

Storytelling in Palestine

Ibrahim Muhawi

Ibrahim Muhawi discusses Palestinian legend (truth) told by men and the folktale (fiction) told by women. Many Palestinian place legends are held in common by Muslims, Christians, and Jews. Since 1947, however, oral histories and heroic tales dealing with the conflict have replaced them as popular storytelling material. The folktale, told by women in the home, survives. Muhawi shows how several of these tales function in the women's world.

To Women the Folktale, to Men the Legend

Given Palestine's exalted place in the sacred geography of the monotheistic religions, it is home to a rich lore of historical and religious legends as well as a highly developed tradition of folktales and fairy tales. The division of genres corresponds neatly with the division in gender. The women appropriate the folktale, which is associated with lies (fiction) and the imagination, and the men, the legend and other genres associated with truth and believability. The legends touch on local sites and holy men (*awliya*) as well as the major figures of all three faiths, including Abraham, Moses, Solomon, David, Jesus, and the Virgin Mary, among others. In the folk imagination prophecy is connected with immortality. The Prophets Abraham and Moses, for example, were favored by God's letting them choose their hour of death. When the moment comes, however, each refuses to surrender his soul and has to be tricked into dying—Abraham by having the angel of death appear to him as a doddering old man, making him wish for death to avoid a similar fate; and Moses, when his eyes are permanently closed by Azrael after he lies down in a grave to resolve an argument about its size.

El-Khadr, the Green One

The wish for immortality that eluded Moses and Abraham was attained by El-Khadr, the Green One, who drank from the Fountain of Youth (Motif D1338.1.2), identified by Muslims with a man of God who appears in a Qur'anic narrative about Moses (18:60–82). A mythological figure shared by the lore of all three faiths, with congeners in other traditions (*Gilgamesh* and *Gawain and the Green Knight*), El-Khadr is the hero of a cycle of legends in which his role is to set things right in the world by helping the needy or the oppressed, as when he magically brings a sack of coins to the Jewish community in Hebron to pay an unjust tax imposed by the Pasha (Hanauer, 46–53). His avatar in Christianity is Mar Jiryis (St. George), and in Judaism, the prophet Elijah, or Mar Elias. In Christian legend he is instrumental in helping Queen Helena find the true cross (Crowfoot and Baldensperger, 127–129). He also saves the sacrificial maiden by slaying the dragon blocking the waters of the spring, and his icon as the dragon slayer graces the walls of most Eastern-rites churches in the country. His main sanctuary (*maqam*) at Mount Carmel, where the sick sought cures, was the site of an extended annual pilgrimage and festival. The versions of the legend associated with Bir Al-Waraqa (Well of the Leaf) inside Al-Aqsa Mosque in Jerusalem—about the man who entered Paradise during his lifetime—clearly belong to the Khadr cycle. A certain person descends into this well to recover his bucket and is met underground by another, who shows him the Garden of Paradise, from which the human plucks a fig leaf that stays green. In Jewish versions (with sources that may go back to Ezek-

344

iel 47:1–12) the hero is identified with Rabbi Joshua ben Levi, or the Prophet Elijah (Shalem, 52–53). El-Khadr's appeal to the folk imagination is such that he crosses the line between legend and folktale. In folktales he retains his status as an immortal, appearing magically in the form of a venerable white-bearded man to grant a boon (MK [Muhawi and Kanaana] Tale 28), but he also appears as the (mortal) hero of a dragon-slayer cycle of tales (AT [Aarne-Thompson] 300, MK T17). Given his potency in the folk hagiology of all three faiths, and judging from the number of shrines in the country dedicated to his cult, El-Khadr should properly be considered the patron saint of Palestine.

Rupture in the Place-Legend Tradition Since 1948

These legends were shared by Muslims, Christians, and Jews, and they present a visionary picture of the country as a place where a communal identity based on the religious significance of the land to each group can be enjoyed, beyond ethnic and national divisions. Sadly, this was not to be. Many of the legends about local saints and haunted springs published by the great Palestinian folklorist Taufik Canaan in the 1920s and 1930s, the religious and historical legends recorded by Hanauer, the haunting stories about fabulous plants and maidens transformed into trees set down by Crowfoot and Baldensperger, and those cited in Dalman's magnificent seven-volume tribute to folk life in Palestine have disappeared or have been forgotten as a result of the rupture in the cultural and historical-geographic continuity of the country that came with the establishment of Israel in 1948 (*Pam al-nakba,* "the year of the catastrophe") and the subsequent loss of the land to the majority of its Arab inhabitants, most of whom became refugees in neighboring countries. The occupation by Israel of the rest of the country in 1967 (*Pam al-naksa,* "the year of the calamity"), which under Jordanian administration had become known as the West Bank (of the River Jordan), brought about the politicization of Palestinian folklore as an expression of national identity, with a concomitant change in the type of legends that became current among the people. If we compare Hanauer's and Canaan's idyllic material with that set down by Kanaana—such as the oral history of the village of Ein Houd, one of 370 Palestinian villages destroyed by the new state of Israel (Ein Houd itself was not destroyed but settled by Jewish artist families after the original inhabitants were made refugees)—and his work on the folklore of the Intifada, particularly the legends in which women assume heroic roles against the Israeli soldiers enforcing the military occupation—we note a shift from stories based on religious history and the topography of the land to those that have an overtly political content or recall the loss of the homeland. The first may not outlast the occupation, but the oral histories will no doubt be remembered for a long time to come.

The Folktale Continues in the Women's Domain

The local legend may have fallen victim to the ravages of uprooting and exile, but the folktale survives in the Palestinian diaspora largely because the tradition is carried on by women within the context of the extended family, an institution that has played a major role in sustaining Palestinian social life and identity even in the most wretched of refugee camps. The "wonderful" content of the tales (which the women narrators say consist entirely of lies—*kullha kizib fi kizib*) and its remoteness from mundane concerns are also contributing factors. We are fortunate that before the tradition fades, Palestinian and other researchers have been able to collect from refugee communities in the East Bank of Jordan (al-Sarisi), the West Bank (Abd al-Hadi, and *passim* in the local folklore journal, *Al-turath wa-al-mujtama?),* both Banks (Sirhan), and from "the crowded tents of the Moslem and Christian refugees from the Holy Land" in Lebanon where Campbell says (p. 12) he came across a great store of folktales. The folktale thrives as well among Palestinians living in historic Palestine, as we see from Muhawi and Kanaana, who selected for extensive analysis 45 tales from more than 200 collected in the Galilee, the West Bank, and Gaza. These, combined with previous collections—Littmann, Hanauer, and Schmidt and Kahle, justly famous for being set down in the dialect of the *fellahin* of Birzeit, and Campbell—provide us with a complete record spanning the twentieth century.

The Palestinian folktale belongs to the great "world" tradition in folk narrative and exhibits its typological variety, including fairy, animal, moralistic, cumulative, formulaic, and humorous tales. Most of the well-known European types (e.g., AT 450, 480, 510, and 707) have Palestinian equivalents. Muhawi and Kanaana provide an account of the Palestinian folktale at a moment at which it still maintains its integrity as a woman's art form, showing that the vitality of the tradition and its uniqueness stem directly from its context: as a household tale serving an important function in the expressive economy of a settled agricultural society organized into extended families with time on their hands during winter evenings. This means, in effect, that the folktale provides a portrait of Palestinian society as seen by women. At the level of form these tales are characterized by a particular style that draws on the syntactic, pragmatic, and stylistic resources of the Palestinian dialect and women's speech patterns to achieve their effect (Muhawi). Women's speech, especially when it takes the form of invocation, has special power in Palestinian and Arab society. A mother calling down curses rather than blessings upon her son's head (MK T4), a daughter putting a curse upon her father's camels if he does not fulfill her wish (MK T12), and a sister cursing her brother with a thorn in his foot that only she can remove (MK T31) are all potent forms of expression that never fail to take effect. And the power to invoke is precisely what is needed to enter verbally into the supernatural world of the folktale. Many Palestinian folktales begin with the traditional lack, which is fulfilled by invocation. "Why of all women am I like this?" complains a childless woman at the beginning of a tale (MK T1). The invocation follows: "May Allah grant me a girl, even if she is only a cooking pot!" And of course her wish is fulfilled, and the tale goes on from there.

Just as women's speech suffuses the texture of these folktales, women's concerns permeate the content. Under the guise of telling lies, the women narrators provide not only a portrait but also a critique of cultural practice, but within acceptable social norms. In Western traditions, many tales revolve around the conflict between stepmothers and stepbrothers and sisters. In the Palestinian tradition, the stepmother is replaced by the co-wife, and the common motif of the motherless children is transformed into plot conflicts involving polygyny. The net result is a relentless commentary on the evils of this practice, whose incidence in the tales far outnumbers its actual occurrence in the society. Further, society at large favors sons, but the women in the Palestinian folktale almost always wish for daughters. We find that females, who in real life are expected to be housebound, are the heroines in the majority

of the tales. Of course, this kind of projection may serve as wish fulfillment, but we must not forget that the tales play an important role in the acculturation of children, who are always present at the telling. To the extent that they paint a portrait, the tales are truthful in showing women as an active force in the management of daily life. The plot in many tales is animated by the conflicts to which women are subject by virtue of their gender and the complex set of situations that an authoritarian, patriarchal society imposes upon them. The mother calls down curses upon her son's head (MK T4) because, in showering her with kindness, he in effect keeps her a prisoner in his household, when what she really wants is a husband.

Such deeply rooted tales put us in touch with the creativity of the women tellers as they weave the universal and the particular: their lives with the larger themes of the folktale, the earthy village geography and the Palestinian landscape beyond with the fantastic landscape of the tale. Like the dialect in which they are told, the landscape suffuses the Palestinian folktale, just as women's lives and daily concerns provide structural paradigms for its content. The seasonal sheep's-milk cheese whose whiteness provides the basic metaphor for the name of a popular tale—*Jbene,* or "cheeselet" (MK T13)—is just one of many household items that fill the world of the Palestinian folktale. With sharp thorns, sweet fruit, and very deep roots that are almost impossible to extirpate, the wild *doum* tree (*Zisyphus spina-christi,* or Christ-thorn, so named from the legend that Christ's crown of thorns came from this tree) in which Jbene is abandoned by her friends is one of the salient features of the Palestinian countryside that dot the landscape of the tales. Others are springs, wells, stone terrace walls, plowed fields, and threshing grounds. This tale, anthologized in nearly all collections, has no parallels outside the country.

When tellers bridge folktale fantasy with reality by locating the action in the village or referring to their neighbors by name or profession (MK T44), they connect the world of the tale, fantastic as it may be, with the ordinary world of daily life. Despite the necessary resort to supernatural paraphernalia, the Palestinian tradition, in which even ghouls are domesticated and kings and queens act more like ordinary people than royalty, demonstrates beyond doubt that the real heroes of the tales are the ordinary folk who form their audience.

Further Reading

Abd al-Hadi, Tawaddud, *Khararif sha?biyah* [Folktales], Beirut, Lebanon: Dar Ibn Rushd, 1980

Campbell, Charles G., *Told in the Market Place*, London: Benn, 1954

Canaan, Taufik, "The Curse in Palestinian Folklore," *Journal of the Palestine Oriental Society (JPOS)* (1935)

——, "Haunted Springs and Water Demons in Palestine," *Journal of the Palestine Oriental Society* (1920–1921)

——, *Mohammedan Saints and Sanctuaries in Palestine*, London: Luzac, 1927

Crowfoot, Grace, and Louise Baldensperger, *From Cedar to Hyssop: A Study in the Folklore of Plants in Palestine*, New York: Macmillan, 1932; London: Sheldon, 1932

Dalman, Gustaf, *Arbeit und Sitte in Palästina*, 7 volumes, Gütersloh, Germany: Bertelsmann, 1928–1942

Hanauer, J.E., *Folk-lore of the Holy Land: Moslem, Christian, and Jewish*, London: Duckworth, 1907; reprint, Folcroft, Pennsylvania: Folcroft Library Editions, 1977

Kanaana, Sharif, *The Destroyed Palestinian Villages: Ein Houd*, Monograph Number 1, Birzeit, Palestine: Birzeit University Center for Documentation and Research, n.d.

——, "The Role of Women in Intifadah Legends," *Contemporary Legend* 3 (1993)

Littmann, Enno, *Modern Arabic Tales*, Leiden, The Netherlands: Brill, 1905

Muhawi, Ibrahim, "On Translating Palestinian Folktales: Comparative Stylistics and the Seniiotics of Genre," in *Arabic Grammar and Linguistics*, edited by Yasir Suleiman, Richmond, Surrey: Curzon, forthcoming

Muhawi, Ibrahim, and Sharif Kana'nah, *Speak, Bird, Speak Again: Palestinian Arab Folktales*, Berkeley: University of California Press, 1989

Sarisi, 'Umar 'Abd al-Rahman, *Al-hikayah al-sha'biyah fi al-mujtama'al-filastini: Al-nusus* [The Folktale in Palestinian Society: The Texts], Amman, Jordan: Dar al-Karmel, 1985

Schmidt, Hans, and Paul Kahle, *Volks-erzählungen aus Palästina*, 2 volumes, Göttingen, West Germany: Vandenhoeck & Ruprecht, 1918, 1930

Shalem, Avinoam, "Bi'r al-Waraqa: Legend and Truth—A Note on Medieval Sacred Geography," *Palestine Exploration Quarterly* 127 (1995)

Sirhan, Nimr, *Al-hikayah al-shu'biyah al-filastiniyah* [The Palestinian Folktale], Beirut, Lebanon: Munazzamat al-Tahrir al-Filastiniyah, 1974

——, *Al-turath wa-al-mujtama?* [Heritage and Society], Al-Birah, Palestine: 1974

Matrilineal Myths, Herbal Healing, and Gender in Tuareg Culture

Susan Rasmussen

Among the Tuareg people of Niger, West Africa, female herbalists trace the origin of their healing to a female ancestress, Tagurmat, and her twin daughters. Susan Rasmussen explores interconnections among the content, context, and function of this etiological mythology, discussing how herbalists "perform" their story both verbally and nonverbally in enacting their healing rituals. She shows how their work and its mythological validation mediates tensions in gender roles and property relations in wider Tuareg society.

The Story of Tuareg Herbal Healing

When I questioned Lala, an elderly woman and the senior herbal medicine woman on top of Mount Bagzan in the Aïr Mountains of Niger, West Africa, about how Tuareg herbal healing began, she explained: "The medicine of *tines-megelen* [literally, "medicine women," from *amagal*, "medicine"] is like "living milk herds" [*akh huderan*]: it is transmitted to, belongs to, and is practiced and managed by women, like property." She then related an etiological myth in order to illustrate this point:

There was a woman who had a very jealous husband. He transferred her very far [away]. They lived so that other men would not see her. One day, he saw people coming toward them on their camels, elaborately decorated. They said, "Look at the men who are going to war." The woman looked and she said, "I see a very

handsome man among these men, one with an indigo robe." As soon as he understood this, the husband killed the woman with a knife and she died. He straightened her body out for burial. The woman's stomach moved. He tore it open and took out two small twin girls. These two little girls, each one brought [out] something in their hands. He cut the umbilical cords. He arranged these girls, and after that he united the people for taking the dead woman to the cemetery. And he told the people afterward, "Look at what is in the hands of the little girls." The people said, "These small objects held, you must hide until the girls grow up to learn about them. If they die, the information will die also." The small objects were in wood. These were hidden until the girls grew up. They replied, "That is the beginning of medicine." They even had medicine of *icherifan* [clans claiming descent from the Prophet], and they taught how the medicine is made: one touches, they explained everything. They were named Fatane and Fatoni. All the women on their side of the family learned to make medicine from them, and taught this to those women who were interested. That was the beginning of healing. Since being taken out of their mother's stomach, these girls held medicines.

Lala, like many herbalists, learned her profession from her mother. She started to watch, apprenticing while she was young, but waited until

348

her mother's death before practicing full-time herself. Another elderly herbalist, Ana, added that "Only women know trees. My medicine is like a secret. It is inherited from the mother of my mother."

Among the Kel Ewey confederation of Tuareg, herbal medicine women traced the origins of herbalism matrilineally to a pair of twin daughters (called by various names) of the local descent-group ancestress called Tagurmat; these twins were said to have started curing because of their inheritance from Tagurmat, which included natural substances used in healing (namely, tree bark), and charcoal, used in Koranic healing.

How exactly are the Tagurmat matrilineal myths used in herbal medicine women's healing and in wider society? In this essay, I explore interconnections among herbal healing, its mythical origins, and gender in Tuareg culture and society. I explore cosmological resources of the matrilineal myths and female-dominated herbalism in terms of the ideological purposes to which these are put, and how. What is the relation between the telling of matrilineal myths and herbalist and Koranic healing among Tuareg? Why have Tuareg Islamic scholars or marabouts not opposed medicine women in the way that the European medieval church opposed herbalists and midwives (Szasz; Chesler)? And how do local residents conceptualize and deploy the mythical matrilineal origins of herbal healing in the management of female biological fertility and cultural descent interests of men and women (Gottlieb; Strathern)? Whence comes the power of this myth in healing, in a society of contemporary and changing relations between the sexes, in the current bilateral system of descent, with patrilineal bias of Islam and sedentization?

The Kel Ewey Tuareg predominate around the Bagzan Massif in the department of Aïr, near the Saharan town of Agadez in northern Niger. They are a seminomadic stock-breeding people who also garden and conduct caravan trading expeditions. They speak a Berber language, Tamacheq, and adhere to Islam but retain many pre-Islamic elements in their ritual, mythology, and cosmology. Precolonial society was organized into hereditary, endogamous, stratified occupational groups. Today, many social stratum-based client-patron relationships are breaking down, although in rural communities the social categories remain salient in ideology; in particular, despite some changes, the smith-noble relationship remains important.[1] Kel

Ewey women, like other Tuareg women, inherit and own livestock and the nuptial tent, and can initiate divorce. Today, however, there are increasing tensions and struggles in property balance between the sexes in sedentization and postmarital residence in many communities.[2]

I show how the matrilineal origin myths of herbalism validate Tuareg herbal medicine women's important roles as mediators between matriliny and patriliny, between pre-Islamic and Islamic ritual and law, and between nature and culture, as these latter are defined locally (MacCormack and Strathern; Gottlieb). Herbal medicine women are central as facilitators. Islam and patrilineal institutions have not co-opted female herbalism or its associated matrilineal mythology, but a compromise has occurred in herbal medicine women's efforts to mediate and translate men's and women's interests in fertility and descent issues. The Tagurmat myth in its text validates this compromise, and in healing and ritual contexts of the medicine women, it reverberates (nonverbally as well as verbally) throughout the wider society. The myth sets the groundwork for herbalists' roles in bridging men's and women's interests.

Tuareg Herbal Medicine Women and Their Profession

Tuareg herbal medicine women predominate around Mount Bagzan in the Aïr. Outside the Aïr, little is known about the healers. There are few references to them in the ethnographic literature.[3] They diagnose by touch, and they treat (predominantly stomach ailments) by tree barks and leaves. They occasionally also practice divination and psychosocial counseling. Most of their patients are women and children, although men, also, sometimes see them. Problems "of the stomach" usually involve gynecologic, fertility, and diarrheic complaints, locally attributed to social tensions and superhuman powers.[4]

Most patients contrasted herbal medicine women to Islamic healers (marabouts and *icherifan*) who use the Koran as a source for healing and divination. Herbalists themselves, however, emphasized their similarities. Marabouts tend to treat mental illnesses caused by spirits possessing the head of the individual.[5] Herbalists and marabouts often refer patients to each other. Many medicine women demonstrated complementarity and cooperation, not only by giving referrals to marabouts but also in the details of their ritual curing symbolism. For example, herbalists pronounce the Islamic benediction *"Bissmillallah"* as they touch the patient's stomach in order to diagnose the illness. Herbalists and patients alike explain herbalists' rotating millet three times around the ill person as being done "in order to obtain God's aid and make the medicines effective." According to Lala, "If a medicine woman herbalist gives anything to someone, even earth, this contains her *al baraka*, the Islamic blessing power." Another herbalist described herbalists and marabouts as "like husband and wife."

Natural and Cultural Substances, Geographic Spaces

Herbal medicine women in effect enact the matrilineal myth ritually throughout their curing, nonverbally as well as verbally. This takes the form of ritual and social acts that mediate forces in Tuareg culture competing with the premises of this mythology. For example, in their practice, medicine women manage substances and cross spaces, both natural and cultural: the earth, ground, and clay (they cannot use iron or other metals); trees and wood (barks); rocks and stones; the stomach and liver, as their primary focus in treatment of the body; and the cereal millet, as an offering (diviners and marabouts offer animals more often). Herbalists' ritual actions include predominantly oral, rather than written, benedictions and counterclockwise circling around *(asoghele)*, rather than the more geometric Islamic ritual pattern. Herbalists gather in the wild during gathering—in the mountains, desert, and oeud (dried riverbed) located outside villages and camps—and heal inside the tent. They combine natural and cultural substances and spaces and, like Tuareg smiths, convert some natural into cultural materials—for example, in some medicines that require cooking over fire. They also combine pre-Islamic and Islamic ritual/mythological/symbolic substances, actions, and spaces. Yet their relation to Islam is ambiguous and, despite explanations emphasizing complementarity, suggests certain tensions.

Ideally, a balance is maintained between herbal medicine women's practice and that of the Islamic scholars called marabouts, but this is an uneasy truce. This is illustrated by certain ritual restrictions and requirements. Herbalists cannot cook medicines on Thursday or Friday, since these are Muslim holy days. If this rule is violated, they will not cure. They cannot gather tree barks during the month of Biano (a holiday commemorating Noah's ark) because during this time there are spirits haunting trees. Those women who specialize in divining in dreams must also, in principle, be authorized by Islam: a famous diviner was rumored to have practiced with both cowrie shells (a pre-Islamic symbol of fertility) and Koranic verses.

Many trees with medicinal value are recurrent in Tuareg folktales and songs with matrilineal themes; for example, they are often animated, and humans communicate with them, asking them for directions on finding lost kinspersons and other information, thereby converting the natural into cultural. Although it takes place in the wild, medicine gathering is firmly implanted in the cultural realm, through the herbalist's "civilized" acts; namely, prayer, benediction, respect, and alms giving. These acts counterbalance the primal act of murder in the Tagurmat myth.

The stomach *(tedis)* in herbal healing, not surprisingly, refers to descent and gender. The stomach is the symbol of the matriline and motherhood. It is also considered, in local medical theories of the body, to be the basis of health. The liver *(tessa)*, also prominent in herbalist healing, is considered an especially vulnerable organ; it can be pierced and dislocated. The liver, in addition, is believed to be the seat of strong sentiments, such as love, fear, and anger. The expression *tehe tessa*, for example, means "you are afraid." Thus, herbalist cures focus upon parts of the body associated with the matriline and maternity, and with strong sentiments. By contrast, marabouts usually heal illnesses attacking the head *(eghef)*, believed to be the seat of logic and intelligence and also the point of entry of Islamic spirits, spirits believed curable by Koranic verses. Spirits attacking the stomach and liver, however, are believed incurable by Koranic verses and require a staging of the spirit-possession exorcist ritual (Rasmussen 1995).[5]

Identity, Fertility, and Continuity

The practice of Tuareg herbalism addresses and manages cultural identity, natural fertility, social reproduction, and, by extension, men's and women's interests of descent and property. The following case of childlessness, followed by sections on Kel Ewey Tuareg descent, inheritance and gender, illustrates how. Many Tuareg women see medicine women herbalists when their menstrual periods stop. Men and women both see them when they are childless. Both men and women also consult marabouts, although many women find marabouts intimidating and thus hesitate to see them unless herbalists refer them to marabouts, or unless their husbands pressure them to see the latter.

One friend and assistant of mine, whom I will call Amo, by the early 1990s had been married to Habiba (also a pseudonym) for about 10 years, and the couple had remained childless. During the early years of their marriage there had been little concern about this, but later the couple became worried. In 1991, although he did not blame his wife directly for infertility and indeed conceded that he himself might be at fault, Amo began joking, in front of his visiting cousins, that he would soon have to contract another, polygynous marriage (to solve this problem of childlessness). Habiba approached me one evening and worriedly asked me whether I had any medicine for conceiving a child. She also saw herbalists, although their treatment produced little effect.

In 1992 Habiba and Amo traveled to the hospital in the town of Agadez, where Habiba underwent a gynecologic examination by Western-trained medical staff. Habiba, like many rural women, tended to be intimidated by outside medical personnel. In contrast to most other rural Tuareg women, however, she spoke some French, having been one of the first two girls to attend the local primary school in the early 1980s, and she had experienced greater-than-average contact with outsiders: she and her husband hosted me in the field, and Amo had previously worked for a French-directed livestock aid development program. Perhaps for these reasons, she willingly submitted to the exam. But she complained to me that the nurses and doctors there "were not nice to Tuareg from the countryside," and that "their medicines [prescribed] were too expensive." The hospital at Arlit, a mining town to the northwest, was reputed to be a better place. The couple did not go there, however, since this was farther away and the route was at the time dangerous, owing to banditry and fighting in the region.[6] The Agadez Hospital examination did not reveal any conclusive evidence of infertility on the part of Habiba.

During the rainy season of 1995, Amo saw several herbalist medicine women. Tekle diagnosed him as having a "cold" illness called *tessmut*.[7] She treated him with her *ilaten* remedies, steeped into a tea she instructed him to drink at home, adding that he should refrain from bathing for 10 days during this treatment. Amo also

saw another herbalist, a very elderly woman, with whom he had a lengthy, intimate conversation in private, during which she questioned him closely about his state of health and his relationship with his wife. In conversations with me afterward, Amo again expressed concern about the couple's childlessness and now indicated that he himself was "in good condition."

About 10 days after Amo's consultations with the herbalists, he arranged for a marabout, Eliman, to visit their home and conduct an examination diagnosing the cause of the couple's childlessness, followed by a ritual cure. Eliman arrived in the morning to perform Koranic divination techniques: *itran* (literally, "the stars," similar to the horoscope) and *alekhustara*, involving taking measurements of the patient and consulting Koranic verses. He also sacrificed a small goat as alms. Amo gave an advance payment of 20,000 Communauté Financiére Africaine francs (about $80) to the marabout. First, Eliman calculated numbers based on Habiba's and Amo's names. He spat three times on the measuring cord. He then measured Habiba's forearm length and also her waist with the cord. Then he calculated in the sand. He felt Habiba's ankle. The cord measure became longer: according to the marabout, "This means that the woman is less than fertile." Eliman stated that the cause was as follows: "it is a blocking from pills and from spirits who are against children." He described her state as "diminished and lacking" because of them.

Next, the marabout sacrificed the animal. This had to be a young, white, male goat of Habiba's, and its meat had to be eaten by the family and marabout at once. The meat must not dry, or this would undo the treatment. In three days, the patient would drink vegetal ink verses prepared by the marabout. The writing must be on a tablet never before used. Following this, the couple would subsequently eat three soft-boiled, shelled eggs (one and a half each) with the same writing on these eggs as on the tablet. This would have to be repeated three more times at intervals afterward. If the treatment was successful, the couple would give the marabout 1,500 francs more as payment later. Habiba would eat the lungs of the sacrificed kid goat.

The marabout slaughtered the goat and then butchered it with the help of Amo and a third party, a male friend of Amo's, distantly related on the paternal side. The marabout took part of the meat home. The intestines and liver were cooked with a little fat in a pot over the fire; these were eaten first. The women of the immediate family grilled the rest of the meat in the compound. They discarded the bladder, large intestine, and stomach contents. These women were Habiba's sisters-in-law, Amo's sisters; the couple had moved away from her parents after the obligatory first few years of postmarital residence there.

Eliman explained, "Childlessness or few children runs through women in certain families; this is inherited. We [marabouts] must do a calculation *[lisafe]* to find out which ones."

During the later stages of this treatment (particularly in the marabout's consultation/treatment ritual), the cause for the couple's childlessness, and the responsibility for curing it, became transferred to the wife. The herbal medicine women, particularly the second, elderly specialist Amo saw, facilitated this transfer.

Amo had earlier acknowledged the possibility of his own sterility, and he saw several herbalists who suspected the "cold" cause of childlessness. Amo seemed reluctant to settle for this diagnosis, however, and he also hesitated to complete the treatment, he told me, because of its requirement that he abstain from washing. Another herbalist, the elderly senior medicine woman, referred him to a marabout. In effect, in the final divination/diagnosis stage of the treatment, the consultation with Eliman transferred responsibility to the wife, Habiba, and also articulated men's interpretations in descent and identity, and reproduction. This is a microcosm of wider tensions and struggles in Tuareg society concerning female and male interests in matriliny, patriliny, pre-Islam, and Islam.

"Children of the Stomach" and "Children of Men": The Descent and Inheritance Conundrum

Kinship among the Kel Ewey, like many other Aïr Tuareg, is traced bilaterally, with vestiges of ancient matriliny combined with patrilineal institutions from Islam (Nicolaisen, *Ecology and Culture;* Murphy, "Social Distance" and "Tuareg Kinship"; Bernus; Casajus; Claudot-Hawad). Women own and inherit the tent constructed by elderly female relatives at their wedding. Men, however, construct, own, and more often inherit the mud house, which is on the increase in more sedentary Kel Ewey communities. The property forms called *akh huderan* (living milk) are intended to counterbalance Koranic inheritance. These include livestock and date palms that go to

sisters, daughters, and nieces and must not be shared, divided, or sold without replacement. They are compared to "alms." Kel Ewey Islamic scholars, however, state that this inheritance must be written specifically, with a witness, before death, or else they are considered Koranic, *takachit*: in this, one woman receives half of what one man receives. Islamic and patrilineal influences extend to political office, which goes from father to son, naming, which officially is Koranic, ideas about children's affiliation and identity, and marriage. Kel Ewey refer to offspring of a polygynous man and one of his co-wives as "children of men." An older form of naming a girl as "daughter of" (*oult*) tends to be disparaged as "only done with an illegitimate child," considered shameful and greatly stigmatizing to the mother. This tension between matriliny and patriliny is apparent in other statements about a child's identity. A child of mixed social origins—for example, of mixed noble and servile descent—takes the affiliation of his/her father. A child belongs to the descent group or clan of his or her father. A few characteristics are believed to be inherited from the same-sex parent (e.g., character), by social stratum (e.g., hair texture), and from maternal uncle (e.g., intelligence). Men insist that the secret Tamacheq name that older women bestow on the child the night before the official name day is "not important; it means nothing," whereas women argue that the latter is as important in the child's identity as the Arabic name from the Koran. A women's bridewealth (one camel) is held in trust for her by her father. Upon divorce, the marabout grants bridewealth reimbursement to whomever he rules is not at fault.

These struggles extend into mythology. Kel Ewey men tend to downplay matrilineal mythology. In discussions of local heroes outside the herbalist curing context, many men expressed admiration for Boulkhou and Kaousan, the former a founding marabout/warrior, the latter leader of the 1917 Tuareg Senoussi Revolt.[8] When one younger schoolboy mentioned Kahena, a Tuareg woman heroine who allegedly fought against Arabs and resisted Islam, older men present quickly dismissed this as "not a true story" and "not important." Only the female healers mentioned Tagurmat to me outright by name. One non-herbalist woman told me this story without pronouncing Tagurmat's name, from respect and also because her husband, a prominent marabout, was present.

Women and Men in
Conflict and Sociability

Despite economic independence and high social prestige of women, and freedom of social interaction between the sexes, long-standing currents—Islam and sedentization—have challenged these patterns. Many Kel Ewey men, in contrast to some other Tuareg, value virginity in brides and disapprove strongly of extramarital affairs. Although single, divorced, and widowed women are not stigmatized, are not necessarily destitute, and may engage in courtship, courtship is ideally supposed to include conversation, music, and poetry, not sexual relations. Women who give birth out of wedlock are ostracized socially, by other women as well as by men.[9] Women who initiate divorce upon a husband's contracting a polygynous marriage are not usually awarded bridewealth, because marabouts do not consider polygyny valid grounds; in such cases, the wife, not the husband, is viewed as being at fault in the Islamic legal ruling. While in principle children are supposed to remain with the mother in divorce, I knew of several men who forcibly removed them from the mother (Rasmussen 1995, 1996).

Men at home as economic middlemen stand between women and the marketplace and tie women more to the home in domestic tasks. For example, women send camels with male relatives on caravans, but unlike some other African women, they do not sell snacks or conduct market trade directly. Furthermore, as Schlegel (pp. 5–6) has pointed out regarding matrilineal societies, the problem anthropologists need to address is the allocation of authority in the domestic group. I noticed that men in more sedentized gardening households tended to give orders to their wives more than men in more nomadic households. Postmarital residence also has an impact upon power relations between the sexes in the household. During the first two to three years of marriage, the couple lives at the wife's natal residence until the husband has completed bridewealth payment and has "pleased" his parents-in-law with gifts of millet and household goods on demand, and sometimes, labor. If all goes well, the couple may then choose to either remain or to move away. Many men attempt virilocal residence at this point for the advantages of being near one's kin rather than one's affines. Many women refuse to follow, leading to eventual divorce, but some women do move near their husband's parents'

home, where the husband owns the land beneath the residential structures in the compound and exercises somewhat greater control over his wife than he would in uxorilocal residence.

The implications of this for young, childbearing-age women, whose fertility is one important focus of ritual curing by herbalist medicine women, are complex. Although maternal kinship remains important, in particular the brother-sister and mother-daughter relationships, among Kel Ewey this is challenged by male offspring of polygynous unions, whom men call "the children of men," and by husbands in virilocal residence and more sedentized households, particularly when the wife has small livestock herds, has given up herding, or even, occasionally, her tent. Elderly female relatives remain influential in arranging official "marriage of the family" (*tedua n eghiwan*), particularly on first marriage. Women often favor marriage between their own and their sisters' children ("family marriage") in order to keep the property within the family. Most marriages, however, are between distantly or unrelated persons, and such matches are often love marriages, particularly after the first marriage. These involve independent choice, but, significantly, Kel Ewey Tuareg of either sex call them "a man's marriage" *(tedua n elis)* and insist that "It is the man who chooses," although a woman may veto an unwelcome suitor, and forced marriages are rare. Some men contract independent marriages in second and third polygynous matches, against the wishes of the first wife, who is more often an arranged match.

Matrilineal Mythology,
Herbal Healing, and Gender

Women's bodies thus provide metaphoric idioms for relatedness and identity, but they also encode conflicts and discordant power currents. In their verbal storytelling and nonverbal enactment of the Tagurmat myth, medicine women convert the sacred and natural resources available to male and female powers into forms that are complementary. They render ancient matriliny more palatable to men, and Islam and patriliny more palatable to women. This collaboration comes at a price, however, for in mediating between natural and cultural forces symbolically associated with women's and men's interests, herbalists sometimes translate women's interests into more "domesticated" forms according to men's interests. But they also remind men of women's interests in repeating, throughout their diagnoses, the importance of female kinship, descent, and property interests.

Notes

Acknowledgements: Data for this article are based upon approximately seven years of residence and research in the Niger Republic, West Africa, between 1974 and 1995. In my projects on Tuareg female spirit possession, aging and the life course, and traditional healing specialists, I am grateful to the following: Fulbright Hays, Wenner-Gren Foundation, Social Science Research Council, National Geographic Society; Indiana University; and the University of Houston.

1. In the countryside, each noble family has a smith family attached to it. The latter sing praise-songs at noble name days and weddings; manufacture and repair tools, weapons, and jewelry for their patron family; dress noblewomen's hair; and serve as important ritual specialists, musicians, oral historians, and intermediaries. In the towns, smiths are tending toward more specialized roles as silversmiths and guides in tourism. For a comparison of Tuareg smiths and Islamic scholars or marabouts, see Rasmussen (1992, pp. 105–128). For a discussion of changing rural and urban Tuareg smith roles, see Rasmussen, "Art as Process," pp. 592–610.
2. See Rasmussen (1995, *Poetics and Politics*, pp. 14–27).
3. Thus far, there are no studies in Tuareg ethnography specifying the roles of herbal medicine women in context; mention is made only of male Islamic scholars and their religious amulets, and there are vague references to ungendered "sorcerers" (Foley; Bernus; Nicolaisen, "Essai," pp. 113–162). For example, Nicolaisen (pp. 150–156), in an early article on Tuareg religion and cosmology, briefly mentions the divining specialty and the "pact with the spirits" but does not explore their role at length, nor does he discuss herbalism at all. Bernus (p. 122) mentions that in certain illnesses, the patient chooses a curer standing in a particular kinship relation—the cross-cousin—or on the basis of a particular characteristic, but he does not elaborate on this or specify with case studies in social context.
4. In the Tamacheq language, there are numerous terms for such forces, reflecting the large number of concepts and categories of ritual/cosmological power: for example, *tehot* or *togershet* approximately denote "evil mouth" or the powers of gossip or speech *(awal)* (the latter is a neutral term but is often used, at least by Kel Ewey, in a negative sense); and smiths' allegedly malevolent mystical powers, activated involuntarily upon nobles' refusal to comply with requests for presents, an obligation in the client-patron relationships (these powers are called, variously, *tezma* and *ettama).* For analysis of the fine distinctions of these forces, see Nicolaisen ("Essai" and *Ecology*), Casajus, and Rasmussen (1989, 1992). In the study of African cosmological power, I am particularly inspired by such works as Buckley and Gottlieb (1988), Arens and Karp (1989), Boddy (1989), and Gottlieb.
5. The head in Tuareg medical and psychiatric theory is associated with intelligence, as opposed, as in some Western formulations, to the sentiments. In female spirit possession, spirits are believed to enter through the stomach and intestines, lodge in the liver for a while, and then proceed up into the head. In cases of spirit possession, herbal medicine women often diagnose this: while feeling the stomach, they find "spirits dancing" there, and they refer such cases to marabouts. In their diagnosis of possession, marabouts measure the head. Some spirits do not respond to Koranic cures, and marabouts thus in turn refer such cases to the musical exorcism ritual specialists. See Rasmussen, *Spirit Possession,* for an ethnography of Tuareg spirit possession rituals called *tende n goumaten,* beyond the scope of this essay.
6. Since the mid-1980s Niger has been suffering economic and political crises. There was a transition from military to parliamentary government, policies toward privatization of the economy and, with the April 1995 pact, regional autonomy. Austerity programs, general shortages of medicines and food, and unemployment have also been serious problems throughout the country, although the northern region became more isolated during the rebellion and suffered from lack of trade and tourism revenues. There followed a military coup d'état in January 1995 and as of this writing, future trends are difficult to predict.

7. This term is a gloss or cover term for "cold illnesses," which include a variety of afflictions opposed to "hot illnesses." Local medical and curing theory resembles the Moorish and Latin American humoral and counteractive theories. "Cold" illness in Tuareg medicine often refers to urinary problems and venereal diseases.

8. Boulkhou was the male founder of the local descent group, Igurmaden, recognized by most men, particularly in the chiefly and maraboutique families. He was a marabout/warrior hero who sank the first well, constructed the first mosque, and resisted enemies by mystical amulets, remaining suspended, according to legend, in a well, hanging by a thread, for 40 days. He is the genealogically traced ancestor of the current local chief, whose family inherited the *ettebel* drum, the chiefly insignia, from him through the paternal line. Men and Islamic scholars encouraged me to collect stories about Boulkhou rather than Tagurmat. Kaousan was the leader of the Tuareg Senoussi Revolt against the French in 1917. See Salifou (1973).

9. See Rasmussen, "Female Sexuality," pp. 433–462).

Further Reading

Bernus, Edmond, *Touaregs Nigériens*, Paris: ORSTOM, 1981

Bird, Charles, and Ivan Karp, eds., *Explorations in African Systems of Thought*, Bloomington: Indiana University Press, 1980

Casajus, Dominique, *La Tente Dans la Solitude: La Société et les Morts Chez les Touaregs Kel Ferwan*, Cambridge, New York, and Paris: Cambridge University Press, 1987

Chesler, Phyllis, *Women and Madness*, Garden City, New York: Doubleday, 1972; London: Allen Lane, 1974

Claudot-Hawad, Hélène, *Les Touaregs: Portrait en Fragments*, Aix-en-Provence, France: Edisud, 1993

Foley, Henry Ti, *Moeurs et Médecine des Touareg de l'Ahaggar*, Algiers: Imprimerie La Typo-Litho, 1930

Gottlieb, Alma, *Under the Kapok Tree: Identity and Difference in Beng Thought*, Bloomington: Indiana University Press, 1992

MacCormack, Carol, and Marilyn Strathern, eds., *Nature, Culture, and Gender*, Cambridge and New York: Cambridge University Press, 1980

Murphy, Robert, "Social Distance and the Veil," *American Anthropologist* 66 (1964)

———, "Tuareg Kinship," *American Anthropologist* 69 (1967)

Nicolaisen, Johannes, *Ecology and Culture of the Pastoral Tuareg*, Copenhagen, Denmark: National Museum of Copenhagen, 1963

———, "Essai sur la religion et la magie touaregues," *Folk* 3 (1961)

Rasmussen, Susan J., "Art as Process and Product: Patronage and the Problem of Change in Tuareg Blacksmith/Artisan Roles," *Africa: Journal of the International Africa Institute* 65:4 (1995)

———, "Female Sexuality, Social Reproduction, and the Politics of Medical Intervention in Niger: Kel Ewey Tuareg Perspectives," *Culture, Medicine, and Psychiatry* 18 (1994)

———, "Lack of Prayer: Ritual Restrictions, Social Experience, and the Anthropology of Menstruation Among the Tuareg," *American Ethnologist* 18:4 (November 1991)

———, *The Poetics and Politics of Tuareg Aging: Life Course and Personal Destiny in Niger*, DeKalb: Northern Illinois University Press, 1997

———, "Ritual Specialists, Ambiguity, and Power in Tuareg Society," *Man: The Journal of the Royal Anthropological Institute* 27:1 (1992)

———, "Speech by Allusion: Voice and Authority in Tuareg Verbal Art," *Journal of Folklore Research* 29:2 (May–August 1992)

———, *Spirit Possession and Personhood Among the Kel Ewey Tuareg*, Cambridge: Cambridge University Press, 1995

———, "The Tent as Cultural Symbol and Field Site: Social and Symbolic Space, 'Topos,' and Authority in a Tuareg Community," *Anthropological Quarterly* 69:1 (January 1996)

Schlegel, Alice, *Male Dominance and Female Autonomy*, New Haven, Connecticut: HRAF, 1972

Strathern, Marilyn, ed., *Dealing with Inequality: Analysing Gender Relations in Melanesia and Beyond*, Cambridge: Cambridge University Press, 1987

Szasz, Thomas, *The Manufacture of Madness: A Comparative Study of the Inquisition and the Mental Health Movement*, New York: Harper & Row, 1970; London: Routledge and Kegan Paul, 1971

Tunisian Storytelling Today

Sabra Webber

Sabra Webber takes a look at the varieties of sto-rytelling in use in Tunisia, with special attention to contemporary women tellers.

The Role of Storytelling in Tunisian Life

The great fourteenth-century historiographer and sociologist Ibn Khaldun whose family were refu-gees to Tunis from Andalusia, recorded oral leg-ends among Bedouin tribes of the Bani Hilal tribes that had thundered into North Africa al-most half a millennium before but had been de-feated for over two centuries. These stories, which can still be found in Tunisia and around the Arab world, are indicative of the role that story-telling has played and still plays in Tunisian cul-ture today. People such as Ibn Khaldun who have been settled and urban-minded for a very long time tell stories that conflict with, problematize, and reinforce their own lifestyles.

Women, most of whom have been secluded un-til the last few decades and who still tend to stay close to home, together imagine life as women warriors of Bedouin tribes; as educated, wealthy women; and as women on a quest, traveling the world seeking justice or a husband and so on. Men who are settled and loath to leave home for a week or a weekend also tell of adventurous times and characters—often these are stories of themselves or friends as young men who left town for employment, as war refugees, as students, and as pilgrims. Men too tell stories of warrior women and of educated, wealthy women. Men and women tell stories of trips into dream worlds and what they brought back with them. In the telling of these stories, the new or different worlds are imagined and tried out while the storyteller re-mains anchored in the familiar. These well-worn

stories are interwoven with innovative verbal constructions, the props at hand, and audience commentary. Every traditional storytelling is bal-anced by its innovative elements.

Officially, colloquial Arabic narratives and most oral colloquial artistic speech (with the possi-ble exception of proverbs) are not held in high es-teem—a fact that has been noted repeatedly in essays on traditional aesthetic culture in the Arab world—but there may be positive as well as nega-tive consequences to this. Because of the rivalry of modern standard and classical Arabic and the tran-scendence of poetry over prose, Tunisian folk nar-rative may stand a better chance of avoiding the co-optation and sterilization by government offi-cials, pedagogues, and others that has befallen oral culture in other parts of the world (such as has be-fallen government-sponsored *malouf* music and Ramadan *rawi* performances in Tunisia). The tales—those subversive "weapons of the weak" (Scott, 1976) provide a vehicle for counterhege-monic discourses and are easily available to women, children, the poor, the colonized, those suffering from oppressive government of one sort or another—are less likely to be noticed or ascribed much importance by the establishment. Still, the self-perceived power of narrators and their self-perceived role in providing a narrative vehicle with which to expand the social world does not seem particularly hidden. "My story goes on and on and your evening meals are all in my stomach," asserts one teller's rhymed, formulaic conclusion. In an ex-cerpt from a formulaic introduction an old crone recites (speaking for all elderly female taletellers?), "I can't bear narrowness, may I never have to put up with it" (Hejaiej, 1996). (On the other hand, the post-independence discouraging of public recit-

356

als of professional male *rawi* storytellers has spun male storytelling into the private, not-for-profit, sphere. Men's stories have moved away somewhat from the fabulous, lengthy, or legendary and toward the personal and the communal—genres more suited to insertion in conversations in coffeehouses, small shops, or living rooms.) Unofficially, anyone with a way with words is distinguished and celebrated while alive and remembered fondly and quoted after their lives have ended. Despite the advent of television and of various public entertainments, social interaction revolving around language is the centerpiece of entertainment.

In Tunisia, storytellers do not mature early. It is unusual for a young man or woman to be able to "story," and storytellers do not usually grow into their art form before the age of 40 or so. Still, younger women, especially, may have developed storytelling skills as they cared for younger siblings or the children of a master, or as an intellectual and emotional outlet when they were prevented from attending school.

Traditional storytelling in Tunisia does not mean 'oral culture' in all cases. There is a good deal of interplay between the oral and written and between the classical (or modern standard) Arabic and colloquial Arabic. Those educated Tunisians with access to stories in written form retell them orally, and often in the evenings educated men read aloud stories like "1001 Nights" to other men or female relatives. Even illiterate women and men can understand something of classical Arabic, especially since the advent of radio and television. Doubtless the three media (oral narrative, silent reading, and reading aloud to an audience) enhance each other as does the exchange of narratives and narrative techniques and talents that take place as large numbers of men (and some women) travel from place to place in search of work or education.

Since the advent of television and especially the satellite dish, storytelling has slipped from a leisure time to a work activity for women. Many stories are told while women are preparing their year's supply of tomato paste, or sweets, or couscous. For men, though, the television in the café seems to have declined as an attraction over the past 20 years. Those who choose to go out to cafés or to get together in their shops seem to be returning to cards, chess and other board games, and conversation; watching television has become more of a household than a public activity because most households now have a television.

There are still "professional storytellers" available for women—the itinerant fortune-tellers, women who still appear routinely in the streets advertising their talent to describe the physical ills and heartaches of their customers and prescribe a proper course of action. Among other stories, riddles or rhymes she might recite, the itinerant fortune-teller may construct stories that feature the women who invite her into their homes—their lives become worthy of her artful telling, set to her odd rhythms and rhymes. By her very presence, a little controlled danger and adventure is introduced into the periphery of a woman's life. A stranger is admitted to the veranda, porch, or courtyard who introduces questionable, perhaps even dangerous, supernatural practices to spice up a rare time of summer afternoon boredom for the mistress of the house and her women friends and relatives. The women's familiar life stories become strange on the lips of a mysterious, dangerous (both because of the reputations of fortune-tellers as thieves and robbers and because of their magical powers) gypsylike woman from who knows where, who travels with a husband and children or a woman companion and sleeps under the stars each night.

Narrative Genres

It should be remembered in a discussion of categories of narrative for any Arab country that regions and even cities have their own categories of classification with significant overlaps from person to person and group to group, and that the categories often do not conform to what are, after all, very recent national boundaries. Even within Tunisia, one has to pay attention to context to decide on the use of any particular term at any particular time. In general, though, one finds oral stories divided into three categories: "true" stories (personal experience narratives, tall tales, or local legends), fantasy stories (resembling fairy tales, folk tales, or märchen), and epics (accounts of tribal heroes and heroines). In Tunisia, the first category of narratives are frequently referred to as *hikayat*, the second as *khurafat*, and the third as *seeyar*. The second and third are festooned with simple or elaborate introductory and closing formulas, but *hikayat* are less heavily guarded—allowing easier transition from conversation to story and back again (Webber, 1991). In addition, of course, there is much overlap among genres so that a story can also be a riddle (a neck riddle, for example) and a proverb can have a story attached to it. True stories can have a dose of the fantastic and vice versa. Lines from stories that people know in common are evoked in everyday conversation, which always produces smiles of recognition at the aptness to a current topic.

A *Khurafah*

In 1974 a young married woman living in Tunis who was from the small Mediterranean town of Kelibia told the following story that contains many elements typical of a traditional *khurafah*.

There was a man and that man didn't have children. He prayed, "Oh God, if I can have a boy or a girl, the wealth that I have will all be spent on the child." (Because he was very rich.) Well, God gave him a son and that son was spoiled, taken wherever he wanted to go, and dressed in the finest clothes. That is to say, all the man's wealth did go to that boy.

Well sirs, the wealth was almost gone and yet he always indulged that boy—dressed him and took him everywhere until his wealth was gone and he became poor. Well, he rented a shop and lived there—he, his wife, and his son. The son said, "Oh father, I still want something." "You still lack something? My wealth has all been spent on you and I promised God I would not keep anything from you." The son said, "I still need something." "What do you lack?" He said, "A horse and a gun." "A horse and a gun? I do not have the money to buy them for you, but I promised God I would not keep any of my resources from you. Take me and sell me and buy a horse and take your mother and buy a gun." The son said, "Oh father, how can I sell you and sell mother?" His father said, "No, never mind, sell me." He went and sold his father and bought a horse and sold his mother and bought a gun with her.

When he rode on the horse he was riding on his father and holding his mother . . . because he sold his mother and bought a gun with her. That boy went out in the country and hunted and traveled around and indulged himself until he no longer wanted to. While he was hunting, he became thirsty, was about to die from thirst, but he found that the horse was drenched with sweat from running so he wiped up the sweat with his hand and drank it. "Well, I've indulged myself enough."

He went and sold his horse and sold his gun and went and rented a small store near a town and bought a lute and sat in the store amusing himself. He slept in the store. When he went into the town he found the castle walls adorned with cut-off heads. The king was cutting off the heads of men. He went to the dry goods store and asked the merchant, "Brother, can you tell me the story of the heads on the castle walls?" "Do you want sugar, do you want tea?" (He didn't want to tell. He was afraid.) He left and found the vegetable seller. He said to him, "Please brother, why are those heads . . . ?" "Do you want some parsley, do you want some onions?" (He didn't want to say.) He left. He thought, "What shall I do? Who will tell me?" He went to the barber. He went to him and said, "Please don't disappoint me . . . I'm a stranger . . . and tell me what the story is." The barber said, "Brother, if the king heard us he wouldn't like it." "Tell me, never mind." "Alright, the daughter of the king is very intelligent and young and beautiful. She told her father she wanted to be engaged and the man to whom she became engaged had to be more intelligent than she. [Because she was very intelligent.] Whoever wanted to become engaged to her was obliged to give her a story and she had to discover to what it alluded. If she did, they would cut off his head and put it on the wall." He said, "Is that all?"

He went home and in the morning when the government opened he went in and said, "Sirs, I heard about you" and so forth and so on. They said, "Are you aware of the story?" He said, "I'm aware." They said, "Have you seen the walls decorated with heads?" He said, "I've seen." They said, "You are playing against that." He said, "I'm willing." They said to him, "Look out, my son, you'll loose your head." "It doesn't matter." They said, "At your service."

They took him into a big room. The judges who were going to write the decision, the cabinet, and the king were there, and the girl was there behind a curtain—not sitting with the people. They were all sitting there and she said, "Give me what you have." He said to her,

It's about he who rode on his father
And held his mother

*And drank water which neither came from the
   earth
Or fell from the sky.*

She paced around, looked through many
books . . . nothing. She couldn't find the answer. She got angry and said to him, "Tomorrow." (She had three days.) Well, he agreed,
left, and the judges inscribed that that day, she
hadn't found the answer.

The next day, he returned. He said, "Do you
want another puzzle or the same one?" She
said, "The same as yesterday." She searched
and searched but couldn't find the answer.
When it was time for him to go home she went
to her servant, a black woman, and said, "Follow him and see where he goes. Let him go and
you stay close behind. When he enters his
house, mark it."

Well, he went along and she followed. She followed until he went in his shop and she
marked it. She went home and said, "Mistress,
he is a foreigner, not from here. He's in a shop
and I marked it." She put on men's clothes and
dressed her servant also in men's clothes and
took horses and guns and snuck away from her
father and left. They got to the shop. (Knock
Knock) He said, "Who is it?" (They were listening to the lute and he was enjoying himself.)
"Who is it?" "Guests of God." "At your service, guests of God. At your service." He
opened the door and brought them in and gave
them all he had to drink. They sat around telling stories and they said to him, "Brother, in
your town, why are the walls decorated with
heads?" "Oh, that daughter of the king believes herself very intelligent. She won't take a
husband unless he is smarter than she is. Everyone who goes to her gives her a question. If
she can answer it, they cut off his head and
decorate the walls with it. I participated in this
story and I'm going to beat her." "Good for
you, by goodness, beat her. Please tell us the
story you gave to her." He told them this and
this and this. He told her the question. They
said, "What is it about?" He told that he had
sold his father and bought a horse and sold his
mother and bought a gun and the water he
drank was the horse's sweat. She understood
everything. They said good-bye, goodnight,
and went home. They said again, "By good-

ness, go beat her, take her." "OK!" Well, they
went out, he shut the door and returned. He
returned and saw her handkerchief had fallen.
He picked it up and knew it was the king's
daughter who came. Her name was written on
it. He put it away and the next morning went
back."

Now she was happy because she was going to
win. He said, "Shall I give you another or do
you want that one?" She said, "The same one
as yesterday." He recited it. She pretended to
search her books (tiff, ton, ton, ton) . . . She
said, "It can only be one thing. He must have
sold his father and bought a horse with him
and sold his mother and bought a gun with her
and the water . . . water . . . water . . . Maybe
he was thirsty and there wasn't water so he
took the sweat of the horse and drank it." He
said to her, "It's not finished." She said,
"What?" He said,

*It's about the little birds that came to us
And with whom we were happy and glad
They went and left us
And let fall a feather from a wing.*

She understood. She said to the judges, "Write
the marriage contract." He got half of the
kingdom of her father and married her. (Because if he took out the handkerchief, her father would have killed her because she
cheated.)

The structure of this "neck riddle" has been
around a long time and is very similar, for example, to the structure of the Biblical neck riddle of
Samson and the honey. Yet, it is timely in its portrayal of female power, especially in 1974 when
the first postcolonial generation of young women
were making choices about marriage, higher education, and so on. Here is an unmarried, educated
princess insisting on choosing a husband, going
out at night disguised as a man (evocative of the
famous medieval ruler of Baghdad going out in
the city at night disguised as a commoner). The
portrayal of boys as overindulged is also timely.
(See Hejaiej 1996 for a discussion of many of
these features in Tunisian tales.)
   This story is one of many that begins with the
wish for a child and rash promises to God or to a
supernatural agent. Sometimes the child is promised to an ogre when the child reaches a certain

age and other times the "child" might take an unusual shape, a cooking pot, for example. In Sirat Beni Hilal, the hero's mother wishes for a child even if it is as black as a blackbird that she encounters at the time of her wish—which subsequently raises paternity issues. In this story, though, the teller rushes through the story of the indulged boy, giving us just enough information to understand the riddle when it comes, and doesn't stop to linger until she reaches the story of the princess. The raconteur's creative energy is put into play only when we encounter the educated, adventurous, husband-seeking princess and her effect on the town and on the young man who "has indulged himself enough." Then she takes her artistic time and slows down to add some nice touches. Here we get a clue as to the teller's aesthetic sensibilities and thus to what she wants foregrounded in her narrative. The lute is a nice touch. Mentioned twice, it is indicative of an indulged boy becoming a young man—sensitive and artistic (the lute), practical, settled, and thrifty (the shop as both home and place of business), but still a confident risk taker (the duel with the princess). The responses of the two merchants are other artistic touches. "Do you want sugar . . ." and the contrasting response of the stereotypical chatty barber. Then, there is the artistic touch of the princess's fake guesses ("and the water . . . water . . . water") and the sound effects as she flips through the books in her library searching for answers that she already knows.

Why did the young teller choose this story to tell to an American scholar in the presence of her own and my Tunisian "mother," both of whom were illiterate? What kinds of issues was she grappling with? Did she regret discontinuing her education and choosing marriage and children at a young age? I do not think she knew yet, but she surely was aware of having made some important choices, and that awareness may have influenced the narrative she chose and how she told it. It is an unfinished story that is told as she is just beginning her own adulthood. She brings up issues that explore or question the possible repercussions of becoming involved with promises to the supernatural, challenges to the powerful (the educated, the rich, rulers), and deception. She introduces timely topics such as choice in marriage, child rearing and children, education—all in the context of two riddles that one cannot answer unless (or until) one has lived them. The story as the young woman uses it is not a static image, but a dynamic

resource for me and for her and other members of the audience "to be modified as future experience dictates" (Braid, 1996, 26). In an exaggerated way, the princess is where we were in those days, on the brink of new experiences.

The Study of Expressive Culture

Folklore, the study of traditional expressive culture, is an important means by which to understand a culture's affective dimension, a culture's sentiment, that centripetal force that holds a culture together (or doesn't) in the face of economic hardships, tyrannies, or natural crises. Yet, the production of artistic speech is also an area in which concepts of the Other are likely to be, "unfamiliar . . . or complicated . . . [and where] the important ones tend to be both." Still, as John R. Bowlin and Peter G. Stromberg observe, the issue facing ethnographic research continues to be one of translation and not a question of fundamentally incomparable psychologies or mindsets (Bowlin and Stromberg, 1997). They argue that "belief and sentiment always come jumbled together . . . [so that] . . . we inevitably think and talk about sentiment by appealing to concepts we employ to think and talk about other things" (131). If "cultures do not . . . have fundamentally different responses to the world," then study of the production of traditional artistic speech such as narrative is fundamental to cross-cultural insight (132). And if, as Dell Hymes and others have argued, narrative is privileged as a way of making sense of experience, including cross-cultural encounters, of course, then I would maintain that narrative processes of one culture cannot finally be studied in isolation from those of other cultures. Studying traditional narrative processes cross-culturally avoids the kind of parochialism that sets in when narratives are isolated and described with little regard to similar processes in other cultures. Careful study and "translation" of sameness and differences in uses of narrative sequences, figures of speech, genre conventions, metanarrative, listeners' expectations, framing, and so on can collapse barriers that we erect if we assume "fundamentally different ethnopsychologies one from another . . . [or] . . . fundamentally different emotional responses to the world" (Bowlin and Stromberg, 1997, 130).

As we attempt to describe cultural constructions of meaning in narrative form, such a comparative approach seeks to find commonality in the storytelling processes and strategies as well as in what stories do for listeners in a community and for their authors and tellers—what they "mean." Such an approach helps avoid "othering" narratives of the non-Western world, and discourages the kind of political posturing, subtle or otherwise, that sometimes accompanies folklore presentations by cultural advocates for one culture or another. A volume such as this one in its very conception recognizes that there exist large areas of commonality among narratives rather than fundamental differences and that these will come into focus as scholars grapple with honest "translations" of the narrative process. Obviously, the young woman who recounted the neck riddle above assumed some commonality with me—some issues that we would both be interested in grappling with given our similar ages and our educations. This volume provides an opportunity to begin to collapse some barriers, to see a particularity in the medium that can be celebrated cross-culturally and thus to pinpoint the differences by comparing not products—narratives—as has been done in the past, but processes (use of rhetorical strategies that include shared histories and other contextual features) and intent, the kinds of truths these strategies are in the service of.

Further Reading

Ayoub, A., "The Hilali Epic: Material and Memory," *Revue d'Histoire Maghrebine* (1984)

Baklouti, Naceur, *Contes populaires de Tunisie,* Sfax, Tunisia: Institut National d'Archéologie et d'Arts, 1988

Benattar, S.C., *Le Bled en lumière Folklore Tunisien,* Paris: Tallandier, 1923

Bouquero de Voligny, R., *Tunis derriere les murs Contes et legends,* Tunis, Tunisia, 1993

Bowlin, John R., and Peter G. Stromberg, "Representation and Reality in the Study of Culture," *American Anthropologist* 99:1 (1997)

Braid, Donald, "Personal Narrative and Experiential Meaning," *Journal of American Folklore* 109:431 (1996)

Guiga, Tahar, *La Geste Hilalienne,* L'Organisation Egyptienne Générale du Livre, 1978

Hejaiej, Monia, *Behind Closed Doors: Women's Oral Narratives in Tunis,* New Brunswick, New Jersey: Rutgers University Press, 1996; London: Quartet, 1996

Hymes, Dell, "The Grounding of Performance and Text in a Narrative View of Life," *Alcheringa* 4:1 (1978)

Laroui, Abdelaziz, *Vieux Contes de Tunise,* Tunis, Tunisia: Maison Tunisienne de l'édition, 1978

Marzuqi, Muhammad, *Al-Adab al-Sha'bi fi Tunis,* Tunis, Tunisia: Maison Tunisienne de l'édition, 1968

———, *Al-Jaziya al-Hilalyya,* Tunis, Tunisia: Maison Tunisienne de l'édition, 1971

———, *Hassuna al-Lili,* Tunis, Tunisia: Maison Tunisienne de l'édition, 1976

Webber, Sabra J., *Romancing the Real: Folklore and Ethnographic Representation in North Africa,* Philadelphia: University of Pennsylvania Press, 1991

———, "Women's Folk Narratives and Social Change," in *Women and the Family in the Middle East: New Voices of Change,* edited by Elizabeth Fernea, Austin: University of Texas Press, 1985

Native America

Storytelling and Teaching: A Cree Example

Kay Stone

Kay Stone discusses the use of story by Cree elder Nathaniel Queskekapow with her university folklore classes. Queskekapow selected stories and prepared questions relating to his tales in a pointed attempt to teach through his stories.

Traditional Tales in a University Setting

The Cree of Manitoba say that traditional narratives are only told in winter so that certain hibernating reptiles and lizards, for example, will not steal the stories. When questioned Nathaniel Queskekapow, a Cree elder from Norway House reserve in north central Manitoba, responded with his usual touch of humor:

Yes, it is not true that lizards would steal away the stories in summer. But now, there are people who love to hear legends and stories and steal away that golden age and sell them and become rich. That is why I don't write down any stories in books. (letter, February 23, 1983)

Nathaniel Queskekapow visited Winnipeg at the invitation of anthropologist Gary Granzberg, who had worked with him in the north.[1] For the next several years he made regular visits for his own purposes, agreeing to tell stories in our classes when he had time. The stories he told included genres that narrative scholars might define, in European-American terms, as personal experience narratives, tall tales, legends, fables, wondertales, and myths (sacred tales). Queskekapow called them all "legends," not for any lack of consciousness about their differences, but as a statement about their connection with truth. Even the narratives that we would consider fictional were, in his words, "false stories with true meaning." He told them in a low-key conversational style with little gesturing or facial expression. He showed no hesitancy in expressing himself even though he was speaking in a foreign language in an unfamiliar setting.

Queskekapow brought his stories south to Winnipeg because he felt that telling and hearing these stories in the proper season would, in his words, "teach white people about what happened to my Cree people." He stressed the educational function of the stories by handing out his own lists of questions after each one. The fact that both he and his narratives were out of their usual cultural context did not bother Queskekapow at all, since his motive was to teach; he used the stories in much the same way when he taught Cree language classes at Rossville school at Norway House. It was the students at the University of Winnipeg who were "out of context" in terms of Cree culture and language, so he adapted his approach by telling the stories in English (and once in Cree as well), often sending his handwritten text in advance with questions that were meant to guide students in understanding the stories; these queries revealed his own perceptions of the stories and underlined his very conscious role as a teacher in our university classes. A letter he wrote to me in 1978 is signed, "from your Cree teacher, Nathaniel Queskekapow." His idiosyncratic English and his lack of formal education beyond elementary school did not make him at all self-conscious in front of university classes; quite the opposite, it gave him opportunities to contrast Cree and white educational traditions and to offer his own method as an alternative, teaching through storytelling.

Queskekapow did not dissuade others from telling his stories as teaching stories; in fact he encouraged the students to do so, but insisted that these never be written down. With this in mind I would like to describe but not reproduce some of the dozen or so that he told over a period of several years and report his comments on them in order to spread his teaching beyond Manitoba.

In order to keep the focus on Queskekapow and his own reasons for choosing to tell certain stories I will present them, as well as I remember, in chronological order. I was not formally studying him or his stories but listening along with my classes, myself a "student" trying to learn what he was teaching. Thus my presentation will by necessity be anecdotal.

The Teller, Nathaniel Queskekapow

Nathaniel Queskekapow was born in 1921 at Norway House reserve on Lake Winnipeg. He has been a hunter and trapper, and fisherman, a teacher of Cree, and a school janitor, among other things. After his mother's death in 1930 his father sent him to a residential school for seven years, which he remembers with both bitterness and humor. He used his experiences there to comment on problems with white and native educational practices.

Queskekapow was in his 50s when I first met him in 1975. He was of medium height and build with an alert face; he wore the well-used baseball cap that came to be a trademark. As a favor to his friend Gary Granzberg he had agreed to tell a story in my folklore class, and we expected a traditional Cree narrative. Instead he began a rambling personal story about taking his family out on a picnic and trying to hunt for food, but having to settle for duck eggs that his children had found. We understood that we were having our collective legs pulled when he described how the duck eggs hatched out and flew away when heated in a kettle of boiling water. When he finished the story he said, "That's the end," and sat down with a smile. I realized that he was testing us to see how much we knew about Cree life—and we knew very little indeed. The very first line describing a picnic would probably have identi-

fied the story as "tall tale" to a Cree listener, but we had to get all the way to the unlikely hatching before we understood. That was the only story he told that day, though when he met my young son Nathaniel he agreed to come back again; he loved telling stories to children who were curious about the world, especially a child with the same name as his own. For him that was no coincidence.

I did not see him again for two years. When he came to my class again (first making certain that "Little Nathaniel" would be there), he told a more traditional legend about a woman who loses her young child and is guided by a raven, who gives her black cotton and instructs her to make a dress that "will never wear out, even though you go in thick bush"; she is firmly instructed: "Unless you obey you will not find it, if you don't believe, your child will be lost forever." She does obey, and on the fourth day finds her son, now a young man, and they return together "full of joy and courage." He had already sent an English text of the story and eight questions to Gary Granzberg with a copy to me. Granzberg wrote an article on this story alone, underlining the symbolic and archetypal depth of the story that makes it applicable to the immediate context and situation (in this case a university classroom) and also the wider context of Cree history and culture.[2] Queskekapow's answers to his own queries all related to education. The last question was, "Why did Raven give the woman black cotton?" and his answer was, "Remember black cotton is Education. Wear it and obey."

Hearing and obeying became a strong theme in all the stories he told over the next decade. In contrast to European tales, in which a protagonist often succeeds by doing exactly the opposite, in many Cree tales protagonists succeed because they do precisely what they are told. Granzberg noted that this story "symbolizes the Cree belief that education cannot work unless there is belief, obedience and fear" (Granzberg 1978, 4), and quoted Queskekapow who felt that white education lacked these qualities.

The next two stories he told also emphasized obedience. Both featured small boys rescued and educated by animals, the first a bear and the second a mouse. In each case the boys were dutiful and respectful, and grew up to become leaders of their people. In his written text of "Mouse Who Saved the Little Boy" he added the subtitle, "Little Things Makes Great." In his list of fourteen questions he answered only the last one about the importance of little things: "Little things make you wealthy, healthy and wise" (handwritten text, 1983). He concluded by asking, "And what is your answer?" emphasizing that education was not only obedience but also interaction and self-reliance.

He underlined balancing obedience with independence in his telling of the traditional Cree narrative of Iyas, variants of which are found from Labrador through the Canadian prairies.[3] In this lengthy and complex heroic adventure, a young man abandoned by his father is aided by various supernatural beings—giant gulls, an underwater monster, and a red fox who instructs him to pay attention to his dreams (visions); he returns to save his mother, defeat his evil father, and destroy the world with arrows of fire, after which he and his mother transform themselves into birds that herald the coming of the new world—spring—every year. In this classic narrative, the protagonist is victorious because he follows the advice of his helpers and also because he uses his own resources and follows his visions. Here Queskekapow mentioned the vision quest that used to be central in Cree culture before white education replaced traditional teaching.[4]

Two or three years passed before Queskekapow was able to tell stories at the university again. His narratives moved from the world of two-legged humans to four-legged animals; in the next two years he told stories in which moose were the central characters. Each expressed his belief that traditional Cree teaching and white schooling were both essential.

The first story, written down by Queskekapow in 1985, was very specific in expressing his belief that traditional Cree methods alone were not enough to prepare young people to live in the contemporary world. His text began with an implied riddle: "Here is the story about the left and right, with sticks and string and the blade." The moose are assembled in council, awaiting the appearance of a mysterious figure, Left and Right. The bull moose warns the others not to accept the pipe that Left and Right will offer. A bull calf disobeys and takes the pipe, leaps up and runs away, is chased and wounded by Left and Right, but lives to tell the tale.

Queskekapow had seven questions for this enigmatic story, and this time he answered them himself—but also asked students to send him their own answers. His questions reveal that Left and Right is a man walking on two legs and his

weapons (bow and arrow, knife) are dangerous; moose can no longer accept the pipe from humans. The young moose who disobeys suffers, but survives to teach. The sixth question, "What is the pipe for?" is answered by Queskekapow in no uncertain terms: "The pipe is for temptation."

The story he told the following year was equally enigmatic, and also featured moose, a primary source of meat for the Cree. On the surface it was a simpler story, but carried even greater symbolic weight for Queskekapow than did the previous tale. Two moose are walking in the woods when they are startled by a strange noise (gunfire) and begin to run; one moose is struck on the antler and loses it, wants to retrieve it but is told by the other moose, "Don't be crazy! Run for your life!" The questions Queskekapow wrote out were even longer than the story, and had their own title: "In your own thinking regarding of the native tradition and culture." The questions detailed the ways in which the Cree people lost their culture, language, and traditional ways of teaching their children, losses he equated with the moose losing an antler to the unknown hunter. He made it clear that the loss of culture and language was devastating, but that it was a mistake to go backwards to find the lost antler—or to be tempted by the traditional pipe.

The last story Nathaniel Queskekapow told in our anthropology and folklore classes was more surprising than the previous moose narratives. The text he sent in advance was in Cree syllabics and illustrated with marginal sketches, but it was a European tale. He titled it "Maski Parch (Half Chick)" but the text was "Chicken Little." He did not refer to its European origin—it was, for him, simply another narrative available for symbolic interpretation. His text, which he read in Cree and then told in English, was only nine lines long. A leaf falls on Half Chick's head and he goes to tell the king that the sky is falling; the king, dressed in a uniform that a looks like the RCMP (Canadian Mounties) says, simply and firmly, "You're a liar." In this concise story Queskekapow managed to express how the sky fell on the Cree but the white world denied the reality of the loss of the traditions world (the lost antler). This simple tale is a forceful example of how stories express objective reality in symbolic ways.

As I thought back over these stories and reflected on their significance in teaching, it seemed to me as if the characters in them matured each year: young boys in the first stories were in early stages of education where fear, obedience and respect were central; in the story of Iyas the protagonist is older and thus needs to do more than simply obey; in the moose stories there is a struggle to adapt Cree and white educational values. In "Chicken Little," the most pessimistic of his teaching stories, it seems that the loss is irreparable. The inadequacy of white education in particular was underlined by Granzberg, who noted that, according to Queskekapow, it failed because Cree values were absent: "There is nothing that they believe in and fear, nothing to guide them" (Granzberg 1978, 4).

Each of these stories has a wealth of symbolic levels of meaning, relevant in both general and specific situations and contexts. As sacred legends they retain their power by remaining applicable to the times in which they are told and relevant to the people who hear them and tell them. For Queskekapow the same tales had quite different implications in my folklore classes, where stories were paramount, and in Granzberg's anthropology classes, where Cree culture was more central. This observation is beyond what I can discuss in a brief article, but it is worth keeping in mind.

I can hardly begin to describe the many ways that Nathaniel Queskekapow has been a teacher to me and to my students from the mid-1970s to the late 1980s. This was true of stories and questions, and also drawings that sometimes accompanied his texts. Queskekapow was also a teacher for himself, as he revealed in comments he prepared for students in Gary Granzberg's anthropology class after telling "Left and Right":

"Be careful of your life, don't be wiser than Left and Right; before you take another step, stop and think, which way to go now?" [He added, philosophically,] "I am trying to find—here, now—which way to go, why I am here." (note, Granzberg, 1985)

I cannot escape the discomfort of presenting his words in print since for him face-to-face contact was critical in education, so much so that he insisted that books by themselves were ineffective without an actual teacher present to explore and explain them. When I spent a year telling stories in a small school on Block Island, Rhode Island, Queskekapow sent me stories, questions, and drawings for the classes I visited, underlining that these were not for me but "for your students," to be read in his words and not told in my own. When the children responded by sending him drawings and questions, he responded by tracing his hand and sending it along with the instruction to "shake hands students and all." We all placed our hands on the sketch and then sent him tracings of our hands to complete the long-distance handshake. This is how he would have greeted each child if he had been present. Touch, voice, and personal communication are, for Nathaniel Queskekapow, how education really happens. A told story is one way to bring these all together, as he continues to do.

Notes

1. Granzberg met Queskekapow when he went north to study the effects of the proposed Churchill River hydroelectric project on Cree land. Later that year Queskekapow came south to reciprocate by speaking to Granzberg's anthropology class about Cree mythology. He only agreed to come to my folklore classes as a favor to Granzberg.

2. Granzberg, Gary, "A Cree Example of the Revelational Meanings of Symbols in Myth," *The Western Canadian Journal of Anthropology,* Vol. VIII, 1978.

3. For two fine examples see Stith Thompson, *Tales of the North American Indians* (Bloomington, Indiana: Indiana University Press, 1968), 116–220; and James R. Stevens, *Sacred Legends of the Sandy Lake Cree* (Toronto: McClelland and Stewart, 1971), 110–120.

4. He lectured at some length on this topic to Granzberg's classes but it was not central in his presentations in any of my classes.

What's in an Ending? Indian Storytelling of the Inland Northwest

Rodney Frey

Frey discusses two endings used with Coeur d'Alene tales. As Coeur d'Alene tellers perform their stories for non–Coeur d'Alene audiences, Frey wonders what effect this will have on the stories themselves.

Telling at the College

He began in a low but confident voice. As the narrative continued, the storyteller's hands and eyes moved, and the pitch of his voice modulated, placing emphasis on Coyote's particular actions, identifying the direction in which he traveled or contrasting his character with that of other Myth People. Despite the narrative's numerous and seemingly disjointed subplots, the rhythm with which the raconteur told the story did not vary. It was a story remembered, not memorized. The narrative came alive, and many who moments before had been listeners now traveled with Coyote. The 25-minute-long story ended as it had begun, with each of the 15 college students, Indian and non-Indian alike, quietly returning to the reality of the classroom. The story of "Coyote Losing His Eyes" was as true to form and content as it had been when the 20-year-old storyteller first heard it told to him by his Coeur d'Alene grandmother. With the exception of its being told in English, this 1997 retelling was also virtually identical to the story conveyed in 1927 to Gladys Reichard by an elder about 70 or 80 years old (Reichard, pp. 89–95).

Storytelling by the Coeur d'Alene, as with the Nez Perce, Crow, Spokane, Colville, Bitterroot Salish, and other tribes of the Inland Northwest of Idaho, Washington, and Montana, continues. It is certainly and typically the elders who are keeping the stories alive. They are told at family gatherings, quilting bees, evenings of drumming and singing, meals celebrating birthdays, and wakes, and in elementary school, high school, and college classrooms. But in increasing numbers, it is the young people and students in those same classrooms who are telling the ancient stories.

The various storytelling techniques used by raconteurs today, as exemplified by the 20-year-old Coeur d'Alene, and as employed in the past, all coalesce to attempt to bring the listeners into the story as participants. There are also changes, however, such as the stories being told in English as opposed to the native language, or told year-round as opposed to only in association with the winter ceremonial season.

One curious change is a contrasting type of narrative ending. In the instance of Coeur d'Alene narratives, some raconteurs conclude with *hinxux^{w}a'tpalqs* (the end of the trail) and others end with "that's why . . ."—as, for example, "that's why Lake Coeur d'Alene is blue!" Both endings are evident today, but the former is more characteristic of past usage and the latter is more frequently heard today. I believe these contrasting types of endings are indicative of more pervasive changes in the understanding and use of narratives, as well as changes in their associated worldviews.

The first ending, "the end of the trail," reflects

a narrative and storytelling style that functions as a vehicle "to travel the trail" of the mythic landscape. The listener becomes a participant in that world, as the reality of the narrative and the larger experiential world are one and the same. In this sense there is no objectified world separate from that of the mythical-narrative reality.

The second ending, "that's why . . . ," is associated with a narrative that functions to explain something. An explanatory role presupposes "something" separate from the narrative, to which an explanation is applied. It is a worldview based upon a dualist, objectified reality. The mythic world has existence only in a story, and is estranged from the experiential world. The listener in this is not so much a participant of the world as he is a distant observer of it.

Today the narratives of the Inland Northwest Indians are being rendered more accessible to a wider audience. In the process, however, are many of the more esoteric and spiritual meanings of these narratives, as well as their very functions, also being compromised as the worldview of the dominant society filters into the stories and worlds of Indian peoples?

Further Reading

Frey, Rodney, ed. *Stories That Make the World: Oral Literature of the Indian Peoples of the Inland Northwest as told by Lawrence Aripa, Tom Yellowtail and other Elders.* Norman and London: University of Oklahoma Press, 1995.

Reichard, Gladys. *An Analysis of Coeur d'Alene Indian Myths.* Philadelphia: American Folklore Society, 1947. Reprint, New York: Kraus Reprint, 1969.

Analysis of a Hupa Storytelling Event*

Ruth Seiman Bennett

Using linguistic analysis, Ruth Seiman Bennett examines a Hupa tale, giving in-depth attention to one variant with references to 13 other variants.

David Peter, Hupa Storyteller

I discuss in this paper a story that was recorded in natural conversation as told to me by an 87-year-old native Hupa speaker, David Peter, who was born and currently lives on the Hupa Indian Reservation in northwest California. The story is called O-HUL-WOH.[1]

I am going to try to talk about this story in a way that is consistent with David's view of what it is all about. In other words, this will be an analysis of a storyteller's intention. It seems to me that the best way to approach such an analysis is to think of the story as a speech event, since this is a way to be able to talk about what is actually happening between speaker and listener as the story is being told. "Speech event" has been defined by Dell Hymes as a rule-governed activity in which the rules identify particular norms for the use of speech (Hymes, 1972). The key word here is *activity,* which implies a series of actions and distinguishes the speech event from the speech act. Table 1 lists typical speech events in the Hupa culture and is intended to provide you with some sort of a picture in which the particular speech event of storytelling can be viewed.

When speech events are delineated according to whether the turn-taking structure is relatively fixed and predetermined or relatively flexible, then the story event can be considered fixed. In this sense, it is more similar to ceremonies, speeches, games, and prayers than to more casual conversational situations such as personal narratives. There is prescribed speaker and prescribed listener behavior when a story is being told. Speakers always introduce their stories in some way; listeners try to keep their attention on the storyteller and they keep their verbal contributions limited to encouraging utterances such as laughter, exclamations of surprise, or nods of agreement. It just so happens that many of the speech events with a predetermined speaker-listener structure are also formally identified with names by people in the Hupa tribe. "Story" is used to refer to traditional oral narratives (traditional referring to something handed down from one generation to the next). David says that O-HUL-WOH has been handed down in his family for 200 years at least, according to his knowledge of who passed it on to who. The story may be much older.

O-HUL-WOH is one of the types of stories that are associated with a character (Table 2). Other stories that are identified similarly are "Coyote Story," "Skunk Story," and "Panther

*Reprinted with permission of the Berkeley Linguistics Society. This article first appeared in *Proceedings of the Third Annual Meeting of the Berkeley Linguistics Society*, February 19–21, 1977, pp. 182–193.

Story"; most of these stories feature animal characters, and frequently there are several stories about the same character. O-HUL-WOH is somewhat unusual in this respect because there is only one story about him. He is also never referred to as an animal, although he is closely associated with sun imagery. O-HUL-WOH is a story that fits into several topical categories, as is typical. It is a story recalling an unusual event: what happened to a baby who arrived after a girl dug a twin potato. It is a story told in the daytime in the spring. And, for the versions that David has told me, it is a love medicine story.

As a result of listening to O-HUL-WOH on five different occasions from 1973 to 1976, and after studying the various 14 versions of the story that have been collected from northern California tribes since 1895 when Jeremiah Curtin collected the first version in Wintu, I have come to the conclusion that there are rules for structuring the story and that many of these rules relate to sequencing. This is consistent with the observations of Susan Ervin-Tripp and Claudia Mitchell-Kernan about speech event rules. They speak of sequential rules being successively embracing since they are constituent structures hierarchically organized. In this sense, sequencing rules are also rules for the relationship between abstract and surface structure. It is most appropriate to Hupa stories (and to all of the many northern California Indian stories I have listened to) to think of three kinds of rules as affecting sequences in discourse: Introductory Rules, Rules for Plots, and Rules for Formulas. I will discuss these three as they apply to the fourth version of O-HUL-WOH that I heard. This was told to me in July 1976, and was the first version I heard in the Hupa language. I will also discuss the 13 other versions of the story where they are relevant.

Introductory Rules

It is customary for a storyteller to spend some time, sometimes hours, talking with his listener (giving a speech or telling personal narratives), before he tells a traditional story. The reason for this is that stories are told only by story*tellers:* storytelling is a profession and the storyteller establishes or reaffirms his qualifications before he begins so that the listener will appreciate the nature of the speech event that he is participating in. Although there are situational differences such as ages of participants, degree of familiarity, and

type of story that account for different introductory content (which particular personal narrative gets told, for example), there is always some sort of introduction.

I recall one time when a Hupa storyteller, a 64-year-old man whom I had just met, spent four hours telling me personal narratives before he told a Coyote Story. He showed me the boundaries of his land, which we could see and which comprised several acres stretching from a road to a river. He told me how he came to own this land; he explained that he had traded some forested land with his brother in order to have some land he could use for gardening. He told me about several other accounts from his past experience, such as his life in the off-reservation school he attended. He was the only Native American in the class. He often felt alone because his clothes were shabby; one time he couldn't go to school at all because he didn't have any shoes.

David Peter introduced the first Hupa-language version of O-HUL-WOH with a speech he called "Business Talk." I considered this to be a somewhat unusual introduction, not the least because he gave it a title. The kernel of what he said is as follows:

> I am going to talk about something. You write on paper to whoever I talk to. . . . I am going to talk about something good. . . . What I'm going to say, they have to listen to me. . . . We are going to tell the across-the-ocean people . . . . That's all.

In addition to presenting a statement of intention that his story be talked about in such circumstances as exist today, David offers clear-cut evidence of how the introduction functions to assert the storyteller's qualifications. A necessary qualification is to be engaging in an activity of enhancing one's prestige. If a storyteller is recognized by an increasingly larger audience as being a good storyteller, it can be assumed that his stories are pretty good. A brief statement of the Introductory Rule is this:

> Talk in such a way as to assert the necessary qualifications. Keep in mind that prestige is one of the most necessary because it is evidence that you have a large audience (since it can be assumed that many people will gather around a prestigious person and listen to what he has to say). Telling a personal narrative or making

a prediction are particularly effective because they establish prestige through the medium of storytelling itself.

In both introductions I have sketched, aspects particular to the situation have played a part in defining the form. In the first instances, the storyteller is speaking to an outsider, someone who may not be familiar with Hupa family territorial boundaries, with prestigious Hupa families, or with the plight of Indian people related to off-reservation experiences. He asserts his qualifications in such a way as to affirm his prestige within the tribe while at the same time he demonstrates his proficiency at telling personal narratives. Anybody who can tell narratives for four hours and keep his audience interested must be a good storyteller. The surface form reveals a deeper intent.

David's "Business Talk" speech is also cast in narrative form. It has a plot, albeit directed toward the future. One reason why David might choose not to tell a personal narrative prior to this version of O-HUL-WOH is that by this time we have known each other for five years and he has told me hundreds of personal narratives. Because telling the story in his own language is something special to him, it makes sense that he would want to preface it with a special kind of introduction. His prediction is a prophecy that directly involves his listener. If and when it comes true, it is living evidence of his powers. In addition to being a storyteller, David is an Indian doctor, a medicine man, and prophecy is one of the abilities he claims to have. Prestige as a storyteller is thus linked to prestige as a doctor. The implication is that someone who is a good medicine man is a good storyteller as well. As above, situation influences form, differences in form being explained by differences in age and parallel occupations engaged in by the storyteller as well as differences in familiarity with the listener. In terms of Sequencing Rules, introductions contain linear sequences that define narrative intention.

Rules for Plots

As I discuss plot sequencing, I will be concerned with internal sequences and will be drawing from the resource of the 14 available versions of the O-HUL-WOH story. In addition to the three English and the two Hupa versions David has told me, there is another Hupa version, collected in 1901 by Pliny Earle Goddard, a colleague of Alfred Kroeber at the University of California, Berkeley, and another one of the pioneers in the field of linguistic anthropology. In addition, there are three Yurok versions, two Wintu versions, and Wiyot, Shasta, and Achomawi versions. The fact that so many versions of the same story exist suggests that people regard it as a very good story; otherwise so many storytellers wouldn't have chosen to tell it. The multiple versions also suggested that this story is at least several hundred years old since it takes time for a story to spread across tribes. This is especially true when all of the tribes cannot be assumed to have had direct contact with each other. Only the Hupa, Yurok, and Wiyot are in northwest California; the Shasta and the Wintu are located in mid-northern California; and the Achomawi are in the northeast.

Plot is the basis for internal sequencing in Alan Dundes's analysis of the structure of North American Indian folktales (Dundes, 1964). His view is that the story consists of a series of actions, as opposed to distinct, possibly unrelated actions. His is the structuralist approach of conceiving of related units and of units of analysis in the most general terms possible. The structuralist assumption is that abstract interrelated units are what is most basic to meaning. In identifying these units, Dundes relies on the concept of the motifemic sequence, which is based on the motifeme.[2] These units contrast with motifs, which are mere labels and which may refer to actions, characters, or objects within a story. Motifemes are necessarily actions and are linked with other actions on a similarly abstract level. The concept of the motifemic sequence can best be described in terms of a particular story. O-HUL-WOH can be analyzed as two motifemic sequences:

First Sequence

Equilibrium: A female goes out digging roots every morning.

Interdiction: A mother tells her daughter (the female) not to dig a root under certain conditions.

Violation: She digs a root.

Consequence: A boy baby cries, and grows up.

Attempted escape: The boy follows his mother to the place where she goes, or she follows him.

Second Sequence

Disequilibrium: The boy, now a man, meets a girl or two girls.

Task: He engages in a series of tasks, all of which are related to the display of masculine powers, and all of which are tests or contests.

Task accomplished: He wins.

Equilibrium: He marries.

Explanatory motif: That's why something in nature is here today.

According to a motifemic analysis, these examples would be considered to be the rules of plot for all of the versions of the O-HUL-WOH story because they constitute the rules as they are manifested in the most extensive versions of the story. But the point to be made immediately is that not all of the events listed above are reported explicitly in every version; there is a real question about whether some of the motifemes are present even implicitly in some of the versions, although all of the versions contain most of the motifemes.

In deciding which stories were versions of O-HUL-WOH, I eliminated some stories that also demonstrated similarities to the versions I included because they did not contain what I intuitively felt to be an adequate number of the motifemes as they are found across the versions that contain most or all of the motifemes. There is a Pomo story, for example, in which Coyote is reported going off to see why the sun does not rise and travel all across the skies, and Coyote sets off in a journey much like O-HUL-WOH. There are also tests in this story, but because the first motifemic sequence is absent, I did not include it. I rejected a Wailaki story for similar reasons. Thus, a motifemic analysis is useful for getting at versions of a story that *show* a considerable degree of consistency and a similar linear sequence from beginning to end. But it is questionable whether such an analysis really gets at the storyteller's intention for the very reason that the structuralist aims at the most general meaning possible while the storyteller weaves his tale out of specific details. It would seem that the analyses of a speech event, once having discovered the bare bones of the structure, would do well to get back as closely as possible to the story's specifics in order to be more in accord with the story as understood by the storyteller himself. For this purpose, I present the motifemes of the story along with repetitions and variations of specific actions across versions:

First Sequence

Equilibrium: The only relevant difference across versions is that in most versions the female is a girl, whereas in the Wintu versions, she is an old woman. There is another difference: some versions report the woman going out "every morning" whereas other versions say "all the time." This kind of a difference, a variation in reporting habitual aspect, does not seem to be significant. It is one of the primary tasks of the analyst, when getting back to the details of the story, to sort out what the relevant differences are. One of the ways to do this is to look at the relationship between the detail and the motifeme, and between details within one motifeme and another.

Interdiction: In the versions where the woman is young there is an explicit interdiction, although the specifics of the interdiction may vary: in the Hupa versions, she is not to dig twin-stalked ones; in the Wiyot version, she is not to dig a single-leafed one; in a Yurok version, she is not to dig one that grows in the middle of the prairie.

Violation: Same across versions, although it may be questionable whether the digging activity can be considered a violation in the Wintu versions, where there is no interdiction. An interesting fact of the two Wintu stories is that both contain an Interdiction-Violation sequence later on in the story, at a point at which no other versions have it.

Consequence: A baby cries in every version. A point that I may as well make here as any other place is that the storytellers do not usually link actions explicitly. In no version of the story does the storyteller say, "she dug one, and this resulted in a baby crying." Sometimes cause and effect chains are implied through connectives, however, and in David's versions, certain implications can be drawn also from gestures and other non-verbal behavior. (This could form the basis for an entire study in itself.)

Attempted escape: There is considerable variation here. In the Hupa versions, the girl, who is now called the mother, is reported to leave every morning and return every evening; after this goes on for awhile, the boy follows her. According to Dundes's scheme, it is appropriate to refer to an action reported as a pursuit as an escape, because what is important is the abstract unit of action. In the Yurok versions, the girl pursues the boy. In the Wintu versions, the boy leaves after violating an interdiction given by the old woman. She tells him not to go east, and that is exactly where he goes.

Second Sequence

Disequilibrium: In the Hupa, Shasta, and Wintu versions, the now grown O-HUL-WOH meets two girls. In the Achomawi version, he meets Flower-Maiden. This can be considered a disequilibrium motifeme because it sets up a sequence of actions wherein the hero tries to prove himself.

Task: There are always a series of tasks, rather than one task, and they are always different from storyteller to storyteller even within tribes, although there is the least amount of variation within one tribe, and David's versions are always the same. In his versions, O-HUL-WOH catches a salmon filled with dentalium, he shoots an eagle that falls to the ground full of dentalium, and finally he engages in a shinny contest first with Fox and then with Thunder.[3] The order of the tasks and of the subtasks is always the same. In the 1901 Hupa version, the tasks include the shinny contest, but instead of the salmon and eagle tasks, O-HUL-WOH eats two baskets of dentalium that Indians can't swallow and he carries wood to 10 sweathouses. In versions from other tribes there are other contests: in the Achomawi and Shasta versions, the contest consists of teetering on the pole and trying to dislodge the opponent who is either Moon or Grizzly Bear; the Wintu versions contain a series of tests, but no contests. In the Wiyot version, there is only a shinny contest; in general, across motifemes, this version of the story is the most sparse. This version does not contain the attempted escape, for example, perhaps because the Wiyot storyteller lost his mother in infancy when she was killed in the Gunther Island massacre (Reichard, 1925).

Task accomplished: In every version, he wins.

Equilibrium: There is always a return to a regular, implicitly normative state of affairs, although specifics differ. In most of the versions there is reference to the Sun and other heavenly bodies following their courses. In the Hupa versions, we are told that O-HUL-WOH and his family still live in heaven having fun today.

Explanatory motif: There is no "that's why . . ." in the Hupa versions, but in the others there is. In the Shasta version, "that's why" an arch now exists at a certain spot in the Salmon River. It is really the petrified body of O-HUL-WOH lying there with his arms and legs uplifted.

There is enough consistency across versions to suggest that if motifemic sequences may not actually be there in the storyteller's mind as he tells the story, at least these sequences are useful to reflect plot structure. Thus they can be used as the basis for sequential rules for plots. The important point to be made is that these rules are applicable to the storyteller's intention because they provide a way of relating specific actions to each other in the story. The assumption here is that related actions are what is most basic to the story because through actions characters make manifest their natures. What I have tried to do in adding a more specific level of generalization to the rules is to get closer to what can be assumed to be the meaning of the story to the storyteller, since it is getting closer to the language he actually uses.

Rules for Formulas

The third kind of sequential rule focuses on formulaic expressions. To paraphrase Albert Lord's definition, formulas can be defined as saying the same thing the same way (Lord, 1960). Lord's criteria include having the same metrical conditions governing a group of words as well as having semantic equivalence. One might add that there are frequent nonverbal equivalences as well. The sheer frequency of formulas in Hupa stories makes it likely that they are related to the storyteller's intention, that they are readily available phrases that the storyteller can call on to put his story together as he thinks of what he is to say (as he must do) during the actual performance.

As we consider how formulas might function in terms of sequencing rules, we will take a passage directly from David Peter's O-HUL-WOH and look at some of the things formulas are doing. Because formulas occur throughout the story, any passage would do; the following passage occurs immediately before the part of the story in which O-HUL-WOH decides to follow his mother up to where she goes:

1. Pretty soon, he's getting big.
2. A squirrel sits on a rock.

3. He killed that same squirrel
4. With that same bow and arrow.
5. They grow up with him.
6. He grows up with it.
7. He killed with that bow and arrow.
8. And he grows bigger.
9. That bow grows a little longer.
10. While he's growing, too. Getting bigger.
11. It grows too, that bow.
12. And then he only had one arrow.
13. And he killed with it.
14. It had a point on it.
15. Pretty soon the boy grows up.
16. He goes off and hunts.
17. A little fawn he shot with the bow.
18. He killed.
19. And then his mother goes off someplace,
20. She went up to heaven,
21. She's picking acorns up there.
22. He goes off.
23. Pretty soon, a large one, a big one, a buck.
24. He killed that buck, then.
25. The grandmother has it in that carrying basket.
26. She packs it in. She has it in that basket.
27. She packs it in. Big buck.
28. The mother talks to him, her son.
29. When he had tasted the deer meat.
30. So she talked to him after eating deer.
31. Pretty soon, after eating deer, they talked.
32. He's growing up to be a young man.
33. Then he thought he wanted to find out
34. Where she goes.

The above passage has been arranged into lines that are consistent with the metrical patterns of David's speech; ends of lines reflect intonational signals and pauses.

One of the ways for formulating sequential rules for formulas is to find a formula that reoccurs and to look at the conditions for reoccurrence. For example, there are four occurrences of "pretty soon" in the above passage and these co-occur with the four actions reported. This rule could be put as follows:

Pretty soon: he shoots a squirrel
Pretty soon: he shoots a little fawn
Pretty soon: he shoots a large one, a buck
Pretty soon: they talk (the boy and the mother)

Putting the rule in this form makes it possible to see that the formula "pretty soon" co-occurs

with the four separate actions reported in the passage. But note that this rule does not really describe the relationship between the formula and the actions as they are actually reported. Although "pretty soon" occurs at the beginning of the first three actions, it does not occur until the fourth action has been going on for three lines (at line 31). Even though it is a linking formula, related to sequence does not occur in parallel ways in relationship to all of the actions. One of the interesting things about this is that there is no way to predict the embedded nature of "pretty soon" within the fourth action. If one were to devise the rule that the fourth time is a variation, one could hardly expect this to hold true across passages across stories. In fact, one of the ways in which formulas function in these stories is to provide the storyteller with a way of creating a new experience with each telling. The phrases themselves are well-known; thus their appearance, in terms of linear sequences, can be something new. This is why there can be no sequential rules written for the formulas themselves.

There are certain types of patterns, however, that can describe various orders of occurrences for formulas. For example, one could look at specific points in a story, such as beginnings, middles, and ends, and note what formulaic expressions are appropriate. In Hupa stories, there are certain formulaic ways of beginning: a Hupa storyteller may use Ɔ+-XÓL-ɔWE-DÓN' (before creation) or H'ó-YO'-Ɔ+-DÉL-TCE'. (They were living there.) There are formulaic ways of ending: X̄UT Hó-Y+X̱ HWO-NE (That's all) or Hó-YO NǪN-D+K̄k̄. (The end.) Also, certain connective formulas appear in linking actions. Besides ŃE-ĴO-X̱x́Oǫ-M+H (which can mean either "pretty soon" or "after a while"), there is Hó-YOH (therewith). One thing that can be said about predictability of occurrence is that some formulas found in stories are found across versions of the same story, across stories told by the same storyteller, across stories within a tribe, and across stories in other modes of discourse. Other formulas are more restricted. Hó-YOH is used elsewhere but is associated particularly with storytelling and with ceremonial recitatives. Victor Golla notes that Hó-YOH or any variation thereof can be expected to introduce almost every sentence in a formal recitation, Hó-YOH is a very frequently used locative phrase and connective in this context (Golla, 1964).

But although it is possible to talk about formulaic occurrences descriptively, such as the "pretty soon" in the above passage, and to talk generally and prescriptively about some kinds of formulas, such as connectives, there are many formulas that cannot be adequately described by sequential rules of discourse. In David's stories, in addition to formulas for beginnings, for ending, and for linking actions, there are formulaic ways of describing characters, or recounting actions, or describing particular places. If one were to take a structuralist approach to analyzing these formulas, one could write up rules based on Franz Boas's approach to North American Indian art. He says that "rhythmic repetition" is basic to "decorative form" and that decorative form is the most important feature of this art (Boas, 1955). Formulas can be thought of as rhythmic repetition, since there is co-occurrence of syntactic repetition with prosodic and stress identities. And within one story, formulas referring to a character will be interwoven with formulas referring to his actions and both these formulas will be repeated. If one were to write up rules for such sequences, they could look like the rules Boas writes for visual formulas: AXAYA or AXYAAB. But the problem with rules such as these is that they are unable to distinguish one set of formulas from another. Because formulas are intricately related to the concrete details of the story (they *are* the concrete details of the story), they can be assumed to be an essential part of the storytelling event as it is told and as it is experienced by storyteller and listener.

In making this sort of assumption, I am taking the view that the storyteller himself views the story as a performance in context, and that he sees that context to consist of both the words and nonverbal language of the story and of the immediate social situation of the storyteller and listener and the cultural and personal background that the storyteller and listener share to varying degrees. That this is the case is demonstrated by the differences in the stories that are told to strangers and those that are told to people who have had either a long acquaintanceship with the Hupa people or who are Hupa themselves and who have grown up in the culture.

To take my own experiences as example, it was four years before I heard any stories in the Hupa language, and this was only after I had demonstrated that I was learning to speak the Hupa language. The stories I heard first were much shorter than the ones I heard after years of knowing David and other Hupa storytellers. One of the key differences was that the stories I heard earlier lacked the same degree of formulaic repetition and variation. I don't want to underestimate the amount of formulaic repetition in the earlier stories I heard, however, because David has always told me stories in the same style. But because I lacked the understanding of what he was doing, or lacked the recognition of some of the formulas as *being* formulas in the earlier stories, he was not free to expand on the formulas or to repeat them with the knowledge that I would recognize his repetitions as being formulaic. Much of the storyteller's intention revolves around his ability to recycle, as it were, many of the formulas, and to thereby play with his listener's sense of what the linear sequence of the story actually is.

Within the passage quoted above, there are ambiguities about linear sequence that are only resolved because of the listener's knowledge of formulas. Take the line, "And then he only had one arrow" (line 12). This occurs immediately after the line referring to a growing bow. Since we usually think of bows and arrows going together, and of "and then" as linking two events in time, at first glance it might not seem appropriate to insert the connective at this point. Why not just say "he only had one arrow"? The reason is that the connective functions as a signal to the listener that the boy is getting ready to shoot. The listener who knows the O-HUL-WOH story knows that "having only one arrow" must refer to the character O-HUL-WOH because "only having one" is a formulaic way to refer to him, and is what distinguishes him from all the other males in the story, none of whom are able to get the hunting prey or the fishing catch with "just one." Because of the "and then" in line 12, the listener expects the killing action that is reported in line 13.

There is a similar level of understanding that can be reached only by the listener who knows the formula in line 16 that reports: "He goes off and hunts." This might seem to be redundant with line 3 where the boy is reported killing a squirrel, but knowing the formula, "he goes off" we know that this is a marker of an advance in the boy's growth because now he is "going off " or leaving his immediate surroundings when he does his hunting. Similarly, knowing the meaning of the formula "a large one, a big one" in line 23, we know that again there is a sequential development in the growth of the boy. Now, instead of hunting relatively small prey, such as squirrels and fawns, he is after "the large one." We may not know exactly what type of animal it is—it may be an elk, a deer, or some other large animal—but we know what the significance is in terms of plot development and in terms of the growth of the boy.

There are clear formulas in this passage, aside from those relating specifically to sequences, as in line 26, "she packs it in." This refers here to the grandmother putting the remains of the buck in her basket so she can carry home the meat, but it has the general meaning of someone packing anything they want to carry, be it fish, deer meat, or basket-making materials. Any Hupa knows this. There is one more point to be made regarding formulas, and that is that when formulaic repetitions occur, especially within a passage, the storyteller is telling the listener something beyond the fact that he is repeating the formula. There is always new information implicit in the formulaic repetition. An example of this can be seen in the lines that refer to the mother talking to the son (lines 28–31). This is an important talk because it is the event that separates the character O-HUL-WOH's boyhood from his manhood. Up until the point when this talk occurs, he has been "getting big," "growing bigger," "growing up." After the talk "he's growing up to be a young man." The talk between mother and son is all the more unusual because up until this point in the story they have not talked at all. We are told earlier that the grandmother raised the boy, that the girl who was his mother ran away from him when she first heard him cry, and that as he grew into boyhood she continued her daily activities, leaving him with his grandmother. Now, at this point in the story, she talks to him, and we are meant to understand by this that she acknowledges him as her son. We are not told this explicitly by the storyteller, but by the use of his repetition, we are given to know. Our implicit knowledge is reinforced by the next line, which reports the boy getting ready to follow the mother to where she goes. Throughout the story, the listener's knowledge of what is occurring, what has happened, and what is to happen, is communicated by the storyteller in much the same way as in the passage I have just discussed.

The important point to be made is that the storyteller cannot get across his intention unless he is assured of a high degree of shared knowledge on the part of his listener. This is because in addition to getting across a plot and to demonstrating his skill in manipulating formulas, one of the primary aspects of storyteller intention relates very directly to maintaining a shared experience with his listener. The basis for this sharing rests on the fact that meanings do not have to be made explicit; the storyteller tells the story, he does not interpret. A high degree of explicitness in a story would amount to interpretation, and this would alter the nature of the relationship between the storyteller and the listener, and this is something the storyteller does not want to do. Thus it would seem that the "interactive process" (a term used by Jenny Gumperz and John Gumperz relative to contextualization and social goals in a nonnarrative context [1976]) is present in a storytelling event and that any sequential rules that are developed for stories must ultimately take this into account as an important aspect of the storyteller's intention. In the process of taking this into account, the analyst discovers that abstract, structuralist rules are useful; that, furthermore, getting back to the most specific level possible for various versions of a story can be useful as well; and that in handling rules for formulas, each story has to be considered on its own terms, which consists of recognizing what is traditional about it, what is present because of the previous experience of the storyteller and the listener, and what is being signaled through the storyteller's largely unpredictable manipulation of formulas as he proceeds.

Another way of saying this is that the audience is an important consideration in the analysis of a storyteller's intention. This reminds me of A.L. Becker's distinction between the essential and the nonessential audience, in which the nonessential audience are those who happen to be around and who may or may not hear the narrative, and the essential audience are the ones to whom the story is really told (Becker, 1976). In Becker's analysis the essential audience is thought to be the spirits of the ancestors; one major distinction between the Javanese narratives he writes about and the Hupa stories I have heard is that in the Hupa stories, the essential audience is the immediately present and available listener. The listener may throw off his role and choose not to listen, but this would not be congruent with the intention of the storyteller. There are a number of cues I have been given that this is the case: once, when I left momentarily because of having to handle a problem involving some children in the next room, I discovered upon my return to hear the rest of the story that David had no more to tell.

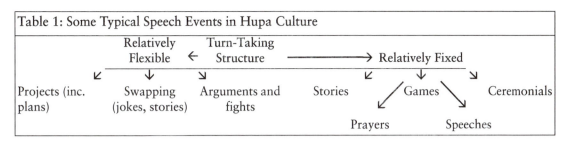

Table 1: Some Typical Speech Events in Hupa Culture

	Relatively Flexible	← Turn-Taking Structure ——————→		Relatively Fixed	
Projects (inc. plans)	Swapping (jokes, stories)	Arguments and fights	Stories	Games	Ceremonials
				Prayers Speeches	

Table 2: How Hupa Storytellers Topicalize Their Stories

Stories Recalling Unusual Events	Ceremonial Occasions	Character-Centered	Medicine	Season	Time of Day
Dreams and Visions*	How to perform	Coyote	Bear	Spring	Daytime
Catastrophes	Why a dance is done	Skunk	Deer	Summer	Evening
Miracles		Fox O-HUL-WOH	Love	Fall Winter	Night

*These examples are intended to be illustrative, not all-inclusive.

Notes

1. O-HUL-WOH is the name of the central character and is a Hupa word that literally means "take-it-out" and refers to human birth. The orthography I am using here and throughout the paper is the Indian Unifon developed for the Northern California Indians and currently in use by them. [Editor's note: We were not able to reproduce Bennett's hand written orthographic notations exactly in this reprinting.]

2. As he acknowledges, Dundes got his theory of the motifeme by combining Propp's "function" with Kenneth Pike's "-emic" unit.

3. Shinny is called "stick game" by Hupas. It is played somewhat like lacrosse on a rectangular grassy field with two teams and matched pairs of offending-defending players. The object is to take a stick wrapped with deer hide and get it across the field.

Acknowledgments

I want to acknowledge the people who gave me suggestions that I incorporated into my paper.

These include David and various other storytellers in the village at Campbell Creek and elsewhere in the Hupa Valley; people at the University of California, Berkeley: Adrian Bennett, Georgette Stratos, Susan Ervin-Tripp, Lily and Charles Fillmore, Herb Simons, Wallace Chafe, Robin Lakoff, and Dan Melia; and lectures by John Searle.

Further Reading

Becker, A.L., *Text-Building, Epistemology, and Aesthetics in Javanese Shadow Theatre,* Ann Arbor: University of Michigan, 1976

Boas, Franz, *Primitive Art,* new edition, New York: Dover, 1955

Burns, L.S., "Digger Indian Legends (Shasta)," *Land of Sunshine* 14 (1901)

Curtin, Jeremiah, *Creation Myths of Primitive America in Relation to the Religious History and Mental Development of Mankind,* Boston: Little, Brown, 1898; London: Williams and Norgate, 1899

Dundes, Alan, *The Morphology of North American Indian Folktales,* Helsinki, Finland: Suomalainen Tiedeakatemia, 1964

Ervin-Tripp, Susan, and Claudia Mitchell-Kernan, *Child Discourse,* New York: Academic Press, 1977

Goddard, Pliny Earle, ed., *Hupa Texts,* Berkeley: University of California Press, 1904

Golla, Victor, *Hupa Grammar* (Ph.D. diss., University of California, Berkeley), 1964

Gumperz, Jenny, and John Gumperz, "Context in Children's Speech," working paper, Language Behavior Research Laboratory, University of California, Berkeley, 1976

Hymes, Dell, "Models of the Interaction of Language and Social Life," in *Directions in Sociolinguistics,* by John Gumperz and Dell Hymes, New York: Holt, Rinehart and Winston, 1972

Kroeber, Alfred, *Yurok Myths,* Berkeley: University of California Press, 1976; London: University of California Press, 1978

Lord, Albert B., *The Singer of Tales,* Cambridge, Massachusetts: Harvard University Press, 1960

Merriam, C. Hart, *An-Nik-A-Del, the History of the Universe as Told by the Modes-se Indians of California,* Boston: Stratford, 1928

Reichard, Gladys, *Wiyot Grammar and Texts,* Berkeley: University of California, 1925

Towendolly, Grant, *A Bag of Bones: The Wintu Myths of a Trinity River Indian,* edited by Marcelle Masson, Oakland, California: Naturegraph, 1966

Traditional Storytelling at San Juan Pueblo

Sue-Ellen Jacobs
Esther Martinez (P'oe Tsawa)

Esther Martinez and Sue-Ellen Jacobs discuss contemporary storytelling at San Juan Pueblo in New Mexico, particularly its use with children.

Sacred and Public Storytelling

At San Juan Pueblo, New Mexico, storytelling serves both sacred and secular purposes. Sacred storytelling is usually performed by men in the kivas as part of ceremonial preparation, initiation of the young, and other matters requiring private communication concerning religious matters. None of the kiva stories is ever told in public. Both women and men tell secular stories in various public settings. Public storytelling used to be done only in the wintertime, but by the 1990s traditional storytellers could be found telling many different types of stories throughout the year in schools, at health and other types of conferences, at intertribal gatherings, and at storytelling festivals.

San Juan Pueblo people who are "traveling" storytellers include Clarence Cata, Peter Garcia, and Esther Martinez (who is usually booked under her Téwa name, P'oe Tsawa [Blue Water]). At the Senior Center, a place where people gather for social and recreational time on the reservation, some elders recount stories of their lives as well as stories they heard from their grandparents and parents as they were growing up. This kind of storytelling is part of everyday life for many children and adults at San Juan Pueblo. There are some homes where "formal" storytelling is not done, yet even in these homes parents will tell stories about what happened to them at work during the day or when they went on a trip. In other words, storytelling is a central part of life, even when it seems that "traditional" stories are not being told.

When it is time for the community to prepare for a ceremonial event, generally referred to as "dances," the people will be told that a ceremony is to take place on a certain day. About one week before that day, the elders explain to everyone who comes to practice how the ceremony came to be, why it is being done, what the meaning is, and how everyone is supposed to think about the ceremony as well as behave during it. The explanations are told in the form of stories, some long and some quite short. The point is to get everyone ready spiritually and physically for the full day of ceremonial dance. Some of the dances are stories, but the songs that accompany them are always stories. These song stories may describe events in nature, relationships between people and the spiritual world, some aspect of pueblo history, or other events. There is no age limit for participation in these ceremonial events.

"Each Child Is Its Own Story"

In preparation for a ceremonial event, such as the 1996 Yellow Corn Dance, the children tell stories about their own efforts to acquire the special clothing and other items they must wear, about

381

being afraid of going out to dance the actual performance of the ceremony in public for the first time, and about how good they feel about participating in a community-wide event of such importance. The elders always tell the children how much they appreciate their performance.

Stories Recorded

In the 1970s a number of stories were recorded from elders who were raised in traditional Téwa storytelling practices. This was an important community project because traditional storytelling was on the wane. As in other communities, television and other imported media distracted family and larger community audiences from local stories; in an effort to preserve them, "old" stories were collected from elders by various family members, friends, and anthropologists, and by Esther Martinez, the founder and director of the bilingual program at the San Juan Pueblo Community School (formerly San Juan Pueblo Day School, under the direction of the Bureau of Indian Affairs). The majority of the stories were recorded on audiotape, and some were recorded on videotape. These recordings were to form the core of a cultural preservation program, but, sadly, most were destroyed in a cataclysmic fire at the school in 1983. Now we are involved in an effort to reclaim and restore stories collected by others during that period and subsequently. At this time we are working with 40 stories, some of which have their origins in the late 1800s, with language and culture preservation and restoration goals in mind. Readers who are interested in Téwa stories collected in the early 1900s will want to read Parsons, *Tewa Tales.*

Performing in Schools and Conferences for Native and Nonnative Audiences

When P'oe Tsawa tells stories to children at the school, the teachers prepare the children by having them sit in a circle, often on the floor, while she sits on a chair. Most of her stories are told in English, even though they are based on original Téwa stories. Her stories cover those that are best suited for teaching children about nature, solving personal problems (including peer problems), the history of everyday community life in years past, and aspects of contemporary life. When telling stories to a large audience of adults—for example, to people attending health conferences—P'oe Tsawa usually stands and at health conferences tells stories intended for healing. These stories include those having to do with losing family members, disappointments, sorrow, loneliness, happiness, and overcoming or otherwise taking care of other forms of stress. Such stories are similar to those told in Téwa by people at the pueblo to help with healing.

Audience response varies according to the type, style, context, and function of the story being told. Ceremonial events are not performed for an audience, yet people from the pueblo and outsiders gather to witness the performance. They become an audience in the theatrical sense of the word, but they are not expected to respond audibly unless invited to do so by the dancers, singers, leaders, or other officials. The job of the "audience" generally is to be a silent and respectful participant; applauding is considered inappropriate. A similar ambiance (mood, behavior, environment) is expected when a storyteller commences and gives the story whether to small children, young people, or adults. The job of the "audience" again is to be silent and respectful unless invited to answer a question. When a story is completed the audience may ask questions, verbally thank the storyteller, or applaud, in some circumstances.

Depending on the situation, a storyteller may dress in everyday clothes or in traditional clothing. When P'oe Tsawa goes to tell stories in nonnative environments, she wears formal traditional clothing such as is worn by women during ceremonial dances or on feast days. This is done to give her audiences the additional gift of seeing her special clothing. When stories are to be told at the school or at other places in the pueblo, she dresses in her everyday clothes.

In our work together we are trying to build a bridge from the past to the future using the cultural traditions we each have been given. Because storytelling has been such an integral part of these traditions, we are exploring the use of various visual and other means to convey a sense of old-fashioned storytelling through the medium with which the present generations seem to be enchanted—namely, computer technology. We do not expect, however, that this new technology will replace the power and wonder children of all ages experience when a storyteller gives her or his story to an audience in person.

Further Reading

Parsons, Elsie Clews, ed., *Tewa Tales,* New York: American Folklore Society, 1926; reprint, Tucson: University of Arizona Press, 1994

Lushootseed Language and Story Revival

Vi (taqʷšəblu) Hilbert

Upper Skagit Elder Vi (taqʷšəblu) Hilbert comments on the revival of Lushootseed language and story. As founder and director of the Lushootseed Research Center, Vi Hilbert is responsible for much of this revival. Vi has transcribed hours of collected Lushootseed tapes, compiled a Lushootseed lexicon, and published many stories in both Lushootseed and English. She hosts an annual gathering of Lushootseed tellers to encourage the revival of this tradition.

Our Tradition

Because the culture of the First People of America (the Native Americans), has been greatly affected by many changes in our world over the past 100 years, our old ways have been endangered. Our traditional stories educated and informed our people, young and old. Our stories taught us about our history, our origins. Our spiritual leaders and historians were honored for their ability to gently pass on valued information. They presented their families with epic stories and family songs that spoke with pride about our ability to keep the most important information of our past in the oral tradition that we could indeed pass down to coming generations. The most important qualities of our culture live through the dynamics of our old stories and our songs.

Our present generation has not been completely aware of the importance of their oral traditions. Over the years the practice of telling stories has been asleep. We were told that a new way of educating our youth was now the law. Our obedient people acquiesced and allowed their primary teaching tools to become dormant.

Thanks are due to the marvelous medium of tape recording. Some of our talented storytellers were captured, at least, in that way.

Stories Are Best Appreciated When Heard in Their Own Culture's Language

We are fortunate to have many hours of our stories told in the beautiful ancient languages of this area in Washington State. Students at the University of Washington, Evergreen State University, and many other institutions have benefited by listening to the rhythm of our very talented people talking in the voice of this land. They have been able to hear the heartbeat of the story as they hear a traditional teller give us a taste of her or his way of presenting through the simple dynamics of the story itself. We hear the pathos, the gentleness, the emotions reflected through the different qualities present in the vocal cords of human beings. Those vocal cords of the First People were heard best when they used the ancient voice of their languages.

Today our young people are hearing some of their culture's stories being told again. They are reading the stories in translation, but they can also hear some of them told in the languages of the original storytellers. Naturally, this is the very best way to hear. This is the very best way to tell. Language programs are presently in progress and it is my belief that in a few years, our young people will be telling their stories again in the language. It is possible.

We have a representative number of tellers being heard in many places today. They are invited to public schools, primary grades and high schools and colleges. Churches and businesses also invite us.

Storytelling within our own communities does not seem to be sought at present. It is my belief that our language classes may create a change here. Students will be encouraged to present storytelling sessions at community gatherings. Family pride will surface as our young people gain fluency and are encouraged to memorize special stories in the language.

Traditional storytellers practiced styles that were immediately recognizable. My Aunt Susie Sampson became the voice of the characters in her stories. She spoke for them in their personalities. My nephew Johnny Moses practices that same technique. His repertoire ranges through countless numbers of stories. His stories can be brief or epic. Some tell me that he tells epic stories that take three to four days each. His audiences enjoy some of his classics and never tire of hearing "Octopus Lady," "The Bicycle," or "The Upside-Down Face." Johnny also becomes each character in the story. Crow always knows it all, and audiences spontaneously shout in the familiar nasal voice of Crow, "I know!" As our young people get acquainted with the master storytellers of the past, they will discover such wealth to learn from and to emulate.

We shy away from the most X-rated of our stories to tell in public. The playful, naughty element has always been shared and enjoyed as we chuckle over the expected position of Skunk, or the troubles Coyote can always get himself into and out of. (Oh, but does he?)

Songs have, in the past, been an important part of our stories. We are fortunate to hear these on our audiotapes. Some of our contemporary storytellers create songs around their stories; some preface the storytelling session with a prayer song from our ancient traditional spirituality. It is my practice to invite this inclusion from practitioners of these areas of our culture.

Because the most important qualities of our culture live through the dynamics of our old stories and songs, we are blessed with the current technology that includes the CD-ROM and the world of the Internet. Through these media, our stories can reach all of our youth and be stored safely for the future generations coming. They will still need to learn from the wisdom of their ancestors.

I believe that this covers what I would like to say about the tradition of storytelling as I know it today and expresses to you my hopes for the future.

Further Reading

Bates, Dawn, Thom Hess, and Vi Hilbert, *Lushootseed Dictionary*, edited by Dawn Bates, Seattle: University of Washington Press, 1994

Bierwert, Crisca, *Lushootseed Texts: An Introduction to Puget Salish Narrative Aesthetics*, Lincoln: University of Nebraska, 1996

Hilbert, Vi, *Coyote and Rock and Other Lushootseed Stories*, cassette recording, told by Vi Hilbert, New York: HarperCollins, 1992

_____, *Haboo: Native American Stories from Puget Sound*, Seattle: University of Washington Press, 1985

Peter, Susie Sampson, *Xᵊcusᵊdᵊᵊgʷᵊʷulcᵊ: The Wisdom of a Skagit Elder*, transcribed by Vi (taqʷšᵊblu) Hilbert, translated by Vi Hilbert and Jay Miller, recorded by Leon Metcalf, Seattle, Washington: Lushootseed, 1997

North America

Where Have All the Märchen Gone?: Or Don't They Tell Those Little Stories in the Ozarks Any More?

W.K. McNeil

W.K. McNeil discusses the survival of the Märchen tradition in Arkansas. He notes the works of collectors from the nineteenth century and early in this century who collected märchen but finds none related today. Still he considers this a "shy" genre and is reluctant to declare the form dead.

Märchen Defined

The märchen is a traditional narrative form usually defined as narratives classified in Aarne-Thompson as Types 300–749, "Tales of Magic," but here refers to Aarne-Thompson Types 300–1199 (Aarne-Thompson 1961). This expanded definition includes Tales of Magic, Religious Tales, Novelle (Romantic Tales), and Tales of the Stupid Ogre. Thus, the usage here includes all stories told primarily for entertainment, regarded both by teller and audience as fiction, and not told for laughs. However one defines the word, though, märchen have a lengthy history, conservative estimates dating it back to the early sixteenth century in western Europe and liberal ones assigning it much greater age and geographical range.[1] One reason for this considerable disagreement is that the term is used inconsistently and employed to cover a wide variety of narratives. While there may not be total agreement on what a märchen is, there is considerably greater unanimity that the narrative form is pretty much a dead letter, at least in the United States. There is little published

evidence to refute the claim that there is no living märchen tradition in this country. To date, fewer than 20 American märchen collections have been published and at least some of these are clearly reports of "memory culture."[2] Based on these publications one must conclude that märchen are found in the United States almost exclusively in the southern Appalachians and the Ozarks.

It is not too surprising that the southern Appalachians and the Ozarks have yielded the major American crop of märchen, because these are the regions popularly accepted as folklore's natural habitat, and these evidences of the ancient narrative form can be interpreted as proof of the validity of the popular assumption. What it really proves, though, is that more collecting has been done in the southern mountains than in most other parts of the United States. In any case, one can hardly argue on the basis of published evidence that märchen exist in abundance in either southern Appalachia or the Ozarks. In the latter region the entire printed record is the work of two men, Joseph Carrière and Vance Randolph.[3]

The Ozarks Region

For the benefit of those who may not be overly familiar with the Ozarks and its history it may be wise to briefly discuss the matter. The Ozarks is one of the most poorly defined mountain regions in the United States, perhaps in the world. There are geological guidelines, but in drawing geographical boundaries most people, including academics, pay more attention to cultural features than geological ones. Some experts say the Ozarks consists of portions of two states, most of southern Missouri and most of northern Arkansas, while others expand it to include portions of four or even five states: most of northern Arkansas, most of southern Missouri, a portion of southern Illinois, a segment of southeastern Kansas, and most of eastern Oklahoma. Whether one accepts the most exclusive drawing of the boundary lines or not, there is no doubt that the Ozarks is not, as is often assumed, Appalachia West. It has been settled by numerous peoples, but four major migrations are preeminent in Ozark history. Beginning about 12,000 B.C., American Indians moved into the region. At the beginning of the eighteenth century, Frenchmen established permanent settlements in the northeastern Ozarks, approximately half a century before permanent non-Indian settlements appeared in southern Appalachia. In the 1820s, a mass migration from Germany into the Ozarks occurred, and in the 1840s a large-scale migration from southern Appalachia into the region took place. This last cultural group became the dominant one in the Ozarks, which explains why many people now erroneously assume that Ozark culture is simply an extension of that found in southern Appalachia. The whole matter of Ozark culture is much more complex than that assumption would lead one to believe; it is an amalgam of many parts, some, but not all, of which come from southern Appalachia. Unfortunately, with only a few notable exceptions collectors of Ozark traditions have focused exclusively on those elements of folklore shared with southern Appalachia.[4]

Early Folklore Collecting in the Ozarks

The first person to intentionally collect folklore in the Ozarks was Silas Claiborne Turnbo (1844–1925). Active from 1868–1913 he amassed thousands of pages of material, virtually none of which was published during his lifetime; today, over seventy years after his death, the vast majority of his collection can only be found in various archives scattered throughout the Ozarks.[5] Turnbo's files contain numerous stories and anecdotes, but no märchen. That is typical for of all the other collectors ranging from Octave Thanet in the nineteenth century to Loman Cansler, Max Hunter, Mary Parler, and myself in the twentieth

century. Only three have reported finding märchen in the Ozarks: Joseph Carrière, Ward Dorrance, and Vance Randolph. Of these, only Carrière and Randolph have published a large number of examples. The first two found a märchen telling tradition while doing research in French American communities in the northeastern Ozarks. Dorrance was doing research for a dissertation and concentrated primarily on the local language, ultimately publishing a glossary of words found only in Missouri French.[6] He did, however, collect various elements of folklore, including märchen, and in his 1938 *We're From Missouri* offered a slightly fictionalized account of the context in which such stories were told in the community of Old Mines:

> Sometimes we'd find a group of men around a table playing cards. They were glad to stop if the Uncle would tell them tales. The Uncle was a "conteur." Of them all, he remembered the folklore best. He alone got each of the tricky words just right. It was he who knew how to make silence eloquent, how to sadden with a glance, how to convulse with a wink or nod. And he was very touchy about the whole matter. One had to approach him as one sets about photographing wildlife. One laugh, once show irreverence—Bah! As well try to lure back the deer frightened by the camera flash at night.
>
> When the cards were pushed back, the Uncle would clear his throat. There would be an instant when we heard the moths thud at the lamp, the creek purling about its rocks beneath the window. Then we would hear of the prince whose magic key was swallowed by a fish, and the princess who roamed the golden wheat on the far side of the moon; of Johnny Greenpea; of the Prince White Pig and the Prince Green Snake; of how the rascal Beausoleil tricked the priest, and how Madame the Vulture got a bald head. (Dorrance, 1938)

Unlike Dorrance, Carrière focused on folktales, presenting 75 Creole versions of anecdotes, novellas, farces, animal tales, and jokes in his 1937 volume *Tales from the French Folklore of Missouri*. In 1983, 21 of the 59 märchen collected by Carrière appeared in the volume *It's Good to Tell You: French Folktales from Missouri,* a book edited by Rosemary Hyde Thomas. One passage in Carrière's 1937 book also gives a description of the role of the storyteller in Old Mines:

To beguile the monotony of life in small communities . . . the Creoles had a rich treasure of oral traditions, songs, and tales. A good singer or a good "conteur" was an important character, and enjoyed unusual prestige. There was a great demand for his talent, as no wedding celebration, no family gathering, no social function could be a success without his presence. Not long ago, miners still used to stop their work to sing a song in chorus, or hear one of their comrades tell a tale. Oral traditions had a definite social significance in primitive settlements. They took everyone, young and old, to a country of fairyland and dream, where all could forget for the time being the dire poverty, the ceaseless struggle, and the hard routine of their everyday life. (Carrière, 1937)

Clearly, märchen were at one time told in the Ozarks. Further proof is provided by Vance Randolph, the most prolific of all Ozark folklorists. In his five folktale collections—*Who Blowed Up the Church House?, The Devil's Pretty Daughter, The Talking Turtle, Sticks in the Knapsack,* and *Pissing in the Snow*—he published over 40 märchen texts.[7] The bulk of these volumes consists of jokes, legends, and tall tales, but the inclusion of 40-plus märchen is significant, especially when compared with the paltry number of examples contributed by other active collectors.

The Lack of Märchen in Recent Collecting
The published and unpublished data collected since Carrière, Dorrance, and Randolph offers little indication that the märchen tradition they found still exists in the Ozarks. I have specifically sought out märchen from various Ozark informants, finding out only that they used to hear what many of them refer to as "those little stories" but never told them.[8] Perhaps my failure to find these narratives could be explained away as ineptness on my part or the expected failure of someone from "off" who has only spent a couple of decades in the region. That, however, doesn't explain the failure of Max Hunter, an Ozark native, who has spent all of his 77 years in the mountains, to turn up märchen. A man with a passionate interest in folklore, Hunter spent the better part of two decades collecting various types of Ozark folklore. His collection, almost all of which is unpublished, is noteworthy for its size; even so, it contains no märchen. This seems to corroborate the opinion that these "little stories" are no longer found in the Ozarks.

Why No More Märchen?
What happened to the märchen in the Ozarks? Such a question can not be easily answered, if at all; instead it holds out the possibility of multiple explanations. In a perceptive paper delivered at the 1990 American Folklore Society meeting in Oakland, California, Carl Lindahl offered four possible answers.[9] One is that most of the reported tales never existed in oral tradition; they were simply made up by the collector. Another is that the texts reported to date are simply the relics of a dying tradition. A third is that there has been a shift away from the märchen to the legend or joke. Finally, Lindahl suggests that the märchen has not died; it simply remains to be found. In other words, it is what he has elsewhere called a "shy" traditional.[10] Lindahl's four points merit further discussion.

It is true that Vance Randolph sometimes had a creative mind. For example, when he couldn't recall whom he heard a tale from he often said it was related by his first wife, Marie Wilbur.[11] Moreover, there is little doubt that he provided some creative touches to many of his texts, casting many of the folktales included in his narrative collections in what he considered proper folktale format. Thus, each of the 97 tales in *Sticks in the Knapsack* and all but one of the 91 in *The Devil's Pretty Daughter* begin with the formulaic "one time" opening. Essentially the same ratio holds for the narratives contained in *Who Blowed Up the Church House?, The Talking Turtle,* and *Pissing in the Snow*. It must be remembered, however, that Randolph tape-recorded relatively few of his tales, märchen or otherwise, on field collecting expeditions. He often merely recalled a tale some time after hearing it, in some cases relying on notes made at the time he heard the story. Some creativity was demanded because he did not have the narrator's exact words in hand. Thus, it is only logical that he would resort to an opening formula that a traditional tale teller would use. In any case, it is a long way from providing virtually every tale with a consistent opening to inventing tales out of whole cloth. The texts published by Carrière also have consistent formulaic opening phrases, in this instance "it's good to tell you." If Randolph is to be accused of wholesale invention of narratives then it seems that Carrière must also be charged with the same. In the absence of any other proof, such a claim stretches credulity. What's more, both men usually name informants and state when they acquired their texts. The claim of fraud, then, seems about as believable as some of the more absurd conspiracy theories regarding the murders of John F. Kennedy and Martin Luther King Jr.[12]

Lindahl's second suggestion, that the texts that have been published are the final relics of a dying tradition, fits perfectly with some views of märchen and folklore itself. According to this view, all tales are survivals from an earlier time that have merely outlasted their period of vitality and are rapidly on their way to extinction. In one sense the longstanding popularity of this belief has proven useful for it has spurred the gathering of many folklore collections, but in another it has been harmful because it has given rise to a belief that folklore is irrelevant because it is something from the past that was once useful but has now lost its usefulness. Is there any validity to the claim that published märchen texts from the Ozarks are the last remains of a dying tradition? Randolph's notes suggest that his informants heard the tales he reports many years before he collected them, usually from grandparents or elders, although Rose Spaulding, his best and most prolific märchen narrator, had a version of Type 780, The Singing Bone, from a little girl in Cassville, Missouri.[13] Carrière refers to the märchen tradition in the past tense, suggesting that even in the 1920s, 1930s, and 1940s when he did his collecting, the märchen tradition he encountered was essentially an example of memory culture.

But in drawing such a conclusion one may be assuming more than the evidence actually implies. For one thing, Randolph and Carrière to some extent felt that they were doing cultural archaeology because they subscribed to the archaist's idea that this tradition was in its final stages and their work represented a salvage mission. As a result they may have unintentionally slanted their findings to reflect such. Beyond that, the history of folklore scholarship is replete with examples that should give anyone caution when making proclamations about the death of traditions. One has only to think of Francis James Child, one of folklore's saints, who was convinced that no one was singing the English and Scottish popular ballads when he began his ten-volume magnum opus in the second half of the nineteenth century. Subsequent history has certainly proved him wrong.

Lindahl's third explanation, that there has been a shift away from märchen to joke and legend, is one with which most scholars would not argue. Such a shift is, of course, not unique to the Ozarks, but can probably be stated with some validity about the narrative tradition of the rest of the United States, if not much of the Western world. Randolph's märchen texts, most of which include magic elements only as a vestige, support this contention. It is also supported by such jokes as the following, which I have collected numerous times from Ozark informants.

> Walter was walking down the road one day and he saw this frog. He picked it up and it said, "Kiss me and I'll turn into a beautiful princess." He just put it in his pocket and walked along. After a while the frog said again, "Kiss me and I'll turn into a beautiful princess."
>
> He just kept walking along with the frog in his pocket. Finally, the frog asked, "Why won't you kiss me?"
>
> "At my age I'd rather have a talking frog than a beautiful princess any day."[14]

Why has this shift occurred? Lindahl argues accurately, I think, that being the most forthrightly artistic oral prose art form found in America, the märchen has an inherent tendency to transform itself into other types of narratives. He might have added that this tendency also exists because märchen are the most complex oral prose art form and the tendency among folk artists in the United States is to go from the more complex and lengthy to the less complex and shorter forms. The joke and the legend are usually briefer and thus have broader appeal to Ozark narrators than the much longer märchen. Also the relative brevity of jokes and legends means that most narrators regard them as less artistic than märchen, an important consideration because, as Lindahl also points out, many American traditional narrators shy away from the "artistic" or folklore forms that bring about the label "artist."

Lindahl's fourth explanation, that the märchen is not dead, it merely remains to be found, is very plausible, especially if one thinks of these narratives as being a subtle tradition. One might think of certain genres of folklore, such as folksongs and jokes, as extroverted because their performance is not tied to specific family functions. Märchen, on the other hand, are and thus can be considered introverted. One reason more folk-songs have been published than märchen is simply that the former are more easily obtainable than the latter. In some instances the easy accessibility of some genres of folklore has led to their not receiving serious attention. For example, the scholarly collection, let alone study, of jokes did not take place until the second half of the twentieth century and even now is still in its infancy.

Other Possible Reasons for a Lack of Märchen in Contemporary Collecting

Although Lindahl's discussion is helpful, there are some other possibilities that he did not consider. One is that collectors assumed the märchen was dead and, not surprisingly, found what they assumed. Such a situation is not without precedent in the history of American folklore studies as the case of Francis James Child demonstrates. Assuming that traditional ballad singing was a dead matter, Child quickly concluded, erroneously as we now know, after making an attempt to find a ballad singing tradition, that his original opinion was correct. Of course, not every collector can be charged with such bias because some did record märchen. Randolph found several texts and, although I have been unsuccessful, I have yet to make the conclusion that the märchen telling tradition has expired in the Ozarks. It also seems unlikely that Mary Parler, Randolph's wife, believed the märchen dead since her husband collected over 40 examples. Also some collectors didn't seek märchen not because they assumed such narratives no longer existed but because they were primarily interested in other matters. This was the case with Silas Turnbo, the most open-minded of collectors. He was literally willing to write down anything informants told him. His collecting ventures, however, were largely focused on farming and outdoor life. Thus, he got many tales about true events such as hunting exploits but very little in the way of fictional entertainments such as märchen.

A second possibility is that the American märchen tradition was never widely popular. There is a tendency to think of a golden age in the past when everyone knew certain types of folklore, but often the golden age never actually existed. Novice ballad collectors often envision a pristine past era when every singer sang Child ballads. The history of ballad collecting in this country, particularly in the first half-century after *The English and Scottish Popular Ballads* appeared,

supports such a view. Most American ballad collections published between 1900 and 1950 contain a heavy emphasis on Child ballads, some editors even going as far as Reed Smith who excluded everything non-Child from his book.[15] Those not going to that extreme still emphasized Child ballads above all others.[16] Evidence now in hand, however, indicates that folksingers typically had many more numbers like "Little Rosewood Casket" than the more prestigious "Death of Queen Jane."[17]

Possibly a similar situation existed with the märchen. Although folklorists may regard these narratives more highly than legends, jokes, and other fare, it is entirely possible that the folk did not. While märchen may have been related in the Ozarks since the early eighteenth century, there was probably never a time when many narrators told such tales. What information exists indicates that although many people may have been passive bearers of such tales, it was a very small percentage of people who were active bearers of these traditions. Dorrance and Carrière got the bulk of their texts from three men and Randolph acquired his from a relatively small number of narrators. Several of these informants had repertoires that included mostly other types of narratives.

A third possibility is that changes have occurred in the Ozark märchen telling tradition that make it more difficult to unearth them. In Europe the narrators were primarily men, in fact travelers who spent their life on the road.[18] One change in this tradition that has been noted by several scholars is that Americans who relate märchen are generally not travelers, but homebodies. This is not the only difference between the Ozark märchen telling tradition and that once commonplace in Europe. With the Old Mines instance standing as an exception, Ozark märchen narrators seem to be mainly women. Hubert Wilkes of Cave City, Arkansas, recalled that his mother told him these "little stories" when he was a child. He also called them "fairy tales" and "moral stories," the latter designation pointing out one of the functions such tales served in his family. In my experience his comments are typical; of all the informants I have asked about these tales over the past 22 years, only one reported having heard such stories from a male narrator, in this instance a grandfather.[19] Furthermore, Vance Randolph's most prolific märchen teller was Rose Spaulding. Such data does not constitute definitive proof that in the Ozarks märchen are primarily conveyed by women, but it does at least make a case for the probability. If my surmise is accurate, then this helps explain why so few märchen have been reported from the Ozarks. Most collectors, whether male or female, have found it more difficult to collect narratives of any kind from Ozark women. Only Randolph and Max Hunter, both of whom spent over 50 years in the region, have had much luck collecting narratives from women. Whether this situation results from a deeply ingrained belief that tale telling is the proper province of men, or some other reason, is unknown to me. Most likely it is due to a variety of reasons, one being that these tales are regarded as primarily for family use or for very specific non-public performance.

For several centuries the imminent demise of folklore has been predicted. Yet, despite the assurances of impending death the funeral has never taken place. This fact alone should give anyone cause for caution in pronouncing the märchen dead in the Ozarks, or anywhere else. Even though no less a critic than Stith Thompson once said the age of the "little stories" is past, it still seems unwise to toll the funeral bell just now.[20]

Notes

1. Albert Wesselski, for example, concluded, in his *Versuch einer Theorie des Märchens* and other places, that the form does not go back before the sixteenth century, being essentially a product of the Renaissance. However, as Stith Thompson says (1977, p. 22) "In the life history of any of our most popular folktales, one must usually go farther back than the sixteenth century and much farther afield than western Europe."

2. John Burrison, Marie Campbell, Isabel Gordon Carter, Richard Chase, Emlyn Gardner, Henry Glassie, Charles Perdue, Vance Randolph, and Leonard Roberts have all published field collected märchen texts or ones that were based on field recorded materials. In the case of Chase his narratives were often greatly reworked to fit with his ideas of folksiness. Of these several collections only Gardner's comes from a non-southern mountain region.

3. This matter is discussed in greater detail in my book *Ozark Country* (1995).

4. The major exceptions are Joseph M. Carrière, Ward A. Dorrance, and the Missouri Friends of the Folk Arts, a group of folklore enthusiasts from St. Louis, who concentrated on collecting French American traditions in the northeastern Ozarks.

5. For an account of the various institutions now housing portions of Turnbo's collection see my introduction to Keefe and Morrow (1994).

6. See Dorrance, 1935.

7. These titles were published in 1952, 1955, 1957, 1958, and 1976.

8. This is a phrase used by more than one informant that I have asked. It seems to be the most commonly used name.

9. See Lindahl, 1990.

10. See Lindahl, 1990 and 1994.

11. Randolph himself told me on several occasions during 1976–1980 that he did this.

12. It should be pointed out that Lindahl was not seriously advocating that Randolph invented the narratives, merely offering it as one possible explanation. It was not a possibility Lindahl put any credence in.

13. See Randolph, 1957, pp. 16–17.

14. I have heard this numerous times over the past 20 years. The version reported here was collected October 11, 1997, from John Taylor, Fox, Arkansas. The Walter referred to is Walter Gosser, Mt. View, Arkansas.

15. See Smith, 1928.

16. See, for example, Randolph 1946–1950, which has the first volume of his mammoth work reserved for variants and versions of Child ballads.

17. Most ballad collections consist of a greater number of the non-classic, i.e., non-Child, ballads than they do of variants and versions of Child's classics. For example, three of the four volumes of Randolph 1946–1950 are devoted to non-Child material. Only in situations where everything but Child items are excluded do the classics dominate number-wise.

18. See Dégh, 1969, pp. 63–93.

19. In 1978 while interviewing a rather shy woman in Cabot, Arkansas (who requested not to be identified) about some of her craft traditions, she mentioned that her grandfather had told her the "little stories" several years earlier when she was a child. She no longer recalled anything more than the broad general outlines of a few tales.

20. See Thompson, 1977, p. 461, where he says, "The folktale has gone the way of the bow and arrow."

Further Reading

Aarne, Antti, *The Types of the Folktale: A Classification and Bibliography,* edited and translated by Stith Thompson, second revision, Helsinki, Finland: Academia Scientarum Fennica, 1961

Burrison, John A., *Storytellers: Folktales and Legends from the South,* Athens: University of Georgia Press, 1989

Campbell, Marie, *Tales from the Cloud Walking Country,* Bloomington: Indiana University Press, 1958

Carrière, Joseph M., *Tales from the French Folklore of Missouri,* Evanston, Illinois: Northwestern University Press, 1937

Carter, Isabel Gordon, "Mountain White Folklore: Tales from the Southern Blue Ridge," *Journal of American Folklore* 38 (1925)

Chase, Richard, *American Folk Tales and Songs,* New York: New American Library, 1956

_____, *Grandfather Tales: American-English Folk Tales,* Boston: Houghton Mifflin, 1948

_____, *The Jack Tales,* Boston: Houghton Mifflin, 1943

Dégh, Linda, *Folktales and Society: Story-telling in a Hungarian Peasant Community,* Bloomington: Indiana University Press, 1969

Dorrance, Ward Allison, *The Survival of French in the Old District of Sainte Genevieve, Missouri,* Columbia: University of Missouri Press, 1935

_____, *We're From Missouri,* Richmond: Missourian, 1938

Glassie, Henrie, "Three Southern Mountain Jack Tales," *Tennessee Folklore Society Bulletin* 30 (1964)

Lindahl, Carl, "Jack: The Name, the Tales, the American Traditions," in *Jack in Two Worlds: Contemporary North American Tales and Their Tellers,* edited by William Bernard McCarthy, Chapel Hill: University of North Carolina Press, 1994

_____, "Vance Randolph and the Ozarks Märchen," paper presented at the annual meeting of the American Folklore Society, Oakland, California, 1990

McNeil, W.K., *Ozark Country,* Jackson: University Press of Mississippi, 1995

Perdue, Charles L., Jr., *Outwitting the Devil: Jack Tales from Wise County, Virginia,* Santa Fe, New Mexico: Ancient City, 1987

Randolph, Vance, comp., *The Devil's Pretty Daughter, and Other Ozark Folk Tales,* New York: Columbia University Press, 1955

_____, *Ozark Folksongs,* 4 volumes, Columbia: State Historical Society of Missouri, 1946–1950; revised edition, Columbia: University of Missouri Press, 1980

_____, ed., *Sticks in the Knapsack, and Other Ozark Folk Tales,* New York: Columbia University Press, 1958

_____, ed., *The Talking Turtle, and Other Ozark Folk Tales,* New York: Columbia University Press, 1957

_____, ed., *Who Blowed Up the Church House? and Other Ozark Folk Tales,* New York: Columbia University Press, 1952

Roberts, Leonard, comp., *Old Greasybeard: Tales from the Cumberland Gap,* Detroit, Michigan: Folklore Associates, 1969

_____, *Sang Branch Settlers: Folksongs and Tales of a Kentucky Mountain Family,* Austin: University of Texas Press, 1974

_____, *South from Hell-fer-Sartin: Kentucky Mountain Folk Tales,* Lexington: University Press of Kentucky, 1955

Smith, Reed, *South Carolina Ballads, with a Study of the Traditional Ballad To-day,* Cambridge, Massachusetts: Harvard University Press, 1928

Thomas, Rosemary Hyde, *It's Good to Tell You: French Folktales from Missouri,* Columbia: University of Missouri Press, 1981

Thompson, Stith, *The Folktale,* New York: Dryden, 1946; reprint, Berkeley: University of California Press, 1977

Turnbo, S.C., *The White River Chronicles of S.C. Turnbo: Man and Wildlife on the Ozarks Frontier,* Fayetteville: University of Arkansas Press, 1994

Jack Tales

Carl Lindahl

Carl Lindahl traces the American "Jack Tale" from the early 1400s in England to its present-day use as a staple of professional touring storytellers in the United States.

"Jack Tales" Defined

Jack Tales is a label applied to various overlapping types of stories in English-language tradition. For some, Jack Tales refers generally to traditional narratives, principally märchen, told throughout the English-speaking world. For others, the term refers more particularly to a series of North Carolina mountain tales told by the Harmon-Hicks family of the Southern Appalachians and made famous by Richard Chase's published collection, *The Jack Tales* (1943). Still others define Jack Tales as a body of narrative particularly representative of American folk values. Jack Tales are probably most significant as a means of bringing traditional narrators and revivalist storytellers in contact with one another.

The Far-flung Tradition of the Name Jack

As a folktale hero's name, "Jack" is both unique to the English-speaking world and broadly characteristic of worldwide märchen tradition. Jack is a diminutive of "John," the most popular name for a male hero in many European and American storytelling communities. Thus, in Grimms' tales, Hans—a diminutive of Johann or Johannes—is a common hero's name. In Spanish-language tales in both the Old and New Worlds, Juan Oso, or "John the Bear," is a popular stock character, and in France, French Canada, and Cajun Louisiana, Tit-Jean, or "Little John," and Jean Sot, or "Foolish John," stand among the most popular heroes. The Russian Ivan, the Scot-tish Ian, and the Irish Sean—all forms of John—are popular names for heroes in their respective European traditions.

Currently, Jack is the most popular name for folktale protagonists in much of the English-speaking world. Among the 150 full-length folktales published in Halpert's and Widdowson's exhaustive *Folktales of Newfoundland*, 63 (42 percent) feature a protagonist named Jack. Similarly, a leading figure named Jack appears in 8 of the 39 (21 percent) märchen published by Leonard Roberts in *South from Hell-fer-Sartin*, and in 6 of 22 (27 percent) of the prose narratives in a collection of tales told by Scottish Traveller Duncan Williamson *(A Thorn in the King's Foot)*.

Jack's popularity possesses time depth. As far back as English language märchen can be traced there are stories about Jack. From the early 1400s survives a northern English–rhymed tale, "Jack and His Stepdame," in which Jack is an only child mistreated by his stepmother. After Jack shares food with an old beggar, the stranger grants him three magic wishes that allow him to punish the stepmother; this is the oldest known version of the internationally known tale type, The Dance among Thorns (AT 592).

Three centuries would pass between the hand-written "Jack and His Stepdame" and the appearance of the first printed Jack tale. But during this long hiatus, scraps of tales emerged to hint strongly that Jack was thriving in oral tradition. For example, Thomas Nashe's Renaissance drama, *Haue with You to Saffron-Waldon*, published in 1596, contains a version of the rhyme later associated throughout the world with Jack's most imposing foe, the giant:

. . . Fy, fa, fum,
I smell the bloud of an Englishman.

We can assume that the rhyme and the giant killer stories were old even in Nashe's time, for he warns that only a pedant would speculate on the "first inuention of Fy, fa, fum."

Only in the early eighteenth century do the oldest surviving printed Jack-and-giant tales first appear: "The History of Jack and the Giants" was published in Newcastle in 1711 and "The History of Jack and the Bean-Stalk" in London in 1734. These works, popular with all classes of English, attracted the admiration of Joseph Fielding, Samuel Johnson, and James Boswell, though Nicholas Amhearst complained that too many professors of history "never read any thing" other than stories of Jack and Tom Thumb. As the cheaply priced chapbooks of the eighteenth century became the elaborate storybooks of the nineteenth century, farmer Jack appeared in the nurseries of wealthy Victorians; all English people knew something of Jack.

Elsewhere in the British Isles, Jack's name thrived. In Scotland and Ireland, even among Gaelic-speaking narrators, the name has long been popular. Among the most prolific contemporary tellers of Jack Tales are the "travelling people," migratory families of Scotland. Narrator Duncan Williamson states that Jack is a hero among the travellers, who often change the names of heroes of borrowed tales to create new adventures for Jack.

The Appalachian Jack Tales

Jack's popularity grew throughout Britain at the time Britain's empire was growing. From the eighteenth century forward, immigrants from Britain and Ireland have brought their tales of Jack and the giants to Britain's colonies, including the Caribbean, where African Americans continue to narrate stories in which Jack appears. In twentieth century Bahamian tradition, animal tales are the most popular fantasy narratives, but Jack is the most popular human character.

For all the popularity of the name Jack, there is little evidence that folktales were generally identified as Jack Tales until relatively recently. True, in Appalachia as elsewhere in English-language tradition, Jack was a favored name for male folktale characters. True as well, his exploits were so popular that tales about him were used to identify an entire genre of oral storytelling. As early as 1760, in what is now West Virginia, the

young boy Charles Doddridge heard folktales performed throughout the frontier:

Dramatic narration's, chiefly concerning Jack and the Giant, furnished our young people with another source of amusement during their leisure hours. Many of those tales were lengthy, and embraced a considerable range of incident. Jack, always the hero of the story, after encountering many difficulties and performing many great achievements, came off conqueror of the Giant. These dramatic narrations . . . were so arranged as to the different incidents of the narration, that they were easily committed to memory. (Perdue 1987)

Doddridge wrote on that these tales had already been swept away by "civilization," which had substituted in their place the novel and the romance. But the Jack tales continued to be told among the mountain people, a fact that folklorists did not rediscover until the 1920s—a century and a half after Doddridge heard them performed—when Isabel Gordon Carter asked a celebrated ballad singer if she knew any folktales.

The singer was Jane Gentry of Hot Springs, North Carolina. She knew a dozen long narratives, which she identified by the name "Jack, Will, and Tom Tales"—often told in her family—but she expressed utter astonishment that any outsider would want to hear them. Yet they were told often and with animation within the group, and most often in situations of group labor for the purpose of entertaining children into working harder.

Clearly, something had happened between the 1760s and the 1920s: what had once been a popular and public art form entertaining the entire range of social classes was now a working-class act, inextricably associated with the hard labor that characterized the mountain poor. This was a private, stay-at-home affair that, no matter how lively inside its native boundaries, remained shy and elusive to the outsider.

The Jack Tale and the American Storytelling Revival

But all this was to change in 1943, when Richard Chase published *The Jack Tales,* easily the most popular and influential collection of American folktales ever compiled, a book in print continually for more than half a century since first published. Tapping the same family to which Jane Gentry belonged, the Harmon-Hicks family of North Carolina, Chase produced a book whose popularity helped perpetuate two fallacies: that American märchen were largely the legacy of one family, and that their sole subject was a boy named Jack.

Chase assigned names and a family pedigree to the tradition behind his tales, but his typical m.o. was to conflate the stories of as many as ten different tellers—many from other families and regions—into one composite form, which he rendered in his own words, thus subordinating the diverse artful voices of his sources to his personal esthetic. The working contexts and the local references that made these tales so much the special province of the Appalachians are largely lost in his versions. Chase was searching not for a family, or even a regional, but a national folk soul, and his task in *The Jack Tales* was to present his nation with a character embodying the American folk soul. As Chase says in the book's introduction: "Jack . . . is . . . the unassuming representative of a very large part of the American people." Many readers bought his line. Jack was taken as a national hero, his book became in the words of one evaluator, "an American folktale classic," and Chase enjoyed great success. As he absorbed the family art of the Harmons and Hickses into his generic vision, Chase promised the family money that he never paid, copyrighted their stories under his own name—the tales may belong to everyone, and represent the entire nation, but only Chase profited from them.

The earliest collections of Jack tales—those of Carter, Chase, and Long—constitute the repertoire of one extended family, the descendants of Council Harmon of North Carolina, a fact that led some to conclude that the Jack Tales are an isolated regional tradition. Nevertheless, the research of Leonard Roberts in eastern Kentucky and parallel versions found by Vance Randolph in the American Ozarks demonstrate a much broader tradition of "Jack tales" than was once supposed. Stories about a character named Jack are found not only in North Carolina, but also in Virginia, West Virginia, Tennessee, Kentucky, New York, Pennsylvania, Missouri, Arkansas, and elsewhere.

Chase's collection exerted enormous influence on both the study and the popular enjoyment of American folktales. Few American storybooks have had greater effect throughout the country than has Chase's. Especially among storytellers' guilds, librarians, and child listeners, Jack Tales has become a household label. Even though his methods were resented by folk artists and folklorists alike, Richard Chase affected the performance and appreciation of storytelling in the mountains as well as in the country at large. Chase visited schoolrooms to perform Jack Tales in eastern Kentucky and western Virginia and North Carolina. In Kentucky, he met future folklorist Leonard Roberts, and in North Carolina he told tales in the classroom of young Donald Davis. Both would go on to become major storytellers themselves. Roberts would perform principally for his students in his Kentucky college classrooms, while Davis would become a professional storyteller purveying Jack Tales to popular audiences throughout the country.

Through Leonard Roberts and others, Chase wrought considerable influence upon the scholarly world. Inspired by *The Jack Tales,* Roberts began reading Chase's stories aloud to settlement school students at Berea, Kentucky, in the late 1940s. His students responded by telling tales—many about a boy named Jack—learned from their parents and grandparents in their Cumberland Mountain homes. These Roberts collected and published in a series of major anthologies: *South from Hell-fer-Sartin* (1955), *Old Greasybeard* (1969), and *Sang Branch Settlers* (1974).

Chase's taped collections of folktales and ballads can be found today in the Archives of Folk Culture in the Library of Congress, where his influence is also measurable in the small number of oral märchen found on deposit there. Nearly all the British-American märchen housed in the Library of Congress were collected from the Harmon-Hicks family of North Carolina, the same family tradition that Chase tapped to record the Jack Tales.

As listeners listened less to Chase and more to the families from whom he had gotten the tales, the Jack Tales of North Carolina exerted an enormous influence on American popular perceptions of storytelling. In 1973, fully three decades after *The Jack Tales* was first published, the National Storytelling Festival in Jonesborough, Tennessee, was inaugurated, and Ray Hicks, a descendent of the Harmon-Hicks family members who had told their tales to Richard Chase, held forth telling Jack Tales. Hicks was to return annually to Jonesborough for the next 25 years. Through his live and taped performances, and such video productions as *Fixing to Talk about Jack* (1975), Ray Hicks influenced thousands of seasoned and fledging performers from around the country, becoming in the process the most famous traditional narrator in the United States.

Ray Hicks's success wrought its influence on other narrators from the Appalachian region, who surfaced to revive Jack Tales heard in their childhood and reshape them for the pleasure of distant audiences. Among the most popular current performers is Donald Davis, a native of North Carolina whose *Jack Always Seeks His Fortune* (1988) is currently popular on the storytelling circuit. William Bernard McCarthy's *Jack in Two Worlds* discusses the performances of Davis and other recently popular performers of Jack Tales.

What makes a Jack Tale distinctive? Early British scholars traced the giant-killer tales back to Germanic myth and legend and contended that Jack was the vestige of an ancient racial or culture hero. Twentieth-century Scottish traveller narrator Duncan Williamson says that Jack is an underdog who presents a heroic figure for children to emulate. Various interpreters of American Jack have sought in him a national personality. Others, like Paige Gutierrez, find him a regional hero, lucky, "hard working, intelligent, and self reliant." Though some claim that Scottish traveller Jack and Appalachian Jack are consistent characters, the majority of British and American tales about Jack cannot be tied firmly to either tradition. Most often, Jack is simply a generic name. Like German Hans, Spanish Juan Oso, French Tit-Jean, Jack is a popular title attached to many varied folktale characters.

Further Reading

Chase, Richard, *The Jack Tales,* Boston: Houghton Mifflin, 1943

Davis, Donald, *Jack Always Seeks His Fortune: Authentic Appalachian Jack Tales,* Little Rock, Arkansas: August House, 1988

Gutierrez, C. Paige, "The Jack Tale: A Definition of a Folk Tale Sub-Genre," *North Carolina Folklore Journal* 26 (1978)

Halpert, Herbert, and J.D.A.Widdowson, eds., *Folktales of Newfoundland: The Resilience of the Oral Tradition,* 2 volumes, New York: Garland, 1996

Isbell, Robert, *The Last Chivaree: The Hicks Family of Beech Mountain,* Chapel Hill: University of North Carolina Press, 1996

Lindahl, Carl, "Who Is Jack? A Study in Isolation," *Fabula* 29:3–4 (1988)

Long, Maud, *Jack Tales,* 2 LP records, AAFS L47, L48, Washington, D.C.: Library of Congress, 1955

McCarthy, William B., *Jack in Two Worlds: Contemporary North American Tales and Their Tellers,* Chapel Hill: University of North Carolina Press, 1994

Nicolaisen, William F.H., "English Jack and American Jack," *Midwestern Journal of Language and Folklore* 4 (1978)

Perdue, Charles, *Outwitting the Devil: Jack Tales from Wise County, Virginia,* Santa Fe, New Mexico: Ancient City, 1987

Roberts, Leonard, ed., *South from Hell-fer-Sartin: Kentucky Mountain Folk Tales,* Lexington: University Press of Kentucky, 1955

Williamson, Duncan, and Linda Williamson, *A Thorn in the King's Foot: Folktales of the Scottish Travelling People,* New York and Harmondsworth, England: Penguin, 1987

Cowboy Poetry and Other Occupational Folk Poetry

Jens Lund

Jens Lund gives us background on the cowboy poetry tradition, mentions several popular contemporary cowboy poets and provides sources for exploration of this genre.

Occupational Folk Poetry

Cowboy and logger poetry (as well as the poetry of other physically demanding occupations, such as fishers, sailors, or miners) and their performance are modern manifestations of an ancient tradition. In the ancient world, the Homeric epics were orally composed and recited.

Although not as widely studied as ballad singing or the telling of fairy tales, the practice of telling a story from memory, in rhyme and/or meter, to entertain and enlighten an audience, is a significant part of Anglo- and Irish-American folk tradition. Recitation is often closely connected with the singing of ballads. The same piece may be recited as a poem in some instances and sung as a ballad in others. In the English-speaking world, the Oxford English Dictionary cites examples of public recitation in the seventeenth century. William Butler Yeats refers to a "gleeman," who entertained in Ireland's pubs in the late eighteenth and early nineteenth centuries.

The traditions of occupational poetry were strengthened by teaching methods used in the early years of public education. Many lessons, such as geography, history, or literature, were taught by having pupils learn recitations. A person spending any time in a nineteenth-century British or American public school would have been taught to memorize and recite.

The work of certain nineteenth- and early-twentieth-century poets has had a particular appeal to men because of their masculine subject matter. These works include Samuel Taylor Coleridge's "The Rime of the Ancient Mariner," Alfred Lord Tennyson's "The Charge of the Light Brigade," Rudyard Kipling's "Barrack-Room Ballads" series, and Robert Service's "Spell of the Yukon," "Ballads of a Cheechako," and "Carols of an Old Logger" series. Individuals with a taste for attention from their peers could memorize such material and share it at appropriate times.

Recited poetry as a medium of popular entertainment has survived well into recent times. Cowboy poetry is the best-known example. Recitations also performed and recorded by Country music entertainers, such as Hank Williams, Porter Wagoner, and Johnny Cash, or by actors, such as Andy Griffith, Sebastian Cabot, and Walter Brennan.

Paralleling the recitation tradition is that of folk poetry itself. By definition, folk poetry is informal communication in vernacular language, composed by individuals in local communities, using rhyme and/or rhythm. It may or may not be intended for recitation, but to quote Roger deV. Renwick, it represents the poet's "bounded and knowable world." In modern times, folk poetry is often self-published or published in newspapers, newsletters, and trade journals.

The above elements have contributed to the popularity of poetic composition and recitation among groups of men working in isolated conditions. Most important, however, may simply have been isolation itself. In the pre-electronic era, groups of men working on the range, water, or woods had no entertainment other than what they made for themselves. They sang and recited material they had learned elsewhere, parodies of the former, and sometimes original material.

Although that of cowboys is the best-known genre of occupational folk poetry, there are also less-studied poetry traditions among other dangerous and predominantly male occupational groups. Mining ballads were widely collected in the early twentieth century, especially in the Appalachian coalfields. The hard-rock miners of the West seem to have preferred recited poetry, perhaps influenced by the recitation traditions of neighboring cowboys and loggers.

Cowboy Poetry

By definition, cowboy poetry is the poetry of the cowboy or the western North American ranching milieu. Strictly speaking, it would be the poetry of authentic cowboys, of ranch hands who work directly with cattle. However, cowboy poetry is also composed and recited by ranchers, Western farmers, ranch owners, and those who work in the cattle industry in capacities other than as cowboys, and by people in associated occupations such as large-animal veterinarians or rodeo performers.

More broadly defined, cowboy poetry can include poetry about ranching and about life in the rural North American West, past or present. Folklorist Alan Lomax has noted that songs and stories describing the hazards and triumphs of the work of tending animals are common among many herding cultures and can often be traced back for centuries.

Cowboy poetry is, however, not defined solely by its content or by the vocations of those who compose and recite it. It is also defined by its style. Traditionally, cowboy poetry consists of rhymed couplets, usually in a narrative that tells a story in a straightforward way. Less often, it can evoke a mood, or describe a person, a place, or a situation.

Older examples of cowboy poetry are invariably stanzas of rhymed metered couplets, offering a highly linear narrative. The repertoire of the post-1985 cowboy poetry revival, however, is far more varied in structure and content and much more likely to be evocative, rather than narrative.

The origins of cowboy poetry reflect the diversity of the people who settled the North American West. Much of it is similar to, and probably derived from, the ballad tradition of the British Isles.

Many of the techniques and much of the occupational jargon of Western ranching are derived from Mexico, a nation that also has a strong narrative ballad tradition. It is the corrido, a type of narrative ballad, often describing a situation of conflict. Corridos have been especially prevalent along the U.S.-Mexican border.

During the late nineteenth century, many cowboys were former slaves. They brought to the West the African-American tradition of the "toast," a humorous and mocking form of narrative.

Both the ballads of the British Isles and those of Mexico were probably sung more often than recited. Likewise, the material in cowboy poetry has as often been sung as it has been recited. Many cowboy poems are better known as cowboy songs and vice versa.

The great Texas and New Mexico cattle drives that comprise the beginning of Western cowboy culture began in the late 1860s. The earliest examples of cowboy poetry were probably never published. The Victorian era's taste for expressions of nostalgia and homesickness dominates many of the earliest cowboy poems and songs, such as the ever-popular "Bury Me Not on the Lone Prairie."

The first non-oral venue for the dissemination of cowboy poems was the ranching trade periodicals and the local newspapers of ranching areas. Published poems about ranch life first became numerous during the 1870s. In the next decade, much of the West began to be homesteaded and the open cattle drives of the late 1860s and 1870s became a focus of nostalgia. This seems to have increased the composition and dissemination of cowboy poems, perhaps also by creating a class of more sedentary ranchhands with access to the possibility of writing and distributing their expressions.

Although the majority of itinerant ranchhands were probably poorly educated and from lower economic classes, Western ranches also attracted their share of adventurous intellectuals from the upper social and economic classes of eastern North America and Europe. An important aspect of early cowboy poetry is that some was composed by these literate people, educated in the classics, who brought their cosmopolitan perspective to this genre. Because of their influence, cowboy poetry has had, from the start, a higher literary quality than other genres of occupational poetry.

Many early classic cowboy poems—those composed in the late nineteenth and early twentieth centuries, that became part of the West's oral tradition—were written by individuals whose connection with ranching was tenuous at best. One of the oldest still-recited poems about cowboy life, "Lasca," was written in the 1880s by an English theater critic. It became part of the traditional repertoire of the cowboy reciter after its appearance in *Montana Stock Growers Journal* in 1888. In 1893, Lawrence Chittenden, a New York newspaper reporter, who had moved to Texas to become his rancher uncle's business partner, published *Ranch Verses,* the first widely distributed book of cowboy poems.

In 1905, the National Live Stock Historical Association planned to publish a three-volume series of prose and poetry about ranching history, but due to lack of funds, the second and third volumes, which were supposed to contain the poetry, never saw print. As folklorist David Stanley has noted, the fact that the material was assembled and readied for publication indicated that a significant body of this material was already in circulation.

Ranching journals and local newspapers continued to be the main print venue for cowboy poetry well into the twentieth century. However, the continued traditions of recitation and ballad-singing facilitated transmission by oral means.

Poems that found their way into the oral tradition were the first that came to general public attention. N. Howard "Jack" Thorp, worked as a cowboy and collected ranching poems and songs beginning in 1889. He published the seminal *Songs of the Cowboy,* at his own expense in 1908. Texan John Avery Lomax, who grew up on a ranch, was inspired by a ballad course he took at Harvard to publish a compilation, in 1910, of cowboy songs and poems that he had collected over a period of years. His *Cowboy Songs and Other Frontier Ballads* became widely popular, both among those interested in the West, and among Westerners themselves. It informed the general public that cowboy verse existed. It may also have helped to create the stereotype of "the singing cowboy," a staple of matinee films in the 1930s. It is important to note that most cowboys, like most of any random group of people, were neither singers not reciters. The popularity of Lomax's book, east and west, undoubtedly helped to spread the verses that it contained. Lomax published another widely distributed collection, *Songs of the Cattle Trail and Cow Camp,* in 1919.

Cowboy scholar Hal Cannon, originator of the Elko, Nevada, Cowboy Poetry Gathering, writes of a "Golden Age" of cowboy poetry composition, roughly 1900–1930. During this time such renowned folk poets as S. Omar Barker, Charles Badger Clark, Curley Fletcher, Gail I. Gardner, and Bruce Kiskaddon, composed most of the classic poems still rendered by cowboy reciters to this day.

A high degree of literacy is reflected in their works, and most of these poets, except Fletcher and Kiskaddon, were people from ranch society's upper classes. Kiskaddon, who had been a real cowboy, wrote some of his best-known works while working as a Los Angeles hotel bellhop, after his planned career as a Hollywood screen cowboy never materialized.

As the automobile ended the isolation of ranch life and the electronic media replaced homemade entertainment, cowboy recitation declined, but never died out. The composition of cowboy poetry was once again kept alive by ranching periodicals and local newspapers in Western communities.

The Elko Cowboy Poetry Gathering and Contemporary Cowboy Poets

By the late 1970s, ranch people had become concerned about the presentation of the image of ranching to the outside world. This was due in part to the rise of environmentalism, the animal rights movement, and vegetarianism, as well as various economic crises that affected American agriculture at that time. This concern coincided with a project by folklorists in the Western states to collect and present cowboy poetry to a wider public.

Although many ranch people were suspicious of the folklorists' motives at first, the folklorists' efforts led to an annual Cowboy Poetry Gathering, held in Elko, Nevada, every January since 1985. Public attention to this event and its participants caused a major revival of interest in cowboy poetry. People who had written cowboy poetry in secret now came off the range, and many rural Westerners who had never before tried to compose a rhyme, began trying their hand at it. The post-Elko generation of cowboy poets include a significant number of ranch women, some of whom, such as Georgie Sicking and Virginia Bennett, are recognized as leading poets and reciters. There are now approximately 150 cowboy poetry events held in the United States and Canada.

In today's cowboy poetry scene there are obvious stars, such as Baxter Black, Wallace McRae, Larry McWhorter, Waddie Mitchell, Rod McQueary, Buck Ramsey (who passed away in 1998), and Paul Zarzyski. Some of them, such as

Ramsey, composed poetry that is widely appreciated, but not generally recited, except by their authors. Others, such as McRae and Mitchell, have written pieces that are now as much a part of traditional recitation as are the early "classics."

One example of a recent poem becoming part of many reciters' repertoire is McRae's "Reincarnation," a hilarious and mildly scatological musing about what happens to a cowboy's remains as they return to the earth.

Although cowboy poetry has had two separate eras of creativity, it is nonetheless correct to say that it forms a single corpus of expression. Today's poets and reciters are acutely aware of what they have inherited from the days of Fletcher and Kiskaddon. Many know at least a few of the classics by memory and can recite them at will. Thus one can still generalize about the genre, as a whole.

Cowboy poetry's content consists of a large dose of humor, often ironic. It seems likely that nearly half of the repertoire is, at least partially, humorous. Even poems that are didactic, such as Wayne Nelson's "Snowville," describing an African-American cowboy's retaliation against a saloon that refused him service, do so, cloaked in bitter humor. Contemporary political poems use irony to satirize government bureaucrats, public range policy, unfair taxation, the animal rights movement, environmentalism, and vegetarianism.

A more serious category of cowboy poetry consists of poems that romanticize or sentimentalize ranch life or life in the rural West in general. These poems often display a reverence bordering on the religious, or are frankly religious in content. They specifically refer to God's role in the natural or the human world. Poems that affirm rural Western values, such as Badger Clark's "A Cowboy's Prayer," also tend to be serious. Poems that extol nature typically do so in reverential tones.

Dangers of ranch work are reflected in the tragic poems. Perhaps because it is safer in modern times, there are fewer poems like Jack Thorp's "Little Joe, the Wrangler" and D.J. O'Malley's "When the Work's All Done This Fall" written today. However both of these poems, and many similar ones, are still part of cowboy reciters' traditional repertoire.

Poems about the technical aspects of ranch work are less common today than they were during the classical period. This may reflect the fact that contemporary cowboy poetry is often intended for a general audience, whereas that of the early days was primarily esoteric.

Bawdy cowboy poetry is an important part of the genre, but it is usually only recited in small all-male groups in private situations, often fueled with alcohol. It is rarely published.

Although the wider popular enthusiasm for cowboy poetry generated by the Elko Gatherings may not persist, cowboy poetry will probably continue to be written and recited by people associated with ranching, to the extent that ranching, as we know it, continues to exist. Economic and ecological factors are likely to further limit the participation of people in the ranching industry, and the production of beef may become as "high tech" as dairy and chicken farming have become today. This may lead to cowboy poetry becoming a purely nostalgic phenomenon. On the other hand, as long as people tend herds of cattle and build a way of life around such work, cowboy poetry will reflect the life of ranchers and their families.

Sources for Cowboy Poetry Material

There are many sources of classic cowboy poems published as songs. John Avery Lomax's *Cowboy Songs and Other Frontier Ballads,* originally published in 1910, has been republished in a 1986 edition, edited and with an introduction by Alan Lomax, and published by Collier, of New York. N. Howard "Jack" Thorp's 1908 *Songs of the Cowboy,* was republished, with an introduction by Guy Logsdon, by University of Nebraska Press in 1984. The rare bawdy material can be found in *"The Whorehouse Bells Were Ringing" and Other Songs Cowboys Sing,* edited by Guy Logsdon, published by University of Illinois Press in 1989. A series of essays about cowboy poetry can be found in *On'ry Propositions: Cowboy Poets and Cowboy Poetry,* edited by David Stanley and Elaine Thatcher, University of Illinois Press, 1999.

Most cowboy poetry volumes are privately or locally published. A substantial collection of cowboy poetry, both published and unpublished, is held at the Fife Folklore Archive in the library of Utah State University, Logan, UT 84322, where it can be accessed. Many of the in-print volumes of cowboy poetry, including some that are privately published, can be ordered from the Western Folklife Center, P.O. Box 1570, Elko, NV 89803, or through their Web site, <www.westfolk.org>. The Western Folklife Center, which is the organizer and sponsor of the Cowboy Poetry Gathering, also sells numerous cassette tapes (and some CDs) of cowboy poetry recitations and cowboy songs. A series, titled The Cowboy Poetry Gathering, includes many of the best Elko performances. Many of the leading poets have produced their own cassettes, and many are available from the Western Folklife Center through their catalogue and their Web site.

Elko Gathering founder Hal Cannon has edited several good representative collections of cowboy poetry, including *Cowboy Poetry: A Gathering,* Salt Lake City: Peregrine-Smith, 1985; *New Cowboy Poetry: A Contemporary Gathering,* Peregrine-Smith, 1990; and, co-edited with Thomas West; *Buckaroo: Visions and Voices of the American Cowboy,* New York; Simon & Schuster, 1993. For poetry of ranch women, see Teresa Jordan, ed., *Graining the Mare: The Poetry of Ranch Women,* Peregrine-Smith, 1994. Another excellent contemporary collection, compiled by Warren Miller, is *Cattle, Horses, Sky, and Grass: Cowboy Poetry of the Late 20th Century,* Flagstaff, Arizona: Northland, 1994. The substantial Mormon contribution to cowboy poetry and song can be seen in *Saints of Sage and Saddle,* edited by Austin and Alta Fife, Bloomington: Indiana University Press, 1956. A fine collection of contemporary Great Basin and Mormon material is *Cowboy Poetry of Utah,* edited by Carol Edison, and published by the Utah Folklife Center of the Utah Arts Council in 1988.

Further Reading

Brunvand, Jan Harold, ed., *American Folklore: An Encyclopedia,* New York: Garland, 1996

Colcord, Joanna, *Songs of American Sailormen,* New York: Norton, 1938; London: Putnam, 1938

Cunningham, Keith, ed., *The Oral Tradition of the American West: Adventure, Courtship, Family, and Place in Traditional Recitation,* Little Rock, Arkansas: August House, 1990

Korson, George, *Coal Dust on the Fiddle: Songs and Stories of the Bituminous Industry,* Philadelphia: University of Pennsylvania Press, 1943

_____, *Minstrels of the Mine Patch: Songs and Stories of the Anthracite Industry,* Philadelphia: University of Pennsylvania Press, 1938

Renwick, Roger DeV., *English Folk Poetry: Structure and Meaning,* Philadelphia: University of Pennsylvania Press, 1980; London: Batsford Academic and Educational, 1980

Service, Robert, *Collected Poems of Robert Service,* New York: Dodd-Mead, 1940; London: E. Benn, 1978

Del Ringer and His Tales of Salmon River, Idaho

Marjorie Bennett

Marjorie Bennett shares tales from former Idaho rancher Del Ringer and discusses his repertoire.

Local Characters

"Local characters? That country was full of them. Why there was the Berlinghoffs, and Old Jewett lived right next to us" (September 1973). So said Del Ringer, referring to the Salmon River country of Idaho, where he spent his youth. I began recording Del Ringer of North Bend, Washington, when he was 76, in 1973. I had come to know Del and his wife, Martha, when I was teaching school in North Bend. Although Del had lived in North Bend for almost 50 years, his stories returned again and again to his youth, when his family homesteaded and ranched along the Salmon River. I was so enchanted by Del's stories of life along the Salmon at the turn of the century that I recorded him in five storytelling sessions from 1973 to 1985. I found his stories about local characters particularly appealing.

Del was born in Colfax, Washington, on July 3, 1897. When he was 15 Del moved to Slate Creek, Idaho. His father was foreman on the ranch of Frank Wyatt, "the Cattle King of Idaho." Del worked a while for "Old Man Wyatt," as he always called him. One of the first things I learned about Del Ringer's storytelling style was that he often referred to his characters as "Old" no matter what their age.

The first day I met Del, his wife said, " Tell her the Before and Behind story, 'The Hayracks'."

"The Hayracks" (September 1973)[1]

Well,
    Old Man Wyatt hired the Berlinghoffs
      to help in haying.
They wanted to know how to make the hayracks.
He told 'em,
    "Just make a flatbed on the hay wagon
      and make a tailgate,"
    (not to put any side boards on 'em or
      anything).
So they made 'em.

Well,
    they couldn't figure out
      how they was going to tell
        which was which.
And they made 'em,
      and there was stirrups went on the
        wagon,
on the cross feet
    in front and behind.
"You just pick 'em up
    and set 'em down in them damn
      stirrups."

They couldn't tell how
    they was going to tell
      the before from the behind.

Finally Jake,

he come up with a bright idea.
"We'll just put B for before, Frank."

"Yeah, Jake,
    and we'll put B for behind."
So they laid 'em out by the wagons.

There was five of them damn wagons,
    and Old Man sent over the next
        morning.
He said,
    "Go put the tailgates on, boys,
    we'll be over."
He was going to have 'em pitch in the field.

They went over to the teams,
    and Old Man he was over in the field.
They didn't come, and they didn't come,
    and finally the guys with the teams
    was getting such a kick out of it.
They were so damned tickled
    at them trying to figure out which end
        was which.

The night before,

    Clay Davis and I passed the old barn
    where they'd built the hay wagons,
and by gosh,
    we'd seen what they'd done.
    We took and piled 'em all up together
        you see.
By gosh,
they was all piled up together.
    And they couldn't tell
        the befores from the behinds.
Old Man,
he went over and said:
    "What's the matter with you guys?"
    "Why aren't you getting over there,
        and getting 'em on,
        and let the boys bring the wagons
            over?"

"Well," they said,

    "We had 'em laid out
    and we marked 'em B for before
        and B for behind.
    We had 'em laying
        front and back of the wagons.
    And somebody come along in the night
    last night and piled 'em all in one pile.

Now we can't tell
    the before from the behind."

Old Man says,

    "You damn crazy bitches
    you didn't have to mark them.
    All you had to do was to set them
    up there on them stirrups.
They are all made the same."
    They couldn't figure that out.

    And the boys with the teams
        they was just came near dying,
            had to laugh at 'em
        thinking how funny it was.

They weren't the brightest boys.

Them stirrups were just the same,
    and the crosspiece in front and back
        were just the same.
They were set the same distance.

When I asked Del if he had any more stories about the Berlinghoffs, he told the following dance story about them. It appears that not only did the boys bungle on the job, they did not do much better on the social front either.

"Dance with the Berlinghoffs"
(September 1973)[2]
The Berlinghoff boys,
There was a dance across the river on Saturday
        night,
and the Beans went.
Guy, the brother,
    and there was two girls.

Guy, and the little fellow,
    his name was Ray.
Guy, he was about my age,
    and one of the girls and I used to be
            pretty good friends.

Annie, the oldest girl,

was kind of a sympathetic girl.
Over at Seth Jones'
    one night,
        they had a dance.

She kind of took pity on Jake and Frank.

They were settin' back in the corner
    go and ask some girl to dance
      and they'd make an excuse.
Annie told two girls that was cousins of hers,
    and turned 'em down and make
      excuses
    "You girls are ornery."
They said,
    "Well, bet you wouldn't dance with 'em."

    "If you just wait and see!"

So pretty soon,

      one of 'em went and asked Annie.
      She got out, and danced with him.
      She hadn't more than finished the
    dance
        'til the next one went, so
        she danced with him.
GOD!
They just about like to
    run her to DEATH that night,
      you know!

So Guy and I told 'em—
    "Kind of think Annie's
      got a case on you guys.
    You better come over tomorrow
      and see her."
We didn't think anything about it.
It was eight miles from their place to town.
It was spring, and the roads was bad.
It was breakin' up,
    and I was goin' from downtown home.
Went by Beans
    and
    By Gosh!
There on the front porch was the two Berling-
    hoffs.
      And Annie standing by the door
      waitin' for 'em.
They had on a pair of old muddy bib overalls.
There was mud on them overalls,
    prettinear to their knees,
    and overshoes,
    them dirty,
    dirty overshoes,
    and them muddy overalls on the front
      porch.
So they went, and got 'em off,

and went into the house.
I waved at Annie when I went by,
    and she looked over that way, and
      looked foolish as the dickens.

Next morning I got a hold of Guy and said,
    "Don't you think
      we ought take the Berlinghoffs
      to Sunday school and church?"
And Guy said,
    "Yeah, a good idea."

So they went with us.
They was a-lookin' at the hymn book,
    and I don't remember what hymn
      was
    the preacher asked to be sung,
    but anyhow,
    the chorus the second time around
      was omitted.
It was wrote there
    "OMIT."
They wanted to know
    "What's that word?"
      and we told 'em.

Guy was settin' on one side of 'em, and
    I was settin' on the other.
We kept diggin' 'em in the ribs,
saying—
    "SING, SING."
    Whispered to 'em to
    "Sing louder."
    They just sounded
      like a couple of bulls a-bellerin'.

They come to where the chorus
    was to be omitted.
Sang—
    "AND OMIT!"

The preacher was so damn tickled,
    he had to laugh.
Annie said,
    "You dirty devils,
    if ever you do me
      a trick like that again,
    I'm going to have a brother,
      and a friend of his
    that's AMONG THE MISSING!"
But they stayed all day
and stayed until it was getting dark,
    before they started back home,

and
> they'd walked
>> that eight miles over to White
>> Bird.

CHARACTERS IS RIGHT!

Everyone always begged Del to tell stories about the Jewetts. Old Jewett, Old Lady Jewett, and their son Bill, had the homestead adjacent to the Ringers'.

"Jewett's Saddle" (September 1975)[3]
Old Bill brought a new saddle.
Christ,
in the wintertime
he was riding that damn mule of his
and he was riding it BAREBACK.

"How come, Bill?"
"What have you done with your saddle?"

Bill,
he said,
"I'm not doing to put that new saddle
on that damn mule,
and have it go
ass over teakettle."

Here is one of Del's local character stories from the Salmon in which he expressed approval for a character.

"The Walnuts" (July 1973)
> Old Henry Ricke,
He was up between Riggins and Lucile
> on the Salmon.
He took a little homestead there,
> and there were rocks.
> Gosh almighty,

That little old bar where he took homestead
> was rocky.

There was a little old creek come down,
well,
> during the night
>> it'd dry up.
Old Henry set out a bunch of walnuts there.

God,
everybody in the county laughed at him
> setting out a bunch of walnut trees.

The first year they bore $1200 worth.
He laughed and said,
> "Henry Ricke ain't such a damn fool
>> even if his clothes don't fit!"

He planted them damn trees,
A lot of 'em he had to use a crowbar
> to get down between the rocks.
Planted 'em in there.
> I know.
We was up there.
> It's been six, seven years ago.
> Went over to Martha's brother's,
>> and up to the Salmon,
>> and stopped there at Riggins.
But when we went by Old Henry's place
I told Roper,
> "I see where Old Henry lived."

The walnut trees was still there.
> I don't know who had the place.
Got to be pretty good-sized trees.

He had a little old one-room cabin.
> Wasn't big enough to
> CUSS A CAT IN!

All in all I recorded some 40 repeated stories from Del Ringer, enough to let me make general observations about his stylistic preference in story-telling. At the grammatical level it was apparent that Del used a fairly small number of concrete words to tell his stories. The most prevalent nouns were the names of the characters and the basic items necessary for the story. There was nothing distinguishable about these common words. The charm lay in what he did with them to create his humor, as in the statement "the cabin wasn't big enough to cuss a cat in." There were favorite words that marked his style, such as *prettinear, old* before names, and fillers such as *by gosh* and *boy*. When the occasion allowed, he used some profanity, or expressions such as *God,* or *damn bitches,* or the slightly off-color *ass over teakettle.*

The literary styling varied as appropriate to the story. The actual percentage of dialogue varied from story to story, but in all stories dialogue was a strong feature. These lines served as highlights of the stories and were also used to delineate character. Another distinctive feature of his style was what I have come to call his synecdoche or cartoon style in his use of description. It was sparse but compelling, leading to the creation of scenes and characters in broad strokes rather than in precise detail. He also used repetition, which gave a poetic quality and rhythm to the stories. Occasionally he used simile or metaphor, but the use of these literary devices did not mark his style. The use of exaggeration was prevalent, and irony used as humor seemed a critical marker of his style. Many of his stories involved the idea of someone knowing something that someone else did not.

In actual performance Del's stories showed variation in length on various occasions, but there was no evidence to show that he lengthened or embellished his stones with time. He was definitely aware that he was performing, presenting his stories dramatically, with full vocal and facial characterization where appropriate, yet he did not use many gestures or larger movements. He used a slow, deliberate speaking rate, with significant pauses.

The stories were complete with his evaluative comments, which served as vehicles for Del's attitudes and views on life. I suspected that the themes and attitudes he presented were representative of those prevalent in the northwest United States at the turn of the twentieth century. Since I found that many of the stories could be indexed with familiar folkloric motifs, undoubtedly these worldviews have much wider distribution. Del's stories were full of scorn for bunglers and rowdies, and admiration for those who succeeded through skill, perseverance, and hard work. His listeners learned the marks of gentlemen who knew how to dance, behave, and talk with the ladies, and of the foolishness of those who lacked these abilities. We learned of appreciation for those who were skilled at common tasks and who could turn their professional skills into an occasional practical joke. Above all, we learned that the adventures of life along the Salmon at the turn of the century were always good grist for story making.

Notes

1. "The Hayracks" is related to motif J 1922, "Marking the Place" and also to J 2700, "The easy problem made hard." Motifs may be located in Stith Thompson, *Motif-Index of Folk-Literature*, revised and enlarged edition, Bloomington: Indiana University Press, 1955–58.
2. "Dance with the Berlinghoffs" is related to K 1210, "Humiliated or ruffled lovers," and also to K 1006, "Dupe induced to incriminate himself, taught incriminating song or persuaded to wear incriminating clothes."
3. "Jewett's Saddle" is related to J 2500, "Foolish Extremes."

Further Reading

Attebery, Louie W., ed., *Idaho Folklife: Homesteads to Headstones,* Salt Lake City: University of Utah Press, 1985; Boise: Idaho State Historical Society, 1985

Carrey, John, and Cort Conley, *River of No Return,* Cambridge, Idaho: Backeddy, 1978

Chedsey, Zona, and Carolyn Frei, eds., *Idaho County Voices: A People's History from the Pioneers to the Present,* Idaho: Idaho County Centennial Committee, 1990

Elsensohn, M. Alfreda, *Pioneer Days in Idaho County,* Caldwell, Idaho: Caxton, 1947

Fifty Functions of Storytelling

Margaret Read MacDonald

Margaret Read MacDonald examines the uses of story in a southern Indiana farming community and suggests some of the functions of story and the storytelling event.

Scipio Storytelling

From 1979 to 1989 I made biannual trips to Scipio, Indiana, to tape the talk of Spiv Helt and his friends. Spiv was then in his 80s and had long been deemed the master storyteller of this small farming community. As my father, Murray Read, often said, "No one can tell 'em like Spiv tells 'em." After transcribing around 200 hours of taped talk and thinking about story in the lives of these Scipio storytellers and in the lives of myself and my storytelling friends, I began to set down a list of those things story does for us, both as tellers and as audience. William Bascom is known for his four functions of folklore, namely: amusement, validation of culture, education, and maintaining conformity to accepted patterns of behavior. Here are my suggestions for Scipio's 50 functions of storytelling.

Any discussion of the function of storytelling is complicated by the multiplicity of ways in which story can function. What does the individual story *content* do for the teller, for the audience, for the group? What does the story *event* do for these? What about the very existence of story as a *format*, storytelling as a *tradition*? There are psychological, social, perhaps even physical results from the use of story. And all this without even beginning to discuss the function of various elements within the tale and the function of the tale's performance itself.

Let's look at some of the things story does for Scipio. Though I suggest only 50 functions here, it must be possible to extrapolate even more ways in which story serves the individual and the group. The reader may create his own list!

The Storytelling Tradition

In a moment we will discuss the functions of the storytelling *event*, functions of the *individual story*, and functions of the story *format*. First a word about the functions of the tradition that extend beyond those components. The very existence of a *tradition of coming together to tell stories* functions in certain ways for the group and the individual.

For the Group

1. *The Storytelling Tradition Anticipates Play.* The ongoing tradition of storytelling means that when the group gets together to talk, they do so with an expectation that play will occur. They approach small group gatherings in a playful mode.
2. *The Storytelling Tradition Encourages the Formation of Conversational Groups.* The expectation that storytelling will traditionally occur whenever a small group gathers encourages individuals to form themselves into such groups in the hope that story may happen. The usual format for a Scipio evening's visit, for example, calls for all members of the group to be involved in a single conversation. This format facilitates the storytelling that the group so enjoys. During an evening in a home, all individuals present join into one storytelling group once the dishes are done and the women are free to come to the living room. However, at church socials or family reunions, whenever there is time to be passed, the men tend to clus-

ter in storytelling groups that are separate from the women's groups. On these occasions the master teller's group draws in listeners.

3. *The Storytelling Tradition Provides a Clear Pattern for Storytelling Events.* This allows everyone to move easily within the storytelling event, performing their own roles with assurance. Because the traditional patterns of expectation are clear, everyone can relax and perform with confidence as both listener and teller. A newcomer unfamiliar with the storytelling traditions of this place must align himself carefully with the group in order to not make a false move in his responses as a listener.

4. *The Storytelling Tradition Provides a Set of Criteria for Evaluating Storytelling Events.* A set of criteria for excellence is clearly delineated by tradition. This facilitates group agreement about which tellers should be defined as master tellers and it gives novice tellers clear guidelines to improve their artistry.

For the Individual

5. *The Storytelling Tradition Encourages the Individual to See Life as Story Material.* Because storytelling is an ongoing tradition, the individual can expect to have use for his own life stories in the future. He therefore watches for good story material in his daily existence. The storyteller tends to formulate his own experience into a story format. Interestingly, some individuals retell their story in a humorous light, others retell their life story as tragedy. Their own interpretive bents perhaps affect their perception of reality as well as reflect it.

6. *The Storytelling Tradition Selects Some Persons to Take on the Social Identity of Storyteller.* The storytelling tradition calls for certain individuals to be defined by the community as master storytellers. Once an individual has achieved the social identity of master storyteller, the die is cast. This person will be asked to tell again and again. He thinks of himself as a storyteller, begins to build his repertoire, and actively seeks opportunities to share his storytelling skills.

The Story Format

We have discussed functions of the story tradition. Now let's turn to the story format itself. The very existence of a story format enables the group and the individual to discuss experience in certain useful ways.

7. *The Story Format Fixes the Remembered Content of an Experience by Framing Segments of Experience, Defining Segments of Experience as Significant, and Providing a Mnemonic Device for Experience.* Through story the group can select certain segments of their experience for analysis and perhaps immortalization in story. The teller sets a frame around the story setting it apart from the rest of existence. This making of story lends significance to the event recounted. The highlighted, storified event is now more memorable than before it was solidified into story. Thus the story format has a mnemonic function. Setting the event in story fixes the remembered content, creating an "official" version of the event.

8. *The Story Format Colors the Way Individuals Shape Their Tales.* The kind of storytelling format popular within the group will affect the way the individual restructures his life stories for telling. He may frame his stories as humorous anecdotes, tales of misery, or explanatory tales. He may fill his tale with lengthy psychological elaboration, with flowery description, or he may deliver it as concisely as possible. The story format preferred by the teller's group will affect his telling.

9. *The Story Format Affects the Way the Individual Talks to Himself.* The group's traditional ways of framing story will affect the way we form our own stories. Since much of our thinking about our lives consists of telling stories to ourselves, the biases of our group's storytelling tradition will affect the way we talk to ourselves and will affect the way we frame our own reality.

10. *The Story Format Provides a Vehicle for Talking Without Owning One's Words.* One of the most important functions of the story format is that it allows the speaker to "say without saying." The storyteller is merely telling a story. The attitudes expressed are those of the story. Tradition accepts that the teller is bound by the format and content of the story itself. If the tale forces him to use unsuitable language or to express attitudes not normally appropriate for group expression, that is not the teller's fault. He is not held responsible. He just told it like it was. Thus story functions as an important vehicle for letting the group explore taboo topics and discuss things they cannot deal with openly. It is an important way to talk about things without talking about them.

11. *The Story Format Allows the Production of an Aesthetically Pleasing Product.* Because the format of a good story is stable, it is possible for virtually every speaker in the community to master its requirements and produce aesthetically pleasing stories from time to time. Some receive much more praise for their performance than others, but this is a form in which everyone can feel achievement once in a while. Though the shy teller may share his story with only one individual at a time, the sense of telling his story well can still be felt. During one New Year's Eve party in Scipio, reticent Bill Byford talked quietly to one conversational partner during most of the evening. His storytelling style was similar to that of those master tellers who held the floor, but he chose not to perform his stories for an audience larger than one or two individuals. An understanding of the group's accepted story format allowed Bill to comfortably perform stories in his chosen intimate venues.

12. *The Story Format Allows for the Group to Assist in Production of the Story Through Vocalized Encouragements and Asides.* The clearly understood story format allows the group to work as a whole in story creation, tossing in comments, adding to stories, evidencing at times a kind of group ownership of the tales. This group ownership of the story is common in Scipio storytelling events, especially when a master teller is performing a story the group has heard before and called for. Asides, additions, overrides, and encouraging remarks are called in from every side as the master teller progresses through the story. The master teller, confident in his hold on the "floor," accepts, encourages, and uses these remarks as he or she leads the group in group play.

The Storytelling Event

We have seen ways in which the tradition of story and the format of story function. Let's look now at the storytelling event.

For the Group

13. *The Storytelling Event Provides a Play Experience.* Through the storytelling event the group's members are able to submerge their own egos with that of the group, pass some of the personal responsibility for their speech over to the nature of the event and the format of story, and experience the joy of participation in a group creation during an aesthetic instant. In the end the group and most of its members may achieve that pleasing state that is sometimes called "flow."

This is perhaps the most important use of story in Scipio. In a fairly straitlaced community with no lavish festival traditions and with little release through music or dance, group talk becomes especially important as a means of communal play.

14. *The Storytelling Event Affirms Group Identity.* Through story the group reaffirms its identity, recognizes itself as a skillfully functioning whole, and feels pride individually and collectively. The use of story as play lends itself to this sense of pleasure in the group.

15. *The Storytelling Event Allows Listeners to Express and Acknowledge Emotions Within the Group Dynamics.* Laughter begets laughter; tears allow other tears to flow. Emotions that are not normally brought to the surface may be shared within the context of shared story. In the context of Scipio living room conversational storytelling, laughter is evoked much more often than pathos. Yet when a neighbor afflicted with Alzheimer's disease is mentioned and a brief story is told of his wandering the highway at night, a spontaneous moment of group silence occurs that functions almost as a prayer on his behalf.

For the Teller

16. *The Storytelling Event Allows the Teller to Assert Membership in an Exclusive Group.* Contributing stories to a story-swapping session is one way of "joining the club," of asserting one's membership in an exclusive group. During the 1984 New Year's Eve party enjoyed by Spiv Helt and his friends at Bill Byford's house, every male in the room except Spiv contributed a story of the first time he smoked a cigar . . . with bilious results. Even the quieter tellers, who stayed out of the storytelling arena most of the time, came forth with a story for this round of "initiation into manhood" tales. Perhaps Spiv, as senior member of the group, was not obliged to reaffirm his membership through story at this point.

17. *The Storytelling Event Is a Vehicle for Creating Status.* Through story content one can easily brag a bit, show oneself off in a good light. Spiv tells a lengthy story of his trip west to work in the wheat harvest when he was a

young man. This narrative is clearly designed to raise Spiv's status in the eyes of his listeners. Though it is scarcely needed now, it must have functioned well in his younger days. In the story Spiv is seen as brave, adventuresome, hardworking, and physically strong. Yet one can hardly be accused of "bragging" when one is simply telling a story of a wild adventure.

18. *The Storytelling Event Is a Vehicle for Endearing Oneself to the Group.* In her dissertation, "The Personal Narrative as Folklore Genre" (Indiana University, 1975), Sandra Stahl points out that the very act of telling endears the teller to the group. She is thinking particularly of personal narratives whose sharing calls for a certain bond of trust and affection between teller and listener. She suggests that the audience appreciates the gesture of the teller's offer of story. Certainly story is used to manipulate identity in this way. During the 1989 New Year's Eve party I told a lengthy, humorous narrative of my husband's feud with a mole in our yard. Though I had no thought of this at the time, I can hear from the tapes that this offering served to bond me with the group, which included two couples I knew only slightly until that evening.

19. *The Storytelling Event Provides Ego Reinforcement for the Teller.* In addition to the obvious joy derived from performing well, even the novice teller receives the pleasure of being heard. Usually the audience provides the teller with attention, consideration, praise, and other indications of approval and caring. They might be said to nurture their teller.

20. *The Storytelling Event Provides an Opportunity to Nurture Others.* The teller is in a position to openly show caring for his audience. He assumes responsibility for their entertainment throughout his telling, and caretakes them, usually affectionately.

21. *The Storytelling Event Provides a Vehicle for Influencing Others.* Story can be offered for explicit didactic use; an exemplary tale can be thrown into the conversation in hopes that the intended recipients will take the hint. At times a story already told will be pointed at someone in the audience almost as an afterthought. After Spiv told of Bruce McConnell having a heart attack from overwork, Spiv's wife, Esther, added, "I think some people struggle a little too hard for their own good." She then turned and gave me a meaningful stare. I had

stayed up late the night before to type and was really going at this tale-collecting business too hard. Her glance turned the preceding narrative into a cautionary tale for my benefit.

22. *The Storytelling Event Provides a Vehicle for Passing on Information.* Tales are sometimes told with the specific intent of passing on information, but tales are informative far beyond any didactic intent on the part of their tellers. For example, Spiv's tales of travel offer tantalizing glimpses of other lifestyles. His fishing and hunting stories are full of useful information for the young out-of-doorsman. His nephews hear Spiv's hunting and fishing stories over and over and no doubt make use of the information in their own attempts.

23. *The Storytelling Event Provides an Opportunity to Exercise Control Over an Event, Over Oneself, Over a Group.* The storytelling event provides an opportunity for the teller to "take control" of a group. If he performs well, his self-control is a source of personal pleasure. Even if the storyteller performs poorly, just "holding a group" through story gives a pleasurable sense of power.

24. *The Storytelling Event Gives Pleasure in the Aesthetics of Using Language Well.* There is a definite joy in speaking aloud in a patterned, carefully stylized way. The teller takes joy in using language in a manner that tradition has deemed aesthetic.

25. *The Storytelling Event Allows Play.* The storytelling event offers the teller an opportunity to put aside his usual identity and take on the playful identity of storyteller. As storyteller he can speak as he would not normally speak and perform as he would not normally perform. The storyteller is also released from the usual sanctions that govern his relationships with the individual members of his audience. The storyteller can now relate to them in new and unusual ways . . . playfully.

26. *The Storytelling Event Can Provide a "Flow" Experience.* All of the pleasures of the storytelling event may combine to provide for the teller that exceptional state that anthropologists have termed "flow." Flow might be defined as a high the teller reaches when he is completely engrossed in his performance. It might be described locally as being "on a roll." Jack McConnell recounted a lengthy and hilarious story during the Scipio 1983 New Year's Party. His tale moved rapidly, without break, from

the breaking of a suitcase on vacation and its return to the store, to the breaking of an umbrella on a windy Indianapolis day and *its* return. This tale string showed Jack definitely on a roll. His audience was laughing until their sides hurt and egging him on at every turn.

Flow, however, depends as much on *teller* feedback as on audience feedback. The teller knows he is good. His self-feedback is all the reinforcement he really needs at this point. The teller does not always reach this stage early in his career. But once the teller has achieved flow he will be "turned on" to telling and will look for opportunities to perform again.

27. *The Storytelling Event Can Lead to Improved Mental and Physical Health.* In the next section we will discuss functions of the specific *story* for the teller: discovering feelings, validating feelings, interpreting reality, and restructuring the life story. These may help to maintain good mental health. The retelling of life story has become a useful tool in helping the elderly integrate their lives and, when necessary, prepare for death. It would be interesting to examine the importance of the social identity of "storyteller" to mental and physical health. The satisfaction achieved through storytelling has obvious implications for the mental health of the individual.

For the Individual Listener

The listener, of course, participates in the ways that story is used by the group. Still, some uses of the individual listener deserve separate attention.

28. *The Storytelling Event Gives a Sense of Belonging to a Group.* Story listening requires no skills and little personal experience. At a church social, for example, anyone can walk up to a story listening group and join without invitation, temporarily becoming part of an in-group.

29. *The Storytelling Event Affords an Opportunity to Get to Know the Teller Better.* The teller reveals his person through story. The listener watches and learns. The listener ends by feeling that he knows this individual better. This may result in a slightly lopsided social relationship between master tellers who dominate the floor and reticent individuals who seldom speak. The shy person feels that he knows the master teller well, but the master teller has not had the same kind of exposure to the persona of the nonteller.

30. *The Storytelling Event Allows a Voyeuristic Experience.* The listener has the opportunity to sit back and observe another individual without having to offer any personal revelations of his own. The listener is in a position to take without giving. It is possibly fear of this potential imbalance that demands that the listener keep up a steady flow of supportive utterances during tellings.

31. *The Storytelling Event Encourages the Listener to Identify with Another Individual.* The auditor is seduced into putting himself in the speaker's shoes. The listener sees things for a moment through another person's eyes. This, in turn, functions to foster intergroup understanding and caring.

32. *The Storytelling Event Provides Aesthetic Pleasure.* We have talked already of the joy of being part of an artistic creation. The storytelling event would not be complete without the audience's participation. As we listeners chortle, kibitz, and toss out asides we contribute to the perfect whole. Our chorus of supportive utterances enfolds the story and gives it luster.

33. *The Storytelling Event Offers Release and Allows for Play.* Through aesthetic pleasure, submerging of the self in the group, the joy of humor, the act of identifying with others, we escape from our personal realities in a moment of pure release. Related to this release is the "breakthrough into play" that occurs in many storytelling events. The individual loses self-consciousness and merges with the audience in a stream of injected comments, unself-conscious body language, and laughter.

34. *The Storytelling Event Can Lead to Improved Mental and Physical Health.* Through entering the story trance of the listening experience, through shared emotional release, through the joy of experiencing story play, and through personal insights of the moment, both mental and physical health may be improved.

The Individual Story

Each story will fill certain needs of the group and the individual. Not all stories will function in the same way, but specific stories will fill a variety of needs.

For the Group

35. *A Story Can Fix in Memory a Historical Event.* Story is a way to remember the past. The story frame acts as a mnemonic device

that enables the event to be called forth intact and replayed at a later date. Spiv tells stories of the general store in Scipio's early days. His stories of the events that took place there serve as the community's memory. They have fixed Scipio's history permanently in the form in which Spiv retells it.

36. *A Story Can Pass on Specific Information that the Group Considers Important.* Spiv's stories were full of information about the wildlife of the Scipio woods, fields, and streams. Both Scipio's young and the uninformed outsider could learn much basic information about the region should they take the trouble to listen carefully. Several of Spiv's stories dealt with the "city slickers" who came to Scipio for only brief stays and knew none of these basic facts about the Scipio environment.

37. *A Story Can Socialize Members.* Story can act as a boundary definer for the group and can serve as a cautionary tale that is useful in socializing new community members, either outsiders or the community's own youth. Spiv tells many tales of pranking at the general store, practical jokes played on outsiders, and "old codgers" who were the butt of much humor. All of these serve to remind the group of just where the boundary between "insider" and "outsider" lies. New group members learn by listening how to keep their own actions on the "inside" of the group.

38. *A Story Can Express and Define a Worldview.* This function might include socialization of members and fixing history but goes beyond them. The attitudes held by the group, its very outlook on life, is expressed and sometimes *determined* through story.

Story is a way for the group to talk to itself, to see what it thinks. This is a way for the group to think out loud and see just what kind of consensus its ideas really have. The New Year's Eve 1983 party yielded a mild example of this kind of groupthink. Jack's suitcase and umbrella stories both dealt with the return of merchandise under somewhat dubious conditions. The group's comments make it clear that, while this was funny and probably okay under the circumstances, the returning of merchandise for spurious reasons does not really meet the group's moral standards. Jack's tales were followed by a storytelling round among the women that related stories of persons who had obviously misused the right

of returning merchandise. The women's stories revealed their agreement that this was shocking behavior.

39. *A Story Can Permit Nonpermissible or Out-of-Character Behavior.* Related to its play function is the story's use as a way to sneak in otherwise nonpermissible behavior. Within his story Spiv can cuss, "That God-damned son-of-a-bitch," quoting his character. Within the context of a storytelling session, normally taboo subjects can be slipped in. Though the Scipio group (at least when the women were present) never touched on sexual or scatological topics, during an evening storytelling event Spiv's brother, Pert Helt, was able to slip in a joke he had heard about a German girl who had written to her American soldier boyfriend in code, after having his babies, "Kraut, Kraut, Kraut. One with wiener, two without." Thus he knew that she had borne a boy and two girls.

40. *A Story Can Permit Socially Awkward Comments.* This function also allows the teller (and in effect his supportive audience) to say things they might not ordinarily say about people and events. Opinions too delicate for normal airing might be expressed through story. As we have said, story can be a way of saying without saying. Views can be clearly expressed through story without ever being explicitly stated.

For the Teller

41. *A Story Can Enable One to Discover Feelings.* Through talk one discovers the way one feels. Story can be a valuable tool to analyze one's own experience. Spiv tells of being visited by the preacher while he was in the hospital for open-heart surgery. The preacher's religious comments annoyed Spiv, and as he tells of this, perhaps for the first time, one can see that he is examining his own feelings about the event.

42. *A Story Can Enable One to Interpret Reality.* By selecting a particular frame for one's life experiences, one interprets reality. We have already noted that the way one chooses to retell the story might affect as well as reflect one's outlook. Esther Helt tells a story of how Spiv ran over her foot with a wheelbarrow full of rocks. The story could have been about Spiv's insensitivity, bumbling, or cruelty. But in Esther's telling the story became one of Spiv's caring and kindness as he apologized and looked after her bruised foot.

43. *A Story Can Provide a Framework for Re-structuring Life Remembrances.* Story helps make sense of existence. Retelling one's life story is a way of framing it and organizing events to make them "read" the way one wants. Storying is one way of making sense of our lives. Spiv tells a story of his family's move to California when he was a child and their return to live in Scipio, Indiana. He structures the tale to show how fortunate it is that they moved back to Scipio.

44. *A Story Can Be Used to Test One's Ideas Against Those of the Group.* Story functions to validate one's feelings. As the group responds to the attitudes expressed in story, the teller learns whether or not he or she is in rapport with the group. Most tellers in an intimate culture such as Spiv's can read their audience well, but an occasional discordant note does occur. One evening Spiv's young nephew, Jeff Swisher, tried to tell a ghost story about the homeplace of Esther's grandfather. Spiv and Esther responded negatively at once. Jess realized that teen scare stories of ghosts in Esther's sacred homeplace would not be tolerated.

45. *A Story Can Place Oneself in Space and Time.* Space: Story seems a way of laying claim on the environment. Spiv tells many tales of his relationship to features of the Scipio landscape. He tells a tale of another individual who stole honey from a bee tree that he could see from his home. Though the tree was on a neighbor's property, it is clear that the telling of this story gives Spiv a certain feeling of proprietary right over that bee tree. In some sense, Spiv owns a piece of that tree by virtue of having told the tree's story over and over. Through story Spiv claims much of Geneva Township as his own. Time: Through story Spiv also places himself in time. His stories reveal Spiv witnessing the history of Scipio. He was there when Helt's Mill fell in the flood; he was there when Charlie Butler got his first car; he was there when old George Waughtel got boxed up at McConnell's store. Spiv Helt existed in all of these times, and has a story to prove it.

For the Listener
In addition to those things that the story tradition and the story format allow, the individual story may provide specific things to the listener.

46. *The Individual Story Can Provide a Model Against Which to Examine One's Own Life*

Story. As they hear Spiv's story of his youthful trek west to work in the wheat harvest, his young nephews may wonder about their own avenues for such adventures.

47. *The Individual Story Can Provide a Metaphor for One's Own Life Experiences.* Within the Scipio experience Bible stories and psalms are often referred to as one attempts to make sense of one's own life. The Twenty-third Psalm's image of a shepherd guarding his sheep is often held up as a metaphor for one's own troubling times. If the frightened sheep is like oneself, then, like the needy sheep, one can expect to be guided through a dark time of adversity.

48. *The Individual Story Can Provide Escape.* As the individual enters into story, he escapes briefly from the realities of the physical world and enjoys the freedom of moving in the plane of the imagination. Though Scipio's stories are not of the dragons and princes variety, they do allow for an escape drifting down Sand Crick in search of fish or tramping the winter woods in search of coon.

49. *The Individual Story Can Provide an Opening of the Emotions.* In experiencing the emotions of others vicariously, the listeners' own emotions become entangled and released. We tense with excitement as Spiv struggles with a thorny catfish stuck in a hollow log, and sigh with pleasure as he extracts it without harm.

50. *The Individual Story Can Provide Insight and Inspiration.* Seeing through the eyes of another, moving in an alternative imaginary world, the individual sometimes is struck with moments of insight and inspiration. These private moments occur internally and are seldom made known to the teller or to the group.

In Conclusion–Still More Functions
We have seen how the storytelling tradition, the story format, the storytelling event, and the story itself function for teller, listener, and group. Clearly the uses of story are many. Perhaps this paper will spur further examination of the ways in which story and its telling serve us.

Further Reading
Bascom, William R., "Four Functions of Folklore," *Journal of American Folklore* 67 (1954)

Janson, William Hugh, "Purpose and Function in Modern Local Legends in Kentucky," in *Varia*

Folklorica, edited by Alan Dundes, The Hague, The Netherlands, and Chicago: Mouton, 1978

MacDonald, Margaret Read, "'It Don't Take Long to Look at a Horseshoe': The Humorous Catch-Phrase as Proverbial Saying," *Indiana Folklore and Oral History* 14:2 (1986)

_____, *Scipio, Indiana: Threads from the Past,* Fairfield, Washington: Ye Galleon, 1988

_____, *Scipio Storytelling: Talk in a Southern Indiana Community,* Lanham, Maryland, and London: University Press of America, 1996

Stahl, Sandra, *The Personal Narrative as Folklore Genre* (Ph.D. diss., Indiana University), 1975

"If We Don't Joke with Each Other, We Won't Have No Fun, Will We?" Storytelling in the Richard Family of Rangeley, Maine

Margaret Yocom

Margaret Yocom discusses the storytelling repertoire of members of a family of Maine woodsmen, the Richards. Sample tales of both male and female family members are given and the tales are discussed as an interrelated part of an entire family corpus of tale-telling.

The Richard Family Tales

In the family of western Maine loggers and woodcarvers, homemakers and knitters whom I first met in 1975, storytelling can erupt at just about any time and in just about any place. Stories about work in this mountain region, stories about carving and knitting, and stories about relatives and townspeople—the Richards tell them all. The family is the "social base" of folklore, as Karen Baldwin reminded us in 1975; it is that "first folk group, the group in which important primary folkloric socialization takes place and individual aesthetic preference patterns for folkloric exchange are set."[1] Exploring a family as a site of tradition also allows us to see how interwoven stories become, since stories from different workplaces get told at home, and they mix with stories from the town, from the wider family, and from a family member's own personal experiences. Because of this mixture, William Wilson—writing of his mother's tales—counsels

us to think of one story in relation to all the other stories in a family: "Really to understand one of these stories, then, one has to have heard them all and has to bring to the telling of a single story the countless associations formed from hearing all the stories."[2] Listening in on a family storytelling session also teaches how the intimacy of a home setting influences the way a story gets told. Finally, my presence as a willing listener with—and without—a tape recorder also makes itself felt in these stories. So, all these elements combine—occupation, region, family, outsider story collector—to influence the way a story gets told. We see this rich melding happen in the Richard family.

William and Rodney Richard, like other fathers and sons of the timber woods, exchanged stories with their workmates and then brought the stories—or at least some of them—home to their families. When William (who lived from 1900 to 1993) worked the woods in New Brunswick and Maine, he and others lived in winter-long logging camps. By Rodney's time (1929–), woods work meant daily trips to the stands of spruce and fir—with, sometimes, a week or a weekend away from home.

William remembered clearly the evening after work in the woods at the Gray Farm near Phillips when he first heard Steve Smith of Lewiston tell about Henry Mayeux, an unusually strong French logger whose power waxed and waned with the moon. It was 1921. William had just come with his cousin Steve to the United States from their Acadian hometown of Village Ste. Pierre, New Brunswick. As the years passed, William would listen to others tell about Henry who, in the end, was killed by loggers who feared his uncanny strength. Rodney remembers first hearing the stories when he and William worked together in the woods. Rodney's three sons can hardly remember a time when they didn't know about Henry. I, too, remember when I first heard this cycle of legends from William. They are not stories that any of us can easily forget, especially since, like objects of memory that recall a treasured person now dead, they remind us of William, who kept the tales alive for so long.[3]

In 1984, in the living room of Rodney and Lucille's home, I turned on my tape recorder and asked William to tell us the tales again. All ears turned his way as he began with one of his favorites, "Henry Mayeux and the fight like to kill 'em all." We joined in with questions and comments, the way we always did when William told his tales:

He worked round *Rangeley* here for years, down to *Kennebago*,[4]
over to *Oquossoc*—
years *ago*,
as far as I *know.*
> Peggy: Yeah.

The night that he had the big fight like to kill 'em all,
that was, uh, over to *Bemis.*
> Rodney: *Oh*! Is that *right*?
Yeah, it was a lumber *camp* there.

I'm telling you *just* the way I *heard* it.
There was an *old man*[5]
work up the farm, uh, *Gray Farm*, with us.
And,
somebody mentioned Henry May*eux.*
He said, " *Yes,*" he said, "I *know* that *man.*"
He said, "I was taking *charge*
of a certain place there in, uh—

Bemis.
And," he said, "I had *half* Irishmen
and *half* French.
They don't EAT TOGETHER.
> Peggy: Oh!
They *fight.*"

So,
the Irish—
the *cook* was Irish.
And, uh, they had *half* the table,
one end the table
for the *Irish* and half for
the *French.*

So Henry come *in*,
for to work.
He sat on the *end* of the *table*,

and there weren't hardly anything to *eat* on their end of the table and on the *other end* they had
    EVERYTHING.
And he done let that go for one meal, you know?
And he asked the fellows *why*
they was acting THAT way.

"Well, the *Irishmen,*" they said,
"don't want us,
"don't want 'ssociate with us at *all.* That's *all.*
"And they want everything their own way."
"*Oh, oh, oh,*" he said. "*Now* I *know,*" he said, "what the trouble *is.*"
He said, "TONIGHT we're going to have something to EAT or
            NONE at all."

So,
when he set on the table on the *end,* 'twas just the same.

He hollered to one them other fellows there,
"*Irish,* pass me certain *thing* there."
"If you *want it, come and* GET IT!"
"OK!" He gets right up and walks on the table, went over *there.* Of course by the time he
    got *there,* everybody's *off* the *table,*
            Peggy: [Laughs ^^]
fighting.
And he *told* the *French,* he said,
"*Hide* all the things that they could *reach,*
so they won't *get* it.
They won't *hit* us then."
There was a *bench* back the *camp there,* the *long window.*
Just as soon's he got over there, by jeez, he begin to throw 'em right through that
    window,
just as fast as he could grab 'em.
Well,

some of them got *away.*
When they see what he was *doin',*
they got *away.*
And,
they called up the—

Rumford,
for the *police,*
to come *up.*
He *like* to kill *some* of them, you know.
Well, they *deserved* it anyway.
            Peggy: Ummm.
But, uh,

the *police* come *up* and *got* 'em.
Took 'em to *Rumford.*
Went before the *judge.*
The judge asked him WHY he had that *fight.*
Well, he *told* them the *whole work.*

"Well," he said, "I don't *blame* you, but," he said, "you shouldn't have *done* what you *did*! You, you almost *killed some* of 'em."
"*Too* BAD," he said, "I didn't KILL 'EM ALL!"
        Peggy: ^^

^^ So,

the judge *told* him, he said,
"*Don't do* that *again*," he said. "I'm gonna let you go *free*
because—you didn't kill anybody. But,"
he said, "the story you told me,"

he said, "is hard take it."

So that's the way—the old man who was tellin' us that he was
        shakin' all over, he was so scared.
He wasn't an Irishman, he was an American.
He was the *boss*!
        Peggy: Oh?
Oh, yeah!
And I *know* it come—*straight* from *that* because he was the *boss*.
He *worked* with us, oh,
pretty near a *month*.
He was loadin' *cars*—
and he was *shovelin'* a little *snow*. He was an *old man, anyway*.

And *that's* the way I *heard* it about *Henry* May*eux*.[6]

In another story, William told how Henry saved a 400-pound hog—a winter's supply of pork for a logging camp—from death by fire, and how Henry lifted a boulder-sized rock for a road crew in Rumford. As William himself said of Henry at different times, "Oh, he was *something*! Weren't *nothing* that he couldn't do.[7] He was a *man* all right."[8]

"But," William added, hinting at why the loggers grew wary of Henry, "nobody knew how he done it."[9] Some, William explained, thought Henry got his strength from the devil; others said it was the moon. William talked on that afternoon, telling about Henry's murder and then reviving him again, through words, to share with us Henry's other adventures among the loggers of the western Maine mountains.

Chain Saw Dangers
Like other woodsmen,[10] William and Rodney also tell stories about their own experiences working in the timber woods, especially stories about the tools

they have used—the same tools they have featured in their woodcarvings of tools and of loggers holding tools that stand from five inches to larger-than-life size. Although Rodney values the old-time tools as his heritage, chain saws have enabled him to work better and more comfortably. They have given him a scare or two, but they have not cost him—or any in his family—life or limb. Hearing, yes, but not life or limb. He is also aware of how he identifies, even merges with, his power machines: "Some people have no feel. . . . You know, they don't . . . have that feel for the machinery, that [you're] a part of the machine and if that breaks, it hurts, you know, that's the way it is." Perhaps because woodsmen literally put their lives in their own hands when they use chain saws, stories about the early ones emphasize danger and survival. These tales also combine admiration for what the tool can do with recognition of the tool's trickster-like nature. One snowy February night in 1985, Rodney told William, Rodney Jr., and me about working with chain saws:

Rodney: And then I bought [that 12A Mall]. We were working up on Day Mountain down in Strong [cutting timber spruce]; and Phil Caron had that 12A Mall before I did, remember?
William (asks, his hearing bad from his many years spent around screeching factory and woods

equipment): Who?

    Rodney (speaks noticeably louder and slower): Phil Caron.

The thing kicked,

and it come out,

and it cut him right across both legs.

Almost ruined the family jewels in the process.

And put him in the hospital.

And while he was in the hospital,

I bought the saw because he said he wasn't ever going to use it again.

Brand new chain saw.

He had it a month.

And I didn't have that son of a bitch much more than a month,

and it kicked back and it caught—

    William: Took your pants right off! ^^^

    Rodney: ^^^Whooo! Did it ever!

It caught in the clips on my boots—

you know?

Those hooks that you hook your lacings in?

And tore one right out.

And it bent two more,

and it punched a hole the whole length of my leg,

and it got caught in my pant leg,

and it turned end for end

and drove in my groin—

             Peggy: God!

and I was sitting on my ass on the ground, just—

bang—

like that.

So goddamned quick you wouldn't hardly know which end you was standing on.

And—

I sit there, you know,

and turn the chain backwards until I got my pant leg out of it,

and I got up,

and I sawed the tree up,

and I threw that goddamned saw just as far as I could throw it,

down the mountain—

    William (his voice heavy with disgust for chain saws): Oh, Jesus.

And I had to walk,

Christ, half,

three-quarters of a mile down to camp.

Jesus Christ.

I couldn't sit in the chair and pick my leg up—

    William (easing himself and his son out of the memories of what could have been a fatal accident): That was close to, that pond there [Day Mountain Pond]?

    Rodney: Well no. We were . . . going the other way. Remember that big clump of timber spruce—

    William: Yeah.

    Rodney: —we had up there—

    William: Yeah.

    Rodney: —that we cut? The steady pile all the way up, just a tassel on the top? And that was the year I got drafted into the army. That was like the fall of '50, that happened.[11]

Hunting Stories

Like chain saw tales, hunting stories also tell of dangers in the woods. In the Richard family, though, such narratives also tell of peoples' relationships with one another, their appreciation for the animals around them, and their admiration for the skills that have to be learned if one is to bring home food. Hunting and trapping for William were necessities; he kept food on his family table and brought in some much-needed money during the Great Depression. Rodney and his brothers added to the family larder, but Rodney's sons have not turned toward hunting. Their animal tales feature traveling the roads, looking for wildlife. Rodney Jr. and Stephen tell of seeing moose or red fox; John delights in remembering the time he locked his brothers outside when they watched the bears at the town dump amble closer and closer to the car.

One evening, William and Rodney told Rodney Jr., Lucille, and me about their hunting adventures, and, as usual, between the two of them with their friendly banter, they hammered the stories together, remembering when Rodney shot his first deer, a rite of passage in a young man's life. Rodney worked hard in this storytelling session to get the facts down right: he wanted his father to remember this event exactly as he, Rodney, did. They questioned each other, yelled out the same words at the same time, shared the spotlight, and competed for attention—all within about five minutes' time. These stories are born from the comfortable telling of two people who are used to team-telling their stories to this family audience and an interested newcomer or two.

Rodney: I never did *that* much trapping, . . . I never got turned on to *trapping.* I used to *hunt* quite a lot. Why, I started hunting when I was—(Rodney turns to William, and speaks very loud).

How *old* was I when I started hunting? I wasn't more than *nine* years old, *was* I, when I took the *.22* and went *down* in the *pasture there?*

William: Oh, the time you was gonna go get a *rabbit*—
Rodney: Yeah— ^
William: —and [you] come back, and you said, "I got you a *rabbit?*" ^
And I said, "*Yes,*" I said, "a rabbit that *high?!*" ^^^
       (William raises his hand four feet off the floor).
He had *a deer!* ^^
He *hollered* back the house—That was *closed season,* you know?
He *hollered* back the house—The *weeds* was way up.
And he dropped him in there.
And, Mortimer, I guess, went over to get it.
^ [Rodney] had set [the deer] *right* on a *hornets' nest!* ^^
Rodney: ^^^^
William: Oh, *you're* the one they *chased?!*

Rodney: I don't remember.
William: [Rodney] was scared of hornets, but, uh—
Rodney and William (together): *Mortimer wasn't!!*
Rodney: Yeah, it was amazing.
William: [Mortimer] could sit *right side* of a *nest* and *tear* it all *out,* you know.
They *wouldn't sting* him.

Rodney: Yeah, but *before* that, when I *first hunted*—I used to take the .22 and go down the, oh, jeez—
William: Well, that's the *one* I *mean.*
Rodney: Yeah, but—When I *first* went *hunting,* I didn't *shoot* anything for a *year.* ^^ I was *only* about nine years *old.*
William: Yeah. Well, I *guess* so.
Rodney: Yeah. . . .

William (to Peggy): You know what? The first deer he ever shot?

Peggy: Huh?

William: He and Mortimer went up in the orchard above the house—

Rodney: Unhh, I was *alone* that *time*. Mortimer—The time *he* went with me is the time he got *buck* fever and *jacked* the *shells* out of the *gun*.

Remember the *first* one *I shot?* I took your *.33*, and you *only* give me *five shells*.

William: Who was with *you* when you shot your *first deer?*

Rodney: *Nobody*. I was *alone*.

William: He *hollered*, and I went up to *get* him—To *help* him. He was dragging him by *hind feet*.^^

Rodney: ^^^^ He gave me *five* shells and the *big rifle*—*first time* I'd ever *hunted* with the *big* rifle. And—

he said, "If you can't hit it with *five* shots, for*git* it." ^^

So I went *up*, and I *shot* the *deer.*

And the *first* shot, I just *wounded* him.

And then, the *next* shot,

he started *running*,

and I *shot* him in the *back*

and *broke* his *back* so he couldn't *go*.

And then I *run* up there and I *filled him full of lead*.

And then I took, ^^ I took my *knife* cut him full of holes ^^^ to make *sure* he was dead.

A great, *nice big buck*, ^^ you know?

And *then* I started *dragging* it down the hill by the *hind* feet. ^^^^

I was so *excited!* ^^ They could hear me *hollering* half a mile across to the house, ^^ there. Oh, *jeez!*[12]

"You've heard of *bobcats*, huh?" William asked me, as he went on with several more hunting tales. Not all of the Richards' stories of men and animals in the wild are laced with danger, however. Some have the soft edges of a man very much in love with the beauty of the land around him. A month later, in March of 1985, as William and I sat in his apartment in his son Lewis' home, he told me about the day he held a baby beaver in his arms:

I used to go over *there* [to a pond, down the Weld Road] and get a few fish, you know?
> Peggy: "You did?"
So one day I went over *there*—

and—

I see something on the shore.
Course, it was a kind of *rainy*,
wet day. So—

I was looking for *greens*.
Fiddle*heads*.

So—

I got over there, and I see where's a beaver hauled a *limb*
to use the water,
with *leaves* on it, you know.
And there was *five little beaver*,
just about that long,
> (William spreads his hands a foot apart)

eatin' on there. When they *saw* me they never *moved,*
they sat right there.
I went over there and *picked* one up,
and *held* him in my arm.
He was *lookin'* at me, you know.
And the others never moved.

So after a while I thought I better put him down or the old *woman* might come over and
chew my *heel.*
So I,
I put that one down and I,
I took off slow, you know.
And they kept lookin' at me, and when I got far ^ enough,
they *went* ^^ for the *water.*
        Peggy: ^^
But they can have their swim when they're little,
they'll turn on their *back* ^ and every *which* way.
But, of course, that's *natural* for them *anyway.*
But they was just about that long.
Cunningest damn things ^ you ever saw.

"They look just like that," William told me as he pointed to a beaver that Rodney had chainsawed
for him out of a piece of white pine.[13]

Lucille's Stories of Knitting

In the Richard family, live animals and carvings, stories and artwork mesh together easily. Lucille, too, a knitter especially of dolls and children's clothes, used a story to tell me why she favors making knit goods for the small ones, rather than adults. It has to do, she said, with her memories of her mother and sitting by her side, learning to knit as a young girl on a rural Maine farm with her six sisters and two brothers. Lucille's story about the time her family's house burned down and she saved her one big doll emphasizes the importance of dolls in her life:

Because I remember *sitting* with my *mother.* . . . She used to knit our mittens and she used to knit sweaters without patterns. . . . She *often* did make *cloth dolls*—[the baby-doll type]—and *dolls' clothes* FOR ME because most of my sisters liked the outdoor work, and they really could care less about dolls. . . .

And [my mother] had no *patterns* or anything. She did everything by *newspapers.* . . . She would just take *newspapers* . . . and make the shape of the doll's *head,* and the *arms,* and legs. I think she made them all *separate* and then sewed the *legs* on, and the *arms* on, and the *head* on. But she would use an *old sheet* . . . for the doll.

And I *really* don't remember what we used for *stuffing.* It was probably some *old* cotton, like maybe old pillowcases or sheets, again.

She would *embroidery* the face, and then she would take *yarn* for the *hair,* and she would either make the *curls* or the *pig tails.*
They were *quite big.*
We *might* have used some small *baby* clothes because it was—

I remember *one* in *particular.*
It was a pretty *big* one,
so it might have even
taken,
you know, six-months or baby-sized clothes.

'Cause I remember we had a *fire* at our house, and ^
my mother ^ never got *over* it—

that was the *first* thing I *grabbed* of all ^^
the things to grab
to save, ah!
The doll,
the big doll was the thing that I *picked up first.* ^^
Oh!
And my *father* either: (in a high, shrill voice) "Of *all* the *things* to *save,* you *saved that thing!*"
Oh!
But I *suppose* maybe I hadn't *had* it that long *either.* ^
You know, maybe she hadn't *made* it that long ago.
That was *quite* a number of years ago.[14]

The worlds of knitting and logging often intertwine. William took yarn to the logging camps so he could mend mittens, and Rodney learned to knit from his mother. Their friend Elijah "Tiger" White of Carthage—former logger and river driver—swears that knitted mittens saved his life when they stuck fast to the wet edge of an ice shelf the day he fell through Weld Pond.[15] Knitters also raise money for injured woodsmen: in 1988, Lucille told me how she donated a teddy bear with a knit outfit for a raffle to benefit her nephew Randy Brackett, who was almost killed two years earlier in a logging accident:

I had the little teddy bear, and I dressed it.
A little knitted suit.
It seems like it was in the fall,
near a holiday season,
and I made his outfit out of red or green.

[Randy] drove a big truck.
He had parked his truck,
and it was on a little bit of ice,
and when the sun came down in early afternoon,
it [melted and] moved the truck.
It was his big logging truck.
And he went to jump down off'n it
to keep it from rolling,
and when he did,
this big piece of wood from the guy loading (a man on the bucket loader was loading
wood into the bed of the logging truck)
struck the back of his head
and knocked him down.

It was about an hour and a half before the ambulance could get there to get him to the
hospital, then another two hours to drive him down.

He was really quite critical.
They didn't expect him to live at first.
And he still has a hearing problem to this day.
Very bad.
He hears very little.
He mostly reads lips.
But he's lucky to be alive because it cracked his skull in two places.

Must have been two years ago,
at least two years ago.
It was real serious.

It was in Bemis,
way in the back shore of Bemis,
and it would have been harder except that they have radio towers,
and so there was somebody right there at the garage that they called right into to get the ambulance started down,
otherwise you'd have to wait until somebody could get to a phone
or get somewhere to get help,
and it would have been many hours later.

It was a serious accident.[16]

Story Audiences for the Richards

The Richards, of course, have many more stories. They also tell tales about their woodcarving and about the summer people who come to buy—or just look at—the animals and other objects that they bring out of Maine pine and cedar with their jackknives and chain saws. The woodcarvings themselves tell stories: Rodney's "Kind Woodsman," for example, shows a logger gently lifting a fallen baby bird back into its nest. Other stories also celebrate the extended family who gather at the Haley and Calden and Wing reunions as summer draws to a close in the north country.

Living in a town where a good story is savored as much as a tasty venison steak keeps the Richards in good storytelling practice. They tell stories about local characters, miraculous feats, sportsmen from "away" whom locals guide on the region's lakes and rivers: in Rangeley, stories are a way of life. Before, during, and after work,

at church, at the American Legion, at beano and cribbage, or at any number of local gathering places such as Fitzy's Donut Shop, Pine Tree Frosty, Dockside, and the M&H Logging garage, Rangeley people share the news of the day and the tales of yesterday. One February day in 1985, over lunch at the Wagon Wheel Diner, owned by Lucille's sister Virginia and her husband, Ralph White, Rodney and his townsmen got to rehearsing the stories of the notorious Eldon Collins. Eldon had left for Alaska several years earlier, but not before leaving behind a whole cycle of stories that are enjoyed over and over again by those who work both in and out of the woods. One of the favorites tells of the time Eldon shot his bulldozer, but in the back-and-forth of one conversation, Rodney's friend Dick added a new piece of information that changed forever the way the story was told. Rodney set the group remembering:

Rodney: Eldon got over on the south shore there,
wasn't it?
Yeah, up in back of Dill's somewhere, wasn't it?
He was yarding wood up there.
I think it was up—
Oh, Jesus!
Yeah, it was up in back of Dill's there.
He came down off the mountain there.
Eldon got way the hell up in the woods there,
and he either lost the track off [his bulldozer],
or something.
And it was in the fall of the year.
He had a .45 revolver with him in case he saw a deer.
And he jumped out and wound a hole in the radiator with it,
and he had to sack the radiator out and get Perly Philbrick to solder it.
  Dick Thompson: Eldon didn't sack it out.
  Rodney: He didn't?
  Dick: Perly Philbrick went right up there and fixed it.
  Rodney: Perly went up there?
  Dick: When I bought Perly's garage over there,
Perly told me.

I was telling him about Eldon shooting his goddamned radiator with a .45,
and Perly says, "That what happened to it?
The son of a bitch told me he stuck a stub through it.
Yeah," he said, "if I'd 've known that—
it was 30 below that morning—
I never would of gone up there and fixed it."

      Rodney: Jesus!
One day down at Fitzy's,
just before Eldon went to Alaska,
we were in there,
and I said, "Eldon,
sometime," I said,
"I want to sit down with you with my tape recorder,
and I'd like to get your version of the day you shot your bulldozer."
And *Jesus,* I got thrown right out the goddamned door.
Bodily!

"You son of a bitch," he said.
He had a violent, violent temper.
'N, just like that,
he was over it, you know?
      Stephen Richard: Yeah, he threw Pinky out the door.
      Dick: Yeah. And Delbert Green—
      Rodney: Delbert's the same way!
      Dick: —the old tractor wouldn't start, and he took the chain saw and tried to saw the track off.
      Rodney: Oh, yeah!
      Stephen: And then there was the time Carl Searles. . . .[17]

On and on the stories go. It would be wrong, however, to see these tales as just being about logging or hunting or knitting or family. Instead, these narratives that live in one family's repertoire feature the valued confluence of family, friends, work, creativity, and place. They are, above all, stories of connection and relationship, of lives lived in partnership with others and with the land of lakes and mountains in western Maine.[18]

Notes

1. Karen L. Baldwin, "Down on Bugger Run: Family Group and the Social Base of Folklore," Ph.D. diss. University of Pennsylvania, 1975.
2. William A. Wilson, "Personal Narratives: The Family Novel," *Western Folklore* 50:127–149, 1991.
3. For a discussion of objects of memory and the study of folklore, see Kirshenblatt-Gimblett.
4. In editing the Richards' stories, I've used several ethnopoetic practices. Line breaks indicate that tellers paused in their telling; spaces between lines indicate longer pauses. *Italics* denote stressed words; CAPITALS, more loudly stressed words. Circumflex marks [^] [^^^] indicate laughter, in varying intensities. I've edited out some false starts and some repetitions of single words.
5. In an earlier version of this story, William names the "old man" working on the Bemis operation with Henry Mayeux as Rowe Smith of Lewiston, Maine. [William Richard, interview by Stephen Richard, tape recording #T1525, Northeast Archive of Folkore and Oral History, Phillips, Maine, 22 July 1980].
6. William, Rodney, Lucille, Stephen, John Richard family, interview by author, tape recording WM1, Rangeley, Maine, 10 March 1985.
7. Richard family, interview, WM1.
8. Richard family, interview, WM5.
9. Richard family, interview, WM1.
10. Several articles and books record stories of families who also make their living in the timber woods. Stories often detail the

relationships between fathers and sons—either as work partners or as people who did not get along with one another. They always describe the changing world of work as different technologies entered the woods. Many tales tell of accidents, often fatal ones, and men's stories and women's stories find their way into some of these studies, but often such tales are in the minority. Finally, some narratives show how much work in the woods meant to men who, like John Lamberton of Vermont, chose a sawmill stone as his tombstone. See Beck, Ives, James-Duguid, Meader, Mitchell, Perreault, and Roberts.

11. William, Rodney, Lucille, Rodney Jr. Stephen, and John Richard, interviews with author, tape recordings WM12 and T13, Rangeley, Maine, 13 February and March 1985.

12. William and Rodney Richard, interview with author, tape recording WM8, Rangeley, Maine, 16 February 1985.

13. William Richard, interview with author, tape recording WM9, Phillips, Maine, 6 March 1985.

14. Lucille Haley Richard, interview with author.

15. Elijah "Tiger" Calvin, Charles, and Wayne White, interview with author, tape recording EW-97-8-6, Carthage, Maine, August 1997.

16. Lucille Haley Richard, interview with author, tape recording LR-88-8-1-1, Rangeley, Maine, 1 August 1988.

17. Rodney Richard and a group of Rangeley residents at the Wagon Wheel Restaurant, interview with author, tape recording EP5, Dallas Plantation, Maine, 13 February 1985.

18. For longer discussions about storytelling and human relationships, see Narayan. On storytelling and people's relationship to the land, see Hufford.

Further Reading

Baldwin, L. Karen, *Down on Bugger Run: Family Group and the Social Base of Folklore* (Ph.D. diss., University of Pennsylvania), 1975

Beck, Jane C., "Just Keep the Saw Cutting," *Northeast Folklore* 30 (1995)

Hufford, Mary, *Chaseworld: Foxhunting and Storytelling in New Jersey's Pine Barrens*, Philadelphia: University of Pennsylvania Press, 1992

Ives, Edward, *George Magoon and the Down East Game War: History, Folklore, and the Law,* Urbana: University of Illinois Press, 1988

_____, *Joe Scott, The Woodsman-Songmaker,* Urbana: University of Illinois Press, 1978

James-Duguid, Charlene, *Work as Art: Idaho Logging as an Aesthetic Moment,* Moscow: University of Idaho Press, 1996

Kirshenblatt-Gimblett, Barbara, "Objects of Memory: Material Culture as Life Review," in *Folk Groups and Folklore Genres: A Reader,* edited by Elliott Oring, Logan: Utah State University Press, 1989

Meader, John T., "Dell Turner: The Stories of His Life," *Northeast Folklore* 27 (1988)

Mitchell, Roger E., "'I'm a Man That Works': The Biography of Don Mitchell of Merrill, Maine," *Northeast Folklore* 19 (1978)

Narayan, Kirin, *Mondays on the Dark Night of the Moon: Himalayan Foothill Folktales,* New York: Oxford University Press, 1997

Perreault, Gene N., *Memories Grow on Trees/ L'Arbre Des Mémoires,* Durham: National Materials Development Center for French, Department of Media Services, Dimond Library, University of New Hampshire, 1986

Richard, William, Interview by Stephen Richard, tape recording #T1525, Northeast Archives of Folklore and Oral History, Phillips, Maine (July 22, 1980)

Richard, William, Rodney Richard Sr., Lucille Richard, Rodney Richard Jr., John Richard, and Stephen Richard, Interviews by Margaret Yocom, tape recordings, Rangeley and Phillips, Maine (1984, 1985, 1988)

Roberts, Leonard W., *Up Cutshin and Down Greasy: Folkways of a Kentucky Family,* Lexington: University Press of Kentucky, 1959

White, Elijah "Tiger," Charles White, Calvin White, and Wayne White, Interview by Margaret Yocom, tape recordings, Carthage, Maine (August 6, 1997)

Wilson, William A., "Personal Narratives: The Family Novel," *Western Folklore* 50:2 (April 1991)

Yocom, Margaret R., "Exuberance in Control: Dialogic Discourse in the Repertoire of Wood Carver and Storyteller William Richard," *Northeast Folklore* (1998)

_____, "Family Folklore," in *Folklore: An Encyclopedia of Forms, Methods and History,* edited by Thomas A. Green, Santa Barbara, California: ABC-Clio, 1997

Stories of Emergency Medical Responders

Timothy R. Tangherlini

Timothy Tangherlini shows the various functions of personal narratives among emergency medical responders.

Emergency Medical Responders' Storytelling Traditions

Storytelling among emergency medical responders is a well-developed, yet little-studied, occupational tradition. The majority of emergency medical responders in the United States are trained as emergency medical technicians (EMTs) and work as ambulance personnel who respond to calls for assistance primarily through the national 911 emergency telephone system. Medics tell stories as part of their work. Sometimes their stories mimic the official report that they provide the emergency room staff. At other times their stories emerge during less formal interactions and concentrate on particular aspects of a problematic call. In many cases, however, their stories are elaborate personal experience narratives that focus on a particularly memorable call. In these stories, they present themselves as competent authorities able to handle crises so extraordinary that others around them blanch. At the same time, they provide a running commentary on the state of health care in the United States, the problems with urban decay and the breakdown of the family, the challenges of overcoming racism, the dangers of their work environment, the deficiencies in the dispatch system, the inability of field supervisors to provide meaningful leadership, the surprising incompetence of other emergency responders, and the remarkably random ways in which death can intrude into our daily lives.

Media Representations of the Medic

Most people's impressions of emergency medicine come from popular television programs, the best known of these being *Emergency!* from the 1970s. In more recent years, fictional occupational series have been replaced by an ever-growing number of television programs referred to as "reality television." Perhaps the most popular reality television program dealing with the work of emergency medicine is *Rescue 911*. Like many programs in this genre, it relies on recreations of medical emergencies, followed by post-incident interviews with the various medical responders and their patients. In general, these television programs focus exclusively on those calls where patients are snatched from the gaping jaws of death and thereby disregard the fact that most 911 calls are not of an emergency nature. These representations of emergency medical response are universally derided by medics in their storytelling:

[Lars]: John was supposed to do an episode for *Rescue 911*. And they came out, and had this whole script and wanted to change everything around. But he said, "you either do it the way it happened or we don't do it at all." They have you act in ways you'd never act. And they often make the paramedics too stiff. They want drama, it's a drama entertainment show, that's what entertains, you know medics running up to the patient and all that. They wanted to film

428

his ambulance at the garage, and pretend it was a station, and all that, and that's just not true. Nothing is really "real" about those shows. They completely redo the whole story. But he wouldn't play their game, he said, "No way, we either do it my way or not at all." So they left.

Popular media representations of emergency medical response deny medics the opportunity to speak for themselves. Indeed, when medics are allowed to speak, it is either within the framework of a highly structured studio interview or in short sound bites. Furthermore, the programs focus primarily on the mechanics of the job—driving, arriving on scene, talking on the radio, starting intravenous lines, administering medications, and defibrillating cardiac arrest patients. There is no mention of the downtime—waiting at tedious post assignments, cleaning and restocking the ambulance between calls, and filling out paperwork—that fills the majority of the ambulance personnel's workday. It is during these long gaps that medics share with each other their perspectives on the job and that their storytelling tradition develops. Unlike the stories presented in the popular media, ones that contribute to a master narrative of the paramedic as a silent hero "just doin' my job," the story tradition presents a different view. The stories address topics ranging from the problems facing urban America, the status of emergency medical services, and the problems with health care, to the difficulties, frustrations, and rewards of the job.

In-Group Narratives

Medics, over the course of repeated narrative sessions, develop their own personal storytelling styles. The storytelling traditions of these emergency personnel (medics) are not easily accessed by nongroup members, an exclusion similar to firefighter and police narrative traditions (Manning and Van Maanen; McCarl). One strategy that medics often employ to exclude uninitiated listeners is the use of specialized jargon:

[Jenny]: We rolled on this one woman, Code Three for the auto-ped. Turned out it wasn't that at all—it was this woman in cardiogenic shock. It wasn't pure cardiogenic shock, she sort of pulled out of it. She was tacky at 150, afib with wide ventricular with a modal branch. Then we hyperventilated her and she

went from 150 down to 80 and her pressure started coming up, so just with the hyperventilation she started moaning and moving her arms—she was getting better. We got her in the rig, by the time we hit the ER, she was actually AO times four, and she was sitting up talking a little tiny bit. But then while I was cutting my paper she crashed.

Cynicism in Narrations: The Medic as Antihero

Most stories focus on extraordinary situations and are told with a degree of ironic detachment. Cynicism informs a great deal of the storytelling, and the typical self-deprecatory stance adopted by many medics in their storytelling undermines the concept of these workers as silent heroes:

[Jerry]: The county fair a few months ago, they had this big bungee jump tower. And there was this guy who was apparently talking a lot of crap to his wife and her girlfriend, saying, "I wanna do it, I wanna do it, I wanna do it." And the wife was like, "No way, we can't afford it," and he's like, "I wanna do it, I wanna do it, I really wanna do it. God, I wanna do it!" So she said, "Okay, do it." So they put out the $65 or whatever and he went up to the top, looked down, said, "No way, I'm not gonna do it." Well, they stay up there for a long time and they're coaxing him, "Just do it, just jump. Once you get up there, just jump, and that's it, you know? It looks scary to do, but once you're flying, it's over." So he's like, "No way, no way!" So he gets up there, gets to the rails, can't do it, can't do it, can't do it. Everyone on the ground is like, "Go! Go! Go!" And he was up there for about ten or 15 minutes while they bring him back down. He comes down and then everyone gives him crap.

Then half an hour or so later, he goes back up to the jump, he goes back up to the top. There he is again for about 15 minutes, people yelling, "Go! Go! Go! Go! Go!" And he's out there and he's out there and he's out there and they tell him the best way to really do it is to just go off backwards. He says, "You don't even know, you just let yourself fall backwards. And you end up falling the perfect way once you get to the bottom," they tell him. So he said alright. So finally he jumped, he lets himself go, and as the cage is going by he grabs onto the cage, he's screaming, "Pull me back up! Pull me back up!" So they're like, "We can't, man. You've just gotta let yourself go now. You can't hang on forever, you gotta let yourself fall." He's like, "No, pull me back, pull me back up!" Finally he lets go. And he reaches for the bungee cord! He comes sliding all the way down to the bottom on the rubber band! He had severe rope rash on his inner thighs, his inner arms, and his chest. We got to him, we laughed! Everybody laughed at him! And they gave him another jump for free! What a dork! We laughed at him so hard! What an idiot.

In contrast to the expectation that medics will treat their patients with compassion, in their storytelling medics often deride the "stupidity" of their patients, make light of human suffering, and laugh at the incongruities produced by traumatic accidents.

The "hero" stories of the popular media are generally omitted from medic storytelling; indeed, those few medics who attempt to tell stories that valorize their own accomplishments are quickly derided by their peers. Some medics take great delight in telling stories of decidedly unheroic activity:

[Darryl]: We used to go around and there was this fad, fashion I guess you'd call it, and people would have all these little tails or they'd have the little dreadlocks or some other hairdo craziness going on. Well if they were drunk and passed out, we'd scalp them! We'd take the tail or a little bead or a dreadlock or something or other. And we had them all up in the front of the ambulance—just like rows of them. It was like, "We take 'em scalp." And we'd look at each other and we always had to look at each other and it'd be like some drunk and he had this tail or something or other, and we'd make this cutting motion and we'd know what we were going to do!

Cooperative Telling and One-upmanship Telling

Medic storytelling usually takes place between partners in the long periods of downtime between calls. Some partners have heard each other's stories very often or have their own additions to the stories, so that the narrative becomes a cooperative endeavor, in much the same way that treating a critical patient on scene is a cooperative endeavor.

At other times, medics congregate near emergency room ambulance loading areas, as this is one of the few places where they have a chance to socialize. In these situations, it is not uncommon for several medics to jump into the storytelling and then the storytelling takes on a competitive feel, with paramedics trying to "outdo" each other:

[John]: I haven't been attacked specifically. Other people from the company have. There was this one guy . . .
[Larry]: Well, I've heard about paramedics that have been attacked.
[John]: Someone just got attacked last week . . .
[Larry]: This one paramedic I know got beat up on the 4th of July. They broke his nose.

In these situations, the general rule of telling stories with firsthand authority does not apply and, in the spirit of competition, medics may tell stories about calls that their partners have had or, in rarer instances, calls that they have "heard about."

Storytelling as a Means of Exerting Control over the Narrated Event

Storytelling also gives medics a chance to exert control over the narrated events. Through their stories they can retell the events and impose order on what are often chaotic, unstructured scenes. Frequently in their stories, the medics place themselves in a position of calm at the center of a storm:

[Lars]: We picked up this no-big-deal call, we had this guy, you know, who felt ill, felt weak. You know, I was driving so I didn't pay too much attention to what his problem was. And we're driving along to the hospital, driving up Seminary Avenue and kind of out the corner of my eye I see a car smashed into a pole. And I'm like, "Oh, there's a car wreck. Oh, there's a guy laying on the front lawn. Oh jeez, I guess that I should probably stop!" And there's all these people waving and yelling, so I stop and I get out, and I walk over to the guy and he's laying on this front lawn and his car is wrecked and he's conscious. So I start checking the guy out, and he's saying "Oh, my chest, my chest," and I ask, "Did you have your seat belt on?" And he says, "Oh yeah, yeah," and I say, "Did you hit the steering wheel?" Meanwhile, I'm cutting off his clothes and I realize that all under his arm is covered with blood! And I say, "Jeez, buddy, you're covered with blood!" and he says, "Oh yeah, I've been shot." Sure enough, up under his arm, he'd been shot. The bullet entered up under his armpit. And I'm thinking "That's pretty weird," 'cause there's no damage to his arm, just in his armpit.

So we call for another ambulance. Meanwhile we've got this old guy sitting in the back of our ambulance going, "Oh wow, this is weird." Now, in the meantime all these people have gathered. There's people running around everywhere, and this group of guys gathers around us, and they start saying to the guy, "What you need to do is that you need to pray to God. You need to pray to Jesus. Come on everybody, let's pray!" And these guys make a little circle of people and they all start praying to Jesus. Now they've got the patient going, and they're all going, "Oh Jesus help me! Oh Jesus help me!" Then all the guys start speaking in tongues! So you've got this circle of people going, "Ubbba burrba lubba dubbba!" This guy's saying, "Oh Jesus help me!" And then the police cars pull up.

It turns out that, laying on this guy's car seat, is a .45-caliber handgun cocked and ready to shoot. This guy was about to do a drive-by shooting, he was about to blow somebody away, and so he was leaning out the driver's side window with his hand out with the gun. But the guy he was about to shoot had a gun too, and shot him before he could shoot them. So it's sort of the Wild West thing you know, whoever's got the quickest draw wins. And this guy didn't. So then the guy went careening out of control and slammed into a telephone pole. So we're on scene with this guy who's been shot, this loaded gun on the seat and this circle of people singing Oh Jesus and speaking in tongues. The patient's yelling, "Oh Jesus help me! Oh Jesus help me!" The cops are running around all over the place, the firemen, when they hear about the gun, run back to their trucks to stage or hide or whatever, we've still got this poor old guy in the back of the ambulance going, "Oh great," and me and my partner are just watching the insanity unfold. It was the funniest thing.

The Presentation of Self Through Story

Medics' stories can be seen as a political act, with the presentation of self taking on strategic impor-

tance. Addressing the presentation of self in personal-experience narratives, Robinson notes, "We may grant that narrators will often endeavor to portray themselves as more clever, skillful, resourceful, or of higher moral character than their antagonists. This attitude is not to be disparaged, for it is not merely an attempt to exploit a social interaction to further one's self esteem. It is a semi-ritualized means of reaffirming both one's personal identity and socially sanctioned beliefs and values, particularly those that ascribe responsibility, hence blame or praise." Through their storytelling, ambulance personnel can comment on the organization of their work environment, the relative competence of the personnel from other agencies with whom they interact, and the merits or faults of other ambulance services.

Apart from firefighters, one of the most derided groups in the medics' stories are nurses:

[Lars]: Me and Bob did three cardiac arrests in the course of the night, but one of them was in the ER [emergency room]. We're sitting in the ER, just hanging out, there's this guy in there for stomach problems. And he's in a room and one of the nurses looks at his heart monitor at the nurses station and goes, "What's wrong with the monitor? It's doing funny things. That almost looks like V-fib!" [ventricular fibrillation] And another nurse says, "Well, go and look at him," and one of them goes in and she comes out screaming, "It's a code! It's a code!" This guy had gone into cardiac arrest for some reason.

So now, look out! Ten people race in there—they grab a crash cart and go racing in there. And it turns instantly into a three-ring circus—they've got too many people in there. Now, the guy needs to be defibrillated—shocked. That's the first thing you do with V-fib—you should walk up and hit him in the chest, do a quick cardial thump, because that will shock the heart back into normal rhythm. And then you should defibrillate—that's the definitive care.

Well, one of the nurses is doing CPR but she's doing it like she's giving him a rub-down. The family's in there, freaking out, and we're sitting at the end of the hall, thinking, "What the hell's going on?" So one of the nurses turns to us and says, "Get the family out of here!" And I'm thinking, "My uniform doesn't say 'Security'," you know?

So we're watching and they've got the guy now on yet another heart monitor, which also shows V-fib. And the doctor says, "Oh, we've got to defibrillate!" Except that the monitor they have on this crash cart did not have regular defibrillator paddles—it had special patches that you put on, so you can stand back and defibrillate. Thing is, they didn't have the cables, they didn't have the patches, they couldn't do it! And one of the nurses says, "Go get the paddles off the other defibrillator."

Finally, my partner, Mark says, "That's it. We have to go in there." And he goes in there and says, "I'll take over the compressions," and he starts doing real chest compressions. I go over to the other crash cart where the nurse is pulling on the paddles and I say, "They don't come off." She's like, "Yes they do." I'm like, "No, trust me. Paddles, they do not come off. They're permanently attached." So I take the crash cart, wheel it into the room, and everyone's yelling, "Defibrillate! Defibrillate!" And I say, "Wait a second, aren't you going to put on the gel pads so we don't light this guy on fire?" And so I put on the pads and charge up to 200 joules and zap him. Nothing, still in V-fib. By this time, the doctors have put an endotracheal tube in him and they're trying to ventilate him, someone's trying to get an IV. I'm like, "All right, clear again," zap him at 300, still in V-fib. All right. Go up to 360, clear, make sure I've got good contact and BOOM! I zap him! And right as I zap him, out of the endotracheal tube shoots this big clot of blood. It comes flying out—bleah!—it hits me right in the arm. I drop the paddles and, at the same time, the guy pops into a normal sinus rhythm, his pulse comes back, and a few second later, he's breathing. That was our cardiac arrest in the ER.

Other stories concerning incompetent physicians, truculent police officers, unhelpful firefighters, and power-happy supervisors abound. By narrating, the storyteller bolsters his position vis-à-vis cohorts, managers, and other emergency responders.

Story as a Way to Exchange Information

Ambulance personnel also use storytelling as an opportunity to exchange information. Stories about combative patients, unexpected hazards, or surprising outcomes provide paramedics with important experiential information:

[Darryl]: I've seen, believe it or not, a head-on accident in the parking lot of a Macy's sale. The parking lot was completely empty, except for these two cars that hit each other head-on. This little old lady and some other idiot. How do you, in an empty parking lot, slam into another car like that? Somehow they managed to hit each other head-on. Well, it was just enough trauma to kill her. Barely any damage but a little old lady driving a big car with a big old steering wheel. That's enough to kill an elderly person.

And then you get these drunks who just mangle their car and they wrap it around a telephone pole and split it in half and it's upside down and you can't even identify what kind of car it was, let alone what color it was. And you walk up and ask, "Where's the patient?" And it's the guy standing next to you and there's nothing wrong with him! At all! It's incredible!

To some degree, the medics' stories serve a didactic purpose. Stories are often offered as anecdotal evidence concerning the treatment of certain patients, the dangers of certain neighborhoods, and the attitudes and abilities of firefighters, emergency room personnel, supervisors, and managers.

Story Builds Solidarity

Stories also build solidarity among medics. In the give-and-take of their storytelling, medics develop commonly held views, debate beliefs, and reinforce occupational norms, and thus develop an occupational cultural ideology. In this way the storytelling contributes to their sense of shared community. Medics also enculturate new medics through storytelling. By participating in repeated storytelling sessions, the new medic learns both the occupational expectations of other medics—how to behave on scene and how to react to certain situations—as well as their storytelling expectations. As he/she gains both medical and storytelling experience, the new medic is able to engage more and more as an active narrator in these sessions. Just as he/she develops his own style of paramedicine, he/she also develops his/her own style of storytelling.

Storytelling as Stress Reliever

Storytelling can be seen in part as an informal form of debriefing. One of the most highly touted developments in emergency medical services is the critical incident stress debriefing (CISD), a formal interaction in which medics discuss aspects of a call among themselves—they narrate their personal experiences of a particularly difficult call and discuss their feelings about the deaths of their patients. Because attending CISD is considered a sign of weakness, many medics are reluctant to request it. In its place, cohort storytelling acts as a much-needed outlet for many of the emotions engendered by seeing people die.

Although many of the stories paramedics tell are devoid of the expected emotions engendered by encountering human suffering and death, it is misleading to suggest that all medic stories are flip. Indeed, stories about pediatric patients tend to be solemn performances:

[Mary]: On our first call of the day, we get an MVA (motor vehicle accident). We get there and it's a mother and her three children. The mother is of course OK, even though everyone was ejected from the car. This is on Bancroft, which is a pretty busy area, or pretty busy street in Oakland. I guess she came flying down the street, swerved to miss another car, hit a pole, and everyone just flew out the windows of this old Impala. And there were three kids and I think the oldest one was maybe three years old. And they were all unconscious, one was more or less dead. The kid that we were working on was in and out of consciousness. It was so sad to see those little kids— bright, sunny day, and then this stark scene, like the bright baby clothes colors against the dark asphalt. That was just one of the most horrendous days I've ever had in my life.

When medics narrate, they tend to present the most extreme of all cases they have encountered. Accordingly, when they tell a sad story, they tell the saddest story they can think of. Among medics, stories of lives cut short fill that role.

Further Reading

Belkin, Lisa, *First, Do No Harm*, New York: Simon & Schuster, 1993; London: Hodder and Stoughton, 1994

Manning, Peter K., and John Van Maanen, eds., *Policing: A View from the Street*, Santa Monica, California: Goodyear, 1978

Mannon, James M., *Emergency Encounters: A Study of an Urban Ambulance Service*, Port Washington, New York: Kennikat, 1981; also published as *Emergency Encounters: EMTs and Their Work*, Boston: Jones and Bartlett, 1992

McCarl, Robert, *The District of Columbia Fire Fighters' Project: A Case Study in Occupational Folklife*, Washington D.C.: Smithsonian Institution, 1985

Metz, Donald L., *Running Hot: Structure and Stress in Ambulance Work*, Cambridge, Massachusetts: Abt, 1982

Post, Carl, *Omaha Orange: A Popular History of EMS in America*, Boston: Jones and Bartlett, 1992

Robinson, John A., "Personal Narratives Reconsidered," *Journal of American Folklore* 94:371 (1981)

Tangherlini, Timothy R., *Talking Trauma: Paramedics and Their Stories*, Jackson: University Press of Mississippi, 1998

Storytelling Style and Community Codes Among the Swiss Volhynian Mennonites

John McCabe-Juhnke

John McCabe-Juhnke, himself a third-generation Swiss Volhynian Mennonite, provides brief historical background and suggests that storytelling is used in this community to help foster Gemeinde, or community, a basic construct of Swiss Volhynian Mennonite life. McCabe-Juhnke discusses the use of dialect to suggest humor in joking, and he notes the importance of establishing family connections with the tale's characters.

Creating a Sense of Community (*Gemeinde*) Through Storytelling

The Swiss Volhynian Mennonites who settled in central Kansas in the 1870s migrated primarily as church congregations and made their living as farmers in isolated rural areas. Sustained by their Anabaptist Christian beliefs, these Mennonites worked to establish a community of mutually accountable believers that was independent of the social and political structures of mainstream society. In their native language of German, they called this idea of community *Gemeinde*. As a result of living in *Gemeinde*, a distinctive cultural identity has endured among the Swiss Volhynians, as evidenced by their ethnic foodways, Swiss-German dialect, and religious orientation.

A careful examination of Swiss Volhynian oral narration reveals that a primary function of narrative performance is to give momentary substance to a continually evolving sense of community. In other words, by affirming community connectedness, reinforcing community values, and some-times questioning the norms and expectations of the community, the Swiss Volhynian Mennonites enact Gemeinde in their storytelling.

As a third-generation descendant of Swiss Volhynian immigrants, the author of this article combined a scholarly interest in interpreting the narrative behaviors of this group with a personal interest in recapturing a disappearing ethnic heritage. These coinciding interests require a special effort to maintain an acceptable balance between participation in and analysis of Swiss Mennonite oral tradition.

A Historical Sketch of the Swiss Volhynian Mennonites

The Swiss Mennonites migrated to the United States from the province of Volhynia in Polish Russia in the 1870s. The greatest number of Swiss Mennonites originally came from Bern canton in Switzerland, where they were persecuted for their Anabaptist beliefs.

In order to escape religious prosecution and to seek new agricultural opportunities, the Swiss Mennonites moved from Switzerland to southern Germany, and then to Volhynia. (Actually, the term "Swiss Mennonite" is something of a misnomer, since the cultural identity of this group developed during several centuries of experience in Europe and Russia rather than in Switzerland.) In 1861 a Swiss Mennonite congregation was founded in the small town of Kotosufka in Volhynia. However, the passing of the military conscription law during the reign of the Russian czar Alexander required yet another emigration. On August 6, 1874, 78 Swiss Mennonite families (nearly everyone in the village) left Kotosufka for New York. Nineteen families chose to settle in South Dakota, while the remaining 59 settled on the prairies of central Kansas. There the Kotosufka congregation established the Hopefield Church and became some of the most significant founding members of the Moundridge community.

Mennonite historian Harley J. Stucky observes that these Russian Mennonites

> tried to establish their own unique communities based on common faith, dialect, [and] occupation. . . . They tried to perpetuate communities similar to those in the old world primarily on the basis of congregational affinity. (p. 33)

For the Swiss Volhynians of the late 1800s, the church was the community and the community was the church. This was the essence of *Gemeinde*—the notion that members in the church community were wholly interdependent. Although having been in the United States for more than a century has diminished the sense of *Gemeinde* for the Swiss Volhynians, prevalent traces of this idea remain in the oral culture of the Mennonites in the Moundridge community. Richard Schrag, a retired Mennonite farmer, remembers it this way:

> [W]e were conscious of the fact that to misbehave—there may be punishment, and to fall out of favor with the community—the church family—was a real disgrace. And you'd really feel isolated. . . . We were considered, at that time—when I was growing up—we were considered a closed group. (McCabe-Juhnke, p. 229)

Although practice of the *Bann* had been abandoned years before, the social exclusion of those who offended the community was still prevalent in Schrag's childhood experience. The formal structures of church discipline in Russia had been transformed into an informal system of social isolation and chastisement.

Richard Schrag was one of the 34 people from the Moundridge community who were interviewed for this study, 30 of whom were either first- or second-generation descendants of the em-

igrants from Volhynia. As a result, the perceptions of "community" as they emerge in this study are those of a specific group of older Swiss Mennonites, who range from 60 to 98 years of age.

This particular group of Swiss Mennonites is a transitional group. They learned English as a second language. They spoke German to their parents and siblings in their childhood homes, but they speak English to their own children. They have seen remarkable changes in farming practices, from the primitive methods of the horse-drawn plow to the modern technology of motorized tractor. Whereas their childhood experience was limited to activities in an isolated rural community, they now have the freedom and mobility that modern forms of transportation provide. Although their experiences with religion, social life, work, education, and family relationships have altered significantly in the course of their lifetimes, they interpret each of these aspects of contemporary life in light of the clearly defined expectations of their youth.

The Reluctant Storyteller in Swiss Volhynian Culture

A search for storytellers with established reputations in the Moundridge community can be fraught with false leads, disorientation, and a general lack of information. In the rare instance that individuals identify others as good storytellers, the "storytellers" themselves deny the distinction.

Several fundamental assumptions of Swiss Volhynian religion and culture undoubtedly contribute to this reticence to acknowledge participation in a storytelling tradition. An oral narrator who has been reared in a religious tradition that, according to Solomon Stucky, values the "practical life, stressing the dangers of pride and admonition to lead holy lives" (p. 101) has plausible reasons for a bias against storytelling, which is associated with frivolity, self-presentation, and secularism. In addition, the Kotosufka congregation's migration en masse to America perpetuated the custom of the closed community by enabling the Swiss Volhynians to maintain the congregational self-sufficiency they had practiced for nearly two centuries in Europe and Russia. Although their interdependence as a congregation has dissipated with acculturation to American society, a measure of clannishness of the Swiss Mennonites in Moundridge has endured. Speaking in 1949 at the seventy-fifth year celebration of the Swiss Volhynian migration, R.C. Kauffman identified the Swiss Mennonites' most obvious characteristic—"that, namely, of a strong in-group feeling—the denominational loyalty and separateness that characterizes us" (p. 54). Even today, after a century of acculturation to American society, the Swiss Mennonites in Moundridge are often perceived as a clannish people.

With such a strong cultural bias toward separateness, the Swiss Mennonites have maintained a community in which the concern for activities and experiences of those within the group dominates the oral culture of the group. Moundridge native J.O. Schrag characterizes the narrow scope of Swiss Mennonite oral narration when he observes, "[W]e developed a lot of little stories [when we were together with our cousins], but no one—they didn't amount to anything outside of your group" (McCabe-Juhnke, p. 258). Thus, storytellers in the Moundridge community cannot be distinguished by their vast repertoire of traditional folktales. Rather, oral narrators tell personal-experience stories, family reminiscences, and stories about unusual community events or personalities. It is not surprising, then, that Swiss Mennonites consider storytelling—in the traditional sense—to be an activity foreign to the Moundridge community.

After dismissing the notion of a folk tale tradition in the Moundridge community, Schrag goes on to address what he sees at the heart of Swiss Mennonite oral narration.

> But, there are stories. Sometimes you have to dig a while till you get them out. But there are some stories that have been—especially in their own experiences, you know. . . . So, they created their own stories. (p. 257)

Indeed, "creating one's own story" is a primary function of Swiss Volhynian oral narration. Drawing from personal experience, narrators not only can affirm their personal identities in oral narration, they can also adhere to expectations of truthfulness, thereby upholding the integrity of narrative discourse.

Despite the absence of a generally acknowledged forum for sharing stories among the Swiss Volhynians, storytelling is pervasive in Swiss Mennonite culture. Ozzie Goering, a participant in a series of storytelling workshops held at the Moundridge Senior Citizens Center, characterized the storytelling practices of the Swiss Volhynians in the following way.

> I think if you were to tell this group that you would like . . . to hear us tell stories about Eli Schrag [Ozzie's uncle, who was often the butt of jokes] and about people like that, that you would find a wealth of stories bubbling out that there wouldn't be time for them all. I think where you are right is that due to the perceived humility factor or something, the Swiss do not want to be identified as being *the* storyteller. But you get a group together and get them started talking, there's stories galore about what all has happened. (Goering, pp. 55–56)

As Goering's comment suggests, for Swiss Mennonites the "traditional" corpus of narratives includes personal-experience stories and community anecdotes rather than standard folktales, legends, or ballads. Stories of community experiences both preserve the "humility factor" and encourage widespread participation in narrative interactions.

The Schweitzer Dialect

A fundamental characteristic of the style and structure of Swiss Volhynian storytelling is the use of the Schweitzer dialect. The term "Schweitzer," derived from the German word *Schweizer* (Swiss), is used by both community insiders and members of other German Mennonite groups to refer to the Swiss Volhynian people and their language. The Schweitzer dialect exhibits a rich interplay among several national languages, or polyglossia (Bakhtin, p. 58). As Adina Krehbiel points out, the Swiss German dialect "isn't like the [German text]book. . . . We had Polish and Russian and German in our language which is so easy for us" (pp. 220–221). The Mennonites' sojourn through southern Germany and Polish Russia has obviously contributed to the multilingual nature of their dialect. Victor Goering gives a clear example of the Polish influence on the Schweitzer dialect in his discussion of the traditional after-harvest celebration, which his family called *objinky*. For years, he assumed that *objinky* was just a family word for the post-harvest event. However, when he and his wife sponsored some Polish trainees, they discovered that the Polish word for harvest festival is *dovzhinky* (p. 403). No doubt the Swiss Mennonites' experience in Polish Russia fostered an assimilation of Polish nuances in their dialect. In the same manner, after more than a century of experiences in the United States, Swiss Mennonites have incorporated American English into their dialect as well. One often hears

"Germanized" pronunciations of English words when listening to the Schweitzer dialect.

Polyglossia abounds in Swiss Mennonite oral narrative. Often, when storytellers render reported speech in dialect, the quoted passage has a special intensity or significance to the event being described. Notice, for instance, William Juhnke's fervent plea to his neighbor for help with the runaway horses.

> [Val Krehbiel] saw that my horses were running. And . . . I yelled, "*Stop mei Geil! Stop mei Geil!*" ["Stop my horses! Stop my horses!"] . . . He couldn't stop them. (p. 245)

In the face of an apparently life-threatening situation, the young William called out in desperation. At this point in the story, a measure of intensity appropriate to the impending danger accompanies the verbal command, and the shift into dialect highlights the urgency of the moment for the narrator.

Swiss Mennonite storytellers also use the Schweitzer dialect to highlight the punch line of a story. Especially for the older Swiss Volhynian storytellers, memorable conversational encounters are those in which the dialect is used to poke fun at someone. J.O. Schrag laughed about Fred Grundman, who finally managed to start his dilapidated car after repeated efforts and then triumphantly exclaimed, "*Entlich uf hoch!*" ["Finally I'm on high!"] (p. 260).

The humor of a punch line spoken in dialect is sometimes elusive when the phrase or sentence is translated into English. J.O. Schrag tells a story about a member of the Hopefield Church choir, John Strauss, who was "the butt of a lot of stories":

> He couldn't sing very well but then, he would try it. Well, we had a cantata. And at the dress rehearsal . . . John Strauss wasn't there. So at the time for the rendition he was there. Now, then he walked up and he said, "Where do I sit?" And at that time Ed P. Goering was still alive. . . . And Ed P. said, "*Das Wees nurre der Gott und der Neuenschwander.*" Now, Neuenschwander was our preacher. "Only God and Neuenschwander knows where you're going to sit." (p. 259)

On the surface, the literal translation of Mr. Goering's comment seems marginally humorous at best. Yet the oral narrator chuckled heartily when he finished the telling. Of course, some of the humor arises from knowing the people involved in the incident, but the oral narrator's direct quotation indicates an interest as well in the specific phraseology of the comment. Indeed, part of what makes the punch line funny is the fact that it is stated in dialect. Typically, Schweitzers enjoy the special finesse that the Swiss dialect lends to the spoken word, and they acknowledge that funny statements frequently lose their humor when translated into English.

The Swiss Mennonites' appreciation of the distinct character of the German language is demonstrated in a reluctance among storytellers to offer English translations of reported speech without acknowledging that the quotations were originally spoken in German. Notice Richard Schrag's story about trying to refuse wine gracefully from his wife's grandfather.

> So I thought, "maybe I can wiggle out of it because of my stomach trouble." So I said, "Well, I don't want to [drink wine] on account of my stomach." He said, "The Apostle Paul"—he said it in German—"The Apostle Paul told Timothy to take a little wine for his stomach's sake." And I was stuck. (p. 270)

Here the narrator interrupts himself to acknowledge the original language of the quotation, almost as if he failed to recognize the inadequacy of the translation until he uttered it aloud. Swiss storytellers typically reveal a reticence to delete completely the influences of the German language on the oral culture of their people.

Schrag's story further indicates that for previous generations of Swiss Mennonites the German language was vested with religious authority. Prior to World War I, the Mennonite churches in Moundridge used German for Sunday morning worship services. Although their education in American schools had fostered the general adoption of English for communication in the home and at work, Swiss Volhynians continued to worship, pray, and read the Bible in German. Therefore, the grandfather's quotation from the Bible would naturally have been spoken in German rather than English. Richard's need to acknowledge the German original no doubt arises from a keen awareness of the significance in earlier years of using German in all forms of religious discourse.

The diminishing influence of the German language among contemporary Swiss Mennonites is revealed in a joke that has circulated in Mennonite circles. The joke tells of an old Mennonite minister who argued vehemently that God spoke in German. In order to prove the fact, the minister pointed to the passage in his German Bible in which God says to Adam, *"Adam, wo bist du?"* While the joke attests to the reverence with which the German language has been viewed, it affirms a new attitude of enlightenment by showing the obvious absurdity of the minister's argument. Stephen Stern's research into the function of ethnic folklore suggests that American-born ethnics often use dialect jokes to distinguish themselves from their "backward" predecessors (p. 23). In the same manner, the joke about the Mennonite minister helps the progressive Mennonite to ease the embarrassment about his or her backward ancestors and disparages the exalted position of the German language. For the "new" generation of Swiss Mennonites, knowledge of German is more novelty than necessity.

Although the play between the two languages is most frequently illustrated by the juxtaposition of German and English phrases, some instances of language play involving double meanings do occur. For example, two storytellers recounted the experience of a Mennonite farmer who asked a neighboring "English" [non-Mennonite] woman for a *Kisse* (pillow) for his sore buttocks. Both accounts develop in a similar fashion: After several hours of riding on a stone sled (or lumber wagon, in one version), the Mennonite farmer began to be irritated by the metal seat. So he decided to stop at a roadside farmhouse and ask for a pillow to ease his sore buttocks. When he called at the door, an "English" woman answered. Suddenly, the farmer panicked, not able to remember the English word for pillow. He said, "Excuse me miss, but I wonder if you could give me a *Kisse*." From her shocked response, the farmer could tell he had made a grave error. So he added, "Oh, no, no, no. Not a *Kisse* here [pointing to lips]. A *Kisse* there [pointing to buttocks]."

These forms of play between English and the Swiss dialect typify the way bilingualism contributes to language play in other immigrant cultures. Rosan Jordan, who has studied Mexican-American immigrants in the southwestern United States, observes that "the power to play with both languages suggests the power to control both cultures and hence to deal effectively with

one's biculturalism" (p. 260). Although Jordan's study involves groups that have migrated more recently than the Swiss Mennonites, her premise that bilingual language play demonstrates a tension between cultures has significant applications in the study of Swiss Mennonite oral culture.

A fundamental tension arises in Swiss Mennonite stories in the play between languages. The prevalence of the dialect and of "Germanized" English expressions in their stories demonstrates the Swiss Volhynians' enduring awareness of their status as an immigrant culture. Their dialect affirms the Schweitzers' identification with their Russian ancestors and reveals an abiding level of separation from American society. At the same time, their facility in American English attests to the Swiss Mennonites' unapologetic participation in the current of contemporary American society. Like Jordan's Mexican American immigrants, Swiss Volhynians in Moundridge demonstrate their command of both languages in their wordplay, and thus bring about a "subliminal merging" of two cultures (Jordan, p. 263). However, the interplay of languages in Swiss Mennonite oral discourse reflects a different tension than that of the Mexican-Americans in Jordan's study.

The need for a "psychological reconciliation of opposites" (Jordan, p. 263) is less intense among Swiss Mennonites. Of course, this need has diminished in part because of the reduced tension between the Swiss Volhynian and American cultures after more than a century of assimilation. Swiss Mennonites, however, differ from other immigrant cultures on a more fundamental level. After their immigration in 1874, a primary goal for Swiss Mennonites was to remain separate from American culture rather than to assimilate into it. They established their own congregational community in the hope of maintaining the way of life that they had established in Kotosufka. In a sense, Swiss Mennonites have assimilated in spite of themselves. Indeed, their oral discourse reflects an abiding preference for separateness over integration. At the same time, it demonstrates a need to renegotiate *Gemeinde* in the context of newly evolving cultural assumptions in their identity as native-born United States citizens.

Minimalist Style and Insider's Code

Another distinguishing feature of Swiss Mennonite oral discourse is the noticeable minimalism that pervades these narratives. Stories are seldom embellished with careful descriptive phrases.

With a few exceptions, storytellers recount incidents in brief statements, sometimes using only two or three short sentences to tell a story. Perhaps this practice is in keeping with the values of truthfulness and modesty: better to err on the side of sparseness than to embellish and run the risk of wavering from the absolute truth.

Often the storyteller uses specific names, especially in discussing family members, without explaining the relationship of the narrator to the person named. Adina Krehbiel remembered Dan Waltner's storytelling antics, suggesting that he spoke "like Carl does a little bit, too" (p. 225). She did not mention that Carl Waltner was a nephew of hers who is at best distantly related to Dan Waltner. William Juhnke referred to the owners of the Alta Mill, saying simply that the mill was run by "Ransom Stucky's father and uncles" (p. 234). Jacob Goering talked about Gilbert and Victor working in the field without mentioning that they were his sons (p. 254). Swiss Mennonite stories are full of these unexplained references that reveal an insider's code in the use of language—a kind of "Schweitzer Shorthand." These storytellers assume (sometimes mistakenly) that their interviewer, who is a community insider, knows these family relationships. Again, these stories evoke *Gemeinde* by assuming a relationship with the listener that depends on the shared knowledge of family and community members.

Storytellers typically use Schweitzer shorthand to orient the listener to the people or places that the story involves. In some instances, efforts to ensure that the listener knows exactly to whom an incident happened or exactly where it occurred supersedes the storyteller's account of the event itself. For example, William Juhnke interrupted the first line of "Uncle Wesley's Hay Story" to ask his wife about the man with whom his uncle was working (p. 248). William was not satisfied with simply identifying the man as "a Wedel." He wanted to know, "Now, which Wedel was that?" Only after his wife identified the man as "John Wedel's older brother" could William proceed with his story. When he finished the story, William added that his Uncle Wesley was the brother to my grandfather.

For some storytellers, this process of making connections errs on the side of obsessive and the shorthand turns to longhand. In a story about a Mennonite farmer who was tarred and feathered for refusing to buy war bonds, Art Goering tried to relate the man's name to his contemporary descendants.

Of course, you take this John Schrag, better known as *Krike Hannes* [Creek John]. You know who I'm talking about. John Schrag, he was Dan and Herman's father, and Pete and Jake, the Schrag boys, you know. There's only three living now, I guess. Pete and Herman and Adam. *Ja*, the three out of nine boys. *Ja*, their father—who, incidentally, was direct uncle to my mother. Mrs. Schrag and my mother's mother were sisters. So, my mother and the Schrags were first cousins. But, uh, John Schrag, he was actually tarred and feathered during that time. (p. 349)

After establishing what he evidently perceived to be a necessary link, he resumed the story, which took only two sentences to tell. In this case the storyteller not only makes an association for the listener, he also demonstrates his own relationship to the protagonist of the story. In so doing, he virtually eclipses the story itself. Swiss Mennonites easily become preoccupied with such digressions. In fact, the "Mennonite Game" (as this activity of making associations has been affectionately labeled) is a commonly acknowledged form of verbal play for Swiss Mennonites in Moundridge as well as for ethnic Mennonites across the country. When Swiss Mennonites shift into the association game, their verbal activity regularly delays or even replaces narration in their oral interactions.

Code words other than specific names of people or family relationships also indicate an in-group relationship. Mennonites in Moundridge often speak a few words or phrases to refer to stories that "everyone" knows. A person may recite a catch phrase as a substitute for telling the story thus demonstrating the story's relevance to a similar situation. J.O. Schrag recalls the origin of the phrase "*grümm Strück Vereiss*" (grim broken rope):

. . . what would that mean to anyone else? Well, it happened that Victor Goering was visiting Uncle Dan's and somehow we fooled around with a rope in the barn. He was involved where he was irritated, he was grim. He was angry about it. [Laughs] And the rope broke, see? Well, so we would just say, "*grümm Strück vereiss,*" and that was our story. We knew what was going on. (p. 259)

Families often share a broad repertoire of such phrases. An actual telling of the story surrounding the phrase's origin seldom occurs within the closed context of the family. Instead, Swiss Mennonites tell these stories to people outside the family who may hear family members use the phrase with each other but are unfamiliar with the context surrounding it.

The microstructure of Schweitzer shorthand is perhaps the most prevalent example of Swiss Mennonite narrative distinctiveness. This narrative component, called "linking," functions to orient the listener to the time, place, and characters in the story in a special way; it links the listener with the characters in the story and with the narrative community. For example, Art Goering told about seeing a Swiss-German play that explored the theme of agricultural progress. After a brief introductory comment that introduced the story frame ("I recall that the Swiss gave a play to that effect"), Art began linking.

A: I don't know whether you heard [the play] or not.
J: No.
A: Phil Waltner was in on—. Of course, Phil died young, you know. Waldo Waltner's oldest brother. And in the play. . . . (p. 355)

In one sense, linking clauses set the scene for the story, but they do so in a special way. Linking attempts to connect the teller and listener by demonstrating shared knowledge of community relational structure. The narrator asserts a community relationship in his assumption that the listener either knows the characters in the story personally or knows someone from the characters' families. Thus, linking invokes "peoplehood" by highlighting the interrelationship of speaker and listener within the context of shared experience.

The frequency with which linking occurs in Swiss Volhynian narrative discourse indicates the fundamental nature of this structural component in Swiss Mennonite narrative form. In many Schweitzer stories, connecting the listener with the characters and relationships in the story is as vitally important as demonstrating the story's point. In fact, sometimes linking becomes the primary goal, as it did in Art Goering's Krike

Hannes story. Although others may view these structures as digressions, Swiss Mennonites deem them central.

The fact that linking often delays or even replaces narrative activity in Swiss Mennonite oral discourse reveals the abundant appeal of this formal structure among Swiss Mennonites. It is one of the most apparent distinguishing components of Swiss Volhynian narrative texts. One can easily identify the similarities between the microstructure of linking and the macrostructure of Swiss Mennonite sociocultural experience. In fact, Swiss Mennonite community is founded on a system of linkages. Community members interconnect in ways that establish a collective system of interaction that is at the same time mutually understood and individually meaningful.

Indeed, Swiss Volhynian oral narration reflects the inevitability of contextual overtones within story texts. The storyteller's participation in community life is apparent in the preponderance of dialect, which promotes an in-group identity. The minimalist style of narration, which frequently utilizes Schweitzer shorthand and insiders' code words, demonstrates a concern for the economy and integrity of speech. The predominance of community anecdotes, family reminiscences, and personal-experience stories demonstrates an overriding interest in life within the fairly limited scope of community experience.

Clearly, the linguistic structure of Swiss Mennonite oral narratives has been shaped by community experience. In addition to reflecting a broad spectrum of community concerns, structural elements function to locate story action within a mutually understood context of people and places. Thus, even an analysis that focuses specifically on textual considerations of Swiss Mennonite oral narrative reveals that narrative structures function both to recall and to evoke the essence of Swiss Volhynian *Gemeinde.*

Further Reading

Bakhtin, M.M., *The Dialogic Imagination: Four Essays,* edited by Michael Holquist, translated by Caryl Emerson and Michael Holquist, Austin: University of Texas Press, 1981

Goering, Ozzie, Storytelling Workshop, Moundridge Senior Center (March 18, 1993)

Jordan, Rosan A., "Tension and Speech Play in Mexican-American Folklore," in '*And Other Neighborly Names': Social Process and*

Cultural Image in Texas Folklore, edited by Roger D. Abrahams and Richard Bauman, Austin: University of Texas Press, 1981

Kauffman, R.C., "A Critical Evaluation of Ourselves (The Swiss Mennonites)," in *Addresses and Other Items of Interest Connected with the Seventy-fifth Anniversary Services of the Swiss Mennonites (Schweitzer-Mennoniten) Held on September 5, 1949,* edited by Harley J. Stucky, 1950

McCabe-Juhnke, John, *Narrative and Everyday Experience: Performance Process in the Storytelling of the Swiss Volhynian Mennonites* (Ph.D. diss., Louisiana State University), 1990

Stern, Stephen, "Ethnic Folklore and the Folklore of Ethnicity," *Western Folklore* 36 (1977)

Stucky, Harley J., *A Century of Russian Mennonite History in America: A Study of Cultural Interaction,* North Newton, Kansas: Mennonite, 1973

Stucky, Solomon, *The Heritage of the Swiss Volhynian Mennonites,* Waterloo, Ontario: Conrad, 1981

Storytellers and the Art of Storytelling in the Mexican Culture

Rosario S. Morales

Rosario Morales discusses the lives of six story-tellers and briefly notes their use of story. She then turns to a discussion of the genres of the Mexican folktale.

Storytellers have played a very special role in history by preserving the oral tradition of their cultures. The storytellers of my Mexican heritage became the basis for my doctoral dissertation at the University of San Francisco in 1992. The study focused on the storytellers' lives, their stories, and the storytelling process, and provided an opportunity for the storytellers to share their experiences with a wider audience and reflect about storytelling. The six traditional Mexican storytellers I met, three women and three men, ranged in age from 60 to 75 years. Two were from Mexico and resided in small communities outside of Guadalajara, in Jalisco, Mexico, and four were from California.

The Storytellers

Doña Carmen is 60 years old and lives in Los Angeles. She was born in Valladolid, Yucatán, Mexico. She and her husband have lived in the United States for 35 years and have eight children and 15 grandchildren. Doña Carmen is unusual because she is trilingual, speaking Spanish, Maya, and English. Her pride in her Maya heritage is evident in the way in which she relates her family history to the Maya legends she tells. She is knowledgeable about the history of the Mayas and passes this on to her children and grandchildren.

During storytelling sessions she often stops to explain the meaning of a Maya word or how an item was used by the Mayas as part of their livelihood. This added historical information provides her storytelling with significant background information for her listeners to understand the world of the Mayas.

Born in Tucson, Arizona, Doña Isabel is 75 years old and lives in Pasadena, California. She has 5 children, 14 grandchildren, and 9 great-grandchildren. She is bilingual in Spanish and English, but she feels more comfortable speaking English. Friendships are important to her, and she enjoys knitting and taking walks in her neighborhood. Her two birds keep her company during the day.

Doña Isabel comes from a family of storytellers. Both her parents, her cousin Billy, and her sisters told stories. Storytelling is a family tradition that she has passed on to her daughter, Vibiana. One story that she especially enjoys telling is the legend of La Llorona (The Weeping Woman).

Doña Jessie is 73 years old and now lives in Kingsburg, California, but she grew up living in different parts of California, following the cosechas (crops) as a farmworker. She has five children and several grandchildren. She is bilingual in Spanish and English but prefers to speak Spanish.

Doña Jessie worked with Cesar Chavez and the United Farmworkers Union all her life, She worked alongside her husband most of these years, but he died a few years ago. Now she is re-

442

tired and spends time as a volunteer for the union translating letters and other documents and going to the fields to inform the new farmworkers about their labor rights.

Doña Jessie learned her storytelling from her grandmother. Today when her grandchildren come to visit her, she often tells them the stories she remembers from her childhood. She translates her stories into English now because her grandchildren have forgotten how to speak Spanish.

Don Refugio is 73 years old and lives in Ajijic, Jalisco, Mexico. He was born in Totatlán, which is 70 miles east of Guadalajara. This area is known as Los Altos and was heavily settled by the Spaniards. He himself is the eldest of 14 children and has 11 children and 31 grandchildren. Many of his children have moved north and live in California.

People in Ajijic call Don Refugio "Don Cuco." He is a property caretaker and is well known in town. He learned his storytelling from two young men who came from the state of Guanajuato to live in his town. He is a soft-spoken man who tells *mentiras* (fantasy stories), *advinanzas* (riddles), and *chistes* (jokes). He enjoys telling stories to the children in the neighborhood as a form of entertainment.

Don Trino is 70 years old and was born in Ajijic, Jalisco. He had 17 children, but one of his sons died in 1980. It was then that he decided to bring his family to live in California, and he now has 51 grandchildren and 4 great-grandchildren. Some of his children and grandchildren live with him and his wife, Aurora, in Santa Ana, California. Don Trino worked as a farmworker for part of his life; then he became a gardener. Now he is retired and spends much of his time reading and writing.

He enjoys composing songs and writing poetry and consejos (advice), which he has developed into short stories that teach values. Don Trino believes in the importance of the family, religion, and values. His life revolves around these three important aspects of his world, and they have made him happy. Storytelling has been part of Don Trino's life, and the meaning of the stories have become lessons in his own life. He learned storytelling from some ancianitos (old men) who lived in the community and gave him consejos. He now tells his grandchildren stories, following the stories with consejos that apply the lessons to life experiences as was done for him as a young boy. He enjoys telling folktales and religious stories, especially the story of La Virgen de Guadalupe (The Virgin of Guadalupe).

Don Cuco and Don Trino are compadres (godfathers, a term that refers to the relationship between the father of a child and a male friend). The father selects a special friend to baptize or christen his child. Traditionally, the friend or relative takes on the responsibility of raising the child in case of an emergency or the death of the parents. The female counterpart is the comadre (godmother). In the Mexican tradition the relationship between compadres and comadres is a very close one.

Padre Macias is 67 and a Roman Catholic priest who managed an orphanage called Niños y Jóvenes (Children and Young Adults) in San Juan Cosolá, which is adjacent to Ajijic, near Lake Chapala. Padre Macias is from a family of storytellers who tell stories whenever people are gathered. He takes pride in stories told to the children under his care or in church as part of his sermons. Padre Macias is a very animated storyteller. He mesmerizes his listeners with his exaggerated gestures, voice, and use of words. He learned many stories from his grandparents and inherited his *gestos* (gestures) from his mother. The children are very familiar with all his storytelling techniques.

The stories he likes to tell are folktales, but he also enjoys entertaining the children with *advinanzas* (riddles). The reason he tells stories is to teach the children lessons, but he feels that children teach adults also. He stated, "*Al final de la vida nosotros dizque educamos a los niños pero también ellos nos educan de verdad a nosotros*" (At the end of life we say that we have educated children, but they have actually educated us).

For these storytellers, their stories are well integrated into their lives. They do not refer to themselves as storytellers, but as people who like to tell stories when it is appropriate. It is a natural activity. Each story has a special message and is told for entertainment or to teach a lesson. The storytellers' message to others who are interested in storytelling is to enjoy the experience and to tell stories from the heart.

Historical Background of the Mexican Folklore

In studying Mexican folklore, it is important to understand the historical origins of the stories. As in other cultures, folklore in Mexico serves as a means to celebrate special events, honor heroes and heroines, and vent the fears, frustrations, and contradictions in life. The folklore of Mexico is grounded in the beliefs, values, history, and traditions of its people. When the Spaniards colonized Mexico, they brought with them their religion and beliefs as well as the Spanish language and their own oral tradition, which ultimately blended with the lives, beliefs, and languages of the indigenous communities, contributing to Mexico's rich oral tradition. Aboriginal myths, legends about religious saints, historic heroines and heroes, folktales, fables, and everyday proverbs of the people have all been handed down from generation to generation.

Because of close proximity to the Mexican-U.S. border, the continuous emigration and visitation of the Mexican people to the U.S., and the people's pride in their heritage, the folklore of Mexico has spread to the southwestern United States. (The states of California, Texas, Arizona, Colorado, and New Mexico have an especially high concentration of people of Mexican heritage.) There are fables, folktales, jokes, and twisters, but the prominent genre is the legend. The corrido, which is a musical narration, has historically depicted the folklore related to the border and the Mexican-American experience (Rocard). The themes of the legends in the U.S. southwest include religion, ghosts, heroes, the missions, the family, traditional beliefs, the supernatural, and romance. Because of the history of colonization by the Spaniards and life in the southwest, the legends varied from raids, ambushes, searches for buried treasure, and tragic tales to romantic episodes and ghostly adventures (Hallenbeck and Williams).

Legends based on traditional beliefs are used by parents and the community to maintain and reinforce particular religious and moral beliefs or to warn and admonish wrongdoers, such as a drunkard or wife abuser. Supernatural tales frequently involve a transformation of the devil into human form. The role of the devil in legends has been questioned by many. Robe provides a characteristic description of the devil: "He is frequently a sympathetic character who is not all bad. He is rarely on the side of sin and evil but rather is ready to punish those who violate moral codes or Christian principles" (*Hispanic Legends,* p.15).

Folktales, Myths, and Legends

Storytelling in the Mexican culture is, as in many cultures, a family tradition in which the heritage of the culture is passed on from generation to generation. In the Mexican culture, this folklore includes folktales, myths, legends, and proverbs that have their roots in history and are influenced by both the indigenous and the Spanish ancestry in Mexico.

The traditional Mexican storytellers in this study were persons in the family or in the community who had told stories that were handed down by their relatives. Some stories that are told within their families today have become part of the family's history. Storytelling reflects cultural knowledge, concepts, and values.

Many scholars interested in storytelling of the Mexican culture have collected stories, folktales, and legends from traditional storytellers in various parts of Mexico and the southwestern United States. The works of Campos, Paredes, Campa, Rael, Espinosa, and Robe have added significantly to the study of Hispanic literature and folklore.

Storytelling, or *decir cuentos,* in Mexico, although a long-held tradition, has been negatively affected by radio, television, and movies (Barton and Booth; Smith; Robe, *Mexican Tales*). Robe's study of the people of Los Altos from Jalisco in the late 1940s found storytelling to be very prevalent at that time. He attributed the survival of the folktales and the practice of storytelling to the strong heritage of the people. Storytelling was done for amusement as well as for the instruction of the young. This was done through a special religious legend called the *ejempla*. The settings for storytelling were gatherings of family and neighbors as well as at bedtime for the children. Storytellers were usually the mother, an older sister, a grandmother, or an older person in the community who told stories to children and neighbors. Men often engaged in storytelling at work or gathered at neighborhood stores to share their stories. Robe (*Mexican Tales*) found that *los alteños* (the people from Los Altos) passed on their stories and the practice of storytelling to the younger generation.

Barlow has provided categories for tales told in Latin America which are applicable to those found in Mexico. These include creation tales, metamorphosis, explanatory tales, tales of animals and birds, post-Columbian folktales, religious tales, and humorous tales about animals and humans. Robe (*Mexican Tales; Antologia*) includes proverbs, riddles, jests, anecdotes, Don Cacahuate stories, and numbskull cycles.

Creation tales are the myths of the aboriginal people, including the Aztecs, the Mayas, the Zapotecas, the Olmecs, and numerous other cultures and their ancestors. Myths about the creation of the world, gods, and the supernatural are based on religious, philosophical, and cosmological concepts. They are concerned with the material needs of the people as well as their understanding of the meaning of life. Some of the themes found in these myths are time and eternity, heaven and hell, immortality and the soul, and nature (Nicholson).

Metamorphosis tales involve a transformation; usually, a human is transformed into a bird or animal. These are common in both myths and legends from South America, especially Paraguay and Argentina (Barlow). In Mexico, the term *nahualismo* refers to this type of conversion (Robe, *Mexican Tales*). The origin of the legend of La Llorona (The Weeping Woman) may be indigenous, as some tales include this feature in the tale.

Tales of birds and animals are abundant in Mexican folklore and are found in myths, folktales, and fables. The eagle has been a symbol of Mexican heritage and is part of the country's flag. The Aztecs tell the tale of their gods who promised them a new home. They were told to find a sign of an eagle perched on a *nopal* (cactus) in the middle of a lake, which would signify the site of their new capital. When they found it, they built their new city and named it Tenochtitlán, which is now called Mexico City (Beals).

Animal tales such as El Conejo y el Coyote (The Rabbit and the Coyote) tell how the rabbit tricks the coyote time and time again. The smaller animal, the rabbit, through cleverness and wit manages to escape the predator, the coyote. The rabbit-coyote stories are pre- and post-conquest tales and have also been part of the South American and Native American folklore (Radin). These stories bear some resemblance to one another and in some cases may have been influenced by the African-American stories of Brer Rabbit. In Peru they exist as La Zorra y el Cuy (The Fox and the Guinea Pig).

Folktales are universal and have been transmitted to various parts of the world by people who attempt to maintain their folkways. Some stories found in Mexico are similar to the those in the United States and Europe. Maria Ceniza (Cinder Mary) is a fairy tale from Azqueltin, Jalisco, collected by J.A. Mason (p. 192) from the Tepecano aborigines. The story reflects the Spanish in-

fluence on the Mexican folktales, as evidenced by the inclusion of incidents and customs that were closely related to European traditions and were foreign to the life of the native people. The theme is similar to that of the familiar Cinderella folktale, but the plot, characters, and ending are different. These provide a means by which adults can teach children values such as self-reliance, obedience, truthfulness, trust, caring, and love.

In contrast to folktales, legends are believed to be true. Religious tales as well as legends about heroes, heroines, and other subjects make up a popular genre throughout Mexico. They are also a large part of the Mexican-American folklore in the southwestern United States. Many legends support the people's beliefs, values, and traditions, including the values of the close-knit family and Catholicism (Robe, *Hispanic Legends*).

Religious tales are about saints, spirits, and miracles. The religious story of the Virgin of Guadalupe who appeared to Juan Diego, an Aztec native, in 1531 has made her the patroness of Mexico, and she is also revered by many Chicanos in the United States. The merger of the Spanish-Catholic and Aztec Indian heritages has been attributed to the apparition, an event that greatly affected Mexican history and folklore (Dorson; Paz; West). Dorson, along with many other anthropologists, has labeled the Virgin a "symbol of the Mexican people" because of the numerous miracles attributed to her and the beliefs and loyalty of the people (Dorson, p. xxvi). A fiesta is held yearly in her honor. The fiesta is a special celebration in Mexico. It integrates the folklore of the people as it combines all the folk arts: dance, song, music, sculpture, cuisine, carnival, ritual decoration, folklore, myths, and legends. West summarizes the story:

> The official miracle relates how a lady appeared to a lowly Indian, Juan Diego, in December 1531 on a hill outside Mexico City—a hill sacred to the worship of Tonantzín, an Indian "Mother of Heaven" cult figure. The lady told Juan that she wanted a chapel built on that spot, and sent him to inform the bishop. As might be expected, Bishop Zumárraga doubted that the Virgin would use such a lowly messenger and asked for a sign. When Juan returned to the hill, the lady received the bishop's reply and told the Indian to take his *tilma* (cape) and gather up the roses that had appeared on the rocky hillside—in cold De-

cember—and carry them to the bishop. When the load of roses tumbled out on the floor before the bishop, the *tilma*'s rough surface contained a picture of the Virgin—and the sign was received as genuine. (p. 68)

Another famous but very different legend is the legend of La Llorana (The Weeping Woman), about a ghost who cries endlessly for her lost children by rivers and lakes. Many versions of this legend are found in Mexico, Latin America, and the southwestern United States. It is thought that

this legend originated from the time of Hernán Cortés, the Spanish conquistador, and his mistress, La Malinche, an Aztec princess. She was considered by many to be a traitor to Mexico because, as a translator for Cortés, she aided him in the conquest of Mexico. The story is told that after La Malinche had a child by Cortés she was replaced by a Spanish wife, and this drove her to acts of vengeance against the Spaniards. In other versions, it is a love story in which the woman is betrayed (West). The following is one version of this story.

La Llorona (The Weeping Woman)
La Llorona was a beautiful woman who did not want her first child when it was born. She threw it into a stream and did so successively with her other three children as they were born.

She died and as penitence was ordered to gather her abandoned children. She has not been able to find them. Consequently she wanders along streams at the edge of towns and in wooded places. Her hair is long and her dress reaches the ground. Many have heard her wailing: "Oh, my children!" (Robe, *Mexican Tales*, p. 108)

There are various versions of La Llorona, and each portrays her in a different light. She can be seen as a murderess, irresponsible and self-indulgent, or as vengeful, haunting men who are unfaithful to their wives. Still other versions have depicted her as a victim of circumstance. Kearney and Jones have analyzed these stories and themes and concluded that they depict some of the real-life experiences of the people who tell them. Peoples' feelings of inadequacies as parents and oppressive marital situations have been related to this legend. La Llorona has thus become a social symbol and is believed to provide an outlet for some of the frustrations and struggles of the women's roles in life. The legend has also been used to prevent children from wandering out at night and to warn people of the importance of maintaining the social ethos of the culture.

Reviewing the storytelling process and literature on Mexican storytelling and having conversations with the storytellers is an enriching experience. As these storytellers are acknowledged for their creativity and gifts of stories, they also serve as role models for all whose heritage has embodied the art of storytelling as an important and valued human experience.

Further Reading

Barlow, Genevieve, "Latin American Folklore and the Folktale," in *Folklore and Folktales*

Around the World, edited by R.K. Carlson, Newark, Delaware: International Reading Association, 1972

Barton, Bob, and David Booth, *Stories in the Classroom: Storytelling, Reading Aloud and Role Playing with Children,* Markham, Ontario: Pembroke, 1990; Portsmouth, New Hampshire: Heinemann, 1990

Beals, Carleton, *Stories Told by the Aztecs Before the Spaniards Came,* New York and London: Abelard-Schuman, 1970

Campa, Arthur L., *Hispanic Folklore Studies of Arthur L. Campa,* New York: Arno, 1976

Campos, Rubén, *El Folklore Literario de México,* Mexico City, Mexico: Talleres gráficos de la nación, 1929

Espinosa, Aurelio M., *The Folklore of Spain in the American Southwest: Traditional Spanish Folk Literature in Northern New Mexico and Southern Colorado,* Norman: University of Oklahoma Press, 1985

Hallenbeck, Cleve, and Juanita Williams, *Legends of the Spanish Southwest,* Glendale, California: Clark, 1938

Jones, Pamela, "'There Was a Woman': La Llorona in Oregon," *Western Folklore* 47:3 (July 1988)

Kearney, Michael, "La Llorona as a Social Symbol," *Western Folklore* 28 (1969)

Mason, J.A., "Four Mexican-Spanish Fairy-tales from Azqueltan, Jalisco," *Journal of American Folklore* 25:95 (July–September 1912)

Nicholson, Irene, *Mexican and Central American Mythology,* London: Hamlyn, 1967; New York: Peter Bedrick, 1985

Paredes, Americo, comp., *Folktales of Mexico,* Chicago: University of Chicago Press, 1970

Paz, Octavio, *The Labyrinth of Solitude: Life and Thought in Mexico,* New York: Grove, 1961; London: Evergreen, 1962

Radin, Paul, "The Nature and Problems of Mexican Indian Mythology," *American Journal of Folklore* 57 (1944)

Rael, Juan B., *Cuentos Españoles de Colorado y Nuevo Mexico,* second edition, Santa Fe: Museum of New Mexico Press, 1977

Robe, Stanley, *Amapa Storytellers,* Berkeley: University of California Press, 1972

_____, *Antologia del Saber Popular: A Selection from Various Genres of Mexican Folklore Across Borders,* Los Angeles: Atzlan, 1971

_____, *Hispanic Folktales from New Mexico: Narratives from the R.D. Jameson Collection,* Berkeley: University of California Press, 1977

_____, *Hispanic Legends from New Mexico: Narratives from the R.D. Jameson Collection,* Berkeley: University of California Press, 1980

_____, comp., *Mexican Tales and Legends from Los Altos,* Berkeley: University of California Press, 1970

Rocard, M., *The Mexican-American Frontier: The Border in Mexican-American Folklore and Literature,* Berkeley, California: Atzlan, 1989

Smith, Charles A., *From Wonder to Wisdom: Using Stories to Help Children Grow,* New York: New American Library, 1989

West, John O., *Mexican-American Folklore: Legends, Songs, Festivals, Proverbs, Crafts, Tales of Saints, of Revolutionaries, and More,* Little Rock, Arkansas: August House, 1988

Traditional Storytelling Among French Newfoundlanders

Gerald Thomas

Gerald Thomas contrasts performance styles of both public and family storytellers. Through a detailed discussion of the meanings of Aarne-Thompson Type 313 (The Girl as Helper in the Hero's Flight), he shows us the use of story in acculturating the young.

Newfoundland and the Memorial University Archives

Newfoundland, the most recent and most anglophone of provinces to join the Canadian confederation, did so in 1949. Nonetheless, it counts about 2,000 Francophones in its population of approximately 550,000. The majority of Newfoundlanders of French descent live on the province's west coast. The principal communities where the French language is still spoken are Cape St. George-Degras, Mainland (or La Grand' Terre), and Black Duck Brook-Winterhouses (L'Anse-à-Canards-Maisons-d'Hiver), situated on the rugged but picturesque Port-au-Port Peninsula. The French population is a mixture of Acadians and the descendants of French and Breton fishermen who deserted the French fishery that lasted in parts of Newfoundland until 1904. English, Irish, and Scottish settlers came, like the French, throughout the nineteenth century, and an admixture of Micmacs further contributed to a rich ethnic mix.

Serious, in-depth research on the traditional culture of French Newfoundlanders began in 1970, and by 1975 Memorial University's Centre d'Etudes Franco-Terreneuviennes was founded, an archive built chiefly by my own fieldwork and supplemented in substantial ways by research undertaken by my graduate and undergraduate students. A major focus of research was on traditional storytelling, and this article will address some of the important features that characterize the narrative tradition.

An Adult Märchen Tradition

To begin at the beginning, it must be stressed that storytelling was, and remains, an adult activity. This does not mean that children were excluded from storytelling occasions, but simply that children were not the primary audience. Secondly, it should also be stressed that while the telling of märchen, or fairy tales, still goes on, it does so now in a world much changed from its heyday, which lasted from the early decades of the nineteenth century until the 1940s. Thereafter, major social developments began to gnaw away at the vigor of the *veillée,* the winter evenings devoted to storytelling in many lamp-lit, wood-heated kitchens.

Confederation with Canada, the introduction of electricity (and with it radio and then television), and the paving of roads were among the first changes to exercise a deleterious effect on storytelling, since they all provided inducements to enjoy novel forms of entertainment. But tradition is tenacious, and the Port-au-Port Peninsula remains one of the last enclaves in North America where it is still possible to hear—and watch—the telling of long and entertaining folktales.

Although French Newfoundlanders, like most of their fellow Newfoundlanders, enjoy the sharing of personal-experience stories, shiver together at the telling of stories about ghosts, the devil, the fairies, laugh together at the telling of jokes and humorous anecdotes, it is, and always was, the telling of märchen that had pride of place in their narrative repertoire.

It is thus stories like Cinderella, Puss-in-Boots, and Jack the Giant Killer—although they were not known by these names and were often quite different from the versions published by the Grimm brothers, Perrault, and later collectors—that formed the substance of the storytelling repertoire. Furthermore, many such tales are not at all widely known to the general public, remaining in our largely urbanized society the domain of scholars and the lucky few with access to a living storytelling tradition.

Storytelling usually took place during the long, cold winter nights. In the summer, fishing dominated life and was a dusk-to-dawn activity often involving the whole family. In the winter, however, there was more time to relax. Thus, if the weather permitted, neighbors would hasten to gather at someone's home if they learned that such-and-such a storyteller would be present. For in the heyday of storytelling, a handful of individuals were known as fine storytellers; they had reputations as people who could tell stories all night long and entertain their audiences with all the skills of a gifted dramatic actor.

These *public* storytellers, as I have dubbed them, were actors, able to judge the mood of their audience and to a large degree control and manipulate their emotions. Public storytellers—and they are not yet all gone—spoke of their storytelling as an art, a craft to be mastered, to which they might add their own individual comic or dramatic genius. Within the context of folktale telling, however, there were certain rules to be obeyed if one was to achieve such a reputation.

The first requirement was the stamina to tell a tale that might last several hours. Audiences appreciated long stories: the longer, the better. At the same time, given that the number of such stories was nonetheless finite within a given community, the audiences would sooner or later know all the stories habitually told. Thus novelty and suspense, characteristics demanded of contemporary forms of entertainment, were not especially important. The pleasure derived from a storytelling session came from the skill and artistry of the teller. Part of the skill was "getting the story right"—that is to say, not deviating from the plot

as it was known within the community. Audiences knew, of course, that there were variants of their tales, but they would note that such-and-such a teller "didn't tell it the same way," or perhaps, depending on their loyalties, "didn't tell it the right way."

"The Girl As Helper in the Hero's Flight"

A characteristic feature of such tales is, of course, the frequency of repetition of elements, often going in threes. In a well-known tale on the Port-au-Port Peninsula, known to scholars as Aarne-Thompson 313, *The Girl As Helper in the Hero's Flight,* the hero, having lost all his possessions and his soul gambling with the devil, has to find the devil's castle within a year and a day. On his quest he encounters three sisters, each 100 (or 1,000) years older than the previous one, and each of whom provides the hero, Jack, with a gift—of seven-league boots, or a never-emptying sack of food, or a magical, talking eagle. This last gift takes Jack to the devil's lands where, deposited beside a lake, he spies three beautiful girls, the devil's daughters, as they fly down to the lake, removing their bird costumes in order to bathe.

Later, the youngest advises Jack as he prepares to confront the devil, and when the devil sets Jack three impossible tasks to perform, it is the daughter who performs them for him. As a result, Jack and the youngest daughter are married, but, wishing to return to Jack's home, they have to escape. The daughter bakes three magical, talking cakes, which serve to fool the devil and his wife while they escape. The devil catches on, however, and sets off in pursuit. Each time he is about to catch the couple, the daughter places a magical obstacle in his way, and they succeed in escaping.

They set up home not far from Jack's village, but his wife warns him, as he prepares to visit his family, not to let anyone kiss him or else he will forget everything. He is kissed, and does forget everything, and is soon to be married anew to a princess. Jack and two comrades inadvertently visit his real wife while inviting everyone to the forthcoming wedding. Each of the three men decides he would like to spend the night with this beautiful and apparently single woman, and each tries. Each is foiled in turn. Finally, using her magical power, the real wife helps restore Jack's memory, and by telling the story of the gold and iron keys, Jack succeeds in having his original marriage sanctioned.

Stylistic Devices of the Public Storyteller

Clearly, it was important for the storyteller not to omit any of the episodes, because his audience appreciated the repetition. It also added, of course, to the length of the tale. One of the tricks of the storyteller's trade—the use of lively dialogue between the characters—also allowed him to lengthen his tales. A good narrator could take a short motif—say, the daughter coming to help Jack in one of his tasks—and by creating dialogue in which Jack bewails his lot and the heroine berates him for not following her advice, make a sentence of a few seconds into a "paragraph" of a minute or so.

Even without extensive conversation there were features of the narrative which, by their formulaic nature, characterize the good storyteller. They include opening and closing formulas—"There was a time, not in my time and not in your time, but a long time ago, and there was a man and a woman and they had one son ," or "And if they're not dead, they're living yet"; internal formulas, often used to indicate the passage of time, such as "He walked and walked and walked"; and, sometimes, whole sentences or conversations, repeated almost word for word, at each of the three appropriate occasions.

Finally, the public storyteller—almost always a man—was an actor. He would match his actions to his words. If Jack was fighting a seven-headed monster, the narrator would be up on his feet, swinging an imaginary sword, roaring out his defiance to the monster. If the storyteller was momentarily in the role of a coy heroine, he would simper, cast down his eyes, and speak in a high-pitched voice. The good storyteller could always play the part of all his characters. It was this that audiences appreciated, for it brought the tales to life in a way no book version ever can. There was always an immediacy, an intimate presence, the more so because in a crowded kitchen, the listener had to be careful of being trampled by an exuberant storyteller. If such a thing happened, as it inevitably did, the audience's laughter might be enhanced by some aside made by the narrator; for, contrary to folktales as they appear in books, there was always some element of interplay between storyteller and audience in a tale-telling, always a degree of spontaneity. The audience were friends and relatives, and the narrator was part of the same community.

The public narrator has been singled out here because in French Newfoundland tradition, the curious researcher would be pointed in the direction of the well-known narrator, whether or not the narrator was, at least by the early 1970s, still interested in telling tales. This generous attitude in fact veiled a certain shyness on the part of many individuals who also knew folktales but did not want to tell them. They did not think of themselves as storytellers, whom they defined with characteristics of the public storyteller.

The Private, Family Storyteller

As I quickly discovered from 1970 on, there were far more individuals who could tell tales but did not want to, at least to an outsider, than there were public storytellers. It took a fair amount of time to be accepted within a community before such individuals relented, and then it was possible to observe the private or family storyteller at work.

There are several differences to be noted between the two types of narrator. First, there was the context: the public narrator performed before anyone who was able to get to the home in which he was performing. Although the private or family narrator told his or her tales in the same kitchen, it was to a different audience. Now it might be two old friends spending the evening together; now, a grandmother entertaining children and any family member who might be present. But it was a very informal audience; there would be comings and goings, interruptions of all kinds, and questions addressed to the narrator in the middle of the tale.

In this kind of intimacy, and without the pressures of a reputation to uphold, the storyteller was intent on telling the story but without feeling obligated to follow all the rules. Cuts could be made, two repetitions given instead of the normal three, whole episodes omitted, formulas mangled or omitted altogether. There was little exuberant gesture, little or no acting, certainly no props as some public narrators occasionally used. The private or family narrator's performance was low-key, informal.

It served an important purpose, however, in the days when public storytellings were still highly esteemed social gatherings. It introduced the content of tales, and the very notion of storytelling, to the next generation, the new audiences and, at times, the next public storytellers. As children heard the tales, they would be told by a modest grandmother, "Ah, but wait till you see so-and-so tell that story! Now there's a man for the stories, my dear!" And perhaps she might suggest some of the things the storyteller did, inadvertently introducing the younger generation to the community's aesthetic of storytelling. For although the very concept of aesthetics is an elitist one, it does not mean that ordinary people do not have notions of excellence in the realm of artistic expression. They may rarely articulate that aesthetic in a coherent fashion, but over time the attentive observer takes note of comments, remarks, and observations, all of which can be construed as pertaining to standards of excellence in storytelling—or, indeed, in any other traditional, expressive activity. In a similar vein, the constituents of a rural community aesthetic may be very different from those of a sophisticated elite, but that does not mean its aesthetic is invalid or nonexistent.

Much of the foregoing suggests that one of the prime purposes of storytelling was entertainment, and there is no doubt that this has always been so; but the telling of märchen, as mentioned above with reference to community aesthetics, is by no means restricted to entertainment. The genre can have other functions, other meanings, less evident to both the observer and the participant.

One of the characteristics of a good storyteller, male or female, is that he or she stamps a personal mark upon the narration without altering the story as such. Personal comments and reflections are usually scattered throughout the narrations, and since they reflect both individual and community values, they therefore have a didactic function. Clearly, the lesson would not be lost on a young child, nor on an older one, if a storyteller emphasizes how loyal, faithful, kind, trusting, and generous one daughter may be, in contrast to her elder stepsister, as illustrated in the tale by her actions—for example, giving her last crumb of bread to a starving fox and then learning through her kindness that the fox is enchanted, can turn stream water into wine, and talk—and if the story ends, because of the good daughter's virtues, in marriage to the fox, now disenchanted back into a prince.

Covert Messages in "The Girl As Helper in the Hero's Flight"

Folktales are, in Franco-Newfoundland tradition, replete with such examples. But there may be an even more covert message present, of particular utility to the youths who might begin their courting during a winter *veillée*. A good example of this can be found in the tale outlined earlier, *The*

Girl As Helper in the Hero's Flight. Careful analysis shows that the tale may be interpreted as an exercise in maturation, chiefly of the hero in that particular tale. He first appears in the story as a youthful braggart, soon reduced after his encounter with the mature and adult devil to a bumbling, inept, immature youth. As the tale unfolds, he learns useful lessons that help his growth. Fearful of the old sisters as he encounters them, he nonetheless overcomes his fear of the old and the ugly and is properly respectful. He is rewarded with gifts that are, in fact, external realizations of his own innate abilities.

When he meets the three girls, he demonstrates his inability to relate to the opposite sex in a typically immature fashion. To draw attention to himself, he steals the youngest daughter's clothes while she is swimming. The help provided to him by the same daughter can even be interpreted (given the symbolism of the tasks he is called upon to perform—emptying a pond with a basket full of holes, cutting down trees for the devil with a paper axe, scaling a glass tower to retrieve an egg for the devil) as developments of his sexuality. He is, in fact, initiated into manhood by a more knowledgeable, a more empowered female. "By my *power*," she exclaims, as *she* empties the pond, chops down the trees, and enables the hero to scale the glass tower.

She, too, matures, particularly in her relationship with her father. She has to free herself from her ties to him in order to set out on the path of starting a new family unit. The conflict of generations, real enough in all communities, is expressed in the tale in her conflict with her father and, to a lesser extent, with her mother.

During the escape of the young couple, the heroine throws three objects to the ground, transforming herself and her husband into, respectively, a church and a priest, a forest and a woodcutter, a pond and a drake. The pursuing father encounters each but cannot identify his daughter or the hero. It is possible to interpret the encounters as failed attempts by the father to reassert paternal authority over his daughter; he reluctantly accepts the fact that his daughter and her husband have become autonomous. Subsequent events—the failed attempts at seduction, the pseudo-marriage, the final assertion of independence by the hero—illustrate the attainment of maturity by the couple.

There are other symbols that might resonate in the minds of a young, Franco-Newfoundland audience. Food plays a not-insignificant role in the story, and it is always a female who provides it. The hero is given food by his mother as he leaves on his quest. The three sisters feed him, and in one instance, one provides him with a magical sack that gives him whatever he wishes to eat and drink. The heroine brings the hero his food while he sits awaiting his fate, unable to complete the tasks set by the devil. The heroine bakes three talking cakes to facilitate the escape. In French Newfoundland tradition, as elsewhere, the male provides raw foods, but it is the female who transforms the raw into the cooked; she symbolizes, one might say, the civilizing influence of the female.

Although these examples do not exhaust the interpretive possibilities of the tale, they serve to illustrate the original point that deeper meanings can be read into a seemingly straightforward folktale. The question is, does such an interpretation have any relevance in the context of French Newfoundland culture? The answer is affirmative. In the first instance, in the days when such tales flourished in the local culture, young men and young women took on adult responsibilities at an early age; by their mid-teens, many were already thinking of marriage and a future family. The kind of lesson they might learn in a *veillée* would not be lost on them.

Young men would be warned against too much youthful confidence and taught to respect their elders; they would understand that difficult tasks lay ahead of them, one of which was the resolution of conflict between themselves and the adult generation. In realistic terms, it was not uncommon for a young couple, upon marriage, to live for a while with their parents, a situation they would try to escape as soon as they were able. They would be advised of the problems to be encountered with the opposite sex and learn to trust, and cooperate with, womenfolk. They would learn of the process by which they would attain maturity. Young women would learn of their power and of their responsibilities.

The lessons, of course, were presented in this fictional form, embedded in symbols, and might not be immediately understood. But an explanation of this kind is necessary to account for the longevity of such tales in tradition, measured not in tens or hundreds of years, but in thousands. And they were lessons incorporated in a highly entertaining, artistic, expressive form; the highest form, perhaps, of oral art in Western culture.

Further Reading

Halpert, Herbert, and J.D.A. Widdowson, *Folktales of Newfoundland: The Resilience of the Oral Tradition*, New York: Garland, 1996

Thomas, Gerald, *The Two Traditions: The Art of Storytelling Amongst French Newfoundlanders*, St. John's, Newfoundland: Breakwater, 1993

Logger Poetry

Jens Lund

Jens Lund examines the history of logger poetry, discusses some of the genres employed by contemporary logger poets, and points the way to numerous logger poetry print and audio sources.

Early Logger Poetry

Logger poetry is part of the heritage of occupational poetry, traditionally composed and then recited or sung by those in hazardous and demanding outdoor occupations. The roots of this tradition are centuries old and are discussed in detail in this volume's "Cowboy Poetry and Other Occupational Folk Poetry" entry.

Possibly the earliest known example of logger poetry in the United States is "Lines Upon the Death of Two Young Men," which appeared in a Maine newspaper in 1815. Logging ballads collected by folklorists Phillips Barry, Franz Rickaby, and Edith Fowke earlier in the twentieth century had their origins in the Northeast and upper Midwestern United States, and eastern Canada. They were often sung and just as often recited. A poem still recited in the Northeast today is "The Falling of the Pine," which appeared in print in Maine in 1825. As the men in the isolated logging camps made their own entertainment, they celebrated humorous incidents or commemorated tragic ones in their songs and recitations. Bunkhouses sometimes had a "camp bard" who entertained his mates with stories, poems, and songs.

The early twentieth century radical union the Industrial Workers of the World (IWW) used locally composed poems and songs to get its message to loggers and farmworkers, thereby encouraging the practice of composing and reciting commentaries about events in the workplace. Conversely, an organization formed after World War I in the Northwest to combat the IWW, the Loyal Legion of Loggers and Lumbermen (4L), also promoted logger poetry. One of the best-known logger poets of the 1920s and 1930s was Charles Olaf Olson of Salem, Oregon, a regular contributor to *4L Bulletin*. On a visit to the Northwest in the 1930s, poet Carl Sandburg wrote about enjoying an evening listening to Olson and his friend, Oregon writer and journalist James Stevens, swap stories, songs, and poems.

As the camps closed and loggers became family folks who commuted to the woods, the recitation tradition faded. A few individuals kept it alive, often men whose fathers and grandfathers had composed and recited logger poetry. Robert E. Swanson of Vancouver Island, British Columbia, himself a protégé of Yukon bard Robert Service, published several pocket-sized books of logger poetry during the 1940s and 1950s. Loggers, as well as cowboys, bought these books and committed Swanson's poems to memory. In the Pacific Northwest, where ranching and forestry are in close proximity, many people have worked in both industries, and some poets have written pieces in both traditions, sometimes lampooning cowboy life from a logger's perspective or vice versa.

A Logger Poetry Revival

In the 1970s, Oregonian Buzz Martin made a career as a singing logger, appearing on the Grand Ole Opry and traveling with Johnny Cash. But two of his most-requested pieces, "Used Log Truck" and "Where There Walks a Logger There Walks a Man," were musically-accompanied recited poems. They stayed on rural jukeboxes in the Northwest throughout the 1970s and 1980s.

Timber industry publications, such as *Loggers World and American Timberman & Trucker,* have continued to publish logger poems to this day. In the 1990s, inspired by the cowboy poetry revival, a few logger poets have begun to revive the tradition of public recitation. Timber industry banquets, political rallies in timber communities, logging shows, and local fairs are a few of the venues where logger poetry is recited today.

Although logger poetry has traditionally been a male expression, today some of the best logger poets are women. Although few women, even at the end of the twentieth century, actually perform the physical work of the logger, logger poetry is written by loggers' wives and by the women who are business partners in mom-and-pop logging companies.

Contemporary Logger Poetry
Form and Themes

Like most English-language folk poetry, logger poetry is usually written in the form of rhymed couplets. It generally takes a linear narrative form, telling a straightforward story. Less often, it may describe a person or thing, or evoke a mood. What makes it logger poetry is its content—the fact that it concerns people, places, things, and events associated with logging and derived from the experience of the logger or from those closely associated with the logger. In that sense it follows Roger DeV. Renwick's characterization of folk poetry, as closely tied to the poet's "bounded and knowable world." One representative collection of 65 of the older lumberjack ballads from eastern North America, Edith Fowke's *Lumbering Songs of the Northern Woods,* includes 26 about work, 17 about tragedy, eight that are humorous, and seven about love.

Occupational poetry, and probably most folk poetry, expresses the worldview of both the individual writer and of the community to which he or she belongs. The 1980s and 1990s have been a time of profound change and challenge in Northwest timber communities as mechanization, resource depletion, and environmental concerns made the logging trade a far less secure living than earlier in the century. At the same time, the very legitimacy of timber cutting was called into question, particularly in the mass media. Loggers and their families, who had taken it for granted that the public appreciated their difficult and dangerous work, now found themselves the subject of negative caricature as brutal "tree-killers" and

"land-rapers." This is despite the fact that the per capita appetite for wood and its products was never higher in our nation's history.

In 1986, folklorist Robert E. Walls studied contemporary Northwest logger poetry published in timber industry periodicals. He found that contemporary logger poetry affirmed the traditional worldview of the logging community. He noted six general themes that appeared repeatedly. These were (1) the unshakable love of the lifestyle that logging, as the ultimate outdoor work, requires; (2) the constant reminder of the dangers involved when working in the woods; (3) respect and awe of the mysterious and potential for the unexpected in nature, including its beauty; (4) admiration for those who can prove themselves beyond all doubts, strictly by their efforts in the woods, whether through the use of sheer strength, tenacity, intelligence, or skills; (5) respect and envy of those who represent—in both the past and the present—the "code" of the logger, wherein one never hesitates to demonstrate his masculinity by drinking, fighting, and womanizing to excess; and (6) the continuous conflict between logger and authority.

Walls also noted that number 5 was, particularly in more recent years, often contradicted by the emergence in poetry of the "changing" logger—a family man, mindful of a "greater wisdom" and fundamental Christian values. Since the shutdown, in the early 1990s, of much of the timber harvest in the Northwest, spurred by protection of the endangered northern spotted owl, two more themes have appeared. They are (7) the idea of the logger as steward of the environment, the notion that a properly-managed timber harvest is an improvement over nature, and (8) frank political protest, sometimes sarcastic or aggressive, other times plaintive, toward the political forces, largely urban, that are perceived to have ruined the economy of timber communities.

A theme which appears explicitly in a number of contemporary logging poems is that of "Logger's Heaven." In a typical example, a logger dies and goes to heaven and is sent to hell for his roughness and rebelliousness, but hell cannot hold him and St. Peter eventually relents and lets him in, even providing him with a forest to log. In other examples, perhaps borrowing from the idea of Valhalla in Norse mythology, the Lord knows that the logger will not be happy unless he is allowed to continue doing the work he loves. He provides the logger with a forest that regrows as fast as it is cut down. There are many similar examples of "cowboy heaven" in cowboy poetry.

Many sociological and technological factors have led to the decline and near extinction of recited logger poetry and sung logger ballads in the twentieth century. Yet, in the late twentieth century, other factors, including a feeling of being besieged, have led to an increased sense of identity among loggers and their families. A generation of retired loggers, sometimes prematurely retired by economic circumstances, have sought what Northwest folklorist Marjorie Bangs Bennett calls "ego integrity" through story and poetry as an alternative to the despair of old age or underemployment. Inspired by their awareness of the revival of cowboy poetry recitation and the general popularity of the spoken word, loggers and their family members, at least in the Northwest, have begun to compose and recite poems derived from their work and life experiences again.

Sources to Explore Logger Poetry

Timber industry newspapers, *American Timberman & Trucker,* P.O. Box 1006, Chehalis, Washington 98532, and *Loggers World,* 4206 Jackson Highway, Chehalis, Washington 98532, still often publish logging poems. The books of Robert E. Swanson, long out of print, have been reissued in a single volume, *Rhymes of a Western Logger,* by Harbour Publishing of Madeira Park, British Columbia, Canada. Collections of poems by Washingtonians Woodrow Gifford (*Timber Bind*) and Lon Minkler (*The Tall and the Uncut and Logger Lon*) as well as Swanson's volume, and an anthology of logger prose and poetry, *Loggers World: The First Ten Years, 1964–1974,* edited by Finley Hays, are available from The Rigging Shack, 664 Oppelt Road, Chehalis, Washington 98532. British Columbia poet Peter Trower's work, including *Bush Poems* and *Goosequill Snags,* are also published by Harbour Publishing. Virgil "The Old Woodsman" Wallace's *Ramblings of a Logger* is also sold by *American Timberman & Trucker.* An available anthology of contemporary logger poetry is Volume 32, number 2 (1990) of *Cowlitz Historical Quarterly,* 405 Allen St., Kelso, Washington 98626. Most contemporary volumes of logger poetry are self-published. Their authors sometimes advertise them in timber industry periodicals. Most of the old collections of lumberjack ballads from the Midwestern and northeastern United States, and eastern Canada are out of print, although they can often be found in university librar-

ies. Look for volumes compiled by Phillips Barry, Earl Clifton Beck, William Main Doerflinger, Edith Fowke, Roland Palmer Gray, Edward D. Ives, and Franz Rickaby. Compilations of American folk song assembled by John and Alan Lomax and Carl Sandburg also contain a number of lumberjack ballads. Edith Fowke's *Lumbering Songs of the Northern Woods* has been reprinted in recent years by NC Press, of Toronto, Ontario, Canada, as have Beck's *Lore of the Lumber Camps and Songs of the Michigan Lumberjacks.* Both are available from University of Michigan Press Books on Demand, Beck's *They Knew Paul Bunyan* from Ayer Publications, and Doerflinger's *Songs of the Sailor & Lumberman* from Meyerbooks. Although Buzz Martin's LP and 45-rpm records from the 1970s are all out of print, a compact disc compilation of many of his songs and recited poems is available from The Rigging Shack. *Caulk Boots and Marlin Spikes,* a two-audiocassette evening of logging poetry, stories, and song, recorded live at the Tidemark Theatre on Vancouver Island, is available from Strathcona-Discovery Entertainment, 355 Leeward Sq., Campbell River, British Columbia, Canada V9W 1X9.

See also the entry for "Cowboy Poetry and Other Occupational Folk Poetry" in this volume.

Further Reading

Brunvand, Jan Harold, ed., *American Folklore: An Encyclopedia,* New York: Garland, 1996

Cunningham, Keith, ed., *The Oral Tradition of the American West: Adventure, Courtship, Family, and Place in Traditional Recitation,* Little Rock, Arkansas: August House, 1990

Ives, Edward D. , *"Suthin'": It's the Opposite of Nothin': An Oral History of Grover Morrison's Woods Operation at Little Musquash Lake, 1945–1947,* Orono, Maine: Northeast Folklore Society, 1978

Kearney, Lake Shore, *The Hodag and Other Tales of the Logging Camps,* Wausau, Wisconsin: Democrat, 1928

Renwick, Roger DeV., *English Folk Poetry: Structure and Meaning,* Philadelphia: University of Pennsylvania Press, 1980; London: Batsford Academic and Educational, 1980

Service, Robert, *Collected Poems of Robert Service,* New York: Dodd-Mead, 1940; London: E. Benn, 1978

———, *Later Collected Verse,* New York: Dodd-Mead, 1965; London: E. Benn, 1979

Stanley, David, and Elaine Thatcher, eds., *On'ry Propositions: Cowboy Poets and Cowboy Poetry,* Urbana: University of Illinois Press, 1999

Walls, Robert E., "Logger Poetry and the Expression of Worldview," *Northwest Folklore* 5:2 (Spring 1987)

South America

Argentinian Folktale: A Genetic Approach

Maria Palleiro

Maria Palleiro discusses ways in which the narrator sets the tale in the audience's locale through allusions, comparisons, descriptions, and metaphors. The veracity of the tale is asserted through asides and through reference to the voice of the community in phrases such as "it is said."

The Influence of the Cultural Environment on the Telling of a Tale

In this paper I propose an approach to folk-narrative analysis based on the study of the contextual changes introduced by different speakers into standard narratives. This approach enables us to examine the influence of the cultural environment on the genetic process of the folktale. The proposal is based on the study of Argentinian oral folk narratives collected in fieldwork from 1985 to 1994 in our "General *Corpus* of Argentinian Folk Narratives." This corpus contains almost 100 versions, whose texts were established according to dialectological criteria of spelling and transcription. The first results of this research have already been discussed in my doctoral thesis, "The Dynamics of Variation in the Folktale." In this thesis I characterize the folk-narrative text as a complex discourse that expresses the cultural blending process of a heterogeneous community.

Setting the Folktale in the Teller's Locale

According to this approach, I consider the folk-narrative situation in the colloquial interaction in which it takes place. In this situation the narrator and the audience share an enunciative context as well as a historical and cultural environment that acts as a dynamic factor in the constructive process of the folk text. We see in the versions of our Argentinian corpus transformations in narratives—for instance, in Cesar Soria's tale, "The Youth Who Wanted to Learn What Fear Is" (Aarne-Thompson [AT] type 326):

Y . . . qu'el gaucho y el diablo han estado peleaando, ahí . . . y que . . . al último . . . le ha plantado el cuchillo *acá*, 'l gaucho, al diablo, y se ha desaparecido . . . (El narrador coloca su mano derecha sobre el pecho, para indicar el lugar donde le fue clavado el cuchillo al diablo.) Y dicen que por eso desde entonces asustaaban esos ahí, a todo el que se atrevía a entrar en el rancho, *ahí*, en las casas de los Aguirre. . . .

[So the "gaucho" and the Devil kept on fighting there . . . And, at last, the "gaucho" stabbed a knife *here,* into the Devil, and then, he vanished. (The narrator puts the right hand on his chest to point out the place where the knife was stabbed into the Devil .) As soon as he had done this, the devilish body vanished (. . .) And thus it said that, from that moment on, people who dare to enter the ranch are scared by such devilish beings, *there,* at the Aguirre's. . . .]

We observe in this quotation the blending process of a folktale matrix with a local situation. In fact, the characters of the narrative are people who actually do exist in that community, such as the "Aguirre." The tale is also related to the cultural background of the group by means of an allusion to the supernatural. Thus the narrator refers to the community's belief in ghostly apparitions that once scared people who happened to pass by there at night. Such a linkage with the contextual background is emphasized by the connector "thus," which establishes a cause-effect relationship between the general narrative pattern and the local case. This relationship is also reinforced by the deictic system and by a corporal gesture that brings the narrative action closer to the enunciative situation ("the 'gaucho' stabbed a knife *here* . . .[The narrator puts the right hand on his chest . . .] . . . *there,* at the Aguirre's . . .").

Strategies to Hold Audience Attention

The audience serves an important function in the construction of the narratives. The fluctuations of the receiver's attention are perceived by the narrators, who frequently introduce certain changes in the tales in order to guarantee reception of the message. In fact, we can observe in the recorded version of this narrative that the speaker adopts a high-pitched tonal register. This change in the narrator's intonation is used with the purpose of persuading the audience to the narrator's point of view. Such argumentative strategy is related to an identification with the set of beliefs in ghostly apparitions that constitutes the referential point of the tale. This fact is connected with the presentation of the general narrative as a localized tale connected with the cultural background of a specific community.

The Tale as Truth

Another argumentative strategy is the employment of modalizing clauses in evaluative sequences that reveal the speaker's subjective engagement in the narrative world. Such evaluative clauses, studied by Labov and Waletzky in oral versions of personal experience, are used here as indexical resources that reveal the speaker's insertion in his own discourse. In this text such evaluative clauses are linked to the insertion of a case, which may also be considered in a certain way as a personal experience, as we can see in the following quotation:

> *Esto es la pura verdaad . . . Que es cieerto . . .* Eso tan raro pasó en el ranchito eese, en lo de los Aguirre. . . .

> [*This is absolutely true . . . It is true . . .* Such a strange event happened in that small ranch, at the Aguirre's. . . .]

This clause, introduced by alethic modalizing particles, is used in order to convince the receivers of the tale's truth. The truths proposed do not actually refer to empirical validation of the event's historical occurrence but to reinforcement of the community's axiological set of values and beliefs. This is the way the narrative world is presented to the audience as a valid cultural pattern, supported by group consensus. This consensus is introduced in the folktale by means of an aside, as we notice in this quotation:

> *Y dicen* que, por eso, desde ese momento, son las ánimas del diablo, que asuustan, ahí, de nooche, a los que se atreven a entrar en el ranchito eese, ahí, en lo de los Aguirre. . . .

> *Y dicen* ahí que por eso es que los Aguirr'eran condenados por el diablo. . . . *Que dicen* qu'ellos, que vivían allá 'n el ranchito, que vendían las almas al diablo y que eran ya condenados. . . .

> [*And* thus *it is said* that . . . from that moment on, people who dare to enter the ranch at night are scared by such devilish beings, there, at the Aguirre's. . . .]

> [And *it is said* that was the reason why the Aguirre were damned by the Devil. . . . *It is said* that those who lived in that small ranch had sold their souls to the Devil and so they became naughty people. . . .]

This reference to the group voice operates as a source of testimonial authority as well as a strategy that confirms the message's social dimension.

The Tale Matrix as Pre-Text

The intratextual analysis of these oral versions selected from our corpus enables us to observe the contextual transformations of narrative patterns. These analyses confirm a narrative matrix whose main characteristic is its essential permeability. This permeability enables each narrator to introduce contextual transformations such as the ones we have just studied in Cesar Soria's version. In terms of genetic criticism, this flexible matrix acts as a "pre-text," used in order to produce a textual message that expresses the differential identity of a social group with its own set of cultural values.

We can recognize in our versions the employment of allusions, comparisons and enumerative descriptions. We also notice the use of metaphoric elements and specific contextual transformations. The genetic process of the message depends on these transformations. They enable each speaker to introduce different changes into a standardized pre-text, conserved in his or her memory as an initial narrative pattern. In Joaquín Peralta's version, "Pedro Ordimán and the Golden Partridge" (AT 1528) we observe the following use of some of these strategies:

> Y había ahí un pencal aalto, como los que saben haber aquí. . . . Y el cura hacía asií . . . los dedos. . . . Y que se había pegado en una penca. . . .

> [And there was a tall "pencal," like the ones that can often be seen around, over here. . . . And . . . the priest made like this . . . with his fingers and that he hit in a "penca". . . .]

We notice in this quotation an obvious analogical connection between the textual and the contextual referents. The mention of the "penca," a regional cactaceous vegetable, is employed as an allusion in order to establish a resemblance between both referential universes. Such resemblance is reinforced by means of a comparative connection ("like the ones") and by the use of the deictic "here," which implies a precise indication of the mentioned place. This analogical linkage brings the narrative message closer to the audience's cultural patterns. It also constitutes a strategy to persuade the receivers of the truth of the tale. This eagerness for verisimilitude is congruent with the presentation of the tale as a historic case, related to the cultural set of values and beliefs of a specific Argentinian rural community.

Descriptive Phrases Give a Sense of Place
Another strategy is employed by the narrators—inserting local descriptions into the narrative. Enumerative description enables the insertion of the spatial environment in speech, as we observe in Isabel Vera's version, "The Three Brothers and the Queen's Golden Apple" (AT 610):

> Y . . . donde vivía la reina . . . er'una finca graande . . . con muchos animaales: gallinas, pollos, de toodo. . . . Y que tenía plantadas vides, olivos, y toodo. . . .

> [And . . . the place where the queen lived . . . was a large farm . . . with a lot of animals:

hens, chickens, everything. . . . And there were grapevines and olive trees, and everything. . . .]

Grapevine and olive trees are certainly crops typical of the area where the tale was compiled, and they are also the settler's main means of support along with the breeding of domestic fowl. Even the noun *finca* (farm) is a lexical use of the area. The semantic field of this word is related precisely to the suitable space for cultivation and cattle rearing. Thus, the descriptive technique is used as a discursive strategy in order to insert those elements linked to the agrarian activity of the regional environment in the narrative text, by means of an extensional enumeration. This strategy serves also an argumentative function, oriented to underline the effect of reality.

Metaphor
Another resource used in order to insert the enunciative context in the text is the metaphoric technique. Such technique is related to the condensation of several meanings linked to the community's animist beliefs, as we can see in César Soria's narrative. In this text, the noun "skeleton" *(esqueleto)* condenses a series of animist properties referring to the semantic area of the supernatural, such as the ability of motion attributed to motionless elements:

> . . . y se aparece un esqueleto . . . que es el diablo . . . que asusta, de noche, ahí, donde está enterrado. . . .

> [. . . and a skeleton appears. . . . It is the Devil himself . . . that scares people at night, there, where he is buried. . . .]

This paradoxical connection between motion and motionless elements refers to the metaphoric identification of the skeleton with the Devil. Such identification constitutes in itself a sort of combination through which different properties that correspond to heterogeneous semantic areas join together according to an equivalence principle. This metaphoric technique is related to the contextual belief in an identification between the natural and the supernatural worlds.

Legends Reported in the Media
In television news, and even in local newspapers, these ghostly apparitions that once scared people at night are often heard and written about in con-

nection with cases of strange events that take place in haunted houses or desert zones. One of these local cases was mentioned, for example, in the Argentinian newspaper *Clarín,* in Buenos Aires, March 1992. In the first two weeks of this month and year, there were several pieces of news related to haunted houses and ghostly apparitions in Argentinian rural areas such as Madariaga. Another local newspaper, *El Independiente* of La Rioja (August 10–15, 1991), mentioned another case related to a haunted house. Both cases were widely commented on in the television news, especially by the Channel 9 reporters. These references to local cases mentioned in journals and television news confirm the inclusion of folktale matrices in the mass media. Such inclusion reveals another role of the folktale in a changing society in which different channels of discourse are open both to written and oral communication. This role is related to a sort of "new oralism" in which the interactive voice of a whole community is reinserted in mediatic channels of discourse by means of technological resources.

Conclusion

This short analysis of Argentinian oral versions collected in different situations enables us to characterize the folktale as a complex message whose referential content reflects the heterogeneous identity of a social group. The enunciative context acts as a dynamic factor in the genetic process of the folktale. Allusions, comparisons, and enumerative descriptions as well as metaphoric procedures are the main discursive strategies used to insert the referential context in the folk text. We can also observe some changes in the deictic system, as well as the inclusion of modalizing particles and the insertion of the polyphonic voice of the local community in the narrative discourse. All these changes introduce transformations in the genetic matrix of the folk text, whose essential permeability enables it to express the differential identity of a changing society. This permeability also favors the insertion of folktale constructive patterns in different channels of discourse, even in the mass media and other audiovisual means of communication.

Appendix: "The Youth Who Wanted to Learn What Fear Is"

My grandfather Pablo told me that, when he was a young boy, a gaucho (horseman) went to a small ranch where nobody dared to enter.

He stayed there during the whole day, and when the night arrived, he fell asleep. At midnight, a mysterious voice awoke him. This strange voice came from the ceiling, and he heard its scaring sound repeating:

"Can I fall down from the ceiling?"

And the gaucho felt no fear, so he answered, "Please, fall down!"

As soon as he said this, a leg of this mysterious being fell down the ceiling, and then the other. And then one of his arms, and then the other. And so on. . . . One by one, all the other pieces of this body went on and on falling during the whole night.

When the pieces finished falling, they joined all together into a devilish shape. In fact, the Devil appeared. . . . It was the Devil himself. . . . This is absolutely true. . . . My grandfather assured it. . . . It was really the Devil, the one who fell down the ceiling.

The gaucho recognized his enemy and, without any hesitation, he went toward him to fight. They kept on fighting all the time until the night was over, until the sun rose up.

It is said that when the morn broke, the gaucho was really tired and full of pain, but he was not even scared. . . . So the gaucho and the Devil kept on fighting there, in that small ranch, during the whole night. . . . And, at last, the gaucho stabbed a knife *here,* into the Devil. As soon as he had done this, the devilish body vanished. . . . [The narrator puts the right hand on his chest to point out the place where the knife was stabbed into the Devil.]

And thus the Devil vanished, in that small ranch, and then the gaucho went away. . . .

It is said also that, a few months later, the gaucho returned to that place and he found a skeleton there, in that small ranch, where the Aguirre used to live once upon a time. . . . But the gaucho did not fear when he saw the skeleton, as he had not even been scared when he recognized the Devil falling down the ceiling the first time. . . . The skeleton belonged to his body, where the gaucho stabbed his knife.

It is true. . . . Such a strange event happened when my grandfather was a young boy, a long time ago, there, in that small ranch, at the Aguirre's, at "La Maravilla". . . . And thus it is said that from that moment on, people who dare to enter that ranch at night are scared by such devilish beings, there, at the Aguirre's. . . .

The place where these strange events happened and continued to happen is a small, white, abandoned house . . . a little ranch, where the

Aguirre used to live once. . . . But at last, even the Aguirre went away, and the ranch remained abandoned. . . .

And it is said that was the reason why the Aguirre were damned by the Devil. . . . It is said that those who lived in that small house had sold their souls to the Devil and so they became naughty people. . . .

And it is also said that, from that moment on, everyone who passes by is scared by those ghostly creatures . . . and a skeleton appears. . . . It is the Devil himself, who can assume different shapes. . . . One of these shapes is the skeleton, that scares people at night, there, where he is buried, just there, at the Aguirre's ranch, there, in La Maravilla. . . .

Narrator: Cesar Soria.

Age: 16 years old.

Date: 9/24/1986.

Local area: El Barreal (rural area).

Department/state/country: Rosario Vera Peñaloza, La Rioja, Argentina.

Emic classification of the narrative (classified by the narrator himself): local case.

Aarne-Thompson's tale type: 326. "A youth who does not know what fear is, goes out to find it. He tries various frightful experiences: staying in a haunted house where a dead man's members fall down the chimney, etc."

Further Reading

Aarne, Antti, *The Types of the Folktale: A Classification and Bibliography,* edited and translated by Stith Thompson, second revision, Helsinki, Finland: Academia Scientarum Fennica, 1961

Abrahams, Roger, "Introductory Remarks to a Rhetorical Theory of Folklore," *Journal of American Folklore* 81 (1968)

Barthes, Roland, *Lo verosímil,* translated by Beatriz Dorriots, Buenos Aires, Argentina: Tiempo Contemporáneo, 1970

Bauman, Richard, "Verbal Art as Performance," *American Anthropologist* 77 (1975)

Bausinger, H., "On Contexts," in *Folklore on Two Continents: Essays in Honor of Linda Dégh,* Bloomington, Indiana: Trickster, 1980

Ben-Amos, Dan, and Kenneth Goldstein, *Folklore: Performance and Communication,* The Hague, The Netherlands: Mouton, 1975

Bennett, Philip, et al., *The Editor and the Text,* Edinburgh: Edinburgh University Press, 1990

Benveniste, Emile, *Problèmes de linguistique générale,* 2 volumes, Paris: Gallimard, 1966

Bevan, D.G., et al., *Sur la génétique textuelle: études,* Amsterdam, The Netherlands, and Atlanta, Georgia: Rodopi, 1990

Britton, Bruce, et al., *Narrative Thought and Narrative Language,* Hillsdale, New Jersey, and Hove, England: Erlbaum, 1990

Clifford, James, *The Predicament of Culture: Twentieth Century Ethnography, Literature, and Art,* Cambridge, Massachusetts: Harvard University Press, 1988

Dégh, Linda, and Andrew Vázsonyi, "Legend and Belief," in *Folklore Genres,* edited by Dan Ben-Amos, Austin: University of Texas Press, 1976

Fine, Elizabeth C., *The Folklore Text: From Performance to Print,* Bloomington: Indiana University Press, 1984

Goody, Jack, *Literacy in Traditional Societies,* Cambridge: Cambridge University Press, 1968; New York: Cambridge University Press, 1975

Grésillon, Almuth, *Eléments de critique génétique: lire les manuscrits modernes,* Paris: Presses Universitaires de France, 1994

Grésillon, Almuth, Jean-Louis Lebrave, and Catherine Viollet, *Proust à la lettre: Les intermittences de l'écriture,* Tusson, Charente, France: Du Lérot, 1990

Gumperz, John, *Discourse Strategies,* Cambridge and New York: Cambridge University Press, 1982

Hay, Louis, ed., *De la lettre au livre: Sémiotique des manuscrits littéraires,* Paris: Editions du CNRS, 1989

Hay, Louis, and Péter Nagy, eds., *Avant-texte, texte, après-texte,* Paris: Editions du CNRS, 1982

Hay, Louis, et al., *Les manuscrits des écrivains,* Paris: Éditions du CNRS, 1993

Hendricks, William, *Semiología del discurso literario,* Madrid, Spain: Cátedra, 1976

Jackendoff, Ray, *Semantics and Cognition,* Cambridge, Massachusetts: MIT Press, 1983

Jason, Heda, and Dimitri Segal, eds., *Patterns in Oral Literature,* The Hague, The Netherlands, and Chicago: Mouton, 1977

Kozzloff, Sarah, "Narrative Theory and Television," in *Channels of Discourse: Television and Contemporary Criticism,* edited by Robert Allen, Chapel Hill: University of North Carolina Press, 1987; London: Routledge, 1987

Labov, W., and J. Waletzky, "Narrative Analysis: Oral Versions of Personal Experience," in *Essays on the Verbal and Visual Arts*, Seattle: University of Washington Press, 1967

Martin, Robert, *Langage et croyance,* Brussels, Belgium: Mardaga, 1987

Ong, Walter, *Presence of the Word,* New Haven, Connecticut: Yale University Press, 1967

Palleiro, Maria, *The Dynamics of Variation in the Folktale* (Ph.D. diss.), 1991

Perelman, Chaim, and L. Olbrechts-Tyteca, *Traité de l'argumentation: La nouvelle rhétorique,* Paris: Presses Universitaires de France, 1958

Scheub, Harold, "Body and Image in Oral Narrative Performance," *New Literary History* 8 (1977)

Tannen, Deborah, "Oral and Literate Strategies in Spoken and Written Narratives," *Language: Journal of the Linguistic Society of America* 58:1 (1982)

Urban, Greg, "Speech About Speech in Speech About Action," *Journal of American Folklore* 97:385 (1984)

Voigt, Vilmos, "Textologie du folklore en Hongrie," in *Avant-texte, texte, après-texte,* edited by Louis Hay and Péter Nagy, Paris: Éditions du CNRS, 1982

White, Hayden, *Metahistory: The Historical Imagination in Nineteenth-Century Europe,* Baltimore, Maryland, and London: Johns Hopkins University Press, 1973

Wilgus, D.K., "The Text is the Thing," *Journal of American Folklore* 86 (1973)

The Art of Bahamian Narration

Daniel J. Crowley

The Bahama Islands

The Bahama Islands lie not in the Caribbean but in the Atlantic's Gulf Stream, east of Florida and north of the Greater Antilles. Half the population of 270,000 lives in the capital, Nassau, and are largely West African in origin, mixed with European and Native American ancestry. Twelve percent of the people are local whites called Conchy Joes, who descend from Scottish and Irish dissenters, sailors, and pirates; another 8 percent are British, Lebanese, Greeks, Cantonese, Americans, and others who have moved in with the development of tourism and gambling.

In their distinctive dialect, Bahamians often proclaim, "I could talk Old Story good," showing both their desire to be recognized as artful narrators and their recognition that their tales are ancient and traditional, rather than created by recent generations. They are enthusiastic storytellers, competing with one another even as children to get the best responses out of their audience.

"Bunday!"

If one wants to tell a story, whether in a traditional evening setting or at another time, one must shout, "Bunday!" If someone nearby answers "Bunday!" or "Ehhh!," people will gather around and the narrator can begin, but if no response is heard to his signal "Bunday!," it is assumed that no one is available or interested in hearing his story just then, so he desists.

If his "Bunday!" is answered, he repeats it, and adds a traditional nominee:

Once upon a time, was a wery [or merry] good time,

Monkey chew tobacco and he spit white lime,
Cuckero [cockroach] jump from bank to bank,
And his ten-quarter never touch water till sunset!
Ehhh! Bunday! Ehhh!

Another popular beginning nominee is

Once upon a time, was a wery good time,
Not in my [or your] time,
Was in old people time,
when they used to take fish scale to make shingle,
And fish bone to made needle [or nail].

Then he begins his tale, usually with, "Now this was a time, it have t'ree [three] woman . . . ," and throughout the tale he will inject an occasional "Bunday!" and wait until one or more of his hearers enthusiastically repeats it before continuing, asking, in effect, for a sign of approval from his audience. Similarly, if there is an interruption, a noise in a nearby street, new people arriving, or other distraction, he will call out "Bunday!" and stop talking until another "Bunday!" is heard. In the same way, members of the audience are free to comment on his story or even to offer praise or criticism, such as "B'Jack too chupid [stupid], yes!"

Attention-Holding Devices

A particularly artistic narrator will have many tricks to keep or intensify the attention of his audience. One is to use props, common objects made into magical ones—for instance, an old pencil: "I . . . and Jack stab B'Devil like this . . . ,"

465

as the storyteller stabs the pencil in the air. Even more appreciated is the use of accidental sounds or happenings, such as a loud noise in the distance—"There go B'Jack now"—or when an ant crawls across the floor—"There he go right there."

Another ploy is to address one person in the audience as a story character; for instance, the story hero says (in the person of the narrator) to a shy but pretty young girl in the audience, "Now me pretty li'l princess, I come for to court ya na." Still another skill of great narrators is the use of a song, making the tale into a chante-fable by singing something such as

> Mary go up so high, and he [she] hit the sky,
> Mary go down so low, and he [she] come down
>   bum bye.

One or more songs may be used at crucial moments throughout a story.

Ending Formula

When the story is over, the narrator adds:

> And I was passin' by, and I say,
> [a reference to the story plot, such as]
> B'Jack, you shouldn't do people so,
> And the kick he kick at me
> Causin' me to come here tonight
> To tell you this wonderful story [or big lie].

Another ending formula brings in a member of the audience:

> E Bo En, My Old Story is end,
> If you don't believe my old Story is true
> Aks [ask] the captain of the longboat crew,
> Or aks Mr.____, he could tell you better.

And another:

> They live in peace, die in peace,
> And bury in a pot of candle grease.

And still another:

> I'll never tell a lie like that again!

Unique Adaptations

All of these are techniques for presenting the story, enlivening it with humor and drama, decorating it with songs and rhymes, and keeping great rapport with the audience throughout. They are also aesthetic aspects of the narrative style, as are the characteristics of the Bahamian distinctive dialect of English. But the actual content of the tales is also open to creative embellishment. Characters can be fully and wittily described or made to act foolish or clever, and the story itself can be modified drastically to fit a particular audience or situation.

This brings up one of the most important aspects of Bahamian narrative artistry, the fact that their tales are virtually all shared with U.S., Caribbean, European, and African storytellers, as documented in the Aarne-Thompson tale and motif indexes. Yet Bahamians make them their own by using local names and places and sometimes changing the plot to give it local directness. A case in point is the widely known tale of Tarbaby, a sticky figure made to catch garden thieves that usually gets slapped or kicked because it does not answer when addressed by one of the thieves. In the Bahamas, however, Tarbaby is a pretty girl, "had lip rouge and everything," and of course the thief gets stuck when he hugs her, a version both more logical and more amusing. Similarly, sly Bahamian narrators can sometimes tell a multilevel tale, perceived differently by different members of the audience. For example, a tale about a pair of rabbits is seen by children as a cute story about pretty little animals; the adults in the audience perceive the sexual innuendo in their relationship; and one or two individuals in the audience recognize that the narrator is commenting obliquely on their activities.

For audience interplay and witty manipulation of traditional narration in both content and style, the Bahamian narrators are true artists, and proud of it.

Further Reading

Aarne, Antti, *The Types of the Folktale: A Classification and Bibliography*, edited and translated by Stith Thompson, second revision, Helsinki, Finland: Academia Scientarum Fennica, 1961

Crowley, Daniel J., *I Could Talk Old-Story Good: Creativity in Bahamian Folklore*, volume 17 of Folklore Studies, Berkeley: University of California Press, 1966

Thompson, Stith, *Motif-Index of Folk-Literature*, Bloomington: Indiana University Press, 1932

"Fattening" in Belizean Creole Storytelling

Ervin Beck

Ervin Beck shows examples of the Belizean Creole storytelling tradition known as "fattening." An audience member can "fatten" a tale through a variety of formulaic interruptions. The teller responds with clever repartee. Fattening can even lead the group into a singing and dancing interruption in the story.

The Audience "Fattens" the Tale

In traditional English Creole culture in Belize, a highly interactive form of storytelling persists in the practice of a few narrators and in the memories of many more. Resembling some elements found in the work of Daniel Crowley in Barbados and confirming other generalizations made by Melville Herskovits for Suriname and Roger Abrahams for the West Indies culture area, the Belizean conventions apparently derive from the African origins of the people who still use them.

Members of the audience collaborate in shaping the narrative experience by interrupting the narrator and introducing material of their own choosing. Belizeans call this conventionalized pattern of turn-taking "fattening," and they call a person who interrupts a "fattener." The fattening seems to serve at least four different functions: (1) it keeps the audience actively involved in the event; (2) it tests the narrator's composure and ability to improvise; (3) it emphasizes the fictional nature of the stories being told and the sanctioned "lying" of the narrator who is performing them; and (4) it creates a festive atmosphere by making room for other performance genres during the narrative event.

The discussion that follows is based on explanations given by narrators and, more important, on my own observations during three different performance sessions: one by Edward Bevans, retired woodcutter, with family and friends in a lower-class neighborhood in Belize City; one by Eulalio Smith for an audience of villagers in Rancho Dolores; and one by Adelia Dixon for her fellow singers following a rehearsal of the Excelsior Women's Chorus of Wesley Methodist Church in Belize City. The last venue was arranged by a seasoned raconteur, Magistrate Oswald Sutherland, in order to show me a traditional Belizean Creole storytelling session, although most of the interaction that occurred with the chorus was also present or latent in the first two sessions.

During the Bevans session, I recorded this classic, formulaic interruption by Christabel of a *märchen* about a seven-headed giant being told by her husband Edward:

Christabel: You mi di deh? [You were there?]
Edward: Right deh, man! [Right there, man!]
Christabel: You mi see? [You saw it?]
Edward: Sure, I was right deh.

Christabel and Leonie White sing:
Man born fi lie. [Man was born to lie.]
Tamango yeggeh yeggeh.
Man no lie, e no live. [If a man doesn't lie, he
    doesn't live.]
Tamango yeggeh yeggeh.
Man born fi trouble,

Tamango yeggeh yeggeh.
Man di born fi lie.
Tamango yeggeh yeggeh.
Man no lie, e no live.
Tamango yeggeh yeggeh.
Christabel: Heave ahn long shore! [Heave it along the shore!] Let's go!

Whereupon Edward, who had sat mute during the interruption, resumed the telling of his story. As the concluding metaphoric formula implies: he took up the "oar" of storytelling again and moved the "boat" (Creole *dorey*) of his story away from the "shore" where it had become stalled during the interruption by his audience. As they sang their call-and-response song, Christabel and her middle-aged daughter Leonie White drummed an intricate rhythm on the table with their knuckles.

The content of this most typical kind of fattening concerns both literary fiction and moral conduct. In regard to performance genre, fattening constantly reminds the audience that it is listening to oral fiction rather than nonfiction; that is, fattening is conventional only for stories that are not to be taken as true, "Anancy" stories, whether they concern the spider trickster hero, other animals, clever Jack, or the little boy or girl hero of *märchen*. Using terminology from dramatic criticism, one could say that fattening ensures an "alienation effect" in the audience, which keeps it fully aware—and critical—of the story and the frequently amoral conduct of its hero.

Such fictional narratives are usually also marked by conventional openings (e.g., "Crick! Crack!") and closings (e.g., "Pin never bend, Nancy story never end"). Fattening is not appropriate for the telling of traditional legends, first-person experiences, or short anecdotes and jokes—all of which have their own distinctive openings.

The ability to respond properly to such conventionalized audience interruption marks the initiated storyteller in Belize. During the session with Eulalio Smith in Rancho Dolores, Eniilio Sutherland, a teenage boy—hitherto mute—suddenly began telling his own story. The audience listened respectfully and quietly for a considerable time, until Eulalio suddenly said: "You mi di deh?" At first, the boy ignored the interruption and continued his narration, but then suddenly he paused and responded. "Right deh with the man." To this minimal response Eulalio added,

"Beautiful"—apparently in approval of the boy's narrative skill.

Joking Fattening

Fattening may be more jokingly opportunistic and also less formulaic in its introduction. After Adelia Dixon referred to "forty-eleventeen pick-nys (pickaninnies)" and one listener immediately interrupted to demand how many "forty-eleventeen" would really be, Adelia responded, "Forty-eventeen? Eleventeen-forty!" without skipping a beat and continued her tale.

Such joking may become more elaborately improvised. At one point, Oswald Sutherland interrupted Adelia with:

Oswald S.: Didn't they have Haulover Bridge in those days?
Adelia D.: This wasn't Haulover Bridge. This is Salsipuedes.
Helen L.: Where is Salsipuedes?
Oswald S.: Back of yonder. Back of Tataduhende.
Adelia D.: Right! But, my cousin, how do you know that?
Oswald S.: I was there back of you, man.
Adelia D.: [You are] Tataduhende, for sure!

This interruption begins in historical reality—Haulover Bridge links two parts of downtown Belize City—and moves into nonsense (Salsipuedes means "get out if you can") and joking fantasy (Tataduhende is a scary, supernatural jungle creature). Oswald's seemingly factual question serves as the prompt for a complex repartee of four joking comments by Oswald and Adelia.

The narrator can even disrupt her own narrative illusion in order to show her comic genus. For instance, Adelia Dixon suddenly addressed her audience: "I tell you! You look like you don't believe me. I was right there. If I wasn't, how could I tell you? I'm ten years older than my ma, so I must know how the thing went." Perhaps she interrupted her own narrative because she grew tired of waiting for the formulaic challenge—"You mi di deh?"—that would naturally have prompted her joke.

Later on, in the middle of her story about the devil and his young bride, Adelia even took the initiative in asking her audience if they wanted to see how the devil danced at the wedding. "Show you motion!" they begged, whereupon Adelia stood and danced with another woman, all the time singing the devil's song as accompaniment.

Fattening as Dance
Indeed, a fattening from the audience may even expand the storytelling session into a group dance performance:

> Oswald S.: Take you time, Sis. Weh e tie that big mouth with? (What did he tie that big mouth with?)
> Adelia D.: Titie (reed used in basketry).
> Oswald S.: Titie grass di grow.
> Palmer William, William Palmer
> Show me Grampa walk.
> *Tamango yeggeh yeggeh tamango—*

Oswald's query led to his introduction of the ring-game song, "Palmer William," into the storytelling event. Sung to the same call-and-response tune as "Man born fi lie," the song assumes a standing audience that acts out each caricature named by the caller—in this case, how an old man walks. Other variant commands might include

> Show me how you mommy walk.
> Show me how you sister walk.
> Show me how you auntie run.
> Show me how you use to creep.
> Show me how you auntie iron.
> Show me how you grampa kiss.

Sung in a fattening, this song encourages the audience to form a ring and join in a group dance. The song and dance may continue for a long time, stopping only when the caller's imagination or the audience's stamina flags. Or, this one song may lead to another. In fact, one informant recalled groups of 25 to 30 people dancing in story interruptions of up to 30 minutes' length, after which they settled down and listened to the rest of the story. Such long interruptions make believable one informant's memory of a story that took four nights to tell.

Refusal to Accept Fattening
Although some interruptions may dispense with the formulaic question "You mi di deh?", not all interruptions are honored or thought proper. A younger woman who increasingly interrupted Adelia was eventually permanently ignored by Adelia. That she never used the formulaic ques-

tion was not the reason; rather, she interrupted too often and too gracelessly and had no interesting joking to add to the event once Adelia responded to her interruption. She may also have been ignored because, as a younger member of a long-established chorus of women older than herself, she lacked social status in the group.

A Functional Interaction
Belizean Creole storytelling sessions thus replicate much that we know is typical of traditional cultures in Africa. The narrator and audience interact in a kind of call and response, with the narrator giving the story as "call" and the audience giving jokes, songs, and even dance in the formulaic "response." The interactive storytelling also integrates many genres of folklore—narrative, proverb, joke, riddle, song, dance, even mime—into a festival-like performance typical of African folk arts performances, which seldom give one genre exclusive attention.

These Belizean Creole narrative events are integral to a very different kind of social milieu than is typical of Belizean Creole culture today, especially Belizean urban culture. They assume a special time set aside for storytelling to a relatively large group of willing, attentive people. The groups I observed comprised from 10 to 20 people. Wakes, church harvest celebrations, evening boat rides in the bay, and picnics and soirees in the countryside or on the cayes were typical venues for such events longer ago.

The Fading of Fattening
With the fading use of such events, with smaller groups serving as the base for more social interaction (especially in cities), and with even the smallest, most isolated rural settlement now using radio, television, CDs, and VCRs for an evening's entertainment, the bravura performance of a storyteller in front of an attentive audience ready to create their share of the fun has become a thing of the past. It is tenuously maintained in only a few venues, such as the church social, although mainly in a self-conscious, revival mode. The telling of Anancy stories in academic classrooms or in storytelling contests at the Bliss Institute features only one person telling a story to a largely mute audience.

As in many other modern cultures, Belizean Creole storytelling in the 1990s consists mainly of conversational narratives such as short legends, personal experience stories, or jokes—all told to one or a few friends in a small group that has formed for some other purpose. No interruptive fattening is appropriate in everyday conversational exchange.

Conversational narratives and contexts no doubt serve modern Belizean Creoles as well as the longer, more formalized events served their ancestors. But they do so in the absence of the communal values that fattened storytelling both reflected and helped sustain.

Further Reading

Abrahams, Roger, "The Shaping of Folklore Traditions in the British West Indies," *Journal of Inter-American Studies* 9 (1967)

Beck, Ervin, "Call and Response in Belizean Creole Folk Songs," *Belizean Studies* 8 (March 1980)

———, "On Saving Anancy," *Belizean Studies* 20 (October 1992)

———, "Telling the Tale in Belize," *Journal of American Folklore* 93 (1980)

Crowley, Daniel, *I Could Talk Old-Story Good: Creativity in Bahamian Folklore,* volume 17 of Folklore Studies, Berkeley: University of California Press, 1966

Hadel, Richard, "Anansi Stories and Their Uses," *National Studies* 1 (January 1973)

———, "Five Versions of the Riding-Horse Tale: A Comparative Study," in *Folklore Annual* 2, Austin: University of Texas, 1970

Herskovits, Melville, Frances Shapiro Herskovits, and Mieczyslaw Kolinski, *Suriname Folk-Lore,* New York: Columbia University Press, 1936

Hunter, Charles T., "The Web of Anancy, Super Spiderman," *Brukdown* 7 (1978)

Poliner, Sharlene May, "The Exiled Creature: Ananse Tales and the Search for Afro-Caribbean Identity," *Studies in the Humanities* 11:1 (June 1984)

Holding on to the Past: Maya Storytelling in Belize

David Pendergast

David Pendergast discusses three functions of contemporary Maya storytelling: the use of story to lighten work, the importance of story in maintaining tradition, and story as a factor in cultural solidarity.

Functions of Telling in Maya Culture

For the Belize Maya with whom I have worked in archaeological excavations since 1961, traditional storytelling has three distinct functions, only one of which is given overt recognition by both the teller and the audience. One of the three functions, the providing of diversion in the work setting, has very probably existed since Maya culture first took shape, perhaps as early as 2000 B.C. The second, the maintenance of tradition, has almost certainly been a feature of storytelling from the outset as well. The third, which involves storytelling in the establishment of solidarity or resistance, is certainly a post-Conquest feature, and may in fact largely be a product of relatively recent social forces. Whatever the time and form of their origin, however, all three functions are played out in today's Maya world, especially since the mid-1980s, each time a session of raconteurship begins. I say "raconteurship" because only a few individuals, recognized for their knowledge of traditional tales and for their speaking abilities, adopt the role of principal storyteller and are expected to hold forth whenever appropriate circumstances arise.

Loss of the Mayan Language

In today's Belize Maya world the recounting of all stories, whether ancient or modern in content, occurs in Spanish rather than Mayan. Within the past four generations the Maya have suffered severance of communications of a type common in situations of language loss, which often results in loss of oral tradition. Individuals of the great-grandparental generation, of whom none remain today, generally spoke only Mayan, whereas their children, now few in number, utilize Mayan as their principal domestic operating language and Spanish only for broader contacts. Some members of the third generation retain limited knowledge of Mayan but do not use the language as a real medium of communication; their children in turn are Spanish-speakers who almost universally retain no knowledge of Mayan. Thanks to translation by the second generation, however, tales once told purely in Mayan can now be appreciated and absorbed by young people for whom their ancestral language has taken on the quality of a foreign tongue.

Scope of This Paper

It is not my intention to explore in this brief presentation the content of modern Maya stories in Belize, but rather to consider the meanings of stories and storytelling in the context of Maya life in a late-twentieth-century developing country, and to review a few aspects of content that illustrate change in the significance of storytelling over time. Many ethnographic studies of individual communities both in the lowlands and in the highlands contain information on story content and function that illustrates the richness and variety of tales both ancient and modern. I do not pretend to present a comprehensive study of the existing literature on the topic here, but instead I seek to characterize Maya storytelling as I have seen it, heard it, and participated in it over the past three-and-a-half decades.

Storytelling in the Work Setting

In Belize Maya storytelling, the definition of a specific appropriate context for the sole function of storytelling that is openly recognized by the participants serves to establish both the physical and the psychological conditions in which the telling will take place. As a result, in most instances such definition also identifies the type of delivery to be employed, the class of tales on which to focus, and sometimes the very stories that should or must be recounted, as well as the responses expected from the audience. The principal context of such activity is the world of physical labor, especially work that is of long duration or is particularly mind-numbing or arduous.

In the work setting, the storyteller provides relief from the tedium of the task at hand and at the same time helps to set the pace of the effort. Many of the tales woven in such circumstances are those likely to be found among any group of males with a broad spectrum of shared experience: stories of hunting luck, rather than prowess, may dominate one session, whereas in another the focus may be on the vagaries of slash-and-burn agriculture and the risks to life and limb inherent in work with ax and machete in places often far from home. Such tales will generally receive the short, often monosyllabic, responses that are nearly universal in contexts of this type. This tale-and-response balance will continue until one of the listeners, stimulated by his ability to augment or shift the flow of the stories, enters the lists with a tale of his own. Each shift of this sort permits the new storyteller not only a moment in the limelight but also a moment of rest from his labors, and hence it is usually true that the men more senior in age or in status will speak up first, and the more junior individuals will join in the exchange later, usually with much shorter stories. No matter how many the shifts may be, in almost every circumstance, all participants tacitly recognize that the stage will ultimately be handed back to the principal raconteur, who will continue to lead both the telling and the labor to which the stories lend richness and timing.

Storytelling and the Maintenance of Tradition

The second function of storytelling emerges as the content of work tales moves from common recent experience to events of the distant past. This type of shift is always, in my experience, orchestrated by the principal teller, who is usually the only individual who knows the stories, or at least the only one who can recount them in full. Some tales of this class are instructional, such as those that speak of means of escaping the dangers that lurk in the forest. The instruction is not, however, couched in formal terms but rather is conveyed through stories of creatures that inhabit the land and will snatch the unwary passerby away either into a different world or to the creature's dinner table. Today, in a pattern that has probably existed since the sixteenth or seventeenth century, Maya belief is commingled with Christian, with the result that the dangers of the weekdays are compounded on the Sabbath. The general nature of such tales is, however, surely a survival from times long before the Conquest.

Cautionary tales are sometimes interspersed with, but more commonly succeeded by, stories presented as purely historical in content, and seem to have no particular lesson to impart. Among such stories, one of the more interesting is the saga of King Canek and Princess Nicte-ha, which recounts all manner of events both plausible and clearly impossible in the world of reality. The combination of native and European elements makes the story a reflection of post-Conquest Maya history, but the greatest interest lies in the fact that, whereas the princess cannot be linked to the known past, Canek is the name or title of a series of rulers who held sway at the Guatemalan Peten community of Tayasal, the final Itza Maya capital, until the end of the seventeenth century. Neither the tellers nor the audiences with whom I have spent time were aware of the concordance between the tale and ethnohistoric documentation; my introduction of the information was met with genuine interest, but, of course, it had no effect whatsoever on the validity of the tale, which had long since been fully established by the force of oral tradition.

The function of tales that embody elements from the past goes beyond that of instruction to the seemingly obvious one of maintaining a body of cultural information. The function seems obvious, but in truth, neither raconteur nor listener conceives of the experience in this way; it is left to outsiders to make of a simple, enjoyable experience something more complex than the participants perceive. The term "maintenance" is particularly apposite and poignant because so much of Maya belief and practice has been lost or diluted over the centuries since the Conquest. The Conquest was, however, not the only disruptive event; in the southern lowlands, including most parts of Belize, the period of dilution and loss unquestionably began with the dispersal of population following the tenth-century collapse of almost all major Maya political and economic centers. Yet, despite internal and external pressures, the remaining body of stories serves to embed information and attitudes from the past in the thinking of the modern Maya, and clearly, in the case of the acknowledged historical tales, to link the people conceptually to their distant ancestors.

Storytelling as Solidarity

Out of the links with the past comes the third function of storytelling, which is to bind the Maya together in a world that very largely ignores, except for purposes of tourism development, the amazing durability of the people and some aspects of their ancient culture. The Maya survive today in numbers not greatly different from those of peak times a millennium and a half ago, in lands that may not now be seen as theirs in courts of law but that have reverberated to Maya footsteps for four thousand years and more. Yet in the midst of such an enduring tradition, the Maya generally occupy the lowest rung of the social ladder, and find their pattern of life very frequently under siege. To remember the achievements of their ancestors gives the modern Maya a sense of place and pride that helps to offset the indifference of much of the surrounding world. Tales that speak of past glories, like archaeologists' retrieval of such glories from the ground, give real force to the remembering of things past, and hence serve to buttress the sense that the Maya experience is larger and stronger than any that has succeeded it in the Maya lands.

It is characteristic of the Maya, as it surely always has been, that the focus on the serious issues bound up in storytelling is leavened with humor. Punning, word substitution, and general language play are the very stuff of Maya discourse, and it is impossible to imagine the telling of even the most serious tale without some small excursion into the playful world that the Maya love so much. Nowhere is this phenomenon more visible than in the relationship recognized by the modern Maya between themselves and their predecessors; this is a matter much discussed, and it is always the individuals of today who are found wanting when comparisons are drawn. Workers striving to move huge stones in an ancient building will be reminded by the raconteur, often with a supporting chorus of remarks from others, that their ancestors put the blocks in place without the aid of modern technology. Those who bear names known from the few surviving ancient records or from ethnohistoric documentation will be forced to acknowledge how great their lineage was, and to what depths it has descended. Chaffing of this sort sometimes springs from elements from stories just told, and in others involves citation of such tales as evidence of how much, and how unfortunately, things have changed.

In all such verbal horseplay, which often involves transformation of modern names into apparent ancient ones and may digress into multiple Mayan/Spanish/English word games on the subject, the surface message is how far the butt of the joking has fallen. Yet the underlying message is at once more complex and more bittersweet; in speaking of past grandeur and present vicissitude, it traces the unhappy course of Maya life over the past five centuries, and yet, at the same time, it ennobles all participants by tying them to their ancestors as it binds them together in modern times. From such ennoblement comes a sense of solidarity that has frustrated many a governmental effort to, as one Belize official so carefully put it, "bring the Amerindian into Western civilization."

Although, as I have shown, all three functions are present in workplace storytelling, I cannot say that all come to the fore with similar strength when tales are recounted in other settings. It is clear, however, that whenever and wherever stories are told by the Maya in Belize, the function of tales in creating a sense of solidarity will be present. It is this relatively new function that gives to traditional Maya storytelling in Belize a broader role than the original—one that will, if Maya durability thus far is any indicator, survive despite the ever-increasing onslaughts of North American television-purveyed culture on all aspects of the country's traditional life.

Further Reading

Craig, Meg, *Characters and Caricatures in Belizean Folklore*, Belize: Belize UNESCO Commission, 1991

Farriss, Nancy M., *Maya Society Under Colonial Rule: The Collective Enterprise of Survival*, Princeton, New Jersey: Princeton University Press, 1984

Graham, Elizabeth, "A Spirited Debate," *Rotunda* 28 (1995)

Hammond, Norman, *Ancient Maya Civilization*, Cambridge and New York: Cambridge University Press, 1981

Jones, Grant D., *Maya Resistance to Spanish Rule: Time and History on a Colonial Frontier*, Albuquerque: University of New Mexico Press, 1989

Pendergast, David M., "The Historical Content of Oral Tradition: A Case from Belize," *Journal of American Folklore* 101:401 (July–September 1988)

———, "The Southern Maya Lowlands Contact Experience: The View from Lamanai, Belize," in *The Spanish Borderlands in Pan-American Perspective*, volume 3 of *Columbian Consequences*, edited by David Hurst Thomas, Washington, D.C., and London: Smithsonian Institution, 1991

———, "Stability Through Change: Lamanai, Belize, from the Ninth to the Seventeenth Century," in *Late Lowland Maya Civilization: Classic to Postclassic*, edited by Jeremy A. Sabloff and E. Wyllys Andrews, Albuquerque: University of New Mexico Press, 1986

———, "Worlds in Collision: The Maya/Spanish Encounter in Sixteenth and Seventeenth Century Belize," in *The Meeting of Two Worlds: Europe and the Americas, 1492–1650*, edited by Warwick Bray, Proceedings of the British Academy 81, Oxford: Oxford University Press, 1993

Redfield, Robert, *The Folk Culture of Yucatan*, Chicago: University of Chicago Press, 1941

Sharer, Robert, *The Ancient Maya*, fifth edition, Stanford, California: Stanford University Press, 1994

Thompson, John Eric Sidney, *Ethnology of the Mayas of Southern and Central British Honduras*, Field Museum of Natural History Publication 274, Anthropological Series 17:2, Chicago: Field Museum, 1930

Tozzer, Alfred M., *Survivals of Ancient Forms of Culture Among the Mayas of Yucatan and the Lacandones of Chiapas*, Proceedings of the 15th International Congress of Americanists, New York

Function and Performance of the Chilean Folktale Today

Manuel Dannemann

Manuel Dannemann discusses eight themes of the folktale popular in Chile. He gives an example of each and notes the function of the tale in Chilean society.

Functions of the Folktale

The functions of the basic themes of the Chilean folktale constitute, by exercise of the narrative art, a conception of human beings and their world and of the people who cultivate the genre. These particular functions come together in the primary function, fundamentally pleasant, of enjoyment, elevation of the soul. This function is interpretative as well as didactic.

The most recent research, resulting from fieldwork on the folk narrative in Chile, has allowed us to increase to eight the functional themes within this genre. They are spicy anecdotes, riddle tales, animal tales, formula tales, marvelous tales, knavish tales, religious tales and advice tales (Dannemann; Dannemann and Quevedo, 311–341).

The examples that follow have been obtained by the author from the Chilean folk tradition.

Spicy Anecdotes

A woman hides some doughnuts when she is visited by a neighbor, in order not to share them with her. During the conversation, the stingy woman's cat eats all the doughnuts.

Function: humorous relaxation. This type of tale is very simple and direct. Destined to produce hilarity, it often also serves a didactic function.

Riddle Tales

A silly must solve a king's riddle in order to marry one of his daughters. He succeeds through a metaphoric game. For example: "I ate meat roasted with words."—The meat was roasted with the flames of a burning book. Or, "I drank water that didn't come from the sky or from the earth."—The speaker drank the sweat of a donkey. Another, "I went to the hill and I caught three hares."—In a room, he abused the candor of three women, without them realizing that their actions would result in damage to themselves. "I took off the skin and I set them free alive."—He took off the chemise and let them go.

Function: Enigmatic game. The problem to be solved requires previous correct knowledge; otherwise, one continues with mere conjecture.

Animal Tales

A hornet and a fox bet which will arrive first at a fixed place. The hornet wins by riding on the top of the fox's tail and gives the fox a surprise final attack.

Function: self-criticism through conferring human attributes to animals. This gives humans more freedom of judgment over their own behaviors since it is not easy to judge oneself.

Formula Tales

Though folklorists use this term, the tellers themselves do not. They simply refer to each tale by its own name, for example, *La Hormiguita que se*

Metió en el Granero (The Little Ant Who Got into the Barn): One little ant carries a little grain, another comes and does the same, and so on, endlessly. These tales are also called never-ending tales in the folk culture.

A subclass is the enumerative tale, in which people, animals, or things increase or decrease. For example, *El del Real y Medio*:

> I had one *real* and a half; with the *real* and a half I bought a chicken and the chicken laid some eggs. I had the chicken, I had the eggs and I still have the *real* and a half.
>   I had one *real* and a half, with the *real* and a half I bought a cow and the cow gave me a calf. I had the cow and I had the calf, I had the chicken, I had the eggs and I still had the *real* and a half. And so on.

Function: Ordering. Tales of this type are generally used with children from four to ten years old.

Marvelous Tales

The word "lie" is the only one in the folk culture that designates this kind of tale. "Lie" in this context means fabulous, unreal, enormous, magical—notions that move in the orbit of what is marvelous. It does not mean deceitfulness or wicked intention.

A young man must agree to carry out superhuman works. He carries them out with the help of the youngest daughter of a king. Both run away, and after her father pursues them twice and her mother once, they arrive at another kingdom. But the queen's curse makes the young man forget his love. Just as he is about to marry another woman, the princess restores his memory and he recovers her love.

Function: Recreation. This type of tale elaborates the symbolic achievements of the protagonists.

Knavish Tales

This conventional name is used by researchers. Its folk nomenclature derives from its stock characters. Knavish tales are told of Pedro Urdemales, the most conspicuous and famous; of Quevedo, who is really Don Francisco de Quevedo y Villegas; of Bertoldo Bertoldino y Cacaseno; of the soldadillo.

Pedro Urdemales cheats a greedy person, making him believe that under a hat there is a par-

tridge of gold, but what is really hidden is excrement.

Function: Satiric social criticism.

Religious Tales

No generic folk term. Each tale is called by its own name.

St. Peter aids a blacksmith who has given the only bread he had to Christ, to another apostle, and to him. He asks Jesus for glory for the blacksmith. But the blacksmith requests magic objects and supernatural powers to rid himself of the demon with whom he had made a pact.

Function: Manifestation and defense of the Catholic faith.

Advice Tales

Folk narrators speak of "advice tales" and "teaching tales." These contain lessons of the ancestors of elderly people. They bring useful examples of how to face difficulties.

A dying father gives three pieces of advice to his son: 1.) Do not adopt strange children; 2.) Do not plant trees that don't give fruit; 3.) Do not tell a secret to your wife.

To test this advice, the son kills a pig, stains his hands with the animal's blood, and buries it close to an orange tree. He arrives home and pretends to be drunk. When faced with the insistence of his wife, he tells her that he has killed a person.

A few days later he again pretends to be drunk, argues with this wife, and punches her. She escapes, shouting, "Assassin, you already killed one and now you want to kill me!"

He comes before the judge and is condemned to die by hanging. A five-year-old child whom they have adopted runs to look for a rope to hang him. He is to be hanged from a willow, a tree which does not bear fruit. He himself planted this tree.

The condemned now tells of his father's advice. He shows the pig he has buried and reports what has happened with his wife. He thus saves himself.

Function: This has a moralizing function.

Function Not Always Realized

Narrators and their audiences are not always aware of the functions of these tales. Still a study of these functions can show them to be a worthy tool for cultural understanding.

Further Reading

Dannemann, Manuel, *Cuentos Folklóricos Chilenos para los Niños de Chile,* Santiago, Chile: FONDART, 1994

Dannemann, Manuel, and Maria Isabel Quevedo, "El Cuento Folklórico en Chile," *Revista Chilena de Historia y Geografía* 158 (1990)

Lira Popular *in Chile:*
Between Traditional Poetry and Popular Urban Versifying

Marcela Orellana

Marcela Orellana presents a historical account of one genre of Chilean oral literature, showing us how the traditional oral poet of the people adapted his art to the cheaply printed sheets called lira popular. *These sheets were sold on the streets of Santiago in the second half of the nineteenth century. Orellana elaborates on one* lira popular, *a report of the San Francisco earthquake, to show how this printed poem is actually composed of verses from the oral tradition.*

Lira Popular

In the second half of the nineteenth century, a form of cheap literature known as *Lira Popular* (the People's Lyre) sprang up in Santiago, and to a lesser extent in other Chilean towns such as Valparaiso, Concepcion, and Talca. It was printed on quarter- or half-sheets of the poorest quality paper and contained rhyming ten-line stanzas with crude etchings for illustrations. These sheets were sold profusely at locations crowded with people, such as marketplaces, railroad stations, and horse-drawn tram terminals.

The verses printed in *Lira Popular* were narrative poems telling a wide variety of stories, where religious subjects shared space with news of natural disasters, murders, and such traditional topics as the topsy-turvy world and like exaggerations.

This practice originated in the oral tradition of poetry that came to Spanish America with the Conquistadors and settlers, took root, and lived on for centuries thanks to poets who recreated their works time and time again by repeating them to the inhabitants of tiny settlements scattered over an extensive territory. *Lira Popular* itself, however, was a purely urban phenomenon and began to flourish around 1863. This was a time when towns sprouted strongly in the American landscape as a result of economic and social changes. Large waves of migration aided speedy growth. In the case of Santiago, the population rose from 10 percent in 1813 to 42.8 percent 100 years later. Such transformations explain the rise of *Lira Popular,* which originated partly from the encounter of the peasant poet with urban surroundings, and partly from the difficulty of adapting traditional poetic language, with its rigid metric and rules of composition, to new discursive requirements.

The Country Poet's Adjustment to Town Life

We focus first on the artist rather than his work because the changes the artist had to face would subsequently affect his poetry. In the case of traditional poetry, poet and poem formed an established unit that renewed itself over time with no internal rifts. The people surrounding the traditional poet saw him as the true guardian of their values and, more important, as the memory of those who lacked any knowledge of writing to give such values a form of permanence. This poetic practice recreated ancient themes and was part of a notion of time governed by the cycles of farming, which gave daily life a sense of stable and immobile course.

In the second half of the nineteenth century, lured by the city and new prospects of employment, waves of migrants began to leave the countryside. Among them were many cultivators of traditional poetry, but their art would inevitably undergo a change in this new context. Understanding the introduction of rural poetry into town life is therefore essential to understanding how traditional oral poetry became this literature printed on loose sheets.

The Physical City

Socially and economically speaking, Santiago was growing and changing. Development put a new face on the old town. On the one hand, large mansions and impressive residences were built in the French style, of which José Luis Romero said, "With the prosperity that Santiago enjoyed between 1840 and 1870, the great splendor of the wealthy class was reflected in the extensive houses or *petits hotels* that the most powerful exponents of that class had built." On the other hand, slums mushroomed on the outskirts, all of them strongholds of poverty and crowding, worsened by lack of sanitation and clean drinking water.

Such were the conditions that greeted the rural poets, who witnessed and experienced the contrasts described above between poverty and crowded living quarters and signs of development that included gas lighting in the streets by 1857, city transportation by horse-drawn trams that same year, and, in 1863, railroads that began to travel from the capital city to other towns.

The Cultural City

The natural turmoil of a growing city was accompanied by a cultural movement that followed the romantic sensibility prevailing in Spanish America in the second half of the nineteenth century. Most notable were the emerging press and diversified cultural events. Different audiences attended the opera at Teatro Municipal and the zarzuela at Teatro del Cerro. The intelligentsia were active in both culture and politics. Political leadership in the press and literature shared the writer's efforts equally. There was no notion as yet of any difference among various cultural practices. Thus literary work was not seen as a specific activity obeying rules of its own, nor were writers distinguished from poets; both were various facets of the "man of letters." The function of literature "was defined as predominantly one of political edification; it was seemingly called to

promote the improvement of republican and democratic life, to instruct the citizenry, to denounce and castigate the deformations of the prevailing political leanings or the remains of the *Ancien Regime.*" (Goic, vol. 2, 63). There is thus a close relationship between awareness of the moment in history and literary expression.

The poet of oral tradition had no place here. To begin with, this poetic practice could not fill the role it had enjoyed in rural surroundings where cultural unity prevailed and where he was appreciated by landowners and peasants alike. In addition, his new audience, the urban people, no longer required a poet to be their memory, for their history as an urban people was just beginning; everything was new. Under these changed circumstances, the old rural view of cyclical time no longer applied. Urban life was marked by linear time; change was a primary element, bringing the unpredictable with it. The rural poet found himself submerged in a new dimension of history, to which he would endeavor to adapt with new themes peculiar to city life in its wide variety of personalities, events, places.

At the same time, a clear cultural and social difference arose between the group of intellectual and political leaders and the majority of the people. The rural poet and his wisdom were consigned to the people, who lacked the channels of expression available to the leading classes. His poetic practice did not belong in the prevailing notion of "literature."

The Press

The press was to play a major role for the poet and his poetry in his new surroundings. The press had belonged by tradition to political groups and was thus by definition an instrument for indoctrination. Gradually, in the second half of the century, publishers began to emphasize news over politics.

Papers were easily available, and the poet, by reading them, gained access to an entirely novel world composed of news of political developments, current events in Chile together with items from abroad. Journalism extended to serial novels known as *folletines* after the French *feuilleton,* and descriptive period pieces. Through the newspapers, the poet gained access to the thinking of the leading class, to what was considered valid literature; in brief, the press spread out in front of him a vast tissue of places and events, completely different from his most deeply rooted notions.

Traditional Poetry and *Lira Popular*

The change of the context in which the artist wrote his poems and his place in the new framework affected both the poet and the principles that guided his work. The basic rules of his form of poetry were questioned, as was the role that poetry ought to fill in society. The figure of the poet and his place in society were also questioned.

Deviations from Tradition and Emergence of *Lira Popular*

A significant number of the leaflets of *Lira Popular* were given over to disputes among poets. The *paya* (duel in verse), a long-standing traditional form, had its own rules as to subject and composition. Two poets took turns to improvise verses around a set subject and continued until one of them gave up. In *Lira Popular,* the debate took place in writing and the traditional themes gave way to disputes and rivalries, enmities and mutual recriminations. These verbal attacks took shape in a broader context, where the issue was not so much petty rivalries among poets but poetry itself, a sign that writers perceived changes in poetic tradition but failed to see where these changes were leading and were concerned. For Daniel Meneses, a renowned loose-leaf poet, whoever deviated from tradition was a poor poet, not noticing, however, that he himself was doing precisely that, that circumstances had changed and poetry was not proof against such change.

> If you are fain to write poetry
> you need a good deal of talent,
> memory and much understanding,
> grammar and a good deal of knowledge.

> *Para escribir poesia*
> *se necesita talento*
> *memoria y entendimiento*
> *gramatica y conocimiento.*

Although acknowledging the arduous effort involved in writing poetry, Meneses denounced the ignorance of great themes or "fundamentals" among writers of leaflets.

> These trumpets are not aware
> of even one fundamental.

> *No saben estos trompetas*
> *ni siquiera un fundamento.*

He accused them of altering the meter and rhyme:

> Watch your singular and plural
> and as you progress along
> do not overlook your rhyme
> which you're doing very badly.

> *En singular y plural*
> *si marchas hacia adelante*
> *cuidate del consonante*
> *que te esta saliendo muy mal.*

He also criticized the order of words and symmetry in their stanzas, as in the following example:

> They also neglect the plurals.
> Of symmetry they know nothing.
> In their verses there is lack
> of all attention to grammar.

> *No arreglan ni los plurales*
> *ni saben las simetrias.*
> *Faltan en sus poesias*
> *los temas gramaticales.*

These and other quarrels in verse bore witness to the changes that traditional poetry was undergoing and also to the distance that urban popular poetry had traveled from tradition. Tradition was no longer the source of poems printed on loose sheets. Speech was rarely mentioned, and writing was now stressed as the poet's habitual practice.

> The pen trembles in my hand
> when I this drama describe.

> *La pluma llega a temblar*
> *al describer este drama.*

The press played a significant part in this clear change in traditional poetry. The poet drew on it to obtain new material for his verses, referring to news of Santiago and other places in Chile and abroad. This helped to create a new space where reference to reality prevailed over the fictional space of traditional verse. The notion of news, as of information on a novel happening, something unlikely, though close to the reader, influenced the popular poet to such an extent that news items became the subject of his verses, doing away with the traditional norm of re-creating traditional themes.

This crime that I shall relate
leaving not a detail out.
If anyone chance to doubt
that this is well-proven truth,
it was printed in the paper
in all its little details
and it was, gentlemen all,
the news we heard of last week.

El crimen lo doi a ver
sin una cosa faltar
si alguien llega a dudar
de esa verdad comprobada
fue en el diario narrada
con todos sus pormenores
y ha sido el tema senores
de la semana pasada.

New Role of Poets and Their Poetry

The new city space, the press the poet read, writing itself, indeed the place of the poet in the new context brought about a gradual definition of the poet and poetry in society. The poet of *Lira Popular* now focused on daily life, current events, urban surroundings, all of which little by little displaced traditional matters. The printed press became a source of inspiration for the poet, who picked out news items from the papers and rewrote them in rhyme for his loose leaflets. The rest was taken from his own experience of the city while keeping up the traditional repertory, though to a lesser extent. The object of publishing verses in looseleaf form was primarily to instruct the people. The poems provided information on political events, on unexpected happenings (e.g., natural disasters and certain occurrences of city life, including crime in the streets).

In this context, the poet arose as a mediator between the educated press and the people, for he took from the papers the themes for the ten-line stanzas addressed to his public, who in turn learned by this means about the latest news and concerns of the leading class as published in the newspapers. The loose sheets thus provided contact between distant groups of society that lived and acted in very different sections of the city.

This revision in verse of items from the papers also entailed a change in the selected material. The voice of the poet, together with his own view of the events described, would be the one heard in the pages of *Lira Popular*. For instance, news of executions by firing squad, which were common enough at the time, were printed in the papers with an effort at objectivity; the story was told soberly with emphasis on the fact that justice was done. *Lira Popular*, however, would tell the tale from the standpoint of the victim, very often in the first person, as presumably spoken by the man about to be shot, either to explain things his way or to take leave of those who surrounded him in life. The news is the same, but the voice of the narrator is different.

This fact led to a radical change from traditional poetry to the verses of *Lira Popular*. In traditional poetry, the voice of the storyteller usually spoke in the third person, retelling tales inherited from the distant past, where the speaker was not personally involved. *Lira Popular*, however, indulged in the first person. The poet spoke in his own name and stated a position in regard to matters of concern to him, from crime to the death penalty, the elections, and so on. The *Lira* poet became personally involved and committed to his subject when required. The new aim to provide information, the truly urban subject matter, gave rise to another, hitherto unconsidered, objective: the actual truth. The poet of *Lira Popular* insisted that he told "the truth as it happened," a nonexistent concern in traditional poetry, where the sole valid truth was the consistency of the tale.

And lastly, in what I am telling,
reader, do not be astonished,
here I shall give you the names
so that you know it is true.
But I say that it was so,
everything that has been told
was what happened recently
in the neighborhood of del Plata.
And gentlemen when I speak
every time I speak the truth
because my morals require me
not to invent anything.

Por ultimo en lo que advierto,
lector por que no te asombres,
voi a darte aqui los nombres
Para que veas que es cierto.
Mas yo dire que ha sido
gran verdad lo relatado
esto es ha desarrollado
En la vecina del Plata.
Al fin senores yo cuento
todas las veces verdad
porque en mi moralidad
ninguna cosa invento.

The Traditional Poetic Language and its Adjustment to New Discursive Requirements

The new objects that the poet of *Lira Popular* set himself, namely, the truth of his statements and consequently his new function in society of telling about urban life, about events, about actual circumstances encountered an obstacle that proved almost insurmountable. This was traditional poetic language, which for centuries had kept up the retelling of topics pertaining to oral poetry. It had its metric requirements, ten-line rhyming stanzas to which the poet had to adapt his new plots: one four-line stanza followed by four ten-line stanzas plus another ten-line stanza of farewell. The last verse of each of the first four stanzas must be the same as the corresponding verse of the opening four-line stanza. So the last verse of the first ten-line stanza must be the same as the first verse of the four-line stanza, the last verse of the second ten-line stanza must be the same as the second verse of the four-line stanza, and so on. A language with a style of composition, the form style was based on the use of verse formulas interspersed in the poem, according to subject and metric requirements, in such a way that each traditional theme had formulas to which the poet might resort. These he was constantly facing in the process of improvising.

In the new urban phase in which the poet wrote his compositions, the form style would hinder the poet's attempts to achieve the new objectives. Indeed, in dealing with original plots, the poet, from habit and without meaning to do so, employed forms proper to some traditional theme. This fact alone emphasized deviation of the topic from its original purpose to the traditional theme. We shall illustrate this with an example of disaster verses employing traditional verses on the end of the world.

If the poet sought to relate an actual disaster, the San Francisco earthquake, the practice of oral poetry and its own style of composition in its traditional form interfered with and prevented proper completion of the primary objective of relating an actual event.

"Complete Description of the Great Disaster of San Francisco, California"

A very flourishing city
was felled and rolled into darkness
owing to grievous disaster

was left completely in ruins.
An awful thundering tremor
destroyed village and towns.
The earth was shaken asunder
with fear and terror prevailing.
The people wailed and lamented,
clamored for mercy from heaven.
The Almighty was merciless then
and turned deaf ears to their pleas.
And that is why fire spread through
a very flourishing city.
The land all shook and trembled
from the palace to the farmyard.
In San Francisco the people
were begging and crying for mercy.
The flames spread through the city
leaving all else in the dark
and the people, with great fluidity
fled and escaped to the desert.
The cable says that the port
was felled and rolled into darkness.
The hungry element, fire,
was spreading little by little.
The flames grew wilder and fiercer
with the wind that blew upon them.
The firemen, greatly contented,
showed their patriotism.
The flames, with great cynicism,
sent all into oblivion.
A catastrophe that came
owing to grievous disaster.
The houses came tumbling down
and everyone was astonished,
that men and women were buried
in the rubble and the ruins.
The very few who escaped
fled overland to the east.
If you want to hear the story
you must listen carefully,
how this very handsome city
was left completely in ruins.
From the sea at last you saw
what was happening on land
and one who was there declares
it was horrible to see.
Everything reduced to ashes,
that is what everyone says.
The cable knows all the news
and gives every single detail,
the poor people are now
in a most ruinous way.

Un ciudad floreciente

rodo y cayo al abismo
por causa de un cataclismo
se arruino completamente.
Un formidable temblor
a los pueblos asolo.
La tierra se remecio
causando espanto y terror.
La gente, con gran dolor,
clamo al omnipotente.
Pero el Dios inclemente
sus ayes no escucho.
Por eso es que se incendio
una ciudad floreciente.
La tierra se remecia
desde el palacio al aprisco.
Y la gente en San Francisco
misericordia pedia.
La gran poblacion ardia
dejando el oscurantismo
y el pueblo con gran lirismo
escapo hacia el desierto.
Y el cable dice que el puerto
rodeo y cayo al abismo.
El gran voraz elemento
de a poco cundia,
se avivaba y se crecia,
protegido por el viento.
Los bomberos con contento
mostraban su patriotismo.
El fuego, con gran cinismo
todo echaba en olvido.
Le catastrofe he sido
por causa de un cataclismo.
Las casas de desplomaban
causando grandes asombros
en medio de sus escombros
a los hombres sepultaban.
Los pocos que se escapaban
huian hacia el oriente.
Si yo quieren que les cuente,
ponganme mas atencion
y esa bella poblacion
se arruino completamente
Al fin del mar se divisa
lo que en tierra sucedio,
y uno que alli se encontro
me aprueba que horroriza.
Todo ha quedado en ceniza,
segun se dice y se opina.
el cable que todo atina
cosa por cosa detalla
y la gente pobre se halla
en una completa ruina.

This version is intended to tell a piece of news—the San Francisco earthquake. The poet takes up the position of a reporter and properly gives his sources, like a newspaper would ("the cable says that the port / was felled and rolled into darkness"; the cable knows all the news and gives every single detail). The influence of the press is evident. In addition to newspaper sources, he further refers to an eyewitness ("and one who was there declares / it was horrible to see") to emphasize the truth of the tale. Notwithstanding, it is easy to spot inconsistencies between the "actual" earthquake and a recurrence of the traditional theme of "the end of the world."

The end of the world is a fundamental, a subject of traditional poetry, and as such, has its own unchanging features. To sing the tale of the end of the world is to warn about its manifold unmistakable signs: tremor, fire, noise, darkness, the total extension of the tragedy, fear of God. Regardless of the poet, the same formulas repeat themselves from one poet to another. For instance, one formula is "the people wailed and lamented, / clamored for mercy from heaven," which has many variants consistent with the requirements of rhyme: the people clamored to heaven, heaven they must beseech, we shall cry to God divine, we must cry for help from heaven, and so on.

The binary composition of parts of the stanza is a kind of formula too. Destruction and terror are described as follows: "the earth was shaken asunder / with fear and terror prevailing." There are several variations on this theme: "terrible troubles will come / with much horror and confusion," or "troubles, confusion, and horror / will very terrible be," or "howls of terror and confusion will be for all to hear."

Other elements linked to the end of the world connect it with the San Francisco earthquake. The impression of total catastrophe "was left completely in ruins," "everything [was] reduced to ashes," and "the tongues of fire were cynical and sent all into oblivion," as well as other signs of the end, including earthquake "an awful thundering tremor," "the land was shaking and trembling," fire "the flames spread through the city," "the hungry element, fire," "the tongues of fire were cynical and sent all into oblivion"; fear of God "the people wailed and lamented, / clamored for mercy from heaven, / the Almighty was merciless then / and turned deaf ears to their pleas."

The report of the San Francisco earthquake is in fact an illustration of a traditional fundamental. The use of forms appropriate to the theme of the end of the world pulls the poet toward that topic, keeping him away from the subject of his original concern, and the San Francisco earthquake becomes an illustration of verses sung *a lo divino* (on a religious subject), about the end of the world.

Another aspect of this *Lira* that interferes with the tale of events in San Francisco is the use of forms appropriate for the traditional religious verses on Moses. This episode describes the flight of the terror-stricken population:

> the flames spread through the city
> leaving all else in the dark
> and the people who were lyrical
> fled and escaped to the desert
> . . . .
> The very few who escaped
> fled overland to the east.

This flexible formula of text strategy, which allows set phrases to be inserted at will as the composition requires, accounted for the interweaving of traditional topics into the new poetic creations of the popular poet. Using forms appropriate for oral reciting out of their natural context, causes interferences and inconsistencies to appear in the poetic tale. In the present case, the story of an actual earthquake becomes a tale of global disaster of biblical dimensions, very far from the intention of reporting an actual event, which was the original intent of the poet of *Lira Popular*.

Conclusions

The rural poet who migrated to the city found himself in an unknown and unexpected world. Having recently emerged, the development of major cities, especially Santiago, was a complex matter and opulence was found side by side with poverty. Cultural life also was affected by signs of change, a new press focusing on news rather than political doctrine as it had earlier.

The popular poet who arrived here was sensitive to the urban environment and city life would determine his experience of poetry. The questions arising in his mind in respect to the urban public, the new circumstances, together with the press to which he had natural access, began to shape a new attitude of the poet in society and new objectives for his poetry. The rural poet, who recreated an oral tradition according to strict rules

of composition and was restricted to a certain number of topics, was now left behind. Gradually from the exercise of his calling, an urban poet emerged, intent on giving his poetry a hitherto unknown purpose—to report events through his verses, to report of the city and its inhabitants, the manifold happenings that made news, both close at hand and in far-off places.

This objective was multifaceted. Using the first person singular, he gave voice to a group deprived of access to official channels of communication. Through *Lira*, a view of the events narrated that had lacked a voice acquired one. *Lira* was thus the voice of those who had no channels to make their voice heard in society. Reality, however, resisted *Lira Popular*. The poet who recited traditional poetry performed according to a particular style of composition pertaining to oral poetry and practiced a formal style that subsequently prevented the poet from developing a new poetry, and so by giving traditional treatment to a new subject matter, the new theme deviated towards the traditional form. The resulting verses were a hybrid between the centuries-old oral tradition and a new written production seeking new topics, between the fiction of traditional themes and the actual circumstances that the new verses endeavored to impose.

Further Reading

Goic, Cedomil, *Del romanticismo al modernismo,* volume 2 of *Historia y Crítica de la Literatura Hispanoamericana*, Barcelona, Spain: Editorial Crítica, 1990

Lord, Albert Bates, *The Singer of Tales,* Cambridge, Massachusetts: Harvard University Press, 1960

Ramón, Armando de, *Santiago de Chile: caracteristicas historico,* London: Monografias de Nueva Historica, 1985

Rojas, Manuel, *Los costumbristas chilenos,* Santiago, Chile: Zig-Zag, 1957

Romero, José Luis, *Latinoamérica: las Ciudades y las Ideas,* third edition, Mexico: Siglo Veintiuno Editores, 1984

Salazar Vergara, Gabriel, *Labradores, Peones y Proletarios: formación y crisis de la sociedad popular chilena del siglo XIX*, Santiago, Chile: Ediciones Sur, 1985

Santa Cruz, Eduardo, *Análisis Histórico del Periodismo Chileno,* Santiago, Chile: Nuestra América Ediciones, 1988

Uribe-Echevarría, Juan, *Cantos a lo divino y a lo humano en Aculeo folklore de la Provincia de Santiago,* Santiago, Chile: Editorial Universitaria, 1962

Zumthor, Paul, *Introduction à la Poésie Orale,* Paris: Seuil, 1983

Discourse and Storytelling in Otavalo Song: Resonance and Dissonance in San Juanitos

Linda D'Amico

D'Amico introduces us to the Otavalans and shows how one songwriter, Galo Maigua, uses traditional music as a vehicle for his own social commentary. The stories his songs tell are accepted because he clothes them in a traditional musical form.

Introduction

These pages describe features of indigenous Otavalan culture and change as reflected in the discourse of three contemporary songs. The songs studied highlight aspects of individual creativity and repertoire within the context of storytelling in traditional Otavalan San Juan music. Galo Maigua, noted for his lyrical skills, spins tales woven from poignant descriptions of the ironies and mundaneness of quotidian life. He has created narratives that inspire enormous audience response, stories of affirmation and dissonance created from real-life images and actions that mirror cultural ethos, the deviation from which generates antiheroes. Maigua frames and performs his songs within traditional San Juan rhythms.

The Otavalans

Otavalans are an indigenous group who inhabit the inter-Andean valley about 20 miles north of the equator in Ecuador. They number about 40,000 and traditionally make their living as agriculturists and textile artisans. During the past 25 years, as a consequence of the influx of outsiders (tourists, missionaries, development workers, and social sci-entists), and transnational migrations of indige-nous peoples owing to international commerce in native handicrafts and the performance of folk mu-sic, community lifeways have been transfigured. Such cultural transformations underscore the in-teraction between innovations within persisting cultural systems. Song, as evidenced in this article, eloquently manifests the reformulation of cultural representations within changing boundaries.

San Juanito Music

Traditional San Juanito music endures as an ex-pression that helps to inscribe indigenous Otava-lan identity. The genre takes its name from Saint John's Day, June 24. According to archaeological and ethnohistorical evidence, the festival is rooted in pre-Colombian harvest and summer solstice rites. In Otavalo today, the holiday punctuates the end of harvest and the beginning of the dry and windy summer. The most prominent public ritual of the entire year, the San Juan celebration both constructs the present jubilantly and activates the collective memory and ethnic cohesiveness. "San Juanitos are like a message from the ancestors. They have always been an expression for indige-nous dance [and music]," commented an older musician. During the rural festival, elaborately costumed dancers perform, courtyard to court-yard, continuously for three or four days and nights. The rhythm of the extravaganza reso-nates; performers' bodies become idiophonic in-struments harmonizing with high-pitched song, mouth organs, charangos, guitars, panpipes, flutes, and drums. Dancers whirl their paths in circles clockwise and counterclockwise, piercing the earth and heavens with repetitive song in a trancelike spell.

The intensity and rhythm of the occasion resounds in people's memories not only during these days at the end of June each year, but throughout all the months of the calendar, in performances marking rites of passage in local communities and in recordings aired on the radio. To think of San Juan is to feel collectively and to establish a moral continuity with the past. By remembering San Juanitos, indigenous people actively construct a social reality that opposes hegemonic forms. San Juanitos have become a genre of music that interweaves meaning into the norms of daily as well as ritual life; they reaffirm traditions in the face of domination. San Juanitos outline the musical landscape as they touch the heart and soul of native sentiments; to read the past is to imagine the future.

Songwriter Galo Maigua has stated, "I feel our rhythm very strongly, the San Juánito, we indigenous people use it, and I have tried to create music for the future." Maigua encapsulates in song much of the emotional quintessence of Otavalan personhood by combining the familiar beat with standard and inventive discursive topics. Moreover, his music is a kind of audio forum, where some of the realities of a plural society are publicly discussed, and later commented upon, from an indigenous perspective. As his music resounds on the radio or at parties, it travels across the boundaries of cultural difference and helps to create a wider discursive field in multiethnic Ecuador.

"Ilumán Tío," A Song by Galo Maigua

Maigua is a very articulate man, married with seven children, who owns agricultural lands and looms. He lives in a sprawling housing compound with his father, brothers, and all their families. He started playing and composing music relatively late in life, when his wife gave him a guitar as a wedding gift, "with her own money." At that time, in 1973, Otavalan folk music was just beginning to be recognized internationally. His first composition, "Ilumán Tío," came to him after a very grave illness. He commented that it came to him as a result of being flat on his back and for some time lingering near death's door. Then inspiration struck him, "Why shouldn't I invent some-

thing, so when I die, people will dance and not be sad." A creative rebirth came after this close brush with death, and as a consequence of this life-threatening illness came Maigua's first song, "Ilumán Tío," and full recovery.

> *Ilumán tiu carani.*
> *Ilumán tiu nijungui.*
> *Soltere cashpa, paya cashpa*
> *nuca tunpi bailapai.*

> *Yo soy el indio de luman.*
> *Por eso toco este lindo Sanjuánito*
> *Para que bailen toditos,*
> *Para que bailen toditos.*

I was the comrade from Ilumán.
You said, comrade from Ilumán?
Young women, old women
please dance to my music (song).

I'm the Indian from Ilumán.
That's why I play this beautiful San Juánito
So that everyone may dance,
So that everyone may dance.

"Ilumán Tío," Maigua's first composition, is a bilingual (Quichua and Spanish) commemoration of indigenous identity through the repetitive beat of song, music, and dance. Maigua implies that his legacy may contribute to the affirmation of indigenous culture through joyous festivities. The appearance of this song in 1973 reflects the upsurgence of ethnic consciousness and marks a pivotal date in the indigenous movement. The music captivates interest and seemingly beats with a collective pulse. Many other musicians offer interpretations of this song, and it is especially popular today performed on the electric piano at weddings, baptisms, and housewarming parties. "Ilumán Tío" has become a classical San Juánito that has a lasting resonance in popular Quichua culture.

"Antonio Mocho," A Song by Galo Maigua

> *Antonio Mocho machashca yalicun*
> *Rosa milpac istancupi machashca.*
> *Huarmita macangapac rijushca.*
> *Jose Mono machashca jarcecun.*
> *Alcandi cani nishcami fahuacun.*

Antonio Mocho is really drunk

Drunk in Rosa Mila's bar.
He went to beat his wife.
A drunken Jose Mono is stopping him.
He is jumping about crying "I am the mayor!"

"Antonio Mocho" is a favorite song among Otavalans. It recounts the disharmonious behavior of the protagonist, who has become a kind of antihero in popular Quichua culture. Listeners respond to the piercing narrative in a very interested manner. The song relates an incident in the life of the community president, painting him as a drunken wife beater. The town official becomes the butt of public ridicule with Maigua's blatant social criticism.

Specifically the narrative informs the public of the questionable behavior of a public figure. The song frames events common in community life, and describes discord associated with drinking and between the sexes. Maigua commented that Antonio Mocho's wife is very grateful that he wrote the song because now Antonio Mocho seldom mistreats or beats her. Maigua went on to say that he might be performing at a wedding party, where of course there is always ritual drinking. He related that on the way home there were bound to be drunks who might mistreat their wives or behave in a dysfunctional fashion, but "in front of me there is no way!" His biting social commentary is celebrated by other music groups and in recordings.

"Lucita," A Song by Galo Maigua

Lucitagulla Tiagulla
Camba tunuta candinimi
Siquiera chaynishca mando
Ama nucata cungahuaychu.

Runa jintita saquishcapac
Gringo cuanhuan puricungul
Gringo cunhuan purishpaca
Gushtu gushtu me raugangui.

Dear companion, dearest Lucita
I sing your song
For all I have told you
Don't forget me.

Leaving your friends
you go around with gringos

And hanging out with them
you become fat like them.

Maigua's story, about and for Lucita, is entirely in Quichua. It is about a young woman who formerly headed the dance troupe of Grupo Ilumán, Maigua explained. Lucita stopped participating in dance and music when the gringos arrived, in this case the Mormons. She began to emulate Mormon ways and became fat and selfish. As a result of her new alliances with the Mormons, she does not even greet the members of the music group when she meets them on the street. Maigua pitied Lucita and wrote the song for her.

This song clearly illustrates some of the tensions produced when outside ideologies infiltrate rural communities. Mormons stress the importance of the individual, an idea that opposes the traditional Andean ethos of reciprocity and mutual cooperation. The song "Lucita" is a public shunning or informative commentary aimed to dissuade those who might assimilate gringo ways.

Discourse Cloaked in An Amicable Beat

Maigua's three songs give us intimate glimpses into contemporary issues and represent interesting facets of storytelling in Otavalo today. The genre of San Juanitos has a lasting resonance in indigenous culture and Maigua cloaks his discourse with the amicable beat well known to indigenous people, an effective communication strategy. His songs represent an example of alternative voices in cultural production on local and global levels. "Ilumán Tío" endorses the expression of indigenous identity through San Juanitos by outlining the link of music, song, and dance to generational continuity and celebration. "Antonio Mocho" represents some of the possible dissident perspectives within a culture. "Lucita" stands out as a critique of hegemonic influences in indigenous cultural production. Thus surveyed, the landscape of Otavalan culture is not uniform; rather, as expressed in Maigua's songs, it is contested from within and from outside pressures. The examples above are cultural expressions within the flow of historical time. The creative genius of Maigua lies in the mode of communication through which he makes Quichua voices heard in a pluricultural society.

Further Reading

D'Amico, Linda, *Expressivity, Ethnicity and Renaissance in Otavalo* (Ph.D. diss., Indiana University), 1993

D'Amico, Linda, and Alberto Muenala, *AY Taquicqu!* [Oh dear Musicmaker], Video, 1991

Guaranitic Storytelling

Martha Blache

Martha Blache discusses five Guaraní legends of the supernatural and shows how each functions in Guaraní society.

Guaraní Storytelling

Guaraní is the generic name for one of the most widespread ethnic groups in South America. Since the fourteenth century, the Guaraní have inhabited the eastern region of what is now Paraguay and adjacent areas of Brazil and Argentina. Interbreeding between Spaniards and Guaraníes occurred during the colonization period, and by the end of the eighteenth century a well-established mestizo population existed. Modern Paraguay still claims a strong Guaraní heritage and it is the largest bilingual country in Latin America. Since the middle of this century, political and economic conditions have brought about the emigration of increasing numbers of Paraguayans, particularly to Argentina.

Guaranitic storytelling enjoys full acceptance in Paraguay, where it is part of a collective tradition that has been registered by authors including Fortunato Toranzos Bardel, Eloy Fariña Núñez, Ramón Bejarano, Darío Gómez Serrato, and León Cadogán. We will refer to a portion of this Guaranitic storytelling tradition corresponding to what has been classified as mythical legends. They were collected among Paraguayan immigrants living in Buenos Aires, Argentina. The narrators came from small rural communities with a common cultural identity. Through the numerous variants of each legend, it was possible to reveal different aspects of the physical and cultural world of the original communities of the Paraguayan immigrants. It was possible as well to discern a structured system of beliefs, norms, values, and attitudes by means of which people give meaning to social interaction. The analysis of the narrative repertoire allowed us to distinguish what Annikki Kaivola-Bregenhoj has designated as cultural and cognitive context ("The Context of Narrating," pp. 153–166). The first refers to the culture in which the narrator operates and the world he discusses; the latter refers to the chain of mental associations of narrator and audience, since legend is a collective tradition. On the basis of these contexts, in this entry we will take into consideration three aspects of the mythical legends analysis: 1) the values each legend stresses, 2) the way the function of some social institutions is reinterpreted by the people, and 3) the cognitive mechanism each narrative mobilizes.

The *Pora*

One of the mythical legends is the *Pora*, considered to be the spirit of a person who, as a general rule, has died violently or tragically, as a consequence of a criminal act. It usually appears at night in certain fixed places. It can assume uncertain shapes or may present itself as an animal or human being that suddenly appears and disappears. Not only does it engender fear, but it may also cause physical or psychological damage. From the sanctions attributed by the community to the *Pora*, punishable forms of guilt can be deduced. Unlike the law, which is not concerned with an individual's life after death, custom assumes the responsibility for punishing transgression even after the death of the transgressor. Essentially, this belief story is concerned with the taking of life, either through suicide or murder. It implies that there is a superior force that regulates life, and that the individual may not decide his own fate.

The values that the *Pora* exhibits are the tragic manner of dying, the survival of the spirit, and the existence of another world similar to ours in that its sanctions are applied against transgressors. The function performed by the Catholic Church is to deliver into the world of the dead the tortured spirit that wanders in the world of the living. It achieves this through a Mass, the great liturgical act of the Roman Catholic Church. Some religious practices, such as carrying a religious medal or a crucifix, making the sign of the Cross, or praying, may contribute to deter the presence or the actions of the *Pora*. In the cognitive process of this mythical figure, we find that the two opposites, life and death, may be reconciled by means of an agreement and brought into harmony. The performance of a Mass, a prayer, or an act of charity contribute to the reconciliation.

The *Yasy Yateré*

The *Yasy Yateré* is a small being with childish aspect, pretty and fair-haired, who carries a golden walking stick in his hand. He announces himself by uttering a birdlike whistle, from which sound his name is derived. He appears at noon and coaxes the children who do not sleep at siesta to follow him into the forest, where he then deserts them. In a tropical climate, the siesta is the time of day in which all activity is suspended. At noon, after having lunch, people rest at home where they are protected from the strong sun and the intense heat. The *Yasy Yateré* stories promote the value of obedience to the elders by children who, tireless and overflowing with energy, resent interrupting their games in order to have a siesta. The role of the Roman Catholic Church is to bless or to "baptize anew" the child abducted by the *Yasy Yateré* so he may recover his speaking powers, mental faculties, understanding, or tranquillity. By these religious practices, the child is absolved of the disobedient act and reincorporated into society. The cognitive mechanism functioning in this legend shows that people justify a child's transgression by maintaining that it is involuntary. Here there is a double justification: the parents are not responsible because they were asleep at siesta, and the children are not responsible because they were irresistibly tempted to disobey their parents' warnings. Like all other societies, Paraguayan society recognizes that children are in the process of learning. They are being molded in accordance with social rules in order to become adults accustomed to these rules. Because chil-dren are still learning to adapt to their culture, they may be forgiven for occasional disobedience.

The *Pombero*

Another supernatural figure is the *Pombero,* who is described as a small, hairy, black being who usually appears at night. Even if he is not actually seen, he may be identified by his whistling or cheeping noises. His relationship with people is either inimical or friendly. His friendship may be acquired by simply leaving outside the house an offering of tobacco, honey, or alcohol. The *Pombero* reciprocates by offering various kinds of protection. He accompanies men along the intricate paths of the forest and assists them or protects them from risks. His enmity may be aroused through insult or provocation. If affronted, the *Pombero* retaliates by inflicting psychological or physical harm to the culprit or to his domestic animals. From time to time he may impregnate girls. The sexual relationship that the *Pombero* establishes is peculiar in that the woman is not aware of the fact that she has had sexual contact, even though she becomes pregnant. Offspring are attributed to the *Pombero* when paternity is unknown. The value that this belief story exhibits is the fear of darkness, which is fraught with insecurity and risk. Just as they are afraid of darkness, people are afraid of a social behavior that is not clearly defined, as in cases where people are "in the dark" about a child's paternity. The function of the Roman Catholic Church is to deter the *Pombero's* action by means of a prayer, the sign of the Cross, or the Baptism sacrament. In the cognitive mechanism, people coalesce the dangerous darkness that disturbs them in the *Pombero* story. This coalescence or concentration allows the individual to change what is amorphous and diffuse into the delineated so that he can better handle the risk, either through the support given by the church or through an ancestral rite. The people have two different systems to which they may appeal for help. If they appeal to the Guaraní heritage, they may win *Pombero's* favor, while if they resort to Hispanic practice, they avert his action. These different attitudes apparently express the characteristics the community attributes to the two main groups that constitute the present Paraguayan society.

The *Luisón*

The *Luisón* (a type of werewolf) is the seventh son of an uninterrupted series of boys. He transforms himself into a dog, usually on a Friday night, by rolling on the ground, in sand or ashes, and at dawn he resumes human form and returns home. His transformation does not occur of his own volition; he cannot prevent it although he may try. As a dog, he goes to the cemetery where he feeds on dead human bodies. In animal form, he attacks humans and tries to pass on his evil. As a person the *Luisón* is considered harmless, and he is easily seen in daily life. He is described as being of pronounced pallor, a weak and ill man. His behavior is unsociable; he runs away from people and his habits are aberrant: he does not work and rejects sexual relationships. He eats decomposed and rejected materials. In his human shape, the *Luisón* is a victim of collective suspicion and he ends up by behaving just as expected. The community that controls him in human form cannot control him in his animal form, thus it is involved in its own confabulation. The value that is stressed in this mythical legend is the fear of deviation from normal behavior. The individual who deviates from conventional patterns of behavior represents a risk for the community. The *Luisón* as such disintegrates the social codes applicable to speech, eating, work, or sex. At a symbolic level, the narratives show the community's necessary rejection of those members who stray or break its social codes. Through this belief legend people manifest support of social institutions—in particular, the church and its sacraments. The church may defeat destiny by baptizing the seventh son, having the president of the republic act as his godfather, or by blessing the bullets used by the police to kill the *Luisón*. The latter two possibilities show the dependence of government agents (the president and the police) on the church in order to be effective. The cognitive structure shows that society has created an individual upon whom it can unload the sanctions that would fall on disruptive members of society. The severe punishment that the *Luisón* has to suffer serves as a warning to all community members.

Hidden Treasure

The belief in *Hidden Treasure* gathered strength during the war Paraguay waged against Brazil, Uruguay, and Argentina in 1870. According to the legend, the Paraguayan government and individual citizens hid money in different places to avoid its sacking by the invading army. Often those who buried the treasure were shot to pre-vent divulgence of where they had hidden their wealth. The *Treasure* was and still is guarded by either the spirit of the owner or of the executed person. The presence of this spirit makes almost all search for the *Treasure* a dangerous enterprise. The *Hidden Treasure* shows itself by a profusion of visual, auditory, tactile, or olfactory perceptions but gives itself to whomever it chooses, having previously put the chosen person to a test. The values articulated through this narrative are the desire to obtain the well-being that riches may give and the striving for change. The limited function of the church in this legend is only that of intervener during the moment of the *Treasure's* actual extraction. Through religious mediatory action, the seeker avoids the *Hidden Treasure's* aggression. In the cognitive structure of this belief legend, there are certain latent analogies. Contained in the explicit desire to obtain the well-being that riches may give is the less obvious wish to recapture the prosperity reached by Paraguay during the nineteenth century, when it became one of the Latin American countries with the most opportunities for development. This era of power and glory has remained in popular memory as a period when Paraguay kept enormous riches in its coffers. With the war that destroyed Paraguay, prosperity came to a sudden stop. Before the war, rural workers were not particularly concerned with their social immobility because the context in which they lived was one of abundance. Today, they are still immobilized in their social stratum but also overcome by a widespread poverty, which stresses even more their marginal condition. Since the country's fate is out of the people's control, they center their potential personal well-being on the *Hidden Treasure*.

Other Mythical Legends

The mythical legends already mentioned are just a portion of the extensive repertoire concerning supernatural beings in force in the Guaranitic area. Many more legends live on, among which the most popular are *Curupí*, *Mala Visión*, and *Payé*, as collected by Fortunata Toranzos Bardel, Ramón Bejarano, León Cadogán, Nasim Yampey, Darió Gómez Serrato, Ernesto Ezquer Zelaya, and this author. All these folk narratives provide an insight into Paraguayan rural workers' worldview. Besides reflecting their cultural background, the mythical legends show the danger people attribute to certain environmental situations, and the uneasiness the individual feels about his subordination to forces of destiny, which he nevertheless tries to manipulate. The legends also disclose the attitude people have toward their social code; what behavior is subject to group disapproval; what happens to those individuals who deviate from the rules; the common attitude toward death and evil; and the people's reactions toward social change and institutional pressures. The folk narratives also reveal the role and function that the people assign to social institutions and how they evaluate their Guaraní and Spanish heritage.

Further Reading

Bejarano, Ramón, *Caraí Vosá*, Asunción, Paraguay: Editorial Toledo, 1960

Blache, Martha, *Estructura del Miedo: Narrativas Folklóricas Guaraníticas*, Buenos Aires, Argentina: Plus Ultra, 1982

Cadogán, León, "Chono Kybwyra: Aportes al Conocimiento de la Mitología Guaraní," in volume 3 of *Suplemento Antropológico de la Revista del Ateneo Paraguayo*, Asunción, Paraguay: Ateneo Paraguayo, 1968

Dégh, Linda, "Folk Narrative," in *Folklore and Folklife: An Introduction*, edited by Richard Mercer Dorson, Chicago: University of Chicago Press, 1972

Ezquer Zelaya, Ernesto, *Payé*, Buenos Aires, Argentina: El Ateneo, 1943

Fariña Núñez, Eloy, *Conceptos Estéticos, Mitos Guaraníes*, Buenos Aires, Argentina: Talleres Gráficos, M. Pastor, 1926

Gómez Serrato, Darío, "Del Folklore Paraguayo," *Folklore Americano* 16 (1969–70)

González, Gustavo, "Mitos, Leyendas y Supersticiones Guaraníes del Paraguay," in volume 2 of *Suplemento Antropológico de la Revista del Ateneo Paraguayo*, Asunción, Paraguay: Ateneo Paraguayo, 1967

Kaivola-Bregenhoj, Annikki, "The Context of Narrating," in *Folklore Processed: In Honour of Lauri Honko on His 60th Birthday, 6th March 1992*, Helsinki, Finland: Suomalaisen kirjallisuuden seura, 1992

Toranzos Bardel, Fortunato, *Alma Guaraní*, Asunción, Paraguay: América Sapucai, 1915

Yampey, Nasim, "Análisis de dos Mitos Sudamericanos: Kurupí y Yasy Yateré," in volume 4 of *Suplemento Antropológico de la Revista del Ateneo Paraguayo*, Asunción, Paraguay: Ateneo Paraguayo, 1969

We Are the Real People: Tzotzil-Tzeltal Maya Storytelling on the Stage

Robert Laughlin

Robert Laughlin discusses the 1983 formation of Sna Jtz'ibajom, The House of the Writer. *This is a Maya cultural cooperative in Chiapas formed to produce bilingual publications in Spanish and Tzotzil or Tzeltal. A puppet theater was formed to present these works to a wider audience. Well-known folktales were used at first, but later, humorous spoofs with didactic aims were added. In 1989, a live theater group continued the work.*

The Words of Long Ago

For the Tzotzil and Tzeltal Mayas of Chiapas, Mexico, whose glyphic books were burned by a seventeenth-century bishop, history has been kept alive through the spoken word, the woven textile, and religious dramatic expression.

"The word of long ago" includes what we would call myth, legend, folktale, fairy tale, and personal reminiscence. It ranges, then, from native folktales, including scenes from the *Popol Vuh*, spread throughout the Maya area, to accounts by the Conquistadors and Dominican friars of the travails of Cinderella and of Christ, transfigured by the Mayas in marvelous ways to conform to their worldview. Although much of the narrative is in ordinary everyday speech, there may be passages in formal speech, i.e., in semantic couplets.

The words of long ago may be told by grandparents and parents around the hearth, or, as in Zinacantán, by men when they travel to lowland cornfields where they spend the night. Although there are no official storytellers, particular individuals come to be known as skillful raconteurs.

Sna Jtz'ibajom, the House of the Writer

In 1982, after the Harvard Chiapas Project had terminated, three of its Tzotzil collaborators whom we had trained to be literate in their mother tongue came to me in distress. With the aid of the renowned Mexican poet Jaime Sabines, they had received funding from the poet's brother Juan, governor of Chiapas, to establish a writers' cooperative. But after publishing two bilingual booklets, their funds were exhausted. They had been sitting in the dark, for the light in their office was cut, and the governor's term was ending.

By chance, I was about to codirect a conference, "Forty Years of Anthropological Research in Chiapas," there, in San Cristóbal de las Casas. I urged them to plead their case before this assemblage of anthropologists and linguists, primarily from Europe and North America.

They spoke with passion of how the anthropologists who had studied in their towns had given them a new awareness of the value of their culture. Anthropologists had paid them to learn about their culture and their language, and had treated them with respect—not the treatment they received daily from the mestizos of San Cristóbal.

They assumed that our studies were good ones, but knew this was only an assumption since the studies were published in distant countries, in languages they couldn't read. Worse yet, in their towns where many changes were occurring, the younger generation, attending school, thought they were smarter, and though they didn't know a quarter of what their grandparents knew about their culture, their grandparents were taking their knowledge to the grave. For the sake of their children and their grandchildren, they asked the scholars to help them in their mission to record, at least on paper, the history of their lives, their customs, and their beliefs.

With a grant of $3,000 seed money from Cultural Survival, Inc., *Sna Jtz'ibajom* (The House of the Writer) was born in 1983, the first cultural cooperative in Chiapas, and one of the first in the nation to be run by Indians. The founders laughed over the name they had chosen, how no mestizo would be able to pronounce it. They have seen since how no editor has been able to spell it. For their logo, they adopted fittingly the figure of a classic Maya scribe.

Teatro Lo'il Maxil, Formation of a Puppet Theater

Because the Mexican government had virtually abandoned bilingual education, our booklets were read, if at all, only in Spanish. Perhaps presenting their contents in puppet theater would attract a readership. (It did not.) After a two-week workshop directed by Amy Trompetter of the Bread and Puppet Theater, where she trained the writers to make papier-mâché hand puppets, we were on the road.

Twenty-five years before, the government, with the aid of the novelist Rosario Castellanos, had introduced puppet theater to "civilize" the Indian. Despite its popularity, it conferred no prestige on the Indian puppeteer.

Our *Teatro Lo'il Maxil* (Monkey Business Theater), to establish its Indian identity, began with well-known folktales, such as the newlywed whose wife's head disappears at night mysteriously to eat corpses. Gradually, didactic pieces were added to spoof monolingual education, alcoholism, and both traditional and modern medicine. But at first, one of the writers, a highly respected shaman, was so nervous that not only did he not wish to be seen in his community in the role of a puppeteer, but he did not even want his voice to be heard and recognized. The members limited their participation to showings in communities where they were not known. Despite this, they remember being so nervous that they cowered behind the curtain, their bodies soaked with

sweat as they gulped down cane liquor to give them courage.

But the personalities of the puppets became an integral part of our society. When a representative of the Inter-American Foundation came to inspect our project they provided her with "an unorthodox profile" of their members, drawing on the characters of a tale in which Zinacantec merchants are castrated by the Guatemalans and then saved by a team of animals and natural forces:

Maryan—Thunderbolt, who makes so much noise, but is, indeed, the strongest leader.

Antzelmo—Whirlwind, who rushes around to make sure that everything is in order.

Xun—Fog, who approaches each problem from every conceivable angle until we are so befogged that we always accept his solution as being the best.

Xap—Hawk, who dives down, knocking us aside to do what he knows is right.

Machyo—Blowfly, who eagerly tackles all the dirty jobs, washes his hands clean and cheerfully begins again.

Tziak—Butterfly, who glides about silently, observing everything, and then keeps us well informed.

The puppeteers write the dialogue in Tzotzil, Tzeltal, and Spanish and learn the lines by heart, but there is tremendous liberty, creative invention, and improvisation when the puppets are in action. Some of the puppeteers are adept at including the public by having the puppet direct questions to them. And at the end of the performance, a puppet demands that the public clap hands.

Presentation of the theater in the communities required in the beginning the approval of the civil officials and cooperation from the schoolteachers, who often provided benches for the audience and announced the theater's arrival over their loudspeaker. Before long, the theater had gained such popularity that it was receiving 15 to 20 invitations a month. Generally, it is set up at the courthouse door or in what in many communities is the social center of the town—on the cement basketball court. The children sit or stand in front, behind them the men, and in the rear, the women, sometimes on school benches. For a time, the puppet theater became a basic ingredient of school holidays. The daylong basketball tournament would be followed by the puppet theater, often in very remote hamlets that could only be reached on foot.

At a linguistic meeting in Antigua, Guatemala, after our puppetry was roundly applauded, Nicholas Hopkins and Kathryn Josserand shoved a stack of papers at us, saying that this was a Ch'ol folktale and that the puppeteers had performed so well they should act out the tale the next day. The Indians' response was, "How dare they?" As we ate our lunch in the market, our one mestizo member enthusiastically read with determination a synopsis of the folktale, but no one would listen, as they called for basket after basket of the tiny Guatemalan tortillas. Retiring to the hotel room, he began to read the story. Soon the puppeteers were sitting up, listening to the dialogue, and when he got on the floor and demonstrated the paddling of a canoe, everyone became a paddler. They learned the lines, acted out their parts, giving the role of Thunderbolt to the senior member, who threatened to act his part naked unless he were given some cane liquor first. Lacking a woman performer, one of the group was chosen to be Frog, wearing a green dress. They decided I should be the Crocodile and rolled me up in blue plastic sheeting, instructing me to take a bite out of Thunderbolt's leg. It was the memory of this performance that a year later bolstered the puppeteers' confidence enough that they considered becoming actors in live theater.

Working together in San Cristóbal and traveling together with the theater created an atmosphere then very rare in Chiapas; differences of town origin, nationality, race, language, age, and gender, although always apparent, lost much of their divisive impact.

Febrero Loco Live Theater

In 1989, we brought Ralph Lee, director of the Mettawee River Company in New York, to initiate a program whereby, every *"Febrero Loco (Crazy February),"* as the month is known locally, he would direct the creation of a new play based on local material. Each morning, standing in a circle, everyone joined Ralph as he shook, stretched, and swirled his head, torso, and limbs, stuck out his tongue, jumped, and emitted every sound imaginable, some at full volume. Or bent at the waist, their arms sweeping the floor, he had them trying to look like elephants snuffling after peanuts. For Mayas who are trained to keep their voices low and their gestures measured, this was a difficult introduction to the theater. Next, one member was to choose an improvisation, enact it in the center, then pass it on to another who would mirror it and create his or her own to be passed on again.

Particularly for the women, at first, the exercise was an embarrassing, fearsome experience that sometimes was enacted in the privacy of the rehearsal room, but often in a green meadow where Indian passersby would stop and gape.

Gradually, their inhibitions and the personal preoccupations they brought with them each morning receded. Physical awkwardness was replaced by ease of movement, and they projected their voices strongly. There was also a growing camaraderie, uniting everyone.

The scripts are developed collaboratively, theoretically by every member of the group. They are written in Spanish, for although the Tzeltal writers have learned Tzotzil, the Tzotzil writers are only bilingual. With no warning, and no hesitation, the actors may shift a performance from Spanish to Tzotzil. The veteran actors have become so sophisticated that when revising the scripts they will say, "A comma is needed there!" to permit a pause.

Personal Impact

For a Mayan woman to agree to work with a group of males and to present herself to the public on stage takes tremendous courage. The father of one actress asked her, "Why don't you get a decent job and be a maid?" This, even though it is common knowledge that Indian maids frequently are sexually abused by their mestizo employers. The first time a woman acted in one of the plays, an Indian spectator exclaimed, "You must have bought her!"

For men it has been difficult performing the role of a saint or of Christ as they fear that the Mayan audience will accuse them of perverting their Mayan Catholicism or of using it for personal gain. Cultural constraints have been very strong. A woman refused to be rolled up in a straw mat because, although this was a scene in a traditional folktale, in her town they used to bury the dead in that manner. In a play that chronicles the life of Christ, they did not dare hang Our Lord on the cross for that would be competing with Good Friday's religious ceremony in the churches. One actor was deeply disturbed by a scene in a play recreating the Spanish conquest where the friar orders the general to burn the Indian leader. "But I am a Catholic, too!"

It is exciting to behold the gradual development of confidence; before long, individuals who have been cautious or shy suddenly begin to flourish in many endeavors: writing, photography, radio, weaving, community affairs. Two of *Sna Jtz'ibajom's* actresses became Mexico's first Indian women playwrights. Raised to suffer in silence, the women realized that they had gained a new voice, a new strength.

Social Impact

The actors believe that it is very important for a play to have a message and to create a dialogue with the audience. As with the puppet theater, the live theater's first productions were based on folktales. The first two plays' messages pointed to traditional values: industriousness, respect, proper religious belief. The third play was based not on myth, but on gossip—a case where two brothers murdered their sisters to gain their land. In this play, the traditional goal of settling disputes within the community was championed, as was justice for women, but in the course of the play, modern Maya women's complaints were aired. Perhaps influenced by this play, the two actress/playwrights began to take a more prominent role in the association. The men from Zinacantán would not perform in a play written by Petrona de la Cruz that focused on domestic abuse, saying that these were her personal problems. Unthinkingly, we had dressed the actors in the clothing of Zinacantán so that Petrona's fellow Zinacantecs felt that this was a direct attack on their town.

Eventually the two women, believing that they were the butt of male discrimination, defiantly established their own all-female cooperative and theater, *La Fortaleza de la Mujer Maya* (The Empowerment of Mayan Women), (FOMMA), in which women took the male roles and addressed these problems with their own voices. This precluded the Zapatista women's demands for cultural change in what is still a markedly patriarchic society.

Unlike *Sna Jtz'ibajom's* productions, which always laced the dark scenes with a Brechtian humor, the women's first plays were deadly serious. "Domestic abuse is not a laughing matter!" they protested. But now they have rebounded with humor. Even the plays' titles have evolved from *Una mujer desesperada* (A Desperate Woman), to *Infierno y Esperanza* (Hell and Hope).

After the Zapatista Rebellion broke out, some of *Sna's* men now wanted to address social issues comprehensively. With considerable resistance by the Zinacantecs, who wished to steer clear of politics and focus on the safe issue of ecology, they explored the possibility of creating a play devoted to the causes of the Zapatista Rebellion. Finally, *De todos para todos* (From All for All) dramatized how mestizo rule had destroyed the relationship between man and nature, and man and the gods. Performing this play in Chiapas, and witnessing the audience's often passionate response, even the cautious Zinacantecs were soon espousing the demands of the Zapatistas. In the scene where the Indian woman turns to the men and cries out, *"¿A poco ustedes no son hombres?"* ("You mean you aren't real men?") and pledges to unite the women in resistance to the government, the entire audience, both sexes, invariably cheers. Within the cooperative and without, attitudes are changing.

Continuing their social concern, the theater has traveled to Immokalee, Florida, where it has trained the Guatemalan, Mexican, and Haitian fieldhands to create their own theater. Together, the members of *Sna* and the Coalition of Immokalee Workers produced a play, *Don Tomate y sus Coyotes* (Mr. Tomato and his Coyotes), that dramatizes the fearful border crossing, the agonizing van ride across the country, the bloody violence, and economic exploitation of the workers, culminating in the workers' protests and creation of the Coalition. This play is to be revised and performed in Chiapas to demonstrate that it is not so easy to get a pot of gold across the border.

Just as in traditional Maya oral literature, oral history continuously adapted important events, important themes to current realities, so, too, does theater. The words of long ago and the words of today, at home or on the stage, pronounce with conviction and with a laugh, "We are the real people!"

Further Reading

Breslin, Patrick, "Coping with Change, the Maya Discover the Play's the Thing," *The Smithsonian Magazine* (May 1994)

Collier, George, and Elizabeth Quaratiello, *Basta!: Land and the Zapatista Rebellion in Chiapas*, Oakland, California: Food First Book, The Institute for Food and Development Policy, 1994

Wilson, Carter, *Crazy February,* Philadelphia: Lippincott, 1965

_____, *A Green Tree and a Dry Tree*, New York: Macmillan, 1972

Fragments From the Past: The Politics of Storytelling in Morelos, Mexico

JoAnn Martin

JoAnn Martin takes us to Morelos, Mexico, first circa 1984 and again in 1991. We see the ancianos, the elders, effecting controls over the distribution of land, using story to demonstrate their points. By 1991 the ancianos *and their stories were no longer an effective part of the political scene.*

Morelos, Mexico 1984, 1991

The United States is currently enjoying a resurgence of storytelling. Local libraries offer children's story hours while universities and colleges encourage adults to enroll in courses devoted to writing biographies. Witnessing this resurgence in my own community, I am moved to tell a story of stories and their decline in the community of Morelos, Mexico, where I have conducted research since 1984. When I first visited Morelos, I was moved by the passionate tales elders told during political meetings and by the fact that the respect these tales garnered gave elders a continuing power in the community. But, by 1991, when I returned to Morelos to carry out additional research, these tales were no longer part of the daily public practices of community life. How did this happen, and what changes in Morelos politics accompanied this shift in the position of the storyteller? The answer may be instructive for broadening our understanding of the contemporary resurgence of storytelling.

Storytelling as Defense

I did not go to Buena Vista to study storytelling, but I soon understood that storytelling nurtured passions that inspired the struggle to defend communal land, land that by law could be inherited, but not bought or sold. Prices of private property had risen exponentially in the 1980s, and Buena Vistans correctly reasoned that if all land entered the private property market, their children and grandchildren would be unable to remain in the town. Despite this strong sense of the importance of communal land, the struggle to defend communal land confronted many obstacles, not the least of which was the questionable status of the legal category of "communal" land.

Mexican agrarian law up until 1991 protected a category of communal land tenure usually defined as *ejido* land. *Ejidos* were formed by the Mexican government after the revolution (1910–1920). As Arturo Warman points out in *"We Come to Object": The Peasants of Morelos and the Nation State,* the postrevolutionary state used the formation of *ejidos* to co-opt the revolutionary struggle in Morelos and to solidify control of the national government over land. But, although the postrevolutionary state developed its own narrative about land redistribution in which the state figured as the hero, the government could not control the alternative versions of the history of land redistribution that survived in the words of storytellers in Morelos.

Buena Vistan storytellers stress that their rights to land depend not on government largesse but on the historic struggles of their ancestors, who defended the town's land. In distinction to the Mexican state's version of history, Buena Vistans trace their communal land to a declaration of Emiliano Zapata, leader of the Mexican revolution in the south. They represent the revolution as another battle in the town's long history of defense of land. Because their land is not, then, a gift from the government, but an inheritance from their ancestors, they are obliged to defend the land even against government development projects. The storytellers in the Committee to Defend Communal Land reinforced this sense of obligation to the past and the loyalties to community it inspired.

A young teacher exerted a good deal of influence within the Committee, but Committee meetings were run by a group of three *ancianos* (male elders) who seasoned discussions of contemporary conflicts with brief, and often not-so-brief, tales of the past. *Ancianos* represented the past as a period of uncontested bravery in defense of community, the embodiment of timeless moral truths, in which families and neighbors treated one another with respect and those in official position cared about the community. The Committee drew on the memories of the elders in handling conflicts over communal land. For example, when an outsider (someone not born and raised in Buena Vista) argued that he had purchased private property legally, the young teacher informed him that the land he had purchased could not have been private property. The teacher explained, "In Cuernavaca they [bureaucrats in the Department of Agrarian Reform] cannot distinguish between private property and communal land. The reason you were called in was because some old people who know Buena Vista's history remembered that there was a road there. They know what is communal land and what isn't and these old people said that there was a road there."

The *Ancianos* Speak in 1984

In 1984, *ancianos* never hesitated to interrupt meetings with richly woven tales of past struggles, often deployed didactically to inform the resolution of contemporary problems. Three months into my research, Margarita, a young woman in her early 20s with three children and no husband, began to come to the Office of Communal Resources on a regular basis to request a plot of land. Each time, the commissioner told her that there was no land available. She began assisting the Committee in its inspections of communal land, and gradually opinion shifted toward an understanding that Margarita deserved land. The

vice commissioner, a man in his late 70s, spoke in favor of her request and, when a large landowner was caught taking over communal land, pointed to Margarita's case: "How can some have so much and this poor woman does not even have a piece of land on which to build her house?!"

One day when Margarita asked if she could have a plot of land, the vice commissioner replied,

> I remember how we started the Colonia Esperanza. Doña Juanita had been kicked out of the house that she was renting. She went to the Commissioner of Communal Resources and asked for a plot of land, but he told her that there was none. Then, she came to me. I told her to get her things together and we would go up on the Mountainside and build her a house. She brought all kinds of things: sticks, iron, whatever scraps she could find. We built her a house. Then, we went to the commissioner and told him to come up and measure the piece of land. There was nothing he could do but give her the land because with her flimsy house she had demonstrated her need. That was the beginning of the Colonia Esperanza. Today there are twenty families living there.

Margarita heard this story several times before she finally realized that she was being told how to get land. One day when the Committee took back communal land from a wealthy man, she took her wood and corrugated iron and a few cardboard boxes to the spot. There she built her house. When I asked the vice commissioner about her actions, he told me the story of the settlement of Colonia Esperanza, concluding, "there is nothing we can do—she has demonstrated her need."

In contrast to the state's emphasis on the role of government in solving problems, the *ancianos* stressed ordinary people who through bravery and perseverance resolved their own problems. These local-level narratives accorded significance to the little things that Buena Vistans do in their everyday lives. When Doña Juanita went to Colonia Esperanza to build her house, she was only a poor woman who had no place to live. Today, in the tales of Buena Vistans, she is the founder of a *colonia*. Told in the context of Margarita's present-day housing problem, the story of Doña Juanita becomes a reminder of Margarita's connection to the past struggles and her potential in the town's history.

While the narratives of the *ancianos* subverted

the power structure of the state, they reinforced a different power structure, one in which *ancianos* wielded power in the name of preserving tradition. The *ancianos* who held power in the Committee to Defend Communal Land were a privileged group who had gained considerable rhetorical skills in the 1930s and 1940s when each had served as commissioner of *ejido* land, a government position. These skills were clearly visible in their storytelling practices. After listening carefully for some time to heated discussions an *anciano* leader would stand and request the floor—a request that was not really a request. "Listen youngsters, I remember when . . ." The tale that followed was a total performance involving not only language play, but also a choreographed mime in which sombreros might be thrown on the ground, bodies straightened in confrontation with an imagined bureaucrat, and drinks downed as agreements were vividly recalled for a captive audience. The youngsters— some of whom were in their 40s—listened while the *ancianos* reminded them of a better day when the people were united and brave in their confrontations with the wealthy and with the state.

The *anciano* leaders donned the garments of poor peasants and rejected the outward manifestations of wealth such as indoor plumbing, but while serving as *ejido* commissioners many had accumulated land. As one *anciano* explained, "Of course I took a little for myself because I knew that I loved the land and would protect it." Too old to farm the land they had accumulated and with most of their children now engaged in salaried professions, they lent land to poorer newcomers who in turn gave their political loyalties to their newfound patrons.

1988, a New Democracy

By 1988 the politics of Buena Vista had changed drastically, partly in response to events taking place at the national level. For the first time in more than seventy years, the power of the Institutional Revolutionary Party to control the national presidential elections was questioned. The son of former president Lazaro Cardenas, Cuauhtemoc Cardenas, had left the Institutional Revolutionary Party to challenge its designated presidential candidate, Salinas de Gortari, with a campaign based on a return to his father's commitment to poor, peasant farmers. Buena Vistans found themselves drawn to a new promise of democracy as newspaper articles and radio and television broadcasts began to discuss the possibility that the ruling party would be defeated. The Committee to Defend Communal Land, which by 1988 had been transformed into an umbrella organization for a host of local-level, self-help groups, was renamed the Democratic Coordinator. The new name reflected deeper shifts in power. A group of young people, most schooled in the radical democratic ideals of liberation theology, had emerged as the new community leaders. Meetings were more tightly organized with an emphasis on prompt arrival and moving through a set agenda. Those who led the meetings encouraged everyone to speak, often begging for participation from members who had little practice in public speaking. Incontrast to the male-dominated structure of the Committee to Defend Communal Land, most members of the Coordinator were women, and women participated in running meetings.

The emerging participatory democracy seemed at odds with the old culture that revered the *ancianos*' tales of the past. As one *anciano* leader of the Committee had told me on numerous occasions, "In the old days there were no divisions here. When it came time to choose a new mayor, the *ancianos* came together and chose the person. Then they announced to the people who the mayor would be and everyone applauded. It was not until the Parties came that the community was divided, and then we could not get anything done. Now there is no respect."

Many of the *ancianos* no longer attended meetings, claiming that they had tired of politics or had stopped attending meetings when confrontations with other Buena Vistan political groups became violent. Those who did attend the meetings listened quietly at the doors rarely offering a story or volunteering to speak. As one *anciano* complained, "They want everyone to speak but not everyone has the same knowledge. Sometimes the people need to hear from those who know more." When speakers did initiate what promised to be a lengthy dialogue, they were politely reminded by those running the meeting that others in the room also had things to say. At one meeting between the Coordinator and an ecological group, an 80-year-old member of the Committee/Coordinator began to explain the history of the town's land struggles starting with the Mexican revolution. He was not far into his story when the young leader of the ecological group interrupted him with reassurances that his knowledge would be of great value in this struggle but at this time the group really needed to move on with its agenda.

Stories of the past had not disappeared entirely from the landscape of Buena Vista political practices, but the stories and their tellers slipped from the main stage of politics to the shadows. Now, *ancianos* shared stories amongst themselves or with members of their immediate families. But the aura that surrounded public storytelling—its compelling invocation of truth, its ability to command moral authority and its power to inculcate passionately held political agendas—seemed to have been lost.

The *Ancianos* Stories as a Disrupter of the Social Order

My purpose in telling this tale of stories and their demise is not to lament the passing of a tradition. As pointed out, the *ancianos* who told these tales were a privileged minority and their invocations of tradition, although useful for subverting the state, reinforced a power structure in which older men dominated younger men and women. Meetings did run more efficiently when they followed an agenda and perhaps the increases in attendance reflected support for the changes. Moreover, as Womack's book on the revolutionary leader Emiliano Zapata suggests, changes in the form and style of leadership have been an ongoing part of Morelos politics. Nonetheless, I think the decline of storytelling in the context of meetings is instructive for broadening our understanding of narrative.

As Paul Ricoeur has noted, the structure of narrative has the power to take a listener or reader through the passage of time. I find a marked difference, though, between the spontaneous generation of stories in the context of contemporary conflicts and the setting aside of a story time. Clearly, the ritualized telling of stories, complete with rules about when and where and in whose company historical narratives should be told, is not at odds with the preservation of a sense of history, but the unruly telling of stories as part of everyday practices lends those stories a doubly subversive quality. In Buena Vista, the stories of

ancianos did not just remind their listeners of the passage of time. Rather, the *ancianos'* stories disrupted a social order that was becoming increasingly dominated by a pragmatic and rational use of time. The importance of the *ancianos'* stories was not so much embedded in the themes of the story as in the practice of telling the story, a point made quite eloquently by Michel de Certeau.

As De Certeau stresses, memory is an invisible fund of knowledge that in the form of a story of the past, intervenes in and disrupts power arrangements. The art of narrative is not only in the telling of the tale but also in the discerning eye and ear that seizes the perfect moment for a story, taking full advantage of the surprise element that forever transforms the situation (pp. 77–90).

As my three-year-old rushes gleefully into storytime, where he will listen intently to a remarkably skilled storyteller, I find myself wondering how we might cultivate a less orderly telling of tales. I always ask that he repeat the stories to his father and grandmother when he comes home, but I find that I cannot teach, although perhaps I can model, that wonderful seizing-of-the-moment I had the privilege to observe in Buena Vista in 1984.

Further Reading

Certeau, Michel de, "Story Time," in *The Practice of Everyday Life*, Berkeley: University of California Press, 1984

Price, Richard, *First-Time: The Historical Vision of an Afro-American People*, Baltimore, Maryland: Johns Hopkins University Press, 1983

Ricoeur, Paul, *Time and Narrative*, translated by Kathleen Blamey and David Pellauer, Chicago: University of Chicago Press, 1984

Warman, Arturo, *"We Come to Object": The Peasants of Morelos and the National State*, translated by Stephen K. Ault, Baltimore, Maryland: Johns Hopkins University Press, 1980

Womack, John, *Zapata and the Mexican Revolution*, New York: Knopf, 1969; London: Thames and Hudson, 1969

Storytelling and Mental Representation Among Totonac Indians (Mexico)

Annamária Lammel

Annamária Lammel discusses historical legends and religious myths of the Totonac-speaking people. She shows how these legends and myths are played out in the lives of the people through ritual, dance, and community action and suggests the function of myth and legend in community identity.

Fieldwork in Totonac Communities

This article studies the topic of storytelling and mental representation among Totonac Indians today. The Totonac Indians live in the state of Veracruz and in the northern part of the state of Puebla in Mexico. They are agriculturalists. The Totonac language is spoken by approximately 120,000 persons. Because of the absence of a larger social structure the Totonac communities undertook to safeguard their language and culture separately in different communities. These communities, which appear homogeneous from the outside, have an intricate inner organization that is indispensable to their survival in the mestizo Mexican environment. This article is based on data gathered in fieldwork (1982, 1985/86, 1991, 1992, 1993, 1995) mainly in two villages (Coahuitlan and Plan de Hidalgo) in the state of Veracruz (Lammel and Nemes 1988; Lammel 1994, 1995, 1997).

From the important storytelling activities of the Totonacs we will present some principal aspects of the mythical historical storytelling practices.

Storytelling, Mental Ideas, and External Representations

The majority of the narrative stories of today's Totonacs are still myths. We consider myths to be products of human logical thinking that organize and explain the nonexperimental, fundamentally belieflike elements of cultural knowledge. Among the Totonacs, as in all societies, concrete, practical-experimental knowledge completes the mythical one. Thus the mythical representations of the world complete experimental-empirical representations. The two types of knowledge can of course appear in mixed forms, and it often occurs that the two kinds of representation turn up within the same text that is regarded as mythical.

In the framework of recent cognitive research mental representations of narratives are not equal to the linguistic representations of narratives but are a larger semantically coded system of ideas that reflect the real or imaginary world of the narrative stories (Garnham 1987; Harré and Gillet 1994). Traditional knowledge is a mentally integrated system of ideas that determines the verbal, ritual, social, and everyday behavior of the members of a culture. The mental representation of mythical narrative knowledge is determined on one hand by logical, linguistic, and figurative organization in *mental models* and on the other hand by *mental ideas* that are semantic units and rules for the regulation of behavior.

The mythical side of thinking is also apparent in external representations other than myths. Besides the so-called myth, mythical ideas can become manifest in many other verbal forms. The discourse named as "myth" by anthropologists is identified by the local people as "ancient talk," "wise talk," "talk believed to be true," "advice," etc. Today's storytelling practices among the Totonacs consist not only in the oral transmission of myths or other narratives but also in the transmission of mythical ideas by rituals and other activities.

Research in mythology has directed attention to the correlation between mythical texts and rites, or between mythical stories and figurative representations. Each of these forms can transmit the same system of ideas in a different external form. They can perform the same kind of mythical story in another way.

But the mythical ideas that we observe in Totonac culture do not get stuck at the level of festive representations, since they have a role in everyday activities. Totonacs tell stories with their everyday activities. For example, myth instructs people how to make maize grow faster and yield more. As they work day by day, agriculturalists are engaged in putting a mythical idea into practice; agricultural practices follow the instructions of mythical stories.

The mythical idea can regulate the behavior of a community. The idea of collective representation, another way to understand the idea of the behavior of a community, has been given increasing attention in the field of social psychology. A mythical idea may be correlated with the institutional forms.

A scheme of what has been stated so far is shown in the box below:

Research on Totonac populations shows that the mythical narrative idea has a kind of autonomous existence and that it can be activated in different external forms as required by individuals or the entire society. So storytelling is a larger activity than the simple oral transmission of narratives.

The Mythical Historical Ideas and Their External Representations

On examining the historical knowledge of the Totonacs no concepts in the Western sense should be expected. The mythical historical narrative includes all topics past and present and even into the future. However, these topics do not unfold in a linear fashion; time's dimensions are relative and interchangeable in the mythical narrative. Accordingly, the topics encompassed in mythical historical narrative in today's Totonac culture are as follows:

1. The history of the natural world around us.
2. The history of humankind.
3. The common history of humankind and of the supernatural world.
4. The history of the humanmade world.
5. The history of the events of humankind.
6. The personally experienced history.

Our analyses suggest that the mythical historical mental representations function differently for text, rites, images as follows the logical, inherent potentialities of the mental models in the external form of representation.

The objective of the mythical historical narrative is to present changes that have occurred through time in our world. In essence, all mythical historical representations present at least one important change in the state of the world. This change in the state of the world's processes is the time itself.

External representations of the mythic narrative mental idea and their relationship

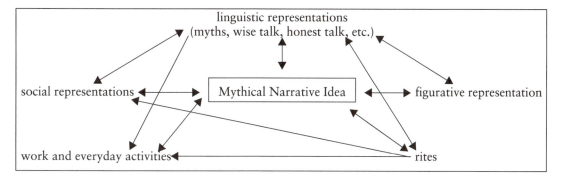

Oral Storytelling of Historical Myths and Today's Social Reality: Processes of Symbolization and Concretization in the Myth of the Conquest of Mexico

I will present a short analysis of an interesting historical myth that I call the myth of Aktzini. The Totonac Indians have lengthy narratives that describe historical events that took place after the Great Flood. These texts are closed formal and contextual units, their beginning and end separate them from everyday language. The members of the community are familiar with these narratives, but naturally not all of them are able to relate them. The stories can only be told in the Totonac language.

My analysis is built on a single myth; the essential features of any phenomenon can be demonstrated on the basis of one sample.

There lived a king, Aktzini, with his body made from water, who punished his disobedient subjects by devouring them. The king/chief wanted his daughter to sleep with his brother-in-law, Kuahtemek, who was at the same time her maternal uncle. But the girl was repulsed by the idea and was scared of being devoured. The girl's mother also wanted to talk her into obeying her father's intention and the girl was in deep distress and did not want to live anymore. She went to Santa Cruz (Mexico) and moaned below a crucifix. An eagle descended next to her and asked her why she was so sad. The girl told the eagle the reason for her distress. The eagle offered to save the girl if she brought him her father's pair of glasses, which he kept in bed. The girl fulfilled his request and at dawn she set off on the wings of the eagle and arrived in Spain. In Spain the people did not know where the girl had come from. She could not tell where she had come from either because she had not seen anything while flying on the eagle's wings.

She was taken to the house of Hernan Cortés. The girl refused to eat boiled meat, she only ate raw meat. Four masses were said for her, after which she was willing to eat boiled meat and she was baptized, too. She was asked what her homeland was like and she answered that it was more beautiful than Spain. Then she took the pair of glasses of her father and the people saw through them Mexico, which was beautiful and the houses were built from gold.

Cristobal Colon set out on board his ship to have a look at Mexico. The trip took very long

and the Spaniards wanted to kill the girl because they had been sailing for two months without seeing any dry land. But then the water drifted tree leaves to the ship and then a carved stick which indicated that they had come to a region populated by people. The Spaniards disembarked with the girl in Veracruz. Here they started to explode buildings, including the office of Veracruz where power was situated. The Spanish only wanted to rob. This was soon realized by Kuahtemek who had become king following the death of Aktzini. He too devoured people. Hernan Cortés engaged in war with Kuahtemek. Cristobal Colon and Cortés began to argue. They only robbed. Kuahtemek saw that these were bad lords and ordered his people not to give them anything to eat or drink. The Indians burnt the bridge and threw stones at the Spanish. Hernan Cortés managed to escape only with great difficulty. The robbed money was all lost in the lake. Cortés cried sadly under a tree called Awuawete. (A more complete version was told in Cohuitlan in 1986 by Antonio Jimenez in the Totanac language in an hour and a half session. "Kuahtemek" is the Totanac name of the historical figure Cuauhtémoc.)

The Totonac Indians, as they told us, regard this story as one of the moments of their history; they believe that it is true. The story is not a myth for them, but an example of "honest talk." I use the term myth here in the traditional anthropological sense. The majority of researchers define the so-called historical myths, like myths in general, as narratives that represent beliefs related to the world, gods, and people. Others, diametrically opposed to this view, emphasize the value of historical myths; moreover, they consider them as history.

I think that a historical myth can be the fruit of the symbolic interpretation of reality and that it can also be constituted by events that actually took place and have been preserved by oral tradition. In Aktzini's myth historical facts (described by scientific history) play as important a role as do the symbols. The transfer of the profane into the myth does not result in its symbolization. Bases of knowledge of a different origin stand behind the two types of process. One is the historical knowledge based on symbolization that follows the internal time and space rules of the mythical narratives, while the other knowledge is to be taken at face value, or eventually interpreted in metaphors.

The Symbols and the Connection of Symbols

The story of Aktzini contains both independent symbols and symbols in relation to certain moments of the story or the whole text. To interpret these symbols is a difficult task, as there are very few publications about the narrative of the Totonacs. (Horcasita 1962; Ichon 1969; Oropeza 1947; Williams Garcia 1980). A more extensive meso-American comparison offers a hypothetical indirect explanation.

The independent symbols are grouped around the four Mexican actors of the story: Aktzini, the girl, Kuahtemek, and the eagle. The meaning of the name Aktzini was not known by the storyteller. "Pos lak katsi, xman Aktzini, Rey." (Well, do not anything else, Aktzini, king.) Among the Totonacs on the seashore the word Aktzini means lightning, thunder. In this myth Aktzini represents violence, and by devouring people probably represents the power derived from human sacrifice—Aktzini was willing to sacrifice his own daughter. A similar role is played by Kuahtemek. He too symbolizes power, devouring people and presenting human sacrifices. His role in connection with the Spanish will be discussed later.

Aktzini's daughter escapes from incest. She can be the symbol of innocence. She can symbolize also the refusal to obey, even betrayal.

The figure of the eagle is intertwined with the sun in Aztec mythology (Sahagún 1956, 2:258–62). At the same time the eagle symbolizes warriors; one of the Mexican military units was named eagle (Robelo 1980, 1:141). But in this story the eagle plays the role of the magic helper. He is the one to plan the escape; he talks the girl into stealing the spectacles. These actions precipitate war with Spain and the end of the Aztec empire.

There is in Aztec mythology a goddess, a female eagle who is the goddess of war (Robelo 1980, 2:128). It may assumed that the girl and the eagle symbolize war together. Although the eagle devoured people, it is a creature who could also partake in power at some level. If we take into account that Aktzini and Kuahtemek represent the power of the king who is feared by everyone, then the girl and the eagle symbolize the tribes that riot against the Aztecs and support the Spanish.

The incestuous situation from which the girl escapes is also a symbol. The obligation to have sexual intercourse with the maternal uncle may refer to a society that lacks any order. Her escape from such a society may even authorize the girl to bring about conquest. At the same time this fear of incest may simply symbolize shrinking from becoming a victim (of sacrifice).

Another symbol is the crucifix below which Aktzini's daughter cries. It may even be the inversion of the "*kwuawuete,*" the tree under which Cortés bemoans the loss of the treasures. The "cruz" is in all probability identical with the crucifix of Christ, though the symbol of the cross existed in the pre-Columbian civilizations too. (Robelo 1980, 1:132–33.) This is the crucifix introduced by the Spanish. The Totonac Indians interpret crucifixion in a very specific way, as do other aboriginal groups on the American continents. As testified by a text collected among the Totonacs, they believe that the crucified Jesus ran from one crucifix to the other (Ichon 1969, 63–81), thereby justifying the meaning of the crucifixes set up along the roads. This crucifix of Santa Cruz cannot merely symbolize the sacrifice of Christ, but probably also symbolizes the Spaniards, who represent escape for the girl.

It is easy to interpret the binary opposition of cooked and raw meat known so well in American mythology (Lévi-Strauss 1968). In all probability, this symbol means opposition to civilization and the state of savagery: the raw meat is the symbol of uncivilized people, while the boiled meat symbolizes civilized Spain with its order and discipline.

The symbolization process lasts until Aktzini's daughter shows Mexico to the Spaniards. The actions merge into the symbols: devouring people, giving orders, moaning, disobeying the order, asking for help, escaping, arriving in Spain, baptizing. Thus, there is a series of events, the majority of which can be interpreted in their concreteness as well. This series of events is executed by the persons who operate as symbols; they impart meanings to the actions that are different from those manifested.

Each of the discourse segments closes with an event that may be considered concrete. These events carry on the narrative: the obligation to commit incest, the arrival in Spain, baptizing. This event will be the axis to which the second part of the discourse may be connected.

The Spanish Word

In the Aktzini myth told in the Totonac language, the objects, persons, places, and concepts related to Spanish are indicated with Spanish nouns, such as <u>objects</u>: *anteojo*/pairs of glasses, *bandera*/flag, *barco*/boat; <u>persons</u>: *cristiano*/Christian man, *general*/general, *cura*/priest, *soldado*/soldier; <u>concept</u>: *misa*/mass, *seña*/sign, *poder*/power.

Although the meaning of these words may change in the text, the change is always related to one of the properties of the original meaning and is not a change concerning the essence of the meaning. These words are all nouns, and all of them are of key importance in the text. They belong to the range of experienced knowledge.

In the second part of the Aktzini myth many elements of the sixteenth-century chronicles on the conquest of Mexico constitute the framework of the discourse (Sahagún, 1956, 4:13–165; 167–185). All the sixteenth-century chronicles consider the ruthless slaughtering by the Spanish on the feast of Uitzlipochtli as the starting point of the Tenochtitlán conflict. The reply of the Aztecs was to starve and lock up the Spaniards. When the Spaniards tried to escape, the Aztecs discovered the attempt and tried to hinder the escape, and many people died in the water. The historians themselves resorted to mythical sources.

The part of Aktzini's myth that describes the actions of the Spanish could be one of the versions of the events surrounding the conquest. The sixteenth-century history of Mexico's conquest could easily survive among the Totonac Indians almost in the form in which it was related by the chronicles. I have already mentioned that this sphere of Totonac knowledge was not subject to symbolic transformation.

Storytelling of Aktzini and the Present Situations of the Totonacs

We could ask the question, "Why do today's Totonacs need to listen to and to transmit their version of the history of the conquest?" The children already learn at school the official version. But the Totonac version in a very sophisticated way changes the historical role played by Indians and Spaniards, and gives a Totonac-centered interpretation of the present situation. In the Aktzini myth the borrowed Spanish words are mostly used to describe aggression. This kind of aggression is constantly experienced by the inhabitants of Coahuitlan, where I collected the Aktzini myth. The village is situated on the top of a hill bordered by precipices, and has only two narrow roads down to the valley in a northwest direction. Only a few hundred meters away from one of the exits

there is a mestizo (for the Indians, a Spanish) village called Progresso de Zaragoza, whose inhabitants have grabbed the power over Coahuitlan, thus creating an intolerable situation for the Totonacs there. The people of Progreso de Zaragoza regularly hold up the Indians who travel along the only good road and attack them even in their huts.

In Totonac ideology, power and money are on the side of evil. The rich (mestizo Spanish) go hand in hand with evil and sell away their souls. At the beginning of the myth, the wicked Indians (man-eaters, raw meat-eaters, nonbaptized, and rich) keep changing their ways by learning how to cook meat and getting baptized. They also lose their money. Having become decent people in that manner, they have every right to mount a resistance to the marauding and power-hungry Spaniards.

The Aktzini myth ends with the final victory of the Indians and the lamentations of Cortés. In other historical Totonac myths and dances one often comes across the phenomenon of regarding the present as being transformed through a transformation of the past. Almost any desirable state of affairs seems to be attainable to them by interchanging the levels of time; in this way they are able to transform the past. By ending the story with the Spaniards' defeat they can prove their own superiority. Consequently, their pride in the face of the Spaniards has its roots in their historical past.

Storytelling by the Rituals: Ritualized Historical Representation, Changing the Past, and Imitation

In the ideas of the Totonac Indians, the same kind of events of the past (e.g., battles and the appearance of foreigners) are intertwined, irrespective of the time of their occurrence, thus becoming interchangeable. The perception of time of the inhabitants of Coahuitlan and Plan de Hidalgo is not horizontal, as in the occidental perception, but cyclic. This mythical perception of historical time is also represented in actions. The actions reflect the idea that if the past is present in our days, our present actions must have some effect on the past and, consequently, on the present. The order of the world that has taken shape can only survive through regularly repeated rituals. By means of sacred actions and ritual dances, the Totonacs can get back to the earliest times, where they can again secure cosmogonic relations. The famous dance of the Totonac Indians called Volador (Flier) serves the same purpose.

The birth of the Sun is a highly important event in the Totonac history. The rays of light are often identified with the birds (mainly the eagle) winging in the air among South American Indians. According to many researchers, the dancers of the Volador are actually embodying birds, creatures that are incarnating the light. Some researchers consider the Chaporral, which dances on the top of the pole of Volador, to be the Sun, and their companions to be the rays of light or the four directions. The light, the Sun, the quarters of the heaven, and the rain all play some roles in the symbolism of Volador.

The dance essentially consists of four dancers jumping off the top of a 30-meter-high pole, while a fifth dancer keeps bowing toward the quarters of the heavens and the sun while playing the flute and rolling a drum. The dance is preceded and followed by rituals. The erection of the pole is accompanied by rites: previous to inserting it into a hole in the ground, an animal sacrifice must be offered up to the god of the mountains (Kiwilkholo). This is made by giving a hen some alcohol to drink, making it walk along a pole, and then cutting its throat and painting 12 crosses on the pole with its blood. Thereafter, they pray over the hen and bury it in the hole made for the pole. As it is the symbol of death, the hen delivers the dancers from the fatal dangers of jumping off the top of the high pole. Only men authorized by the community may become Volador dancers; they must strictly observe certain regulations, practice abstinence for a week before and after the dance, offer a sacrifice, and in general be worthy of the ritual whose function is to maintain the historical cosmic order. Regular functioning of the Sun, safe arrival of the winds, rain, and the seasons of the year are ensured by the dances that are performed during the feast of the village. In all likelihood, Volador has its roots in pre-Columbian times, but it is almost equally possible that it is of Totonac origin, and that its beginnings were merely lost in the fog of history.

Interpretation of the dance is fairly controversial. According to Fewkes (1907), the Volador dancers of Papantla are dressed as birds, and the dance itself, along with the rites that accompany it, are identical with those I observed: "An old woman, a witch, offers copal, brandy and a hen as a sacrifice, putting it into the hole made in the ground to receive the pole" (Fewkes 1907, 249). Other interpretations (Krickeberg 1993, 74–75) view the shooting stars as symbolizing partly the

sacrifices and partly the dropping of heavenly bodies on the earth.

To another ritual dance of the Totonacs, the so-called Quetzal-dance, is attributed a similar function. The quetzal bird can symbolize the rays of the Sun, whereas the richly decorated dancers revolving on a cross-shaped structure denote the quarters of the heavens.

These dances cannot be regarded as pure fertility magic, because they are detached from the everyday agricultural cycle and are scheduled on the name day of the village's patron saint. Accordingly, they serve to maintain a general order and the "good history" of the universe.

The memories of human historical events are safeguarded by narrative dances. The inhabitants of Coahuitlan dance the drama of the conquest year after year. The fight between the Spaniards and the Indians, soothing in the dances depicting the victory over the Saracens at morisma (Spain), ends in an appeasement that has never taken place in "real history."

The praying women (*rezandera*) offer the dancers into the gods' mercy by chanting the following prayer:

Where the Spaniards live, where the foreigners
    live,
        where Kuahtemek lives.
Where the Spaniards live, where the foreigners
    live,
        where Kuahtemek lives.
Where the people living beyond the sea have
    their towns,
Where the Spaniards live,
        where Kuahtemek lives.
Where the foreigners live.
Oh, my God!
Will they now start fighting?
Now they encounter each other.
But they should not suffer any injury, and the
        might of their swords be not become
        weaker!
The end of the fight should be won by them.
They should not suffer any loss,
        so as not to have to put up with any
        sorrow.
These fighters should feel well,
        be powerful and have great might.
Send them fulfillment of thine will
        from one of thine temples, from God's
        Mother,
        from a master god,

along with thine thanks, amazement,
and full power.
(Prayer by Francisca Maria in Totanac
language, collected in Coahuitlan,
1985)

The equality of forces made manifest in the course of the ritual fencing of richly decorated fighters finally leads to peace. Unable to gain victory over the Indians, the Spaniards can go on living with them in peace. The quoted hymn includes some motifs that run parallel to Spanish conquest, e.g., the role of Kuahtemek and the reference to the two belligerent people living on the opposite shores of the ocean. The power of sacred dancing and the events symbolized by the dances must have made clear for everyone that the Spaniards could not possibly gain the upper hand there. The events transposed into the past are actualized just as they are in textual representations. The dances that are repeated year after year represent history altered retroactively in a clear fashion that is easily understandable to every onlooker.

The retroactive insertion of equality of rank into the past provides for the possibility of the future emancipation of the Totonacs. This is one symbolic meaning of the dance in which the light (Mexican Indians) struggles against the darkness (Spaniards). Thus the dance fits into a relativistic way of thinking according to which the goal of the Totonacs is not identification with the Spaniards but the achievement of emancipation through defining themselves and retaining their identity.

The dance called Malinche also tells a story of the time of Spanish conquest. The topic is the marriage of Cortés. Malinche was a high-born Indian woman who lived in sorrow with 12 servant girls after her husband's death. Cortés was also a widower who also grieved his deceased wife without comfort. A meeting of Malinche and Cortés generated deep love, and the story ends with their happy union.

This beautiful dance, performed by girls between 8 and 12 and a boy around 12, also points toward emancipation by stepping back into the distant past; the mighty warlord of the conquerors finds an Indian woman worthy of marriage for love.

The historical dances play an active role in maintaining the Totonac identity. One of the goals of these dances is probably to make the present situation acceptable. Although reality fails to corroborate the conditions depicted by the dances, it strengthens the internal distancing and self-assurance that a relativistic way of thinking brings. Thus, in the final analysis, the practical goal of sacred dances is to provide cosmological security in the natural world and the historical origins of self-esteem for Totonacs.

Storytelling Through Everyday Life and Work Activities: Imitation and Analogy

In this section, some aspects of the mythical historical idea appearing in transposed forms in everyday life will be presented.

Some behaviors are explained by the Totonacs as the imitations of the activities of dramatis personae of historical narratives. For example, we know from the report of Olmos (1912, 205–215) that those wishing to obtain healing for a relative refrain from sexual intercourse for 18 days before appealing to supernatural powers for intervention.

Today's Totonacs regard abstinence from sexual life as a prelude to purging. Previous to performing their ritual dances Totonac dancers live under a common roof for seven days, and were any of them to visit his wife during that period he would risk being bitten by the snake referred to in the dance, or being horned by a bull, or being bewitched by his mask.

The Totonacs told me that it is the imitation of the Sun's behavior that lies behind those beliefs. The Sun, who had become a heavenly body out of a young, weak man, could overtake the Moon with ease. Although the Moon was the older and the stronger, he made love before the competition, and as a result he was unable to catch up with the Sun. The Totonacs say that the Sun, as a former human being, is imitated during the practice of abstinence. This is an example of the use of a mythical historical narrative idea in everyday life.

The Great Flood myth can help us understand some other storytelling practices related to everyday life. After the flood had passed, the people who had been kept alive by the Hare braved the gods by laying a fire and frying men turned into fish on it. (Ichon 1969, 119). Thus fire became a link between heaven and earth. The gods took notice of man's disobedience. The presence of fire indicated the end of the flood. Thus, the rites often include laying fires with the goal of giving signals of the gods. Danger, water, and darkness can only be kept off by fire. According to Sahagún (1929–1930, 3:61) and Alvarado Tezozómoc (1878, 31), fires were always burning in the temples. The same phenomenon was observed in Latin America by Lévi-Strauss, who reported that fire had been looked upon as a mediator between heaven and earth. (Lévi-Strauss 1968).

Fires were incessantly burning also in the temples of Totonacapan, where tending fires was the duty of the lower clergy. The circular structures found on Cempoala were in all likelihood fireplaces. This supposition is supported by an observation of the Spanish conquerors in Puerto de Lema (Bernal Diaz 1904, 173), who made mention of huge piles of firewood beside the temple.

Today's Totonacs also keep fires going. Whenever they leave their homes, they carefully shut the doors and leave enough embers to rekindle their fires. Fires flicker all night and may only be tended by women who always knot up their long hair before doing anything near the fireplaces. Some of the rites associated with fires can be regarded as imitations of the activities described in the historical mythical ideas.

Some external representations of mythical historical ideas have either no mythical connections at all, or only fragmented ones. The agrarian rites are historical in nature beyond a doubt. Cortés, who did not want to batter away the trust of the Totonac allies, started demolishing the idols only when he deemed his victory absolutely certain. On seeing the soldiers throwing themselves upon the idols, the Totonacs protested in despair, fearing the end of the world. They believed that the gods would deny their corn and that the crops would be devastated by insects, hail, storm, and drought (Diaz 1904; Gómara 1749). After a lapse of 500 years, the Rezanderas prayed for deliverance from the same kind of perils as the chronicles described in the sixteenth century. Let us see how the Totonacs pray for protection against pests in our days:

Oh, you planting, sowing, and creating gods,
You, who water every single plant,
Please take care not to let pests attack us
To devastate our plants,
To chew off the leaves,
To do away with plants,
Do keep them off.
Please make good things into reality,
Let plants tended by us grow
And bear fruits.
　　(Prayer by Francisca Maria in Totanac
　　language, Coahuitlan, 1985)

The following text is a prayer against storm and hail:

You clever creatures,
You men turned into gods!
You tip over, making a big noise. Do not stay here,
Do not have a rest at this place!
You, there, you will roll off the hill,
And you there, you will drop off in the small wood.
You all will arrive on the ground, having a rest there.
We do not want you to fall on a village!
Do not be stupid,
Show due regard for us,
Since it would be of no good for you to fall on a village!
You will have to clear off, please go away,
Shift further off!
You, fathers, lords, clever creatures,
You men turned into gods.
　　(Prayer by Gracia Rosa in Totanac language,
　　collected in Coahuitlan, 1985)

The prayers do not name any of the gods, but from the references made to them we may conclude that the prayers are directed to cultural heroes very similar to former human beings such as the Sun.

The agrarian rites can be the external representations of complicated mythological historical ideas. For example, the historical record states that "when the seeds were sown, when the corn field started to yield produce, the people acquired slaves for sacrificing them" (Krickeberg 1993, 96). The cult was likely aimed at the Goddess of the heaven, Tlazotoatl, who was also known as the maize goddess, Cinteotl, and "Our Flesh," Tonavayo. According to Krickeberg (1993, 96), the sacrificing ceremonies were the "kill-with-arrows" type, and it is assumed that also the Volador dance was included. The sacrifices described in the early years of the twentieth century involved the killing of turkeys; Totonacs identified those birds with fire (Ichon 1969, 70), and fire is a herald between heaven and earth.

The Totonacs of Santa Maria arrange feasts on a certain day of the year to ensure good crops and fine weather for the whole year. The ceremonies are guided by an old woman in a big house, and the Sun, the Moon and the stars are symbolized by gilded paper decorations. People dance in the house and sprinkle the ground with turkey blood. On the second day of the festivities, maize and beans are offered to the gods, and the gilded paper decorations are painted crosswise with blood. At the end of the ceremony, children throw arrows at the decorations until all of them are destroyed. Finally, every participant takes a handful of earth and some seeds to ensure a high yield on the land (Starr 1900, 187–88).

In Krickeberg's interpretation, that series of rituals clearly indicate the Sun's role and its unlimited power (the Sun achieves the victory over the stars, the stars are destroyed in order to let the Sun overcome the other heavenly bodies) (Krickeberg 1993, 77).

The ritual actions adopted by the Totonacs to improve the yield of corn begin with the purification of the corn from the evil forces. Some of the seeds are sprinkled with turkey blood and mixed with the rest to transfer their purity to them. After they have been moistened with blood and soaked in water, corn seeds can be planted. Over and above that magic, seeds may be consecrated also by the Church. The day of planting and sowing is of importance as well, since there are sacred days that provide protection and common days on which corn should not be planted. The Totonacs want to achieve the best yield possible, and strongly believe that the name days of certain saints strengthen the effects of the other rites.

Purified seeds may, thus, only be planted into a soil that has been properly consecrated by sacrificial rites. The people engaged in planting should also be cleansed in a similar manner. Let us now take a look at one example of today's Totonac practices. While in Plan de Hidalgo, I suddenly saw a group of men running down the street. All passersby who were walking in the opposite direction gave way to them, since the men had to be home on time. As it happened, Carlos, a healer who has the fame of a sorcerer, was hurrying home with his peons so as to be able to place the remnants of the food taken to the field that morning on their private altars at 1:00 P.M. sharp. The goal was to let the patron saints take away the food so that they would assist them in their work. Thus the peasants said their thanksgiving prayers and returned to their fields in haste to begin their work.

Consecration of the soil is a highly important rite, both in Coahuitlan and at Plan de Hidalgo. As with almost all rites of vital importance, sacrifices are performed, mostly turkeys, out of which some festive food is made. The so-called *mole* dish is placed on the ground in the middle of the plot earmarked for planting seeds. This is done at noon. The men who are working the land cleanse their hands and faces with some brandy, then they all drink a little of the spirit, and pour out the rest on the soil to gain the goodwill of the god of the earth. After lunch they go home as fast as they can to pray. That rite is only made on the first day of sowing and planting; repetition is only necessary when starting work at a new plot of land. The men returning from work continue their days with merrymaking at home.

It is apparent from what has been stated so far that the Totonacs offer their sacrifices to the very supernatural powers that their ancestors turned to with the same intention: the gods of the Sun (*Chichini*), the Earth (*Et'iyat*), the wind (*un*), the rain (*s'in, chchut*), and of course the corn (*staku*).

In their historical myths about the birth of the corn, sprinkling corn with blood and blood sacrifice is a very important element. The blood sacrifice indicates the worship of Sun. The Sun and the corn as divine beings are often identified with each other in the mythology of Central Americans. Consequently, the presentation of blood that accompanies corn planting denotes a sacrifice performed to the Sun and to the plant alike. The god of Earth (male and female at the same time) is also that of the soil. The Earth, and for that reason all essential geographical objects and natural phenomena, can be identified with a divine being who has taken the shape of a man.

The agrarian rites of the Totonacs are practical storytelling practices of ritual events described in myths. These rites are external representations intertwined with a multitude of symbols that often overlap each other. The rites revolve around surrounding a "historical idea," with which to bring forth the changes necessary to maintain human life in earth.

Review

I have briefly presented some external representations of historical mythical ideas as linguistic units and as rules for the regulation of behavior. In the framework of this article I could not analyze the very complicated mental models that provide the logical, linguistic organization of the historical mythical ideas.

I have shown that the traditional storytelling practice among Totonacs does not consist only in oral transmission, but also in rituals, dances, and everyday behaviors. The stories told in this way offer an important range of appropriate responses to the everyday situations Totonacs encounter in the mestizo Spanish environment. This kind of storytelling permits a collective practice of behaviors that are regulated by a long historically constructed knowledge. Finally we can see that among the Totonacs there is a living connection between narrative ideas and experiences that permit them the symbolic (mythic) transformation of a frequently painful reality.

Further Reading

Alvarado Tezozómoc, Fernando, *Cronica mexicana*, Mexico: Impr. y. litog. de I. Paz, 1878

Borofsky, Robert, *Making History: Pukapukan and Anthropological Constructions of Knowledge*, Cambridge and New York: Cambridge University Press, 1987

Carr, David, *Time, Narrative, and History*, Bloomington: Indiana University Press, 1986

Díaz del Castillo, Bernal, *Historia verdadera de la Conquista de la Nueva España*, 2 volumes, Mexico: Oficina Tipográfica de la Secretaría de Fomento, 1904; also published as *The True History of the Conquest of New Spain*, London: Hakluyt Society, 1908; also published as *The True History of the Conquest of Mexico: Written in the Year 1568*, New York: McBride, 1927

Fewkes, Jesse, *Certain Antiquities of Eastern Mexico*, Washington, D.C.: Government Printing Office, 1907

García Payón, C., "Evolución histórica del Totonacapan," in *Huaxtecos y totonacos: Una antología histórico-cultural*, edited by Lorenzo Ochoa, Mexico City, Mexico: Consejo Nacional para la Cultura y las Artes, 1989

Garnham, Alan, *Mental Models as Representations of Discourse and Text*, New York: Halsted, 1987; Chichester, West Sussex: Horwood, 1987

Guenther, R. Kim, *Human Cognition*, Upper Saddle River, New Jersey: Prentice Hall, 1998

Harré, R., and Grant Gillet, *The Discursive Mind*, Thousand Oaks, California: Sage, 1994

Ichon, Alain, *La religion des Totonaques de la Sierra*, Paris: Éditions du Centre national de la recherche scientifique, 1969

Jackendoff, Ray, *Patterns in the Mind: Language and Human Nature*, New York: Harvester Wheatsheaf, 1993

Krickeberg, Walter, *Los Totonaca: contribución a la etnografía histórica de la América Central*, Mexico: Talleres gráficos del Museo nacional de arqueología, historia y etnografía, 1993

Lammel, Annamária, "La categorisacion de personajes históricos," in *El cambio de la mitología entre las Indigenas de América*, edited by J. Bottasso, Quito, Ecuador: Abya-Yala, 1994

———, "La Naturaleza Totonaca: Percepción, representación y gestión," in *Cuadrante, 11–12*, Mexico: Universidad de San Luis Potosi, 1995

———, "Los colores del viento y la voz del arcoiris: Percepción del clima entre los Totonacas (México)," in *Antropología del clima en el mundo hispanoamericano*, edited by Esther Katz, Marina Goloubinoff, and Annamária Lammel, Quito, Ecuador: Abya-Yala, 1997

Lammel, Annamária, and Cs. Nemes, *Les Indiens des Déesses Mères*, Budapest, Hungary: Akadémiai, 1988

Lévi-Strauss, Claude, *L'origine des manières de table*, Paris: Plon, 1968; also published as *The Origin of Table Manners*, New York: Harper and Row, 1978; London: Cape, 1978

López Gómara, Francisco, *Historia de las Indias y Conquista de México: Zaragoza, 1552*, Mexico: Centro de Estudios de Historia de México Condumex, 1978

Melgarejo Vivanco, José Luis, *Los totonaca y su cultura*, Xalapa, Mexico: Universidad Veracruzana, 1985

Olivera de Bonfil, Alicia, *La tradición oral sobre Cuauhtémoc*, México: UNAM, 1980

Olmos, A., "Proceso seguido por fray Andrés de Olmos en contra del cacique de Matlatlan," in *Procesos de Indios Idolatras y Hechiceros*, volume 3 of *Publicaciones del Archivo general de la Nación*, edited by Luis González Obregon, Mexico: Tip. Guerrero Hnos., 1912

Oropeza, C.M., "El diluvio Totonaco," *Tlalocan* 2 (1947)

Robelo, Cecilio A., *Diccionario de Mitologia Nahuatl*, 2 volumes, Mexico City, Mexico: Editorial Innovación, 1980

Sahagún, Bernardino de, *Historia general de las Cosas de Nueva España*, edited by Angel María Garibay, 4 volumes, Mexico: Porrúa, 1956

Siran, Jean-Luis, *L'illusion mythique*, Paris: Institut Synthélabo pour le progrès de la connaissance, 1998

Starr, Frederick, *Notes upon Ethnography of Southern Mexico*, Davenport, Iowa: Putnam Memorial Publication Fund, 1900

Vansina, Jan, *Oral Tradition as History*, Madison: University of Wisconsin Press, 1985; London: Currey, 1985

Williams Garcia, R., *Tradicion oral en Tajin*, Jalapa, Mexico, 1980

Exemplary Ancestors and Pernicious Spirits: Sibundoy Concepts of Cultural Evolution

John H. McDowell

John H. McDowell juxtaposes Sibundoy personal experience stories of encounters with spirits with Sibundoy mythic traditions.

Taita Bautista Juajibioy Narrates:

Hee heeee.
 ffffffttttt.

Hee heeee.
 fffffttttttt.

Hee heeee.
 fffffffttttt.

With these sounds the distinguished Kamsá elder, taita Bautista Juajibioy, conveys the eerie presence of a menacing spirit. Taita Bautista tells of two ambitious travelers who have left behind the familiar contours of the Sibundoy Valley to wander in search of gold in the spiritual wilderness of its wooded mountainous fringe. First the men hear a distant shout from above; then they feel the breeze pass beside them. Each successive shout emanates from a closer point, and each time the breeze that follows close upon it is stronger. At last the spirit actually becomes visible: the shape of a puma, dressed in white. As the spirit appears, the moon goes behind a cloud and the fire is extinguished. The two men, thrown into a primordial darkness, are left crushed with fright.

Taita Bautista, six-time governor of the Kamsá community, is noted for his verbal skills and knowledge of the old days; he animates the story with dramatic effects and we huddle a little closer to the embers of the evening fire. His narrative tactics seem to bring the *mal vienta*, the evil wind, right to the margins of the fire's glow, and we all feel perilously vulnerable to the *mala hora,* the evil hour, the point of contact with the spiritual underground.

In Bautista's story the arrival of the spirit is foretold, like all significant events in the Sibundoy Valley, in a dream the previous night. One of the men experiences a warning: "Damn, I am going to pass by today, so get out of the way." He alerts his companion: "A puma or something like that might be coming." The storyteller does not leave this event unexplained: he tells us that the evil wind was a soul, an *ado,* or drowned one. In a similar story, Bautista tells us that the souls of purgatory require our prayers and that they become angry at "those who don't know how to pray for them." But this slant toward Roman Catholicism is suspect: a lifelong Catholic, Bautista in his dotage has become tremendously devout. When I visit him a few years later, he will tell no *cuentos pajosos,* foolish stories, and insists on narrating stories from the Bible exclusively.

Encounters with Bad Spirits

The Sibundoy Valley of southwestern Colombia is the home of two indigenous communities, the Kamsá (whose language is the sole remnant of the language of the archaic Quillasinga federation) and the Ingano (speakers of the northernmost dialect of Quechua). In the narratives of both communities spirits appear relentlessly to focus on experiences of the modern-day people. They evince a peculiar obsession with human affairs and their influence is invariably baneful. These intrusive spirits may take many forms: a black shadow; a moving, shapeless bulk (*bulto*); an irascible elder whose feet don't touch the ground, and who offers a cold hand and a colder warning: "Be careful, Nephew!"; a group of floating lights that carry a person across a field.

Recountings and dramatizations of personal encounters with spirit presences have a pervasive nightmarish quality. My compadre Francisco Tandioy, an Ingano who has become a professor of English and Inga at the Universidad de Nariño in Pasto, recalls vividly an experience from his childhood:

I left town around seven in the evening, maybe a bit later, and then in a bad spot where there was a landslide, I almost turned back, I remembered what my mother had told me about the souls of the departed. And just then I heard a loud noise, it sounded like a large ox. Then I began to run and when I tried to run I couldn't do it. And then after that I saw it, you know, a firefly came along and then it turned into a dog, the dog turned white and it wouldn't let me pass. And so I arrived at my house, but the next day I awoke with fever. I woke up very sick. I was in bad shape. They had to go and bring a native doctor. They told me that I had received a bad wind.

The framing is important here: the protagonist is passing by a bad spot, *mal punto;* these are places marked by topographical contrast and are often the site of previous human tragedy. Moreover, we are told that it is seven in the evening, dusk, a period of transition into nighttime when spirits are likely to be abroad. Francisco's story conveys the terrifying self-transformative powers of these spirit presences, whose mutability denies the stability of material substance. A story by Justo Jacanamijoy, my adopted Kamsá father, reinforces this feature: he is out on a path at night and senses a dark form, about the size of a dog, brush past him; it returns going the other way, this time the size of a cow. The child Francisco

awakes from his experience with a fever and his parents are obliged to send for a native doctor. The family's diagnosis is unequivocal: *mal viento,* or spirit sickness, has struck their youngster.

The spirits do not physically assault those who chance upon them so much as disorient them: their mere proximity triggers a psychic disintegration that can be fatal and that routinely causes severe illness. Sibundoy Indians refer to this malady as spirit sickness, and they believe that only Catholic prayer and the spiritual ministry of the native doctors can stop the advance of its symptoms, which include loss of appetite and color, severe vomiting and diarrhea, fever, rash, coughing, and chills.

What are we to make of these curious accounts? I do not intend here to offer an externally based rationale, bringing in, for example, psychological or sociological models, though these options might produce useful results. Instead, I propose to work largely within the context of Sibundoy thought itself. My treatment of Sibundoy spiritual beliefs and practices will be lamentably brief in this paper (McDowell 1989).

The Meaning of Spirit Encounters in Sibundoy Understanding

Let's begin by asking: How do Sibundoy natives understand these transcendental experiences? What kinds of native testimony might be available for scrutiny?

In the first place, Sibundoy natives routinely discuss the spirit realm, which constitutes, after all, a crucial influence on their well-being. Statements like the one to follow are common:

We believe that all places are full of spirits. These spirits, at certain hours, are not congenial one might say. And so when they are not in a good humor, they attack people. One can speak of the evil wind of the cemetery, of the rivers and streams, of the cliffs, one can speak of the evil wind of the forest. So the world is full of spirits, sometimes even in our houses.

This discourse identifies an overall domain, a spirit realm labelled *binyea* in Kamsá and *huayra* in Inga, each term meaning literally "wind" but connoting the vast domain of spiritual forces. The spirit realm, we soon discover, is composed of two kinds of spirits, the spirits of the forest ("who never were human") and the souls of the departed. Spirits are said to flourish at certain places and times; we have already happened upon the indigenous concepts of the bad hour, the bad spot. But native exegesis is pragmatic in nature, geared to the successful manipulation of this realm. The native doctors recognize specific categories of forest spirits (for example, the masters of different animal species and natural domains), but their discourse also reflects the practical goal of providing spiritual remedies.

In coming to a fuller appreciation of this spiritual system that so colors life in the Sibundoy Valley, we will find it useful to draw upon what I would term a Sibundoy theory of the origin and evolution of civilization, exposited most clearly in another branch of Sibundoy narrative, the mythic narrative, but also manifest in the folk medicinal system aimed at securing precious spiritual health.

Kaka Tempo

The same Bautista, on one of my early visits to the valley, provided me with an overview of the succession of cosmic epochs in Sibundoy thought.

> They tell about it, you know?
> The time of darkness, *yibets tempoka.*
> And then, the time of light, *binyea tempoka.*
> And then another one, *kaka tempoka,* the raw time,
>
> they ate everything raw, *kaka tempo* [laughs]
>
> All during the raw time, they ate everything raw.
> all fruits, everything, raw, raw, raw,
> since previously there was no fire.
> That's why its called *kaka tempo,* the raw time.
> Later there was fire and they learned how to cook.
>
> I used to like to hear these things,
> since there were many tales,
> and the elders would be conversing among themselves,
> and oneself just listening to everything.
>
> Before the arrival of the missionaries.

This account identifies a series of cosmic moments: a primordial, inaccessible time of darkness which yields to the time of light with the first rising of the sun (the Kamsá word *binyea* means "dawn" as well as "wind" and "spirit"); the en-

suing raw time, which is treated with some amusement; and its sequel, the time of fire. Lastly, we can deduce a time of the missionaries, by which he means the Capuchin Order that became established in the valley just before the turn of the century (Bonilla 1972).

Bautista's account is skeletal; he produces it for my sake from his reminiscences as a child auditor. But during a year's residence in the Sibundoy Valley, I was privileged to become an auditor in my own right, and I heard numerous performances from a narrative tradition that is carefully segregated in Sibundoy thought, labelled *antioj palabra* in Inga, *antewa parlo* in Kamsá. The defining feature of this narrative category is its focus on the times and doings of the ancestors, in Inga *nujpam-andacuna,* the first people. Sibundoy ancestors are not reckoned in family or clan lines; they are not conceived of as specific progenitors of modern social groupings. Instead they are a hypothetical early stratum of humanity, specifically the stratum that "made the world safe for civilization."

The Raw Time

Ancestral period begins when the very first people appear in the time of light, and it recedes only with the establishment of appropriate social forms in the time of fire. The body of mythic narrative depicts the gradual transition from a primordial epoch during which the celestial deities interact directly with the first people and the earth is dominated by a substrate population known as *aucas* in Inga and *yembas* in Kamsá (terms that could be translated as "heathen savages"), to the modern period with its familiar patterns of human civilization. Much of this narrative centers on the pivotal movement from the raw time to the time of fire, a formative period when the exemplary deeds of the ancestors established precedents for behavior that remain in force to the present moment.

Sibundoy mythic narrative is heard when people assemble in the evenings with gourds of chicha in their hands. Its episodes flesh out taita Bautista's skeletal inventory of world-forming epochs. We hear, in alternating strains of reverence and hilarity, how the weasel danced before Wangetsmuna to obtain fire; how the mouse procured cornseed for planting; how death and hardship entered the world; and, at the most recent extension of mythic time, how taita Tamoabioy left his lands in perpetuity to his descendants, the indigenous peoples of the valley.

Wangetsmuna

In this imposing corpus there is one myth, actually a series of episodes clustered around the cultural hero Wangetsmuna, that conveys the full trajectory of the civilizing process in the Sibundoy Valley. Wangetsmuna is now an obscure figure; like Viracocha in the Central and Southern Andes, he appears both as cultural hero and deity. Even remembrance of his name is fading in the Sibundoy valley; his people are forgetting him. But the elders recall his deeds and narrative bits continue to cling to this shrouded figure.

I have in my possession four tellings of the full cycle, another telling of the death of Wangetsmuna (which assimilates him to the Christian model of martyrdom), and a multitude of narrative fragments depicting isolated moments in the overall cycle. The name *Wangetsmuna* is Kamsá; it has no precise meaning to modern-day Kamsá people, but incorporates a root similar to the word for "beak." We can speculate that Wangetsmuna was once a birdlike deity, perhaps the master of the feathered protagonists that populate Sibundoy mythic narrative. In order to sample the world of the ancestors, allow me to walk you through some key moments in the Wangetsmuna cycle, drawing on excerpts from tellings by two outstanding Kamsá storytellers, Mariano Chicunque and Estanislao Chicunque.

The story begins with the original human beings: a miner, his younger brother who cooks for him, and in some variants, their sister who spins thread. The miner encounters a trail and leaves a trap there. He dreams that night of a young woman caught in the trap, and sure enough, the next day he finds her there entangled in its vines. She scolds him, he lets her go, and then they decide to marry. The identity of this woman, and of her father, is made very clear:

> Then she took that miner to her house.
> And it turned out, so they say, to be the home of the sun.
> Now this is what we call *bngabe taita,*
> which means 'Our Lord,' so it's like saying 'the Father.'
> "My father," she said, "my father, my father is the sun."
> *"Taitana,"* she said. "I am his daughter."
> She is the moon, it turned out, she is the moon.

The initial phase of the Wangetsmuna cycle transports us to an early moment in cosmic time, a moment when the celestial deities interacted directly with the very first ancestors of the modern people.

They agree to marry, and the miner follows her home, only to experience the uncomfortable proximity of her solar father:

> They arrived after a long time, and when they sat down,
> by the edge of a large body of water, when they sat down,
> truly, heaven forbid, suddenly those carts came roaring
> to the edge of the water, and that water completely dried, yes sir,
> and that beach was nothing but beads,
> composed of beads, of beads was that beach.
>
> Fine, then they hid, that woman and her husband-to-be,
> for they had agreed to marry,
> they hid in a large jar that was there,
> and inside it they were able to sit down.
> And then hen droppings were scattered all about there,
> the sun's droppings were scattered all about.
>
> There they took refuge, and as they were hiding there,
> heaven forbid, the sun arrived to eat,
> he stopped off there as he went on his rounds.
> And inside there it was getting very hot, inside,
> saintly God, it was getting very hot.
>
> Then, in order to eat, every serving a bushel,
> every serving a bushel, as much as three bushels to eat,
> three bushels he ate, and three bushels he ate.
>
> And then, then he said to her:
> "Why, why does it smell of moss here?"
> Then that daughter answered:
> "I went to the woods, and there was moss on the tree.
> I went to gather firewood. That's the odor."
> Be careful. He came over to take the lid off,
> but then he stopped. Aha.
>
> Surely he sat down again and that machine roared,
> and then that water there just completely dried up.
> And like that, that body of water disappeared.

And the sun, as he went off to some other
place,
that water came together again there.

In one of the most remarkable passages in Sibundoy mythology, the awesome sun deity is portrayed as driver of an immense machine, and
consumer of enormous quantities of food to fuel
his journey across the sky. Sibundoy exegesis of
these episodes makes clear their exemplary character: the sun's droppings account for the presence of gold in the world, and the sands that are
beads reveal the origin of the colorful seed *chagu-
ira* that are worn with pride by members of the indigenous communities.

But returning to the plot: if the sun is portrayed as hostile to humankind, too pervasive in
his fiery persona to be endured, his daughter the
moon is far more accommodating. In human
form she agrees to marry the miner, and she proposes the following arrangement:

Aha. Fine. Then that woman spoke to him,
they came to an agreement, so they could
marry.
Then: "Take this wad of cotton.
This evening I will come to you."

She took out some cotton, she rubbed it back
and forth,
that woman, and she gave it to him.
And in the old days they carried those sacks,
and like that he had it slung over his shoulder
there,
and she stuffed it with that cotton. Fine.

And truly she remained inside there, with the
older brother.

Cotton, portrayed here as the medium of spiritual communication, plays an important spiritual
role in the practice of the native doctors as an
agent for retaining spiritual essence. In the mythical context, this unusual mode of association
triggers a seminal episode in the myth—the transformation of the younger brother into the infant
Wangetsmuna. The younger brother hears the
sound of people conversing during the night, and
goes about inspecting the older brother's gear to
discover the secret:

Fine. And then he went to put out that bed-
ding,

he began to search through it, looking all
around. And that spirit was there, but he
didn't notice it. She went to the mine to tell
him about it.
That woman arrived at the mine:
"Your younger brother is looking for me. He
almost found me."
Then he said: "By Our Lord, appear to him. I
wonder what will become of him."

The next day the younger brother finds the
cotton, which he rubs all about his body, including the crotch area. This action has the effect of
turning him into a woman. In an attempt to return him to his original gender, the older brother
has him (her) lie down beside a river and allow
all the animals to approach, each one taking a
lick at the vagina. The younger brother is to remain silent. All goes well until the last beast
comes by, identified as one with very sharp
claws—very likely the small bear that used to be
found in the vicinity of the Sibundoy Valley. The
younger brother cries out in pain, and throws
this beast off of him. Now all the beasts must return, this time not to take a lick but to take a bite.
The narrator makes this agony iconic: the beasts
come "taking a bite, taking a bite, taking a bite,
taking a bite."

Eventually, all that remains of the younger
brother is a head, and this head becomes vexa-
tious to the miner in the manner of the "rolling
head" that appears in a number of American Indian mythologies (Lévi-Strauss 1978; Niles
1981), reminding us that important clusters in
our small-scale settings have a pan-Andean or
even pan-Amerindian presence. The head proposes a solution: the older brother must take the
wooden drum from the wall, place the head inside, tie the cover of the drum back on, and throw
it into the river. The drum, with the head inside,
disappears downstream.

Far below, the heathen women are out washing clothes. One of them spots the drum and takes
it out of the water. She opens it and finds a tender
infant, the young Wangetsmuna, inside. The celestial bodies, the sun and the moon, play no further role in this myth; we have entered a
subsequent cosmogenic phase—the dawn of the
present creation, marked by the emergence of
Wangetsmuna. The tender infant grows rapidly
and becomes a pivotal force in this Native American account of the movement from savagery to
civilization.

Some Unusual Attributes of Early Man

The heathens lack specific faculties essential to civil society in the modern creation: they have fire, but they are without the anus, and therefore cannot eat food; and they exhibit a very odd form of sexuality, involving the mustering of a collective penis. These shortcomings are described as follows in one telling of the myth:

Eating Habits
Then they had nothing in the way of an anus,
    nothing.
As for eating, they couldn't eat anything.
And they had turkeys, lots of them.
They would kill a fine turkey, pluck it, and put
    it in the pan.
And they would eat like this, only the steam,
    that steam they would gulp.
That's how they nourished themselves.

Sexuality
Heaven forbid, it was by the edge of a large
    river,
and that long thing, that penis would pass by
    there.
Then the husband of those heathen women
    would lie there,
and so truly, to speak in a vulgar way,
that's how they would copulate.

It is possible that the inappropriate customs described in these passages encode an ethnocentric highland perception of certain lowland customs, such as the maintenance of separate men's and women's quarters. In any case, Wangetsmuna sets about correcting this state of affairs. In the place where the anus should be, the heathens have a mark. They see Wangetsmuna enjoying the pleasure of eating, and beg him to open their anuses so that they might eat also:

And so they decided on it. They made up their
    minds,
and on that mark, with a knife, he opened
    them,
and a medicine, some medicine,
he chewed some bark and rubbed that on
    them.
And truly some of them did well and healed,
they began to eat well, they shat, truly.
Aha. But others died.

Wangetsmuna plays the part of the first native

doctor and introduces proper eating habits among the heathens.

His attempt to correct the peculiar sexual practices of the heathens meets with less success. He sets a trap along the path where the collective penis travels to cross the river and copulate with the heathen women. This organ is crushed as it activates the trap: the earth shakes and a loud groan is heard. The storytellers are quite graphic about what they clearly perceive to be a sexual perversity; two heathen men walk along carrying their damaged organ coiled around a long pole.

Wangetsmuna is advised to run to the house of his grandfather, who turns out to be the thunder. And so another celestial deity enters the story. The thunder, a major figure in Andean cosmologies (Cobo 1956; Rowe 1946; Demarest 1981), is portrayed in this myth cycle much as he appears in classical Andean sources: a powerful deity given to spinning a sling about and sending off destructive peals of thunder and bolts of lightning.

At this juncture in the story he appears as a kindly grandfather who agrees to hide his grandson and then obliterates the heathen men when they insist on searching for the one who abused them:

That sling he picked up. He whirled it about,
and the lightning bolts completely finished
    them off.
Then that rock of gold, that ball of gold,
spun about and completely destroyed them.

With this episode a mythical network is completed: the miner, who searches for gold (the sun's droppings) provides the balls of gold for the thunder deity's sling. Wangetsmuna enters the scene as a catalyst, and his caprice results in the eradication of the heathens and the preparation of the world for the establishment of modern human society.

The narrative shifts gears here, and Wangetsmuna is sent off (much like his counterpart from the southern Andes, Viracocha) to visit the world and report back to his grandfather after a year's time. Wangetsmuna goes about "pronouncing judgments," giving the animals their voices and characteristics, and eventually establishing for all time the boundary between animals and humans:

Then the grandfather sent him into the world.
"With this trumpet you are to visit the world,
to every region you will travel.

You will be called Wangetsmuna.
Thus from this day you will go among the animals,
and you will defend yourself from the beasts with an incantation.
And so prepare yourself, so you must travel.

In this way, you will make the weasel laugh,
Wangetsmuna, in this way the squirrel.
In this way you will make the monkey laugh.
In this way, the chkuro surely kills the hen.
And that rump is the first part eaten.
That one then squealed at her.
The weasel is like that, like that she kills the hen,
like that she squeals at her.
There she turned out to be harmful that weasel.
So a curse you must lay on her.
The monkey, no, the monkey just on that rope, on the vine he must hang.
Like the wind he must fly, thus he is to fly."

At the next dawn he had to sound the trumpet.
Whatever day it happened to be,
we humans became as we are in God's world,
we humans, human, and from that day on,
the animals remained animals.

In his travels Wangetsmuna sustains a series of rather biblical encounters with people in different places. In some tellings the Wangetsmuna cycle concludes with the cultural hero returning to abide with his grandfather; in others, perhaps influenced by the Christian story, the unfortunate hero falls victim to ravenous beasts here on earth. We can see that the sequence of episodes included in this mythic narrative cycle spans a crucial moment in cosmic time: the transition from the preancestral period, when the proto-people interacted directly with the celestial bodies, to the dawn of the ancestral world, when the first people began to live in society according to "civilized" norms.

The mythic narratives that feature Wangetsmuna make up the primary foundation myth of the Sibundoy natives. The narratives depict the vanquishing of the heathens, whose inappropriate modes of living had to yield to civilized customs; the establishment of the boundary between people and animals; and the origin of many practices, objects, and habits constitutive of the modern-day social and natural worlds. They carry us from a remote "time before time" to a tangible prehistory composed of familiar patterns of behavior.

The Ancestral Presence

I hope that this brief excursion into Sibundoy mythic narrative convincingly suggests its role in formulating the civilizing process in one Andean setting. There is a temporal and a spatial dispensation to this gradual taming of brute spiritual power. Along the timescale, early encounters with spiritual elements produce knowledge, wisdom, power and order; later encounters, especially as we approach modern times, produce the disintegrative effects of spirit sickness. The first people have the mettle to withstand such encounters and profit from them; contemporary mortals are less resilient. In the ancestral period, spirituality lies at the heart of world action; later it is banished to the byways.

The myths trace a three-tiered spiritual topography: the Sibundoy Valley at the center, a vibrant point of tension between order and chaos; the highland wastes above it (the *paramo*), a bleak region of destructive spiritual influences; and the lowland jungle below, a region of potent spirituality. Following the trajectory of Wangetsmuna, Sibundoy native doctors travel to the lowlands to learn from renowned Siona and Kwakier shamans.

The Sibundoy corpus of mythic narrative presents a charter, not so much for social structure as in Malinowski's formulation of this concept, but for the pursuit of individual and collective health and happiness in the modern period. The ancestral model represents the best hope for survival in a precarious existence. It is lauded in Kamsá ceremonial speeches, which routinely proclaim loyalty to the ancestors through this formula (see McDowell 1983):

ts-ye-ts-a-shekwastona
I am following in the footsteps of the ancestors

The ancestors are not as remote as one might think; in fact, they persist in an eternal present that lies just outside the margins of normal, wakeful experience. Sibundoy natives use a variety of channels to recover access to the ancestors, and to enlist their aid in combating the onslaught of deleterious spiritual forces.

Fragments of ancestral wisdom are preserved in the sayings of the ancestors, Inga *nujpamandacuna imasa rimascacuna*, "how the first people used to speak," brief statements that link perceived signs to spiritual consequences. Images that occur in dreams as well as wakeful observations trigger an association between sign and consequence whose validity is attributed to the authority of the ancestors. These sayings encompass the entire fabric of life in the Sibundoy setting yet they tend to concentrate on spiritual health. The sayings are part of a folk medicinal system that seeks to avoid spiritual sickness; they allow for self-diagnosis of impending vulnerability to malevolent spiritual forces.

For Sibundoy natives, dreams are a precious channel of communication that link the individual to the ancestors. Dreaming is not a casual experience, nor is it something that arises in the psychodynamics of the self. Instead, as the Ingas say (using the causative suffix *-chi*), we *are made* to dream: dreams come from a source external to the individual, the spiritual underground, and the ancestors have left a code, carefully passed along from one generation to the next, that elucidates their meaning.

Another channel allows not for a recovery of ancestral wisdom, but for communion with ancestral spirits: the visionary drug experience managed by the native doctors of the valley. Two hallucinogenic substances, *yage* (Banisteriopsis caapi and related species) and *borrachero* (Brugmansia), are prepared and administered for medicinal purposes. *Yage* is more frequently used: every Sibundoy will take a dose at least once a year as a kind of spiritual tonic. Special curing ceremonies occur in the cases of spiritual sickness, accidental injury, or in association with planting and other routine activities. *Borrachero* is a stronger psychodyslepic agent and its use is confined largely to cases of heinous sorcery.

It is believed that these visionary experiences transport patient and doctor to the ancestral domain where they benefit from the direct intervention of ancestral spirits in their predicaments. The native doctors call on spirit helpers and seek to banish negative spiritual influences that might have entered the picture. Here the ancestral impact is not mediated through a traditional code: rather, the modern people come face-to-face with the ancestors and assimilate some small portion of their spiritual prowess.

There is one additional recourse to the ancestors: during the Sibundoy carnival people gather to dance, make music, and consume large quantities of *chicha*, the home-brewed corn beer.

Dressed in their feathered coronas or crowns, "the modern-day people impersonate ancestors and heathens in a striking enactment of cosmology" (McDowell 1987). As each musician-dancer moves within a vibrant envelope of sound, the ancestors appear to walk the earth once again, and the modern people renew their contract with the ancestral model.

Conclusion

What I have done in this presentation is to bring together two prominent forms of Sibundoy discourse, personal experience narratives about encounters with rampant spirits, and mythic narratives about the times of the ancestors, in the effort to portray Andean cosmology in one microcosm. These two narrative modes contrast on many counts: the stories are told in casual, often intimate settings by people of all ages, whereas the myths are performed in more formal gatherings by elders; the stories well forth from the actual experience of the speaker, whereas the myths transport us to ancestral times.

In spite of these contrasts, the two narrative traditions form interlocking segments of one comprehensive story, and they constantly reference and revive one another. The pernicious spirits of the modern frame emerge from the fabulous cosmological scaffolding constructed and reconstructed in the myths; this cosmology in turn is validated and renewed with each new account of a spirit encounter.

Pernicious spirits as well as exemplary ancestors remain a critical influence in the lives of modern Sibundoy Indians. Once this spiritual tapestry is revealed, it becomes clear that the Sibundoy experience is largely conditioned by this vast panorama of cosmic struggle that so often intrudes upon the human sphere of action. What the uneducated eye might perceive as a mere crest in a hill, the initiated mind knows to be a *mal punto*, a spiritually charged interstice; the odd behavior of a bird, or a striking image in a dream, provides evidence of significant spiritual dynamics. And people are constantly on the lookout for pugnacious souls of the departed or unworldly forest spirits.

Juxtaposing personal experience stories about modern-day encounters with spirits and mythic narratives about the doings of the ancestors allows us to grasp the underlying dynamic that animates the Sibundoy concept of world history—a perpetual quest for control over unruly spiritual forces, played out in the collective effort to achieve civilization and in the daily striving for spiritual health. Each phase in the cosmic succession brings a new extension of spiritual control: darkness is replaced by light; rawness is replaced by cooking; the heathens are vanquished by the first people; proper norms of subsistence and sexual reproduction replace the previous models. The advent of the missionaries is easily assimilated into this grand scheme of things: their blessing is but another instrument for warding off the disintegrative influences of unrestrained spiritual vitality, which constantly threatens to overwhelm the fragile conventions that preserve a realm for human development.

From a paper presented at the Andean Studies Group Symposium, "Andean Cosmologies Through Time: Persistence and Emergence," Bloomington, Indiana, October 22–23, 1988.

For a longer version of this paper, see Andean Cosmologies Through Time: Persistence and Emergence, *edited by Robert H.V. Dover, Katharine E. Seibold, and John H. McDowell, Bloomington: Indiana University Press, 1992*

Further Reading

Bonilla, Victor Daniel, *Servants of God or Masters of Men—The Story of a Capuchin Mission in Amazonia,* Harmondsworth, England: Penguin, 1972

Cobo, Bernabé, *Historia del Nuevo Mundo,* 2 volumes, Madrid, Spain: Ediciones Atlas, 1956

Demarest, Arthur, *Viracocha: The Nature and Antiquity of the Andean High God,* Cambridge, Massachusetts: Peabody Museum of Archaeology and Ethnology, Harvard University, 1981

Lévi-Strauss, Claude, *L'origine des manières de table,* Paris: Plon, 1968; as *The Origin of Table Manners,* New York: Harper and Row, 1978; London: Cape, 1978

McDowell, John H., "Kamsá Music-Making: An Andean Musical System," in *Andean Musics,* volume 3 of *Andean Studies Occasional Papers,* edited by Robert V.H. Dover and John H. McDowell, Bloomington: Center for Latin American and Caribbean Studies, Indiana University, 1981

———, *Sayings of the Ancestors: The Spiritual Life of the Sibundoy Indians,* Lexington: University Press of Kentucky, 1989

———, "The Semiotic Constitution of Kamsá Ritual Language," *Language in Society* 12:1 (1983)

———, *"So Wise Were Our Elders": Mythic Narratives of the Kamsá,* Lexington: University Press of Kentucky, 1994

Niles, Susan, *South American Indian Narrative, Theoretical and Analytical Approaches: An Annotated Bibliography,* New York: Garland, 1981

Rowe, John, "Inca Culture at the Time of the Spanish Conquest," in *The Andean Civilizations,* volume 2 of *Handbook of South American Indians,* edited by Julian Steward, Washington, D.C.: Government Printing Office, 1946

Saramaka Maroon Folktales in Comparative Afro-American Perspective

Richard Price and Sally Price

The Prices describe contemporary Maroon tales and compare them with related traditions in other African American cultures. Their interpretation shows how the Maroons' heritage of resistance to slavery produced characters and plots and morals that differ from those in the tales of African Americans whose ancestors remained in slavery until emancipation.

Maroon Communities

For more than four centuries, the communities formed by runaway slaves—Maroons—dotted the fringes of plantation America, from Brazil to the southeastern United States, from Peru to the American southwest. These new societies ranged from tiny bands that survived less than a year to powerful states encompassing thousands of members and surviving for generations or even centuries. Today their descendants still form semi-independent enclaves in several parts of the hemisphere—Suriname, Jamaica, French Guiana, Colombia, and elsewhere—remaining fiercely proud of their Maroon origins and, in some cases at least, faithful to unique cultural traditions that were forged during the earliest days of Afro-American history. The English word "maroon," like the French and Dutch *marron*, derives from the Spanish *cimarrón*—itself based on an Arawakan/Taino root. *Cimarrón* originally referred to domestic cattle that had taken to the hills in Hispaniola, and soon after to American Indian slaves who had escaped from the Spaniards as well. But

by the end of the 1530s, it was used primarily to refer to Afro-American runaways, and the word had taken on strong connotations of "fierceness," of being "wild" and "unbroken."

Afro-American folktales told at wakes to honor the dead reflect subtle contrasts between the way Maroons (the descendants of slaves who rebelled and escaped) and other Afro-Americans (the descendants of slaves who became "free" only upon general emancipation) think about their place in the world and act upon it. Part of the same plantation world but facing it from distinctive perspectives, Maroons and slaves gradually elaborated the same initial stock of folktale materials into overlapping but significantly different repertoires. Today these tales, as told by Maroons and by other Afro-Americans, bear the marks both of a shared Afro-American heritage and an important divergence in historical experiences.

Roger Abrahams has viewed Afro-American folktales within a broad historical and comparative context, writing that "together, they demonstrate a wholeness in this folk literature, an integrity of theme, a consistency of style and pattern that owes much to its African origins, even while it breathes with a life of its own" (p.18). He goes on to suggest that it is often in focusing on the ways Afro-Americans have reshaped African or European patterns to their own ends that the deeper meaning and significance of New World tale-telling emerges.

In the folktales of the Saramaka Maroons of Suriname, the stock characters number in the scores and have a wide range of historical provenances. Some, like the "scrawny little kid" (usually the youngest sibling who saves his sister from disaster), appear, albeit in different guise, throughout Afro-America. Others, like the giant, oafish "devils," have at least partial Christian/European roots. Still others, like Anasi the Spider (and his numerous progeny) or, more remarkably, Elephant (an animal whose memory is preserved by Saramakas at a remove of three centuries) are African to the core.

Saramakas' Anasi—at once man and spider—is, above all, outrageous. As Abrahams notes, writing of Afro-America more generally, we can see his "tremendous ingenuity in stirring things up and keeping them boiling; how he gets into a stew of his own making on many occasions, and how, as often as not, he uses his wits to get out of this trouble. . . . [His] unbridled egotism runs as high as his clever wit" (p. 180). He is admired for his creativity in meeting the boundless demands of his own ego and is much appreciated for the entertainment that his incorrigible naughtiness contributes to an evening of tale-telling. Even in tales about other sets of characters, Anasi often makes a cameo appearance, jumping briefly into the action to stake his claim when there are spoils to be had (a princess's hand in marriage, the prestige of having slain a monster, etc.). Win or lose, Anasi epitomizes the valued Saramaka (and Afro-American) strategy of trying things out, keeping multiple options open, and relying largely on one's wits to stay a step ahead of the competition.

However, the bulk of the denizens of Saramaka folktale-land are either humans, more or less like Saramakas themselves, or familiar animals of their own South American rain forest—Bushfowl, Jaguar, Howler Monkey, Deer, Hummingbird, Cayman, Anaconda, and a host of others. If Lion is king in much of Africa, it is Jaguar who reigns over the other animals in the rain forest of Suriname. Saramakas underscore his absolute authority in folktale-land by repeating the formulaic "all the animals called him 'mother's brother'" (*tío*, the ultimate authority in this matrilineal society). But though chief of all the animals, and physically powerful, Jaguar—like his less-exotic counterparts elsewhere in Afro-America (and like Lion himself in Africa)—often comes up short in the end, being tricked by smaller but smarter creatures such as Shrimp, Turtle, or Hummingbird.

In addition, Maroon folktales feature frequent cameo appearances by special figures such as Death and the Great God. One memorable character is the mysterious stranger whose impressive dancing inspires Anasi to offer him a congratulatory embrace; only after the damage has been done does he, along with the other spectators who smell his soiled body, realize that the stranger was none other than Shit himself. The characters who inhabit folktale-land are familiar to all Saramakas, and their individual gifts and foibles are frequently alluded to, by way of comparison, in everyday discourse about the here and now.

The Saramaka "Scrawny Little Kid" and the West Indian "Chiggerfoot Boy"

But Saramaka (and other Maroon) folktale characters are differentiated from those elsewhere in Afro-America less by their bare identities than by the roles and significance they take on for tellers and listeners. For example, the "scrawny little kid" of Saramaka tales is a direct parallel to the Chiggerfoot (or Jiggerfoot) Boy of Anglophone West Indian tales, described by Abrahams as

> an almost invisible character . . . a "dark" figure: an "Old Witch Boy," a dirty and diseased misfit, a mysterious member of the [white] king's family. . . . He lives at the margins between the family and the wilds, and can be seen as something of a contaminating anomaly, and . . . the upsetter of order. Described variously as "dirty," "smelly," "covered with ashes" (like Cinderella), he is best known for his ugly foot, which is described alternatively as diseased, constantly surrounded by fleas and nits . . . or as a clubfoot. . . . [He is] contrasted with the king's beautiful daughter, ostensibly his sister. (pp. 22–23)

In certain important ways the Saramaka kid (*makisá míi*) and his West Indian counterpart are the same. In Saramaccan, *makisá* means crushed, mashed up, messed up, weak, frail, and generally in a dilapidated state that could be regarded as either pitiable or laughable, depending on the sympathies of the observer; *míi* is the word for child, kid, or boy. So, the two are physically alike. But there is also a crucial difference between them.

As Abrahams glosses a common West Indian plot involving the Chiggerfoot Boy:

The daughter [the white princess] is courted by many of the best men in the land, but she rejects them all until one man comes riding by with whom she falls madly in love. Their courtship and marriage is therefore quickly achieved, and her new bridegroom carries her off with him to his home in the bush. The boy, through snooping or using one of his witching powers, is able to follow the couple and discover that his sister has married an animal or bush spirit that has been able to transform itself into human form. The boy also discovers how the transformation is brought about—it is commonly a song—and he persuades his father to accompany him to witness what he has discovered. The boy sings the song, the bridegroom is transformed, and the king then does what he must do. (p. 22)

Here, the West Indian audience is meant to empathize and identify, at least to a point, with this rather bizarre royal family; it is the princess whose life is in danger, and her brother who is the hero.

But in Saramaka, this ubiquitous character is the younger brother, not of a white princess in the family of a king, but of "normal" Saramaka sisters. From a Saramaka perspective, he is one of "us," not one of "them." The difference is cardinal and points to an ideological contrast that helps us understand how Maroon tales, while in general very much a part of the Afro-American tale-telling world, also stand alone in that comparative context. Although white kings and princesses occasionally appear in Saramaka tales, they are consistently portrayed as part of an alien, foreign world. Indeed, in the most fully developed Saramaka depiction of a princess that we know, she appears as a prototypical bitch—self-centered, fickle, spoiled, condescending, and nasty. And the scrawny little kid, who in Saramaka as elsewhere in Afro-America saves his sister(s) from disaster, always saves *black*, "normal" sister(s), not—as in the West Indian cases—a strange white one.

More generally, the folktales of Saramaka Maroons contrast with those of other Afro-Americans in portraying the white world (with its kings and princesses, palaces and cannon, horses and coaches, ships and sailors, slavemasters and wage-labor bosses) as decidedly other, fully beyond the boundaries of Saramaka society. When Bajans or Nevisians or Alabamians depict those same characteristics, they are talking about a much more in-

tegral—if still in many ways distant—part of their own social universe. In this sense, then, the contrast in folktale conventions reflects the different social realities of the descendants of Maroons and the descendants of plantation slaves. In this broader Afro-American context, the special ideological stance of Saramakas toward whitefolks renders unique the specific transformations that they have effected on African, other Afro-American, and European tales.

A Saramaka Hero Tale Compared With Its Afro-American Counterpart

Another contrast occurs in what Abrahams calls "Afro-American 'In the beginning' stories." These, he argues, "underscore the value of accommodating yourself to the way things are (and always will be) . . . [and] underscore the fact that [one must accept that] life isn't usually very fair" (p. 39). But while the West Indian Chiggerfoot Boy, through his cleverness or witching powers, saves his sister or solves some other *domestic* problem, his Saramaka counterpart solves *community-wide* problems. Many Saramaka tales describe how a particular individual—often the scrawny little kid—refuses to accept a difficult, unfair status quo and sets out to alter it, changing some aspect of the world into the (better) way it now is. In various tales, heroes render a particular stretch of forest, which had been inhabited by devils or monsters, safe for humans; in others, through their courage and initiative, they introduce central aspects of life—drums, fire, polygyny, all-night dancing—into the Saramaka world. The contrasts seem clear: "slaves vs. maroons, tales of playful antagonism within a world of social inequities vs. genuine hero tales."

One ideologically central Saramaka tale may serve as an illustration of these contrasts:

There was a great hunter called Bási Kodjó. He had hunting dogs that were killing off all the Bush Cows in the forest. [The Bush Cow is a mythical animal, resembling, but fiercer than, a tapir.] Finally, the Bush Cows held a council meeting. They said, "What can we do to kill this man? Soon there will be none of us left." One of them, a female, spoke. "I'll go to him. I have a plan to lure him back here so we can kill him." And she changed herself into a beautiful woman in order to trick Bási Kodjó. She arrived in his village with a basket on her head, saying that the man who could knock it to the ground would become her husband. She was really beautiful! No one could do it. Finally Bási Kodjó tried, and the basket fell. So this beautiful woman became his wife. Every night, when they were in their hammock, making love, she would ask Bási Kodjó what his secret was, how it was that he was able to kill so many Bush Cows without their ever hurting him. Each night she asked, and each night he told her a little more. She was so beautiful!

Often, during the night, the woman would go out behind the house to stare at the row of Bush Cow skulls that her husband had nailed against the rear wall as trophies. She would weep and weep, silently, for her dead relatives. When she had finished crying, she would return to the house, and Bási Kodjó would ask, "Where have you been?" "I went to urinate," she would say. But every few minutes she would go back out and just stare at those skulls and weep.

Every night, she asked Bási Kodjó over and over, "Those animal skulls at the back of your house. How in the world did you kill those animals? They're fiercer than any animal alive!"

One night, Bási Kodjó finally told her, "Woman, those animals live in savannahs. I go all the way to the middle of the savannah and fire my gun. When they come charging, I toss my gun aside and climb an awara [palm] tree. The animals circle round and furiously chew at the trunk to fell it. Meanwhile, my mother is back in the village, stirring the boiling pap that she feeds to my hunting dogs at the proper moment, to excite them. When I see that the palm tree is about to fall, I turn myself into a chameleon, sitting on the trunk, and I call out, '*fííí*,' and this makes the trunk grow even thicker than it was at first. I do this until I know that the dogs have had time to gobble up all the boiling pap, and really feel it. Then I let the tree fall. By then, the Bush Cows have realized that I am the chameleon, so I turn into a spot of sand. When they try to eat that up, I use my final disguise and turn myself into a . . ." Just then, Bási Kodjó's mother shrieked from her house, "Bási Kodjó. Bási Kodjó. Hurry. Snake. Snake!" [It was really the god in her head that was calling out.] Bási Kodjó jumped out of his hammock and ran to kill the snake. When he got to his mother's house, she pulled him close and whispered, "There's no snake. But I must

warn you. That beautiful woman is not really a woman! Don't tell her the last thing you know how to turn yourself into. Instead, tell her that you become a *nóuna*." Bási Kodjó returned to his wife. She said, "That thing you were about to tell me, the very last thing you turn yourself into, when the Bush Cows come charging at you, what is it?" He said, "I become a *nóuna* [a nonsense word, a word with no meaning]." At last, she was satisfied. They slept.

In the middle of the night, the woman arose very quietly and went to her basket and took out a razor. She prepared to cut Bási Kodjó's throat. Bási Kodjó's gun said, "I will shoot her *kpóó*!!" His machete said, "I will cut her *vélevélevélevéle*!" His magical belt [*óbiatatái*] said, "I will tie her *kílikílikílikíli*." All the posts of the house groaned loudly, "*hiiiiii*." Bási Kodjó awoke with a start, saying, "What's going on?" She answered, "I have no idea. I was asleep." Not a single thing in the house slept during the rest of the night.

At dawn, the beautiful wife asked Bási Kodjó to go off to the forest with her to collect awara palm seeds. He told his mother to prepare the pap for the dogs. And they set off. The woman led them deeper and deeper into the forest until they finally reached the savannah. Bási Kodjó climbed the awara tree and began picking fruit. Suddenly, the woman turned back into her natural form, a Bush Cow, and called out to her relatives. In a moment, the savannah was black with Bush Cows, all coming to eat Bási Kodjó. Quickly, he turned himself into a chameleon. She told them he was now the chameleon. So they began felling the tree. When it finally fell, they couldn't find the chameleon. She said, "Eat that spot of sand. *It* is Bási Kodjó." After a while, they could not find the sand. Bási Kodjó had turned himself into a tiny awara palm thorn, and hidden himself by sticking himself into a leaf. She said, "Destroy the *nóuna*. He's turned himself into a *nóuna*." The Bush Cows milled around in confusion. None of them knew what a *nóuna* was!

Meanwhile, Bási Kodjó's hunting dogs, who by then had finished eating their boiling pap and had been untied, arrived on the scene and they ripped every last Bush Cow to shreds. Except for one. Bási Kodjó saw that this last Bush Cow was pregnant, and he called off the dogs. This Bush Cow was hiding in a cave near a stream. She called out, "Bási Kodjó, have mercy. You're about to kill your own offspring!" He grabbed her by one side, ripping off the whole leg, and then shoved her back into the cave.

Now you know the importance of *nóuna*. Note that the rhetorical structure of this version of *nóuna* (considerably condensed from two 1978 tellings by the late Kandámma, then ailing and in her hammock) almost exactly parallels that of a central First-Time historical account—the story of the faithful slave/spy, Kwasímuk-ámba, who arrived in Saramaka feigning friendship, *almost* learned the secret of Saramaka invulnerability, "escaped" back to the whites to lead a giant whitefolks' army against the Saramakas, and in the final battle was maimed by the Saramaka chief in an ultimate act of vengeance. (Price, 159)

In the common West Indian plot glossed by Abrahams, a white princess is seduced by an evil animal in disguise; the action unfolds on a purely domestic plane involving personal dangers and triumphs, and the central characters are empathetic (if somewhat strange) whitefolks. In the Saramaka *nóuna* tale (and others of its genre), two worlds are pitted in mortal battle—"our" world (that of Maroons) and another (rhetorically that of bush cows, historically and structurally that of the plantation and whitefolks); the seduction is carried out in the service of the bush cow state; and the renunciation of the beautiful "woman" and her eventual destruction are carried out by the Saramaka hero on behalf of his people.

Even where clear variants of the *nóuna* tale exist elsewhere in Afro-America, the common elements they include are limited to a monster (witch, bush spirit, animal) becoming a beautiful seductress, her requiring a vessel to be knocked off her head, the old mother tending the dogs back home while the hunter goes off to gather fruit with his changeling lover, the lover calling out helpers to fell the fruit tree, and the dogs eventually massacring her. In none of these variants is the lover a disguised enemy of the people. In none does she try to extract a secret. And in none is she merely maimed (rather than killed) by the hero, as a way of showing his ultimate disdain. Among the more than twenty variants we have seen from Africa (Bascom, 134), only one—from Dahomey—includes an animal in disguise/spy who tries to extract a secret from her hunter husband. (Herskovits and Herskovits, 186–90)

Although the other Afro-American tales are largely entertainment, the Maroon story (in addition to its entertainment value) encodes Saramakas' strongest ideological concern—community betrayal, treason vis-à-vis whitefolks, and the fear that "those times [the days of whitefolks' slavery] shall come again." (Price, 1–12)

Folklore and the Contemporary Political Scene

In the 1990s, these folktale contrasts take on a poignant political charge. For it could be argued that both the recent civil war in Suriname (1986–1992) and the Maroons' ongoing struggle against the national government's attempts to auction off their lands to transnational logging and mining companies represent the continued playing out of precisely these contrasts between slave and Maroon definitions of reality, between differing ideological stances toward Western authority. Saramaka folktales, like the spirit that inspired the Maroon Jungle Commandos fighting against the national army of Suriname, are infused with a firm sense of Afro-American differentness, a recognition that Maroons fought and died (and continue to do so) for a place on the fringes of the Western world where they can maintain their dignity and moral independence. Today's Maroon leaders do not seek political independence or separation from the national state any more than their eighteenth-century ancestors wished to cut themselves off from the plantation society of the coast. In both cases, Maroons have been well aware of their dependence on the coastal society for a panoply of material goods, and have maintained intimate contacts through kinship and other ties with people on the coast. The contest today, as two hundred years ago, might ultimately be said to be about identity and the right to control one's own destiny. These ideologically charged folktales, then, far from being some sort of fossilized survivals from Africa, speak directly to the Maroons' current predicament (which so resembles that of their First-Time ancestors). And in seeking a satisfactory solution to ongoing Maroon-Creole conflicts in Suriname, it would be wise not to forget the importance, to Maroons themselves, of the lessons their ancestors encoded in the exploits of such characters as Anasi, the princess, and the scrawny little kid.

Further Reading

Abrahams, Roger D., *Afro-American Folktales: Stories from Black Traditions in the New World,* New York: Pantheon, 1985

Arrom, José Juan, "Cimarrón: Apuntes sobre sus primeras documentaciones y su probable origen," in *Cimarrón,* by José Juan Arrom and Manuel A. García Arévalo, Santo Domingo, Dominican Republic: Fundación García-Arévalo, 1986

Bascom, William, *Ifa Divination; Communication Between Gods and Men in West Africa,* Bloomington: Indiana University Press, 1969

Colchester, Marcus, *Forest Politics in Suriname,* Utrecht, The Netherlands: International, 1995

Gates, Henry Louis, Jr., *The Signifying Monkey: A Theory of Afro-American Literary Criticism,* New York: Oxford University Press, 1988

Herskovits, Melville J., and Frances S. Herskovits, *Dahomean Narrative: A Cross-Cultural Analysis,* Evanston, Illinois: Northwestern University Press, 1958

Price, Richard, "Executing Ethnicity: The Killings in Suriname," *Cultural Anthropology* 10:4 (1995)

————, *First-Time: The Historical Vision of an Afro-American People,* Baltimore, Maryland: Johns Hopkins University Press, 1983

Price, Richard, and Sally Price, *Two Evenings in Saramaka,* Chicago: University of Chicago Press, 1991

Tanna, Laura, *Jamaican Folk Tales and Oral Histories,* Kingston: Institute of Jamaica, 1984

The Art of Storytelling: Field Observations in Venezuela

Daniel Mato

From 1985 to 1987 Daniel Mato observed 65 tellers in 37 sites throughout Venezuela. He discusses the varieties of performers and performance styles, drawing on his own experience as storyteller and researcher and applying theories from the semiotics of theater and body language.

Basis for the Field Research

This field research was carried out during the period 1985 to 1987 and covered a total of 65 storytellers in 37 places throughout Venezuela that included the capital city of Caracas and other cities of different kinds and sizes in 12 of the country's states. Because of the objectives of the investigation no narratives were compiled. Instead, reports about performances, events, contexts, and the narrators and their craft were made.

Some fundamental goals of the research were:

a. To identify the social meaning and ways of existence of storytelling in each community instead of assuming any preconceived image of the ways in which it exists.

b. To identify the patterns of appreciation of storytelling in each community instead of using others from different cultural frames.

c. To identify the persons who are well known as storytellers in each community instead of deciding this based on external criteria.

d. Not to believe the existence of some "true" circumstances and of others that are "not true." Every circumstance that occurs is, by virtue of its existence, true. Each performance acquires meaning in relationship to a kind of event. Each kind of event acquires its meaning in relationship to a certain cultural context. Of course, I am conscious that the fieldworker has an inevitable part in segregating these performances, events, and contexts from the continuity of everyday life.

e. To assume the cultural differentiation between researcher and community, rejecting the naïveté of believing that the mimesis with the members of any community is possible; it is not even desirable.

Because in this particular case the researcher was also a storyteller, it was assumed that the similarity of occupation was the basis of the relationships that would form as a storyteller from another area traveled to meet other narrators. This practice is common among narrators of diverse social environments. The peculiarity in my case, which I explicitly communicated, was that the traveler-narrator came from a large city and was writing a book about storytelling.

Interviews with performers and other people in each community have let me produce information about functions of storytelling, patterns of appreciation, genres of tales, styles of performance, etc. Interviews with narrators also enabled me to produce information about professional "secrets," processes by which the craft is learned, and the relationship of storytellers to print and audiovisual media.

A descriptive sociosemiotic model has helped me to observe and make reports of the performances. This model was an original analytical device created mainly from some specific developments in the fields of the semiotics of theater and body language, and from other more generic semiotic formulations that I adapted from my own experience as a storyteller. This model has allowed me to produce systematic and comparative descriptions of each performance in terms of types of tales and kinds of personal devices, such as vocalization (imitation of voices and sounds, modulation), gesture (types and parts of the body involved in the different kinds of gestures), use of space, representation of characters, use of objects, management of interaction, and exploitation of emerging circumstances.

I used this model to systematically observe and describe almost one hundred performances of 65 narrators (indigenous, Afro-Venezuelan, peasant, "popular," and professional urban storytellers) in about 30 settlements (rural and urban) of 12 states of Venezuela. Most observations were of typical performances. Some of them were performances that were induced by the researcher telling the first story.

Patterns of Appreciation and Learning Processes

In every community that was studied, certain individuals were recognized as having a special *don* (gift) of telling stories. For this reason they were chosen by their attendants and special attention was paid to their narrating. This gift was variously called *gracia* (grace), *sabor* (flavor), *sal* (salt), *pimienta* (pepper), or *chispa* (spark).

When people were asked to explain these expressions, their answers, with a few exceptions, referred to the nonverbal aspects of the storyteller's art. The representation of characters, the gesticulation, the imitation of voices and sounds, and stage mastery were most frequently mentioned. The inventiveness and the scope of the repertoire were mentioned secondarily. With less frequency the importance of the *labia* (fluency of speaking) was emphasized, except in the Andean region (western Venezuela) where it receives primary importance.

Some particular remarks about the two Indian groups included in the research are necessary. In these indigenous communities the knowledge of ethnic tales was especially valued. Among the Guayúu people the ability to imitate voices and different sounds is also highly valued, while the

importance given to gesture is in a certain way contradictory. Indeed, in the epic stories called *jaiechi,* which are sung, no importance at all is given to gesture. In other kinds of stories gesture is preferred by some people, while content is emphasized by others. This diversity of opinions is also a significant feature among the Kariña people.

In any case, I am not trying to reduce the idea of grace as a part of gestures and representations. This grace does not seem to be easily contrasted at an empirical level. Although it is related to the management of certain personal resources, these do not in themselves constitute grace. Displaying them is not necessarily an indication that the storyteller has grace, nor does not showing them indicate the contrary. Furthermore, on some occasions, a highly stylized attitude might indicate this particular gift. However, the majority of the narrators emphasized that the most important thing was not the story, but how it was told. Many of them insisted that there was no such thing as "bad" stories and "good" stories. A bad narrator can murder the best story and a good narrator can do wonders with any tale.

Practically all the interviewed storytellers said that they had begun their apprenticeship as children. Usually they began by observing adults in their family or social circle; little by little they began to practice with their peers. Normally this process took a long time until they became recognized as storytellers in their own right. Generally speaking, it began as an unconscious work by observing and listening to consummate narrators. But from a certain point this process became more and more conscious. In some way this process is similar to that of learning how to do anything in nonscholarly aspects of life. I observed the activities of apprentices, observing and participating with their narrations on no less than a dozen cases. Often tellers would proudly introduce their apprentices to me.

Among the Guayúus and the Kariñas there is no formalized process, but most adults pay very special attention to the children who are learning the tales of their ethnic tradition. Guayúu children also learn those of their clan. Some peasant storytellers pay particular attention to stimulating and facilitating the apprenticeship of a son, nephew, or even a young neighbor that they believe has a special talent. Caracas storytellers follow formal courses, which is a remarkable difference between the learning process of the rest of the storytellers in my research.

Most of the narrators said that this process usually consisted of first learning the plots and trying them out in front of their young friends. The style of performance usually was developed later, partly by imitating some of the devices of their model adults, and partly by introducing their own devices. But the learning process seems to be continuous, or overlapped with the creative process, as with any artistic activity. Many adult and consummate narrators have told me that they still spend a lot of time analyzing audience reactions and adjusting their styles accordingly. The exposure to situations of competence when jousting with other narrators was especially mentioned as one that leads to learning and the development of style.

Imagination, Verisimilitude, and the Work of Inventing Stories

The majority of the narrators studied, apart from narrating stories that they have learned from others, create their own stories. Some of them are completely fictional, but most of them are created by arranging material from their careful observation of daily life in the community and from the personal experiences of the narrators.

Many of these stories are generated from a visual image (e.g., the way someone fell, or the reaction to any kind of *susto* [scare], etc.). These visual images also give the narrator the opportunity for acting the part, of course exaggerating the circumstances, and also for imagining and adding new body images in the creative process. But the importance of visual images in the work of narrators is not confined to the generation of body images alone. Narrators were also reported as having a key role in generating verbal images, and in evoking and retelling stories.

The anecdotes usually refer to people who are well known in the community, though they may also refer to others who presumably are known only by the storyteller. Anecdotes are usually created by simply restructuring and exaggerating actual circumstances. But in some cases a good deal of falsification is introduced. However, whether they be exaggerations or fabrications, anecdotes have to seem true. In the majority of the communities that I visited, if anecdotes were not verisimilar, they were not considered anecdotes.

The anecdotes are called *cachos* in Oriente (the east coast of the country) and in Los Llanos Occidentales, two regions that are a long way from each other and are ethnically and culturally very different. In both areas the *cacho* is proudly assumed to be a treasure of regional heritage. Similarly, in both areas many people *echa cachos* (tell anecdotes), and to be a well-known *cachero* (teller of anecdotes) is a very important social distinction.

In the same way in Yaracuy State, which is not included in either of the two aforementioned regions, tales of this kind are very frequently told among Afro-Venezuelan communities. Here they are simply called *cunetos* (stories).

The *cachos* are usually funny tales, but sometimes they can be tragic. Obviously, not only the names of stories, but also the criteria of classification vary from one region to another, and eventually from one community to another. But verisimilitude is a significant differentiating factor between the *cacho,* or humorous anecdote, and the *chiste,* or joke. Verisimilitude also distinguishes the anecdote from the *embuste* (innocent, intentional, and extremely exaggerated lie). The *embuste* is a genre that is usually told by people who do not tell tales of other genres. These people are called *embusteros* and they only tell *embustes,* obstinately believing in their own lies. Nobody else believes their stories, but many people like to listen to their tales, sometimes even for hours.

Performance Style

It seems very important to emphasize that the style of performance of each narrator shows not only cultural differences but also personal differences. Furthermore the same narrator not only tells the same tale in different ways according to the event's variations, but also tells different kinds of tales, which of course call for different styles. It is, however, possible to make some generalizations.

Eye contact: Almost all of the narrators keep eye contact with their audience while performing. There are some exceptions. Usually when the tellers take the part of a character they break eye contact. This allows them to look at relevant points of their "stage," which are imaginary representations of the scenes in the story. This use of the narrators' gaze is indicative of their imaginative work at the same time that it stimulates spectators' imaginations. A significant exception is the case of most Guayúu narrators, who have a tendency to look anywhere but at their audience when telling.

Imitative sounds: Almost all narrators frequently used onomatopoeia, imitated sounds, and altered their voices according to the needs of the story. But only about half of the narrators in the study markedly imitated the voice and speaking manner of their characters. Others only slightly differentiated their tones as they imitated the character's ways of speaking. But this is not only a matter of personal style. On the contrary, this imitating seems to be linked more with the genres of tales and the types of events.

Body language: Most narrators often made expressive and indicative gestures. In the semiotic model of observation, I have called expressive those gestures that have an undefined verbal meaning. Self-contact gestures of various sorts, a particular kind of expressive gesture, often indicated the breakthrough into performance of the narrator. I have called indicative those gestures that give information about place, time, manner, etc. About half of the narrators also used illustrative gestures. This term describes any gesture that illustrates a specific action of a character. The majority of these storytellers involved almost their whole bodies to illustrate the actions that were called for, when the physical space and the social circumstances allowed. I also observed that, in general, the same narrators that performed illustrative gestures also acted the parts of their characters. The use of these two devices seems to depend not only on the personal style of the storyteller but also on the genres of tales and kinds of events. Some genres, for example humorous tales, frequently call for the playing of the part of characters. It must be emphasized that between making illustrative gestures and acting the part of the characters there is a substantive difference in the function and imaginative work that the storyteller—and, more generally speaking, any person—plays.

Teller position: About two-thirds of the storytellers in this study remained standing during most of their performances or at least stood up when the narration called for them to do so. They also made good meaningful use of stage space. Even those narrators who generally remained sitting during their performances eventually stood up when they had a particular need to illustrate or represent an action of a character. Some of these narrators would make fortuitous use of the chair they sat on. For example, using the chair as a prop, they raised both legs at the same time.

One teller, two events: I observed significant changes in general expressive behavior, particularly in gesture and use of stage space when narrators were performing at different kinds of events, or when they were telling different genres of tales. Some narrators confirmed this observa-

tion. For example, two Afro-Venezuelan female narrators in the east coast region told märchen to children in a quiet, gentle manner while sitting and without acting the parts of characters, simply using illustrative gestures. In complete contrast, the same narrators telling *cachos* to adults would adopt a much more energetic style, would play the parts of their characters, would stand up, and would make meaningful use of stage space.

Props and audience interaction: Some narrators used different incidental objects during their performances to symbolically represent different things in the story they were narrating. Most narrators readily accepted or sometimes deliberately provoked verbal or physical interaction with their spectators. Some would skillfully blend these audience interventions into the story. Very few narrators included songs or recitations in their performances.

Storytelling and Print and Audiovisual Media

The majority of the narrators stated that they had learned their tales from other narrators or that they themselves had created them. In the particular case of Caracas narrators, books were reported as being the main source of their repertoire. These were books of tales by both literary authors and collections of oral literature from various countries. As a secondary source these narrators mentioned their own creations.

The fact that urban and modern narrators used books as a source is hardly surprising. However, at least 11 of the nonurban storytellers used tales that came from books as part of their repertoire. An interesting feature was that some illiterate storytellers had learned some of their stories from listening to other people, usually children, read. Some of the tales learned in this way were by Latin American authors, but others were from collections of oral literature from many different countries. But books are not the only sources of tales. There was one storyteller who used to tell a story that was his personal version of one Tío Conejo tale that had been included in a booklet of a fire prevention campaign.

Another storyteller used to tell a long tale that he called "*El un sólo ojo*" ("The One-eyed Man"). The story was his own particular version of the life of the Greek hero Odysseus; the title he used was a reference to the Cyclops. He told this tale with remarkable realism, as if he had been actually there. But, in fact, his source for this story was a movie that he had seen many years ago on one of his infrequent visits to a nearby city. Another narrator used to tell some folktales that he had learned from a cassette produced by a storyteller from another Latin American country. He had never been in this other country, nor even did he know which country it was. The cassette had been given to him as a gift by a friend.

Four storytellers used to tell jokes that they had learned from television programs. Another would narrate tales about national political history and aspects of the life of the Venezuelan national hero, Simon Bolívar. These he had learned by listening to the radio. Finally, it should be emphasized that radio and television have not only influenced the content of the tales but also the styles of performances. Some narrators commented that they had learned some of their gestures or vocal devices by the careful observation of television actors and/or radio performers.

The Storyteller and the Intrusion of the Researcher

I have borrowed the idea for the title of this section from an article by George Carey in which he reflected about how his intrusion in the life of a storyteller had changed the storyteller's life (Carey 1976). I wonder to what extent collectors' intrusions have changed styles. Continuous visits of someone obsessively interested in "hunting" for stories could have changed the storyteller's perception of what is more and what is less important in his or her performances.

I wonder about this in my own field experience. My tape recorder was an ostensible participant only when I was interviewing narrators and on a few other occasions that were intentionally devoted to observing personal reactions and variations in the dynamics of the events. In other cases it was reduced to fulfilling the role of aide-de-mémoire, working inside a bag or under a chair. Its existence was always communicated to the performers, sometimes before and sometimes after the performance. But on every occasion when I made my tape recorder visible the behavior of the narrator and that of the audience changed. Two consequences were most frequent. One consequence was that the narrator began to treat the tape recorder as a privileged participant, and therefore keep closer to the machine, diminishing his or her movements and changing the focus. The other consequence was that the participating audience became a nonparticipating

audience. Olivia Torres, a narrator who had been engaged in the preparation of a book of tales with a collector, spontaneously made some comments that confirm these observations. I wonder to what extent the reflections of some performance-centered text collectors about the neutrality of their tape recorder are excessively innocent.

On the other hand, I wonder to what extent the use of video cameras to record performances could be neutral. I have used a still photo camera with a lot of care, but I could see how, when I used it repeatedly, it stimulated or inhibited body expression. I am not proposing that we should not make any kind of record. What I argue is that we can not be so innocent, and therefore that, apart from being very conscious about how and when to use this equipment, we only can use those records for illustrating partial aspects of the performances.

About the Narrators' Ages and Social Environments

Despite the widely held notion that storytellers are usually old people, my research established that many recognized storytellers are in fact younger people. Among those included in this research there are storytellers of all ages: nine were in their 70s, thirteen were in their 60s, seventeen were in their 50s, twelve were in their 40s, five were in their 30s, and the remaining nine were in their 20s.

Another preconception related to storytelling is the belief that only among peasant and indigenous people can the best storytellers be found, and that the best storytellers are illiterate. Only a small proportion of the narrators in this study were illiterate, although they live in areas that have a high rate of illiteracy. On the other hand, in Caracas, in addition to an unknown number of traditional narrators, there are some 60 modern and professional storytellers, the majority of whom have completed high school; some of them are university graduates. Most of them are widely known because they perform in parks, libraries, museums, theaters, and other public places and their shows are often announced in the newspapers. A few of them have had radio shows, and others have appeared occasionally on television. Six of these storytellers are included in this research.

The other 59 narrators included in the research are well known only in their own communities, with the exception of three who have a wider reputation. Forty of them live in small towns, villages, and cities with 100 to 10,000 inhabitants. The majority of them are agricultural workers, but they also include store workers and owners, musicians, artisans, domestic workers, and building workers. In addition, this group includes a witch doctor, a policeman, a regional chronicler, and a librarian. The latter is a German woman who is a semiprofessional storyteller. She has had many stories published in local newspapers, has performed in cultural institutions in Caracas, and has produced a cassette of some of her stories. In addition, six of this group are indigenous: one is a Kariña Indian, and the other five are Guayúus. Only two of these are illiterate. Another six of this group are Afro-Venezuelan, five of whom live in Afro-Venezuelan communities a long way apart; the other lives in a mestizo community. Another group of 11 storytellers live in cities with populations of 10,001 to 30,000; another eight live in state capitals. This group includes an economist, a maid, a Guayúu teacher (who is also a writer and a well-known official of the Ministry of Education), musicians, artisans, and the only full-time professional storyteller in Venezuela. He has had two records made of his tales, has appeared on television, and frequently performs in folk festivals and clubs in many parts of the country.

Various Genres Told

The research deliberately excluded the narration of myths as they occur in ritual contexts. The study of this kind of phenomena should be approached from a different perspective. Nevertheless the narration of tales of mythological characters was included when it occurred in ordinary contexts. This phenomenon was particularly observed among the Guayúu Indians. During the get-togethers held in the *enramadas* (bowers), the meeting place par excellence of their houses, they often tell tales that refer to their mythological heroes. During such events they also tell jokes, anecdotes, and even a few folktales they have incorporated from their interactions with creole people. It is even possible to observe that each of these genres has its own time during the event. In the same event it is also possible that a *jaiechi* (epic song) would be sung, but because of its length and other characteristics, the *jaiechi* is more often performed during events on its own.

As other researchers have pointed out, the same tale is often told in different ways by differ-

ent narrators. It is also known that this does not happen because some of them commit mistakes in telling a so-called original tale. On the contrary, this happens because each storyteller is not only an arranger or re-creator of an orally transmitted text but also a true creator from the point of view of the art of storytelling. Moreover, the research allows us to verify that the same narrator tells the same tale in very different ways according to his personal and social circumstances (e.g., among same-gender friends, at home, at a wake, etc.). This means that the storyteller recreates the tale each time, according to the context.

Types of Events

The types of storytelling events vary little from one region of the country to another. In most small towns and villages they take place during journeys of all sorts, working, family and other get-togethers, popular festivals, and meetings and jousts of narrators. Some storytellers expressed the view that jousting with others was an important stimulus for their performances. Some attached importance to the element of competition itself and others said it helped their memories. This latter in many different regions is usually expressed by the formula *cuento saca cuento* (one tale draws out another).

In the particular case of professional narrators the spectrum of events includes those that take place in festivals, theaters, museums, schools, and other social places. A good number of Caracas storytellers often perform in duets, trios, and quartets.

Personal Motivation

The most frequent causes of personal motivation are to entertain, to give amusement and to be amused, the desire to share, the desire to make people happy, the enjoyment of personal contacts, and other kinds of emotions. In some cases other causes were revealed: to spread diverse kinds of knowledge, to put forward and to resolve interpersonal conflicts, to help motivate people at work, and to obtain payment.

The particular interest in the spreading of knowledge was especially observed among indigenous communities and some peasant communities, in some of which the preservation of cultural heritage was also referred to as a motivation. The use of storytelling to put forward and to resolve interpersonal conflicts was observed especially among narrators of *cachos* and among the Guayúus.

Genres of Tales

Most of the storytellers I studied not only tell different kinds of folk tales that can be included in the Aarne-Thompson Index but also others that can not be included in the index. These are tales of animals, jokes and anecdotes, and historical tales related to political and military conflicts of their area.

In addition to the anecdotes, the most widespread stories are those of the Tío Conejo cycle (literally Uncle Rabbit—Brer Rabbit in the United States), with Tío Tigre (Uncle Tiger) as his favorite victim. This cycle, originating from Africa, is told in most of the regions of the country. In the region of Los Andes (in the west of the country) the cycle of Pedro Rimales is the most widespread; this character originates from Spain. Tales of this cycle are also told in other regions of the country, but less frequently. Another widely disseminated cycle that also originates from Spain is one whose principal character is called Quevedo. The majority of the tales of this cycle are socially regarded as obscene. In different regions of the country tales from "The One Thousand And One Nights" are also told, as are tales about different kinds of ghosts, specters, and other supernatural phenomena.

Purpose and Orientation of this Research

I have assumed, and my research has confirmed, that in any culture, the performers of this art that are valued as being of high quality involve specific creative and expressive skills. These skills allow storytelling events to be differentiated from other arts and from low-quality performances. The identification, description, and study of these skills and of their ways of learning have been the main goals of my research. I am speaking of storytellers who are clearly recognized by their audience as being, in some way, masters in their art. I am not speaking about what researchers usually call informants, nor about good connoisseurs of "the old stories," nor about occasional storytellers.

The collecting and publishing of tales, legends, and myths that emerge from such performances may be an adequate strategy for establishing some partial aspects of the cultural dynamics. This perpetuates them as cultural heritage and ensures their availability for posterity and for social groups with reading habits. These activities are currently associated with the idea of rescue. The making of those collections do not require identifying the best narrators, only the best connoisseurs of the old stories.

The contextual interpretation of performances and events and their analysis as communicative phenomena can be useful for highlighting social and political play and its meaning in a particular social context. Interpretations can provide useful notations about the nonverbal aspects of these performances. Unfortunately, little research has been done using this relatively new perspective, particularly in Venezuela, where the art of storytelling has a vigor that current methods of research have been unable to reflect.

Researching and analyzing the diverse ways in which storytelling exists, examining aspects of the appreciation of the art of storytelling, and studying its techniques and ways of learning can be adequate strategies for learning about the specificity and the cultural and social variability of this kind of expressive form. In other words we should compare the various forms of storytelling, rather than compare oral tales to written literature. This may also contribute to learning more about the human experience and may challenge the established stereotypes about so-called fine and popular arts. This approach can also be useful to narrators who practice their (our) art with the freedom of going beyond socially established images of what is traditional and what is not. It has at least proved to be useful in this regard for myself and a few colleagues who have adopted it. Finally, this approach has also been useful in teaching this art.

Further Reading

Baumann, Richard, *Story, Performance and Event: Contextual Studies of Oral Narrative,* Cambridge and New York: Cambridge University Press, 1986

Carey, George, "The Storyteller's Art and the Collector's Intrusion," in *Folklore Today: A Festschrift for Richard M. Dorson,* edited by Linda Dégh, Henry Glassie, and Felix Oinas, Bloomington: Indiana University, Research Center for Language and Semiotic Studies, 1976

Finnegan, Ruth, *Oral Poetry: Its Nature, Significance, and Social Context,* Cambridge and New York: Cambridge University Press, 1977

Georges, Robert, "Toward an Understanding of Storytelling Events," *Journal of American Folklore* 82 (1969)

Mato, Daniel, *El arte de narrar y la noción de literatura oral: Protopanorama intercultural y problemas espistemológicos,* Caracas: Universidad Central de Venezuela, 1990

———, *Cómo Contar Cuentos: El arte de narrar y sus aplicaciones educativas y sociales,* Caracas, Venezuela: Monte Avila Editores Latinoamericana, 1991

———, "Criterios Metodológicos para la Investigación Intercultural y Reactivación de las Formas Tradicionales del Arte de Narrrar," *Folklore Americano* 50 (1990)

———, "Cuenteros Afro venezolanos en accion," *Oralidad* 2 (1990)

———, *Cuenteros, Cuentahistorias y Cacheros del Oriente Venezolano,* Barcelona, Venezuela: Fondo Editorial del Caribe, 1993

———, "Especificidad de la Narracion Orogestual," *Imagen* (1986)

———, "Interculturalidad y transposicion de lenguajes en la constitucion y difusion de la literatura oral," *Escritura* 15:29 (1990)

———, *Narradores en Acción: Problemas Epistemológicos, Consideraciones Teóricas y Observaciones de Campo en Venezuela,* Caracas, Venezuela: Academia Nacional de la Historia, 1992

———, "La nocion de literatura oral: obstaculo epistemologico para el estudio del arte de narrar," in *Anuario Fundación de Etnomusicología y Folklore: Año I,* Caracas, Venezuela: La Fundación, 1990

———, "Para una Etnografía de las Formas Escénicas en Latinoamerica," *Gestos* 5:10 (1990)

———, "Sobra la Importancie del Gesto, la Proxemia y la Voz en el Arte de Narrar," *Ludo* (1997)

Theory

Children's Telling of Ghost Stories

Sylvia Grider

Sylvia Grider discusses the uses of ghost stories among elementary age children and displays several sample texts.

American Children and the Ghost Story

American children maintain a lively reservoir of traditional tales of the supernatural, commonly known as ghost stories.[1] Throughout the elementary school years (roughly ages seven through twelve), children learn and pass on these ghost stories in a variety of settings, ranging from sleepovers and Halloween parties to school classrooms and recess. The tales are so audience- and performance-oriented that fairly large groups of children engage in these sometimes rowdy but always entertaining communal storytelling sessions, usually without adult supervision or input. Due in part to this general lack of adult input, this traditional tale repertoire remains unusually stable.

Ghost story is a popular term that is really too broad for technical or professional use by folklorists. Nevertheless, the term is used so widely in American popular culture that we must deal with it whenever we encounter this particular narrative set or subcategory. Among American children, the term denotes any scary story that deals with revenants, monsters, haunted houses, or evil and demented humans. Even at a very young age, children learn the formulaic and stylistic cues of these stories well enough to recognize them as fiction. A ghost story is distinct from the category of story that children call fairy tales or fantasy stories that deal with magic. The standard folklore terms of legend, folktale, memorate, and such are

not, of course, part of the lexicon of American children.

The American experience—including a rural landscape and population, deserted country roads, public school education, and a shared ethos of "the good old days" of the nineteenth century—has a significant bearing on the development of the ghost story as it is told among many American children. The context and content of these stories harks back to an idealized period of small towns, peaceful predictability, and relative homogeneity. Unlike the European märchen, or folktale, exemplified by the tales of the Grimm Brothers and popularized by Walt Disney, the ghost stories so cherished by American children depict local landscapes, settings, and characters. Whereas the märchen depicts exotic castles, fairy princesses, witches, and dragons, the ghost story is at home in the backyard, the deserted house down the street, or the darkened basement. The ghosts and other antagonists of the oral ghost story are vague, shadowy creatures of the imagination rather than the well-described, clearly articulated villains and monsters so familiar from storybook illustrations and animated cartoons. Their lack of visual definition makes the ghosts that stalk the children in the narratives psychologically much more frightening than the images from TV screens or comic books.

By the time children enter public school at around age six or seven, their language abilities are generally well developed enough that they can tell and appreciate fictional and made-up stories. In fact, it is not uncommon for children as young as four years of age to master the rudiments of oral storytelling, such as logical plot sequencing and character development. Because language development is one of the main objectives of elementary school instruction, schools provide one of the main venues for the telling of stories of all kinds, including traditional narratives such as ghost stories, jokes, and riddles.

Since young children are not literate, oral expression is paramount. As a result, storytelling expertise is highly valued among peers; prestige is definitely associated with virtuoso storytelling. The virtuoso storyteller who can keep all of the plot and setting elements in order as well as entertain with vocal sound effects and gestures is a popular and influential child. The gender of the teller of ghost stories seems to make no difference at all to most children. Girls are as likely to tell gory tales as boys are. Not surprisingly, children practice their storytelling and imitate the accomplished storytellers that they know. Children who cannot master the storytelling techniques or who otherwise violate the group's aesthetic parameters are openly criticized by their peers, so the less talented children consistently defer to their more talented friends and classmates. A new child who moves into the school community and who is a good storyteller who knows new variants of favorite stories is immediately popular and much sought after. The folklorist immediately recognizes in such dynamic interaction the transmission of tradition within the folk group and the role of active and passive bearers in the maintenance of the narratives.

The Proper "Legend Climate" for Telling Ghost Stories

Although recess and other informal gatherings at school are common settings for learning ghost stories, children are very responsive to the so-called legend climate when telling ghost stories for entertainment. Sleepovers and Halloween parties provide the best storytelling conditions because the children can manipulate the storytelling environment to conform more to the content and aesthetic of the ghost stories. In order for the ghost stories to be really effective, the children like to sit in a darkened room with a lighted candle at the center of their circle. Sometimes a flashlight held by the narrator works just as well. Campouts are a favorite setting for ghost stories, especially if the children can be outside at night around a campfire. Otherwise, dorms and bunkhouses, especially after lights out, are perfect settings for telling ghost stories. Apparently being

safe in bed while listening to the stories adds to the overall ambiance of the storytelling sessions. As if mimicking this real-life setting, one favorite story type, "The Stolen Liver," (discussed in detail below) frequently features a child protagonist crouched in bed with the bedcovers over his head as the disembodied ghost approaches.

When they are away from the school context children are much more likely to punctuate their storytelling sessions with screaming and loud laughter as well as open criticism if they object to any aspect of the performance. The children are also more prone to talk all at once and interrupt and correct each other if they are away from school and classroom rules of decorum, which include politeness, talking one at a time, raising hands for attention, and so forth. Memorable storytelling sessions are often marked by knocking over the furniture, screaming and yelling, and ultimately having to turn on the lights and stop the session before it gets too far out of control. Generally the narrators are careful not to scare one another too badly because it would spoil the fun and camaraderie if any of the children cried from fright or needed adult consolation and intervention. A virtuoso storyteller will modify the ghost story according to the audience; if very young or impressionable children are present, the telling will be less intense. Likewise, among peers and as a show of bravado, the storyteller can create a genuinely frightening scenario. The dramaturgy of a storytelling session can be heightened by prearranged pranks, such as having someone run through the group or set off firecrackers at an appropriate point in the story. Such pranks usually put an end to the storytelling session.

Halloween is crucial to the maintenance of this storytelling tradition because ghost stories are an integral feature of the holiday. One might even speculate that the telling of ghost stories throughout the rest of the year is simply a prelude to the one season of the year when the stories are showcased. The costume parties, which are a regular feature of the observance of Halloween, are the most common context for storytelling.

The Child-to-Child Conduit for Passing on Tales

Children apparently learn ghost stories from one another more readily than from adults such as teachers or day-care supervisors. Perhaps one reason for this is that within the child-to-child conduit there is more room for innovation and peer approval without a concern for getting the story "right" according to adult standards. Furthermore, the children know that the content of many of the stories is regarded by adults as inappropriate, off color, and otherwise forbidden. This is especially the case among younger children who still revel in scatological stories that they don't want adults to hear.

Although the child-to-child conduit is the most common and effective mode of transmission for these stories, of course children can and do learn stories from adults. Camp counselors and family members are more effective as transmitters of the tradition than teachers and librarians because of the artificial storytelling context of schools and libraries and the rules of decorum that reign there. Camp counselors in particular often go to great pains to set up their young charges for a good, entertaining scare by manipulating the storytelling environment and mixing staged pranks into the storytelling session. Children who participate as audience members in these elaborate participatory dramas often attempt to recreate these episodes later, often when they become camp counselors themselves, which is another example of how this tradition is perpetuated. Parents and other family members who are recognized tellers of ghost stories can be equally effective in more intimate family settings, such as campouts and backyard sleepovers. On the whole, however, this vital storytelling tradition is unaffected by classroom presentations conducted by teachers and other authority figures.

Another, more complicated means by which these stories are transmitted and reinforced is through the various media, both electronic and printed. Publishers and video producers have used traditional ghost stories in countless spin-offs. Children who are talented tellers of ghost stories pick up plots and motifs to enhance their stories from a wide variety of sources. This phenomenon creates a kind of cross-fertilization whereby oral tradition provides the basis for a storybook or TV program, which in turn inspires a storyteller to modify his or her repertoire of oral stories accordingly. The amazingly popular Goosebumps series of easy-reading ghost and horror stories for children is the most current example of the savvy marketing of oral tradition.[2]

Some Popular Ghost Story Types

The ghost stories that generation after generation of American children have told and enjoyed clus-

ter around only a few well-known types. Perhaps the best known of all American ghost stories is "The Stolen Liver," which was popularized by Mark Twain as "The Golden Arm."[3] The story is a distinct American variant of Aarne-Thompson tale type 366, "The Man from the Gallows": "A man steals the heart (liver, stomach, clothing) of one who has been hanged. Gives it to his wife to eat. The ghost comes to claim his property and carries off the man." The following is a transcript of a child telling a typical version:

> This boy's mom told him to go to the store and get him some, get her some liver. But by the time he got to the store the store was closed. So there was a graveyard beside the store and so he went over there and dug up a person and got the liver out of him and took it home and they ate it that night. And that night he heard something. He heard a voice, "Johnny, I'm on the first step; Johnny, I'm on the second step; Johnny, I'm at the third step; Johnny, I'm in the hall; Johnny, I'm by your door; Johnny, I'm opening your door; Johnny, I'm in your room; Johnny, I'm by your dresser; Johnny, I'm by your posters; Johnny, I'm by your bed; Johnny, I got ya!"[4]

The next most common ghost stories can be classified as "Speaking Ghosts," and are structurally and aesthetically distinctive because although they start out as typical ghost stories, they conclude with the ironic twist of a jokelike punch line. The key character in these stories is a disembodied voice that typically identifies itself as either "The Ghost of the White Eye" or the "Ghost of the Bloody Fingers," or a similar name.[5] Since the child protagonist in these stories is unafraid, they can be considered as forms of Aarne-Thompson tale type 326, "The Youth Who Wanted to Learn What Fear Is": "A youth who does not know what fear is goes out to find it."

The following transcript is a typical version of "The Ghost of the White Eye":

> There's this baby and he was going across the floor and he dropped his bottle down the stairs and so he went and told his big brother, "Big brother, will you go get my bottle?" And so the big brother started down there and the ghost goes, "I'm the Ghost of the White Eye." And so the big brother ran up there and so the baby told his second biggest brother, and he goes, "Second biggest brother, will you go get my

bottle?" And so he gets down there and the ghost goes, "I'm the Ghost of the White Eye." So he runs back up there and the baby tells his next to the biggest brother and goes, "Next to the biggest brother, will you go get my bottle?" So he goes down there and comes back up because of the ghost saying, "I'm the Ghost of the White Eye." And so the baby goes down there and goes, and the ghost goes, "I'm the Ghost of the White Eye." "You better shut up or you're going to be the Ghost of the Black Eye!"[6]

The story of "Bloody Fingers" is structurally similar, as the following transcription demonstrates:

There was these, there was this guy and he went to a hotel and he goes, "I want to rent a room." And the guy says, "Well, we only have one room left and it's haunted. There's already been one guy killed in there." But he said, "I'll take it anyway." And he went up there and he heard somebody saying, "Bloody Fingers." And, um, and it scared him, you know, real bad, so he jumped out the window and killed hisself. And there's this, another guy come and he said, "I want to rent a room." And he said, "We only have one and there's been two people killed in there." And he says, "Oh well, I don't care." And he goes in there and he hears, "Bloody Fingers." And he jumps out the window and kills hisself. And then the hippie comes in, he says, "I want to rent a room." And he says, "We're all filled up and three men have already been killed in there." "Oh, I don't give a darn." And so he goes up to this room and hears, "Bloody Fingers." "Band-Aids in the bathroom."[7]

Another popular ghost story among American children has previously been classified by Jan Brunvand as "Shaggy Dog" story #100, "The Encounter with a Horrible Monster."[8] It is common enough to have its own distinct motif number in the Baughman index: Z13.4(i): "Escaped inmate from insane asylum chases man. They run and run until the pursued falls. The inmate with a long knife approaches, touches victim with free hand and says, 'Tag!'"[9] The following transcription is an example of this children's ghost story:

It's about this farmer and this city guy comes to the house and says, "I'm a traveling sales-man. Can I sleep here awhile? There's only one hotel in town and it's all filled up." And he goes, "OK, but beware of my daughter." And he said, "OK." So he, he took him to his room and he said, "Now lock all of the windows and all the doors." He said, "OK." And so he, um, all of a sudden, um, he was in bed and all of a sudden he heard this coming up by the window and it was her and he, he, he wanted to let her in because it was so cold outside so, um, so the door, the door to the hallway was close to the window so he unlocked the door and all of a sudden he let her in and she came in and he got out in the field and he was dodging through all the wheat and everything and he came up to these woods and he was dodging the trees and everything and she was still right on his tail and then they got down to the road. He was still running but he was about half pooped and everything so she was getting closer and closer and all of a, he goes, he dropped down on the road and he goes, "OK, I give up. What do you want?" And she goes, "Tag, you're it!"[10]

A related category of supernatural stories told by and among American children are the rambling, stream-of-consciousness tales of visits to haunted houses, encounters with monsters, and oral renditions of movie plots that deal with gruesome murders, accidents, and so forth. Children frequently distinguish this body of stories from those discussed above by calling them "real stories" or "true stories" instead of "ghost stories." They identify the media-derived narratives by introductory statements such as, "I saw this on TV," or "We rented this video the other night."[11] These stories depend more on the shock effect of the descriptions than on plot logic. In most storytelling sessions, the children intermingle the traditional tales mentioned above with these more diffuse, spur-of-the-moment descriptive narratives.

Possible Functions of the Telling of Ghost Stories

Folklorists, child development specialists, and educators have all contributed to the dialog concerning the function of traditional ghost stories in the lives of American children. Most agree that these stories apparently function for the children on a wide range of levels. From the linguistic and aesthetic points of view, telling and listening to the stories enables children to learn the basic literary structure of plot sequence and development. Most of these stories are so short that proper sequencing is essential if the story is to make any sense. Those stories that end with a humorous punch line depend on logical plot development for the concluding ironic punch line to make sense and therefore be funny. As with any joke, in telling these stories, timing is everything.

Narrative technique is also important for these stories to be effective. As they listen to and learn these stories, the young narrators master the techniques of responsiveness to audience reaction. They learn to extend or contract episodes in response to audience reaction and to use the special effects that are inherent to good storytelling, such as gestures and voice modification, to differentiate moods and characters.

On a broader scale, familiarity with ghost stories teaches children to distinguish between fantasy and reality. Although the stories deal with fearsome subject matter, the lightheartedness of the comic punch line diffuses any real fear and causes the children to look forward to a well-told tale because through the formulaic ending "everything will turn out all right." These stories also help introduce each new generation of children to the pervasive American fascination with the supernatural and the paranormal, ranging from Dracula and Frankenstein to haunted houses and UFOs. The inherent structure of the narratives also enables storytellers to create emotional distance and exert control over the fearful content. Perhaps the best example of this phenomenon in all of the ghost story repertoire is the ever-popular "Stolen Liver" stories. The storyteller controls the progress of the unseen ghost up the stairs and determines the exact point at which the ghost pounces on the young human protagonist; likewise, the storyteller decides when to fuse reality with fantasy by screaming and lunging at an unsuspecting member of the audience just as the ghost in the story attacks the fictional child.[12]

Although publishers and video producers have exploited supernatural subject matter for children until many adults feel that the market is saturated, the unsupervised telling of traditional ghost stories by American children goes on unabated. The annual observance of Halloween and the ongoing enculturation of children through the schools help maintain this storytelling tradition decade after decade in America.

Notes

1. A detailed study of children's storytelling behavior is Sylvia Grider, *The Supernatural Narratives of Children,* Indiana University: Ph.D. dissertation, 1976.
2. The Goosebumps series of short paperback novels for children by R.L. Stine began in 1992 with the publication by Scholastic Magazine of *Welcome to Dead House.* There are now 62 of these books in print, as well as numerous spinoff series and associated merchandise.
3. Mark Twain, *How to Tell a Story and Other Essays,* New York: Harper's, 1897.
4. Grider, pp. 198–99.
5. For further information about these distinctive stories see: John M. Vlach, "One Black Eye and Other Horrors: A Case for the Humorous Anti-Legend," *Indiana Folklore* 4 (1971): 95–140.
6. Grider, pp. 212–13.
7. Grider, pp. 217–18.
8. Jan H. Brunvand, "A Classification for Shaggy Dog Stories," *Journal of American Folklore* 76 (1963): 42–68.
9. Ernest Baughman, *Type and Motif Index of the Folktales of England and North America,* The Hague: Mouton, 1966.
10. Grider, pp. 228–29.
11. Elsewhere I have designated these media-inspired renditions as "media narraforms." See Grider, pp. 345–459.
12. Baughman classifies these plot components as Motif # Z13.1, "The teller scares the listener. The teller uses part of the dialogue of the story, shouting it at a crucial point to scare the listener; or he grabs the listener and yells 'Boo', etc. at an exciting point;" and Motif #Z13.1(a), "Man coming to get girl calls out from each step of the stairs that he is coming. Final line: 'Sally I have hold of thee!' (Here the teller grabs the listener.)"

Further Reading

Brunvand, Jan H., "A Classification for Shaggy Dog Stories," *Journal of American Folklore* 76 (1963)

Grider, Sylvia, *The Supernatural Narratives of Children,* 2 volumes (Ph.D. diss., Indiana University), 1976

Vlach, John M., "One Black Eye and Other Horrors: A Case for the Humorous Anti-Legend," *Indiana Folkore* 4 (1971)

Organizational Storytelling

Richard Raspa

Richard Raspa examines ways in which corporate storytelling functions to encapsulate the corporate code.

The Corporate Code in Story

Human beings tell stories at work. Managers, accountants, engineers, doctors, teachers, knowledge and craft workers, hourly employees—all experience much of work life through narrative performance. Stories allow us to make sense of organizational problems and expectations. They are maps for maneuvering through the obstacles and challenges that mark landscapes of work. They also provide information for making decisions and reveal the sometimes unconscious and tacit assumptions employees have about every aspect of the organization—its products, services, values, operating philosophy, structures, customers, competition, vendors, and fellow employees. Even assumptions about what is possible, what is reasonable, and what is good or evil in the company are embedded in stories. We come to know the corporate code, the specific techniques for doing the job, and the sanctioned ways of communicating, through listening and telling stories. Narratives reveal the rules for living in organizations.

IBM: A Tale of Democratic Principles

Corporate stories are expressions of the folk wisdom and lore of the organization. They function in much the same way stories function in traditional societies. They encode the best practices of the community and create a sense of shared identity. Stories, for instance, about legendary Chief Executive Officer of IBM Thomas Watson Sr. instantly reveal the life of the organization in a way that business reports and statistical studies are unable to do. Stories transform recorded events of an organization's history into aesthetic form that can often delight and instruct an audience. One story, in particular, illustrates a rule for living in the IBM corporate village. A 24-year-old woman was assigned security detail at the entrance to a restricted work area at an IBM plant. No one could enter unless she or he could present the certified green card. On one occasion, surrounded by a group of his vice presidents, Thomas Watson Sr. was marching toward the door. The woman, recognizing Watson, shivered, then refused Watson permission to enter because he did not have the proper identification. When those surrounding the CEO protested, Watson contained their outrage and calmly waited until someone retrieved a green card for him before entering. The story reveals a dramatic episode in the history of the organization and offers a rich set of symbolic enactments that disclose the nature of the IBM corporation. Democratic principles structure the work environment. The story suggests that even a new employee is able to survive when she exercises the right to confront the chief executive when key values are violated.

Survival is the central theme of both traditional and organizational stories, though each type is inflected differently. Survival in traditional tales consists in maintaining continuity with the past and transmitting customary ways of being and doing as ideal and normative. The past is revered; history becomes destiny. Corporate stories, in contrast, esteem the future. Innovation is praised. Indeed, the past is often seen as an obstacle to success. The power to predict emergent market forces and identify areas of growth is the source of survival. Change rather than persistence and continuity is encouraged. Change may provoke anxiety, but the corporation ultimately welcomes it as the catalyst for creativity and success. The model for corporate storytelling is not history but biology—the capacity of living systems to adapt and change. Biology becomes corporate destiny.

3M: A Tale of Innovation

At 3M corporation, for example, the story of how Post-it Notes were invented has moved into the popular business literature and serves as an example of organizational change and creativity. The engineer who invented Post-it notes, Art Fry, sang in his church choir. He was frustrated by the slips of paper marking the songs for the service falling out of his hymnal. If only a glued marker could be invented that could identify the page and yet not destroy it when lifted. He remembered that a particular glue developed at 3M might offer possibilities, though it had been discarded as a failure because it was too soft for any current use. When he began to experiment with the glue at work, he meet with resistance from his associates because, he was told, everybody knew the research the company had conducted on the glue yielded no practical results. So why was Art Fry wasting his time with useless material? Fry carried on his experiments surreptitiously, and, ultimately, shepherded Post-it Notes to the marketplace where they not only served the church choir but proved to have unforeseen uses in business, education, hospitals, and other industries; in fact, it is difficult to imagine how work was accomplished before the invention of Post-it Notes.

The Art Fry story represents the workplace culture to the 3M corporation and to the world. It situates the main character in the organizational process and reveals the collective history and the values of the organization. The story suggests that innovation and creativity are valued at 3M. And even when common sense dictates one path of action, creativity can prevail and push the organization into new areas of performance and success. Creative action sometimes requires the courage to challenge deeply held beliefs about the way things are and should be.

Organizational stories can be understood structurally as well as functionally. Thematic approaches to organizational stories reveal the influence of sports analogies and motifs in describing desired behavior. Managing is represented as a coaching activity; employees train to become a championship team—the premier provider of service and products in the field. An unexpected challenge might be called a curve ball. Through the filter of the game metaphor, organizational competence is defined as the ability to deal adequately with a surprise, as if working were playing a game, and work associates were teammates. Other themes from popular psychological literature classify organizational stories more ominously in terms of predator/prey analogies and include stories of organization life as a horror tale, with abusive, sadomasochistic leaders who direct fearful, dysfunctional employees in mind-dulling work practices.

The Apollo Space Mission as Epic

Research has also yielded literary classification schemes to help us understand the nature of organizational fables. Genres—like the epic depicting heroic action in the face of terrifying conditions, or tragedy revealing arbitrary action and the defeat of possibilities, or comedy enacting the mythic process of subverting obstacles and renewing energy—can characterize organizational storytelling. President John F. Kennedy's announcement of the Apollo space mission is an often cited example of an epic story. In 1961, President Kennedy declared to the world that Americans would travel to the moon before the end of the decade. Many politicians, media representatives, and corporate and government leaders regarded Kennedy's declaration as foolish, even grandiose. The Russians had launched Sputnik in 1957, which was evidence for some that the United States had fallen behind in space exploration, and, hence, the United States was losing the ideological war with the Soviets. Like epics from antiquity, the story unfolded over almost a decade, and in that time, many organizations in the aerospace industry were inspired by Kennedy's vision to develop flight and engineering innovations that made the lunar voyage possible. When Neil Armstrong walked on the moon in 1969, the epic was complete. What began as a possibility embodied in a science-fiction story authored by President Kennedy ended in a new reality: manned space travel to the moon. Stories do not merely represent reality. They have the power to evoke it as well.

Storytelling evocation occurs in the context of other conversational genres of discourse in the workplace. Organizational stories are not necessarily fully formed narrative structures, with beginnings, middles, and ends. More often, they are truncated anecdotes, without the complete suite of traditional folktale forms and motifs, like tricksters, numskulls, ogres, villains, heroes, tests, trials, and supernatural helpers. More often, they are presented rhetorically as fragments at critical points in a conversation: as evidence to support a position, as a way to clarify an ambiguity, a way to imagine the outcome of decisions.

Domino's Pizza as Domino Game

An organization has a repertoire of stories that represents it to the world, even to itself. Everyone, from executive suite to shop floor, shares in tale telling with varying influences on listeners. Sometimes, corporate stories are also told by insiders, like public relations specialists, to outsiders, as when reinterpreting an event or story to cast the organization in a favorable light, putting what has been popularly called a spin on the tale. Frequently, outsiders, like consultants, tell stories to insiders about outsiders, other organizational tales to decode organizational problems and help reconfigure the corporation. Some theorists argue that all the stories told by an organization are really one archetypal story that permeates every aspect of the workplace and endows the organization with its characteristic identity.

Domino's Pizza, Inc., for instance, has a story embedded in its name. Dominoes is a board game, one in which players try to match opponents' sets. This play action is a motif that informs the operating structures and conduct of the entire Domino's organization. One of the ways of looking at Domino's Pizza is as a story of entrepreneurial success with founder Tom Monahan as hero. Monahan shares the background of poverty that many American entrepreneurial heroes, like Horatio Alger, have. As a child Monahan lived for a time in an orphanage. After military service, in the early 1960s he bought Dominick's pizza parlor in Ypsilanti, Michigan. Knowing nothing about pizza or the food industry, Monahan, nonetheless, had one brilliant marketing idea: bringing pizza to the customer quickly rather than requiring the customer to come to the pizza parlor and wait 45 minutes or more for the pizza—an idea that over time helped invent a new industry that would be exported around the world—fast foods.

To appreciate the entrepreneurial power of this strategy, one needs to understand the logo—dominoes. Dominoes is a matching game. In each franchise, Domino's had a glossy photograph of the ideal pizza—21 slices of thin pepperoni, two ladles of tomato sauce, and three handfuls of grated mozzarella spread on each 12-inch pizza. Each pizza maker tries to match the pizza she or he is making with the glossy photo. Monahan also tells employees that each of them can become just as successful as he is. They can match his success and wear $200 Hennes neckties and $12,000 Rolex watches, which Monahan customarily hands out as bonuses to managers who do well. The game plan in each pizza shop is to match the pizza makers and the drivers against the clock. The entire transaction, from telephone order to house delivery, has to be executed in less than 30 minutes or the customer gets a free pizza. From frontline employee to CEO, everyone plays the Domino's game.

Telling stories is working. The act of working is listening to stories—those I have constructed as well as those others have—stories about how to do something or stories about how to be in the organization, and then taking action based upon those stories. Working is telling tales about oneself and the other. We constitute our lives at work as well as at play and at home in the stories we hear and tell. Organizational stories provide the codes for survival in one of the worlds we inhabit.

Further Reading

Armstrong, David, *Managing by Storying Around*, New York: Doubleday, 1992

Boje, David, "The Storytelling Organization: A Study of Story Performance in an Office-Supply Firm," *Administrative Science Quarterly* 36:1 (March 1991)

Feldman, Steven, "Stories as Cultural Creativity: On the Relation Between Symbolism and Politics in Organizational Change," *Human Relations* 43:9 (September 1990)

Gabriel, Yiannis, "Turning Facts into Stories and Stories into Facts: A Hermeneutic Exploration of Organizational Folklore," *Human Relations* 44:8 (August 1991)

Jones, Michael Owen, Michael Moore, and Richard Snyder, eds., *Inside Organizations: Understanding the Human Dimension*, Newbury Park, California: Sage, 1988

Mitroff, Ian, and Ralph Kilmann, "Stories Managers Tell: A New Tool for Organizational Problem-Solving," *Management Review* 64:7 (1975)

Morgan, Gareth, *Images of Organization*, Beverly Hills, California: Sage, 1986

Neuhauser, Peg, *Corporate Legends and Lore: The Power of Storytelling as a Management Tool,* New York: McGraw-Hill, 1993

Raspa, Richard, "The CEO as Corporate Myth-Maker: Negotiating the Boundaries of Work and Play at Domino's Pizza Company," in *Symbols and Artifacts: Views of the Corporate Landscape,* edited by Pasquale Gagliardi, Berlin and New York: Walter de Gruyter, 1990

The Role of Traditional Stories in Language Teaching and Learning

Martha S. Bean

Martha Bean suggests ways in which traditional stories can be used to enhance learning in the ESL classroom.

The Universality of Story Structure

From the linguist's viewpoint, traditional stories come close to having a "universal template," a similar general structure, in all cultures and languages (Mandler and Johnson). Broadly speaking, traditional stories, like other narratives, can be reduced to a situation and main character, a sequence of events that poses some kind of problem, efforts to solve that problem, and a resolution. The universality of this structure makes narratives one of the most easily accessible vehicles for language learning since language learners from all cultures are familiar with stories. Yet, there is a great deal of cultural variability in traditional stories. Such stories may play a greater or lesser role from culture to culture and vary according to whom the tellers are and the style and occasion of the telling. In addition, traditional stories embody a repertory of themes important in a given culture and, in the tacit lessons and morals they provide, point to qualities and characteristics esteemed in that culture. Although certain fables and tales exist in many cultures and preserve themes understood across cultures, a listener from one culture hearing a story from another culture may miss its meaning because he or she lacks cultural background information. Still, in terms of language learning, traditional stories

can be used as familiar pedagogical springboards since the benefit of the universality of such stories far outweighs any possible local misunderstandings, and these can easily be addressed in face-to-face communication situations like the language classroom.

The Value of Traditional Stories in Language Teaching and Learning

By drawing characters, settings, situations, and lessons, traditional stories map a culture. Inasmuch as language is culture, listening to or reading stories from a particular culture provides language learners with cultural icons and constructs that help them enter more fully into the traditions and thought patterns of the speakers of the new language (Polanyi). Thus, students can explore language and culture simultaneously by listening to and/or reading a series of stories from the target culture. As specific characters or types of characters recur, students learn the vocabulary with which to talk about and clarify the meanings of the stories. Each culture offers special animals and stock characters, such as Coyote in Mexican culture, Kalulu the rabbit in some cultures of East Africa, or White Spirit Woman in Japanese culture. Similarly, one learns much about Chinese culture through exposure to excerpts from the story of the young boy who grows up in the epic Chinese story "A Dream of the Red Chamber" or about Japanese culture from the *Tale of Genji*. By coming to know such characters, language learners taste the culture of the language they are studying and learn to construct and respond to references to these well-known characters and events.

On a deeper psychological level, stories provide a metaphor for cultural stresses that may parallel the stresses experienced by language learners. Traditional stories, whether featuring animals or people, typically entail a struggle for survival in a challenging situation, not unlike the struggles faced by language learners as they grapple with the new idiom (Stahl). Although what language learners wish to express and accomplish often lies just beyond the pale of their level of acquisition, their desire to say and do motivates them to persist in the face of this challenge. To that end, language learners frequently find themselves symbolically in the stories that they encounter as they monitor their own progress in learning the new language. In addition, in allowing learners to enter simultaneously into the target language and culture, traditional stories in particular do synergistic work. Students learn not only how to understand and express themselves in the new language but also how to talk of things intimately known by speakers of the language. Stories from the Bible, for example, form an important part of the cultural repertory of many Western countries, providing anchor points to which Westerners may make ready reference.

Specific Ways in Which Language Teachers Work with Traditional Stories

The classroom use of stories has broad appeal, since, in the language-learning setting, it is especially important that students feel relaxed and engaged with the material at hand. Because of the universal nature and familiarity of traditional stories, learners feel that they are on common ground when the language classroom turns to stories. They generally know something of the stories of their own culture and are curious about the stories of other cultures.

A primary way in which language teachers use traditional stories in their classes is by becoming storytellers themselves (Morgan and Rinvolucri). Traditional stories can fruitfully be used from beginning to advanced levels and with children and adults alike. A teacher of English as a Second Language might tell the story of "The Boy Who Cried Wolf"; a teacher of French might have students memorize the cadences of the La Fontaine fable, "Le corbeau et le renard" (The Crow and the Fox); and a teacher of Spanish might share with students the archetypal Mexican legend of "La Llorona (The Weeping Woman)," or stories of the crafty Coyote. In telling such a story, the teacher first introduces key vocabulary words through pictures, gesture, mime, and explanation in the target language and then proceeds to give a dramatic telling of the story at a level that the students can grasp. Students are first asked to answer key questions about the story and later encouraged to retell the story in groups, with learners helping each other reconstruct the story until it can be retold with relative ease. The teacher also helps the students explore the meanings and messages of the story as well as situations in which the story might be told. For example, "The Boy Who Cried Wolf" cautions children to be moderate in their demands for attention and is thus popular with parents; the story of the fox and the crow shows that those who are vain fall easy prey to flatterers, a lesson applicable to adults as well as children.

An expansion of the activity above has students giving versions of the same or a similar story from their own culture. The story of Cinderella, for example, appears in many cultures but with variant details and twists of plot that reflect different emphases. Cinderella might be a stepdaughter, as in U.S. culture, or another relative in some other culture. Yet another activity variation finds students conversing in groups of three or four and telling stories to the others in their group in the target language. When language learners become storytellers, everyone is challenged, listeners as well as speakers. Speakers must struggle to describe characters, places, things, and sequences of action, and listeners must struggle to grasp the cast of characters and the characteristics of each, the story line, and the explicit or implicit moral. In this setting, the storytellers become the teachers, calling on as many linguistic and nonlinguistic resources (pictures, mime, and so on) as needed to communicate their meanings. The listeners must practice their "strategic competence" by asking clarification questions and generally ensuring that they know who is doing what in the teller's story. In this manner, students improve their language skills while gaining glimpses into the lore of their classmates' cultures. Likewise, Spanish teachers from Spain or Mexico teaching Spanish in the United States learn from U.S. students such traditional stories as the tale of Paul Bunyan and his blue ox, Babe, or the story of

Johnny Appleseed and his apple-growing habits, and teachers from the U.S., England, or Australia teaching English in Korea meet the woodsman who lost his axe or the crane who came to dinner.

Writing Out a Story Script and Performing It

A further expansion of the above activity into reading and writing may find students working in small groups to dramatize a traditional story. In such an activity, students pass around a piece of paper to record what the characters in a given story might say, including a narrator who fills in the details of setting or action needed to provide the framework for the dialogue. After this exercise, the teacher assists the students by providing missing vocabulary or correcting grammatical errors. A corrected copy of the "script" is given to each student and the students rehearse the story in groups as they read the script that they themselves have produced in the target language. The students may then prepare to perform their skits either with or without scripts or props. In such dramatizations, language learners tend to leave themselves behind and adopt the persona, probable gestures, actions, and intonations of the characters of their story. Such an activity allows students to abandon the shyness and hesitancy that characteristically surround production in a second language and to emerge from behind the mask of their character as fluent speakers capable of sharing both information and emotion in the new language. If a camcorder is available, students may be videotaped so that learners can view their fluency in places where the new language flows smoothly and naturally and discuss how to improve areas where hesitations occur.

Making Traditional Stories "Traditional" in the Language Classroom

Just as traditional stories have become traditional because they have struck a cultural chord and endured throughout decades or even centuries within a given group, so too can stories become traditional in a new sense in the language classroom. As students gain exposure to the repertory of stories either from the target culture or an array of cultures, they can then individually or collectively "adopt" certain characters and contextualize them more fully. Individuals in many Native American cultures feel kinship with a certain animal; in the same way, learners can be asked with which traditional characters they feel the most kinship. They can describe these characters, their physical characteristics as well as their personalities, in imaginative detail. A traditional story can become the foundation for ongoing innovations by language learners when teachers invite them to embellish their chosen character and to speculate on what other experiences this character might have. Learners may likewise wish to adopt a character as a mascot or totem. Traditional stories take on new flavors as the class develops its own versions of the stories, using the story first heard as a starting point. Learners can change the ending of a story or create another story that resembles or takes off from the original. Story characters who are unnamed can be named and provided with interesting friends, families, and wardrobes (e.g., "Let's name the tortoise and the hare," "Do you think the tortoise was married?" or "What do you think the hare was wearing on the day of the race?").

Illustrating Stories

Language learners can also illustrate their favorite stories by creating pictures, collages, or murals on butcher block paper with paints, markers, or crayons. As in the drama activity above, the artistic activity of converting a story into an illustration involves much cooperative effort and task-based talk among learners that itself supports the acquisition of the new language. The emotional experience of creating art, like drama, takes students' attention off the language they are learning, freeing them from self-consciously delivered drills and exercises and leading them into spontaneous talk about the content and task at hand. Such story-based art provides a powerful linguistic mnemonic as well, for the pictures created are then displayed in the classroom where they help learners recall the language of the story as well as the language of the task of creating the story visually. These picture products also help create a classroom environment conducive to student integration into the target culture.

Few language teachers use traditional stories exclusively. However, because of their universal familiarity and appeal, traditional stories can easily be used either to supplement the lessons of beginning language learners or to form one of the cores of a more advanced course that integrates the skills of listening, speaking, reading, and writing. Already widespread in the study of classical languages, the use of traditional stories in the teaching of modern languages is steadily gaining ground as teachers and learners discover, explore, and develop an appreciation for their abundance of cultural themes and their endless possibilities for adaptation and expansion in the language classroom.

Further Reading

Mandler, Jean M, and Nancy S. Johnson, "Remembrance of Things Parsed: Story Structure and Recall," *Cognitive Psychology* 9 (1977)

Morgan, John, and Mario Rinvolucri, *Once Upon a Time: Using Stories in the Language Classroom*, Cambridge and New York: Cambridge University Press, 1983

Polanyi, Livia, *Telling the American Story: A Structural and Cultural Analysis of Conversational Storytelling*, Norwood, New Jersey: Ablex, 1985

Stahl, Sandra K.D., *Literary Folkloristics and the Personal Narrative*, Bloomington: Indiana University Press, 1989

The Storytelling Revival *

Joseph Sobol

Joseph Sobol discusses the current revival of storytelling by educators, professional storytellers, and others who find the art form useful in their lives and their work. The growth of the National Storytelling Association as a focus and a support for this movement is examined.

The Emergence of the Storytelling Revival

Much as "The Folksinger" did in the early 1960s, "The Storyteller" has developed a certain mythic resonance in popular culture and language—perhaps more in the way of a poetic conceit than an anthropologically specific role. Yet it depends for its emotive force on the idea that somewhere, sometime, there was, or even is such a role—a role with expressive, didactic, oracular, cathartic, and community-binding functions. Enough people have resubscribed to the idea over the last 20 years to have created little subcultural pockets of what performance theorist Richard Schechner calls "restored behaviors" (Schechner, 35–116). These pockets, taken collectively, constitute what is known within them as "the storytelling community," and "the storytelling revival."

Storytelling festivals around the country have projected the image of the fireside folkteller onto a popular stage, framed by tents and spotlights, magnified by public relations machinery, amplified by the latest sound technology, all to satisfy mass hunger for a restored sense of rootedness. In all 50 states of the United States, in Canada, in many countries of Western Europe, and Australia as well, professional storytellers have multiplied in public schools, libraries, and state-funded community arts programming. Support groups of amateurs and professionals have banded together to swap tales and potluck suppers and to create local, regional, and national networks for promoting one another's work.

The storytelling revival community has developed its own kind of psychic geography over the years—the mutable map of what sociologist Howard Becker calls an "artworld." The self-proclaimed (and still) capital of the storytelling world is the town of Jonesborough, Tennessee, where the first national festival devoted exclusively to the many facets of storytelling performance was founded in 1973. The National Association for the Preservation and Perpetuation of Storytelling (known to intimates as NAPPS, though in 1994 it trimmed its name to the National Storytelling Association, or NSA), also headquartered in Jonesborough, emerged in 1975 from the enthusiasm surrounding the first National Storytelling Festivals, and has developed into the nearest thing that this artistic movement has to an institutional base.

NAPPS/NSA puts out a directory of professional storytellers, storytelling events, groups, and educational programs nationwide. Criteria for listing in the storytellers' section are a willingness to advertise one's professional services, to

*This article is based on a chapter in *The Storytellers' Journey: An American Revival*, by Joseph Daniel Sobol, Urbana: University of Illinois Press, 1999. Reprinted with permission of The University of Illinois Press.

pay the required fee, and to affiliate with the national community as represented by the organization. This excludes traditional and community storytellers who have not learned or chosen to translate their art into economic terms, as well as those performers who are disinterested in NAPPS for a variety of personal, professional, or political reasons. The 1994 edition listed nearly 600 storytellers in 45 states and the District of Columbia, as well as a handful in Canada, the Caribbean, England, Ireland, France, Australia, Israel, and Africa (the 1997 directory showed about the same number). The 1994 directory also listed 304 local or regional storytelling organizations, groups, or guilds in the United States (the 1997 directory had only 227—as much, perhaps, because of increased directory fees as because of actual attrition in the movement).

NAPPS-Affiliated Touring Tellers Evolve from Diverse Beginnings

Among those NAPPS-affiliated storytellers, there are a small number, between 20 and 50 depending on the reckoning, who regularly headline festivals around the country and who are able to draw substantial audiences in well-publicized performances beyond their local or regional bases. These "national performers," or "stars," would include people like Jackie Torrence; David Holt; Barbara Freeman and Connie Regan-Blake (who until 1995 made up the storytelling duo The Folktellers); Donald Davis of North Carolina; Jay O'Callahan; Bill Harley of Massachusetts; Diane Wolkstein, Laura Simms, and Heather Forest from New York; and Diane Ferlatte and David Novak from California. Most of the tellers in the NSA directory, like most small performing arts entrepreneurs generally, make a full- or part-time living doing performances and residencies through local and regional networks of schools, libraries, and arts councils. Many have come to storytelling after some previous training and identification with other arts or arts-related crafts—like music, theater, poetry, dance, or journalism. Many moved to storytelling from professions that dealt with cultural conservation and transmission, like teaching or library work; and many came from helping professions with strong expressive components, like social work, therapy, or ministry.

Brother Blue, for example, came out of both the Harvard Divinity School and the Yale School of Drama in the 1960s and was steeped in the civil rights and social justice ferment of that time. He began telling stories in Harvard Square, in jails, and on street corners around the country, developing a rhyming, chiming "street style" drawn from African-American rapping, toasting, and preaching traditions blended with material from his elite university training—he would perform 20-minute jive versions of "Hamlet" or "Othello"—and he has influenced most of the next generation of professional storytellers.

Gioia Timpanelli was teaching junior high school literature during the day and at night was a painter, deeply involved with the New York visual art world. She became a storytelling literature teacher on New York's public television station in the late 1960s, going on to become an important performer and teacher in the emerging storytelling world. Her repertoire has included folktales from her Sicilian grandmother but also tales from the Brothers Grimm, Sufi teaching tales, Tibetan folktales, and other international tales.

Diane Wolkstein studied mime with Etienne Decroux in the mid-1960s, but found that what she most enjoyed was telling folktales to children at a variety of church and synagogue jobs. When she began telling stories in the New York City parks in 1967, her instinctive use of her training in physical theater marked a clear stylistic break from the formalities of public library storytelling up to that time. Her repertoire has evolved to include biblical and epic material, from the stories of Ruth, Esther, and Joseph to the Sumerian epic of Innana.

Jay O'Callahan was a struggling apprentice novelist in the early 1970s, and he also found that what was most alive for him creatively were not the novels he was writing during the day but the stories he was making up and telling to his children at night. He began to tell in libraries and schools around the Boston area, eventually becoming a major influence on the national scene. His performances feature an extravagance of vocal and physical characterization and explosiveness of comic and dramatic timing that further extended the vocabulary of the art form.

Two librarian cousins from Chatanooga, Tennessee, Barbara Freeman and Connie Regan-Blake, drove up to Jonesborough to attend the first National Storytelling Festival in 1973. What they experienced there inspired them eventually to leave their library jobs and take to the road as freelance performers. Their 20-year partnership, christened The Folktellers, helped to link the already established circuit of folk music festivals to the growing storytelling scene, and to open new conduits between them, both of audiences and of performers.

Beyond their mere professional affiliation, what unites these and many other artists into a storytelling community is a shared sense that storytelling endows one with, not just a job, but a mission: that it is an art form with revitalizing potential for individuals as well as for the culture as a whole. This conviction permeated the growing storytelling scene like the steel reinforcing rods in poured concrete.

The Jonesborough Mythos

As befits a movement that privileges the mythic and the marvelous, the spirit of the storytelling revival is fueled by a distinctive mythos, within which Jonesborough plays a central part. While storytellers were awakening to their vocations in isolated epiphanies all over America, the arc of the national movement could be plotted in synchrony with developments in the little Tennessee town. The founding of the first storytelling festival there in 1973 provided a touchstone for a widespread awakening of cultural missionary spirit. Over the next decade, this spirit used Jonesborough and its accomplice citizens as an administrative and ritual center of gravity, as each region of the country developed its own coteries of storytelling activists and touring professional performers. All of these continue, to some extent, to look to the national association and the national festival as vessels of public and personal identity-formation, policy-making, and communal realization. Meanwhile, the town of Jonesborough used storytelling as a vehicle to form a new economic and cultural identity in a changing tourism- and service-based regional economy. For Jonesborough, storytelling has become the flagship industry of its own civic revival.

Other Folklore-Based Cultural Revivals

The storytelling revival of the 1970s and 1980s is far from an isolated event. It is part of a longstanding pattern of folklore-based cultural revivals, and it bases itself firmly upon its predecessors. These include—just to name a few— the fairy tale vogue at the court of Louis XV, which produced the works of Charles Perrault, Madame D'Aulnoy, and others; the Hasidic movement in eighteenth- and nineteenth-century Judaism, which gave such instrumental roles to oral cultural expressions such as storytelling,

folk music, and folk dance, in contrast to the rabbinic fixation on the written word (Buber); the German romantic movement, fueled by the articulate enthusiasms of J.G. Herder, Achim Von Arnim, Clemens Brentano, and Jacob and Wilhelm Grimm (Kamenetsky, 39–68, 181–214); and the romantic nationalist movements in Western European literature and music, which produced great collections of regional folklore in nearly every European country during the nineteenth century as well as literary and musical works based upon folk forms and themes from such major figures as Walter Scott, Hans Christian Andersen, Joel Chandler Harris, Oscar Wilde, W.B. Yeats, or Antonín Dvořák, Jean Sibelius, Béla Bartók, R. Vaughan Williams, Aaron Copland, and many more.

In the United States in the twentieth century we have witnessed a continual reappropriation of folk material on the part of popular movements with diverse and often conflicting cultural and political goals—from the library-based storytelling movement of the early years of the century, with its explicit social service agenda of socializing immigrant children within a western cultural norm (Alvey, 15–18, 396–432), to the racist Anglo-Saxon nativist ideology surrounding the White Top Folk Festival in the 1930s (Whisnant, 181–252), to the use of folk song in the Communist labor movement of the 1930s and 1940s (explored from opposing political viewpoints by R. Serge Denisoff and Robbie Lieberman). The folk music revival of the 1950s, purged of its explicit dependence on old-Left ideology, provided an alternative community of identification to the gray-flannel juggernaut of the Eisenhower years. Later it bred iconography for the civil rights movement and provided a medium of solidarity for the youth rebellion of the 1960s (an evolution exhaustively charted by Robert Cantwell in *When We Were Good*). It was in the dwindling phase of this cycle of folk cultural revivalism that the storytelling movement took wing in Jonesborough and in communities throughout the United States.

Revitalization Movements

The most comprehensive and useful taxonomic framework for examining the dynamics of cultural revivals is in Anthony F.C. Wallace's 1956 article, "Revitalization Movements." Wallace places revival movements as one genus of a broad and significant class of cultural transformations. "A revitalization movement," he writes, "is defined as a deliberate, organized, conscious effort by members of a society to construct a more satisfying culture" (p. 265). Using the analogy of society as organism, he regards revitalization movements as homeostatic responses to cultural stress:

> [A] society will work, by means of coordinated actions (including "cultural" actions) by all or some of its parts, to preserve its own integrity by maintaining a minimally fluctuating, life-supporting matrix for its individual members, and will, under stress, take emergency measures to preserve the constancy of its matrix. Stress is defined as a condition in which some part, or the whole, of the social organism is threatened with more or less serious damage. (p. 265)

Wallace uses the term "mazeway" to denote the image of self, society, nature, and culture as perceived by individuals and groups and suggests that this mazeway of perception is the medium out of which the social organism constructs its reality. To change the mazeway, in these terms, is to change social reality. He distinguishes several subclasses of revitalization movements:

> "Nativistic movements". . . are revitalization movements characterized by strong emphasis on the elimination of alien persons, customs, values, and/or material from the mazeway. . . . "Revivalistic" movements emphasize the institution of customs, values, and even aspects of nature which are thought to have been in the mazeway of previous generations but are not now present. . . . "Vitalistic movements" emphasize the importation of alien elements into the mazeway. . . . "Millenarian movements" emphasize mazeway transformation in an apocalyptic world transformation engineered by the supernatural. "Messianic movements" emphasize the participation of a divine savior in human flesh in the mazeway transformation. . . . These and parallel terms do not denote mutually exclusive categories, for a given revitalization movement may be nativistic, millenarian, messianic, and revivalistic all at once; and it may (in fact, usually does) display ambivalence with respect to nativistic, revivalistic, and importation themes. (p. 267)

According to this classificatory scheme, the revitalization movement gathered under the term "storytelling revival" contains a mixture of revivalistic, vitalistic, and nativistic elements. Though most storytellers promote the revival of an art form presumed to have flourished in an ideally imagined past, many tellers are also eagerly importing traditions and repertoires that had no part in their own particular backgrounds. Still others are performing nativistic exercises, selectively representing in their storytelling the traditions of their own ethnic ancestors, yet often, quite naturally, wielding those traditions on behalf of explicitly contemporary political and cultural programs.

An "Anti-Environment"

In 1969, in the book, *The Feast of Fools,* Harvey Cox wrote:

> We cannot really "see" something if it fills in our whole visual environment. We need an "anti-environment" against which to make out its profile. The background or field is an essential element in perception. Music on a concert stage we listen to. Music pumped into every closet and corridor by Muzak we may vaguely hear, but we do not really *listen* to. Conversely, an old automobile attracts our attention and becomes a work of "art" when it is removed from the highways and set on a display pedestal at a fair. (p. 44)

The "anti-environment" of the storytelling revival was the cultural turbulence of the 1960s. Accelerating changes in the technological, social, and economic organization of mainstream America all seemed to be enforcing a rapid decline in conditions supportive of traditional storytelling and story-listening. Chief among those changes were the shift from rural to urban and suburban communities, the shift from extended to nuclear families, increasing social mobility leading to a decline in local, regional, and ethnic particularity, and the increasing dominance of electronic media and consequent decline in the cultural value of the spoken and written word.

The political and cultural mass movements of the 1960s—the sexual revolution, the anti-war, civil rights, feminism, and hippie movements—can all be seen as homeostatic responses on the part of the social organism to critical levels of stress. The tenor of those movements, however, was overwhelmingly antagonistic. The issues raised were framed in such violently oppositional cultural narratives that they threatened to tear society apart. New cultural revival movements emerged in the years that followed as a kind of camouflage—artistic sublimations that allowed psychic heat to diffuse itself in ritual and ceremony. One such sublimation was the storytelling movement.

In the 1970s, after Woodstock and Altamont, the traumatic spate of political assassinations and massacres, the whimpering end to the Vietnam War, and the national catharsis of Watergate, the wider public environment went into a cooling period. In small groups and private refuges, however, the culture was simmering away. There was an instinctive sense that radical changes in community and self were tragically frail without disciplines of awareness and communication. There was a surge of meditation practices, personal-growth and encounter groups, and intentional communities. Images of healing and connectedness began to unseat images of revolution and destruction in the iconography of a generation. The counterculture was turning to the difficult task of cultivating sustainable community. The antagonistic tone of the mass movements of the previous decade turned agonistic, confronting the demons of the personal psyche, often through the mechanisms of communal encounter, ritual, and celebration.

As Harvey Cox put it in *The Feast of Fools:* "I have become aware that there is an unnecessary gap between the world-changers and the life-celebrators" (p. viii). He wrote:

> The epochal crisis of Western consciousness which we call the death of God is not just a passing fad. It is the result of a cumulative history that includes industrialization and the ascent of technology, pluralism, modern science, and cultural self-consciousness. Most importantly, however, the vivid cultural experience of God's absence, disappearance, or death occurred in a civilization where festivity in all its forms was in a state of steady decline. (p. 27)

The shift for Connie Regan-Blake, for example, from being an organizer of the Tennessee chapter of the National Organization for Women (NOW) in the early 1970s to being a traveling storyteller and proselytizer for NAPPS, encapsulates the shift from the revolutionary rhetoric of the 1960s (We want it *NOW!*) to the evolutionary dreamtime of the 1970s (Sleep on it: *NAPPS*). The difference between the confrontational drama of a street theater performance and the guided inner fantasy of a storytelling event is emblematic. In leaving their jobs as children's librarians in order to "spend their lives at a festival," they were answering a Dionysian call that still resounded in the culture from the 1960s. They were buoyed by a sense of plenty and protection that lingered from the postwar boom of our childhoods. But their careers, and those of many of their storytelling companions, have been dedicated to the service of festivity itself. Storytelling has been a vessel through which festival could incarnate in our culture, not explosively, as at Woodstock, but sustainably, as at Jonesborough.

From Text to Performance

Folklore collectors of the nineteenth and twentieth centuries had done yeoman work to preserve many of the world's tribal and regional folktale stocks in print, even as those stocks themselves drastically declined or disappeared from living tradition. This had the effect, from the end of the nineteenth century until the 1960s, of making librarians the chief public custodians of that part of our cultural inheritance, a duty they performed in good faith. But as the dominant technology by which we store, process, and experience cultural information shifted from print to electronic media, this situation was bound to change.

In the field of folklore, the change was signaled in the shift of its dominant analytic model from text to performance. Audio and video recording devices made it possible for performance features to be recorded, along with a much fuller reproduction of textual features than had ever been captured by dictation. The new technology, then, made certain ways of knowing possible and necessitated the creation of ideological frameworks to accommodate them. One of the new frameworks declared that it was inadequate to look at folklore as text—that we needed to look at the entire dynamic of performance in its cultural context in order to understand the form. This led certain key folklorists in the 1970s, like Dell Hymes, Dennis Tedlock, and Barre Toelken, to experiment with performance themselves in order to understand the dynamics of folklore from within (efforts that were summarized and consolidated by Elizabeth Fine in *The Folklore Text*). There was considerable academic resistance to this, but it was an inevitable ferment as our technological extensions altered the sensory envelope by which we experienced ourselves and our environment. In the field of storytelling, the same adjustments were in process, as conservators of culture were pressed beyond the performance prism of the book. There was a need to compete for the attention of the young, using the kinds of dynamics in which their environment had already soaked them: color, movement, music, vocal characterization, and sound—what Marshall McLuhan called "the reoralization of culture."

A Mythic Quality

The concept of a storytelling revival can be useful, as Wallace wields it, as a category of sociological change; in its common use by enthusiasts of the movement, however, it quickly reveals an element of myth. In the eyes of its partisans, myth is not untruth—though the words are used interchangeably in the popular press—but a story, which in the telling acts to align the worlds of imagination and emotion with the world of social action and so shapes our human world. The death-and-resurrection narrative that is woven into the language of revival, for example, is powerfully generative. It was retold constantly in NAPPS's publications, and in the ritual form of its events. The mythic imagery and atmosphere accumulating like a magnetic field around storytelling communities, and particularly around Jonesborough, in the 1970s and 1980s, produced a revitalization movement's defining quality of fervor.

A resident of Jonesborough who turned one of the restored antebellum houses into a bed-and-breakfast told me about her first exposure to storytelling at an early NAPPS festival: "It was like a religious experience," she said. She went on:

> You know we get a lot of the Institute people staying here over the summer. And we get a lot of people who are new to this storytelling stuff, and somebody's told them that they really ought to do this, and they're really, you know: "I don't know about this. . ." And I love to watch these people come back here over the course of the week, and they're just *glowing*. And they say, "I've *never* had an experience anything *like* this, it's so *wonderful!*" It's like getting into some kind of cult or something.

This cultic atmosphere was generated partly by design and partly by a kind of unconscious collaboration of human agents with intangible forces—like those that previous romantic movements have named "the *zeitgeist*," and "the spirit

of place." This quality of fervor—which Martin Buber, writing of the Hasidic movement, called by its Hebrew name of *hitlahavut*—is an essential element in cultural revitalizations. "*Hitlahavut* can appear at all places and all times," writes Buber. "Each hour is its footstool and each deed its throne. Nothing can stand against it, nothing hold it down; nothing can defend itself against its might which raises everything corporeal to spirit" (Buber, 75). It is a locus of psychological value so powerful that an encounter with it can reshape an art form, a community, or a life.

Socioeconomic and Political Aspects of the Storytelling Movement

There is certainly a sociological as well as a mythological dimension to the storytelling movement. The storytelling revival has been a mechanism for transforming the socioeconomic organization of the storytelling profession in this country. In the early 1970s, as Richard Alvey's dissertation made clear, organized storytelling was almost exclusively the province of librarians, educators, and recreation directors, with a few figures working on the margins between those fields and the print and electronic media industries. Traditional storytelling—storytelling based in community, family, and ethnic traditions—had no presence whatsoever within the field of U.S. economic life. It was an unexploited, "natural" resource. In the years since, a resurgent mythological imagining of the storyteller as artist and cultural healer provided the impetus for storytellers to move out of those institutional settings, on the one hand, and out of their family and community backgrounds, on the other, and to form themselves into a network of freelance professional performers.

These new professionals are supported in large part by those earlier institutional bases—libraries, schools, and recreation centers—but also by a national network of storytelling festivals, modeled on the national festival in Jonesborough. In the process, they have developed a web of connections among support personnel in previously established "artworlds"—publishers, media producers, arts councils, arts journalists, and public sector folklorists. All of these interlocking networks of storytellers and support people have come to constitute an "artworld" of its own, in Becker's sense—a "storytelling world." In addition, storytelling has been seized upon by community activists and civic boosters in a variety of towns and cities—paradigmatically by Jonesborough itself—as a tool to identify themselves through distinctively local cultural productions. Storytelling festivals transform familiar settings into liminal frames in which threads of local and national, individual and communal identity can be unbound and rewoven.

Politically, the contemporary storytelling movement grew out of the cultural radicalism of the 1960s and the 1960s' inward-turning politics of personal growth. It can certainly be viewed as a sublimation of politics within the realm of performance, a retreat to a constructed communal dreamworld in which intractable issues that were rending American society—issues like war and peace, ecological destruction, or racial and ethnic strife—could be faced and overcome in imaginative transport, bypassing the physical realm of bullets and blood, in the hope of advancing the healing process to a point where more gruesome turns of plot could be avoided. If the folksong revivals of the twentieth century have been artistic wedges of the labor movement, the civil rights movement, and the peace movement, the storytelling revival has helped give form to various ethnic identity movements, to the human potential movement, multiculturalism, environmentalism, the men's movement, and the goddess branch of feminism. The seminars, tapes, and books of Idries Shah, Robert Bly, Sam Keen, Michael Meade, Jean Houston, Merlin Stone, Clarissa Pinkola Estes, Brooke Medicine Eagle, Alex Haley, Matthew Fox, Joseph Bruchac, Gary Snyder, and many of their colleagues and followers form intersecting circles of revitalistic activity, all of which feed and feed upon the fervor of the storytelling revival.

A Documented Contemporary Tradition Relying on Traditional Modes

In dealing with the contemporary storytelling revival, documentary facts are plentiful. The National Storytelling Festival and the National Storytelling Association are quintessential media phenomena. They function as elaborate mechanisms for amplifying an oral, face-to-face communal art into the arenas of modern print and electronic consumer culture. Since the inception of the festival and the organization, their preoccupation has been with representing and interpreting their mission to the media and to their membership. In so doing they have generated an ever-expanding archive of print, audio, and video documentation of the movement's evolution, in plainly marked historical sequence (most of which is now stored at the National Storytelling Resource Center, or NSRC, at NSA headquarters in Jonesborough). But what is most striking about much of this material is how insistently it is structured by traditional modes of narrativization and ritualization. When we turn to the personal, autobiographical tellings of the storytelling revivalists, the pattern is just as clear: the storytelling revival has provided a channel for the psychological urgency of myth and ritual to flow into this world.

Further Reading

Alvey, Richard G., *The Historical Development of Organized Storytelling to Children in the United States* (Ph.D. diss., University of Pennsylvania), 1974

Becker, Howard S., *Art Worlds,* Berkeley: University of California Press, 1982; London: University of California Press, 1984

Buber, Martin, *Hasidism and Modern Man,* New York: Harper & Row, 1958

Cantwell, Robert, *When We Were Good: The Folk Revival,* Cambridge, Massachusetts: Harvard University Press, 1996

Cox, Harvey, *The Feast of Fools,* Cambridge, Massachusetts: Harvard University Press, 1969

Denisoff, R. Serge, *Great Day Coming: Folk Music and the American Left,* Urbana: University of Illinois Press, 1971

Fine, Elizabeth C., *The Folklore Text: From Performance to Print,* Bloomington: Indiana University Press, 1984

Kamenetsky, Christa, *The Brothers Grimm and Their Critics: Folktales and the Quest for Meaning,* Athens: Ohio University Press, 1992

Lieberman, Robbie, *"My Song Is My Weapon": People's Songs, American Communism, and the Politics of Culture, 1930–1950,* Urbana: University of Illinois Press, 1989

National Directory of Storytelling, Jonesborough, Tennessee: National Association for the Preservation and Perpetuation of Storytelling, 1994

Schechner, Richard, *Between Theater and Anthropology,* Philadelphia: University of Pennsylvania Press, 1985

Wallace, Anthony F.C., "Revitalization Movements," *American Anthropologist* 58 (1956)

Whisnant, David, *All That Is Native and Fine: The Politics of Culture in an American Region,* Chapel Hill: University of North Carolina Press, 1983

Preadolescent Girls' Storytelling

Elizabeth Tucker

Elizabeth Tucker discusses the psychological uses of horror narratives among preteen girls. She outlines several popular plots.

Horror and the Preadolescent

Preadolescence—roughly defined as the age span from 9 to 11 or 12 years old—is a time of widening social awareness and increasing competence in the art of storytelling. For American girls, preadolescent storytelling becomes a forum for expressing fears related to the vulnerabilities of both childhood and adolescence: cruel parents, menacing male attackers, and threats from the realm of the supernatural. While many preadolescent girls' stories are suffused with a blend of fear and excitement, some are playful and lighthearted in tone. The strong vein of traditionalism in girls' stories frequently undergoes creative variation. Narratives used as examples here were collected from preadolescent girls in southern Indiana and New York State, from the mid-1970s to the early 1990s.

American girls find opportunities to tell stories at slumber parties, at camp, at informal get-togethers with friends, and on the playground at school. Halloween, with its haunted house exhibits, parties, and trick-or-treat preparations, provides a stimulus for narrating scary stories. The symbiosis of oral tradition, popular literature, television, and film has reinforced both girls' and boys' telling of scary stories at the preadolescent stage. In particular, R.L. Stine's Goosebumps books have encouraged children to read and talk about frightening plot twists. Weekly television shows such as *Are You Afraid of the Dark?* have further reinforced children's appreciation of scary stories as exciting entertainment that stretches the boundaries of what society considers to be safe, normal, and permissible.

Younger preadolescents tend to prefer simple folktales with happy or "catch" endings. While these narratives begin with scary noises or other kinds of threats to the child protagonists, they end with positive, humorous punch lines that provide comic relief. One popular tale of this sort begins with a little girl and boy walking through the woods, hearing the ghostly cry, "It floats!" Finally summoning the courage to ask what floats, the girl and boy hear the ghost's reply: "Ivory soap, you dope!" Another tale tells of a little boy discovering a mysterious chest in the middle of a haunted hotel. From the chest comes a terrifying noise: "Rap! Rap!" When the boy dares to open the chest, he finds wrapping paper. Other examples of tales about worrisome noises or utterances are "Bloody Fingers," "One Black Eye," and "Now I Gotcha Where I Wantcha, Now I'm Gonna Eatcha." Although their plots vary, there is a consistent pattern of action for the child character: hearing something scary, offering a verbal solution or putdown, and ending with a laugh.

One very popular folktale is the story of "The Stolen Liver." Conforming to Aarne-Thompson Folktale Type 366, "The Man from the Gallows," this story includes many motifs, principally E235.4.4, Return from Dead to Punish Theft of Liver from Man on Gallows. The child protagonist who steals the liver, trying to make up for having spent all available funds on candy, is sometimes a boy and sometimes a girl. Gender distinctions seem relatively minor in this kind of story, although it should be noted that the mother who cooks the liver for dinner takes on the role of an unwittingly cannibalistic nurturer. At the end of the story the ghost goes after Johnny or Susie, concluding the tale with a rousing "I GOTCHA!" (With this shout, the young storyteller grabs whoever is closest.) Following a very similar plot, "The Golden Arm" tells of the ghost of a woman who pursues her husband, trying to get back the golden arm that he stole from her. This vengeful female ghost, doing her best to regain what is rightfully hers, has greater significance in terms of gender than does the ghost in "The Stolen Liver." Both boys and girls enjoy "The Golden Arm," often recalling it as a favorite story from camp or overnight parties.

Witches and Mothers

More fanciful and less bound to a particular tale type are stories about cruel parents, especially mothers. According to Dorothy Bloch, psychoanalyst and author of *So the Witch Won't Eat Me*, young children fear engulfment by their parents. Preadolescent girls, moving toward the end of the latency period of their development, may feel especially worried about being swallowed up by their mothers. This pattern emerges in stories about witches or witchlike mothers who cut off their children's heads, cook them on the stove, and serve them to other family members for dinner. The cannibalistic witch takes her prototype from "Hansel and Gretel," AT 327A, where the children narrowly escape being consumed through their own cleverness. Similarly, in girls' tales of voracious mothers, the central female character must use her wits to escape a dreadful death. The witch's danger is complicated by her deceptively kind behavior; she may offer candy to the little girl or say something friendly like "Take a nice hot bath." Sometimes the little girl must kill the witch in order to escape alive; other times she can simply sneak away. In any case, victory over the cruel witch/mother represents a major triumph of independence and self-assertion against a powerful parental figure.

Home Alone—The Slumber Party

Although dangerous mothers are significant characters in the repertoire of preadolescent girls, menacing male figures are much more common. "The Slumber Party" is one story in which a group of girls suffers from the attack of a "crazy man" who breaks into the house. In the midst of a pizza party, the girls run to hide in different places; no parents are there to protect them. Suddenly, most of the girls hear someone making a

strange noise on the stairs: "Click-click. Sh-sh! Click-click. Sh-sh! Click-click. Sh-sh! Click-click. Sh-sh!" The "click-click" turns out to be the sound of one poor victim's legs, cut off at the knees, while the "sh-sh" is the sound of her arms cut off at the elbows. Such horrifying dismemberment represents the fear of being victimized, maimed by an attacker who preys upon young women and makes them lose their wholeness as individuals. "The Slumber Party" functions as a cautionary tale, showing what disastrous consequences can result from preadolescent party giving with no adults around. Part of the story's structure comes from AT 123, *The Wolf and the Kids*, in which a wolf takes advantage of a mother goat's absence to devour her babies. As in "Red Riding Hood" (AT 333), the wolf is a predatory male pursuing female victims. Feelings of vulnerability at the hands of a male attacker are frequently expressed in stories by girls of this age group. Since actual attacks upon girls at slumber parties have been reported in newspapers, "The Slumber Party" derives some of its impact from known tragedy. Like "Hansel and Gretel," it warns girls to watch out for threatening figures and to protect themselves as much as possible.

The Babysitter

Another warning about what can happen in an unprotected house comes from the legend of "The Babysitter." The heroine of this story, alone in a house at night with young children, gets a series of phone calls from a man who threatens to kill her. The climax of the story occurs when the operator, asked to trace the calls, says, "You'd better get out of the house right now, because he's on the basement extension!" In some versions of this legend the babysitter escapes, but the children die at the hands of the intruder. Like "The Slumber Party," this story mirrors fear of what can happen when a male assailant discovers a girl alone: a scenario that has sexual connotations as well as threatened violence. "The Babysitter" features a heroine who is not only deprived of adult protection but also responsible for safeguarding younger children. When the killer pursues her and the children, he violates her effectiveness as a substitute mother as well as her personal safety. Preadolescent girls tend to be very interested in babysitting, as the popularity of the "Baby-Sitters Club" books shows. Babysitting brings authority, challenge, and financial gain; it can also bring loss of control, as the legend shows. One "Babysitter" subtype tells of a hippie teenager who, after taking drugs, puts the baby in the oven and places a turkey in the baby's crib. This story teaches young listeners that peril doesn't only come from intruders; it can also come from one's own mind in an altered state of consciousness.

Date Terror

Contrasting with the stories girls tell about babysitting are the ones they tell about boys and girls going out on dates. In these texts the emphasis is not on maintaining a motherly role but on exploring relationships with the opposite sex. "The Boyfriend's Death" is an especially popular legend with broad national dissemination. In this story the boyfriend, driving through woods or a park, runs out of gas and goes in search of more. Before leaving, he cautions his girlfriend to stay inside the car. Although she hears a scream and some frightening noises—"drip-drop" and "scritch-scratch"—she stays in the car and avoids looking out. The next morning a policeman tells her, "Lady, lady, drive your car away and don't look behind you." Of course, the girl looks back anyway, her concern overriding the policeman's admonition, and sees a terrible sight: her boyfriend hanging above the car, with his blood falling "drip-drop" and his toenails going "scritch-scratch" on the roof of the car. This story has a male victim and a female survivor who must figure out how to assert herself. Even though two male authority figures, her boyfriend and a policeman, have told her to remain passive, she takes the risk of looking at the gory scene. Unlike Lot's wife in the Bible, she is not changed into a pillar of salt or otherwise punished for not following orders. Since staying in the car saves her life, "The Boyfriend's Death" bears mixed messages about choosing to be passive or assertive. In any case, it shows that going out on a date can become a perilous venture.

Another well-known legend about a date is "The Hook," in which a boy and a girl just barely escape with their lives. While parking on Lover's Lane, they hear a frightening announcement on their car radio: "Escaped lunatic from an insane asylum! He has a hook for a hand!" Reluctant at first to leave, the boy finally yields to his girlfriend's request to drive her home. As he opens the car door for her, he finds a hook stuck to the handle. Alan Dundes has aptly pointed out that the boy in this legend is "all hands" and that the hook itself is a phallic symbol. Typifying the anxiety that girls feel about early sexual encounters, "The Hook" has been dominant in preadolescents' repertoires for several generations. It has also been satirized in youth-oriented television shows like *South Park,* in which the dangerous lunatic has a piece of celery on his arm instead of a hook.

The China Doll

While dangers from human beings tend to receive particular attention in preadolescent girls' stories, threats from supernatural or otherwise inexplicable forces also come to the fore. One favorite legend of this kind is "The China Doll," sometimes called "The Purple Doll." This legend features a beautiful, finely dressed doll that has been purchased by a sailor father in China as a gift for his little daughter. Although the doll has a lovely smile and a pretty purple dress, she turns out to be a killer who attacks all the members of the little girl's family in rapid succession. Each murder is signaled by a frightening sound: "Hrrrunch!" This sound effect, like those in "The Slumber Party" and "The Boyfriend's Death," gives young storytellers a chance to practice their histrionic skills. The doll's murderous power is all the more frightening because she seems inanimate to all but her victims. Both folktales and legends have explored the enigma of "living dolls," with some of the most destructive dolls arising from sacrilegious acts of creation. Contemporary children's literature has continued to develop this theme, with books such as R.L. Stine's *Night of the Living Dummy* (1993). Preadolescent girls may especially enjoy "The China Doll" because it so eerily brings danger from a familiar plaything that will soon be discarded as the teen years arrive.

Sometimes girls tell personal experience narratives about things that have happened at slumber parties, campouts, or other get-togethers. Narratives about Ouija board use are especially prominent: mysteriously spelled names, sudden noises, and other strange occurrences become the focal points of stories attempting to show that the supernatural really does exist. Some of these accounts frighten listeners so much that just hearing the words "Ouija board" makes them leave the storytelling group. Somewhat less frightening are the stories about seances and other supernatural games. In "Mary Worth," sometimes known as "Mary Wolf," girls may combine the narration of a legend with an attempt to make a traffic accident victim materialize in the mirror of a darkened bathroom. Other stories spring from the game "Levitation," alternatively named "Light as a Feather," in which girls lift a friend using only two fingers from each hand.

Through folktales, legends, and personal experience narratives, preadolescent girls express their trepidations and excitement about moving toward adulthood. Telling stories about confrontations with cruel mothers, hook-handed assailants, and ghosts helps tellers and listeners to develop a sense of strength in vicariously handling new challenges. This storytelling process also encourages verbal artistry, contributing to girls' expressive skills as they enter the teenage years.

Further Reading

Bloch, Dorothy, *"So the Witch Won't Eat Me": Fantasy and the Child's Fear of Infanticide,* Boston: Houghton Mifflin, 1978; London: Burnett, 1979

Dégh, Linda, "The Boy Friend's Death" and "The Hook," *Indiana Folklore* 1 (1968)

Dundes, Alan, "On the Psychology of Legend," in *American Folk Legend; a Symposium,* edited by Wayland D. Hand, Berkeley: University of California Press, 1971

Langlois, Janet, "Mary Whales, I Believe in You," in *Indiana Folklore: A Reader,* edited by Linda Dégh, Bloomington: Indiana University Press, 1980

An Analysis of Five Interviews with Storylisteners to Determine How They Perceive the Listening Experience

Brian Sturm

Brian Sturm interviewed five storytellers about their storylistening experiences. He examines the vocabulary they use to describe listening to stories and draws some conclusions regarding a trance-like state into which some enter during storytelling events.

An Interview Model to Study the Storytelling Trance

The modern storytelling event is usually a staged affair to which listeners come with the sole intention of hearing stories. Whether told to children or to adults, stories have the power to entrance listeners, to captivate them, if they are good stories well told. Sometimes this enchantment is so extensive, listeners enter "an altered state of consciousness verging on hypnosis: the 'storylistening trance'" (Stallings, p. 6). Listeners sit immobile, breathing slows, and eyes widen as the story unfolds. These characteristics are similar to those exhibited by hypnotized clients: "pupil dilation, flattened cheeks, skin pallor, lack of movement, slowed blink and swallowing reflex, [and] lowered and slowed respiration" (Lankton and Lankton, p. 66).

Storytelling is increasingly accepted as an adjunct to psychotherapy. Clinical psychologists now incorporate storytelling into therapeutic treatment programs, often tracing the practice back to Milton Erickson, the father of hypnotherapy. Storytelling has been used to reduce the pain

children feel while undergoing treatment for leukemia (Kuttner, 1988); it is used to enable abused children to speak about their trauma without re-enacting it (Rhue, 1991); and it is used with other clients to give a vicarious, metaphoric experience that enables the clients to manipulate the stories, shape the outcomes, and thereby gain control, first over the story and then over their own lives. These last therapeutic techniques rely on the metaphoric quality of the stories; the first seems to rely on the listener's absorption in the story to the exclusion of the pain.

There seems to be, then, an exceptional power in a story well told, but often a listener hears a tale without becoming involved or entranced by it. The listener remains on the periphery of it, aware of its storyness, not experiencing it as real. Katharine Young (1987) distinguishes the Tale-world, a state in which a listener becomes actively involved in the world in which the characters live and act, from the Storyrealm, in which the listener is not yet a part of the story's world. A listener who encounters a story but retains a sense that it is a story experiences the Storyrealm, but the listener so caught up in the story that quotidian reality fades experiences the Taleworld. The story comes alive for these listeners, and they see the setting and action unfolding in their minds.

This entrancing power of storytelling was the subject of this investigation. Rather than write a survey in my words and with my preconceptions, I conducted a set of interviews to explore the vocabulary and concepts storylisteners use. The choice of candidates to interview was not random. I applied the concept of "expert participants" as discussed by Romney, Weller, and Batchelder (1986). In this article, the authors present the idea that members of small cultural units (e.g., tennis players or eight-ball pool players) exhibit common behaviors and perceptions, and that there exist within the subculture quantifiable patterns of behavior that members understand and use. In order to express these common perceptions, the members develop "an associated semantic domain that provides a way of classifying and talking about the elements in the culture pattern" (Romney, p. 315). Not only do the members of a group or subculture exhibit similar behavior patterns, but they also use similar words to describe them, words with meanings understood and agreed upon by the members. Knowing the usage of these terms within a particular culture enables a researcher to ask questions using terminology familiar to the group's members. Respondents, then, are able to understand the questions more completely, and the responses are more precise and more consistent. Posing questions from a common vocabulary eliminates much of the ambiguity inherent in communication.

I chose five people who were all part of a local subculture of storylisteners. Two were children's librarians who have attended many storytelling events, were storytellers themselves, and had been part of the storytelling culture for years. The other three people were members of a storytelling class, which was nearing completion at the time of the interviews. These people too had been involved in storytelling for several years. The reason for choosing people who were also storytellers was that knowledge and familiarity with a subject often enables one to talk about it in more depth. The questions capitalized on this knowledge of stories and storytelling. A storylistener without this background may not have been able to discuss the points of interest in as much detail. Though this assumption certainly influenced the results, my purpose of exploring the vocabulary and experiences of experienced storylisteners warranted the choice.

The questions posed to the informants were open-ended and intended to evoke their individual perceptions of the storylistening experience. The following list of questions is indicative,

though not prescriptive, of those asked during the interviews. Every effort was made to listen to the words the informant used, and questions were phrased as much as possible using their words in order to avoid prescribing a vocabulary while encouraging them to explore and use their own.

1. What are your general impressions of listening to stories? Like/dislike? Why?
2. How does listening to stories make you feel?
3. What kinds of stories do you like/dislike? Why?
4. Do you get involved in the stories to which you listen? In what way?
5. Can you remember a time when you were deeply involved in a story? Explain that experience.
6. What was it that got your attention so completely?

a. Story	Specific character
	Event
	Setting
	Plot
	Descriptions/Imagery
b. Teller	Dress
	Gestures
	Choice of words
c. Telling	Rhythm
	Style
d. Context	Dark or light
	Noisy or quiet
	Stage, circle of chairs, around a table

7. Looking back on the experience, can you describe how it felt? What were you aware of?
8. Describe the "ideal" environment that would help your involvement in a story.

The interviews were conducted from December 1 to December 10, 1991. One librarian interview was conducted while she worked at the reference desk, the other in the library's programming room. The interviews with the students took place in isolated rooms around the college campus. Distractions and disruptions were minimal except for the librarian interview at the reference desk. Each interview was tape recorded for later transcription and analysis. Each transcription was then coded according to emergent categories of information.

The analysis of the five interviews yielded six areas of interest: how listeners describe the entrancing experience; those things that augment a storytelling's ability to entrance the listeners; those things that hinder such involvement; the sensations and emotions involved in being entranced; who controls the experience; and, which aspect of a storytelling is most important.

Words Used to Describe Becoming Entranced

Most of the verbs used to describe the experience of becoming involved or entranced with a story were passive: "pulled into," "drawn into," "taken into," "swept away," "bounce in and out," "drift way out," "wrapped up in a story." None of these requires effort on the part of the listener, who perceives him- or herself as being acted upon by the experience, as though the control lies outside the listener.

The only active verbs used by any of the interviewees were to "break into a story," or to "go back into a story." These imply that an effort is necessary to become involved. One participant alluded to this effort in the form of active concentration. He felt that he must work at concentrating up to a certain point until the story took over. Perhaps this explains the use of these active verbs. The other participant who responded using an active verb, used it not in the context of entering a story for the first time, but to describe what happens when one "comes out of it" before the conclusion and wants to return to the involved state. At that point, effort is needed to refocus attention on the story rather than on other things.

The informants used many phrases that imply that the storytelling trance is a "place," a plane of existence, an alternate reality perhaps, which one can enter and exit. The image arises of a box or container that represents the story. Viewed from the outside, the story remains distant, an other, yet as soon as a listener climbs inside the box and views it from inside, the view is restricted to the space within. The external world outside the box is imperceptible ("you're oblivious to the world around you") and reality becomes the box or the story itself. This quality of story place or space recalls the terms used by Katharine Young, Storyrealm and Taleworld. Both appear to listeners as somewhere.

Another word that signals this enclosed space is "in" or "into," which was used repeatedly to describe the engrossed state. "Pulled into,"

"taken into," "journey into," "break into," "bounce in," and "get gone into" are some examples. The implication here is that there is some form of tangible boundary that must be crossed before the story "works." This boundary is not impenetrable, nor is it particularly strong. It allows both entry and egress, but it seems to require a guide to enter while one easily may exit alone. The guide is the thing (whether animate or not) that pulls or draws a listener into the space of enchantment.

There seems to be, then, a time during a storytelling when a listener becomes a passive entity who releases control of the story or the images and allows him- or herself to be led on by the story or the storyteller. Having released control, the listener becomes oblivious to quotidian reality; reality for that listener is the story being told ("it's real for you"). Sometimes a listener "pops back out" of the story and realizes that "I haven't been concentrating" (consciously) on the story. If the listener can "go back in," a change occurs "from conscious analysis to unconscious analysis of the story," and the listener once again relinquishes control.

Things That Augment One's Ability to Be Entranced

Five aspects of the storytelling event seem to influence the listener's ability to become involved in a story: the story, the telling or presentation, the teller, the context or physical environment of the storytelling event, and the listener.

The Story

The story itself needs to be well structured so that it presents a logical and coherent message. Too much diversion from the basic sequence of events (plot) in the story seemed counterproductive. While the progression needed to be logical, the conclusion should not be obvious. As one interviewee put it, "Suspense helps." This suspense may manifest itself in a surprise ending or an unexpected punch line. Just as a good joke capitalizes on a surprise twist at the end, so, too, a good story that is "engaging" seems to include this revelatory quality; it concludes with an "Aha!" This revelation is the quality of a story that enables the listeners to "learn something more about themselves or the world."

An engrossing story is multisensory. It evokes in the listener's mind a visual picture complete with the sounds and smells that accompany it. Interviewees claimed that when they were engrossed in a story they could "vividly" "see what's going on," and they could "envision things." There was a sense of physically "being in" a story; the events were actually happening. Richard Schechner (1985) claims that during a performance, "the performer goes from the 'ordinary world' to the 'performative world,' from one time/space reference to another, from one personality to one or more others." (pp. 125–126) Add to this concept that of Robert Georges (1969), who claims that during a storytelling, the roles of storyteller and storylistener become indistinct and merge as the two cocreate the story—and the potential becomes clear for the listener to follow the performer as he or she changes worlds. As one interviewee expressed it, "I was there." The story did not remain an intellectual or intangible encounter; it became an experiential one, and "the realness of it" became important.

While most informants expressed the need for a story to be multisensory, some also said that for a story to be entrancing it must be "rich in emotion." It must evoke a strong emotional response in the listener. The "mood" of a story was mentioned in this context. Whether the mood must parallel that of the listener, or whether it must be appropriate to the setting, or both, is an area for further research, but some emotional response to the story or identification with the story was necessary.

Finally, the interviewees claimed that they were more easily engrossed in the story if they could identify with the story's setting, characters, or character types. One participant was familiar with Chinese culture and prosodic style. He found an Asian story engrossing because of this familiarity. Another participant claimed that a story was entrancing for her if the story's characters were undergoing similar experiences as she. This identification with a character's experiences, the "human element" of a story, augmented the story's power to involve her.

The data suggest that for a story to be entrancing it should have five characteristics: it should have a logical plot progression; it should be suspenseful; it should appeal to many senses; it should involve the emotions; and it should reflect or refract the experiences of the listeners.

The Telling

The way the story is told has an impact on the listener's ability to become engrossed in a tale. Of primary importance to the people inter-viewed was the natural quality of the presentation. One person described this quality as a "natural flow, not forced." For him, a storytelling was engrossing if "the performer isn't even there, and it's just the story." Another interviewee claimed that she was drawn into a story "because she [the storyteller] wasn't necessarily performing it." If the storytelling seemed to be effortless, the listeners were more easily caught up in the story. Visible effort on the part of the storyteller caused listeners to "focus on what was going on in the present rather than what's going on in the story." This idea will return later when considering distractions.

Though the storyteller should perform without visible effort, he or she should also, according to one participant, appear to be "enjoying and loving the telling of the tale" because that "is something I end up sharing in." The storyteller's interest and involvement was infectious; listeners enjoyed the story because the teller visibly did. A sense of "camaraderie" developed between the listener and the teller, a bond. This bond was very personal; it existed not between the teller and the audience, but between the teller and each individual member of the audience. Listeners reported that during a good storytelling, it felt "as if the story was being told directly to them," despite the 300-500 other members of the audience. "It was a more personal experience, even though she wasn't just telling it to me, she was telling it to everybody in the group," explained one participant. The telling of the story must enable listeners to feel individual ownership of the story.

Finally, there must be an even rhythm to the story. One participant described this as "soothing" while another said that an entrancing story was "very smooth." The rendition had a practiced, polished quality, which freed it from awkward pauses or ruptures in the rhythm. The tellers seemed to have "told it many times before," or "read it quite a few times." There seems to be a cadence that draws listeners into the story and lulls them into accepting the reality or presence of the story. This does not mean a monotonous "recitation" of the story; it must have "vigor," or intensity, but this intensity must be constrained by a deeper rhythmic quality.

The rendering of a story that is most effective for entrancing a listener is effortless and rhythmical, and the storyteller should enjoy telling the story and be able to make it very personal for each listener.

The Teller

Besides what is included in the previous section, one aspect of the storyteller was mentioned that could augment the storytelling's power to entrance listeners: his or her apparent authenticity. One participant described being entranced by a Vietnamese tale. He was familiar (from previous encounters) with Chinese literature, and so in his mind he "made it [the Vietnamese story] a Chinese story." He then went on to say that "that would be a great story to hear from an ancient Chinese type, someone with a little bit of an accent, that would make it seem like the storyteller was an actual member of the story." This listener wanted the story to be visually represented before him. The story would come to life in the presence of the storyteller. Though this opinion may seem directly to contradict the previously mentioned invisible nature of the storyteller ("the performer isn't even there"), the two opinions are actually complementary. The performance quality was absent from both. A Chinese storyteller telling a Chinese story appears natural, unforced, and effortless. He or she is authentic. A Caucasian American teller dressed up as a Chinese storyteller would have the opposite effect. Attention would focus on the performance quality of the storytelling, the acting, and the listeners would not be entranced. This has important ramifications for the use of dialect when telling a story; perhaps it should only be used if the storyteller could believably use that dialect in real life. A red-headed Caucasian using an African-American dialect would draw attention to the performance itself, although that same person, whether Irish or not, might be able to use an Irish dialect with the appearance of authenticity, and thereby augment the story's enchanting power.

The Context

The context, the physical environment in which a storytelling event took place, affected the listeners' ability to become engrossed in a story. Similar responses were given when asked about the "ideal" setting for a storytelling event: informants wanted bodily comfort, peace of mind, and the ability to see and hear the storyteller without distractions.

The environment had to be comfortable. Listeners wanted to have a "full stomach" ("not hungry"), to feel "warm," (a "fireplace" was mentioned), and to feel "safe." They wanted "dim lights," "soft lighting with a few shadows," or "darkness." "Evening" was judged to be the best time for storytelling by one participant, perhaps because of these other factors (after dinner and soft light). They saw themselves "sitting on a big pillow," or in a "chair, kind of soft," somewhere where they could "sit back and get comfortable."

Informants also wanted peace of mind. They did not want to be bothered by "anything on the back of your mind to worry about," because they wished to be "able to give your whole mind to that kind of thing [story]."

They wanted to be able to see and hear the storyteller. Small to medium-sized audiences were preferred over large ones. Proximity to the teller was mentioned as the reason for a small group. "Staging, where the teller is in relation to the audience, also makes a difference," according to one participant, while another drew in the air a semicircle of listeners around the storyteller to describe the ideal stage setup since it allows unobstructed viewing and listening. The acoustics of the building or area in which the storytelling took place also needed to be good so that no effort was needed to hear.

Finally, the listeners wanted the environment free of distractions and interruptions so that they could "hear the story and nothing else." This would give them the "ability to concentrate" on the story so "you can really focus."

The best context, then, was one in which one's basic needs were met, and the setting was intimate and with few distractions.

The Listeners

The listeners played a crucial role in the entrancing quality of a story. Not only were they the ones who experienced the process, they could also be predisposed to it. The attitudes of the listener upon entering the storytelling event influenced whether or not he or she became enchanted. "It depends largely on my mood what kind of story I'm into." A happy mood might increase the likelihood of becoming engrossed in a happy story, just as a sad story could enrapture a listener in a disconsolate mood.

The interests of the listener factored into the experience. A listener fascinated by trains might become entranced by a railroad story, or a person whose passion was exploration might find an adventure story irresistible. This idea is reminiscent of the previously mentioned concept of the parallel between a person's life and the events of the story. If the timing of the story coincided with a similar event in the listener's life, it was more likely that the listener would become involved in that story. On the other hand, a need or unfulfilled desire that was evident in a story could also trigger that deep involvement. One participant whose parents had gone through divorce and who had felt neglected and unloved found solace in a story filled with caring and motherly protection. He filled his needs "from the story rather than from my parents." The listener's life experiences, then, dispose him or her to become engrossed in a story.

The dynamics of the audience must also be considered. "There's a group dynamic . . . that is maybe intensified by an audience experience, being with others." At first glance this quotation seems self-evident: group dynamics, of course, are intensified by the presence of people. However, the participant who made the statement seemed to be equating group dynamic with group entrancement, in which case the presence of some people being swept into a story helped others become swept up as well; a kind of bandwagon or domino effect. The power of the group to create its own reality is well known. Mob psychology is a potent force.

Finally, the listener was responsible for reaching the threshold where the story took control. One participant said that he had to concentrate actively, to engage his will and put forth effort, in order to reach the point of entrancement. Without the effort on his part, the involvement would never happen. A listener may need to make a conscious effort to reach the boundary between being "outside" a story and being "in" it. Perhaps any storytelling has the power to entrance its listeners if they willingly suspend their grasp of quotidian reality in order to imbue the story reality with vitality.

Things That Hinder One's Ability to Be Entranced

Often a storytelling event fails to entrance its listeners. The reasons, given by the informants in these interviews, seem to fall into four categories: distractions caused by the context of the event, distractions caused by the storyteller, breaks in the rhythm of the telling, and the predisposition of the listeners.

Distractions caused by the context were those that could be attributed to the physical environment in which the storytelling took place. If the place was "uncomfortable," "cold," or "windy," then it was hard to focus on the story. If there were many people in the audience and listeners were

constantly "being pushed or jostled," or if the acoustics or the sound system were inadequate so that the listeners "can't hear," then again the story was submerged by a host of quotidian concerns, and it was "hard to keep my train of thought going." The environment must fade into the background of the listener's consciousness before the story's environment can become prominent.

The storyteller, too, could be a distraction if too much attention were focused on him or her. If the storyteller did "too much," made "melodramatic motions," or was "being too ethereal, or overly sentimental or affected" then the emphasis was on the teller and not the story. The teller should remain as unobtrusive as possible. "As long as people don't go, 'Aha! You're doing that,'" as long as the listeners don't recognize they are being entranced, then they may allow it to happen. As soon as the intention or effort becomes obvious, the opportunity is lost.

Once a listener became involved, there were moments that could abruptly end the involvement; "something jolts the story." Some examples of such jolts were an abrupt transition from one visual image to another, a "time shift" that confuses the listener, a story element that "kind of surprised me and popped me back out," "[the storyteller's] body moved and [his] voice changed," or "there's a stumble over a word." All of these examples highlight the rupture that occurred in a listener's involvement when the expected rhythm of the story was broken. The enchantment seemed to rely heavily on the maintenance of a natural and even cadence in the rendition of the story.

The fourth type of hindrance to which informants referred could be called listener bias or predisposition. Two of the informants who are practicing storytellers claimed that they were often "busy looking at technique . . . and not allowing [themselves] to be taken into the story." They were predisposed to critique the event or empathize with the storyteller to the point that they were distracted from the story. Just as the mood of one of the informants determined what he found entrancing (and probably affected his ability even to be entranced), the personal biases or private agendas of each listener will influence his or her degree of involvement.

So far I have addressed how listeners described the process of becoming entranced and the things that promoted and hindered that process. I now turn to the fourth area of interest, the period of entrancement itself and the participants' descriptions of that time.

Descriptions of the Period of Entrancement

The descriptions of the state of entrancement given by the informants fall into three categories: feelings of excitement, feelings of preoccupation and relaxation, and various degrees of isolation and community.

Some informants found the experience of being entranced an "exciting" one. "There's a feeling of electricity," a charge of energy that seemed to resonate within listeners. Another informant referred to this phenomenon as "the chills that you get" when you listen to a good story. "It's something that somehow reaches your core." Perhaps this excitement is the product of such deep-seated emotion. Just as a dream can leave the awakening dreamer shaking because of its intensity, a well-told story might touch the listener in a very intense way. It may be that the intensity of the emotion is brought about by the deeply personal nature of the story; on the other hand, it may be that "something is being satisfied that is universal to humankind." What causes this excitement bears further inquiry.

The most often-cited feeling that accompanied this deep involvement was a relaxed, preoccupied one. It was a "kind of lilting, almost floating" that required "no effort, no concentration, it just flows." Informants described it as a very "passive" experience in which the listener felt "dependent on the teller to keep the story going." The listener's "mind just goes on hold for a bit," and "you don't have to think about anything." But the listeners didn't "realize it until after it's been going on for a while." The present became less distinct. Awareness of the physical environment and even one's own feelings grew dim. "During the story I don't remember the classroom," explained one informant, and "for a large amount of time I think I ignore feelings, and I'm able to ignore them." These feelings seemed to be those connected with quotidian reality because the same informant expressed the idea that listeners empathized with the story characters' emotions to the point of identity with them. During the process of getting involved in a story, all the trappings of quotidian reality were left behind. On a symbolic level, this process is very similar to ritual washing in which the "soiled" nature is cleansed and renewed. This, too, is an exciting area for further research.

The informants found it difficult, but possible, to describe the feelings involved when entranced. One informant described this state as a "feeling of 'aaahhh,' of group approval, satisfaction and fulfillment." She accompanied her description with a relaxing of her shoulders, a slow, deep breath, and a brief, unfocused stare off into the room. Another informant used the same word and a similar bodily response. He identified the entrancing period of the story as "that's when you really, 'aaahhh.'" He slumped back in his chair, put his hands behind his head, let out a deep breath, and crossed his legs. A third informant described watching the others in the audience become entranced. "People were just kind of 'blaaahh,'" he explained, and he made his eyes big, round, and glassy as he stared off into space. He also wobbled his head slowly in a circle with his jaw slack and his mouth slightly open. There seems to be a fair amount of agreement about the physical manifestations of being engrossed in a story, symptoms that closely parallel those exhibited by hypnotized people.

The third aspect of the state of involvement was the degree of isolation felt by the informants. One described it as "you're to yourself, you're not invading anyone else's space or having your space invaded; it's a very safe type of feeling." The primary focus of this listener was inward. Another informant made a similar comment when he answered a question about whether the mood of the story was created by a rapport among the audience. He replied, "It's more personal for me. I think I can detach myself from that for the most part." Again the focus was internal. A third informant, however, claimed that he could "feel a real bond with the teller." His story space, for want of a better word, was large enough to include the storyteller; while the others felt withdrawn, he felt connected.

An engaging storytelling is an exciting experience, yet one that deeply relaxes. It is an experience that joins one with other listeners and with the teller, yet it focuses one inward. Perhaps it is the dynamic between these extremes—excitement versus relaxation and community versus isolation—that makes the storytelling experience so powerful.

Who Controls the Experience

There seemed to be two stages in an entrancing story encounter. The first stage was one in which the storyteller began to describe the story, or as one informant phrased it, "the picture is being begun for you." Another informant said that the listener was "dependent on the storyteller to keep the story going." Not only were the visual images in the hands of the storyteller, "part of that [the mood of the experience] should be worked up by the teller." So the storyteller began the experience in control. This control, however, began to shift to the listener as the story unfolded and the listener became involved. "The storyteller gets you going; it's for you to take it from there." The listener must "paint the picture yourself." As a listener, "you create the story as you go."

The first stage parallels Katharine Young's description of the Storyrealm in which the story is still an external object. The story exists in another reality, in another space/time reference. The storyteller is describing a scene over which he or she has complete control. As the listener begins to take responsibility for creating his or her own images (or reality) from the words of the storyteller, control shifts, and the listener enters the second stage. This is the Taleworld in which the story reality overshadows quotidian reality. The listener exists within the story frame. Yet, just as when one is hypnotized, a part of the mind seems to remain unaffected, a third party observer, so when one is entranced by a story, a part of the mind is able to "bounce in and out" and observe the listener in trance.

One comment by an informant added a third possibility to the understanding of control. He said that, "the listener puts in a lot of effort until it takes over." He never explained the "it." "It" could represent the trance, which seems to take control of the listener and ease the effort needed to visualize the story. "It" could represent the rhythm of the telling that lulls the listener into relaxation. "It" could also mean the story reality itself, which seems to sweep over the listener. Perhaps neither the storyteller nor the listener is in control of the experience. Maybe the story itself is in control. This concept is supported by the ideas expressed by the children's librarians who are also active storytellers. They claim that for a story to be really good, it must be involving for the storyteller as well. Perhaps the story itself is at the base of the enchantment. The listener needs the teller, and the teller needs the story.

The Importance of Various Aspects of the Storytelling Experience

The informants differed in their opinions of the importance of the various aspects of a storytelling event. Some felt that the "story line or plot" was of primary importance: the "listener and the story have to click" in order for them to become deeply involved. Others felt that the primary influence on the listener's ability to become engrossed in a story was "how it's told." "The story can go anywhere it wants for a while so long as the telling is smooth." A third opinion was that the emotional connection with the story was the principal influencing agent. One informant summed up the relative importance of the story, the listener, and the telling by saying that "any failure of one part of it is going to keep the people from being involved." Perhaps there is no principal agent that controls the involvement of the listeners. Instead, the varying aspects must all intermingle to create the entrancing experience.

Conclusions

The purpose of this study has been to begin to explore the perceptions of listeners as they try to describe the entrancing power of storytelling. The conclusions of this study are not meant to be definitive, nor are they generalizable to any other population. One cannot explain any cause and effect relationships among the various elements described in this research; that has not been the intent. Instead, the intent has been to identify common themes and words used by storylisteners so that more detailed studies can be conducted.

One of the most powerful influences on the involvement of listeners is the presence or absence of distractions. Whether they are due to breaks in the rhythm of the presentation, uncomfortable qualities of the physical environment, or prior moods and expectations, distractions are the greatest hindrance to becoming involved. This implies that concentration is vital. The more intense the concentration of the listener, the more involving the story becomes. This is similar to trance. "Medical scientists now believe that trance is a normal and very common altered state of consciousness, an intense form of focused attention" (Stallings, p.7). If storytelling is indeed a form of trance, a conclusion that the descriptions of the informants would seem to support, then storytellers must become aware of it. This study lays the foundation for continued research into the perceptions of storylisteners. Their descriptions, which research seems to have ignored (until recent developments in reader response research), need to be considered. In doing so, a better understanding of the experience of, or encounter with, storytelling will develop.

Further Reading

Georges, Robert, "Toward an Understanding of Storytelling Events," *Journal of American Folklore* 82 (1969)

Kuttner, Leora, "Favorite Stories: A Hypnotic Pain-Reduction Technique for Children in Acute Pain," *American Journal of Clinical Hypnosis* 30 (April 1988)

Lankton, Stephen R., and Carol H. Lankton, *The Answer Within: A Clinical Framework of Ericksonian Hypnotherapy*, New York: Brunner/Mazel, 1983

Rhue, Judith W., and Steven Jay Lynn, "Storytelling, Hypnosis and the Treatment of Sexually Abused Children," *The International Journal of Clinical and Experimental Hypnosis* 39:4 (1991)

Romney, A. Kimball, Susan C. Weller, and William H. Batchelder, "Culture as Consensus: A Theory of Culture and Informant Accuracy," *American Anthropologist* 88 (1986)

Schechner, Richard, *Between Theater and Anthropology*, Philadelphia: University of Pennsylvania Press, 1985

Stallings, Fran, "The Web of Silence: Storytelling's Power to Hypnotize," *The National Storytelling Journal* (Spring/Summer 1988)

Young, Katharine Galloway, *Taleworlds and Storyrealms: The Phenomenology of Narrative*, Dordrecht, The Netherlands, and Boston: Nijhoff, 1987

Urban Legends

Jan Harold Brunvand

Jan Harold Brunvand defines the urban legend, discusses the study of the genre, and shows various examples of one urban legend, "The Hook." He notes the use of urban legends as a reliever of social fears, discusses early prototypes of some contemporary legends, and notes an origin based on fact for one urban legend.

Urban Legend Defined

An urban legend is an apocryphal contemporary story told as true but incorporating traditional motifs and usually attributed to a friend of a friend (FOAF). Urban legends are somewhat bizarre unverifiable stories, plausible nonetheless because they are grounded in certain verifiable facts, such as the existence of shopping malls, the dangers of crime, and the hazards of everyday life. The characters in urban legends are generic types—a housewife, a student, or a businessman, for example. The plots are neatly organized, often with ironic or well-deserved outcomes for the persons said to be involved. There is no significant character development, background, or aftermath in most urban legends; they are just economically phrased accounts of something that supposedly happened that build to a climax and then abruptly conclude. In a nutshell, urban legends are contemporary "true stories" that are really too good to be true.

Formerly, such stories were termed "urban belief tales," and presently they are also called "contemporary legends," "modern legends," and "modern urban legends." While neither the subject matter nor the circulation of urban legends is necessarily "urban," the stories do usually reflect themes of modern life in cities or suburbs. Urban legends are about family life, pets, travel, companies, professions, crime, technology, current events, sex, academe, government, celebrities, and many other topics. Some of these so-called "modern urban legends" are clearly *not* modern, *not* urban, and *not* always told as true, but at least *some* variants of the stories thus classified must fit these criteria, although other versions of modern urban legends may have ancient and/or rural prototypes and may sometimes be told merely for entertainment, usually in the form of jokes. Still, the term "urban legend" is used by many folklorists, and it has become the generic usage among members of the public and journalists, although media writers sometimes employ the less accurate term "urban myth."

Folklorists Study the Urban Legend

Although some folklorists in England and the United States collected and studied individual urban legends earlier, the American folklorist Richard M. Dorson first focused attention on the whole genre in the last chapter ("Modern Folklore") of his 1959 textbook *American Folklore*. Since then, folklorists have collected, identified, and studied hundreds of urban legends, and the subject has interested numerous scholars and storytellers as well as the general public.

The widespread popularity of American urban legends and some interpretations are suggested in my series of books, The *Vanishing Hitchhiker* (1981), *The Choking Doberman* (1984), *The Mexican Pet* (1986), *Curses! Broiled Again!* (1989), *The Baby Train* (1993), and *Too Good to Be True* (forthcoming), all published by W.W. Norton & Co. Similar collections of urban legends have been published in England, Scandinavia, Germany, The Netherlands, South Africa, Australia, and elsewhere. The genre is truly international, and the International Society for Contemporary Legend Research (ISCLR) was formed in 1988 to promote collection and study of urban legends worldwide. ISCLR grew out of a series of annual seminars that began at the University of Sheffield, England, in 1982; the society publishes a newsletter, *FOAFtale News,* and an annual journal, *Contemporary Legend.*

Some Types of the Urban Legend

The 10 major headings of the "Type-Index of Urban Legends" included in my 1993 book—along with a sample legend title from each—demonstrate the range of stories to be found among urban legends: automobiles ("The Slasher Under the Car"), animals ("The Microwaved Pet"), horrors ("The Babysitter and the Man Upstairs"), accidents ("The Exploding Toilet"), sex and scandal ("The Girl on the Gearshift Lever"), crime ("The Kidney Heist"), business and professions ("The Procter and Gamble Trademark"), government ("The Wordy Memo"), celebrities ("The Elevator Incident"), and academe ("The One-Word Exam Question"). These and hundreds of other stories circulate by word of mouth among adolescents at slumber parties and bull sessions, among office and factory workers during breaks, and among just about everybody at car pools, parties, dinners, and other social gatherings.

The Telling of Urban Legends

The telling of urban legends in folk tradition (similar to telling nearly any legend) is often more a situation of groups debating the possible truth of an odd story than of a single storyteller "performing" a complete plotted narrative. Someone may mention a rumor he or she has heard about gang members driving without headlights at night to provoke other drivers to flash their own lights. Listeners to this report may then contribute what they have heard about the gangsters pursuing the "flashers" to kill them, as part of a gang initiation. Someone else in the group may have heard where the incident is supposed to have occurred and how many people were killed. Yet another person may have seen an anonymous photocopied flier warning people about the supposed crime wave, which, however, is entirely fictional. Thus, by word of mouth, a simple rumor that reflects a contemporary crime concern may develop narrative elements and grow into a legend with at least

a modicum of plot. (In some versions of "Lights Out!" even the name of the police officer who supposedly first investigated the incident is cited, but no such person can be found by legend researchers, or if the named person is real, he or she took no part in spreading the story.)

"The Hook"

In terms of style, structure, and detail, "The Hook" defines the classic modern horror legend in the way that *Psycho,* for many people, defines the horror film. Both of these thrillers have compelling atmosphere, gripping suspense, realism, and a shocking ending. If Alfred Hitchcock had made up urban legends, he might have composed something like "The Hook." But we have no idea who invented this story; we only know that it has been told for more than 40 years, yet it remains many people's favorite urban legend. Each version has certain features in common, but still they're all slightly different.

Here's how a ninth-grade girl wrote her version of it recently:

> There was a young couple who were parking, and as they were making out a news flash came over the radio saying that a man with a hook had escaped from the prison. "Lock your windows and doors!" they said.
>
> They thought nothing of it for a second, but then the girl got scared. The boy said, "Don't worry about it," but the girl wanted to go home.
>
> So they locked the doors and started to roll up the window, but before she finished rolling it up, a hook stopped it!

That's probably not quite the way most people have heard the story because usually the hookman has escaped from an asylum, and the severed hook is found on the door handle when the boyfriend, after driving home, walks around the car to open it for the girl. Another variation, from a young boy, claimed that the girl got so scared by the warning that she had to go to the bathroom. She went into the woods, and when she returned, "She found her boyfriend dead, with blood all over the car, and a hook on the door handle."

Whatever its specific details, "The Hook" usually seems believable when it is told, despite discrepancies in the plot: Would a dangerous maniac be given a hook? Why would he try to open the door with his hook? Could a car accelerate fast enough to tear off the hook? Wouldn't the couple hear it rattling as they drove home? Perhaps the toughest questions are: How could the radio announcement be timed so perfectly to occur just when the hookman was lurking outside the car? Why would the boy walk politely around to open the car door after being frustrated in his lovemaking?

"The Hook" has moved from oral tradition into popular culture and literature. For example, Bill Murray told it in his film *Meatballs*, the 1992 film *Candyman* featured the hookman as the title character, Gary Larson referred to it in a "Far Side" cartoon, and several fiction writers have alluded to it.

In a 1986 anthology called *Sudden Fiction*, a story titled "Blind Girls," by Jayne Anne Phillips, presents this lurid version:

> It got darker and the stories got scarier. Finally she told their favorite, the one about the girl and her boyfriend parked on a country road on a night like this, with the wind blowing and then rain, the whole sky sobbing potato juice.
>
> Please let's leave, pleads girlie. It sounds like something scratching at the car.
>
> For God's sake, grumbles boyfriend, and takes off squealing. At home they find the hook of a crazed amputee caught in the door.
>
> Jesse described his yellow face, putrid, and his blotchy stump. She described him panting in the grass, crying and looking for something.

The Hook in Parody
A funny plot reversal appeared in a three-paragraph story titled "Hooked," by Ron Coulthard, that appeared in the 1985 Appalachian State University annual *Cold Mountain Review*. The story describes a man with a hook in place of his right arm walking home from work:

> One dark night as he was walking on a dirt road sometimes used as a Lover's Lane, something very strange happened. As he hurried past a black clump of trees, he felt something catch on his hook and give it a hard tug.
>
> He took off running as fast as he could, but he couldn't escape the feeling that something was pulling on his hook. He still felt it as he jumped into bed and covered his head.
>
> His first thought when he awoke the next morning was that it was just a bad dream.

Then he looked down at his hook hanging off the side of his bed.

Attached to it was a small sports car containing two horrified teenagers.

Urban Legends Penetrate Popular Culture
As this discussion of "The Hook" illustrates, urban legends have penetrated popular culture. Such legends appear regularly in the press, especially in tabloids, and they are further disseminated via photocopies, faxes, and the Internet. The stories are repeated on radio and television talk shows, and they have inspired sitcoms, films, and even serious literature. The New York City legend "Alligators in the Sewers" is depicted on a T-shirt sold by the city Department of Environmental Protection. A cartoon allusion to the legend on the shirt is captioned "The Legend Lives." The same story has been the subject of comic books, children's literature, and a Hollywood film (*Alligator*, 1980), and it was a major theme in Thomas Pynchon's 1963 novel *V.* A large comic-book style anthology, *The Big Book of Urban Legends*, was published in 1994.

New Urban Legends Appear
New urban rumors and legends regularly appear. For example, in the summer of 1995 a story suddenly began to circulate about a woman found sitting terrified in her scorching-hot car in a supermarket parking lot, slumped over the steering wheel with one hand held to the back of her head. When a bystander offered to help her, the woman said, "I've been shot in the head! My brains are coming out! Call the police and an ambulance!" The rescuers discovered that a cannister of Pillsbury Poppin' Fresh biscuit dough had exploded in her grocery bag placed on the back seat. When the lid of the container and the top biscuit struck her head, the woman, startled by the loud popping sound, put her hand to her head, felt the gooey dough, and immediately drew the wrong conclusion. Folklorists dubbed this story "The Brain Drain" or "The Biscuit Bullet" and have identified some prototypical elements of it in older traditional folktales.

The Mexican Pet as a Reflection of Social Themes
"The Mexican Pet" legend illustrates how variations of a widespread urban legend reflect different social or cultural themes. The first versions noted by folklorists described an American family

vacationing in Mexico who adopted a stray Chihuahua dog and smuggled it home, only to learn from their veterinarian that the creature was a sewer rat not a dog. This version depicts kind-hearted, if lawbreaking, tourists traveling in a country with lower standards of public cleanliness. Later versions of the story claimed that the rat/dog was found at a major seaport (Baltimore, New York, Los Angeles, etc.) and had come off a ship from a developing country; thus, unclean conditions seemed to be invading the United States.

In Europe the counterpart story was told about tourists from "clean" northern countries (Sweden, The Netherlands, England, etc.) who adopted the pet while traveling in a "dirty" southern or eastern country (Spain, Egypt, Thailand, etc.). In the latest American versions the "dog" is found floating on a piece of driftwood off the coast of Florida or northern California, but it turns out to be a rat from either Haiti (Florida) or China (California); thus, the stray animal has become a symbol of refugees attempting to enter the United States illegally.

Although the "meanings" of urban legends are best interpreted with reference to individual stories and their specific histories, a number of general themes appear repeatedly in legends. One such theme is "jumping to conclusions," as in "The Brain Drain" mentioned above, and in such popular urban legends as "The Poisoned Pussycat at the Party." In this classic story, the family cat nibbled at a poached salmon on the buffet table at a party. When the cat later was found dead, the partygoers assumed it was the result of food poisoning and rushed to the hospital to have their stomachs pumped. Later it was learned that the cat had been killed by a passing car and that a neighbor had placed its body on the porch, intending to report the pet's demise after the party. Another popular theme is "just deserts," or the workings of poetic justice. For example, when hunters cruelly attach a stick of dynamite to a jackrabbit they have captured and light the fuse, the animal runs beneath their camper and blows it to pieces.

Centuries-Old European Prototypes of Some Urban Legends

Rumors and legends have probably always been a feature of urban life, and sometimes virtually the same "modern" tale can be documented from very early writings. For instance, "The Robber Who Was Hurt" story, in which a would-be burglar is identified by an injury to his hand suffered during the assault, turns out to be an updating of a much older traditional supernatural legend. In the prototype story, a witch in animal form attacked a person who defended himself by stabbing the raging beast's paw with a knife. Later the neighbor was seen with a bandaged hand, implying that this was the witch back in human form. The "Choking Doberman" legend, although including such modern aspects as a veterinarian, a telephone, and a contemporary crime situation, is actually a recent variation of an ancient fable that was first transmuted into a European legend and later adopted contemporary details as the story spread to the New World. (The doberman legend also seems to echo "The Robber Who Was Hurt" in that it too is a tale in which a hand is mutilated during a robbery attempt, in this instance by a watchdog.)

A True Origin for One Urban Legend

Most urban legends either originate from unknown sources or are derived from older traditional legends, but occasionally one can be traced to an actual event. A good example is "The Heel in the Grate" story that stemmed from an incident in a church in Dayton, Ohio, in 1949. The heel of a woman's shoe became stuck in a floor grating as she marched forward in the church choir during the processional. Another singer tried to pick up the shoe, but it remained firmly stuck, and the grate itself came loose in his hand. A third choir member fell into the opening. The incident was reported in the local press, and two individuals involved in it were interviewed by folklorists. The story spread further via printed sources, including *Reader's Digest,* and eventually it was repeated by readers and became an anonymous urban legend describing a supposed mishap taking place at an unknown location during a wedding procession.

Further Reading

AFU & Urban Legends Archive (http://www.urbanlegends.com)

Bennett, Gillian, and Paul Smith, *Contemporary Legend: A Folklore Bibliography,* New York: Garland, 1993

Brunvand, Jan Harold, "Dorson and the Urban Legend," *The Folklore Historian* 7 (1990)

Fine, Gary Alan, *Manufacturing Tales: Sex and Money in Contemporary Legends,* Knoxville: University of Tennessee Press, 1992

Fleming, Robert Loren, *The Big Book of Urban Legends: Adapted from the Works of Jan Harold Brunvand,* New York: Paradox, 1994

Turner, Patricia, *I Heard It Through the Grapevine: Rumor in African-American Culture,* Berkeley: University of California Press, 1993; London: University of California Press, 1994

Urban Legends Reference Pages (http://www.snopes.com)

Cross-Culture, Cross-Class, Crossed Wires: A Case Analysis of an Etic/Emic Storytelling Event

Wendy Welch

In this first-person account, Wendy Welch describes her use of storytelling in an urban Virginia housing project.

A Storyteller in Residence in a Housing Project

When I heard the job description, I laughed. "You don't want a storyteller; you want a martyr!" The woman on the phone, now defensive, continued to describe the setup.

A literacy center in a housing project located in urban Virginia sought a professional storyteller for a one-year residency. The successful candidate would design and implement programs to increase academic skills and self-esteem among participants, who would range from preschool age through senior citizens. Not necessarily in the same programs, of course, the disembodied voice added. Of course, I agreed, rolling my eyes.

For what could be described as a slight salary, the job required, among other things, intense dedication (read unpaid overtime). And, incidentally, the storyteller was also in charge of the computer lab.

The drop-in center was on-site in a housing complex of about 300 people. The facility sported a one-room library, the previously mentioned computer lab, and a play area with educational toys. The administrating government agency poured on the statistics: 75 percent of the families were one-parent; 95 percent of the mothers drew Aid to Families with Dependent Children. Before I had even signed the contract, barricades of numbers cut me off from objective observation. I understood from the outset: poor mothers are bad mothers.

The first lesson I learned in de-stereotyping came from the flashbulbs on cameras held by proud parents watching their children perform in the center's "production." Productions, held monthly, were complex-wide extravaganzas at which children performed folktales. We rehearsed three consecutive afternoons using all the children who wanted to participate. The performances on the third evening were followed by a potluck featuring really good food, so these events were well attended.

At each audition we talked over proposed story plots; the children's suggestions ran heavily to Disney and the horror movie genre. In the beginning I edited heavily and we did simple pieces, working up to larger epics (such as "Sleeping Beauty") as the children and I got to know one another better.

Discovering what the children did and did not know from the Western canon proved enlightening and disheartening. I was naively surprised to learn that, in an urban community with 78 percent illiteracy, oral tradition meant something completely other than what I had in mind. Most

577

of the children knew only those versions of stories Disney had produced. They knew nothing about princes and heroines with three impossible tasks and a chance to marry well, and they were initially bored by these until the dragons appeared. My purist attitudes melted before the need to engage these kids in something besides Freddy Krueger's latest misdeeds. It had mattered greatly in folktale classes back at the university whether AT 333 ("Little Red Riding Hood") included a red cape in its ur-form; it did not matter here.

The unfamiliarity with Western culture classics stemmed from several circumstances; certainly there were disinterested parents, but there were also those with such limited literacy that they felt uncomfortable reading in front of their children. There was also the factor of purchase prices for books; one mother was pleased to find the Disney Golden Book of "Cinderella," at a remarkably reduced rate, because she wanted her child to "know the stories I knew when I was growing up." My friend had bought the Golden Book of "Cinderella" because she did not trust herself to do the story correctly from memory. In a community where self-esteem was at a low ebb, the self-confidence to produce an entire narrative for one's own child was practically nonexistent.

The oral tradition in this community was significantly other than what I had expected to find in my romantic view of illiteracy as a breeding ground for narrative-collecting, and it caused some serious shuffling of my perspective toward folklore's love affair with nonliterate populations. Where were those creative throngs of underpaid folk-art inheritors, placidly altering ballad chords on their guitars and remembering whole narratives at a single reciting?

Thus my etic expectations dissolved daily into the reality of the complex's atmosphere, concerns, and activities, but the best was yet to come. The day a production finally connected with the identity of the community rather than simply offering entertainment and activity was the day sparks flew.

The Community Assumes Ownership

About nine months into the residency, a church up the street approached the center about "doing something" for the complex. What did they have in mind, we asked cautiously, not wishing to appear cynical yet acutely aware of the difference between "up the street" and "in the projects." They had in mind a storytelling event involving puppets and children's theater and a special meal for the entire complex. The parents of our storytelling kids were excited about the visitors; they thought we should do a production as part of the event. I pointed out that there really was not time to rehearse the children effectively in a new production.

"No," said Terry, who had made the suggestion, "I mean us, the parents. We'll put on a production for them."

Adult storytelling was not new at the center, but it was unusual. We had events parents and children were encouraged to attend ("Come to Bedtime Stories every Tuesday evening at the center, followed by cookies and milk; all parent-child participants receive a free book to take home and read together!") and events for the older crowd ("Teatime Stories this Wednesday; come and share a favorite memory!"), but our only venture into an adult production had been about two months before.

That production had developed through a set of strange circumstances. The driver of a car seen circling the complex reportedly had repeatedly attempted to entice a six-year-old boy with candy. The boy, well trained, fled to his mother. Rumors about the car circulated and escalated in true oral-tradition fashion throughout the afternoon and evening; the actual car returned the following day, the driver attempting the same scenario on a mentally handicapped girl. Fortunately, other children playing nearby stopped the child, and the police were called. They never arrived; housing projects are not civil servants' favorite places to go.

With that situation fresh in their minds, some parents sitting around the center began talking a few days later, and without really knowing how it happened, an all-adult production of "Little Red Riding Hood" was on the next playbill. The children were suitably impressed, especially as the parents rewrote the woodcutter into a center employee and included dire warnings from Red's mother of the consequences of talking to strange wolves in the city, particularly wolves with candy.

Apparently this earlier production had given confidence to the parental core group, for it was their idea to welcome the visitors with a story. "What would you tell?" I asked, and Andrea's eyes lit up. A vivacious woman with a physically handicapped daughter who required home care, Andrea was renowned for her wicked sense of humor. "The Three Little Pigs," she said with a grin, "the way you do it, Wendy."

Uh-oh, I thought. As part of a stay-in-school campaign, I had done that story at a school fair. The first little pig dropped out of high school; the second little pig dropped out, but went back to get her GED, etc., etc. Andrea had been volunteering at her son's school when I performed it, but I had avoided this story at the center, thinking it might cut too close to the quick.

The other moms were not overly enthusiastic, but as Andrea outlined the idea, they began to respond. When Andrea described the first little pig, Susan said, "That's me." I started a list—Susan, first little pig. "No," Sue said, "I mean, that's me. I dropped out of school because I was pregnant and I never went back."

Embarrassed, I crossed out her name, but she began to laugh. "Yeah," she said, "put me down for that. I wanna play the first little pig." The other moms caught the spirit of the moment. The second little pig graduated from high school, married a substance abuser, and was now unable to enter the job market because of her children. The third little pig was intelligent and quick, and the center staff had helped her with the paperwork for community college. Then her teenage daughter was diagnosed with a severe mental condition, and the situation escalated rapidly until she felt she could not handle both pressures simultaneously. She swore she would go back to school someday.

The storytelling extravaganza was a sight to behold; a giant puppet stage went up in the courtyard; pizza and people were everywhere. When the tumult was finally brought under control, the guests presented their message. It was kindly meant, if a bit stiff, and the audience was appreciative. Then the Pig Sisters appeared.

The sight of well-known complex members wearing Styrofoam-cup snouts fastened with rubber bands was enough to start the audience laughing. The guests from up the street smiled. The first little pig explained who she was and that she was building her house of straw "because I couldn't buy anything better because it's two weeks until my check comes again." The audience gave an appreciative snort; the church group looked aghast.

The second little pig really hammed it up. "If I had just gone to college, even if I'd just paid attention in English class 'stead of spending all my time thinking about that boy across the aisle, I could

get me a job that paid something 'stead of this stupid part-time job at Burger King!" The community howled; the guests shuffled their feet and averted their gazes.

The third little pig was apologetic. She was not better than anybody else, she said softly through her snout; she knew it did not make her a better person to have gone to school. She just knew if she was gonna give her little piglets anything in life, she was gonna have to work at it; so she had finished night school even though it was terribly hard, and now she was so pleased she had, because she was renting her own two-bedroom house on a quiet street, and it even had a garden in back where she grew her own tomatoes. The residents were quiet but smiling; the people from up the street looked confused. By the time the Big Bad Wolf had resolved to give up smoking and go back to school, half the audience members were laughing so hard they were crying, while the other half looked as if they wanted to cry.

Why did the story work this way on its dichotomous audience? Perhaps it was because the performers were members of the community who knew what life was like for the half of the audience the other half had come to preach to. The puppet show was an etic attempt to impose not necessarily values but a false heartiness, a contrived understanding, and an empty empathy on people who felt they did not need the sympathy the guests were pretending not to offer.

It is not in any way my intention to malign or belittle the guests who came that day; they came, after all, and some of them continue to come as volunteers with the tutorial program. The focus of this article is, rather, the simple misperceptions that develop between groups when perspectives are not informed by actual experience. This case study does not attempt to draw forceful conclusions, only to point out that interest in and sympathy for a community does not make one a member of the same, and it behooves us, particularly as storytellers or social scientists, to remember this. Outsider status does not prohibit a person from telling stories to or from another group; it does mean the person has to be careful, perhaps more careful than he or she thinks.

In essence—let the gentle reader draw from it what he or she will—this is merely the description of one time when the story went full circle.

The Nature of Women's Storytelling*

Linda Dégh

Linda Dégh discusses the role woman play as tellers of tales and examines the repertoires of women tellers in an article that provides citations to much of the current literature on women's storytelling.

It has been repeatedly stated through history by authors of many persuasions that storytelling is a preeminently feminine occupation. Without specifying the kinds of stories, authors claimed that women by nature and by vocation as mothers, nurses, homemakers, and domestic workers narrate to children, adolescent girls, and their own female associates. Although women may learn stories from their fathers and brothers, and may also invite men to their winter evening work circles for story entertainment, it historically has been their family role to narrate. Women use their diverse kinds of narratives for diverse purposes when addressing their household audiences. In addition to pure entertainment, stimulating laughter, excitement, emotion, or fright, women's stories discipline and socialize children and teach girls proper behavior in preparation for future life-roles as well as comfort adult women in their daily domestic drudgery.

On the other hand, sources indicate an equal number of male storytellers who perform for mixed audiences or exclusively for work and leisure gatherings of men (Dégh, 1983). Several authors observed that women are more creative in lyric genres, whereas men excel in elaborate epics, the märchen in particular (Böckel, 1913; Katona, 1980). In fact, as reported by field researchers in traditional communities within the classic märchen distribution area of Europe, Asia, and immediate contact territories and faraway colonies, storytelling can be considered a par excellence male occupation. It is migrant workers who exchange stories at distant working places and temporary residences and who further embellish and disseminate their repertoires while on the road and back to their hometowns. Marginal men—exiles, beggars, peddlers, discharged soldiers, and preachers—were welcome guests treated generously by village families in exchange for stories, as were the craftsmen who did necessary repairs while entertaining the womenfolk at the fireside. The arrival of itinerants thus highlighted the dull winter life of villagers (Dégh, 1969 and 1989). These *wissende Leuten, Durchreisenden*, were the men from whom N.O. Winokurowa learned the majority of her tales (Azadovskii, 1926). Indeed, most of the other noted female narrators who became community entertainers beyond the confines of the family also gave credit to the men who brought their stories home to the family circle. More fathers and grandfathers than mothers and grandmothers are referred to as sources of prominent female personalities (Delargy, 1945) such as the East Prus-

---

*This essay is the original English version of the entry "Frauenmärchen" in the *Enzyklopädie des Märchens* (Dégh, 1985).

sian Trude Lenz (Tolksdorf, 1980), the Bukovina Székely Zsuzsanna Palkó (Dégh, 1969), Mária Fábián (Sebestyén, 1979–86), and the Transylvanian Klára Györi (G. Nagy, 1978), to name some of the most recent.

Nevertheless, these facts would not suggest male prominence over women in narrating but rather a certain functional division in sex roles, given by family and occupational distinctiveness. Thus, in discussing the concept of female folktales, two main issues may be raised:

1. What is the distinctive role of women as tellers of tales?

2. Do women develop a specifically feminine repertoire to serve their female audiences?

The woman appears as the natural storyteller through her traditional position in the family dating from classical antiquity; arching over subsequent historic epochs, social systems, and religious ideologies; and cutting across folk and elite groups of complex civilizations. The image of the woman-narrator seems both ambiguous and mutable in different situations. Prior to the Grimms, commentaries refer to *Ammenmärchen, contes de ma mère l'oye, contes de vieilles et de nourrices,* and *Mährleins mütterchen,* and signify the low public opinion and discreet nature of both tellers and stories (Bolte and Polívka, 1913–32; Schenda, 1983). The women's tales are plain, naive, unremarkable, and unpretentious, tied to everyday private occasions in which hired domestic servants and wet nurses entertain, put to sleep, discipline by rewarding or, in turn, scare young children.

Yet the elite authors were deeply impressed by their childhood memories and enthusiastically reported their first exposure to nursery tales. Diaries, private letters, and literary works expressed admiration for narrating nurses, upgrading their image and turning them into literary models. The reported repertoire of stories was a miscellany of genres: fable, formula tale, Schwank, exemplum, märchen, horror story, supernatural and religious legend, not infrequently also from written sources, as well as occasionally invented or personally experienced. Nevertheless, the märchen— magic or novelesque—became the recognized and fashionable pastime story of women. During the eighteenth and nineteenth centuries, not only the telling of nursery stories was reported but also the

exchange of *Weiber Märchen* among spinning, quilting, and knitting women. On the other hand, urban elite ladies killed their boredom with "winter tales," enjoying each other's company and narrating skill. Among the known raconteurs were the mothers of Aleksandr Pushkin and Maksim Gorky and the grandmothers of Leo Tolstoy and Charles Dickens. Johann von Goethe's mother was particularly noted as a narrator. Her way of retelling newly learned pieces is featured in her letter from 1807. "Ich habe mir die Geschichte (von Fortunatus) zusammengezogen, alles überflüssige weggeschnitten und ein ganz artiges Märchen deraus geformt" (Bolte and Polívka, 1913–32).

The märchen, that is, the *contes des fées,* or *contes merveilleux,* as a feminine literary genre was already established since the time of Charles Perrault. A line of women authors popularized the märchen in France in the course of the eighteenth century, to the tastes of the feudal aristocracy as well as the educated urban classes. This specific märchen became the tool of child and adolescent women's education, intended to supply "Kinder mit Normen und Geselschaftsmodellen class sie sich vorstellen konnten, durch Verdrängung und Konformismus ihr eigenes Glück zu finden zu zivilisieren" (Zipes, 1983). No wonder that by the time of the debut of the Grimm brothers, sophisticated tale enthusiasts knew that tales belong to women and the household. Thus, the Grimms named their scientifically intended collection *Kinder- und Hausmärchen* (KMH) and presented it to the broader urban elite as an *Erziehungsbuch* to be used selectively for their children. This made perfect sense because, for the most part, both collectors and narrators were women who learned their stories from other women in their childhood homes. The most cherished Märchenfrau of the Grimms, the widow K.D. Viehmann, was also presented to fit the image of the old nurse storyteller. The collection, as a whole, identified as "Gattung Grimm," did not, however, deviate from the miscellany of earlier household narrators. It included magic tales, novellas, Christian legends, chain and catch tales, lies, and *Schwanke.* It is quite remarkable how little there was in this rich treasury for mothers and nurses actually to select for the bedtime entertainment of youngsters following the advice of the Grimms. While Johannes Bolte and Jirí Polívka list a total of 18 titles of children's stories (Bolte and Polívka, 1913–32), later authors also identified the *Warn- und Schreckmärchen* category (Rumpf, 1955; Zipes, 1982) intended for child control. Along with the rest, meant to be good reading for women of all ages and retelling material, the KHM became the ultimate sourcebook for the märchen disseminated in the world.

The seemingly anachronistic märchen was given new lease on life by the editorial hand of the Grimms, successfully incorporating and solidifying the whimsically floating oral folk tradition of previous centuries in a structurally and stylistically balanced and standardized literary form. While consistent and multiple media dissemination of this standardized stock of narratives helped reinvigorate fading peasant tradition in the twentieth century into a socially significant educational institution. Educators and child psychologists recognized overt and covert meanings of tales and their beneficial effects on personality development (Bühler and Bilz, 1961; von Franz, 1970; Piaget, 1929; Bettelheim, 1976) and encouraged storytelling in public schools and at home. Drawing on the *Viehmäbbub* model, and exploiting a relatively limited selection of booktales from Perrault, Grimm, Andrew Lang, Hans Christian Andersen, and *The Thousand and One Nights* (Dégh, 1983), a new cast of professional and lay female storytellers emerged, mostly in Germany, France, and the United States. Young audiences were the primary recipients: story hours were instituted for different age groups of children and adolescents in day care centers, kindergarten playgrounds, summer camps, schools, and libraries, and furthermore for gifted, handicapped, delinquent, and other special groups. The storytellers—educators, counselors, librarians—availing themselves of materials from special sourcebooks (Eastman, 1926; Ireland, 1973; Clarkson and Cross, 1980; Janning, 1983; Betz, 1983) obtained their training in narrating courses and workshops in teachers' colleges and university library schools (Baker and Greene, 1977). Their goal was to provide entertainment, broaden experiences, instigate desired values and ideals, and keep alive cultural heritage.

Beyond storytelling for children, there is a growing, nostalgic interest in the reintroduction of the märchen to adult urban audiences as a more human substitute for mass media entertainment. Female raconteurs are known to perform at clubs, resorts, art programs, military camps, retirement homes, etc. Storyteller Felicitas Betz describes her way of restoring modern-day *Märchenerzählgemeinschaft* by telling (or reading) *Buchmärchen* creatively when addressing different groups of listeners (Betz, 1983; Görög-Karady and de la Salle, 1979). The Europäische Märchengesellschaft has held annual international encounters for storytellers and researchers—laymen, artists, and scholars—since 1956 to maintain the märchen tradition.[1] Storytelling guilds began to multiply at the same time in the United States, with a predominantly female membership between the ages of 20 and 70. In celebrating the bicentennial anniversary of the nation, the Smithsonian Institution launched a festival movement and also established annual weeklong storytelling festivals with competing members. The art of storytelling was also taught through radio programs.[2]

Innumerable local groups study and practice narration at weekend get-togethers[3] and communicate with newsletters and magazines.[4] Their repertoire includes international classical forms as well as local oral stories, learned or spontaneously invented, by narrators of both folk and elite extraction. Development of genre specialization may be observed between the sexes: the märchen and the ghost stories became almost exclusively feminine, whereas men became the tellers of jokes, lies, and humorous and adventurous occupational and personal narratives (Dégh, 1983). If mothers and nurses nurture children of both sexes with märchen, there is a considerable division in narrative preference past the märchen age. Traditional Muslim society prescribes that adolescent boys stop listening to female tales and join their elders in devoting themselves to pious life, engaging in the narration of saints' legends and exempla (Abdelsalam, 1983). Even without such strictures, boys reject the märchen repertoire that women continue to use for feminine audiences beyond childhood in modern urban society (Stone, 1975b, 1983). This repertoire consists of narratives about the adventures of female heroes from rags to riches.

But, in reference to our second question, can we speak of tales with specifically feminine themes told by women to other women? In traditional societies, two groups of narratives have been identified as tales of women: (a) complex magic and romantic tales with women protagonists, and (b) *Schwanke* in which the education of young women is offered by humorous exempla, criticizing socially unacceptable conduct. Additionally, a much less sizable category, relevant to both old-fashioned rural and modern urban societies, has only recently been discovered by *Märchenbiology* and performance-oriented fieldworkers: autobiographical episodes of great variety circulating among women groups outside the household.

In a worldwide distribution, the Aarne-Thompson index lists 92 heroine tales compared to 207 hero tales, twice as many, whereas the Grimm collection, a secondary source for the modern urban tale repertoire, contains 44 heroine and only 70 hero tales (Stone, 1975). A further increase of heroine tales and decrease of hero tales in storybook selections during the last century indicate that the märchen has become more and more a woman-oriented genre, addressed to girl education and socialization beyond the unisex märchen age of children. If märchen heroines previously exhibited a variety of characteristics in the tales in which they had starring roles as mirror images of male protagonists (such as in AaTh 327, 328, 510/532), tricksters (874, 875, 879, 882), shrewd manipulators, and achievers of power (881, 884, 888, 890, 940), then in our time women seem to be more popular in their submissive and helpless roles. A small but extremely popular repertoire of tales evolved and persist with innocent beauties in the title role. Their fate is to be abused, tortured, banished, persecuted, corrected, and reformed in order to conform to the female image of patriarchal family systems. Subservience, patience, endurance, passivity, devotion, and industry are the virtues of women in "Aschenbrödel," "Schneewittchen," "Dornröschen," "Rapunzel," "Froschkönig," "Rotkäppchen," "Frau Holle," "Gänsemagd," "Sieben Raben," "Hansel und Gretel," and others (Lüthi, 1979; Stone, 1975, 1983; Dégh, 1983). The almost symptomatic acceptance of these role models by women has been noted by feminist authors as well as psychiatrists (Berne, 1973; de Beauvoir, 1953; Dowling, 1981; Meyer zu Capellen, 1980).

On the other hand, the repertoire of traditional rural female storytellers does not show the same attraction to the same group of tales (Fabré and Lacroix, 1974). As a randomly selected example, drawn from the märchen repertoires of Hungarian women community raconteurs, no such preference is indicated. Székely Zsuzsanna Palkó (Dégh, 1969 and 1989) told 16 heroine and 22 hero tales, Mária Fábián 23 heroine and 61 hero tales (Sebestyén, 1979–86), and Julie Szöke-Tót 16 heroine and 27 hero tales (Dobos, 1962). Two of these women gave their sources as their fathers or other male relatives and the third cited her grandfather and his old cronies. The ratio is similar within the repertoire of men: Péter Pandur narrated 19 heroine and 20 hero tales (Dégh, 1940), Lajos Ámi 26 heroine and 58 hero tales (Erdész, 1968). This conforms with the international distribution in the Aarne-Thompson index. Alessandro Falassi's description of a storytelling event at a Tuscan *veglia* further weakens the exclusivity of female hero tales as Frauenmärchen. In the company of adults and children, feminine tales (AaTh 333, 403, 440, 510A and 510B in three versions) were recited by two women, a man, and a grandson (Falassi, 1980).

In general terms, *Schwankenerzähler* are held to be men (Neumann, 1964); nevertheless, female work and leisure groups enjoy as much joking as their male counterparts. Male village jokesters have a choice of sexual jests at their disposal to entertain and tease young married women, while older women spice dull manual work by exchanging dirty jokes among themselves. Except for jokes told by extraordinary women of comic talent (G. Nagy, 1978), however, the feminine *Schwank* repertoire is what Ágnes Kovács characterizes as "girl-raising tales" (Sebestyén, 1979), passed from woman to woman in the family. As a child, Mária Fábián was often instructed by her relatives with didactic tales for young girls: "Mind you, the same thing might happen to you" (Kovács, 1980), and women at evening gatherings often request some of their favorite pieces (Dégh, 1969 and 1989). These themes are more variable locally than Aarne-Thompson numbers would suggest, satirizing bad conduct of newlywed women and girls of marriageable age. The targets of ridicule are laziness combined with ignorance of feminine duties (AaTh 822, 902, 1371), stubbornness (1365), vanity (902), bad manners (1458), gossipiness (1381 D), stupidity (1387, 1450), and bodily defect (1456, 1457). By their very nature, these stories can easily be adjusted to local events and are open to improvisation.

Narratives of a personal nature, featured in terms of life history episodes or current experience accounts, belong to the contemporary interests of folk narrativists. Earlier, though, more attention was paid to the experience stories of mobile men than homebound women; and except for solicited autobiographies, or analytic reconstruction of life histories of outstanding personalities (Pentikäinen, 1978), little is known about this most functional, spontaneous female form. Personal stories began to attract attention when post-World War II industrial growth forced rural women out of their villages in search of jobs elsewhere. It was found that peasant women released from household obligations easily adjusted their narrative competence to absorb new experiences. Some women, inspired traditional storytellers among them, developed new repertoires of personal experience accounts drawn upon the most memorable events of their past everydays from childhood to adulthood, highlighting episodes of first love and family life; they also drew upon new adventures experienced during migration and work (Dobos, 1962, 1978, 1981). The audience—work and leisure companions—likewise displaced from their hometowns, shared in the exchange of life experiences, satisfying their need to express the longing for their lost homes, their desire to integrate into a new group, and the need for cultural learning and entertainment. Similar narratives have also resulted from other types of temporary or permanent detachment (Tolksdorf, 1980), employment in other countries, and emigration in modern urban America. Closely related to the upsurge of the feminist movement in recent years, women's associations have emerged as political action groups for women's rights. These groups have developed their specific "collaborative" folk narratives, a new brand of women-stories declaring women's claims in the public arena. Susan Kalčík (1975) describes a unique genre developed in conversation at consciousness-raising rap sessions. Other female conversational storytelling appears to be less organized but nevertheless spontaneously therapeutic, such as rape stories circulated among the abused who seek solace in each other's company. Within the broad category of crime narratives, on the basis of 400 items collected from women in Brooklyn, Eleanor Wachs (1988) gave a detailed account of the nature of stories told by victims of mugging, rape, and robbery as a shared "warning system" among women.

Evidently, women's märchen cannot be defined simply by relating to one type of tale told by women to other women. It must be considered a mutable concept, subject to change in time and space. Researchers analyzing the märchen repertoire of traditional peasant women saw the feminine nature of the märchen not so much in the choice of themes but in the stylistic featuring of their stories. When Asadowskij spoke of the "be-

sonderen Eigenschaften der Weiblichen Volksdichtung," he meant "die liebevolle Schilderung des eigene weiblichen Lebens . . . in den von Frauen erzählten Märchen sich die Herrschaft des Gefühlvollen Tones geltend macht" (Asadowskij, 1926). With reference to earlier Russian collectors, Onchukov also observes that women have their own "'womanish' ancient tales. . . . [I]n relating any tale, a woman involuntarily reflects in it that which especially interests her, everything that touches her everyday mode of life. The woman storyteller, relating a folk tale, among other things, always describes in detail and with special fondness the everyday life that she knows so well, as well as the life of a woman" (Sokolov, 1950). Furthermore, "the special social and everyday conditions of the life of the woman . . . have placed their imprint on the tales which were related by women" (Sokolov, 1950).

It thus is not the preference for heroine tales that makes a märchen a woman's märchen but the elaboration, stressing the feminine point of view in any kind of märchen. This has been illustrated by Asadowskij, discussing Winokurowa's narration; by Dégh (1969 and 1989), discussing Székely Zsuzsanna Palkó; by Á. Kovács, comparing Palkó and Mária Fábián's different ways to use and manipulate their life experiences in tale construction; and by Adams (1972), comparing Winokurowa and Palkó to Tzune Watanabe's featuring tales. By comparing versions of the same tale type told by men and women, we may be able to isolate specific male and female subtypes of the same tale, as has been suggested by El-Shamy and Swahn (El-Shamy, 1979, 1984; Swahn, 1955).

Notes

1. "Märchenpflege' bedeutet, der modischen Märchenschwämme die echten Volksmärchen entgegenzusetzen, die Erzählgelegenheiten und Erzählgemeinschaften von heute zu fördern" (Flyer from 1981).
2. For example, "The Spider's Web" is a nationally broadcast noncommercial radio program (WGBH in Boston) for family audiences.
3. The widely publicized Lexington (Kentucky) Storytelling Weekend (June 22–24, 1984) is a good example of a weekend get-together for storytellers.
4. For example, *Swapping Ground* is the newsletter of the Chicago Storyteller's Guild. A

quarterly, *National Storytelling Journal*, has been published by the National Association for the Preservation and Perpetuation of Storytelling in Jonesborough, Tennessee, since 1984. Interestingly, *Die Märchen Zeitung: Informationen des Märchen, Folklore, Fantasy* was also instituted in 1984 for the "Friends of the Märchen" by Hans-Christian Kirsch in West Germany.

Further Reading

Abdelsalam, Sharafeldin E., *A Study of Contemporary Sudanese Muslim Saints' Legends in Sociocultural Contexts* (Ph.D. diss., Indiana University), 1983

Adams, Robert J., *Social Identity of a Japanese Storyteller* (Ph.D. diss., Indiana University), 1972

Azadovskii, Mark, *Eine sibirische Märchenerzählerin*, Helsinki, Finland: Suomalainen Tiedeakatemia, Academia Scientiarum Fennica, 1926

Baker, Augusta, and Ellin Greene, *Storytelling: Art and Technique*, New York: Bowker, 1977

Beauvoir, Simone de, *The Second Sex*, translated by H.M. Parshley, New York: Knopf, 1952; London: Cape, 1953

Berne, Eric, *What Do You Say After You Say Hello? The Psychology of Human Destiny*, New York: Grove, 1972; London: Deutsch, 1974

Bettelheim, Bruno, *The Uses of Enchantment: The Meaning and Importance of Fairy Tales*, New York: Knopf, 1976; London: Thames and Hudson, 1976

Betz, Felicitas, "Der Märchenerzähler nach dem Ende der Mündlichen Überlieferung," in *Märchenerzänler, Erzählgemeinschaft*, edited by Rainer Wehse, Kassel, West Germany: Röth-Verlag, 1983

Böckel, Otto, *Psychologie der Volksdichtung*, second edition, Leipzig, East Germany: Teubner, 1913

Bolte, Johannes, and Jirí Polívka, eds., *Anmerkungen zu den Kinder-und Hausmärchen der Brüder Grimm*, 5 volumes, Leipzig, East Germany: Weicher, 1913–1932

Bühler, Charlotte, and Josephine Bilz, *Das Märchen und die Phantasie des Kindes*, second edition, Munich, Germany: Barth, 1961

Clarkson, Atelia, and Gilbert B. Cross, *World Folktales*, New York: Scribner, 1980

Dégh, Linda, *Folktales and Society: Story-Telling in a Hungarian Peasant Community*, translated by Emily M. Schossberger, Bloomington: Indiana University Press, 1969; expanded edition, Bloomington: Indiana University Press, 1989

_____, *Narratives in Society: A Performance-Centered Study of Narration*, Bloomington: Indiana University Press, 1995

_____, *Pandur Péter hét bagi meséje* [Seven Tales from the Bag by Péter Pandur], Budapest, Hungary: Officina, 1940

_____, "Zur Rezeption der Grimmschen Märchen in den USA," in *Über Märchen für Kinder von heute: Essays zu ihrem Wandel und ihrer Funktion*, edited by Klaus Doderer, Weinheim, Germany: Beltz, 1983

Delargy, James, *The Gaelic Story-Teller, with Some Notes on Gaelic Folk-tales*, London: Cumberlege, 1945

Dobos, Ilona S., *Áldozatok*, Budapest, Hungary: Kozmosz Könyvek, 1981

_____, *Egy somogyi parasztcsalád meséi* [Tales of a Peasant Family of Somogy], Budapest, Hungary: Akadémiai Kiadó, 1962

_____, "True Stories," in *Studies in East European Folk Narrative*, edited by Linda Dégh, Bloomington, Indiana: American Folklore Society, 1978

Dowling, Colette, *The Cinderella Complex: Women's Hidden Fear of Independence*, New York: Summit, 1981; London: Joseph, 1982

Eastman, Mary Huse, *Index to Fairy Tales, Myths, and Legends*, second edition, Boston: Faxon, 1926

El-Shamy, Hasan M., *Brother and Sister, Type 872: A Cognitive Behavioristic Analysis of a Middle Eastern Oikotype*, Bloomington: Folklore Publications Group, Indiana University, 1979

_____, "Vom Fisch geboren," in *Enzyklopädie des Märchens: Handwörterbuch zur historischen und vergleichenden Erzählforschung, Band 4*, New York: de Gruyter, 1984

Erdész, Sándor, ed., *Ámi Lajos meséi* [Tales of Lajos Ámi], 3 volumes, Budapest, Hungary: Akadémiai Kiadó, 1968

Fabré, Daniel, and Jacques Lacroix, *La Tradition Orale du Conte Occitan: Les Pyrénées Audoises*, 2 volumes, Paris: Presses Universitaires de France, 1974

Falassi, Alessandro, *Folklore by the Fireside: Text and Context of the Tuscan Veglia,* Austin: University of Texas, 1980; London: Scolar, 1980

Franz, Marie-Luise von, *An Introduction to the Psychology of Fairy Tales,* New York: Spring Publications, 1970

Görög-Karady, Veronika, and Bruno de la Salle, "Qui conte en France? L'apparation de quelques nouveaux types de conteurs," lecture at the Seventh Congress of the International Society for Folk Narrative Research, Edinburgh, 1979

Ireland, Norma Olin, *Index to Fairy Tales, 1949–1972,* Westwood, Massachusetts: Faxon, 1973

Janning, Jürgen, "Märchenerzählen: Lässt er sich lernen—Kann man es lehren?," in *Märchenerzänler, Erzählgemeinschaft,* edited by Rainer Wehse, Kassel, West Germany: Röth-Verlag, 1983

Janz, Trude, *Eine ostpreussische Volkserzählerin: Geschichten, Geschichte, Lebensgeschichte,* Marburg, West Germany: Elwert, 1980

Kalčík, Susan, "'. . . like Ann's gynecologist or the time I was almost raped': Personal Narratives in Women's Rap Groups," *Journal of American Folklore* 88 (1975)

Katona, Imre, "Mannesfolklore— Weibesfolklore: Analyses der verschiedenen Gattungen," in *Congressus Quintus Internationalis Fenno-Ugristarum,* Turku, Finland: Suomen Kielen Seura, 1980

Kovács, Agnes, "A Bukovinian Szekler Storyteller Today," in *Folklore on Two Continents: Essays in Honor of Linda Dégh,* edited by Nikolai Burlakoff and Carl Lindahl, Bloomington, Indiana: Trickster, 1980

Lüthi, Max, *Märchen,* seventh revised edition, Stuttgart, West Germany: Metzler, 1979

Meyer zu Capellen, Renate, "Das Schöne Madchen: Psychoanalytische Betrachtungen zur 'Formwendung der Seele' de Mädchens," in *Und wenn sie nicht gestorben sind: Perspektiven auf das Märchen,* edited by Helmut Brackert, Frankfurt am Main, West Germany: Suhrkamp, 1980

Nagy, Géza, "Personality and Community as Mirrored in the Formation of Klára Györi's Repertoire," in *Studies in East European Folk Narrative,* edited by Linda Dégh, Bloomington, Indiana: American Folklore Society, 1978

Pentikäinen, Juha, *Oral Repertoire and World View: An Anthropological Study of Marina Takalo's Life History,* Helsinki, Finland: Suomalainen Tiedeakatemia, 1978

Piaget, Jean, *The Child's Conception of the World,* New York: Harcourt, Brace, 1929; London: K. Paul, Trench, Trubner, 1929

Rumpf, Marianne, *Ursprung und Entstehung von Warn- und Schreckmärchen,* Helsinki, Finland: Suomalainen Tiedeakatemia, 1955

Schenda, Rudolf, "Märchen Erzählen, Märchen verbreiten: Wandel in den Mitteilungsformen einer populären Gattung," in *Über Märchen für Kinder von heute: Essays zu ihrem Wandel und ihrer Funktion,* edited by Klaus Doderer, Weinheim, Germany: Beltz, 1983

Sebestyén, Ádám, *Bukovinai Székely népmesék* [Székely Folktales from the Bukovina], 4 volumes, Szekszárd, Hungary: Tolna megyei Tanács V.B. Könyvtára, 1979–1986

Sokolov, Iurii, *Russian Folklore,* translated by Catherine Ruth Smith, New York: Macmillan, 1950

Stone, Kay, "Missbrauchte Verzauberung: Aschenputtel als Wseiblichkeitsideal in Nordamerika," in *Über Märchen für Kinder von heute: Essays zu ihrem Wandel und ihrer Funktion,* edited by Klaus Doderer, Weinheim, Germany: Beltz, 1983

_____, *Romantic Heroines in Anglo-American Folk and Popular Literature* (Ph.D. diss., Indiana University), 1975

Swahn, Jan Öjvind, *The Tale of Cupid and Psyche,* Lund, Sweden: C.W.K. Gleerup, 1955

Wachs, Eleanor, *Crime-Victim Stories: New York City's Urban Folklore,* Bloomington: Indiana University Press, 1988

Zipes, Jack, "Klassische Märchen im Zivilisationsprozess: Die Schattenseite von 'La Belle et la Béte'," in *Über Märchen für Kinder von heute: Essays zu ihrem Wandel und ihrer Funktion,* edited by Klaus Doderer, Weinheim, Germany: Beltz, 1983

_____, *Rotkäppchens Lust und Leid: Biographie eines Europäischen Märchens,* Cologne, West Germany: Diederich, 1982

Notes on Contributors and Editors

Notes on Contributors and Editors

Abu Shardow Abarry is an associate professor and graduate director in the Department of African Studies at Temple University, Philadelphia. Born in Accra, Ghana, he studied for the B.A. and M.A. degrees at the University of Ghana (Legon), specializing in English and African Literature. Since obtaining his Ph.D. from the State University of New York at Buffalo in the late 1970s, he has taught English, communication, and African American Studies at SUNY–Buffalo, the University of Nebraska at Omaha, and the University of Jos, Nigeria. His several articles and books on African languages and literature include *African Intellectual Heritage* (with Molefi Asante) published by Temple University Press.

Ezekiel B. Alembi was born in Ebwiranyi Village in Bunyore, Kenya, and went to primary school in Ziwani and Ebwiranyi before attending high school in Kakamega between 1977 and 1981. Between 1982 and 1983 he attended Kangaru High School, Embu. In 1985 he joined Kenyatta University, after working as an untrained teacher at Goibei Girls High School. At Kenyatta University he studied English, literature, and education, and in 1988 he graduated with a Bachelor of Education (Arts) degree. In 1990 he embarked on an M.A. degree in literature at Kenyatta University, graduating in 1992. His M.A. thesis was on Abanyole children's oral poetry. He has published widely for children and in oral literature. His published works include *Understanding Poetry: A Guide to Understanding, Looking for a Rain God and Other Stories; Telling Tales: The Use of the Oral Narrative in Religious Sermons in Kenya; Fine Feathers; High Adventures; The Cry of a Goat; Yellow Mangoes; Mistaken Identity; Selly; Settling the Score;* and *The Winner and Other Stories: A Reader's Guide.* He has traveled widely in Australia, India, China, Germany, and Finland giving lectures and attending conferences. Currently he is a lecturer at Kenyatta University and is working on his doctoral dissertation in oral poetry. He hopes to graduate from the University of Helsinki in 1999. He is vice president in charge of Africa for the International Society of Folk Narrative Research and is secretary general of the society's conference in the year 2000.

Richard W. Anderson is an adjunct faculty member at Oregon State University and Linfield College specializing in Japanese/East Asian religion, history, and culture. His primary research interests center on Japanese new religions, religious narrative, and ritual. He is currently rewriting a book-length manuscript on his four-year experience living in and working at the largest Buddhist temple complex in Tokyo.

Chukwuma Azuonye is a professor in the Department of Africana Studies, University of Massachusetts at Boston. Azuonye is author of many articles on Igbo narrative and is at work on *The Hero in Igbo Life and Literature.*

Hinekahukura Barrett-Aranui is an elder (*kuia*) of the Ngaati Uekaha, Parekahuki, Te Kanawa, Waiora subtribes of the Maniapoto tribe of the Tainui Confederation of tribes. She is a life member of the New Zealand Association of Counselors and in 1993 initiated the formation of a National Association of Maori Counselors under the group name of Te Whariki Tautoko. This name reflects the image of the Maori woven mat, where people sat with their elders to resolve personal, family, and tribal issues. As a child, sitting on the very same woven mats, Hinekahukura heard her elders recite and relate many stories. They were related as symbolic directions to discipline and direct the energies and initiatives of the education paths invented by the elders. With encouraging nudges from her elders she became a teacher, a facilitator for learning, and a counselor for all people. Even in her retirement, she continues to challenge the education systems to include and value the treasures and related stories of the Maori, which helped her to achieve her aspirations. Today she is dedicating her time to writing some of the stories she heard, for the many "grand-children" all over the world.

Martha S. Bean teaches intercultural communication in the M.A. program in Teaching English to Speakers of Other Languages. She has lived and worked in Malawi, Honduras, Peru, and China, as well as New York and Los Angeles. Her interests include oral discourse analysis, literacy, and minority education. She believes that both cultures and individuals use stories to script their lives and uncover their values. She is associate professor in the Department of Linguistics and Language Development, San Jose State University, San Jose, California.

Ervin Beck is professor of English at Goshen College in Indiana. He has published extensively on folklore and folk arts, especially from Belize, England, northern Indiana, and Mennonite and Amish communities.

Stephen Belcher has taught at the University of Nouakchott and at the Pennsylvania State University. He has coedited (with John W. Johnson and Thomas Hale) an anthology of African epics and has a study forthcoming. He is now working on book projects involving African mythology.

Mark Bender is assistant professor of Chinese in the Department of East Asian Languages and Literatures at Ohio State University. The author lived in China for a number of years and has produced articles and translations on the oral performing arts and folklore of various cultures of East Asia, traditional performance in East Asia, and ethnic minority literature in China.

Marjorie Bennett became interested in folklore in the 1950s and 1960s as a young folksinger hosting public television series on folklife for WHA–Madison, Wisconsin; KRMA–Denver, Colorado; and KCTS–Seattle, Washington; as well as radio series for Radio-Innsbruck, Austria, and KING-FM, Seattle. She received her Ph.D. in folklore from the University of Washington in 1986, specializing in personal narratives. She has served on the advisory boards to the Washington State Folklife Council, the Washington State Folklorist, and Northwest Folklife. A retired teacher, she now is folklorist in the Schools for the Washington State and Idaho arts commissions. In this work she brings local folk artists into the schools for weeklong residencies.

Ruth Seiman Bennett, University of California at Berkeley.

Megan Biesele received her Ph.D. in social anthropology from Harvard University in 1975. Since then she has taught anthropology part-time as a self-employed academic at the University of Texas at Austin and Rice University in Houston and has lectured at the University of Cape Town, South Africa. She helped form one of the earliest anthropological advocacy groups, the Kalahari Peoples Fund, in 1973 and currently serves as its coordinator. She worked for 10 years in Botswsana and Namibia in applied research and indigenous rights advocacy. Her interests include religion, belief systems, and verbal and visual art of hunting-gathering societies; cognitive systems and environmental resource use; and human rights of indigenous peoples. Her most recent book (with Richard Katz and Verna St. Dennis) is *Healing Makes Our Hearts Happy: Spirituality and Cultural Transformation Among the Kalahari Ju/'Hoansi.*

Martha Blache has a Ph.D. in folklore from Indiana University and taught for many years at the University of Buenos Aires, Argentina, where she also serves as director of the Folklore Division in the Anthropological Department and was in charge of the Folklore Series. Her folklore studies deal particularly with theory, folk narrative, and festivals. Currently she is conducting folklore research studies at the National Research Council of Argentina and is director of the Revista de Investigaciones Folkloricas.

Donald Braid teaches folklore, English, and anthropology at Butler University in Indianapolis, Indiana. His research interests include narrative theory and performance, especially as they intersect issues of worldview, cultural identity, meaning, and belief. He has worked with the Travelling People of Scotland since 1985, focusing primarily on Traveller storytelling and ballad singing traditions. His publications include "Personal Narrative and Experiential Meaning," in *Journal of American Folklore* 109 (1996); "'Did it happen or did it not?': Dream Stories, Worldview, and Narrative Knowing," in *Text and Performance Quarterly* 18 (1998); and "The Ethnography of Performance in the Study of Oral Traditions" (coauthored with Richard Bauman), in *Teaching Oral Traditions*, edited by John Miles Foley (New York: MLA Press, 1998). He is currently working on a book on Traveller storytelling that is tentatively titled *Lives Shaped Through Stories: The Role of Narrative in One Traveller Community*.

Jan Harold Brunvand is the author of five books on urban legends (with at least two more forthcoming) and general editor of *American Folklore: An Encyclopedia* as well as *The Study of American Folklore*, the standard textbook in the field (4th ed., 1998). He retired as professor of English and folklore at the University of Utah after 32 years of service.

Sory Camara was born in Kankan in the Republic of Guinea in West Africa. His first book, *People of the Word*, received the Grand Prix Littéraire d'Afrique Noire in 1976. This book was reissued in an edition by Kathala in Paris in 1990. He also has published *Paroles Très Anciennes ou le Mythe de l'Accomplissement de l'Homme* in an edition by Pensée Sauvage à Grenoble in 1982. Professor Camara is director of the Department of Social and Cultural Anthropology at the University of Bordeaux.

Pauline E. Campbell-McLeod is one of Australia's leading Aboriginal storytellers. After completing her training at the Eora Centre for Performing Arts in Redfern, she worked as a freelance performer for seven years. Popularly known as "Pauline from Playschool," she is one of the first Aboriginal performers to appear regularly on a television show. Since 1990 Pauline has appeared on *Playschool* and other television shows with ABCTV and SBSTV. She has been a regular cultural educator/storyteller/performer since 1992 in the Yirribana

Gallery at the Art Gallery of New South Wales in Sydney as well as from 1996 to 1998 poet and storyteller at Reconciliation forums throughout Sydney. She has worked as guest lecturer in Aboriginial studies at TAFE colleges and universities throughout New South Wales. She is director and founder of Kirka Marri Theatre and writer and director of the Nallawilli 7* project, which presents Aboriginal culture as entertainment in a respectful and culturally correct manner. Several of her retellings of Aboriginal stories have been published for educators in New South Wales, and a collection will be published in the United States in 1999 by Libraries Unlimited.

Isabel Cardigos was born in Lisbon, Portugal. She lived for more than 20 years in London where she completed a master's degree and a Ph.D. in King's College London on Portuguese studies. The thesis and the dissertation were on fairy tales. Back in Portugal since 1993, she teaches at the University of the Algarve, where she created a research center for oral literature—Centro de Estudos Ataide Oliveira—and an annual journal, *Estudos de Literatura Oral (Studies on Oral Literature)*. She is a member of the International Society for Folk Narrative Research and an associate member of the Folklore Fellows. A revised edition of her dissertation, "In and Out of Enchantment: Blood Symbolism and Gender in Portuguese Fairytales," was published in the series *Folklore Fellows Communications*, Helsinki, Finland: Academia Scientiarum Fennica, 1996.

Inta Gale Carpenter was born in Latvia but grew up in the United States after spending her first five years in refugee camps after World War II. After completing a B.A. in sociology at Chatham College in Pittsburgh, she worked briefly as a social worker in Colorado before pursuing graduate degrees in folklore at Indiana University. She currently is associate research scholar in the Folklore Institute. Her publications have focused primarily on issues of exile identity and nationalism, both in (and between) the native land and the diaspora, but more generally she has been concerned with narrative as a resource in social life.

Daniel J. Crowley was associate professor of anthropology and art and chairman of the Department of Anthropology at the University of California at Davis. He received a bachelor's degree from Northwestern University in 1943, a master's from Bradley University in 1948, and a Ph.D. from Northwestern University in 1956. He was associate professor at the University of California at Davis in 1961 and chair of the Department of Anthropology after 1966. He is the author of *I Could Talk Old-Story Good: Creativity in Bahamian Folklore* and contributed to many journals, including *American Anthropologist, Journal of American Folklore, Journal of Aesthetics and Art Criticism, Ethnomusicology,* and *Présence Africaine.*

Linda D'Amico is a cultural anthropologist and Latin Americanist who has lived and worked extensively in Mexico and Ecuador. She is presently visiting assistant professor in the Department of Anthropology and Sociology at West Chester University in West Chester, Pennsylvania.

James Danandjaja is professor in anthropology and folklore at the Department of Anthropology, School of Social and Political Sciences, at the University of Indonesia. He has published books on Indonesian (Javanese and Balinese) and Japanese folklore and written numerous essays on Indonesian folklore and Balinese ethnography based on fieldwork in Indonesia and Japan.

Manuel Dannemann is a professor at the University of Chile in the Department of Anthropology of the Faculty of Social Sciences. He directs the Interfaculty Seminar on Folklore as Culture and the Revista of Anthropology. He is academic vice-rector of Universidad Educares. He has been visiting professor at Universidad Nacional de Salta and Universidad Nacional de Comahue in Argentina, at the University of Indiana, and at the Instituto Interamericano de Ethnomusicología y Folklore in Caracas, Venezuela. He is on the editorial board of the *Rivista de Investigaciones Folklóricas de Argentina, Folklore Americana,* and *Oralidad* and has contributed many articles. Among his many books are *Bibliografía del Folklore Chileno* (1952–65), *Bibliografía del Folklore Chileno* (1966–76), *Bilbiografía de la Artesanía Tradicional Chilena, Il Congreso Chileno de Estudiosos del Folklore, La*

Disciplina del Folklore en Chile, El Romancero Chileno (with Raquel Barros), *Cuentos Folklóricos Chilenos para los Niños de Chile, Tipos Humanos en la Poesía Folklórica Chilena, Ensayo Filológico, Antropológico y Sociológico,* and his most extensive work *Enciclopedia del Folklore de Chile* (Editorial Universitaria, 1997).

Linda Dégh, distinguished professor of folklore at Indiana University in Bloomington, is a folklorist and field ethnographer who specializes in traditional and modern Western civilization and ethnic relations in Europe and North America. Her books and essays discuss folk belief and ideology as expressed in narratives, tales, legends, and personal accounts. Focusing on the creativity of storytellers guided by tradition and community suggestions, she seeks understanding of the processes of variation and stabilization in the spatial and temporal spread of stories.

Robert Knox Dentan is author of *The Semai: A Nonviolent People of Malaya* and coauthor of *Malaysia and the "Original People": A Case Study of the Impact of Development on Indigenous Peoples* (Allyn and Bacon) as well as many articles and chapters. He is currently writing a book about the interplay of violence and nonviolence in Semai life, of which the chapter in *Traditional Storytelling Today* is an excerpt. Other excerpts from this work have appeared in the *American Anthropologist,* the *Journal of Asian Folklore,* and the *Review of Indonesian and Malaysian Affairs.* Denton is affiliated with the Department of American Studies and the Department of Anthropology at State University of New York/University at Buffalo.

Joyce Burkhalter Flueckiger is an associate professor in the Department of Religion at Emory University in Atlanta, Georgia. She received her Ph.D. in South Asian language and literature from the University of Wisconsin–Madison. She specializes in performance studies, with a particular interest in gender. She has carried out extensive fieldwork in India, working with both Hindu and Muslim popular traditions. She is currently writing an ethnographic study on a Muslim female folk healer in South India. She is the author of *Gender and Genre in the*

Folklore of Middle India (1996) and is the co-editor of *Oral Epics in India* (1989) and *Boundaries of the Text: Epic Performances in South and Southeast Asia* (1991).

Rodney Frey received his Ph.D. in cultural anthropology from the University of Colorado in 1979. He taught at Carroll College in Helena, Montana; Lewis-Clark State College in Coeur d'Alene, Idaho; and joined the Department of Sociology and Anthropology at the University of Idaho in 1998. He has been involved in several applied research projects beginning on the Crow Indian Reservation in 1974 and on the Coeur d'Alene Indian Reservation since 1989. Among his publications are *The World of the Crow Indians: As Driftwood Lodge* and *Stories That Make the World: Oral Literature of the Indian Peoples of the Inland Northwest as Told by Lawrence Aripa, Tom Yellowtail and other Elders.*

Barbara Gobrecht was born in 1953 in Berlin, Germany. She studied French, Russian, German, Spanish, and Italian literature in Berlin; Boulder, Colorado; and Zurich, Switzerland. Her 1979 thesis was "Fairy Tale Elements in the Opus of Jules Verne." Her 1994 Ph.D. thesis was "Successful European Comedies from 18th Century." Since 1985 she has been a freelance author of the *Encyclopedia of Fairy Tale* and *Fabula* and has contributed to numerous scientific and journalistic publications about fairy tales and storytelling. She is a guest lecturer at the University of St. Gall in Switzerland. Her 1996 book is entitled *Märchenfrauen* (about strong and weak women in fairy tales). She is a member of the executive board of the Swiss Fairy Tale Society and a member of the scientific advisory board of the European Fairy Tale Society. The foci of her research is women in fairy tales and German, Russian, Italian, and Swiss compilations.

Veronika Görög-Karady is a senior research fellow of the French National Center for Scientific Research in Paris. She teaches at the Institut National des Langues Orientales and is one of the editors of the *Cahiers de Littérature Orale.* Her main fields of interest are African and Hungarian oral literature. She is author of several books, including *L'univers familiale dans les contes africains* (1997).

Sylvia Grider is associate professor of anthropology at Texas A&M University, where she teaches graduate and undergraduate courses in folklore, cultural anthropology, and history. One of her primary research interests is the legend, and she has published widely on children's ghost stories and haunted houses as well as on historical legends, primarily about Texas. She is past president of both the American Folklore Society and the Texas Folklore Society.

Lindsey Harlan is associate professor of religious studies at Connecticut College. She is the author of *Religion and Rajput Women: The Ethic of Protection in Contemporary Narratives* (Berkeley: University of California Press, 1992) and coeditor (with Paul Courtright) of *From the Margins of Hindu Marriage: Essays on Gender, Culture, and Religion* (New York: Oxford University Press, 1995). She is currently writing a book on hero worship in India, tentatively titled *The Goddess' Henchmen: Gender and Masculinity in Contemporary Hero Veneration,* and working on a project on shamanic narratives.

Vi (taqʷšəblu) Hilbert is founder and director of the Lushootseed Research Center in Seattle, Washington. She has compiled a Lushootseed lexicon and coauthored *Lushootseed Dictionary.* She has transcribed and translated hours of Lushootseed language tapes, and her publications include *Haboo: Native American Stories from Puget Sound; Huboo;* and *xəcusədəagʷəʷulcə: The Wisdom of a Skagit Elder: Aunt Susie Sampson Peter.* She has contributed to *Lushootseed Texts: An Introduction to Puget Salish Narrative Aesthetics.* Hilbert is also widely renowned as a storyteller, has performed at the National Storytelling Festival, and has released a tape *Coyote and Rock and other Lushootseed Stories.*

Kamal el dien Hussien is a professor of folkdrama on the Faculty of Kindergarten at Cairo University in Egypt.

Sue-Ellen Jacobs has been professor of women studies and adjunct professor of anthropology and music at the University of Washington since 1974. She has been involved in research with various cultural experts at San Juan Pueblo, New Mexico, since 1970 and has published articles related to her research there. In addition, she has published books and articles based on anthropological research she has conducted in other communities.

Annikki Kaivola-Bregenhøj is professor of folkloristics at the University of Turku in Finland. In addition to oral narrating, her studies have covered enigmatology, popular dream interpreting, and old wedding customs. She has done fieldwork in Finland, among Finns living in Sweden, and among the old Finnish population around St. Petersburg, Russia, and in Karelia. She has published books and articles in English and in the Scandinavian languages.

Deborah A. Kapchan is director of the Center for Intercultural Studies in Folklore and Ethnomusicology and assistant professor of anthropology at the University of Texas at Austin. Her first book is entitled *Gender on the Market: Moroccan Women and the Revoicing of Tradition* (University of Pennsylvania Press, 1996). She is currently working on a second book about ethnography, charlatanism, and intentionality in language.

Gabriela Kiliánová was born in Bratislava, Slovakia, in 1951. She studied ethnology at Comenius University in Bratislava and received a Ph.D. in folklore studies in 1977 and a Ph.D. in (European) ethnology in 1990. Since 1991 Kilianova has been senior research fellow in the Institute of Ethnology of the Slovak Academy of Sciences in Bratislava. Since 1993 she has been deputy director at the Institute of Ethnology and lecturer at Comenius University, at the Academia Istropolitana Nova Institute for Advanced Studies in Bratislava, and at the University of Vienna in Austria. Publications include *Rozpravac Alojz Kovac z Riecnice* (*Storyteller Alojz Kovac from Riecnica*) (Cadca, 1984); "Folk Narrative, Chapter XII" in *Slovakia: European Context of Folk Culture*, edited by R. Stolicna (Bratislava, 1997); (joint editor with E. Krekovicova) *Folklore, Folklorism and National Identification: The Slovak Cultural Context* (Bratislava, 1992), and many other books and articles on ethnic and national identities in Central Europe and on Central European cultural traditions.

Vincent Muli Wa Kitumba is a native of Kenya. He was educated in Africa and the United States and earned his Ph.D. from the University of Wyoming in 1991. He is author of *East African Folktales for All Ages from the Voice of Mukamba, Multicultural Folktales for All Ages, The School with No Walls, Buffaloes in the Workplace,* and *Hold It for Me So That I Can Make the Bed.* He is an award-winning motivational speaker and a storyteller. His Web page is at <www.kituku.com>.

Yordanka Kotseva was graduated from the University of Sofia, Bulgaria, in 1968. She received her Ph.D. in 1977 with a dissertation on "Taboos in Bulgarian Fairy Tales." Kotseva has worked at the Institute of Folklore in Sofia since 1975. Her publications are dedicated to folktales and fairy tales. She was responsible for the chapter "Fairy tales" (AT 300–750) in the *Catalog of the Bulgarian Folk Tale* (1994).

Annamária Lammel earned her Ph.D. in 1990. She is a Hungarian anthropologist and psychologist living since 1987 in Paris, where she is professor at the University of Paris VIII (University of Vincennes at Saint-Denis). She has done research among the Totonac Indians (from 1982 to 1998), among Igloolik Eskimos, and with Hungarian peasants. Her research area is traditional knowledge transmission and representation about history and natural phenomena in different cultures. With Ilona Nagy she is studying the Hungarian peasant Bible tradition. She is author of several books and articles.

Robert Laughlin received a master's degree and a Ph.D. in anthropology from Harvard University. Since 1962 he has been an ethnologist with the Bureau of American Ethnology at the Smithsonian Institution. From 1973 Laughlin has been curator of the Department of Anthropology. He is author of more than 50 articles on Mayan folklore and is literary coordinator of more than 21 publications of Chamula and Zinacantan material by the Dirección General de Culturas Populares in Mexico City and the Subsecretaria de Cultura y Recreacion in Tuxtla Gutiérrez. Among his publications are *Mayan Tales from Zinacantan: Dreams and Stories from the People of the Bat,* with Carol Karasik (Smithsonian Institution Press, 1996), and "The Great Tzotzil Dictionary of San Lorenzo Zinacantan," *Smithsonian Contributions to Anthropology* 19 (1975).

Michael Lieber is professor of anthropology at the University of Illinois at Chicago. Trained in folklore at Indiana University and in anthropology at the University of Pittsburgh, Lieber has done field research with African Americans in the United States, with western Shoshone in central Nevada, with the Polynesian people of Kapingamarangi Atoll, and with the resettled Kapingamarangi communities on Pohnpei Island in the Federated States of Micronesia. He is currently conducting program evaluation of university-community partnerships in Chicago. In addition to teaching anthropology and folklore courses, he is also a professional musician.

Carl Lindahl is professor of English and folklore at the University of Houston. Lindahl is series editor of the World Folktale Library, coeditor of *Swapping Stories: Folktales from Louisiana,* and author of some 30 publications on contemporary and medieval folk narrative, including a book on Chaucer's use of folk traditons, *Earnest Games: Folkloric Patterns in the Canterbury Tales.* He is currently at work on a study of the märchen-telling tradition in the southern Appalachians and on an anthology of folktales housed in the collections of the Library of Congress.

Jens Lund holds a Ph.D. in folklore from Indiana University. He has taught at Southern Illinois University, Indiana University–Purdue University at Indianapolis, the University of Washington, and Linfield College. He is the author of *Flathead and Spooneys: Fishing for a Living in the Ohio Valley* (University Press of Kentucky, 1995), *Folk Arts of Washington State* (Washington State Folklife Council, 1989), and more than 40 articles about folklore and local history. He was involved in developing the first Elko, Nevada, Cowboy Poetry Gathering and has organized several logger poetry events in Washington State and California. From 1984 through 1990 he was the Washington State folklorist. Lund has been a consultant for the Smithsonian Institution, the Library of Congress, and many other museums and historical organizations. He is presently developing folklore tour guides for the states of Washington and Utah.

Patricia Lysaght is a native of County Clare, Ireland. Her academic background is in law and the classics as well as in Irish language and literature and Irish and comparative folklore. She is a senior lecturer in the Department of Irish Folklore at University College in Dublin. Her work has appeared in major international publications, and she has lectured widely at academic conferences and institutions in Europe, the United States, and Canada, as well as in parts of Asia. She is a member of the International Society for Folk Narrative Research and is the Irish representative of Société Internationale d'Ethnologie et de Folklore, the International Commission for the Study of Religion in Everyday Life, and the European Ethnocartographic Working Group. She is currently president of the International Commission for Ethnological Food Research. Lysaght was an Alexander von Humboldt scholar at Westfälische Wilhelms–Universität in Münster, Germany, in 1987–88. She was guest international scholar at the Hungarian Academy of Sciences in 1995 and guest professor of folklore at Seminar für Volkskunde at Georg-August-Universität Göttingen in Germany in 1996–97 and at Seminar für Volkskunde at Westfälische Wilhelms-Universität in Münster, Germany, in 1998–99.

Margaret Read MacDonald is children's librarian at the King County Library System in Seattle, Washington. MacDonald holds master's degrees in library science (University of Washington) and education (University of Hawaii) and a Ph.D. in folklore from Indiana University. She is author of more than 20 books on storytelling and folklore topics, including *The Storyteller's Sourcebook: A Subject, Title, and Motif-Index to Children's Folktale Collections* (Gale, 1982) and *The Folklore of World Holidays* (Gale, 1992). Born and raised in southern Indiana, MacDonald has provided a community history for her hometown, *Scipio, Indiana: Threads from the Past* (Ye Galleon, 1988), and has analyzed their storying in *Scipio Storytelling: Talk in a Southern Indiana Community* (University Press of America, 1996). During 1995–97 she was a Fulbright scholar at Mahasarakham University in Thailand, and she has toured widely in Asia, Australia, New Zealand, and South America as a professional storyteller and as a presenter of workshops on the art of storytelling for librarians and educators.

Raouf Mama is an internationally known story-teller who performs indigenous English tales from his native Benin. Drawn from one of the richest oral traditions in Africa, Mama's stories have strong connections to African cultures on both sides of the Atlantic. His first book, *Why Goats Smell Bad and Other Stories from Benin* (Linnet Books, 1998), was hailed by *School Library Journal* as "a fascinating collection of 20 traditional folktales that make the Fon culture come alive." A second book, *The Barefoot Book of Tropical Tales,* is to be published in England in 1999. Raouf Mama is a graduate of the University of Michigan with an M.A. and a Ph.D. in English. He is fluent in English, French, Fon, and Yoruba and is proficient in Spanish and German. He teaches English at Eastern Connecticut State University.

Ljiljana Marks is an associate member of the Institute of Ethnology and Folklore Research in Zagreb, Croatia. She received her Ph.D. in Croatian folk narratives (contemporary and traditional tales and legends). She contributes regularly to the journal *Narodna umjetnost,* to the *Croatian Journal of Ethnology and Folklore Research,* to the *Enzyklopaedie des Märchens,* and to many other folkloristic and philological publications. She is the author of the book *Vekivecni Zagreb: Zagrebacke price i predaje* (Eternal Zagreb-Story and Legends from Zagreb, 1994).

JoAnn Martin is associate professor of anthropology at Earlham College. She has written and published extensively on storytelling and its role in political processes and is the coauthor with Carolyn Nordstrom of *The Paths to Domination, Resistance and Terror* (University of California Press). She is currently working on a book entitled *The Passions of Place: The State, Politics and Identity in Contemporary Mexico.*

Esther Martinez, an enrolled tribal member of San Juan Pueblo, New Mexico, is a retired schoolteacher, a former director of bilingual education at the San Juan Pueblo Day School, compiler and editor of the *San Juan Pueblo Tewa Dictionary,* and a world-renowned storyteller. In 1997, she won the National Congress of American Indian Woman of the Year Award for her work since 1995 with children, elders, and teachers for the Tewa Language Project to build a new dictionary and the interactive multimedia CD-ROM for that project. Other names by which she is known are Blue Water and Estafanita Martinez. She was born in 1912, and in 1998 she continued as an active consultant to numerous university and other scholars in matters associated with indigenous language and culture preservation and the craft of storytelling.

Lee-Ellen Marvin has explored the art of story-telling as performer, producer, teacher, and organizer since 1976. She is the founding director of the Sharing the Fire storytelling conference—still held annually in Boston, Massachusetts—and is pursuing a Ph.D. in folklore from the University of Pennsylvania. She is the program manager for the Constance Saltonstall Foundation for the Arts in Ithaca, New York.

Daniel Mato is the director of the Program on Globalization, Culture, and Sociopolitical Transformations at the Universidad Central de Venezuela, where he teaches at the Center for Postdoctoral Studies. He has been a visiting professor at various U.S. and Latin American universities and has published numerous research books and articles both on storytelling and on current cultural and sociopolitical processes in Latin America. His books include *Crítica de la Modernidad Globalización y Construcción de Identidades* (Universidad Central de Venezuela, 1995); *Narradores en Acción* (Academia Nacional de Historia, 1992); *El Arte de Narrar y la Noción de "Literatura Oral."* His most recent edited volumes are *Teoría y Política de la Construcción de Identidades y Diferencias* (UNESCO-Nueva Sociedad, 1994) and *América Latina en Tiempos de Globalización* (UNESCO-ALAS-Universidad Central de Venezuela, 1996). He has been a storyteller and a consultant with UNESCO and several indigenous peoples' organizations.

John McCabe-Juhnke is a native of Moundridge, Kansas, where he completed his public school education. In 1978 he received his bachelor of arts degree in English and speech/drama from Bethel College in North Newton, Kansas. He holds a master's degree in speech communication from the University of Illinois and a doctorate in performance studies from Louisiana State University. He is currently the chair of the Communication Arts Department at Bethel College, where he has been teaching speech and theater since 1986. He resides in North Newton, Kansas, with his wife, Karen, son, Austin, and daughter, Taylor.

Barbara McDermitt is a research fellow and part-time lecturer on Scots and Appalachian oral traditions at the School of Scottish Studies (S.S.S.), University of Edinburgh. American by birth, she received her master's degree in theater arts from Northwestern University and stayed to teach for 10 years before moving to Scotland to pursue her doctorate in folklore at the S.S.S. She has written professional papers and articles for such journals as *Tocher* (S.S.S.), *The North Carolina Folklore Journal, The Scandinavian Yearbook of Folklore, The Second International Turkish Folklore Congress,* and *Explor.* A founder member of the Scottish Storytelling Forum, Barbara is an active storyteller who performs in schools, libraries, community centers, and festivals in the United Kingdom and abroad. She also works with a partner to sign stories for hearing-impaired audiences. In addition to her university and storytelling activities she regularly writes stories for the BBC's educational and religious radio programs for children. She is married to a Scottish harp maker and lives in the tiny hamlet of Silverburn.

John H. McDowell is a folklorist at Indiana University's Folklore Institute. He specializes in the verbal and expressive traditional arts of Latin American peoples, with particular emphasis on mythic narrative and heroic balladry. He is the author of three research monographs: *Children's Riddling* (Indiana University Press, 1979), the two-volume set *Sayings of the Ancestors: The Spiritual Life of the Sibundoy Indians* (University Press of Kentucky, 1989), and *So Wise Were Our Elders: Mythic Narratives of the Kamsa* (University Press of Kentucky, 1994). He is currently completing two monographs on the Mexican *Corrido,* a popular ballad form deeply entwined with Mexican history.

W.K. McNeil is folklorist at the Ozark Folk Center, a position he has held since 1976. Prior to that he was administrator-folklorist for the Division of Performing Arts at the Smithsonian Institution and prior to that a historian for the Office of State History with the New York State Education Department. He also served as a VISTA volunteer in southeastern Kentucky. McNeil's B.A. in history and German is from Carson-Newman College, his M.A. is in museology and American folklore from the Cooperstown Graduate Program of State University of New York–Oneonta, and his Ph.D. is in folklore and American studies from Indiana University. McNeil is the author of 15 books, including *Ghost Stories from the American South; The Charm Is Broken: Readings in Arkansas and Missouri Folklore;* and *Appalachian Images in Folk and Popular Culture.* He has written 100 articles and 750 reviews for a variety of folklore and history journals. From 1986 to 1994 he was editor of *Old Time Country* and from 1988 to 1994 editor of *Rejoice: The Gospel Music Magazine.* Since 1977 he has written a column on Ozark folksongs for *The Ozarks Mountaineer,* a regional magazine. He is a former president of the Ozark States Folklore Society and book review editor of the *Journal of American Folklore* and *Mid-America Folklore.* For 14 years he was on the board of the National Council for Traditional Arts and since 1978 has served on the advisory board of *Appalachian Journal.* He has produced several recordings and was nominated for a Grammy in 1993 for his *Smithsonian Collection of Classic Blues.* In 1995 he was elected to the Fellows of the American Folklore Society.

Kuʻualoha Meyer-Hoʻomanawanui was born on Oahu and raised both on Oahu and Lanai. She is *hapa* (part) Hawaiian and proudly traces her lineage to the islands of Kauai, Maui, and Hawaii. She is also a descendant of both chiefly and kahuna families in the districts of Kohala, Kaʻū, and Puna on the island of Hawaii. Kuʻualoha attended Kauai Community College before transferring to the University of Hawaii at Mānoa, where she graduated from the Center for Hawaiian Studies with a B.A. in traditional culture and arts and a minor in English. In 1997 she earned a degree in Hawaiian religion, with an emphasis on nineteenth-century Hawaiian-language Pele texts. She is currently a doctoral candidate in English literature with a focus on nineteenth-century Hawaiian literature, children's literature, and the development of methods to evaluate Hawaiian literature from a native perspective. She has taught at the Center for Hawaiian Studies, Kapi'olani Community College, and Chaminade University. She is a member of Hālau Hula o Kūkunaokalā, having studied the hula under *kumu hula* John Ka-imikaua. She is a *haku mele* (composer) whose work appears on the compact discs of several Hawaiian artists, and she has written and illustrated two children's stories written from a Hawaiian perspective.

Rosario S. Morales is an assistant professor in the Curriculum and Instruction Division and the Charter School of Education at California State University, Los Angeles (CSLA). Morales teaches various courses in the teacher credentialing program and in the master's in early childhood program. She specializes in multicultural education and literacy and has been a presenter and speaker at numerous statewide, national, and international conferences. She consults with school districts and conducts seminars for teachers and parents in the area of early literacy through storytelling and writing books with children. Currently, she is the director of the California Beginning Teacher Education and Assessment Program at CSLA where she works closely with new teachers and trains mentor teachers in several school districts. She received her doctorate in the area of international and multicultural education from the University of San Francisco.

Ibrahim Muhawi was born in Palestine in 1937 and received his primary and secondary education there and his higher education at the University of California, where he specialized in English. He has taught English literature in Canada, Jordan, Palestine, and Tunisia and Arabic folklore and rhetoric at the University of California at Berkeley. He is currently with the Department of Islamic and Middle Eastern Studies at the University of Edinburgh, where he teaches courses in modern Arabic literature, translation studies, and comparative literature. His love for the folktale was rekindled as an adult while teaching English literature at Birzeit University in his native land. His current research combines literary and folkloristic concerns with a focus on the rhetoric and comparative stylistics of the Arabic oral tradition.

Ilona Nagy was born in 1944 in Nagyfoedemes, Hungary. She earned a degree in ethnography and Latin philology in 1968 from Eotvoes Lorand University in Budapest. She received a Herder-stipendium at the University of Vienna in 1972–73. In 1985 Nagy received the Pitre-Salomone Marino prize "per i meriti" in Palermo, Italy. From 1989 to 1998 she was vice president for Europe of the International Society for Folk-Narrative Research. Nagy has been a research fellow at the Ethnographical Institute of the Hungarian Academy of Sciences since 1968. She is editor of a folktale series at the Publishing House of the Hungarian Academy, New Collection of Hungarian Folk Poetry and Tales-Legends-Stories, and is the author of numerous publications on the folktale and on folk legend research.

Siegfried Neumann studied in Rostock, East Germany, and received his doctorate in ethnology and German from the Humboldt University at Berlin in 1961. From 1957 until 1991 he was a scholar at the German Academy of Sciences in Berlin. Since 1988 he has headed the Institute für Volkskunde (Institute of Ethnology) in Mecklenburg-Vorpommern (Wossidlo-Archiv) in Rostock. He has written and edited more than 20 books and numerous articles in German, Polish, Russian, Bulgarian, Italian, French, and English on folklife and folk culture in northern Germany, on the history of German literature and folklore, and on subjects relating to proverbs and to folk narratives such as fairy tales, comical tales, stories of saints, and everyday storytellings (Alltagserzählungen).

Ode Ogede, a professor of English at North Carolina Central University, held an Andrew Mellon Faculty Fellowship at the University of Pennsylvania. He has taught at Ahmadu Bello University in Nigeria and at Lincoln University in Pennsylvania. Among his numerous publications are *Art, Society, and Performance: Igede Praise Poetry* (University Press of Florida, 1997); *Ayi Kwei Armah: Radical Iconoclast, Pitting Imaginary Worlds Against the Actual* (Heinemann, 1998); and *Chinua Achebe and the Politics of Representation;* as well as contributions to *The Cambridge History of African and Caribbean Literatures, The Foreign Woman in British Literature, Postcolonial Afri-*

can Writers: A Bio-bibliographical Critical Sourcebook, and other edited collections, including more than two dozen journals in Africa, Australia, Canada, Denmark, England, Germany, and the United States.

Mahmoud Omidsalar was born in 1950 in Iran. He studied in the United States, where he received his Ph.D. in Near Eastern studies from the University of California at Berkeley in 1984. He studied folklore with Alan Dundes, who also served as the adviser and chairman of his Ph.D. dissertation. He has been a consulting editor on folklore to the *Encyclopaedia Iranica,* edited at the Center for Iranian Studies at Columbia University, and is currently editing the sixth volume of the new critical edition of the *Shahnama,* of which the first five volumes, edited by Professor Khaleghi-Motlagh of Hamburg University, have already been published. Omidsalar was the Visiting Lady Davis Professor of Iranian Studies at the Hebrew University of Jerusalem during the spring quarter of 1998, where he did research for a book on the logic of the *Shahnama* narrative. He has published more than 100 papers in Iran, Europe, and the United States on classical Persian literature and folklore. Currently, he works as the Stacks Supervisor at the John F. Kennedy Memorial Library of the California State University, Los Angeles.

Teresa Omidsalar was born in Cuba in 1954. She studied in the United States where in 1979 she received her master of library science degree from the Graduate School of Library and Information Science at UCLA. She worked as a reference librarian at UCLA for 17 years before accepting a position as a reference librarian with the John F. Kennedy Memorial Library of the California State University, Los Angeles. She and Mahmoud Omidsalar have coauthored a number of papers on Persian folklore.

Mohammed Taib Osman, Datuk Professor Emeritus Dr. Mohammed Taib Osman received his M.A. from the University of Malaya and his Ph.D. from Indiana University. He is currently professor emeritus at the University of Malaysia and is a fellow of Berita Harian Sdn. Bhd.

Marcela Orellana received her bachelor's degree in Roman languages at the Université Catholique de Louvain in Louvain-la-Neuve, Belgium (1980) and her Ph.D. at the École des Hautes Études en Sciences Sociales in Paris in 1985. She is currently associate professor in the Spanish Department at the Universidad de Santiago de Chile, where she coordinates the bachelor's degree in Spanish literature. Her major research interests deal with oral and popular literature from Chile.

Maria Palleiro is professor in the Hispanic Philology Institute at Buenos Aires University in Buenos Aires, Argentina.

Chan E. Park, assistant professor of Korean language, literature, and folklore at The Ohio State University, is a performer and ethnographer of *p'ansori,* an oral narrative tradition of Korea. For the past decade, Park has worked toward inventing and theorizing the global presentation of *p'ansori* outside its local context. Her work on the ancient narrative art integrates the multiple disciplines in the science of humanity.

David Pendergast is an archeologist with 37 years' experience in the excavation and study of ancient Maya remains in Belize. He is vice president for collections and research at the Royal Ontario Museum in Toronto. Pendergast was educated in California (B.A., University of California at Berkeley, 1955; Ph.D., UCLA, 1961), and following six years as a faculty member in anthropology at the University of Utah he has been on the Royal Ontario Museum staff since 1967. He is the author of 230 publications, including books, monographs, book chapters, scholarly and popular articles, and reviews, of which more than 200 deal with the Maya. In addition to his ongoing research in Belize, he is currently carrying out archaeological work at a Taino site on the north coast of Cuba.

Nigel Phillips was born in Jinan, China, in 1934. He received a B.A. in classics from Cambridge University in 1956 and a Ph.D. in Indonesian literature in 1979. From 1956 to 1958 he was in the Russian interpreter's course with the Royal Navy. He has been a lecturer and senior lecturer in Austronesian Languages at the School of Oriental and African Studies of London University from 1967 to the present. His main interest is the oral literature of West Sumatra, Indonesia.

Sally Price and **Richard Price** have been learning and writing about the Afro-Caribbean for more than 30 years. They divide their time between the College of William and Mary in Williamsburg, Virginia, where they each hold a professorial chair, and rural Martinique, where they live for eight months of the year. Sally Price's books include *Co-Wives and Calabashes* and *Primitive Art in Civilized Places*. Richard Price's books include *First-Time, Alabi's World,* and *The Convict and the Colonel.* Their most recent jointly authored books, both about the arts of the Suriname Maroons, are *Enigma Variations* (a novel) and *Maroon Art: Cultural Vitality in the African Diaspora.*

Susan Rasmussen is associate professor of anthropology at the University of Houston. She has conducted extensive field research in Niger among the Tuareg people on female spirit possession, the life course and aging, healing specialists, and smiths/artisans. She has published numerous articles on religion, gender, cosmology and symbolism, and aging and two books, *Spirit Possession and Personhood Among the Kel Ewey Tuareg* (Cambridge University Press, 1995) and *The Poetics and Politics of Tuareg Aging: Life Course and Personal Destiny in Niger* (Northern Illinois University Press, 1997). Other of her interests are ethnographic analysis and African humanities. Her experience in Africa includes teaching for the Peace Corps and the Ministry of Education in Niger. She is currently writing a book about women and health care.

Richard Raspa is professor of humanities at Wayne State University in Detroit, Michigan. His areas of interest include folk narratives and organizational culture. He is the coauthor of three books on communication and folklore, one of which, *Italian Folktales in America,* with Elizabeth Mathias, was awarded the Botkin Prize.

Christiane Seydou (née Mazzoni) was born in Oran, Algeria, in 1934 and is of French nationality. She is director of research for CNRS (UMR 7594, Langage, Langues et cultures d'Afrique noire). Seydou earned degrees in French, Latin, and Greek from the Sorbonne in 1958 and received a degree in the classics from the University of Algeria in 1954 and a diploma in Greek in 1955. She received diplomas from the Institute National des Langues et Civilisations Orientales in Paris in 1964 (*langue peule*) and 1966 (*langue haoussa*) and a doctorat de troisième cycle en ethnologie from the Institute National des Langues et Civilisations Orientales in 1968. Seydou was professeur de lettres classiques at the Lycée de Rouen from 1958 to 1961 and has been at the Centre National de Recherche Scientifique (CNRS-Paris) since 1965.

Joseph Sobol has worked since 1981 as a professional storyteller, musician, and folklorist. He has an M.A. in folklore from the University of North Carolina and a Ph.D. in performance studies from Northwestern University. His writings on traditional and contemporary storytelling include essays in the volumes *Jack in Two Worlds: Contemporary North American Tales and Their Tellers* (edited by William Bernard McCarthy, University of North Carolina Press, 1994) and *Who Says: Pivotal Issues in Contemporary Storytelling* (edited by Carol Birch and Melissa Meckler, August House, 1996). The article in this book is excerpted from *The Storytellers' Journey: An American Revival* (University of Illinois Press, 1999).

Ramadan Sokoli is a professor in Tiranë, Albania.

Cathy Spagnoli, professional storyteller and writer, has given storytelling performances and workshops in the United States, Canada, and Asia for more than 20 years. Funding from The Japan Foundation, The Korea Foundation, USIA, and other organizations have allowed her to collect many Asian tales and to document Asian storytelling techniques. Cathy's collected stories are also shared through her books of Asian folktales, her storytelling cassette tapes, and many articles published in the United States and abroad. Cathy, her husband, Indian sculptor Paramasivam, and their son, Manu, live on an island off Seattle, Washington, in a home that they built themselves.

Kay Stone is a folklorist with a special interest in wonder tales and a storyteller who has been telling them professionally for two decades. She has published widely on women in folktales and on contemporary stories and storytellers. Her recent book *Burning Brightly: New Light on Old Tales Told Today* brings the two professions together. She has taught folklore and techniques of storytelling at the University of Winnipeg since 1971.

Brian Sturm is an assistant professor for the School of Information and Library Science at the University of North Carolina at Chapel Hill. He received his master's in library science and his Ph.D. from the Indiana University School of Library and Information Science. He has been a storyteller for many years and has a long-standing interest in the power of stories and their potential for healing.

Timothy R. Tangherlini is assistant professor at the University of California at Los Angeles in the Scandinavian Section and the Department of East Asian Languages and Cultures. He is affiliated with the Interdepartmental Program in Folklore and Mythology. He has carried out fieldwork in Denmark, Korea, and the United States. His most recent book is *Talking Trauma: Paramedics and Their Stories* (University of Mississippi Press, 1998).

Gerald Thomas is the author of several books and numerous articles on folk narrative. He is a professor and former head of Memorial University of Newfoundland's Department of Folklore, from which he retired in 1996 after a 32-year career. Most of his research and writing has focused on the French enclave of Newfoundland's west coast. In recognition of this work, the government of France named him, in 1996, Chevalier dans l'Ordre des Palms Academiques.

Barre Toelken was born and raised in Massachusetts. He received his education in the west (B.S., Utah State University, 1958; M.A., Washington State University, 1959; Ph.D. in medieval literature, University of Oregon, 1964). Currently he is professor of English and history at Utah State University, where he is director of both the graduate program in American studies and the interdisciplinary Folklore Program. His publications include *The Dynamics of Folklore, the Ballad and the Scholars* (with D.K. Wilgus), *Ghosts and the Japanese:*

Cultural Experience in Japanese Death Legends (with Michiko Iwasaka), *Morning Dew and Roses: Nuance, Metaphor and Meaning in Folksongs*, and a number of scholarly and popular essays on folklore, balladry, worldview, medieval literature, intercultural perspective, and Native American traditions.

Diane Tong is author of *Gypsy Folk Tales* (Harcourt Brace Jovanovich, 1989). She has spent much time studying and photographing Gypsy culture. She lives in New York City.

Wajuppa Tossa is assistant professor of English and American literature at Mahasarakham University in Mahasarakham, Thailand. She is also director of the Mahasarakham University Storytelling Project. She received her Ph.D. in English and American literature from Drew University in 1986. She is recipient of two grants from the Wittner Byrner Foundation for Poetry to translate Isan folk verse into English verse and recipient of several Fulbright awards as student, as scholar, and as sponsor. She is a Fulbright visiting scholar at the University of Oregon, where she is engaged in a research project, "Thai/Lao Folktales and Storytelling in Language Classrooms," and in preparation of two verse translations, "Kamphra Phinoi, the Orphan and the Little Ghost" and "Kaew Na Ma, a Horse-Face Woman Warrior."

Lukas D. Tsitsipis is professor of anthropology and linguistics at the Aristotle University of Thessaloníki in Greece. Tsitsipis holds a Ph.D. in anthropology from the University of Wisconsin at Madison (1981) and two M.A.s from the same university in anthropology and linguistics. Special research interests include narrative performance, linguistic anthropology of language shift, the ethnography of speaking, the political economy of language, polyphonic discourse, and language and ideology. His articles have appeared in *Journal of Pragmatics, Word, Language in Society, International Journal of the Sociology of Language, Anthropological Linguistics*, and elsewhere. He has published *A Linguistic Anthropology of Praxis and Language Shift: Arvanitíka (Albanian) and Greek in Contact* (Clarendon Press, 1998).

Elizabeth Tucker is associate professor of English

at Binghamton University, where she has taught since 1977 when she received her doctorate from the Folklore Institute at Indiana University. Her main areas of research and publication have been children's folklore, women's traditions, and folklore of the supernatural. In her work as faculty master of one of the residential colleges at Binghamton University, she often has enjoyed leading storytelling sessions and encouraging students to organize storytelling events of their own.

Kristin Bervig Valentine and Eugene Valentine: Kristen Bervig Valentine is a professor of communication and women's studies at Arizona State University, where she teaches performance studies and oral traditions. Eugene Valentine teaches applied linguistics at Arizona State University. Together they have been actively researching Galician oral traditions since 1978. Their research is informed by ethnographically sensitive participant-observation fieldwork conducted in Spain in 1982–83, 1989–90, and 1994. During their fieldwork they lived and worked in the cities of Santiago de Compostela and La Coruña, attending cultural festivals throughout Galicia and conducting in-depth audio interviews with more than 50 women and men about oral traditions, folklore, legends, and culturally significant stories. In addition to contributing chapters to various books dealing with oral traditions, they have contributed articles to *Europa, Southern Folklore,* and the *Encyclopedia of World Cultures.*

Ülo Valk was born in 1962 and was graduated from the University of Tartu as a folklorist in 1986. He received his Dr. Philol. degree at the same university for his thesis on the image of the devil in Estonian folklore. He is a professor of Estonian and comparative folklore at the University of Tartu, and his current research interests include folk religion, legends, and comparative mythology.

Kira Van Deusen is a Canadian storyteller and researcher of Siberian shamanic oral traditions. She is concerned with the preservation of indigenous languages and cultures. Her publications include *Shyaan Am! Tuvan Folk Tales* and *Raven and the Rock: Oral Traditions and Spiritual Geography of Chukotka.*

Sabra Webber is an associate professor in the Department of Near Eastern Languages and Cultures and the Division of Comparative Studies in the Humanities at The Ohio State University. She received her Ph.D. in anthropology and folklore from the University of Texas at Austin and her M.A. from the University of California at Berkeley. From 1990 to 1995 she served as the first chair of the new Division of Comparative Studies. She is a specialist in folklore, ethnography, and the Arab world, especially Egypt and the Maghreb. Her most recent book, the prizewinning *Romancing the Real: Folklore and Ethnographic Representation in North Africa* (University of Pennsylvania Press, 1991), demonstrates the crucial role contemporary folklore theory plays in both historical and ethnographic studies, including studies in the third and postcolonial world. She has published articles on a range of issues, including canonicity, subaltern studies, and the position of women in the Middle East, and is the recipient of several research awards, including fellowships from Fulbright and from the Social Science Research Council.

Wendy Welch is conducting her Ph.D. studies in folklore at Memorial University of Newfoundland. With a background in journalism and a master's degree in storytelling, she writes a weekly newspaper column on stories and other folklore issues. Her publications include articles in *Now and Then, Storytelling World Journal, Digest,* and *Southern Folklore.* She is the author of an audiocassette entitled *Story Sampler* and is the founder of the Greene-Spring Storytelling Festival. The recipient of a travel grant to study uses of storytelling in tourism, Wendy divides her time between the United States and the United Kingdom, telling and listening to stories and ideas of how they are used in the heritage industry. She is the convener of the American Folklore Society's special interest section on storytelling.

Linda White has a Ph.D. in Basque studies with a specialization in language and literature. She is coauthor of a Basque-English/English-Basque dictionary, has translated five books about Basques, and is currently the assistant director of the Basque Studies Program at the University of Nevada at Reno. She speaks Basque, Spanish, French, Russian, and English.

Sabine Wienker-Piepho studied German and American studies and history with Lutz Röhrich at the University of Freiburg im Breisgau in the field of folk culture with a dissertation on female hero-patterns. After working for 10 years in the German Folksong Archives and teaching in universities both in Germany and in other countries, most recently in Minsk (Belarus), she has submitted her thesis on "Kulturgeschichte der Intellektuellenfeindlichkeit in Deutschland" to the University of Göttingen. Her primary area of interest is storytelling research, and she is also the chief editor of the magazine *Märchenspiegel.* She lives in Freiburg.

Margaret Yocom received a Ph.D. in English from the University of Massachusetts at Amherst in 1980. She is a specialist in family folklore, oral narrative, material culture, and gender studies. She is an associate professor at George Mason University in Fairfax, Virginia. She has conducted fieldwork in her home Pennsylvania German culture, with the Inuit of northwestern Alaska, and in several northern Virginia communities. Her major field site is a north Appalachian mountain community in Maine where she also serves as folklorist to the Rangeley Lakes Region Logging Museum. She has published articles with accompanying photographs on ethnographic fieldwork, regional study, ethnopoetics, family folklore, gender, and material culture. Her most recent work includes "'Awful Real': Dolls and Development in Rangeley Maine" (1993), "The Yellow Ribboning of the USA: Contested Meanings in the Construction of a Political Symbol" (1996), and an article on storytelling and wood carving in *Northeast Folklore.* She is the assistant editor of *Ugiuvangmiut Quiliapyuit: King Island Tales* (1988), and in 1994 she edited, produced, and wrote most of the text of *Logging in the Maine Woods: The Paintings of Alden Grant.* She is writing a book on the traditional arts of the Richards of Rangeley, Maine, entitled *Generations in Wood.* A storyteller herself, she has served on the board of the Washington Storytellers Theater.

Index

Index

Abarry, Abu Shardow 589
  Ga folktales 18–24
Abdellah, Moulay 341–343
Abdoullov, Ibryam 197, 200
Aboriginal Australia
  Dreamtime stories 155–159
Abraham
  storytelling in Palestine 344
Abrahams, Roger 522, 523
abu-aha
  Igbo folk epics 26
Abu-Lughod, Lila 342–343
a Búrc, Éamon
  modern Irish storytelling 266–
    267
Achebe, Chinua
  Beninese storytelling 10
  Igbo storytelling 35, 36
adivasi
  middle India performances 106,
    108
Africa
  Beninese storytelling 9–12
  Central African epics 6–8
  Dogon creation stories 48–53
  Egyptian peep-show
    storytelling 325
  French storytelling 229
  Fulani epics 13–17
  Ga folktales 18–24
  hunters' narratives 3–5
  Igbo storytelling 25–32, 33–40,
    41–47
  Igede storytelling 54–58
  Ju/'hoan folktales 59–64
  Kamba storytelling 65–67
  Kenyan storytelling 68–70
  Mandenkan storytelling 71–81
  matrilineal myths in Tuareg
    culture 348–355
  Moroccan storytelling 341–343
  Tunisian storytelling 356–361
Ainu (people)
  traditional Japanese folktelling
    119
akam
  Savitri performances 95

Aktzini
  Totonac storytelling 504–506
ákúkó
  Igbo storytelling 33
ákúkó-àlà
  Igbo storytelling 33–36
ákúkó-ifo
  Igbo storytelling 33, 36–38
Álá (goddess)
  Igbo storytelling 33
álá (story genre)
  Igbo storytelling 34
Albania
  Arvanítika 247–251
  folk teller's stories 181–184
aldeas 230
Alembi, Ezekiel B. 589
  Kenyan storytelling 68–70
Algarve (Portugal) 281–284
"Alligators in the Sewers" 574
aloha 'āi-na
  Hawaiian storytelling 164
ambulance
  paramedic stories 428–433
Ameke Okoye
  Igbo folk epics 28–30, 31
American Folklore (Dorson) 572
American Folklore Society 389
Amma
  Dogon cosmology 49–52
Amoogu
  Igbo folk epics 27
Amur (Russia) 286
Anambra
  Igbo folk epics 30, 34
Ananu the Spider
  Ga folktales 20, 21
Anasi the Spider
  Maroon folktales 523
ancestor. *See also* genealogy
  Colombia storytelling 513–521
  Maori storytelling 173, 174
  Mayan storytelling 471–473
ancestor tales
  Hungarian storytelling 257–
    258
  Igbo storytelling 34, 36

Igede storytelling events 57
Rajasthani hero legends 92
Russian storytelling by women
  286
anciano
  Mexican storytelling 499–501
Anderson, Richard W. 589
  Japanese religious tales 114–
    118
Anderson, Walter 207
Andes Mountains
  Colombian spirit stories 513–
    521
  Otavalo song 486, 488
anecdote 530
Anggun Nan Tungga 134
animal tales
  Bulgarian folktales 190–191
  Chilean folktales 475
  Colombian spirit stories 519
  Igbo storytelling 37, 43–44
  Latvian storytelling 274
  Russian storytelling by women
    286
*Annals and Antiquities of
  Rajasthan*
  hero legends 92
Anthills of the Savannah
  Igbo storytelling 40
anti-environment 555
anti-fairy tale 254–255
"Antonio Mocho" (Maigua) 487
Apollo program 545
apostrophic refrains 42–43
Appalachian Mountains
  fairy tales 387
  Jack Tales 395–396
Appleseed, Johnny 550
apprenticeship
  Indonesian storytelling 113
  Iranian epic storytelling 333
  Maori storytelling 174–175
  Venezuelan storytelling 529
Arabic language
  Tunisian storytelling 357
"Arber's Great Year"
  Albanian folktales 182

Archives of Folk Culture (U.S. Library of Congress)
Jack Tales 396
Argentina
folktales 459–464
Guaranitic storytelling 490–493
"Ark of the World." *See* "Boat of the World"
Aro (people) 26
Arvanítika
Greek-Albanian storytelling 247–251
Asia
Hmong antiphonal epics 88–90
Indian storytelling 91–93, 94–97, 98–101, 102–105, 106–109
Indonesian storytelling 110–113
Japanese religious storytelling 114–118
Korean storytelling 122–129
Malaysian tales 130–133, 138–141
Suzhou chantefable tradition 85–87
Thai storytelling 142–143, 144–152
traditional Japanese folktales 119–121
West Sumatran storytelling 134–137
Atanassov, Dimo
Bulgarian folktales 199, 200
aucas
Colombian spirit stories 515
audience, *or* listeners
Africa
Fulani epics 17
Ga folktales 20, 23
Igbo storytelling events 38–39
Igede storytelling events 58
Kenyan Storytellers 69
Mandenkan storytelling 73–77
Asia
Chinese chantefable tradition 86
Indian storytelling 99, 108
Iranian epic storytelling 337
Japanese religious stories 115
Malaysian storytelling traditions 139

p'ansori 122
Savitri performance 95–96
West Sumatran storytelling 137
Europe
Albanian folktales 183
formulation of narrative 218–220
French storytelling 227, 228
German storytelling 235
Scottish storytelling 293, 295, 298–299, 305
Hawaiian storytelling 164–165
Native America
Hupa storytelling 378
Téwa storytelling 382
North America
children's ghost stories 539, 543
French Newfoundland storytelling 450–451
function of storytelling 410, 412–413, 414
listening experiences 563–571
Maine family stories 425–426
Swiss Volhynian storytelling 439–440
South America
Argentinean folktales 459, 460
Bahamian narration 466
Belizean storytelling 467, 471
Mexican storytelling 501
Venezuelan storytelling 531
Australia
Dreamtime stories 155–159
Australian Aborigine
Dreamtime stories 155–159
Awang Selampit, *or* Tok Selampit
Malaysian storytelling traditions 140
Aztec (people) 505–506
Azuonye, Chukwuma 589
Dogon creation stories 48–53
Igbo storytelling 33–40, 41–47

Babalawo or Bokonon
Beninese storytelling 10
"Babysitter, The" 560–561
Bahama Islands, the 465–466
bakaba 111
Baldwin, James 11
ballad

Chinese chantefable tradition 86
Igbo storytelling devices 43
Ozark tales 391
Bangkok Thai
Thai storytelling 148
bankekumo
Mandenkan storytelling 74
BaNyanga (people)
Central African epics 6
Baptista, Dona Salvina 282–283
Barandiarán Irizar, Luis de 186
Barandiarán, José Miguel de 186
Barlow, Genevieve 444
Barrett-Aranui, Hinekahukura 589–590
Maori storytelling 171–175
basajauna
Basque storytelling 187
bas git
middle Indian narrative performance 108
Bási Kodjó
Maroon folktales 524–526
basket weaving
Portuguese storytelling 281
Basque (people) 185–189
battle songs
Igbo folk epics 26
Bayhaqî
Iranian epic storytelling 330
Bean, Martha S. 590
storytelling in the ESL classroom 548–551
bebom-mvett
Central African epics 6–8
Beck, Ervin 590
Belizean Creole storytelling 467–470
Becker, A.L. 378
Bedouin
Tunisian storytelling 356–361
Beh N!a'an
Ju/'hoan storytelling 60
Belcher, Stephen 590
Central African epics 6–8
hunters' narratives 3–5
Belize
Creole storytelling 467–470
Mayan storytelling 471–474
Belye, *or* Fudin 286
Ben-Amos, Dan 277
Bender, Mark 590
Chinese chantefable tradition 85–87
Hmong antiphonal epics 88–90

Benin 9–12, 34

Beninese (people) 10–12

Bennett, Marjorie 590
    Idaho ranching stories 403–407

Bennett, Ruth Seiman 590
    Hupa storytelling 371–380

bertsolaritza 186, 188

Betz, Felicitas 582

Bhakti 186
    Savitri performances 95

bhomiya
    Rajasthani legends 92

bhopa
    Rajasthani legends 92–93

binyea tempoka
    Colombian spirit stories 515

Biesele, Megan 590
    Ju/'hoan folktales 59–64

Binu 52

Bir Al-Waraqa 344

Bird, Charles 4

"Biscuit Bullet, The" 574

Blache, Martha 590
    Guaranitic storytelling 490–
    493

Black Folktales (Lester)
    power of folktales 11

"Blind Girls"(Phillips) 574

"Bloody Fingers" 542

Boas, Franz 377

"Boat of the World," *or* "Ark of
    the World"
    Dogon creation story 50

Bogdanka, *or* Galenka 195

Bokonon, or Babalawo 10

bomoh 139

book
    Indian storytelling 103
    Venezuelan storytelling 531

Borneo 138

Borneo Literature Bureau 139

borrachero
    Colombian spirit remedies 520

Botswana 59

Bowlin, John R.
    Tunisian storytelling 360

"Boyfriend's Death, The" 561

"Boy Who Cried Wolf, The" 549

Braid, Donald 590–591
    Scottish Travellers' stories 301–
    309

"Brain Drain, The" 574

Brazil 490–493

Brer Rabbit 534

Bridge of Arta, The 254

Brother Blue 553

Brothers Grimm
    translation and storytelling 317,
    320
    women's storytelling 581

Brunold-Bigler, Ursula 318

Brunvand, Jan Harold 591
    urban legends 572–576

Bubu Ardo Galo
    Fulani storytelling 15

Buddhism
    Japanese storytelling 114–118
    Thai storytelling 142

"Bueb mit dem isige
    Spazierstecke, Der"
    translation and storytelling 319

Buena Vista (Mexico) 498

Bulgaria 190–202

bu mai
    Miao antiphonal epics 88–90

Bunday 465

"Bun Phawet." *See* "Thet
    Mahachaart"

Bunyan, Paul 549

Burkina Faso 48

business
    organizational storytelling
    544–547

Butterfly Mother
    Miao creation tales 89–90

cachero 530

cacho 530

call-and-response
    Belizean Creole storytelling 468

Camara, Seydou 4

Camara, Sory 591
    hunter's narratives 4
    Mandenkan storytelling 71–81

Cameroon 6–8

Campbell-McLeod, Pauline E.
    591
    Dreamtime stories 155–159

Canaan, Taufik 345

Canada
    Cree storytelling 365–368
    storytelling in French
    Newfoundland 448–452

Candaini
    Indian storytelling 107–108

Canek, King
    Mayan stories 472

Cannon, Hal 400

cantrik
    Indonesian storytelling 113

Cao Cao
    p'ansori 125

Caracas (Venezuela) 529, 531,
    532

Cardenas, Cuauhtemoc 500

Cardigos, Isabel 591
    Portuguese storytelling 281–284

Caribbean 465–466

carnival 520

Carpenter, Inta Gale 591
    Latvian storytelling 273–280

Carrière, Joseph 388–390

catch-tales
    Igbo storytelling 38

cattle breeders 15

"Cattle Raid of Cooley." *See*
    "Táin Bó Cuailnge"

cautionary tales
    function of storytelling 413
    Malaysian stories 130–133
    Mayan storytelling 472
    preadolescent girls' storytelling
    560
    storytelling in the ESL
    classroom 549

ceh
    Sumatran storytelling 111

Central Am
    Creole storytelling
    Mayan storytelling 471–474

Central Thai language 146

Certeau, Michel de 501

chain saw
    Maine logging stories 419–420

chajinmori 127

changdan 126

ch'anggŭk 123

chant
    Albanian folktales 182
    Igbo folk epics 31
    Polynesian tale telling 177

chantefables
    Chinese traditions 85–87
    Igbo storytelling 38

Chaporral 507

Chase, Richard 395–396

che 17

Chetak
    Rajasthani hero legends 91–92

Chhattisgarh (India) 106

Chiappas (Mexico) 494

"Chicken Little"
    Cree storytelling 367

Chiggerfoot, *or* Jiggerfoot
    Maroon folktales 523, 523

Child, Francis James 390, 391
children
  Beninese storytelling 9
  Brothers Grimm 317
  Bulgarian folktales 190, 191,
    198
  Egyptian peep-show
    storytelling 325
  ghost stories 539–543
  Indian storytelling 99, 101
  Javanese storytelling 110–113
  matrilineal myths in Niger 350–
    352
  Mexican storytelling 446
  Polynesian tale telling 178
  preadolescent girls' storytelling
    559–562
  Russian storytelling by women
    288
  Scottish storytelling 291
  Semai cautionary tales 130–133
  Thai storytelling project 149–
    152
  Venezuelan storytelling 529
  women's storytelling 582
"Children with a Star on their
    Foreheads, The"
  Portuguese storytelling 283
Chile
  folktale performance and
    function 475–477
  Lira Popular 478–485
China
  chantefable tradition 85–87
  Maio antiphonal epics 88–90
"China Doll, The," or "The
    Purple Doll" 561
chinyang 127
chiste
  Venezuelan storytelling 530
Chittenden, Lawrence 400
cho 127
"Choking Doberman, The" 575
chorus
  Igbo storytelling 41–47
  Igede storytelling events 58
  Malaysian storytelling 139
  Mandenkan storytelling 72
Christianity 344–347
Chukotka 287
Ch'unhyang 123
chungjungmori 127
chungmori 127
Cinderella
  ESL stories 549

Mexican storytelling 445
city
  cross-cultural storytelling 577–
    579
  Lira Popular in Chile 479–484
  urban legends 572
click language. *See* Khoisan
    language
Clifford, Hugh 140
coding
  Savitri performance 96
  Swiss Volhynian storytelling
    438–440
  switching in Arvanítika stories
    247–251
Coeur d'Alene (people) 369–370
coffeehouse
  Iranian epic storytelling 331–
    332
Collins, Eldon 425–426
Colombia 513–521
colonialism 10
comic tales
  German storytelling 235
  Greek Gypsy narrative 254
  Idaho ranching stories 406
  Igbo storytelling 35–36
  Slovakian storytelling 313
  Venezuelan storytelling 530
Committee to Defend Communal
    Land (Mexico) 500
community
  cross-cultural storytelling 578
  function of storytelling 408–
    409, 410–413
  Gemeinde in Mennonite stories
    434–441
  Greek Gypsy narrative 252
  Mexican storytelling 498–501
  paramedic stories 432
  storytelling revival 556, 558
  Totonac Indian stories 503
  translation and storytelling 318
  Travellers' stories 302–305
  Venezuela 528, 529–530
complementary refrains 46
conduit theory 261–262
Conejo y el Coyote, El
  Mexican storytelling 445
Confucianism
  ancient Korean storytelling 123
contemporary legends. *See* urban
    legends
contes des fées 581
contes merveilleux 581

conversation
  Arvanítika 248–249
  functions of storytelling 408
  Igede storytelling events 57
  Mandenkan storytelling 72–73
Conversations with Ogotemmeli
    (Gridaule)
  Dogon creation story 51
corn
  Totonac storytelling 510
corrido
  Cowboy poetry 399
  Mexican storytelling 444
Cortés, Hernán
  Mexican storytelling 446, 504,
    506, 508–509
cosmology
  Colombian spirit stories 515–
    517
  Dogon stories 48–53
  Igbo themes 34, 38
  Iranian epic storytelling 326
  matrilineal myths in Niger 348
costume 69
Côte d'Ivoire 3
cotton
  Colombian spirit stories 517
Coulthard, Ron 574
Cowboy poetry 398–402
  logger poetry 453, 455
Cowboy Poetry Gathering (Elko,
    Nevada) 400
*Cowboy Songs and Other
    Frontier Ballads* (Lomax)
    400, 401
"Cowboy's Prayer, A" (Clark) 401
Cox, Harvey 555, 556
Coyote
  Coeur d'Alene stories 369
  Hupa storytelling 372, 374–375
  Mexican storytelling 445
crack 302
creation tales. *See also* cosmology
  Dogon stories 48–53
  Igbo cosmology 34
  Mexican storytelling 445
  Miao antiphonal epics 88–90
Cree (people) 365–368
Creole (people) 467–470
Croatia 203–206
Crow 384
Crowley, Daniel J. 591–592
  Bahamian narrative 465–466
Cú Chulainn, *or* Hound of
    Culainn

modern Irish storytelling 264
cuckoo
    Albanian folktales 182
cuento saca cuento 533
cultural revitalization
    Hawaiian language 165
    story revival 557
Custódio, Idália 281

daari
    Fulani epics 15
Dainihonkoku Hokekyôkenki
    Japanese religious tales 115
dalang
    Indonesian storytelling 110
Dalmatia (Croatia) 203–205
Dama 52–53
D'Amico, Linda 593
    Otavalo song 486–489
Danandjaja, James 593
    Indonesian storytelling 110–
        113
dance
    Belizean Creole storytelling 469
    Téwa storytelling 381–382
    Totonac storytelling 507–508
"Dance among Thorns, The"
    Jack Tales 394
Dannemann, Manuel 593
    Chilean folktales 475–477
dating
    preadolescent girls' storytelling
        561
Davis, Donald 397
death. *See also* mourning
    Dogon rituals 52–53
Dechepare, Bernat 185
decir cuentos
    art of Mexican storytelling 444
declamation
    Fulani epics 14
Decolonizing the Mind (Ngugi)
    Beninese storytelling 10
dege
    Dogon cosmology 51, 52
Dégh, Linda 593
    conduit theory of storytelling
        261–262
    women's storytelling 580–586
Déirdre and the Sons of Uisneach
    modern Irish storytelling 264
Delaney, James G.
    modern Irish storytelling 269
del Real y Medio, El 476
Democratic Coordinator 500

dendang Pauah
    West Sumatran storytelling
        135–137
Dentan, Robert Knox 593
    Malaysian stories 130–133
desgarrada
    Portuguese storytelling 281
Desjarlais, Robert 342
De todos para todos
    Tzotzil-Tzeltal storytelling 497
devil
    Argentinean storytelling 459,
        462–463
    Estonian legends 208–209
    Mexican storytelling 444
Devil's Pretty Daughter, The
    (Randolph) 389
dialogue
    Chinese chantefable tradition
        86
didactic stories. *See* teaching tales
didong
    Sumatran storytelling 111
Diego, Juan 445
Dieterlen, Germaine 51
díkē
    Igbo storytelling 35
dikir rebana
    Malaysian storytelling 141
Dimitrova, Maria Stancheva
    Bulgarian folktales 200
divided earth
    Mandenkan storytelling 78
Di//xao
    Ju/'hoan storytelling variations
        61
Doddridge, Charles 395
Dogon (people) 48–53
doll 561
Domino's Pizza 546
Don Tomate y sus Coyotes
    Tzotzil-Tzeltal storytelling 497
Dorrance, Ward 388, 389
Dorson, Richard M. 572
doum
    storytelling in Palestine 346
Dreaming, the
    Aboriginal Australia
        storytelling 156–159
"Dreamtime, the"
    Aboriginal Australia
        storytelling 155–159
Dryanovets (Bulgaria) 190
Duala (people)
    Central African epics 6

Dusuns
    Malaysian storytelling
        traditions 139
Dyougou Serou
    Dogon creation story 49

eagle
    Totonac storytelling 504
Eastern School. *See Tongp'yonche*
East Java 112
echo, *or* parrot refrain
    Igbo storytelling devices 44–45
Ecuador
    Otavalo song 486–489
Edinburgh University 289
education. *See also* didactic tale;
        moral tale; teaching tale
    fairy tale preservation in
        Germany 241
    Portuguese storytelling 283
    Saneguruji Storytelling
        Academy 98–101
    Scottish travelers' stories 290
    storytelling in the ESL
        classroom 548–551
Egbele
    Igbo folk epics 27
Egypt 325
ejempla
    Mexican storytelling 444
ejido
    politics of storytelling 498
Ekoi (people) 26
elder
    Latvian storytelling 273
    Maori tradition 174–175
    Mexican storytelling 499–501
    Polynesian storytelling 177
elegy
    Basque storytelling 186
    Igbo storytelling devices 46
Elibe Aja
    Igbo folk epics 27
Elijah, *or* Mar Elias
    storytelling in Palestine 344
emaki
    Japanese religious tales 115
embroidery
    Slovakian storytelling 313
embuste 530
embustero 530
emergencies
    paramedic stories 428–433
emergency medical technician, *or*
        EMT 428–433

"Encounter with a Horrible Monster, The" 542
engi
  Japanese religious tales 115
Englert-Faye, Curt 319, 320
English as a Second Language, *or* ESL
  storytelling as teaching tool 548–551
"Eochair mac Rí in Éirinn," or "Eochair, a King's Son in Ireland"
  modern Irish storytelling 267
epic
  African hunters' narratives 4
  Basque storytelling 185–186
  Central Africa 6–8
  Fulani storytelling 13–17
  Igbo folktales 25–32
  Iranian epics 326–340
  Malaysian storytelling traditions 139, 140–141
  Rajasthani legends 93
erisiak
  Basque storytelling 186
erotic tales
  Bulgarian folktales 195
ESL. *See* English as a Second Language
Estonia 207–211
ethnography
  French storytelling 227
  Moroccan storytelling 342
Europe
  Albanian folk teller's stories 181–184
  Basque storytelling 185–189
  Croatian storytelling 203–206
  Estonian legends 207–211
  formulation of narrative 212–226
  French storytelling 227–229
  Galician storytelling 230–233
  Germany 234–238, 239–246
  Greek-Albanian storytelling 247–251
  Gypsy narratives 252–256
  Latvian storytelling 273–280
  modern Irish storytelling 264–272
  northeastern Bulgaria 190–202
  Portuguese storytelling 281–284
  Russian stories told by women 285–288

Scottish storytelling 289–300, 301–309
  Slovakian storytelling 310–315
  Swiss storytelling 316–321
  urban legends 575
Euskal Herria
  Basque storytelling 185
Euskara
  Basque storytelling 185

fairy tales. *See also* magic tales; märchen
  Bulgarian folktales 191–192, 198
  children's ghost stories 539
  German storytelling 236, 242–246
  Scottish storytelling 297
  Swiss storytelling 316–321
family
  Bulgarian folktales 198
  Igede storytelling events 54–58
  Japanese religious storytelling 117
  Maharashtran storytelling 100–101
  Maine woods 416–427
  matrilineal myths in Niger 348–354
  Mexican storytelling 444
  Polynesian storytelling 178
  Rajasthani hero legends 92
  Scottish storytelling 296
  Semai cautionary tales 130–133
  storytelling in middle-class India 102–105
  Swiss Volhynian storytelling 439–440
Fang (people) 6–7
Fara Makan
  hunters' narratives 4
fasting
  Indian storytelling 103
fattening
  Creole storytelling 467–470
Favorite Folktales from around the World (Yolen)
  power of folktales 11
fear
  Semai cautionary tales 130–133
Feast of Fools, The (Cox) 555, 556
Febrero Loco
  Tzotzil-Tzeltal storytelling 496
Fenian Lays
  modern Irish storytelling 265

Fianna
  modern Irish storytelling 264–265
Finland 212, 215
Finnish School
  Estonian legends 207
Finn Tales
  modern Irish storytelling 266
Fionn MacCumhaill
  modern Irish storytelling 265
fire
  Colombian spirit stories 518
  Totonac stories 509
fishing tales
  Fulani epics 15
  Igbo folk epics 30–31
  Polynesian tale telling 177
Flueckiger, Joyce Burkhalter 592–593
  Middle Indian narrative performance 106–109
flying fox 158–159
FOAF. *See* friend of a friend
focus formula 28
folklor 231
folk medicine 520
folk music 554
folk song 235
folktales
  Albania 181–184
  Basque storytelling 187
  Beninese 10–12
  Bulgaria 190–202
  Ga 18–24
  Germany 235
  Greek Gypsy narrative 252, 254–255
  Igbo storytelling 37
  Igede 56
  Ju/'hoan 59–64
  Kamba 66
  Mexican 445
  Palestine 344
  Polynesia 178
folletines
  Lira Popular in Chile 479
fools
  Bulgarian folktales 195
Foragers, Tricksters, and Trancers (Guenther)
  Ju/'hoan storytelling 61
forestry 416–427, 453–456
formula
  Bahamian narration 466
  Basque storytelling 186

Belizean Creole storytelling 469
Bulgarian folktales 193
children's ghost stories 539, 543
Chilean folktales 475–476,
    482, 484
French Newfoundland stories
    450
Hupa storytelling 375–379
Igbo storytelling devices 27–28,
    43
Iranian epic storytelling 336
Ozark folklore 389
Scottish storytelling 291
Venezuelan storytelling 533
Fortaleza de la Mujer Maya, La
    Tzotzil-Tzeltal storytelling 497
Fortis, Alberto 204
Forty Brothers and the Bridge,
    The
    Greek Gypsy narrative 254
Fowke, Edith 454
fox 190–191
Fox and the Crow, The
    Travellers' stories 305–308
France
    Basque storytelling 185–189
    new storytelling 227–230
    women's storytelling 581
Franco, Franciso
    cultural repression 230
"Frau Holle"
    translation and storytelling
    317–318
Freeman, Barbara 553
Frey, Rodney 593
    Couer d'Alene tales 369–370
friend of a friend (FOAF)
    urban legends 572–576
Fry, Art 545
Fudin. *See* Belye
Fulani (people) 13–17
Fulbe (people) 13–17
Fulfulde, *or* Pulaar
    Fulani epics 13
funny tales. *See* comic tales
furusato
    Japanese folktelling 120
Futuwwat Nâma-yi Sultânî 335
Fuulu Faala Fukho, *or* Plateau of
    the Narrative
    Contemplation
    Mandenkan storytelling 75–76

Ga (people) 18–24
Gaelic language 291–292, 293

Gaj Ljudevit
    Croatian storytelling 204
Galenka. *See* Bogdanka
Galicia (Spain) 231–233
Gan-aboot folk. *See* Traveller
Gandhi, Mahatma 99
Ganeva, Yana Gancheva 200
Gayo (people) 111
Gelajo, Samba 14
Gemeinde
    Mennonite stories 434–441
gender
    Chhattisgarhi narrative
        performance 109
    far eastern Russia stories 285–
        288
    Hungarian folktales 257–264
    matrilineal myths in Niger 348–
        355
    storytelling in Palestine 344–
        347
    women's storytelling 580–586
"Gender and Sexuality"
    (Lövkrona) 262
genealogy
    Hungarian storytelling 257–
        258
    matrilineal myths in Niger 348–
        354
    Scottish storytelling 296, 297
Gentry, Jane 395, 396
German language
    Swiss Volhynian storytelling
        436–438
    translation and storytelling 319
German-Swiss fairy tale
    translation and storytelling 317,
        319
Germany
    fairy tale preservation in
        Germany 239–246
    storytelling in the northeast
        234–238
    women's storytelling 582
Gesellschaft zur Pflege de
        Märchengutes der
        europäischen Volker, *or*
        Society for Taking Care of
        Fairy Tale Materials of
        European Peoples 241
Ghazzâlî, -al 334
ghost
    Argentinean storytelling 461
    children's stories 539–543
    Galician storytelling 231

modern Irish storytelling 269–
    270
"Ghost of the White Eye, The"
    541
Gidbole, Anile 98
gid so
    Dogon creation story 51
Giltzu, Dominica 187
Giraffe Medicine Dance
    Ju/'hoan storytelling 60
girl
    preadolescent storytelling 559–
        562
"Girl as Helper in the Hero's
    Flight"
    French Newfoundland stories
        449, 451
Glasgow (Scotland) 298
goaa heihei noo
    Polynesian storytelling 178
goana
    Aboriginal Australia
        storytelling 157–158
Gobrecht, Barbara 593
    Swiss storytelling 316–321
Goering, Ozzie
    Swiss Volhynian storytelling
        436
"Golden Arm, The" 560
"Golden, Children, The" 283
Gondoriah
    West Sumatran storytelling 134
Goosebumps 541
Görög-Karady, Veronika 593
    French storytelling 227–230
gôsân
    Iranian epic storytelling 327–
        328
"Granary of the Master of Pure
    Earth"
    Dogon creation story 51
Grandad Radko 196
grandmother
    Basque storytelling 186
    storytelling in India 100–101,
        104–105
Great Britain 572
Great Flood, the
    Totonac storytelling 504, 508
Great Spirit, the
    Aboriginal Australian
        storytelling 158–159
Great Tradition
    Malaysian storytelling
        traditions 138–139

Greece
  Arvanítika 247–251
  Gypsy narratives 252–256
Gridaule, Marcel 51
Grider, Sylvia 593
  children's ghost stories 539–543
grief. *See* mourning
Grimm Brothers. *See* Brothers
    Grimm
griot
  Fulani epics 13
  Mandenkan storytelling 79
Guaraní (people) 490–493
Guayúus (people) 529, 530, 533
Guimba the Tyrant 4
Guizhou (China) 88–90
Gunther, Mathias 61
Gutierrez, Paige 397
Gypsy
  Greek narrative tradition 252–
    256
  Travellers' stories 301–302
Gypsy and the Giant
  Greek Gypsy narrative 255

Haidouk Rada
  Bulgarian folktales 194
ha'i 'ōlelo
  Hawaiian storytelling 160–170
hālau 165
hālau hūla
  Hawaiian storytelling 164
"Half Chick." *See* "Maski Parch"
Halloween
  childrens' ghost stories 540
Ham-Bodejo
  Fulani epics 15
"Hamster Tale, The" 66–67
Hanauer, J.E. 345
"Hansel and Gretel" 560
hapa-haole
  Hawaiian storytelling 165
Hare 508
Hârith, Nadr Ibn 328–329
Harlan, Lindsey 593
  Rajasthani hero legends 91–93
Haue with You to Saffron-Waldon
  394
Hawaii
  language revival through stories
    160–170
Hawaiian creole
  Hawaiian storytelling 165
Hawaiian cultural renaissance
  165

Hawaiian language. *See kā 'olelo
    Hawai'i*
Hawai'i Children's Opera Chorus
  Hawaiian storytelling 167
healing. *See also* herbal healing;
    medicine woman; shaman
  matrilineal myths in Niger 348–
    354
hearth
  Igede storytelling 57
"Heel in the Grate, The" 575
Heikki
  formulation of narrative 214–
    216, 217, 219, 222
heke
  Maori storytelling 173
hela
  Hawaiian storytelling 161
Helali, Abo Zeed El 325
Helena, Queen 344
Helt, Spiv 408–414
Henderson, Hamish 289, 302
herbal healing
  matrilineal myths in Niger 348–
    354
hero, *or* heroine
  Albanian folktales 181
  Bulgarian folktales 192, 193
  Central African epics 7
  French Newfoundland
    storytelling 449, 451
  Fulani epics 14–17
  Igbo storytelling 25–31, 34–39,
    46, 47
  Iranian epic storytelling 327
  modern Irish storytelling 265
  organizational storytelling 545
  Rajasthani legends 91–93
  Russian stories 286
  women's storytelling 583
Hicks, Ray 397
hidden treasure
  Guaranitic storytelling 492
highwaymen
  Bulgarian folktales 194
hijiri
  Japanese religious tales 115
hikayat
  Malaysian storytelling traditions
    138
  Tunisian storytelling 357
Hikayat Seri Rama
  Malaysian storytelling 141
Hilbert, Vi (taqʷšəblu)
  Lushootseed stories 383–84

Hindi
  Middle Indian performances
    106–109
Hinduism
  non-religious storytelling in
    India 99
Hindutva
  non–religious storytelling in
    India 99
Hokkaido Island 119
Holo Mai Pele
  Hawaiian storytelling 165, 167
Homeric epic
  Igbo folk epics 27
"Hook, The" 561
  urban legends 573–574
"Hooked" (Coulthard) 574
horror stories
  preadolescent girls' storytelling
    559–562
  urban legends 573–575
Hound of Culainn. *See* Cú
    Chulainn,
Hua Mulan
  Chinese chantefable tradition 86
hua 'ōlelo
  Hawaiian storytelling 161
hula
  Hawaiian storytelling 161, 164,
    165, 166–167
humorous tales. *See* comic tales
Hūngbu
  p'ansori 124
hunters' narratives 3–5
hunting
  African storytelling 3–5
  Maine stories 421–423
  Russian storytelling by women
    287
  Saramaka tales 524–526
Hupa (people) 371–380
Hussein, Kamal El dien 593
  Egyptian peep-show
    storytelling 325
hwimori
  p'ansori 127
Hyena 21

Ibibio (people) 26
IBM 544
Ibn al-Muqaffa
  Iranian epic storytelling 330
icherifan
  matrilineal myths in Niger 349–
    352

Idaho 403–407
identity
    Albanian folktales 184
    Latvian storytelling 273
    listening experiences 569
    Maroon folktales 526
    matrilineal myths in Niger 350–352
    middle-class storytelling in India 102
    Moroccan storytelling 342
    organizational storytelling 544–547
    performances in Chhattisgarh 106, 107
    storytelling in Palestine 345
    storytelling revival 558
    Swiss Volhynian storytelling 434–440
    Totonac storytelling 508
    translation and storytelling 317
    Travellers' stories 302, 305–307
ideophones
    Igbo storytelling 39–40, 45–46
Ìdúù
    Igbo storytelling 34, 38
Ifa
    Beninese storytelling 10
ífò
    Igbo storytelling 36
Igbo (people)
    folk epics 25–32
    meaningless refrains 41–47
    stories and storytelling 33–40
Igede
    storytelling event 54–58
iji
    Igbo folk epics 30
íkpa úbùbò
    Igbo storytelling 36
ikperikpe ogu
    Igbo folk epics 26
Ilio'ulaokalani
    Hawaiian storytelling 168
ílú
    Igbo storytelling 33
"Ilumán Tío" (Maigua) 487–488
immigrant
    Swiss Volhynian storytelling 438
India
    Malaysian storytelling traditions 141
    middle-class families 102–105
    narrative performances 106–109

Rajasthani hero legends 91–93
Saneguruji storytelling Academy 98–101
Savitri performances 94–97
Indonesia 110–113, 134–137
infertility 350–352
Ingano (people) 514
interjections
    Igbo storytelling devices 43–45
International Society for Contemporary Legend Research, *or* (ISCLR) 573
International Society for Folk Narrative Research, *or* ISFNR
    fairy tale preservation in Germany 242
Introductory Rule
    Hupa storytelling 372–373
Iran 326–340
Ireland
    Jack Tales 395
    modern storytelling 264–272
iri-aha
    Igbo folk epic 25
Irish Folklore Commission 267
Irish language 265
irony
    urban legends 572
Isan (people) 142–143
Isan (Thailand) 144
ISCLR. *See* International Society for Contemporary Legend Research
ISFNR. *See* International Society for Folk Narrative Research
Islam
    Iranian epic storytelling 328, 330
    Malaysian storytelling traditions 141
    matrilineal myths in Niger 349, 350, 352, 353
    storytelling in Palestine 344–347
    women's storytelling 582
Island Talk Story Festival (Hawaii) 168
Istria (Croatia) 205
ita
    Igbo storytelling 25, 36
Ito Takeyo
    Japanese folktelling 120
itu-afa
    Igbo folk epics 26
"Itumbi ya Nyaa"

Kamba storytelling 65
Iyas
    Cree storytelling 367, 368

Jacanamijoy, Justo 514
"Jack and His Stepdame" 394
Jackson, Kenneth 267
Jack Tales 394–397
    Newfoundland stories 449
Jacobs, Sue-Ellen 593–594
    San Juan storytelling 381–382
Jagif, Vatroslav 205
Jaguar
    Maroon folktales 523
jaiechi
    art of Venezuelan storytelling 529, 533
Jang Vang 90
Japan
    religious tales and storytelling 114–118
    traditional folktelling 119–121
Jason, Heda
    Portuguese storytelling 282
jataka
    Thai storytelling 142
Java
    children and storytelling 110
Jeerige Yelen 77
Jeki
    Central African epics 6
jemblung. *See* kentrung
Jentila
    Basque storytelling 187
Jhumjharji
    Rajasthani legends 92
Jiggerfoot. *See* Chiggerfoot
Jiija, *or* shadow
    Mandenkan storytelling 77
Jimbe, Bala 4
jokes
    Belizean Creole storytelling 468
    Bulgarian folktales 196
    German storytelling 236
    Hungarian storytelling 262
    Mayan storytelling 473
    urban legends 572
    Venezuelan storytelling 530
    women's storytelling 583
Joko Tingkir
    Indonesian storytelling 112
Jones, Pamela 446
Jonesborough (Tennessee)
    storytelling revival 552, 554, 557

Juajibioy, Bautista 513
Judaism
    French storytelling 229
    storytelling in Palestine 344–347
Ju'/hoan (people) 59–64
Jura (Switzerland) 317

kaba
    Indonesian storytelling 111, 134, 137
Kabuki theater
    Hawaiian language 167
Ka Ha'i 'Ana O Nā Mo'olelo Maoli
    Hawaiian storytelling 166
Kahalaopuna
    Hawaiian storytelling 167
Kahn, Walter 242
Kaho'olawe
    Hawaiian storytelling 165
Ka Huli'ana 165
Kaivola-Bregenhøj, Annikki 594
    Estonian legends 212–226
    Guaranitic storytelling 490
    Hungarian storytelling 260
kaka tempoka, or the raw time
    Colombian spirit stories 515
Kalahari Desert (Africa) 3
Kalaji Rathor
    Rajasthani legends 93
Kalevala
    memory and narration 212
Kaluaiko'olau
    Hawaiian storytelling 166
Kamba (people) 65–67
Kambili (Camara)
    hunters' narratives 4
Kamenovo (Bulgaria) 198
Kamsá (people) 513–514
Kanaana, Sharif 345–346
kanaka maoli
    Hawaiian storytelling
kanjin hijiri
    Japanese religious tales 115
Kansas
    Mennonite storytelling 434
ka 'ōlelo Hawai'i, or Hawaiian language
    Hawaiian storytelling 160–170
kaona
    Hawaiian storytelling 161–162
Kapantsi (people) 191, 194

Kapchan, Deborah A. 594
    Moroccan storytelling 341–343
Kariñas (people) 529
Kâshifî, Mullâ Husayn-i
    Iranian epic storytelling 335
kathani kuha
    Chhattisgarhi narrative performance 108
kaumatua
    Maori storytelling 173
Kayan (people) 139
Keaomelemele
    Hawaiian storytelling 168
Kearney, Michael 446
Kel Ewey Tuareg (people) 349
Kelkar, Gajanan 98
Kennedy, John F. 545
kentrung, or tempting, or rumpling, or kemplinq, or jemblung
    Indonesian storytelling 112
Kenya
    Kamba storytelling 65
    storytellers 69–71
Kenyah (people) 139
Kerins, Michael 298
Khadr, El- 344–345
Khoi-San, *or* Khoisan (people)
    hunters' narratives 3
    Ju'/hoan folktales 60
Khoisan, *or* click language
    Ju'/hoan storytelling 60
Khorenats'i, Moses 328
khurafat
    Tunisian storytelling 357–360
Kilianova, Gabriela 594
    Slovakian storytelling 310–315
King Country (New Zealand) 172, 173
Kintsch, Walter 213
kirtan
    Savitri performances 95
kirtankar
    Savtri performances 95–96
kisaeng
    p'ansori 128
Kitumba, Vincent Muli Wa 594
    Kamba storytelling 65–67
kiva
    storytelling in San Juan Pueblo 381
knavish tales 476
knitting
    Maine stories 423–425
    women's stories 581

Kojiki (Phillippi)
    Japanese religious tales 114
Konjaku monogatari
    Japanese religious tales 115
Konjobi Seerango. See Metallic Blackbird
Konole
    Ga folktales 21
Kopla zaharrak
    Basque storytelling 186
Korea 122–129
koroua
    Maori storytelling 174
"Kostandin and Doruntina"
    Albanian folktales 182
Kotseva, Yordanka 594
    northeastern Bulgaria stories 190–202
Koushkoundalevo (Bulgaria) 192
Krickeberg, Walter 509
Krivnya (Bulgaria) 192
kuaha 173
kuia 174
kuldevi 93
Kumulipo 162–163
kunju 86
kuti 123
kwangdaei 123, 128
Kwasímukámba 526
kyemmyŏnjo 127
Kysuce (Slovakia) 310–314

Lā'eikawai 167
Lā Ho'olilo 167
Lā Kukahekahe
    Hawaiian storytelling 167
lamina
    Basque storytelling 187
Lammel, Annamária 594
    Totonac storytelling 502–512
Lanser, Susan 96
Lao
    cultural preservation through storytelling 144–145
"Lasca" 400
Latvia 273–280
"Latvian Storyteller: The Repertoire of Jānis Pḷavnieks, A" 274, 279
Laughlin, Robert 594
    Tzotzil-Tzeltal storytelling 494–497
laziness
    Bulgarian folktales 195
    Greek Gypsy narrative 252

legend
    Albanian folktales 182, 184
    Basque storytelling 186
    Bulgarian folktales 193–194
    Cree storytelling 365
    Estonian legends 207–211
    Fulani epics 14–16
    Ga folktales 18
    German storytelling 236
    Greek Gypsy narrative 253–254
    Guaranitic storytelling 490
    Igbo storytelling 34
    Iranian epic storytelling 326
    Maori storytelling 171–175
    Mexican storytelling 444
    Palestinian storytelling 344
    Russian stories 286
    Swiss storytelling 316
    urban storytelling 572–576
Lester, Julius 11
"Levitation," *or* "Light as a
    Feather"
    preadolescent girls' storytelling
        559–562
librarian
    storytelling revival 556
    women's storytelling 582
Lieber, Michael 595
    Polynesian storytelling 176–
        178
lies. *See also* marvelous tales
    Moroccan storytelling 341–342
    Venezuelan storytelling 530
"Light as a Feather." *See*
    "Levitation"
"Lights Out!" 573
Lindahl, Carl 595
    Jack Tales 394–397
    Ozark folklore 389–390
Linguae Vasconum Primitiae
    Basque storytelling 185
linguistics
    children's ghost stories 542–543
    critical study of language 247
    ESL teaching tools 548–551
    Schweitzer dialect in
        storytelling 436–438, 440
linking
    Swiss Volhynian storytelling
        440
Lira Popular
    Chilean poetry 478–485
literacy
    Indian storytelling 101, 102,
        103

Malaysian storytelling
    traditions 141
"Little Ant Who Got into the
    Barn, The" 476
*Little Black Snake: A Plains Story
    of New South Wales, The*
    Dreamtime stories 157–158
Little Flying Fox, The
    Aboriginal Australian
        storytelling 158–159
Little Tradition
    Malaysian storytelling
        traditions 138–139
Liu Bei
    ancient Korean storytelling 125
Llorana, La, or The Weeping
    Woman
    Mexican storytelling 446
"Logger's Heaven" (Walls) 454
logging
    Maine stories 416–427
    poetry 398, 453–456
Lomax, Alan 399
Lomax, John Avery 400, 401
Lord, Albert 27
Lövkrona, Inger 262
Luison
    Guaranitic storytelling 491
*Lumbering Songs of the Northern
    Woods* (Fowke) 454
Lund, Jens 595
    Cowboy poetry 398–402
    logger poetry 453–456
Lura (Albania) 183
Lushootseed language 383–84
lute
    Fulani epics 16, 17
Lüthi, Max 254, 256
Lutz-Röhrich Prize 243
luupainaja
    Estonian legends 210
lyreme
    Igbo storytelling devices 46
Lysaght, Patricia 595
    modern Irish storytelling 264–
        272

maabo
    Fulani epics 16
Mac Coisdeala, Liam 267
MacDonald, Margaret Read 595
    function of storytelling 408–415
magic tales. *See also* fairy tales
    fairy tale preservation in
        Germany 242

gender in Hungarian
    storytelling 257
    Ozark fairy tales 387
    Russian stories 285–286
Mahabharata
    Chhattisgarhi genre variation
        107
    Indian storytelling 103
    Saneguruji Storytelling
        Academy 99
    Savitri origins 95
Maharashtra (India)
    Saneguruji Storytelling
        Academy 98
    storytelling in middle-class
        families 102
Maigua, Galo 486–488
Maine
    family storytelling 416–427
makisá miíi
    Maroon folktales 523
mala hora
    Colombian spirit stories 513
Malaysia
    cautionary tales 130–133
    storytelling traditions 138–141
Mali
    Dogon creation stories 48
    Fulani epics 13, 15
Malinche, La
    Mexican storytelling 446
    Totonac storytelling dances
        508
mal punto 514, 520
mal vienta, or spirit sickness 513
mal viento 514, 520
Mama, Raouf 596
    Beninese storytelling 9–12
mana 164
Manczal, Etelka, or Károly
    Matlaha
    gender and storytelling 257–
        263
Manczal, Feri 258–263
Manczal, József 258–263
Mande (people) 4
Mandenka (people) 71–81
"Man from the Gallows, The "
    541
Manitoba 365–368
Maori (people) 171–175
marabout
    matrilineal myths in Niger 349
marae
    Maori storytelling 173–174

Marathi language
   Saneguruji Storytelling
     Academy 98
märchen, *or* fairy tale
   Belizean Creole storytelling 467
   children's ghost stories 539–543
   German storytelling 239–246
   Jack Tales 394–397
   Newfoundland stories 448
   Ozark stories 387–393
   women's storytelling 581–585
Märchenkreis 241
Märchenspiegel 243
Märchen-Stiftung Walter Kahn
   242
Märchenzentren 240
Marcuse, Herbert 247
Mardândukht
   Iranian epic storytelling 337
Mar Elias. *See* Elijah
Mari
   Basque storytelling 188
Maria Ceniza
   Mexican storytelling 445
Mar Jiryis
   storytelling in Palestine 344
Marks, Ljiljana 596
   Croatian storytelling 203–206
Maroon (people)
   folktales 522–527
marriage
   matrilineal myths in Niger 353
Martin, Buzz 453
Martin, JoAnn 596
   Mexican storytelling 498–501
Martinez, Esther, *or* P'oe Tsawa
   596
   storytelling in San Juan Pueblo
     381–382
marvelous tales
   Chilean folktales 476
Marvin, Lee-Ellen 596
   Saneguruji Storytelling
     Academy 98–101
   Savitri performances in India
     94–97
   storytelling in middle-class
     Indian families 102–105
"Mary Worth," *or* "Mary Wolf"
   preadolescent girls' storytelling
     561
"Maski Parch," *or* "Half Chick"
   Cree storytelling 367
Massina Fulani
   epic storytelling 15

mastersinger
   African hunter narratives 4
Matlaha, Károly, Mrs. *See*
   Manczal, Etelka
Mato, Daniel 596
   art of Venezuelan storytelling
     528–535
matriarchy
   Igbo storytelling 33
matriliny
   myths in Niger 348–354
Maxwell, W.E. 140
Maya (people)
   Belizean storytelling 471–474
   Mexican storytelling 442
   Tzotzil-Tzeltal storytelling
     494–497
Mayeux, Henry 417–419
Mbe
   Igbo storytelling 37, 43
McCabe-Juhnke, John 596
   Kansan Mennonite stories 434–
     441
McCarthy, William Bernard 397
McDermitt, Barbara 597
   Scottish storytelling 289–300
McDowell, John H. 597
   Colombian animistic stories
     513–521
   functions of storytelling 408–
     415
McGlynn, Jenny 269–270
McNeil, W.K. 597
   Ozark fairy tales 387–393
McRae, Wallace 400–401
mea ha'i 'ōlelo
   Hawaiian storytelling 164
mea oli
   Hawaiian storytelling 164
Mecklenburg (Germany) 234–
   238
medical emergencies 428–433
medicine woman
   matrilineal myths in Niger 348–
     354
melismata
   Igbo storytelling devices 43
memory
   formulation of narrative 212
   function of storytelling 412–
     413
   Iranian epic storytelling 333
   Mandenkan storytelling 76
   Mexican storytelling 501
   Travellers' stories 302, 303

men
   Bulgarian folktales 199
   Chhattisgarhi narrative
     performance 109
   far eastern Russian stories 285–
     286
   gender and repertoire in
     Hungarian telling 257–264
   Igbo storytelling 33
   Maori storytelling 173–174
   matrilineal myths in Niger 353
   modern Irish storytelling 265
   Polynesian storytelling 177
   Rajasthani hero legends 92
   Slovakian storytelling 313
   storytelling in Palestine 344–
     347
   Tunisian storytelling 357
Meneses, Daniel 480
Mennonites (people)
   Swiss Volhynian stories 434–
     441
Metallic Blackbird. *See Seerango*
metamorphosis tales
   Mexican storytelling 445
metaphoric indirection
   Savitri performance 96
"Mexican Pet, The" 574
Mexico
   art of storytelling 442–447
   corrido 399
   politics of storytelling 498–501
   Totonac Indian stories 502–512
   Tzotzil-Tzeltal storytelling
     494–497
Meyer-Ho'omanawanui,
   Ku'ualoha 597–598
   Hawaiian storytelling 160–170
Micronesia 176–178
Middle East
   Egyptian peep-show
     storytelling 325
   Iranian epics 326–340
   Palestine 344–347
Midwives' Day
   Bulgarian folktales 195
migrant workers
   women's storytelling 580
Miller, Baker 255
Minangkabau
   Indonesian professional
     storytelling 134–137
   kaba storytelling 111
mining
   ballads 399

miracle stories
  Croatian storytelling 204
mîrzâ
  Iranian epic storytelling 332
Mission House Museum
      (Honolulu, Hawaii)
  Hawaiian storytelling event
      167–168
Mister Johnson 10
mist-folk. *See* Traveller
Mitchell, Waddie 400–401
modern legends. *See* urban
      legends
Mohammed Taib Osman 138–
      141
Mokoli'i
  Hawaiian storytelling 163
Monahan, Tom 546
monk
  Thai storytelling 142–143, 148
mo'olelo
  Hawaiian storytelling 163
Moon
  Colombian spirit stories 516–
      517
  Maio creation tales 89
  organizational storytelling 545
  Totonac storytelling 508
Moon and the Hare
  Ju/'hoan storytelling variations
      61–64
moose
  Cree storytelling 367, 368
Morales, Rosario S. 598
  Mexican storytelling 442–447
moral tale. *See also* teaching tale
  Igede storytelling 57–58
Morelos (Mexico)
  politics of storytelling 498–501
Morocco
  storytelling 341–343
Moses
  storytelling in Palestine 344
Moses, Johnny 384
mother
  preadolescent girls' storytelling
      560
mother-in-law
  Greek Gypsy narrative 252
motifeme
  Hupa storytelling 373–375
motto
  Fulani epics 16–17
mourning. *See also* elegy
  Greek Gypsy narrative 254

Igbo storytelling devices 43, 46
  Maori storytelling 174
Moussa Gname
  hunters' narratives 4
muhaddith
  Iranian epic storytelling 330
Muhawi, Ibrahim 598
  storytelling in Palestine 344–
      347
Munnelly, Tom 269
murana
  Albanian folktales 181
Murphy, Michael J. 269
murshid
  Iranian epic storytelling 333
musha'widin
  Moroccan storytelling 341
music. *See also* song
  Chinese chantefable tradition 86
  Fulani epics 16–17
  Mandenkan storytelling 74
Musumbi Kitumdumo
  Kamba storytelling 66
mvett
  Central African epics 7
myths
  Ga folktales 18
  Maori storytelling 171–175
  matrilineal myths in Niger 348–
      354
  Mexican storytelling 445, 502–
      512
  storytelling revival 557

Nagy, Ilona 598
  gender and folktale repertoire
      257–263
nahualismo
  Mexican storytelling 445
nā mea Hawai'i
  Hawaiian storytelling 165
Namibia 59
NAPPS. *See* National Association
      for the Preservation and
      Perpetuation of Storytelling
naqqâl
  Iranian epic storytelling 332,
      333, 334
narration. *See* performance
narrator. *See* storyteller
Nastradin Hodja. *See* Sly Peter
National Association for the
      Preservation and
      Perpetuation of Storytelling
      (NAPPS) 242

storytelling revival 552
National Storytelling Association,
      or NSA 552
Native Americans
  Coeur d'Alene tales 369–370
  Cree storytelling 365–368
  Hupa storytelling event 371–
      380
  Lushootseed stories 383–384
  Téwa storytelling 381–82
Ndong Ndoutoume, Tsira 7
Neumann, Siegfried 598
  German storytelling 234–238
Newfoundland 448–452
New Mexico
  Cowboy poetry 399
  Téwa stories 381–382
New Religions
  Japanese storytelling 116–117
newspapers
  Lira Popular in Chile 479–484
New Zealand 171–175
Ngaati Maniapoto
  Maori storytelling 172–173,
      175
Ngoma, Mwatu Wa
  Kamba storytelling 65–67
Ngugi wa Thiong
  Beninese storytelling 10
Nias
  Indonesian storytelling 111
Nic an Luain, Anna
  modern Irish storytelling 268
Nicte-ha, Princess
  Mayan storytelling 472
Niger 348–355
Nigeria
  Igbo folk epics 25, 33, 42
  Igede storytelling 54–58
night
  Igede storytelling events 56–57
  Mandenkan storytelling 78–79
nightmare
  Estonian legends 210
"Night of the Living Dummy"
      561
Nihon ryôiki
  Japanese religious tales 114–
      115
Nihon Shoki (Aston)
  Japanese religious tales 114
Nkuu'
  Semai cautionary tales 133
Nnobi
  Igbo storytelling 34

Nommo
  Dogon creation story 49
North America
  children's ghost stories 539–543
  Cowboy poetry 398–402
  cross-cultural storytelling 577–
    579
  ESL stories 548–551
  functions of storytelling 408–
    415
  Idaho stories 403–407
  Jack Tales 394–97
  Kansan Mennonite stories 434–
    441
  listening experiences 563–571
  logger poetry 453–456
  Maine family stories 416–427
  Mexican storytelling 442–447
  Newfoundland storytelling
    448–452
  organizational storytelling
    544–547
  Ozark fairy tales 387–393
  paramedic stories 428–433
  preadolescent girls' storytelling
    559–562
  storytelling revival 552–558
  urban legends 572–576
  women's storytelling 580–586
nóuna
  Maroon folktales 525, 526
Nová Bystrica (Slovakia) 311–313
"Novelist as a Teacher, The"
  (Achebe)
  Beninese storytelling 10
novella
  Bulgarian folktales 194
Nri (people)
  Igbo storytelling 34
NSA. *See* National Storytelling
  Association
ntu 25, 36
nurse 431–432
nyabei 139
nyama 51–52

O'ahu (Hawaii)
  Hawaiian storytelling 163
O'Callahan, Jay 553
Oceania
  Hawaiian storytelling 160–170
  Polynesian storytelling 176–
    178
Ó Conaill, Seán 265–266
Ó Dálaigh, Seósamh 267

Odysseus
  Venezuelan storytelling 531
Ogede, Ode 598–599
  Igede storytelling events 54–58
Ogo, *or* Yo Ogo, *or* Yurugu
  Dogon creation story 49
Ohafia
  Igbo storytelling 26, 34
Ó hEalaoire, Stiofán 266
ÓhEochaidh, Seán 268
O-HUL-WOH
  Hupa storytelling 371–380
Ojaadili
  Igbo folk epics 31
ojah
  Igede storytelling events 56
Okpewho, Isidore 41–42
Oksanen, Juho 212–223
'olapa
  Hawaiian storytelling 164
Old Woman's Reflections, An
  modern Irish storytelling 267–
    268
Olson, Charles Olaf 453
Omalinze
  Igbo storytelling devices 42
òménààlà
  Igbo storytelling 35
Omidsalar, Mahmoud 599
  Iranian epics 326–340
Omidsalar, Teresa 599
  Iranian epics 326–340
Onicha Igbo (people) 34
Ŏnmori 127
onomatopoeia
  Ga folktales 20
  Igbo storytelling 39–40, 42, 44
Ono Niha (people) 111
*On'ry Propositions: Cowboy
    Poets and Cowboy Poetry*
  (Stanley and Thatcher) 401
opera
  Hawaiian language 167
oral literature, *or* oral tradition
  Basque storytelling 185–189
  Belizean Creole storytelling 468
  Beninese storytelling 11
  cross-cultural storytelling 578
  French storytelling 227, 228
  Ga folktales 18–24
  gender in Hungarian
    storytelling 257
  German storytelling 236
  Greek Gypsy narratives
  Igbo storytelling 27, 35

Ju/h'oan folktales 59
  Kamba 65
  Lushootseed stories 383
  Mayan storytelling 471
  modern Irish storytelling 267
  Portuguese storytelling 283
  Scottish storytelling 290, 297
Orellana, Marcela 599
  Chilean Lira Popular 478–485
organizational storytelling 544–
    547
organ napping
  Semai cautionary tales 131–133
Oruluk
  Polynesian storytelling 177
Osman, Mohammad Taib 599
  Malaysian storytelling 138–141
Ossenets (Bulgaria) 196
Otavalan (people) 486–489
Ouija board
  preadolescent girls' storytelling
    561
Ozarks (U.S.)
  fairy tales 387–393
Ozidi Saga
  Central African epics 6–8
Ozoemena Ndive 31

Pabuji
  Rajasthani legends 93
Pacific
  Hawaiian storytelling 160–170
  Polynesian storytelling 176–
    178
Page, Mary Ellen 336
Palestine 344–347
Palleiro, Maria 599
  Argentinean folktales 459–464
Panchatrantra
  Indian storytelling 103
Pandvani
  Indian storytelling 107–108
panjak
  Indonesian storytelling 113
p'ansori
  ancient Korean storytelling
    122–129
pantun
  Indonesian storytelling 111–
    112, 135
Papahānaumoku
  Hawaiian storytelling 164
Paraguay 490–493
parda
  Rajasthani hero legends 92

Park, Chan E. 599
  ancient Korean storytelling
    122–129
Parler, Mary 391
parrot dance. *See sua nac*
parrot refrain. *See* echo refrain
Parry, Milman 27
pastorales
  Basque storytelling 186, 188
patriliny
  matrilineal myths in Niger 352,
    353
patter
  Scottish storytelling 298
pawang
  Malaysian storytelling 139
paya
  Lira Popular 480
Pearl Pagoda, The
  Chinese chantefable tradition
    87
"Pedro Ordimán and the Golden
    Partridge" (Peralta) 461
Pedro Rimales 534
Pekaan, or Pekkaafi
  Fulani epics 15, 17
Pele
  Hawaiian storytelling 163, 166
Pendergast, David 599
  Mayan storytelling 471–474
penglipur lara
  Malaysian storytelling 139, 140
penungun
  Sumatran storytelling 111
performance, *or* storytelling event.
    See also audience;
    storyteller
  Africa
    Central African epics 6–7
    Fulani epics 16–17
    Ga folktales 18–23
    hunters' narratives 4
    Igbo storytelling events 36–
      40
    Igede stories 55–59
    Kenyan Storytellers 69
  Asia
    Chinese chantefable tradition
      86–87
    Indian storytelling 100, 104,
      106–109
    Indonesian storytelling 110–
      113
    Iranian epic storytelling 334
    Korean storytelling 122

Saneguruji Storytelling
    Academy 100
  Savitri and women 94–97
  Thai storytelling 142–143,
    149, 152
  West Sumatran storytelling
    134–137
  Europe
    Albanian genres 183–184
    Arvanítika 248–250
    Basque storytelling 186
    Bulgarian folktales 193, 198–
      202
    Croatian storytelling 205–
      206
    Estonian legends 209
    fairy tale preservation in
      Germany 241
    formulation of narrative
      223–225
    French storytelling 227–229
    gender in Hungarian
      storytelling 257, 258–263
    German storytelling 234–238
    Slovakian storytelling 313,
      314
    Travellers' stories 302–308
  Native America
    Hupa storytelling event 371–
      380
    Lushootseed storytelling 383
  North America
    children's ghost stories 540,
      543
    Cowboy poetry 398
    function of storytelling 410–
      412
    Idaho ranching stories 407
    listening experiences 563–
      571
    storytelling revival 556
    Swiss Volhynian storytelling
      438–440
    urban legends 573
  Pacific
    Hawaiian storytelling 165
    Maori storytelling 172
  South America
    Chilean folktales 475–477
    Venezuelan storytelling 528–
      534
Perrault, Charles 581
Persian language
  Iranian epic storytelling 329
Persian *Rivâyât*

Iranian epic storytelling 327
Peter, David 371–380
Peterson, George 296, 297
Phadaeng Nang Ai
  cultural preservation in Isan
    144
Phillips, Nigel 599–600
  Sumatran storytelling 134–137
Phya Khankhaak
  cultural preservation through
    storytelling 144
pinghua
  Chinese chantefable tradition
    85
pingtan
  Chinese chantefable tradition
    85
Pissing in the Snow (Randolph)
    389
Plateau of the Narrative
    Contemplation. *See* Fuulu
    Faala Fukho
Pḷavnieks, Jānis 273–279
poetry
  Chilean Lira Popular 478–485
  Cowboy tradition 398–402
  Igbo folk epics 31
P'oe Tsawa. *See* Martinez, Esther
Pohnpei Island
  Polynesian storytelling 176–
    178
"Poisoned Pussycat at the Party,
    The" 575
Polynesia 176–178
Pombero
  Guaranitic storytelling 491
Pora
  Guaranitic storytelling 490–
    491
Portugal 281–284
Post-it Notes
  organizational storytelling 545
poupou
  Maori storytelling 173
poutokomanawa
  Maori storytelling 173
praise naming
  Igbo folk epics 26, 28
Pratap, Rana
  Rajasthani hero legends 91–92
prayer 283
Price, Richard 600
  Maroon folktales 522–527
Price, Sally 600
  Maroon folktales 522–527

priest 115–117
"Prince and the Storm, The" 283
Protect Kaho'olawe 'Ohana
    Hawaiian storytelling 165
Puebla (Mexico) 502
Pulaar, *or* Fulfulde
    Fulani epics 13
Pune (India)
    Saneguruji Storytelling
        Academy 98–101
    storytelling in middle-class
        families 102
puppet
    Albanian folktales 183
    Egyptian peep-show
        storytelling 325
    Tzotzil-Tzeltal storytelling
        495–496
puram
    Savitri performance 95
"Purple Doll, The." *See* "China
    Doll, The"

qacida
    Fulani religious epics 15
qâss
    Iranian epic storytelling 335
Queixeiro Crego, Dóres 231
Queskekapow, Nathaniel 365–368
Quetzal-dance
    Totonac storytelling 507
Quevedo 534
Quichua language
    Otavalo song 487, 488
Quran
    storytelling in Palestine 344–347

rabab Pasisia
    West Sumatran storytelling
        136–137
rabbit 445
Radnor, Jo 96
ragi
    narrative performances in India
        107
Raikova, Fidana 201
Rajan, Rajeswari
    Savitri performances 95
Rajasthan
    hero legends 91–93
Rama V 146
Ramanujan, A.K. 95
Ramayana
    Indian storytelling 103
    Malaysian storytelling 141

Ramsey, Buck 400–401
ranching
    Cowboy poetry 399–402
    Idaho stories 403–407
    logger poetry 453
Randolph, Vance 389–391
Ranke, Kurt 240
Rashid al-Dîn al-Watwât
    Iranian epic storytelling 331
Rasmussen, Susan 600
    matrilineal myths in Niger 348–
        355
Raspa, Richard 600
    organizational storytelling
        544–547
ratib saman
    Malaysian storytelling 141
ratijaa
    Rajasthani legends 93
ratijaga
    Rajasthani legends 92
raven
    Cree storytelling 366
raw time, the. *See kaka tempoka*
Razgrad (Bulgaria) 190–198
Reboleiro Grandal, Domingo 231
recitation. *See* also performance
    Cowboy poetry 398
    Igbo folk epics 25, 28
"Red Riding Hood" 560
refrain
    Igbo storytelling 41–47
Regan-Blake, Connie 553, 556
religion
    Basque storytelling 185
    Chilean folktales 476
    Croatian storytelling 203
    Estonian legends 208
    Fulani epics 15
    Japanese storytelling 114–118
    Mexican storytelling 445
    Portuguese storytelling 282–
        283
    Savitri performances 95
    storytelling in Palestine 344–347
Rescue 911
    medical emergency stories 428
"Revitalization Movements"
    (Wallace) 554
Richard family 416–427
Ricouer, Paul 501
riddle
    Chilean folktales 475
    Ga folktales 19
    Greek Gypsy narrative 252

Ringer, Del 403–407
river 34
"Robber Who Was Hurt, The"
    575
Roberts, Leonard 396
Robertson, Stanley 294, 295, 296
Rodger, W.R. 267
Roman Catholicism
    Colombian spirit stories 514
    Guaranitic storytelling 491
    Tzotzil-Tzeltal storytelling 496
Romani
    Greek Gypsy narratives 252
romantic tale
    Greek Gypsy narrative 255
    Igbo folk epics 31
Rozafa
    Albanian folktales 182
Ruch, Barbara 115, 116
Rumelhart, David E. 213
rumpling. See kentrung
Russia
    women's stories 285–288
Rustam and Suhrâb
    Iranian epic storytelling 336
Rustam Nâma
    Iranian epic storytelling 333

Sabah (Malaysia)
    Malaysian storytelling
        traditions 138–139
sagasji
    Rajasthani legends 92
Sagasji Bavji
    Rajasthani legends 92
Sakonji Masae
    traditional Japanese folktelling
        120
salvation
    Mandenkan storytelling 79–80
Samak-i `Ayyâr
    Iranian epic storytelling 337
Sambô-e
    Japanese religious tales 115
San
    Ju/'hoan folktales 59
Sandouk El Donia, or Sifira Aziz
    Egyptian peep-show
        storytelling 325
San Francisco earthquake
    Lira popular 482–484
Sang Kancil
    Malaysian storytelling 141
Sanguruji Storytelling Academy
    98–101

San Juanito music
    Otavalo song 486–487
San Juan Pueblo (New Mexico)
    381–382
Santa Compaña
    Galician storytelling 231
Saramaka (Suriname) 522–527
Sarawak (Malaysia) 138–139
Savitri
    contemporary performances
    94–97
sawura
    Mandenkan storytelling 77
Sayers, Peig 267
scéalaí
    modern Irish storytelling 264
Schechner, Richard 552, 566
Schwanke 582
Schwankenerzähler 583
Schweitzer dialect
    Swiss Volhynian storytelling
    436–440
Schwyzerdütsch
    translation and storytelling
    318–320
Scotland
    Jack Tales 395
    storytelling traditions 289–
    300
    Travellers' stories 301–309
Scottish Storytelling Forum 290
"Scrawny Little Kid"
    Maroon folktales 523
Seerango, or Konjobi Seerango, or
    Metallic Blackbird
    Mandenkan storytelling 72–73,
    76
seeyar
    Tunisian storytelling 357
Seira Al
    Egyptian peep-show
    storytelling 325
Semach'I
    p'ansori 127
Semai
    Malaysian cautionary tales
    130–133
Senegal 13, 14, 17
Senovo (Bulgaria) 191, 192,
    193
Seydou, Christiane 600
    Fulani epics 13–17
shadow. *See Jiija*
shadow plays
    Albanian folktales 183

Sháhnáma
    Iranian epic storytelling 326–
    337
shaman
    Rajasthani legends 93
    Russian stories 285
Shasekishû
    Japanese religious tales 115
shastric
    Indian narrative performances
    106
Shaw, John 292
Shetland Islands
    Scottish storytelling 289, 296,
    298
Shintoism
    Japanese religious tales 116
Shirasawan Nabe
    traditional Japanese folktelling
    119–120
Shkodra (Albania) 183
Siberia
    women's stories 285–288
Sidundoy Valley (Colombia)
    spirit stories 513–521
*Sifira Aziza. See Sandouk El
    Donia*
Sigui
    Dogon cosmology 52
Siikala, AnnaLeena
    formulation of narrative 215
sijobang
    West Sumatran storytelling
    134–135, 136
Silimaka
    Fulani epics 15
Sim Ch'ŏng
    ancient Korean storytelling
    125–126
singing. *See* song
singing cowboy 400
sipatuang sirah
    West Sumatran storytelling 136
Sirius
    Dogon cosmology 52
Skanderberg
    Albanian folktales 182
slavery
    Maroon folktales 522–527
sleepover
    children's ghost stories 540
Slovakia
    contemporary storytelling 310–
    315
"Slumber Party, The" 560

Sly Peter, *or Nastradin Hodja*
    Bulgarian folktales 196
Sna Jtz'ibajom
    Tzotzil-Tzeltal storytelling 494
snake 157–158
"Snowville" (Nelson) 401
Sobol, Joseph 600
    storytelling revival 552–558
Society for Taking Care of Fairy
    Tale Materials of European
    Peoples. *See* Gesellschaft
    zur Pflege de Märchengutes
    der europäischen Volker
so dayi
    Dogon creation story 51
Sokoli, Ramadan 600
    *Albanian folk teller's stories
    181–184*
song. *See also* music
    Chhattisgarhi narratives 107,
    108
    Chinese chantefable tradition 86
    Cowboy poetry 399
    Ga folktales 20–23
    hunters' dirges 4
    Igbo folk epics 25–27, 31, 41–
    47
    Indonesian storytelling 111,
    112
    Korean storytelling 122–129
    Lushootseed stories 384
    Mandenkan storytelling 72, 74
    Maori storytelling 174
    Miao antiphonal epics 88–89
    Otavalan storytelling 486–489
    Savitri performance 96
    West Sumatran storytelling
    134–137
Song of Ch'unhyang 123–124
Song of Hŭngbu 124
Song of Sim Ch'ŏng 125–126
"Song of the Ancient Sweet Gum"
    89–90
Song of the Red Cliff 124–125
Song of the Underworld Palace
    126
Songs of the Cowboys (Thorp)
    400, 401
sŏngŭm 127
Sŏp'yŏnche, or Western School
    127
sorgina 187
sòrómchìá 35
So the Witch Won't Eat Me
    (Bloch) 560

South America
  Argentinean folktales 459–464
  Bahamian narration 465–466
  Belizean Creole storytelling
    467–470
  Belizean Mayan storytelling
    471–474
  Chilean folktales 475–477,
    478–485
  Colombian spirit stories 513–
    521
  Guaranitic storytelling 490–493
  Otavalo song 486–489
  politics of storytelling 498–501
  Suriname Maroon folktales
    522–527
  Totonac Indian storytelling
    502–512
  Tzotzil-Tzeltal storytelling
    494–497
  Venezuelan storytelling 528–
    535
Spagnoli, Cathy 600
  traditional Japanese folktellers
    119–121
Spain
  Basque storytelling 185–189
  Galician storytelling 230–233
Spanish Conquest, the
  Mayan storytelling 472
  Mexican storytelling 444
  Totonac storytelling 504–509
Spanish language 444
"Speaking Ghosts" 541
spider 20, 21, 523
spinning
  Basque storytelling 186–187
spirit
  Colombian stories 514–521
spirit sickness. *See mal viento*
sports
  organizational storytelling 545
Stanev, Peter Stanchev 194, 200
Stanley, David 400
"starke Hans, Der"
  translation and storytelling
Stewart, Essie 291–292
Stewart, Sheila 296
Sticks in the Knapsack (Randolph)
  389
Stojanovic, Mijat 205
"Stolen Liver, The"
  children's ghost stories 541, 543
  preadolescent girls' storytelling
    559–562

Stone, Kay 600–601
  Cree storytelling 365–368
Storyrealm
  listening experiences 563, 570
storyteller, *or* teller, *or* narrator, *or*
    singer
  Africa
    Beninese storytelling 11
    Central African epics 6–7
    Ga folktales 19–23
    Igbo storytelling 38–39
    Igede storytelling events 55–
      56, 57–58
    Ju/'hoan storytelling 60–64
    Kenya 68–70
    Mandenkan telling 72–80
  Asia
    Chinese chantefable tradition
      85, 86
    Indian storytelling 100–101,
      104–105, 107–109
    Indonesia 110–113
    Iranian epic storytelling 331,
      335
    Japanese religious tales 115–
      117
    Malaysian storytelling 139–
      140
    p'ansori 122–123, 126–128
    Savitri performance 95–96
    West Sumatran
      storytelling 135, 136
  Australia and the Pacific
    Dreamtime stories 156
    Hawaiian storytelling 164
    Maori storytelling 174–175
    Polynesian storytelling 177
  Europe
    Albanian folktales 183
    Arvanítika 248–251
    Basque storytelling 186–187,
      188
    Bulgarian folktales 194, 198,
      199
    Croatian storytelling 205
    formulation of narrative
      212–226
    French storytelling 227–229
    gender and repertoire in
      Hungarian storytelling
      257–264
    German storytelling 236,
      237
    Greek Gypsy narrative 254,
      255

    growing consciousness 273–
      279
    Latvian storytelling 274–76
    modern Irish storytelling
      264–272
    Scottish storytelling 289–300
    Slovakian storytelling 312–
      315
    translation and storytelling
      317, 318
  Native America
    Hupa storytelling 372–373,
      378
    Lushootseed stories 383–384
    Téwa storytelling 382
  North America
    children's ghost stories 540,
      541, 543
    French Newfoundland 449,
      450–451
    function of storytelling 410–
      412, 413–414
    listening experiences 567,
      570
    Mexican storytelling 442–
      447
    paramedic stories 428–433
    social identity 409
    storytelling revival 557
    Swiss Volhynian storytelling
      439–440
  South America
    Argentinean folktales 459,
      460
    Bahamian narration 465–
      466
    Belizean Creole storytelling
      467–470
    Mayan storytelling in Belize
      471, 472
    politics in Mexican
      storytelling 500–501
    Venezuelan storytelling 528–
      553
storytelling. *See also* audience;
    performance; storyteller
  ESL teaching tools 548–551
  functions of storytelling 408–
    415
  listening experiences 563–571
  narrative formulation 212–226
  revival 552–558
storytelling event. *See*
    performance
Straparola, Giovanni 204

Stromberg, Peter G. 360
structuralism
 Hupa storytelling 373–375
Sturm, Brian 601
 listening experiences 563–571
sua nac, or parrot dance
 Chhattisgarhi narrative
  performances 108
Subalbe
 Fulani epics 15
Sudden Fiction 574
Sumatra
 didong performers 111
 professional storytelling 134–
  137
Sumumgo
 Mandenkan storytelling 72–73
Sumunkaro koyo
 Mandenkan storytelling 79
Sun
 Colombian spirit stories 516–
  517
 Maio creation tales 89
 Totonac storytelling 507–510
Sundanese (people)
 Indonesian storytelling 111–
  112
supernatural stories
 Argentinean storytelling 460,
  461
 Basque storytelling 187
 children's ghost stories 539–543
 Colombian spirit stories 513–
  521
 Estonian legends 209–211
 Galician storytelling 232–233
 Igbo storytelling 37–38
 Mexican storytelling 444
 modern Irish storytelling 269–
  270
 preadolescent girls' storytelling
  559–562
 Scottish storytelling 297
 Slovakian storytelling 312, 313
 storytelling in Palestine 346
Suriname 522–527
Suzhou chantefable
 Chinese oral tradition 85–87
Swiss Volhynians
 Mennonite stories 434–441
Switzerland
 translation and storytelling
  316–321
 Volhynian Mennonite stories
  434–441

syair
 Malaysian storytelling
  traditions 139
Syokimau
 Kamba storytelling 65

Taalilaala
 Mandenkan storytelling 72–79
taboo
 function of storytelling 409,
  413
 Igede storytelling 57
Tagurmat
 matrilineal myths in Niger 349
tahuuhuu 173
taiken 116
Tai languages 145–152
"Táin Bó Cuailnge," *or* "Cattle
  Raid of Cooley"
 modern Irish storytelling 264
tale-and-response
 Mayan work stories 472
Taleworld 563, 570
Talking Turtle, The (Randolph)
  389
tanci 85
Tandioy, Francisco 514
Tangherlini, Timothy R. 601
 paramedic stories 428–433
tangi 174
tanmori 127
Tarbaby
 Bahamian narration 466
Tartu, University of
 Estonian legends 207
teaching
 storytelling in the ESL
  classroom 548–551
teaching tale. *See also* education;
  moral tale
 Bulgarian folktales 191
 Chilean folktales 476
 Indian storytelling 99
 Russian storytelling 286
 storytelling in Palestine 346
Teatro Lo'il Maxil
 Tzotzil-Tzeltal storytelling
  495–496
technology 556
television
 German storytelling 235, 237
 Indian storytelling 101, 103
 Venezuelan storytelling 532
Tellabration
 Thai storytelling 152

telling, *or* telling situation. *See*
  performance
Temante dula
 Mandenkan storytelling 78
tempting. See kentrung
Tessin (Switzerland) 316
Te Tookanganui-a-noho
 Maori storytelling 172
Téwa (people)
 storytelling in San Juan Pueblo
  381–382
Tewa Tales 382
Texas
 Cowboy poetry 399
Thailand
 cultural preservation in Isan
  144–152
 Thet Siang performance 142–
  143
Thessaloníki (Greece)
 Greek Gypsy narratives 252
"Thet Mahachaart," *or* "Bun
  Phawet"
 Thai storytelling 142
Thet Siang
 Thai storytelling 142–143
Things Fall Apart (Achebe)
 Igbo storytelling 35
Thomas, Gerald 601
 storytelling in French
  Newfoundland 448–452
Thorp, N. Howard "Jack" 400,
  401
"Three Brothers and the Queen's
  Golden Apple, The" (Vera)
  461
3M Company
 organizational storytelling 545
thumpling. See kentrung
Thunder God
 Colombian spirit stories 518
 Maio creation tales 90
 Semai cautionary tales 133
tikanga
 Maori storytelling 173
Timpanelli, Gioia 553
tingkeban
 Indonesian storytelling 112
tinker. *See* Traveller
Tio Conejo 534
Tio Tigre 534
Tlazotoatl
 Totonac storytelling 509
toast
 Cowboy poetry 399

Tod, James 92
Toelken, Barre 601
Tok Selampit. *See* Awang Selampit
Tong, Diane 601
    Gypsy narratives 252–256
Tongp'yŏnche, or Eastern School
    127
tonum 127
Topolinsky, Kaha'i 167
toro 52
Tortoise 37, 43
Tossa, Wajuppa 601
    Thai storytelling 142–143,
        144–152
Totonac Indians (people)
    storytelling in Mexico 502–512
trance
    listening experiences 563, 565–
        566, 568, 569, 570
translation
    problems in Swiss storytelling
        316–321
    Tunisian storytelling 360
Traore, Karim 4
Traveller, *or* tinker, *or* mist-folk,
    or Gan-aboot folk, *or*
    tinker-gypsy
    Jack Tales 395
    Scottish storytelling 289–300,
        301–309
trickster tales
    Central African epics 7
    Igbo storytelling 37
    Ju/'hoan storytelling 64
    Malaysian storytelling 141
    Moroccan storytelling 341
trowly tales
    Scottish storytelling 297
Tserovets (Bulgaria) 194, 196
Tsitsipis, Lukas D. 601
    Greek-Albanian storytelling
        247–251
Tuareg (people)
    matrilineal myths in Niger 348–
        355
Tucker, Elizabeth 601–602
    preadolescent girls' storytelling
        559–562
Tukang Cerita
    Malaysian storytelling 140
tukang hoho 111
tukang kaba 111, 134
tukang rabab 136
tukang sijobang 134–135
Tukulor (people) 14

tukutuku 173
Tulloch, Laurence 296–297
tûmâr-khânî
    Iranian epic storytelling 334
Tunisia 356–361
Turkey 252–256
Turks (people)
    Bulgarian folktales 199, 200
    Greek Gypsy narratives 252–
        256
Turnbo, Silas Claiborne
    Ozark folklore 388
tuupuna 173
txapelketa 188
Tyam, Mohammadu Aliyu 15
Tzeltal Maya (people) 494–487
Tzotzil Maya (people) 494–497

úbùbó 33–40
ufiem 26–27
Uji shû monogatari
    Japanese religious tales 115
ujo 127
Ujwoh 56
Ukxa N!a'an
    Ju/'hoan storytelling variations
        61
Ulster Cycle
    modern Irish storytelling 264
un solo ojo, El
    Venezuelan storytelling 531
United States
    children's ghost stories 539–
        543
    Cowboy poetry 398–402
    cross-cultural storytelling 577–
        579
    ESL stories 548–551
    functions of storytelling 408–
        415
    Idaho stories 403–407
    Jack Tales 394–397
    Kansan Mennonite stories 434–
        441
    listening experiences 563–571
    logger poetry 453–456
    Maine family stories 416–427
    Mexican storytelling 444
    organizational storytelling
        544–547
    Ozark fairy tales 387–393
    paramedic stories 428–433
    preadolescent girls' storytelling
        559–562
    storytelling revival 552–558

urban legends 572–576
    women's storytelling 580–586
!Unn/obe
    Ju/'hoan storytelling variations
        62–63, 64
urban legends, *or* contemporary
    legends, *or* modern legends
    572–576
    preadolescent girls' storytelling
        559–562
urupa
    Maori storytelling 173
'uwehe
    Hawaiian storytelling 161

Vale Judeu (Portugal)
    Portuguese storytelling 281–
        284
Valentine, Eugene 602
    Galician storytelling 230–233
Valentine, Kristen Bervig 602
    Galician storytelling 230–233
Valk, Ülo 602
    Estonian legends 207–211
Van Deusen, Kira 602
    Russian stories told by women
        285–288
Vatasavitri
    contemporary Savitri
        performances 94
Velkova, Danka Ivanova 198
Venezuela 528–535
Veracruz (Mexico)
    Totonac Indian storytelling 502
View from a Witch's Cave, A
    Basque storytelling 186
vir
    Rajasthani hero legends 91
Virgin of Guadalupe 445
"Vogel Greif"
    translation and storytelling
        320
voice
    Mandenkan storytelling 74
    Maori storytelling 174
    p'ansori 122, 126–128
Volador
    Totonac storytelling 507
Volkschochschule
    fairy tale preservation in
        Germany 241
von Sydow, Carl 35

wahi pana
    Hawaiian storytelling 163

waka
    Maori storytelling 173
Wallace, Anthony F.C. 554, 557
Walls, Robert E. 454
Wangetsmuna
    Colombian spirit stories 516–519
war dance 26
war songs 26
Watson, Thomas, Sr. 544
wayang golek
    Indonesian storytelling 112
Webber, Sabra 602
    Tunisian storytelling 356–361
We Come to Object: The Peasants of Morelos and the Nation State 498
wedding 313
Weeping Woman, The. *See Llorana, La*
Welch, Wendy 602
    cross-cultural storytelling 577–579
We're from Missouri
    Ozark folklore 388
Wesselski, Albert 239–246
West, the
    Cowboy poetry 399–402
    Idaho stories 403–407
Western School. *See Sop'yonche*
West Indies
    Maroon folktales 523, 526
West Java 111–112
West Pomerania (Germany) 234–238
West Sumatra 134–137
whaikorer 174
whanaungatanga 172
whanau pani 174
wharekai 173
wharenu 171
White, Linda 602
    Basque storytelling 185–189
White Ethiopian
    Bulgarian folktales 198
Why Goats Smell Bad and Other Tales from Benin (Mama) 9
why so stories
    Igbo storytelling 38
Who Blowed Up the Church House? (Randolph) 389
Whyte, Betsy 293
Wienker-Piepho, Sabine 603
    fairy tale preservation in Germany 239–246

Wilkes, Hubert 391
Williamson, Duncan
    Jack Tales 397
    Scottish storytelling 293, 305, 308
Williamson, Jimmy 294–295, 298
Winograd, Terry 213
witch
    Basque storytelling 187
    Iranian epic storytelling 337
    preadolescent girls' storytelling 560
"Witches of Xuritegui, The"
    Basque storytelling 187
witness
    Mandenkan storytelling 72–73, 76
Wolf and the Kids, The 560
Wolkstein, Diane 553
Wolof (people)
    Fulani epics 14
women. *See also* matriarchy
    Africa
        Igbo storytelling 27, 33
        matrilineal myths in Niger 348–354
        Tunisian storytelling 356
    Asia
        Indian storytelling 104–105, 106–109
        Japanese religious storytelling 117
        Korean storytelling 123
        Rajasthani hero legends 92
        Savitri performances 94–96
        storytelling in Palestine 344–347
    Europe
        Arvanítika stories 248–251
        Basque storytelling 186–187, 195
        Bulgarian folktales 191, 198
        far eastern Russian stories 285–288
        gender and storytelling 257–264
        Portuguese storytelling 281
    Maori storytelling 173–174
    North America
        French Newfoundland storytelling 451–452
        Mexican storytelling 446
        nature of storytelling 580–586
        Ozark tales 392

Tzotzil-Tzeltal storytelling 496
Women Like Meat
    Ju/'hoan storytelling 63
woodcarving 425–426
woods
    logger poetry 453–456
    Maine stories 416–427
working bee 198, 200
work tales 472
world tales 228
Wossidlo, Richard 234

Xoan N!a'an
    Ju/'hoan storytelling variations 62
Xong Jang
    Maio creation tales 89

yage 520
yala 52
yarnin 297
yarn spinning 198, 199
Yashts
    Iranian epic storytelling 327–340
Yasy Yateré
    Guaranitic storytelling 491
Yellow Corn Dance
    Téwa storytelling 381–382
yembas
    Colombian spirit stories 515
Yocom, Margaret 603
    Maine family stories 416–427
Yokoyama Sachiko 120–121
Yolen, Jane 11
Yo Ogo. *See* Ogo
Young, Katherine 563, 570
"Youth Who Wanted to Learn What Fear Is, The" (Soria) 462
Yugoslavia 203
yukara 120
yûnân 327–328
Yurugu. *See* Ogo

Zagreb (Croatia)
    Croatian storytelling 205
Zamzami dan Marlaini
    West Sumatran storytelling 136
zanana 92
Zapata, Emilio 499
Zarîrî, Murshid Abbas 333, 334, 336, 337
Zhuge Liang 125